## Business & Company Resource Center (BCRC) Exercises

Boone & Kurtz keep you and your students up to date and continually interacting with the business world by providing online exercises that point students to current articles located in our BCRC. These exercises ask students to read the articles and answer questions, encouraging them to apply their knowledge of concepts to the ideas discussed in the article. Each student who purchases *ThomsonNOW* for the Boone & Kurtz text will automatically receive access to the BCRC database. View a guided tour of the Business & Company Resource Center at http://www.gale.com/BusinessRC.

## Introducing – *The Second City* – Boone & Kurtz's New Integrated Video Case

It is no wonder why Boone & Kurtz chose *The Second City* to show how business works in the real world. Throughout the text, the new video cases combine the entrepreneurial and creative spirit with which *The Second City* was founded with the reality of a successful working business model. In these videos students will examine the history of the theater company as well as the successful business practices that have allowed for expansion and growth.

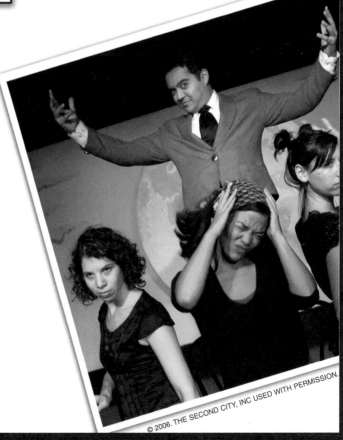

# Contemporary Business

## 12th Edition

**David L. Kurtz**
Distinguished Professor and
R.A. and Vivian Young Chair
of Business Administration
University of Arkansas

THOMSON
SOUTH-WESTERN

Australia · Brazil · Canada · Mexico · Singapore · Spain · United Kingdom · United States

## Contemporary Business, Twelfth Edition

Louis E. Boone and David L. Kurtz

**VP/Editorial Director:**
Jack W. Calhoun

**Publisher:**
Neil Marquardt

**Acquisitions Editor:**
Erin Joyner

**Senior Developmental Editor:**
Rebecca von Gillern

**Marketing Manager:**
Kimberly Kanakes

**Marketing Communications Manager:**
Sarah Greber

**Content Project Manager:**
Amy Hackett

**Manager of Technology, Editorial:**
Vicky True

**Technology Project Manager:**
Kristen Meere

**Senior Manufacturing Coordinator:**
Diane Gibbons

**Production House:**
Lachina Publishing Services, Inc.

**Printer:**
RR Donnelley
Willard Manufacturing Division

**Art Director:**
Stacy Jenkins Shirley

**Internal and Cover Designer:**
Mike Stratton

**Cover Image:**
© Getty Images/Michael Stratton

**Photography Manager:**
John Hill

**Photo Researcher:**
Seidel Associates

Library of Congress Control Number:
2006934271

For more information about our products, contact us at:
Thomson Learning Academic Resource Center
1–800–423–0563

**Thomson Higher Education**
5191 Natorp Boulevard
Mason, OH 45040
USA

# Moving Business Forward...*Faster*

MOVING

FORWARD

FASTER

*Contemporary Business* is moving forward faster, making Boone &

Kurtz still the most current and comprehensive text and package on the

market! This edition is packed with resources that will help YOU move

forward into the world of business! The authors have incorporated a new

business case throughout the text, focusing on *The Second City*, a world-

renowned comedy troupe that launched such stars as Bill Murray, Chris

Farley, Tina Fey, Stephen Colbert, and Steve Carell. Not only that, this

edition offers you more ways to learn about the different aspects of business

through a variety of study materials including *ThomsonNOW*™ and the

Business & Company Resource Center (BCRC)!

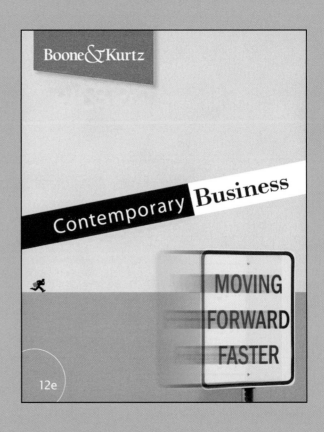

# How Are We Moving Forward Faster?

**For YOU, the Student** – You will benefit from using *ThomsonNOW* as you determine how you learn material most efficiently and study the concepts you have not mastered through a personalized learning path. And, with the Business & Company Resource Center, you can read relevant and exciting articles that will keep you interested in important business concepts.

**For YOUR Instructor** – Boone & Kurtz can help your instructor move forward faster while he or she prepares for and teaches your course. Our new *ThomsonNOW* integrated homework system helps instructors plan, manage, teach, and grade assignments faster than ever before!

## Moving Forward Faster in the Business World

Throughout the 12th edition, you will find this small icon of a businessperson. This icon moves through the book with you, representing today's businessperson on the move in our fast-paced business world, just as you will be better prepared to move forward faster into the business world after using Boone & Kurtz.

## New Features to Keep YOU Moving Forward... Faster

### ThomsonNOW™ **for** *Contemporary Business 12e*

*ThomsonNOW* is a completely online product that is comprised of *prepopulated* homework, assessments with a personalized learning path, an *eBook*, and other learning resources. When you purchase *ThomsonNOW* for the 12th edition, you automatically receive access to the Business & Company Resource Center (BCRC) database. In addition to questions about articles in the BCRC, *ThomsonNOW* includes a set of comprehensive questions that help you test your knowledge of chapter concepts.

### Business & Company Resource Center (BCRC)

Included with your purchase of *ThomsonNOW* for *Contemporary Business 12e* is access to the BCRC. BCRC allows you to research company histories, articles, industry data, company financials, and much more. Boone & Kurtz keep you up to date and continually interacting with the business world by providing online exercises in *ThomsonNOW* that point you to current articles located in the BCRC.

### The Second City – Continuing Video Cases

It's no wonder why Boone & Kurtz chose *The Second City* to show how business works in the real world. "The modern purveyors of sketch and improvisational comedy, including SNL, SCTV, and MADTV, all owe a debt to *The Second City*. After 45 years of being one of Chicago's most enduring comedy institutions their members have grown up to be some of the top names in American Comedy." Throughout the text, new video cases illustrate how the entrepreneurial and creative spirit of *The Second City* exemplifies the best of modern business practices.

**Assessment Checks** – Found at the end of each section, these quick questions allow you to check your knowledge of the chapter material before continuing on to the next topic.

**Project and Teamwork Applications** – Designed to be a more in-depth learning experience, many of these exercises can be used to promote team building.

**Launching Your Business Career** – This brand-new feature, which can be found at the end of each Part, gives you an understanding of all the many different jobs that are a part of each function in a business – and the job path that you may take from entry-level positions to high-level management positions in each of these functional areas. At the end of each of these features are Career Assessment Exercises and projects that help you gauge your interest in and natural predisposition for certain careers.

**Audio CDs** – Included with every purchase of a new copy of the 12th edition are the ever-popular audio chapter review CDs. These CDs give you a quick overview of the main chapter concepts, allowing you to review in the car, on foot, at the gym—anywhere! These audio chapter reviews will also be available for download within the *ThomsonNOW* product.

**Introducing – *The Second City* – Boone/Kurtz's New Integrated Company**

"The modern purveyors of sketch and improvisational comedy, including SNL, SCTV, and MADTV, all owe a debt to *The Second City*. After 45 years of being one of Chicago's most enduring comedy institutions their members have grown up to be some of the top names in American Comedy: John Belushi, Bill Murray, Betty Thomas, Alan Arkin, Tina Fey, Chris Farley, Bonnie Hunt, Steve Carell, and Stephen Colbert, just to name a few."

**"*The Second City* also has touring troupes that take our shows on the road, a Training Center that teaches improvisation, acting, writing, and other skills, and a corporate communications division that services the business world."**

It is no wonder why Boone & Kurtz chose *The Second City* to show how business works in the real world. Throughout the text, the new video cases combine the entrepreneurial and creative spirit with which *The Second City* was founded with the reality of a successful working business model. In these videos you will examine the history of the theater company as well as the successful business practices that have allowed for expansion and growth.

*The Second City*

## *ThomsonNOW*™ for Boone/Kurtz's *Contemporary Business 12e*

Designed BY instructors and students FOR instructors and students, *ThomsonNOW* for Boone & Kurtz's *Contemporary Business 12e* gives you what you want to do, how you want to do it. From extra practice questions to a personalized learning path that helps you study the way you learn best... *ThomsonNOW* delivers!

**Access to a Unique Database** – When you purchase *ThomsonNOW* for the Boone & Kurtz text, you will automatically receive access to the BCRC database. This access allows you to apply concepts to real business articles while also opening up a database in which you can research company histories, articles, industry data, company financials, and more!

**Efficient Paths to Success** – *ThomsonNOW* gives you a personalized learning path that helps you focus on what you still need to learn, as well as the opportunity to select activities, videos, animations, web links, text pages, and audio lectures that best match your learning style.

**Delivering the Results You Deserve** – Students like you report that they do better on exams and come to class better prepared when using *ThomsonNOW*. They also feel they are studying more efficiently and feel more confident taking exams. And both instructors and stu-

dents report that *ThomsonNOW* gets them the results they want FAST.

To get started with *ThomsonNOW*, log in at www.thomsonedu.com/login or if you need to purchase access, go to www.ichapters.com.

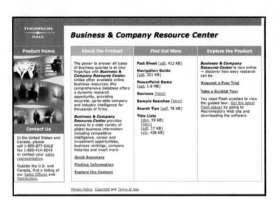

## Business & Company Resource Center (BCRC) Exercises

Boone & Kurtz keep you up to date and continually interacting with the business world by providing online exercises that point to current articles located in our BCRC. These exercises ask you to read the articles and answer questions, encouraging you to apply your knowledge of concepts to the ideas discussed in the article. When you purchase *ThomsonNOW* for the Boone & Kurtz text, you will automatically receive access to the BCRC database. This access allows you to apply concepts to real business articles while also opening up a database in which you can research a wide variety of global business information, including competitive intelligence, career and investment opportunities, business rankings, company histories, and much more. View a guided tour of the Business & Company Resource Center at http://www.gale.com/BusinessRC.

# Preface

Boone & Kurtz . . . continuing a legacy of excellence and MOVING BUSINESS FORWARD FASTER!

A part of every business is change; now more than ever, business moves at a pace that is unparalleled. Just like the ever-changing business world, so are there changes in the process of writing a textbook. This 12th edition of *Contemporary Business* is the first edition written without the collaboration of my longtime co-author, Louis E. (Gene) Boone. As with every good business, though, the patterns of innovation and excellence established at the beginning remain steadfast. The goals and standards of Boone & Kurtz, *Contemporary Business,* remain intact and focused on excellence, as always. I present to you a text and supplement package that will not only move your COURSE FORWARD FASTER but also move your STUDENTS FORWARD FASTER into the new business era.

**Moving instructors forward . . . faster.** This new edition's supplement package is designed to propel the instructor into the classroom with all the materials needed to engage students and help them understand text concepts. All the major teaching materials have been combined into one resource—the Instructor's Manual. While this might not sound revolutionary, good businesses know that the heart of the business is in its ability to keep track of all of its units. In the same way, our new Instructor's Manual combines all of the most important teaching materials into one stellar item. We've included collaborative learning exercises directly in the lecture outlines, so you'll know best where to use them. We've also included references to the Power-Point slides throughout the lecture notes for your convenience. The Second City Theater, Inc., our brand-new continuing case, is highlighted in all-new part videos, while chapter videos showcase a stellar list of companies, including standard-bearers such as BP Oil Company and companies doing business with a brand new set of ideals such as American Apparel. We've heard your appreciation for our PowerPoint presentations and have gone one step further: the PowerPoint presentations for this edition are tailored to meet the needs of all instructors, offering three versions: our Expanded collection, the Basic collection, and a student version available on our Web site. In addition, our new certified test bank, verified separately by two different sources, gives instructors that extra edge needed to drive home key concepts and ignite critical thinking, as well as confidence and assurance when creating and issuing tests. We also listened to your feedback and have incorporated more material on the business plan within the ThomsonNOW product. Past users will note that the new edition is less theme driven and designed to emphasize the very best concepts in the business world today.

**Moving students forward . . . faster.** With *contemporary* being the operative word, we've showcased a new, exciting company, The Second City Theater, Inc., a comedy corporation that has produced stars of *Saturday Night Live* and other comedy venues, such as John Belushi and Tina Fey—a company that students can really finding interesting! As always, every chapter is loaded with up-to-the-minute business issues and examples to enliven classroom discussion and debate, such as how Jones Soda is rebuilding and reorganizing its business as well as a completely new discussion on the Central American Free Trade Agreement (CAFTA), which President Bush signed in 2005. Processes, strategies, and procedures are brought to life through videos highlighting real companies and employees, an inventive business model, and collaborative learning exercises. And to further enhance the student learning process, we've developed an Introduction to Business–focused technology product, ThomsonNOW, that integrates personalized learning along with a research database of articles.

# HOW BOONE & KURTZ BECAME THE LEADING BRAND IN THE MARKET

For more than three decades, *Contemporary Business* has provided the latest in content and pedagogy. Our *current* editions have long been the model for our competitors' *next* editions. Consider Boone & Kurtz's proven record of providing instructors and students with pedagogical firsts:

- *Contemporary Business* was the first introductory business text written specifically for the student—rather than the instructor—featuring a motivational style students readily understood and enjoyed.
- *Contemporary Business* has always been based on marketing research, written the way instructors actually teach the course.
- *Contemporary Business* was the first text to integrate computer applications—and later, Internet assignments—into each chapter.
- *Contemporary Business* has always employed extensive pedagogy—such as opening vignettes and boxed features—to breathe life into the exciting concepts and issues facing contemporary business.
- *Contemporary Business* was the first business text to offer end-of-chapter video cases as well as end-of-part cases filmed by professional producers.
- *Contemporary Business* was the first to use multimedia technology to integrate all components of the Introduction to Business ancillary program, videos, and PowerPoint CD-ROMs for both instructors and students—enabling instructors to custom-create lively lecture presentations.

## Pedagogy

The 12th edition is packed with new pedagogical features to keep students interested and bring the text topics to life:

- Business Etiquette: The 12th edition contains a new box feature focusing on business etiquette, addressing the trend of more and more schools to add business etiquette to the curriculum.
- Assessment Checks: In every business department in the country, assessment and assurance of learning among students has become increasingly important. As a result, we've provided you with assessment checks after every main head in every chapter.
- New End-of-Chapter Self-Quizzes: In addition to ensuring that students are learning throughout the chapter, we've taken assessment one step further by incorporating new end-of-chapter self-quizzes called Review Questions. These questions are designed to quickly assess whether students understand the basic concepts in the chapter.
- Teamwork: Teamwork is at the core of every modern business's success, and today's student needs to be well trained on working in a team. To further prepare students to enter business and MOVE FORWARD FASTER, we've incorporated new teamwork exercises at the end of each chapter.
- NEW Launching Your Career: While students often have an amazing ability to understand chapter concepts and intellectually understand business and what a business career entails, they are very often unprepared to take the next step and understand in a real-life sense what a career in each aspect of business may involve. We've added a brand-new feature at the end of each part of the book that helps students understand how to launch a real business career for themselves.

# Continuing to Build the Boone & Kurtz Brand

Because the business world is constantly MOVING FORWARD FASTER, the Introduction to Business course must keep pace. Trends, strategies, and practices are constantly changing, and students must understand how to perform business in today's world.

You've come to trust *Contemporary Business* to cover every aspect of the business world with a critical but fair eye. Let's face it: there are best business practices and those we'd never want to repeat. However, both provide learning opportunities and we've always chosen to take a critical look at the way business is being done in the world and help students understand what they need to know in order to have a long and illustrious business career. Keeping this in mind, here are just a few of the important business trends and practices we've focused on for this new edition to help move students forward into a great business career:

- Launching Your Business Career (section preceding Chapter 1): This popular Boone & Kurtz feature has been revised to rely less on annual salary data than in the past, and instead concentrate on the lifetime value of education. Students in Introduction to Business courses must keep up with the newest trends and shifts in career fields. The 12th edition of *Contemporary Business* helps them answer the question, "Where do I fit in the business world?"
- Chapter 1 now includes information on outsourcing, offshoring, and nearshoring as a part of the discussion on the framework of business today.
- The discussion on business ethics in Chapter 2 has been completely reworked to provide a more relevant explanation of how businesses and individuals incorporate their beliefs and standards into everyday business as well as how the Sarbanes-Oxley Act is changing the very essence of reporting.
- International fiscal policy is a new concept for Chapter 3, which also explains the core inflation rate.
- CAFTA and the so-called Doha Round of trade negotiations are now discussed in Chapter 4.
- A discussion of college-based entrepreneurship programs has been added in Chapter 6.
- Given that today's students have grown up with the Internet, Chapter 7 has been substantially revised and now focuses on the business function of the Internet.
- Chapter 9 includes new coverage of cognitive ability tests, family-friendly benefits, and dependent-care spending as well as a new section on goal-setting theory and new information on the federal government's Pension Benefit Guaranty Corporation.
- Chapter 10 now covers problem-solving teams, action learning teams, team level, team diversity, cognitive conflict, and affective conflict and has a new section on crisis management, including the steps companies and managers should take when dealing with a public crisis regarding their organization.
- Chapter 11 now includes an explanation of the six-sigma concept.
- Chapter 12 includes the American Marketing Association's new definition of *marketing* and a short discussion of why the definition was changed.
- More in-depth coverage of the importance of good credit management, including the pros and cons of student loan consolidation, has been included in the personal finance appendix.

# The Second City Theater, Inc. Continuing Video Case

Almost no business started in 1959 can still say today that it moves business forward in a new and different way each day. You've come to expect only the best from us in choosing our continuing video case company, and we've taken it one step further with our new choice. No other company combines Second City Theater's unique brand of social and political satire with successful and proven business practices in the same way that has helped The Second City grow from a small but successful comedy troupe into a large international business. With several theaters in two countries, troupes performing every day all over the world, and performances on international cruise lines, The Second City has found a way to turn comedy into business—and in the process they've had fun! Students and instructors alike know and love many of the famous faces that started performing at Second City—John Belushi, Dan Aykroyd, John Candy, Gilda Radner, Chris Farley, Tina Fey, and the list goes on and on. But how many students realize just how important good business practices are in keeping a comedy business that started in 1959 thriving and growing all the way into 2007 and beyond? We've focused on all the aspects of The Second City Theater's business that students need to know in a way that's interesting and fun for them to learn. So sit back, get some popcorn, and enjoy the show!

Written case segments at the end of each part of the text contain critical-thinking questions designed to provoke discussion and interaction in the classroom setting. Answers to the questions can be found in the Instructor's Manual, as can a complete video synopsis, a list of text concepts covered in the videos, and even more critical-thinking exercises.

## End-of-Chapter Video Cases

In addition to a stellar new continuing video case, we've also produced a whole new batch of video cases for each and every chapter, designed to exceed your every expectation. Students need to know the basics about life in the real world of business and how businesses succeed and grow, but they don't need a bunch of talking heads putting them to sleep. So while we admit that you will indeed see a few talking heads—they're just there because they really do know what they're talking about—they have something important for students to hear. But do trust us . . . the videos we've created for this new edition of *Contemporary Business* contain so much more!

A complete set of written cases accompanies these chapter videos and can be found in the end-of-book video case appendix. The written segments contain discussion questions. As with the Second City cases, answers to the questions can be found in the Instructor's Manual, as can a complete video synopsis, a list of text concepts covered in the videos, and even more critical-thinking exercises. The video cases are as follows:

Chapter 1: Peet's Coffee & Tea Brews Good Business
Chapter 2: Ford Turns Green with Clean Energy
Chapter 3: BP Meets Global Energy Challenges Head-On
Chapter 4: Cold Stone Creamery Cools off Consumers around the World
Chapter 5: The UL Mark of Approval
Chapter 6: Culver's: Great Food from a Good Business
Chapter 7: Manifest Digital: Putting the User First
Chapter 8: Made in the USA: American Apparel
Chapter 9: Allstate Employees Are in Good Hands
Chapter 10: Meet the People of BP
Chapter 11: Washburn Guitars: Sound Since 1883
Chapter 12: Harley-Davidson: An American Icon Cruises into Its Second Century
Chapter 13: High Sierra Climbs to New Heights
Chapter 14: Wild Oats Promotes Local Foods
Chapter 15: Peet's Coffee & Tea: Just What the Customer Ordered
Chapter 16: Taking Account: The Little Guys
Chapter 17: JPMorganChase Lends a Hand to Small Business
Chapter 18: A.G. Edwards: Helping Business Grow

# THE CONTEMPORARY BUSINESS RESOURCE PACKAGE

Since the first edition of this book was published, Boone & Kurtz has exceeded the expectations of instructors, and it quickly became the benchmark for other texts. With its precedent-setting learning materials, *Contemporary Business* has continued to improve on its signature package features—equipping students and instructors with the most comprehensive collection of learning tools, teaching materials, and innovative resources available. As expected, the 12th edition continues to serve as the industry benchmark by delivering the most extensive, technologically advanced, user-friendly package on the market.

## For the Instructor

**ThomsonNOW (ISBN: 0–324–53974–6)**  Designed *by* instructors and students *for* instructors and students, ThomsonNOW gives you what you want to do, how you want to do it. ThomsonNOW is an integrated online suite of services and resources with proven ease of use and efficient paths to success, delivering the results you want—NOW! ThomsonNOW includes pre-populated homework, assessments with a personalized learning path, an e-book, and more. In the new edition of *Contemporary Business,* students will receive access to the Business Company and Resource Center automatically with their ThomsonNOW product, allowing them to answer homework questions and conduct research for their own projects.

**Instructor's Manual with Collaborative Learning Exercises and Media Guide (ISBN: 0–324–53664–X)**  The 12th edition of *Contemporary Business* has a new, extremely easy-to-use Instructor's Manual. This valuable tool completely integrates the various supplements and the text. A detailed lecture outline provides guidance about how to teach the chapter concepts. Collaborative learning exercises are included for each chapter, which give students a completely different way to apply chapter concepts to their own lives. References to the PowerPoint slides are included in the chapter outline. You'll also find answers to all of the end-of-chapter materials and various critical-thinking exercises. Full descriptions of the ThomsonNOW product and BCRC exercises can be found in the Media Guide along with complete video synopses, outlines, and extra questions.

**Chapter Video Cases on DVD (ISBN: 0–324–53659–3)**  New end-of-chapter video cases for every chapter of the text focus on successful real companies' processes, strategies, and procedures. Real employees explain real business situations with which they have been faced, bringing key concepts from the chapter to life.

**The Second City Theater, Inc. Continuing Case Video on DVD (ISBN: 0–324–53660–7)**  This brand-new continuing video case combines the entrepreneurial and creative spirit with which Second City was founded with the reality of a successful working business model. Rarely has a creative enterprise so uniquely brought real business savvy to its success. In these videos, we examine the history of the theater company as well as the successful business practices that have allowed for its expansion and growth. The written and video cases are divided into seven sections and are created to be used at the end of each part of the text.

**Test Bank (ISBN: 0–324–53665–8)**  Containing more than 4,000 questions, this is the most accurate test bank we've had in years. For the first time we've put our test bank through a complete verification process. Every question and answer has been read and reviewed for correctness. Each chapter of the test bank is organized by chapter objective, and each question is categorized by difficulty level, type of question, and text page reference, and has also been tagged for AACSB requirements.

### Basic and Expanded PowerPoint Presentations on CD (ISBN: 0–324–53662–3)

After reviewing competitive offerings, we are convinced that our PowerPoint presentations are the best you'll find. We offer two separate collections. The Basic PowerPoint collection contains 10 to 20 slides per chapter. This collection provides a basic outline of the chapter, with Web links that are used to bring chapter concepts to life. The Basic collection includes figures and tables from each chapter as well as teaching notes for instructors in the "Notes" view. The Expanded PowerPoint collection includes 20 to 40 slides per chapter and provides a complete overview of the chapter. The Expanded collection includes figures and tables from each chapter, Web links, video links, and teaching notes for instructors.

### Instructor's Resource CD (ISBN: 0–324–53661–5)

The IRCD includes electronic versions of all of the instructor supplements: Instructor's Manual, Collaborative Learning Exercises, Media Guide, Test Bank, and Examview Testing Files and Software.

### Examview Testing Software on IRCD (ISBN: 0–324–53663–1)

Examview Testing Software is a Windows-based software program that is both easy to use and attractive. We can say with confidence that this is the most accurate test bank we've had in years because it has been through our certification process and every question and answer has been verified. Each chapter of the test bank is organized by chapter objective, and each question is categorized by difficulty level, type of question, and text page reference, and has also been tagged for AACSB requirements.

### Contemporary Business, 12th Edition Web Site

Our text Web site (http://www.thomson edu.com/introbusiness/boone) is filled with a whole set of useful tools. Instructors will find all the key instructor resources in electronic format: Test Bank, Basic PowerPoint Presentations, Instructor's Manual with Collaborative Learning Exercises, Media Guide, and BCRC Exercises. Students will also find a host of valuable resources.

### Resource Integration Guide (RIG)

The RIG is written to provide the instructor with a clear and concise layout to all of the ancillaries that accompany the text as well as how best to use these items in teaching an Introduction to Business course. Not only are all of the book's ancillaries organized clearly for you, but we also provide planning suggestions, lecture ideas, and help in creating assignments. This guide will help instructors prepare for teaching the course, execute teaching plans, and evaluate student performance. The RIG can be found on the text Web site (http://www.thomsonedu.com/introbusiness/boone) in the Instructor's Resource section.

## For the Student

### ThomsonNOW (ISBN: 0–324–53974–6)

Designed *by* instructors and students *for* instructors and students, ThomsonNOW gives you what you want to do, how you want to do it. ThomsonNOW includes pre-populated homework, assessments with a personalized learning path, an e-book, and more. In the new edition of *Contemporary Business,* students will receive access to the Business Company and Resource Center automatically with their ThomsonNOW product, allowing them to answer homework questions and conduct research for their own projects.

**Contemporary Business, *12th Edition Web Site*** Our text Web site (http://www.thomsonedu.com/introbusiness/boone) is filled with a whole set of useful tools. Students will find a host of valuable resources, including key terms with definitions, quizzes for each chapter, chapter summaries in both English and Spanish, and recent business news tied directly to chapter concepts.

***Chapter Audio Reviews*** These audio reviews, provided on CD-ROM (and available on the Web site for download) contain short summaries of the chapter objectives and major concepts in each chapter and are a good review of reading assignments. Listen to them before you read the chapter as a preview of what's to come or after you read the chapter as a reinforcement of what you've read. Listen to them on the way to class as a refresher before the lecture or after you've left class as a review of what the instructor just discussed. However you choose to listen to them, these concise summaries will help reinforce all the major concepts for each chapter.

# ACKNOWLEDGMENTS

*Contemporary Business* has long benefited from the instructors who have offered their time as reviewers. Hundreds of people have contributed their suggestions over the years. I am most appreciative of their efforts and thoughts. Previous reviewers have included the following people:

Jamil Ahmad
*Los Angeles Trade–Technical College*

Sylvia Allen
*Los Angeles Valley College*

Kenneth F. Anderson
*Borough of Manhattan Community College*

Andrea Bailey
*Moraine Valley Community College*

Norman E. Burns
*Bergen Community College*

Diana Carmel
*Golden West College*

Barbara Ching
*Los Angeles City College*

Ron Colley
*South Suburban College*

Scott Colvin
*Naugatuck Community College*

Peter Dawson
*Collin County Community College*

Dr. Richard L. Drury
*Northern Virginia Community College*

John A. Fawcett
*Norwalk Community College*

Dr. Barry Freeman
*Bergen Community College*

Richard Ghidella
*Fullerton College*

Ross Gittell
*University of New Hampshire*

Clark Hallpike
*Elgin Community College*

Carnella Hardin
*Glendale College—Arizona*

Britt Hastey
*Los Angeles City College*

Dave Hickman
*Frederick Community College*

Nathan Himelstein
*Essex County College*

Scott Homan
*Purdue—West Lafayette*

Howard L. Irby, Jr.
*Bronx Community College*

Robert Ironside
*North Lake College*

Charlotte Jacobsen
*Montgomery College*

Bruce Johnson
*College of the Desert*

Judith Jones
*Norwalk Community College*

Marce Kelly
*Santa Monica College*

Gregory Kishel
*Cypress College—Santa Ana College*

Patricia Kishel
*Cypress College*

Andy Klein
*DeVry*

Mary Beth Klinger
*College of Southern Maryland*

John S. Leahy
*Palomar College*

Delores Linton
*Tarrant County College—Northwest Campus*

Stacy Martin
*Southwestern Illinois College*

Theresa Mastrianni
*Kingsborough Community College*

Bob Matthews
*Oakton Community College*

Hugh McCabe
*Westchester Community College*

Tricia McConville
*Northeastern University*

Rebecca Miles
*Delaware Tech*

Linda Morable
*Richland College*

Linda Mosley
*Tarrant County College*

Carol Murphy
*Quinsigamond Community College*

Andrew Nelson
*Montgomery College*

Greg Nesty
*Humboldt College*

Linda Newell
*Saddleback College*

Emmanuel Nkwenti
*Pennsylvania College of Technology*

Paul Okello
*Tarrant County College*

Lynn D. Pape
*Northern Virginia Community College—
Alexandria Campus*

Charles Pedersen
*Quinsigamond Community College*

John Pharr
*Cedar Valley—Dallas County Community
College District*

Jeff Podoshen
*DeVry*

Sally Proffitt
*Tarrant County College Northeast*

Jude A. Rathburn
*University of Wisconsin—Milwaukee*

Levi Richard
*Citrus College*

Joe Ryan
*Valley College*

Althea Seaborn
*Norwalk Community College*

John Seilo
*Orange Coast Community College*

Pat Setlik
*Harper College*

Richard Sherer
*Los Angeles Trade–Technical College*

Gerald Silver
*Purdue University—Calumet*

Leon Singleton
*Santa Monica College*

Malcolm Skeeter
*Norwalk Community College*

Robert Smolin
*Citrus College*

Darrell Thompson
*Mountain View College*

Sandra Toy
*Orange Coast College*

Phil Vardiman
*Abilene Christian University*

Sal Veas
*Santa Monica College*

Gina Vega
*Merrimack College*

Michelle Vybiral
*Joliet Junior College*

Rick Weidmann
*Prince George's Community College*

S. Martin Welc
*Saddleback College*

Steve Wong
*Rock Valley College*

A number of other colleagues at colleges and universities throughout the United States participated in focus group sessions. They provided invaluable recommendations for this new edition. They include the following people:

Greg Akins
*Lansing Community College*

Ken Anderson
*Boro of Manhattan Community College*

Nancy Bailey
*Middlesex Community College*

Mary Barnum
*Grand Rapids Community College*

Sherry Bell
*Ferris State University*

Ellen Benowitz
*Mercer Community College*

Mike Bento
*Owens Community College*

Pat Bernson
*County College of Morris*

Trudy Borst
*Ferris State University*

David Braun
*Pierce College*

David England
*John A. Logan College*

Barry Freeman
*Bergen Community College*

Eric Glohr
*Lansing Community College*

Karen Hawkins
*Miami Dade Community College*

Nate Himelstein
*Essex Community College*

Kim Hurns
*Washtenaw Community College*

Dmitriy Kalyagin
*Chabot College*

Elias Konwufine
*Keiser College*

Carl Kovelowski
*Mercer Community College*

Pierre Laguerre
*Bergen Community College*

Stacy Martin
*Southwestern Illinois College*

Duane Miller
*Utah Valley State College*

Ed Mitchell
*Hillsborough Community College*

Frank Novakowski
*Davenport University*

Tom Passero
*Owens Community College*

Tom Perkins
*Lansing Community College*

Robert Reck
*Western Michigan University*

Paul Ricker
*Broward Community College*

Jenny Rink
*Community College of Philadelphia*

Susan Roach
*Georgia Southern University*

Edith Strickland
*Tallahassee Community College*

Keith Taylor
*Lansing Community College*

Joyce Thompson
*Lehigh-Carbon Community College*

Bob Urell
*Irvine Valley College*

Richard Warner
*Lehigh-Carbon Community College*

David Woolgar
*Santa Ana College*

Chuck Zellerbach
*Orange Coast College*

Thanks also to all of our colleagues who have assisted us in previous editions in our continuing efforts to make the best business text even better. The new edition continues to reflect so many of their recommendations. Among the hundreds of reviewers and focus group participants who contributed to the book during previous editions, we acknowledge the special contributions of the following people:

Alison Adderly-Pitman
*Brevard Community College*

David Alexander
*Angelo State University*

Kenneth Anderson
*Mott Community College*

Charles Armstrong
*Kansas City Kansas Community College*

Donald B. Armstrong
*Mesa College*

Nathaniel Barber
*Winthrop University*

Alan Bardwick
*Community College of Aurora*

Keith Batman
*Cayuga Community College*

Robb Bay
*Community College of Southern Nevada*

Charles Beem
*Bucks County Community College*

Carol Bibly
*Triton College*

Daniel Biddlecom
*Erie Community College—North Campus*

Joseph Billingere
*Oxnard College*

Larry Blenke
*Sacramento City College*

Paula E. Bobrowski
*SUNY Oswego*

Charlane Bomrad Held
*Onandaga Community College*

Brenda Bradford
*Missouri Baptist College*

Steven E. Bradley
*Austin Community College*

Willie Caldwell
*Houston Community College*

Barney Carlson
*Yuba College*

Bonnie Chavez
*Santa Barbara City College*

Felipe Chia
*Harrisburg Area Community College*

Rowland Chidomere
*Winston-Salem State University*

Marie Comstock
*Allan Hancock College*

Ronald C. Cooley
*South Suburban College*

Suzanne Counte
*Jefferson College*

Robert Cox
*Salt Lake Community College*

Pam Crader
*Jefferson College*

Norman B. Cregger
*Central Michigan University*

Dana D'Angelo
*Drexel University*

Dean Danielson
*San Joaquin College*

Kathy Daruty
*Los Angeles Pierce College*

David DeCook
*Arapahoe Community College*

Richard L. Drury
*Northern Virginia Area Community College—Annandale*

Linda Durkin
*Delaware County Community College*

Lance J. Edwards
*Otero Junior College*

William Ewald
*Concordia University*

Carol Fasso
*Jamestown Community College*

Jodson Faurer
*Metropolitan State College at Denver*

Jan Feldbauer
*Austin Community College*

Sandie Ferriter
*Harford Community College*

Steven H. Floyd
*Manatee Community College*

Nancy M. Fortunato
*Bryant and Stratton*

John G. Foster Jr.
*Montgomery College—Rockville*

William D. Foster
*Fontbonne College*

Blane Franckowiak
*Tarrant County Community College*

Edward Friese
*Okaloosa-Walton Community College*

Atlen Gastineau
*Valencia Community College—West Campus*

Milton Glisson
*North Carolina A&T State University*

Bob Googins
*Shasta Community College*

Robert Gora
*Catawba Valley Community College*

Don Gordon
*Illinois Central College*

Gary Greene
*Manatee Community College*

Blaine Greenfield
*Bucks County Community College*

Stephen W. Griffin
*Tarrant County Community College*

Maria Carmen Guerrero-Caldero
*Oxnard College*

Annette L. Halpin
*Beaver College*

Michael Hamberger
*Northern Virginia Area Community College—Annandale*

Neal Hannon
*Bryant College*

Douglas Heeter
*Ferris State University*

Paul Hegele
*Elgin Community College*

Chuck Henry
*Coastline Community College*

Thomas Herbek
*Monroe Community College*

Tom Heslin
*Indiana University, Bloomington*

Joseph Ho
*College of Alameda*

Alice J. Holt
*Benedict College*

Vince Howe
*University of North Carolina, Wilmington*

Eva M. Hyatt
*Appalachian State University*

Kathy Irwin
*Catawba Valley Community College*

Gloria M. Jackson
*San Antonio College*

Ralph Jagodka
*Mount San Antonio College*

Chris Jelepis
*Drexel University*

Steven R. Jennings
*Highland Community College*

Geraldine Jolly
*Barton College*

Dave Jones
*LaSalle University*

Don Kelley
*Francis Marion University*

Bill Kindsfather
*Tarrant County Community College*

Charles C. Kitzmiller
*Indian River Community College*

B. J. Kohlin
*Pasadena City College*

Carl Kovelowski
*Mercer Community College*

Ken Lafave
*Mount San Jacinto College*

Rex Lambrecht
*Northeastern Junior College*

Fay D. Lamphear
*San Antonio College*

Bruce Leppine
*Delta College*

Thomas Lloyd
*Westmoreland County Community College*

Jim Locke
*Northern Virginia Area Community College—Annandale*

Paul Londrigan
*Mott Community College*

Kathleen J. Lorencz
*Oakland County Community College*

John Mack
*Salem State College*

Paul Martin
*Aims College*

Lori Martynowicz
*Bryant and Stratton*

Michael Matukonis
*SUNY Oneonta*

Virginia Mayes
*Montgomery College—Germantown*

Joseph E. McAloon
*Fitchburg State College*

James McKee
*Champlain College*

Michael McLane
*University of Texas, San Antonio*

Ina Midkiff
*Austin Community College*

Rebecca Mihelcic
*Howard Community College*

Richard Miller
*Harford Community College*

Joseph Mislivec
*Central Michigan University*

Kimberly K. Montney
*Kellogg Community College*

Gail Moran
*Harper College*

Linda S. Munilla
*Georgia Southern University*

Kenneth R. Nail
*Pasco-Hernando Community College*

Joe Newton
*Buffalo State College*

Janet Nichols
*Northeastern University*

Frank Nickels
*Pasco-Hernando Community College*

Sharon Nickels
*St. Petersburg Junior College*

Nnamdi I. Osakwe
*Livingstone College*

Tibor Osatreicher
*Baltimore City Community College*

George Otto
*Truman College*

Thomas Paczkowski
*Cayuga Community College*

Alton Parish
*Tarrant County Community College*

Jack Partlow
*Northern Virginia Area Community College—Annandale*

Jeff Penley
*Catawba Valley Community College*

Robert Pollero
*Anne Arundel Community College*

Alton J. Purdy
*Solano Community College*

Surat P. Puri
*Barber Scottia College*

Angela Rabatin
*Prince George's Community College*

Linda Reynolds
*Sacramento City College*

Brenda Rhodes
*Northeastern Junior College*

Merle Rhodes
*Morgan Community College*

Pollis Robertson
*Kellogg Community College*

Robert Ross
*Drexel University*

Benjamin Sackmary
*Buffalo State College*

Catherina A. Sanders
*San Antonio College*

Lewis Schlossinger
*Community College of Aurora*

Gene Schneider
*Austin Community College*

Raymond Shea
*Monroe Community College*

Nora Jo Sherman
*Houston Community College*

Leon J. Singleton
*Santa Monica College*

Jeff Slater
*North Shore Community College*

Candy Smith
*Folsom Lakes College*

Solomon A. Solomon
*Community College of Rhode Island*

R. Southall
*Laney College*

Martin St. John
*Westmoreland County Community College*

E. George Stook
*Anne Arundel Community College*

James B. Stull
*San Jose State University*

Bill Syverstein
*Fresno City College*

Thomas Szezurek
*Delaware County Community College*

Daryl Taylor
*Pasadena City College*

John H. Teter
*St. Petersburg Junior College*

Gary Thomas
*Anne Arundel Community College*

Michael Thomas
*Henry Ford Community College*

Frank Titlow
*St. Petersburg Junior College*

Roland Tollefson
*Anne Arundel Community College*

Sheb True
*Loyola Marymount University*

Robert Ulbrich
*Parkland College*

Ariah Ullman
*SUNY Binghamton*

Sal Veas
*Santa Monica College*

Steven Wade
*Santa Clara University*

Dennis Wahler
*San Jacinto Evergreen Community College District*

W. J. Walters
*Central Piedmont Community College*

Timothy Weaver
*Moorpark College*

Richard Wertz
*Concordia University*

Darcelle D. White
*Eastern Michigan University*

Jean G. Wicks
*Bornie State University*

Tom Wiener
*Iowa Central Community College*

Dave Wiley
*Anne Arundel Community College*

Richard J. Williams
*Santa Clara University*

Joyce Wood
*Northern Virginia Community College*

Gregory Worosz
*Schoolcraft College*

Martha Zennis
*Jamestown Community College*

## Special Acknowledgment

With Gene Boone's passing, I reached out to two experienced textbook authors for help in getting this edition out on time. I am grateful that Douglas Hearth of the University of Arkansas and Chuck Williams of the University of the Pacific were willing to lend their considerable expertise to this project.

Doug and Chuck have each written their own successful books in finance and management. Their writing and editorial skills blended perfectly with the approach that Gene Boone and I have always employed. I am very appreciative of their efforts.

## In Conclusion

I would like to thank Karen Hill of Elm Street Publishing and Katie O'Keeffe-Swank of Lachina Publishing Services. Their unending efforts on behalf of *Contemporary Business* were truly extraordinary.

Let me conclude by noting that this new edition would never have become a reality without the outstanding efforts of the Thomson editorial, production, and marketing teams. My editors Melissa Acuna, Neil Marquardt, Erin Joyner, Rebecca von Gillern, Amy Hackett, and Vicky True produced another *Contemporary Business* winner!

Dave Kurtz

# About the Author

During Dave Kurtz's high school days, no one in Salisbury, Maryland, would have mistaken him for a scholar. In fact, he was a mediocre student, so bad that his father steered him toward higher education by finding him a succession of backbreaking summer jobs. Thankfully, most of them have been erased from his memory, but a few linger, including picking peaches, loading watermelons on trucks headed for market, and working as a pipefitter's helper. Unfortunately, these jobs had zero impact on his academic standing. Worse yet for Dave's ego, he was no better than average as a high school athlete in football and track.

But four years at Davis & Elkins College in Elkins, West Virginia, turned him around. Excellent instructors helped get Dave on a sound academic footing. His grade point average soared—enough to get him accepted by the graduate business school at the University of Arkansas, where he met Gene Boone. Gene and Dave became longtime co-authors; together they produced more than 50 books. In addition to writing, Dave and Gene were involved in several entrepreneurial ventures.

Today, Dave is back teaching at the University of Arkansas, after tours of duty in Ypsilanti, Michigan; Seattle, Washington; and Melbourne, Australia. He is the proud grandfather of five "perfect" kids and a sportsman with a golf handicap too high to mention. Dave, his wife, Diane, and four demanding canine companions (Daisy, Lucy, Molly, and Sally) live in Rogers, Arkansas. Dave holds a distinguished professorship at the Sam M. Walton College of Business in nearby Fayetteville, home of the Arkansas Razorbacks.

# Brief Contents

# Contents

## Chapter 6

## STARTING YOUR OWN BUSINESS: THE ENTREPRENEURSHIP ALTERNATIVE

# Part 3

## Chapter 9

## Chapter 10

# IMPROVING PERFORMANCE THROUGH EMPOWERMENT, TEAMWORK, AND COMMUNICATION    318

## Chapter 11

# PRODUCTION AND OPERATIONS MANAGEMENT    344

# Part 4

## Marketing Management — 377

### Chapter 12

## CUSTOMER-DRIVEN MARKETING — 378

**Opening Vignette**
Whole Foods Market: A
Whole New Kind of
Grocery Store 379

**Hit & Miss**
One Company Makes a
Cereal Killing 384

**Hit & Miss**
Marketers Fall Short
When It Comes to Older
Consumers 395

**Solving an Ethical
Controversy**
Are Gift Cards
Really a Gift? 400

**Business Etiquette**
Thank-You Notes
Do Count 401

# Part 5

## Managing Technology and Information   481

### Chapter 15

## USING TECHNOLOGY TO MANAGE INFORMATION   482

## Chapter 16

## Part 6

## Chapter 17

# Launching Your Business Career

You'll be hitting the job market soon—if you haven't already. Regardless of what industry you want to work in—financial services, marketing, travel, construction, hospitality, manufacturing, wireless communications—you need an education. Attending college and taking a business course like this one gives you an edge because business skills and knowledge are needed in many different fields. But education comes in many forms. In addition to taking classes, you should try to gain related experience, through either a job or participation in campus organizations. Cooperative-education programs, internships, or work-study programs can also give you hands-on experience while you pursue your education. These work experiences will often set you apart from other job seekers in the eyes of recruiters or human resources professionals—people who hire employees.

Every one of you will be responsible for making a living once you leave school. Education influences that, as well. As a graduate with an associate's or bachelor's degree, over your lifetime of work, you will earn between 40 and 80 percent more than someone with a high school degree. That translates to about $500,000 (for an associate's degree) and $1 million (for a bachelor's degree) in your bank account over a lifetime. If you go on for an advanced degree, the figure could double to $2 million.[1] However, keep in mind that while a degree may help you get in the door for certain job interviews and may put you on a path for advancement, it doesn't guarantee success; you have to achieve that yourself.

Companies plan their hiring strategies carefully in order to attract and keep the most productive, creative employees and avoid the cost of rehiring. So soon-to-be graduates still need to be on their toes. But creativity has never been in short supply among business students, and by the time you finish this class—and college—you will be well equipped to take on the challenge. You'll be able to think of your hunt for employment as a course in itself, at the end of which you will have a job. And you will be on your way toward a rewarding business career.

During the next few months you will be introduced to all the functional areas of business. You will learn how firms are organized and operated. You'll find out who does what in a company. Gradually you will identify industries and disciplines—such as sales, finance, or product design—that interest you. And you'll learn about many organizations, large and small—who founded them, what products they offer, how they serve their customers, and what types of decisions they make.

Choosing a career is an important life decision. It sets you on a path that will influence where you live, how much money you earn, what type of people you encounter, and what you do every day. And whether your goal is to operate an organic farm or to rise high in the ranks of a major corporation, you'll need to understand the principles of business. Even if you think you're headed down a different

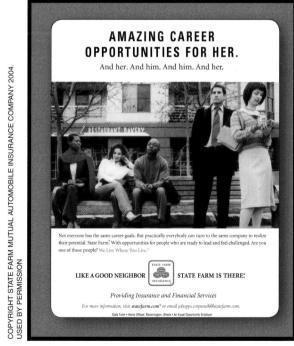

No matter what career you choose, you need an education. State Farm Insurance tells students from diverse backgrounds that it values their contribution to its company.

path, business skills may prove to be important. Consider the $40 billion biotech industry. "Scientists often underestimate the importance of business skills," notes a professional in the biotech field.[2] That's why *Contemporary Business* begins by discussing the best way to approach career decisions and to prepare for an *entry-level job*—your first permanent employment after leaving school. We then look at a range of business careers and discuss employment opportunities in a variety of fields.

## INTERNSHIPS—A GREAT WAY TO ACQUIRE REAL-WORLD EXPERIENCE

Many business students complete one or more *internships* prior to completing their academic careers. Some arrange internships during the summer, while others work at them during a semester away from college. An internship gives you hands-on experience in a real business environment, whether it's in banking, the hotel industry, or retailing. Not only does an internship teach you how a business runs, but it can also help you decide whether you want to pursue a career in a particular industry. You might spend a summer interning in the admissions department of a hospital and then graduate with your job search focused on hospital administration. Or you might decide you'd much rather work for a magazine publisher or a construction company.

When you apply for an internship, don't expect to be paid much, if at all. The true value of an internship lies in its hands-on experience. An internship bridges the theory-practice educational gap. It will help carry you from your academic experience to your professional future. Also keep in mind that, as an intern, you will not be running the company. People may not ask for your input or ideas. You may work in the warehouse or copy center, at least for a while. But it is important to make the most of your internship. Because many companies make permanent job offers—or offers to enter paid training programs—to impressive interns, you'll want to stand out. Start your professional attitude now. Here are some tips for a successful internship experience. These guidelines are also helpful for your first job.

- *Dress like a professional.* Dress appropriately for your future career. During an interview visit, look around to see what employees are wearing. If you have any questions, ask your supervisor.
- *Act like a professional.* Arrive on time to work. Be punctual for any meetings or assignments. Ask questions and listen to the answers carefully. Complete your work thoroughly and on time. Maintain good etiquette on the phone, in meetings, and in all interactions with other people.
- *Stand out.* Work hard and show initiative, but behave appropriately. Don't try to use authority that you do not have. Show that you are willing to learn.
- *Be evaluated.* Even if your internship does not include a formal evaluation, ask your employer how you are doing to learn about your strengths and weaknesses.
- *Keep in touch.* Once you complete your internship, stay in touch periodically with the firm so people know what you are currently doing.

Internships can serve as critical networking and job-hunting tools. In many instances, they lead to future employment opportunities, allowing students to demonstrate technical proficiency while providing cost-effective employee training for the company. According to a survey by the National Association of Colleges and Employers, 80 percent of employers say they hire recent grads with internship or co-op experience.[3] An excellent source of information about the nation's outstanding internships can be found at your local bookstore—*America's*

*Top 100 Internships* by Mark Oldman and Samer Hamadeh. New editions are published annually by Villard Books.

In addition to an internship, you can build your résumé with work and life experience through volunteer opportunities, extracurricular activities, and summer or off-campus study programs.

# SELF-ASSESSMENT FOR CAREER DEVELOPMENT

You are going to spend a lot of time during your life working, so why not find a job—or at least an industry—that interests you? To choose the line of work that suits you best, you must first understand yourself. Self-assessment involves looking in the mirror and seeing the real you—with all your strengths and weaknesses. It means answering some tough questions. But being honest with yourself pays off because it will help you find a career that is challenging, rewarding, and meaningful to you. As you get to know yourself better, you may discover that helping other people really makes you happy. You may realize that to feel secure, you need to earn enough to put away substantial savings. Or you might learn that you are drawn to risks and the unknown, characteristics that might point you toward owning your own business someday. Each of these discoveries provides you with valuable information in choosing a career.

Many resources are available to help you in selecting a career. They include school libraries, career guidance and placement offices, counseling centers, and online job-search services. They include alumni from your college, as well as friends, family, and neighbors. Don't forget the contacts you make during an internship—they can help you in many ways. Ask questions of anyone you know—a shopkeeper, banker, or restaurant owner. Most people will be happy to speak with you or arrange a time to do so.

If you are interested in a particular industry or company, you might be able to arrange an informational interview—an appointment with someone who can provide you with more knowledge about an industry or career path. This type of interview is different from one that follows your application for a specific job, although it may ultimately lead to that. The informational interview can help you decide whether you want to pursue a particular avenue of employment. It also gives you some added experience in the interview process—without the pressure. To arrange an interview, tap anyone you know—friends of your parents, local businesspeople, or coordinators of not-for-profit organizations. Colleges often have databases of graduates working in various fields who are willing to talk with students on an informational basis, so be sure to start your search right at your own school.

## The Self-Assessment Process

For a thorough assessment of your goals and interests, follow these steps:

1. *Outline your career interests.* What field or work activities interest you? What rewards do you want to gain from work?
2. *Outline your career goals.* What do you want to achieve through your career? What type of job can you see yourself doing? Where do you see yourself in a year? In five years? Do you have an ultimate dream job? How long are you willing to work to reach it? Write your goals down so you can refer to them later.
3. *Make plans to reach your goal.* Do you need more education? Does it require an apprenticeship or a certain number of years on the job? Write down the requirements you'll need to meet in order to reach your goal.

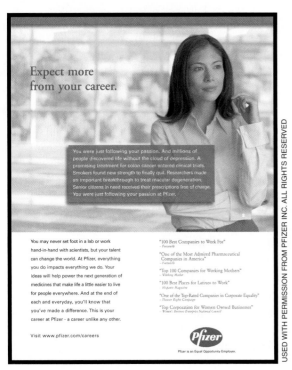

Expect more from your career.

You were just following your passion. And millions of people discovered life without the cloud of depression. A promising treatment for colon cancer entered clinical trials. Smokers found new strength to finally quit. Researchers made an important breakthrough to treat macular degeneration. Senior citizens in need received their prescriptions free of charge. You were just following your passion at Pfizer.

You may never set foot in a lab or work hand-in-hand with scientists, but your talent can change the world. At Pfizer, everything you do impacts everything we do. Your ideas will help power the next generation of medicines that make life a little easier to live for people everywhere. And at the end of each and everyday, you'll know that you've made a difference. This is your career at Pfizer - a career unlike any other.

Visit www.pfizer.com/careers

"100 Best Companies to Work For"
- Fortune®

"One of the Most Admired Pharmaceutical Companies in America"
- Fortune®

"Top 100 Companies for Working Mothers"
- Working Mother

"100 Best Places for Latinos to Work"
- Hispanic Magazine

"One of the Top-Rated Companies in Corporate Equality"
- Human Rights Campaign

"Top Corporation for Women Owned Businesses"
- Women's Business Enterprise National Council

**Pfizer**

Pfizer is an Equal Opportunity Employer.

Find a job—or an industry— that you would love as a start to your career search. Pfizer discusses some of the breakthrough medicines that were developed by people who were passionate about solving health problems.

4. ***List your skills and specific talents.*** Write down your strengths— job skills you already have, as well as skills you have developed in life. For instance, you might know how to operate financial software, and you might be good at negotiating with people. In addition, your school's career development office probably has standardized tests that can help determine your aptitude for specific careers. However, take these only as a guideline. If you really want to pursue a certain career, go for it.

5. ***List your weaknesses.*** This can be tough—it can also be fun. If you are shy about meeting new people, put shyness on your list. If you are quick to argue, admit it. If you aren't the best business letter writer or think you're terrible at math, confess to yourself. This list gives you an opportunity to see where you need improvement—and take steps to turn weaknesses into strengths.

6. ***Briefly sketch out your educational background.*** Write down the schools, colleges, and special training programs you have attended, along with any courses you plan to complete before starting full-time employment. Make a candid assessment of how your background matches up with the current job market. Then make plans to complete any further education you may need.

7. ***List the jobs you have held.*** Include jobs that paid, internships, and volunteer opportunities. They all gave you valuable experience. As you make your list, think about what you liked and disliked about each. Maybe you liked working with the general public as a supermarket cashier. Perhaps you enjoyed caring for animals at a local shelter.

8. ***Consider your hobbies and personal interests.*** Many people have turned hobbies and personal pursuits into rewarding careers. Jake Burton Carpenter earned a bachelor's degree in economics, but he loved winter sports. So he started a snowboard manufacturing company. Bonnie Kelly and Teresa Walsh turned their passion for sterling silver jewelry into a successful direct-sales company featuring the jewelry they love, called Silpada Designs.[4]

## **"They Said It"**

"The best career advice given to the young is, 'Find out what you like doing best and get someone to pay you for doing it.'"
—Katharine Whitehorn
(b. 1926)
British columnist

# JOB SEARCH GUIDELINES

Once you have narrowed your choice of career possibilities to two or three that seem right for you, get your job search under way. Because the characteristics that made these career choices attractive to you are also likely to catch the attention of other job-seekers, you must expect competition. Locate available positions that interest you; then be resourceful! Your success depends on gathering as much information as possible.

## Register at Your Career Center

Register at your school's career center. Establish an applicant file, including letters of recommendation and supporting personal information. Most placement offices send out periodic lists of new job vacancies by e-mail, so be sure to get your name and e-mail address on the list. Visit the office regularly and become a familiar face. Find out how the office arranges interviews with company representatives who visit campus. If your school has a career-oriented event, be sure to attend.

## Preparing Your Job Credentials

Most placement or credential files include the following information:

1. Letters of reference from people who know you well—instructors and employers
2. Transcripts of course work to date
3. Personal data form to report factual information
4. Statement of career goals

The career center will provide you with special forms to help you to develop your file. Often these forms can be completed online. Prepare the forms carefully, because employers are always interested in your written communication skills. Keep a copy of the final file for later use in preparing similar information for other employment sources. Check back with the career center to make sure your file is in order and update it whenever necessary to reflect additional academic accomplishments and work experiences.

Letters of reference are very important, because they give prospective employers both personal and professional insights about you. They can influence a hiring decision. So make a careful list of people who might be willing to write letters of reference. Your references should not be family members or close friends. Instead, choose a coach, an instructor, a former employer, or someone else whose knowledge could contribute to your job application. A soccer coach could vouch for your hard work and determination. A music teacher might be able to detail how well you accept instruction. A former employer might describe your punctuality and ability to get along with others. If possible, include someone from your school's business faculty on your list of references, or at least one of your current instructors.

Always ask people personally for letters of reference. Be prepared to give them brief outlines of your academic preparation, along with information about your job interests and career goals. This information will help them prepare their letters quickly and efficiently. It also shows that you are serious about the task and respect their time. Remember, however, that these people are very busy. Allow them at least a couple of weeks to prepare their reference letters; then follow up politely on missing ones. Always call or write to thank them for writing the letters.

## Finding Employment through the Internet

The Internet plays an important role in connecting employers and job seekers. Companies of all sizes post their job opportunities on the Web, both on their own sites and on job sites such as Monster.com and HotJobs .com. Some sites are free to applicants, while others charge a subscription fee. Figure 1 provides a sampling of general and more focused career sites.

Career Web sites typically offer job postings, tips on creating an effective résumés, a place to post your résumé, and advice on interviews and careers. If this sounds easy,

**Figure 1**

Internet Job Sites

**General**

Monster.com

HotJobs.com

**Industry or Employer Focused**

USAJOBS and Federaljobs.com—job listings by the federal government

eFinancialCareers.com—jobs in the financial industry

WomensJobList.com and WomenSportsJobs.com—listings open to both men and women

Recruiting.com and hrcareerpage.com—jobs in human resources

SalesJobs.com—jobs in sales

Msajobs.com and MedZilla.com—sales jobs in the medical and biotechnical industries

Technicalsalesjobsblog.com—jobs in computers and telecommunications

**Source:** Sarah E. Needleman, "Pounding the Pavement on Wall Street, Virtually," *CollegeJournal*, accessed May 26, 2006, http://www.collegejournal.com.

keep in mind that these sites may receive hundreds of thousands of hits each day from job hunters, which means you have plenty of competition. This doesn't mean you shouldn't use one of these sites as part of your job search; just don't make it your sole source. Savvy job seekers often find that their time is better spent zeroing in on niche boards offering more focused listings. Naturally, if a particular company interests you, go to the firm's Web site, where available positions may be posted. If you are interested in Timberland, visit the firm's site at http://www.timberland.com; if you want a job at energy giant Southern Company, go to http://www.southerncompany.com.

Newspapers, the source for traditional classified want ads, also post their ads on the Web. Job seekers can even visit sites that merge ads from many different newspapers into one searchable database, such as CareerPath (http://www.careerbuilder.com). Some sites go a step further and create separate sections for each career area. For example, entire sections may be devoted to accounting, marketing, and other business professions. Searches can then be narrowed according to geographic location, entry level, company name, job title, job description, and other categories.

As mentioned earlier, you can connect with potential employers by posting your résumé on job sites. Employers search the résumé database for prospects with the right qualifications. One commonly used approach is for an employer to list one or more *keywords* to select candidates for personal interviews—for example, "field sales experience," "network architecture," or "auditing"—and then browse the résumés that contain all the required keywords. Employers also scan résumés into their human resources database, and then when a manager requests, say, ten candidates, the database is searched by keywords that have been specified as part of the request. Job seekers can respond to this computer screening of applicants by making sure that relevant keywords appear on their résumés.

The *Contemporary Business* Web site hosts a comprehensive job and career assistance section. The site is updated frequently to include the best job and career sites for identifying and landing the career you want, as well as current strategies for getting the best results from your Web-based career-search activities.

## Finding Employment through Other Sources

We've already mentioned the importance of registering at your college's career planning or placement office. If you have completed formal academic coursework at more than one institution, you may be able to set up a placement file at each. In addition, you may want to contact private and public employment services available in your location or in the area where you would like to live.

### Private Employment Agencies

These firms often specialize in certain types of jobs—such as marketing, finance, sales, or engineering—offering services for both employers and job candidates that are not available elsewhere. Many private agencies interview, test, and screen job applicants so that potential employers do not have to do so. Job candidates benefit from the service by being accepted by the agency and because the agency makes the first contact with the potential employer.

A private employment agency usually charges the prospective employer a fee for finding a suitable employee. Other firms charge job seekers a fee for helping find them a job. Be sure that you understand the terms of any agreement you sign with a private employment agency.

### State Employment Offices

Don't forget to check the employment office of your state government. Remember that in many states, these public agencies process unemployment compensation applications along with other related work. Because of the mix of duties, some people view state employment agencies as providing services for semiskilled or unskilled workers. However, these agencies *do* list jobs in many professional categories and are often intimately involved with identifying job finalists for major new facilities moving to your state. In addition, many of the jobs listed at state employment offices may be with state or federal government agencies and may include professionals, such as accountants, attorneys, health-care professionals engineers, and scientists.

## Learning More about Job Opportunities

Carefully study the various employment opportunities you have identified. Obviously, you will like some more than others, but you can examine a variety of factors when assessing each job possibility:

- Actual job responsibilities
- Industry characteristics
- Nature of the company
- Geographic location
- Salary and opportunities for advancement
- Contribution of the job to your long-range career objectives

Too many job applicants consider only the most striking features of a job, perhaps its location or the salary offer. However, a comprehensive review of job openings should provide a balanced perspective of the overall employment opportunity, including both long-run and short-run factors.

# BUILDING A RÉSUMÉ

Regardless of how you locate job openings, you must learn how to prepare and submit a *résumé*, a written summary of your personal, educational, and professional achievements. The résumé is a personal document covering your educational background, work experience, career preferences and goals, and major interests that may be relevant. It also includes such basic information as your postal address, e-mail address, and telephone number. It should *not* include information on your age, marital status, race, or ethnic background.

Your résumé is usually your formal introduction to an employer, so it should present you in the best light, accentuating your strengths and potential to contribute to a firm as an employee. However, it should *never* contain embellishments or inaccuracies. You don't want to begin your career with unethical behavior, and an employer is bound to discover any discrepancies in fact—either immediately or during the months following your employment. Either event typically results in short-circuiting your career path.

## Organizing Your Résumé

The primary purpose of a résumé is to highlight your qualifications for a job, usually on a single page. An attractive layout facilitates the employer's review of your qualifications. You can prepare your résumé in several ways. You

TOM STRICKLAND/BLOOMBERG NEWS/LANDOV

Identifying your skills is an important step to locating a great job. RadioShack notifies prospective job seekers that it is looking for people who value teamwork, pride, trust, and integrity for its Sales Management program in its retail chain.

**Figure**

**2** Chronological Résumé

**FELICIA SMITH-WHITEHEAD**
4265 Popular Lane
Cleveland, Ohio 44120
216-555-3296
Felicia_SW@aol.com

**OBJECTIVE**

Challenging office management position in a results-oriented company where my organizational and people skills can be applied; leading to an operations management position.

**WORK EXPERIENCE**

*ADM Distribution Enterprises, Cleveland, Ohio*                                    2006–Present
Office Manager of leading regional soft-drink bottler. Coordinate all bookkeeping, correspondence, scheduling of 12-truck fleet to serve 300 customers, promotional mailings, and personnel records, including payroll. Install computerized systems.

*Merriweather, Hicks & Bradshaw Attorneys, Columbus, Ohio*                         2004–2006
Office Supervisor and Executive Assistant for Douglas H. Bradshaw, Managing Partner. Supervised four clerical workers and two paraprofessionals, automated legal research and correspondence functions, and assisted in coordinating outside services and relations with other firms and agencies. Promoted three times from Secretary to Office Supervisor.

*Conner & Sons Custom Coverings, Cleveland, Ohio*                                  2000–2004
Secretary in father's upholstery and awning company. Performed all office functions over the years, running the office when the owner was on vacation.

**EDUCATION**

Mill Valley High School, Honors                                                     2000
McBundy Community College, Associate's Degree in Business                           2004

**COMPUTER SKILLS**

Familiar with Microsoft Office and Adobe Acrobat

**LANGUAGE SKILLS**

Fluent in Spanish (speaking and writing)
Adequate speaking and writing skills in Portuguese

**PERSONAL**

Member of various community associations; avid reader; enjoy sports such as camping and cycling; enjoy volunteering in community projects.

---

may use narrative sentences to explain job duties and career goals, or you may present information in outline form. A résumé included as part of your credentials file at the career center on campus should be quite short. Remember to design it around your specific career objectives.

Figures 2, 3, and 4 illustrate different ways to organize your résumé—by *reverse chronology*, or time; by *function*; and by *results*. Regardless of which format you select, you will want to include the following: a clearly stated objective, your work or professional experience, your education, your personal interests such as sports or music, and your volunteer work. While all three formats are acceptable, one study showed that 78 percent of employers preferred the reverse chronological format—with the most recent experience listed first—because it was easiest to follow.

## Tips for Creating a Strong Résumé

Your résumé should help you stand out from the crowd, just as your college admissions application did. A company may receive hundreds or even thousands of résumés, so you want yours to be on the top of the stack. Here are some do's and don'ts from the pros:

*Do:*

- State your objective clearly. If you are applying for a specific job, say so. State why you want the job and why you want to work at this particular company.
- Use terms related to your field, so that an electronic scanner—or busy human resources manager—can locate them quickly.
- Provide facts about previous jobs, internships, or volunteer work, including results or specific achievements. Include any projects or tasks you undertook through your own initiative.
- Highlight your strengths and skills.
- Write clearly and concisely. Keep your résumé to a single page.
- Proofread your résumé carefully.[5]

Figure

3

## Don't:

- Offer any misleading or inaccurate information.
- Make vague statements, such as "I work well with others," or "I want a position in business."
- Include a salary request.
- Make unreasonable demands.
- Highlight your weaknesses.
- Submit a résumé with typos or grammatical errors.
- Include pictures or graphics, or use fancy type fonts.[6]

Take your time with your résumé; it is one of the most important documents you'll create during your career. If you need help, go to your school's career center. If you are dealing with an employment agency, a counselor there should be able to help as well.

Keep in mind that you will probably have to modify your résumé at times to tailor it to a particular company or job. Again, take the time to do this; it may mean the difference between standing out and being lost in a sea of other applicants.

## Preparing Your Cover Letter

In most cases, your résumé will be accompanied by a *cover letter*. This letter should introduce you, explain why you are submitting a résumé (cite the specific job opening if possible), and let the recipient know where you can be reached for an interview. An effective cover letter will make the recipient want to take the next step and read your résumé. Here are a few tips for preparing an outstanding letter:

**Functional Résumé**

Enrique Garcia
Five Oceanside Drive, Apt. 6B
Los Angeles, CA 90026
215-555-7092
EGARCIA@hotmail.com

**OBJECTIVE**

Joining a growth-oriented company that values highly productive employees. Seeking an opportunity that leads to a senior merchandising position.

**PROFESSIONAL EXPERIENCE**

*Administration*
Management responsibilities in a major retailing buying office; coordinated vendor-relation efforts. Supervised assistant buyers.

*Category Management*
Experience in buying home improvement, and sport and recreation categories.

*Planning*
Chaired a team charged with reviewing the company's annual vendor evaluation program.

*Problem Solving*
Successfully developed a program to improve margins in the tennis, golf, and fishing lines.

**WORK EXPERIENCE**

| | |
|---|---|
| Senior Buyer for Southern California Department Stores | 2005–Present |
| Merchandiser for Pacific Discount Stores, a division of Southern California Department Stores | 2003–2005 |

**EDUCATION**

| | |
|---|---|
| *Bachelor's Degree* California State University—San Bernardino | 2001–2003 |
| *Associate's Degree* Los Angeles City College | 1999–2001 |

- Write the letter to a specific person, if possible. A letter addressed "to whom it may concern" may never reach the right person. Call the company or check its Web site for the name of the person to whom you should send your letter. Be sure to spell the person's name correctly.
- Introduce yourself and explain the purpose of your letter—to apply for a job.
- Include a few sentences with information about yourself that is not on your résumé—perhaps describe a project you are currently working on that may be relevant to the job.
- Without boasting, explain why you think you are the right candidate for the job.

**Figure**

**4** Results-Oriented Résumé

ANTONIO PETTWAY
101 Beverly Road
Upper Montclair, NJ 07043
820-555-1234
apettway@sbcglobal.net

**OBJECTIVE**

To apply my expertise as a construction supervisor to a management role in an organization seeking improvements in overall production, long-term employee relationships, and the ability to attract the best talent in the construction field.

**PROFESSIONAL EXPERIENCE**

DAL Construction Company, Orange, NJ                                               2006–Present
　Established automated, on-site recordkeeping system, improving communications and morale between field and office personnel, saving 400 work hours per year, and reducing the number of accounting errors by 20 percent. Developed a crew selected as "first-choice crew" by most workers wanting transfers. Completed five housing projects ahead of deadline and under budget.

NJ State Housing Authority, Trenton, NJ                                               2004–2006
　Created friendly, productive atmosphere among workers, enabling first on-time job completion in 4 years and one-half of usual materials waste. Initiated pilot materials delivery program with potential savings of 3.5 percent of yearly maintenance budget.

Essex County Housing Authority, Montclair, NJ                                               2004
　Produced information pamphlets, increasing applications for county housing by 22 percent. Introduced labor-management discussion techniques, saving jobs and over $29,000 in lost time.

Payton, Durnbell & Associates Architects, Glen Ridge, NJ                                               2003–2004
　Developed and monitored productivity improvements, saving 60 percent on information transfer costs for firm's 12 largest jobs.

**EDUCATION**

Montclair State University, Business                                               1999–2003

**COMPUTER SKILLS**

Familiar with Microsoft Office and Adobe Acrobat

**PERSONAL**

Highly self-motivated. Willing to relocate. Enjoy tennis and hiking.

- Request an interview.
- Thank the person for his or her time and consideration.
- Make sure all your contact information is in the letter— name, address, home phone number, cell phone number, and e-mail address.
- Proofread your letter carefully.[7]

## Submitting through Automated Systems

Many large—and small—organizations have moved to automated (paperless) résumé processing and applicant-tracking systems. As a result, if you write and design a technology-compatible résumé and cover letter, you'll enjoy an edge over an applicant whose résumé and cover letter can't be added to a database. Also, remember that résumés are often transmitted electronically and then placed in a company database with an automated applicant-tracking system. Here are a few rules for submitting your résumé by e-mail:

- Use the words in your "Subject" line carefully. Don't just say "seeking employment." If possible, use the job title or a few words from the job description. If you are responding to a published job advertisement, include the job code from the advertisement.

- Include your cover letter in the e-mail.
- Send your résumé following the directions in the instruction.
- If you are answering an ad, read the instructions for application and follow them to the letter.[8]

# THE JOB INTERVIEW

Congratulations! You've prepared an effective résumé, and you've been contacted for an interview. An interview is more than a casual conversation. During an interview, at least one company manager will learn about you, and you'll learn more about the company and the job.

Although you may feel nervous about the interview, you can control some of its outcome by doing your homework: planning and preparing for this important encounter with your potential employer. Before you meet with an interviewer, learn everything you can about the firm. The simplest way to do this is to visit the company's Web site. You can also check with your school's career center. If you know anyone who works for the company, you may ask the person about the firm. Try to learn the answers to the following questions about the organization:

- What does the firm do—manufacture clothing, market snack foods, produce films, sell cars? If you are applying for a job at a large corporation, zero in on the division for which you would be working.
- What is the company's mission? Many firms include a statement about their purpose in the business world—to supply affordable energy to communities, to serve fresh food, to make communication easier. Understanding why the company exists will help you grasp where it is headed and why.
- Where, when, and by whom was the company founded? Learn a little about the history of the firm.
- What is its position in the marketplace? Is it a leader or is it trying to gain a competitive advantage? Who are its main competitors?
- Where is the firm based? Does it have facilities located around the country and the world, or is it purely local?
- How is the company organized? Are there multiple divisions and products?

Learning about the firm indicates to the interviewer that you have initiative and motivation, as well as an interest in the firm's culture and history. You have taken the time and effort to find out more about the organization, and your enthusiasm shows.

## Tips for Successful Interviewing

An interview is your personal introduction to the company. You want to make a good impression, but you also want to find out whether you and the firm make a good fit. Although the interviewer will be asking most of the questions, you will want to ask some, as well. People who conduct interviews say that the most important qualities candidates can exhibit are self-confidence, preparedness, and an ability to communicate clearly.

When you are contacted for an interview, find out the name(s) of the person or people who will be interviewing you. It's also appropriate to ask whether the initial interview will be with a human resources manager, the person to whom you would be reporting on the job, or both. Many people who conduct initial job interviews work in their firms' human resources divisions. These interviewers act as gatekeepers and can make recommendations to managers and supervisors about which individuals to interview further or hire. Managers who head the units in which an applicant will be employed may get involved later in the hiring process. Some hiring decisions come from human resources personnel together with the immediate supervisor of the prospective employee. In other cases, immediate supervisors make the decision alone. At your interview, keep in mind the following:

- *Dress appropriately.* Dress as if it is your first day of work at the firm. Conceal any tattoos or body piercings and wear simple jewelry.
- *Arrive a few minutes early.* This gives you time to relax and take in the surroundings. It also shows that you are punctual and care about other people's time.
- *Introduce yourself with a smile and a handshake.* Be friendly, but not overly familiar.
- *Be yourself—at your best.* Don't suddenly adopt a new personality. But try to be confident, polite, respectful, and interested in the people who are spending time with you. Be sure to thank each person who interviews you.[9]

In a typical format, the interviewer tries to talk as little as possible, giving you a chance to talk about yourself and your goals. You want to present your thoughts clearly and concisely, in an organized fashion, without rambling on to unrelated topics. The interviewer may wait until you are finished or prompt you to talk about certain subjects by asking questions. Be as specific as possible when answering questions. The questions that interviewers ask often include the following:

- "Why do you want this job?"
- "Why do you want to work in this field?"
- "What are your short-term goals? Long-term objectives?"
- "What are your strengths? What are your weaknesses?"
- "What motivates you?"
- "What problem have you solved recently, and how?"
- "Why should my firm hire you?"
- "Are you considering other jobs or companies?"[10]

At some point, the interviewer will probably ask you whether you have any questions of your own. It's a good idea to come prepared with some questions, but others may arise during the interview. Try to keep your list concise, say three or four of your most important questions. The questions you ask reflect just as much about you as the answers you give to the interviewer's questions. Here is a sample of appropriate questions for the initial interview:

- "Could you clarify a certain aspect of the job responsibilities for me?"
- "Do people who start in entry-level jobs at this company tend to develop their careers here?"
- "In what ways could I perform above and beyond the job requirements?"

At some point during your conversation, the interviewer may give you an idea of the salary range for the job. If not, he or she will do so during a subsequent interview. You may ask about the range, but do not ask exactly how much you will be paid if you get the job. Keep in mind that usually there is little or no negotiation of an entry-level salary. However, you may ask if there is a probationary period with a review at the end of the period. Here are a few other questions *not* to ask:

- "When will I be promoted?"
- "How much time off do I get?"
- "When will I get my first raise?"

A successful first interview often leads to a second. The purpose of this interview is to better determine your specific qualifications and fit with the company. You may be introduced to more people—potential co-workers, people in other divisions, or sales staff. You may have another meeting with human resources staff members in which you'll learn more about salary, employee benefits, the firm's code of ethics, and the like. Depending on the type of job, you might be asked to take some skills tests. If you are entering a training program for a bank, you might be required to take some math-oriented tests. If you are going to work for a publisher, you might be asked to take an editing test or do some proofreading. If you are applying for a job as a sales representative, you may be given a test that assesses your personality traits. Don't be intimidated by these tests; just do your best.

## *Making the Employment Decision*

After receiving your résumé, conducting one or two interviews, and administering a skills test, a potential employer knows a lot about you. You should also know a lot about the company. If the experience has been positive on both sides, you may be offered a job. If you have interviewed at several companies and are offered more than one job, congratulations! You may receive a phone call, followed by a letter outlining the offer in writing. Whether you receive one offer or several, thank the person making the offer. If you choose to accept immediately, feel free to do so. If you have doubts about the job or need to decide between two, it is appropriate to ask for 24 hours to respond. If you must decline an offer, do so promptly and politely. After all, you may end up working for that firm sometime in the future. If you get a few rejections before you receive an offer, don't give up. Every application and interview adds to your experience.

As you think about an offer, consider the aspects that are most important. You'll want to choose a job that comes closest to your career interests and objectives. But don't rule out the element of surprise—you might wind up with a job you like in an industry you'd never considered before. Don't worry too much about the salary. The point of an entry-level job is to set you on a forward path. And keep in mind that your first job won't be your last. Once you have accepted an offer, you'll be given a start date as well as the name of the person to whom you should report on arrival. Congratulations, you are now a member of the workforce!

# NONTRADITIONAL STUDENTS

Take a quick glance around your class. You'll likely see classmates of all ages. Some will fall into the traditional college age group of 18 to 22, but many don't. Perhaps you are a veteran returning from military duty overseas. Maybe you have been engaged in a full-time career but want to broaden your education. Students who fall outside the 18-to-22 age group are often referred to as *nontraditional students*, but these students have become the norm on many campuses. Homemakers returning to school to freshen up their résumés before returning to the workforce and workers who have been laid off due to an economic downturn are other examples of nontraditional students. As diverse as this group is, they share one thing in common: they are older than traditional students. This means that they face different challenges—but also enjoy some advantages over their younger classmates.

One major challenge faced by nontraditional students is scheduling. Often they are juggling the responsibilities of work, school, and family. They may have to study at odd times—during meals, while commuting, or after putting the kids to bed. If they are switching careers, they may be learning an entirely new set of skills as well. But nontraditional students have an important advantage: experience. Even experience in an unrelated field is a plus. Older students know how organizations operate. Often they have developed useful skills in human relations, management, budgeting, and communications. Even a former stay-at-home parent has skills in all of these areas. Through observing other people's successes and failures—as well as living through their own—they have developed an inventory of what to do and what not to do. So in some ways, these students have a head start on their younger counterparts. But they also face the reality that they have fewer years in which to develop a career.

# THE JOB MARKET: WHERE DO YOU FIT IN?

The industry you choose, and the career you follow within it, are part of a bigger picture. They reflect the needs of society, changing populations, developing technology, and the overall economy. For instance, the U.S. population is expected to increase at a slower rate of growth than during the previous two decades. The U.S. workforce will continue to become more diverse, with Hispanics accounting for the largest share of jobs among minorities, while Asians represent the fastest-growing group of employees. The number of women in the workforce is still growing at a faster rate than that of men.[11]

All of these facts combine to shape a picture of the needs of U.S. society and the work-force available to serve it. As the baby boom generation ages, the United States will need more healthcare services as well as services for the leisure and hospitality industries. We could see the addition of 4.4 million new jobs in healthcare and social assistance fields, along with about 500,000 new positions in leisure and hospitality. Professional and business services are expected to increase nearly 50 percent by 2012, adding 5 million new jobs.[12]

Careers in environmental engineering and science are already hot—and expected to get hotter, as the United States and countries around the world place more emphasis on solving and preventing environmental problems. "We expect the U.S. to start exporting environmental expertise to Europe and Asia, including to emerging markets like India," predicts one industry watcher. Fields that require advanced computer skills such as network systems analysts, personal financial advisors, database administrators, and software engineers are on the rise as well.[13] Registered nurses, postsecondary teachers, retail salespeople, and customer service representatives can expect an increase in opportunities. But farmers and ranchers, word processors, and stock clerks can expect a decline.[14]

As the population changes and technology automates certain tasks or simply alters the way they are accomplished, opportunities will grow or shrink. As you plan your career, it is wise to stay up-to-date on the job market.

# A LONG-RANGE VIEW OF YOUR CAREER

As we said earlier, choosing a career is an important life decision. A career is a professional journey—regardless of whether you want to run an art gallery or a branch bank, whether you are fascinated by language or math, whether you prefer to work with animals or people. In the end, you hope to contribute something good to society while enjoying what you do—and make a reasonable living at it.

Throughout your career, it is important to stay flexible and continue learning. Challenging new skills will be required of managers and other businesspeople during these first decades of the 21st century. Remain open to unexpected changes and opportunities that can help you learn and develop new skills. Keep in mind that your first job will not be your last. But tackle that first job with the same enthusiasm you'd have if someone asked you to run the company itself, because everything you learn on that job will be valuable at some point during your career—and someday you may actually run the company.

Finally, if you haven't already started your career search, begin now. Do this by talking with various resources, lining up an internship, looking for a part-time job on or off campus, or volunteering for an organization. Register with the campus career center long before you graduate. Then, when you reach your final semester, you'll be well on your way to beginning the career you want.

We are confident that this textbook will present a panorama of career options for you. Whatever you decide, be sure it is right for you—not your friends, your instructors, or your parents. As the old saying goes, "You pass this way just once." Enjoy the journey!

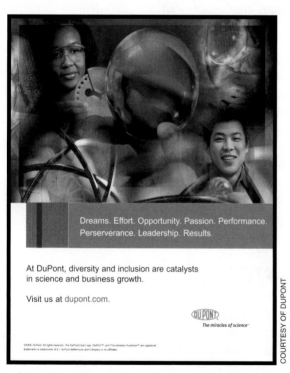

Following your dreams can lead you to an exciting career. DuPont looks for a wide variety of people who can contribute to its success while fulfilling theirs.

## More Career Information on the Contemporary Business Web Site

More career information is available to students using *Contemporary Business* at the following Web site: http://www.swlearning.com/business/boone. The "Management Careers" section on the Web site enables you to learn more about business careers and to locate currently posted job opportunities. The site provides a vast number of career resources such as links to job sites and career guidance sites. Many links include extensive career information and guidance, such as interviewing techniques and tips for résumé writing.

1. Prepare your résumé following the procedures outlined earlier in this section. Ask your instructors, friends, and relatives to critique it. Then revise and proofread it.
2. Talk with someone in your community who is working in a profession that interests you. Write, call, or e-mail to request an appointment. The interview should take no more than 15 to 20 minutes. Come prepared with questions to ask. Report to your class about what you learned.
3. Prepare answers to each of the questions that interviewers most often ask. Discuss your answers in class.
4. Select a partner and take turns interviewing each other for a job in front of the class. Use the interview questions mentioned earlier, and develop two or three of your own. After completing the interviews, ask the class to give you feedback on how you looked and acted during your interview. Would they advise you to do or say anything differently?
5. Pick a Web site dealing with careers. Select an employment field and prepare a report on what you learned from the Web site. What jobs are available? From your perspective, were they in desirable locations? What did these jobs pay? Did the information in the Web site agree or conflict with your initial perceptions of the job?

**"They Said It"**

"Once you say you're going to settle for second, that's what happens to you in life, I find."
—John F. Kennedy
(1917–1963)
35th president
of the United States

# Business in a Global Environment

# Part 1

# Chapter 1

## The Framework of Contemporary Business

### Learning Goals

1. Distinguish between business and not-for-profit organizations.

2. Identify and describe the factors of production.

3. Describe the private enterprise system, including basic rights and entrepreneurship.

4. Identify the six eras of business and explain how the relationship era—including alliances and technology—influences contemporary business.

5. Explain how today's business workforce is changing.

6. Describe how the nature of work itself is changing.

7. Identify the skills and attributes that managers need to lead businesses in the 21st century.

8. Outline the characteristics that make a company admired by the business community.

AP PHOTO/TOM UHLMAN

You toss your laundry in the washing machine with a scoop of Tide. You pour Iams dry pet food into your dog's food dish. You use Crest Whitestrips while getting ready for a big date. You are loyal to these product brands, but you might not think about the company behind them: Procter & Gamble. P&G, as it is known throughout the business community, has been around for nearly 170 years. Its products are a part of millions of consumers' daily lives. Items such as Glad Press 'n Seal Wrap, the Swiffer duster, Dawn dish detergent, Pampers diapers, and Olay Daily Facials are put into shopping carts every day. Since P&G's acquisition of Gillette, brand names such as Oral-B, Braun, and Duracell are now included in the firm's shopping cart list.

# Procter & Gamble: Innovation Drives Business Success

Procter & Gamble is a huge, U.S.-based corporation headed by chief executive A. G. Lafley. Its size has in the past made the company seem lumbering—unable to change quickly in response to shifting consumer preferences, new technology, and marketplace demands. But the firm has been getting back in shape and is now flexing its innovative muscles regularly. With its stream of unique new products, consumers and competitors alike are taking notice.

Lafley's vision for the future of his company is one of problem solver—he wants his firm to provide consumer products that offer solutions to every problem in the home, from laundry to food storage to personal care. This vision relies on innovation, technology, and alliances—all geared toward building relationships with customers. Several years ago, P&G purchased the high-end pet-food manufacturer Iams. Industry watchers predicted the downfall of Iams's quality and prestige within such a huge corporation. But P&G marketers conducted surveys to find out what Iams customers wanted, then put its vast scientific resources to work. As a result, P&G launched a new line of Iams foods aimed at lengthening the lives of pets—weight control formulas, antioxidant food blends, and foods blended with tartar-fighting ingredients. The result? Iams has

moved from the number 5 pet food brand to number 1. Its worldwide sales have doubled to $1.6 billion, and its profits have tripled. Why are these products so successful? "We're offering consumers peace of mind," explains Lafley, who just happens to own a dog and two Maine Coon cats.

Tide laundry detergent has been a marketplace leader for 40 years, which could lead you to remark, "If it isn't broken, don't fix it." But sales in general of laundry detergent have been somewhat stale, growing at less than 1 percent per year industry-wide. So P&G looked for ways to freshen the brand by offering more choices. Today, consumers have their choice of everything from Tide Coldwater, designed for washing clothes in cold water, to Tide Kick—a combination measuring cup and stain remover. Because P&G is as adept at forming alliances among its own divisions as it is at building relationships through new acquisitions, it can adapt good ideas company-wide. One example of this cross-fertilization is the Tide StainBrush, a new electric brush for removing stains that is based on the same mechanism used for the Crest SpinBrush Pro toothbrush—another P&G brand.

Procter & Gamble employs 7,500 people in research and development, located in 20 technical facilities in 20 countries. The firm depends on these employees—as well as everyone else in the firm—to think critically and creatively. It also encourages employees to communicate ideas—that's how the Tide StainBrush was developed. Diane Dietz, who heads the North American oral care division, notes that the ideas for Crest's new flavors actually came from aroma experts who work on Millstone coffee and Herbal Essences shampoos. Colleagues can post or review new ideas on P&G's internal Web site and attend special internal trade shows to learn more about products in other divisions. And if one division needs a few creative thinkers from another division to develop a new product, it "borrows" them for awhile. A. G. Lafley conducts annual "innovation reviews" of each business unit, evaluating the amount of idea sharing among marketers and scientists. He believes that the future of his company—which is number 6 on *Fortune's* worldwide list of most admired companies—lies in the minds of his own employees. "People get as much credit for giving good ideas as for receiving them," says Lafley.[1]

The U.S. has rebounded from the challenges of terrorism, recession, and war. Consumers have regained confidence and are spending again, particularly in the one of the hottest housing markets in the nation's history. Spurred by mortgage rates that have held steady for several years, more people are jumping into the housing market or taking the opportunity to upgrade to that dream home. Despite high gasoline prices, travelers have taken to the roads and skies in record numbers—during one recent holiday weekend, an estimated 37 million drivers hit the road, while the number of air travelers is now actually challenging the capacity of the skies, creating new challenges for the Federal Aviation Administration (FAA) and airlines. And it's not just vacationers seeking getaways; business travel has experienced a tremendous comeback.[2] American Express's Travel Related Services recently reported a 20 percent increase in its revenues, including a significant boost in charges by business travelers on their travel and expense cards.[3]

Perhaps the best evidence of a new outlook among companies is the rate at which they are investing in students—their future employees—particularly in the areas of technology and service. At several high schools in Massachusetts, biology students now dissect DNA as part of their course work, thanks to funding by local biotech companies such as Genzyme and Serono. "It's very philanthropic, but it's also selfish," explains Una Ryan, chair of the Massachusetts Biotechnology Council and CEO of Boston-area vaccine maker Avant Immunotherapeutics Inc. "We need people who are better trained."[4]

In short, business in many sectors is booming—and *Contemporary Business* is right there with it. This book explores the strategies that allow companies to grow and compete in today's interactive marketplace, along with the skills that you will need to turn ideas into action for your own success in business. This chapter sets the stage for the entire text by defining business and revealing its role in society. The chapter's discussion illustrates how the private enterprise system encourages competition and innovation while preserving business ethics.

## WHAT IS BUSINESS?

What comes to mind when you hear the word *business*? Do you think of big corporations like General Electric or Microsoft? Or does the local bakery or shoe store pop into your mind? Maybe you recall your first summer job. The term *business* is a broad, all-inclusive term that can be applied to many kinds of enterprises. Businesses provide the bulk of employment opportunities, as well as the products that people enjoy.

**business** all profit-seeking activities and enterprises that provide goods and services necessary to an economic system.

**Business** consists of all profit-seeking activities and enterprises that provide goods and services necessary to an economic system. Some businesses produce tangible goods, such as automobiles, breakfast cereals, and computer chips; others provide services such as insurance, banking, and entertainment ranging from Six Flags theme parks and Broadway plays to rap concerts.

Business drives the economic pulse of a nation. It provides the means through which its citizens' standard of living improves. At the heart of every business endeavor is an exchange between a buyer and a seller. A buyer recognizes a need for a good or service and trades money with a seller to obtain that product. The seller participates in the process in hopes of gaining profits—a main ingredient in accomplishing the goals necessary for continuous improvement in the standard of living.

**Profits** represent rewards for businesspeople who take the risks involved in blending people, technology, and information to create and market want-satisfying goods and services. In contrast, accountants think of profits as the difference between a firm's revenues and the expenses it incurs in generating these revenues. More generally, however, profits serve as incentives for people to start companies, expand them, and provide consistently high-quality competitive goods and services. Consider the role of profits among companies in the travel industry. During one recent year, the average rate of occupancy in hotels rose nearly 4 percent, as did the average price of a hotel room, representing greater profits for those hotels. In turn, the owners of those hotels might choose to reinvest those profits in expansions and improvements in order to grow.[5]

The quest for profits is a central focus of business because without profits, a company could not survive. But businesspeople also recognize their social and ethical responsibilities. To succeed in the long run, companies must deal responsibly with employees, customers, suppliers, competitors, government, and the general public.

## Not-for-Profit Organizations

What do Ohio State's athletic department, the U.S. Postal Service, the American Heart Association, and C-SPAN have in common? They are all classified as **not-for-profit organizations**, businesslike establishments that have primary objectives other than returning profits to their owners. These organizations play important roles in society by placing public service above profits, although it is important to understand that these organizations need to raise money so that they can operate and achieve their social goals. Not-for-profit organizations operate in both the private and public sectors. Private-sector not-for-profits include museums, libraries, trade associations, and charitable and religious organizations. Government agencies, political parties, and labor unions, all of which are part of the public sector, are also classified as not-for-profit organizations.

Not-for-profit organizations are a substantial part of the U.S. economy. Currently, 1.5 million nonprofit organizations are registered with the Internal Revenue Service in the United States, in categories ranging from arts and culture to science and technology.[6] These organizations control more than $1 trillion in assets and employ more people than the entire federal government and all 50 state governments combined. In addition, millions of volunteers work for them in unpaid positions. Not-for-profits secure funding from both private sources, including donations, and government sources. They are commonly exempt from federal, state, and local taxes.

Although they focus on goals other than generating profits, managers of not-for-profit organizations face many of the same challenges as executives of profit-seeking businesses. Without funding, they cannot do research, obtain raw materials, or provide services. Habitat for Humanity cannot build new houses for poor families without lumber and tools. The Children's Miracle Network, illustrated in Figure 1.1, could not help children with life-threatening injuries or diseases without raising nearly $250 million for 170 North American children's hospitals in a recent year through telethons, radiothons, corporate donations, and local fund-raising efforts. Without donations from every corner of the world, organizations such as Save the Children and the World Health Organization could not provide much-needed relief to survivors of the

**profits** rewards for businesspeople who take the risks involved to offer goods and services to customers.

**Figure**

1.1

Children's Miracle Network: Helping Fight
Childhood Injury and Illness

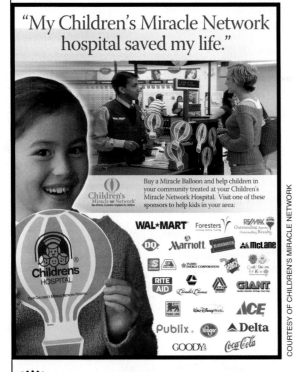

COURTESY OF CHILDREN'S MIRACLE NETWORK

**Table**

1.1

**assessment check**

1. What activity lies at the heart of every business endeavor?
2. What are the primary objectives of a not-for-profit organization?

**factors of production**
four basic inputs for effective operation: natural resources, capital, human resources, and entrepreneurship.

recent deadly tsunami that struck Southeast Asia. In an unprecedented effort to raise money for food, shelter, clothing, medical care, and ultimately rebuild Indonesia and other hard-hit countries, former U.S. presidents George H.W. Bush and Bill Clinton traveled together to the region, made television commercials, and conducted personal appeals for contributions. Within two months of the disaster, experts estimated that more than $1 billion had been raised from the U.S. private sector, in addition to the nearly $1 billion pledged by the U.S. government.[7]

Some not-for-profits sell merchandise or set up profit-generating arms to provide goods and services for which people are willing and able to pay. College bookstores sell everything from sweatshirts to coffee mugs with school logos imprinted on them, while the Sierra Club and the Appalachian Mountain Club both have full-fledged publishing programs. The Lance Armstrong Foundation has sold more than 40 million yellow Live Strong wristbands in the United States and abroad, with the money earmarked to fight cancer and support patients and families.[8] Handling merchandising programs like these, as well as launching other fund-raising campaigns, requires managers of not-for-profit organizations to develop effective business skills and experience. Consequently, many of the concepts discussed in this book apply to not-for-profit organizations as much as to profit-oriented firms.

## Factors of Production

An economic system requires certain inputs for successful operation. Economists use the term **factors of production** to refer to the four basic inputs: natural resources, capital, human resources, and entrepreneurship. Table 1.1 identifies each of these inputs and the type of payment received by firms and individuals who supply them.

**Natural resources** include all production inputs that are useful in their natural states, including agricultural land, building sites, forests, and mineral deposits. The sawmill operated by Willamette Industries in the little town of Dallas, Oregon, takes 2,500-pound second-growth logs from Oregon's hillsides and cuts them into boards. Other companies use natural resources after they have been processed by companies like Willamette. Natural resources are the basic inputs required in any economic system.

**Capital**, another key resource, includes technology, tools, information, and physical facilities. *Technology* is a broad term that refers to such machinery and equipment as computers and

Factors of Production and Their Factor Payments

| Factor of Production | Corresponding Factor Payment |
| --- | --- |
| Natural resources | Rent |
| Capital | Interest |
| Human resources | Wages |
| Entrepreneurship | Profit |

Figure

1.2

software, telecommunications, and inventions designed to improve production. Information, frequently improved by technological innovations, is another critical factor because both managers and operating employees require accurate, timely information for effective performance of their assigned tasks. Technology plays an important role in the success of many businesses. Sometimes technology results in a new product, such as hybrid autos that run on a combination of gasoline and electricity. Both Honda and Toyota are successfully marketing these hybrids. Ford has introduced a hybrid version of its Escape SUV, and General Motors offers Chevy trucks with hybrid engines, as illustrated by Figure 1.2.

GM's Hybrid Trucks

Sometimes technology helps a company improve a product. Recently, Microsoft came up with a wireless ergonomic keyboard designed to reduce fatigue on users' wrists and fingers. Its Wireless Comfort Keyboard is curved to allow more natural movement of the fingers and wrist. Logitech claims it has built a better cordless mouse by using lasers. Logitech's MX1000 Laser Cordless Mouse uses a tiny laser instead of a light-emitting diode (LED), making it more precise.[9]

And sometimes technology helps a company operate more smoothly by tracking deliveries, providing more efficient communication, analyzing data, or training employees. Unisys offers software to businesses called 3D Visible Enterprise, which creates three-dimensional "blueprints" of the potential outcomes of business decisions. Xerox helped its business customer Dow Chemical gain better access to its more than 5 million pages of archived research and development documents. The latest generation of high-speed wireless networking technology, called WiMax, will soon help businesses communicate more efficiently. SBC Communications is testing a prototype with two of its major corporate customers, while Nortel Networks and LG Electronics have announced plans to develop WiMax-enabled phones.[10]

To remain competitive, a firm's capital needs to be continually acquired, maintained, and upgraded, so businesses need money for that purpose. A company's funds may come from investments by its owners, profits plowed back into the business, or loans extended by others. Money then goes to work building factories; purchasing raw materials and component parts; and hiring, training, and compensating workers. People and firms that supply capital receive factor payments in the form of interest.

**Human resources** represent another critical input in every economic system. Human resources include anyone who works, from the chief executive officer (CEO) of a huge corporation to a self-employed auto mechanic. This category encompasses both the physical labor and the intellectual inputs contributed by workers. Companies rely on their employees as a valued source of ideas and innovation, as well as physical effort. Some companies solicit employee ideas through traditional means, such as an online "suggestion box" or in staff meetings. Others encourage creative thinking during company-sponsored hiking or rafting trips or during social gatherings. Effective, well-trained human resources provide a significant competitive edge because competitors cannot easily match another company's talented, motivated employees in the way they can buy the same computer system or purchase the same grade of natural resources. Discount airline JetBlue has a mandatory training program in leadership

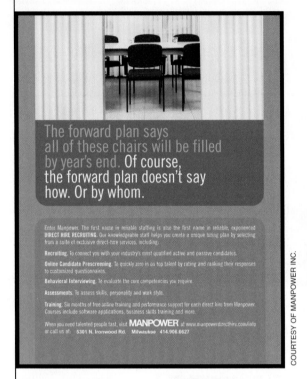

The forward plan says all of these chairs will be filled by year's end. **Of course, the forward plan doesn't say how. Or by whom.**

Enter Manpower. The first name in reliable staffing is also the first name in reliable, experienced **DIRECT HIRE RECRUITING.** Our knowledgeable staff helps you create a unique hiring plan by selecting from a suite of exclusive direct-hire services, including:

**Recruiting.** To connect you with your industry's most qualified active and passive candidates.

**Online Candidate Prescreening.** To quickly zero in on top talent by rating and ranking their responses to customized questionnaires.

**Behavioral Interviewing.** To evaluate the core competencies you require.

**Assessments.** To assess skills, personality and work style.

**Training.** Six months of free online training and performance support for each direct hire from Manpower. Courses include software applications, business skills training and more.

When you need talented people fast, visit **MANPOWER** at www.manpowerdirecthire.com/info or call us at: **5301 N. Ironwood Rd.   Milwaukee   414.906.6627**

COURTESY OF MANPOWER INC.

**a**ssessment **c**heck

1. Identify the four basic inputs to an economic system.
2. List four types of capital.

qualities. CEO David Neeleman claims that the results have included happier workers and more satisfied customers. He believes that his managers must earn the respect of their employees, and that all managers should teach by example. "We want people to follow our leaders because they respect us, not because they've been told to," says Neeleman.[11]

Figure 1.3 emphasizes the importance of human resources to organizational goals—that people make the business what it is. Manpower provides staffing services to a wide range of companies, helping firms "staff up with skilled, experienced people, fast."

**Entrepreneurship** is the willingness to take risks to create and operate a business. An entrepreneur is someone who sees a potentially profitable opportunity and then devises a plan to achieve success in the marketplace and earn those profits. Kathy Ireland used to be a supermodel. Today, she is a super businesswoman, having been named Businesswoman of the Year by the National Association of Women Business Owners. Ireland is the CEO and chief designer of her own company, Kathy Ireland Worldwide, which sells its own lines of home furnishings and clothing targeted mainly to busy women on a budget. Ireland is proud of her company's accomplishments, including its recent licensing agreement that allows the firm to reproduce "The Quilts of Gee's Bend"—museum-quality folk art quilts made by a group of African American women from Alabama. "Real brands require infrastructure, leadership, and a strong, committed sales and distribution force," says Ireland. "We've built our brand from the ground up."[12]

U.S. businesses operate within an economic system called the *private enterprise system*. The next section looks at the private enterprise system, including competition, private property, and the entrepreneurship alternative.

GETTY IMAGES

AP PHOTO/CHITOSE SUZUKI

Kathy Ireland (shown in photo at left) is an entrepreneur who started her business by selling socks and has built it into the $1 billion dollar a year in sales revenue—Kathy Ireland Worldwide. The company recently beat out Donna Karan and Calvin Klein for the right to reproduce the acclaimed "The Quilts of Gee's Bend," based on the fine art folk quilts handmade by Mary Lee Bendolph (shown in photo at right) and her women friends in Gee's Bend, Alabama.

# THE PRIVATE ENTERPRISE SYSTEM

No business operates in a vacuum. All operate within a larger economic system that determines how goods and services are produced, distributed, and consumed in a society. The type of economic system employed in a society also determines patterns of resource use. Some economic systems, such as communism, feature strict controls on business ownership, profits, and resources to accomplish government goals.

In the United States, businesses function within the **private enterprise system**, an economic system that rewards firms for their ability to perceive and serve the needs and demands of consumers. The private enterprise system minimizes government interference in economic activity. Businesses that are adept at satisfying customers gain access to necessary factors of production and earn profits.

Another name for the private enterprise system is **capitalism**. Adam Smith, often identified as the father of capitalism, first described the concept in his book *The Wealth of Nations*, published in 1776. Smith believed that an economy is best regulated by the "invisible hand" of **competition**, the battle among businesses for consumer acceptance. Smith thought that competition among firms would lead to consumers' receiving the best possible products and prices because less efficient producers would gradually be driven from the marketplace.

The "invisible hand" concept is a basic premise of the private enterprise system. In the United States, competition regulates much of economic life. To compete successfully, each firm must find a basis for **competitive differentiation**, the unique combination of organizational abilities, products, and approaches that sets a company apart from competitors in the minds of consumers. Businesses operating in a private enterprise system face a critical task of keeping up with changing marketplace conditions. Firms that fail to adjust to shifts in consumer preferences or ignore the actions of competitors leave themselves open to failure. In the very competitive food-manufacturing industry, General Mills and Kellogg have been duking it out for decades. When Kellogg cereals grew soggy in the sales bowl, the firm promoted Carlos Gutierrez to CEO in the hope that he could add a crisp snap, crackle, and pop to Kellogg's revenues. Gutierrez immediately took stock of the cereals that consumers preferred, those that had been copied by other companies, and those that were the most profitable. He created a strategy called Volume to Value, in which Kellogg's allocated more of its resources to products such as Special K, which appeals to weight-conscious women; Kashi, for health food consumers; and Nutri-Grain bars, for those who want breakfast or a snack on the go. These products, priced higher than cereals such as Corn Flakes, would generate more profits, which would then be plowed back into research and development for new competitive products. So far, the plan has been successful. Kellogg's share of sales from new cereal products, now at about 18 percent, has rocketed past that of the industry as a whole. Gutierrez's star also rose: from his CEO post at Kellogg, he was tapped to become the 35th U.S. secretary of commerce.[13]

Throughout this book, our discussion focuses on the tools and methods that 21st-century businesses apply to compete and differentiate their goods and services. We also discuss many of the ways in which market changes will affect business and the private enterprise system in the years ahead.

**private enterprise system** economic system that rewards firms for their ability to identify and serve the needs and demands of customers.

**competition** battle among businesses for consumer acceptance.

## "They Said It"

*"All strategy depends on competition."*
—*Bruce D. Henderson (1915–1992) American educator and founder of the Boston Consulting Group*

## Basic Rights in the Private Enterprise System

For capitalism to operate effectively, the citizens of a private enterprise economy must have certain rights. As shown in Figure 1.4, these include the rights to private property, profits, freedom of choice, and competition.

The right to **private property** is the most basic freedom under the private enterprise system. Every participant has the right to own, use, buy, sell, and bequeath most forms of property, including land, buildings, machinery, equipment, patents on inventions, individual possessions, and intangible properties.

The private enterprise system also guarantees business owners the right to all profits—after taxes—they earn through their activities. Although a business is not assured of earning a profit, its owner is legally and ethically entitled to any income it generates in excess of costs.

Freedom of choice means that a private enterprise system relies on the potential for citizens to choose their own employment, purchases, and investments. They can change jobs, negotiate wages, join labor unions, and choose among many different brands of goods and services. People living in the capitalist nations of North America, Europe, and other parts of the world are so accustomed to this freedom of choice that they sometimes forget its importance. A private enterprise economy maximizes individual prosperity by providing alternatives. Other economic systems sometimes limit freedom of choice to accomplish government goals, such as increasing industrial production or military strength.

The private enterprise system also permits fair competition by allowing the public to set rules for competitive activity. For this reason, the U.S. government has passed laws to prohibit "cutthroat" competition—excessively aggressive competitive practices designed to eliminate competition. It also has established ground rules that outlaw price discrimination, fraud in financial markets, and deceptive advertising and packaging. Not long ago, the Securities and Exchange Commission (SEC), along with internal New York Stock Exchange (NYSE) investigators, discovered that some of the NYSE's in-house floor traders had engaged in "improper proprietary trading" of 2.2 billion shares of stock over a three-year period, resulting in unfair competitive advantage and profits. The subsequent legal charges sparked the reform of certain trading regulations.[14]

## The Entrepreneurship Alternative

**entrepreneur** person who seeks a profitable opportunity and takes the necessary risks to set up and operate a business.

The entrepreneurial spirit beats at the heart of private enterprise. An **entrepreneur** is a risk taker in the private enterprise system. You hear about entrepreneurs all the time—two college students starting a software business in their dorm room or a mom who invents a better baby carrier. Many times their success is modest, but once in a while, the risk pays off in huge profits, as described in the "Hit & Miss" feature. Individuals who recognize marketplace opportunities are free to use their capital, time, and talents to pursue those opportunities for profit. The willingness of individuals to start new ventures drives economic growth and keeps pressure on existing companies to continue to satisfy customers. If no one were willing to take economic risks, the private enterprise system wouldn't exist.

By almost any measure, the entrepreneurial spirit fuels growth in the U.S. economy. Of all the businesses operating in the United States, about one in seven firms started operations during the past year. These newly formed businesses are also the source of many of the nation's new jobs. Every year, they create more than one of every five new jobs in the economy. Most measures of entrepreneurship look at the smallest or youngest businesses on the assumption that they are the enterprises in which entrepreneurship is most significant. These companies are a significant source of employment or self-employment. Of the 20 million U.S. businesses currently in operation, 15 million are self-employed people without any employees. Nearly 12 million U.S. employees currently work for a business with fewer than ten employees.[15] Does starting a business require higher education? Not necessarily, although it can help. Figure 1.5 presents the results of a survey of small-business owners, which shows that about 24 percent of all respondents had graduated from college, and 19 percent had postgraduate degrees.

# HIT & MISS

## Airborne Takes Off

It's a marketer's dream come true: the cure for the common cold. Airborne may not technically be a cure, but the latest remedy for head colds is nothing to sneeze at. Developed by entrepreneur Victoria Knight-McDowell, the herbal remedy contains many traditional cold-fighting ingredients—vitamins C, E, and A, along with zinc, ginger, and echinacea.

Like many entrepreneurs, Knight-McDowell came up with the idea for Airborne because she needed the product herself. A substitute teacher, she found she was catching too many colds in the classroom. So she headed to her own kitchen to come up with a concoction to help relieve the symptoms. In six months she had come up with a prototype recipe, which she tried on herself, her family, and her friends. It seemed to work. So Knight-McDowell and her husband Rider decided to market the new product directly from their home. The first year, Airborne brought in $25,000—the same as Victoria's teaching salary.

Eight years later, Airborne is making $21 million annually, thanks in part to Knight-McDowell's appearance on *The Oprah Winfrey Show* and endorsements from such celebrities as Kevin Costner and Sarah Jessica Parker. But Knight-McDowell also credits her own and her husband's business sense. "One of the keys to our success is that I'm used to operating on a shoestring budget," she says. "Once a teacher, always a teacher. Now I can be in the classroom and enjoy being with the children, without worrying about money." Airborne's whimsical and humorous packaging is also a factor. Its distinctive yellow box with cartoon-style drawings is pleasing to consumers. And of course, the fact that Knight-McDowell is a teacher is a vital marketing point; everyone trusts a teacher's word.

### Questions for Critical Thinking

1. How does Victoria Knight-McDowell embody the entrepreneurial spirit?
2. What might be the next step for Knight-McDowell's company?

**Sources:** "The Secrets of Success," *The Oprah Winfrey Show,* accessed May 26, 2006, http://www.oprah.com; "Unconventional Cold Remedies Big Sellers," NewsMax.com, May 26, 2006, http://www.newsmax.com; Kerry Fehr-Snyder, "Herbal Cold Remedy Goes Airborne after Oprah Plug," *The Arizona Republic,* May 26, 2006, http://www.azcentral.com.

---

Besides creating jobs and selling products, entrepreneurship provides the benefits of innovation. In contrast to more established firms, start-up companies tend to innovate most in fields of technology that are new and uncrowded with competitors, making new products available to businesses and consumers. Because small companies are more flexible, they can make changes to products and processes more quickly than larger corporations. Entrepreneurs often find new ways to use natural resources, technology, and other factors of production. Often, they do this because they have to—they may not have enough money to build an expensive prototype or launch a nationwide ad campaign. Sometimes an entrepreneur may innovate by simply tweaking an existing idea. Curves is a chain of no-frills fitness clubs across the nation started by a husband-and-wife team. In the 15 years it has been in existence, the business for single-gender, quick-exercise gyms has shot upward, now accounting for nearly 25 percent of the entire fitness club market in the United States. Enter Scott Smith, a former Curves franchise owner who wanted to give himself and his friends the same kind of deal. So he launched Blitz, a male-only, quick-fitness gym complete

Figure

1.5

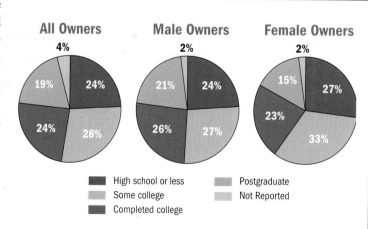

Education Levels of Small-Business Owners

**Note:** Numbers may not total to 100 percent due to rounding.
**Source:** Data from "Survey of Business Owners (SBO): Owner's Education Levels at Start-Up, Purchase, or Acquisition of the Business," U.S. Census Bureau, accessed May 26, 2006 http://www.census.gov/csd/sbo/edu.html.

with mock boxing rings and punching bags. Smith, who now has 86 Blitz locations in the United States and Canada, says his customers love the quick pace of the workouts. And he swears by the results. "I don't care what your size or strength is, at the end of two 10-minute circuits, you'll wear yourself out and get blitzed," he promises.[16]

Entrepreneurship is also important to existing companies in a private enterprise system. More and more, large firms are recognizing the value of entrepreneurial thinking among their employees, hoping to benefit from enhanced flexibility, improved innovation, and new market opportunities. Jim Throneburg runs his family's North Carolina sock-manufacturing firm, Thorlo. The company has been around for a long time, and Throneburg makes certain it continually innovates and changes. A few decades ago, he noticed that American consumers had begun buying different athletic shoes for different sports. "If the shoe changed for function, I figured I needed to design a sock that complemented the shoe," he recalls. His figuring resulted in a thick-soled hiking sock and later a padded sock for the military. Since then, Thorlo has created more than 25 varieties of sport socks. Throneburg invests heavily in research—in search of new markets and new technologies. Research helped the firm identify what it calls the "7 Elements of Comfort" for footwear and then develop its Comfort Science program. Thorlo has spent millions on developing new yarns and designs and responded to requests from its customers for new products. Throneburg likes to differentiate his firm from its competitors. "Thorlo does not make socks. There are lots of companies that do that. At Thorlo, all our resources are dedicated to improving the quality of our consumers' lives by providing the most protective sock products in the world."[17]

As the next section explains, entrepreneurs have played a vital role in the history of American business. They have helped create new industries, developed successful new business methods, and improved U.S. standing in global competition.

## assessment check

1. What is an alternative term for private enterprise system?
2. What is the most basic freedom under the private enterprise system?
3. What is an entrepreneur?

# SIX ERAS IN THE HISTORY OF BUSINESS

In the roughly 400 years since the first European settlements appeared on the North American continent, amazing changes have occurred in the size, focus, and goals of U.S. businesses. As Figure 1.6 indicates, U.S. business history is divided into six distinct time periods: (1) the Colonial period, (2) the Industrial Revolution, (3) the age of industrial entrepreneurs, (4) the production era, (5) the marketing era, and (6) the relationship era. The next sections describe how events in each of these time periods have influenced U.S. business practices.

## The Colonial Period

Before the U.S. Declaration of Independence from England in 1776, Colonial society emphasized rural and agricultural production. Colonial towns were small compared with European cities, and they functioned as marketplaces for farmers and craftspeople. The economic focus of the nation centered on rural areas, because prosperity depended on the output of farms and plantations. The success or failure of crops influenced every aspect of the economy.

Colonists depended on England for manufactured items as well as financial backing for their infant industries. Even after the Revolutionary War (1776–1783), the United States maintained close economic ties with England. British investors continued to provide much of the financing for developing the U.S. business system, and this financial influence continued well into the 19th century.

Figure

1.6

Six Eras in Business History

| Era | Main Characteristics | Time Period |
|---|---|---|
| Colonial | Primarily agricultural | Prior to 1776 |
| Industrial Revolution | Mass production by semiskilled workers, aided by machines | 1760–1850 |
| Industrial entrepreneurs | Advances in technology and increased demand for manufactured goods, leading to enormous entrepreneurial opportunities | Late 1800s |
| Production | Emphasis on producing more goods faster, leading to production innovations such as assembly lines | Through the 1920s |
| Marketing | Consumer orientation, seeking to understand and satisfy needs and preferences of customer groups | Since 1950s |
| Relationship | Benefits derived from deep, ongoing links with individual customers, employees, suppliers, and other businesses | Began in 1990s |

## The Industrial Revolution

The Industrial Revolution began in England around 1750. It moved business operations from an emphasis on independent, skilled workers who specialized in building products one by one to a factory system that mass-produced items by bringing together large numbers of semiskilled workers. The factories profited from the savings created by large-scale production, bolstered by increasing support from machines over time. As businesses grew, they could often purchase raw materials more cheaply in larger lots than before. Specialization of labor, limiting each worker to a few specific tasks in the production process, also improved production efficiency.

Influenced by these events in England, business in the United States began a time of rapid industrialization. Agriculture became mechanized, and factories sprang up in cities. During the mid-1800s, the pace of the revolution was increased as newly built railroad systems provided fast, economical transportation. In California, for example, the combination of railroad construction and the gold rush fueled a tremendous demand for construction.

## The Age of Industrial Entrepreneurs

Building on the opportunities created by the Industrial Revolution, entrepreneurship increased in the United States. In 1900, Arthur R. Wilson and several partners paid $10,000 in gold coins for a 27-acre parcel of granite-rich land in California. This natural resource was the basis for the Granite Rock Co., which provided the material for roads and buildings in California's booming economy. The company, now called Graniterock, evolved in response to technological, competitive, and marketplace demands and continues to survive in the 21st century. Today the firm, which has stores throughout California, offers consumer products such as granite countertops as well as many "green" products made from recycled materials.[18]

Inventors created a virtually endless array of commercially useful products and new production methods. Many of them are famous today:

- Eli Whitney introduced the concept of interchangeable parts, an idea that would later facilitate mass production on a previously impossible scale.
- Robert McCormick designed a horse-drawn reaper that reduced the labor involved in harvesting wheat. His son, Cyrus McCormick, saw the commercial potential of the reaper and launched a business to build and sell the machine. By 1902, the company was producing 35 percent of the nation's farm machinery.
- Cornelius Vanderbilt (railroads), J. P. Morgan (banking), and Andrew Carnegie (steel), among others, took advantage of the enormous opportunities waiting for anyone willing to take the risk of starting a new business.

The entrepreneurial spirit of this golden age in business did much to advance the U.S. business system and raise the overall standard of living of its citizens. That market transformation, in turn, created new demand for manufactured goods.

## The Production Era

As demand for manufactured goods continued to increase through the 1920s, businesses focused even greater attention on the activities involved in producing those goods. Work became increasingly specialized, and huge, labor-intensive factories dominated U.S. business. Assembly lines, introduced by Henry Ford, became commonplace in major industries. Business owners turned over their responsibilities to a new class of managers trained in operating established companies. Their activities emphasized efforts to produce even more goods through quicker methods.

During the production era, business focused attention on internal processes rather than external influences. Marketing was almost an afterthought, designed solely to distribute items generated by production activities. Little attention was paid to consumer wants or needs. Instead, businesses tended to make decisions about what the market would get. If you wanted to buy a Ford Model T automobile, your color choice was black—the only color produced by the factory.

## The Marketing Era

The Great Depression of the early 1930s changed the shape of U.S. business yet again. As incomes nose-dived, businesses could no longer automatically count on selling everything they produced. Managers began to pay more attention to the markets for their goods and services, and sales and advertising took on new importance. During this period, selling was often synonymous with marketing.

Demand for all kinds of consumer goods exploded after World War II. After nearly five years of doing without new automobiles, appliances, and other items to contribute to the war effort, consumers were buying again. At the same time, however, competition also heated up. Soon businesses began to think of marketing as more than just selling; they envisioned a process of determining what consumers wanted and needed and then designing products to satisfy those needs. In short, they developed a **consumer orientation**.

Businesses began to analyze consumer desires before beginning actual production. Consumer choice skyrocketed. Today's automobiles no longer come just in black; instead, car buyers can choose from a wide range of colors and accessories.

Businesses also discovered the need to distinguish their goods and services from those of competitors. **Branding**, the process of creating an identity in consumers' minds for a good, service, or company, is an important marketing tool. A **brand** can be a name, term, sign, symbol, design, or some combination that identifies the products of one firm and differentiates them from competitors' offerings.

One of the early masters of branding was Ray Kroc, who was the franchising agent for a small hamburger chain started in San Bernardino, California. Kroc opened his first restaurant in the chain in Des Plaines, Illinois. A few years later, he bought out the owners, the McDonald brothers, and built the franchise into the famous McDonald's restaurant chain. Kroc insisted that every one of his restaurants follow the same operating procedures and offer similar menu items, reinforcing the nationwide image of the growing restaurant franchise in consumer minds across the country. Today, the "golden arches" are among the best-known company symbols in the world.

The marketing era has had a tremendous effect on the way business is conducted today. Even the smallest business owners recognize the importance of understanding what customers want and the reasons they buy.

## The Relationship Era

As business continues in the 21st century, a significant change is taking place in the ways companies interact with customers. Since the Industrial Revolution, most businesses have concentrated on building and promoting products in the hope that enough customers will buy them to cover costs and earn acceptable profits, an approach called **transaction management**.

In contrast, in the **relationship era**, businesses are taking a different, longer-term approach to their interactions with customers. Firms now seek ways to actively nurture customer loyalty by carefully managing every interaction. They earn enormous paybacks for their efforts. A company that retains customers over the long haul reduces its advertising and sales costs. Because customer spending tends to accelerate over time, revenues also grow. Companies with long-term customers often can avoid costly reliance on price discounts to attract new business, and they find that many new customers come from loyal customer referrals.

Business owners gain several advantages by developing ongoing relationships with customers. Because it is much less expensive to serve existing customers than to find new ones, businesses that develop long-term customer relationships can reduce their overall costs. Long-term relationships with customers enable businesses to improve their understanding of what customers want and prefer from the company. As a result, businesses enhance their chances of sustaining real advantages through competitive differentiation. Figure 1.7 illustrates one way that Citibank creates long-term customer relationships—through its Thank You rewards program that offers benefits to Citi credit card users, such as free hotel stays and airline tickets, college savings programs, and electronic gifts.

The McDonald's "golden arches" are one of the most recognizable brand symbols in the world.

**brand** name, term, sign, symbol, design, or some combination that identifies the products of one firm and differentiates them from competitors' offerings.

Citibank: Creating Long-Term Customer Relationships

**Figure**
1.7

An almost staggering array of rewards cards.

You must have been awfully good in another life.

citi
Live richly.

## Dress for Success

Congratulations—you've got a job interview! You're accustomed to wearing whatever you want to class—jeans, a T-shirt, sneakers. But in the working world, those clothes won't get you very far. In fact, employment experts warn that your appearance can make or break your chances of getting the job you want. While prospective employers care most about your skills, experience, and attitude, they also evaluate the way you present yourself to the world, even if you won't be dealing directly with customers. So an important first step in your career is to assess your wardrobe and make some purchases if necessary. You want to make the best first impression you can.

- Invest in one good-quality suit and wear it with a solid-color shirt or blouse. Men should wear a conservative tie; women might opt for a nice silk scarf or plain gold necklace. Make sure your shoes are clean, simple, and polished—the same goes for your purse or briefcase. If you are interviewing in a cold climate, invest in a good, conservative coat. Don't be tempted to throw on a ski jacket over your nice suit.
- Get a haircut before your interview. Neatly styled hair makes you look pulled together. Don't try giving your hair a radical new color—natural is best. Make sure

the rest of your grooming is meticulous—including teeth and fingernails.

- Avoid any visible body piercings, tattoos, or other decorations. Women may wear simple studs or small hoop earrings; men should leave these at home.
- Leave plenty of time to shower and dress before your interview, then check yourself in a full-length mirror before you head out the door.

Remember that you are dressing for the position you want; an interviewer should be able to visualize you in the job. Although your current budget may be tight, purchasing one good outfit is truly an investment in your career. Retailers are now focusing on post-college consumers for this very reason. Gap and Express are jumping into the career market, as is Abercrombie & Fitch. Department stores and value chains such as Kohl's, Target, and Wal-Mart are always a good bet for career apparel as well.

**Sources:** "Dress for Interview Success," CollegeGrad.com, accessed May 26, 2006, http://www.collegegrad.com; Randall S. Hansen, "When Job-Hunting: Dress for Success," *Quintessential Careers*, accessed May 26, 2006, http://www.quintcareers.com; Calvin Bruce, "Dress for Success," *Black Collegian*, accessed May 26, 2006, http://www.black-collegian.com; Lorrie Grant, "Trendy Retailers Get Dressed for Work," *USA Today*, May 26, 2006, p. B3.

The relationship era is an age of connections—between businesses and customers, employers and employees, technology and manufacturing, and even separate companies. The world economy is increasingly interconnected, as businesses expand beyond their national boundaries. In this new environment, techniques for managing networks of people, businesses, information, and technology are critically important to contemporary business success. As you begin your own career, you will soon see how important relationships are, beginning with your first job interview, as described in the "Business Etiquette" feature.

## Managing Relationships through Technology

Increasingly, businesses focus on **relationship management**, the collection of activities that build and maintain ongoing, mutually beneficial ties with customers and other parties. At its core, relationship management involves gathering knowledge of customer needs and preferences and applying that understanding to get as close to the customer as possible. Many of these activities are based on **technology**, or the business application of knowledge based on scientific discoveries, inventions, and innovations. In managing relationships with customers, technology most often takes the form of communication, particularly via the Internet.

Stonyfield Farm is the largest organic yogurt company in the world, and it relies on technology to help build and maintain relationships with its customers. Using one of the latest forms of Internet communication—Web logs, or blogs, which are online journals that the public can access—Stonyfield reinforces its relationships with consumers. The firm has hired a full-time blogger, Christine Halvorson, to create five different blogs on its Web site, including the Strong Women Daily News, the Bovine Bugle, and Creating Healthy Kids. Halvorson posts various news items, health and fitness tips, and other information on the blogs, to which consumers can respond. Stonyfield CEO Gary Hirshberg believes that giving customers this kind of access to his firm helps develop an emotional connection with them.[19]

**relationship management** collection of activities that build and maintain ongoing, mutually beneficial ties between a business and its customers and other parties.

## THE BUCK STOPS HERE: WHO SHOULD PAY FOR PROFESSIONAL SPORTS STADIUMS?

*It sounds great to sports fans: their team gets a new stadium or ballpark, or their city gets a new team. Or both happen at once.*

This was the case with baseball's Montreal Expos, as they were trying to move to Washington, D.C., to become the Nationals. Meanwhile, Las Vegas has been attempting to lure a Major League Baseball team. While sports buffs are cheering, fellow taxpayers are moaning—who pays for the new stadium? Often, professional sports team owners negotiate for as much of the cost as possible to be shouldered by the city or state. Mayors and state officials may agree to the terms because they envision long-term benefits to their cities and local businesses. But critics argue that professional sports stadiums should be built with private funds, including those of team owners and leagues.

**Should professional sports stadiums be funded with public money?**

### PRO

1. An updated or new professional sports stadium attracts visitors who spend money at the stadium and surrounding businesses, and enhances the image of the city.
2. Using public money makes the general public feel more like

owners and encourages them to attend games and functions.

### CON

1. In most cases, public funds are not even necessary. According to one estimate, a team can recoup half the cost of construction within the first 5 years, and all of it within 12 years.
2. A study of the economics of building stadiums concludes that consumers are not spending more money at surrounding businesses. "As sport- and stadium-related activities increase, other spending declines because people substitute spending on sports for other spending," notes the study. So, the surrounding community does not necessarily benefit economically.

### Summary

Government officials, team owners, professional leagues, and taxpayer groups continue to haggle over who foots the bill for new stadiums. In recent years, some officials have begun to take a tougher stand against the practice of public funding. A member of the Washington,

D.C., city council stood firm against the original financial plan and reduced the public payout to half the cost of construction. In addition, a Boston legislator recently blocked a deal in which Massachusetts taxpayers would have paid for a new ballpark for the Boston Red Sox. "The bottom line is that these new stadiums generate sufficient revenue to pay for themselves," argues one economics professor who has studied the situation. "If the stadium pays for itself internally, that should be sufficient motivation for the owners to build it."

**Sources:** Eric Fisher, "Stadium Labor Deal Reached," *The Washington Times*, accessed May 26, 2006, http://www.washingtontimes.com; Doug French, "Taxpayer-Financed Sports Stadiums: Deals Benefit Teams, Not Public," *Las Vegas Review-Journal*, accessed May 26, 2006, http://www.reviewjournal.com; Eric Fisher, "District Strikes Stadium Deal," *The Washington Times*, accessed May 26, 2006, http://www.washingtontimes.com; "Public Financing of Stadiums Unnecessary, Study Shows," *CBS SportsLine*, accessed May 26, 2006, http://cbssportsline.com.

## Strategic Alliances and Partnerships

Businesses are also finding that they must form partnerships with other organizations to take full advantage of available opportunities. A **partnership** is an affiliation of two or more companies that help each other achieve common goals. One such form of partnership between organizations is a **strategic alliance**, a partnership formed to create a competitive advantage for the businesses involved. While alliances are usually formed to benefit both parties, sometimes the balance appears to be one-sided, as discussed in the "Solving an Ethical Controversy" feature.

E-business has created a whole new type of strategic alliance. A firm whose entire business is conducted online, such as eBay or Amazon, may team up with traditional retailers that

**"They Said It"**

*"It's our customers who have built eBay."*
—Meg Whitman (b. 1956)
CEO and president, eBay

contribute their expertise in buying the right amount of the right merchandise, as well as their knowledge of distribution. Bloomingdale's, Home Depot, and Motorola all have one thing in common: an arrangement with eBay in which they sell excess or outdated merchandise on its Internet site called eBay Stores. With this agreement between retailers and the Web marketing giant, everyone wins: Consumers get good prices, the retailers get more return on the dollar than they'd earn in a clearance or liquidation sale, and eBay gets a cut.[20] Pepsi and Apple Computer recently joined forces in a short-term promotional effort in which Pepsi agreed to distribute up to 200 million free songs through the Apple iTunes Music Store when consumers bought Pepsi products that contained codes for the free songs. Consumers who participated also had chances to win free Apple iPod minis.[21]

Each new era in U.S. business history has forced managers to reexamine the tools and techniques they formerly used to compete. Tomorrow's managers will need creativity and vision to stay on top of rapidly changing technology and to manage complex relationships in the global business world of the fast-paced 21st century.

**assessment check**

1. What was the Industrial Revolution?
2. During which era was the idea of branding developed?
3. What is the difference between transaction management and relationship management?

# TODAY'S BUSINESS WORKFORCE

A skilled and knowledgeable workforce is an essential resource for keeping pace with the accelerating rate of change in today's business world. Employers need reliable workers who are dedicated to fostering strong ties with customers and partners. They must build workforces capable of efficient, high-quality production needed to compete in global markets. Savvy business leaders also realize that the brainpower of employees plays a vital role in a firm's ability to stay on top of new technologies and innovations. In short, a first-class workforce can be the foundation of a firm's competitive differentiation, providing important advantages over competing businesses.

## Changes in the Workforce

Companies now face several trends that challenge their skills for managing and developing human resources: aging of the population, a shrinking labor pool, growing diversity of the workforce, the changing nature of work, and new employer-employee relationships.

*Aging of the Population*  Members of the baby boom generation, people born between 1946 and 1965, are nearing the peaks of their careers, and the oldest of them have begun to retire. So employers must deal with issues arising from reliance on older workers, such as retirement, disability programs, retraining, and insurance benefits. By 2030, the number of Americans who are age 65 or older will reach 71 million—nearly double what it is today. These seniors will represent nearly 20 percent of the U.S. population. For every five working-age adults in the year 2000, there was one person age 65 or older, but by the year 2030, there will be only three working-age adults for every senior citizen.[22] As Table 1.2 illustrates, the U.S. Census Bureau has even identified the median population age of individual states—Maine has the oldest median population age at 40.6, while Utah has the youngest at 27.9.

A similar trend is occurring on a global scale. The worldwide population of seniors is expected to double by 2030 as well, from 420 million to 973 million. In fact, other countries are aging faster than the United States because of low birth rates and improved healthcare services. The median age in Japan is 42.9; in Europe it is 40.7.[23]

Table

1.2

Twenty States with the Oldest and Youngest Median Ages

| Oldest | | | Youngest | | |
|---|---|---|---|---|---|
| Rank | State | Median Age | Rank | State | Median Age |
| 1 | Maine | 40.6 | 1 | Utah | 27.9 |
| 2, 3 | Vermont | 40.2 | 2 | Texas | 32.8 |
| | West Virginia | 40.2 | 3 | Alaska | 33.3 |
| 4 | Montana | 39.5 | 4 | Georgia | 33.8 |
| 5 | Florida | 39.3 | 5, 6 | Arizona | 34.1 |
| 6 | Pennsylvania | 39.2 | | Idaho | 34.1 |
| 7 | Connecticut | 38.8 | 7 | California | 34.2 |
| 8–10 | Iowa | 38.0 | 8 | Colorado | 34.3 |
| | Rhode Island | 38.0 | 9 | Mississippi | 34.7 |
| | Wyoming | 38.0 | 10 | Louisiana | 34.9 |

**Source:** Data from U.S. Census Bureau, as cited in Haya El Nasser and Paul Overberg, "Youthquakes Shake Up Gray-Haired States," *USA Today*, March 10, 2005, p. 3A.

Because of these changes, companies are increasingly seeking—and finding—talent at the extreme ends of the working-age spectrum. Teenagers are entering the workforce sooner, and some seniors are staying longer—or seeking new careers after retiring from their primary careers. Companies that once encouraged early retirement are now developing incentives to keep workers on longer. Many older workers work part-time or flexible hours. Monsanto has a program that allows retired workers to return part time without giving up their retiree benefits. Procter & Gamble and Eli Lilly founded YourEncore, a service company that contracts retired scientists, engineers, and product developers out to other firms that need part-time or short-term help.[24]

*Shrinking Labor Pool* Today's managers face the opposite problem: a shrinking labor pool. Some economists predict that the U.S. workforce could fall short by as many as 10 million by 2010. More sophisticated technology has intensified the challenge by requiring workers to have more advanced skills. Although the pool of college-educated workers has doubled in the last 20 years, the demand is still greater than the supply of these individuals.

The challenge of a shrinking labor pool is especially great in developed nations, where the birthrate has shrunk to less than the rate of deaths. Particularly in Europe, the population of some countries is expected to decline over the first half of this century. The same forecasts predict continued growth in the U.S. population because immigration more than makes up for the low birthrate. In the future, as in the past, immigrants will provide a significant share of U.S. labor and entrepreneurship. Currently, immigrants represent one of every seven U.S. workers, and one of every two workers who are new to the workforce.[25]

*Increasingly Diverse Workforce* Reflecting these immigration trends, the U.S. workforce is growing more diverse. In the last decade, California and Florida received the most immigrants, although Colorado, North Carolina, and Kentucky experienced the greatest *percentage*

**1.8** ABN AMRO's Commitment to Diversity

"I want a bank rooted in the community. Not implanted."

COURTESY OF ABN AMRO

of growth in foreign-born residents. In addition, the two fastest-growing populations in the United States are those of Hispanic and Asian origins. Currently, Hispanics represent about 14 percent of the United States population and Asians represent about 4 percent.[26] Many of these individuals are looking for jobs, and companies are willing to train them. Managers must also learn to work effectively with diverse ethnic groups, cultures, and lifestyles to develop and retain a superior workforce for their company.

**Diversity,** blending individuals of different genders, ethnic backgrounds, cultures, religions, ages, and physical and mental abilities, can enhance a firm's chances of success. Several studies have shown that diverse employee teams and workforces tend to perform tasks more effectively and develop better solutions to business problems than homogeneous employee groups. This difference is due in part to the varied perspectives and experiences that foster innovation and creativity in multicultural teams.

To benefit from diversity, executives of many companies develop high-profile strategies to encourage and manage multiculturalism. UPS is one such firm. Minorities account for 35 percent of the company's 317,000 employees in the United States. Top leaders at UPS believe that "diversity is a valuable, core component of UPS because it brings a wider range of resources, skills, and ideas to the business." The firm has a UPS Diversity Steering Council that oversees the commitment to diversity, including equal opportunity and promotion programs, team building, and employee stock ownership. UPS has received many awards for its focus on diversity, including being ranked on *Fortune*'s list of "50 Best Companies for Minorities" several years running.[27] The ad for ABN AMRO in Figure 1.8 illustrates the worldwide banking group's commitment to diversity with its 110,000 employees in 60 countries.

Also, practical managers know that attention to diversity issues can help them avoid costly and damaging legal battles. Employee lawsuits alleging discrimination are a major legal issue that employers face. Losing a discrimination lawsuit can be very costly, yet in a recent survey, a majority of executives from racial and cultural minorities said they had seen discrimination in work assignments.

### assessment check

1. How does the aging workforce affect businesses?
2. How can businesses benefit from a diverse workforce?

*Outsourcing and the Changing Nature of Work* Not only is the U.S. workforce changing, but so is the very nature of work. Manufacturing used to account for most of U.S. annual output, but the scale has now shifted to services such as financial management and communications. This means that firms must rely heavily on well-trained service workers with knowledge, technical skills, the ability to communicate and deal with people, and a talent for creative thinking. Different work lifestyles, such as telecommuting, are also becoming common in business life. Many employers allow job flexibility so employees can meet family and personal needs along with job-related needs. Employers are also hiring growing numbers of temporary and part-time employees.

The Internet has made possible another business tool for staffing flexibility—**outsourcing**, using outside vendors to produce goods or fulfill services and functions that were previously handled in-country or in-house. For example, if you dial the call center for America Online, your call most likely will be answered by someone in India. Companies outsource certain functions for several reasons, among them reduction of labor or production costs and improvement in the quality or speed of software maintenance or development. In the best situation, out-

**outsourcing** using outside vendors to produce goods or fulfill services and functions that were previously handled in-country or in-house.

sourcing allows a firm to concentrate its resources on the things it does best. It also provides access to expertise that may not exist within the firm. But outsourcing also creates its own challenges, such as differences in language or culture. When Dell Computer received numerous complaints from customers who were frustrated by the outsourcing of its help line to a firm in India, Dell began to roll back some of its customer service operations to the United States.

**Offshoring** is the relocation of business processes to lower-cost locations overseas. This can include both production and services. In recent years, China has emerged as a dominant location for production offshoring for many firms, while India has become the key player in offshoring services. Some U.S. companies are now structured so that entire divisions or functions are developed and staffed overseas—the jobs were never in the United States to start with. According to one survey, nearly 40 percent of start-up companies employ engineers, marketers, and other workers in India and other countries. Google began hiring outside the United States only three years after it opened its virtual doors, and a significant number of its 3,000 employees are located in offices in Toronto, London, Tokyo, Paris, Milan, Sydney, Dublin, and other cities.[28]

Another trend has developed in some industries—**nearshoring,** which involves outsourcing production or services to locations near firm's home base. For example, western European companies have discovered a talented labor pool in the eastern European countries of Bulgaria and Romania. German software giant SAP has a research lab in Bulgaria, where nearly 200 engineers write software for SAP's products. The United States has also benefited from nearshoring by locating offices and factories in Mexico and the Caribbean to tap nearby labor forces.[29]

*The New Employer-Employee Partnership*  The old relationship between employers and employees was pretty simple: workers arrived at a certain hour, did their jobs, and went home every day at the same time. Often the two were tied together for their working lifetime. Companies rarely laid off workers, and employees rarely left for a job at another firm. But all of that—and more—has changed. Employees are no longer likely to remain with a single company throughout their entire careers. In fact, you probably can't imagine working for one company your entire life. On the other hand, you probably expect to work more than the traditional 8-hour workday. You don't necessarily expect lifetime loyalty from the company you work for, but you don't expect to give it either. Instead, you are looking forward to building your own career however and wherever you can.

These changes mean that employers and employees must forge new partnerships. As the nature of work and the workforce are changing, so is the nature of the relationship between employers and employees. Many firms now recognize the value of a partnership with employees that encourages creative thinking, problem solving, and innovation. Managers are being trained to listen to and respect employees. Companies now routinely share financial data and reward employees with benefits such as stock and profit sharing so that they feel more committed to contributing to their firm's success. In addition, employees often receive training geared toward career advancement in the hope that they will remain with the firm that trains them. Microsoft focuses on recruiting employees who are capable of innovative thinking in both business and technology. Founder Bill Gates believes that fostering a culture of creativity among employees has allowed his firm to grow and to take risks on future products.[30]

**assessment check**

1. Define outsourcing, offshoring, and nearshoring.
2. Describe the new employer-employee partnership.

# THE 21ST-CENTURY MANAGER

Today's companies look for managers who are intelligent, highly motivated people with the ability to create and sustain a vision of how an organization can succeed. The 21st-century manager must also apply critical-thinking skills and creativity to business challenges and steer change.

## Importance of Vision

To thrive in the 21st century, businesspeople need **vision**, the ability to perceive marketplace needs and what an organization must do to satisfy them. Forty years ago, Amar Bose saw an opportunity in the marketplace when he invented the sound system that still bears his name. He continues to run his firm with the same kind of vision he had when he began: Bose secures his company's place in the future by reinvesting a large portion of its $1.7 billion earnings into the research and development of new products. One of the firm's latest innovations is a super-smooth automobile suspension system. Bose realizes that bringing his firm's products to market involves taking a risk. But he believes in his company. "We just know that we have a technology that's so different and so much better that many people will want it," he says.[31]

It takes vision to turn a tiny handbag shop located in a New York apartment into a $125 million design business that offers shoes, fragrances, china—and, of course, handbags. But Kate Spade and her husband Andy have managed to do exactly that. Once their bags became popular, they decided to take a chance. "We knew we had a window of opportunity, but the point was to get into a category that had a growth prospect, and not for growth to simply be the byproduct," says Kate.[32] Note that the founders of both of these companies understand the importance of following through with sound business and marketing practices.

## Importance of Critical Thinking and Creativity

Critical thinking and creativity are essential characteristics of the 21st-century workforce. Today's businesspeople need to look at a wide variety of situations, draw connections between disparate information, and develop future-oriented solutions. This need applies not only to top executives, but to midlevel managers and entry-level workers as well.

**Critical thinking** is the ability to analyze and assess information to pinpoint problems or opportunities. The critical-thinking process includes activities such as determining the authenticity, accuracy, and worth of information, knowledge, and arguments. It involves looking beneath the surface for deeper meaning and connections that can help identify critical issues and solutions. Without critical thinking, a firm may encounter serious problems, as described in the "Hit & Miss" feature.

**Creativity** is the capacity to develop novel solutions to perceived organizational problems. Although most people think of it in relation to artists, musicians, and inventors, that is a very limited definition. In business, creativity refers to the ability to see better and different ways of doing business. A computer engineer who solves a glitch in a software program is executing a creative act; so is a shipping clerk who finds a way to speed delivery of the company's overnight packages. Companies must constantly find innovative ways to communicate with and attract new customers, while keeping the interest of established customers. Howard Schultz, founder of Starbucks, looks to all of his employees for new ideas—particularly those who interact with customers in Starbucks stores every day. He loves to tell the story of the Starbucks store manager in West Los Angeles who "was fooling around one day in our store, blending beverages with a blender she bought on her own." The company distributed samples of one of the beverages throughout several southern California stores, and both managers and customers gave it a positive review. "We tested it, named it, and Frappuccino today is a multi-hundred-million dollar business in our stores," says Schultz.[33]

Some practice and mental exercise can cultivate your own ability to think creatively. Here are some exercises and guidelines:

- In a group, brainstorm by listing ideas as they come to mind. Build on other people's ideas, but don't criticize them. Wait until later to evaluate and organize the ideas.
- Think about how to make familiar concepts unfamiliar. A glue that doesn't stick very well? That's the basis for 3M's popular Post-it notes.

## HIT & MISS

### How Jones Soda Regained Its Fizz

Entrepreneurs must be willing to take risks—it is part of the job. Often, they make mistakes simply from lack of experience. But the lessons they learn from those mistakes can eventually strengthen their businesses. That's what happened to Peter van Stolk, founder of Jones Soda.

Twenty years ago, van Stolk squeezed fresh fruit juices on the streets of Canada. He was so successful that his company, Urban Juice & Soda, grew to $6 million in sales. Within five years it went public on the Vancouver stock exchange and later began trading in the United States. In 2000, the company's name was changed to Jones Soda. The firm was on a steady climb to fame and fortune. "It all seemed simple," recalls van Stolk, perhaps a bit wistfully.

Then the soft-drink bubble burst. The firm had to recall 1 million bottles because ingredients were breaking down too quickly. That year "was pretty much shot because of that," says van Stolk. He sued the supplier and eventually received a $4 million settlement, but that didn't replace lost sales or confidence in the product. When Jones Soda moved its headquarters to Seattle, few distributors agreed to handle the drinks because they'd never heard of Jones and competition from the larger soft-drink companies was intense. Van Stolk kept spending money on advertising and incentives to distributors until his marketing expenses topped $7.6 million. The company was literally giving away cases of soda. "The only thing that mattered to us was the top line," explains van Stolk. "We were building the company to be sold."

But no one wanted Jones. Meanwhile, Jones botched a potentially lucrative deal with Pepsi by hastily delivering a mislabeled product, resulting in a $400,000 loss, and five of its distributors went bankrupt. "Store shelves were going empty, and our competitors were quick to fill them," notes van Stolk.

Just when Jones couldn't seem to get any flatter, Panera Bread approached the firm and agreed to carry some of its products in their restaurants. Barnes & Noble followed and now carries Jones Naturals juices and teas in all 500 of its cafes. Then Starbucks came through—Jones drinks are now in 4,000 Starbucks shops across the United States. Finally, van Stolk persuaded Target to purchase Jones in concentrated form, then do its own bottling. Target accounts for $1 million of Jones Soda's annual earnings. By selling 22 percent of its beverages directly to retailers instead of dealing with distributors, Jones Soda has returned to profitability with an increase in profits of nearly 300 percent in one year. Van Stolk has learned that haste—as in the case of the Pepsi deal—often makes waste and that business is never simple. But the fizz is back in Jones Soda.

### Questions for Critical Thinking

1. Do you think van Stolk had a clear vision when he started his firm? Why or why not?
2. How might critical thinking have helped Jones Soda avoid some of its pitfalls? How might it help the firm in the future?

**Sources:** Jones Soda Web site, accessed May 26, 2006, http://www.jonessoda.com; Christopher Steiner, "Soda Jerk," *Forbes*, May 26, 2006, pp. 74–75; "Jones Soda Co. Announces Record Fourth Quarter and 2004 Year-End Financial Results," *Yahoo!*, accessed May 26, 2006, http://biz.yahoo.com; "Soda Company Serves Up Feast in a Bottle," *(Danbury, CT) News-Times*, accessed May 26, 2006, http://www.newstimes180.com.

- Plan ways to rearrange your thinking with simple questions such as, "What features can we leave out?" or by imagining what it feels like to be the customer.
- Cultivate curiosity, openness, risk, and energy as you meet people and encounter new situations. View these encounters as opportunities to learn.
- Treat failures as additional opportunities to learn.
- Get regular physical exercise. When you work out, your brain releases endorphins, and these chemicals stimulate creative thinking.
- Pay attention to your dreams and daydreams. You might find that you already know the answer to a problem.

Creativity and critical thinking must go beyond generating new ideas, however. They must lead to action. In addition to creating an environment in which employees can nurture ideas, managers must give them opportunities to take risks and try new solutions.

## 1.9  Aetna's Health Fund Insurance Plans: Staying Ahead through Innovation and Change

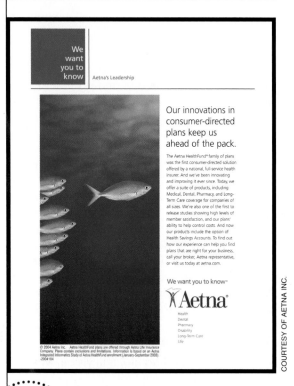

## Ability to Steer Change

Today's business owners must guide their employees and organizations through the changes brought about by technology, marketplace demands, and global competition. Managers must be skilled at recognizing employee strengths and motivating people to move toward common goals as members of a team. Throughout this book, real-world examples demonstrate how companies have initiated sweeping change initiatives. Most, if not all, have been led by managers comfortable with the tough decisions that today's fluctuating conditions require. For the past decade, managers in the fast-food industry have been searching for ways to create healthier, better-tasting menu offerings that consumers will actually buy and eat. They've had more failures than successes—hardly anyone cared about McDonald's McLean burgers or McSalad Shakers, and Taco Bell's Border Lights didn't light up the cash registers. But they keep trying. "My job has become a lot harder," says the vice president of menu marketing at Jack in the Box.[34]

Factors that require organizational change can come from both external and internal sources; successful managers must be aware of both. External forces might include feedback from customers, developments in the international marketplace, economic trends, and new technologies. Internal factors might arise from new company goals, emerging employee needs, labor union demands, or production problems. Figure 1.9 illustrates health insurance firm Aetna's response to consumer demands for change.

# WHAT MAKES A COMPANY ADMIRED?

Who is your hero? Is it someone who has achieved great feats in sports, government, entertainment, or business? Why do you admire the person—does he or she run a company, earn a lot of money, or give back to the community and society? Every year, business magazines and organizations publish lists of companies that they consider to be "most admired." Companies, like individuals, may be admired for many reasons. Most people would mention solid profits, stable growth, a safe and challenging work environment, high-quality goods and services, and business ethics and social responsibility. *Business ethics* refers to the standards of conduct and moral values involving decisions made in the work environment. *Social responsibility* is a management philosophy that includes contributing resources to the community, preserving the natural environment, and developing or participating in nonprofit programs designed to promote the well-being of the general public. You'll find business ethics and social responsibility examples throughout this book, as well as a deeper exploration of these topics in Chapter 2. Figure 1.10 illustrates medical technology firm Becton, Dickinson's socially responsible commitment to diabetes research.

As you read this text, you'll be able to make up your own mind about why companies should—or should not—be admired. *Fortune* publishes two lists of most-admired companies each year, one for U.S.-based firms and one for the world. The list is compiled from surveys and other research conducted by the Hay Group, a global human resources and organizational consulting firm. Criteria for making the list include innovation, financial soundness, use of corporate assets, long-term investment, people management, quality of management, social responsibility,

**assessment check**

1. Why is vision an important managerial quality?
2. What is the difference between creativity and critical thinking?

**assessment check**

1. Define business ethics and social responsibility.
2. Identify three criteria used to judge whether a company might be considered admirable.

Table 1.3

Figure 1.10

*Fortune's* Top Ten Most Admired U.S. Companies

| 1 | General Electric | 6 | Johnson & Johnson |
|---|---|---|---|
| 2 | FedEx | 7 | Berkshire Hathaway |
| 3 | Southwest Airlines | 8 | Dell |
| 4 | Procter & Gamble | 9 | Toyota Motor |
| 5 | Starbucks | 10 | Microsoft |

**Source:** Data from http://www.timeinc.net/fortune/information/Presscenter/ 0,,20060221_mostadmired,00.html, accessed June 13, 2006.

Becton, Dickinson's Fight to Cure Diabetes: Commitment to Social Responsibility

and quality of products and services.[35] Table 1.3 lists the top ten U.S. firms for one recent year.[36]

# WHAT'S AHEAD

As business speeds along in the 21st century, new technologies, population shifts, and shrinking global barriers are altering the world at a frantic pace. Businesspeople are catalysts for many of these changes, creating new opportunities for individuals who are prepared to take action. Studying contemporary business will help you prepare for the future.

Throughout this book, you'll be exposed to the real-life stories of many businesspeople. You'll learn about the range of business careers available and the daily decisions, tasks, and challenges that they face. By the end of the course, you'll understand how marketing, accounting, finance, and management work together to provide competitive advantages for firms. This knowledge can help you become a more capable employee and enhance your career potential.

Now that this chapter has introduced some basic terms and issues in the business world of the 21st century, Chapter 2 takes a detailed look at the ethical and social responsibility issues facing contemporary business. Chapter 3 deals with economic challenges, and Chapter 4 focuses on the challenges and opportunities faced by firms competing in global markets.

## SUMMARY OF LEARNING GOALS

**1 Distinguish between business and not-for-profit organizations.**

Business consists of all profit-seeking activities that provide goods and services necessary to an economic system. Not-for-profit organizations are business-like establishments whose primary objectives involve social, political, governmental, educational, or similar functions—instead of profits.

### Assessment Check Answers

**1.1 What activity lies at the heart of every business endeavor?**

At the heart of every business endeavor is an exchange between a buyer and a seller.

**1.2 What are the primary objectives of a not-for-profit organization?**

Not-for-profit organizations place public service above profits, although they need to raise money in order to operate and achieve their social goals.

**2 Identify and describe the factors of production.**

The factors of production consist of four basic inputs: natural resources, capital, human resources, and entrepreneurship. Natural resources include all productive inputs that are useful in their natural states. Capital includes technology, tools, information, and physical facilities. Human resources include anyone who works for the firm. Entrepreneurship is the willingness to take risks to create and operate a business.

## Assessment Check Answers

**2.1 Identify the four basic inputs to an economic system.**
The four basic inputs are natural resources, capital, human resources, and entrepreneurship.

**2.2 List four types of capital.**
Four types of capital are technology, tools, information, and physical facilities.

**3 Describe the private enterprise system, including basic rights and entrepreneurship.**
The private enterprise system is an economic system that rewards firms for their ability to perceive and serve the needs and demands of consumers. Competition in the private enterprise system ensures success for firms that satisfy consumer demands. Citizens in a private enterprise economy enjoy the rights to private property, profits, freedom of choice, and competition. Entrepreneurship drives economic growth.

## Assessment Check Answers

**3.1 What is an alternative term for *private enterprise system*?**
*Capitalism* is an alternative word for *private enterprise system*.

**3.2 What is the most basic freedom under the private enterprise system?**
The most basic freedom is the right to private property.

**3.3 What is an entrepreneur?**
An entrepreneur is a risk taker who is willing to start, own, and operate a business.

**4 Identify the six eras of business and explain how the relationship era—including alliances and technology—influences contemporary business.**
The six historical eras are the Colonial period, the Industrial Revolution, the age of industrial entrepreneurs, the production era, the marketing era, and the relationship era. In the Colonial period, businesses were small and rural, emphasizing agricultural production. The Industrial Revolution brought factories and mass production to business. The age of industrial entrepreneurs built on the Industrial Revolution through an expansion in the number and size of firms.

The production era focused on the growth of factory operations through assembly lines and other efficient internal processes. During and following the Great Depression, businesses concentrated on finding markets for their products through advertising and selling, giving rise to the marketing era. In the relationship era, businesspeople focus on developing and sustaining long-term relationships with customers and other businesses. Technology promotes innovation and communication, while alliances create a competitive advantage through partnerships.

## Assessment Check Answers

**4.1 What was the Industrial Revolution?**
The Industrial Revolution began around 1750 in England, and moved business operations from an emphasis on independent, skilled workers to a factory system that mass-produced items.

**4.2 During which era was the idea of branding developed?**
The idea of branding began in the marketing era.

**4.3 What is the difference between transaction management and relationship management?**
Transaction management is an approach that focuses on building, promoting, and selling enough products to cover costs and earn profits. Relationship management is the collection of activities that build and maintain ongoing ties with customers and other parties.

**5 Explain how today's business workforce is changing.**
The workforce is changing in several significant ways: (1) it is aging; (2) the labor pool is shrinking; and (3) it is becoming increasingly diverse.

## Assessment Check Answers

**5.1 How does the aging workforce affect business?**
An aging workforce requires businesses to hire workers at both extreme ends of the working-age spectrum.

**5.2 How can businesses benefit from a diverse workforce?**
A diverse workforce can enrich a company's chances of success because diverse groups tend to perform tasks more effectively and develop better solutions. They also tend to foster greater innovation.

**6 Describe how the nature of work itself is changing.**
The nature of work has shifted toward services and a focus on information. More firms now rely on outsourcing, offshoring, and nearshoring to produce goods

or fulfill services and functions that were previously handled in-house or in-country. In addition, new employer-employee partnerships are being forged.

## Assessment Check Answers

**6.1 Define *outsourcing*, *offshoring*, and *nearshoring*.**
Outsourcing involves using outside vendors to produce goods or fulfill services and functions that were once handled in-house or in-country. Offshoring is the relocation of business processes to lower-cost locations overseas. Nearshoring is the outsourcing of production or services to locations near a firm's home base.

**6.2 Describe the new employer-employee partnership.**
The new employer-employee partnership encourages creative thinking, problem solving, and innovation. Managers are trained to listen to and respect employees. Companies now routinely share financial data and reward employees with certain financial benefits.

**7 Identify the skills and attributes that managers need to lead businesses in the 21st century.**
Managers in the new century need vision, the ability to perceive marketplace needs and how their firm can satisfy them. Critical-thinking skills and creativity allow managers to pinpoint problems and opportunities and plan novel solutions. Finally, managers are dealing with rapid change, and they need skills to help steer their organizations through shifts in external and internal conditions.

## Assessment Check Answers

**7.1 Why is vision an important managerial quality?**
Managerial vision allows a firm to innovate and adapt to meet changes in the marketplace.

**7.2 What is the difference between creativity and critical thinking?**
Critical thinking is the ability to analyze and assess information to pinpoint problems or opportunities. Creativity is the capacity to develop novel solutions to perceived organizational problems.

**8 Outline the characteristics that make a company admired by the business community.**
A company is usually admired for its solid profits, stable growth, a safe and challenging work environment, high-quality goods and services, and business ethics and social responsibility.

## Assessment Check Answers

**8.1 Define *business ethics* and *social responsibility*.**
Business ethics refers to the standards of conduct and moral values involving decisions made in the work environment. Social responsibility is a management philosophy that includes contributing resources to the community, preserving the natural environment, and developing or participating in nonprofit programs designed to promote the well-being of the general public.

**8.2 Identify three criteria used to judge whether a company might be considered admirable.**
Criteria in judging whether companies are admirable include solid profits, stable growth, a safe and challenging work environment, high-quality goods and services, and business ethics and social responsibility.

## Business Terms You Need to Know

| | | |
|---|---|---|
| business 4 | private enterprise system 9 | brand 15 |
| profits 5 | competition 9 | relationship management 16 |
| factors of production 6 | entrepreneur 10 | outsourcing 20 |

## Other Important Business Terms

| | | |
|---|---|---|
| not-for-profit organizations 5 | private property 9 | strategic alliance 17 |
| natural resources 6 | consumer orientation 14 | diversity 20 |
| capital 6 | branding 14 | offshoring 21 |
| human resources 7 | transaction management 15 | nearshoring 21 |
| entrepreneurship 8 | relationship era 15 | vision 22 |
| capitalism 9 | technology 16 | critical thinking 22 |
| competitive differentiation 9 | partnership 17 | creativity 22 |

1. Why is business so important to a country's economy?
2. In what ways are not-for-profit organizations a substantial part of the U.S. economy? What challenges will not-for-profits face in the next decade or two?
3. Identify and describe the four basic inputs that make up factors of production. Give an example of each factor of production that an auto manufacturer might use.
4. What is a private enterprise system? What are the four rights that are critical to the operation of capitalism? Why would capitalism have difficulty functioning in a society that does not assure these rights for its citizens?
5. In what ways is entrepreneurship vital to the private enterprise system?
6. Identify the six eras of business in the United States. How were businesses changed during each era?
7. Describe the focus of the most recent era of U.S. business. How is this different from previous eras?
8. How might a supermarket chain use technology to assist in its relationship management?
9. Define *partnership* and *strategic alliance*. How might a motorcycle dealer and a local radio station benefit from an alliance?
10. Identify the major changes in the workforce that will affect the way managers build a world-class workforce in the 21st century. Why is brainpower so important?
11. Identify four qualities that the "new" managers of the 21st century must have. Why are these qualities important in a competitive business environment?

1. The entrepreneurial spirit fuels growth in the U.S. economy. Choose a company that interests you—one you have worked for or dealt with as a customer—and read about the company in the library or visit its Web site. Learn what you can about the company's early history: Who founded it and why? Is the founder still with the organization? Do you think the founder's original vision is still embraced by the company? If not, how has the vision changed?
2. Brands distinguish one company's goods or services from its competitors. Each company you purchase from hopes that you will become loyal to its brand. Some well-known brands are McDonald's, Coca-Cola, Hilton, and Old Navy. Choose a type of good or service you use regularly and identify the major brands associated with it. Are you loyal to a particular brand? Why or why not?
3. More and more businesses are forming strategic alliances to become more competitive. Sometimes, businesses pair up with not-for-profit organizations in a relationship that is beneficial to both. Choose a company whose goods or services interest you, such as Timberland, Patagonia, General Mills, or Wal-Mart. On your own or with a classmate, research the firm on the Internet to learn about its alliances with not-for-profit organizations. Then describe one of the alliances, including goals and benefits to both parties. Create a presentation for class.
4. This chapter describes how the nature of the workforce is changing: the population is aging, the labor pool is shrinking, the workforce is becoming more diverse, the nature of work is changing, and employers are forging new partnerships with their employees. Form teams of two to three students. Select a company and research how that company is responding to changes in the workforce. When you have completed your research, be prepared to present it to your class. Choose one of the following companies or select your own:

   - Costco
   - Whole Foods Market
   - Nordstrom
   - Marriott
   - Dell Computer

## Under Armour: Built with Sweat Equity

You've heard the term *sweat equity*—businesses built with lots of work and little cash. Under Armour, founded by college student Kevin Plank, was built on this concept. Plank, and his college football teammates at the University of Maryland, got tired of wearing soggy, shapeless cotton T-shirts. The clammy shirts made them feel uncomfortable as they played, but Plank couldn't find anything better.

Plank was determined to find an answer to the problem. A natural entrepreneur—he'd already started a floral delivery service from his dorm—Plank began combing fabric stores for something that would give a snug, smooth fit and carry away moisture at the same time. He found a slinky synthetic fabric, bought it, and paid a tailor $400 to sew several prototypes for his teammates to try. They loved it. "They said the shirt was great for football—and baseball and lacrosse, too," recalls Plank. "I realized this wasn't just a shirt but a marketing opportunity."

Once Plank had graduated from college, he pursued his dream full time. Working from the basement of his grandmother's home, he borrowed $40,000 on his credit cards to get started and later received a $250,000 small-business loan. Plank didn't have a sales force, so he took his shirts from school to school, and from pro team to pro team, where some of his college football teammates were now playing. When sports fans started to see Under Armour apparel on pro football players, they wanted the same thing. Then Plank had to find a factory to make more shirts.

Today, Under Armour dominates the market for "tight-fitting compression wear," as it is called, with more than $200 million in sales per year. "When people ask for compression gear, they ask for Under Armour, like Scotch tape or Xerox machines," says Ron Menconi, vice president of the sporting goods

chain G.I. Joe's in Oregon and Washington. Under Armour is currently the official supplier of compression apparel to Major League Baseball and Major League Soccer, and its clothing is worn by players on 30 NFL teams and nearly 100 Division 1-A college football teams, including Plank's alma mater, the University of Maryland. Plank also makes certain that his firm gives something back to the community. As chairman of the Baltimore City Fire Foundation, he uses his firm's popularity to help raise funds for the fire department.

In addition to the original T-shirt, Plank's firm now makes everything from shorts and leggings to knit caps, headbands and wristbands, socks and gloves, and even gym bags. Plank's products are so innovative that competing manufacturer Neal Caplowe of Sport Science calls them "the new mousetrap." Caplowe explains, "Whether it's product innovation, packaging or right-time, right-place or all of the above, they basically were able to light the fuse."

### Questions for Critical Thinking

1. Identify specific examples of factors of production that Under Armour requires for effective operation.
2. Explain how innovation, creativity, and critical thinking have all played a role in the development of Under Armour as a company.

**Sources:** Under Armour Web site, accessed May 26, 2006, http://www.underarmour.com; "ESPN, Under Armour Sign Deal," Brandweek.com, accessed May 26, 2006, http://www.brandweek.com; Jane Bennett Clark and Kimberly Lankford, "How to Make a Million," *Kiplinger's*, February 2005, pp. 69–74; Barbara De Lollis, "No Sweat: Idea for Athletic Gear Takes Him to the Top," *USA Today*, December 13, 2004, pp. B1, B2.

---

## VIDEO **Case 1.2**

### Peet's Coffee & Tea Brews Good Business

This video case appears on page 608. A recently filmed video, designed to expand and highlight the written case, is available for class use by instructors.

# Chapter 2

## Business Ethics and Social Responsibility

DIGITAL VISION/GETTY IMAGES

When a small café in Waitsfield, Vermont, opened for business in 1981, owner Bob Stiller didn't expect that his fresh-roast business would grow into a $137 million firm or become one of the nation's largest specialty-coffee manufacturers. But that's exactly what happened. Thanks to the high quality of Green Mountain's fresh-roasted blends and its commitment to a set of highly ethical guiding principles, the company has more than 7,000 wholesale clients and thousands of mail-order and Internet customers around the country. Its ethical guidelines put the health of the environment second only to passion for coffee—and rank ethics above all. The company's Web site emphasizes Green Mountain's social conscience: "We create the ultimate coffee experience in every life we touch

PHOTODISC/GETTY IMAGES

## Green Mountain Cares about More Than Coffee

from tree to cup, transforming the way the world understands business."

As the company has grown, Green Mountain Coffee Roasters has expanded the range of its commitments to include not only making wise use of the world's resources but also safeguarding the welfare of all those it deals with, from customers at home to coffee farmers far away. When it comes to the environment, Green Mountain, now headquartered in Waterbury, Vermont, has three core values:

- to consider the environmental impact of its actions in every decision
- to seek continuous environmental innovation in its products and programs
- to promote employee awareness of and participation in environmental efforts

The company works hard to put these values into practice. For instance, National Wildlife Blend and National Wildlife Decaf are two certified organic blends Green Mountain developed in cooperation with the National Wildlife Federation. These coffees offer consumers an alternative to inexpensive commercial coffees that must be grown in full sun, which means large-scale land clearing for coffee-growing areas and the destruction of bird and other wildlife habitats. The National

Wildlife cobranded coffees are made from shade-grown beans harvested by trusted small-scale farms in Mexico and Peru. Green Mountain is also a staunch supporter of fair trade pricing, which guarantees farmers fair prices for their crops so that "they can afford to feed their families, keep their kids in school and invest in the quality of their coffee."

To contribute to the communities in which it operates, Green Mountain encourages its nearly 600 employees to volunteer their time and expertise. Its Community Action for Employees (CAFÉ) program provides paid time off for community service, including in a recent year nearly 2,000 hours of employee time donated to schools, fire departments, rescue squads, and other community organizations. Employees even volunteer to visit Mexican and Central American coffee farms to help farmers improve their families' and their communities' healthcare and housing.

Green Mountain's corporate-wide efforts to help its communities include financial support for charitable organizations such as the United Way, the Salvation Army, and the Red Cross, as well as for many local organizations such as libraries, schools, and food programs. The company also created two matching funds to supplement the money donated by employees to aid relief of the 2004 tsunami that struck Sumatra, where many coffee growers live and work, and it continues to plan long-term strategies to provide assistance there. In addition to such efforts, the company each year contributes at least 5 percent of its pretax profits to social programs, and it has been frequently recognized for its good works by *Forbes* magazine in its annual list of "200 Best Small Companies" and *Business Ethics* magazine's "100 Best Corporate Citizens."

Within its organization, Green Mountain upholds the values of open dialogue and communication. The firm appreciates employee differences and tries to find opportunity in conflict and continuous learning. Teamwork, shared ownership and use of resources, and a commitment to personal excellence that includes self-awareness and respect all encourage leadership throughout the organization. Last but not least in this company's set of guiding values is to be "a force for good in the world." But good business decisions remain paramount. Says CEO Stiller, "To help the world, we have to be successful. If we help the world and go out of business, we're not going to help anybody."[1]

The values that drive Green Mountain's operations at home and abroad are not unique in the world of business. Many firms are concerned about the environment and their societies. Sometimes that means growing more slowly than they might or reducing short-term profits for longer, sustained benefits. Even Green Mountain faces tough decisions, for example, if one of its small-scale suppliers produces beans the firm must reject for quality reasons or because it has reached its production limit.

But although most organizations strive to combine ethical behavior with profitable operation, some large and prominent organizations have struggled to overcome major ethical lapses in recent years. Ethical failures in a number of large or well-known firms led to lawsuits, indictments, fines, guilty pleas, pleas of ignorance, jail sentences for high-profile executives, the financial failures of several powerful U.S. businesses, job losses for thousands of former employees at these firms, and the loss of billions of dollars in investors' savings that had been held as stock shares in these companies. Troubled firms included Enron, Tyco, MCI (formerly WorldCom), Global Crossing, the investment firm Credit Suisse First Boston, and even the venerable auction house Sotheby's.

The image of the CEO—and of business in general— suffered as the evening news carried dramatic pictures of the so-called perp walk—in which indicted and handcuffed corporate executives were paraded before the media in an exercise previously reserved for local criminals. Following a series of disclosures made in congressional investigations and in civil and criminal investigations conducted by state attorneys general, in 2002 Congress enacted the **Sarbanes-Oxley Act** to correct these abuses by adding oversight for the nation's major companies and a special oversight board to regulate public accounting firms that audit the financial records of these corporations. In 2004 the Federal Sentencing Commission strengthened its guidelines for ethics compliance programs, and more and more firms began to pay attention to formulating more explicit standards and procedures for ethical behavior. Companies were also forced to recognize the enormous impact of a good example, as it became clear that stated ethical values mean little if they are not being strictly followed at the very highest levels of the organization.

As we discussed in Chapter 1, the underlying aim of business is to serve customers at a profit. But most companies try to do more than that, looking for ways to give back to customers, society, and the environment. Sometimes they face difficult questions in the process. When does a company's self-interest conflict with society's and customers' well-being? And must the goal of seeking profits conflict with upholding high principles of right and wrong? In response to the second question, a growing number of businesses of all sizes are answering no.

# CONCERN FOR ETHICAL AND SOCIETAL ISSUES

An organization that wants to prosper over the long term cannot do so without considering **business ethics,** the standards of conduct and moral values governing actions and decisions in the work environment. Businesses also must take into account a wide range of social issues, including how a decision will affect the environment, employees, and customers. These issues are at the heart of social responsibility, whose primary objective is the enhancement of society's welfare through philosophies, policies, procedures, and actions. In short, businesses must find the delicate balance between doing what is right and doing what is profitable.

In business, as in life, deciding what is right or wrong in a given situation does not always involve a clear-cut choice. Firms have many responsibilities—to customers, to employees, to investors, and to society as a whole. Sometimes conflicts arise in trying to serve the different needs of these separate constituencies. The ethical values of executives and individual employees at all levels can influence the decisions and actions a business takes. Throughout your own business career, you will encounter many situations in which you will need to weigh right and wrong before making a decision or taking action. So we begin our discussion of business ethics by focusing on individual ethics.

Business ethics are also shaped by the ethical climate within an organization. Codes of conduct and ethical standards play increasingly significant roles in businesses in which doing the right thing is both supported and applauded. This chapter demonstrates how a firm can create a framework to encourage—and even demand—high standards of ethical behavior and social responsibility from its employees. The chapter also considers the complex question of what business owes to society and how societal forces mold the actions of businesses. Finally, it examines the influence of business ethics and social responsibility on global business.

# THE NEW ETHICAL ENVIRONMENT

Business ethics are now in the spotlight as never before. High-profile investigations, lawsuits, arrests, and convictions, as well as business failures due to fraud and corruption, have created a long string of headline news. While these events have brought about rapid change in many areas and new laws to prevent them from happening again, they have also obscured for many people the fact that most companies and their leaders are highly ethical. The National Business Ethics Survey found that more than 80 percent of employees believed top management in their organizations kept promises and commitments, and most believed that honesty and respect were more prevalent than a few years ago.[2]

Most business owners and managers have built and maintained enduring companies without breaking the rules. One example of a firm with a longstanding commitment to ethical practice is Johnson & Johnson, the giant multinational manufacturer of healthcare products. The most admired pharmaceutical maker and the ninth-most-admired company in the world, according to *Fortune*, Johnson & Johnson has abided by the same basic code of ethics, its well-known Credo, for more than 50 years. The Credo, reproduced in Figure 2.1, remains the ethical standard against which the company's employees periodically evaluate how well their firm is performing. Management is pledged to address any lapses that are reported.[3]

Many CEOs personify the best in management practices and are highly respected for their integrity, honesty, and business ethics. Jeff Immelt, General Electric's CEO, lists four things needed to keep the company at the top of the "most valuable" and "most admired" lists: Virtue first, followed by execution, growth, and great people. Immelt began by appointing the company's first vice president of corporate citizenship, Bob Corcoran, who started a program for reviewing more than 3,000 of GE's overseas suppliers for compliance with labor, health, and safety standards. In its other workforce programs, the company now offers domestic partner benefits to gay employees and has recently won awards for promoting women and African

**assessment check**

1. To whom do businesses have responsibilities?
2. If a firm is meeting all its responsibilities to others, why do ethical conflicts arise?

**"They Said It"**

"Don't major in P.E. and try to run a major company."
—Jim Blackwood Laid-off WorldCom employee, on the conviction of former CEO Bernard Ebbers

**"They Said It"**

"Start with what is right rather than what is acceptable."
—Peter Drucker (1909–2005) American business philosopher and author

**Figure**

**2.1** | Johnson & Johnson Credo

**Our Credo**

We believe our first responsibility is to the doctors, nurses and patients, to mothers and fathers and all others who use our products and services. In meeting their needs everything we do must be of high quality. We must constantly strive to reduce our costs in order to maintain reasonable prices. Customers' orders must be serviced promptly and accurately. Our suppliers and distributors must have an opportunity to make a fair profit.

We are responsible to our employees, the men and women who work with us throughout the world. Everyone must be considered as an individual. We must respect their dignity and recognize their merit. They must have a sense of security in their jobs. Compensation must be fair and adequate, and working conditions clean, orderly and safe. We must be mindful of ways to help our employees fulfill their family responsibilities. Employees must feel free to make suggestions and complaints. There must be equal opportunity for employment, development and advancement for those qualified. We must provide competent management, and their actions must be just and ethical.

We are responsible to the communities in which we live and work and to the world community as well. We must be good citizens—support good works and charities and bear our fair share of taxes. We must encourage civic improvements and better health and education. We must maintain in good order the property we are privileged to use, protecting the environment and natural resources.

Our final responsibility is to our stockholders. Business must make a sound profit. We must experiment with new ideas. Research must be carried on, innovative programs developed and mistakes paid for. New equipment must be purchased, new facilities provided and new products launched. Reserves must be created to provide for adverse times. When we operate according to these principles, the stockholders should realize a fair return.

**Source:** "Our Company: Our Credo," Johnson & Johnson Web site, accessed June 7, 2006, http://www.jnj.com.

Americans to executive positions. It began an extensive healthcare project in Ghana and purchased companies that purify water, manufacture solar-energy equipment, and produce wind energy—overall doubling its research budget for investigating environmentally sound technologies. "Good leaders give back," says Immelt. "The era we live in belongs to people who believe in themselves but are focused on the needs of others."[4]

However, not all companies set and meet high ethical standards. A survey by Public Agenda and the Kettering Foundation found that typical Americans, interviewed in focus groups, thought that greed and poor values had led many companies astray from their moral bearings, and that a major ethical priority for business should be preserving jobs. Executives interviewed for the study believed that jobs were a business, rather than an ethical, issue.[5]

With passage of the Sarbanes-Oxley Act of 2002, which establishes new rules and regulations for securities trading and accounting practices, a company is also required to publish its code of ethics, if it has one, and inform the public of any changes made to it. The new law may actually motivate even more firms to develop written codes and guidelines for ethical business behavior. The federal government also created the U.S. Sentencing Commission to institutionalize ethics compliance programs that would establish high ethical standards and end corporate misconduct. The requirements for such programs are shown in Table 2.1.

The current ethical environment of business also includes the appointment of new corporate officers specifically charged with deterring wrongdoing and ensuring that ethical standards are met. Ethics compliance officers, whose numbers are rapidly rising, are responsible for conducting employee training programs that help spot potential fraud and abuse within the firm, investigating sexual harassment and discrimination charges, and monitoring any potential conflicts of interest. In some firms, such as Molson Coors, the ethics training program is closely linked to the audit department and the integrity of the company's financial statements.[6] This last responsibility is more important than ever, now that the Sarbanes-Oxley Act requires financial officers and CEOs to personally certify the validity of companies' financial statements.

## Individuals Make a Difference

In today's business environment, individuals can make the difference in ethical expectations and behavior. As executives, managers, and employees demonstrate their personal ethical principles—or lack of ethical principles—the expectations and actions of those who work for and with them can change.

What is the current status of individual business ethics in the United States? Although ethical behavior can be difficult to track or even define in all circumstances, evidence suggests

Table

2.1

Minimum Requirements for Ethics Compliance Programs

- **Compliance standards and procedures.** Establish standards and procedures, such as codes of ethics and identification of areas of risk, capable of reducing misconduct or criminal activities.

- **High-level personnel responsibility.** Assign high-level personnel, such as boards of directors and top executives, the overall responsibility to actively lead and oversee ethics compliance programs.

- **Due care in assignments.** Avoid delegating authority to individuals with a propensity for misconduct or illegal activities.

- **Communication of standards and procedures.** Communicate ethical requirements to high-level officials and other employees through ethics training programs or publications that explain in practical terms what is required.

- **Establishment of monitoring and auditing systems and reporting system.** Monitor and review ethical compliance systems and establish a reporting system employees can use to notify the organization of misconduct without fear of retribution.

- **Enforcement of standards through appropriate mechanisms.** Consistently enforce ethical codes, including employee discipline.

- **Appropriate responses to the offense.** Take reasonable steps to respond to the offense and to prevent and detect further violations.

- **Self-reporting.** Report misconduct to the appropriate government agency.

- **Applicable industry practice or standards.** Follow government regulations and industry standards.

**Sources:** "An Overview of the United States Sentencing Commission and the Federal Sentencing Guidelines," U.S. Sentencing Commission, accessed June 7, 2006, http://www.ussc.gov; "The Relationship between Law and Ethics, and the Significance of the Federal Sentencing Guidelines for Organizations," Ethics and Policy Integration Center, accessed June 7, 2006, http://www.epic-online .net; U.S. Sentencing Commission, "Sentencing Commission Toughens Requirements for Corporate Compliance and Ethics Programs," USSC news release, April 13, 2004.

that some individuals act unethically or illegally on the job. A survey of British employees found that more than a third admitted to spending up to 30 minutes a day using the Internet and the World Wide Web for personal business when they should have been working. This amount of time may not seem abusive, but it adds up to as much as two weeks a year.[7] In another poll, the main types of unethical behavior observed by employees were lying, withholding information, abusing or intimidating employees, inaccurately reporting the amount of time worked, and discrimination. Related to personal ethics in the workplace is the broader issue of being considerate to co-workers and using common office courtesy. The "Business Etiquette" feature explores these issues.

Technology seems to have expanded the range and impact of unethical behavior. For example, anyone with computer access to data has the potential to steal or manipulate the data or to shut down the system, even from a remote location. Often the people who hack into a company's computers are employees, and some observers consider employee attacks the most expensive. Such attacks often result in the theft of intellectual property, such as patented or copyrighted information.

Nearly every employee, at every level, wrestles with ethical questions at some point or another. Some rationalize questionable behavior by saying, "Everybody's

**assessment check**

1. What role can an ethics compliance officer play in a firm?

2. What factors influence the ethical environment of a business?

## Being Considerate of Co-Workers

Working brings us into close and frequent contact with others. The physical environment of many workplaces—especially those with cubicles—makes few concessions to employee privacy or desire to avoid noise and distractions. If you find yourself occupying a cubicle, here are some ways to ensure that you are as considerate of others as you would wish them to be of you.

1. Respect others' privacy. Pretend cubicles have full walls and doors; avoid glancing in when you walk by and always knock before entering. If the person you need to see is occupied, don't wait in the doorway; come back later.

2. When you are in someone else's office or cubicle, keep your eyes off the computer screen. If the other person's phone rings, excuse yourself and come back later.

3. If you want to listen to music while working and if it is permitted, wear headphones to avoid distracting others.

4. Set the volume low on your computer, and use a screen saver option without sound effects.

5. Answer your phone promptly and keep your voice down. Set the ring tone on low volume, and if you use a speakerphone, keep it on low. If you must make a personal call, remember that you can probably be heard.

6. Be aware that some people are sensitive to strong or excessive perfumes, colognes, and sprays, and apply them sparingly and before you leave home.

7. Keep personal touches to your space in line with company standards and take care not to offend or distract co-workers, clients, or other visitors with inappropriate posters, cartoons, or trinkets.

8. If an impromptu meeting or gathering begins outside someone's workspace, move to a conference room or common area such as the lunchroom to avoid disturbing others.

9. If you need to borrow something from another person's office, ask permission first, and always return or replace the item.

10. Avoid habits that distract others, such as popping gum, humming, tapping things on the desk, taking shoes off, eating food with strong odors, and leaving refuse and leftovers out.

**Sources:** Mary Lebeau, "The Fine Art of 'Cube-tiquette,'" JobWeb, accessed June 7, 2006, http://www.jobweb.com; Jill Bremer, "Cubicle Etiquette," Bremer Communications, accessed June 7, 2006, http://www.bremercommunications.com; "Cubicle Culture Isn't Necessarily Very Private," (Sioux Falls, SD) Argus Leader, accessed June 7, 2006, http://www.herald-dispatch.com.

doing it." Others act unethically because they feel pressured in their jobs or have to meet performance quotas. Yet some avoid unethical acts that don't mesh with their personal values and morals. To help you understand the differences in the ways individuals arrive at ethical choices, the next section focuses on how personal ethics and morals develop.

## Development of Individual Ethics

Individuals typically develop ethical standards in the three stages shown in Figure 2.2: the preconventional, conventional, and postconventional stages. In the preconventional stage, individuals primarily consider their own needs and desires in making decisions. They obey external rules only because they are afraid of punishment or hope to receive rewards if they comply.

In the second stage, the conventional stage, individuals are aware of and act in response to their duty to others, including their obligations to their family members, co-workers, and organizations. The expectations of these groups influence how they choose between what is acceptable and unacceptable in certain situations. Self-interest, however, continues to play a role in decisions.

The postconventional stage, the final stage, represents the highest level of ethical and moral behavior. The individual is able to move beyond mere self-interest and duty and take the larger needs of society into account as well. He or she has developed personal ethical principles for determining what is right and can apply those principles in a wide variety of situations.

An individual's stage in moral and ethical development is determined by a huge number of factors. Experiences help shape responses to different situations. A person's family, educational, cultural, and religious backgrounds can also play a role, as can the environment within the firm. Individuals can also have different styles of deciding ethical dilemmas, no matter what their stage of moral development.

To help you understand and prepare for the ethical dilemmas you may confront in your career, let's take a closer look at some of the factors involved in solving ethical questions on the job.

Figure 2.2

# On-the-Job Ethical Dilemmas

In the fast-paced world of business, you will sometimes be called on to weigh the ethics of decisions that can affect not just your own future but possibly the futures of your fellow workers, your company, and its customers. As already noted, it's not always easy to distinguish between what is right and wrong in many business situations, especially when the needs and concerns of various parties conflict. Some CEOs recently accused of wrongdoing have claimed they did not know that crimes were being committed, but this defense has not always been effective (see the "Hit & Miss" feature).

Many manufacturers that utilize factories overseas have faced criticism at home over the poor working conditions found there. Concerned that pulling their business from overseas suppliers often leaves workers in developing countries without employment, some firms have turned instead to efforts to improve working conditions abroad. Reebok International developed software to monitor working conditions at the factories that manufacture the company's brand-name shoes and clothing. Other manufacturers grew interested in the Human Rights Tracking System, which tracks such factors as wages, air quality, and building safety features. So Reebok's chief information officer and vice president of human rights programs set up a nonprofit organization to share the software with other firms, which pay only a subscription fee to help fund research and improvements to the software. The nonprofit Fair Factories Clearinghouse maintains a global database about workplace and factory conditions around the world that member companies can share.[8] And in yet another ethical corporate stand, Reebok has refused to do any business in Burma, an Asian country notorious for its government's widespread brutality and human rights abuses. The company is urging other businesses to **boycott** the country to pressure it to reform.[9]

Solving ethical dilemmas is not easy. In many cases, each possible decision can have unpleasant consequences and positive benefits that must be evaluated. The ethical issues that confront manufacturers with overseas suppliers are just one example of many different types of ethical questions encountered in the workplace. Figure 2.3 on page 39 identifies four of the most common ethical challenges that businesspeople face: conflict of interest, honesty and integrity, loyalty versus truth, and whistle-blowing.

### Stage 1: Preconventional

Individual is mainly looking out for his or her own interests. Rules are followed only out of fear of punishment or hope of reward.

### Stage 2: Conventional

Individual considers the interests and expectations of others in making decisions. Rules are followed because it is a part of belonging to the group.

### Stage 3: Postconventional

Individual follows personal principles for resolving ethical dilemmas. He or she considers personal, group, and societal interests.

**conflict of interest** situation in which an employee must make a decision about a business's welfare versus personal gain.

## Conflict of Interest

A **conflict of interest** exists when a businessperson is faced with a situation in which an action benefiting one person or group has the potential to harm another. Conflicts of interest may pose ethical challenges when they involve the businessperson's own interests and those of someone to whom he or she has a duty or when they involve two parties to whom the businessperson has a duty. Lawyers, business consultants, or advertising agencies would face a conflict of interest if they represented two competing companies: a strategy that would most benefit one of the client companies might harm the other client. Similarly, a real estate agent would face an ethical conflict if he or she represented both the buyer and seller in a transaction. In general, the buyer benefits from a low price, and the seller benefits from a high price. Handling the situation responsibly would be possible, but it would also be difficult. A conflict may also exist between someone's personal interests and those of an organization or its customers. An offer of gifts or bribes for special treatment creates a situation in which the buyer, but not necessarily his or her company, may benefit personally.

**assessment check**

1. What is the preconventional stage in the development of ethical standards?

2. What is the difference between the conventional and the postconventional stages?

# HIT & MISS

## Failure at the Top

It seemed the scandals and ethical failures would never end, as top executives faced charges ranging from fraud to conspiracy to perjury and obstruction of justice. What happened to them? Here's an update.

Bernard Ebbers, former CEO of WorldCom, was convicted of fraud and conspiracy in a huge accounting fraud at the company now called MCI. He still claims ignorance of accounting methods, but he was sentenced to 25 years in prison.

L. Dennis Kozlowski and Mark Swartz, former CEO and chief financial officer (CFO) of Tyco International, were convicted of looting more than $600 million from company coffers to pay for personal items, such as extravagant parties, a glitzy Manhattan apartment, and artwork. Both were convicted on 22 charges, including grand larceny, falsifying business records, and securities fraud. They still say they were unaware of any wrongdoing at the company.

John Rigas, founder of Adelphia Communications, was convicted of conspiracy and fraud in the theft of about $100 million from the firm. He denied wrongdoing and shifted blame to his son Timothy, former CEO, who was also convicted. Rigas was sentenced to 15 years in federal prison and his son received a 20-year sentence.

Before his death in July of 2006, Kenneth Lay, former Chairman and CEO of Enron, was convicted on six counts of fraud, insider trading, lying to investors and auditors, and inflating Enron's assets. Lay maintained that he didn't know of any misdeeds and blamed former CFO, Andrew Fastow. Due to his death preceding his sentencing, Lay's convictions will likely be overturned. However, Jeffrey Skilling, former CEO of Enron, who was also convicted on the same counts as Lay, will not be so lucky. Despite the fact that he still maintains his innocence, his convictions will stand.

Martha Stewart, CEO and founder of her namesake company, served five months in prison and five months confined to her home for conspiracy, obstruction of justice, and making false statements after selling her stock in ImClone Systems. She has returned to work at her namesake company.

### Questions for Critical Thinking

1. Is it possible for top executives to be unaware of ongoing fraud and other crime in their firms if they are not experts in accounting, taxation, or law?
2. How can CEOs of large companies ensure that everyone in the organization is consistently behaving in an ethical manner?

**Sources:** Erin McClam, "WorldCom's Ebbers Weeps at 25-Year Sentence," *Yahoo! News,* accessed June 7, 2006, http://news .yahoo.com; Associated Press, "Ex-Tyco CEO Dennis Kozlowski Found Guilty," *MSNBC,* accessed June 7, 2006, http://msnbc .msn.com; Mary Flood and Purva Patel, "WorldCom Case May Be Omen for Lay," *Houston Chronicle,* accessed June 7, 2006, http://www.chron.com; "Status of High-Profile Corporate Scandals," *USA Today,* accessed June 7, 2006, http:// www.usatoday.com; Daren Fonda, "After Bernie, Who's Next?" *Time,* March 28, 2005, pp. 44–46.

## "They Said It"

"It's easy to have principles when you're rich. The important thing is to have principles when you're poor."

—Ray A. Kroc (1902–1984) founder, McDonald's Corporation

A former U.S. Air Force acquisition executive, Darleen Druyun, was sentenced to nine months in prison, fined $5,000, and ordered to perform 150 hours of community service after her conviction in a conflict-of-interest case. Druyun was negotiating a new job with aerospace firm Boeing while she was also negotiating contracts with the company for the Air Force. Her son-in-law also worked for Boeing. She admitted that she did favor Boeing in some of her contract negotiations by increasing the dollar amounts of some contracts, which cost her employer, the Defense Department.[10]

Ethical ways to handle conflicts of interest include (1) avoiding them and (2) disclosing them. Some companies have policies against taking on clients who are competitors of existing clients. Most businesses and government agencies have written policies prohibiting employees from accepting gifts or specifying a maximum gift value of, say, $25 or so. Or a member of a board of directors or committee might abstain from voting on a decision in which he or she has a personal interest. In other situations, people state their potential conflict of interest so that the people affected can decide whether to get information or help they need from another source instead.

## Honesty and Integrity

*Honesty and Integrity* Employers highly value honesty and integrity. An employee who is honest can be counted on to tell the truth. An employee with **integrity** goes beyond truthfulness. Having integrity means adhering to deeply felt ethical principles in business situations. It includes doing what you say you will do and accepting responsibility for mistakes. Behaving with honesty and integrity inspires trust, and as a result, it can help build long-term relationships with customers, employers, suppliers, and the public. Employees, in turn, want their managers and the company as a whole to treat them honestly and with integrity.

Unfortunately, violations of honesty and integrity are all too common. Some people misrepresent their academic credentials and previous work experience on their résumés or job applications. Others steal from their employers by taking home supplies or products without permission or by carrying out personal business during the time they are being paid to work.

The Employment Law Alliance recently asked nearly 800 workers about their Internet use at work. Nearly a quarter said they or a co-worker had used their employer's computer for "romance/sexual purposes," which for about 6 percent included engaging in "sexually explicit chatting/instant messaging." Surprisingly, more than half the respondents said such computer use "is not having a negative impact on productivity."[11] Despite this view, most employers find such misuse of company equipment and other offenses, such as the use of e-mail for downloading pirated software at work, serious enough to make electronic monitoring and surveillance increasingly widespread in the workplace. Compliance with laws regarding the privacy and security of client information is another major reasons given for the continuing increase in such monitoring.[12]

## Loyalty versus Truth

*Loyalty versus Truth* Businesspeople expect their employees to be loyal and to act in the best interests of the company. But when the truth about a company is not favorable, an ethical conflict can arise. Individuals may have to decide between loyalty to the company and truthfulness in business relationships. People resolve such dilemmas in various ways. Some place the highest value on loyalty, even at the expense of truth. Others avoid volunteering negative information but answer truthfully if someone asks them a specific question. People may emphasize truthfulness and actively disclose negative information, especially if the cost of silence is high, as in the case of operating a malfunctioning aircraft or selling tainted medicine.

## Whistle-Blowing

*Whistle-Blowing* When an individual encounters unethical or illegal actions at work, the person must decide what action to take. Sometimes it is possible to resolve the problem by working through channels within the organization. If that fails, the person should weigh the potential damages to the greater public good. If the damage is significant, a person may conclude that the only solution is to blow the whistle. **Whistle-blowing** is an employee's disclosure to company officials, government authorities, or the media of illegal, immoral, or unethical practices.

A whistle-blower must weigh a number of issues in deciding whether to come forward. Resolving an ethical problem within the organization can be more effective, assuming higher-level managers cooperate. A company that values ethics will try to correct a problem, and staying at a company that does not value ethics may not be worthwhile. In some cases, however, people resort to whistle-blowing because they believe the unethical behavior is causing significant damage that outweighs the risk that the company will retaliate against the whistle-blower. Those risks have been real in the past. State and federal laws protect whistle-blowers

**Common Business Ethical Challenges**

Figure 2.3

**whistle-blowing** employee's disclosure to company officials, government authorities, or the media of illegal, immoral, or unethical practices committed by an organization.

in certain situations, such as reports of discrimination, and the Sarbanes-Oxley Act of 2002 now requires that firms in the private sector provide procedures for anonymous reporting of accusations of fraud. Under the act, anyone who retaliates against an employee for taking concerns of unlawful conduct to a public official can be prosecuted. Whistle-blowers who still experience retribution for their actions have recourse thanks to the act—those who have been fired, demoted, threatened, or harassed have 90 days to file a complaint with the U.S. Department of Labor.

Not all whistle-blowing cases are straightforward. Douglas Durand cooperated with the government to build a fraud case against TAP Pharmaceutical Products for several years after he left his job there as vice president of sales. Durand charged that TAP conspired with doctors to overcharge Medicare tens of millions of dollars. TAP eventually paid the government a fine of $885 million, several times the amount it was accused of making through fraudulent claims. Under a 1986 law that awards whistle-blowers up to 30 percent of any amount the government recovers in their case, Durand was awarded $126 million, but all the defendants in the TAP case were recently exonerated. Supporters of the law that rewards whistle-blowers say it is the only way to combat fraud in government contracts. "Financial incentives are what bring people forward," admits the director of the Justice Department's civil fraud department. But, he concludes, the facts of the case are then brought to light in the investigation that follows.[13]

Obviously, whistle-blowing and other ethical issues arise relatively infrequently in firms with strong organizational climates of ethical behavior. The next section examines how a business can develop an environment that discourages unethical behavior among individuals.

# HOW ORGANIZATIONS SHAPE ETHICAL CONDUCT

**code of conduct** formal statement that defines how the organization expects employees to resolve ethical issues.

No individual makes decisions in a vacuum. Choices are strongly influenced by the standards of conduct established within the organizations where people work. Most ethical lapses in business reflect the values of the firms' corporate cultures.

As shown in Figure 2.4, development of a corporate culture to support business ethics happens on four levels: ethical awareness, ethical reasoning, ethical action, and ethical leadership. If any of these four factors is missing, the ethical climate in an organization will weaken.

**Figure 2.4** Structure of an Ethical Environment

## Ethical Awareness

The foundation of an ethical climate is ethical awareness. As we have already seen, ethical dilemmas occur frequently in the workplace. So employees need help in identifying ethical problems when they occur. Workers also need guidance about how the firm expects them to respond.

One way for a firm to provide this support is to develop a **code of conduct,** a formal statement that defines how the organization expects employees to resolve ethical questions. Johnson & Johnson's Credo, presented earlier, is such a code. At the most basic level, a code of conduct may simply specify ground rules for acceptable behavior, such as identifying the laws and regulations that employees must obey. Other companies use their codes of conduct to identify key corporate values and provide frameworks that guide employees as they resolve moral and ethical dilemmas.

Canada-based Nortel Networks, an international telecommunications giant with customers in 150 countries, uses a code of conduct to define its values and help employees put them into practice. The code of conduct defines seven core values that Nortel requires as it strives to become known as a company of integrity. The code also defines standards for conduct among employees and between employees and the company's shareholders, customers, suppliers, and communities. Employees are expected to treat one another with respect, including respect for individual and cultural differences; protect the company's assets; and fulfill whatever commitments they make. The code of conduct also states that each employee is responsible for behaving consistently with its standards and for reporting possible violations of the code. Nortel provides each employee with a copy of this code of conduct and also posts it on its Web site.[14]

Other firms incorporate similar codes in their policy manuals or mission statements; some issue a code of conduct or statement of values in the form of a small card that employees and managers can carry with them. Harley-Davidson has developed a brief code of ethics that employees can apply both at work and in their personal lives. It reads: "Tell the truth, keep your promises, be fair, respect the individual and encourage intellectual curiosity."

## Ethical Reasoning

Although a code of conduct can provide an overall framework, it cannot detail a solution for every ethical situation. Some ethical questions have black-and-white answers, but others do not. Businesses must provide the tools employees need to evaluate the options and arrive at suitable decisions.

Many firms have instituted ethics training programs. Lockheed Martin has developed a training program in the form of interactive lessons that employees can access online. The sessions include cases performed by actors, plus tests in the form of multiple-choice questions. They cover a variety of business-related topics, from security to sexual harassment. The company also tracks which employees have completed which training sessions. In addition, Lockheed Martin uses a game called the Ethics Challenge, in which the players use cards and tokens to read about and resolve ethical quandaries based on real-life situations. Everyone in the company, from hourly workers to the chairman, is required to play the Ethics Challenge once per year.

Many authorities debate whether ethics can actually be taught, but training can give employees an opportunity to practice applying ethical values to hypothetical situations as a prelude to applying the same standards to real-world situations. Similar strategies are being used in many business school ethics programs, where case studies and practical scenarios work best.[15]

## Ethical Action

Codes of conduct and ethics training help employees recognize and reason through ethical problems. In addition, firms must also provide structures and approaches that allow decisions to be turned into ethical actions. Texas Instruments gives its employees a reference card to help them make ethical decisions on the job. The size of a standard business card, it lists the following guidelines:

- Does it comply with our values?
- If you do it, will you feel bad?
- How will it look in the newspaper?
- If you know it's wrong, don't do it!
- If you're not sure, ask.
- Keep asking until you get an answer.

Goals set for the business as a whole and for individual departments and employees can affect ethical behavior. A firm whose managers set unrealistic goals for employee performance may find an increase in cheating, lying, and other misdeeds, as employees attempt to protect themselves. In today's Internet economy, the high value placed on speed can create a climate in which ethical behavior is sometimes challenged. Ethical decisions often require careful and quiet thought, a challenging task in a business moving at warp speed.

Some companies encourage ethical action by providing support for employees faced with dilemmas. One common tool is an employee hotline, a telephone number that employees can call, often anonymously, for advice or to report unethical behavior they have witnessed. Nortel Networks, for example, operates a Business Ethics Advice Line. Employees from around the world can contact the advice line via phone or e-mail to ask for advice in applying the code of conduct in specific situations. Ethics compliance officers at some firms, as mentioned previously, guide employees through ethical minefields.

## Ethical Leadership

Executives must not only talk about ethical behavior but also demonstrate it in their actions. This principle requires employees to be personally committed to the company's core values and be willing to base their actions on them. One important way for business leaders to model ethical behavior is to admit when they are wrong and correct their organization's mistakes and problems. Citigroup, the world's largest financial services group, provides banking, investment banking, insurance, and other financial services in more than 100 countries. But its recent impressive growth has been tainted by financial scandals in Germany, the United Kingdom, and Japan, among other countries. CEO Charles Prince denounced the wrongdoing by its London bond-trading desk as "completely knuckleheaded." He not only apologized for failing to prevent wrongdoing by clients in Japan but also fired the top executives who were involved. Despite ongoing legal and regulatory problems for Citigroup around the world, Prince continues to weed out errant managers and calls it a "key priority for this management team to take these open issues off the table." A recent annual report promises that the financial giant will develop "best practice" standards: "We need to be clear about this subject; because of our size and scope, because of our position of business leadership, we are held to a higher standard. We accept this responsibility."[16]

However, ethical leadership should also go one step further and charge each employee at every level with the responsibility to be an ethical leader. Everyone should be aware of problems and be willing to defend the organization's standards. The Nortel Networks guidelines specifically communicate these responsibilities. The company tells employees they are expected to "ask questions when we're unsure of the appropriate course of action in any situation" and "report violations or concerns to . . . someone who has no connection to the activity in question and who can make an objective evaluation."[17]

Unfortunately, not all organizations are able to build a solid framework of business ethics. Because the damage from ethical misconduct can powerfully affect a firm's stakeholders—customers, investors, employees, and the public—pressure is exerted on businesses to act in acceptable ways. But when businesses fail, the law must step in to enforce good business practices.

Many of the laws that affect specific industries or individuals are described in other chapters in this book. For example, legislation affecting international business operations is discussed in Chapter 4. Laws designed to assist small businesses are examined in Chapter 5. Laws related to labor unions are described in Chapter 9. Legislation related to banking and the securities markets is discussed in Chapters 17 and 18. Finally, for an examination of the legal and governmental forces designed to safeguard society's interests when businesses fail at self-regulation, see the Part 1 Appendix, "The Legal Framework for Business."

**"They Said It"**

"It's up to us to use our platforms to be a good citizen . . . it's a business imperative."
—Jeff Immelt (b. 1956)
CEO, General Electric

**assessment check**

1. What is a code of conduct?
2. How does ethical leadership contribute to ethical standards throughout a company?

# ACTING RESPONSIBLY TO SATISFY SOCIETY

A second major issue affecting business is the question of social responsibility. In a general sense, **social responsibility** is management's acceptance of the obligation to consider profit, consumer satisfaction, and societal well-being of equal value in evaluating the firm's performance. It is the recognition that business must be concerned with the qualitative dimensions of consumer, employee, and societal benefits, as well as the quantitative measures of sales and profits, by which business performance is traditionally measured. Businesses may exercise social responsibility because such behavior is required by law, because it enhances the company's image, or because management believes it is the ethical course of action.

Historically, a company's social performance has been measured by its contribution to the overall economy and the employment opportunities it provides. Variables such as total wages paid often indicate social performance. Although profits and employment remain important, today many factors contribute to an assessment of a firm's social performance, including providing equal employment opportunities; respecting the cultural diversity of employees; responding to environmental concerns; providing a safe, healthy workplace; and producing high-quality products that are safe to use.

A business is also judged by its interactions with the community. To demonstrate their social responsibility, many corporations highlight charitable contributions and community service in their annual reports and on their Web site. Deere & Company of Illinois, for example, sells agricultural, construction, and lawn care equipment all over the world, but it also recently donated $1.5 million in land and facilities to its neighbor, Western Illinois University. The firm is also working with local community colleges to recruit hundreds of new employees over the next few years.[18]

Some firms measure social performance by conducting **social audits**, formal procedures that identify and evaluate all company activities that relate to social issues such as conservation, employment practices, environmental protection, and philanthropy. The social audit informs management about how well the company is performing in these areas. Based on this information, management may revise current programs or develop new ones.

Outside groups may conduct their own evaluations of businesses. Various environmental, religious, and public-interest groups have created standards of corporate performance. Reports on many of these evaluations are available to the general public. The New York–based Council on Economic Priorities is "committed to making available to the public information about corporate social responsibility in areas such as the environment, community outreach, advancement of women and minorities, charitable giving, family benefits, and animal testing."[19] Other groups publicize their evaluations and include critiques of the social responsibility performance of firms. The Center for Science in the Public Interest evaluates the healthfulness of the foods marketed to consumers.[20]

As Figure 2.5 shows, the social responsibilities of business can be classified according to its relationships to the general public, customers, employees, and investors and other members of the financial community. Many of these relationships extend beyond national borders.

**social responsibility**
business's consideration of society's well-being and consumer satisfaction, in addition to profits.

**assessment check**

1. What is meant by social responsibility and why do firms exercise it?
2. What is a social audit?

**Figure**

**2.5**

Responsibilities of Business

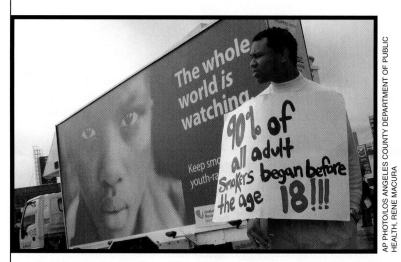

Under the settlement that the U.S. government made with tobacco companies, the industry must work to avoid targeting young people. Part of that effort also involves smoking prevention programs. This photo of a Los Angeles county youth advocate was taken just prior to a youth rally held in Los Angeles.

## Responsibilities to the General Public

The responsibilities of business to the general public include dealing with public health issues, protecting the environment, and developing the quality of the workforce. Many would argue that businesses also have responsibilities to support charitable and social causes and organizations that work toward the greater public good. In other words, they should give back to the communities in which they earn profits. Such efforts are called *corporate philanthropy*.

**Public-Health Issues**   One of the most complex issues facing business as it addresses its ethical and social responsibilities to the general public is public health. Central to the public-health debate is the question of what businesses should do about dangerous products such as tobacco and alcohol. Tobacco products represent a major health risk, contributing to heart disease, stroke, and cancer among smokers. Families and co-workers of smokers share this danger as well, as their exposure to secondhand smoke increases their risks for cancer, asthma, and respiratory infections.

Exposure to viruses is harder to control, although vaccines exist for many diseases. Complications from the flu cause up to 36,000 U.S. deaths each year. However, shortages of flu vaccines can cause unexpected havoc, as happened recently when the U.S. supply fell short of the amounts needed at the height of the flu season. Contamination during vaccine production halted shipment of the supply expected from England and forced the government to appeal to the public to save the remaining vaccine for those most at risk. The vaccine takes months to prepare, so additional quantities could not be manufactured in time. In the wake of the shortage, the three vaccine manufacturers issued production estimates for the following season; the company whose products had been contaminated then lowered its estimates by several million doses due to a lag in increasing its capacity.[21]

Substance abuse is another serious public health problem worldwide. The recent revelations of the use of illegal steroids by many athletes, particularly in professional baseball, highlights the difficulty of devising accurate tests for performance-enhancing and muscle-building drugs and fairly evaluating the results. Many of the drugs in question are so similar to compounds naturally present in the body that identification is extremely difficult. With regard to drug testing, athletes' individual rights to privacy have been questioned, particularly due to their widespread influence on youthful fans. Steroid use is on the rise among high school athletes, despite the wide publicity about the dangers of such drugs. Tougher penalties for professional players who fail drug tests are being formulated but are sure to be controversial for the beleaguered sports industry.[22]

**Protecting the Environment**   Businesses consume huge amounts of energy, which increases the use of fossil fuels such as coal and oil for energy production. This activity introduces carbon dioxide and sulfur into the earth's atmosphere, substances that many scientists believe will result in dramatic climate changes during the 21st century. Meanwhile, the sulfur from fossil fuels combines with water vapor in the air to form sulfuric acid. The acid rain that results can kill fish and trees and pollute groundwater. Wind can carry the sulfur around the entire globe. Sulfur from U.S. factories is damaging Canadian forests, and pollution from London smokestacks has been found in the forests and lakes of Scandinavia. Other production and manufacturing methods leave behind large quantities of waste materials that can further pollute the environment and fill already bulging landfills. Some products themselves, particularly electronics that contain toxins such as lead and mercury, are difficult to reuse or recycle. Few manufacturers are really equipped to deal with recycled materials; some refurbish junked products and sell them abroad—where later recycling is even less likely. Hewlett-Packard, however, is making its scanners with a combination of new and recycled plastics, and lead, mercury, and cadmium will soon be banned from new equipment manufactured in Europe.[23]

For many managers, finding ways to minimize **pollution** and other environmental damage caused by their products or operating processes has become an important economic, legal, and social issue. The solutions can be difficult—and expensive. It costs computer makers up to $20 to recycle each old computer, for instance.[24] Drivers may face high costs, too. Hybrid cars use a combination of gas and electricity to power their engines and promise much better fuel efficiency than conventional autos. As gasoline prices soared, sales of U.S. hybrids reached nearly 7,000 a month. Most of the purchasers chose the Toyota Prius hybrid, followed by the Honda Civic. Hybrid pickups and SUVs are on the market, and many more models are on the way. The fuel saving enjoyed by hybrid owners isn't cheap; experts figure that adding the electric system to the car also adds about $3,000 to $4,000 to the vehicle sticker price.[25]

Despite the difficulty, however, companies such as Green Mountain Coffee Roasters, profiled at the beginning of the chapter, are finding that they can be environmentally friendly and profitable, too. A "totally biodegradable and nontoxic plastic" has been developed for Motorola by a Dutch lab, Pvaxx Research and Development. Although the polymer has many possible uses, Motorola is considering using it first in snap-on cell phone covers. Researchers in Britain have also come up with an unusual method of recycling plastic. They have devised a way to embed a sunflower seed in a phone cover, which would use the polymer's waste products as nutrients to grow after the phone is discarded.[26]

Another solution to the problems of pollutants is **recycling**— reprocessing used materials for reuse. Recycling can sometimes provide much of the raw material that manufacturers need, thereby conserving the world's natural resources and reducing the need for landfills. Several industries are developing ways to use recycled materials, although in many cases getting the public to bring used products in is the first hurdle. A recent drive to collect old cell phones in Westchester County, New York, home to about 900,000 people, yielded only 32 units. And according to the Silicon Valley Toxics Coalition, as much as 60 to 80 percent of material intended for recycling "is being dumped in containers and sent to China." But companies such as Collective Good and ReCellular are taking in tens of thousands of cell phones a day and recycling and refurbishing them. TechCycle, in Colorado, recycles all kinds of used equipment and parts, even shipping old computer monitors to China to be made into televisions.[27]

According to the Environmental Protection Agency, discarded electronic units now make up as much as 40 percent of the lead in landfills in the United States, and the International Association of Electronics Recyclers estimates that consumers and businesses will be disposing of 400 million such units by 2010. Manufacturers and federal agencies are struggling to come up with a way to pay for a voluntary system for managing the problem; one possibility is a surcharge consumers would pay on each electronics purchase. In

"They Said It"
**"They Said It"**

"The nation behaves well if it treats the natural resources as assets which it must turn over to the next generation increased, and not impaired, in value."
—Theodore Roosevelt (1858–1919) 26th president of the United States

**recycling** reprocessing of used materials for reuse.

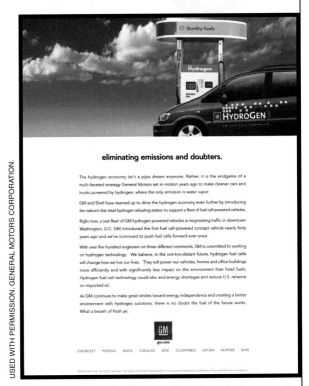

As part of a research effort to reduce the pollution caused by traditional gasoline vehicles, General Motors is testing hydrogen-powered engines. If you are in Washington, D.C., you may see one of these test cars in downtown traffic. GM has more than 500 engineers on three continents working to make hydrogen power a reality.

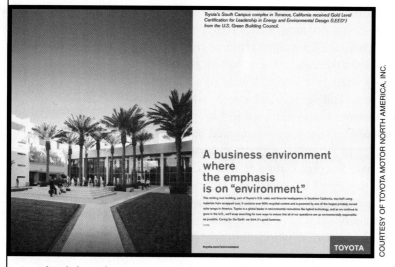

COURTESY OF TOYOTA MOTOR NORTH AMERICA, INC.

A business environment
where
the emphasis
is on "environment."

*This striking new building, part of Toyota's U.S. sales and financial headquarters in Southern California, was built using materials from scrapped cars. It contains over 90% recycled content and is powered by one of the largest privately owned solar arrays in America. Toyota is a global leader in environmental innovations like hybrid technology, and as we continue to grow in the U.S., we'll keep searching for new ways to ensure that all of our operations are as environmentally responsible as possible. Caring for the Earth: we think it's good business.*

TOYOTA

toyota.com/environment

Recycling helps reduce garbage, which makes for a cleaner environment. Toyota's U.S. sales and financial headquarters in Southern California was built from scrapped cars, with more than 90 percent of the content coming from recycled materials. The building also uses solar power for much of its energy needs.

the meantime, Staples accepts all gadgets for recycling no matter where they were purchased, and Hewlett-Packard and Dell have agreed not to send waste materials overseas. Opportunities are opening up for firms such as RetroBox of Columbus, Ohio, which recycles used electronic products and shares the profits with the customers who bring them in.[28]

Many consumers have favorable impressions of environmentally conscious businesses. To target these customers, companies often use **green marketing,** a marketing strategy that promotes environmentally safe products and production methods. A business cannot simply claim that its goods or services are environmentally friendly, however. The Federal Trade Commission (FTC) has issued guidelines for businesses to follow in making environmental claims. A firm must be able to prove that any environmental claim made about a product has been substantiated with reliable scientific evidence. In addition, as shown in Figure 2.6, the FTC has given specific directions about how various environmental terms may be used in advertising and marketing.

Other environmental issues—such as finding renewable sources of clean energy—are the focus of many firms' efforts. Ocean Power Delivery has harnessed the power of ocean waves to supply energy to 500 Scottish homes, and Verdant Power hopes to supply power to a market on New York City's Roosevelt Island through the use of experimental turbines placed under the East River. Similar projects are under consideration by the Environmental Department of San Francisco, which is surrounded by water on three sides.[29]

*Developing the Quality of the Workforce* In the past, a nation's wealth has often been based on its money, production equipment, and natural resources. A country's true wealth, however, lies in its people. An educated, skilled workforce provides the intellectual know-how required to develop new technology, improve productivity, and compete in the global marketplace. It is becoming increasingly clear that to remain competitive, U.S. business must assume more responsibility for enhancing the quality of its workforce, including encouraging diversity of all kinds.

In developed economies like that of the United States, most new jobs require college-educated workers. With demand greatest for workers with advanced skills, the difference between the highest-paid and lowest-paid workers has been increasing. Among full-time workers in the United States, the top 10 percent earn an average of $1,200 per week, compared with just $275 for the average worker in the bottom 10 percent. Twenty years ago, a college graduate on average earned 38 percent more than someone with only a high school diploma, but today the typical college graduate earns 71 percent more.

**Figure**

**2.6** FTC Guidelines for Environmental Claims in Green Marketing

| If a business says a product is... | The product or package must . . . |
| --- | --- |
| **Biodegradable** | break down and return to nature in a reasonably short period of time. |
| **Recyclable** | be entirely reusable as new materials in the manufacture or assembly of a new product or package. |
| **Refillable** | be included in a system for the collection and return of the package for refill. If consumers have to find a way to refill it themselves, it is not **refillable**. |
| **Ozone Safe/Ozone Friendly** | must not contain any ozone-depleting ingredient. |

In fact, over a span of 40 years, a person with a college degree can earn more than $2.1 million.[30] Clearly, education is essential to the well-being of the workforce. Businesses must encourage students to stay in school, continue their education, and sharpen their skills. Target contributes funds to hundreds of students each year through partnerships with the Hispanic Scholarship Fund and the United Negro College Fund and also supports Reach Out and Read, a national program designed to encourage young children to read by distributing books through local children's health clinics.[31] Companies must also encourage employees to learn new skills and remain competitive.

Organizations also face enormous responsibilities for helping women, members of various cultural groups, and those who are physically challenged to contribute fully to the economy. Failure to do so is not only a waste of more than half the nation's workforce but also devastating to a firm's public image. Some socially responsible firms also encourage diversity in their business suppliers. Retail giant JCPenney's Partnership Program is designed to foster relationships with minority- and women-owned businesses—an effort the company has worked at for more than 30 years.

Through a commitment to developing employee diversity, ChevronTexaco has rebounded from a racial discrimination lawsuit. When information that the company's top managers had engaged in racist behavior became public, the company (then known simply as Texaco) was embarrassed, and its stock price tumbled. It quickly agreed to settle the lawsuit and crafted a plan to place more value on diversity among employees. Recruiting methods were revised to reach a more diverse pool of applicants, and scholarship programs were launched to develop talented minorities interested in key careers such as the physical sciences and international business. The company set specific goals for hiring and promoting qualified minority employees, and to achieve those goals, it included women and minorities on human resources committees and established mentoring programs. Within three years, the company had increased its recruiting of minorities to more than four of every ten new hires, and minorities accounted for one of every five promotions.

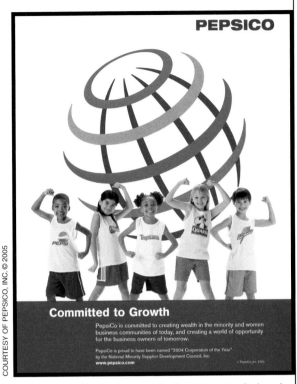

COURTESY OF PEPSICO, INC. © 2005

Diversity is an important way for businesses to find and employ the best workers possible. PepsiCo's forward-looking practices of using minority- and women-owned businesses as its suppliers helps create wealth in their communities—and benefits future workers as well. PepsiCo has received many awards for its diversity efforts over the years.

**Corporate Philanthropy**   As Chapter 1 pointed out, not-for-profit organizations play an important role in society by serving the public good. They provide the human resources that enhance the quality of life in communities around the world. To fulfill this mission, many not-for-profit organizations rely on financial contributions from the business community. Firms respond by donating billions of dollars each year to not-for-profit organizations. This **corporate philanthropy** includes cash contributions, donations of equipment and products, and supporting the volunteer efforts of company employees. Recipients include cultural organizations, adopt-a-school programs, community development agencies, and housing and job training programs.

**corporate philanthropy** act of an organization giving something back to the communities in which it earns profits.

Corporate philanthropy can have many positive benefits beyond the purely "feel-good" rewards of giving, such as higher employee morale, enhanced company image, and improved customer relationships. General Mills, for instance, is a major contributor to the Susan G. Komen Breast Cancer Foundation, through its line of yogurt products marketed under the Yoplait brand name. Yoplait's target market is health-conscious women, the same group most likely to know of or become involved with the Komen Foundation's fund-raising efforts.[32]

Companies often seek to align their marketing efforts with their charitable giving. Many contribute to the Olympics and create advertising that features the company's sponsorship. This is known as *cause-related marketing*. In a recent survey nearly nine out of ten young people said they believed companies had a duty to support social causes, and nearly seven in eight said they would switch brands in order to reward a company that did so. "Writing checks is not enough," says the director for research and policy development at Boston College's Center for Corporate Citizenship.[33]

Another form of corporate philanthropy is volunteerism. In their roles as corporate citizens, thousands of businesses encourage their employees to contribute their efforts to projects as diverse as Habitat for Humanity, the United Way, and Red Cross blood drives. In addition to making tangible contributions to the well-being of fellow citizens, such programs generate considerable public support and goodwill for the companies and their employees. In some cases, the volunteer efforts occur mostly during off-hours for employees. In other instances, the firm permits its workforce to volunteer during regular working hours. Sometimes companies help by contributing resources to promote worthy causes, such as Concern Worldwide's mission to help poverty-stricken people around the world.

Habitat for Humanity is one of many organizations that benefit from corporate philanthropy and partnerships. Organizations like this benefit through a corporation's ability to raise public awareness, volunteer manpower, product donations, and financial support.

*KEVIN DIETSCH/UPI/LANDOV*

## Responsibilities to Customers

**consumerism** public demand that a business consider the wants and needs of its customers in making decisions.

Businesspeople share a social and ethical responsibility to treat their customers fairly and act in a manner that is not harmful to them. They can even encourage harried customers to slow down for a rejuvenating ritual such as a cup of tea, as the "Hit & Miss" feature explains. **Consumerism**—the public demand that a business consider the wants and needs of its customers in making decisions—has gained widespread acceptance. Consumerism is based on the belief that consumers have certain rights. The most frequently quoted statement of consumer rights was made by President John F. Kennedy in 1962. Figure 2.7 summarizes these consumer rights. Numerous state and federal laws have been implemented since then to protect these rights.

Figure

2.7

Consumer Rights as Proposed by President Kennedy

Right to Be Heard

Right to Be Safe

**Consumer Rights**

Right to Choose

Right to Be Informed

*The Right to Be Safe*   Contemporary businesspeople must recognize obligations, both moral and legal, to ensure the safe operation of their products. Consumers should feel assured that the products they purchase will not cause injuries in normal use. **Product liability** refers to the responsibility of manufacturers for injuries and damages caused by their products. Items that lead to injuries, either directly or indirectly, can have disastrous consequences for their makers.

Many companies put their products through rigorous testing to avoid safety problems. Still, testing alone cannot foresee every eventuality. Companies must try to consider all possibilities and provide adequate warning of potential dangers. When a product does pose a threat to customer safety, a responsible manufacturer responds quickly to either correct the problem or recall the dangerous product. For example, General Motors recently recalled more than 300,000 SUVs and trucks to correct problems with a turn signal even though no injuries or damage had been reported.[34]

# HIT & MISS

## No Passport Needed to Visit the Republic of Tea

Would you like to visit the Republic of Tea and join those who are learning the "Sip-by-Sip life," one of health, balance, and well-being? All you need do is visit one of the 20,000 specialty stores and upscale restaurants that offer the company's certified organic full-leaf teas or place a mail or Internet order and enjoy their exotic blends at home.

Based in California, the quirky private firm offers only full-leaf tea, made from "simple, natural . . . hand-picked young shoots" to retain the essential oils that make each flavor unique and aromatic. The Republic has grown rapidly in the last ten years and now ships hundreds of orders a day from its more than 170 different product lines, which include not only teas such as Silver Rain, Dragon Well, and Moroccan Mint and caffeine-free herbal teas but also the occasional CD of soothing music to sip by. At prices of $10 or more for 50 bags, Republic of Tea blends are unlikely to show up in your local supermarket anytime soon. But sales of specialty teas have been rising to a record 20 percent of total tea sales, and Republic's managers have seen their business quadruple to more than $10 million a year.

The company is thriving by offering high-quality products, marketing them in the same way producers of fine wine do, and creating an unusual working atmosphere. Its human resource policies are attuned to its philosophy of promoting a balanced lifestyle that honors the sharing of tea as a ritual of "hospitality and nourishment for both body and soul." Every year several of its salespeople and managers travel to India, China, or South Africa to see the tea being made and to pick it themselves. "It's so motivating," said one employee of his trip to China. "It's the trip of a lifetime."

### Questions for Critical Thinking

1. In what way is Republic of Tea's focus on lifestyle an ethical choice the company has made? What values does this choice suggest?
2. Does the Republic of Tea demonstrate any ethical responsibilities to its employees? How? How might that contribute to the company's success?

**Sources:** "High Time for Tea in America," *BusinessWeek Online*, accessed June 14, 2006, http://www.businessweek.com; Republic of Tea Web site, accessed June 7, 2006, http://www.republicoftea.com; "What Motivates Me," *Sales & Marketing Management*, September 2004, p. 20.

---

***The Right to Be Informed*** Consumers should have access to enough education and product information to make responsible buying decisions. In their efforts to promote and sell their goods and services, companies can easily neglect consumers' right to be fully informed. False or misleading advertising is a violation of the Wheeler-Lea Act, a federal law enacted in 1938. The FTC and other federal and state agencies have established rules and regulations that govern advertising truthfulness. These rules prohibit businesses from making unsubstantiated claims about the performance or superiority of their goods or services. They also require businesses to avoid misleading consumers. Businesses that fail to comply face scrutiny from the FTC and consumer protection organizations. In one case, the FTC responded to complaints by filing charges against Star Publishing Group, which under the name National Consumer Services placed want ads promising as much

Honda goes beyond product testing to help prevent and reduce injuries related to accidents—not only for passengers but also for pedestrians. The company created a test dummy called POLAR II to analyze the force and types of impacts in car-person accidents. As a result, Honda developed energy-absorbing bumpers and hoods and modified its windshield wiper design to reduce the injuries from impact.

COURTESY OF AMERICAN HONDA MOTOR CO. INC.

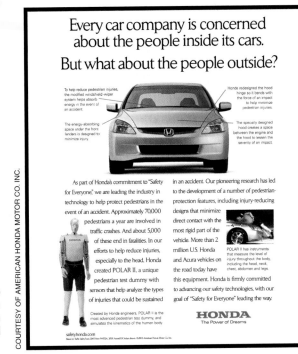

as $800 per week for starting a home-based business. Consumers who called the toll-free number in the ad reached a recording selling a guide to start a business that the recording falsely implied would involve government work.

The Food and Drug Administration (FDA), which sets standards for advertising conducted by drug manufacturers, eased restrictions for prescription drug advertising on television. In print ads, drug makers are required to spell out potential side effects and the proper uses of prescription drugs. Because of the requirement to disclose this information, prescription drug television advertising was limited. Now, however, the FDA says drug ads on radio and television can directly promote a prescription drug's benefits if they provide a quick way for consumers to learn about side effects, such as displaying a toll-free number or Internet address. The FDA also monitors "dietary supplements," including vitamins and herbs. These products may make claims about their general effect on health but may not claim to cure a disease, unless the company has presented the FDA with research and received the agency's approval. For instance, a product may say it helps the body maintain a healthy immune system but not that it fights colds.

The responsibility of business to preserve consumers' right to be informed extends beyond avoiding misleading advertising. All communications with customers—from salespeople's comments to warranties and invoices—must be controlled to clearly and accurately inform customers. Most packaged-goods firms, personal-computer makers, and other makers of products bought for personal use by consumers include toll-free customer service numbers on their product labels so that consumers can get answers when they have questions about a product.

To protect their customers and avoid claims of insufficient disclosure, businesses often include warnings on products. As Figure 2.8 shows, sometimes these warnings go far beyond what a reasonable consumer would expect.

**The Right to Choose**   Consumers should have the right to choose which goods and services they need and want to purchase. Socially responsible firms attempt to preserve this right, even if they reduce their own sales and profits in the process. Brand-name drug makers have recently gone on the defensive in a battle being waged by state governments, insurance companies, consumer groups, unions, and major employers such as General Motors and Verizon. These groups want to force down the rising price of prescription drugs by ensuring that consumers have the right and the opportunity to select cheaper generic brands.

**The Right to Be Heard**   Consumers should be able to express legitimate complaints to appropriate parties. Many companies expend considerable effort to ensure full hearings for consumer complaints. The eBay auction Web site assists buyers and sellers who believe they

Figure

2.8

Wacky Warning Labels

CAUTION:
Do not spray
in eyes.

WARNING:
Never use hair dryer
while sleeping.

WARNING:
Do not drive with
sunshield in place.

This towel has been tested
to withstand significantly
strong winds. But please be
advised that during a
hurricane or other severe
weather conditions, this
product should not be
used to secure yourself
or anything of value.

To protect themselves from product liability lawsuits, businesses have become more careful about including warnings on products. However, some companies may go overboard, as demonstrated by these actual product warning labels.

were victimized in transactions conducted through the site. It deploys a 200-employee team to work with users and law enforcement agencies to combat fraud. The company provides all users with insurance coverage of up to $200 per transaction, with a $25 deductible. It operates a feedback forum where it encourages users to rate one another. The auction site operates a software program that tracks individuals' bidding performance, looking for patterns associated with fraudulent behavior. And when it receives complaints of fraud, eBay forwards them to the FTC. So, although eBay cannot prevent all instances of fraud, it does provide an environment in which buyers and sellers feel protected.[35]

## Responsibilities to Employees

Companies that can attract skilled and knowledgeable employees are better able to meet the challenges of competing globally. In return, businesses have wide-ranging responsibilities to their employees, both here and abroad. These include workplace safety, quality-of-life issues, avoiding discrimination, and preventing sexual harassment and sexism. Today, they also have to accommodate office workers who fear working in tall buildings.

*Workplace Safety*  A century ago, few businesses paid much attention to the safety of their workers. In fact, most business owners viewed employees as mere cogs in the production process. Workers—many of whom were young children—toiled in frequently dangerous conditions. In 1911, a fire at the Triangle Shirtwaist Factory in New York City killed 146 people, mostly young girls. Contributing to the massive loss of life were the sweatshop working conditions at the factory, including overcrowding, blocked exits, and a lack of fire escapes. The horrifying tragedy forced businesses to begin to recognize their responsibility for their workers' safety.

The safety and health of workers on the job is now an important business responsibility. The Occupational Safety and Health Administration (OSHA) is the main federal regulatory force in setting workplace safety and health standards. These mandates range from broad guidelines on storing hazardous materials to specific standards for worker safety in industries such as construction, manufacturing, and mining. OSHA tracks and investigates workplace accidents and has the authority to fine employers who are found liable for injuries and deaths that occur on the job.

Although businesses occasionally complain about having to comply with too many OSHA regulations, ultimately management must set standards and implement programs to ensure that workers are safe in the workplace. The Jewel-Osco food-drug chain, the Midwest division of SuperValu, shows employees training videos about safe practices. The videos teach about fire safety, germs transmitted in blood, and actions to take if the store is robbed. The store makes special efforts to protect teenage employees. They are expected to read and sign a statement that they will not use any machinery, lift equipment (including the elevator), or meat slicers. Use of power equipment is limited by law to employees age 18 or older, and those employees must undergo training before the store permits them to use the equipment. Laws also extend extra protection to teenage workers by limiting the number of hours they work and the number of trips they may make away from their primary place of employment each day. Protection of young workers is

The Occupational Safety and Health Administration (OSHA) is the main federal agency responsible for workplace safety and health. The organization provides many resources for employers and employees, including this poster, to help reduce workplace accidents and injuries.

# DO YOU SMOKE? YOU'RE FIRED.

*Weyco, a Michigan health benefits administrator, plans to randomly test its workers for tobacco use once a year and suspend or fire them if they fail—or even if they refuse to be tested. In fact, four employees who refused to take Weyco's test were fired.*

Weyco also claims the right to search employee belongings if it suspects they contain tobacco. The policy created an uproar, but Weyco is not alone in its efforts to control worker behavior with an eye toward the bottom line. More than 440,000 tobacco-related deaths occur every year, with medical costs estimated at more than $75 billion.

*Should employers have the right to prohibit smoking and other risky behavior away from the workplace?*

## PRO

1. Companies have a right to promote the health of their workers because they have invested time and effort to hire and train them. "The main goal is to elevate the health status of our employees," says Weyco's chief financial officer.
2. Firms need to control their skyrocketing health-care costs whenever possible, and smoking is a major

factor in health claims. Lowering the cost of benefits improves profits, which is a gain for all stakeholders in the organization.

## CON

1. What employees do on their own time is their own business. Work should not invade employee privacy at home.
2. Enforcing smoking bans could trigger other invasive monitoring. Such policies will encourage employers to prohibit still other off-site activities that have no relationship to performance of the job.

## Summary

In states with "at-will" employment laws, employees can be fired for any or no reason. More than 20 states prohibit discrimination against workers (including firing) based on their lifestyle. One smokers' rights advocate says, "You're creating a class

of unemployable citizens. It won't stand." But some companies are either refusing to hire, firing, raising health-insurance premiums for, or denying insurance coverage to employees who smoke, are overweight, have high cholesterol, or participate in risky activities. Investors Property Management in Seattle won't hire smokers, and Alaska Airlines' no-smoking policy includes testing new hires for tobacco use. Such rules have led some employees to quit smoking, but further challenges are sure to be thrown from both sides.

**Sources:** Barbara Wieland, "Grounds for Firing: Just About Anything," *Lansing (MI) State Journal*, accessed June 7, 2006, http://www.lsj.com; Stephanie Armour, "Trend: You Smoke? You're Fired!" *USA Today*, May 12, 2005, p. 1A; Karen Springen, "Smoking: Light Up and You May Be Let Go," *Newsweek*, February 7, 2005.

solving an **ETHICAL** controversy

especially significant because almost one workplace injury in three involves employees with less than a year's experience.[36] Some firms have gone a step further and want to protect workers off the job as well as on, as the "Solving an Ethical Controversy" feature discusses.

*Quality-of-Life Issues* Balancing work and family is becoming harder for many employees. They find themselves squeezed between working long hours and handling child-care problems, caring for elderly parents, and solving other family crises. A *sandwich generation* of households, those caring for two generations—their children and their aging parents—has arisen. As the population ages, the share of American households providing some type of care to a relative or friend age 50 or older has grown dramatically in the early years of the 21st century. At the same time, as married women spend more time working outside the home, they have fewer hours per week to spend on family. The employees juggling work with life's other demands aren't just working mothers. Childless couples, single people, and men all express frustration with the pressures of balancing work with family and personal needs. Peter Brand, a senior manager at PricewaterhouseCoopers, is determined to spend time with his two young children after work, even though it's a struggle to leave his office by 6 p.m. when his wife, Marcy, a manager at Southwest Airlines, picks the youngsters up on her way home. He is not alone in his desire for balance between work and family; 70 percent of the men in a recent study by the Families and Work Institute said they would accept less pay to spend more time with their families, and nearly half would rather have family time than a promotion.[37]

Helping workers find solutions to these quality-of-life issues has become an important concern of many businesses, but finding answers isn't always easy. Some companies offer flexible work arrangements to support employees. Other firms offer benefits such as subsidized child care or on-site education and shopping to assist workers trying to balance work and family. Some employees are carving out agreements with their firms that allow them to work part time.[38]

Another solution has been to offer **family leave** to employees who need to deal with family matters. Under the Family and Medical Leave Act of 1993, businesses with 50 or more employees must provide unpaid leave annually for any employee who wants time off for the birth or adoption of a child, to become a foster parent, or to care for a seriously ill relative or spouse. The law requires employers to grant up to twelve weeks of leave each year, and leave may be taken intermittently as medical conditions make necessary. This unpaid leave also applies to an employee who has a serious illness. Workers must meet certain eligibility requirements. Employers must continue to provide health benefits during the leave and guarantee that employees will return to equivalent jobs. The issue of who is entitled to health benefits can also create a dilemma as companies struggle to balance the needs of their employees against the staggering costs of health care.

### Ensuring Equal Opportunity on the Job
Businesspeople face many challenges managing an increasingly diverse workforce in the 21st century. Technological advances are expanding the ways people with physical disabilities can contribute in the workplace. Businesses also need to find ways to responsibly recruit and manage older workers and workers with varying lifestyles. In addition, beginning with Lotus Development in 1982, companies have begun to extend benefits equally to employees, regardless of sexual orientation. In particular, that means the company offers benefits such as health insurance to unmarried domestic partners if it offers them to spouses of married couples. Companies that now offer these gender-neutral benefits include Boeing, Citigroup, Disney, General Mills, and Prudential. This treatment reflects the view that all employee groups deserve the right to work in an environment that is nondiscriminatory.

To a great extent, efforts at managing diversity are regulated by law. The Civil Rights Act (1964) outlawed many kinds of discriminatory practices, and Title VII of the act specifically prohibits discrimination in employment. As shown in Table 2.2, other nondiscrimination laws include the Equal Pay Act (1963), the Age Discrimination in Employment Act (1967), the Equal Employment Opportunity Act (1972), the Pregnancy Discrimination Act (1978), the Civil Rights Act of 1991, and numerous executive orders. The Americans with Disabilities Act (1990) protects the rights of physically challenged people. The Vietnam Era Veterans Readjustment Act (1974) protects the employment of veterans of the Vietnam War.

The **Equal Employment Opportunity Commission (EEOC)** was created to increase job opportunities for women and minorities and to help end discrimination based on race, color, religion, disability, gender, or national origin in any personnel action. To enforce fair-employment laws, it investigates charges of discrimination and harassment and files suit against violators. The EEOC can also help employers set up programs to increase job opportunities for women, minorities, people with disabilities, and people in other protected categories.

Fair treatment of employees is more than a matter of complying with EEOC regulations, however. Like white male employees, women and people of color want opportunities to excel and rewards for excellence. They also want to be treated with respect. A minority employee

Table

2.2    Laws Designed to Ensure Equal Opportunity

| Law | Key Provisions |
|---|---|
| Title VII of the Civil Rights Act of 1964 (as amended by the Equal Employment Opportunity Act of 1972) | Prohibits discrimination in hiring, promotion, compensation, training, or dismissal on the basis of race, color, religion, sex, or national origin. |
| Age Discrimination in Employment Act of 1967 (as amended) | Prohibits discrimination in employment against anyone age 40 or older in hiring, promotion, compensation, training, or dismissal. |
| Equal Pay Act of 1963 | Requires equal pay for men and women working for the same firm in jobs that require equal skill, effort, and responsibility. |
| Vocational Rehabilitation Act of 1973 | Requires government contractors and subcontractors to take affirmative action to employ and promote qualified disabled workers. Coverage now extends to all federal employees. Coverage has been broadened by the passage of similar laws in more than 20 states and, through court rulings, to include people with communicable diseases, including AIDS. |
| Vietnam Era Veterans Readjustment Act of 1974 | Requires government contractors and subcontractors to take affirmative action to employ and retain disabled veterans. Coverage now extends to all federal employees and has been broadened by the passage of similar laws in more than 20 states. |
| Pregnancy Discrimination Act of 1978 | Requires employers to treat pregnant women and new mothers the same as other employees for all employment-related purposes, including receipt of benefits under company benefit programs. |
| Americans with Disabilities Act of 1990 | Makes discrimination against the disabled illegal in public accommodations, transportation, and telecommunications; stiffens employer penalties for intentional discrimination on the basis of an employee's disability. |
| Civil Rights Act of 1991 | Makes it easier for workers to sue their employers for alleged discrimination. Enables victims of sexual discrimination to collect punitive damages; includes employment decisions and on-the-job issues such as sexual harassment, unfair promotions, and unfair dismissal. The employer must prove that it did not engage in discrimination. |
| Family and Medical Leave Act of 1993 | Requires all businesses with 50 or more employees to provide up to twelve weeks of unpaid leave annually to employees who have had a child or are adopting a child, are becoming foster parents, are caring for a seriously ill relative or spouse, or are themselves seriously ill. Workers must meet certain eligibility requirements. |
| Uniformed Services Employment and Reemployment Rights Act of 1994 | Prohibits employers from denying employment benefits on the basis of employees' membership in or obligation to serve in the uniformed services and protects the rights of veterans, reservists, and National Guard members to reclaim their jobs after being absent due to military service or training. |

who misses out on a plum assignment may miss out on the big raise that goes with it. As the employee's salary grows more slowly, managers may eventually begin to use the size of the salary as an indicator that the employee contributes less to the organization. Chapter 9 takes a closer look at diversity and employment discrimination issues as part of a discussion of human resources management.

*Age Discrimination*    With the average age of U.S. workers steadily rising, the government expects more than half the workforce to be age 40 or older by 2010. Yet some employers find it less expensive to hire and retain younger workers, who generally have lower medical bills as well as lower salary and benefits packages. At the same time, many older workers have training and skills that younger workers have yet to acquire. The Age Discrimination in Employment Act of 1967 (ADEA) protects individuals who are age 40 or older, prohibiting discrimination on the basis of age and denial of benefits to older employees.

Ruling in a recent lawsuit brought under ADEA, the Supreme Court determined that employers can be held liable for age discrimination against older workers even if they intended no harm. At the same time, the court allowed employers to use "reasonable" factors such as cost cutting to defend business practices that might have more severe impacts on older than on younger workers.[39]

### Sexual Harassment and Sexism

Every employer has a responsibility to ensure that all workers are treated fairly and are safe from sexual harassment. **Sexual harassment** refers to unwelcome and inappropriate actions of a sexual nature in the workplace. It is a form of sex discrimination that violates the Civil Rights Act of 1964, which gives both men and women the right to file lawsuits for intentional sexual harassment. More than 15,000 sexual harassment complaints are filed with the EEOC each year, of which about 12 percent are filed by men. Thousands of other cases are either handled internally by companies or never reported.

Two types of sexual harassment exist. The first type occurs when an employee is pressured to comply with unwelcome advances and requests for sexual favors in return for job security, promotions, and raises. The second type results from a hostile work environment in which an employee feels hassled or degraded because of unwelcome flirting, lewd comments, or obscene jokes. The courts have ruled that allowing sexually oriented materials in the workplace can create a hostile atmosphere that interferes with an employee's ability to do the job. Employers are also legally responsible to protect employees from sexual harassment by customers and clients. The EEOC's Web site informs employers and employees of criteria for identifying sexual harassment and how it should be handled in the workplace.

Preventing sexual harassment can be difficult because it involves regulating the conduct of individual employees. Sometimes victims, especially young employees, are intimidated or unaware of their rights, but the EEOC has set up a Youth@Work program (http://youth.eeoc.gov) to ensure that young workers can learn about the various types of discrimination and ways to avoid them. The agency recently announced the settlement of a sexual harassment suit against a Missouri Burger King franchise brought by seven women, six of whom were teenagers.[40]

To avoid sexual harassment problems, many firms have established policies and employee education programs aimed at preventing such violations. An effective harassment prevention program should include the following measures:

- Issue a specific policy statement prohibiting sexual harassment.
- Develop a complaint procedure for employees to follow.
- Create a work atmosphere that encourages sexually harassed staffers to come forward.
- Investigate and resolve complaints quickly and take disciplinary action against harassers.

Unless all these components are supported by top management, sexual harassment is difficult to eliminate.

Sexual harassment is often part of the broader problem of **sexism**—discrimination against members of either sex, but primarily affecting women. One important sexism issue is equal pay for equal work. On average, U.S. women earn 76 cents for every dollar earned by men. In the course of a working lifetime, this disparity adds up to a gap of almost $426,000. The percentage of women who hold managerial and professional positions has grown to 50 percent. But that trend has not necessarily reduced the pay gap. And while men with children earn about 2 percent more than average, women with children earn 2.5 percent less than childless women. In terms of pay, full-time female employees in most industries—ranging from engineering, education, and banking to law, medicine, and technology—lag behind men. Female advertising executives earn $49,000 on average while men earn $56,000, and retail salespeople earn more than $31,000 if they are men compared with just less than $20,000 if they are women.[41]

In some extreme cases, differences in pay and advancement can become the basis for sex discrimination suits, such as those filed against Wal-Mart Stores and Morgan Stanley, the Wall Street brokerage house. Morgan Stanley recently settled the sex discrimination suit brought by the EEOC for $54 million; Wal-Mart is charged with discriminating against women in hiring, pay, and promotion decisions in an ongoing class-action suit.[42]

## Responsibilities to Investors and the Financial Community

Although a fundamental goal of any business is to make a profit for its shareholders, investors and the financial community demand that businesses behave ethically as well as legally. When firms fail in this responsibility, thousands of investors and consumers can suffer.

State and federal government agencies are responsible for protecting investors from financial misdeeds. At the federal level, the Securities and Exchange Commission (SEC) investigates suspicions of unethical or illegal behavior by publicly traded firms. It investigates accusations that a business is using faulty accounting practices to inaccurately portray its financial resources and profits to investors. Regulation FD ("Fair Disclosure") is an SEC rule that requires publicly traded companies to announce major information to the general public, rather than first disclosing the information to selected major investors. The agency also operates an Office of Internet Enforcement to target fraud in online trading and online sales of stock by unlicensed sellers. Recall that the Sarbanes-Oxley Act of 2002 also protects investors from unethical accounting practices. Chapter 18 discusses securities trading practices further.

## WHAT'S AHEAD

The decisions and actions of businesspeople are often influenced by outside forces such as the legal environment and society's expectations about business responsibility. Firms also are affected by the economic environments in which they operate. The next chapter discusses the broad economic issues that influence businesses around the world. Our discussion will focus on how factors such as supply and demand, unemployment, inflation, and government monetary policies pose both challenges and opportunities for firms seeking to compete in the global marketplace.

## SUMMARY OF LEARNING GOALS

**① Explain the concepts of business ethics and social responsibility.**

Business ethics refers to the standards of conduct and moral values that govern actions and decisions in the workplace. Businesspeople must take a wide range of social issues into account when making decisions. Social responsibility refers to management's acceptance of the obligation to consider profit, consumer satisfaction, and societal well-being of equal value in evaluating the firm's performance.

### Assessment Check Answers

**1.1 To whom do businesses have responsibilities?**
Businesses are responsible to customers, employees, investors, and society.

**1.2 If a firm is meeting all its responsibilities to others, why do ethical conflicts arise?**
Ethical conflicts arise because business must balance doing what is right and doing what is profitable.

**2** **Describe the factors that influence business ethics.**

Among the many factors shaping individual ethics are personal experience, peer pressure, and organizational culture. Individual ethics are also influenced by family, cultural, and religious standards. Additionally, the culture of the organization where a person works can be a factor.

## Assessment Check Answers

**2.1 What role can an ethics compliance officer play in a firm?**
Ethics compliance officers are charged with deterring wrongdoing and ensuring that ethical standards are met.

**2.2 What factors influence the ethical environment of a business?**
Individual ethics and technology influence the ethical environment of a business.

**3** **List the stages in the development of ethical standards.**

In the preconventional stage, individuals primarily consider their own needs and desires in making decisions. They obey external rules only from fear of punishment or hope of reward. In the conventional stage, individuals are aware of and respond to their duty to others. Expectations of groups, as well as self-interest, influence behavior. In the final, postconventional stage, the individual can move beyond self-interest and duty to include consideration of the needs of society. A person in this stage can apply personal ethical principles in a variety of situations.

## Assessment Check Answers

**3.1 What is the preconventional stage in the development of ethical standards?**
In the preconventional stage the individual looks out for his or her own interests and follows rules out of fear of punishment or hope of reward.

**3.2 What is the difference between the conventional and the postconventional stages?**
In the conventional stage, the person considers the interests and expectations of others, and in the postconventional stage, he or she considers personal, group, and societal interests.

**4** **Identify common ethical dilemmas in the workplace.**

Conflicts of interest exist when a businessperson is faced with a situation in which an action benefiting one person has the potential to harm another, as when the person's own interests conflict with those of a customer. Honesty and integrity are valued qualities that engender trust, but a person's immediate self-interest may seem to require violating these principles. Loyalty to an employer sometimes conflicts with truthfulness. Whistle-blowing is a possible response to misconduct in the workplace, but the personal costs of doing so are high.

## Assessment Check Answers

**4.1 What are honesty and integrity and how do they differ?**
Honesty is the trait of telling the truth; integrity goes beyond truthfulness and means adhering to deeply felt ethical principles.

**4.2 How can loyalty and truth come into conflict for an employee?**
Truth and loyalty can come into conflict when the truth about a company or situation is unfavorable.

**5** **Discuss how organizations shape ethical behavior.**

Employees are strongly influenced by the standards of conduct established and supported within the organizations where they work. Businesses can help shape ethical behavior by developing codes of conduct that define their expectations. Organizations can also use this training to develop employees' ethics awareness and reasoning. They can foster ethical action through decision-making tools, goals consistent with ethical behavior, and advice hotlines. Executives must also demonstrate ethical behavior in their decisions and actions to provide ethical leadership.

## Assessment Check Answers

**5.1 What is a code of conduct?**
A code of conduct is a formal statement defining the way the organization expects and requires employees to resolve ethical questions that arise at work.

**5.2 How does ethical leadership contribute to ethical standards throughout a company?**
Employees more readily commit to the company's core values when they see that leaders and managers

behave ethically and when the ethics program is not seen as a way to protect top executives from being blamed for wrongdoing.

### 6 Describe how businesses' social responsibility is measured.

Today's businesses are expected to weigh their qualitative impact on consumers and society, in addition to their quantitative economic contributions such as sales, employment levels, and profits. One measure is their compliance with labor and consumer protection laws and their charitable contributions. Another measure some businesses take is to conduct social audits. Public-interest groups also create standards and measure companies' performance relative to those standards. Consumers may boycott groups that fall short of social standards.

## Assessment Check Answers

**6.1 What is meant by social responsibility and why do firms exercise it?**
Social responsibility is management's acceptance of its obligation to consider profit, consumer satisfaction, and societal well-being to be of equal value when evaluating the firm's performance. Businesses exercise it because it is required by law, because it enhances the company's image, or because management believes it is ethical to do so.

**6.2 What is a social audit?**
A social audit is a formal procedure to identify and evaluate all company activities that relate to social issues such as conservation, employment practices, environmental protection, and philanthropy.

### 7 Summarize the responsibilities of business to the general public, customers, and employees.

The responsibilities of business to the general public include protecting the public health and the environment and developing the quality of the workforce. Additionally, many would argue that businesses have a social responsibility to support charitable and social causes in the communities in which they earn profits. Business also has a social and ethical responsibility to treat customers fairly and protect consumers upholding the rights to be safe, to be informed, to choose, and to be heard. Businesses have wide-ranging responsibilities to their workers. They should make sure that the workplace is safe, address quality-of-life issues, ensure equal opportunity, and prevent sexual harassment.

## Assessment Check Answers

**7.1 What is green marketing?**
Green marketing is a marketing strategy that promotes environmentally safe products and production methods.

**7.2 What is corporate philanthropy?**
Corporate philanthropy includes cash contributions, donations of equipment and products, and support for the volunteer efforts of company employees.

**7.3 What are the four main consumer rights?**
The four main consumer rights are the right to be safe, to be informed, to choose, and to be heard.

### 8 Explain why investors and the financial community are concerned with business ethics and social responsibility.

Investors and the financial community demand that businesses behave ethically as well as legally in handling their financial transactions. Businesses must be honest in reporting their profits and financial performance to avoid misleading investors. The Securities and Exchange Commission is the federal agency responsible for investigating suspicions that publicly traded firms have engaged in unethical or illegal financial behavior.

## Assessment Check Answers

**8.1 Why do firms need to do more than just earn a profit?**
Firms need to do more than just earn a profit because the law requires them to behave in a legal and ethical manner and because investors and shareholders demand such behavior.

**8.2 What is the role of the Securities and Exchange Commission?**
Among other functions the Securities and Exchange Commission investigates suspicions of unethical or illegal behavior by publicly traded firms.

## Business Terms You Need to Know

Sarbanes-Oxley Act 32
business ethics 32
conflict of interest 37
whistle-blowing 39

code of conduct 40
social responsibility 43
recycling 45
corporate philanthropy 47

consumerism 48
sexual harassment 55

## Other Important Business Terms

boycott 37
integrity 39
social audit 43
pollution 45

green marketing 46
product liability 48
family leave 53

Equal Employment Opportunity
Commission (EEOC) 53
sexism 55

## Review Questions

1. What do the terms *business ethics* and *social responsibility* mean? Cite an example of each. Who are the main constituents that businesses must consider?

2. Identify and describe briefly the three stages in which individuals typically develop ethical standards. What are some of the factors that determine the stage of moral and ethical development an individual occupies at any given time?

3. What are the four most common ethical challenges that businesspeople face? Give a brief example of each.

4. What are the four levels of development of a corporate culture to support business ethics? Describe each briefly.

5. How do organizational goals affect ethical behavior? How might these goals interfere with ethical leadership? Give an example.

6. What basic consumer rights does the consumerism movement try to ensure? How has consumerism improved the contemporary business environment?

7. What are some of the major factors that contribute to the assessment of a company's social performance?

8. Identify the major benefits of corporate philanthropy.

9. What are some of the responsibilities that firms have to their employees?

10. What are quality-of-life issues? How can companies best meet them?

11. What laws protect employees from age discrimination? From sexual harassment?

12. How does a company demonstrate its responsibility to investors and the financial community?

## Projects and Teamwork Applications

1. Write your own personal code of ethics, detailing your feelings about ethical challenges such as lying to protect an employer or co-worker, favoring one client over another, misrepresenting credentials to an employer or client, and using the computer for personal purposes while at work. What role will your personal ethics play in deciding your choice of career and acceptance of a job?

2. "Everybody exaggerates when it comes to selling products, and customers ought to take that with a grain of salt," said one advertising executive recently in response to a complaint filed by the Better Business Bureau about misleading advertising. "Don't we all have a brain, and can't we all think a little bit, too?" Do you agree with this statement? Why or why not?

3. Imagine that you work for a company that makes outdoor clothing, such as L.L. Bean, Timberland, or Patagonia. Write a memo describing at least four specific ways in which your company could practice corporate philanthropy. Include the benefits you think the company and the community would realize from such actions.

4. Imagine that you are the human resources director for a company that is trying to establish a written policy to outline its responsibilities to its employees. Choose one of the responsibilities described in the chapter—such as workplace safety—and write a memo describing specific steps your company will take to fulfill that responsibility.

5. Suppose that you own a small firm with twelve employees. One employee tells you in confidence that he has just learned he is HIV positive. You know that healthcare costs for AIDS patients can be disastrously high, and this expense could drastically raise the health insurance premiums that your other employees must pay. What are your responsibilities to this employee? To the rest of your staff? Explain.

## Case 2.1

## U.S. Federal Sentencing Guidelines: The Carrot and the Stick

The U.S. Federal Sentencing Guidelines were originally designed to help the government find meaningful and consistent ways to sentence organizations—including public and private companies and not-for-profits—convicted of crimes. After discovering that similar cases had been resolved differently by the courts, the Sentencing Commission enacted guidelines that rely on what legislators call the stick-and-carrot approach to corporate ethics: The financial penalties that the courts can impose for wrongdoing are the stick, while the existence of an effective ethics program can reduce the fines the courts can set, which serves as the carrot.

The guidelines make organizations subject to sentencing, fines, and probation if they are convicted of violations of antitrust, securities, bribery, fraud, money laundering, criminal activities, extortion, embezzlement, or conspiracy laws. Because organizations are liable for the offenses committed by their officers, the guidelines were intended to provide for just punishment, deterrence, and the creation of internal company policies to prevent unlawful behavior.

To define what an "effective" ethics program looks like, the guidelines identify seven elements it should include:

1. standards and procedures, such as a code of ethics, to prevent or detect wrongdoing
2. responsibility at all levels and oversight at a high level, such as an ethics officer
3. due care in the delegation of authority

4. communication of the code of ethics, such as training, at all levels
5. auditing, monitoring, and reporting systems, such as an ethics hotline free of internal repercussions
6. enforcement of established ethical standards, including incentives and disciplinary measures
7. appropriate response to any wrongdoing that is found, including prevention of any recurrence

Thousands of U.S. companies have responded by creating new or enhancing existing ethics programs. Even organizations abroad have reacted, such as the CBIC, a bank in Canada, and the Bank of Tokyo, which has adopted the guidelines as the centerpiece of its own compliance program. Surveys of employees find that the changes are making themselves felt in the workplace, and observers believe they are occurring primarily in the areas of ethics training, the establishment of ethics offices and appointment of ethics officers, and the creation of ethics hotlines. Codes of ethics appear to have been affected the least, mostly because according to one survey, about 93 percent of firms already had such a code in place.

After tracking responses for about ten years, the Sentencing Commission strengthened the criteria in order to reflect "best practices" among organizations that had applied them since enactment and the Sarbanes-Oxley Act. These revisions were meant to provide an even clearer model of the "corporate good citizen" and make it easier for organizations both large and small to comply. Some of the changes increase the responsibility of boards of directors and top executives to demonstrate ethical leadership, require the organization to show due diligence in fulfilling the guidelines, and require it to cultivate an organizational culture that encourages ethical conduct and a commitment to compliance with the law. Firms must also periodically assess the risk that criminal behavior might occur in their organizations.

## Questions for Critical Thinking

1. Which do you think will be more effective in ensuring that organizations act in ethical ways, the carrot or the stick? Why?
2. Do you think the Sentencing Guidelines provide a sound basis for creating and maintaining a corporate ethics program? Why or why not? If not, how would you modify them?

**Sources:** "An Overview of the United States Sentencing Commission and the Federal Sentencing Guidelines," U.S. Sentencing Commission, accessed June 7, 2006, http://www.ussc.gov; Dove Izraeli and Mark S. Schwartz, "What Can We Learn from the U.S. Federal Sentencing Guidelines for Organizational Ethics?" European Institute for Business Ethics, accessed June 7, 2006, http://www.itcilo.it/english; Stanley A. Twardy, "Compliance Programs to Detect and Prevent Crime: Amended Federal Sentencing Guidelines," FindLaw, accessed June 7, 2006, http://library.findlaw.com.

## VIDEO Case 2.2

### Ford Turns Green with Clean Energy

This video case appears on page 609. A recently filmed video, designed to expand and highlight the written case, is available for class use by instructors.

# Chapter 3

## Economic Challenges Facing Global and Domestic Business

### Learning Goals

1. Distinguish between microeconomics and macroeconomics.

2. Explain the factors that drive demand and supply.

3. Describe each of the four different types of market structures in a private enterprise system.

4. Compare the three major types of economic systems.

5. Identify and describe the four stages of the business cycle.

6. Explain how productivity, price level changes, and employment levels affect the stability of a nation's economy.

7. Discuss how monetary policy and fiscal policy are used to manage an economy's performance.

8. Describe the major global economic challenges of the 21st century.

You probably won't be involved in a police car chase anytime soon. But as a businessperson, you might be interested in the story of the police car itself. For years, Ford Motor Company has dominated the police car market with its special model Crown Victoria Police Interceptor. That souped-up model has accounted for about 85 percent of all police cars sold in the United States. But all that is changing. Police departments now have a choice about what vehicles they purchase, and DaimlerChrysler is in hot pursuit of their dollars.

DaimlerChrysler announced that its Dodge division is unveiling a police model of its classic Dodge Charger. The firm also plans to produce a law enforcement edition of its Magnum, but the Charger is expected to compete directly with

AFP/GETTY IMAGES

version of its Intrepid, but officers did not feel comfortable with front-

# Dodge Tries to Dethrone Ford's Crown Victoria

Ford's Crown Victoria. While many police departments claim loyalty to Ford, some are beginning to look at alternatives because of high-profile accidents with the Crown Victoria. According to reports, nearly 20 officers died in fiery explosions that resulted when their cruisers were hit from behind. Some departments have even sued the automaker. The bad publicity has created a window of opportunity for competitors.

While Ford is taking steps to increase the safety of its cars by installing fire suppression devices and gas tank protectors, Dodge is rolling out its new cars. The new Charger has enhanced brakes and a 340-horsepower Hemi engine, features that take direct aim at the Crown Victoria. The Magnum, which is a sport wagon, is expected to attract some interest. But 75 percent of police departments prefer sedans, so the Charger is the flagship model. Dodge developed both cars knowing they will face some tough testing by organizations such as the California Highway Patrol and the Michigan State Police. Both agencies put any prospective police cars through difficult maneuvers and publish the results, which influence the purchase decisions made by many police departments. Dodge has also listened to customers and learned from its previous mistakes. Several years ago, it introduced a police

wheel drive at high speeds or when making tight turns. So it's back to rear-wheel drive for the Charger. "With all of this, we know we'll hit the sweet spot," predicts Eric Ridenour, executive vice president of product development for Chrysler.

Dethroning the Crown Victoria won't be easy, though. Police departments have been comfortable with the auto for years. Officers report that they like the Crown Victoria's roomy interior, which can hold laptop computers, papers, and all the other equipment that they need to haul around on the job. Purchasing managers like to order a single type of vehicle so that officers can swap cars easily, if necessary, and maintenance is more efficient with one type of part to supply. So it is typical for departments to outfit an entire fleet with a single model. But with budgets always in mind, police departments are opening up to the possibility of a new vehicle. "We're excited that there's another competitor out there," says John Alley, fleet administrator for the San Diego Police Department. He manages a fleet of 550 Crown Victorias at about $21,000 to $23,000 each. "We're hoping the new Dodge will be cheaper." DaimlerChrysler marketers hope that when police dispatchers send out the alert, "calling all cars," they'll be talking about the Charger.[1]

When we examine the exchanges that companies and societies make as a whole, we are focusing on the *economic systems* operating in different nations. These systems reflect the combination of policies and choices a nation makes to allocate resources among its citizens. Countries vary in the ways they allocate scarce resources.

**Economics,** which analyzes the choices people and governments make in allocating scarce resources, affects each of us, because everyone is involved in producing, distributing, or simply consuming goods and services. In fact, your life is affected by economics every day. When you decide what goods to buy, what services to use, or what activities to fit into your schedule, you are making economic choices.

**economics** social science that analyzes the choices people and governments make in allocating scarce resources.

The choices you make may often be international in scope. If you are in the market for a new car, you might visit several dealers in a row on the same street—Ford, Chrysler, Honda, Toyota, and Saturn. You might decide on Toyota—a Japanese firm—but your car might very well be manufactured in the United States, using parts from all over the world. Although firms sometimes emphasize the American origin of their goods and services in order to appeal to consumers' desire to support the U.S. economy, many products are made of components from a variety of nations.

Businesses and not-for-profit organizations also make economic decisions when they choose how to use human and natural resources; invest in equipment, machinery, and buildings; and form partnerships with other firms. When a police department decides whether to purchase a Ford or a Dodge for its officers to drive, it is making an economic choice.

**microeconomics** study of small economic units, such as individual consumers, families, and businesses.

Economists refer to the study of small economic units, such as individual consumers, families, and businesses, as **microeconomics.** On a broader level, government decisions about the operation of the country's economy also affect you, your job, and your financial future. A major feature of the recent Sarbanes-Oxley Act was to limit the consulting services that accounting firms can provide for a company whose financial records they audit. The new law affected the entire accounting profession.

**macroeconomics** study of a nation's overall economic issues, such as how an economy maintains and allocates resources and how a government's policies affect the standards of living of its citizens.

The study of a country's overall economic issues is called **macroeconomics** (*macro* means "large"). Macroeconomics addresses such issues as how an economy uses its resources and how government policies affect people's standards of living. Macroeconomics examines not just the economic policies of individual nations but the ways in which those individual policies affect the overall world economy. Because so much business is conducted around the world, a law enacted in one country can easily affect a transaction that takes place in another country. Although macroeconomic issues have a broad scope, they help shape the decisions that individuals, families, and businesses make every day.

This chapter introduces economic theory and the economic challenges facing individuals, businesses, and governments in the global marketplace. We begin with the microeconomic concepts of supply and demand and their effect on the prices people pay for goods and services. Next we explain the various types of economic systems, along with tools for comparing and evaluating their performance. Then we examine the ways in which governments seek to manage economies to create stable business environments in their countries. The final section in the chapter looks at some of the driving economic forces currently affecting people's lives.

**assessment check**

1. Define microeconomics.
2. Define macroeconomics.

# MICROECONOMICS: THE FORCES OF DEMAND AND SUPPLY

Think about your own economic activities. You shop for groceries, you subscribe to a cell phone service, you pay college tuition, you fill your car's tank with gas. Now think about your family's economic activities. When you were growing up, your parents might have owned a home or rented an apartment. You might have taken a summer family vacation. Your parents may have shopped at discount clubs or at local stores. Each of these choices relates to the study of microeconomics. They also help determine both the prices of goods and services and the amounts sold. Information about these activities is vital to companies because their survival and ability to grow depends on selling enough products priced high enough to cover costs and earn profits. The same information is important to consumers who must make purchase decisions based on prices and the availability of the goods and services they need.

At the heart of every business endeavor is an exchange between a buyer and a seller. The buyer recognizes that he or she needs or wants a particular good or service—whether it's a hamburger or a haircut—and is willing to pay a seller for it. The seller requires the exchange in order to earn a profit and stay in business. So the exchange process involves both demand and supply. **Demand** refers to the willingness and ability of buyers to purchase goods and services at different prices. The other side of the exchange process is **supply,** the amount of goods and services for sale at different prices. Understanding the factors that determine demand and supply, as well as how the two interact, can help you understand many actions and decisions of individuals, businesses, and government. This section takes a closer look at these concepts.

**demand** willingness and ability of buyers to purchase goods and services.

**supply** willingness and ability of sellers to provide goods and services.

## Factors Driving Demand

For most us, economics amounts to a balance between what we want and what we can afford. Because of this dilemma, each person must choose how much money to save and how much to spend. We must also decide among all the goods and services competing for our attention. Suppose you wanted to purchase a camera phone. You'd have to choose from a variety of brands and models. You'd also have to decide where you wanted to go to buy one. After shopping around, you might decide you didn't want a camera phone at all. Instead, you might purchase something else, or save your money.

Demand is driven by a number of factors that influence how people decide to spend their money, including price. It may also be driven by outside circumstances or larger economic events. And it can be driven by consumer preferences. Recently, McDonald's decided to introduce a new fruit-and-walnut salad in response to consumer demand for more healthful meal choices. Naturally, McDonald's hopes that people will buy the new salad. But so do the nation's apple growers. If the fruit-and-walnut salad proves popular, McDonald's will order more apples from growers. "Obviously, it's a big boon," says Dave Carlson, president of the Washington Apple Commission. "If we get several other fast-food chains involved as well, it could certainly turn into being a significant factor in the industry."[2]

© SUSAN VAN ETTEN/PHOTOEDIT

Consumers have many choices on how to spend their money. Their choices determine the demand for products, such as high-tech electronics sold at Best Buy.

Figure

3.1 Demand Curves for Gasoline

**A. Demand Curve for Gasoline and Change in Quantity Demanded**

**B. Shift in the Demand Curve for Gasoline—Change in Demand**

Demand can also increase the availability of certain types of software. As more and more information on consumers is stored in databases, identity theft has been on the rise. Criminals are willing to pay for confidential information about consumers, such as credit history, bank account and credit card numbers, and Social Security numbers. Recently, hackers stole millions of Discover, MasterCard, and American Express numbers from one card-processing company in Atlanta. These numbers were then sold to individuals who wanted to use the information for fraudulent purchases. This situation not only created an uproar among consumers but also increased demand for new information security products to protect against data theft.[3]

In general, as the price of a good or service goes up, people buy smaller amounts. In other words, as price rises, the quantity demanded declines. At lower prices, consumers are generally willing to buy more of a good. A **demand curve** is a graph of the amount of a product that buyers will purchase at different prices. Demand curves typically slope downward, meaning that lower and lower prices attract larger and larger purchases.

Gasoline provides a classic example of how demand curves work. The left side of Figure 3.1 shows a possible demand curve for the total amount of gasoline that people will purchase at different prices. When gasoline is priced at $2.79 a gallon, drivers may fill up their tanks once or twice a week. At $3.19 a gallon, many of them may start economizing. They may combine errands or carpool to work. So the quantity of gasoline demanded at $3.19 a gallon is lower than the amount demanded at $2.79 a gallon. The opposite happens at $2.39 a gallon. More gasoline is sold at $2.39 a gallon than at $2.79 a gallon, as people opt to drive to work or take a weekend trip. However, as mentioned earlier, other factors may cause consumers to accept higher prices anyway. They may have made vacation plans in advance and do not want to cancel them. Or they may be required to drive to work every day.

Economists make a clear distinction between changes in the quantity demanded at various prices and changes in overall demand. A change in quantity demanded, such as the change that occurs at different gasoline prices, is simply movement along the demand curve. A change in overall demand, on the other hand, results in an entirely new demand curve. Businesses are constantly trying to make predictions about both kinds of demand, and a miscalculation can cause problems. In one recent year, experts predicted a 7 percent increase in Chinese demand for oil, when in fact the growth in demand only reaches 5 percent. The overestimation resulted in a drop in investor confidence in the industry.[4]

As American household incomes have risen and lifestyles have changed, many American consumers have chosen to purchase SUVs, which consume large amounts of gasoline. At the same time, in developing countries like India and China, consumers have been able to afford cars for the first time. These changes have increased the demand for gasoline at all prices. The right side of Figure 3.1 shows how the increased demand for gasoline worldwide has created a new demand curve. The new demand curve shifts to the right of the old demand curve, indicating that overall demand has increased at every price. A demand curve can also shift to the left when the demand for a good or service drops. However, the demand curve still has the same shape.

Although price is the underlying cause of movement along a demand curve, many factors can combine to determine the overall demand for a product—that is, the shape and position of the demand curve. These influences include customer preferences and incomes, the prices of substitute and complementary items, the number of buyers in a market, and the strength of their optimism regarding the future. Changes in any of these factors produce a new demand curve. Despite high gasoline prices, soaring airfares, and rising hotel rates, U.S. consumers are traveling more than ever, according to the Travel Industry Association of America. "Usually when prices are high and the dollar is low people stay home," says one travel agent. "But the opposite is true [right now]." Demand for flights to popular locations has been so high that consumers have been forced to travel to other destinations or make plans for another time. Obviously, factors other than price—such as an improved U.S. economy or the urge for adventure—are driving the demand for travel.[5]

Changes in household income also change demand. As consumers have more money to spend, firms can sell more products at every price. This means the demand curve has shifted to the right. The price of related goods and services also can influence demand. As the price of gasoline rose recently, the demand for SUVs fell somewhat, and the demand for hybrid vehicles such as Toyota's Prius increased.[6] Table 3.1 describes how a demand curve is likely to respond to each of these changes.

For a business to succeed, management must carefully monitor the factors that may affect demand for the goods and services it hopes to sell. In setting prices, firms often try to predict how the chosen levels will influence the amounts they sell. The Coca-Cola Company experimented with smart vending machines, adjusting prices to such variables as the weather. If the temperature was hot outside, the machines could automatically raise the price. If the vending machine contained too many cans of root beer and restocking was five days away, the machine

**Table**

**3.1**

Expected Shifts in Demand Curves

| | Demand Curve Shifts | |
| Factor | to the Right *if:* | to the Left *if:* |
| --- | --- | --- |
| Customer preferences | increase | decrease |
| Number of buyers | increases | decreases |
| Buyers' Incomes | increase | decrease |
| Prices of substitute goods | increase | decrease |
| Prices of complementary goods | decrease | increase |
| Future expectations become more | optimistic | pessimistic |

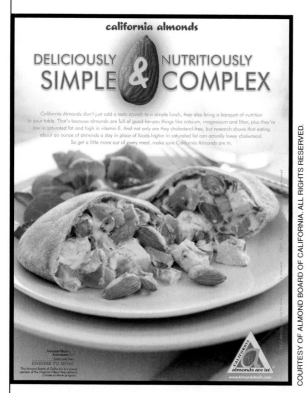

The Almond Board of California hopes to increase demand for its product by promoting its healthful benefits. Not only do almonds taste great, but they also are packed with vitamins and fiber and may help reduce cholesterol.

could lower the price of root beer. Organizations also try to influence overall demand through advertising, free samples and presentations at retail stores, sales calls, product enhancements, and other marketing techniques.

## Factors Driving Supply

Important economic factors also affect supply, the willingness and ability of firms to provide goods and services at different prices. Just as consumers must decide about how to spend their money, businesses must decide what products to sell, and how.

Sellers would prefer to charge higher prices for their products. A **supply curve** shows the relationship between different prices and the quantities that sellers will offer for sale, regardless of demand. Movement along the supply curve is the opposite of movement along the demand curve. So as price rises, the quantity that sellers are willing to supply also rises. At progressively lower prices, the quantity supplied decreases. In Figure 3.2, a possible supply curve for gasoline shows that increasing prices for gasoline should bring increasing supplies to market.

Businesses need certain inputs to operate effectively in producing their output. As discussed in Chapter 1, these *factors of production* include natural resources, capital, human resources, and entrepreneurship. Natural resources include land, building sites, forests, and mineral deposits. Capital refers to resources such as technology, tools, information, physical facilities, and financial capabilities. Human resources include the physical labor and intellectual inputs contributed by employees. Entrepreneurship is the willingness to take risks to create and operate a business.

Factors of production play a central role in determining the overall supply of goods and services. A change in the cost or availability of any of these inputs can shift the entire supply curve, either increasing or decreasing the amount available at every price. If the cost of land increases, a firm might not be able to purchase the site for a more efficient manufacturing plant, which would lower production levels, shifting the supply curve to the left. But if the company finds a way to speed up the production process anyway, allowing it to turn out more products with less labor, the change reduces the overall cost of the finished products, which shifts the supply curve to the right. Table 3.2 summarizes how changes in various factors can affect the supply curve. Sometimes forces of nature can affect the supply curve. When a hurricane swept along the coast of Venezuela, oil exports from the country's ports were halted until the storm passed, reducing the supply of oil for several days.[7] The agriculture industry has often experienced shifts in the supply curve. U.S. apple growers suffered from several years of oversupply and flat prices, losing an estimated $1.7 billion over a period of five years. But the increasing interest in healthful foods and discovery of the health benefits of apples in particular has helped reduce the oversupply.[8] The "Solving an Ethical Controversy" feature describes the debate over the supply of oil and whether the United States should drill for this resource in Alaska.

**Figure**

**3.2** Supply Curve for Gasoline

# TO DRILL—OR NOT TO DRILL—FOR OIL IN ALASKA?

*The debate has been raging for decades over whether the United States should begin drilling for oil in the Arctic National Wildlife Refuge in Alaska. It's a complex issue involving many factors, including the impact that drilling would have on the surrounding environment, the potential reduction of American dependence on foreign oil, a possible boost in productivity for the United States, and debate over who would pay for—and benefit from—the drilling activities. Politicians, businesspeople, and average taxpaying citizens all have strong views on the topic.*

*Should the United States expand oil drilling in Alaska's Arctic National Wildlife Refuge?*

### PRO

1. "This project will keep our economy growing by creating jobs and ensuring that businesses can expand," noted President George W. Bush in a statement. "And it will make America less dependent on foreign sources of energy, eventually by up to a million barrels of oil a day."
2. Experts argue that today's drilling technology, along with tight environmental restrictions, will dramatically limit the effect on Alaska's tundra, protecting the wildlife habitat.

### CON

1. Opponents say that the amount of oil the United States can retrieve from Alaska—and the ten years it will take to reach the market—will have minimal impact on global markets, high gasoline prices, or U.S. dependence on foreign oil.
2. Others argue that the United States should be spending more on developing renewable energy sources such as solar and wind power, as well as producing more fuel-efficient cars, trucks, and other vehicles.

### Summary

While legislators, businesspeople, and environmentalists continue the argument, a recent survey revealed that U.S. citizens are split in their views: 42 percent of respondents said that drilling should proceed, while 53 percent said that it should not. Most likely, many people echo the view of Senator Pete Domenici of New Mexico: "Some people say we ought to conserve more. They say we ought to conserve instead of producing this oil. But we need to do everything. We have to conserve and produce where we can."

**Sources:** "Most Americans Oppose Alaska Oil Drilling," Angus Reid Consultants, accessed June 8, 2006, http://www.angus-reid.com; H. Josef Hebert, "Senate OKs Plan to Allow Oil Wells in Alaska Refuge," *Deseret Morning News*, accessed June 8, 2006, http://www.deseretnews.com; James Kuhnhenn, "Alaska Oil Drilling Gets Boost from Senate," *Detroit Free Press*, accessed June 8, 2006, http://www.freep.com.

Table 3.2

Expected Shifts in Supply Curves

| Factor | Supply Curve Shifts | |
| --- | --- | --- |
| | to the Right *if:* | to the Left *if:* |
| Costs of inputs | decrease | increase |
| Costs of technologies | decrease | increase |
| Taxes | decrease | increase |
| Number of suppliers | increases | decreases |

## How Demand and Supply Interact

**assessment check**

1. What is a demand curve?
2. What is a supply curve?
3. How do factors of production influence the overall supply of goods and services?

Separate shifts in demand and supply have obvious effects on prices and the availability of products. In the real world, changes do not alternatively affect demand and supply. Several factors often change at the same time—and they keep changing. Sometimes such changes in multiple factors cause contradictory pressures on prices and quantities. In other cases, the final direction of prices and quantities reflects the factor that has changed the most.

Figure 3.3 shows the interaction of both supply and demand curves for gasoline on a single graph. Notice that the two curves intersect at *P*. The law of supply and demand states that prices (*P*) are set by the intersection of the supply and demand curves. The point where the two curves meet identifies the **equilibrium price,** the prevailing market price at which you can buy an item.

If the actual market price differs from the equilibrium price, buyers and sellers tend to make economic choices that restore the equilibrium level. So how do we explain the shortages of vaccines to protect against such diseases as tetanus, diphtheria, whooping cough, measles, mumps, and chicken pox? Why did many of the 75 million adults seeking flu shots in a recent flu season encounter delays in obtaining flu shots? Part of the answer lies with the federal government, which pays vaccine makers between 38 and 60 percent of the going price for these vaccines in the global marketplace. The result is a reduction in product supply. In recent years, the number of commercial makers of the flu vaccine dropped dramatically, so when one manufacturer's vaccines were discovered to be contaminated and unusable, the supply decreased and consumers could not obtain vaccinations.

In other situations, suppliers react to market forces by reducing prices. To fight off flagging sales and increase demand for its autos, General Motors offered its employee discount to the general public. Sales rebounded. Not surprisingly, Ford and DaimlerChrysler followed suit with similar pricing programs.[9]

As pointed out earlier, the forces of demand and supply can be affected by a variety of factors. One important variable is the larger economic environment. The next section explains how macroeconomics and economic systems influence market forces and, ultimately, demand, supply, and prices.

**"They Said It"**

*"You don't make more oil."*

—*Sam Shelton (b. 1940) Director, Strategic Energy Initiative at Georgia Tech*

**Figure**

**3.3** Law of Supply and Demand

## MACROECONOMICS: ISSUES FOR THE ENTIRE ECONOMY

Every country faces decisions about how to best use the four basic factors of production. Each nation's policies and choices help determine its economic system. But the political, social, and legal environments differ in every country. So no two countries have exactly the same economic system. In general, however, these systems can be classified into three categories: private enterprise systems, planned economies, or combinations of the two, referred to as mixed economies. As business becomes an increasingly global undertaking, it is important to understand the primary features of the various economic systems operating around the world.

## Capitalism: The Private Enterprise System and Competition

Most industrialized nations operate economies based on the *private enterprise system*, also known as *capitalism* or a *market economy*. A private enterprise system rewards businesses for meeting the needs and demands of consumers. Government tends to favor a hands-off attitude toward controlling business ownership, profits, and resource allocations. Instead, competition regulates economic life, creating opportunities and challenges that businesspeople must handle to succeed. In your career, one area of business that you will encounter in the private enterprise system that is completely unregulated is tipping. Read the "Business Etiquette" feature for hints on how to tip appropriately.

The relative competitiveness of a particular industry is an important consideration for every firm because it determines the ease and cost of doing business within that industry. Four basic degrees of competition take shape in a private enterprise system: pure competition, monopolistic competition, oligopoly, and monopoly. Table 3.3 highlights the main differences among these types of competition.

**Pure competition** is a market structure, like that of small-scale agriculture or fishing, in which large numbers of buyers and sellers exchange homogeneous products and no single participant has a significant influence on price. Instead, prices are set by the market itself as the forces of supply and demand interact. Firms can easily enter or leave a purely competitive market because no single company dominates. Also, in pure competition, buyers see little difference between the goods and services offered by competitors.

Fishing and agriculture are good examples of pure competition. The wheat grown and sold by one farmer in the Midwest is virtually identical to that sold by others. As rainfall and temperatures affect the crop growth, the price for this commodity rises or falls according to the law of supply and demand. The same concept applies to the fishing industry gathering clams and mussels off the coast of New England. The region's notorious "red tide" of algae sometimes contaminates part of the season's supply of shellfish just when summer tourists want them the most—and prices skyrocket.

## (b)usiness (e)tiquette

### Tips on Business Tipping

When you eat out, take a cab, or stay in a hotel, you're faced with a dilemma. Whom—and how much—should you tip? If you find tipping a mystery, here are a few guidelines to help you solve the puzzle.

- At a restaurant, it is customary to tip your waiter between 15 and 20 percent of the bill. You may calculate the tip before tax or alcohol, but many people simply base the tip on the total bill. Naturally, if the service is outstanding, you'll want to tip at the upper end of the scale.
- If you check coat(s) at a restaurant or event, tip the person $1 per coat.
- Tip the bellhop $1 to $2 per bag for carrying your luggage.
- Give a valet or parking attendant $1 to $2 for parking or retrieving your car.
- Add a 10 to 15 percent tip to the fare for a taxi ride, or $1 to $2 for a free shuttle.
- If the hotel concierge provides you with special service such as arranging a meeting space or making dinner or theater reservations, tip that person around $5. If he or she has provided an extraordinary service, a tip of $20 is not out of line.

Of course, before you tip, make sure that a service charge has not already been included. Some upscale restaurants and hotels have begun automatically including fees ranging up to 20 percent.

While these guidelines should be helpful, before you make any calculations, remember that service personnel usually try their best to make your experience a good one. "When in doubt, I always operate under the premise that you tip for a service performed with excellence, and you tip more generously for something that exceeds your expectations," advises Amy Ziff of Travelocity Business. "And remember the saying, 'what goes around comes around,' and that in business a little good tipping karma can never hurt."

**Sources:** "Tipping Etiquette," FindaLink.net, accessed June 8, 2006, http://www.findalink.net; "Proper Tipping Etiquette," Essortment, accessed June 8, 2006, http://msms.essortment.com; "Travelocity Business Makes Travel Easier with Hints on Tipping," *Business Wire*, accessed June 8, 2006, http://www.corporate-ir.net; Laura Bly, "The Tipping Point," *USA Today*, August 26, 2005, p. 1D; "Tipping Etiquette: Travel," AllSands.com, accessed May, 4, 2005, http://www.allsands.com.

Table

3.3    Types of Competition

## Types of Competition

| Characteristics | Types of Competition | | | |
| --- | --- | --- | --- | --- |
| | Pure Competition | Monopolistic Competition | Oligopoly | Monopoly |
| Number of competitors | Many | Few to many | Few | No direct competition |
| Ease of entry into industry by new firms | Easy | Somewhat difficult | Difficult | Regulated by government |
| Similarity of goods or services offered by competing firms | Similar | Different | Similar or different | No directly competing products |
| Control over price by individual firms | None | Some | Some | Considerable in a pure monopoly; little in a regulated monopoly |
| Examples | Small-scale farmer in Indiana | Local fitness center | Boeing aircraft | Rawlings Sporting Goods, exclusive supplier of major-league baseballs |

**Monopolistic competition** is a market structure, like that for retailing, in which large numbers of buyers and sellers exchange relatively well-differentiated (heterogeneous) products, so each participant has some control over price. Sellers can differentiate their products from competing offerings on the basis of price, quality, or other features. In an industry that features monopolistic competition, it is relatively easy for a firm to begin or stop selling a good or service. The success of one seller often attracts new competitors to such a market. Individual firms also have some control over how their goods and services are priced.

An example of monopolistic competition is the market for pet food. Consumers can choose from private-label (store brands) and brand-name products in bags, boxes, and cans. Producers of pet food and the stores that sell it have wide latitude in setting prices. Consumers can choose the store or brand with the lowest prices, or sellers can convince them that a more expensive offering is worth more because it offers better nutrition, more convenience, more information, or other benefits.

An **oligopoly** is a market situation in which relatively few sellers compete and high start-up costs form barriers to keep out new competitors. In some oligopolistic industries, such as paper and steel, competitors offer similar products. In others, such as aircraft and automobiles, they sell different models and features. The huge investment required to enter an oligopoly market tends to discourage new competitors. The limited number of sellers also enhances the control these firms exercise over price. Competing products in an oligopoly usually sell for very similar prices because substantial price competition would reduce profits for all firms in the industry. So a price cut by one firm in an oligopoly will typically be met by its competitors. However, prices can vary from one market to another, as from one country to another. OPEC, which controls much of the world's supply of crude oil, is considered by many to be a successful oligopoly, as described in the "Hit & Miss" feature.

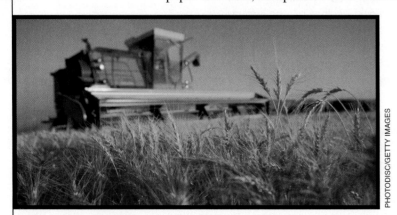

PHOTODISC/GETTY IMAGES

Farmers produce their crops in a purely competitive market, so the prices of their crops are determined by the laws of supply and demand.

## HIT & MISS

### OPEC: A Successful Oligopoly

By the time you finish this chapter, you'll know what an oligopoly is; you'll even be able to pronounce it. But can you name successful oligopolies around the world? OPEC—the Organization of Petroleum Exporting Countries—is one. If you aren't sure how OPEC affects you, think of gas prices, which recently have soared. OPEC controls much of the supply of crude oil that is produced in the world, which ultimately affects the cost of heating homes and filling gas tanks in your hometown.

OPEC was founded in 1960 by five nations—Iran, Iraq, Kuwait, Saudi Arabia, and Venezuela. The group was later joined by eight more countries—Qatar, Indonesia, Libya, United Arab Emirates, Algeria, Nigeria, Ecuador, and Gabon. According to the organization's Web site, "OPEC's objective is to coordinate and unify petroleum policies among member countries, in order to secure fair and stable prices for petroleum producers; an efficient, economic and regular supply of petroleum to consuming nations; and a fair return on capital to those investing in the industry."

OPEC nations have worked together to control the supply of their products to the world for nearly 50 years, despite criticism from watchdog agencies such as the International Energy Agency and internal blunders, including exceeding their own production quotas. In what has become a very complex oil market, the cur-rent discussion centers on a simple argument: whether the planet is running out of oil. OPEC insists that, although it is pumping at a high capacity to meet high demand, it still has the capacity to produce more. Some scientists and other experts warn that, in fact, the earth is rapidly being depleted of its total supply of oil. Falling somewhere in the middle of the debate, oil and gas analyst Adam Sieminski of Deutsche Bank AB in London says, "It's not a crisis. If a little more is needed, [OPEC] can bring it on. The market is aware of the fact that demand seems to be rising pretty much in line with OPEC [supply]."

### Questions for Critical Thinking

1. Why is OPEC a successful oligopoly?
2. Describe several ways you think this oligopoly affects your daily life.

**Sources:** OPEC Web site, accessed June 8, 2006, http://www.opec.org; Kevin Morrison, "IEA Says Supply Tightness to Remain," *Financial Times*, accessed June 8, 2006, http://news.ft.com; David Lazarus, "OPEC Still Sings Same Tune," *San Francisco Chronicle*, accessed June 8, 2006, http://www.sfgate.com; Jim Efstathiou, "Attiyah Sees Tough Choices for OPEC," *(Doha, Qatar) Gulf Times*, accessed June 8, 2006, http://www.gulf-times.com.

---

Cement is another product for which an oligopoly exists. Mexican-based Cemex SA is the third-largest cement manufacturer in the world and the largest seller of cement in both the United States and Mexico. It holds 60 percent of the market share in Mexico. Cement is usually sold in bulk in the United States, like a commodity. However, it is sold as a branded product in Mexico. Cemex's prices are too high for many Mexican families to afford, which often means they must put plans for home building on hold. Because Cemex is also Mexico's largest seller of concrete, which is made with cement, those prices remain high as well. Although large construction companies in the United States can force cement manufacturers to drop their prices, Mexican construction companies are smaller and have little clout, so they end up paying higher prices.[10]

The final type of market structure is a **monopoly,** in which a single seller dominates trade in a good or service for which buyers can find no close substitutes. A pure monopoly occurs when a firm possesses unique characteristics so important to competition in its industry that they serve as barriers to prevent entry by would-be competitors. Microsoft has held a near monopoly in the Internet browser market with its Internet Explorer for quite a while. Recently, its share of the total U.S. market for all operating systems dipped below 90 percent after consumers became alarmed at Internet Explorer's reported security flaws. Another reason for the decrease in market share percentage is the increased competition from Firefox, an open-source

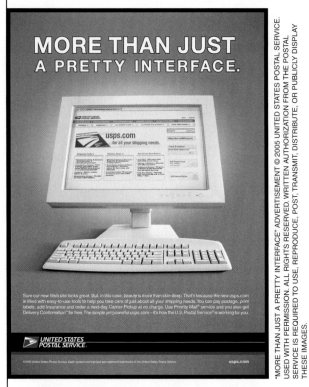

The U.S. Postal Service now offers services at its Web site to help it compete against such firms as UPS, FedEx, and DHL. With its new Click-N-Ship program, customers can calculate rates, print labels, pay postage, and get free delivery confirmation.

## assessment check

1. What is the difference between pure competition and monopolistic competition?

2. Distinguish between oligopoly and monopoly.

browser developed by the Mozilla Foundation. Other browsers based on the Mozilla code such as America Online's Netscape and GNOME's Epiphany have also increased market share in the last 2 years.[11]

Many firms create short-term monopolies when research breakthroughs permit them to receive exclusive patents on new products. In the pharmaceuticals industry, drug giants such as Merck and Pfizer invest billions in research and development programs. When the research leads to successful new drugs, the companies can enjoy the benefits of their patents: the ability to set prices without fear of competitors undercutting them. Once the patent expires, generic substitutes enter the market, driving down prices.

Because a monopoly market lacks the benefits of competition, the U.S. government regulates monopolies. Besides issuing patents and limiting their life, the government prohibits most pure monopolies through antitrust legislation such as the Sherman Act and the Clayton Act. The U.S. government has applied these laws against monopoly behavior by Microsoft and by disallowing proposed mergers of large companies in some industries. In other cases, the government permits certain monopolies in exchange for regulating their activities.

With *regulated monopolies*, a local, state, or federal government grants exclusive rights in a certain market to a single firm. Pricing decisions—particularly rate-increase requests—are subject to control by regulatory authorities such as state public service commissions. An example is the delivery of first-class mail, a monopoly held by the U.S. Postal Service (USPS). The USPS is a self-supporting corporation wholly owned by the federal government. Although it is no longer run by Congress, postal rates are set by a Postal Commission and approved by a Board of Governors.

During the 1980s and 1990s, the U.S. government favored a trend away from regulated monopolies and toward **deregulation.** Regulated monopolies that have been deregulated include long-distance and local telephone service, cable television, cellular phones, and electric utilities. Long-distance companies such as MCI are now allowed to offer local service. The idea is to improve customer service and reduce prices for telephone customers through increased competition. Deregulation of electric utilities began when California opened its market in 1998. Several years later, about half the states were on board. In those states, private companies could compete with utilities to sell electricity and natural gas.

## Planned Economies: Communism and Socialism

In a **planned economy,** government controls determine business ownership, profits, and resource allocation to accomplish government goals rather than those set by individual businesses. Two forms of planned economies are communism and socialism.

The writings of Karl Marx in the mid-1800s formed the basis of communist theory. Marx believed that private enterprise economies created unfair conditions and led to worker exploitation because business owners controlled most of society's resources and reaped most of the economy's rewards. Instead, he suggested an economic system called **communism,** in which all property would be shared equally by the people of a community under the direction of a strong central government. Marx believed that elimination of private ownership of property and businesses would ensure the emergence of a classless society that would benefit all. Each individual would contribute to the nation's overall economic success, and resources would be distributed according to each person's needs. Under communism, the central government owns the means of production, and the people work for state-owned enterprises. The government determines what people can buy because it dictates what is produced in the nation's factories and farms.

A number of nations adopted communist economic systems during the early 20th century in an effort to correct abuses they believed to be present in their previous systems. In practice, however, communist governments often give people little or no freedom of choice in selecting jobs, purchases, or investments. Communist governments often make mistakes in planning the best uses of resources to compete in the growing global marketplace. Government-owned monopolies often suffer from inefficiency.

Consider the former Soviet Union, where large government bureaucracies controlled nearly every aspect of daily life. Shortages became chronic because producers had little or no incentive to satisfy customers. The quality of goods and services also suffered for the same reason. When Mikhail Gorbachev became the last president of the dying Soviet Union, he tried to improve the quality of Soviet-made products. Effectively shut out of trading in the global marketplace and caught up in a treasury-depleting arms race with the United States, the Soviet Union faced severe financial problems. Eventually, these economic crises led to the collapse of Soviet communism and the breakup of the Soviet Union itself.

Today, communism exists in just a few countries, such as the People's Republic of China, Cuba, and North Korea. Even these nations show signs of growing openness toward some of the benefits of private enterprise as possible solutions to their economic challenges. Since 1978, China has been shifting toward a more market-oriented economy. The national government has given local government and individual plant managers more say in business decisions and has permitted some private businesses. Households now have more control over agriculture, in contrast to the collectivized farms introduced with communism. In addition, Western products such as McDonald's restaurants and Coca-Cola soft drinks are now part of Chinese consumers' lives.

A second type of planned economy, **socialism,** is characterized by government ownership and operation of major industries such as healthcare and communications. Socialists assert that major industries are too important to a society to be left in private hands and that government-owned businesses can serve the public's interest better than can private firms. However, socialism also allows private ownership in industries considered less crucial to social welfare, such as retail shops, restaurants, and certain types of manufacturing facilities. Scandinavian countries such as Sweden and Finland have socialist characteristics in their societies, as do many African nations and India.

## Mixed Market Economies

Private enterprise systems and planned economies adopt basically opposite approaches to operating economies. In reality though, many countries operate **mixed market economies,** economic systems that draw from both types of economies, to different degrees. In nations generally considered to have a private enterprise economy, government-owned firms frequently operate alongside private enterprises.

France has blended socialist and free enterprise policies for hundreds of years. The nation's energy production, public transportation, and defense industries are run as nationalized industries, controlled by the government. Meanwhile, a market economy flourishes in other industries. Over the past two decades, the French government has loosened its reins on state-owned companies, inviting both competition and private investment into industries previously operated as government monopolies.

The proportions of private and public enterprise can vary widely in mixed economies, and the mix frequently changes. Dozens of countries have converted government-owned and -operated companies into privately held businesses in a trend known as **privatization.** Even the United States has seen proposals to privatize everything from the postal service to Social Security. Governments may privatize state-owned enterprises in an effort to raise funds and improve their economies. The objective is to cut costs and run the operation more efficiently. For most of its existence, Air Canada was a state-owned airline. But in 1989 the airline became fully privatized, and in 2000 the firm acquired Canadian Airlines International, becoming the world's tenth-largest international air carrier. Recently, Air Canada announced a major agreement with the People's Republic of China to expand passenger and cargo services between the two countries.[12] Table 3.4 compares the alternative economic systems on the basis of ownership and management of enterprises, rights to profits, employee rights, and worker incentives.

**a**ssessment **c**heck

1. On which economic system is the U.S. economy based?
2. What are the two types of planned economies?
3. What is privatization?

**Table 3.4** Comparison of Alternative Economic Systems

| System Features | Capitalism (Private Enterprise) | Planned Economies | | |
| | | Communism | Socialism | Mixed Economy |
| --- | --- | --- | --- | --- |
| Ownership of enterprises | Businesses are owned privately, often by large numbers of people. Minimal government ownership leaves production in private hands. | Government owns the means of production with few exceptions, such as small plots of land. | Government owns basic industries, but private owners operate some small enterprises. | A strong private sector blends with public enterprises. |
| Management of enterprises | Enterprises are managed by owners or their representatives, with minimal government interference. | Centralized management controls all state enterprises in line with three- to five-year plans. Planning now is being decentralized. | Significant government planning pervades socialist nations. State enterprises are managed directly by government bureaucrats. | Management of the private sector resembles that under capitalism. Professionals may also manage state enterprises. |
| Rights to profits | Entrepreneurs and investors are entitled to all profits (minus taxes) that their firms earn. | Profits are not allowed under communism. | Only the private sector of a socialist economy generates profits. | Entrepreneurs and investors are entitled to private-sector profits, although they often must pay high taxes. State enterprises are also expected to produce returns. |
| Rights of employees | The rights to choose one's occupation and to join a labor union have long been recognized. | Employee rights are limited in exchange for promised protection against unemployment. | Workers may choose their occupations and join labor unions, but the government influences career decisions for many people. | Workers may choose jobs and labor union membership. Unions often become quite strong. |
| Worker incentives | Considerable incentives motivate people to perform at their highest levels. | Incentives are emerging in communist countries. | Incentives usually are limited in state enterprises but do motivate workers in the private sector. | Capitalist-style incentives operate in the private sector. More limited incentives influence public-sector activities. |

# EVALUATING ECONOMIC PERFORMANCE

Ideally, an economic system should provide two important benefits for its citizens: a stable business environment and sustained growth. In a stable business environment, the overall supply of needed goods and services is aligned with the overall demand for those goods and services. No wild fluctuations in price or availability complicate economic decisions. Consumers and businesses not only have access to ample supplies of desired products at affordable prices but also have money to buy the items they demand.

Growth is another important economic goal. An ideal economy incorporates steady change directed toward continually expanding the amount of goods and services produced from the nation's resources. Growth leads to expanded job opportunities, improved wages, and a rising standard of living.

## Flattening the Business Cycle

A nation's economy tends to flow through various stages of a business cycle: prosperity, recession, depression, and recovery. No true economic depressions have occurred in the United States since the 1930s, and most economists believe that society is capable of preventing future depressions through effective economic policies. Consequently, they expect a recession to give way to a period of economic recovery.

Both business decisions and consumer buying patterns differ at each stage of the business cycle. In periods of economic prosperity, unemployment remains low, consumer confidence about the future leads to more purchases, and businesses expand—by hiring more employees, investing in new technology, and making similar purchases—to take advantage of new opportunities.

During a **recession**—a cyclical economic contraction that lasts for six months or longer—consumers frequently postpone major purchases and shift buying patterns toward basic, functional products carrying low prices. Businesses mirror these changes in the marketplace by slowing production, postponing expansion plans, reducing inventories, and often cutting the size of their workforces. During past recessions, people facing layoffs and depletions of household savings have sold cars, jewelry, and stocks to make ends meet. During the most recent recession, they did this as well but with a twist: they turned to eBay. There, they sold everything from old books to kitchen knickknacks, contributing to their own success as well as that of eBay.

If an economic slowdown continues in a downward spiral over an extended period of time, the economy falls into depression. Many Americans have grown up hearing stories about their great-grandparents who lived through the Great Depression of the 1930s, when food and other basic necessities were scarce and jobs were rare and precious.

In the *recovery stage* of the business cycle, the economy emerges from recession and consumer spending picks up steam. Even though businesses often continue to rely on part-time and other temporary workers during the early stages of a recovery, unemployment begins to decline as business activity accelerates and firms seek additional workers to meet growing production demands. Gradually, the concerns of recession begin to disappear, and consumers start eating out at restaurants, booking vacations, and purchasing new cars.

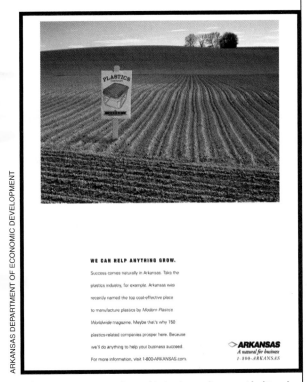

Arkansas promotes its favorable business climate with this ad featuring the growth and prosperity of its plastics industry.

**recession** cyclical economic contraction that lasts for six months or longer.

## "They Said It"

"It's a recession when your neighbor loses his job; it's a depression when you lose your own."
—Harry S. Truman (1884–1972) 33rd president of the United States

### assessment check

1. Which stages of the business cycle indicate a downturn in the economy?
2. Which stages point to an upswing?

# Productivity and the Nation's Gross Domestic Product

**productivity** relationship between the number of units produced and the number of human and other production inputs necessary to produce them.

**gross domestic product (GDP)** sum of all goods and services produced within a country's boundaries during a specific time period, such as a year.

**inflation** rising prices caused by a combination of excess consumer demand and increases in the costs of raw materials, component parts, human resources, and other factors of production.

An important concern for every economy is **productivity,** the relationship between the goods and services produced in a nation each year and the inputs needed to produce them. In general, as productivity rises, so does an economy's growth and the wealth of its citizens. In a recession, productivity stalls or even declines.

Productivity describes the relationship between the number of units produced and the number of human and other production inputs necessary to produce them. So productivity is a ratio of output to input. When a constant amount of inputs generates increased outputs, an increase in productivity occurs.

Total productivity considers all inputs necessary to produce a specific amount of outputs. Stated in equation form, it can be written as follows:

$$\text{Total productivity} = \frac{\text{Output (goods or services produced)}}{\text{Input (human/natural resources, capital)}}$$

Many productivity ratios focus on only one of the inputs in the equation: labor productivity or output per labor-hour. An increase in labor productivity means that the same amount of work produces more goods and services than before. Many of the gains in U.S. productivity are attributed to technology, and in recent years the United States alone appears to be enjoying the fruits of technology and productivity. No other industrial nation has experienced the rapid growth of the United States.[13] During the last decade, output per worker has increased at the fastest rate in 40 years. Some analysts believe that the industry that has benefited the most from this increase is healthcare.[14]

Productivity is a widely recognized measure of a company's efficiency. In turn, the total productivity of a nation's businesses has become a measure of its economic strength and standard of living. Economists refer to this measure as a country's **gross domestic product (GDP)**—the sum of all goods and services produced within its boundaries. The GDP is based on the per-capita output of a country—in other words, total national output divided by the number of citizens. As Figure 3.4 shows, the U.S. GDP remains the highest in the world, almost double that of second-ranked China. However, productivity in the United States is suffering in certain areas of the Midwest, where young, educated workers are departing for jobs elsewhere. This situation is described in the "Hit & Miss" feature.

In the United States, GDP is tracked by the Bureau of Economic Analysis (BEA), a division of the U.S. Department of Commerce. Current updates and historical data on the GDP are available at the BEA's Web site (http://www.bea.gov).

## Price-Level Changes

Another important indicator of an economy's stability is the general level of prices. For most of the 20th century, economic decision makers concerned themselves with **inflation,** rising prices caused by a combination of excess consumer demand and increases in the costs of raw materials, component parts, human resources, and other factors of production. The **core inflation rate** is the inflation rate of an economy after energy and food prices are removed. This measure is often an accurate prediction of the inflation rate that consumers, businesses, and other organizations can expect to experience during the near future.

**Figure**

**3.4** Nations with Highest Gross Domestic Products

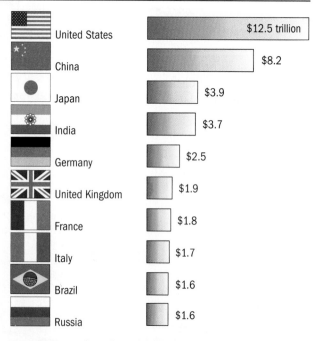

| | |
|---|---|
| United States | $12.5 trillion |
| China | $8.2 |
| Japan | $3.9 |
| India | $3.7 |
| Germany | $2.5 |
| United Kingdom | $1.9 |
| France | $1.8 |
| Italy | $1.7 |
| Brazil | $1.6 |
| Russia | $1.6 |

**Source:** Central Intelligence Agency, "Rank Order—GDP," *World Factbook*, accessed June 12, 2006, http://www.cia.gov.

# HIT & MISS

## Is the Midwest Losing Its Brainpower?

Excellent colleges and universities are located in the Midwest, along with beautiful countryside and friendly towns in which to live. Then why have so many Midwestern counties—particularly in rural areas—lost more residents than they have gained in the last half century? According to one survey, Iowa and North Dakota have lost many young, well-educated workers because they want an urban lifestyle and a warmer climate. They are also looking for better pay in professional jobs, which is typically 20 to 50 percent better elsewhere, although this can be offset by a higher cost of living. Colleges and universities in these states are producing highly educated, well-trained workers who leave to find better opportunities in other parts of the country. Experts who study demographics fear that states such as Indiana, Kansas, Iowa, and North Dakota will face a drastic labor shortage within the next 20 years.

Government and business leaders have not ignored the problem, but they haven't yet found a solution. Iowa has abolished its state income tax for workers under age 30. North Dakota has programs to create jobs, increase wages, and keep taxes low. Some towns in Kansas are giving away land to attract new residents. The U.S. Congress is even considering a New Homestead Act, which includes an extensive list of benefits to people who choose to live and work in rural Midwestern areas. Still, the so-called brain drain continues.

But the picture is not entirely bleak. North Dakota has the nation's lowest unemployment rate, which is a huge relief to workers from other regions looking for jobs. And its small cities, Bismarck and Fargo, are actually growing. Technology companies are beginning to invest in the area. Microsoft recently purchased Great Plains Software of Fargo for $1.1 billion, which should attract college graduates who want to stay in the area. Public officials remain optimistic. North Dakota agriculture commissioner Roger Johnson declares, "We're the last undiscovered great place to live."

### Questions for Critical Thinking

1. Describe two incentives you think might help recent college graduates stay to work in rural Midwestern areas. Explain why you think these would be successful.
2. How does loss of young, educated workers affect the productivity of these states?

**Sources:** Tim Swanson, "A Midwestern Brain Drain," Ludwig von Mises Institute, accessed June 8, 2006, http://blog.mises .org; Les Christie, "Stopping the Great Plains Brain Drain," CNN Money, accessed June 8, 2006, http://money.cnn .com; Dennis Cauchon, "Big Cities Lure Away North Dakota Youth," *USA Today*, accessed June 8, 2006, http://www .usatoday.com.

---

Excess consumer demand generates what is known as *demand-pull inflation*; rises in costs of factors of production generates *cost-push inflation*. America's most severe inflationary period during the last half of the 20th century peaked in 1980, when general price levels jumped almost 14 percent in a single year. In extreme cases, an economy may experience *hyperinflation*—an economic situation characterized by soaring prices. This situation has occurred in South America, as well as in countries that once formed the Soviet Union.

Inflation devalues money as persistent price increases reduce the amount of goods and services people can purchase with a given amount of money. This is bad news for people whose incomes do not keep up with inflation or who have most of their wealth in investments paying a fixed rate of interest. Inflation can be good news to people whose income is rising or those with debts at a fixed rate of interest. A homeowner during inflationary times is paying off a fixed-rate mortgage with money that is worth less and less each year. Over the last decade, inflation helped a strong stock market drive up the number of millionaires to more than 8 million. But because of inflation, being a millionaire does not make a person as rich as it once did. To live like a 1960s millionaire, you would need almost $6 million today.

When increased productivity keeps prices steady, it can have a major positive impact on an economy. In a low-inflation environment, businesses can make long-range plans without the constant worry of sudden inflationary shocks. Low interest rates encourage firms to invest in

If oil and gas prices continue to climb, they may force consumers to look for alternative-fueled vehicles. Some natural-gas-powered cars can already be refueled right in owners' garages through a wall-mounted appliance that taps into a home's natural-gas line.

research and development and capital improvements, both of which are likely to produce productivity gains. Consumers can purchase growing stocks of goods and services with the same amount of money, and low interest rates encourage major acquisitions such as new homes and autos. Despite the recent good news in the U.S. economy, some economists have cautioned that inflation may be "flickering on the horizon." The mounting cost of oil—which is used to produce nearly every product—is a continuing concern. Businesses need to raise prices to cover their costs. Also, smaller firms have gone out of business or have been merged with larger companies, reducing the amount of competition and increasing the purchasing power of the larger corporations. However, other factors signal that inflation will not reach alarming proportions.[15]

The opposite situation—**deflation**—occurs when prices continue to fall. In Japan, where deflation has been a reality for several years, shoppers pay less for a variety of products ranging from Big Macs to apartments. While this situation may sound ideal to consumers, it can weaken the economy.

*Measuring Price Level Changes*  In the United States, the government tracks changes in price levels with the **Consumer Price Index (CPI),** which measures the monthly average change in prices of goods and services. The federal Bureau of Labor Statistics (BLS) calculates the CPI monthly based on prices of a "market basket," a compilation of the goods and services most commonly purchased by urban consumers. Figure 3.5 shows the categories included in the CPI market basket. Each month, BLS representatives visit thousands of stores, service establishments, rental units, and doctors' offices all over the United States to price the multitude of items in the CPI market basket. They compile the data to create the CPI. So the CPI provides a running measurement of changes in consumer prices.

## Employment Levels

People need money to buy the goods and services produced in an economy. Because most consumers earn that money by working, the number of people in a nation who currently have jobs is an important indicator of how well the economy is doing. In general, employment has been on the rise in the United States the past few years: the Bureau of Labor Statistics projects a total increase of 21.3 million jobs, or 15 percent.

Economists refer to a nation's **unemployment rate** as an indicator of its economic health. The unemployment rate is usually expressed as a percentage of the total workforce who are actively seeking work but are currently unemployed. The total labor force includes all people who are willing and available to work at the going market wage, whether they currently have jobs or are seeking work. The U.S. Department of Labor, which tracks unemployment rates, also includes so-called discouraged workers in the total labor force. These individuals want to work but have given up looking for jobs, for various reasons. Unemployment can be grouped into the four categories shown in Figure 3.6: frictional, seasonal, cyclical, and structural.

*Frictional unemployment* applies to members of the workforce who are temporarily not working but are looking for jobs. This pool of potential workers includes new graduates, people who have left jobs for any reason and are looking for other employment, and former workers who have decided to return to the labor force. *Seasonal unemployment* is the joblessness of workers in a seasonal industry. Construction workers, farm laborers, fishery workers, and landscape employees may contend with bouts of seasonal unemployment when wintry conditions make work unavailable.

## "They Said It"

"Inflation might almost be called legal counterfeiting."
—Irving Fisher
(1867–1947)
American economist

Figure

3.5

Contents of the CPI Market Basket

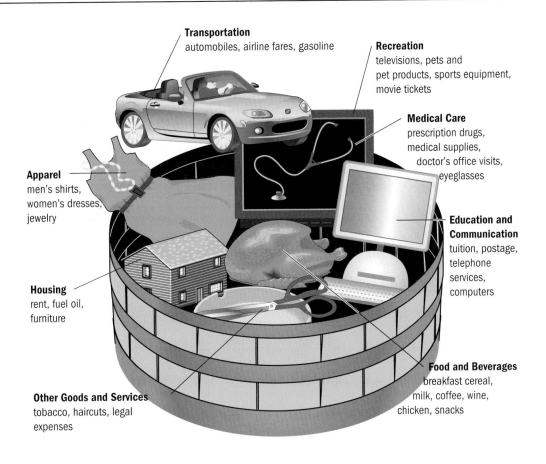

**Transportation**
automobiles, airline fares, gasoline

**Recreation**
televisions, pets and
pet products, sports equipment,
movie tickets

**Medical Care**
prescription drugs,
medical supplies,
doctor's office visits,
eyeglasses

**Apparel**
men's shirts,
women's dresses,
jewelry

**Education and
Communication**
tuition, postage,
telephone
services,
computers

**Housing**
rent, fuel oil,
furniture

**Other Goods and Services**
tobacco, haircuts, legal
expenses

**Food and Beverages**
breakfast cereal,
milk, coffee, wine,
chicken, snacks

**Source:** Information from Bureau of Labor Statistics, "Consumer Price Indexes: Frequently Asked Questions," accessed June 8, 2006, http://www.bls.gov/cpi.

*Cyclical unemployment* includes people who are out of work because of a cyclical contraction in the economy. During periods of economic expansion, overall employment is likely to rise, but as growth slows and a recession begins, unemployment levels commonly rise. At such times, even workers with good job skills may face temporary unemployment. Workers in high-tech industries, air travel, and manufacturing have all faced unemployment during economic contraction.

*Structural unemployment* applies to people who remain unemployed for long periods of time, often with little hope of finding new jobs like their old ones. This situation may arise because these workers lack the necessary skills for available jobs or because the skills they have are no longer in demand. For instance, technological developments have increased the demand for people with computer-related skills but have created structural unemployment among many types of manual laborers.

# MANAGING THE ECONOMY'S PERFORMANCE

As recent years have vividly demonstrated, a national government can use both monetary policy and fiscal policy in its efforts to fight unemployment, increase business and consumer spending, and reduce the length and severity of economic recessions. The Federal Reserve System can

**assessment check**

1. What is productivity?
2. How does the U.S. government track changes in price levels?
3. Identify the four categories of unemployment.

Figure

3.6 Four Types of Unemployment

**Frictional Unemployment**
- Temporarily not working
- Looking for a job
**Example:** New graduates entering the workforce

**Seasonal Unemployment**
- Not working during some months
- Not looking for a job
**Example:** Farm laborers needed only when a crop is in season

**Structural Unemployment**
- Not working due to no demand for skills
- May be retraining for a new job
**Example:** Assembly line workers whose jobs are now done by robots

**Cyclical Unemployment**
- Not working due to economic slowdown
- Looking for a job
**Example:** Executives laid off during corporate downsizing or recessionary periods

increase or reduce interest rates, and the federal government can enact tax cuts or propose other reforms.

## Monetary Policy

A common method of influencing economic activity is **monetary policy,** government actions to increase or decrease the money supply and change banking requirements and interest rates to influence spending by altering bankers' willingness to make loans. An *expansionary monetary policy* increases the money supply in an effort to cut the cost of borrowing, which encourages business decision makers to make new investments, in turn stimulating employment and economic growth. By contrast, a *restrictive monetary policy* reduces the money supply to curb rising prices, overexpansion, and concerns about overly rapid economic growth.

In the United States, the Federal Reserve System ("the Fed") is responsible for formulating and implementing the nation's monetary policy. It is headed by a chairman and board of governors, all of whom are nominated by the president. The most well-known chairman, Alan Greenspan, recently retired after heading the Fed for nearly two decades. All national banks must be members of this system and keep some percentage of their checking and savings funds on deposit at the Fed.

The Fed's board of governors uses a number of tools to regulate the economy. By changing the required percentage of checking and savings accounts that banks must deposit with the Fed, the governors can expand or shrink funds available to lend. The Fed also lends money to member banks, which in turn make loans at higher interest rates to business and individual borrowers. By changing the interest rates charged to commercial banks, the Fed affects the interest rates charged to borrowers and, consequently, their willingness to borrow. That commercial lending rate reached a 46-year low of 1 percent in January 2004, but the Fed later raised rates in a series of quarter-point moves.[16]

## Fiscal Policy

Governments also influence economic activities by making decisions about taxes and spending. Through revenues and expenses, the government implements **fiscal policy.** This is the second technique that officials use to control inflation, reduce unemployment, improve the general standard of living, and encourage economic growth. Increased taxes may restrict economic activities, while lower taxes and increased government spending usually boost spending and profits, cut unemployment rates, and fuel economic expansion.

*International Fiscal Policy* Nations in the industrial world, including the United States, are currently struggling to find ways to help developing nations modernize their economies. One proposal is to "forgive" outright the debts of some of these countries, particularly those in Africa, to stimulate their economies to grow. But not all fiscal experts agree with this idea. They suggest that any debt forgiveness should come with certain conditions so that these countries can build their own fiscal policies. Countries should encourage and allow citizens to own property, lower their tax rates, avoid devaluing their currencies, lay a path for new businesses to start up, and reduce trade barriers.[17]

## "They Said It"

"The nine most terrifying words in the English language are 'I'm from the government, and I'm here to help.'"

—Ronald Reagan
(1911–2004)
40th president
of the United States

**monetary policy** government actions to increase or decrease the money supply and change banking requirements and interest rates to influence bankers' willingness to make loans.

***The Federal Budget*** Each year, the president proposes a **budget** for the federal government, a plan for how it will raise and spend money during the coming year, and presents it to Congress for approval. A typical federal budget proposal undergoes months of deliberation and many modifications before receiving approval. The federal budget includes a number of different spending categories, ranging from defense and Social Security to interest payments on the national debt. The decisions about what to include in the budget have a direct effect on various sectors of the economy. During a recession, the federal government may approve increased spending on interstate highway repairs to improve transportation and increase employment in the construction industry. During prosperity, the government may allocate more money for scientific research or the arts.

The primary sources of government funds to cover the costs of the annual budget are taxes, fees, and borrowing. Both the overall amount of these funds and their specific combination have major effects on the economic well-being of the nation. One way governments raise money is to impose taxes on sales and income. But increasing taxes leaves people and businesses with less money to spend. This might reduce inflation, but overly high taxes can also slow economic growth. So governments try to balance taxes to give people necessary services without slowing economic growth.

Taxes don't always generate enough funds to cover every spending project the government hopes to undertake. When the government spends more than the amount of money it raises through taxes, it creates a **budget deficit.** To cover the deficit, the U.S. government borrows money by selling Treasury bills, Treasury notes, and Treasury bonds to investors. All of this borrowing makes up the **national debt.** Currently the Government Accountability Office (GAO) estimates that the national debt is $43 trillion.[18] One of the factors contributing to the budget deficit is the war in Iraq and related military operations. If the government takes in more money than it spends, it is said to have a **budget surplus. A balanced budget** means total revenues raised by taxes equal the total proposed spending for the year.

Achieving a balanced budget—or even a budget surplus—does not erase the national debt, which must be paid off. U.S. legislators continually debate how fast the nation should use revenues to reduce its debt. Most families want to wipe out debt—from credit cards, automobile purchases, and college. But for the federal government, the decision is more complex. When the government raises money by selling Treasury bills, it makes safe investments available to investors worldwide. If foreign investors cannot buy Treasury notes, they might turn to other countries, reducing the amount of money flowing into the United States. U.S. government debt has also been used as a basis for pricing riskier investments. If the government issues less debt, the interest rates it commands are higher, raising the overall cost of debt to private borrowers. In addition, the government uses the funds from borrowing, at least in part, to invest in such public services as education and scientific research. As a society, if we decide our economy needs these services, debt reduction may not always be the best use of government funds. However, it can also be argued that paying down the national debt will free up more money to be invested by individuals and businesses.

**fiscal policy** government spending and taxation decisions designed to control inflation, reduce unemployment, improve the general welfare of citizens, and encourage economic growth.

**budget** organization's plan for how it will raise and spend money during a given period of time.

**assessment check**

1. What is the difference between an expansionary monetary policy and a restrictive monetary policy?

2. What are the three primary sources of government funds?

3. Does a balanced budget erase the federal debt?

# GLOBAL ECONOMIC CHALLENGES OF THE 21ST CENTURY

Businesses face a number of important economic challenges in the 21st century. As the economies of countries around the globe become increasingly interconnected, governments and businesses must compete throughout the world. Although no one can predict the future, both governments and businesses will likely need to meet several challenges to maintain their

Table

3.5    Global Economic Challenges

| Challenge | Facts and Examples |
|---|---|
| International terrorism | Assistance in locating and detaining known terrorists by dozens of nations. |
| | Cooperation in modifying banking laws in most nations in an effort to cut off funds to terrorist organizations. |
| | Concerns over the safety of mass-transit systems following bombings in London and elsewhere. |
| Shift to a global information economy | Half of all American workers hold jobs in information technology or in industries that intensively use information technology, products, and services. |
| | Software industry in India is growing more than 50 percent each year. |
| | Internet users in Asia and western Europe have more than doubled in five years. |
| Aging of the world's population | Median age of the U.S. population is 35 plus, and by 2025, more than 62 million Americans will be age 65 or older—nearly double today's number. This will increase demands for health-care, retirement benefits, and other support services, putting budgetary pressure on governments. |
| | As baby boomers, now beginning to reach their mid- to late 50s, begin to retire, businesses around the globe will need to find ways to replace their workplace skills. |
| Improving quality and customer service | In today's global marketplace, every company will have to achieve world-class performance in product quality and customer service. |
| Enhancing competitiveness of every country's workforce | Leaner organizations (with fewer supervisors) require employees with the skills to control, combine, and supervise work operations. |
| | Employers must provide training necessary to develop the increased skills they require of their workforce. |

global competitiveness. Table 3.5 identifies five key challenges: (1) the economic impact of the continuing threat of international terrorism, (2) the shift to a global information economy, (3) the aging of the world's population, (4) the need to improve quality and customer service, and (5) efforts to enhance the competitiveness of every country's workforce.

No country is an economic island in today's global economy. Not only is an ever-increasing stream of goods and services crossing national borders, but a growing number of businesses have become true multinational firms, operating manufacturing plants and other facilities around the world. As global trade and investments grow, events in one nation can reverberate around the globe.

Despite the risks of world trade, global expansion can offer huge opportunities to U.S. firms. With U.S. residents accounting for less than 1 in every 20 of the world's nearly 7 billion people, growth-oriented American companies cannot afford to ignore the world market. U.S. businesses also benefit from the lower labor costs in other parts of the world, and some are finding successful niches importing goods and even services provided by foreign firms. Still, it is extremely important for U.S. firms to keep track of the foreign firms that supply their products. A recent trend toward the use of overseas service call centers by U.S. firms such as American Express, Sprint, General Electric, and IBM has had mixed results. Despite training in language and other skills, customer service representatives in India often struggle to serve frustrated customers. "Many callers refuse to speak to Indians and ask for an American right away," reports one call center employee.[19]

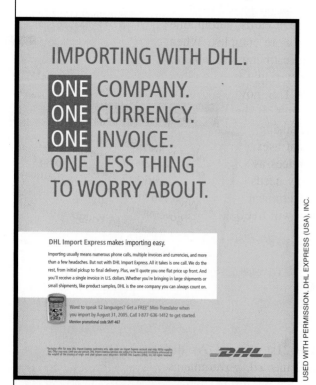

DHL simplifies global business by offering firms a single source for importing services.

U.S. firms must also develop strategies for competing with each other overseas. In the huge but fragmented snack chip industry, Frito-Lay International currently claims 30 percent of the market outside North America, considerably more than its closest competitor, Procter & Gamble, has captured. Coca-Cola still edges out Pepsi as the top-selling cola worldwide.

# WHAT'S AHEAD

Global competition is a key factor in today's economy. In Chapter 4, we focus on the global dimensions of business. We cover basic concepts of doing business internationally and examine how nations can position themselves to benefit from the global economy. Then we describe the specific methods used by individual businesses to expand beyond their national borders and compete successfully in the global marketplace.

**assessment check**

1. Why is virtually no country an economic island these days?
2. Describe two ways in which global expansion can benefit a U.S. firm.

## SUMMARY OF LEARNING GOALS

**1 Distinguish between microeconomics and macroeconomics.**

Microeconomics is the study of economic behavior among individual consumers, families, and businesses whose collective behavior in the marketplace determines the quantity of goods and services demanded and supplied at different prices. Macroeconomics is the study of the broader economic picture and how an economic system maintains and allocates its resources; it focuses on how a government's monetary and fiscal policies affect the overall operation of an economic system.

### Assessment Check Answers

**1.1 Define *microeconomics*.**
Microeconomics is the study of economic behavior among individual consumers, families, and businesses whose collective behavior in the marketplace determines the quantity of goods and services demanded and supplied at different prices.

**1.2 Define *macroeconomics*.**
Macroeconomics is the study of the broader economic picture and how an economic system maintains and allocates its resources.

**2 Explain the factors that drive demand and supply.**

Demand is the willingness and ability of buyers to purchase goods and services at different prices. Factors that drive demand for a good or service include customer preferences, the number of buyers and their incomes, the prices of substitute goods, the prices of complementary goods, and consumer expectations about

the future. Supply is the willingness and ability of businesses to offer products for sale at different prices. Supply is determined by the cost of inputs and technology resources, taxes, and the number of suppliers operating in the market.

### Assessment Check Answers

**2.1 What is a demand curve?**
A demand curve is a graph of the amount of a product that buyers will purchase at different prices.

**2.2 What is a supply curve?**
A supply curve shows the relationship between different prices and the quantities that sellers will offer for sale, regardless of demand.

**2.3 How do factors of production influence the overall supply of goods and services?**
A change in the cost or availability of any of the inputs considered to be factors of production can shift the entire supply curve, either increasing or decreasing the amount available at every price.

**3 Describe each of the four different types of market structures in a private enterprise system.**

Four basic models characterize competition in a private enterprise system: pure competition, monopolistic competition, oligopoly, and monopoly. Pure competition is a market structure, like that in small-scale agriculture, in which large numbers of buyers and sellers exchange homogeneous products and no single participant has a significant influence on price. Monopolistic competition is a market structure, like that of retailing, in which large numbers of buyers and sellers exchange differentiated products, so each participant has some control over price. Oligopolies are market situations, like those in the steel and airline industries, in which relatively few sellers compete and high start-up costs form barriers to keep out new competitors. In a monopoly, one seller dominates trade in a good or service, for which buyers can find no close substitutes. Privately held local water utilities and firms that hold exclusive patent rights on significant product inventions are examples.

## Assessment Check Answers

**3.1 What is the difference between pure competition and monopolistic competition?**
Pure competition is a market structure in which large numbers of buyers and sellers exchange homogeneous products. Monopolistic competition is a market structure in which large numbers of buyers and sellers exchange differentiated products.

**3.2 Distinguish between oligopoly and monopoly.**
An oligopoly is a market structure in which relatively few sellers compete, and high start-up costs form barriers to new competitors. In a monopoly, one seller dominates trade in a good or service.

**4** **Compare the three major types of economic systems.**
The major economic systems are private enterprise economy, planned economy (such as communism or socialism), and mixed market economy. In a private enterprise system, individuals and private businesses pursue their own interests—including investment decisions and profits—without undue governmental restriction. In a planned economy, the government exerts stronger control over business ownership, profits, and resources to accomplish governmental and societal—rather than individual—goals. Communism is an economic system without private property; goods are owned in common, and factors of production and production decisions are controlled by the state. Socialism, another type of planned economic system, is characterized by government ownership and operation of all major industries. A mixed market economy blends government ownership and private enterprise, combining characteristics of both planned and private enterprise economies.

## Assessment Check Answers

**4.1 On which economic system is the U.S. economy based?**

The U.S. economy is based on the private enterprise system.

**4.2 What are the two types of planned economies?**
The two types of planned economies are socialism and communism.

**4.3 What is privatization?**
Privatization is the conversion of government-owned and -operated agencies into privately held businesses.

**5** **Identify and describe the four stages of the business cycle.**
The four stages are prosperity, recession, depression, and recovery. Prosperity is characterized by low unemployment and strong consumer confidence. In a recession, consumers often postpone major purchases, layoffs may occur, and household savings may be depleted. A depression occurs when an economic slowdown continues in a downward spiral over a long period of time. During recovery, consumer spending begins to increase and business activity accelerates, leading to an increased number of jobs.

## Assessment Check Answers

**5.1 Which stages of the business cycle indicate a downturn in the economy?**
Recession and depression indicate a downturn.

**5.2 Which stages point to an upswing?**
Prosperity and recovery point to an upswing.

**6** **Explain how productivity, price level changes, and employment levels affect the stability of a nation's economy.**
As productivity rises, so do an economy's growth and the wealth of its citizens. In a recession, productivity stalls or possibly declines. Changes in general price levels—inflation or deflation—are important indicators of an economy's general stability. The U.S. government measures price-level changes by the Consumer Price Index. A nation's unemployment rate is an indicator of both overall stability and growth. The unemployment rate shows the number of people actively seeking employment who are unable to find jobs as a percentage of the total labor force.

## Assessment Check Answers

**6.1 What is productivity?**
Productivity is the relationship between the goods and services produced in a nation each year and the inputs that produce them.

**6.2 How does the U.S. government track changes in price levels?**

The U.S. government tracks changes in price levels with the Consumer Price Index (CPI), which measures the monthly average change in prices of goods and services.

**6.3 Identify the four categories of unemployment.**
The four categories of unemployment are frictional, seasonal, cyclical, and structural.

**7  Discuss how monetary policy and fiscal policy are used to manage an economy's performance.**

Monetary policy encompasses a government's efforts to control the size of the nation's money supply. Various methods of increasing or decreasing the overall money supply affect interest rates and therefore affect borrowing and investment decisions. By changing the size of the money supply, government can encourage growth or control inflation. Fiscal policy involves decisions regarding government revenues and expenditures. Changes in government spending affect economic growth and employment levels in the private sector. However, government must also raise money, through taxes or borrowing, to finance its expenditures. Because tax payments represent funds that might otherwise have been spent by individuals and businesses, any taxation changes also affect the overall economy.

## Assessment Check Answers

**7.1 What is the difference between an expansionary monetary policy and a restrictive monetary policy?**
An expansionary monetary policy increases the money supply in an effort to cut the cost of borrowing. A restrictive monetary policy reduces the money supply to curb rising prices, overexpansion, and concerns about overly rapid economic growth.

**7.2 What are the three primary sources of government funds?**
The U.S. government acquires funds through taxes, fees, and borrowing.

**7.3 Does a balanced budget erase the federal debt?**
No, a balanced budget does not erase the national debt; it just doesn't increase it. The government must pay off the debt just as consumers pay off their charge accounts.

**8  Describe the major global economic challenges of the 21st century.**

Businesses face five key challenges in the 21st century: (1) the threat of international terrorism, (2) the shift to a global information economy, (3) the aging of the world's population, (4) the need to improve quality and customer service, and (5) efforts to enhance the competitiveness of every country's workforce.

## Assessment Check Answers

**8.1 Why is virtually no country an economic island these days?**
No business or country is an economic island because many goods and services travel across national borders. Companies now are becoming multinational firms.

**8.2 Describe two ways in which global expansion can benefit a U.S. firm.**
A firm can benefit from global expansion by attracting more customers and using less expensive labor and production to produce goods and services.

## Business Terms You Need to Know

economics 64
microeconomics 64
macroeconomics 64
demand 65

supply 65
recession 77
productivity 78
gross domestic product (GDP) 78

inflation 78
monetary policy 82
fiscal policy 82
budget 83

## Other Important Business Terms

demand curve 66
supply curve 68
equilibrium price 70
pure competition 71
monopolistic competition 72
oligopoly 72
monopoly 73

deregulation 74
planned economy 74
communism 74
socialism 75
mixed market economy 75
privatization 76
core inflation rate 78

deflation 80
Consumer Price Index (CPI) 80
unemployment rate 80
budget deficit 83
national debt 83
budget surplus 83
balanced budget 83

1. Distinguish between macroeconomics and micro-economics. Give at least one example of issues addressed by each.

2. Draw supply and demand graphs that estimate what will happen to demand, supply, and the equilibrium price of pizza if these events occur:
   a. A widely reported medical report suggests that eating cheese supplies a significant amount of the calcium needed in a person's daily diet.
   b. The price of flour increases.
   c. The state imposes a new tax on restaurant meals.
   d. The biggest competitor leaves the area.

3. Describe the four different types of competition in the private enterprise system. In which type of competition would each of the following businesses be likely to engage?
   a. a 100-acre Wisconsin dairy farm
   b. Stop & Shop supermarkets
   c. Southwest Airlines
   d. the U.S. Postal Service
   e. Microsoft

4. Describe the two types of planned economies and give an example of each. What is a mixed market economy?

5. What are the four stages of the business cycle? In which stage do you believe the U.S. economy is now? Why?

6. Define *productivity*. Why is it an important concern for every economy?

7. What are the effects of inflation on an economy? How does the Consumer Price Index (CPI) work?

8. Describe the four types of unemployment, and give an example of each. Which type might signify that an economy is in a downturn?

9. Explain the difference between monetary policy and fiscal policy. How does the government raise funds to cover the costs of its annual budget?

10. What are the benefits of paying down the national debt? What might be the negative effects?

1. Describe a situation in which you have had to make an economic choice in an attempt to balance your wants with limited means. What factors influenced your decision?

2. On your own or with a classmate, visit a large general merchandise retailer—such as a Target or Wal-Mart store. (Alternatively, you can visit a retailer online.) List five different goods sold by the retailer. Note also one or two major competitors, if there are any, on the shelves nearby. (If you are online, note one or two brands you think might be competitors.) Classify each good in terms of the competitive environment. Be sure to note the characteristics you used to make each classification. Create a chart illustrating your findings. Include each of the goods, its competitors, its classification of competitive environment, and the characteristics you used to make the classification. Present your chart to the class.

3. Some businesses automatically experience seasonal unemployment—beach or ski resorts, construction companies, ice-cream stands. Choose a "business partner" from among your classmates and select a business that interests you that experiences seasonal unemployment. Then develop a plan for increasing demand for your business during the off-season. Present your plan to the class.

4. In the past, many proposals have been made for privatizing certain federal or state-run agencies such as Social Security, Medicare, and the U.S. Postal Service. On your own or with a classmate, select one of these agencies and go online to research more about how it is run. Do you favor privatization of this agency? Why or why not? Discuss your findings with the class.

5. Consider your economic lifetime to date. What stages of the business cycle have you experienced? In what ways have these stages affected your—and your family's—lifestyle? (You might want to talk with your parents, grandparents, siblings, and other relatives about their views.)

## Case 3.1

### General Motors Staggers under the Weight of Healthcare Costs

General Motors is the world's largest auto manufacturer, and it may claim the world's largest healthcare costs to match. GM insures 1.1 million current employees, retirees, and even their widows and widowers as part of the benefits plan it negotiated with the United Auto Workers (UAW) and began implementing over 50 years ago. The plan cost $5.2 billion in a recent year, contributing to losses. Healthcare costs were so significant that GM executives had to search frantically for a solution.

Richard Wagoner, GM's chairman and CEO, charged that U.S. companies and workers pay more for healthcare—and receive less—than their counterparts in other countries. "In the U.S., healthcare costs are rising at an annual rate of 14 percent to 18 percent and already account for 15 percent of our gross domestic product—50 percent higher than the next most expensive country," he argued. Even if he was correct, it didn't solve GM's problem. "Our foreign-based competitors have just a fraction of these costs because they have few retirees in this country and in their own country where the bulk of their people are, their governments pay a much greater proportion of their employee and retiree healthcare costs," Wagoner pointed out. GM was faced with a future cost of $77 billion to cover its current workers and retirees, but had only $20 billion in the bank to cover it. The firm had to come up with a creative answer—and fast.

One possibility was to increase revenues by cutting out discount sales to rental-car agencies and to employees themselves. But the firm recently launched a marketing campaign offering cars to retail consumers at the employee discount to boost lagging sales. To boost revenues, GM could also increase sales, but the firm makes so many models of cars and trucks that its design and engineering teams can't redesign or improve them as often as some of the smaller manufacturers do. This cycle makes GM look sluggish and unresponsive to consumer preferences—and buyers go elsewhere for their cars, reducing demand for GM vehicles. Wagoner began to order the closing of some assembly plants and the retirement of certain brands—such as Oldsmobile—in order to trim down, and convinced the UAW that it had to shoulder more of the healthcare costs to survive. GM succeeded in convincing the UAW that it had to shoulder more of the healthcare costs to survive. After the company reported a staggering $1.6 billion loss in one quarter, the union realized that bankruptcy was a real possibility. So with the cuts to its healthcare coverage, GM estimated it could save $3 billion a year—a significant contribution to its bottom line.

### Questions for Critical Thinking

1. How might a positive change in demand for GM's products affect its overall financial picture? What steps might GM take to create that demand?
2. Do you think GM workers and retirees were right to agree to help pay more for their own healthcare costs? Why or why not?

**Sources:** "GM's $1.1 Billion Loss to Impact UAW," *Washington Times*, accessed June 8, 2006, http://www.washingtontimes.com; Rick Popely and Jim Mateja, "GM, UAW Come to Terms," *Chicago Tribune*, October 18, 2005, section 3, pp. 1, 7; Jonathan Fahey, "Black Hole," *Forbes*, April 11, 2005, p. 54; David Welch, "Running Out of Gas," *BusinessWeek*, March 28, 2005, pp. 28–30.

## VIDEO Case 3.2

### BP Meets Global Energy Challenges Head-On

This video case appears on page 610. A recently filmed video, designed to expand and highlight the written case, is available for class use by instructors.

# Chapter 4

## Competing in Global Markets

PHOTODISC/GETTY IMAGES

A U.S. shoe manufacturer that can make work boots trendy among young European and Asian consumers must be unusual, and Red Wing Shoe Company certainly is. The 100-year-old firm, which is based in the small Minnesota town that shares its name, has become a standout in its industry, and not just for its growing fashion sense. About 98 percent of the footwear sold in the United States today is imported from somewhere else in the world, which means Red Wing is one of the very few domestic shoe manufacturers still making its products on American soil.

It hasn't always been a smooth ride for the company, which is privately owned and profitable, with annual sales at about $375 million. Competition from lower-priced merchandise has been eating into its market, and Red Wing has worked hard to control costs and expand its product lines in order to remain competitive. Other boot

LON C. DIEHL/PHOTOEDIT

The company makes about 200 different boot models, some of which are tailored for the needs and hazards of particular jobs and industries. For instance, boots for iron-

# These Boots Are Made for Working—Internationally

makers such as Timberland and Doc Martens have pushed ahead on the fashion frontier, while Red Wing has stayed close to the blue-collar workers who have always made up the largest part of its customer base. "Would I say we're the best-looking boot in the world?" asks president and CEO David Murphy. "No, but we're getting better."

Getting better, however, means branching out from the company's classic designs, many of which have remained the same for decades. With new designers on board, the company is now making women's shoes and motorcycle boots. The steel-toed boots needed by young blue-collar workers also come styled like hiking shoes or sneakers. And Red Wing has succeeded in cracking the international market with a new brand of footwear called "Euro Classics," which use special leathers and distinctive stitching to appeal to fashion-conscious youth in Europe and Asia. Says Murphy, "The reason they sell so well in those places is because we're such a genuine American name; you can't create that—it just is or it isn't." About 15 percent of Red Wing's annual sales now come from international markets, and the company recently created a new position—vice president of international and strategic development—to highlight the growing role of international sales in its corporate strategy.

workers have soft soles so that wearers can feel the steel beams under their feet while working on building construction sites. Farmers in the southeastern United States need boots that grip despite slippery floors but don't pick up the sticky clay of the region. But regardless of the industry, one of Red Wing's biggest selling points is the fact that its products come in enough sizes to fit almost anybody—from 4B to 18EE in some models.

Although it's very conscious of the importance its U.S. customer base places on Red Wing's homegrown pedigree, the company also imports some shoes from China that it markets under other brand names, and it imports some of the leather uppers used to make its Red Wing brand products. But Red Wing's managers know that its U.S. customers include many union workers who appreciate products "Made in the U.S.A." The company plans to keep serving them, even though they are, ironically, a customer base that's shrinking as manufacturing jobs continue to move overseas, where labor is cheaper. And, in fact, "the willingness of the American worker to buy American . . . gets less all the time," says Murphy. "In today's world, the young consumer has never worn a shoe made in America." But "we do look beyond pure economics. I think most great companies do."[1]

Consider for a moment how many products you used today that came from outside the United States. Maybe you drank Brazilian coffee with your breakfast, wore clothes manufactured in Honduras or Malaysia, drove to class in a German or Japanese car fueled by gasoline refined from Venezuelan crude oil, and watched a movie on a television set assembled in Mexico for a Japanese company such as Sony. A fellow student in Germany may be wearing Levi's jeans, using a Dell computer, and drinking Coca-Cola.

U.S. and foreign companies alike recognize the importance of international trade to their future success. Economic interdependence is increasing throughout the world as companies seek additional markets for their goods and services and the most cost-effective locations for production facilities. No longer can businesses rely only on domestic sales. Today, foreign sales are essential to U.S. manufacturing, agricultural, and service firms as sources of new markets and profit opportunities. Foreign companies also frequently look to the United States when they seek new markets.

Thousands of products cross national borders every day. The computers that U.S. manufacturers sell in Canada are **exports**, domestically produced goods and services sold in markets in other countries. **Imports** are foreign-made products and services purchased by domestic consumers. Together, U.S. exports and imports make up about a quarter of the U.S. gross domestic product (GDP). U.S. exports recently set a record high of more than $1.1 trillion, and annual imports hit another new high of nearly $1.8 trillion. That total amount is more than double the nation's imports and exports from just a decade ago.[2]

**exports** domestically produced goods and services sold in other countries.

**imports** foreign goods and services purchased by domestic customers.

Transactions that cross national boundaries may expose a company to an additional set of environmental factors such as new social and cultural practices, economic and political environments, and legal restrictions. Before venturing into world markets, companies must adapt their domestic business strategies and plans to accommodate these differences.

This chapter travels through the world of international business to see how both large and small companies approach globalization. First, we consider the reasons nations trade, the importance and characteristics of the global marketplace, and the ways nations measure international trade. Then we examine barriers to international trade that arise from cultural and environmental differences. To reduce these barriers, countries turn to organizations that promote global business. Finally, we look at the strategies firms implement for entering foreign markets and how they develop international business strategies.

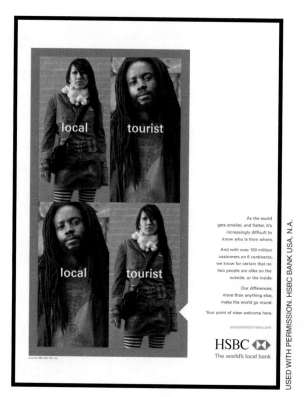

Businesses that are thinking of going global need to understand and appreciate local customs and culture. Banking firm HSBC has offices in 77 countries and territories—in Europe, the Americas, the Middle East, and Africa. The company uses its local knowledge to provide personal service no matter where its banks are.

# WHY NATIONS TRADE

As domestic markets mature and sales growth slows, companies in every industry recognize the increasing importance of efforts to develop business in other countries. Wal-Mart operates stores in Mexico, Boeing sells jetliners in Asia, and soccer fans in Britain watch their teams being bought by U.S. billionaires. These are only a few of the thousands of U.S. companies taking advantage of large populations, substantial resources, and rising standards of living abroad that boost foreign interest in their goods and services. Likewise, the U.S. market, with the world's highest purchasing power, attracts thousands of foreign companies to its shores.

International trade is vital to a nation and its businesses because it boosts economic growth by providing a market for its products and access to needed resources. Companies can expand their markets, seek growth opportunities in other nations, and make their production and distribution systems more efficient. They also reduce their dependence on the economies of their home nations.

## International Sources of Factors of Production

Business decisions to operate abroad depend on the availability, price, and quality of labor, natural resources, capital, and entrepreneurship—the basic factors of production—in the foreign country. Indian colleges and universities produce thousands of highly qualified computer scientists and engineers each year. To take advantage of this talent, many U.S. computer software and hardware firms have set up operations in India and many others are outsourcing information technology and customer service jobs there, as we'll see later in this chapter.

Trading with other countries also allows a company to spread risk because different nations may be at different stages of the business cycle or in different phases of development. If demand falls off in one country, the company may still enjoy strong demand in other nations. Companies such as Toyota and Sony have long used international sales to offset lower domestic demand.

## Size of the International Marketplace

In addition to human and natural resources, entrepreneurship, and capital, companies are attracted to international business by the sheer size of the global marketplace. Only one in five of the world's nearly 7 billion people lives in a relatively well-developed country. The share of the world's population in the less developed countries will increase over the coming years because more developed nations have lower birthrates. But the U.S. Census Bureau says the global birthrate is slowing overall, and the average woman in today's world bears half as many children as her counterpart did 35 years ago.[3]

As developing nations expand their involvement in global business, the potential for reaching new groups of customers dramatically increases. Firms looking for new revenue are inevitably attracted to giant markets such as China and India, with respective populations of nearly 1.3 billion and 1.1 billion each. However, people alone are not enough to create a market. Consumer demand also requires purchasing

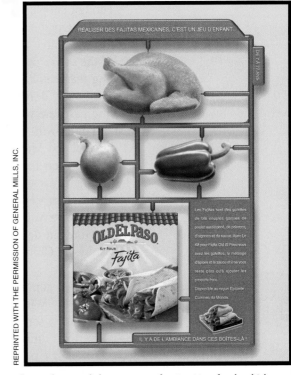

REPRINTED WITH THE PERMISSION OF GENERAL MILLS, INC.

Even the French have a taste for Tex-Mex food—chicken fajitas, to be specific. Old El Paso sells its fajita kits there, saying it's "child's play" (un jeu d'enfant) to make them.

Table

4.1

The World's Top Ten Nations Based on Population and Wealth

| Country | Population (in Millions) | | Country | Per-Capita GDP (in U.S. dollars) |
|---------|------------------------|---|---------|----------------------------------|
| China | 1,299 | | Luxembourg | $55,100 |
| India | 1,065 | | United States | $37,800 |
| United States | 293 | | Norway | $37,800 |
| Indonesia | 238 | | Bermuda | $36,000 |
| Brazil | 184 | | Cayman Islands | $35,000 |
| Pakistan | 159 | | San Marino | $34,600 |
| Russia | 144 | | Switzerland | $32,700 |
| Bangladesh | 141 | | Denmark | $31,100 |
| Japan | 127 | | Iceland | $30,900 |
| Nigeria | 126 | | Austria | $30,000 |

**Sources:** Data from U.S. Census Bureau, International Database, "Top 50 Countries Ranked by Population," accessed June 11, 2006, http://www.census.gov; Central Intelligence Agency, "GDP—Per Capita," *World Factbook*, accessed June 11, 2006, http://www.cia.gov.

power. As Table 4.1 shows, population size is no guarantee of economic prosperity. Of the ten most populous countries, only the United States appears on the list of those with the highest per-capita GDPs.

Though people in the developing nations have lower per-capita incomes than those in the highly developed economies of North America and Western Europe, their huge populations do represent lucrative markets. Even when the higher-income segments are only a small percentage of the entire country's population, their sheer numbers may still represent significant and growing markets.

Also, many developing countries have posted high growth rates of annual GDP. For instance, over the past few years, U.S. GDP has grown at an annual rate of about 4.4 percent. By contrast, GDP growth in less developed countries is much greater—China's GDP growth rate was 9.1 percent, and Malaysia's was 7.1 percent.[4] These markets represent opportunities for global businesses, even though their per-capita incomes lag behind those in more developed countries. Many firms are establishing operations in these and other developing countries to position themselves to benefit from local sales driven by expanding economies and rising standards of living. Wal-Mart Stores is one of those companies. The retail giant has opened dozens of new stores in developing countries from China to Brazil. It is nearly doubling the number of its stores in China, planning to have more than 90 outlets there by the end of 2006.[5]

The United States trades with many other nations. As Figure 4.1 shows, the top five are Canada, Mexico, China, Japan, and the Federal Republic of Germany. With the United Kingdom, South Korea, France, Taiwan, and Italy, they represent more than two-thirds of U.S. imports and exports every year.[6] Foreign trade is such an important part of the U.S. economy that it makes up a large portion of the business activity in many of the country's individual states as well. Texas exports more than $117 billion of goods annually, and California exports more than $109 billion. Other big exporting states include New York, Michigan, Washington, Ohio, and Illinois.[7]

**assessment check**

1. Why do nations trade?
2. Cite some measure of the size of the international marketplace.

Figure 4.1

## Absolute and Comparative Advantage

Few countries can produce all the goods and services their people need. For centuries, trading has been the way that countries can meet the demand. If a country focuses on producing what it does best, it can export surplus domestic output and buy foreign products that it lacks or cannot efficiently produce. The potential for foreign sales of a particular item depends largely on whether the country has an absolute advantage or a comparative advantage.

A country has an *absolute advantage* in making a product for which it can maintain a monopoly or that it can produce at a lower cost than any competitor. For centuries, China enjoyed an absolute advantage in silk production. The fabric was woven from fibers recovered from silkworm cocoons, making it a prized raw material in high-quality clothing. Demand among Europeans for silk led to establishment of the famous Silk Road, a 5,000-mile link between Rome and the ancient Chinese capital city of Xian.

Absolute advantages are rare these days. But some countries manage to approximate absolute advantages in some products. Climate differences can give some nations or regions an advantage in growing certain plants. Saffron, perhaps the world's most expensive spice at around $40 per ounce, is the stigma of a flowering plant in the crocus family. It is native to the Mediterranean, Asia Minor, and India. Today, however, saffron is cultivated primarily in Spain, where the plant thrives in its soil and climate. Attempts to grow saffron in other parts of the world have generally been unsuccessful.[8]

A nation can develop a *comparative advantage* in a product if it can supply it more efficiently and at a lower price than it can supply other goods, compared with the outputs of other countries. China is profiting from its comparative advantage in producing textiles. On the other hand, ensuring that its people are well educated is another way a nation can develop a comparative advantage in skilled human resources. India, for example, has acquired a comparative advantage in software development with its highly educated workforce and low wage scale. As a result, several companies have moved part or all of their software development to India.

Canon has adopted a strategy for research and development based on various nations' comparative advantage in engineering knowledge. Rather than basing all of its research at its Tokyo headquarters, the company operates regional headquarters in Europe and the Americas, each focused on a different area of expertise. In the United States, engineers concentrate on digital and networking technology, whereas Canon engineers in France focus on telecommunications.

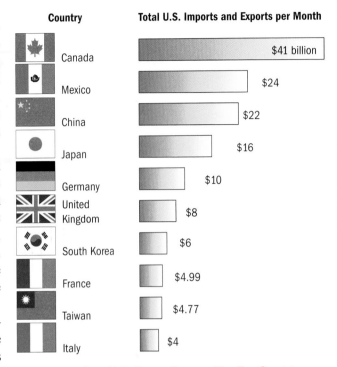

Top Ten Trading Partners with the United States

**Source:** Data from U.S. Census Bureau, "Top Ten Countries with Which the U.S. Trades," accessed June 11, 2006, http://www.census.gov/foreign-trade/top/dst/current/balance.html.

### assessment check

1. Define absolute advantage.
2. How does a nation acquire a comparative advantage?

# MEASURING TRADE BETWEEN NATIONS

Clearly, engaging in international trade provides tremendous competitive advantages to both the countries and individual companies involved. Any attempt to measure global business activity requires an understanding of the concepts of balance of trade and balance of payments. Another important factor is currency exchange rates for each country.

balance of trade differ-
ence between a nation's
exports and imports.

balance of payments
overall money flows into
and out of a country.

A nation's **balance of trade** is the difference between its exports and imports. If a country exports more than it imports, it achieves a positive balance of trade, called a *trade surplus*.
If it imports more than it exports, it produces a negative balance of trade, called a *trade deficit*.
The States has run a trade deficit every year since 1976. Despite being the world's top exporter,
the U.S. has an even greater appetite for foreign-made goods, which creates a trade deficit.

A nation's balance of trade plays a central role in determining its **balance of payments**—
the overall flow of money into or out of a country. Other factors also affect the balance of payments, including overseas loans and borrowing, international investments, profits from such
investments, and foreign aid payments. To calculate a nation's balance of payments, subtract
the monetary outflows from the monetary inflows. A positive balance of payments, or a *balance-
of-payments surplus*, means more money has moved into a country than out of it. A negative
balance of payments, or *balance-of-payments deficit*, means more money has gone out of the
country than entered it.

## Major U.S. Exports and Imports

The United States, with combined exports and imports of nearly $3 trillion, leads the world in
the international trade of goods and services. As listed in Table 4.2, the leading categories of
goods exchanged by U.S. exporters and importers range from machinery and vehicles to scientific and telecommunications equipment. Strong U.S. demand for imported goods is partly a
reflection of the nation's prosperity and diversity.

Although the United States imports more goods than it exports, the opposite is true for
services. U.S. exporters sell more than $338 billion in services annually. Much of that money
comes from travel and tourism—money spent by foreign nationals visiting the United States.
The increase in that figure is especially significant because the dollar has not been worth as
much in terms of foreign currencies in recent years. U.S. service exports also include business
and technical services such as engineering, financial services, computing, legal services, and

**4.2** Top Ten U.S. Exports and Imports

| Exports | Amount (in billions) | Imports | Amount (in billions) |
|---|---|---|---|
| Electrical machinery | $86 | Motor vehicles | $173 |
| Motor vehicles | $63 | Petroleum, petroleum products | $130 |
| Transport equipment | $43 | Electrical machinery | $83 |
| Office machines and data-processing equipment | $41 | Office machines and data-processing equipment | $81 |
| Miscellaneous manufactured articles | $35 | Telecommunications equipment | $71 |
| Power-generating machinery | $34 | Apparel and clothing | $68 |
| General industrial machinery | $32 | Miscellaneous manufactured articles | $64 |
| Professional scientific instruments | $31 | General industrial machinery | $38 |
| Specialized machinery | $25 | Organic chemicals | $33 |
| Telecommunications equipment | $24 | Power-generating machinery | $32 |

**Sources:** Annual data from International Trade Administration, "U.S. Manufacturers Trade: Top Ten Product Exports, Imports,
Balances," U.S. Department of Commerce, accessed June 11, 2006, http://www.ita.doc.gov.

entertainment, as well as royalties and licensing fees. Major service exporters include America Online, Citibank, Walt Disney, Allstate Insurance, and Federal Express, as well as retailers such as The Gap and Starbucks.

Businesses in many foreign countries want the expertise of U.S. financial and business professionals. Entertainment is another major growth area for U.S. service exports. Recently Disney, which already operates theme parks in France and Japan, opened a theme park on Hong Kong's Lantau Island. The company invested $318 million for a 43 percent share of the new Magic Kingdom and its three hotels. It also earns fees for managing the theme park and has announced plans to build one in Shanghai as well.

With annual imports far exceeding $1 trillion, the United States is by far the world's leading importer. American tastes for foreign-made goods—which show up as huge trade deficits with the consumer-goods-exporting nations of China and Japan—also extend to European products. The 25 countries of the European Union (EU) ship more than $220 billion of merchandise, including Audi cars, Saeco espresso machines, Norelco electric shavers, to U.S. buyers.[9]

## Exchange Rates

A nation's **exchange rate** is the rate at which its currency can be exchanged for the currencies of other nations. It is important to learn how foreign exchange works because we live in a global community and the value of currency is an important economic thermometer for every country. Each currency's exchange rate is usually quoted in terms of another currency, such as the number of Mexican pesos needed to purchase one U.S. dollar. About 11 pesos are needed to exchange for a dollar. A Canadian dollar can be exchanged for approximately 79 cents in the United States. The euro, the currency used in many of the EU countries, has made considerable moves in exchange value during its few years in circulation—ranging from less than 90 cents when it was first issued to around $1.27 in American currency in more recent years. European consumers and businesses now use the euro to pay bills by check, credit card, or bank transfer. Euro coins and notes are also used in many EU-member countries.

**exchange rate** value of one nation's currency relative to the currencies of other countries.

Foreign exchange rates are influenced by a number of factors, including domestic economic and political conditions, central bank intervention, balance-of-payments position, and speculation over future currency values. Currency values fluctuate, or "float," depending on the supply and demand for each currency in the international market. In this system of *floating exchange rates*, currency traders create a market for the world's currencies based on each country's relative trade and investment prospects. In theory, this market permits exchange rates to vary freely according to supply and demand. In practice, exchange rates do not float in total freedom. National governments often intervene in currency markets to adjust their exchange rates.

Nations influence exchange rates in other ways as well. They may form currency blocs by linking their exchange rates to each other. Many governments practice protectionist policies that seek to guard their economies against trade imbalances. For instance, national governments sometimes take deliberate action to devalue their currencies as a way to increase exports and stimulate foreign investment. **Devaluation** describes a drop in a currency's value relative to other

AP PHOTO/XINHUA, PANG XINGLEI

After nearly a decade of pegging the foreign exchange rate of the yuan to the U.S. dollar, China changed its policy. It now allows its currency to float more flexibly on a mix of foreign currencies. Such a change might make Chinese imports to the United States more expensive, but it might also make U.S. exports to China cheaper.

currencies or to a fixed standard. In Brazil, a recent currency devaluation made investing in that country relatively cheap, so the devaluation was followed by a flood of foreign investment. Pillsbury bought Brazil's Brisco, which makes a local staple, *pao de queijo*, a cheese bread formed into rolls and served with morning coffee. Other foreign companies invested in Brazil's construction, tourism, banking, communications, and other industries. For an individual business, the impact of currency devaluation depends on where that business buys its materials and where it sells its products. St. Paul, Minnesota–based St. Jude Medical, which develops, manufactures, and distributes heart-monitoring and surgical devices, does about a quarter of its business in western Europe. Declines in the dollar-euro exchange rate made its products more competitively priced with those of competing medical suppliers, boosting revenues and profits. When the dollar began to climb again, the growth in value of the euro slowed.[10]

Business transactions are usually conducted in the currency of the particular region in which they take place. When business is conducted in Japan, transactions are likely to be in yen. In the United Kingdom, transactions are in pounds. With the adoption of the euro among the countries of the EU, the number of foreign currencies in that region has been reduced. (The euro is the common currency adopted by some members of the European Union, which include founding members Belgium, Denmark, France, Germany, Greece, Italy, Ireland, Luxembourg, the Netherlands, and the United Kingdom.) Other countries' currencies include the Australian dollar, the Indian rupee, the Italian lira, the Mexican peso, the Taiwanese dollar, and the South African rand.

Exchange rate changes can quickly create—or wipe out—a competitive advantage, so they are important factors in decisions about whether to invest abroad. In Europe, a declining dollar means that a price of ten euros is worth more, so companies are pressured to lower prices. At the same time, the falling dollar makes European vacations less affordable for U.S. tourists because their dollars are worth less relative to the euro.

On the Internet you can find currency converters such as those located at http://beginnersinvest .about.com/cs/currencycalc/index.htm, which can help in your dollar-for-dollar conversions. It also helps you understand how much spending power a U.S. dollar has in other countries. Currencies that owners can easily convert into other currencies are called *hard currencies*. Examples include the euro, the U.S. dollar, and the Japanese yen. The Russian ruble and many central European currencies are considered soft currencies because they cannot be readily converted. Exporters trading with these countries often prefer to barter, accepting payment in oil, timber, or other commodities that they can resell for hard-currency payments.

The foreign currency market is the largest financial market in the world, with a daily volume in excess of 1.5 trillion U.S. dollars. This is about 50 times the size of the transaction volume of all the equity markets put together, so the foreign exchange market is the most liquid and efficient financial market in the world.

## assessment check

1. Compare balance of trade and balance of payments.
2. Explain the function of an exchange rate.
3. What happens when a currency is devalued?

# BARRIERS TO INTERNATIONAL TRADE

All businesses encounter barriers in their operations, whether they sell only to local customers or trade in international markets. Countries such as Australia, Germany, and New Zealand regulate the hours and days retailers may be open. Besides complying with a variety of laws and exchanging currencies, international companies may also have to reformulate their products to accommodate different tastes in new locations. Frito-Lay exports cheeseless Cheetos to Asia, and Domino's Pizza offers pickled-ginger pizzas at its Indian fast-food restaurants.

Figure

4.2

In addition to social and cultural differences, companies engaged in international business face economic barriers as well as legal and political ones. Some of the hurdles shown in Figure 4.2 are easily breached, but others require major changes in a company's business strategy. To successfully compete in global markets, companies and their managers must understand not only how these barriers affect international trade but also how to overcome them.

## Social and Cultural Differences

The social and cultural differences among nations range from language and customs to educational background and religious holidays. Understanding and respecting these differences are critical in the process leading to international business success. Businesspeople with knowledge of host countries' cultures, languages, social values, and religious attitudes and practices are well equipped for the marketplace and the negotiating table. Acute sensitivity to such elements as local attitudes, forms of address, and expectations regarding dress, body language, and timeliness also helps them win customers and achieve their business objectives. See the "Business Etiquette" feature for some tips about courtesy in other cultures.

*Language*    English is the second most widely spoken language in the world, followed by Hindustani, Spanish, Russian, and Arabic. Only Mandarin Chinese is more commonly used. It is not uncommon for students abroad for whom English is not their first language to spend eight years of elementary and high school in English language classes. Understanding a business colleague's primary language may prove to be the difference between closing an international business transaction and losing the sale to someone else. Company representatives operating in foreign markets must not only choose correct and appropriate words but also translate words correctly to convey the intended meanings. Firms may also need to rename products or rewrite slogans for foreign markets. See the "Hit & Miss" feature for examples of some spectacular failures in this area.

Potential communication barriers include more than mistranslation. Companies may present messages through inappropriate media, overlook local customs and regulations, or ignore differences in taste. Cultural sensitivity is especially critical in cyberspace. Web site developers must be aware that visitors to a site may come from anywhere in the world. Some icons that seem friendly to U.S. Internet users may shock people from other countries. A person making a high-five hand gesture would be insulting people in Greece; the same is true of making a circle with the thumb and index finger in Brazil and a two-fingered peace sign with the back of the hand facing out in Great Britain. Even colors can pose problems. In the Middle East, people view green as a sacred color, so a green background on a Web page would be inappropriate there.

Gift-giving traditions employ the language of symbolism. For example, in Latin America, knives and scissors should not be given as gifts because they represent the severing of friendship.

**"They Said It"**

"If you speak three languages, you are trilingual. If you speak two languages, you are bilingual. If you speak one language, you're American."
—*Anonymous*

# (b)usiness (e)tiquette

## Global Etiquette: Learning about Differences

Committing a social blunder in class or at home is one thing, but committing one in a foreign country may mean the end of your business relationship with your host. Each culture has its own set of rules and customs, and before you head out to dinner with your foreign business associates or venture into their country for a meeting, you'll need to learn all you can about global etiquette and what is and is not appropriate abroad.

For instance, in Iraq you shake hands gently, always with the right hand, and do not use your left hand to eat, gesture, or touch others. If a woman is present, allow her to greet you first. She will shake hands with only her fingertips.

Here are some additional little-known facts about other countries and their customs:

1. In Chile, business gifts should be of good quality but not lavish, and women should not give gifts to men because the gesture can be misunderstood.
2. When in South Africa, dress well in public because your host will expect it.
3. In Iraq, if you must point at something, use your entire hand, not just one finger, which is considered a sign of contempt.
4. The Chinese do not speak with their hands, so do not use large gestures and remember that men should not touch women in public.
5. In Egypt members of the same sex stand much closer to each other than North Americans and Europeans do, but men and women stand farther apart.
6. Avoid casual dress when doing business in Japan and dress to impress, but remember that shoes will be taken off frequently so they should be easy to remove.
7. It is impolite to show the soles of your shoes in Russia.
8. In Germany sudden changes in business transactions are unwelcome even if they are positive, and humor in business settings is not encouraged.

Most important, learn the basic vocabulary and historical background of the country and region, as well as the proper use of greetings and introductions. Pay attention to your physical gestures, facial expressions, dress, and dining and drinking habits. Mastering the details can save you embarrassment and perhaps make or break your career.

**Sources:** International Business Center Web site, accessed June 11, 2006, http://www.cyborlink.com; Peter Edidin, "How to Shake Hands or Share a Meal with an Iraqi," *The New York Times*, March 6, 2005, p. WK 7; "City Tips," *Worth*, March 2005.

Flowers are generally acceptable, but Mexicans use yellow flowers in their Day of the Dead festivities, so they are associated with death.

***Values and Religious Attitudes*** Even though today's world is shrinking in many ways, people in different countries do not necessarily share the same values or religious attitudes. Marked differences remain in workers' attitudes from country to country, for instance.

U.S. society places a higher value on business efficiency and low unemployment than European society, where employee benefits are more valued. The U.S. government does not regulate vacation time, and employees typically receive no paid vacation during their first year of employment, then two weeks' vacation, and eventually up to three or four weeks if they stay with the same employer for many years. In contrast, the EU mandates a minimum paid vacation of four weeks per year, and most Europeans get five or six weeks. In these countries, a U.S. company that opens a manufacturing plant would not be able to hire any local employees without offering vacations in line with a nation's business practices.

U.S. culture values national unity, with tolerance of regional differences. The United States is viewed as a national market with a single economy. European countries that are part of the 25-member EU are trying to create a similar marketplace. However, many resist the idea of being European citizens first and British, Danish, or Dutch citizens second. British consumers differ from Italians in important ways, and U.S. companies that fail to recognize this variation will run into problems with brand acceptance.

Religion plays an important role in every society, so businesspeople also must cultivate sensitivity to the dominant religions in countries where they operate. Understanding religious cycles and the timing of major holidays can help prevent embarrassing moments when scheduling meetings, trade shows, conferences, or events such as the opening of a new manufacturing plant. People doing business in Saudi Arabia must take into account Islam's monthlong observance of Ramadan, when work ends at noon. Friday is the Muslim Sabbath, so the Saudi workweek runs from Saturday through

# HIT & MISS

## Lost in Translation

The fact that product names and marketing slogans don't always translate well from one country or culture to another is widely known. But mistakes still happen. Although Chevrolet denies the popular myth about its Nova flopping in Latin America because *no va* means "won't go" in Spanish, most marketers would agree with British business writer Simon Anholt, who says, "Language is in many respects such a silly little thing, but it has the power to bring marketing directors to their knees. That's where the terror lies."

Here are some recent translation errors made—or avoided—by international automakers.

- Toyota's MR2 is known as the MR in France, because in French "MR-deux" sounds too much like merde, another name for manure.
- Mercedes-Benz shortened "Grand Sports Tourer" to GST, but the initials remind Canadians of an unpopular tax on goods and services dubbed the "gouge and screw tax."
- Ford had to change the name of its Pinto in Brazil, where it connotes part of the male anatomy in Portuguese. The car now goes by the name Corcel.
- Although there was no translation problem, Toyota's Canadian division had international naming troubles of its own. The firm announced plans to introduce its new model, the Celica Tsunami. It quickly backpedaled after the disastrous waves hit Southeast Asia, renaming the car the Celica Sport Package.

Car makers are not alone in their naming troubles. Ikea customers are still wondering who chose the names of the Fartfull workbench. The Mexican firm Corona had to rechristen its beer in Spain, because a winemaker there already bore the same name. Corona was fortunate to adopt Coronita, which is easy to associate with its company name. And Sweden's toffee-and-licorice ice cream product known as Nogger Black has come under fire. "We certainly had no intention that the name 'Nogger' would be associated with any negative word," says its maker, GB Glace.

### Questions for Critical Thinking

1. Consultants advise against relying solely on non-native translators to help marketing campaigns cross international lines because they lack detailed knowledge of the language and culture. "You can be saved by the right secretary in another country reading [your communications]," says one. Do you agree? Why or why not?
2. One marketing executive says that even perfect literal translations will not ring true to those in other countries. What does he mean, and why is that a potential problem?

**Sources:** Timothy Noah, "MooLatte, Bested," *Slate*, accessed June 11, 2006, http://slate.msn.com; "What's in a Name? For Cars, Everything," *Detroit News*, accessed June 11, 2006, http://www.detroitnews.com; Sergio Beristain, "Does Your Brand Register Abroad?" Brandchannel.com, accessed June 11, 2006, http://www.brandchannel.com; Ed Garsten and Brett Clanton, "A Tsunami by Any Other Name," *Time*, January 24, 2005, p. 17; Mark Lasswell, "Lost in Translation," *Business 2.0*, August 2004, pp. 68–70.

---

Thursday. Furthermore, Muslims abstain from alcohol and consider pork unclean, so gifts of pigskin or liquor would be offensive.

Some devout Muslims have raised concern about interest-bearing loans in their nations, such as car loans or home mortgages, which they fear are to be considered usury by the standards of the Qur'an. However, because Muslims have traditionally been traders, and because the Qur'an supports trade, such reservations are slowly being overcome with the help of arguments by Muslim scholars showing that usury implies that the lender is taking unjust advantage of the borrower. Ordinary loans, on the other hand, can help increase the value of the borrowers' assets or property, and they can also help achieve the goal of helping distribute wealth more widely.[11]

## Economic Differences

Business opportunities are flourishing in densely populated countries such as China and India, as local consumers eagerly buy Western products. Although such prospects might tempt American

Lack of infrastructure is a concern for global telecommunications. Chinese firm Huawei Technologies helped develop the industry in China, and it now provides network, data communications, and telecommunications products throughout the world through 8 regional headquarters and 55 branch offices outside China.

firms, managers must first consider the economic factors involved in doing business in these markets. A country's size, per-capita income, and stage of economic development are among the economic factors to consider when evaluating it as a candidate for an international business venture.

*Infrastructure*   Along with other economic measures, businesses should consider a country's **infrastructure.** Infrastructure refers to basic systems of communication (telecommunications, television, radio, and print media), transportation (roads and highways, railroads, and airports), and energy facilities (power plants and gas and electric utilities). The Internet and technology use can also be considered part of infrastructure.

Many consumers in the United States, western Europe, Japan, and Hong Kong own cell phones. Even most of their children have their own phones. So the availability of telecommunications technology creates fertile soil for Internet businesses that use wireless communication. There are about 1.5 billion mobile phone users worldwide, for instance. In rural Kenya, some of the country's 3 million mobile phone users share a phone with several other people, but they enjoy inexpensive text messaging for about a third the cost of sending an e-mail over the country's often unreliable Internet service. A Kenyan firm called OneWorld International has sprung up that puts employers and job seekers in almost instant touch with each other through subscriptions to text messages carried by mobile phone. "The service has an advantage," says a human resource employee for Softa Bottling Company. "It reaches as many people as possible within the shortest time." In fact, about 5,000 people have already signed up for the job search service, which also distributes public health information about AIDS and cancer.[12]

Financial systems also provide a type of infrastructure for businesses. In the United States, buyers have widespread access to checks, credit cards, and debit cards, as well as electronic systems for processing these forms of payment. In many African countries, such as Ethiopia, local businesses do not accept credit cards, so travelers to the capital city, Addis Ababa, are warned to bring plenty of cash and traveler's checks.

*Currency Conversion and Shifts*   Despite growing similarities in infrastructure, businesses crossing national borders encounter basic economic differences: national currencies. Foreign currency fluctuations may present added problems for global businesses. As explained earlier in the chapter, the values of the world's major currencies fluctuate in relation to each other. Rapid and unexpected currency shifts can make pricing in local currencies difficult. Shifts in exchange rates can also influence the attractiveness of various business decisions. A devalued currency may make a nation less desirable as an export destination because of reduced demand in that market. However, devaluation can make the nation desirable as an investment opportunity because investments there will be a bargain in terms of the investor's currency.

## Political and Legal Differences

Like social, cultural, and economic differences, legal and political differences in host countries can pose barriers to international trade. Advocates for children in Britain have long fought to ban television advertising aimed at kids. With concerns for childhood obesity on the rise and blame being laid at the door of fast-food advertising, Turner Broadcasting plans a new cartoon series for British TV that will promote fruit and vegetables to young audiences. The program is offered free to other broadcasters. "We wanted to counter the possible negative effects of advertising on kids' TV," says general manager Richard Kilgariff, "but [the program] quickly developed into a positive project to provide parents and broadcasters with a tool to fight obesity."[13]

To compete in today's world marketplace, managers involved in international business must be well versed in legislation that affects their industries. Some countries impose general trade restrictions. Others have established detailed rules that regulate how foreign companies can operate. The one consistency among all countries is the striking lack of consistent laws and regulations governing the conduct of business.

*Political Climate*   An important factor in any international business investment is the stability of the political climate. The political structures of many nations promote stability similar to that in the United States. Other nations, such as Indonesia, Congo, and Bosnia, feature quite different—and frequently changing—structures. Host nations often pass laws designed to protect their own interests, sometimes at the expense of foreign businesses.

In recent years, the political structures of Russia, Turkey, the former Yugoslavia, Hong Kong, and several central European countries including the Czech Republic and Poland have seen dramatic changes. Such political changes almost always bring changes in the legal environment. Hong Kong's status as part of China makes it an economy where political developments produced changes in the legal and cultural environments. Since the collapse of the Soviet Union, Russia has struggled to develop a new market structure and political processes.

*Legal Environment*   When conducting business internationally, managers must be familiar with three dimensions of the legal environment: U.S. law, international regulations, and the laws of the countries where they plan to trade. Some laws protect the rights of foreign companies to compete in the United States. Others dictate actions allowed for U.S. companies doing business in foreign countries.

The *Foreign Corrupt Practices Act* forbids U.S. companies from bribing foreign officials, political candidates, or government representatives. This act prescribes fines and jail time for U.S. managers who are aware of illegal payoffs. Until recently, many countries, including France and Germany, not only accepted the practice of bribing foreign officials in countries where such practices were customary but allowed tax deductions for these expenses. The United States, France, Germany, and 33 other countries recently signed the Organization for Economic Cooperation and Development Anti-Bribery Convention. This agreement makes offering or paying bribes a criminal offense and ends the deductibility of bribes.[14]

Still, corruption continues to be an international problem. Its pervasiveness, combined with U.S. prohibitions, creates a difficult obstacle for Americans who want to do business in many foreign countries. Chinese pay *huilu*, and Russians rely on *vzyatka*. In the Middle East, palms are greased with *baksheesh*. Figure 4.3 compares 102 countries based on surveys of perceived corruption. This Corruption Perceptions Index is computed by Transparency International, a Berlin-based international organization that rates the degree of corruption observed by businesspeople and the general public.

The growth of online business has introduced new elements to the legal climate of international business. Patents, brand names, trademarks, copyrights, and other intellectual property are difficult to police, given the availability of information on the Internet. However, some countries are adopting laws to protect information obtained by electronic contacts. Malaysia imposes stiff fines and long jail terms on those convicted of illegally accessing computers and using information that passes through them.

*International Regulations*   To regulate international commerce, the United States and many other countries have ratified treaties and signed agreements that dictate the conduct of international business and protect some of its activities. The United States has entered into

Figure

4.3    Corruption in Business and Government

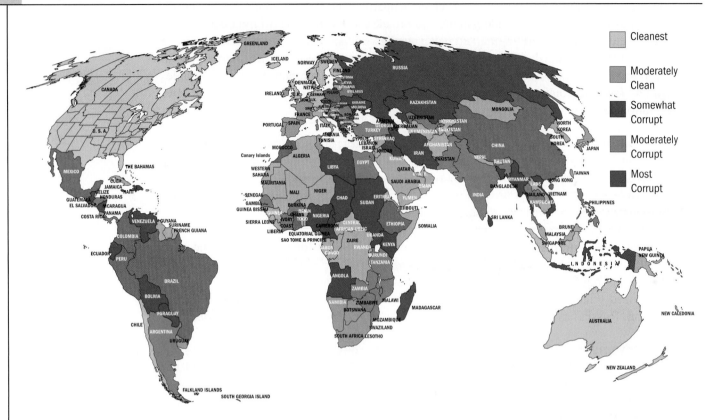

Cleanest

Moderately Clean

Somewhat Corrupt

Moderately Corrupt

Most Corrupt

**Source:** Data from Transparency International, "Transparency International Annual Corruption Perceptions Index," Internet Center for Corruption Research, http://en.wikipedia.org/wiki/Corruption_Perceptions_Index.

many *friendship, commerce, and navigation treaties* with other nations. Such treaties address many aspects of international business relations, including the right to conduct business in the treaty partner's domestic market. Other international business agreements involve product standards, patents, trademarks, reciprocal tax policies, export controls, international air travel, and international communications.

When Congress granted China full trade relations with the United States, China agreed to lower trade barriers, including subsidies that held down the prices of food exports, restrictions on where foreign law firms can open offices, and taxes charged on imported goods. In exchange for China's promise to halve these taxes, called *tariffs*, the United States granted Chinese businesses equal access to U.S. markets enjoyed by most other countries.

Many types of regulations affect the actions of managers doing business in international markets. Not only must worldwide producers and marketers maintain required minimum quality levels for all the countries in which they operate, but they must comply with numerous specific local regulations. Britain prevents advertisers from encouraging children to engage in such unhealthy behavior as overeating or replacing regular meals with candy and snack foods. Malaysia's Censorship Board prohibits nudity and profanity on TV. Germany and France allow publishers to set prices that retailers charge for their books. Because companies such as Amazon.com adhere to the fixed prices, German customers looking for English-language books can get better prices by buying at the U.K. Web site, even with the extra shipping costs.

A lack of international regulations or difficulty in enforcement can generate its own set of problems. Software piracy offers an example, particularly in Asia. More than 90 percent of all software used in Vietnam, for instance, is pirated, making it the biggest offender against intellectual property rights laws and regulations enforced by the World Trade Organization (WTO) worldwide. Close behind Vietnam were Ukraine, China, Zimbabwe, and Indonesia. Translated into dollars, that level of piracy means a loss of about a third of the software industry's annual revenue of $90 billion, according to a regional director for the Business Software Alliance, a worldwide watchdog agency. Contrary to claims that buying software legally is too expensive, the director said, "If you can afford the hardware, you can afford the software." But piracy remains widespread, despite WTO sanctions against offending nations. And with the number of Internet users expected to rise in China alone by about 100 million people over the next few years, enforcement efforts are likely to increase.[15]

## Types of Trade Restrictions

Trade restrictions such as taxes on imports and complicated administrative procedures create additional barriers to international business. They may limit consumer choices while increasing the costs of foreign-made products. Trade restrictions are also imposed to protect citizens' security, health, and jobs. A government may limit exports of strategic and defense-related goods to unfriendly countries to protect its security, ban imports of insecticide-contaminated farm products to protect health, and restrict imports to protect domestic jobs in the importing country.

Other restrictions are imposed to promote trade with certain countries. Still others protect countries from unfair competition. Regardless of the political reasons for trade restrictions, most take the form of tariffs. In addition to tariffs, governments impose a number of nontariff—or administrative—barriers. These include quotas, embargoes, and exchange controls.

*Tariffs*   Taxes, surcharges, or duties on foreign products are referred to as **tariffs**. Governments assess two types of tariffs—revenue and protective tariffs—both of which make imports more expensive for domestic buyers. Revenue tariffs generate income for the government. Upon returning home, U.S. leisure travelers who are out of the country more than 48 hours and who bring back goods purchased abroad must pay import taxes on their value in excess of $200 to $1,600, depending on the country of origin. This duty goes directly to the U.S. Treasury. The sole purpose of a protective tariff is to raise the retail price of imported products to match or exceed the prices of similar products manufactured in the home country. In other words, protective tariffs seek to level the playing field for local competitors.

**tariff** tax imposed on imported goods.

Of course, tariffs create a disadvantage to companies that want to export to the countries imposing the tariffs. In addition, governments do not always agree on the reasons behind protective tariffs. So they do not always have the desired effect. The U.S. imposes a tariff on foreign competitors accused of selling products at lower prices in the United States than U.S. manufacturers charge. The government recently passed a bill giving the money from these tariffs directly to U.S. plaintiff companies, instead of to the Treasury as in the past. In retaliation, U.S. exports of paper, textiles, machinery, farm products, oysters, and other products to Canada, Brazil, Chile, India, South Korea, and Mexico will be subject to punitive tariffs of 15 percent, which may end up costing U.S. exporters as much as $150 million a year, a number some observers say will only grow.[16]

*Nontariff Barriers*   Nontariff, or administrative, trade barriers restrict imports in more subtle ways than tariffs. These measures may take such forms as quotas on imports, restrictive standards for imports, and export subsidies. Because many countries have recently substantially reduced tariffs or eliminated them entirely, they increasingly use nontariff barriers to control flows of imported products.

**Quotas** limit the amounts of particular products that countries can import during specified time periods. Limits may be set as quantities, such as number of cars or bushels of wheat, or as values, such as dollars' worth of cigarettes. Governments regularly set quotas for agricultural products and sometimes for imported automobiles. Although the U.S. government had previously imposed about 1,000 quotas related to clothing imports from various countries, many of them have now been lifted. Recently, however, quotas on three categories of clothing from China were reinstated, following claims by U.S. manufacturers that the lifting of quotas had created a huge flow of inexpensive cotton garments that might endanger thousands of jobs.[17]

Quotas help prevent **dumping,** a practice that developed during the 1970s. In one form of dumping, a company sells products abroad at prices below its cost of production. In another, a company exports a large quantity of a product at a lower price than the same product in the home market and drives down the price of the domestic product. Dumping benefits domestic consumers in the importing market, but it hurts domestic producers. It also allows companies to gain quick entry to foreign markets.

More severe than a quota, an **embargo** imposes a total ban on importing a specified product or even a total halt to trading with a particular country. Embargo durations can vary to accommodate changes in foreign policy. The U.S. government recently rejected a United Nations resolution opposing the United Sates' long-standing trade embargo on Cuba.

Another form of administrative trade restriction is **exchange controls.** Imposed through a central bank or government agency, exchange controls affect both exporters and importers. Firms that gain foreign currencies through exporting are required to sell them to the central bank or another agency. Importers must buy foreign currencies to pay for their purchases from the same agency. The exchange control authority can then allocate, expand, or restrict foreign exchange in accordance with national policy.

**assessment check**

1. How might values and attitudes form a barrier to trade, and how can they be overcome?
2. What is a tariff? What is its purpose?
3. Why is dumping a problem for companies marketing goods internationally?

# REDUCING BARRIERS TO INTERNATIONAL TRADE

Although tariffs and administrative barriers still restrict trade, overall the world is moving toward free trade. Several types of organizations ease barriers to international trade, including groups that monitor trade policies and practices and institutions that offer monetary assistance. Another type of federation designed to ease trade barriers is the multinational economic community, such as the European Union. This section looks at the roles these organizations play.

## Organizations Promoting International Trade

For the 60 years of its existence, the **General Agreement on Tariffs and Trade (GATT),** an international trade accord, sponsored a series of negotiations, called rounds, that substantially reduced worldwide tariffs and other barriers. Major industrialized nations founded the multinational organization in 1947 to work toward reducing tariffs and relaxing import quotas. The last set of negotiations—the Uruguay Round—cut average tariffs by one-third, in excess of $700 billion; reduced farm subsidies; and improved protection for copyright and patent holders. In addition, international trading rules now apply to various service industries. Finally, the new agreement established the **World Trade Organization (WTO)** to succeed GATT. This organization includes representatives from 149 countries.

**World Trade Organization** Since 1995, the WTO has monitored GATT agreements among the member nations, mediated disputes, and continued the effort to reduce trade barriers through-

**World Trade Organization (WTO)** 149-member international institution that monitors GATT agreements and mediates international trade disputes.

out the world. Unlike provisions in GATT, the WTO's decisions are binding on parties involved in disputes.

The WTO has grown more controversial in recent years as it issues decisions that have implications for working conditions and the environment in member nations. Concerns have been expressed that the WTO's focus on lowering trade barriers encourages businesses to keep costs down through practices that may increase pollution and human rights abuses. Particularly worrisome is the fact that the organization's member countries must agree on policies, and developing countries tend not to be eager to lose their low-cost advantage by enacting stricter labor and environmental laws. Other critics claim that if well-funded U.S. firms such as fast-food chains, entertainment companies, and Internet retailers can freely enter foreign markets, they will wipe out smaller foreign businesses serving the distinct tastes and practices of other countries' cultures.

Trade unions in developed nations complain that the WTO's support of free trade makes it easier to export manufacturing jobs to low-wage countries. According to the U.S. Department of Commerce, about a million U.S. jobs are lost each year as a result of imports or movement of work to other countries, and the pace of the migration has increased in the last few years. They are not always minimum-wage jobs either. But many small and midsized firms have benefited from the WTO's reduction of trade barriers and lowering of the cost of trade. They currently make up 97 percent of all firms that export goods and services, according to the Department of Commerce. "Trade is now seamless and global," says Randy Tofteland, CEO of SoftBrands, a Minneapolis firm with 500 employees that sells software for the hospitality industry. "Those that take advantage of it are going to be the long-term winners."[18]

The most recent round of WTO talks was called the *Doha Round* after the city in Qatar where it began. After several years of heated disputes and collapsed negotiations, the eight leading industrial nations committed themselves to successful conclusion of the talks. Under discussion were ways to improve global agricultural trade and trade among developing countries. The leaders worked to reduce domestic price supports, eliminate export subsidies, and improve market access for goods. Such changes should help farmers in developing countries compete in the global market.[19]

Although free trade can indeed contribute to economic growth and change, including the creation of new jobs, concerns about WTO policy have led to protest demonstrations—sometimes violent—beginning with the WTO meeting in Seattle a few years ago.

*World Bank*  Shortly after the end of World War II, industrialized nations formed an organization to lend money to less developed and developing countries. The **World Bank** primarily funds projects that build or expand nations' infrastructure such as transportation, education, and medical systems and facilities. The World Bank and other development banks provide the largest source of advice and assistance to developing nations. Often, in exchange for granting loans, the World Bank imposes requirements intended to build the economies of borrower nations.

The World Bank has been criticized for making loans with conditions that ultimately hurt the borrower nations. When developing nations are required to balance government budgets, they are sometimes forced to cut vital social programs. Critics also say that the World Bank should consider the impact of its loans on the environment and the treatment of workers.

*International Monetary Fund*  Established a year after the World Bank, the **International Monetary Fund (IMF)** was created to promote trade through financial cooperation and, in the process, eliminate barriers. The IMF makes short-term loans to member nations that are unable to meet their expenses. It operates as a lender of last resort for troubled nations. In exchange for these emergency loans, IMF lenders frequently require significant commitments from the borrowing nations to address the problems that led to the crises. These steps may include curtailing imports or even devaluing currencies. Throughout its existence, the IMF has worked to prevent financial crises by warning the international business community when countries encounter problems meeting their financial obligations. Often, the IMF lends to countries to keep them from defaulting on prior debts and to prevent economic crises in particular countries from spreading to other nations.

However, some countries owe far more money than they can ever hope to repay, and the debt payments make it impossible for their governments to deliver desperately needed services to their citizens. The nations of sub-Saharan Africa are hard-pressed to deal with the ravages of AIDS, yet their debt exceeds their GDP and is three times as high as their total annual exports. The so-called Group of Eight economic powers—the United States, Britain, France, Germany, Japan, Italy, Canada, and Russia—recently agreed to offer full debt relief to African countries that are working toward government reforms on behalf of education and welfare.[20]

## International Economic Communities

International economic communities reduce trade barriers and promote regional economic integration. In the simplest approach, countries may establish a *free-trade area* in which they trade freely among themselves without tariffs or trade restrictions. Each maintains its own tariffs for trade outside this area. A *customs union* sets up a free-trade area and specifies a uniform tariff structure for members' trade with nonmember nations. In a *common market*, or economic union, members go beyond a customs union and try to bring all of their trade rules into agreement.

One example of a free-trade area is the **North American Free Trade Agreement (NAFTA)** enacted by the United States, Canada, and Mexico. Other examples of regional trading blocs include the MERCOSUR customs union (joining Brazil, Argentina, Paraguay, Uruguay, Chile, and Bolivia) and the ten-country Association of South East Asian Nations (ASEAN).

## NAFTA

NAFTA became effective in 1994, creating the world's largest free-trade zone with the United States, Canada, and Mexico. With a combined population of more than 435 million and a total GDP of nearly $14 trillion, North America represents one of the world's most attractive markets. The United States—the single largest market and one of the world's most stable economies—dominates North America's business environment. Although fewer than 1 person in 20 lives in the United States, the nation's more than $11 trillion GDP represents about one-fifth of total world output.[21]

Canada is far less densely populated but has achieved a similar level of economic development. In fact, Canada's economy is booming and has been growing at a faster rate than the U.S. economy in recent years. More than two-thirds of Canada's GDP is generated in the services sector, and three of every four Canadian workers are engaged in service occupations. The country's per-capita GDP places Canada in the top ten nations in terms of its people's spending power. Canada's economy is fueled by trade with the United States, and its home markets are strong as well. The United States and Canada are each other's biggest trading partners. About 85 percent of Canada's exports and about 60 percent of its imports are to or from the United States.[22] U.S. business is also attracted by Canada's human resources. For instance, all major U.S. automakers have large production facilities in Canada.

**North American Free Trade Agreement (NAFTA)** agreement among the United States, Canada, and Mexico to break down tariffs and trade restrictions.

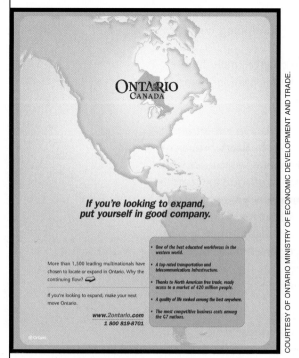

**ONTARIO** CANADA

*If you're looking to expand, put yourself in good company.*

More than 1,500 leading multinationals have chosen to locate or expand in Ontario. Why the continuing flow?

If you're looking to expand, make your next move Ontario.

www.2ontario.com
1 800 819-8701

- One of the best educated workforces in the western world.
- A top-rated transportation and telecommunications infrastructure.
- Thanks to North American free trade, ready access to a market of 420 million people.
- A quality of life ranked among the best anywhere.
- The most competitive business costs among the G7 nations.

COURTESY OF ONTARIO MINISTRY OF ECONOMIC DEVELOPMENT AND TRADE.

This message from Ontario, Canada, promotes the province's favorable business climate. The ad states that more than 1,500 multinational companies are located there and highlights the province's low basic business costs and educated workforce.

Mexico is moving from developing nation to industrial nation status, thanks largely to NAFTA. Mexico's trade with the United States and Canada has tripled since the signing of NAFTA, although 40 percent of the country's 106 million people still live below the poverty line and per-capita income is a quarter that of the United States.[23] But Mexico's border with the United States is busy with a nearly endless stream of traffic transporting goods from Mexican factories into the United States. Along its so-called NAFTA Highway between Nuevo Laredo, Mexico, and Laredo, Texas, $52 billion worth of appliances, auto parts, computers, and other goods made the trip in a recent year—amounting to 38 percent of all Mexican exports to the United States.[24]

By eliminating all trade barriers and investment restrictions among the United States, Canada, and Mexico over a fifteen-year period, NAFTA opens more doors for free trade. The agreement also eases regulations governing services, such as banking, and establishes uniform legal requirements for protection of intellectual property. The three nations can now trade with one another without tariffs or other trade barriers, simplifying shipments of goods across the partners' borders. Standardized customs and uniform labeling regulations create economic efficiencies and smooth import and export procedures. Trade among the partners has increased steadily, more than doubling since NAFTA took effect.

## CAFTA

Passed by Congress and signed by President Bush in 2005, the **Central American Free Trade Agreement (CAFTA)** created a free-trade area among the United States, Costa Rica, the Dominican Republic, El Salvador, Guatemala, Honduras, and Nicaragua. The agreement ends most tariffs on nearly $33 billion in products traded between the United States and its Latin American neighbors. Agricultural producers such as corn, soybean, and dairy farmers stand to gain under the relaxed trade rules. U.S. sugar producers, which were supported by subsidies keeping their prices higher than the rest of the world's, fought against CAFTA's passage. And labor unions complained that the agreement would lower labor standards and export millions more jobs to lower-wage countries. But overall, CAFTA's effects should be positive, increasing both exports and imports substantially, much as NAFTA did.[25]

**Central American Free Trade Agreement (CAFTA)** agreement among the United States, Costa Rica, the Dominican Republic, El Salvador, Guatemala, Honduras, and Nicaragua to reduce tariffs and trade restrictions.

**European Union (EU)** 25-nation European economic alliance.

## European Union

Perhaps the best-known example of a common market is the **European Union (EU)**. The EU combines 25 countries, more than 450 million people, and a total GDP exceeding $12 trillion to form a huge common market.[26] As Figure 4.4 shows, ten countries—Cyprus, Malta, Estonia, Latvia, Lithuania, Hungary, Poland, the Czech Republic, Slovakia, and Slovenia—are the latest EU members. Some observers think the EU's efforts to unite Europe suffered a setback after two countries, France and the Netherlands, voted against the proposed constitution intended to make the organization run more smoothly after its recent enlargement from 15 to 25 states. All 25 must ratify the constitution before it can take effect.[27]

**Figure 4.4**

The 25 Nations of the European Union

Twelve of the European Union member states use the euro (€) and so quote prices in that currency (left). Denmark, Sweden, and Great Britain (£) still use their traditional currency, the pound note.

The EU's goals include promoting economic and social progress, introducing European citizenship as a complement to national citizenship, and giving the EU a significant role in international affairs. To achieve its goal of a borderless Europe, the EU is removing barriers to free trade among its members. This highly complex process involves standardizing business regulations and requirements, standardizing import duties and taxes, and eliminating customs checks so that companies can transport goods from England to Italy or Poland as easily as from New York to Boston.

Unifying standards and laws can contribute to economic growth. But just as NAFTA sparked fears in the United States about free trade with Mexico, some people in western Europe worried that opening trade with such countries as Poland, Hungary, and the Czech Republic would cause jobs to flow eastward to lower-wage economies.

The EU also introduced the euro to replace currencies such as the French franc and Italian lira. For the twelve member states that have already adopted the euro, potential benefits include eliminating the economic costs of currency exchange and simplifying price comparisons. Businesses and their customers now make check and credit card transactions in euros and use euro notes and coins in making cash purchases.

**assessment check**

1. What international trade organization succeeded GATT and what is its goal?

2. Compare and contrast the goals of the World Bank and the International Monetary Fund.

3. Identify the members of NAFTA and briefly explain how it works.

4. What are the goals of the European Union and how do they promote international trade?

## GOING GLOBAL

While expanding into overseas markets can increase profits and marketing opportunities, it also introduces new complexities to a firm's business operations. Before deciding to go global, a company faces a number of key decisions, beginning with the following:

- Determining which foreign market(s) to enter
- Analyzing the expenditures required to enter a new market
- Deciding the best way to organize the overseas operations

These issues vary in importance depending on the level of involvement a company chooses. Education and employee training in the host country would be much more important for an electronics manufacturer building an Asian factory than for a firm that is simply planning to export American-made products.

The choice of which markets to enter usually follows extensive research focusing on local demand for the firm's products, availability of needed resources, and ability of the local workforce to produce world-class quality. Other factors include existing and potential competition, tariff rates, currency stability, and investment barriers. A variety of government and other sources are available to facilitate this research process. A good starting place is the CIA's *World Factbook*, which contains country-by-country information on geography, population, government, economy, and infrastructure.

U.S. Department of Commerce counselors at the agency's district offices offer a full range of international business advice, including computerized market data and names of business and government contacts in dozens of countries. As Table 4.3 shows, the Internet provides access to many resources for international trade information.

## Levels of Involvement

After a firm has completed its research and decided to do business overseas, it can choose one or more strategies:

- Exporting or importing
- Entering into contractual agreements such as franchising, licensing, and subcontracting deals
- Direct investment in the foreign market through acquisitions, joint ventures, or establishment of an overseas division

Although the company's risk increases with the level of its involvement, so does its overall control of all aspects of producing and selling its goods or services.

Companies frequently combine more than one of these strategies. Web portal Yahoo! used joint ventures with local firms to gain a quick presence in Japan, Britain, France, Germany, and South Korea. Only after developing experience as an international company has Yahoo! begun to engage in direct investment by creating foreign subsidiaries. Waiting to develop expertise before moving overseas is risky for online businesses, though, because Web sites are so easy for competitors to copy. Alando, an auction Web site based in Germany, looked remarkably like eBay. Rather than fight the company, eBay entered Germany by acquiring Alando.

**Table 4.3**

International Trade Research Resources on the Internet

| Web Site and Address | General Description |
|---|---|
| Asia, Inc.<br>http://www.asia-inc.com | Business news in Asia, featuring articles on Asian countries from India to Japan |
| Europages<br>http://www.europages.com | Directory of and links to Europe's top 500,000 companies in 33 European countries |
| World Trade Organization<br>http://www.wto.int | Details on the trade policies of various governments |
| CIA World Factbook<br>http://www.cia.gov/cia/publications/factbook | Basic facts about the world's nations, from geography to economic conditions |
| STAT-USA<br>http://www.stat-usa.gov | Extensive trade and economic data, information about trends, daily intelligence reports, and background data (access requires paid subscription to the service) |
| U.S. Commercial Service<br>http://www.export.gov/comm_svc | Information about Commerce Department counseling services, trade events, and U.S. export regulations |
| U.S. Business Advisor<br>http://www.business.gov | One-stop access to a range of federal government information, services, and transactions |
| U.S. State Department<br>http://www.travel.state.gov/travel/cis_pa_tw/tw/tw_1764.html | Listing of the State Department's latest travel warnings about conditions that may affect safety abroad, supplemented by the list of consulate addresses and country information |

*Importers and Exporters*   When a firm brings in goods produced abroad to sell domestically, it is an importer. Conversely, companies are exporters when they produce—or purchase—goods at home and sell them in overseas markets. An importing or exporting strategy provides the most basic level of international involvement, with the least risk and control.

Roots, a Canadian clothing manufacturer, has used its success as the chosen outfitter of the U.S. and Canadian Olympic teams to expand its apparel and sportswear brands into the United States and Asia. The company already has 140 stores in Canada and about 70 in Korea, 12 in Taiwan, and 5 in the United States. Roots earns about $200 million in annual sales and now sells eyewear, watches, and fragrance as well.[28]

Exports are frequently handled by special intermediaries called export trading companies. These firms search out competitively priced local merchandise and then resell it abroad at prices high enough to cover expenses and earn profits. When a retail chain such as Dallas-based Pier One Imports wants to purchase West African products for its store shelves, it may contact an export trading company operating in a country such as Ghana. The local firm is responsible for monitoring quality, packaging the order for transatlantic shipment, arranging transportation, and arranging for completion of customs paperwork and other steps required to move the product from Ghana to the United States.

Firms engage in exporting of two types: indirect and direct. A company engages in *indirect exporting* when it manufactures a product, such as an electronic component, that becomes part of another product that is sold in foreign markets. The second method, *direct exporting*, occurs when a company seeks to sell its products in markets outside its own country, as Red Bull does with its energy drink, which is discussed in the "Hit & Miss" feature. Often the first step for companies entering foreign markets, direct exporting is the most common form of international business. Firms that succeed in exporting their products may then move on to other entry strategies.

In addition to reaching foreign markets by dealing with export trading companies, exporters may choose two other alternatives: export management companies and offset agreements. Rather than simply relying on an export trading company to assist in foreign markets, an exporting firm may turn to an *export management company* for advice and expertise. These international specialists help the exporter complete paperwork, make contacts with local buyers, and comply with local laws governing labeling, product safety, and performance testing. At the same time, the exporting firm retains much more control than would be possible with an export trading company.

An *offset agreement* matches a small business with a major international firm. It basically makes the small firm a subcontractor to the larger one. Such an entry strategy helps a new exporter by allowing it to share in the larger company's international expertise. The small firm also benefits in such important areas as international transaction documents and financing, while the larger company benefits from the local expertise and capabilities of its smaller partner.

*Countertrade*   A sizable share of international trade involves payments made in the form of local products, not currency. This system of international bartering agreements is called **countertrade.**

A common reason for resorting to international barter is inadequate access to needed foreign currency. To complete an international sales agreement, the seller may agree to accept part or all of the purchase cost in merchandise rather than currency. Because the seller may decide to locate a buyer for the bartered goods before completing the transaction, a number of international buyers and sellers frequently join together in a single agreement.

Countertrade may often be a firm's only opportunity to enter a particular market. Many developing countries simply cannot obtain enough credit or financial assistance to afford the

## Red Bull Charges into Global Markets

Few people would expect a drink with a sour berry taste, an outsized price, and ingredients such as amino acid taurine and a carbohydrate called glucuronolactone to capture half of the U.S. energy drink market. But that's exactly what Austrian-based Red Bull has done.

After successfully branching out across Europe, the drink was introduced in the United States with the slogan "Red Bull Gives You Wings." Red Bull packs 80 milligrams of caffeine per 8.3-ounce can, more than twice as much as found in 12 ounces of Coke, and nearly as many calories—110 to the larger Coke's 140. It owes the ingredients taurine and glucuronolactone to the recipe for a tonic discovered in Asia by CEO Dietrich Mateschitz. But the sugar and caffeine, with carbonation added for Western palates, have helped popularize it. College students, club patrons, fans of extreme sports, and truck drivers all pay $2 a can for Red Bull's jolt.

"When we first started, we said there is no existing market for Red Bull, but Red Bull will create it," says Mateschitz. The drink has benefited from an unusual marketing campaign, funded by 30 percent of annual revenues. The Coca-Cola Company, by comparison, spends less than 10 percent of revenues on marketing. Saturating the market with samples, sponsoring hun-

dreds of aspiring athletes, and staging extreme sports events around the world are just a few of the strategies that help increase U.S. sales about 40 percent a year. What could be more appropriate for a hip energy drink than sponsoring a flying contest in which all the flying machines are homemade?

The company is also test-marketing an herbal tea that claims to boost the immune system, and Mateschitz believes many new products lie ahead. "We have the next hundred years in front of us," he says.

### Questions for Critical Thinking

1. Do you think it was a smart move to introduce Red Bull throughout Europe before exporting it to the United States? Why or why not?
2. Red Bull sells well in more than 100 countries. What do you think accounts for its success in so many different cultures?

**Sources:** "Red Bull Founder Rides Wave of Success," 2004 Global Business Influentials, CNN.com, accessed June 11, 2006, http://cnnstudentnews.cnn.com; Christopher Palmeri, "Hansen Natural: Charging at Red Bull with a Brawny Energy Brew," *BusinessWeek*, June 6, 2005, pp. 74–77; Kerry A. Dolan, "The Soda with Buzz," *Forbes*, March 28, 2005, pp. 126–130.

imports that their people want. Countries with heavy debt burdens also resort to countertrade. Russian buyers, whose currency is often less acceptable to foreign traders than the stronger currencies of countries such as the United States, Great Britain, Japan, and EU countries, may resort to trading local products ranging from crude oil to diamonds to vodka as payments for purchases from foreign companies unwilling to accept Russian rubles. Still other countries, such as China, may restrict imports. Under such circumstances, countertrade may be the only practical way to win government approval to import needed products.

**Contractual Agreements**   Once a company, large or small, gains some experience in international sales, it may decide to enter into contractual agreements with local parties. These arrangements can include franchising, foreign licensing, and subcontracting.

**Franchising**   Common among U.S. companies, franchising can work well for companies seeking to expand into international markets, too. A **franchise**, as described in detail in Chapter 5, is a contractual agreement in which a wholesaler or retailer (the franchisee) gains the right to sell the franchisor's products under that company's brand name if it agrees to the related operating requirements. The franchisee can also receive marketing, management, and

Hello Kitty is a worldwide product-licensing phenomenon. Sanrio, the Japanese company that owns the cartoon character, gets nearly $500 million in revenue each year from the furry feline. Shown here perched on a mobile phone, Hello Kitty has also adorned keychains, screen savers, bracelets, pillows, and tens of thousands of other items in its 30-year-plus history.

business services from the franchisor. While these arrangements are common among leading fast-food brands such as McDonald's and KFC, other kinds of service providers also often look to franchising as an international marketplace option.

Domino's Pizza has expanded by about 1,200 franchised stores over the last few years, and two-thirds of them are outside the United States. The pizza company's largest international market is in Mexico, where it is bigger than McDonald's and Burger King combined, and it is also succeeding in Taiwan and Japan. To entice Chinese consumers, who are more interested in dining out than in having food delivered, the chain is trying larger stores with eating areas.[29]

**Foreign Licensing**  In a **foreign licensing agreement,** one firm allows another to produce or sell its product, or use its trademark, patent, or manufacturing processes, in a specific geographical area. In return, the firm gets a royalty or other compensation.

Licensing can be advantageous for a small manufacturer eager to launch a well-known product overseas. Not only does it get a proven product from another market, but little or no investment is required to begin operating. The arrangement can also allow entry into a market otherwise closed to imports due to government restrictions. The popular Hello Kitty cartoon character, for instance, appears on about 22,000 different products around the world at any given time, with hundreds of new items appearing every month as old ones are "retired." Sanrio, the Japanese company that owns the character, produces about 6,000 Hello Kitty items itself. It licenses the wide-eyed cat to other manufacturers such as a winery that makes a Hello Kitty Beaujolais and Mitsubishi, which made a pink Hello Kitty minicar for several years. Other license holders have made Hello Kitty laptops, cell phones, thermoses, and even computer USB hubs and a luxury trailer from Airstream.[30]

**Subcontracting**  The third type of contractual agreement, **subcontracting,** involves hiring local companies to produce, distribute, or sell goods or services. This move allows a foreign firm to take advantage of the subcontractor's expertise in local culture, contacts, and regulations. Subcontracting works equally well for mail-order companies, which can farm out order fulfillment and customer service functions to local businesses. Manufacturers practice subcontracting to save money on import duties and labor costs, and businesses go this route to market products best sold by locals in a given country. Some firms, such as Maryland-based Pacific Bridge Medical, help medical manufacturers find reliable subcontractors and parts suppliers in Asia.[31] Whirlpool, the appliance maker, subcontracts to India and China the manufacture of many of its products, particularly washing machines and refrigerators intended for sale in local markets. These household appliances often require subtle design changes to conform to Asian consumers' needs.[32]

A key disadvantage of subcontracting is that companies cannot always control their subcontractors' business practices. Several major U.S. companies have been embarrassed by reports that their subcontractors used child labor to manufacture clothing.

*Offshoring*  While it is not generally considered a way of initiating business internationally, *offshoring,* or the relocation of business processes to a lower-cost location overseas, has become a widespread practice. China has emerged as the preferred destination for production off-

# ARE MANUFACTURERS TAKING ADVANTAGE OF THE AMERICAN JOBS CREATION ACT?

*The American Jobs Creation Act of 2004 was an attempt to keep manufacturing jobs in the United States The act granted tax relief to U.S. manufacturers based on the portion of income derived from domestic production. The income ceiling was limited to 50 percent of wages.*

The law also created a 9 percent tax deduction to be phased in over six years, repealed export taxes, imposed a one-year moratorium on foreign profits reinvested in the United States, and gave small business capital investment breaks. But lobbyists for various special interests ensured that about 200,000 different manufacturers got the tax breaks, sometimes by stretching the definition of a manufacturing job. For instance, some of the coffee baristas at Starbucks were counted as manufacturing industry workers, along with employees of movie theaters, shopping malls, and NASCAR. The net result in terms of tax revenue lost and jobs created or saved remains to be seen.

*Is it ethical for firms to interpret the American Jobs Creation Act in ways that allow the greatest possible tax break, if the purpose is to save jobs?*

## PRO

1. U.S. manufacturers pay higher tax rates than in any other industrialized country, and they need tax relief to remain competitive and keep jobs at home.
2. The bill is beneficial because it also closes loopholes that allowed businesses to avoid taxes by sending jobs overseas.

## CON

1. It is never ethical to stretch a law for any purpose other than what lawmakers intended.
2. Including industries that are not true manufacturers will deprive the government of revenue it could use to strengthen business and save jobs in other ways such as retraining programs.

## Summary

The law's effect, in terms of tax revenue and jobs, is still uncertain at this point. The National Association of Manufacturers (NAM) is very optimistic, however. "Over the next 10 years, this landmark legislation will save U.S. manufacturers billions of dollars and create hundreds of thousands of new jobs," said NAM president and former Michigan governor John Engler.

**Sources:** "President Bush Signs Important Tax Relief for America's Job Creators," press release, House Committee on Ways and Means, accessed June 11, 2006, http://waysandmeans.house.gov; "NAM Says New Tax Measure Is Great News for American Companies and Workers," National Association of Manufacturers, accessed June 11, 2006, http://www.nam.org; Bill Thomas, "Industry Tax Relief Rewards," *Washington Times*, accessed June 11, 2006, http://www.washtimes.com; "Landmark Business Tax Relief Bill Signed into Law," National Association of Manufacturers, accessed June 11, 2006, http://www.nam.org.

solving an **ETHICAL** controversy

shoring, and India for services offshoring. Many business leaders argue, in favor of offshoring, that global firms must keep their costs as low as possible to remain competitive. But the apparent link between jobs sent overseas and jobs lost at home has made the practice controversial. Legislatures of various states have tried to slow the tide of offshoring through new laws, but many observers believe the real goal should be to improve corporate research and development efforts in the United States. Education reforms, professional retraining, and investment in research and development are among the initiatives cited by a recent survey of professionals in business, government, and higher education.[33] The "Solving an Ethical Controversy" feature considers the effects of the new American Jobs Creation Act, which was intended to slow the loss of jobs to overseas labor markets.

In the meantime, offshoring allows firms such as San Jose–based PortalPlayer, a manufacturer of hardware and software for MP3 media players, to operate almost around the clock. They work with colleagues in India with a twelve-hour time difference. "We keep passing the baton between California and India, and that way, we can cram a lot more work into a 24-hour period," says PortalPlayer's vice president.[34]

**"They Said It"**

"Outsourcing is just a new way of doing international trade."
—N. Gregory Mankiw (b. 1958)
Former chairman, Council of Economic Advisers

*International Direct Investment* Investing directly in production and marketing operations in a foreign country is the ultimate level of global involvement. Over time, a firm may become successful at conducting business in other countries through exporting and contractual agreements. Its managers may then decide to establish manufacturing facilities in those countries, open branch offices, or buy ownership interests in local companies.

In an *acquisition*, a company purchases another existing firm in the host country. An acquisition permits a largely domestic business operation to gain an international presence very quickly. This advantage was probably what made the purchase of IBM's ailing Personal Computing Division so attractive to Lenovo Group, the largest PC manufacturer in China. The acquisition boosts Lenovo's share of the Chinese PC market to about a third; in comparison, Dell has about 8 percent. Anchored by a large investment in the company by the Chinese government, which isn't pushing for the quick profits most Western companies must deliver, Lenovo stands poised to make a big impact both at home and abroad. "This is the big experiment," said an information technology consultant. "China is already the factory of the world. Now they're testing whether they can raise the value of that output."[35]

**Joint ventures** allow companies to share risks, costs, profits, and management responsibilities with one or more host country nationals. H. J. Heinz's European unit recently acquired a majority stake in Petrosoyuz, a top Russian maker of mayonnaise, ketchup, and other condiments and sauces. The two companies formed a new joint venture company to market the products in Russia and its neighbors in Eastern Europe. The CEO of Heinz Europe said of the move, "This joint venture is consistent with our European strategy to build our core businesses in the rapidly emerging markets of eastern Europe. Additionally, it will give Heinz access to local market understanding that will allow us to expand sales of other popular Heinz brands and products throughout Russia."[36]

By setting up an *overseas division*, a company can conduct a significant amount of its business overseas. This strategy differs from that of a multinational company in that a firm with overseas divisions remains primarily a domestic organization with international operations. Panasonic and General Electric, for instance, both rely on overseas divisions. Panasonic's Automotive Systems Company, headquartered in Japan, has overseas divisions in the United States, Mexico, Germany, China, Thailand, Taiwan, and the Czech Republic.[37] General Electric's energy technology company, GE Energy, has headquarters in Atlanta and divisions in Barcelona; Florence, Italy; and Shanghai. Its transportation division has locations in Canada, Italy, and Brazil.[38]

**assessment check**

1. Name three possible strategies for beginning overseas business operations.
2. What is countertrade?
3. Compare and contrast licensing and subcontracting.
4. Describe joint ventures.

## From Multinational Corporation to Global Business

A **multinational corporation (MNC)** is an organization with significant foreign operations. As Table 4.4 shows, firms headquartered in the United States make up half the list of the world's largest multinationals. The United Kingdom and the Netherlands have two companies each, and Japan's Toyota Motor rounds out the top ten.

Many U.S. multinationals, including Nike and Wal-Mart, have expanded their overseas operations because they believe that domestic markets are peaking and foreign markets offer greater sales and profit potential. Other MNCs are making substantial investments in developing countries in part because these countries provide low-cost labor compared with the United States and western Europe. In addition, many MNCs are locating high-tech facilities in countries with large numbers of technical school graduates, such as India.

**multinational corporation (MNC)** firm with significant operations and marketing activities outside its home country.

**Table**

**4.4**

The World's Leading Companies (Based on a Combined Ranking for Sales, Profits, Assets, and Market Value)

| Rank and Company | Business | Country of Origin |
| --- | --- | --- |
| 1. Citigroup | Banking | United States |
| 2. General Electric | Conglomerate | United States |
| 3. Bank of America | Banking | United States |
| 4. American International Group | Insurance | United States |
| 5. HSBC Group | Banking | United Kingdom |
| 6. Exxon Mobil | Oil and gas | United States |
| 7. Royal Dutch/Shell Group | Oil and gas | Netherlands |
| 8. BP (British Petroleum) | Oil and gas | United Kingdom |
| 9. JPMorgan Chase | Financial Services | United States |
| 10. UBS | Financial Services | Switzerland |

**Source:** "The World's Leading Companies," *Forbes*, accessed May 19, 2006, http://www.forbes.com.

# DEVELOPING A STRATEGY FOR INTERNATIONAL BUSINESS

In developing a framework in which to conduct international business, managers must first evaluate their corporate objectives, organizational strengths and weaknesses, and strategies for product development and marketing. They can choose to combine these elements in either a global strategy or a multidomestic strategy.

## Global Business Strategies

In a **global business** (or *standardization*) **strategy**, a firm sells the same product in essentially the same manner throughout the world. Many companies simply modify their domestic business strategies by translating promotional brochures and product-use instructions into the languages of the host nations. Toyota adapts its marketing not only to international markets but to consumer segments within nations. The company's new Scion model is aimed at U.S. youth.[39]

A global marketing perspective can be appropriate for some goods and services and certain market segments that are common to many nations. The approach works for products with nearly universal appeal and for luxury items such as jewelry. But food retailers such as McDonald's, PepsiCo, and KFC have discovered how much they must adapt their products to consumer tastes in China, for instance. Spinach, egg, and tomato soup is on KFC's menu in China, as are red-bean sundaes at McDonald's. PepsiCo's Frito-Lay chips are lemon-flavored and packaged in pastel colors to accommodate Chinese consumers' love of product flavors and designs that suggest coolness in hot weather. The redesigned chips became Lay's best-selling new product in China.[40] Scientific equipment, on the other hand, is not bound by geographical differences.

**global business strategy** offering a standardized, worldwide product and selling it in essentially the same manner throughout a firm's domestic and foreign markets.

## Multidomestic Business Strategies

**multidomestic business strategy** developing and marketing products to serve different needs and tastes of separate national markets.

Under a **multidomestic business** (or *adaptation*) **strategy,** the firm treats each national market in a different way. It develops products and marketing strategies that appeal to the customs, tastes, and buying habits of particular national markets. Companies that neglect the global nature of the Internet can unwittingly cause problems for potential customers by failing to adapt their strategy. European consumers, for instance, were at first hesitant to adopt online ordering of products ranging from books to railroad tickets. But in recent years, Internet use in western Europe has grown dramatically. Companies as diverse as the European divisions of Amazon.com; Egg PLC of London, an online financial services company; and the French national railroad have seen the numbers of visitors to their Web sites climbing, along with Internet revenues.

**assessment check**

1. What is a global business strategy? What are its advantages?
2. What is a multidomestic business strategy? What are its advantages?

# WHAT'S AHEAD

Examples in this chapter indicate that both large and small businesses are relying on world trade, not just major corporations. Chapter 5 examines the special advantages and challenges that small-business owners encounter. In addition, a critical decision facing any new business is the choice of the most appropriate form of business ownership. Chapter 5 also examines the major ownership structures—sole proprietorship, partnership, and corporation—and assesses the pros and cons of each. The chapter closes with a discussion of recent trends affecting business ownership, such as the growing impact of franchising and business consolidations through mergers and acquisitions.

## SUMMARY OF LEARNING GOALS

**1** **Explain the importance of international business and the primary reasons nations trade.**

The United States is both the world's largest importer and the largest exporter, although less than 5 percent of the world's population lives within its borders. With the increasing globalization of the world's economies, the international marketplace offers tremendous opportunities for U.S. and foreign businesses to expand into new markets for their goods and services. Doing business globally provides new sources of materials and labor. Trading with other countries also reduces a company's dependence on economic conditions in its home market. Countries that encourage international trade enjoy higher levels of economic activity, employment, and wages than those that restrict it.

### Assessment Check Answers

**1.1 Why do nations trade?**

Nations trade because trading boosts economic growth by providing a market for products and access to

needed resources. This makes production and distribution systems more efficient and reduces dependence on the economy of the domestic market.

**1.2 Cite some measure of the size of the international marketplace.**

Though developing countries have lower per-capita incomes than developed nations in North America and western Europe, their populations are large and growing. China's population is almost 1.3 billion and India's is roughly 1.1 billion.

**2** **Discuss the concepts of absolute and comparative advantage in international trade.**

Nations usually benefit if they specialize in producing certain goods or services. A country has an absolute advantage if it holds a monopoly or produces a good or service at a lower cost than other nations. It has a comparative advantage if it can supply a particular product more efficiently or at a lower cost than it can produce other items.

## Assessment Check Answers

**2.1 Define *absolute advantage*.**
Absolute advantage means a country can maintain a monopoly in or produce a product at lower cost than any other competitor.

**2.2 How does a nation acquire a comparative advantage?**
Comparative advantage exists when a nation can supply a product more efficiently and at a lower price than it can supply other goods, compared with the outputs of other countries.

**3 Describe how nations measure international trade and the significance of exchange rates.**
Countries measure the level of international trade by comparing exports and imports and then calculating whether a trade surplus or a deficit exists. This is the balance of trade, which represents the difference between exports and imports. The term *balance of payments* refers to the overall flow of money into or out of a country, including overseas loans and borrowing, international investments, and profits from such investments. An exchange rate is the value of a nation's currency relative to the currency of another nation. Currency values typically fluctuate, or "float," relative to the supply and demand for specific currencies in the world market. When the value of the dollar falls compared with other currencies, the cost paid by foreign businesses and households for U.S. products declines, and demand for exports may rise. An increase in the value of the dollar raises the prices of U.S. products sold abroad, but it reduces the prices of foreign products sold in the United States.

## Assessment Check Answers

**3.1 Compare balance of trade and balance of payments.**
Balance of trade is the difference between exports and imports; balance of payments is the overall flow of money into or out of a country.

**3.2 Explain the function of an exchange rate.**
A nation's exchange rate is the rate at which its currency can be exchanged for the currencies of other nations to make it easier for them to trade with one another.

**3.3 What happens when a currency is devalued?**
Devaluation describes a fall in a currency's value relative to other currencies or to a fixed standard.

**4 Identify the major barriers that confront global businesses.**
Businesses face several obstacles in the global marketplace. Companies must be sensitive to social and cultural differences, such as languages, values, and religions, when operating in other countries. Economic differences include standard-of-living variations and levels of infrastructure development. Legal and political barriers are among the most difficult to judge. Each country sets its own laws regulating business practices. Trade restrictions such as tariffs and administrative barriers also present obstacles to international business.

## Assessment Check Answers

**4.1 How might values and attitudes form a barrier to trade, and how can they be overcome?**
Marked differences in values and attitudes, such as religious attitudes, can form barriers between traditionally capitalist countries and those adapting new capitalist systems. Many of these can be overcome by learning about and respecting such differences.

**4.2 What is a tariff? What is its purpose?**
A tariff is a surcharge or duty charged on foreign products. Its purpose is to protect domestic producers of those items.

**4.3 Why is dumping a problem for companies marketing goods internationally?**
Dumping is selling products abroad at prices below the cost of production or exporting products at a lower price than charged in the home market. It drives the cost of domestic products sharply down.

**5 Explain how international trade organizations and economic communities reduce barriers to international trade.**
Many international organizations seek to promote international trade by reducing barriers. Examples include the World Trade Organization, the World Bank, and the International Monetary Fund. Multinational economic communities create partnerships to remove barriers to flows of goods, capital, and people across the borders of member nations. Three such economic agreements are the North American Free Trade Agreement, the Central American Free Trade Agreement, and the European Union.

## Assessment Check Answers

**5.1 What international trade organization succeeded GATT, and what is its goal?**

The World Trade Organization (WTO) succeeded GATT with the goal of monitoring GATT agreements, mediating disputes, and continuing the effort to reduce trade barriers throughout the world.

### 5.2 Compare and contrast the goals of the World Bank and the International Monetary Fund.

The World Bank funds projects that build or expand nations' infrastructure such as transportation, education, and health systems and facilities. The International Monetary Fund makes short-term loans to member nations that are unable to meet their budgets. The fund operates as a lender of last resort.

### 5.3 Identify the members of NAFTA and briefly explain how it works.

NAFTA created a free-trade zone between the United States, Canada, and Mexico by eliminating trade barriers and investment restrictions among them, as well as easing regulations on services such as banking and establishing uniform rules for protection of intellectual property.

### 5.4 What are the goals of the European Union and how do they promote international trade?

The European Union's goals include promoting economic and social progress, introducing European citizenship as a complement to national citizenship, and giving the EU a significant role in international affairs. Unifying standards and laws is expected to contribute to international trade and economic growth.

### 6 Compare the different levels of involvement used by businesses when entering global markets.

Exporting and importing, the first level of involvement in international business, involves the lowest degree of both risk and control. Companies may rely on export trading or management companies to help distribute their products. Contractual agreements such as franchising, foreign licensing, and subcontracting offer additional, flexible options. Franchising and licensing are especially appropriate for services. Companies may also choose local subcontractors to produce goods for local sales. International direct investment in production and marketing facilities provides the highest degree of control but also the greatest risk. Firms make direct investments by acquiring foreign companies or facilities, forming joint ventures with local firms, and setting up their own overseas divisions.

## Assessment Check Answers

### 6.1 Name three possible strategies for beginning overseas business operations.

Strategies are exporting or importing; contractual agreements such as franchising, licensing, or subcontracting; and making direct investments in foreign markets through acquisition, joint venture, or establishment of an overseas division.

### 6.2 What is countertrade?

Countertrade consists of payments made in the form of local products, not currency.

### 6.3 Compare and contrast licensing and subcontracting.

In a foreign licensing agreement, one firm allows another to produce or sell its product or use its trademark, patent, or manufacturing process in a specific geographical area in return for royalty payments or other compensations. In subcontracting a firm hires local companies abroad to produce, distribute, or sell its goods and services.

### 6.4 Describe joint ventures.

Joint ventures allow companies to share risks, costs, profits, and management responsibilities with one or more host country nationals.

### 7 Distinguish between a global business strategy and a multidomestic business strategy.

A company that adopts a global (or standardization) strategy develops a single, standardized product and marketing strategy for implementation throughout the world. The firm sells the same product in essentially the same manner in all countries in which it operates. Under a multidomestic (or adaptation) strategy, the firm develops a different treatment for each foreign market. It develops products and marketing strategies that appeal to the customs, tastes, and buying habits of particular nations.

## Assessment Check Answers

### 7.1 What is a global business strategy? What are its advantages?

A global business strategy specifies a standardized competitive strategy in which the firm sells the same product in essentially the same manner throughout the world. It works well for goods and services that are common to many nations and allows the firm to market them without making significant changes.

### 7.2 What is a multidomestic business strategy? What are its advantages?

A multidomestic business strategy allows the firm to treat each foreign market in a different way to appeal to the customs, tastes, and buying habits of particular national markets. It allows the firm to customize its marketing appeals for individual cultures or areas.

## Business Terms You Need to Know

exports 92
imports 92
balance of trade 96
balance of payments 96
exchange rate 97
tariff 105

World Trade Organization (WTO) 106
North American Free Trade Agreement (NAFTA) 108
Central American Free Trade Agreement (CAFTA) 109

European Union (EU) 109
multinational corporation (MNC) 116
global business strategy 117
multidomestic business strategy 118

## Other Important Business Terms

devaluation 97
infrastructure 102
quotas 105
dumping 106
embargo 106
exchange control 106

General Agreement on Tariffs and Trade (GATT) 106
World Bank 107
International Monetary Fund (IMF) 107
countertrade 112

franchise 113
foreign licensing agreement 114
subcontracting 114
joint ventures 116

## Review Questions

1. How does a business decide whether to trade with a foreign country? What are the key factors for participating in the information economy on a global basis?
2. Why are developing countries such as China and India becoming important international markets?
3. What is the difference between absolute advantage and comparative advantage? Give an example of each.
4. Can a nation have a favorable balance of trade and an unfavorable balance of payments? Why or why not?
5. Identify several potential barriers to communication when a company attempts to conduct business in another country. How might these be overcome?
6. Identify and describe briefly the three dimensions of the legal environment for global business.
7. What are the major nontariff restrictions affecting international business? Describe the difference between tariff and nontariff restrictions.
8. What is NAFTA? How does it work?
9. How has the EU helped trade in European businesses?
10. What are the key choices a company must make before reaching the final decision to go global?

1. When Britain transferred Hong Kong to China in 1997, China agreed to grant Hong Kong a high degree of autonomy as a capitalist economy for 50 years. Do you think this agreement will hold up? Why or why not? Consider China's economy, population, infrastructure, and other factors in your answer.

2. The tremendous growth of online business has introduced new elements to the legal climate of international business. Patents, brand names, copyrights, and trademarks are difficult to monitor because of the boundaryless nature of the Internet. What steps could businesses take to protect their trademarks and brands in this environment? Come up with at least five suggestions and compare your list with your classmates'.

3. The WTO monitors GATT agreements, mediates disputes, and continues the effort to reduce trade barriers throughout the world. However, widespread concerns have been expressed that the WTO's focus on lowering trade barriers may encourage businesses to keep costs down through practices that may lead to pollution and human rights abuses. Others argue that human rights should not be linked to international business. Do you think environmental and human rights issues should be linked to trade? Why or why not?

4. The IMF makes short-term loans to developing countries that may not be able to repay them. Do you agree that the IMF should forgive these debts in some cases? Why or why not?

5. Describe briefly the EU and its goals. What are the pros and cons of the EU? Do you predict that the European alliance will hold up over the next 20 years? Why or why not?

6. Use the most recent edition of "The Fortune Global 500," which is published in *Fortune* magazine normally in late July or early August, or go to *Fortune*'s online version at http://money.cnn.com/magazines/fortune/global500, to answer the following questions.

   a. On what is the Global 500 ranking based (for example, profits, number of employees, revenues)?

   b. Among the world's ten largest corporations, list the countries represented with the number of companies from each nation.

   c. Identify the top-ranked company, along with its Global 500 ranking and country, for the following industry classifications: Food and Drug Stores; Industrial and Farm Equipment; Petroleum Refining; Utilities: Gas and Electric; Telecommunications; Pharmaceuticals.

## Exporting to Afghanistan

In the landlocked country of Afghanistan, devastated by a generation of war and repression, efficient transportation is a rarity. There are only 15 miles of railroad in the country's almost 250,000 square miles, and less than 2,000 miles of paved roads. Despite aggressive efforts by the Ministry of Communication, there are only about 12,000 working telephones in the capital city of Kabul, with a population of nearly 2 million people. Though tens of thousands of refugees have returned during the reconstruction efforts of the last several years, more than 4 million people of the country's population of about 29 million still live outside their country.

The United States is at the head of the massive reconstruction of Afghanistan, and experts believe there will be export opportunities in the recovering nation for years to come. But with almost no business infrastructure such as roads, phones, and hotels, no sales and distribution channels, and little available skilled labor to hire, foreign investment will be painfully slow to flourish. Streamlined licensing procedures and tools for international dispute resolution that are now in place should help.

However, local interpreters and drivers are considered essential for those who know enough about the country, its geography, and its culture and language to transact business on Afghan soil.

The U.S. Department of Commerce warns that limited purchasing power in Afghanistan will dictate the pace of export opportunities. But basic industries that can help Afghans in their reconstruction efforts will likely find markets first. The country desperately needs architectural, construction, telecommunications, and engineering services—as well as goods such as construction materials and building equipment, computer hardware, telecommunications equipment, diesel-powered generators, security and safety equipment, and office furniture. Medium- and long-term needs include aircraft, aircraft parts, and airport and ground-support equipment.

Social change is sure to come, though it may be slow. Exporters should not overlook the chance to do business with Afghan women. "There are barriers," says Sara Rahmani, who runs a new and growing clothing business. "We are recovering from war and devastation and Taliban repression. . . . But there's nothing in Shariah [Islamic law] that says women can't do business."

### Questions for Critical Thinking

1. A Commerce Department task force on Afghanistan warns that "only the most experienced, well-informed, and open-minded traveler should consider visiting Afghanistan." What difficulties do you think a business traveler to Kabul would need to overcome? How could he or she prepare for such a trip and ensure its success?

2. It is expected that lower-cost and possibly lower-quality goods and services from Pakistan and Iran will compete with U.S. exports to Afghanistan in the coming years. What can U.S. companies wishing to export to Afghanistan do to combat such competition?

**Sources:** Matthew Pennington, "Women Go into Business in Afghanistan," *Casper (WY) Star Tribune*, accessed June 11, 2006, http://www.casperstartribune .net; U.S. Department of State, "Background Note: Afghanistan," accessed June 11, 2006, http://www.state .gov; Afghanistan Investment and Reconstruction Task Force, "Traveling to and Doing Business in Afghanistan," U.S. Department of Commerce, accessed June 11, 2006, http://www.export.gov/afghanistan.

---

**VIDEO** **Case 4.2**

### Cold Stone Creamery Cools off Consumers around the World

This video case appears on page 611. A recently filmed video, designed to expand and highlight the written case, is available for class use by instructors.

# The Legal Framework for Business

## CLASS-ACTION FAIRNESS

We've all shopped around for the best deal on a car, computer, or sound system. But have you ever heard of lawyers shopping around for clients willing to sue or for the best state courts for their trials? Certain states or counties did seem to reward plaintiffs filing class-action lawsuits with much higher figures than elsewhere. A *class-action suit* groups a number of small plaintiffs, as many as hundreds of thousands of them, to allow for efficient processing under one lawsuit. And the rules for the location of those trials were loose, allowing lawyers to pick locations with juries likely to be favorable to their suits. Certainly, businesses that create defective products that hurt consumers or commit fraud need to be held accountable, and everyone is sympathetic to those who've been harmed. But the mushrooming of frivolous lawsuits was imposing huge fines on businesses and hampering their ability to compete. Critics also said that the lawyers bringing the suits sometimes benefited much more than their clients, receiving percentages of the entire settlement well beyond the work they did. Eventually, the U.S. Chamber of Commerce, legislators, and others called for a change. It came in the form of the **Class-Action Fairness Act of 2005.**

Before the reform, many companies facing such an action, whether it involved a faulty medication or a defective TV, complained that plaintiffs' lawyers shopped around for sympathetic courts. The Class-Action Fairness Act of 2005 imposes certain restrictions on such suits. First, it automatically moves most large, multistate class actions—those with potential damages exceeding $5 million and in which more than two-thirds of the plaintiffs are geographically dispersed—from state courts into federal courts. This restriction prevents "shopping around" in different states for sympathetic courts but lets cases that belong within a particular state remain there. Second, judges must consider the actual monetary value of any damage done so that plaintiffs receive true compensation for injury instead of large—and perhaps arbitrary—awards.

A third major provision of the law affects the way attorneys receive payment for their legal representation. Under the old system, an attorney would usually receive a percentage of the gross settlement amount, regardless of whether all plaintiffs bothered to collect. Now judges can require that any uncollected rewards be given to charities or government organizations, and attorneys may

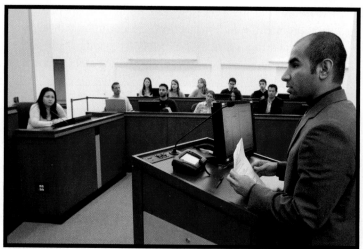

not include those rewards in calculating their fees. Also, if the attorney's fee was not based on a percentage, then it must be based on time actually spent working on the case. Finally, the act ensures that plaintiffs' interests are protected equally with their lawyers'.

Critics of the Class-Action Fairness Act claim that it will suppress legitimate consumer claims, while supporters believe that it will protect jobs and businesses by exposing them to less risk. If it is successful, both consumers and businesses could experience something new: fairness.[1]

# OVERVIEW

The first four chapters of the text show how important the legal environment is to business, government, and the general public and how changes occur to rectify problems. The corporate governance failures discussed in Chapter 2 continue to be addressed throughout the book. In the aftermath of corporate wrongdoing, charges against and convictions of business leaders like Tyco's Dennis Kozlowski and WorldCom's Bernard Ebbers, and the bankruptcies of such firms as Enron and WorldCom, we have seen the passage of new laws designed to end abuses by unethical business executives. In addition, we have seen criminal charges against wayward business leaders end in convictions. Bernard Ebbers, former CEO of WorldCom, was convicted of securities fraud, conspiracy, and filing false documents with regulators.[2] These events have also led to new regulations restricting investment advisors, accountants, and board members in their oversight responsibilities. A business environment of personal greed and excess is being cleaned up to reflect the demands of ethical business leaders, government officials, investors, and the general public.

On a more personal level, you may be frustrated by all the junk e-mail (called *spam*) you receive, in addition to pop-up messages. Also, those annoying telephone solicitations became so pervasive that a Do Not Call law was enacted, making it illegal to call anyone listed on the federal do-not-call roster maintained by the Federal Trade Commission.

Legal issues affect every aspect of business. In fact, most of the remaining chapters will discuss legislation that specifically affects the business functions analyzed in each chapter. Already, an overview of the legal environment was presented in Chapter 2, and legislation affecting international operations was covered in Chapter 4. Chapter 5 discusses laws related to small businesses. Laws regarding human resources management and labor unions are examined in Chapter 9. Laws affecting other business operations, such as environmental regulations and product safety, are one of the topics in Chapter 13, and marketing-related legislation is examined in Chapter 14. Finally, legislation pertaining to banking and the securities markets is discussed in Chapters 17 and 18. In this appendix, we provide an overall perspective of legislation at the federal, state, and local levels, and point out that, while business executives may not be legal experts, they do need to be knowledgeable in their specific area of responsibility. A good dose of common sense also helps avoid potential legal problems.

Despite the best efforts of most businesspeople, legal cases do arise. A dispute may arise over a contract, an employee may protest being passed over for a promotion, or a town may challenge the environmental impact of a new gas station. Unfortunately, the United States has the dubious distinction of being the world's most litigious society. Lawsuits are as common as business deals. Consider Wal-Mart, which is involved in up to 7,000 legal cases at any one time. Even if you are never involved in a lawsuit, the cost still affects you. The average U.S. family pays a hidden "litigation tax" of $2,900 each year because of the costs of lawsuits that force businesses to increase their prices.[3] Small businesses, including doctors' offices, are often the hardest hit and may cut back on their services or close.

On the lighter side, every day there are news reports of proposed new laws intended to protect businesses, consumers, and the general public—but somehow miss the mark. One Texas legislator proposed a law prohibiting weather forecasters from calling themselves "meteorologists" unless they had a certain degree. In Oklahoma, another legislator tried to revive the cockfighting industry—which was banned in his state—by proposing that fighting roosters wear miniature boxing gloves and protective vests. Neither bill was passed.[4]

This appendix looks at the general nature of business law, the court system, basic legal concepts, and finally the changing regulatory environment for U.S. business. Let's start with some initial definitions and related examples.

# LEGAL SYSTEM AND ADMINISTRATIVE AGENCIES

The **judiciary**, or court system, is the branch of government responsible for settling disputes among parties by applying laws. This branch consists of several types and levels of courts, each with a specific jurisdiction. Court systems are organized at the federal, state, and local levels. Administrative agencies also perform some limited judicial functions, but these agencies are more properly regarded as belonging to the executive or legislative branches of government.

At both the federal and state levels, **trial courts**—courts of general jurisdiction—hear a wide range of cases. Unless a case is assigned by law to another court or to an administrative agency, a court of general jurisdiction will hear it. The majority of cases, both criminal and civil, pass through these courts. Within the federal system, trial courts are known as *U.S. district courts*, and at least one such court operates in each state. In the state court systems, the general jurisdiction courts are often called *circuit courts*, and states typically provide one for each county. Other names for general jurisdiction courts are superior courts, common pleas courts, or district courts.

State judiciary systems also include many courts with lower, or more specific, jurisdictions. In most states, parties can appeal the decisions of these lower courts to the general jurisdiction courts. Examples of lower courts are probate courts—which settle the estates of people who have died—and small-claims courts—where people can represent themselves in suits involving limited amounts of money. For example, a landlord might go to small-claims court to settle a dispute with a tenant over a security deposit.

Appeals of decisions made at the general trial court level are heard by **appellate courts.** Both the federal and state systems have appellate courts; for instance, the U.S. Court of Appeals for the Seventh Circuit, located in Chicago, covers Illinois, Indiana, and Wisconsin.[5] The appeals process allows a higher court to review the case and correct any lower court error indicated by the appellant, the party making the appeal.

Appeals from decisions of the U.S. circuit courts of appeals can go all the way to the nation's highest court, the U.S. Supreme Court. Appeals from state courts of appeal are heard by the highest court in each state, usually called the *state supreme court*. In a state without intermediate appellate courts, the state supreme court hears appeals directly from the trial courts. Parties who are not satisfied by the verdict of a state supreme court can appeal to the U.S. Supreme Court and may be granted a hearing if they can cite grounds for such an appeal and if the Supreme Court considers the case significant enough to be heard. In a typical year, the Supreme Court hears roughly 1 percent of the 7,500 cases filed.[6]

While most cases are resolved by the system of courts described here, certain highly specialized cases require particular expertise. Examples of specialized federal courts are the U.S. Tax Court for tax cases and the U.S. Court of Claims, which hears claims against the U.S. government itself. Similar specialized courts operate at the state level.

Administrative agencies, also known as bureaus, commissions, or boards, decide a variety of cases at all levels of government. These agencies usually derive their powers and responsibilities from state or federal statutes. Technically, they conduct hearings or inquiries rather than trials. Examples of federal administrative agencies are the Federal Trade Commission (FTC), the National Labor Relations Board, and the Federal Energy Regulatory Commission. Examples at the state level include public utility commissions and boards that govern the licensing of various trades and professions. Zoning boards, planning commissions, and boards of appeal operate at the city or county level. The FTC has the broadest power of any of the federal regulatory agencies. It enforces laws regulating unfair business practices, and it can stop false and deceptive advertising practices.

# TYPES OF LAW

**Law** consists of the standards set by government and society in the form of either legislation or custom. This broad body of principles, regulations, rules, and customs that govern the actions of all members of society, including businesspeople, is derived from several sources. **Common law** refers to the body of law arising out of judicial decisions, some of which can be traced back to early England. For example, in some states, an unmarried couple who has lived together for a certain period of time is said to be legally husband and wife by common law.

**Statutory law,** or written law, includes state and federal constitutions, legislative enactments, treaties of the federal government, and ordinances of local governments. Statutes must be drawn precisely and reasonably to be constitutional, and thus enforceable. Still, courts must frequently interpret their intentions and meanings.

With the growth of the global economy, a knowledge of international law becomes crucial. **International law** refers to the numerous regulations that govern international commerce. Companies must be aware of the domestic laws of trading partners, trade agreements such as NAFTA, and the rulings of such organizations as the World Trade Organization. International law affects trade in all kinds of industries. Recently, the Canadian government announced it would add a 15 percent surtax on such diverse products as oysters, pigs, and cigarettes from the United States. This action is in response to the Continued Dumping and Subsidy Offset Act (commonly called the Byrd Amendment), which distributes proceeds the United States collects to firms, primarily U.S. steel companies. The World Trade Organization declared the Byrd Amendment illegal. "Retaliation is not our preferred option, but it is a necessary action," stated former Canadian trade minister Jim Peterson. "International trade rules must be respected."[7]

In a broad sense, all law is business law because all firms are subject to the entire body of law, just as individuals are. In a narrower sense, however, **business law** consists of those aspects of law that most directly influence and regulate the management of various types of business activity. Specific laws vary widely in their intent from business to business and from industry to industry. The legal interests of airlines, for example, differ from those of oil companies.

State and local statutes also have varying applications. Some state laws affect all businesses that operate in a particular state. Workers' compensation laws, which govern payments to workers for injuries incurred on the job, are an example. Other state laws apply only to certain firms or business activities. States have specific licensing requirements for businesses, such as law firms, funeral directors, and hair salons. Many local ordinances also deal with specific business activities. Local regulations on the sizes and types of business signs are commonplace. Some communities even restrict the sizes of stores, including height and square footage.

**law** standards set by government and society in the form of either legislation or custom.

**common law** body of law arising out of judicial decisions, some of which can be traced back to early England.

**statutory law** written law, including state and federal constitutions, legislative enactments, treaties of the federal government, and ordinances of local governments.

**business law** aspects of law that most directly influence and regulate the management of business activity.

# REGULATORY ENVIRONMENT FOR BUSINESS

Government regulation of business has changed over time. Depending on public sentiment, the economy, and the political climate, we see the pendulum swing back and forth between increased regulation and deregulation. But the goal of both types of legislation is protection of healthy competition. One industry that has experienced some deregulation in the past is still subject to relatively tight regulations: banking. Despite the relaxation of banking regulations across state lines and the advent of online banking, laws governing everything from stock trading to retirement investing remain strict. Recently, several bills were proposed in Congress to shore up the Pension Benefit Guaranty Corporation, an agency that is running at a $20 billion deficit, particularly after assuming the pensions of some bankrupt companies, including United Airlines. The agency is not funded by tax dollars—instead, it is financed by insurance premiums and investments. But the bills did not pass. When asked later about the agency's ability to continue to absorb such burdens, the chairman of the Federal Reserve noted that the agency's difficulties could be handled within current banking regulations.[8]

Let's look at the issues surrounding regulation and deregulation, and the legislation that has characterized them.

## Antitrust and Business Regulation

John D. Rockefeller's Standard Oil monopoly launched antitrust legislation. Breaking up monopolies and restraints of trade was a popular issue in the late 1800s and early 1900s. In fact, President Theodore Roosevelt always promoted himself as a "trust-buster." The highly publicized Microsoft case of the 1990s is an example of antitrust litigation.

During the 1930s, several laws designed to regulate business were passed. The basis for many of these laws was protecting employment. The world was in the midst of the Great Depression during the 1930s, so the government was focused on keeping its citizens employed. Recently, government officials became concerned with the security aspects of international business transactions, Internet usage, the sources of funds, and their effects on U.S. business practices. So, new regulatory legislation in the form of the USA Patriot Act was enacted in 2001. In 2005, Congress voted to extend most provisions of the Patriot Act indefinitely.[9]

The major federal antitrust and business regulation legislation includes the following:

| Law | What It Did |
| --- | --- |
| Sherman Act (1890) | Set a competitive business system as a national policy goal. The act specifically banned monopolies and restraints of trade. |
| Clayton Act (1914) | Put restrictions on price discrimination, exclusive dealing, tying contracts, and interlocking boards of directors that lessened competition or might lead to a monopoly. |
| Federal Trade Commission Act (1914) | Established the FTC with the authority to investigate business practices. The act also prohibited unfair methods of competition. |
| Robinson-Patman Act (1936) | Outlawed price discrimination in sales to wholesalers, retailers, or other producers. The act also banned pricing designed to eliminate competition. |
| Wheeler-Lea Act (1938) | Banned deceptive advertising. The act gave the FTC jurisdiction in such cases. |
| Patriot Act (2001; extended in 2005) | Limited interactions between U.S. and foreign banks to those with "know your customer" policies; allowed the U.S. Treasury Department to freeze assets and bar a country, government, or institution from doing business in the United States; gave federal authorities broad powers to monitor Internet usage and expanded the way data is shared among different agencies. |

## Business Deregulation

Deregulation was a child of the 1970s whose influence continues today. Many formerly regulated industries were freed to pick the markets they wanted to serve. The deregulated industries, such as utilities and airlines, were also allowed to price their products without the guidance of federal regulations. For the most part, deregulation led to lower consumer prices. In some cases, it also led to a loss of service. Many smaller cities and airports lost airline service for a while because of deregulation. But small and discount airlines such as Southwest and JetBlue began to focus on and serve those locations, with great success.

Following are several major laws related to deregulation:

| Law | What It Did |
| --- | --- |
| Airline Deregulation Act (1978) | Allowed airlines to set fares and pick their routes. |
| Motor Carrier Act and Staggers Rail Act (1980) | Permitted the trucking and railroad industries to negotiate rates and services. |
| Telecommunications Act (1996) | Cut barriers to competition in local and long-distance phone, cable, and television markets. |
| Gramm-Leach-Bliley Act (1999) | Permitted banks, securities firms, and insurance companies to affiliate within a new financial organizational structure; required them to disclose to customers their policies and practices for protecting the privacy of personal information. |

# CONSUMER PROTECTION

Many laws designed to protect consumers have been passed in the last 100 years. In many ways, business itself has evolved to reflect this focus on consumer safety and satisfaction. Following some widely publicized problems with brand-name prescription drugs such as Vioxx, the Food and Drug Administration (FDA) is more closely scrutinizing the accuracy of consumer advertisements for such products. However, the FDA does not have the legal authority to ban all consumer advertising for prescription drugs. It is up to the manufacturers and trade associations such as the Pharmaceutical Research and Manufacturers of America to set industry standards for advertising. Some companies have voluntarily opted to avoid advertising for the first year a prescription drug is available.[10]

The major federal laws related to consumer protection include the following:

| Law | What It Did |
| --- | --- |
| Federal Food and Drug Act (1906) | Banned adulteration and misbranding of foods and drugs involved in interstate commerce. |
| Consumer Credit Protection Act (1968) | Required disclosure of annual interest rates on loans and credit purchases. |
| National Environmental Policy Act (1970) | Established the Environmental Protection Agency to deal with various types of pollution and organizations that create pollution. |
| Public Health Cigarette Smoking Act (1970) | Prohibited tobacco advertising on radio and television. |
| Consumer Product Safety Act (1972) | Established the Consumer Product Safety Commission with authority to specify safety standards for most products. |
| Nutrition Labeling and Education Act (1990) | Stipulated detailed information on the labeling of most foods. |
| Dietary Supplement Health and Education Act (1994) | Established standards with respect to dietary supplements including vitamins, minerals, herbs, and amino acids. |

# EMPLOYEE PROTECTION

Chapters 2 and 9 cover many of the issues employers face in protecting their employees from injury and harm while on the job. But employees must also be protected from unfair practices by employers. Recently, concerned about the cutbacks on retiree medical benefits at age 65—when they are eligible for Medicare coverage—AARP (the American Association of Retired Persons) won a court decision protecting the health benefits of retired workers. Under the Age Discrimination in Employment Act, employers must provide the same coverage to all their retirees, regardless of their age.[11] Some of the relevant laws related to employee protection include the following:

| Law | What It Did |
| --- | --- |
| Fair Labor Standards Act (1938) | For hourly workers, provided payment of the minimum wage, overtime pay for time worked more than 40 hours in a workweek, restricted the employment of children, and required employers to keep records of wages and hours. |
| OSHA Act (1970) | Required employers to provide workers with workplaces free of recognized hazards that could cause serious injury or death and required employees to abide by all safety and health standards that apply to their jobs. |
| Americans with Disabilities Act (1991) | Banned discrimination against the disabled in public accommodations, transportation, and telecommunications. |
| Family and Medical Leave Act (1993) | Required covered employers to grant eligible employees up to twelve workweeks of unpaid leave during any twelve-month period for the birth and care of a newborn child of the employee, placement with the employee of a son or daughter for adoption or foster care, care of an immediate family member with a serious health condition, or medical leave for the employee if unable to work because of a serious health condition. |
| Uniformed Services Employment and Reemployment Rights Act (1994) | Protected the job rights of individuals who voluntarily or involuntarily leave their jobs to perform military service. Also prohibited employment discrimination in such cases. |
| American Jobs Creation Act (2004) | Reduced taxes for manufacturing in the United States, provided temporary tax breaks for income repatriated to the United States, and encouraged domestic job growth. |

# INVESTOR PROTECTION

Chapters 16, 17, and 18 describe the institutions subject to investor protection laws and some of the events that brought the Sarbanes-Oxley law into being. (See the entry in the following table for specific provisions of Sarbanes-Oxley.) Following is a summary of legislation to protect investors:

| Law | What It Did |
| --- | --- |
| Securities Exchange Act (1934) | Created the Securities and Exchange Commission with the authority to register, regulate, and oversee brokerage firms, transfer agents, clearing agencies, and stock exchanges; the SEC also has the power to enforce securities laws and protect investors in public transactions. |
| Bank Secrecy Act (1970) | Deterred laundering and use of secret foreign bank accounts; created an investigative paper trail for large currency transactions; imposed civil and criminal penalties for noncompliance with reporting requirements; improved detection and investigation of criminal, tax, and regulatory violations. |
| Sarbanes-Oxley Act (2002) | Required top corporate executives to attest to the validity of the company's financial statements; increased the documentation and monitoring of internal controls; prohibited CPA firms from providing some types of consulting services for their clients; established a five-member accounting oversight board. |

# CYBERSPACE AND TELECOMMUNICATIONS PROTECTION

Computers and widespread use of the Internet and telecommunications have dramatically expanded the reach of businesses. They have also raised some thorny issues such as computer fraud and abuse, online privacy, and cyberterrorism. Under a recent Supreme Court ruling, Internet file-sharing services are now held accountable if their intention is for consumers to use software to exchange songs and videos illegally. Although lower courts had ruled that file-sharing services such as Grokster and Streamcast couldn't be sued, the Supreme Court unanimously decided that there was enough evidence of unlawful intent on the part of these companies. This ruling also helps protect copyrights, which are covered later in this appendix.[12]

Following are some of the major laws enacted to regulate cyberspace and telecommunications:

| Law | What It Did |
| --- | --- |
| Computer Fraud and Abuse Act (1986) | Clarified definitions of criminal fraud and abuse for federal computer crimes and removed legal ambiguities and obstacles to prosecuting these crimes; established felony offenses for unauthorized access of "federal interest" computers and made it a misdemeanor to engage in unauthorized trafficking in computer passwords. |
| Children's Online Privacy Protection Act (1998) | Authorized the FTC to set rules regarding how and when firms must obtain parental permission before asking children marketing research questions. |
| Identity Theft and Assumption Deterrence Act (1998) | Made it a federal crime to knowingly transfer or use, without lawful authority, a means of identification of another person with intent to commit, aid, or abet any violation of federal, state, or local law. |
| Anticybersquatting Consumer Protection Act (1999) | Prohibited people from registering Internet domain names similar to company or celebrity names and then offering them for sale to these same parties |
| Homeland Security Act (2002) | Established the Department of Homeland Security; gave government wide new powers to collect and mine data on individuals and groups, including databases that combine personal, governmental, and corporate records including e-mails and Web sites viewed; limited information citizens can obtain under the Freedom of Information Act; gave government committees more latitude for meeting in secret. |
| Amendments to the Telemarketing Sales Rule (2003) | Created a national "do not call" registry, which prohibits telemarketing calls to registered telephone numbers; restricted the number and duration of telemarketing calls generating dead air space with use of automatic dialers; cracked down on unauthorized billing; and required telemarketers to transmit their Caller ID information. Telemarketers must check the do-not-call list quarterly, and violators could be fined as much as $11,000 per occurrence. Excluded from the registry's restrictions are charities, opinion pollsters, and political candidates. |
| Check Clearing for the 21st Century Act (2003) | Created a substitute check, allowing banks to process check information electronically and to deliver substitute checks to banks that want to continue receiving paper checks. A substitute check is the legal equivalent of the original check. |

# THE CORE OF BUSINESS LAW

Contract law and the law of agency; the Uniform Commercial Code, sales law, and negotiable instruments law; property law and the law of bailment; trademark, patent, and copyright law; tort law; bankruptcy law; and tax law are the cornerstones of U.S. business law. The sections that follow set out the key provisions of each of these legal concepts.

## Contract Law and Law of Agency

Contract law is important because it is the legal foundation on which business dealings are conducted. A **contract** is a legally enforceable agreement between two or more parties regarding a specified act or thing.

**Contract Requirements**   As Figure 1 points out, the four elements of an enforceable contract are agreement, consideration, legal and serious purpose, and capacity. The parties must reach *agreement* about the act or thing specified. For such an agreement, or contract, to be valid and legally enforceable, each party must furnish *consideration*—the value or benefit that a party provides to the others with whom the contract is made. Assume that a builder hires an electrician to install wiring in a new house. The wiring job and the resulting payment are the considerations in this instance. In addition to consideration, an enforceable contract must involve a *legal and serious purpose*. Agreements made as a joke or involving the commission of crimes are not enforceable as legal contracts. An agreement between two competitors to fix the prices for their products is not enforceable as a contract because the subject matter is illegal.

The last element of a legally enforceable contract is *capacity*, the legal ability of a party to enter into agreements. The law does not permit certain people, such as those judged to be insane, to enter into legally enforceable contracts. Contracts govern almost all types of business activities. You might sign a contract to purchase a car, to do a job for someone as a freelancer or outsourcer, or to lease an apartment.

**Breach of Contract**   A violation of a valid contract is called a **breach of contract.** The injured party can go to court to enforce the contract provisions and, in some cases, collect **damages**—financial payments to compensate for a loss and related suffering.

**Law of Agency**   All types of firms conduct business affairs through a variety of agents, such as partners, directors, corporate officers, and sales personnel. An **agency** relationship exists when one party, called the *principal*, appoints another party, called the *agent*, to enter into contracts with third parties on the principal's behalf.

The law of agency is based on common-law principles and case law decisions of state and federal courts. Relatively little agency law has been enacted into statute. The law of agency is important because the principal is generally bound by the actions of the agent.

The legal basis for holding the principal liable for acts of the agent is the Latin maxim *respondeat superior* ("let the master answer"). In a case involving agency law, the court must decide the rights and obligations of the various parties. Generally, the principal is held liable if an agency relationship exists and the agent has some type of authority to do the wrongful act. The agent in such cases is liable to the principal for any damages.

## Uniform Commercial Code

Most U.S. business law is based on the **Uniform Commercial Code**—usually referred to simply as the UCC. The UCC covers topics such as sales law, warranties, and negotiable instruments. All 50 states have adopted the UCC, although Louisiana also relies on the Napoleonic Code from its French origins. The UCC is actually a "model law" first written by the National Conference of Commissioners on Uniform State Laws, which states can then review and adopt, adopt with amendments, or replace with their own laws. The idea of the UCC is to create at least some degree of uniformity among the states.[13]

**Figure**

**1**   Four Elements of an Enforceable Contract

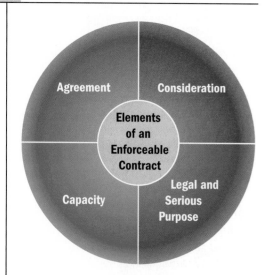

**Sales law** governs sales of goods or services for money or on credit. Article 2 of the UCC specifies the circumstances under which a buyer and a seller enter into a sales contract. Such agreements are based on the express conduct of the parties. The UCC generally requires written agreements for enforceable sales contracts for products worth more than $500. The formation of a sales contract is quite flexible because certain missing terms in a written contract or other ambiguities do not prevent the contract from being legally enforceable. A court will look to past dealings, commercial customs, and other standards of reasonableness to evaluate whether a legal contract exists.[14]

**sales law** law governing the sale of goods or services for money or on credit.

Courts also consider these variables when either the buyer or the seller seeks to enforce his or her rights in cases in which the other party fails to perform as specified in the contract, performs only partially, or performs in a defective or unsatisfactory way. The UCC's remedies in such cases usually involve the award of monetary damages to injured parties. The UCC defines the rights of the parties to have the contract performed, to have it terminated, and to reclaim the goods or place a lien—a legal claim—against them.

*Warranties*   Article 2 of the UCC also sets forth the law of warranties for sales transactions. Products carry two basic types of warranties: an *express warranty* is a specific representation made by the seller regarding the product, and an *implied warranty* is only legally imposed on the seller. Generally, unless implied warranties are disclaimed by the seller in writing, they are automatically in effect. Other provisions govern the rights of acceptance, rejection, and inspection of products by the buyer; the rights of the parties during manufacture, shipment, delivery, and passing of title to products; the legal significance of sales documents; and the placement of the risk of loss in the event of destruction or damage to the products during manufacture, shipment, or delivery.

*Negotiable Instruments*   The term **negotiable instrument** refers to commercial paper that is transferable among individuals and businesses. The most common example of a negotiable instrument is a check. Drafts, certificates of deposit, and notes are also sometimes considered negotiable instruments.

**negotiable instrument** commercial paper that is transferable among individuals and businesses.

Article 3 of the UCC specifies that a negotiable instrument must be written and must meet the following conditions:

1. It must be signed by the maker or drawer.
2. It must contain an unconditional promise or order to pay a certain sum of money.
3. It must be payable on demand or at a definite time.
4. It must be payable to order or to bearer.

Checks and other forms of commercial paper are transferred when the payee signs the back of the instrument, a procedure known as *endorsement*.

## Property Law and Law of Bailment

Property law is a key feature of the private enterprise system. *Property* is something for which a person or firm has the unrestricted right of possession or use. Property rights are guaranteed and protected by the U.S. Constitution. However, under certain circumstances property may be legally seized. In a recent ruling by the U.S. Supreme Court, the city of New London, Connecticut, was granted permission to seize a distressed area of real estate—owned by individual citizens—for future economic development by private business. In response, several states are now proposing laws to ban such practices.[15]

As Figure 2 shows, property can be divided into three basic categories. *Tangible personal property* consists of physical items such as equipment, supplies, and delivery vehicles. *Intan-*

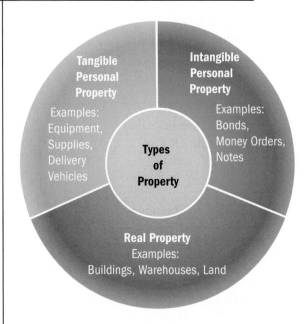

*gible personal property* is nonphysical property such as mortgages, stocks, and checks that are most often represented by a document or other written instrument, although it may be as vague and remote as a computer entry. You are probably familiar with certain types of intangible personal property such as checks or money orders. But other examples include bonds, notes, letters of credit, and warehouse receipts.

A third category of property is *real property*, or real estate. All firms have some interaction with real estate law because of the need to buy or lease the space in which they operate. Some companies are created to serve these real estate needs. Real estate developers, builders, contractors, brokers, appraisers, mortgage companies, escrow companies, title companies, and architects all deal with various aspects of real property law.

The law of bailment deals with the surrender of personal property by one person to another when the property is to be returned at a later date. The person delivering the property is known as the *bailor*, and the person receiving the property is the *bailee*. Some bailments benefit bailees, others benefit bailors, and still others provide mutual benefits. Most courts now require that all parties practice reasonable care in all bailment situations. The degree of benefit received from the bailment is a factor in court decisions about whether parties have met the reasonable-care standards.

Bailment disputes are most likely to arise in business settings such as hotels, restaurants, banks, and parking lots. A series of rules have been established to govern settlement of these disagreements. The law focuses on actual delivery of an item. For instance, a restaurant owner is not liable if a customer's coat or purse is stolen from the back of his or her chair. This is because the customer has not given the item to the restaurant for safekeeping. However, if the customer delivers the coat or purse to the restaurant checkroom, receives a claim check, and the item is stolen, then the restaurant is liable.

# TRADEMARKS, PATENTS, AND COPYRIGHTS

Trademarks, patents, and copyrights provide legal protection for key business assets by giving a firm the exclusive right to use those assets. A **trademark** consists of words, symbols, or other designations used by firms to identify their offerings. The Lanham Act (1946) provides for federal registration of trademarks. Trademarks are a valuable commercial property. For instance, Coca-Cola is considered the world's most widely recognized trademark, so it is very valuable to the company.

If a product becomes too well known, its fame can create problems. Once a trademark becomes a part of everyday usage, it loses its protection as a legal trademark. Consider the fate of *aspirin*, *cola*, *nylon*, *kerosene*, and *linoleum*. All these product names were once the exclusive property of their manufacturers, but they have passed into common language, and now anyone can use them. Companies often attempt to counter this threat by advertising that a term is actually a registered trademark. As more firms expand overseas, unintentional overlap between trademarks occurs. Recently, the Indian software firm Wipro, which holds 180 trademarks in India and 3 registered trademarks in Japan, was served notice by the German advertising firm Wipro Werbeagentur, alleging infringement of the German company's trademark. Wipro software denied the allegations.[16] In another international dispute, India's Jet Airways, which was founded in 1993 and plans to begin service between Mumbai and Newark International Airport in New Jersey, has been accused by another Jet Airways (based in Maryland) of trademark infringement.[17]

A **patent** guarantees an inventor exclusive rights to an invention for seventeen years. Copyrights and patents have a constitutional basis; the U.S. Constitution specifies that the federal government has the power "to promote the progress of science and useful arts, by securing for limited times to authors and inventors the exclusive rights to their respective writings or discoveries." Recently, the patent process and patent laws have been under scrutiny. Congress has approved a fee hike in order to hire 900 more staff in an attempt to speed the patent process. In addition, business trade groups have recommended a review that would allow the patent office instead of courts to deal with complaints. A proposal has also been floated to award a patent to the first person to file—instead of trying to prove who came up with the idea for an invention first.[18]

A **copyright** protects written or printed material such as books, designs, cartoon illustrations, photos, computer software, music, and videos. This class of business property is referred to as *intellectual property*. Copyrights are filed with the Library of Congress. Congress recently extended copyright protection for creative material by an additional 20 years, covering artistic works for the lifetime of the creator plus 70 years; for companies the time is 95 years. Not surprisingly, the Internet has opened up a whole new realm of copyright infringement, ranging from downloading music files to illegally sharing video footage. Recently, people suspected of using the popular BitTorrent file-sharing program to obtain versions of the movie *Star Wars Episode III: Revenge of the Sith* were served search warrants for copyright infringement.[19]

As mentioned earlier, the U.S. Supreme Court has ruled that Internet file-sharing services will be held accountable if they intend for their customers to use the software illegally. "We hold that one who distributes a device with the object of promoting it to infringe copyright, as shown by the clear expression or other affirmative steps taken to foster infringement, is liable for the resulting acts of infringement by third parties," wrote Justice David H. Souter.[20] And the U.S. government is becoming stricter about piracy of U.S. property from overseas. "Before Russia enters the [World Trade Organization], many of us will have to be convinced that the Russian government is serious about cracking down on the theft of intellectual property," said Senator Orrin Hatch, who chairs the Senate copyright subcommittee.[21]

Despite publicity about Internet copyright infringement, many people engage in the practice unintentionally. In an effort to educate children, the director of the U.S. Patent and Trademark Office recently gave a commencement speech to a group of elementary school students in Utah about the seriousness of downloading music, movies, and games illegally from the Internet.[22]

## Law of Torts

A **tort** (French for "wrong") refers to a civil wrong inflicted on another person or the person's property. The law of torts is closely related to the law of agency because a business entity, or principal, can be held liable for torts committed by its agents in the course of business dealings. Tort law differs from both criminal and contract law. While criminal law is concerned with crimes against the state or society, tort law deals with compensation for injured people who are the victims of noncriminal wrongs.

Tort cases are often extremely complex and may result in large monetary awards. It is typical to read or hear about cases in which patients are awarded millions of dollars in compensation for inadequate medical care. But what about pets? Lawsuits have surged around pets, their owners, and veterinarians. In the last few years, courts in several states have awarded damages to pet owners whose pets were lost or injured while under veterinary care. In Kentucky, a jury awarded $15,000 to the owner of a German shepherd that did not survive surgery. In California, a judge awarded $28,000 in general damages to the owner of a Rottweiler that had to have its teeth capped after improper dental surgery.[23]

*Types of Torts*   A tort may be intentional, or it may be caused by negligence. Assault, slander, libel, and fraud are all examples of intentional torts. Businesses can become involved in such cases through the actions of both owners and employees. A security guard who uses excessive force to apprehend an alleged shoplifter may have committed a tort. Under agency law, the guard's employers, such as a shopping mall or retailer, can be also held liable for any damages or injury caused by the security guard.

The other major group of torts result from negligence. This type of tort is based on carelessness rather than intentional behavior that causes injury to another person. Under agency law, businesses can also be held liable for the negligence of their employees or agents. A delivery truck driver who kills a pedestrian while delivering goods creates a tort liability for his or her employer if the accident results from negligence.

*Product Liability*   An area of tort law known as **product liability** has been developed by both statutory and case law to hold businesses liable for negligence in the design, manufacture, sale, or use of products. Some states have extended the theory of tort law to cover injuries caused by products, regardless of whether the manufacturer is proven negligent. This legal concept is known as *strict product liability*.

The business response to product liability has been mixed. To avoid lawsuits and fines, some recall defective products voluntarily; others decide to fight recall mandates if they believe the recall is not justified. Auto manufacturers and toy makers typically issue voluntary recalls, as do drug manufacturers.

## Bankruptcy Law

**bankruptcy** legal non-payment of financial obligations.

**Bankruptcy**, legal nonpayment of financial obligations, is a common occurrence in contemporary society. The term *bankruptcy* is derived from *banca rotta*, or "broken bench," referring to the medieval Italian practice of creditors breaking up the benches of merchants who did not pay their bills.

Federal legislation passed in 1918 and revised several times since then provides a system for handling bankruptcies. Bankruptcy has two purposes. One is to protect creditors by providing a way to obtain compensation through debtors' assets. The second goal, which is almost unique to the United States, is to also protect debtors, allowing them to get a fresh financial start.

Federal law recognizes two types of bankruptcy. Under voluntary bankruptcy, a person or firm asks to be judged bankrupt because of inability to repay creditors. Under involuntary bankruptcy, creditors may request that a party be judged bankrupt.

*Personal Bankruptcies*   With a growing number of individuals amassing large personal debt—often through credit cards—Congress recently revised personal bankruptcy law to make it more difficult for people to erase their debt instead of being held accountable for it. Under the revised law, it will be harder for individuals to file Chapter 7 bankruptcy, which traditionally has wiped out most debt. If their earnings exceed their state's median income, they will instead be required to file Chapter 13 bankruptcy, which sets up a repayment plan as designed by the court. Despite criticism by consumer groups that say that banks and credit card companies have caused the problem by encouraging personal debt, many people agree that the revisions are fair. "This practical reform will help ensure that debtors make a good-faith effort to repay as much as they can afford," said President George W. Bush as he signed the legislation into law. "This new law will help make credit more affordable, because when bankruptcy is less common, credit can be extended to more people at better rates."[24]

*Business Bankruptcies*   Businesses can also go bankrupt for a variety of reasons—mismanagement, plunging sales, an inability to keep up with changes in the marketplace. Under Chapter 11 a firm may reorganize and develop a plan to repay its debts. Chapter 11 also permits prepackaged bankruptcies, in which companies enter bankruptcy proceedings after obtaining approval of most—but not necessarily all—of their creditors. Often companies can emerge from prepackaged bankruptcies sooner than those that opt for conventional Chapter 11 filings. Airlines have managed to accomplish this, as well as large retailers such as Kmart.

## Tax Law

A branch of law that affects every business, employee, and consumer in the United States is tax law. A **tax** is an assessment by a governmental unit. Federal, state, and local governments and special taxing authorities all levy taxes. Appendix B, "Personal Financial Planning," also covers tax law.

**tax** assessment by a governmental unit.

Some taxes are paid by individuals and some by businesses. Both have a decided impact on contemporary business. Business taxes reduce profits, and personal taxes cut the disposable incomes that individuals can spend on the products of industry. Governments spend their revenue from taxes to buy goods and services produced by businesses. Governments also act as transfer agents, moving tax revenue to other consumers and transferring Social Security taxes from the working population to retired or disabled people.

Governments can levy taxes on several different bases: income, sales, business receipts, property, and assets. The type of tax varies from one taxing authority to the other. The individual income tax is the biggest source of revenue for the federal government. Many states also rely heavily on income taxes as well as sales taxes, which vary widely. Cities and towns may collect property taxes in order to operate schools and improve roads. So-called luxury taxes are taxes on items like yachts, and sin taxes are levied on items such as cigarettes and alcohol. During the past decade, the issue of whether to tax different types of Internet services and use has been hotly debated.

## "They Said It"

"I am convinced that if most members of Congress did their own taxes, we would have had tax reform long ago."
—Bill Archer (b. 1928)
American politician

## Business Terms You Need to Know

| | | |
|---|---|---|
| judiciary 126 | business law 127 | negotiable instrument 133 |
| law 127 | contract 132 | bankruptcy 136 |
| common law 127 | agency 132 | tax 137 |
| statutory law 127 | sales law 133 | |

## Other Important Business Terms

| | | |
|---|---|---|
| Class-Action Fairness Act of 2005 124 | breach of contract 132 | copyright 135 |
| trial courts 126 | damages 132 | tort 135 |
| appellate courts 126 | Uniform Commercial Code 132 | product liability 136 |
| international law 127 | trademark 134 | |
| | patent 135 | |

1. Many firms incorporate in Delaware. Such choices are at least partially because Delaware regularly updates its corporate laws. A recent update permits the roughly 500,000 corporations registered in Delaware to hold electronic annual meetings. Delaware also allows annual meetings to be held via Web, e-mail, or fax. What is your opinion of the first state's novel approach to corporate governance? What advantages and disadvantages do you think can result? Discuss your opinions with the class.

2. When a business loses its case in a trial, it may have a chance to appeal to a higher appellate court. That's what the accounting firm Arthur Andersen did after being found guilty of destroying certain documents related to its client Enron as the energy giant fell apart. Specifically, Andersen was convicted of "corruptly persuading its employees to destroy documents." Later, the U.S. Supreme Court overturned the ruling because the jury in the lower court had not been told that, in order to find Andersen guilty, they needed to decide that Andersen had acted "knowingly to subvert an investigation."[25] The court's ruling did little to help Andersen, because its employees left to find other work after the first judgment. Do you agree with the Supreme Court ruling? Do you think that businesses should be able to appeal court decisions based on technicalities such as a person's intent? Why or why not? Discuss your views with the class.

3. On your own or with a classmate, use a Web search engine to select and research a state or federal business-related law enacted during the past year. Why was this legislation passed? What were the arguments for and against it? How do you think the new law will affect businesses? Consumers? Society in general?

4. In place of professional fees—typically billed on an hourly basis—some attorneys accept cases on a contingency basis. The attorney earns nothing if he or she loses the case. If the case results in an award, the attorney collects a contingency fee, which is typically 30 percent or more of the total award. On your own or with a classmate, do online research and construct arguments for and against contingency fees.

5. Because it can copy and distribute material anywhere in the world at lightning speed, the Internet has created a whole new challenge for those who create intellectual property—text, music, videos, software, and the like. Some people argue that old copyright laws are obsolete—they may actually stifle technological creativity. Others claim that creators must be protected at all costs. But some are beginning to think in terms of a new copyright, which preserves some rights but relinquishes others. For instance, music artists might ask for permission and payment for the commercial use of their work, but not for noncommercial use. They might allow a certain amount of sampling before purchase.[26] On your own or with a classmate, use a Web search engine to research examples of companies and cases—such as Napster and Grokster—involving Internet file sharing and copyright. Then write your own opinion about what a "new" copyright should cover.

# The Second City Theater Continuing Case
## Second City: First in Comedy

Writer A. J. Liebling derided the city of Chicago as inferior to what he considered the more appealing cities of Paris, London, and, in particular, New York. Indeed, in his articles for the *New Yorker*, he dubbed Chicago "the second city," after New York, which he considered the country's first city. Chicagoans were understandably offended, but a group of young aspiring performers, including many University of Chicago alumni, embraced Liebling's jab and self-mockingly adopted the name "The Second City" for their new cabaret theater.

Second City opened its doors on December 16, 1959, and the theater's unique brand of social and political satire soon made it a Chicago institution. From the beginning, Second City began building its unique "brand" of theater, reaching larger and larger audiences, and over the years the Second City brand grew to become one of the strongest in comedy. Branding was just getting started at many U.S. businesses in the late 1950s when The Second City was founded. This period would come to be known by business historians as "The Marketing Era," when corporations began to adopt a consumer orientation and to distinguish their brand. The success of Second City in Chicago helped foster the

establishment and growth of dozens of theaters in the city.

Almost from the theater's inception, alumni have garnered critical and commercial triumphs. Early troupe members Alan Arkin, Barbara Harris, and Severn Darden enjoyed film and theater success, and in the 1970s, many Second City actors, including John Belushi and Dan Aykroyd, gained fame on the (then) new weekly television show *Saturday Night Live*. This trend of achievement has continued and accelerated through the last 25–30 years. Today, many of the most famous comedic television and film stars have in some way traveled through Second City's doors. For many people, Second City's name has become synonymous with live comedic theater. Patrons enjoy the "up close" and interactive experience at a Second City performance, and the theater labors to maintain and build a strong sense of relationship with its audience.

Success for the theater has also bred expansion. In the United States, Second City currently operates in Chicago, Detroit, Denver, and Las Vegas, with training centers in Los Angeles and New York. The oldest offshoot of the theater is in Toronto, which opened its doors in 1973. Since then Second City has maintained strong ties to its Canadian

branch. Canada remains Second City's strongest foreign market, where it is currently involved in a significant amount of television and film production, fueled by government funding available for Canadian productions. Also, Second City's Canadian home base of Toronto is the country's media center. Canada is not the only area of international expansion for the company. In 1962, the theater made its first London appearance with an artistic exchange with the English satirical performing group The Establishment. In 1992, Second City began a long-running relationship with the English Theater in Vienna, Austria, and three years later performed in the Edinburgh Fringe Festival in Edinburgh, Scotland.

Kelly Leonard, vice president of The Second City and president of Second City Theatricals, said, "We aren't focused on international growth. However, it's clear that many of our endeavors can potentially translate internationally. Our focus starts on what our base business is, content creation and talent development, and we look at opportunities that grow out of those two core competencies."

Today, three touring companies travel around the globe, bringing Second City performances to remote audiences worldwide. In 2001, one of Second City's touring companies traveled through Saudi Arabia, Kuwait, and the United Arab Emirates, entertaining U.S. troops stationed abroad. In 2002, Second City toured Tokyo, Singapore, Bangkok, and Hong Kong. Recently, the theater has expanded into the high seas, bringing weekly performances to audiences aboard various international cruise lines. These international performances are often attended by English speakers who live on foreign soil, as well as a growing audience of non-native English speakers.

International growth brings increased revenues and audiences but also potential pitfalls. The biggest potential pitfall is relying on an international audience "getting the jokes" created by a U.S.-based theater company. But as foreign audiences learn what makes Americans laugh, the lesson just may come from The Second City—something that might have disappointed A.J. Liebling and others who see Manhattan as the center of the cultural universe.

## QUESTIONS

1. Identify how Second City might use technology to expand its markets. What dangers might it face in its use of technology?
2. What value does a Second City performance bring to its customers?
3. Identify specific factors that might drive demand higher and lower for Second City's products.
4. What unique challenges does Second City face as the company tries to expand internationally?

# Part 1: Launching Your Global Business and Economics Career

In Part 1, "Business in a Global Environment," you learned about the background and current issues driving contemporary business. The part includes four chapters and an appendix covering such issues as business ethics and social responsibility, economic challenges facing global and domestic business, competing in global markets, and the legal framework for business. Business has always been an exciting career field, whether you choose to start your own company, work at a local business, or set your sights on a position with a multinational corporation. But today's environment is especially attractive because businesses are expanding their horizons to compete in a global economy—and they need dedicated and talented people to help them accomplish their goals. In fact, professional and business service jobs are found in some of the fastest-growing industries in the U.S. economy and are projected to grow by nearly 28 percent over a decade.[1]

So now is the time to explore several different career options that can lead you to your dream job. Each part in this text profiles the many opportunities available in business. Here are a few related to Chapters 1 through 4.

If you're good at number crunching and are interested in how societies and companies function, then maybe a career as an *economist* is in your future. Economists study how resources are allocated, conduct research by collecting and analyzing data, monitor economic trends, and develop forecasts. They look into such vital areas as the cost of energy, foreign trade and exchange between countries, the effect of taxes, and employment levels—both from a big-picture national or global viewpoint and from the perspective of individual businesses. Economists work for corporations to help them run more efficiently, for consulting firms to offer special expertise, or for government agencies to oversee economic decision making. Typically, advanced degrees are needed to climb to top-level positions. Economists usually earn about $72,780 per year.[2]

Or perhaps you are interested in global business. Companies increasingly search the world for the best employees, supplies, and markets. So you could work in the United States for a foreign-based firm such as Nokia or Toyota; abroad in Africa, Asia, Europe, or Latin America for a U.S.-based firm such as Microsoft or Wal-Mart; or with overseas co-workers via computer networks to develop new products for a firm such as General Electric. With technology and telecommunications, distance is no longer a barrier to conducting business. Global business careers exist in all the areas you'll be reading about in this text—business ownership, management, marketing, technology, and finance.

Global business leaders are not born but made—so how can you start on that career path? Here are the three areas that businesses consider when selecting employees for overseas assignment:

- **Competence**—including technical knowledge, language skills, leadership ability, experience, and past performance.
- **Adaptability**—including interest in overseas work, communication and other personal skills, empathy for other cultures, and appreciation for varied management styles and work environments.
- **Personal characteristics**—level of education, experience, and social compatibility with the host country.[3]

Solid experience in your field or company ranks at the top of the list of needed skills. Firms want to send employees who have expertise in their business and loyalty to the firm to represent them overseas. Those who obtain their master of business administration (MBA) degree are reaping rewards financially: in a recent year, the average starting salary for someone with an MBA reached $88,600 and often included signing bonuses in the tens of thousands of dollars.[4] But companies are reluctant to send new graduates abroad immediately. Instead, they invest in training to orient employees to the new assignment.

Knowledge of and interest in other languages and cultures is the second-highest priority. Businesspeople need to function smoothly in another society, so they are selected based on their familiarity with other languages and cultures. Because China is a business hotspot, some people have become fluent in Mandarin Chinese to boost their career prospects.[5] Also, some elementary school systems are even beginning to offer Chinese language classes in addition to their standard offerings of French, Spanish, German, and Russian.

Finally, employees are evaluated on their personal characteristics to be certain that they will fit well in their new country. More and more diversity is appearing among global managers, and a person's talent is still foremost in making assignments. As IBM's vice president of global workforce diversity puts it, "We have to be in compliance with a country's laws and sensitive to its local customs, but we also want the very best talent."[6]

## Career Assessment Exercises in Economics and Global Business

1. With the change in the leadership at the U.S. Federal Reserve (the nation's central bank), economists have been highlighted in the news. Alan Greenspan, who retired after eighteen years as head of the Fed, turned over the reins to Benjamin Bernanke. Both men have backgrounds in economics. To get an idea of the role economists play in a federal government agency, research either Greenspan's or Bernanke's background, qualifications, and abilities. Assess how they performed or are performing at the Fed. Now make a list of your own skills. Where is there a match? What do you need to change?

2. To see the effect of the global economy in your town, go to a major retailer. Take a survey of the number of different countries represented in the products on the shelves. Compare your list with those of your classmates to see who found the most countries and what goods those countries provided. Go online to research the career opportunities at the firm's Web site.

3. To learn more about other countries, do research online for a country in which you are interested. Here are two sources that may be useful:

- *The World Factbook*, published by the Central Intelligence Agency, http://www.cia.gov/cia/publications/factbook. This publication, updated yearly, contains a wealth of information about countries—geography and climate, population statistics, cultural and political information, transportation and communications methods, and economic data.

- *The Wall Street Journal's CollegeJournal* Web site, http://www.collegejournal.com. This site has a Global Careers link, which contains articles on international news and trends, country profiles, and career tips for several countries.

Write a one-page summary of what you found. Make a list of abilities you would need to function well as a businessperson in that country. Concentrate on the areas of competence, adaptability, and personal characteristics. Now formulate a plan to gain those skills.

# Starting and Growing Your Business

# Part 2

# Chapter 5

## Options for Organizing Small and Large Businesses

ore than 30 years ago, Don Dionisio Gutierrez and his father, Don Juan Bautista Gutierrez, opened the first Pollo Campero restaurant in their native Guatemala. The new owners probably never thought it would grow into a hugely popular worldwide chain. Yet today Pollo Campero's quick-serve chicken restaurants have millions of ardent fans who love the authentic recipes and nostalgic atmosphere enough to wait in line to get in. Each new-store opening is a big event in its community; when the first Pollo Campero opened in New York City, the mayor attended the ribbon-cutting ceremony.

An immediate hit at home in Guatemala, Pollo Campero—meaning, roughly, "country chicken"—soon became the centerpiece of many well-remembered special occasions, such as family gatherings and celebrations for blue-collar workers and business executives "a brand created and developed in Latin America, featuring the favorite dishes of many Latin American countries and offering top-quality service and product to our loyal customers from home and our new and valued customers in the U.S." Children are always welcome, and

# Pollo Campero Feeds Hungry Fans— and Their Nostalgia for Home

alike. "This is something very special," said one U.S. customer who grew up in Guatemala City. "It's part of all of our childhoods. It's a piece of our homelands." Says another native Guatemalan now living in Texas, "Every time we had extra money or it was someone's birthday, we'd head for Pollo Campero." When customers emigrated, they brought their fondness for Pollo Campero with them.

The chain's unique fried chicken specialty, with its spicy secret ingredients, grew popular in other Latin American countries as well, and the chain opened stores in Ecuador, Honduras, El Salvador, Nicaragua, and Mexico. Soon U.S. customers traveling to Latin America became aware of Pollo Campero's unique appeal. After selling about 3 million take-out orders from airports in Central America, which both Americans and nostalgic Guatemalans were taking home on the plane to their family and friends, the company opened its first U.S. restaurant in Los Angeles in 2002.

Today the chain comprises about 200 restaurants. Almost 20 of them are franchises in the United States. "We are very proud to be the first restaurant of our kind in the U.S.," says president and CEO Juan Jose Gutierrez,

the restaurants and service standards are definitely family friendly. Charity events, community involvement, and top employee benefits help strengthen the chain's image wherever it goes.

Although the quick-serve market is nearly saturated, Pollo Campero franchises in the United States are expected to grow. "The number of sites we open next year is limited only by how quickly we can find sites and build restaurants," said Jose Cofiño, CEO of the master franchisor for the western United States. One reason for the high expectations is that black and Asian customers are discovering Pollo Campero, and as one restaurant consultant noted, the public clearly sees the chain as "something different or better" in the crowded fast-food market. Once people taste the menu, they tend to come back, even when advertising and promotion are minimal.

Cofiño defines the competition not just as other chicken outlets but also as all eateries: "Somebody is eating across the street," he says in speaking of competitors. "Why are they eating there and not here?" If Pollo Campero continues to offer the special recipes that have filled countless airplanes with mouth-watering smells, that question won't need to be asked again.[1]

If you have ever thought of operating your own business, you are not alone. In fact, on any given day in the United States, more people are trying to start new businesses than are getting married or having children. However, before entering the world of contemporary business, an entrepreneur needs to understand its framework and choose the form the business will take, as Pollo Campero's owners did when they expanded the business to the United States as a series of franchises.

Several variables affect the choice of the best way to organize your business:

- How easily can you set up this type of organization?
- How much financial liability can you afford to accept?
- What financial resources do you have?
- What strengths and weaknesses do you see in other businesses in the industry?
- What are your own strengths and weaknesses?

This chapter begins by focusing on small-business ownership, including the advantages and disadvantages of small-business ventures, the contributions of small business to the economy, and why small businesses succeed and fail. We also look at the services provided by the U.S. government's Small Business Administration. The role of women and minorities in small business is discussed in detail, as well as franchising and global opportunities for small-business owners. We then provide an overview of the three forms of private business ownership—sole proprietorships, partnerships, and corporations. Next, the structures and operations typical of larger companies are explored, followed by a review of mergers, acquisitions, and joint ventures. The chapter concludes with an explanation of public and collective ownership.

# MOST BUSINESSES ARE SMALL BUSINESSES

Although many people associate the term *business* with corporate goliaths such as ExxonMobil, Ford, PepsiCo, Pfizer, Microsoft, and Wal-Mart, 89 percent of firms with employees have fewer than 20 people on staff, and 98 percent have fewer than 100 employees.[2] Many U.S. businesses have no payroll at all: more than 15 million people in the United States earn business income without any employees.[3] Almost half the sales in the United States are made by small businesses.[4]

Small business is also the launching pad for entrepreneurs from every sector of the diverse U.S. economy. Thirty-four percent of the nation's 17 million small businesses are owned by women.[5] Hispanic-owned businesses account for 5.8 percent of all U.S. businesses with fewer than 100 employees. Asian Americans own another 4.4 percent, and African Americans own 4 percent.[6]

## What Is a Small Business?

**small business** firm that is independently owned and operated, is not dominant in its field, and meets industry-specific size standards for income or number of employees.

How do you distinguish a small business from a large one? Are sales the key indicator? What about market share or number of employees? The Small Business Administration (SBA), the federal agency most directly involved with this sector of the economy, considers a **small business** to be a firm that is independently owned and operated and is not dominant in its field. The SBA also considers annual sales and number of employees to identify small businesses for specific industries.

- Most manufacturing businesses are considered small if they employ fewer than 500 workers.
- To be considered small, wholesalers must employ no more than 100 workers.
- Most kinds of retailers and other services can generate up to $6 million in annual sales and still be considered a small business.
- An agricultural business is generally considered small if its sales are no more than $750,000 a year.[7]

The SBA has established size standards for specific industries. These standards, which range from $500,000 to $25 million in sales and from 100 to 1,500 for employees, are available at the SBA's "What Is a Small Business" Web page, http://www.sba .gov/size.

An excellent example of a small business—and its owner— is Barbara Kavovit, founder of New York City–based Barbara K! Enterprises, which sells user-friendly tool kits to women who are inexperienced do-it-yourselfers. Kits come in blue-gray cases that contain easy-to-understand instructions plus all the tools and parts needed for household repairs. Roadside safety and dorm survival kits are also available on the company's Web site or at Home Depot and JCPenney stores.[8] Barbara K!—a $5 million company—has an appropriate motto: "If I can do it, so can you."

Because government agencies offer benefits designed to help small businesses compete with larger firms, small-business owners want to determine whether their companies meet the standards for small-business designation. If it qualifies, a company may be eligible for government loans or for government purchasing programs that encourage proposals from smaller suppliers.

Barbara Kavovit started her first small business as a general contractor in New York City and worked for corporate clients such as IBM, Carnegie Hall, and Polo Ralph Lauren. She started Barbara K! to make power tools and do-it-yourself kits easier for women to use.

## Typical Small-Business Ventures

For decades, small businesses have competed against some of the world's largest organizations, as well as multitudes of other small companies. For example, Shoes for Crews, a 160-employee manufacturer of work shoes in West Palm Beach, Florida, competes against much larger shoe companies, such as Wolverine and Timberland, which have more than 5,000 employees and sales of $1 billion and $1.5 billion, respectively. How can it compete against these big firms? By offering a serious nonslip guarantee. If a worker slips and falls while wearing its shoes, it pays up to $5,000 per claim. That guarantee is why the Cheesecake Factory, which employs 25,000 employees in 97 restaurants, encourages its workers to buy from Shoes for Crews. Vice President Kurt Leisure said, "The warranty is obviously a big incentive for us to get as many employees as possible into their shoes. It's very shrewd on their part."[9]

The past fifteen years have seen a steady erosion of small businesses in many industries as larger firms have bought out small independent businesses and replaced them with larger operations. For example, the number of independent bookstores and hardware stores has fallen dramatically as Borders Books, Barnes & Noble, Home Depot, and Lowe's have dramatically increased their stores over the last decade. But as Table 5.1 reveals, the businesses least likely to be gobbled up and consolidated into larger firms are those that sell services, not things; rely on consumer trust and proximity; and keep their overhead costs low.

For centuries, most nonfarming small businesses have been concentrated in retailing and the service industries. Recently many entrepreneurs have started successful businesses by providing time-starved homeowners with customized services such as housekeeping, lawn care, and home and computer repair. The small size of such a business allows it to cater to customers in ways that big companies can't. See the accompanying "Business Etiquette" feature for some ideas about how to manage an operation that requires working in other people's homes and on their property.

Table

5.1

David vs. Goliath: Business Sectors Most Dominated and Least Dominated by Small Firms

| Most Likely to Be a Small Firm | Fewer Than 20 Workers |
| --- | --- |
| Home builders | 97% |
| Florists | 97% |
| Hair salons | 96% |
| Auto repair | 96% |
| Funeral homes | 94% |
| **Least Likely to Be a Small Firm** | **Fewer Than 20 Workers** |
| Paper mills | 25% |
| Nursing homes | 27% |
| Oil pipelines | 33% |
| Electric utilities | 42% |
| Railroad car makers | 42% |

**Source:** U.S. Census Bureau, "Number of Firms, Number of Establishments, Employment, and Annual Payroll by Employment Size of the Enterprise for the United States, All Industries," accessed August 31, 2005, http://www.census.gov.

As Figure 5.1 indicates, small businesses provide most jobs in the construction, agricultural services, wholesale trade, services, and retail trade industries. Retailing is another important industry for today's small businessperson. Merchandising giants such as Target and Wal-Mart may be the best-known retailing firms, but small, privately owned retail stores far outnumber them. Small-business retailing includes stores that sell shoes, jewelry, office supplies and stationery, clothing, flowers, drugs, convenience foods, and thousands of other products. People wishing to form their own business have always been attracted to retailing because of the ability to start a firm with limited funds, rent a store rather than build a facility, create a Web site, and use family members to staff the new business.

Powell's Books, based in Portland, Oregon, is one of the most successful retail bookstores in the United States. In contrast to "big box" superstores such as Barnes & Noble and Books-A-Million, which use their huge buying power to secure lower prices for large orders and Amazon.com's well-known high-tech, stock-everything strategy, Powell's competes by specializing in used, sometimes hard-to-find, books. Through its seven bookstores and its Web site (http://www.powells.com), Powell's serves customers who like buying from an independent store instead of one of the larger chains and who don't mind paying extra to find something special to read. Their unique strategies permit Powell's and Amazon to benefit one another. Powell's buys returned books from Amazon.com at a discount and sells them as used books. Amazon

Figure

5.1

Major Industries Dominated by Small Businesses

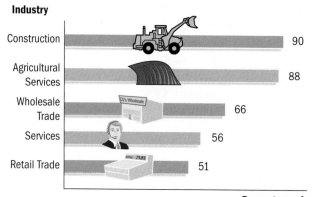

**Industry**

- Construction — 90
- Agricultural Services — 88
- Wholesale Trade — 66
- Services — 56
- Retail Trade — 51

**Percentage of firms with fewer than 500 employees**

**Source:** Office of Advocacy, U.S. Small Business Administration, "Small Business Profile: United States," accessed June 17, 2006, http://www.sba.gov/advo.

fills orders for out-of-print books through Powell's. This strategy will never make Powell's the largest bookseller, but that is just fine with the retailer's founder, Michael Powell.[10]

Small business also plays a significant role in agriculture. Although most farm acreage is in the hands of large corporate farms, most farmers still operate as small businesses. Most U.S. farms are owned by individual farmers or families, not partners or shareholders.[11] The family farm is a classic example of a small-business operation. It is independently owned and operated, with relatively few employees, relying instead on the labor of family members. But today's small farmers must combine savvy business and marketing techniques to thrive, like California-based Earthbound Farm (http://www.ebfarm.com), which grows, packages, and sells organic salads, vegetables, fruits, and dried fruits.

Just over half of small businesses in the United States are **home-based businesses**— firms operated from the residence of the business owner.[12] Between 1960 and 1980, fewer people worked at home, largely because the number of farmers, doctors, and lawyers in home-based practices was declining. But since then, the number of people working at home has more than doubled. A major factor in this growth is the increased availability of personal computers with access to the Internet and other communications devices such as fax machines and cell phones. As computer technology evolves rapidly and more workers prefer the flexibility of working from alternative locations, it is predicted that the number of home-based businesses will grow even faster.[13] Sometimes, however, office space is needed for a meeting or conference or to convey an image of solidity and professionalism. New options for renting such space are springing up in response to the growth of small business, but owners should be wary about projecting an image they can't live up to, as the "Solving an Ethical Controversy" feature discusses.

Lower costs are one of the main reasons that the number of home-based businesses is growing so quickly. Financing a small business is a difficult challenge, so by not leasing or maintaining separate office or warehouse space, a home-based business owner can pour precious

## (b)usiness (e)tiquette

### Tips for Your Small Business When Working in Customers' Homes

A growing number of entrepreneurs are starting businesses that operate in other people's homes. Housekeeping, handyman, home improvement, lawn care, computer repair, and other service-based businesses are experiencing rapid growth, and their owners and employees need to be considerate about working in customers' private spaces. Here are some tips for in-home services of all kinds.

1. Wear (or have employees wear) a uniform, not only to establish a sense of professionalism but also to identify yourself and your business to the customer.
2. Be on time. Allow yourself extra time for traffic or other problems, and phone if a delay is unavoidable.
3. Take two steps backward after ringing the doorbell, remove your sunglasses if any, and present your business card when the door is opened.
4. If no adults are at home, wait in your car or truck until a parent arrives.
5. If the homeowner needs to prepare for your work by clearing up toys from the floor or yard, confining a dog, or making sure the yard or pool is not in use, call the night before to remind the customer to expect you.
6. Keep your eyes to yourself; never pry into customers' belongings or areas that are off-limits. As one owner of a handyman franchise suggests, "Pretend everything you see is perfectly normal."
7. Never use foul language while working in the client's home.
8. Be considerate. Always advise the customer before using any machinery that's noisy, use tarps or drop cloths, and contain and remove any waste or debris. Take special care not to leave any tools or equipment behind.
9. Avoid becoming involved in any conversations that might be going on in the home, particularly disagreements.
10. Remember that satisfying the customer is what a service business is all about. If the customer isn't happy, make whatever adjustments are needed to satisfy the promises you've made.

**Sources:** Gwendolyn Bounds, "Handyman Etiquette: Stay Calm, Avert Eyes," *Wall Street Journal Online*, accessed June 17, 2006, http://www.startupjournal.com; Deborah Crawford, "Great Customer Service," Bella Online, accessed June 17, 2006, http://www.bellaonline.com; "Lawn Care Success Tip of the Week," Lawn Care Success, accessed September 16, 2005, http://www.lawncaresuccess.com.

# IS IT ETHICAL TO MAKE YOUR BUSINESS APPEAR LARGER THAN IT IS?

*What if clients want to visit your office, but you don't have one? Or what if it's damp and dark because it's your basement? Many shoestring entrepreneurs face this problem. A popular new solution is to rent temporary offices equipped with everything from receptionists and bottled water to computers, fax machines, potted plants and paintings, videoconferencing capability, and voice-mail services.*

Some "flex spaces" offer technology support, mail delivery, maintenance, security, and even fellow renters to network with. Convenient leases cost a fraction of what permanent space commands, but while flex space helps start-ups appear large and well established, there are dangers.

"There is a fine line between fraud and puffery," says an ethics professor at UCLA. "When you cross the line is when you have a client with a big project and a lot of money at stake and they're fooled into thinking you're much larger and more capable than you really are."

Tricks that edge entrepreneurs toward that line include filling offices with family members, getting friends to follow up with clients to create the illusion of staff, and printing business cards with different job titles for different occasions.

Should small and entrepreneurial companies try to make themselves seem larger?

## PRO

1. Making a business appear larger is a competitive strategy, and no one is lying to the client.
2. If clients think you're on a shoe-string budget, they may assume you aren't busy, aren't well established, or have financial difficulties.

## CON

1. Clients won't worry about size if you project expertise and reliability. Outsourcing is common these days, so there is nothing to hide or disguise.
2. Pretending you are something you are not is inherently dishonest even if no outright lies are told.

## SUMMARY

Partnering with larger companies, attending trade shows, and using promotional tools such as press releases to get mentioned in industry publications are alternate ways to project a big image. As one public-relations CEO says, "You can look bigger; you can use strategies that play on people's perceptions; but if confronted with a question, you'd best tell the truth."

**Sources:** Kortney Stringer, "Temporary Offices Offer the Best of Both Worlds," *StartupJournal*, accessed June 17, 2006, http://www.startupjournal.com; Geoff Williams, "Creative License," *Entrepreneur*, accessed June 17, 2006, http://www.entrepreneur.com; Nicole Gull, "Move-In Ready," *Inc.*, March 2005, pp. 48, 51.

solving an **ETHICAL** controversy

## "They Said It"

*"Size certainly matters, and not always in a positive way."*
Michael Powell (b. 1941)
Founder and owner, Powell's Books

funds into the business itself. Some home-based business owners have even discovered the benefits of selling their goods through eBay, the online auction site. Ron Jones, who helped his wife Jan start their home-based business, Beads, Creativity, and You, on eBay, said, "If you want to be in business for yourself, it's a great way to do it. It keeps the overhead down—you don't have to have a storefront."[14] The cost of operating from home through eBay is far less than the cost of leasing, staffing, and maintaining a retail store at a high-traffic shopping mall, not to mention the far greater number of consumers eBay reaches.

Other benefits of a home-based business include greater flexibility and freedom from the time and expense of commuting. Drawbacks include isolation and less visibility to customers—except, of course, if your customers visit you online. In that case, they don't care where your office is located.

Many small-business start-ups are more competitive because of the Internet. An estimated three of every five small businesses have an online presence. But the Internet does not automatically guarantee success, as illustrated by the thousands of dot-com failures during the early years of e-commerce. Still, setting up a Web site can be relatively inexpensive and enables a business to reach a huge marketplace.

Tiny Salem Five Cents Savings Bank, a Massachusetts firm with only thirteen branches, has a significant presence on the Internet. It established that presence by acting quickly in the mid-1990s, when Internet banking was still an innovation. Consumers liked the new service and low fees, and before long, Salem Five had attracted thousands of new customers. When bigger banks began adding Internet service, Salem Five honed its focus to New England, where the bank already had a good reputation, and then became the first bank to offer every one of its services, from personal and business banking to mortgages and investing, on the Internet, which earned the company recognition as the Internet Bank of the Year. Today, Salem Five continues to innovate and has opened branches with automated-teller machines and Internet kiosks offering videoconferencing with bank representatives. High technology coupled with concern for customer service keeps Salem Five in business even as the biggest banks spend millions of dollars on advertising.[15]

American business history is filled with inspirational stories of great inventors who launched companies in barns, garages, warehouses, and attics. For young visionaries such as Apple Computer founders Steve Jobs and Steve Wozniak, the logical option for transforming their technical idea into a commercial reality was to begin work in a family garage. The impact of today's entrepreneurs, including home-based businesses, is discussed in more depth in Chapter 6.

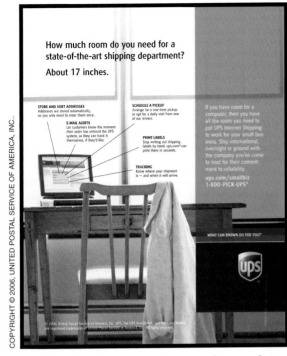

Home-based businesses have low costs because their owners aren't spending precious startup funds on office or warehouse space. And as this UPS promotion shows, the only thing that home-based businesses need to ship their products worldwide is an Internet connection, or "About 17 inches."

# CONTRIBUTIONS OF SMALL BUSINESS TO THE ECONOMY

Small businesses form the core of the U.S. economy. Businesses with fewer than 500 employees generate 39 percent of total U.S. sales and more than half the nation's gross domestic product. Ninety-two of every 100 U.S. businesses are small businesses. In addition, small businesses employ almost half of the nation's private nonfarm workforce.[16]

## Creating New Jobs

Small businesses make tremendous contributions to the U.S. economy and to society as a whole. One impressive contribution is the number of new jobs created each year by small businesses. While it varies from year to year, on average three of every four new jobs are created by companies with fewer than 500 employees.[17] A significant share of these jobs was created by the smallest companies—those with four or fewer employees. Small firms are dominant factors in many of the industries that have added the most jobs: construction trade contractors, wholesale trade, amusement and recreation, service businesses, restaurants, and engineering and management services.[18]

Even if you never plan to start your own business, you will probably work for a small business at some point in your career. Not only do small firms employ about half of all U.S. workers, but they are more likely than large firms to employ the youngest (and oldest) workers. In addition, as detailed in a later section of this chapter, small businesses offer significant opportunities to women and minorities.

Small businesses also contribute to the economy by hiring workers who traditionally have had difficulty finding jobs at larger firms. Compared with large companies, small businesses are more likely to hire former welfare recipients.[19] Driven in part by their limited budgets,

**assessment check**

1. What characteristics does the SBA use to determine whether a business is a small business?

2. Identify three industries in which small businesses are common.

**"They Said It"**

"You may not think you're going to make it. You may want to quit. But if you keep your eye on the ball, you can accomplish anything."
*Hank Aaron (b. 1934)*
*American baseball legend*

small businesses may be more open to locating in economically depressed areas, where they contribute to rehabilitating neighborhoods and reducing unemployment.

## Creating New Industries

The small-business sector also gives entrepreneurs an outlet for developing their ideas and perhaps for creating entirely new industries. Many of today's successful high-tech firms—Microsoft, Dell, Cisco Systems, Yahoo!, and Google—began as small businesses. Most high-tech startups are looking for growth, too, sometimes by moving overseas in creative ways. See the "Hit and Miss" feature for just one example of small business on a global scale.

The growth of new businesses and new industries not only provides new goods and services but also fuels local economies. Tucker Technology provides full-service telecommunications and information technology solutions for *Fortune* 500 companies. Tucker, which is based in Oakland, California, has 132 employees, half of whom live in the local neighborhood. Also, 15 percent of its employees got their jobs when founder Frank Tucker went to community-based organizations that help local people learn new job skills. Tucker said, "I'd see all the human resources on the street corner. Clearly, they had no jobs to go to." So he began hiring them at more than $20 an hour to install network and phone cables in office buildings.[20] For more information on the dramatic effects that small businesses can have on local economies, see http://www.theinnercity100.org.

New industries are sometimes created when small businesses adapt to provide needed services to the larger corporate community. The movement toward corporate downsizing that began in the early 1990s created a demand for other businesses to perform activities previously handled by company employees. Outsourcing such activities as security, maintenance, employee benefits management, and transportation services created opportunities that were often filled by small businesses.

Finally, new industries can be created when small businesses adapt to shifts in consumer interests and preferences. Over the last few years the explosion of wireless Internet access in schools, restaurants, airports, hotels, and cities (some of which are installing wireless access to be used by their entire citizenry) has created tremendous growth opportunities. InterDigital Communications of King of Prussia, Pennsylvania, designs wireless technology chips and devices that are used in mobile phones, personal digital assistants, laptop computers, and other wireless digital devices. With the coming shift to 3G wireless capabilities with speeds up to 2 megabits per second, InterDigital's patents and products will enable consumers to quickly and easily download music, video, and other kinds of digital files and services whenever and wherever they want.[21]

## Innovation

Small businesses are much better than large businesses at developing new and better goods and services. Although the DVD rental market was dominated by Blockbuster Video, Reed Hastings knew that there just had to be a better way. Perhaps it was that $40 late fee he had to pay Blockbuster when he forgot to return *Apollo 13*, but Hastings recalls asking himself, "How come movie rentals don't work like a health club, where whether you use it a lot or a little, you get the same charge?" And from that question, Netflix.com, the first successful online DVD rental service, was born.

Today, after just a few years in business, the Californian heads a company with more than 3 million subscribers, a DVD library of 50,000 titles, and revenue approaching $1.2 billion.[22] DVDs are mailed to subscribers and returned in prepaid postage envelopes provided by Netflix. Because they can rent several movies at a time without late fees, Netflix customers rent twice as many movies per month. Netflix is so successful that Wal-Mart discontinued its DVD

# HIT & MISS

## Tacit Networks Builds a Global Alliance

You've got a hot product or service that you're eager to export overseas. But the problem is that your U.S. operation, while successful, is small—efficient, creative, and experienced, but small. There's no easy way to buy the labor or experience needed to launch overseas operations and deal with differences in language, culture, and legal systems.

That's the problem that faced Tacit Networks, a New Jersey–based technology firm whose software lets networks share files instantly, no matter how far apart they are. With 60 employees and revenue of less than $5 million, Tacit had to come up with a way to build a global business from scratch.

The answer was to find partners first instead of clients. Tacit took its first steps into the European market by contacting technology companies interested in selling just the sort of software Tacit makes. Its first such partner, a London-based tech consulting firm called Solution Centre, agreed to a partnership in which Tacit would sell Solution its software at a 30 to 40 percent discount. Solution sells the software to end users, and Tacit provides tech support. The partnership's first client was the firm that introduced the two partners, and Solution Centre has been helping Tacit look for other business.

Similar partnership deals have since been signed, with tech firms acting as Tacit's resellers in Denmark, Ireland, and Germany. Tacit's overseas partners sign a nondisclosure agreement to protect Tacit's intellectual property. Its latest deal is with a California manufacturer of communications equipment that has a big market in Europe and will sell the file-sharing software preinstalled. "With this kind of partner," says CEO Chuck Foley, "they can't be swayed to the competition as easily."

So how have Tacit's partnerships paid off? Sales have doubled to $10 million as international sales have climbed to 20 percent of Tacit's revenue. Meanwhile, the firm continues to expand; it now has its own offices in England and Australia.

### Questions for Critical Thinking

1. Can Tacit's strategy for moving overseas apply to other small-business efforts? Why or why not?
2. Has Tacit done enough to ensure that its intellectual property will remain secure? Why or why not? What makes such precautions necessary?

**Sources:** Tacit Networks Web site, accessed June 17, 2006, http://www.tacitnetworks .com; Lucas Mearian, "Backing Up the Edge," *Computerworld*, accessed June 17, 2006, http://www.computerworld.com; Laura Kolodny, "Building a Global Alliance," *Inc.*, September 2003, p. 48.

---

rental business, choosing instead to offer Netflix DVD rentals at Wal-Mart.com. Netflix's success has also forced Blockbuster to eliminate the late fees that accounted for most of its profits.[23]

Small businesses are often fertile ground in which to plant innovative ideas for new goods and services. As a chemist in the pharmaceutical industry, Thomas E. D'Ambra saw many exciting ideas neglected because his employer lacked the resources to pursue them. D'Ambra decided that a market existed for a company that would offer research services on a contract basis to firms in the industry. His start-up business, Albany Molecular Research in Albany, New York, focused on obtaining contracts for research and development of new drugs. Today, the company employs 200 chemists and tackles research projects for such industry giants as DuPont Pharmaceuticals and Eli Lilly. With his customers facing a continued shortage of talented chemists, D'Ambra foresees a strong future for Albany Molecular.[24]

In a typical year, small firms develop twice as many product innovations per employee as larger firms. They also obtain more patents per sales dollar than do larger businesses. In addition, the fact that small firms are a richer source of innovations is even more evident than these statistics show because large firms are more likely to patent their discoveries.[25] Key 20th-century innovations that were developed by small businesses include the airplane, the audiotape recorder, double-knit fabrics, the optical scanner, the personal computer, soft contact lenses, and the zipper. One area of innovation that is likely to occupy small businesses

> ## "They Said It"
>
> "When big businesses want to innovate, what do they do? They take a bunch of guys, throw them out, and let them create a small business."
> *Zach Nelson (b. 1971)*
> *President and CEO, NetSuite*

## Steve Lipscomb, Bluffing His Way to the Top

A lawyer with an entrepreneurial frame of mind, Steve Lipscomb has created a new model of televised poker. After winning a $10,000 prize at a local poker tournament in the World Series of Poker, Lipscomb realized that ESPN, which televised the event, was missing a bet. The broadcasts were "worse than watching paint dry," he says.

The world of high-stakes poker already had several big annual events and tournaments. Lipscomb pulled them all together and created the World Poker Tour (WPT), modeled on the PGA Tour in golf. As Lipscomb says, "I created the only sports league in America where you can come out and play. If you could sell spots for people to suit up and play in the NBA finals for, say, $25,000, many people would do it. But you can't. Here, you can pay your money and compete with the best players in the world. And you can win."

Lipscomb made his dream a debt-free reality by acquiring start-up financing and signing on high-profile casinos that already hosted big events. Next, he created graphics to make viewing exciting. Icons of the cards, the players' names, and the amounts of the bets appear on the TV screen, along with a continual update on each player's odds of winning the game. With everything in place, Lipscomb needed just one more thing—a network partner. He found one in the Travel Channel, an unlikely but happy marriage that has brought the WPT a broad audience. Licensed WPT products completed the picture.

WPT's sponsor-funded prize pools recently passed $10 million, and a celebrity tournament helped bring revenue past $17 million. Although competing shows with similar graphics are springing up on channels such as Bravo and Fox Sports, Lipscomb is confident that "we make the best television." And besides, WPT already has casinos such the Bellagio, Foxwoods, Borgata, Commerce, and the Bicycle Casino on board. Says Lipscomb, "*The New York Times* said that 50 million people were playing poker on a regular basis, and no one had branded it. This became our mission."

### Questions for Critical Thinking

1. Which of the steps Lipscomb took to turn an idea into a business would apply to other entrepreneurial ventures? Which were unique to the kind of business he wanted to create?
2. Lipscomb has applied for a patent to protect the graphics he developed for his broadcasts. What else can he do to prevent competitors from adopting too many of his innovations?

**Sources:** Allyn Jaffrey Shulman, "Steve Lipscomb Changes the Face of Poker," *Card Player*, accessed June 17, 2006, http://www.cardplayer.com; Wendeen Eolis, "Lyle Berman and Steve Lipscomb's Confection: A Poker Tournament Season on National Television," PokerPages.com, accessed September 12, 2005, http://www.pokerpages.com; Larry Olmsted, "How Steve Lipscomb Reinvented Poker and Built the Hottest Business in America," *Inc.*, May 2005, pp. 80–92.

---

### assessment check

1. To what extent do small businesses help create new jobs?
2. In what ways do small businesses contribute to the economy?

during the early years of the 21st century is security—whether it's the protection of information or people. The "Hit & Miss" feature presents another hot business venture—the entrepreneur who designed the World Poker Tour.

# WHY SMALL BUSINESSES FAIL

While small businesses benefit the economy by creating new jobs, new industries, and various innovations, small businesses are much more likely to fail than large businesses, especially during economic downturns. Why? Because of management shortcomings, inadequate financing, and difficulty dealing with government regulations. These issues—quality and depth of management, availability of financing, and ability to wade through government rules and requirements—are so important that small businesses with major deficiencies in one or more of these areas may find themselves in bankruptcy proceedings.

Figure

5.2

As Figure 5.2 shows, almost one new business in three will permanently close within two years of opening, half will close within four years, and 62 percent will fail within the first six years of operation. By the tenth year, 82 of every 100 businesses will have failed. Although highly motivated and well-trained business owner-managers can overcome these potential problems, they should thoroughly analyze whether one or more of these problems may threaten the business before deciding to launch the new company.

## Management Shortcomings

Among the most common discoveries at a postmortem examination of a small-business failure is inadequate management. Business founders often possess great strengths in specific areas such as marketing or interpersonal relations, but they may suffer from hopeless deficiencies in others such as finance or order fulfillment. Large firms recruit specialists trained to manage individual functions; small businesses frequently rely on small staffs who must be adept at a variety of skills.

An even worse result occurs when people go into business with little, if any, business training. Some new businesses are begun almost entirely on the basis of what seems like a great idea for a new product. Managers assume that they will acquire needed business expertise on the job. All too often, the result is business bankruptcy.

If you are contemplating starting a new business, heed some words of warning. First, learn the basics of business. Second, recognize your own limitations. Although most small-business owners recognize the need to seek out the specialized skills of accountants and attorneys for financial and legal assistance, they often hesitate to turn to consultants and advisors for assistance in areas such as marketing, where they may lack knowledge or experience.

Founders of new businesses are typically excited about the potential of newly designed products, so they may neglect important details such as marketing research to determine whether potential customers share their excitement. Individuals considering launching a new business should first determine whether the proposed product meets the needs of a large enough market and whether they can convince the public of its superiority over competing offerings.

## Inadequate Financing

Another leading cause of small-business problems is inadequate financing. First-time business owners often assume that their firms will generate enough funds from the first month's sales to finance continuing operations. Building a business takes time, though. Employees must be trained, equipment purchased, deposits paid for rent and utilities, and marketing dollars spent to inform potential customers about the new firm and its product offerings. Even a one-person, home-based business has start-up expenses—such as a new computer or additional phone lines. Unless the owner has set aside enough funds to cover cash shortfalls during the first several months while the business is being established, the venture may collapse at an early stage.

Rate of Business Failures

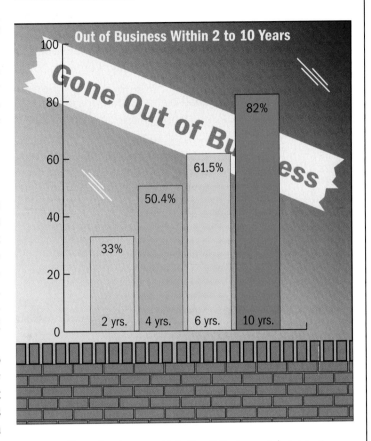

**Source:** Office of Advocacy, U.S. Small Business Administration, "Frequently Asked Questions: Advocacy Small Business Statistics and Research," accessed June 17, 2006, http://app1.sba.gov/faqs; Amy Knaup, "Survival and Longevity in the Business Employment Dynamics Data," *Monthly Labor Review* (Bureau of Labor Statistics), May 2005, p. 50.

After surviving the cash crunch that often accompanies the first months of operation, a business must confront another major financial problem: uneven cash flows. For most small and large businesses, cash inflows and outflows fluctuate greatly at different times of the year. Small retail outlets generate much of their annual sales revenues during the December holiday period. Florists make most of their deliveries during three holidays: Valentine's Day, Easter, and Mother's Day. Large firms may build sufficient cash reserves to weather periods of below-average sales, or they can turn to banks and other lenders for short-term loans. By contrast, small business start-ups often lack both cash reserves and access to sources of additional funds.

Another reason that small businesses are inadequately financed is that they rely less on debt for financing than large businesses do; 47 percent of small businesses have no outstanding loans at all, and another 25 percent have just one loan to pay off.[26] But when small firms need loans, the most frequent source of funding, as shown in Figure 5.3, is trade credit, that is, buying goods and agreeing to pay for them later, usually within 30 to 60 days. The next most commonly used sources of financing are personal credit cards, loans from commercial banks,

Figure

5.3

Sources of Small-Business Financing

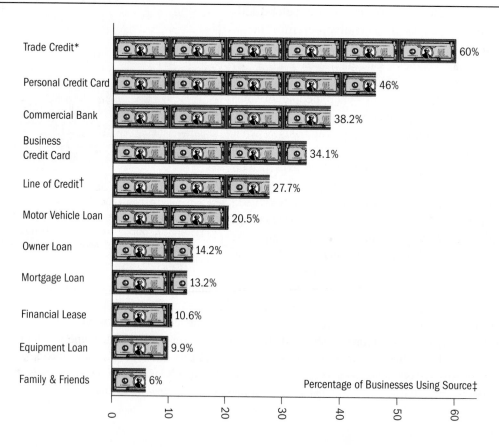

*Trade credit is purchasing goods or equipment from a supplier who finances the purchase by delaying the date of payment for those goods.

†A line of credit is an agreement between a bank and a borrower, indicating the maximum amount of credit the bank will extend to the borrower.

Note: Total exceeds 100 percent because businesses typically use more than one source of financing.

**Source:** Small Business Administration, Office of Advocacy, "Financing Patterns of Small Firms," accessed June 17, 2006, http://www.sba.gov/advo; Susan Coleman, "Free and Costly Trade Credit: A Comparison of Small Firms," Academy of Entrepreneurial Finance, accessed June 17, 2006, http://www.aoef .org/papers.

business credit cards, lines of credit from a bank, motor vehicle loans, owner loans in which the owner lends the business money, and then mortgage loans. Figure 5.3 shows that despite their relatively high interest rates, credit cards are an important source of financing for small businesses. The heaviest users of credit cards for business financing are tiny firms with fewer than ten employees. A small-business owner who has a good credit record with a consumer credit card will have relatively easy approval for a corporate credit card. Even a business owner who doesn't have the best credit history will be more apt to win approval on a credit card than on a traditional business loan.[27] As discussed later in this chapter, small-business owners may have other sources of financing as well.

Inadequate financing can compound management shortcomings by making it more difficult for small businesses to attract and keep talented people. Typically, a big company can offer a more attractive benefits package and a higher salary. During the wave of dot-com start-ups, many people decided to take a chance and work for these companies, which often offered stock options—the right to buy stock in a firm at a lower price—in place of higher salaries or better benefits. If a company succeeded, its employees could become rich. If it failed, its workers were left not only without profits but often without jobs.

With less money to spend on employees, successful small companies need to be more creative. Ronald Richey, who runs Precision Plastics, an injection-molding plant in Columbia City, Indiana, watched one-fifth of his employees quit each year. Lacking sufficient employees to operate the factory, he had to keep some of his machinery idle every week. Richey tried better communication and hiring temporary workers, but nothing worked. Then he thought of an innovative arrangement: If employees would work five 6-hour shifts without lunch breaks, he would pay them 40 hours' wages each week for 30 hours of work. Two weeks into the new plan, turnover plummeted—and quality improved. Even with what is effectively a higher pay scale, Precision's profits have grown.[28]

## *Government Regulation*

Small-business owners often complain bitterly about excessive government regulation and red tape. Paperwork costs alone account for billions of small-business dollars each year. A large company can better cope with requirements for forms and reports. Larger firms often find that it makes economic sense to hire or contract with specialists in specific types of regulation, such as employment law and workplace safety regulations. By contrast, small businesses often struggle to absorb the costs of government paperwork because of their more limited staff and budgets. Some small firms close for this reason alone.

Recognizing the burden of regulation on small businesses, Congress sometimes exempts the smallest companies from certain regulations. For example, small businesses with 49 or fewer employees are exempt from the Family and Medical Leave Act, which gives employees up to twelve weeks of unpaid leave each year to take care of a newborn child, adopt a child, or care for a family member who has serious health problems.[29] Most small-business owners comply with employment and other laws, believing that such compliance is ethically correct and fosters better employee relations than trying to determine which regulations don't apply to a small business. To help small businesses obey employment laws, the U.S. Department of Labor provides forms and guidelines at its "elaws Advisors" Web page (http://www .dol.gov/elaws/). Employers can also file these forms online.

Taxes are another burdensome expense for a small business. In addition to local, state, and federal income taxes, employers must pay taxes covering workers' compensation insurance, Social Security payments, and unemployment benefits. Although large companies have similar expenses, they generally have more resources to cover them.

**assessment check**

1. What percentage of small businesses will still be in business two, four, six, and ten years after starting?

2. How do management shortcomings, inadequate financing, and government regulation make small businesses more likely to fail?

# INCREASING THE LIKELIHOOD OF SMALL-BUSINESS SUCCESS

In spite of the challenges just discussed, many small businesses do succeed. How can a prospective owner gain the many advantages of running a smaller firm while also overcoming the disadvantages? Most successful entrepreneurs believe that two recommendations are critical:

- Develop a business plan.
- Use the resources provided by such agencies as the Small Business Administration, local business incubators, and other sources for advice, funding, and networking opportunities.

## Creating a Business Plan

business plan written document that provides an orderly statement of a company's goals, the methods by which it intends to achieve those goals, and the standards by which it will measure achievements.

Perhaps the most important task a would-be business owner faces is creating a business plan. An effective business plan can mean the difference between a company that succeeds and one that fails. A business plan is a written document that provides an orderly statement of a company's goals, the methods by which it intends to achieve these goals, and the standards by which it will measure achievements.

Business plans give the organization a sense of purpose. They provide guidance, influence, and leadership, as well as communicate ideas about goals and the means of achieving them to associates, employees, lenders, and others. In addition, they set standards against which achievements can be measured. Although no single format best suits all situations, a good small-business plan includes the methods and time frames for achieving specific goals (sales, profits, or changes in market share), as well as cash flow projections (both income received by the business and funds disbursed to pay expenses). Because business plans are essential tools for securing funding, the financial section should be thorough, professional, and based on sound assumptions. A business plan also includes the following components:

- An *executive summary* that briefly answers the who, what, why, when, where, and how questions for the business
- An *introduction* that includes a general statement of the concept, purpose, and objectives of the proposed business
- Separate *financial* and *marketing sections* that describe the firm's target market and marketing plan as well as detailed financial forecasts of the need for funds and when the firm is expected to break even—the level of sales at which revenues equal costs
- *Résumés of principals*—especially in plans written to obtain financing

Business plans are discussed in more detail in Appendix C, "Developing a Business Plan," and on the *Contemporary Business* Web site.

## Small Business Administration

Small Business Administration (SBA) federal agency that aids small businesses by providing management training and consulting, financial assistance, and support in securing government contracts.

Small businesses can benefit from using the resources provided by the Small Business Administration (SBA). The SBA is the principal government agency concerned with helping small U.S. firms, and it is the advocate for small businesses within the federal government. Over 3,000 employees staff the SBA's Washington headquarters and its regional and field offices. The primary operating functions of the SBA include providing financial assistance, aiding in government procurement matters, and providing management training and consulting.

*Financial Assistance from the SBA* Contrary to popular belief, the SBA seldom provides direct business loans. Its major financing contributions are the guarantees it provides for small-business loans made by private lenders, including banks and other institutions. Direct SBA loans are available in only a few special situations, such as natural disaster recovery and energy conservation or development programs. For example, after Hurricane Katrina destroyed homes and businesses in New Orleans and the southern coastal regions of Louisiana, Mississippi, and Alabama, the SBA offered small businesses disaster loans up to $1.5 million to repair or replace damaged buildings, equipment, inventory, and supplies.[30] Even in these special instances, a business applicant must contribute a portion of the proposed project's total cost in cash, home equity, or stocks to qualify. However, in the case of Hurricane Katrina, if everything associated with a small business was destroyed, the SBA used the business's real estate as collateral.

The SBA also guarantees **microloans** of up to $35,000 to start-ups and other very small firms.[31] Microloans may be used to buy equipment or operate a business but not to buy real estate or pay off other loans. These loans are available from nonprofit organizations located in most states. Other sources of microloans include the federal Economic Development Administration, some state governments, and certain private lenders, such as credit unions and community development groups.

AP PHOTO/CHARLIE RIEDEL

C. Ray Bergeron salvages his tire inventory as he cleans out the flood-damaged office of his service station in the lakeside area of New Orleans. Bergeron's business was under eight feet of floodwater after Hurricane Katrina hit. Bergeron managed to salvage about $15,000 worth of tires, but the rest of his business was a total loss.

Small-business loans are also available through SBA-licensed organizations called **Small Business Investment Companies (SBICs),** which are run by experienced venture capitalists. SBICs use their own capital, supplemented with government loans, to invest in small businesses. Like banks, SBICs are profit-making enterprises, but they are likely to be more flexible than banks in their lending decisions. Well-known companies that used SBIC financing when they were start-ups include Apple Computer, Callaway Golf, America Online, Federal Express, Intel, Staples, and Outback Steakhouse.

Another financial resource underwritten by the SBA is *Active Capital,* which matches entrepreneurs looking for start-up capital with potential investors willing to exchange their money and advice for partial ownership of the company. Entrepreneurs post information about their businesses on the Active Capital Web site, where potential investors can review it. Interested parties contact the firms. The goal is to help businesses seeking smaller amounts of capital than those typically handled by bigger investment firms. However, small businesses can raise up to $5 million via Active Capital. Why use Active Capital? Because, as a nonprofit organization sanctioned by the SBA, Active Capital charges a small annual fee of $1,000 but no commissions, which makes it a cheap, safe, and secure way for entrepreneurs and investors to exchange information and do business.[32]

*Other Specialized Assistance* Although government purchases represent a huge market, small companies have difficulty competing for this business with giant firms, which employ specialists to handle the volumes of paperwork involved in preparing proposals and completing bid applications. Today, many government procurement programs set aside portions of government spending for small companies; an additional SBA role is to help small firms secure these contracts. With **set-aside programs** for small businesses, up to 23 percent of certain government contracts are designated for small businesses.[33] Every federal agency with buying authority must maintain an Office of Small and Disadvantaged Business Utilization to ensure that small businesses receive a reasonable portion of government procurement contracts. To help connect small businesses with government agencies, the SBA's Web site offers Central Contractor Registration, which includes a search engine for finding business opportunities as well as a chance for small businesses to provide information about themselves.[34] Set-aside programs are also common in the private sector, particularly among major corporations.

In addition to help with financing and government procurement, the SBA delivers a variety of other services to small businesses. It provides information and advice through toll-free telephone numbers and its Web site, http://www.sba.gov, where you can find detailed information about starting, financing, and managing a small business, along with further information about businesses opportunities and disaster recovery. Finally, through its Small Business Training Network, the SBA offers free online courses; sponsors inexpensive training courses on topics such as taxes, networking, and start-ups in cities and small towns throughout the country; and provides a free online library of more than 200 SBA publications and additional business resources.

## Business Incubators

**business incubator** organization that provides temporary low-cost, shared facilities to small start-up ventures.

Some local community agencies interested in encouraging business development have implemented a concept called a **business incubator** to provide low-cost shared business facilities to small start-up ventures. A typical incubator might section off space in an abandoned plant and rent it to various small firms. Tenants often share clerical staff, computers, and other business services. The objective is that, after a few months or years, the fledgling business will be ready to move out and operate on its own.

Hundreds of business incubator programs operate nationwide. About half are run by not-for-profit organizations, including industrial development authorities. The remainder are divided between college- and university-sponsored incubators and business-run incubators.[35] These facilities offer management support services and valuable management advice from in-house mentors. Operating in an incubator gives entrepreneurs easy access to such basic needs as telephones and human resources experts. They also can trade ideas with one another.

**assessment check**

1. What components should be part of a good business plan?
2. What are the various ways and methods by which the SBA helps small businesses with financing and getting government contracts?

# SMALL-BUSINESS OPPORTUNITIES FOR WOMEN AND MINORITIES

The thousands of new business start-ups each year include growing numbers of women-owned firms as well as new businesses launched by African Americans, Hispanics, and members of other minority groups. The numbers of women-owned and minority-owned businesses are growing much faster than the overall growth in U.S. businesses. The people who start these companies see small-business ownership and operation as an attractive and lucrative alternative to working for someone else.

## Women-Owned Businesses

In the United States today, more than 10.6 million women-owned firms provide jobs for almost 19.1 million people. Forty-eight percent of U.S. businesses are owned by women, compared with one-fourth to one-third of businesses worldwide. One of every five of these businesses is owned by minority women.[36]

Women, like men, have a variety of reasons for starting their own companies. Some are driven by an idea that they believe can help others. Some have a unique business idea that they want to bring to life, such as Kimberly See, an African American business woman who founded Arlington, Texas–based kemse & company, which offers a line of multicultural stationery and invitations designed for women of color.[37] Others decide to strike out on their own when they lose their jobs or become frustrated with the bureaucracies in large companies. In other cases, women leave large corporations when they feel blocked from opportunities for advancement. Sometimes this occurs because they hit the so-called glass ceiling, discussed in Chapter 8. Because women are more likely than men to be the primary caregivers in their families, some may seek self-employment as a way to achieve flexible working hours so they can spend more time with their families.

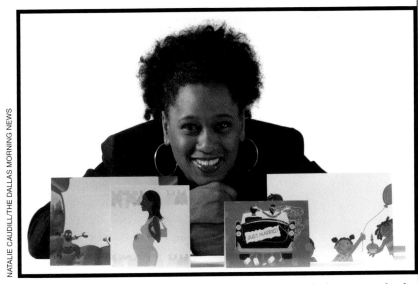

After being unable to find stationery, invitations, or greeting cards showing people of color, Kim See started her own business, kemse & company. "I decided to take matters into my own hands and create a line of paper products, in particular, invitations, to fill that void." Her products have been featured in the *Dallas Morning News* and *Essence* and *O* magazines.

The fastest growth among women-owned firms is occurring in construction, transportation and communications, and agricultural services.[38] One woman who created a successful manufacturing business is Karen Alvarez of Dublin, California. She got her original product idea when she was grocery shopping with her children and one child fell from the shopping cart. To prevent such accidents, which occur to thousands of children every year, Alvarez developed the Baby Comfort Strap, a simple padded strap that parents use to buckle a small child to a cart or stroller. She consulted experienced retailers and manufacturers for help in developing packaging, pricing, and testing. When the Baby Comfort Strap proved to be a reliable seller, Alvarez began a successful strategy to generate publicity about the frequency of shopping carts' resulting in injuries to small children. This led to widespread awareness of the problem—and about how the Baby Comfort Strap could resolve it. This publicity worked, and Alvarez was able to set up distribution throughout the United States.[39]

As the number of female small-business owners has grown, they have also been able to establish powerful support networks in a relatively short time. Many nationwide business assistance programs serve women exclusively. Among the programs offered by the Small Business Administration are the Contract Assistance for Women Business Owners program, which teaches women how to market to the federal government; the Women's Network for Entrepreneurial Training, which matches experienced female entrepreneurs with women trying to get started; and dozens of Women's Business Centers, which offer training and counseling in operating a business.

Springboard Enterprises is a nonprofit organization based in Washington, D.C., that promotes entrepreneurship and acquisition of capital for women entrepreneurs. Amy Millman, president of Springboard, assesses the small-business environment for women this way: "If you are an entrepreneur, it is always the right time to launch a business. There is great opportunity [if you] focus on the fundamentals. Remember, there is no free lunch."[40] In addition, women can find encouragement, advice, and mentors by joining organizations such as Women Entrepreneurs and the Forum for Women Entrepreneurs and Executives, both of which support women who want to start high-growth companies.[41]

**"They Said It"**

"Whatever women do, they must do twice as well as men to be thought half as good. Luckily, this is not difficult."
*Charlotte Whitton (1896–1975) Mayor of Ottawa*

## Minority-Owned Businesses

Business ownership is also an important opportunity for America's racial and ethnic minorities. In recent years, the growth in the number of businesses owned by African Americans, Hispanics, and Asian Americans has far outpaced the growth in the number of U.S. businesses overall. Figure 5.4 shows the percentages of minority ownership in major industries. The relatively strong presence of minorities in the services and retail industries is especially significant because these industries contain the greatest number of businesses.

Hispanics are the nation's largest group of minority business owners, followed by Asian American, African American, and Native American owners.[42] The Small Business Administration attributes some of this pattern to strong population growth among Hispanics, whose disposable income is also growing at twice the rate of non-Hispanics.[43] Even more growth lies ahead for Hispanic-owned businesses during this decade, especially as trade between the United States and Latin America increases under NAFTA and CAFTA (see Chapter 4 for more information on NAFTA and CAFTA).

Historically, large numbers of U.S. immigrants have started businesses. In fact, immigrants own nearly 15 percent of all small businesses.[44] In addition, both male and female immigrants are more likely to own small businesses than are native-born Americans. For example, 8 percent of female immigrants own small businesses compared with 6 percent of women born in

**5.4** Types of Businesses Owned by Racial and Ethnic Minorities

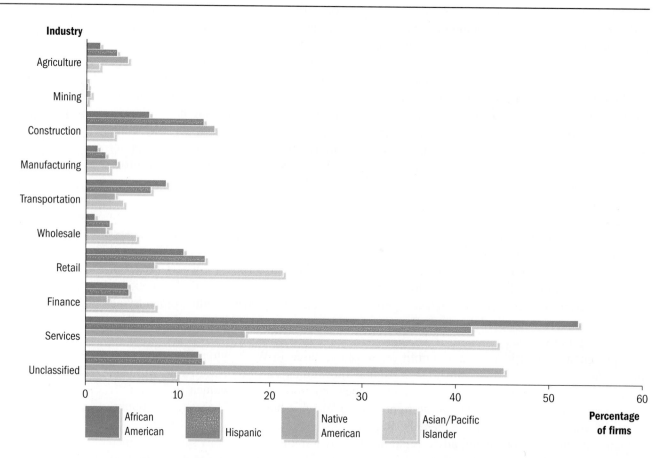

**Source:** Data from Office of Advocacy, U.S. Small Business Administration, "Minorities in Business," p. 17, accessed June 17, 2006, http://www.sba.gov/advo.

the United States.[45] Susana Cook, originally from Peru, who with her husband owns Cook's Natural Foods and Universal Medical Supply in Little Rock, Arkansas, said, "In our countries owning your own business is a struggle; here it's like a dream come true. Here they do not put so many obstacles or red tape in your way."[46]

Despite their progress, minority business owners still face considerable obstacles. Minority entrepreneurs tend to start businesses on a smaller scale and have more difficulty finding investors than other entrepreneurs. They rely less on bank credit than do other business owners, possibly because they have a harder time getting loans from banks. According to the Federal Reserve, bank loan applications of Hispanic- and African American–owned businesses are rejected at twice the rate of white-owned businesses. Not surprisingly, other research finds that roughly half of minority small-business owners don't even apply for bank loans, presumably because they believe their loan requests will be turned down.[47]

# THE FRANCHISING ALTERNATIVE

Franchising is a major factor in the growth of small businesses. **Franchising** is a contractual business arrangement between a manufacturer or another supplier and a dealer. The contract specifies the methods by which the dealer markets the good or service of the supplier. Franchises can involve both goods and services; some well-known franchises are Burger King, KFC, McDonald's, Jiffy Lube, Domino's Pizza, Coldwell Banker Real Estate, and Supercuts.

Starting a small, independent company can be a risky, time-consuming endeavor, but franchising can reduce the amount of time and effort needed to expand. The franchisor has already developed and tested the concept, and the brand may already be familiar to prospective customers.

**franchising** contractual agreement that specifies the methods by which a dealer can produce and market a supplier's good or service.

## The Franchising Sector

Franchising started just after the U.S. Civil War, when the Singer Company decided to build its business by franchising retail sewing machine outlets. The concept became increasingly popular after 1900 in the automobile industry. Automobile travel led to demand for local auto sales and service outlets, as well as gasoline, oil, and tire retailers. Auto manufacturers created systems of franchised distributors and then set up local retailers in each retail location—auto dealers, gas stations, tire stores, and auto parts retailers. Dunkin Donuts, Meineke Muffler, and Super 8 Motels also set up their distribution systems through a network of local and regional franchises.

Today, the franchising concept continues its rapid growth. U.S. franchises generate sales of $1.53 trillion annually and employ more than 18 million people.[48] According to *Entrepreneur*, the Number one franchise is Subway, with Curves (exercise centers for women) coming in second. Quizno's Subs, the Jackson Hewitt Tax Service, UPS Stores, Sonic Drive-In, Jani-King (janitorial services), 7-Eleven, Dunkin' Donuts, and RE/MAX real estate complete the rest of *Entrepreneur*'s top ten list.[49] Areas in which strong growth is likely to continue include technology consulting; products for seniors and kids, both of which are growing population segments; and anything having to do with fitness or weight loss. With weight problems at epidemic proportions, Curves, whose slogan is "No men, no mirrors, no makeup," is growing 37 percent per year, has 4 million members and 9,000 centers after ten years in business, and is planning to open another 8,000 centers in Asia and Europe in the near future. Figure 5.5 shows four of the hottest industries in which franchising growth is currently occurring.

Franchising overseas is also a growing trend for franchisors and franchisees who want to expand into foreign markets. It seems that anywhere you go in the world, you can get a

**"They Said It"**

"The road to success is dotted with many tempting parking spaces."
*Anonymous*

Figure

5.5   The Fastest-Growing Franchises by Industry

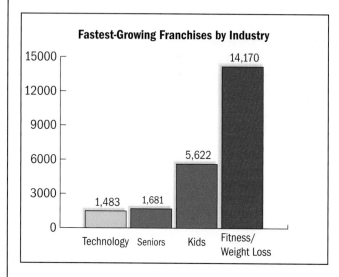

**Fastest-Growing Franchises by Industry**

- Technology: 1,483
- Seniors: 1,681
- Kids: 5,622
- Fitness/Weight Loss: 14,170

**Source:** Sara Wilson, "All the Rage: Wondering What Everyone Will Be Crazy About in the Coming Year? Take a Sneak Peek at the Hottest Franchising Trends for 2005," *Entrepreneur*, accessed June 17, 2006, http://www .entrepreneur.com.

McDonald's burger. But other international franchises, such as Best Western, Pak Mail, Pizza Hut, KFC, Subway, and 7-Eleven, are almost as common.

Some people get into franchising because they can operate their business from home, another continuing trend. Examples of these franchises include ServiceMaster Clean, Chem-Dry Carpet Drapery & Upholstery Cleaning, Snap-On Tools, and Lawn Doctor.[50]

## Franchising Agreements

The two principals in a franchising agreement are the franchisee and the franchisor. The individual or business firm purchasing the franchise is called the **franchisee,** while the small-business owner who contracts to sell the good or service of the supplier is called the **franchisor.** In exchange for some payment (usually a fee plus a percentage of franchise sales) from the franchisee, the franchisor typically provides building plans, site selection help, managerial and accounting systems, and other services to assist the franchisee. Franchisees' total costs can vary over a wide range. The initial fee paid by a franchisee to McDonald's for a new McDonald's franchise is $45,000, but the total start-up costs can run anywhere from $500,000 to $1.6 million. In contrast, the initial fee for a Subway franchise is $12,500, but the total start-up costs range from $70,000 to $220,000.[51] The franchisor also provides name recognition for the small-business owner who becomes a franchisee. This public image is created by their familiarity with the franchise in other geographical areas and by advertising campaigns, all or part of which is paid for by contributions by the franchisees.

Curves, the second-fastest-growing franchise in the United States, uses weightlifting and diet management to help its customers lose weight. For 30 minutes, three times a week, customers build muscles, strengthen joints, and increase flexibility by working their way around a circuit of weight-bearing machines.

Franchise agreements often specify that the franchisee will receive materials, equipment, and training from the franchisor. Charmain and Charles Smith bought a Fruitfull Frozen Fruit Bars franchise from Happy & Healthy Products for $28,000, financing much of the purchase price with an SBA-backed loan. Charmain, with a decade of experience in the food service business, runs the franchise. Her husband, who also has a full-time job as a corporate financial executive, provides accounting and other services. The basic agreement with Happy & Healthy Products provides the franchisees with ten freezers, two pallets of frozen fruit and yogurt bars, and a week of training, which covers sales and the company's products and equipment. The franchisee then sells the product to retailers to be stocked in either Fruitfull freezers or the retailer's own freezers. The Smiths' franchise has accounts in Georgia, including Kroger supermarkets, a chain of health clubs, and school cafeterias.[52]

AP PHOTO/PAT WELLENBACH

# Benefits and Problems of Franchising

As with any other business, a franchise purchaser bears the responsibility for researching what he or she is buying. Poorly financed or poorly managed franchise systems offer opportunities no better than those in poorly financed or poorly managed independent businesses. Although franchises are more likely than independent businesses to succeed, many franchises do go out of business. The franchising concept does not eliminate the risks of a potential small-business investment; it simply adds alternatives.

Advantages of franchises include a prior performance record, a recognizable company name, a business model that has proven successful in other locations, a tested management program, and business training for the franchisee. An existing franchise has posted a performance record on which the prospective buyer can base comparisons and judgments. Earlier results can indicate the likelihood of success in a proposed venture. In addition, a widely recognized name gives the franchisee a tremendous advantage; auto dealers, for instance, know that their brand-name products will attract particular segments of the market.

A tested management program usually allows the prospective franchisee to avoid worrying about setting up an accounting system, establishing quality-control standards, or designing employment application forms. In addition, most franchisors offer valuable business training. McDonald's teaches the basics of operating a franchise at its Hamburger University in Oak Brook, Illinois. Franchise operators quickly learn to meet customer expectations by following strict guidelines for how many seconds to cook the french fries and what words to use when serving customers. By following the franchisor's standards and building on an existing brand name, franchise operators typically can generate profits faster than an independent business owner. That was the case for Joe Grimand 25 years ago. After serving as a pilot in the Air Force, he knew he wanted to run his own business, but he had no business experience. So he bought into a Precision Tune Auto Care franchise, worked long hours, followed the company's advice, and adhered to its management system. Today he owns eight Precision stores, which together generate nearly $5 million in annual revenues. Says Grimand, "Looking back, I never thought it would grow to what it is now."[53]

On the negative side, franchise fees and future payments can be very expensive. As with any business, a franchise may well be unprofitable during its first months and at times thereafter. Payments to the franchisor can add to the burden of keeping the business afloat until the owner begins to earn a profit.

Another potential drawback stems from the fact that the franchisee is linked to the reputation and management of the franchise. If customers are unhappy with their experience at one franchised sandwich shop, they might avoid stopping at another one several miles away, even if the second one is owned and operated by someone else. So a strong, effective program of managerial control is essential to maintain a franchise brand's effectiveness. Before signing on with a franchisor, potential franchisees should carefully study its financial performance and reputation and talk with current franchise owners. Sources of information include the franchisor as well as state consumer protection agencies, the Better Business Bureau, and the Federal Trade Commission. The FTC's Web site includes advice for franchisees and reports of complaints against franchisors. Potential franchisees also should study the franchise agreement carefully to make sure they can succeed within the limitations of the agreement. In some instances, franchisors pursue additional sales by establishing new distribution outlets, which may compete directly with established franchisees. In today's online business environment, it is important to ask whether the franchisor retains the right to sell the same products online that the franchisee is trying to sell through a local outlet.

Even well-known, previously successful franchises can suffer from problems. Most people don't realize it, but auto dealers, just like McDonald's and Burger King stores, are franchises with the exclusive right to resell an auto manufacturer's cars. So when a franchisor like GM suffers, its dealers, that is, its franchises, suffer right along with it. And with its U.S. market share at half of what it was 25 years ago, GM has been suffering a lot, and so have its franchises.[54] For example, 20 years ago, Jeff Wooley's Pontiac dealership in Tampa, Florida, was selling 300 cars a month. Today, however, it's about 50 cars a month.[55] By contrast, since his Nissan dealership, which once sold 100 cars a month, now sells twice that many and will likely sell 300 cars a month within a few years, Wooley tore down his large Pontiac showroom, replacing it with a new $4.5 million showroom for Nissans.

Finally, some people are more suited to the demands of operating a franchise than others. Any person who is considering buying a franchise must think first about whether he or she has the right personality for the endeavor. Chapter 6 features an in-depth discussion of the basic characteristics that entrepreneurs should bring to their new endeavors.

**assessment check**

1. Distinguish between a franchisor and a franchisee.
2. Name some of the largest franchises.
3. What are the benefits and problems of franchising?

# ALTERNATIVES FOR ORGANIZING A BUSINESS

Whether small or large, every business fits one of three categories of legal ownership: sole proprietorships, partnerships, and corporations. As Figure 5.6 shows, sole proprietorships are the most common form of business ownership. Although a much smaller percentage of firms are organized as corporations, corporate revenues are nineteen times as large as the revenues earned by all sole proprietorships. After all, a corporate giant such as Wal-Mart, with annual sales of nearly $320 billion, has a huge impact on the nation's economy.

Each form offers unique advantages and disadvantages, as outlined in Table 5.2. To overcome certain limitations of the traditional ownership structures, owners may also use three specialized organizational forms: S corporations, limited-liability partnerships, and limited-liability companies. Along with the basic forms, this section also briefly examines each of these alternatives.

**sole proprietorship** form of business ownership in which the company is owned and operated by one person.

## Sole Proprietorships

The most common form of business ownership, the **sole proprietorship** is also the oldest and the simplest because no legal distinction separates the sole proprietor's status as an individual from his or her status as a business owner. Although sole proprietorships are common in a variety of industries, they are concentrated primarily among small businesses such as repair shops, small retail outlets, and service providers, such as painters, plumbers, and lawn care operations.

Sole proprietorships offer advantages that other business entities cannot. For one, they are easy to form and dissolve. (Partnerships are also easy to form, but difficult to dissolve.) A sole proprietorship offers management flexibility for the owner, along with the right to retain all profits after payment of personal income taxes. Retention of all profits and responsibility for all losses give sole proprietors the incentive to maximize efficiency in their operations.

Minimal legal requirements simplify entering and exiting a sole proprietorship. Usually, the owner must meet only a few legal requirements for starting one, including registering the business or trade name—to guarantee that two firms do not use the same name—and taking out any necessary licenses. Local

**Figure**

**5.6** Forms of Business Ownership

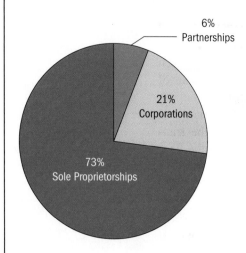

6%
Partnerships

21%
Corporations

73%
Sole Proprietorships

**Source:** Data from U.S. Census Bureau, "Statistics about Business Size (Including Small Business) from the U.S. Census Bureau," http://www.census.gov.

Table 5.2

Comparing the Three Major Forms of Private Ownership

| Form of Ownership | Number of Owners | Liability | Advantages | Disadvantages |
|---|---|---|---|---|
| Sole proprietorship | One owner | Unlimited personal liability for business debt | 1. Owner retains all profits<br>2. Easy to form and dissolve<br>3. Owner has flexibility | 1. Unlimited financial liability<br>2. Financing limitations<br>3. Management deficiencies<br>4. Lack of continuity |
| Partnership | Two or more owners | Personal assets of any operating partner at risk from business creditors | 1. Easy to form<br>2. Can benefit from complementary management skills<br>3. Expanded financial capacity | 1. Unlimited financial liability<br>2. Interpersonal conflicts<br>3. Lack of continuity<br>4. Difficult to dissolve |
| Corporation | Unlimited number of shareholders; up to 75 share-holders for S corporations | Limited | 1. Limited financial liability<br>2. Specialized management skills<br>3. Expanded financial capacity<br>4. Economies of large-scale operations | 1. Difficult and costly to form and dissolve<br>2. Tax disadvantages<br>3. Legal restrictions |

governments require that certain kinds of licenses be obtained before opening restaurants, motels, and retail stores. Some occupational licenses require firms to carry specific types of insurance, such as liability coverage.

The ease of dissolving a sole proprietorship is an attractive feature for certain types of enterprises. This advantage is particularly important for temporary businesses set up to handle just a few transactions. Ownership flexibility is another advantage of a sole proprietorship. The owner can make management decisions without consulting others, take prompt action when needed, and keep trade secrets. You've probably heard people say, "I like being my own boss." This flexibility leads many business owners to prefer the sole proprietorship organization form.

A disadvantage of the sole proprietorship form is the owner's personal financial liability for all debts of the business. Also, the business must operate with financial resources limited to the owner's personal funds and money that he or she can borrow. Such financing limitations can keep the business from expanding. Another disadvantage is that the owner must handle a wide range of management and operational tasks; as the firm grows, the owner may not be able to perform all duties with equal effectiveness. Finally, a sole proprietorship lacks long-term continuity, because death, bankruptcy, retirement, or a change in personal interests can terminate it.

These limitations can make potential customers nervous about buying major goods or services from a sole proprietorship. When they know the form of organization being used by their supplier, they may worry that the sole proprietor will not be around long enough or have the resources to fulfill the agreement. Paulette Thomas, who writes the Startup Q&A column for the *Wall Street Journal*, says that because of that risk, "It makes no sense for such behemoths as BellSouth [or any other large corporation] with its $22.6 billion in annual revenue to parcel out that work to solo operators."[56]

## Partnerships

Another option for organizing a business is to form a partnership. The Uniform Partnership Act, which regulates this ownership form in most states, defines a **partnership** as an association of two or more persons who operate a business as co-owners by voluntary legal agreement. The partnership was the traditional form of ownership for professionals offering services, such as physicians, lawyers, and dentists. Today, most of these service providers have switched to other organizational forms to limit personal liability.

Like sole proprietorships, partnerships are easy to form. The legal requirements consist of registering the business name and taking out the necessary licenses. Partnerships also offer expanded financial capabilities when each partner invests money. They also usually increase access to borrowed funds compared with sole proprietorships. Another advantage is the opportunity for professionals to combine complementary skills and knowledge. In the earlier example of Charmain and Charles Smith's Fruitfull Frozen Fruit Bars franchise, the two franchise owners each contribute important skills. Charmain has experience as a manager in the food service business, and Charles has a financial background.

Like sole proprietorships, most partnerships have the disadvantage of unlimited financial liability. Each partner bears full responsibility for the debts of the firm, and each is legally liable for the actions of the other partners. Partners must pay the partnership's debts from their personal funds if it ceases operations and its debts exceed its assets. Breaking up a partnership is also a much more complicated undertaking than dissolving a sole proprietorship. Rather than simply withdrawing funds from the bank, the partner who wants out may need to find someone to buy his or her interest in the firm.

In many states, partners can minimize some of these risks by organizing as a limited liability partnership. In many respects, such a partnership resembles a general partnership, but laws limit the liability of the partners to the value of their investments in the company.

The death of a partner also threatens the survival of a partnership. A new partnership must be formed, and the estate of the deceased is entitled to a share of the firm's value. To ease the financial strains of such events, business planners recommend life insurance coverage for each partner, combined with a buy-sell agreement. The insurance proceeds can be used to repay the deceased partner's heirs and allow the surviving partner to retain control of the business.

Because partnerships are vulnerable to personal conflicts that can quickly escalate into business battles, you should carefully choose your business partners. Scott Stewart, whose former business partner spent extravagantly, said, "People told me a business partnership is like a marriage. I didn't understand it until now. You have to go through a dating period to find out if you're compatible."[57] Good communication is the key to resolving conflicts before they damage a partnership's chances for success or even destroy it.

## Corporations

A **corporation** is a legal organization with assets and liabilities separate from those of its owner(s). Although even the smallest business can choose the corporate form of organization, most people think of large companies when they hear the term *corporation*. In truth, many corporations are extremely large businesses.

Recently, ExxonMobil, whose annual worldwide sales are nearly $340 billion, passed longtime number one–ranked Wal-Mart to become the largest U.S.-based corporation in terms of sales. ExxonMobil has been ranked third for a number of years, so its move to the number one slot pushed General Motors to number three on the list, ahead of Chevron and Ford Motor Company. The list of the ten largest U.S. corporations contains another manufacturer, General

Electric, as well as banking firm Citigroup, insurance and financial firm AIG, information technology solution provider IBM, and international petroleum giants.[58]

The corporate ownership form offers considerable advantages. First, because a corporation acquires the status of a separate legal entity, its stockholders have only limited financial risk. If the firm fails, they lose only the money they have invested. Protection also applies to legal risk. Class-action suits filed against automakers, cigarette makers, and drug manufacturers are filed against the companies, not the owners of those companies. The limited risk of corporate ownership is clearly reflected in corporate names throughout the world. While many U.S. and Canadian corporations include the designation *Inc.* in their names, British firms use the abbreviation *Ltd.* to identify their limited liability. In Australia, the abbreviation for *proprietary limited*—Pty. Ltd.—is frequently included in corporate names.

Corporations offer other advantages. They can draw on the specialized skills of many employees, unlike the typical sole proprietorship or partnership, for which managerial skills are usually confined to the abilities of their owners and a small number of employees. Corporations gain access to expanded financial capabilities based on the opportunity to offer direct outside investments such as stock sales.

The large-scale operation permitted by corporate ownership also results in a number of advantages for this legal form of organization. Employees can specialize in their most effective tasks. A large firm can generate internal financing for many projects by transferring money from one part of the corporation to another. Long manufacturing runs usually promote efficient production and allow the firm to charge highly competitive prices that attract customers.

One major disadvantage for a corporation is the double taxation of corporate earnings. After a corporation pays federal, state, and local income taxes on its profits, its owners (stockholders) also pay personal taxes on any distributions of those profits they receive from the corporation in the form of dividends. One of the key components of the 2003 U.S. tax cut was the reduction of federal taxes on corporate dividends to 15 percent. Prior to passage of the economic stimulus legislation, people in the highest income bracket would pay more than 38 percent of any dividends received in federal taxes.

Corporate ownership also involves some legal issues that sole proprietorships and partnerships do not encounter. The number of laws and regulations that affect corporations has increased dramatically in recent years.

To avoid double taxation of business income while achieving or retaining limited financial liability for their owners, some firms have modified the traditional corporate and partnership structures. Businesses that meet certain size requirements, including ownership by no more than 75 shareholders, may organize as **S corporations,** also called *subchapter S corporations.* These firms can elect to pay federal income taxes as partnerships while retaining the liability limitations typical of corporations. The tax advantage of S corporations over typical corporations, which incur double taxation, is that S corporations are only taxed once. Unlike regular corporations, S corporations do not pay corporate taxes on their profits. Instead, the untaxed profits of S corporations are paid directly as dividends to shareholders, who then pay the lower 15 percent corporate dividend tax rate. This tax advantage has induced a fivefold increase in the number of S corporations. Consequently, the IRS is closely auditing S corporations for abuse because some businesses that don't meet the legal requirements have formed S corporations to illegally take advantage of the S corporation's lower taxes.[59]

Business owners may also form **limited liability companies (LLCs)** to secure the corporate advantage of limited liability while avoiding the double taxation characteristic of corporations. An LLC is governed by an operating agreement that resembles a partnership agreement, except that it reduces each partner's liability for the actions of the other owners. Professional corporations—such as law offices, accounting firms, and physicians—use a similar approach, with the abbreviation *PC* shown at the end of the name of the business.

## Changing Legal Structures to Meet Changing Needs

Before deciding on an appropriate legal form, someone planning to launch a new business must consider dozens of factors, such as these:

- Personal financial situations and the need for additional funds for the business's start-up and continued operation
- Management skills and limitations
- Management styles and capabilities of working with partners and other members of top management
- Concerns about exposure to personal liability

**assessment check**

1. What are the key differences between sole proprietorships, partnerships, and corporations?
2. What are the advantages and disadvantages of sole proprietorships, partnerships, and corporations?

Although the legal form of organization is a major decision, new business owners need not treat it as a permanent decision. Over time, changing conditions such as business growth may prompt the owner of a sole proprietorship or a group of partners to switch to a more appropriate form. For example, if you have a successful business organized as a limited liability company, but you want to give your children or other family members partial ownership, you can give them shares of the company by switching to a corporation. And you can do this without giving up control of the company or paying a gift tax.[60]

# ORGANIZING AND OPERATING A CORPORATION

One of the first decisions in forming a corporation is determining where to locate its headquarters and where it will do business. This section describes the various types of corporations and considers the options and procedures involved in incorporating a business.

## Types of Corporations

Corporations fall into three categories: domestic, foreign, or alien. A firm is considered a **domestic corporation** in the state where it is incorporated. When a company does business in states other than the one where it has filed incorporation papers, it is registered as a **foreign corporation** in each of those states. A firm incorporated in one nation that operates in another is known as an **alien corporation** where it operates. Some firms—particularly large corporations with operations scattered around the world—may operate under all three of these designations.

## The Incorporation Process

Suppose that you decide to start a business, and you believe that the corporate form offers the best way to organize it. Where should you set up shop? How do you establish a corporate charter? The following paragraphs discuss the procedures for creating a new corporation.

**Where to Incorporate** Location is one of the most important considerations for any small-business owner. Although most small and medium-sized businesses are incorporated in the states where they do most of their business, a U.S. firm can actually incorporate in any state it chooses. The founders of large corporations, or of those that will do business nationwide, often compare the benefits provided in various states' laws to firms in various industries.

The favorable legal climate in Delaware and the speed and simplicity of incorporating there have prompted more than half of the companies in *Fortune* magazine's list of the top

500 companies to set up operations there. Because of this popularity, incorporation has become a $400 million government-run industry in Delaware.

*The Corporate Charter*  Each state mandates a specific procedure for incorporating a business. Most states require at least three *incorporators*—the individuals who create the corporation—which opens incorporation possibilities to small businesses. Another requirement demands that a new corporation adopt a name dissimilar from those of other businesses; most states require that the name must end with the word *Company*, *Corporation*, *Incorporated*, or *Limited* to show that the owners have limited liability. Figure 5.7 lists ten elements of the articles of incorporation that most states require for chartering a corporation.

The information provided in the articles of incorporation forms the basis on which a state grants a **corporate charter**, a legal document that formally establishes a corporation. After securing the charter, the owners prepare the company's bylaws, which describe the rules and procedures for its operation.

## Corporate Management

Depending on its size, a corporation has some or all of the ownership and management levels illustrated in Figure 5.8. At the top of the figure are **stockholders.** They acquire shares of stock in the corporation and so become part owners of it. Some companies, such as family businesses, are owned by relatively few stockholders, and the stock is generally unavailable to outsiders. In such a firm, known as a *closed* or *closely held corporation*, the stockholders also control and manage all activities. In contrast, an open corporation, sometimes called a *publicly held corporation*, sells stock to the general public, establishing diversified ownership and often leading to larger operations than those of a closed corporation.

**stockholder** person or organization who owns shares of stock in a corporation.

*Stock Ownership and Stockholder Rights*  Publicly held corporations usually hold annual stockholders' meetings. During these meetings, managers report on corporate activities, and stockholders vote on any decisions that require their approval, including elections of officers. Wal-Mart holds the nation's largest stockholder meeting in a university's basketball arena. Approximately 18,000 people attend. In addition to standard shareholder business, the Wal-Mart meeting has featured celebrities and entertainers such as Jessica Simpson, Jimmy Buffett, and Will Smith.[61]

Stockholders' role in the corporation depends on the class of stock they own. Shares are usually classified as common or preferred stock. Although owners of **preferred stock** have limited voting rights, they are entitled to receive dividends before common-stock holders. If the corporation is dissolved, they have first claims on assets, once debtors are repaid. Owners of **common stock** have voting rights but only residual claims on the firm's assets, which means they are last to receive any income distributions. Because one share is typically worth only one vote, small stockholders generally have little influence on corporate management actions.

*Board of Directors*  Stockholders elect a **board of directors**—the governing body of a corporation. The board sets overall policy, authorizes major transactions involving the corporation, and hires the chief executive officer (CEO). Most boards include both inside directors (corporate executives) and outside directors—people who are not employed by the organization.

**board of directors** elected governing body of a corporation.

**Figure**

**5.7**

Traditional Articles of Incorporation

- Name and Address of the Corporation
- Corporate Objectives
- Type and Amount of Stock to Issue
- Expected Life of the Corporation
- Financial Capital at the Time of Incorporation
- Provisions for Transferring Shares of Stock among Owners
- Provisions for Regulating Internal Corporate Affairs
- Address of the Business Office Registered with the State of Incorporation
- Names and Addresses of the Initial Board of Directors
- Names and Addresses of the Incorporators

## 5.8 Levels of Management in a Corporation

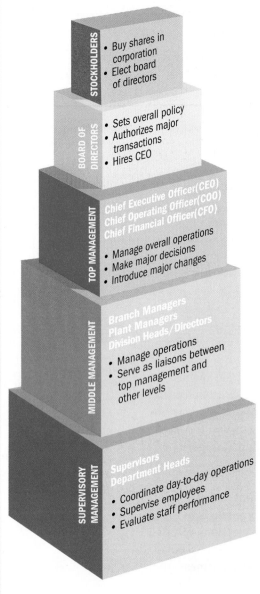

**STOCKHOLDERS**
- Buy shares in corporation
- Elect board of directors

**BOARD OF DIRECTORS**
- Sets overall policy
- Authorizes major transactions
- Hires CEO

**TOP MANAGEMENT**
Chief Executive Officer(CEO)
Chief Operating Officer(COO)
Chief Financial Officer(CFO)
- Manage overall operations
- Make major decisions
- Introduce major changes

**MIDDLE MANAGEMENT**
Branch Managers
Plant Managers
Division Heads/Directors
- Manage operations
- Serve as liaisons between top management and other levels

**SUPERVISORY MANAGEMENT**
Supervisors
Department Heads
- Coordinate day-to-day operations
- Supervise employees
- Evaluate staff performance

Sometimes the corporation's top executive also chairs the board. Generally, outside directors are also stockholders.

***Corporate Officers and Managers*** The CEO and other members of top management, such as the chief operating officer (COO) and chief financial officer (CFO), make most major corporate decisions. Managers at the next level down the hierarchy, middle management, handle the ongoing operational functions of the company. At the first tier of management, supervisory personnel coordinate day-to-day operations, assign specific tasks to employees, and evaluate job performance. The activities and responsibilities of managers at various levels in the organization are described in detail in Chapter 8.

In the past, top managers of corporations have had nearly free rein to guide their companies. The firm's CEO has traditionally played a major role in nominating candidates for board membership and often served jointly as board chairperson and CEO. Recent corporate and accounting scandals were traced to a lack of business ethics, coupled with illegal acts of members of top management and failure of the corporate boards to fulfill their obligations to the firm's investors in providing adequate oversight. These failings among a number of large corporations prompted Congress to pass the Sarbanes-Oxley Act of 2002, which tightened requirements of corporate boards and required CEOs and CFOs of major corporations to certify in writing the accuracy of the firm's financial statements. New criminal penalties were established for corporate wrongdoers. This far-reaching legislation, which focuses on improving corporate governance and increasing the accountability of corporate boards, top executives, and accounting firms, was introduced in the appendix titled "A Legal Framework for Business" following Chapter 4. Its impact on business will be also be discussed in the management, accounting, and finance chapters later in the text.

## Employee-Owned Corporations

Another alternative in creating a corporation is **employee ownership,** in which workers buy shares of stock in the company that employs them. The corporate organization stays the same, but most stockholders are also employees.

The popularity of this form of corporation is growing. Since the mid-1970s, the number of employee ownership plans has grown sevenfold—to approximately 11,400. But the number of employees participating in such plans today is nearly 34 times as many—nearly 10 million people.[62] Several trends underlie the growth in employee ownership. One is that employees want to share in whatever wealth their company earns. Another is that managers want employees to care deeply about the company's success so that they will contribute their best effort. Because human resources are so essential to the success of a modern business, employers want to build their employees' commitment to the organization. Some of the country's most successful public corporations, including Procter & Gamble, Lowe's, and Southwest Airlines, have embraced employee ownership and watched their stock values hold up better than other companies; sales of employee-owned companies are 2.3 to 2.4 percent larger than nonemployee-owned firms.[63] Employee-owned firms are discussed in more detail in Chapter 9.

**assessment check**

1. What is the role of stockholders, the board of directors, and corporate officers and management?
2. Identify all the levels of corporate management.

## Not-for-Profit Corporations

The same business concepts that apply to organizations whose objectives include earning profits also apply to **not-for-profit corporations**—firms pursuing objectives other than returning profits to owners. About 1.5 million not-for-profits operate in the United States, including charitable groups, social-welfare organizations, and religious congregations. This sector includes museums, libraries, religious and human-service organizations, private secondary schools, healthcare facilities, symphony orchestras, zoos, and thousands of other groups such as government agencies, political parties, and labor unions.

A good example of a not-for-profit corporation is the San Francisco Ballet, which has been at the forefront of dance in America since its founding in 1933 as America's first professional ballet company. It is widely regarded as one of the premier ballet companies in the nation. Visitors to its Web site, http://www.sfballet .org, can learn about upcoming performances, purchase tickets, buy gift certificates, and shop online at the gift shop.[64]

Most states set out separate legal provisions for organizational structures and operations of not-for-profit corporations. These organizations do not issue stock certificates, because they pay no dividends to owners, and ownership rarely changes. They are also exempt from paying income taxes.

UPI PHOTO/WILLIAM ALIX/LANDOV

The San Francisco Ballet company was founded in 1933 to train dancers to appear in full-length operas. Today, though, the not-for-profit company is the third-largest ballet company in the United States, and it stages more than 100 performances annually. It also trains approximately 325 ballet dancers per year.

# WHEN BUSINESSES JOIN FORCES

Today's corporate world features many complex unions of companies, not always in the same industry or even in the same country. Many well-known firms have changed owners, become parts of other corporations, split into smaller units, or experienced financial bankruptcy. Current trends in corporate ownership include mergers and acquisitions, and joint ventures.

## Mergers and Acquisitions (M&A)

In recent years, merger mania has hit U.S. corporations. Procter & Gamble paid $54 billion in stock to acquire Gillette. Cingular Wireless paid $41 billion to acquire AT&T Wireless. Sprint paid $35 billion to merge with Nextel Communications. SBC paid $16 billion to acquire AT&T.[65] Typically, 7,000 to 9,000 mergers and acquisitions take place annually.[66]

The terms *merger* and *acquisition* are often used interchangeably, but their meanings differ. In a **merger,** two or more firms combine to form one company; in an **acquisition,** one firm purchases the property and assumes the obligations of another. Acquisitions also occur when one firm buys a division or subsidiary from another firm. Many mergers and acquisitions cross national borders, as managers attempt to enter new markets and improve global competitiveness for their companies. Bermuda-based Bacardi International, one of the world's largest producers of alcoholic beverages, paid $2.29 billion to acquire Grey Goose, a maker of premium vodka ($30+ a bottle) in Cognac, France, from Sidney Frank Importing of New Rochelle, New York. Bacardi not only aims to increase sales of Grey Goose vodka in the United States but wants to double the number of countries around the world in which it is sold.[67]

Mergers can be classified as vertical, horizontal, or conglomerate. A **vertical merger** combines firms operating at different levels in the production and marketing process—the

**merger** combination of two or more firms to form one company.

**acquisition** procedure in which one firm purchases the property and assumes the obligations of another.

combination of a manufacturer and a large retailer, for instance. A vertical merger pursues one of two primary goals: (1) to ensure adequate flows of raw materials and supplies needed for a firm's products, or (2) to increase distribution. Software giant Microsoft is well known for acquiring small firms that have developed products with strong market potential, such as Teleo, a provider of voice over Internet protocol (VoIP) software and services that can be used to make phone calls via the Internet.[68] Likewise, large petroleum companies often try to reduce the uncertainty of their future petroleum supplies by acquiring successful oil and gas exploration firms.

A **horizontal merger** joins firms in the same industry that wish to diversify, increase their customer bases, cut costs, or offer expanded product lines. While P&G and Gillette are both in the global consumer goods business, Gillette was strong in shaving, men's grooming, and oral care and toothbrushes, while P&G excelled in beauty care, laundry and household cleaners, baby products, drugs, and pet care. The combined company features 21 brands with annual sales of $1 billion or more.[69]

A **conglomerate merger** combines unrelated firms. The most common reasons for a conglomerate merger are to diversify, spur sales growth, or spend a cash surplus that might otherwise make the firm a tempting target for a takeover effort. Conglomerate mergers may join firms in totally unrelated industries. A company well known for its conglomerate mergers is GE, which owns television broadcaster NBC and cable programmers CNBC and MSNBC, along with its manufacturing businesses such as appliances, aircraft engines, and industrial products. Experts debate whether conglomerate mergers are beneficial. The usual argument in favor of such mergers is that a company can use its management expertise to succeed in a variety of industries. However, the stock of an acquiring company often falls in price when it makes an acquisition, suggesting that investors doubt the value of this strategy.

## Joint Ventures: Specialized Partnerships

A **joint venture** is a partnership between companies formed for a specific undertaking. Sometimes a company enters into a joint venture with a local firm or government, sharing the operation's costs, risks, management, and profits with its local partner. A joint venture also may enable companies to solve a mutual problem. Four U.S. pipeline companies entered into a joint venture to provide better service to the oil refineries that use their services. Their venture, called Transport4, created an online resource at which 430 oil companies can schedule use of the pipelines and track the delivery of 4.5 million barrels of petroleum per day, which often must pass through more than one company's pipelines to reach its destination. Transport4 collects orders and schedules petroleum shipments for more than 150,000 oil transactions per day through the four pipeline companies' systems. It frees customers from calling each company to negotiate and renegotiate schedules.[70] As discussed in the previous chapter, joint ventures also offer particularly attractive ways for small firms to conduct international business, because they bring substantial benefits from partners already operating inside the host countries.

# PUBLIC AND COLLECTIVE OWNERSHIP

Most business organizations are owned privately by individuals or groups of people, but municipal, state, and national governments own some firms. In addition, groups of people collectively own some companies. Public ownership is common in many industries, both in the United States and abroad. In the United States, more than 350 municipalities offer Internet or cable TV services, competing with private firms that offer those same services.[71]

## Public Ownership

One alternative to private ownership is some form of **public ownership,** in which a unit or agency of government owns and operates an organization. In the United States, local governments often own parking structures and water systems. The Pennsylvania Turnpike Authority operates a vital highway link across the Keystone State. The federal government operates Hoover Dam in Nevada to provide electricity over a large region.

## Government-Owned Corporations

Sometimes public ownership results when private investors are unwilling to invest in a high-risk project. This situation occurred with the rural electrification programs of the 1930s, which expanded utility lines in sparsely populated areas. At other times, public ownership has replaced private ownership of failed organizations. Certain functions, such as municipal water systems, are considered so important to public welfare that government often implements public ownership to protect its citizens from problems. Finally, some nations use public business ownership to foster competition by operating public companies as competitive business enterprises. In Bogota, Colombia, the government runs a TV and radio network, Instituto Nacional de Radio & Television, that broadcasts both educational and commercial programs. Public ownership remains common abroad, despite a general trend toward privatization.

## Customer-Owned Businesses: Cooperatives

Another alternative to traditional private business ownership is collective ownership of a production, storage, transportation, or marketing organization. Such collective ownership establishes an organization referred to as a **cooperative** (or **co-op),** whose owners join forces to collectively operate all or part of the functions in their industry.

Cooperatives allow small businesses to obtain quantity discounts on purchases, reducing costs and enabling the co-op to pass on the savings to its members. Marketing and advertising expenses are shared among members, and the co-op's facilities can also serve as a distribution center.

Cooperatives are frequently found in small farming communities, but they also serve large growers of specific crops. For instance, Blue Diamond Growers is a cooperative that represents California almond growers. Retailers have also established co-ops. Ace Hardware is a cooperative of independently owned hardware stores. Financial co-ops, such as credit unions, offer members higher interest rates on deposits and lower interest rates on loans than other profit-seeking institutions could provide.

**assessment check**

1. What is private ownership? What is public ownership? What is government ownership?
2. Where are cooperatives typically found and what benefits do they provide small businesses?

# WHAT'S AHEAD

The next chapter shifts the book's focus to the driving forces behind new-business formation: entrepreneurs. It examines the differences between a small-business owner and an entrepreneur and identifies certain personality traits typical of entrepreneurs. The chapter also details the process of launching a new venture, including identifying opportunities, locating needed financing, and turning good ideas into successful businesses. Finally, the chapter explores a method for infusing the entrepreneurial spirit into established businesses—intrapreneurship.

**1** **Distinguish between small and large businesses and identify the industries in which most small firms are established.**

Small businesses can adopt many profiles, from part-time, home-based businesses to firms with several hundred employees. A small business is a firm that is independently owned and operated, is not dominant in its field, and meets industry-specific size standards for income or number of employees. Small businesses operate in every industry, but retailing, services, and construction feature the highest proportions of small enterprises.

### Assessment Check Answers

**1.1 What characteristics does the SBA use to determine whether a business is a small business?**
The SBA looks at the number of employees, annual sales, and whether a firm is independently owned and not dominant in its field.

**1.2 Identify three industries in which small businesses are common.**
Construction, wholesale, retail, and service industries are common for small businesses.

**2** **Discuss the economic and social contributions of small business.**

Small businesses create 75 percent of the new jobs in the U.S. economy and employ half of U.S. workers. They provide valuable outlets for entrepreneurial activity and often contribute to the creation of new industries or development of new business processes. Women, minorities, and immigrants find small-business ownership to be an attractive alternative to working in large firms and are starting new companies at a much faster rate than the overall growth in U.S. businesses. Small firms may also offer enhanced lifestyle flexibility and opportunities to gain personal satisfaction.

### Assessment Check Answers

**2.1 To what extent do small businesses help create new jobs?**
On average, three of every four new jobs are created by small businesses.

**2.2 In what ways do small businesses contribute to the economy?**
Small businesses create new jobs, new industries, and better products and services through innovation.

**3** **Describe the reasons that small businesses fail.**

Because of management shortcomings, inadequate financing, and difficulty dealing with government regulations, small businesses are much more likely to fail than large businesses, especially during economic downturns.

### Assessment Check Answers

**3.1 What percentage of small businesses will still be in business two, four, six, and ten years after starting?**
One-third, 50 percent, 62 percent, and 82 percent of small businesses will have failed within two, four, six, and ten years, respectively.

**3.2 How do management shortcomings, inadequate financing, and government regulation make small businesses more likely to fail?**
Founders of new businesses often lack the business expertise and experience needed to grow a small business. Inadequate financing prevents small businesses from handling the inevitable cash shortfalls they face and from attracting and keeping talented people. Government regulation burdens small businesses that have limited staff and budgets with expensive, time-consuming red tape and paperwork.

**4** **Describe how the Small Business Administration assists small-business owners.**

The U.S. Small Business Administration helps small-business owners obtain financing through programs that guarantee repayment of their bank loans or match small-business owners with potential investors. The SBA also helps women and minority business owners obtain government purchasing contracts. It offers training and information resources, so business owners can improve their odds of success. Finally, the SBA advocates small-business interests within the federal government.

### Assessment Check Answers

**4.1 What components should be part of a good business plan?**
A good business plan contains an executive summary, an introduction, separate financial and marketing sections, and the résumés of the principals.

**4.2 What are the various ways and methods by which the SBA helps small businesses with financing and getting government contracts?**
The SBA guarantees business loans, helps small businesses compete for government set-aside programs, and provides business information, advice, and training.

### 5 Explain how franchising can provide opportunities for both franchisors and franchisees.

A franchisor is a company that sells the rights to use its brand name, operating procedures, and other intellectual property to franchisees. Franchising helps business owners expand their companies' operations with limited financial investments. Franchisees, the individuals who buy the right to operate a business using the franchisor's intellectual property, gain a proven business system, brand recognition, and training and other support from the franchisor.

## Assessment Check Answers

**5.1 Distinguish between a franchisor and a franchisee.**
Franchisors permit franchisees to use their business name and to sell their business's goods and services. Franchisors also provide franchisees a variety of marketing, management, and other services in return for various fees and a percentage of the franchisee's sales.

**5.2 Name some of the largest franchises.**
McDonald's, Burger King, KFC, Pizza Hut, Taco Bell, Subway, Curves, Quizno's, Jackson Hewitt Tax Services, UPS, Sonic Drive-In, Jani-King, 7-Eleven, Dunkin' Donuts, and RE/MAX are some of the largest franchises.

**5.3 What are the benefits and problems of franchising?**
Advantages include a prior performance record, a recognizable company name, a business model that has proven successful in other locations, a tested management program, and business training for the franchisee. On the negative side, franchise fee payments can be very expensive, the franchisee is linked to the reputation and management of the franchise, and new franchise outlets may compete directly with established franchises.

### 6 Summarize the three basic forms of business ownership and the advantages and disadvantages of each form.

A sole proprietorship is owned and operated by one person. While sole proprietorships are easy to set up and offer great operating flexibility, the owner remains personally liable for all of the firm's debts and legal settlements. In a partnership, two or more individuals share responsibility for owning and running the business. Partnerships are relatively easy to set up, but they do not offer protection from liability. Also, partnerships may experience problems by the death of a partner or when partners fail to communicate or establish effective working relationships. When a business is set up as a corporation, it becomes a separate legal entity. Investors receive shares of stock in the firm. Owners have no legal and financial liability beyond their individual investments.

## Assessment Check Answers

**6.1 What are the key differences between sole proprietorships, partnerships, and corporations?**
Sole proprietorships expose their owners to unlimited financial liability from their businesses. Corporations shield business owners from financial liability by separating an organization's assets and liabilities from its business owners' assets and liabilities.

**6.2 What are the advantages and disadvantages of sole proprietorships, partnerships, and corporations?**
Sole proprietorships are easy to form and dissolve, and they allow owners to retain all business profits. But they lack long-term continuity, and their owners are personally liable for all business debts and must be capable of handling a wide range of business tasks. Partnerships are easy to form and offer expanded financial capabilities and complementary skills and knowledge. But they are difficult to dissolve, are vulnerable to personal conflicts, and make their owners personally liable for all business debts. Corporations shield owners from financial and legal risks, draw on specialized skills of employees, and can expand financial capabilities by selling stock. However, corporations are more difficult to establish, face double taxation of corporate earnings, and are subject to numerous state and federal laws and regulations.

### 7 Identify the levels of corporate management.

Stockholders, or shareholders, own a corporation. In return for their financial investments, they receive shares of stock in the company. The number of stockholders in a firm can vary widely, depending on whether the firm is privately owned or makes its stock available to the public. Shareholders elect the firm's board of directors, the individuals responsible for overall corporate management. The board has legal authority to change or create the firm's policies. A company's officers are the top managers who oversee its operating decisions.

## Assessment Check Answers

**7.1 What is the role of stockholders, the board of directors, and corporate officers and management?**
Stockholders acquire shares of stock and become corporate owners. At the annual stockholders' meeting, managers report on corporate activities and stockholders vote on any decisions that require their approval, including elections of officers. The board of directors sets overall policy, authorizes major transactions involving the corporation, and hires the chief executive officer (CEO). The CEO and other members of top management make most major corporate decisions and are accountable to the board and shareholders.

**7.2 Identify all the levels of corporate management.**
The levels of corporate management include top management, middle management, and supervisory management.

**8 Describe recent trends in mergers and acquisitions.**
Typically, 7,000 to 9,000 corporate mergers and acquisitions occur each year. U.S. corporations are spending record amounts on mergers and acquisitions. These business combinations occur worldwide, and companies often merge with or acquire other companies to aid their operations across national boundaries. Vertical mergers help a firm ensure access to adequate raw materials and supplies for production or improve its distribution outlets. Horizontal mergers occur when firms in the same industry join to diversify or offer expanded product lines. Conglomerate mergers combine unrelated firms, often to help spend cash surpluses that might otherwise make a firm a takeover target.

## Assessment Check Answers

**8.1 Distinguish between a merger and an acquisition.**
In a merger, two or more firms combine to form one company. In an acquisition, one firm purchases the property and assumes the obligations of another. Acquisitions also occur when one firm buys a division or subsidiary from another firm.

**8.2 What are the different kinds of mergers?**
Mergers can be classified as vertical, horizontal, or conglomerate.

**8.3 What is a joint venture?**
A joint venture is a partnership between companies formed for a specific undertaking.

**9 Differentiate among private ownership, public ownership, and collective ownership (cooperatives).**
Managers or a group of major stockholders sometimes buy all of a firm's stock. The firm then becomes a privately owned company, and its stock is no longer publicly traded. Some firms allow workers to buy large blocks of stock, so the employees gain ownership stakes. Municipal, state, and national governments also own and operate some businesses. This public business ownership has declined, however, through a recent trend toward privatization of publicly run organizations. In a cooperative, individuals or companies band together to collectively operate all or part of an industry's functions. The cooperative's owners control its activities by electing a board of directors from its members. Cooperatives are usually set up to provide for collective ownership of a production, storage, transportation, or marketing organization that is important to an industry.

## Assessment Check Answers

**9.1 What is private ownership? What is public ownership? What is collective ownership?**
Most business organizations are owned privately by individuals or groups of people. Public ownership occurs when a government unit or agency owns and operates an organization. In a cooperative, individuals or companies band together to collectively operate all or part of an industry's functions. The cooperative's owners control its activities by electing a board of directors from their members.

**9.2 Where are cooperatives typically found and what benefits do they provide small businesses?**
Cooperatives are usually set up to provide for collective ownership of a production, storage, transportation, or marketing organization that is important to an industry.

## Business Terms You Need to Know

small business 146
business plan 158
Small Business Administration
   (SBA) 158
business incubator 160

franchising 163
sole proprietorship 166
partnership 168
corporation 168
stockholder 171

board of directors 171
merger 173
acquisition 173

## Other Important Business Terms

home-based business 149
microloans 159
Small Business Investment
   Company (SBIC) 159
set-aside program 159
franchisee 164
franchisor 164
S corporation 169

limited liability company
   (LLC) 169
domestic corporation 170
foreign corporation 170
alien corporation 170
corporate charter 171
preferred stock 171
common stock 171

employee ownership 172
not-for-profit corporation 173
vertical merger 173
horizontal merger 174
conglomerate merger 174
joint venture 174
public ownership 175
cooperative (co-op) 175

## Review Questions

1. What is meant by the term *small business?* What business sectors are most and least likely to be dominated by small firms?

2. What are the most common industries for small businesses? What opportunities do home-based companies and the Internet provide for small business? How do small businesses contribute to a nation's economy in terms of job creation and new industries and innovation?

3. What percentage of small businesses is likely to fail two, four, six, and ten years after starting? Why are small businesses more likely to fail? Explain how poor management, inadequate financing, and government regulations put small businesses at a disadvantage.

4. What are the benefits of a good business plan? Identify the major components of a business plan.

5. What is the Small Business Administration? How does it assist small companies, financially and in other specialized ways? What are business incubators?

6. To what extent are small businesses creating opportunities for women today? Why have Hispanics become the nation's largest group of minority business owners? To what extent are

other minority groups, including immigrants, taking advantage of opportunities to start and run their own businesses?

7. What are the top franchises and the latest trends in franchising? Describe a typical franchising agreement. What are the advantages and disadvantages of a franchising agreement?

8. What are a sole proprietorship, a partnership, and a corporation? How are they different? What are the advantages and disadvantages of each organizational form?

9. What are the three categories of corporations? What are the steps for creating a new corporation? Why does location matter? What is a corporate charter?

10. What are the levels of management in a corporation? What is the difference between employee-owned and not-for-profit corporations?

11. How are mergers and acquisitions different? What are the three kinds of mergers? What is a joint venture?

12. Distinguish among public ownership, government-owned corporations, and customer-owned businesses (cooperatives).

1. Go to Entrepreneur.com and look for information on home-based business franchises. Choose three that interest you. Compare their company backgrounds, the costs and fees of becoming a franchisee, the training and support provided by the franchisor, and Entrepreneur.com's ratings for each franchisor. Also, visit the franchisors' Web sites. Which of the three home-based business franchises would represent the best opportunity for you? Why?

2. Read the business page of your local newspaper and choose a small business that has been profiled or mentioned in the paper. What do you think makes this business successful?

3. Propose an idea for a business incubator in an industry that interests you. Describe where the incubator would be located, how it would function, and what it is intended to accomplish.

4. Livewire International, http://www.livewirekiosk .com, a York, Pennsylvania, firm that provides electronic kiosks for ski lift tickets, has made alliances with businesses such as ski resorts and sports retailers. Describe another type of company that Livewire might make an alliance with. How might this alliance benefit Livewire? What precautions should Livewire take in entering into the alliance?

5. Do you think that consumers benefit from public ownership of such functions as municipal water systems and the postal service? Why or why not?

## Case 5.1

### Armstrong's Supply Rebuilds in the Wake of Hurricane Katrina

Scott Armstrong's family has been in New Orleans since the 1840s, only a generation less than his wife's ancestors. His electrical and lighting supply business, Armstrong's Supply, was founded by a great-uncle there in 1924. So leaving the city after the flooding and other damage wrought by Hurricane Katrina was simply not an option for him.

President and part owner of the electrical services and lighting firm, Armstrong faced numerous problems as New Orleans struggled to dry, clean, and rebuild thousands of ruined homes and businesses. His first priority was to find or account for all of his 32 longtime employees, which included rowing back to the flooded city to check the home of a missing worker. While Armstrong tackled that job, his wife and four other employees raced to every Home Depot and Lowe's in Houston and southern Louisiana to stock up on the electrical service equipment Armstrong's small-business customers and emergency repair crews would soon be asking him for. "I'm trying to make sure that not a single one of my customers has to go to another supplier because we don't

have it," he explained. To ensure he could meet demand, Armstrong also asked his regular wholesale suppliers to rush him shipments of wiring, circuit-breaker panels, and other supplies on credit and to give him six months to pay.

Armstrong then negotiated leases on two buildings, one in a heavily damaged area of the city where he guessed most of the rebuilding would begin. He rented another building near his branch office to take the place of his ruined headquarters, which was inches deep in the flood's toxic mud. Without any means to write a lease, he and the landlord sealed the deal with a handshake. Armstrong had estimated that about 80 percent of his inventory was unsalvageable, along with the company's trucks, computers, and new phone system. So he spent hours on the phone getting the credit limits extended on his personal credit cards to cover necessary business purchases, including $11,000 for new computer equipment.

The next step was rebuilding financial security for the company by taking out short-term loans and wrangling with the insurance company that had protected

Armstrong's business against work stoppages by covering the payroll for up to 90 days. When the insurer explained that his policy didn't cover flooding, Armstrong argued that the government-mandated evacuation had caused the stoppage, along with the city's traumatic power loss and other factors. While waiting for a decision about his insurance settlement, Armstrong struggled to reduce his $25,000 weekly payroll. He contacted suppliers and business acquaintances and asked them to try to give some of his workers jobs. He and two other company executives took an immediate 25 percent pay cut, and workers who returned and whom the firm could still employ were given 10 percent pay cuts. Those who weren't essential for the short term, such as workers in the temporarily defunct retail arm of the business, were being paid half their salaries until further notice. Darren Sixkiller, operations and customer service manager, lost his home in the hurricane and his family was displaced. "Armstrong's Supply is my lifeline right now," he said, "because I have nothing to go back to."

Just days after the storm, Armstrong's Supply had updated its Web site with emergency information for customers and employees and was already selling thousands of devices to connect power lines to individual homes. Because his business computers were down and his records were presumed destroyed, Armstrong asked buyers what they had most recently paid for the same item, and that's what he charged them. Though such sales were encouraging, "It's just not fueling the engine that we have to have fueled," said Armstrong. But on the other hand, he concluded, "If we can survive a month, a month, a month, a month, maybe we will be around."

## Questions for Critical Thinking

1. What do you think accounts for Scott Armstrong's dedication to his business in the face of such adversity? List as many factors as you can.
2. No business can truly plan for the kind of emergency Armstrong's Supply faced. What effect do you think its size had on its ability to take the first steps to recovery? Are there other actions it could take?

**Sources:** Armstrong's SupplyWeb site, accessed June 17, 2006, http://www.armstrongssupply.com; Sarah Rubenstein, "A New Orleans Man Struggles to Rebuild His Small Business," *Wall Street Journal Online*, accessed June 17, 2006, http://online.wsj.com; "Special Report: Katrina Update, Part 3," *Ted Magazine*, accessed September 19, 2005, http://www.tedmag.com.

## VIDEO Case 5.2

### The UL Mark of Approval

This video case appears on page 612. A recently filmed video, designed to expand and highlight the written case, is available for class use by instructors.

# Chapter 6

## Starting Your Own Business: The Entrepreneurship Alternative

### Learning Goals

1. Define the term *entrepreneur* and distinguish among entrepreneurs, small-business owners, and managers.

2. Identify four different types of entrepreneurs.

3. Explain why people choose to become entrepreneurs.

4. Discuss conditions that encourage opportunities for entrepreneurs.

5. Identify personality traits that typically characterize successful entrepreneurs.

6. Summarize the process of starting a new venture.

7. Explain how organizations promote intrapreneurship.

You need a strong stomach to be an entrepreneur. You have to be willing to ride to the top of the roller coaster, take the plunge to the bottom, and ride to the top again. Bill Gross knows this. No matter what happens to the companies he starts, he is prepared for the ups and downs. He figures it's the only way to get to the top.

Gross began his entrepreneurial career in college—when he founded a business that sold solar-based products during the energy crisis of 1973. The profits from that first company helped him pay his tuition, and he went on to start another company with his brother Larry. In the early 1990s, he established Knowledge Adventure, an educational software firm that grew to a $25-million-a-year business before he moved on to launch CitySearch, the first online metro guide. With his

GETTY IMAGES

## Bill Gross: Riding the Entrepreneurial Roller Coaster

string of start-ups, Gross had become a serial entrepreneur, and he'd also caught the attention of celebrity investors such as Steven Spielberg.

But Gross is best known for his firm Idealab, a California-based business incubator for high-tech companies. A decade ago, Idealab appeared to be poised to cash in on the dot-com boom. With 50 start-up companies on its roster, Idealab was on the brink of huge success. But the boom went bust, and with it went many of Idealab's companies. Gross canceled the firm's big plans for an initial public offering (IPO) of stock and closed down its satellite offices in New York, London, and Silicon Valley. Idealab workers lost their jobs, and private investors in the firm counted their financial losses. Company insiders recall this as the "dark time." Company board member Howard Morgan explains, "For all of us, especially Bill, it was a managerial growing up." Gross says, "I never want to be in a position to . . . cut people's jobs again."

Gross is back on the roller coaster again, on his way up. Idealab has cut back on the number of start-ups it funds to about two a year. Each must display true technological

innovation. One such innovation is LaneHawk, vision-recognition software that is being tested at such supermarket chains as Pathmark and Giant Eagle. Internet Brands, which started CarsDirect—an online car-sales firm—is actually making money. And Snap.com enables advertisers such as United Airlines and eBay to pay only when a purchase or transaction takes place because of their ad posting—instead of paying every time someone clicks on the site. Idealab start-ups that survived its early years lend the company credibility as well. Go2.com and Picasa were purchased by Yahoo! and Google, respectively.

Idealab recently completed funding deals with more venture capitalists, indicating that major investors have renewed confidence in Gross. "Bill is starting companies of great promise and of great interest to the venture community," notes Erik Straser, a partner at Mohr Davidow, an investor in the new firm Energy Innovations. "His enthusiasm and passion are still contagious. But now there's a clarity that comes from having to regroup and think about the next wave of companies—and a new ability to take execution to the next level."[1]

Like millions of people, you'd probably love to start and run your own company. Perhaps, just like Idealab's Bill Gross, you've spent time trying to devise a concept for a business you could launch. If you've been bitten by the entrepreneurial bug, you're not alone. More than ever, whether on their own or within an innovative firm, people like you, your classmates, and your friends are choosing the path of entrepreneurship for their careers.

How do you become an entrepreneur? Experts advise aspiring entrepreneurs to learn as much as possible about business by completing academic programs such as the one in which you are currently enrolled and by gaining practical experience by working part or full time for businesses. In addition, you can obtain invaluable insights about the pleasures and pitfalls of entrepreneurship by reading newspaper and magazine articles and biographies of successful entrepreneurs. These sources will help you learn how entrepreneurs handle the challenges of starting their businesses. For advice on how to launch and grow a new venture, turn to magazines such as *Entrepreneur*, *Success*, *Black Enterprise*, *Hispanic*, and *Inc*. Entrepreneurship associations such as the Asso-

ciation of African-American Women Business Owners and the Entrepreneurs' Organization also provide invaluable assistance. Finally, any aspiring entrepreneur should visit these Web sites:

- Center for Entrepreneurial Leadership (http://www.celcee.edu)
- Entrepreneur.com (http://www.entrepreneur.com)
- Kauffman eVenturing (http://www.eventuring.org)
- The Small Business Administration (http://www.sba.gov)
- *Wall Street Journal*, StartupJournal (http://www.startupjournal.com)

In this chapter, we focus on pathways for entering the world of entrepreneurship, describing what entrepreneurs do, the different kinds of entrepreneurs, and why a growing number of people choose to be entrepreneurs. It discusses the business environment in which entrepreneurs work, the characteristics that help entrepreneurs succeed, and the ways they start new ventures. The chapter ends with a discussion of methods by which large companies try to incorporate the entrepreneurial spirit.

# WHAT IS AN ENTREPRENEUR?

**entrepreneur** person who seeks a profitable opportunity and takes the necessary risks to set up and operate a business.

You learned in Chapter 1 that an **entrepreneur** is a risk taker in the private enterprise system, a person who seeks a profitable opportunity and takes the necessary risks to set up and operate a business. Consider Sam Walton, Wal-Mart's founder, who started by franchising a few small Ben Franklin variety stores, and then opened his own Walton Five and Dime stores. Forty-five years later, this small venture has grown into a multibillion-dollar global business that is the largest company on earth.

Entrepreneurs differ from many small-business owners. Although many small-business owners possess the same drive, creative energy, and desire to succeed, what makes entrepreneurs different is their overwhelming desire to make their businesses grow. Sam Walton wasn't satisfied with just one successful Ben Franklin franchise, so he purchased others. And when that wasn't enough, he started and grew his own stores. Entrepreneurs combine their ideas and drive with money, employees, and other resources to create a business that fills a market need. That entrepreneurial role can make something significant out of a small beginning. In preparing its annual list of the 500 fastest-growing U.S. companies, *Inc*. magazine found that 29 percent started with less than $20,000 in the bank, that 14 percent started with less than $10,000, and that 15 percent started with less than $1,000. Yet 34 percent of the 500 CEOs on the list estimated their current net worth at more than $5 million.[2]

## "They Said It"

"It's just paper. All I own is a pickup truck and a little Wal-Mart stock."

—Sam Walton
(1918–1992)
American entrepreneur

Entrepreneurs also differ from managers. Managers are employees who direct the efforts of others to achieve an organization's goals. Owners of some small start-up firms serve as owner-managers to implement their plans for their businesses and to offset human resource limitations at their fledgling companies. Entrepreneurs may also perform a managerial role, but their overriding responsibility is to use the resources of their organizations—employees, money, equipment, and facilities—to accomplish their goals. Indeed, their zeal to make their companies successful, particularly in the start-up stage of a new venture, can often turn entrepreneurs into terrible managers. Jim Ansara, founder of Boston-based Shawmut Design and Construction, now a $500 million construction company, said, "There were problems with my management style, and that started to create morale problems. The people I had were very dedicated—it was a cultlike atmosphere in most of the good ways—but they all would have said I was a complete maniac. I was way too intense, I pushed too hard, I didn't listen, I couldn't be reasoned with. Luckily I had a couple of people who were brave enough to tell me that consistently."[3] A key indication of Ansara's success as an entrepreneur was his willingness to recognize his limitations as a manager. When he finally recognized the negative effect he was having on his business, he hired others who were better suited to lead his business than was he.

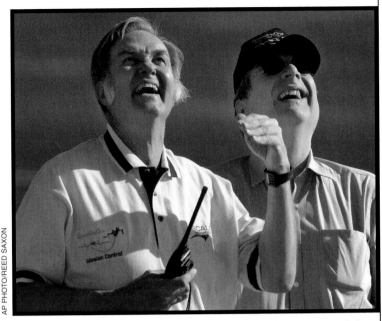

Entrepreneurs are risk takers and people who have a unique vision of the future. Burt Rutan, already a famous aerospace engineer, brought his dream of commercial spaceflight to reality when his SpaceShipOne took humans to the edge of space and back twice. Rutan's 125-person firm, Scaled Composites, achieved its success without government funding or assistance but with help from private funds from Microsoft co-founder Paul Allen, shown here with Burt.

Studies have identified certain personality traits and behaviors common to entrepreneurs that differ from those required for managerial success. One of these traits is the willingness to assume the risks involved in starting a new venture. Some, like Jim Ansara, the founder of Shawmut Design and Construction, leave their jobs to start their own companies and become successful entrepreneurs. Others find that they lack the characteristics required to start and grow a business. Entrepreneurial characteristics are examined in detail in a later section of this chapter.

**assessment check**

1. What tools do entrepreneurs use to create a new business?
2. How do entrepreneurs differ from managers?

## CATEGORIES OF ENTREPRENEURS

Entrepreneurs apply their talents in different situations. These differences give rise to a set of distinct categories of entrepreneurs. As Figure 6.1 shows, four basic categories exist: classic entrepreneurs, serial entrepreneurs, intrapreneurs, and change agents.

**Classic entrepreneurs** identify business opportunities and allocate available resources to tap those markets. The story of Ben Serotta exemplifies the actions of a classic entrepreneur. Serotta is the founder of Serotta Competition Bicycles in Saratoga Springs, New York, which sells custom-made bikes that cost from $2,600 to $15,000. Serotta realized that dedicated cyclists would gladly pay big bucks for his company's bikes, as long as they fit their owners—and no one else—like a glove. Serotta's School of Cycling Ergonomics teaches bike shop

**classic entrepreneur** person who identifies a business opportunity and allocates available resources to tap that market.

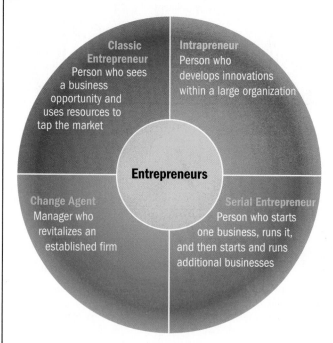

**serial entrepreneur** person who starts one business, runs it, and then starts and runs additional businesses in succession.

**intrapreneur** entrepreneurially oriented person who develops innovations within the context of a large organization.

**change agent** manager who revitalizes an established firm to keep it competitive.

owners how to achieve that custom fit, which usually takes two hours to get right. Kathleen Krumme of Oakley Cycles in Cincinnati, which sells 60 Serotta custom bikes a year, says, "Serotta equips us with the knowledge to sell its products, [and] then trusts us to do it. There isn't another company out there doing that."[4] The "Hit & Miss" feature describes the remarkable story of another classic entrepreneur, John H. Johnson, who created a publishing company and a new industry.

While a classic entrepreneur starts a new company by identifying a business opportunity and allocating resources to tap a new market, **serial entrepreneurs** start one business, run it, and then start and run additional businesses in succession. Stelios Haji-Ioannou, founder of the easyGroup companies, based in London, is a serial entrepreneur. Stelios's first company was easyJet, the low-fare European airline modeled after Southwest Airlines. Four years later, he started easy Internetcafé, which provides low-cost Internet access in high-traffic locations in major cities, such as London, Berlin, and New York, for students, travelers, and anyone else needing high-speed Internet services. Today, in addition to easyJet and easyInternetcafé, Stelios's easyGroup runs easyCar (rentals), easyValue (reviews and price comparisons for online shopping), easyMoney (insurance and credit cards), easyCinema (low-cost movie theaters and online DVD rentals), easyBus, easyHotel, easy4men (toiletries), easyJobs, easyPizza, easyMusic (music downloads by the track), easyCruise, easyMobile (cell phones), and easyWatch (watches for men, women, and children).[5]

**Intrapreneurs** are entrepreneurially oriented people who develop new products, ideas, and commercial ventures within large organizations. For example, 3M develops innovative products by encouraging intrapreneurship among its personnel. Some of 3M's most successful products began as inspirations of intrapreneurs. Art Frey invented the Post-it note, and intrapreneurs Connie Hubbard and Raymond Heyer invented the Scotch-Brite Never Rust soap pad. Intrapreneurship is discussed later in this chapter.

**Change agents**, also called *turnaround entrepreneurs*, are managers who revitalize established firms to keep them competitive in today's marketplace. When Bank of America (BofA) paid $47 billion to acquire FleetBoston, the general assessment was that BofA had "grossly overpaid," especially given FleetBoston's weak profits and customer service. But thanks to Liam McGee, BofA's primary change agent and president of BofA's consumer and small-business division, the critics are turning out to be wrong. McGee has worked with managers and employees at the 1,500 branch banks previously run by FleetBoston to change everything from training to the corporate culture. And those changes are beginning to work. For instance, when McGee visited a bank branch in Boston's historic district, he found the branch manager and customer representatives greeting customers as they entered the branch. Said McGee, "If you'd visited here six months ago, you would have seen all these people hidden back in their offices."[6] Also, thanks to new software that approves or rejects mortgage and home equity loans in just 30 minutes, free checking and online bill paying, extensive training on how to interact and greet customers, and a new bonus system that rewards employees only if customers sign up for and use bank services for at least four months, BofA has added 184,000 new checking accounts and 196,000 new savings accounts at Fleet Boston's old bank branches in the first year, all while cutting more than $900 million in costs.

**assessment check**

1. Why do companies encourage intrapreneurs?

2. What do intrapreneurs and change agents have in common?

# HIT & MISS

## John H. Johnson Creates a Business—and an Empire

When he died at age 87, John H. Johnson had left a huge imprint on the publishing world. One of the most powerful and influential U.S. entrepreneurs, he was the first to recognize the African American market for media and cosmetics. Johnson founded his magazine *Ebony* in 1945, the first general-interest monthly magazine for African Americans. Today its circulation tops 1.7 million. In 1951, he followed with *Jet*, a weekly newsmagazine written from an African American perspective. *Jet*'s current circulation hovers just under 1 million. And in 1973, Johnson established Fashion Fair Cosmetics—skin care and cosmetics formulated especially for African American women. Fashion Fair also sponsored a large touring fashion show run by Johnson's wife, Eunice.

Johnson Publishing Company—an empire that includes publishing, cosmetics, television production, and fashion—is based in Chicago. With revenues of about $500 million, it is the nation's largest black-owned business. Johnson's daughter, Linda Rice Johnson, now the chief executive officer of the firm, describes her late father as "the greatest salesman and CEO I have ever known." Johnson grew up in poverty but did not let that stop him. "I thought my way out of poverty," he once said. "*Ebony* was my passport."

As an entrepreneur, Johnson insisted on controlling his own companies. He never turned them over to others and tried to keep top positions within the family whenever he could. His daughter, Linda, held several executive positions before becoming CEO upon her father's retirement, and his wife, Eunice, remains secretary-treasurer. Johnson Publishing is a privately held firm. As a visible public figure, Johnson endured criticism from workers who thought he drove them too hard and some African Americans who thought he was too oriented toward the middle class. But Lerone Bennett Jr., executive editor emeritus of *Ebony*, points out, "He virtually invented the black consumer market. He was the first publisher I know of who went to Madison Avenue and persuaded them that they had to address the African American market and use African American models. It paid off."

### Questions for Critical Thinking

1. Describe two ways in which you believe John H. Johnson has affected U.S. business in general.
2. Describe ways in which John H. Johnson—and his company—could be considered innovative.

**Sources:** Johnson Publishing Web site, accessed June 17, 2006, www.johnsonpublishing.com; Tara Burghart, "Hundreds Remember Johnson," *Chicago Sun-Times*, accessed June 17, 2006, http://www.suntimes.com; Cora Daniels, "Pioneers," *Fortune*, August 22, 2005, pp. 72–88; Jason George, "Mourners Reflect on Inspiration," *Chicago Tribune*, August 15, 2005, section 1, pp. 1, 14; Charles Storch and Barbara Sherlock, "A Publishing Pioneer," *Chicago Tribune*, August 9, 2005, section 1, pp. 1, 16.

## *REASONS TO CHOOSE ENTREPRENEURSHIP AS A CAREER PATH*

If you want to run your own business someday, you'll have plenty of company. Studies indicate that more than 11 percent of Americans, about one of every nine people, run their own businesses.[7] Surveys, however, generally indicate that many more people, as many as half of Americans, want to start their own businesses. This interest is even stronger among 14- to 19-year-olds; nearly two-thirds want to start and run their own business.[8] While general interest in entrepreneurship is very high, how many Americans are actually taking steps to start their own businesses at any particular time? In an average month, Americans start approximately 550,000 new businesses![9] And, that number is up substantially in recent years.

The past two decades have witnessed a heightened interest in entrepreneurial careers, spurred in part by publicity celebrating the successes of entrepreneurs such as Pierre Omidyar, who founded eBay; Oprah Winfrey, who has used her immensely popular television program

ELLICE PEREZ

Warren Brown started baking to relieve the stress of his day job as a federal litigator in Washington, D.C. From hosting dessert parties with his friends, he moved on to open his small bakery, CakeLove. That business became so successful that the small shop was always jammed with customers. The resolution? Brown's Love Café, which opened across the street.

Figure

6.2 Why People Become Entrepreneurs

| | |
|---|---|
| **Desire to Be One's Own Boss** | **Desire to Succeed Financially** |
| **Desire for Job Security** | **Desire for an Improved Quality of Life** |

as a springboard for ventures into magazine publishing and TV and film production; Michael Dell, who launched what would become personal computer giant Dell following his freshman year at the University of Texas; and Bill Gates, who left Harvard to start Microsoft with friend Paul Allen.

People choose to become entrepreneurs for many different reasons. Some are motivated by dissatisfaction with the organizational work world, citing desires to escape unreasonable bosses or insufficient rewards and recognition. Other people start businesses because they believe their ideas represent opportunities to fulfill customer needs. Luis Espinoza founded a business to meet the unmet demand for Hispanic foods in his new home in northern Indiana. Espinoza had grown up in Texas, where his family enjoyed authentic Mexican foods. Although Espinoza found a significant, growing Hispanic community in Indiana, the local stores didn't know what products to offer these customers. One supermarket chain tried buying foods from a Texas distributor and stocked its shelves with items that appeal to Mexican tastes—in a neighborhood of Puerto Ricans, who prefer less spicy dishes. Espinoza knew he could do better. He learned about local tastes and set up Inca Quality Foods to provide canned goods and spices tailored to stores' local clientele. He convinced a Kroger manager to let him set up a display; when sales increased, he landed a contract to service Kroger stores throughout the area.[10]

As pointed out in Figure 6.2, people become entrepreneurs for one or more of four major reasons: a desire to be their own boss, succeed financially, attain job security, and improve their quality of life. Each of these reasons is described in more detail in the following sections.

## Being Your Own Boss

Self-management is the motivation that drives many entrepreneurs. No entrepreneur matches this portrait of the American independent professional as an individual who has control over when, where, and how she works more than Liz Lange, the 30-something founder and CEO of Liz Lange Maternity.

Lange recognized a real need while working as a designer's assistant. Expectant mothers seeking sophisticated maternity wear quickly discovered that they would have to make do with baby-doll dresses or pants with a hole cut in the front—and a Lycra panel to accommodate their unborn child. Lange found herself offended by what was available. "I looked around the market to see what was out there and was frankly horrified. It was all so un-upscale, and much of it was oversized so that a woman could get through nine months in the same outfit. During her early days, a mother-to-be had nothing she could really fit into. It was all frilly—I mean, you are having a baby, not becoming a baby."[11]

Lange left her job to begin work designing a few basic items to show to retail buyers. They stated that pregnant women would not spend money on high-end maternity clothing. Undaunted, she borrowed $50,000 from family and friends and opened a small New York City office where she sold her made-to-order clothes by appointment. Word of the high-fashion maternity clothing spread like wildfire and led to an article in the *New York Times* Style section. Sales exploded after that, and Lange decided to bypass department stores in favor of selected high-fashion boutiques. Soon her slim pants, cashmere sweaters, and fitted slinky dresses were attracting super stylish expectant moms, including such celebrities as Cindy Crawford and Catherine Zeta-Jones.

Today, Lange runs stores in Beverly Hills, on New York's Madison Avenue, and on Long Island, New York, as well as producing an online catalog (http://www.lizlange.com) and a separate, less-expensive line of clothes marketed at more than 1,300 Target stores nationwide. Annual sales exceed $10 million. Both Lange and her satisfied customers agree that her decision to be her own boss was a wise one.

## Financial Success

Entrepreneurs are wealth creators. Many start their ventures with the specific goal of creating a profitable business and reaping its financial rewards. Why? Because they believe they won't get rich by working for someone else. And studies indicate they're generally right. While only one in five American workers is self-employed, more than two-thirds of all millionaires are self-employed. Consequently, if you run your own business, you're more likely to become wealthy.[12] The business press, of course, is quick to publish stories about the wealth and "self-made" successes of today's entrepreneurs. For example, it's well known that Google founders Sergey Brin and Larry Page made over $14 billion each when Google sold its shares in an initial public offering, and they are worth much more than that today.[13] Less well known, though, are successful entrepreneurs such as Constantino de Oliveira Jr. and his father, who founded Brazil's third largest airline, Gol Linhas Aéreas Inteligentes (Gol Intelligent Airlines), just five years ago. Gol, or *goal* in English, is the most profitable airline in the world, with an operating margin of 37 percent compared with 20 percent for extremely successful Southwest Airlines. Gol achieves those profits with prices so low that it put its major competitor, Transbrasil, out of business in less than a year. By growing from 38 to 76 planes over the next few years, Gol will likely overtake Varig Airlines and become Brazil's second-largest airline. Today, the value of the Oliveira family's share of Gol is worth more than $2.4 billion.[14]

Although entrepreneurs often mention financial rewards as a motive for starting their businesses, the path to riches can be long and uncertain. As you learned in Chapter 5, one-third of newly started small firms are out of business within two years, more than half within four years, 61 percent within six years, and 82 percent within ten years.[15] So there's clearly no guarantee of success. Furthermore, among the CEOs heading America's fastest-growing private companies (the so-called *Inc.* 500), almost one-fourth took no compensation at all from their business during its first five years of operation. For example, at first, Stephen Culp, founder and CEO of Smart Furniture, a modular-furniture company in Chattanooga, paid everyone in his company *but* himself. Culp reasoned, "If I can survive on cereal and take all the cash that I would have spent on a more extravagant lifestyle and put it back into the company, it increases my chances of success."[16]

Entrepreneurs often work long hours to bring their dreams to life. Mexican immigrants Pablo and Juanita Ceja first worked as grape pickers in the Napa Valley fields from before dawn until after sunset. They scrimped and saved and eventually bought their first fifteen acres of grape fields, which they have added to over the years. Thanks to son Armando, who studied winemaking at UC Davis, the family became prize-winning vintners. Says Armando, "It's the American dream."

© ED KASHI/CORBIS

## Job Security

Although the demand for skilled employees remains high in many industries, working for a company, even a *Fortune* 500 firm, is no guarantee of job security. In fact, over the last ten years, large companies sought efficiency by downsizing and actually eliminated more jobs than they created. As a result, a growing number of American workers—both first-time job seekers and laid-off long-term employees—are deciding to create their own job security by starting their own businesses. Why? Because "even if you're the creative director for Disney, Comcast could buy the company, and you could be out of a job," says Mary Furlong, who teaches entrepreneurship at Santa Clara University.[17] While running your own business doesn't guarantee job security, the U.S. Small Business Administration has found that most newly created jobs come from small businesses, with a significant share of those jobs coming from new companies.[18]

The key difference is that an entrepreneur's job depends not on the decisions of employers but instead on the decisions of customers and investors and on the cooperation and commitment of the entrepreneur's own employees. People like Jim Minick, 51, of Smyrna, Georgia, who has been laid off by employers three times in 25 years, would rather work for themselves than for others. Minick, who started his own business, noted, "You don't want to find yourself 55 or 60 with no one wanting to hire you. That's a concern with any 50-year-old."[19] However, many younger workers feel the same way. Twenty-three-year-old pastry chef Sarah Levy quit her high-stress, low-paying restaurant jobs to start her own business, Sarah's Pastries & Candies, in Chicago. Regarding the change, Levy said, "I feel better when I'm working for myself and building a name for myself."[20]

## Quality of Life

**lifestyle entrepreneur** person who starts a business to reduce work hours and create a more relaxed lifestyle.

Entrepreneurship is an attractive career option for people seeking to improve their quality of life. Starting a business gives the founder some choice over when, where, and how to work. Brett Schulte became a **lifestyle entrepreneur,** a person who starts a business to reduce work hours and create a more relaxed lifestyle, after vacationing in Mexico's Baja California. Schulte quit his job at a dot-com company, moved his family to Mexico, and became a Web consultant. Schulte points out how technology has allowed him to be a lifestyle entrepreneur, saying, "Technology is making geography less important. [Internet telephone service] is enabling me to have a U.S. phone number in Mexico."[21] His U.S. clients don't have to know that he's working from his laptop while sitting at the beach.

Despite Brett Schulte's relaxed work environment, most entrepreneurs work long hours and at the whims of their customers. For instance, Eva Rosenberg, who runs a tax accounting business from her home in Irvine, California, began as a lifestyle entrepreneur, working just three days a week. But her business grew so much that she obtained a regular office and began working long hours. Said Rosenberg, "I had so many clients that I was pretty much working almost seven days a week, morning until night. I had an office on Ventura Boulevard, and I was always there. Then somewhere along the way I got married, and I wanted to see my husband."[22] Michelle Tell experienced a similar time crunch when she started her company, Preferred Public Relations & Marketing, in Las Vegas. Tell, who had just left a job with the MGM Grand Hotel and Casino, said, "My goal was to have five clients and take it easy for a while." However, one month after starting her business, she had seven clients. Today, she has 30 clients and seven full-time employees. Says Tell, "Our company took off like a storm, and we find ourselves working seven days a week."[23]

For other lifestyle entrepreneurs, quality of life is not defined by how many hours they work but by their ability to fulfill broader social objectives through their ventures. Darren Patrick founded Rainbow Play Systems in Brookings, South Dakota, when he was 20. Three years later, he was a millionaire. Today, Rainbow makes 64 different kinds of redwood and red cedar residential playground equipment and sells it in 250 stores in the United States, Canada, Mexico, Panama, Spain, and South Korea. This year, the company will ring up more than $500 million in sales, making Rainbow one of the nation's largest consumers of redwood.

And that's what worried Patrick from the start. "Since the onset of our business, we have always been concerned about our lumber purchases and the mills that fulfill them," he states. Rainbow buys lumber only from mills participating in sustained-yield programs that protect the redwood population. The firm goes further by educating purchasers about the benefits offered by such programs. As a result, Patrick says, "Today, we have more redwood trees than ever before."[24]

**assessment check**

1. Are entrepreneurs more likely than employees to achieve financial success?
2. What factors affect the entrepreneur's job security?

# THE ENVIRONMENT FOR ENTREPRENEURS

If you are motivated to start your own company, several factors suggest that now may be the right time to begin. First, as discussed earlier in the chapter, the status of entrepreneurship as a career choice has been rising. Entrepreneurship began moving toward the business mainstream in the early 1980s after Steve Jobs of Apple Computer and other high-tech entrepreneurs gained national attention by going public—that is, selling stock in their companies. And, as discussed later in the chapter, today's entrepreneurs are also reaping the benefits of financial interest among investors. In addition to favorable public attitudes toward entrepreneurs and the growing number of financing options, several other factors—identified in Figure 6.3—also support and expand opportunities for entrepreneurs: globalization, education, information technology, and demographic and economic trends. Each of these factors is discussed in the following sections.

## Globalization

The rapid globalization of business, described in preceding chapters, has created many opportunities for entrepreneurs. Entrepreneurs market their products abroad and hire international talent. Among the fastest-growing small U.S. companies, almost two of every five have international sales. One entrepreneur who sees international opportunities is Mia Abbruzzese, who, after working for Stride Rite developing shoes to be sold at Target department stores, thought to herself, "If I can do this for Target, what's to say that I can't do it for myself?" So Abbruzzese quit her job at Stride Rite, started her own company, and began working her contacts in China to find a factory that was willing to begin production of her new line of Morgan & Milo shoes. Abbruzzese used freelance designers to develop the look she wanted and then found a maker of shoe parts in China that wanted to move up to producing entire shoes. In her first year, her company made 65,000 shoes and had sales of $800,000. Furthermore, her Morgan & Milo line of shoes now sells at Nordstrom's, Macy's, and Zappos.com, a leading Web shoe retailer.[25]

Growth in entrepreneurship is a worldwide phenomenon. The role of entrepreneurs is growing in most industrialized and newly industrialized nations as well as in the emerging free-market countries in central and eastern Europe. However, as shown in Figure 6.4, the level of entrepreneurship

**Figure**

**6.3**

Factors Supporting and Expanding Opportunities for Entrepreneurs

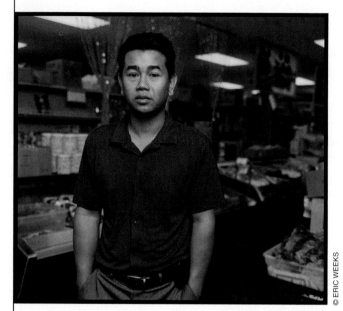

The entrepreneurial spirit thrives in many cultures. Rainsey Ker's family left Cambodia when he was six to flee oppression of the brutal Khmer Rouge government. Ker's Mitpheap Asian Market in Portland, Maine, carries Asian, African, and Hispanic foods. Ker is not content to run his small store, though. He is working part time as a real estate agent and hopes eventually to open his own agency.

© ERIC WEEKS

varies considerably. Worldwide, more than 9 percent of adults are starting or managing a new business. But in Peru, almost four in ten adults are engaged in entrepreneurial activity, followed by Uganda (32 percent), Ecuador (27 percent), Jordan (18 percent), New Zealand (15 percent), and Iceland (14 percent). The United States, with more than 11 percent of adults qualifying as entrepreneurs, is currently in tenth place.[26]

Still, Figure 6.4 also shows that entrepreneurs in many other countries, such as Japan (2 percent), Slovenia and Hong Kong (3 percent each), and Belgium and Sweden (4 percent each), find it much more difficult to start businesses. Obstacles include government regulations, high taxes, and political attitudes that favor big business. In the United Kingdom, which has a below-average rate of entrepreneurship (slightly more than 6 percent), four in ten small-business owners say they would not start a new company because of the heavy burden of government regulations.[27] In addition, cultural values in other countries may differ from those in the United States and other countries, where individualism and risk taking are admired and where high value is placed on seizing a business opportunity.

**Figure**

**6.4**  Levels of Entrepreneurial Activity in 34 Countries

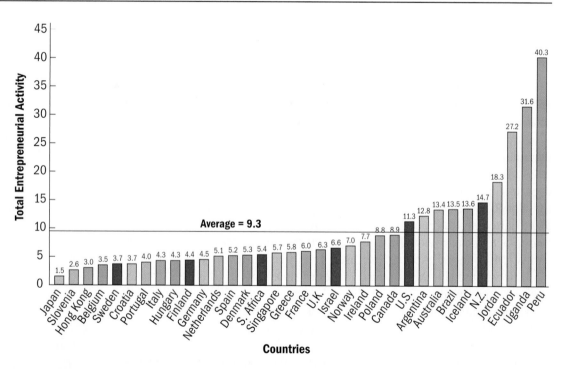

**Source:** Zoltan Acs, Pia Arenius, Michael Hay, and Maria Minniti, "Global Entrepreneurship Monitor: Executive Report," Global Entrepreneurship Monitor Consortium, accessed June 17, 2006, http://www .gemconsortium.org.

## Education

The past two decades have brought tremendous growth in the number of educational opportunities for would-be entrepreneurs. Today, more than 100 U.S. universities offer full-fledged majors in entrepreneurship, another 73 offer an emphasis in entrepreneurship, and hundreds more offer one or two courses in how to start a business.[28] Some schools, including Alfred University, University of St. Thomas, and Miami University of Ohio, offer entrepreneurship courses to nonbusiness students, on the assumption that people in other disciplines will eventually start businesses, too.

Another way business schools are responding to the interest in entrepreneurship is by helping their students start businesses. Babson College has a program in which a few students are permitted to replace several of the usual classes with launching an actual business under coaching from an entrepreneur-turned-professor. At the University of Maryland, entrepreneurship students live together in an exclusive, apartment-style residence hall that, with dedicated meeting rooms, offices, and computer labs, is designed to encourage interaction and ideas. Students are taught by entrepreneurship professors, experienced entrepreneurs, CEOs, and technology specialists from the engineering school and industry. Students in this program are not only expected to start a business but also given responsibility to run the university's business plan competition and technology start-up boot camp.[29]

Besides schools, many organizations have sprouted up in recent years to teach entrepreneurship to young people. The Kauffman Center for Entrepreneurial Leadership offers training programs for learners from kindergarten through community college. The center's Entreprep summer program, which is taught in conjunction with local colleges and universities, teaches high school juniors how to start and manage a company. Students in Free Enterprise (SIFE) is a worldwide not-for-profit organization in which college students, working with faculty advisors, teach grade school and high school students and other community members the value of private enterprise and entrepreneurship.[30] The Association of Collegiate Entrepreneurs has chapters on many college campuses in the United States and Canada.

The question, of course, is whether students who major in entrepreneurship or take entrepreneurship classes are any more likely to successfully start a business. In fact, students who graduate from entrepreneurship programs are three times as likely to be self-employed and three times more likely to help start new companies.[31] Jeffrey Betz, Cecilia Domingos, and Michael Lobsinger started their company, Orca Gear, while in the graduate entrepreneurship program at Rensselaer Polytechnic Institute in Troy, New York. The company designs and manufactures Float Tech outerwear—lightweight all-season jackets with built-in inflatable life jackets; one tug on the rip cord inflates the life jacket. Says Betz, "Our story definitely supports that you can learn entrepreneurship."[32]

## Information Technology

The explosion in information technology (IT) has provided one of the biggest boosts for entrepreneurs. As computer and communications technologies have merged and dropped dramatically in cost, entrepreneurs have gained tools that help them compete with large companies. Information technology helps entrepreneurs work quickly and efficiently, provide attentive customer service, increase sales, and project professional images. New technologies helped Kelly Ford's new company, Oriel Wines, which imports and exports 24 handmade wines from 22 wine-producing regions and countries, to sound, act, and look like a large company. Said Ford, "We're a luxury brand, so customers have to think we're bigger than we really are."[33] But with Ford and just five other employees, Oriel Wines is a tiny company that just looks and acts big, thanks to NetSuite software, which manages inventory, accounting, customer orders, newsletters, and marketing, all from one central computer.

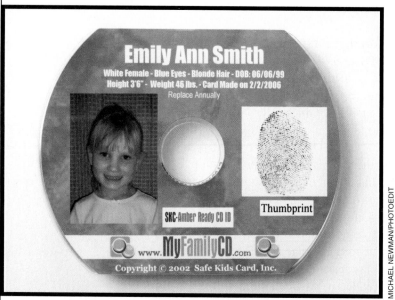

MICHAEL NEWMAN/PHOTOEDIT

Jeremiah Hutchins combined his knowledge of information technology with his desire to help parents and law enforcement officials. The mini-CDs produced by his company, Safe Kids Card, help locate lost or kidnapped children by storing vital statistics and pictures of children.

Advances in information technology have also created demand for new products, and entrepreneurs have risen to the challenge. Some have started businesses that directly apply information technology. After hearing reports about a missing girl, and "all the talk shows . . . saying, 'If only they'd had better identification information about her,'" Jeremiah Hutchins wondered if the mini-CD business cards that he was producing could enable stressed parents to quickly provide police with the information they needed, such as allergies, scars, birthmarks, blood type, height, weight, and photos to identify and track down lost or abducted children. Today, Safe Kids Cards sells mini CDs, about the size of a credit card, through franchises in the United States, Australia, Canada, Ireland, New Zealand, and South Africa.[34]

Yet the Internet is a challenge as well as an opportunity for entrepreneurs. Because customers can go online to check prices and buy from large or small companies anywhere in the world, entrepreneurs need to find a distinctive advantage over big competitors. Raymond Galeotti, president of EvesAddiction.com, which sells jewelry, found that advantage for his small business by pairing with one of the Internet's largest companies, Yahoo! For as little as $30 a month, Yahoo! Small Business Web hosting provides tools to build and maintain his Web site, specialized marketing services that recommend new products to his customers based on their previous purchases, secure purchasing via PayPal and credit cards, and 24-hour toll-free consulting. Most important, though, says Galeotti, "We wanted reliability."[35] And, since he signed on with Yahoo!, his Web site hasn't been down even once.

## Demographic and Economic Trends

Demographic trends, such as the aging of the U.S. population, the emergence of Hispanics as the nation's largest ethnic group, and the growth of two-income families, create opportunities for entrepreneurs to market new goods and services. Entrepreneurs take advantage of such trends to offer everything from retirement homes to grocery delivery services. For example, Alere Medical, based in Reno, Nevada, sells equipment that enables nurses to monitor heart-failure patients from their homes. Patients step onto a biometric device the size of a scale, which monitors and reports the patient's weight and physical symptoms. While standing on the monitor, patients use a small interactive display device to respond to yes and no questions about their health. That information is forwarded to Alere's database, where a nurse analyzes the data and immediately notifies physicians and patients when problems are indicated. With 4.6 million Americans already diagnosed with heart failure, and an aging population, Alere's business, which reduces hospital costs and stays and allows patients to recover and monitor their health at home, will continue to grow.[36]

**assessment check**

1. To what extent is entrepreneurship possible in different countries, and what opportunities does globalization create for today's entrepreneurs?
2. Identify the educational factors that help expand current opportunities for entrepreneurs.
3. Describe current demographic trends that suggest new goods and services for entrepreneurial businesses.

# CHARACTERISTICS OF ENTREPRENEURS

The examples of entrepreneurship you've read about so far suggest that people who strike out on their own are a different breed. Well, they are. Successful entrepreneurs are more likely to have had parents who were entrepreneurs. They also tend to possess unique personality traits. Researchers who study successful entrepreneurs report that they are more likely to be inquisitive, passionate, self-motivated, honest, courageous, flexible, intelligent, and reliable people. The eight traits summarized in Figure 6.5 are especially important for people who want to succeed as entrepreneurs.

## Vision

Entrepreneurs begin with a *vision*, an overall idea for how to make their business idea a success, and then they passionately pursue it. Bill Gates and Paul Allen launched Microsoft with the vision of a computer on every desk and in every home, all running Microsoft software. Their vision helped Microsoft become the world's largest marketer of computer software. It guided the company and provided clear direction for employees as Microsoft grew, adapted, and prospered in an industry characterized by tremendous technological change.

Talk about vision, about the ability to think out of the box; talk about the Thomas Edison of the 21st century and you're not talking about Bill Gates, though. No, these descriptions are for wildly successful inventor and entrepreneur Dean Kamen. The tireless and gregarious father of the first portable insulin pump, heart stent, and stair-climbing wheelchair certainly has vision, but he also keeps a close watch on the bottom line of the numerous successful companies that have resulted from his technological breakthroughs.

His latest creation has met with mixed success. The Segway Human Transporter is a two-wheeled self-balancing electric-powered superscooter that allows people to zip along sidewalks and in large business facilities at eight to twelve miles per hour. While Segway sales have been slower than expected, police and security forces, tour companies (you can take guided Segway tours of Atlanta, Budapest, Chicago, Paris, and Washington D.C.), businesses, and people with disabilities are buying Segways.[37] Shane Latham, who was born without a hip, uses a Segway instead of a wheelchair. The Segway allows him to hold hands with his wife while shopping. Moreover, he says, "I am no longer looking at people's belt buckles when I talk to them. I can look them eye to eye."[38]

## High Energy Level

Entrepreneurs willingly work hard to realize their visions. Starting and building a company require an enormous amount of hard work and long hours. Some entrepreneurs work full time at their regular day jobs and spend weeknights and weekends launching their start-ups. Many devote fourteen-hour days seven days a week to their new ventures. In his ten-year study of entrepreneurs, author Amar Bhidé found that what distinguishes successful entrepreneurs from other

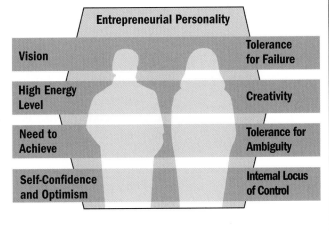

Figure

6.5

Characteristics of Entrepreneurs

**Entrepreneurial Personality**

| Vision | Tolerance for Failure |
| High Energy Level | Creativity |
| Need to Achieve | Tolerance for Ambiguity |
| Self-Confidence and Optimism | Internal Locus of Control |

JONATHAN DRAKE/EPA/LANDOV

The Segway Human Transporter has been a hit for a variety of people—including those with physical handicaps and law enforcement officers. The Segway is just one idea that inventor Dean Kamen has dreamed up and brought to market.

business owners is that they "work harder, hustle for customers, and know that the opportunity may not last for more than six or eight months."[39]

A major reason entrepreneurship demands hard work is that start-up companies typically have a small staff and struggle to raise enough capital. Under these resource constraints, the entrepreneur has to make up the difference. When two engineers started Gilat Satellite Networks in Petah Tikva, Israel, to build satellite systems, they had to work extremely hard to compete with giant corporations like EchoStar. They offered to do whatever was necessary to tailor a system to the client's needs. Gilat's first customer was Rite Aid, the drugstore chain. The company won the contract by agreeing to adapt its satellite system in significant ways. The two founders and four other members of the project's development team put in many nights and evenings to achieve their commitment. Co-founder Amiram Levinberg says simply, "In a high-tech start-up such as Gilat . . . it's a given that there will be some 12-hour days."[40]

With studies indicating that the average entrepreneur works between 52 and 56 hours per week, and that one-fifth of all entrepreneurs work seven days a week, the challenge for entrepreneurs is to balance the hard work with the rest, recreation, and family time that are so essential to good health, quality of life, and continued creativity.[41] Serial entrepreneur Peyton Anderson, CEO of North Carolina–based Affinergy, admits that he thinks about business when with his children. "I have three kids 4 and under. And even while I'm singing to them in the bathtub, in the back of my mind, I'm grinding on stuff at work." Still, Anderson creates time for his children by working after they go to bed, not working one day per weekend, and coming into work late once per week. Said Anderson, "I can do a lot of work from 9 P.M. to midnight using my wireless laptop and sending out e-mails. And I try to keep Saturday [open] all day to do things with the kids. I can [also] come in to work at 9:30 one morning, because I know I'll stay late that night."[42]

## Need to Achieve

Entrepreneurs work hard because they want to excel. Their strong competitive drive helps them enjoy the challenge of reaching difficult goals and promotes dedication to personal success. Entrepreneurship expert Amar Bhidé says successful entrepreneurs have "an almost maniacal level of ambition. Not just ambition to make a comfortable living, to make a few million dollars, but someone who wants to leave a significant mark on the world."[43]

Maria de Lourdes Sobrino's dream was to find success in the United States. A Mexican immigrant, Sobrino moved with her husband and daughter to Los Angeles, where she opened a travel business concentrating on travel between the United States and Mexico. But economic woes in Mexico ended demand for her services, and personal conflicts ended her marriage. Sobrino needed a new way to support herself, and an idea came to her: selling small cups of flavored gelatin, a common treat in Mexico that had not yet found its way to U.S. stores. Identifying retailers willing to take a chance on the new product required persistence. Store managers didn't understand the product, so Sobrino honed the marketing strategy for her company, LuLu's Dessert Factory. She identified Hispanic communities and visited independent stores. Finally, one allowed her to leave gelatin cups, with payment contingent on sales. When Sobrino returned to her spartan office, a message was waiting for her: "Please come back, Señora. Your gelatins are sold."[44] That was the turning point for LuLu's. When her product became popular in local stores, a food broker began to carry it, and Sobrino borrowed money to expand her facilities. Paying off the loans was difficult and took years, but today LuLu's is a $15 million company with 45 products offered in West Coast stores. And she is working with Wal-Mart to export her products to Mexico. Said Sobrino, "Wal-Mart is a very important company to do business with. It will be very exciting to have LuLu's in Mexico."[45]

## Self-Confidence and Optimism

Entrepreneurs believe in their ability to succeed, and they instill their optimism in others. Often their optimism resembles fearlessness in the face of difficult odds. "People thought we were crazy to give up six-figure salaries at investment banking firms to reinvent the earmuff," says Brian LeGette of himself and his business partner Ron Wilson. "They laughed at us." LeGette and Wilson are the founders of 180s LLC, a Baltimore company that got its start with a fleece-covered ear warmer that wraps around the back of the wearer's head. Despite not knowing anything about fabric or sewing, the two business school students put start-up expenses on their credit cards, built a prototype from items they bought at Wal-Mart, and went to work. Within a year, they were a successful start-up, selling their ear warmers for $20 each. Soon they were raising capital to finance growth, hiring additional employees, and adding products. The firm's innovative takes on ordinary products such as sunglasses, beach chairs, and gloves have made 180s into a $50 million firm with 100 employees that sells its products in 18,000 retail stores in 40 countries. One of 180s's latest products is the Quantum Vent, a jacket that allows runners to control their body temperature by pulling cords to lower a vent in the back that draws cool air through a mesh vent. Says LeGette, "We have an inexhaustible desire to question the things that most people think have already been answered. And that's how we succeed in reinventing the wheel."[46]

Sometimes, though, overconfidence can blind entrepreneurs and jeopardize their businesses. This is what happened at 180s. After burning through most of their investors' cash, both LeGette and Wilson have left the company. New investors, who have put $20 million into the company, have now turned the company over to a new CEO with much more experience in the apparel industry.[47]

## Tolerance for Failure

Entrepreneurs often succeed by sheer will and the ability to try and try again when others would give up. They also view setbacks and failures as learning experiences and are not easily discouraged or disappointed when things don't go as planned. Howard Schultz, founder and CEO of Starbucks Coffee, said, "I took Starbucks into the magazine business with *Joe*—my idea. Nobody read it. Since *Joe* failed, I've kept a rack of issues in my office so everyone can see the magazine and realize we shouldn't hide behind our mistakes and we should have the courage to keep pushing by not embracing the status quo. I keep that there as a memento. It was an embarrassing defeat, and we lost a fair amount of money, but sometimes you have to have the courage to fail."[48]

## Creativity

Entrepreneurs typically conceive new ideas for goods and services, and they devise innovative ways to overcome difficult problems and situations. Kenny Kramm struggled in frustration and despair as he watched his infant daughter try to swallow bitter antiseizure medication four times a day. Often Kramm and his wife had to rush their daughter to the emergency room for treatment for the seizures because she had not been able to take enough of the medicine. Kramm improvised at first, giving his daughter mashed banana to help her stomach her medication. Then inspiration struck: He guessed that he wasn't the only parent who had trouble feeding foul-tasting medications to his child. So Kramm concocted harmless additives in his parents' suburban Washington, D.C., pharmacy, where he worked. The additives sweeten the taste and suppress bitterness without diluting the medicine. From a banana flavor, he branched out to other flavors for liquids, pills, and powders. Today, 30,000 pharmacies in the United

States, Canada, Australia, and New Zealand use FLAVORx to make medicine taste better.[49] And thanks to a contract with Walgreen's and other major drugstore chains, revenues grew from $450,000 to $7.8 million in just six years.[50] Is Kramm finished innovating? Not yet. His flavored pet medications are now used at more than 2,000 vet clinics.

Entrepreneurs like Kenny Kramm often achieve success by making creative improvements, rather than single-handedly revolutionizing an industry. Amar Bhidé's research identified a substantial amount of creativity among entrepreneurs "at the tactical level"—in other words, in the ways entrepreneurs built their businesses, more so than in the product itself.[51]

## Tolerance for Ambiguity

Entrepreneurs take in stride the uncertainties associated with launching a venture. Dealing with unexpected events is the norm for most entrepreneurs. Kate and Andy Spade didn't transform their business, Kate Spade, from a small handbag store in New York into a $125 million business by taking unnecessary risks. Kate Spade said, "When we started to have a lot of success with the bags, people said we should expand into this or that category. We knew we had a window of opportunity, but the point was to get into a category that had a growth prospect, and not for growth to simply be the byproduct." In other words, Kate Spade was going to be very careful about which products her company chose to design and sell. Kate's husband, Andy, explains, saying, "If we go into a new category we always ask, 'Do we understand it? Can we design it well?'" And if they don't and can't, they won't design and make those products.[52]

Tolerance for ambiguity is different from the love of risk taking that many people associate with entrepreneurship. Successful entrepreneurship is a far cry from gambling because entrepreneurs look for strategies that they believe have a good chance of success, and they quickly make adjustments when a strategy isn't working. An important way entrepreneurs manage ambiguity is by staying close to customers so that they can adjust their offerings in keeping with customer desires. Amnon Landan, CEO of Mercury, a Mountain View, California–based company that helps banks use information technology to better serve their customers, was named Entrepreneur of the Year by *Forbes* magazine several years ago. Commenting on the importance of being close to customers, Landan says, "It is an overused expression, but the problem is that not too many people are actually exercising it. If you are wise enough to keep close and listen, then you learn about product direction, you learn about the tone of the [customer's] business and where it is moving and shifting." Accordingly, Landan spends 40 percent of his time each year visiting 50 key customers and expects his managers, staff, and especially engineers who design the company's products to spend time with customers, too. Says Landan, "If there is a big deal pending, usually I will not show up to try to close a deal, because you do not learn a lot when you do that. [I go] to our customers to understand how they use the products and what their needs are, and to create communication and trust."[53]

## Internal Locus of Control

Entrepreneurs believe that they control their own fates, which means they have an internal locus of control. You won't find entrepreneurs gazing into a crystal ball, calling psychic help lines, or looking for a four-leaf clover; they take personal responsibility for the success or failure of their actions rather than believing in luck or fate. They neither make excuses for their shortcomings nor blame others for their setbacks and failures. Chris Reeve is one entrepreneur who took a hard look at his abilities in light of the needs of his growing business. He took decisive action to get the company on the right track, as described in the "Hit & Miss" feature.

# HIT & MISS

## Chris Reeve Knives Hunts for a New CEO

Starting a company has been compared to raising a child—at some point, parents must let their grown child enter the world as an independent adult. Entrepreneurs face a similar challenge. Once a business has reached a certain point, its founders may find that their old roles no longer benefit the company, so they struggle to find and fill new ones. They may discover that they enjoy the changes or that they would prefer to move on. The founder of eBay ultimately brought in Meg Whitman to run the company. Yahoo!'s founders tapped Terry Simmel. Chris Reeve, founder of Chris Reeve Knives, finds himself in a similar situation.

Thirty years ago, Chris Reeve established his company in Idaho. His high-end, handmade hunting knives are considered works of art—ranking among the best in the world. Celebrities such as Tom Selleck and Tom Cruise have made purchases. Chris Reeve knives appear in movies and other promotions. But Reeve is no longer sure he's the best person to run his company. "A business like mine that makes something is often started by a very fine craftsman or engineer who is brilliant at what he does," he explains. "That doesn't necessarily translate into being able to run a business and manage and motivate people to do the work properly."

So Reeve is hunting for a new chief. He wants to remain with the firm as its chief designer and inventor—which is how he started out. Several years ago, he tried hiring managers who were friends, or referred by friends—twice. Neither worked out. Reeve understands that the next candidate needs an outside perspective on the company. He also knows that the firm's goals must be made clear. And while he knows he's the best in the world at designing knives, he will have to hire someone who is much better than he is at managing the company—after all, that's the whole point.

### Questions for Critical Thinking

1. What entrepreneurial traits does Chris Reeve seem to have?
2. Do you think it will be beneficial for Reeve to step aside as his firm's chief executive? Why or why not?

**Sources:** Chris Reeve Knives Web site, accessed June 17, 2006, http://www.chrisreeve.com; Perri Capell, "When a Small Company Outgrows Its Founder," *StartupJournal*, accessed June 17, 2006, http://www.startupjournal.com; "Hire People Better Than You," *BusinessWeek*, accessed June 17, 2006, http://www.businessweek.com.

---

After reading this summary of typical personality traits, maybe you're wondering if you have what it takes to become an entrepreneur. Take the test in Figure 6.6 to find out. Your results may help you determine whether you would succeed in starting your own company.

## STARTING A NEW VENTURE

The examples of entrepreneurs presented so far have introduced many ways to start a business. This section discusses the process of choosing an idea for a new venture and transforming the idea into a working business.

### Selecting a Business Idea

In choosing an idea for your business, the two most important considerations are (1) finding something you love to do and are good at doing and (2) determining whether your idea can satisfy a need in the marketplace. People willingly work hard doing something they love, and

**assessment check**

1. What is meant by an entrepreneur's vision?
2. Why is it important for an entrepreneur to have a high energy level and a strong need for achievement?
3. How do entrepreneurs generally feel about the possibility of failure?

**Figure**

6.6

Testing Your Entrepreneurial Potential

**ENTREPRENEUR POTENTIAL ASSESSMENT FORM**

Answer each of the following questions:

Yes   No

☐   ☐   1. Are you a first-generation American?

☐   ☐   2. Were you an honor student?

☐   ☐   3. Did you enjoy group functions in school—clubs, team sports, even double dates?

☐   ☐   4. As a youngster, did you frequently prefer to spend time alone?

☐   ☐   5. As a child, did you have a paper route, a lemonade stand, or some other small enterprise?

☐   ☐   6. Were you a stubborn child?

☐   ☐   7. Were you a cautious youngster, the last in the neighborhood to try diving off the high board?

☐   ☐   8. Do you worry about what others think of you?

☐   ☐   9. Are you in a rut, tired of the same routine every day?

☐   ☐   10. Would you be willing to invest your savings—and risk losing all you invested—to go it alone?

☐   ☐   11. If your new business should fail, would you get to work immediately on another?

☐   ☐   12. Are you an optimist?

Add up your total score. A score of 20 or more points indicates strong entrepreneurial tendencies. A score between 0 and 19 points suggests some possibility for success as an entrepreneur. A score between 0 and −10 indicates little chance of successful entrepreneurship. A score below −11 indicates someone who's not the entrepreneurial type.

Answers: 1. Yes = 1, No = −1; 2. Yes = −4, No = 4; 3. Yes = −1, No = 1; 4. Yes = 1, No = −1; 5. Yes = 2, No = −2; 6. Yes = 1, No = −1; 7. Yes = −4, No = 4 (if you were a very daring child, add another 4 points); 8. Yes = −1, No = 1; 9. Yes = 2, No = −2; 10. Yes = 2, No = −2; 11. Yes = 4, No = −4; 12. Yes = 2, No = −2.

**Source:** Copyright Northwestern Mutual Life Insurance Company. Reprinted with permission.

the experience will bring personal fulfillment. The old adages "Do what makes you happy" and "To thine own self be true" are the best guidelines for deciding on a business idea.

Success also depends on customers, so would-be entrepreneurs must also be sure that the idea they choose has interest in the marketplace. The most successful entrepreneurs tend to operate in industries where a great deal of change is taking place and in which customers have difficulty pinpointing their precise needs. These industries, including advanced technology and consulting, allow entrepreneurs to capitalize on their strengths, such as creativity, hard work, and tolerance of ambiguity, to build customer relationships. Nevertheless, examples of outstanding entrepreneurial success occur in every industry, such as Firefly Mobile, which sells simple five-button mobile phones (Call Mom, Call Dad, Phone Numbers, Hello, and Good-bye) for young children that come with 30 minutes of talking time and let parents restrict incoming and outgoing phone numbers.[54] The following guidelines may help you select an idea that represents a good entrepreneurial opportunity:

- List your interests and abilities. Include your values and beliefs, your goals and dreams, things you like and dislike doing, and your job experiences.
- Make another list of the types of businesses that match your interests and abilities.
- Read newspapers and business and consumer magazines to learn about demographic and economic trends that identify future needs for products that no one yet offers.
- Carefully evaluate existing goods and services, looking for ways you can improve them.
- Decide on a business that matches what you want and offers profit potential.
- Conduct marketing research to determine whether your business idea will attract enough customers to earn a profit.
- Learn as much as you can about the industry in which your new venture will operate, your merchandise or service, and your competitors. Read surveys that project growth in various industries.

Like Kenny Kramm, whose medication-flavoring business was described earlier, many entrepreneurs start businesses to solve problems that they experienced either at work or in their personal lives. When Robert Byerley's $100 dress shirt was ruined at the cleaners, he just wanted his shirt replaced. But when they didn't even apologize, he got the idea for a new business, a premium dry cleaner that stands behind its services. But before he started this business, he did his thinking and his research first. Unable to sleep one night, he created a list of features for the business: "a bank-like drive-through area with curbside delivery; a computerized system that would track clothes all the way through the process and read cleaning preferences off a small bar code; and state-of-the-art, environmentally friendly cleaning processes." Then he spent a week in the library, where he learned that the $16-billion-a-year business is dominated by mom-and-pop businesses. At the Better Business Bureau, he discovered the most common complaint about dry cleaners: not standing behind what they did. Finally, he spent $15,000 to conduct focus groups, asking potential customers to comment on his store's name, features, and advertising and a sample of clothes, which he had taken to the best dry cleaner in town. Today, Byerley's Dallas-based dry cleaning business, Bibbentuckers, has three stores, each of which averages $1 million a year in revenues, four times that of the average dry cleaning store.[55]

While Byerley's Bibbentuckers dry cleaning stores didn't invent a new product or process, many entrepreneurs who start new businesses do. When that happens, the inventor-entrepreneur needs to protect the rights to his or her invention by securing a patent. The U.S. Patent and Trademark Office's Web site (http://www.uspto.gov) provides information about this process, along with forms to apply for a patent. Inventors can also apply for a patent online.

*Buying an Existing Business*    Some entrepreneurs prefer to buy established businesses rather than assume the risks of starting new ones. Buying an existing business brings many advantages: Employees already in place serve established customers and deal with familiar suppliers, the good or service is known in the marketplace, and the necessary permits and licenses have already been secured. Getting financing for an existing business also is easier than it is for most start-ups. Some sellers may even help the buyers by providing financing and offering to serve as consultants.

To find businesses for sale, contact your local chamber of commerce, brokers who sell businesses, and professionals such as lawyers, accountants, and insurance agents. It is important to analyze the performance of businesses under consideration. Most people want to buy a healthy business so that they can build on its success. When Debra Fine decided to start a business making long-lasting, high-end children's toys to be sold at upscale stores, she bought 40-year-old Small World Toys in Culver City, California, which made high-quality wooden castles and dollhouses. Small World Toys became a division in her new business, Small World Kids. In her first year of business, she increased revenues 13 percent to $29.5 million by selling toys at high-end retailers such as Nordstrom, Neiman Marcus, and Learning Express.[56]

In contrast, turnaround entrepreneurs enjoy the challenge of buying unprofitable firms and making enough improvement in their operations to generate new profits. Hancock & Moore, a leather furniture manufacturer in Hickory, North Carolina, chose this route when it purchased Councill Craftsman, a bankrupt furniture manufacturer. Success with a turnaround strategy requires that the entrepreneur have definite and practical ideas about how to operate the business more profitably. After investing $5.1 million in Councill Craftsman for new production equipment that would raise quality and lower costs, Hancock & Moore focused Councill Craftsman's business from three lines of furniture—office, 18th-century reproductions, and high-end—to just one, custom-made furniture.[57]

**Buying a Franchise**  Like buying an established business, buying a franchise offers a less risky way to begin a business than starting an entirely new firm. But as the previous chapter pointed out, franchising still involves risks. You must do your homework, carefully analyzing the franchisor's fees and capabilities for delivering the support it promises. Energetic preparation helps ensure that your business will earn a profit and grow.

## Creating a Business Plan

Traditionally, most entrepreneurs launched their ventures without creating formal business plans. Although planning is an integral part of managing in the world of 21st-century business, entrepreneurs typically seize opportunities as they arise and change course as necessary. Flexibility seems to be the key to business start-ups, especially in rapidly changing markets. Forty-seven percent of the most recent *Inc.* 500 CEOs did not create a formal written plan before launching their companies.[58] Entrepreneurial researcher Amar Bhidé attributes that surprising fact to the types of businesses that today's entrepreneurs start. When businesspeople do not need a large amount of cash to start their businesses, they often do not need financing from outside sources—which usually require plans. Also, the rapid pace of change in some industries reduces the benefit of writing a plan.[59] Still, when an entrepreneur needs additional funds to start or grow a business, a business plan is indispensable.

Although the planning process for entrepreneurs differs from a major company's planning function, today's entrepreneurs are advised to construct business plans following the guidelines presented in Chapter 5 and Appendix C. Careful planning helps the entrepreneur prepare enough resources and stay focused on key objectives, and it provides an important tool for convincing potential investors and employees that the enterprise has the ingredients for success. Entrepreneurial business plans vary depending on the type of start-up, but the basic elements of such a plan—stating company goals, outlining sales and marketing strategies, and determining financial needs and sources of funds—apply to all types of ventures. The Internet also offers a variety of resources for creating business plans. Table 6.1 lists some of these online resources.

## Finding Financing

A key issue in any business plan is financing. How much money will you need to start your business and where will you get it? Requirements for **seed capital,** funds used to launch a

**seed capital** initial funding needed to launch a new venture.

Table
6.1

**Online Resources for Preparing a Business Plan**

| | |
|---|---|
| AllBusiness.com<br>http://www.allbusiness.com | The "Business Advice" page provides links to examples, templates, and tips for writing a plan. |
| Inc.<br>http://www.inc.com | Under "Departments," click "How-To-Guides" and then "Writing a Business Plan," which links to 150+ articles about how to write a business plan. |
| Kauffman eVenturing<br>http://www.eventuring.org | The "Explore Topics" section has links to information and resources for researching and writing a plan, as well as presenting it to lenders or investors. |
| MoreBusiness.com<br>http://www.morebusiness.com | To see a sample plan, select "Business & Marketing Plans" from the list of templates. |

company, depend on the nature of your business and the type of facilities and equipment you need. On average, CEOs of the fastest-growing small businesses raised $1.5 million in seed capital to start their businesses. This average is highly skewed, though, by a few entrepreneurs who raised tens of millions of dollars for their business. The median amount of seed money, $50,000, was significantly below the average of $1.5 million. In fact, 54 percent of entrepreneurs started their businesses with $50,000 or less.[60]

Most entrepreneurs rely on personal savings, advances on credit cards, and money from partners, family members, and friends to fund their start-ups. When Ben David started his Nurses Now! temporary agency, to provide nurses to local hospitals in the Baltimore, Maryland, area, he used every dollar he had to start the business. David took out a second mortgage on his house, borrowed from his 401(k) retirement account, and maxed out all of his credit cards. Today, he's well on his way to paying off those loans as his business, now in its third year, will have revenues of $5 million this year.[61]

*Debt Financing*   When entrepreneurs like Ben David use **debt financing,** they borrow money that they must repay. Loans from banks, finance companies, credit card companies, and family and friends are all sources of debt financing. Although many entrepreneurs charge business expenses to personal credit cards because they are relatively easy to obtain, high interest rates make this source of funding expensive. Annual interest charges on a credit card can run as high as 20 percent, while rates for a home equity loan (borrowing against the value of a home) currently run between 6 and 8 percent. In exchange for a lower interest rate, borrowers with a home equity loan pledge the value of their home, so a borrower who does not repay the loan risks losing the home.

When a business fails and cannot repay its loans, the owner must often declare bankruptcy. Regardless of legal

**debt financing** borrowed funds that entrepreneurs must repay.

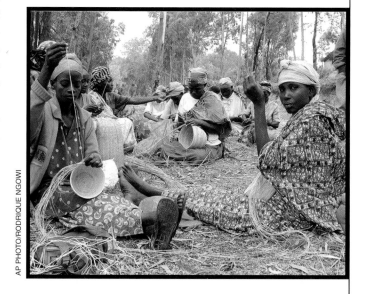

AP PHOTO/RODRIQUE NGOWI

Roberto Milk found a way to serve society through his company, Novica, which sells handcrafted art from artisans around the world. To obtain the funds to start his business, Milk turned to venture capital firms that invested millions of dollars. His buying teams travel the world in search of unique pieces. And when an item is sold, Novica guarantees artists that they will be paid at least 60 percent of the retail price.

# SMALL BUSINESS AND BANKRUPTCY—IS THERE AN ETHICAL RESPONSIBILITY?

*When a small business goes bankrupt, its legal obligations to pay creditors are significantly reduced. Most creditors expect to receive pennies on the dollar. But is there an ethical responsibility to reimburse creditors?*

The National Hockey League's Pittsburgh Penguins once found itself in this situation. The team suffered from poor performance and declining attendance at its games, and its debt totaled $120 million. So the Penguins finally declared bankruptcy. But in an unusual move—including a comeback from retirement by star player Mario Lemieux—the team made a commitment to pay off 100 percent of its debts.

Does a small business have an ethical responsibility to repay debts, even if it does not have the legal responsibility under bankruptcy protection?

## PRO

1. It is more ethical to pay off a debt—even if it takes many months or years—than to negotiate repayments of pennies on the dollar.

2. When a firm goes bankrupt, employees and contract workers, as well as vendors and suppliers, are often hit the hardest. So every effort should be made to compensate them.

## CON

1. Bankruptcy law is designed to help companies cut their losses, pay creditors a reasonable amount, and move on to future success. Tying them down with past debt may cost future jobs and interrupt service to new customers.
2. There is no legal requirement to repay the debt, so there should not be an ethical one.

## SUMMARY

With the help of Lemieux—who agreed to restructure his salary and who found a group of investors willing to buy the team and keep it in Pittsburgh—the Penguins paid their debts. Even during the NHL strike, which meant no revenues, the team continued to make payments. "That's just the way we do business," explained team president Ken Sawyer. "There's absolutely a sense of pride."

**Sources:** Helen Huntley, "Bankruptcy Law Ensnares Businesses," *St. Petersburg (FL) Times*, accessed June 17, 2006, http://www.sptimes.com; Judy Newman, "When Companies Go Bankrupt, Employees and Freelancers Often Hit Hardest," *Wisconsin State Journal*, accessed June 17, 2006, http://www.madison.com/wsj; "Penguins Paying Creditors 100 Percent in Rare Bankruptcy Result," Associated Press, August 20, 2005, http://www.ap.org.

## solving an ETHICAL controversy

## "They Said It"

*"The only thing tainted about money is 'taint mine' or 'taint enough'."*
—Anonymous

requirements, some entrepreneurs who have been forced to declare bankruptcy still feel obligated to repay their debts. The "Solving an Ethical Controversy" feature debates the ethics of repaying creditors.

Many banks turn down requests for loans to fund start-ups, fearful of the high risk such ventures entail. In fact, Ben David, who relied on credit cards and a second mortgage to start Nurses Now!, said, "Anyone who thinks they can draw up a business plan and walk into a bank and ask for money is crazy. Banks aren't going to give you money for just an idea. You need a track record, and you need backers."[62] Only a small percentage of start-ups raise seed capital through bank loans, although some new firms can get SBA-backed loans, as discussed in Chapter 5.

Applying for a bank loan requires careful preparation. Bank loan officers want to see a business plan and will evaluate the entrepreneur's credit history. Because a start-up has not yet established a business credit history, banks often base lending decisions on evaluations of entrepreneurs' personal credit histories. Banks are more willing to make loans to entrepreneurs who have been in business for a while, show a profit on rising revenues, and need funds to finance expansion. Some entrepreneurs have found that local community banks are more interested in their loan applications than are the major national banks.

*Equity Financing*   To secure **equity financing,** entrepreneurs exchange a share of ownership in their company for money supplied by one or more investors. Entrepreneurs invest their own money along with funds supplied by other people and firms that become co-owners of the start-ups. An entrepreneur does not have to repay equity funds. Rather, the investors share in the success of the business. Sources of equity financing include family and friends, business partners, venture capital firms, and private investors.

Teaming up with a partner who has funds to invest may benefit an entrepreneur with a good idea and skills but little or no money. Investors may also have business experience, which they will be eager to share because the company's prosperity will benefit them. Like borrowing, however, equity financing has its drawbacks. One is that investment partners may not agree on the future direction of the business, and in the case of partnerships, if they cannot resolve disputes, one partner may have to buy out the other to keep operating. When Joe Strazza founded WinMill Software in New York City, he reduced his ownership stake in the company from 40 to 20 percent by securing $3 million in equity financing from 100 investors, most of whom were family and friends. These funds allowed the company to grow from one office and three workers to four offices in four cities and 180 workers. When the company was doing well, his investors were happy, but when business dropped from $24 million in revenues to $7 million, numerous investors asked to cash out, but they could not because the company lacked funds. Moreover, other investors opposed management decisions—for example, expanding into other lines of business such as installing wireless networks for cities and hospitals. Strazza said, "People say they believe in you and like you. But then when you're down, you learn it was all about the money. That's a very tough lesson to learn as an entrepreneur. You feel like you're losing your friends."[63]

**Venture capitalists** are business organizations or groups of private individuals that invest in new and growing firms. These investors expect high rates of return, typically more than 30 percent, within short time periods of five years or fewer. Prior to the widespread failures of many dot-coms in the early years of the 21st century, a sizable portion of venture capital flowed into start-up Internet firms. Today, most of the $20 billion that venture capitalists invest annually flows to a very limited number of businesses. Less than one-tenth of firms receiving funds from venture capitalists are start-ups, and most of the remainder are high-tech firms.[64]

**Angel investors,** wealthy individuals who invest money directly in new ventures in exchange for equity, are a larger source of investment capital for start-up firms. In contrast to venture capitalists, angels focus primarily on new ventures. Many angel investors are successful entrepreneurs who want to help aspiring business owners through the familiar difficulties of launching their businesses. Angel investors back a wide variety of new ventures. Some invest exclusively in certain industries, others invest only in start-ups with socially responsible missions, and still others prefer to back only women entrepreneurs. The "Business Etiquette" feature provides tips on a key strategy that entrepreneurs use to interest investors in their ideas: the business dinner.

Because most entrepreneurs have trouble finding wealthy private investors, angel networks form to match business angels with start-ups in need of capital. As you learned in Chapter 5, the Small Business Administration's Active Capital provides online listings to connect would-be angels with small businesses seeking financing. Similar networks try to expand the old-boy network of venture capitalists to new investors and entrepreneurs as well. Venture capitalists that focus on women include Isabella Capital (http://www.fundisabella.com) and Springboard Enterprises (http://www.springboardenterprises.org). Those interested in minority-owned business include the U.S. Hispanic Chamber of Commerce (http://www.ushcc.com).

**equity financing** funds invested in new ventures in exchange for part ownership.

**venture capitalists** business firms or groups of individuals that invest in new and growing firms in exchange for an ownership share.

**angel investors** wealthy individuals who invest directly in a new venture in exchange for an equity stake.

**assessment check**

1. What are the two most important considerations in choosing an idea for a new business?
2. What is the purpose of a patent?
3. What is seed capital?

## Dining for Dollars

Entrepreneurs need money to fund their businesses. Many start with their own savings, but they quickly reach a point at which outside financing is necessary to survive and grow. So being successful means becoming skilled in attracting potential investors. Often the initial courtship occurs over a business meal, which can be a good way to get to know each other in a relaxed setting. But the dinner requires some savvy etiquette. To unravel the mystery of dining for dollars, follow these hints from the experts.

- Before setting up a dinner meeting, think through the mission of the meal. Is it simply to introduce yourself and your business? Are you ready to discuss specific business details? Write down your objectives.
- If possible, choose a restaurant you already know, where you trust the food and the staff. You'll want someplace that is relatively quiet so that you can talk. If you are paying a visit to potential investors outside your own town, research the restaurants ahead of time. You can ask your guests where they would like to eat—but make it clear that you will be the host.
- Arrive at the restaurant ten to fifteen minutes before the reservation time. Let the restaurant host know you are there. Wait in the lobby or near the door for your guests. If the staff prefers to seat you at a table, do not

order drinks or food until your guests arrive.
- Greet your guests upon arrival with a smile and a firm handshake. Keep business papers off the table, and turn off your cell phone. Enjoy dinner and follow proper dining etiquette. Limit your alcohol intake, and don't smoke.
- Don't skip dessert and coffee. Key business discussions and decisions often take place during this part of the meal. It is usually acceptable to refer to any documents you may need for discussion at this point.
- When the check arrives, payment is your responsibility. Do so quickly and quietly. Alternatively, if you arrive early enough, you can give the wait staff your credit card so that it is clear you will be paying the bill.
- Escort your guests to the door, shake hands, and thank them for taking the time to join you. Later, you may want to jot down some meeting notes. Send a written note to your guests within a day or two, thanking them again for their time and consideration.

**Sources:** Naomi Torre Poulson, "Hosting a Formal Dinner," AskMen.com, accessed June 17, 2006, http://www.askmen.com; Scott Reeves, "Hosting a Business Dinner," *Forbes*, accessed June 17, 2006, http://www.forbes.com; Lydia Ramsey, "Sealing the Deal over the Business Meal," *Consulting to Management*, accessed June 17, 2006, http://www.c2m.com.

# INTRAPRENEURSHIP

Established companies try to retain the entrepreneurial spirit by encouraging **intrapreneurship,** the process of promoting innovation within their organizational structures. Today's fast-changing business climate compels established firms to innovate continually to maintain their competitive advantages.

At Cambridge Consultants, a 250-person consulting firm in Boston that helps clients create products for five different industries, the entire company is designed around intrapreneurship. Each year, the company uses 10 percent of its revenues to help employees start and run new businesses. All of the firm's five divisions then use that money for a spin-off budget that employees use to develop initial new product ideas. Roughly 15 percent of initial ideas are then approved for more funds, which are used for marketing research and viability—in other words, to determine the likelihood of selling the new products. Finally, the company's top managers review the research studies and typically select one idea per year that is then spun off into its own new product division. Over the last 45 years, Cambridge has launched an average of one new company per year with an average investment of $1 million. When those new businesses are successful, employees and the companies share the profits. But if they fail, employees get their old jobs back, and the company incurs the loss.[65]

Established companies such as 3M support intrapreneurial activity in varied ways. 3M allows its researchers to spend 15 percent of their time working on their own ideas without approval from management. In addition to allowing time for traditional product development, 3M implements two intrapreneurial approaches: skunkworks and pacing programs. A **skunkworks** project is initiated by an employee who conceives an idea and then recruits resources from within 3M to turn it into a commercial product. **Pacing programs** are company-initiated projects that focus on a few products and technologies in which 3M sees potential for rapid marketplace winners. The company provides financing, equipment, and people to support such pacing projects.

Entrepreneurial environments created within companies can help firms retain valuable employees who might otherwise leave to start their own businesses. The Walt Disney Company is an icon of creativity, and many of its creative people leave to start businesses on their own. Among them is Jake Winebaum, formerly president of Walt Disney Magazine Publishing and intrapreneurial founder of Disney Online. While at Disney, he loved the climate of innovation in which he ran Disney.com, ABCNews.com, ESPN.com, and Go.com. He found the process of starting these operations inside Disney very similar to the process of starting a new company. In fact, the experience reminded him how much he loved being an entrepreneur, and he left to start a business incubator called eCompanies, with the goal of helping businesses move from ideas to operating businesses within a few months. Winebaum credits Disney with helping him learn how to identify business ideas with good potential.[66]

**intrapreneurship**
process of promoting innovation within the structure of an existing organization.

**assessment check**

1. Why would large companies support intrapreneurship?

2. What is a skunkworks?

# WHAT'S AHEAD

The next chapter turns to a realm of business in which many entrepreneurs have been active during the past decade: e-business, or business use of the Internet. The chapter describes the technology behind electronic business. It introduces the challenges and opportunities available to entrepreneurs and other businesspeople who want to communicate with and sell to customers on the Internet. Not many years ago, Internet technology was a novelty except among high-tech firms and tech-savvy individuals. Today it is an integral factor in starting and growing a business.

## Summary of Learning Goals

**1** **Define the term *entrepreneur* and distinguish among entrepreneurs, small-business owners, and managers.**

Unlike many small-business owners, entrepreneurs typically own and run their businesses with the goal of building significant firms that create wealth and add jobs. Entrepreneurs are visionaries. They identify opportunities and take the initiative to gather the resources they need to start their businesses quickly. Both managers and entrepreneurs use the resources of their companies to achieve the goals of those organizations.

### Assessment Check Answers

**1.1 What tools do entrepreneurs use to create a new business?**
Entrepreneurs combine their ideas and drive with money, employees, and other resources to create a business that fills a market need.

**1.2 How do entrepreneurs differ from managers?**
Managers direct the efforts of others to achieve an organization's goals. The drive and impatience that entrepreneurs have to make their companies successful often hurts their ability to manage.

**2** **Identify four different types of entrepreneurs.**

The four categories of entrepreneurs are classic entrepreneurs, serial entrepreneurs, intrapreneurs, and change agents. A classic entrepreneur identifies a business opportunity and allocates available resources to tap that market. A serial entrepreneur starts one business, runs it, and then starts and runs additional businesses in succession. An intrapreneur is an employee who develops a new idea or product within an organizational position. A change agent is a manager who revitalizes an existing firm to make it a competitive success.

## Assessment Check Answers

**2.1 Why do companies encourage intrapreneurs?**
Established companies need intrapreneurs to help develop new products, ideas, and commercial ventures.

**2.2 What do intrapreneurs and change agents have in common?**
Like intrapreneurs, change agents turn around and revitalize established firms to keep them competitive in today's marketplace.

**3 Explain why people choose to become entrepreneurs.**
People choose this kind of career for many different reasons. Reasons most frequently cited include desires to be one's own boss, to achieve financial success, to gain job security, and to improve one's quality of life.

## Assessment Check Answers

**3.1 Are entrepreneurs more likely than employees to achieve financial success?**
While only one in five American workers is self-employed, more than two-thirds of all millionaires are self-employed. Consequently, if you run your own business, you're more likely to achieve financial success.

**3.2 What factors affect the entrepreneur's job security?**
An entrepreneur's job security depends on the decisions of customers and investors and on the cooperation and commitment of the entrepreneur's own employees.

**4 Discuss conditions that encourage opportunities for entrepreneurs.**
A favorable public perception, availability of financing, the falling cost and widespread availability of information technology, globalization, entrepreneurship education, and changing demographic and economic trends all contribute to a fertile environment for people to start new ventures.

## Assessment Check Answers

**4.1 To what extent is entrepreneurship possible in different countries, and what opportunities does globalization create for today's entrepreneurs?**
More than 9 percent of adults worldwide are starting or managing a new business. As for globalization opportunities, entrepreneurs market their products abroad and hire international talent. Among the fastest-growing small U.S. companies, almost two of every five have international sales.

**4.2 Identify the educational factors that help expand current opportunities for entrepreneurs.**
More than 100 U.S. universities offer majors in entrepreneurship, another 73 offer an entrepreneurship emphasis, and hundreds more offer courses in how to start a business. Also, organizations such as the Kauffman Center for Entrepreneurial Leadership, Entreprep, and Students in Free Enterprise encourage and teach entrepreneurship.

**4.3 Describe current demographic trends that suggest new goods and services for entrepreneurial businesses.**
The aging of the U.S. population, the emergence of Hispanics as the nation's largest ethnic group, and the growth of two-income families are creating opportunities for entrepreneurs to market new goods and services.

**5 Identify personality traits that typically characterize successful entrepreneurs.**
Successful entrepreneurs share several typical traits, including vision, high energy levels, the need to achieve, self-confidence and optimism, tolerance for failure, creativity, tolerance for ambiguity, and an internal locus of control.

## Assessment Check Answers

**5.1 What is meant by an entrepreneur's vision?**
Entrepreneurs begin with a vision, an overall idea for how to make their business idea a success, and then passionately pursue it.

**5.2 Why is it important for an entrepreneur to have a high energy level and a strong need for achievement?**
Because start-up companies typically have a small staff and struggle to raise enough capital, the entrepreneur has to make up the difference by working long hours. A strong need for achievement helps entrepreneurs enjoy the challenge of reaching difficult goals and promotes dedication to personal success.

**5.3 How do entrepreneurs generally feel about the possibility of failure?**
They view failure as a learning experience and are not easily discouraged or disappointed when things don't go as planned.

### 6 Summarize the process of starting a new venture.

Entrepreneurs must select an idea for their business, develop a business plan, obtain financing, and organize the resources they need to operate their start-ups.

## Assessment Check Answers

**6.1 What are the two most important considerations in choosing an idea for a new business?**
Two important considerations are finding something you love to do and are good at doing and determining whether your idea can satisfy a need in the marketplace.

**6.2 What is the purpose of a patent?**
A patent protects the rights to a new invention, process, or product.

**6.3 What is seed capital?**
Seed capital is the money that is used to start a company.

### 7 Explain how organizations promote intrapreneurship.

Organizations encourage intrapreneurial activity within the company in a variety of ways, including hiring practices, dedicated programs such as skunkworks, access to resources, and wide latitude to innovate within established firms.

## Assessment Check Answers

**7.1 Why would large companies support intrapreneurship?**
Large firms support intrapreneurship to retain an entrepreneurial spirit and to promote innovation and change.

**7.2 What is a skunkworks?**
A skunkworks project is initiated by an employee who conceives an idea and then recruits resources from within the company to turn that idea into a commercial product.

## Business Terms You Need to Know

entrepreneur 184
classic entrepreneur 185
serial entrepreneur 186
intrapreneur 186

change agent 186
lifestyle entrepreneur 190
seed capital 202
debt financing 203

equity financing 205
venture capitalist 205
angel investor 205
intrapreneurship 206

## Other Important Business Terms

**skunkworks 206**

**pacing programs 206**

## Review Questions

1. What are the similarities and differences among entrepreneurs, small-business owners, and managers? What tools do entrepreneurs use to create a new business?
2. Why do companies encourage intrapreneurs? What do intrapreneurs and change agents have in common?
3. Identify the four categories of entrepreneurs. How are they different from each other?

4. What are the four major reasons for becoming an entrepreneur? Why do you think entrepreneurs are more likely than employees to achieve financial success? What factors affect the entrepreneur's job security?
5. How have globalization and information technology created new opportunities for entrepreneurs? Describe current demographic trends that suggest new goods and services for entrepreneurial businesses.

6. Identify the eight characteristics that are attributed to successful entrepreneurs. Which trait or traits do you believe are the most important for success? Why? Why is it important for an entrepreneur to have a high energy level and a strong need for achievement? How do entrepreneurs generally feel about the possibility of failure?

7. What are the benefits and risks involved in buying an existing business or a franchise?

8. Why is creating a business plan an important step for an entrepreneur?

9. Describe the different types of financing that entrepreneurs may seek for their businesses. What are the risks and benefits involved with each?

10. Why do most entrepreneurs rely on personal savings, credit cards, and money from family and friends? Why is it difficult to obtain bank financing?

11. What is intrapreneurship? How does it differ from entrepreneurship?

## Projects and Teamwork Applications

1. Think of an entrepreneur whom you admire or choose one of the following: Bill Gates of Microsoft, Jeff Bezos of Amazon.com, or Oprah Winfrey of Harpo Productions. Explain why you admire this entrepreneur, including ways in which the person has contributed to his or her industry as well as to the economy.

2. Current demographic and economic trends support entrepreneurs who create new businesses. One of these trends is the willingness of Americans to spend more money on certain goods and services, such as pet care. On your own or with a classmate, brainstorm a trend that may be a good idea for a new business. Write one or two paragraphs describing the trend and how it could be applied to a business.

3. Review the eight characteristics of successful entrepreneurs. Which characteristics do you possess? Do you think you would be a good entrepreneur? Why? Write a paragraph or two listing your strengths.

4. Many entrepreneurs are motivated by working in an area they love. Think about something you love to do that you believe could be turned into a business. What aspect of the activity would actually be turned into a business? For example, if you love to play golf or shop at vintage clothing stores for 1970s-style attire, how would you shape this interest into a business?

## Case 6.1

### Genuine Scooters

Philip McCaleb has always loved riding scooters. When he worked in Europe as a sales manager for a U.S. company, he rode one to his job. It was cheap, maneuverable, and fun. Back home in Chicago a few years later, he began tinkering with the rusty parts of vintage scooters in his basement. He hunted down parts and accessories for old Vespa scooters and painstakingly restored them to life. Before he knew it, he was running a small restoration business called Scooterworks. Although there were a few diehard fans, the two-wheeled vehicles were slow to catch on in the United States. So McCaleb started a Vespa fan club and Internet message board. Today, with more and more consumers taking an interest in vintage scooters, Scooterworks is the largest importer of parts and accessories for the two-wheelers in the United States.

But Scooterworks is now a secondary business for McCaleb. As gas prices have soared, so has interest in alternative forms of travel. Scooters are cheaper than motorcycles, and they don't require a special license. They get anywhere from 50 to 110 miles per gallon, and they can keep up with the flow of general traffic on the road. Consumers who once made fun of scooters—or viewed them as toys—are now taking a second look. Banking on this new interest, McCaleb launched a second company called Genuine Scooter.

In its first three years, Genuine Scooter's popular Stella scooter—designed by McCaleb—has rolled down thousands of driveways. Priced at $2,895, it can reach 55 miles per hour and averages 90 miles per gallon of gas. Customers include urban dwellers, commuters, and even retirees who just want to head into town for lunch or a bag of groceries. But McCaleb emphasizes the fun factor. "A large portion of my market is delayed adolescents, or those looking to return to adolescence," he says with a smile.

As his firm rapidly grows bigger and more successful, McCaleb has a clear understanding of its position in the marketplace. "I always want to grow and compete," he explains, "but there is no way we can compete, or want to compete, with the Hondas or the Yamahas. We carefully look to compete on a scale that focuses on niche, on service, and quality." McCaleb also understands his own role as an entrepreneur. He loves to come up with new ideas, design things, and put them together. But he is not a businessperson. So he hired a consultant to help draw up a formal business plan to achieve the kind of expansion he envisions for Genuine Scooter. "I crave the opportunity to put concepts on the street," says McCaleb. "I'm a horrible bureaucrat and lousy operations guy." With this strategy, McCaleb can focus on what he does best—coming up with ideas for new products and new markets. Recently, Genuine Scooters launched a sidecar that attaches to its scooter and plans to offer a scooter trailer soon. Meanwhile, McCaleb is working on the next generation of scooters, which will be larger and faster. He hopes to win over more consumers who want the ease and flexibility of squeezing through traffic and parking in tight spaces—and who don't mind a little wind in their hair.

## Questions for Critical Thinking

1. What conditions do you think opened the door of opportunity for Philip McCaleb's two companies?
2. What type of entrepreneur is Philip McCaleb? What personality traits does he have that could contribute to his success?

**Sources:** Genuine Scooter Web site, accessed June 17, 2006, http://www.genuine scooters.com; Tara Siegel Bernard, "Scooters' Popularity Offers a Chance for Growth," *Wall Street Journal*, accessed June 17, 2006, http://online.wsj.com; Joe Kafka, "High Prices Pumping Up Scooter Sales," *(Fort Wayne, TX) Journal Gazette*, accessed June 17, 2006, http://www.fortwayne.com/mld/journalgazette; John Schmeltzer, "Sales of Scooters Get in the Fast Lane," *Chicago Tribune*, accessed June 17, 2006, http://www.chicagotribune.com.

## VIDEO Case 6.2
### Culver's: Great Food from a Good Business

This video case appears on page 614. A recently filmed video, designed to expand and highlight the written case, is available for class use by instructors.

# Chapter 7

## E-Business: Doing Business Online

**Learning Goals**

1. Define e-business and discuss how it can help achieve business success.

2. Distinguish between a corporate Web site and a marketing Web site.

3. List the major forms of business-to-business (B2B) e-business.

4. Explain business-to-consumer (B2C) e-business and identify the products most often sold online.

5. Describe some of the challenges associated with e-business.

6. Discuss how organizations use the communication functions of the Internet to advance their objectives.

7. List the steps involved in developing successful Web sites and identify methods for measuring Web site effectiveness.

8. Explain the global scope of e-business.

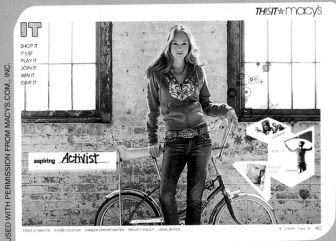

**B**ecause teenagers and young adults already spend a lot of time online, it should be easy for marketers to sell them CDs, games, and high-fashion clothing on the Internet, right? After all, they're already at their computers. Why wouldn't they shop there as their parents do?

Selling online to the youth market isn't quite as simple as just offering a Web site. Teens might actually surf fewer hours a week than their parents, because having access at school is limited or focused on specific tasks, which doesn't bring the same freedom to shop that many adults enjoy. And when online, many teens are busy communicating—sending instant messages, writing and reading blogs, and conversing in chat rooms. Further, many teens are price conscious because their earning power is low

# Reaching the Elusive Teen Market Online

and few have credit cards. These factors combine to make it easier for teens to window-shop than to actually purchase.

Still, retailers see big potential in capturing the attention of this lucrative—and elusive—market. For one thing, credit cards for many teens are only a year or two away, and the purchasing power of this age group is expected to be high. Within the next few years, roughly 34 million people will be in their teens in the United States, so they are an attractive market. Another motivation for venturing online is the opportunity to build customer loyalty, especially for big retail operations like Macy's Thisit.com, Crate and Barrel's cb2.com, and Pottery Barn's pbteen.com. Young people who begin a relationship online with a department store such as Macy's or a home-and-hearth retailer like Pottery Barn may continue to shop there—online, in person, or by catalog—for many years. So how do retail businesses create Web sites that attract teens and young adults?

Macy's partnered with *Teen Vogue* magazine to develop Thisit.com for girls in the 13- to 17-year-old age range. The home page features a picture of Times Square with numbered billboards and a blimp. Hidden behind the numbers are descriptions of the site's contents—in

place of the typical dull navigation bar. In addition to high-fashion clothes for purchase, the site features flashy graphics, music and video clips to download, and fashion and grooming advice. The manager of Macy's online division says the site is "mostly designed to be about their lifestyle and communicating with them versus a hard sell like 'here's the merchandise, it's on sale.'" The site has no housewares or appliances, for instance, although all items on Thisit.com can be accessed, presumably by parents, from the company's main Web site at Macys.com.

Alloy.com, a specialty-clothing site that caters to female teens, packages polls, contests, sweepstakes, message boards, fashion advice, and horoscopes on its site. The site also features tips and news about trends, books, movies, and music and film celebrities. The polls and message boards help give the company feedback; its buyers can spot emerging trends from posted comments. Hip Web site http://hollisterco.com, owned by Abercrombie & Fitch, has separate pages for "Dudes" and "Bettys" in need of fashionable clothes and accessories, as well as trendy features about pop groups with audio and video clips on its "Club Cali" page. In contrast, eBay doesn't have to dress up its Web site very much to draw teens. In fact, it's hard for other companies to compete with eBay when it comes to entertainment value, and eBay and Amazon are already top destinations for teen shoppers.

But making Web sites entertaining and interactive isn't all retailers need to do. They must also draw teens to visit them, often by linking to popular "social networking" sites such as Facebook.com, Quizilla.com, CollegeBoards.com, and Xanga.com. Even the education site SparkNotes.com is considered a good way to reach teens. One reason is that teens consider social and educational sites safe and tend to trust information they find there. Stores are also experimenting with e-mail promotions and ways to use text messaging to reach teens.

Although many teen sites cater to females, retailers must still grapple with a few gender-related differences of Internet users. First, although teenage girls spend about 22 percent more time online than boys, teen boys buy more items online. The kind of merchandise boys buy—videos, music, games, and high-tech items—doesn't need to be tried on. And, as any parent can attest, teen girls simply like the social aspects of shopping together at the mall. But if Thisit.com brings the customer to the mall, Macy's won't be complaining.[1]

Over the past decade few developments in contemporary business have been as monumental as the Internet and its related technologies. The Internet offers businesses and other organizations a source of information, a means of communication, and a channel for buying and selling, all rolled into one. With just a few ticks of the clock and a few clicks of a mouse, the Internet has revolutionized virtually every aspect of business. Consumers use the Internet for a variety of tasks: to pay bills, obtain product information, make purchases, and even consult with their physicians. Businesses use the Internet to exchange information with customers, advertise products, research market trends, and, of course, buy and sell a whole range of goods and services. New words have emerged, such as *blog*, *RSS*, *extranet*, and *wiki*, and old words have new meanings: *Web, search marketing, banner, pop-up,* and *online.*

Electronic business (or e-Business) refers to conducting business via the Internet. The size and scope of e-business is difficult to understate. For instance, during a two-week period leading up to Valentine's Day, U.S. consumers spent close to $4 billion online, a 30 percent increase over the previous year.[2] Sigma-Aldrich, a St. Louis–based chemical company that sells products to biologists, has seen its online sales rise fiftyfold—from $4 million to more than $200 million in less than ten years. Office products retailer Staples reports that more than half its orders are placed via the company's Web site. Meanwhile, Ford Motor Credit recently launched an Internet portal for receiving and processing credit applications. Already the portal is processing around half of all the applications that come from Ford dealers, or more than 150,000 per day.[3]

E-business involves much more than just buying and selling. Some surveys suggest that the Web is the number one medium for new-product information, eclipsing catalogs, print ads, and trade shows. The Internet allows retailers and vendors to exchange vital information, improving the overall functioning of inventory and supply, which lowers costs and increases profits. Moreover, an increasing number of Americans now get their news and information from blogs (short for *Web logs*, which are online journals) rather than from traditional media such as television and newspapers. Consequently, a growing number of businesses use blogs to put human faces on their organizations and communicate directly with customers.

Government agencies and not-for-profit organizations have also embraced the Internet. On college and university Web sites, students can obtain academic program information, register for courses, check grades, and even pay their college bills. Many states now allow residents to renew their car registrations online, saving time and trips to the motor vehicle office.

In the past decade, the number of Internet users in the United States and worldwide has grown dramatically. Today an estimated 200 million Americans—more than 63 percent of the U.S. population—access the Internet at home, at school, at work, or at public-access sites. Active at-home Internet users alone exceed 135 million in the United States today. Worldwide, the number of Internet users is close to 900 million.[4] While some of the initial novelty has worn off, the Internet has become a significant presence in the daily lives of a majority of Americans. For instance, according to recent surveys, the average Internet user spends more time online than watching television.[5] Moreover, over half of all Americans accessing the Internet today use broadband connections—such as DSL or cable modems—which vastly increase reaction times and allow nearly seamless graphics and video displays.[6] Experts believe that the continued growth of broadband is one of the keys to the continued growth and development of e-business.

In spite of the past success and future potential of the Internet, issues and concerns relating to e-business remain. Some highly touted e-business applications have proven less than successful, cost savings and profits have occasionally been elusive, and many privacy and security issues still linger. Nevertheless, the benefits and potential of e-business clearly outweigh the concerns and problems.

This chapter examines the current state and potential of e-business. We begin by discussing the capabilities of e-business, the benefits of e-business, and the ways organizations use the Web. Next, we focus on business-to-business (B2B) transactions, which make up the most e-business transactions today. Then we explore business-to-consumer (B2C) e-business—online shopping sites such as Macy's Thisit.com, described in the opening vignette. We also consider some of the challenges of e-business. Next, we explain how organizations use the Web's communication functions to advance their objectives. The chapter concludes with discussions of how to create and maintain an effective Web presence and the global reach of e-business.

# WHAT IS E-BUSINESS?

Today the term **e-business** describes a wide range of business activities that take place on the Internet using any of the applications that rely on Internet technology, such as e-mail and virtual shopping carts. E-business can be divided into the following five broad categories:

1. e-tailing, or virtual storefronts on Web sites
2. online business-to-business transactions
3. electronic data interchange (EDI), the business-to-business exchange of data using compatible software
4. e-mail, instant messaging, and other Web-enabled communication tools and their use as media for reaching prospective and existing customers
5. the gathering and use of demographic, product, and other information through Web contacts

E-business provides a foundation for launching new businesses, extending the reach of existing companies, and building and retaining customer relationships. A Web presence builds awareness of a company's products and brands, provides the means for one-on-one communication with customers, and permits customers to place orders from anywhere in the world, at any time of day. E-business encompasses all of the following types of activities:

- Legally downloading songs from Apple Computer's iTunes Web site
- Buying a used laptop computer on the online auction site eBay
- Accessing Infotrac (http://www.infotrac.com) through your college's wireless network to find articles to complete a class research assignment
- Researching new-car models on Edmunds.com (http://www.edmunds.com) and getting price quotes from several local dealers

**electronic business (e-business)** conducting business via the Internet.

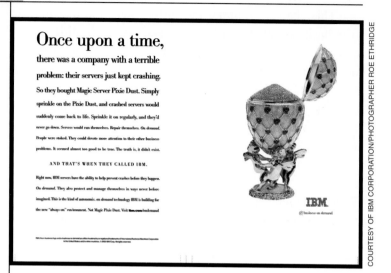

COURTESY OF IBM CORPORATION/PHOTOGRAPHER ROE ETHRIDGE

The growth of e-business has attracted an army of specialized software firms and other service suppliers that provide expertise for firms taking their first steps into this competitive arena. Examples include Accenture, IBM, Microsoft, and Oracle. IBM, for instance, offers its business customers both software and services designed to build virtual stores that go far beyond traditional Web sites. Although IBM was originally known as a producer of computer hardware, it now generates more than half its revenue from e-business and other information technology services.[7] IBM even runs e-business systems for companies that want to outsource this activity. The firm's management believes that much of its future lies in providing e-business services. As a result IBM sold its PC manufacturing business. Figure 7.1 illustrates the types of e-business services offered by IBM.

E-business has also had an impact on governments and others in the not-for-profit sector. For instance, MunicipalNet is a growing e-procurement business based in Boston. It focuses on services to states, local governments, and the businesses that supply them. The city of Torrington, Connecticut, recently signed up for the MunicipalNet service. According to Charlene Antonelli, the city's purchasing agent, the service has generated far more bids and had an impact on prices. "We put a request out for a multimedia projector that previously we had a best price of around $3,700. . . . Through the MunicipalNet service, we got a number of bids in at the $2,000 level," noted Antonelli.[8] MunicipalNet can also help governments set up Web sites at which citizens can register cars, pay taxes, or look for government jobs. By one estimate, more than 15 percent of federal, state, and local taxes will be collected online within the next few years.

## Capabilities and Benefits of E-Business

The last years of the 20th century and the early years of the 21st century witnessed the change from a manufacturing-based industrial economy to its electronic successor—an economy based on information, the Internet, and other related online technologies. Many people see e-business as a major component of growth for the rest of the 21st century. Since the Web first opened for commercial activity in 1993, e-business has had a major impact on both consumers and businesses. It is estimated that in the United States e-business is currently over 2 percent of GDP. This figure is expected to increase to more than 5 percent within the next three to five years.[9] Some recent successes in e-business are summarized in Table 7.1.

E-business offers a wide variety of capabilities and benefits to contemporary businesspeople.

- *Global reach.* The Net allows goods and services to be sold to customers regardless of geographic location. eBay, for instance, is now the nation's largest used-car dealer.[10] Buyers and sellers throughout the country meet in this virtual used-car marketplace, where more than $7 billion worth of used vehicles are bought and sold annually.
- *Personalization.* Only a handful of Dell computers are waiting for customers at any one time. The production process begins when an order is received and ends a day or two later when the PC is shipped to the customer. Not only does this approach better satisfy customer needs, but it also sharply reduces the amount of inventory Dell has to carry.
- *Interactivity.* Customers and suppliers negotiate prices online in much the same manner as at a local flea market or car dealership. The result is the creation of an ideal product at the right price that satisfies both parties.

Table
7.1

**Some E-Business Successes**

- More than 70,000 students are taking courses online at the University of Phoenix. The Web has helped the for-profit institution become the largest private college in the United States.

- FreshDirect—an online supermarket—now has annual revenues exceeding $100 million and is the first online supermarket to turn a profit.

- The Boston Symphony Orchestra's Web site attracts thousands of visitors a day, and online ticket sales are approaching $5 million annually. The orchestra credits the Web for a dramatic increase in the number of young concertgoers and season ticket subscribers.

- Americans book more than $62 billion in online travel annually. This figure is expected to reach $91 billion by 2009. By then one out of every three travel dollars will be booked online.

**Sources:** "About Us," University of Phoenix, accessed July 20, 2006, http://www.uopxonline.com; Erick Schonfeld, "The Big Cheese of Online Grocers," *Business 2.0*, accessed July 20, 2006, http://www.business2.com; Deborah Vence, "Boston Orchestra Tunes Up Net Campaign," *Marketing News*, accessed July 20, 2006, http://www.marketingpower.com; Rob McGann, "U.S. Online Travel Market to Soar," ClickZ Network, accessed June 20, 2006, http://www.clickz.com.

- *Right-time and integrated marketing.* Online retailers, such as Amazon.com and Buy.com, can provide products when and where customers want them. Moreover, the Internet enables the coordination of all promotional activities and communication to create a unified, customer-oriented promotional message.

- *Cost savings.* E-business can markedly reduce the costs associated with operating and starting a business. Ace Hardware says that a Web-based program has reduced inventory costs by around 20 percent.[11]

In addition to the benefits listed here, increasing evidence shows that an effective online presence improves the performance of traditional brick-and-mortar operations. As noted earlier, some surveys suggest that the Web has become the primary source of product information. A study by the Dieringer Group, a marketing and business research firm, found that a significant segment of American consumers—perhaps as many as 83 million—rely on the Internet nearly twice as much for local purchasing information compared with traditional media such as newspaper, local TV, or radio ads. For each dollar these consumers spent online, the study found, they spent $1.60 offline at local stores.[12]

**corporate Web site** Web site designed to increase a firm's visibility, promote its offerings, and provide information to interested parties.

## Business Web Sites

Virtually all businesses today have Web sites. They may offer general information, electronic shopping, and promotions such as games, contests, and online coupons. Type in the firm's Internet address, and the Web site's home page appears on your computer screen.

Two types of company Web sites exist. Many firms have established **corporate Web sites** to increase their visibility, promote their offerings, and provide information for other interested parties. Rather than selling goods and services directly, these sites attempt to build customer goodwill and assist retailers and other resellers in their marketing efforts.

USED WITH PERMISSION FROM FORD MOTOR COMPANY

Ford Motor Company's website is an example of an informational web site as it includes details about Ford's products as well as financial documents, investor relations, and job-related information.

## Tips for Using E-Mail

You are probably aware of the general guidelines about using e-mail responsibly, such as following the rules of grammar and spelling, not typing in all caps, and not sending anyone information you wouldn't mind seeing in the daily newspaper. Here are a few tips that should help ensure that your online business correspondence is always effective and appropriate.

1. Choose a professional-looking format; avoid color, fancy type fonts, and emoticons (smiley faces).
2. Keep your message short and to the point.
3. Always include a specific subject line so that your correspondents know what to expect. For instance, write "Revised schedule for McGregor project" instead of "Schedule."
4. If you are replying to an e-mail, respond as promptly as you would to a phone call on the same subject.
5. Write and reply to all the people who need the information you are sending, but only to those people.
6. If you are writing to a large group of people who don't know one another, use the BCC (blind carbon copy) function to ensure that each person's e-mail address remains private from the others.
7. Let recipients know ahead of time if you are sending a very large attachment, because download times can vary. You might want to break large attachments into several smaller ones to make downloading easier.
8. If a disagreement or argument develops during e-mail communications, stop, calm down, and continue the discussion in person or on the phone.
9. Before you send any e-mail, proofread your message and double-check the "To:" line. Make sure you have attached any needed documents and that you've typed your name at the bottom of the message.
10. Remember that e-mails are considered public documents. Avoid writing anything you wouldn't say in person.

**Sources:** "Email Etiquette," Online Writing Lab at Purdue University, accessed July 20, 2006, http://owl.english.purdue.edu; "Harness E-Mail: E-Mail Etiquette," Learn the Net, accessed July 20, 2006, http://www.learnthenet.com; "Email Etiquette," AllBusiness, accessed July 20, 2006, http://www.allbusiness.com.

For example, the Web site for Levi's jeans offers detailed product information and a chance to view recent commercials. Consumers who want to actually buy jeans, however, can link to the Web sites of retailers such as Kohl's and JCPenney.

In addition to using the Web to communicate product information and build relationships with customers, many companies use their Web sites for a variety of purposes, including disseminating financial information to investors, enabling prospective employees to apply online for jobs, and providing e-mail communication for customers and other interested parties. Some tips for writing and using e-mail in a business setting are listed in the "Business Etiquette" feature.

Although **marketing Web sites** often include information about company history, products, locations, employment opportunities, and financial information, their goal is to increase purchases by site visitors. For instance, the Starbucks Web site contains all of the information traditionally found on a corporate Web site, but it also includes an online store selling everything from coffee to espresso machines. Many marketing Web sites try to engage consumers in interactions that will move them closer to a demonstration, trial visit, purchase, or other marketing outcome. Some marketing Web sites, such as Sony.com, are quite complex. Visitors can go to pages for Sony Pictures Entertainment (with movie trailers and sweepstakes), Sony Music (audio and video clips plus news about recordings), and Sony Online Entertainment (online games plus information about games and gaming systems), among other possibilities.

### assessment check

1. Briefly identify the differences between a corporate Web site and a marketing Web site.
2. Visit the Web site for Specialized (http://www.specialized.com). Is this site a corporate Web site or a marketing Web site?

**marketing Web site** Web site whose main purpose is to increase purchases by visitors.

## BUSINESS-TO-BUSINESS (B2B) E-BUSINESS

FedEx's Web site is not designed to be flashy. There are no fancy graphics or streaming video clips, just lots of practical information to assist the firm's customers. The site enables customers to check rates, compare services, schedule package pickups and deliveries, track shipments, and order shipping supplies. This information is vital to FedEx's customers, most of whom are businesses. Customers access the site thousands of times a day.

**Business-to-business e-business,** known as **B2B,** is the use of the Internet for business transactions between organizations. Although most people are familiar with such consumer-oriented (B2C) online firms as Amazon.com and eBay, B2C transactions are dwarfed by their B2B counterparts. B2B e-business transactions stand at nearly $2.5 trillion. By some estimates, close to 80 percent of all e-commerce activity consists of B2B transactions.[13] In the United Kingdom, more than 30 percent of all businesses purchased goods and services over the Internet in a recent year.[14]

In addition to generating sales revenue, B2B e-business also provides detailed product descriptions whenever they are needed. Payments and other information are transferred on the Web. Moreover, B2B e-business can slash order-processing expenses. Business-to-business transactions, which typically involve more steps than consumer purchases, can be much more efficient on the Internet. Orders placed over the Internet typically contain fewer errors than handwritten ones, and when mistakes occur, the technology can quickly locate them. So the Internet is an attractive option for business buying and selling. In some industries, relying on the Internet to make purchases can reduce costs by almost 25 percent.

B2B e-business activity has become more varied in recent years. In addition to using the Web to conduct one-on-one sales transactions and provide product information, companies use such tools as EDI, extranets, private exchanges, electronic exchanges, and e-procurement.

## Electronic Data Interchanges, Extranets, and Private Exchanges

*Electronic Data Interchange*   One of the oldest applications of technology to business transactions is **electronic data interchange (EDI),** computer-to-computer exchanges of invoices, purchase orders, price quotations, and other sales information between buyers and sellers. EDI requires compatible hardware and software systems to exchange data over a network. Use of EDI cuts paper flow, speeds the order cycle, and reduces errors. In addition, by receiving daily inventory status reports from vendors, companies can set production schedules to match demand.

Wal-Mart was one of the first major corporations to adopt EDI in the early 1990s. In fact, the retailer refuses to do business with distributors and manufacturers that do not use compatible EDI standards. EDI is one of the major reasons Wal-Mart is able to operate with the efficiency that has made it the market leader in retailing. It can buy just the merchandise its customers want and just when it needs to restock its shelves, using a system known as **quick response.** Quick response is the retailing equivalent of *just-in-time inventory,* an inventory management system commonly used in manufacturing. (Just-in-time inventory is discussed in detail in Chapter 11.) Today, most large retailers have adopted variations of Wal-Mart's quick response system.

Early EDI systems were limited due to the requirement that all parties had to use the same computer operating system. So a company using UNIX couldn't easily link up with a company using Windows NT. That changed with the introduction of something called Web

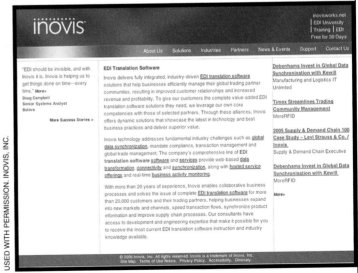

USED WITH PERMISSION. INOVIS, INC.

Inovis is one of many companies that provide a comprehensive line of B2B software and services, including EDI as well as providing Web-based data transformation, real-time business activity monitoring, and exception management capabilities.

services—Internet based systems that allow parties to communicate electronically with one another regardless of the computer operating system used by each individual party. Web services rely on open-source XML (Extensible Markup Language) standards.

**Extranets**  Internet commerce also offers an efficient way for businesses to collaborate with vendors, partners, and customers through **extranets,** secure networks used for e-business and accessible through the firm's Web site by external customers, suppliers, or other authorized users. Extranets go beyond ordering and fulfillment processes by giving selected outsiders access to internal information. As with other forms of e-business, extranets provide additional benefits such as enhanced relationships with business partners. As noted earlier in the chapter, Ford Motor Credit uses an extranet to process credit applications from Ford dealers. Intelsat, which operates global communications satellites, has an extranet called Intelsat Business Network (IBN). More than 2,500 users of IBN log on from more than 400 organizations to check the availability of satellite capacity, view satellite maps, download corporate documents, and participate in discussion groups. Users can personalize their IBN account so that it shows information about only the services they use.[15]

Security and access authorization remain critical issues, and most companies create virtual private networks that protect information traveling over public communications media. These networks control who uses a company's resources and what users can access. Also, they cost considerably less than leasing dedicated lines.

**Private Exchanges**  The next generation of extranets is the **private exchange,** a secure Web site at which a company and its suppliers share all types of data related to e-business, from product design through order delivery. A private exchange is more collaborative than a typical extranet, so this type of arrangement has sometimes been called *c-business.* The participants can use it to collaborate on product ideas, production scheduling, distribution, order tracking, and any other functions a business wants to include. Partners in a private exchange often form strategic alliances, similar to those described in Chapter 4. Wal-Mart Stores has a private exchange it calls a *retail link.* The system permits Wal-Mart employees to access detailed sales and inventory information. Suppliers such as Procter & Gamble and Nestlé, in turn, can look up Wal-Mart sales data and forecasts to manage their own inventory and logistics, helping them better meet the needs of the world's largest retailer and its millions of customers worldwide.

Another variant of extranets is an *intranet,* which provides similar capabilities but limits users to an organization's employees. Intranets are discussed in Chapter 15.

## Electronic Exchanges and E-Procurement

The earliest types of B2B e-business usually consisted of a company setting up a Web site and offering information, as well as products, to any buyer willing to make online purchases. Then entrepreneurs created **electronic exchanges,** online marketplaces that bring buyers and sellers together and cater to a specific industry's needs. One of the earliest electronic exchanges, FreeMarkets, was set up by a former General Electric executive named Glen Meakem. FreeMarkets allowed suppliers to compete for the business of organizational buyers of anything from gears to printed circuit boards. The idea was to improve the efficiency of the purchase process for hundreds of business products.

Initially, many believed that electronic exchanges would become one of the most popular uses of the Internet. It didn't quite work out that way. Something like 15,000 electronic exchanges were launched within a span of a few years. Today, however, less than 20 percent remain. The others either merged or simply disappeared. (FreeMarkets was acquired recently by the e-business software firm Ariba.) Only electronic exchanges specializing in electronic components and transportation services have proven consistently successful.[16]

Why did many electronic exchanges perform so poorly? Experts believe that many suppliers weren't happy with the pressure to come in with the lowest bid each time a satisfied long-term buyer decided to make a new purchase. Moreover, many buyers preferred to cultivate long-term relationships with their suppliers, even those that charged slightly higher prices occasionally. Purchasing agents simply didn't see enough benefits from electronic exchanges to abandon suppliers they knew.[17]

Evolving from electronic exchanges has been something called **e-procurement,** Web-based systems that enable all types of organizations to improve the efficiency of their procurement processes. Ariba, the company that acquired FreeMarkets, offers a variety of e-procurement software products. Many large corporations, such as Saks and Unilever, use Ariba products such as Buyer for purchasing operating goods and services. Unilever reports that Buyer and other Ariba e-procurement software products have saved the company tens of millions of dollars. Saks believes that Buyer has cut the negotiating cycle time from four months to six weeks and saved the company 10 to 20 percent off regular, published prices.[18]

E-procurement also benefits the public sector. For instance, the State of North Carolina has recently instituted a program called *NC E-Procurement,* which combines Internet technology with traditional procurement practices to streamline the purchasing process and reduce costs. State and local governmental agencies, public schools, and state-supported colleges can use the system to purchase products from state-approved vendors. According to the state, "E-Procurement has reduced prices for goods and services through volume discounts, and also enables administrative and operational cost savings by streamlining processing and interactions with vendors/suppliers." One North Carolina county reported saving more than 30 percent on printer supplies by using E-Procurement.[19]

**assessment check**

1. What is B2B e-business? How large is it relative to B2C e-business?
2. What is an EDI? An extranet? A private exchange?
3. Briefly explain how e-procurement works.

# ONLINE SHOPPING COMES OF AGE

One area of e-business that has consistently grabbed news headlines is Internet shopping. Known as **business-to-consumer e-business,** or **B2C,** it involves selling directly to consumers over the Internet. Driven by convenience and improved security for transmitting credit card numbers and other financial information, online retail sales, sometimes called *e-tailing,* now account for around 8 percent of total retail sales in the United States.[20] During one holiday shopping period, over 10 percent of consumer spending took place online, one-third more than in the prior year.[21] At present, about 30 percent of the population shops online. It is estimated that nearly half of American consumers will soon make purchases online.[22]

Most people generally think of the Web as a giant cybermall of retail stores selling millions of goods online. However, service providers are also important participants in e-business. These firms include providers of financial services. Brick-and-mortar banks, such as Wachovia, and brokerage firms, such as Fidelity Investments, have greatly expanded their online services. In addition, many new online service providers are rapidly attracting customers who want to do more of their own banking and stock trading 24/7. Figure 7.2 illustrates some of the benefits of banking online. Airlines, too, have discovered the power of the Web. For example, Southwest Airlines and JetBlue sell more than half of their tickets online, leading the industry in sales via this low-cost channel.[23] Southwest's Web site is the only airline Web site that regularly makes the top rankings for popularity, ease of use, and revenue generation—more than $3 billion annually in air travel is booked through Southwest.com.[24] The success of Southwest.com is described in more detail in the "Hit & Miss" feature.

**business-to-consumer (B2C) e-business** selling directly to consumers over the Internet.

**Figure**

7.2    The Benefits of Online Banking

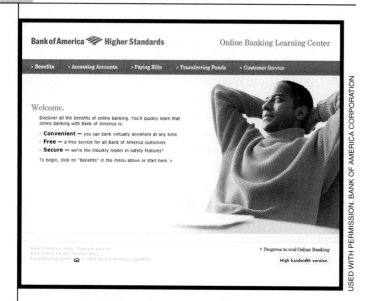

USED WITH PERMISSION. BANK OF AMERICA CORPORATION

**electronic storefront**
company Web site that
sells products to cus-
tomers.

Another point to remember is that there are basically two types of B2C Web sites: shopping sites and informational sites. Williams-Sonoma has a shopping site (http://www.williams-sonoma.com), where customers can view product information and place orders online. By contrast, Toyota's Web site (http://www.toyota.com) is informational only. Consumers can view detailed product information, compare financing alternatives, and even request a price quote from a local dealer. They *cannot,* however, buy a new car online.

## E-Tailing and Electronic Storefronts

Major retailers have staked their claims in cyberspace by setting up **electronic storefronts,** Web sites that sell items to consumers. Wal-Mart received such a positive response to the launch of its electronic storefront a couple of years ago that it expanded online product offerings from 2,500 to more than 40,000 items. Macy's department store has put its bridal registry, personal shopping, and interior-decorating services online. Clothing retailer Lands' End used to generate virtually all of its orders by telephone. A few years ago the company decided to turn to B2C e-business to boost sales and reduce costs. Today, LandsEnd.com is the world's largest apparel Web site and has pioneered several ways to enhance the online shopping experience.[25] Online customers can communicate with customer service representatives in real time, and two customers can even shop on the site simultaneously—just as if they were shopping together in a brick-and-mortar store. Customers can even "try on" clothes using a tool called Virtual Model.

Generally, online retailers—such as L.L. Bean and Barnes & Noble—provide an online catalog where visitors click on items they want to buy. These items are placed in a file called an **electronic shopping cart.** When the shopper indicates that he or she wants to complete the transaction, the items in the electronic shopping cart are listed on the screen, along with the total amount due, so that the customer can review the whole order and make changes before making a payment.

One factor that experts think will have a significant influence on the growth of online shopping is the increased availability of broadband technology. According to data from Nielsen NetRatings, more than 55 percent of American Internet users now have broadband connections. Nielsen projects that 70 percent of all U.S. home Internet users will soon be using broadband. Why is this trend significant for e-tailers? On average, broadband users are online more often for longer periods of time, and, most important, spend more online than narrowband users. Typically, today around 70 percent of all online retail purchases are conducted over broadband connections. Broadband shoppers also spend around 34 percent more online than narrowband shoppers.[26]

## Who Are the Online Buyers and Sellers?

The Pew Internet and American Life Project collects and analyzes data about Americans' Internet usage, including online buying behavior. A recent survey they conducted paints a comprehensive demographic picture of online users and buyers. Some of the key findings of the report are summarized in Figure 7.3 on page 224. While the typical Internet user is still

## HIT & MISS

### Southwest Scores with Its Web Site

Southwest Airlines has solved the problem of communicating great deals to its customers in real time. The company's innovation is no surprise to the travel industry, because Southwest was also the first airline to have its own Web site, now more than ten years old and still one of the most popular Internet sites in any category.

To reach travelers with news about short-term special deals, such as a $33 flight from Chicago to St. Louis that was good for only a three-hour booking window, the innovative carrier created a software program called "DING!," named after the sound some e-mail systems make to announce a new message. Downloading the program from http://www.southwest.com takes a couple of minutes and creates a special icon in the user's system tray at the bottom of the screen. When Southwest has a new rock-bottom special for subscribers a tiny envelope appears on the icon and a "ding" sound is heard. Simply clicking on the icon brings up all the information on the user's computer screen, including a "Book Now" button.

During the registration process, users specify their home city or zip code and receive only information about that destination. Top cities are Baltimore, Chicago, Houston, Los Angeles, Oakland, and Phoenix.

Most offers are available for less than a day and represent savings from $5 to $75 off Southwest's lowest-priced one-way Internet specials. They require fourteen-day advance purchase, and customers have to be near their computers often to take advantage of the short-term offers. But in just the first few months of operation, travelers who like the thrill of getting a great deal booked more than $10 million worth of tickets through DING!, making it a resounding success for the company. "Only Southwest Airlines would dare to offer fares this low," says the publisher of BestFares.com.

#### Questions for Critical Thinking

1. Why do you think customers are willing to download DING! when the low prices are available for such a short period of time?
2. Can you think of any other uses Southwest might consider for its DING! software?

**Sources:** "What Is DING!?" Southwest Airlines Web site, accessed July 20, 2006, http://www.southwest.com; "Southwest Airlines Delivers the Heat with Hot Summer Fares," PRWebDirect, accessed July 20, 2006, http://www.prwebdirect.com; Jessica Labrencis, "Southwest's New Ding Fares: Worth the Download?" SmarterTravel.com, accessed July 20, 2006, http://www.smartertravel.com.

relatively young, highly educated, urban or suburban, and affluent, the demographics of online buyers are apparently changing. For instance, since 2000, Internet penetration—the percentage of a particular group going online—among older Americans has increased faster than it has among younger Americans. Moreover, today there is much less difference among demographic groups in the percentage of Internet users who purchase products online compared with a few years ago. Women, for example, are today just as likely as men to purchase products online. In 2000, men made up the majority of online shoppers.[27]

Realizing that customers would have little or no opportunity to rely on many of the senses—smelling the freshness of direct-from-the-oven bread, touching the soft fabric of a new cashmere sweater, or squeezing fruit to assess its ripeness—early online sellers focused on offering products that consumers were familiar with and tended to buy frequently, such as books and music. Other popular early online offerings included computer hardware and software, and airline tickets.

Figure 7.4 on page 225 lists the five product categories showing the highest growth in online sales during a recent year. The data illustrate how the B2C market has changed in recent years. A few years ago, books, music, and airline tickets were the most popular items sold online. Today, clothing and apparel, toys and video games, and consumer electronics are tops. In fact, online sales of clothing and apparel are growing at an annual rate of more than 40 percent.[28]

Figure

7.3 | Demographics of Internet Users

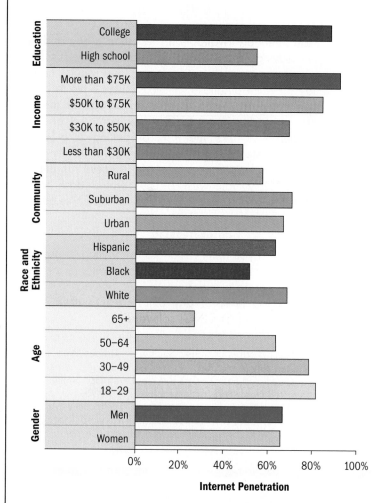

**Internet Penetration**

Internet penetration is the percentage of a certain demographic group that accesses the Internet.

**Source:** Pew Internet and American Life Project, accessed July 20, 2006, http://www.pewinternet.org.

In the coming years online sales of apparel, prescription drugs, and home products will continue to grow rapidly as the demographics of Internet users change. Because women—who spend more money on apparel than men do—will continue to become a larger share of Internet users, online apparel sales are likely to stay hot. Similarly, as the population of online users over age 55 grows, so will the online sales of prescription drugs. Kitchen products, small appliances, and large appliances—which typically are bought more frequently by women and older consumers—will also experience strong growth in the near future.[29]

## Benefits of B2C e-Business

Why do consumers shop online? Three main reasons are most often cited in consumer surveys: price, convenience, and personalization.

*Lower Prices* Many products actually cost less online. Many of the best deals on airfares and hotels, for instance, are found at travel sites on the Internet. If you call Delta Airlines' toll-free number, before you speak to an agent a recorded voice invites you to visit Delta.com, "where lower fares may be available." Visitors to BN.com—the online store of bookseller Barnes & Noble—find that many bestsellers are discounted by up to 40 percent. At the brick-and-mortar stores, bestsellers are marked down only 30 percent. It comes as no surprise to anyone who has ever searched the Web for the best price for software or a newly issued CD that almost 60 percent of Web shoppers cited lower prices as a motivation for shopping online.[30]

The Web is an ideal method for savvy shoppers to compare prices from dozens—even hundreds—of sellers. Online shoppers can compare features and prices at their leisure, without being pressured by a salesperson or having to conform to the company's hours of operation. One of the newer e-commerce tools, **bots,** aid consumers in comparison shopping. Bots—short for *robots*—are search programs that check hundreds of sites, gather information, and bring it back to the sender. Assume you're in the market for a new computer monitor. At Shopping.com, you can specify the type and size of monitor you're looking for, and the Web site displays a list of the highest-ranked monitors, the e-tailer offering the best price on each, and the estimated taxes and shipping expenses. The Web site even ranks the e-tailers by customer experience and tells you whether a particular model is in stock.

*Convenience* A second important factor in prompting online purchases is shopper convenience. Cybershoppers can order goods and services from around the world at any hour of the day or night. Most e-tailers allow customers to register their credit-card and shipping information to streamline future purchases. Customer register with a user name and password, which they enter when they place another order. E-tailers typically send an e-mail message confirming an order and the amount charged to the buyer's credit card. Another e-mail is sent once the product is shipped, along with a tracking number that the customer can use to track the order through the delivery process.

Many Web sites offer customized products to match individual customer requirements. Nike (http://nikeid.nike.com) enables online shoppers the opportunity to customize a running shoe, personalizing such features as the outsole, the amount of cushioning, and the width. The personalized shoe costs about $10 more than buying it off the shelves.

*Personalization* While online shopping often operates with little or no human interaction, successful B2C e-business companies know how important personalization is to the quality of the shopping experience. Customer satisfaction is greatly affected by the firm's ability to offer service tailored to many customers. But each person expects a certain level of customer service. Consequently, most leading online retailers offer customized features on their Web sites.

In the early years of e-commerce, Web marketers cast their nets broadly to land as many buyers as possible. Today, the emphasis has turned toward one-to-one marketing, creating loyal customers who are likely to make repeat purchases. How does personalized marketing work online? Say you buy a book at Amazon.com and register with the site. The site welcomes you back for your next purchase by name. Using software that analyzes your previous purchases, it also suggests other books you might like. You can even choose to receive periodic e-mails from Amazon.com informing you of new products. Many other leading e-tailers have adopted similar types of personalized marketing.

**Figure**

**7.4**

Fastest-Growing Online Retail Categories

**Source:** Enid Burns, "Online Retail Growth Robust," ClickZ Network, accessed July 20, 2006, http://www.clickz.com.

## Developing Safe Online Payment Systems

In response to consumer concerns about the safety of sending credit card numbers over the Internet, companies have developed secure payment systems for e-business. The most common forms of online payment are electronic cash and electronic wallets. Internet browsers, such as Microsoft Internet Explorer, contain sophisticated encryption systems. **Encryption** is the process of encoding data for security purposes. When such a system is active, users see a special icon indicating that they are at a protected Web site.

To increase consumer security most companies involved in e-business use **Secure Sockets Layer (SSL)** technology to encrypt information and verify the identity of senders and receivers (called *authentication*). SSL consists of a public key and a private key—software that encrypts and decrypts information. The public key is used to encrypt information, and the private key is used to decipher it. When a browser points to a domain with an SSL certificate, the technology authenticates (verifies the identity of) the server and the visitor and establishes an encryption method and a unique session key. Both parties can then begin a secure session that guarantees a message's privacy and integrity. VeriSign is one of the leading providers of SSL technology, which is used by more than 90 percent of *Fortune* 500 companies and the ten largest banks in the United States.[31]

An electronic wallet is another online payment method. An **electronic wallet** is a computer data file at an e-business site's checkout counter that contains not only electronic cash but credit card information, owner identification, and address. With electronic wallets, customers do not have to retype personal information each time they make a purchase at that site. Consumers simply click on the electronic wallet after selecting items, and their credit card payment information, name and address, and preferred mailing method are transmitted instantly.

# E-BUSINESS CHALLENGES

Not surprisingly, e-business has had its problems and challenges. Consumers are concerned about protecting their privacy and being victimized by Internet fraud, frustrated with unreliable and hard-to-use Web sites, and annoyed over the inconveniences of scheduling deliveries and returning merchandise. Businesses are concerned about potential conflicts with business partners and difficulty in measuring the effectiveness of Internet-based promotion.

## Privacy Issues

Consumers worry that information about them will become available to others without their permission. In fact, research indicates that privacy is one of the top concerns of Internet users and may impede the growth of e-business.[32] As the earlier discussion of Internet payments explained, concern about the privacy of credit card numbers has led to the use of secure payment systems. To add to those security systems, e-business sites require passwords as a form of authentication—that is, to determine that the person using the site is actually the one who is authorized to access the account. More recently, **electronic signatures** have become a way to enter into legal contracts such as home mortgages and insurance policies online. With an e-signature, an individual obtains a form of electronic identification and installs it in his or her Web browser. Signing the contract involves looking up and verifying the buyer's identity with this software.

Thanks to cookies and spyware, which are automatic data collection methods, online companies can track their customers' shopping and viewing habits. The way that companies use these technologies has the potential both to make visits to the Web site more convenient and to invade computer users' privacy. Amazon.com, for instance, has long employed sophisticated data collection systems to track customer habits. While Amazon sees such data gathering as the best way to keep customers happy and loyal, some believe that the company is getting too close to becoming a type of Big Brother—an all-knowing and all-seeing organization, complete with customer's credit card numbers. The "Hit & Miss" feature describes Amazon's latest technologies designed to better know and predict shopping habits—and the concerns these technologies raise.

Most consumers want assurances that any information they provide won't be sold to others without their permission. In response to these concerns, online merchants protect consumer information. For example, many Internet com-

Amazon.com makes use of its automatic data collection methods in order to provide personalized recommendation pages based on a user's past purchases and the items they have viewed.

COURTESY OF AMAZON.COM, INC. ALL RIGHTS RESERVED.

## HIT & MISS

### Amazon as Big Brother?

Amazon.com, among the biggest and most innovative of online retailers, has been collecting detailed information about its customers' buying habits and preferences for years. Most of that information is crunched by sophisticated software to provide customers with personalized recommendations based on their past searches, browses, and purchases. Amazon recently changed its privacy policies to allow it to share with its suppliers and partners the personal information it collects, and it has launched a new search engine called A9 that can store data on every item a customer has ever searched for.

Amazon, like many other e-tailers, believes its customer-tracking technology is its most important weapon against competition from its rivals—both traditional and Internet retailers. Its storehouse of information about shoppers allows Amazon to suggest new products customers might be interested in, better direct their searches on the site, and even stop them from making duplicate purchases if they're forgetful. All these services come under the heading of "relationship building," according to the company.

But some privacy advocates wish Amazon would ask permission to collect, and share, all the information it gathers. That would allow customers to opt out of these processes if they wished. It might also protect Amazon from charges that it is veering close to the edge of the law, specifically a federal law that limits the gathering of information about children under age 13. Amazon recently received a patent on technology that allows it to track gift-giving habits, including the gift recipient's age. The company says it has not yet used the technology and will not violate any laws.

#### Questions for Critical Thinking

1. Begun as a book-selling Web site, Amazon has branched into electronics, hardware, software, jewelry, tools, toys, cameras, office products, and more. What effect do you think this expansion of its product offerings has had on its need to protect its competitive position? Why?
2. Do you think Amazon is in danger of violating its customers' privacy? Why or why not?

**Sources:** Leslie Walker, "Ad Firms Follow Customers around the Web," *Washington Post*, accessed July 20, 2006, http://www.washingtonpost.com; Allison Linn, "Amazon.com Knows, Predicts Shopping Habits," Yahoo! News, accessed July 20, 2006, http://news.yahoo.com; Rob Tedeschi, "A Web Site for Gift Seekers," *New York Times*, accessed July 20, 2006, http://www.nytimes.com.

---

panies have signed on with Internet privacy organizations such as TRUSTe, shown in Figure 7.5. By displaying the TRUSTe logo on their Web sites, they indicate that they have promised to disclose how they collect personal data and what they do with the information. Prominently displaying a privacy policy is an effective way to build customers' trust.

A policy is only as good as the company publishing it, though. Consumers have no assurances about what happens if a company is sold or goes out of business. Now-defunct Toysmart.com promised customers that it would never share their personal data with a third party. But when the company landed in bankruptcy court, it considered selling its database, one of its most valuable assets. And Amazon.com has told customers openly that if it or part of its business is purchased at some point, its database would be one of the transferred assets.

Such privacy features may become a necessary feature of Web sites if consumer concerns continue to grow. They also may become legally necessary. Already in the United States, the *Children's Online Privacy Protection Act (COPPA)* requires that Web sites targeting children younger

TRUSTe Logo

USED WITH PERMISSION. TRUSTE.

**reviewed by**

**TRUST·e**

**site privacy statement**

**Figure**

**7.5**

than age 13 obtain "verifiable parental consent" before collecting any data that could be used to identify or contact individual users, including names and e-mail addresses.

Security concerns are not limited to consumers. Employees are realizing that their employers can monitor their online behavior and e-mail messages at work. Some companies even specialize in helping employers use such information. Tacit Knowledge Systems builds a database from key terms in employees' e-mail. The primary objective is to help a company identify which employees have knowledge that they can contribute to the company—for example, knowledge about a particular competitor or type of product. Of course, many employees might be uncomfortable with their employer tracking what they write about. So Tacit's software allows employees to decide which aspects, if any, of their personal profile they want to make public.

Companies, too, are concerned about the privacy of their data, and with good reason. For instance, the personal data of almost 60,000 people affiliated with California State University, Chico, were recently stolen by computer hackers.[33] This incident followed closely a similar case of identity theft in which personal data for more than 145,000 people were exposed by a security breach at ChoicePoint, a firm that collects and stores consumer financial data.

To prevent such intrusions, companies install combinations of hardware and software called *firewalls* to keep unauthorized Net users from tapping into private corporate data. A **firewall** is an electronic barrier between a company's internal network and the Internet that limits access into and out of the network. However, an impenetrable firewall is difficult to find. A determined and skilled hacker can often gain access. So it is important for firms to test their Web sites and networks for vulnerabilities and back up critical data in case an intruder breaches security measures.

## Internet Fraud

**phishing** high-tech scam that uses authentic looking e-mail or pop-up ads to get unsuspecting victims to reveal personal information.

Fraud is another barrier to e-business. The Internet Crime Complaint Center (http://www .ic3.gov), run by the FBI, compiles complaints concerning Internet fraud. According to recent statistics, IC3 logged more than 207,000 complaints during a recent year, an increase of 67 percent from the prior year. Online auctions were the number one source of fraud complaints. Around 70 percent of the total Internet-related fraud complaints referred to law enforcement agencies dealt with online auctions. Auction fraud ranges from merchandise that does not match the description the bidder was given, such as fraudulent paintings, to products that were purchased but never delivered. Nondelivery of merchandise, credit and debit card fraud, investment fraud, and identify theft also made up major categories of Internet-related complaints referred to law enforcement agencies, according to the center.[34]

One growing type of Internet fraud, called **phishing,** is a high-tech scam that uses e-mail or pop-up messages claiming to be from familiar businesses or organizations, such as banks, Internet service providers, or even government agencies. The message usually asks the reader to "update" or "validate" account information, often stating that some dire consequence will occur if the reader doesn't respond. The purpose of phishing is to get unsuspecting victims to disclose personal informa-

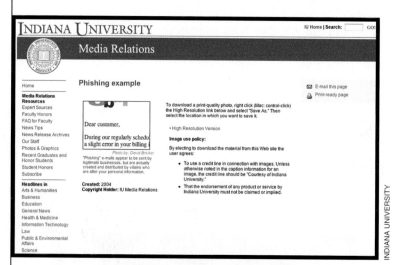

Here is an example of a PHISHING, which has been personalized enough to fool many unsuspecting e-mail users, but still remains generic enough to be spotted by someone who is familiar with this type of internet fraud.

tion such as credit card numbers, bank account numbers, Social Security numbers, or computer passwords. Phishing is also a common method of distributing viruses and malicious spyware programs to computer users. As the Federal Trade Commission advises, if you receive an e-mail or pop-up message that asks for personal information, don't reply or click on the link in the message no matter how authentic the message or pop-up appears. Legitimate companies don't ask for personal or financial information via e-mail or pop-ups.[35] If in doubt, rather than following the link in the suspect e-mail, users should contact the organization directly, either by separately typing the Web address in a browser or by telephone.

Payment fraud is another growing problem for many e-tailers. Orders are placed online, paid for using a credit card, and the merchandise is shipped. Then, the cardholder asks the credit card issuer for chargeback to the e-tailer. The cardholder claims that he or she never made the purchase or never received the merchandise. Some claims are legitimate, but many involve fraud. Because an online purchase doesn't require a customer's signature or credit card imprint, the merchant, not the credit card issuer, bears the liability in most fraud cases. E-tailers are trying to reduce payment fraud by employing software that spots fraud before it happens, using payment verification services offered by credit card companies such as Visa, and even hiring companies who specialize in fighting credit card chargebacks.

## Poor Web Site Design and Service

For e-business firms to attract customers—and keep them—companies must meet buyers' expectations. For instance, customers want to find items without frustration and get questions answered. However, Web sites are not always well designed and easy to use. In fact, around two-thirds of Web shopping carts are abandoned before a customer places an order. In other words, among the people who start selecting items to buy online, most of them change their minds before making a purchase.

System overload is another problem for e-tailers, especially during holiday and other heavy shopping periods. For instance, during one recent holiday shopping period, some customers reported breakdowns during Amazon's one-click checkout process. Others reported errors in the addresses to which items were sent. According to Gomez—a research firm that conducts automated shopping searches across popular online merchants—for about 13 percent of its attempted purchases on Amazon.com the week after Thanksgiving, technical glitches stopped the transaction. During the same period, other popular e-tailing sites, such as L.L. Bean, operated so slowly at times that they were unusable.[36]

Another challenge to successful e-business is merchandise delivery and returns. Retailers sometimes have trouble making deliveries to on-the-go consumers. And consumers don't want to wait for packages to be delivered. Also, if customers aren't satisfied with products, they have to arrange for pickup or send packages back themselves.

Retailers have begun to address these issues. Most Web sites allow customers to track orders from placement to delivery. E-tailers have worked hard on a process known as *reverse logistics*. Detailed directions on how to return merchandise, including preprinted shipping labels, are included in orders. A few, such as Nordstrom's and Chef's Catalog, even pay the shipping cost for returns.

Many of the so-called pure-play dot-com retailers—those without traditional stores or catalogs—didn't survive for very long. They had no history of selling and satisfying customers. Because of expertise in all parts of retailing, companies that combine their brick-and-mortar operations with e-business—such as Old Navy and REI—have generally been more successful than those with little or no retail experience.

The same lesson also applies to other service industries. To be successful at e-business, a firm must establish and maintain competitive standards for customer service. When it began enabling customers to check flight schedules and purchase tickets online, Southwest Airlines worked hard to make sure its Web site had the same high service standards the airline is known for. As noted earlier, Southwest.com has proved both very popular and profitable.

## Channel Conflicts

Companies spend time and money to nurture relationships with their partners. But when a manufacturer uses the Internet to sell directly to customers, it can compete with its usual partners. Retailers often have their own Web sites. So they don't want their suppliers competing with them for sales. As e-business broadens its reach, producers must decide whether these relationships are more important than the potential of selling directly on the Web. Disputes between producers, wholesalers, and retailers are called **channel conflicts.**

Mattel, well known for producing toys such as Barbie, Cabbage Patch dolls, and Matchbox cars, sells most of its products in toy stores and toy departments of other retailers, such as Target and Wal-Mart. The company wants an Internet presence, but it would cut the retailers out of this important source of revenue if it sold toys online to consumers. Mattel cannot afford to lose the goodwill and purchasing power of giant retailers such as Toys "R" Us and Wal-Mart. So the company sells only specialty products online, including pricey American Girl dolls.

Pricing is another potential area of conflict. In their eagerness to establish themselves as Internet leaders, some companies sell merchandise at discount prices. American Leather sells custom leather furniture through upscale retailers, and each dealer serving a geographic area has an exclusive contract for the collections it offers in its area. But at least one dealer began offering American Leather furniture at a discount to customers outside its market area. Other dealers complained, so American Leather established a policy that dealers were not to advertise the company's products on the Internet. Instead, American Leather offered links to local dealers on its own Web site and made plans to allow buyers to order online, with the sale to be directed to the dealer serving the consumer's geographic area.

# USING THE WEB'S COMMUNICATION FUNCTION

The Internet has four main functions: e-business, entertainment, information, and communication. Even though e-business is a significant activity and is growing rapidly, communication still remains the most popular Web function. For instance, the volume of e-mail today exceeds regular mail (sometimes called *snail mail*) by an estimated ten to one. It's not surprising, then, that contemporary businesspeople use the communication function of the Internet to advance their organizational objectives.

Companies have long used e-mail to communicate with customers, suppliers, and other partners. Most companies have links on their Web sites that allow outside parties to send e-mails directly to the most appropriate person or division within the company. For instance, if you have a question concerning an online order from Eddie Bauer, you can click on a link on the retailer's Web site and send an e-mail to a customer service representative. Many online retailers have gone even further, offering their customers live help. Using a form of instant messaging, live help provides real-time communication between customers and customer service representatives. Figure 7.6 illustrates how one online retailer uses live help to better meet the needs of its customers.

Firms also use e-mail to inform customers about such company events as new products and special promotions. While using e-mail in this manner can be quite cost effective, companies have to be careful. A growing number of customers consider such e-mails **spam**—the popular name for junk e-mail. In fact, in a recent survey, one of the leading reasons given by consumers for reducing online shopping was "receiving spam after online purchase."[37] Many Internet users use *spam filters* to automatically eliminate junk e-mail from their in boxes.

## Online Communities

In addition to e-mail, many firms use Internet forums, newsgroups, electronic bulletin boards, and Web communities that appeal to people who share common interests. All of these sites take advantage of the communication power of the Internet which, as noted earlier in the chapter, is still a main reason people go online. Members congregate online and exchange views and information on topics of interest. These communities may be organized for commercial or noncommercial purposes.

**Online Shopping Site with "Live Help" Function**

USED WITH PERMISSION. CRUTCHFIELD CORPORATION.

**spam** popular name for junk e-mail.

Online communities can take several forms, but all offer specific advantages to users and organizations alike. Online forums, for instance, are Internet discussion groups. Users log in and participate by sending comments and questions or receiving information from other forum members. Forums may operate as electronic bulletin boards, as libraries for storing information, or even as a type of classified ad directory. Firms often use forums to ask questions and exchange information with customers. Adobe, which designs such software as Acrobat and Photoshop, operates a "user-to-user" forum on its Web site as a support community for its customers. Customers who share common personal and professional interests can congregate, exchange industry news and practical product tips, share ideas, and—equally important—create publicity for Adobe products.

Newsgroups are noncommercial Internet versions of forums. Here people post and read messages on specific topics. Tens of thousands of newsgroups exist on the Internet, and the number continues to rise. **Electronic bulletin boards** center on a specific topic or area of interest. For instance, mountain bikers might check online bulletin boards to find out about the latest equipment, new places to ride, or current weather conditions in popular biking locations. While newsgroups resemble two-way conversations, electronic bulletin boards are more like announcements.

Online communities are not limited to consumers. They also facilitate business-to-business marketing. Using the Internet to build communities helps companies find other organizations to benchmark against, including suppliers, distributors, and competitors that may be interested in forming an alliance. Business owners who want to expand internationally frequently seek advice from other members of their online community.

## Blogs

Another type of online communication method that is gaining popularity is the **blog.** Short for *Web log*, a blog is a Web page that serves as a publicly accessible personal journal for an individual or organization. Typically updated daily or even more frequently, these hybrid

**blog** online journal written by a blogger.

diary-guide sites are read on a regular basis by almost 30 percent of American Internet users. Using *RSS (Really Simple Syndication)* software, readers are continually kept up-to-date on new material posted on their favorite blogs whenever they are online. Unlike e-mail and instant messaging, blogs let readers post comments and ask questions aimed at the author (called a *blogger*). Some blogs today also incorporate **wikis.** A wiki is a Web page that anyone can edit, so a reader can, in addition to asking questions or posting comments, actually make changes to the Web page. Video blogs—called **podcasts**—are another emerging technology. Bloggers can prepare a video recording on a PC and then post it to a Web site, from which it can be downloaded to any MP3 player. According to the Web site iPodder.org, more than 3,000 podcasts operate worldwide.[38]

With the growing interest in blogs, many companies incorporate blogs in their e-business strategies. GreenCine—a small online DVD rental company—partially credits its blog for a sharp increase in revenues. Films critiqued by the blog's two writers are often snapped up immediately by renters.[39] Moreover, many believe that corporate blogs, if done properly, can also help build brand trust. An example is iLounge.com, a blog hosted by Apple, which lets users discuss their ideas for the next-generation iPod. David Eastman, managing director of Agency.com, believes that iLounge.com benefits Apple in two ways. First, it helps build the iPod brand; second, it gives Apple ideas to improve the design of Apple's most successful product. On the other hand, Eastman says that companies that try to exploit their audiences using blogs will end up hurting their brands. An example was the blog hosted by Cadbury Schweppes for its Raging Cow milk drink. That site didn't come across as particularly genuine because all it featured were product-endorsing comments from children.[40] In fact, many Internet users view most corporate blogs today as being more public-relations vehicles than anything else, and experts advise companies to use blogs with care. Rebecca Blood, author of *The Weblog Handbook: Practical Advice,* advises companies that "repositioning marketing materials on a blog is a waste of time. . . . Those materials already exist. The blog that is powerful is when it is real."[41]

Some people who write blogs muse about their jobs, including co-workers, bosses, and customers. Sometimes employee blogs make employers very nervous. One blogger who was working for a New York public-relations company described late nights in her cubicle "debating semantics with corporate idiots [clients]." In another posting, the blogger wrote, "I wonder how much longer I can deal with the mediocrity and just plain idiocy of corporate America." Even though the blogger didn't name any names, anyone who knew the blogger personally, or knew where she worked, could have identified the targets of her stinging criticism. The firm's managers discovered the blog and forced the blogger to remove it from the Web before any clients found out about the journal. But an employee blog can also benefit a company. Kevin Dugan works as a public-relations consultant and is a blogger. At the top of Dugan's blog is a disclaimer stating that the opinions expressed are his and are not supported by his firm. Dugan and his employer believe that his blog is more than just a soapbox; it indirectly markets the

Blogs, web logs or web-based diaries, are a popular feature on the Internet today.

## SHOULD COMPANIES MONITOR EMPLOYEE BLOGS?

*The explosion of employee blogs (personal Web logs) has unexpectedly brought employers into the spotlight. Mark Jen described his first week at Google, including employee orientation, the cafeteria, and the company's finances. Heather Armstrong wrote colorful anonymous commentary about her boss and co-workers at a California software company. Peter Whitney wrote about his life, his friends, and his work at Wells Fargo. Ellen Simonetti posted revealing photos of herself in her Delta Airlines uniform.*

All of these people were fired when their employers discovered their blogs. Whether they intended to harm their employers, thought anonymity would protect them, or complied with a boss's request to remove relevant posts, these and many other bloggers have learned the hard way that few companies are comfortable being the topic of employee comments on the Internet.

Is it ethical for employers to take disciplinary action based on the postings in employees' blogs?

### PRO

1. Negative comments on the Internet can circulate worldwide and be preserved in many media without offering the injured party an opportunity to respond.
2. Workers have an ethical responsibility not to harm their employer by criticizing the organization publicly or revealing its trade secrets and not to use the Internet to launch demoralizing personal attacks against co-workers. Companies should be able to counteract such postings.

### CON

1. Employees can talk freely about their jobs and co-workers in public places such as parties, commuter trains, and bars; blogs are no different as a form of free speech.
2. Blogs allow employees to reach out to the public, including customers, clients, and recruits, and firms benefit from the humanizing effect of such frank and personal communication. Positive postings can even boost the company's image.

### SUMMARY

A recent study of 526 organizations showed that one in four had guidelines on blogging, and more firms are sure to follow suit. IBM tells employees to state that they don't speak for the firm; Microsoft actively encourages blogs. "It's great," says a Microsoft group manager. "It's instant feedback. We give a lot of support to blogging and . . . how to be a good blogger." Employee blogging is still a gray area, however, and employment consultants advise that if you must blog, ask first.

**Sources:** Matt Villano, "Write All about It (at Your Own Risk)", *New York Times*, accessed July 20, 2006, http://www.nytimes.com; Stephanie Armour, "Warning: Your Clever Little Blog Could Get You Fired," *USA Today*, accessed July 20, 2006, http://www.usatoday.com; "Blog-Linked Firings Prompt Calls for Better Policies," CNN.com, accessed July 20, 2006, http://cnn.technology.com.

solving an **ETHICAL** controversy

firm's work and philosophies.[42] The ethics of employee blogs—and what employers should do about them—is debated in more detail in the "Solving an Ethical Controversy" feature.

## Web-Based Promotions

Rather than relying completely on their Web sites to attract buyers, companies frequently expand their reach in the marketplace by placing ads on sites their prospective customers are likely to visit. **Banner ads,** the most common form of Internet advertising, are typically small messages placed in high-visibility areas of frequently visited Web sites. **Pop-up ads** are separate windows that contain an advertising message. The effectiveness of pop-up ads, however, is questionable. For one thing, scam artists use pop-ups. For another, many Internet users simply hate pop-up ads—even those from legitimate companies. Consequently, most Internet service providers now offer software that blocks pop-up ads. Google and Microsoft also offer free pop-up ad-blocking software.

**search marketing** paying search engines, such as Google, a fee to make sure that the company's listing appears toward the top of the search results.

Another type of online advertising gaining popularity is so-called **search marketing.** Firms make sure that they are listed with the major search engines, such as Google. But that is not enough. A single search for an item—say, plastic fasteners—will yield thousands of sites, many of which might not even be relevant. To overcome this problem, companies pay online search engines to have their Web sites or ads pop up after a computer user enters certain words into the search engine, or to make sure that their firm's listing appears toward the top of the search results. Google and other search engines now include "sponsored links" on the right side of the search results page. When a user clicks on one of the sponsored links, he or she is taken to that site and the company pays the search engine a small fee. Many experts consider search marketing the most cost-effective form of Web-based advertising.

Companies also use online coupons to promote their products via the Web. For instance, customers can visit a company's Web site—such as Procter & Gamble's (http://www.pg.com)—to learn about a new product and then print a discount coupon redeemable at participating retailers. Consumers can also search for virtual coupons using such criteria as business name, location, and keyword, and then download and print them. ValPak Marketing Systems, a longtime leader in the paper coupon industry, now offers the online equivalent at its Web site (http://www.valpak.com).

**assessment check**

1. What are online communities? Explain how online communities can help companies market their products and improve customer service.
2. What is a blog? A wiki? A podcast?
3. Explain the difference between a banner ad, a pop-up ad, and search marketing.

# MANAGING A WEB SITE

Business Web sites serve many purposes. They broaden customer bases, provide immediate accessibility to current catalogs, accept and process orders, and offer personalized customer service. As technology becomes increasingly easy to use, anyone with a computer and Internet access can easily design and then publish a site on the Web. How people or organizations use their sites to achieve their goals determines whether their sites will succeed. Figure 7.7 lists some key questions to consider in developing a Web site.

## Developing Successful Web Sites

Most Web experts agree that it is easier to build a bad Web site than a good one. When judging Web sites, success means different things to different businesses. One firm might feel satisfied by maintaining a popular site that conveys company information or reinforces name recognition—just as a billboard or magazine ad does—without requiring any immediate sales activity. Web sites like those of the *Los Angeles Times* and *USA Today* draw many visitors who want the latest news, and Yahoo!, Google, and ESPN are successful because they attract heavy traffic. Popular Web sites add to their success by selling advertising space to other businesses.

Internet merchants need to attract customers who transact business on the spot. Some companies host Web sites that offer some value-added service to create goodwill for potential customers. Organizations such as the Mayo Clinic and accounting giant Ernst & Young provide useful information or links to related sites that people frequently visit. But to get people to stay at the site and complete a transaction, the site must also be secure, reliable, and easy to use.

*Planning and Preparation*   What is the company's goal for its Web site? Answering this question is the first and most important step in the Web site development process. For discount

Figure

7.7

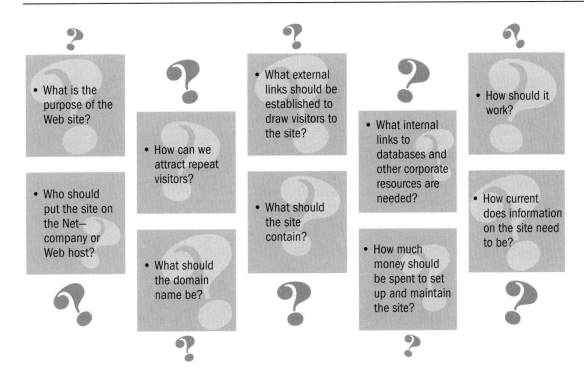

- What is the purpose of the Web site?
- Who should put the site on the Net— company or Web host?
- How can we attract repeat visitors?
- What should the domain name be?
- What external links should be established to draw visitors to the site?
- What should the site contain?
- What internal links to databases and other corporate resources are needed?
- How much money should be spent to set up and maintain the site?
- How should it work?
- How current does information on the site need to be?

brokerage firm Charles Schwab, the primary objective is to sign up new customers. So the Web site designers put a link called "Open an Account" prominently in the upper right-hand corner of the home page. In addition, to reinforce Schwab's image as a respectable investment firm, the site uses a businesslike color scheme.

Objectives for the Web site also determine the scope of the project. If the company's goal is to sell merchandise online, the site must incorporate a way for customers to place orders and ask questions about products, as well as links to the company's databases to track inventory and deliveries. As in this example, the plan includes not only the appearance of the Web site but also the company's behind-the-scenes resources for making the Web site deliver on its promises.

Other key decisions include whether to create and maintain a site in-house or to contract with outside experts. Some companies prefer to retain control over content and design by producing their own sites. However, because acquiring the expertise to develop Web sites can be very time-consuming, hiring specialists may be more cost-effective. Often companies such as Yahoo!, Google, or IBM are enlisted to provide both software and consulting services to clients for their Web sites.

Naming the Web site is another important early step in the planning process. A domain name should reflect the

Yahoo offers many web-related services besides just Internet searches. A successful Web site, such as Yahoo!, requires planning not only for the interest of the site, but also on the business end.

company and its products and be easy to remember. For U.S. companies, the last part of the domain name identifies an affiliation category. Examples include .com for businesses, .org for organizations, .gov for government sites, and .edu for educational institutions. For companies outside the United States, the last part of the domain name identifies the country of origin, such as .ca for Canada and .jp for Japan. In addition to the original .com, .gov, and .org addresses, several new suffixes have been added to the Internet's naming system, including .aero, .biz, .coop, .info, .museum, .name, and .pro. These suffixes were created to alleviate overcrowding in the .com domain and represent the first major addition of Internet addresses in more than a decade. With millions of domain names already registered, the search for a unique, memorable, and easily spelled name can be difficult.

**Content and Connections**   Content is one of the most important factors in determining whether visitors return to a site. People obviously are more inclined to visit a site that provides material that interests them. Many e-business Web sites try to distinguish themselves by offering information or online communities along with a chance to buy. For example, Williams-Sonoma's Web site lures traffic to the site with weekly menu planners; printer-ready recipes; and features that convert menus between metric and U.S. measurement systems, adjust measurements for different numbers of servings, and create shopping lists for menus. Many sites offer links to other sites that may interest visitors.

Standards for good content vary for every site, but available resources should be relevant to viewers, easy to access and understand, updated regularly, and written or displayed in a compelling, entertaining way. When the World Wide Web was a novelty, a page with a picture and a couple of paragraphs of text seemed entertaining. But such "brochureware" falls far short of meeting today's standards for interactivity, including the ability to accept customer data and orders, keep up-to-the-minute inventory records, and respond quickly to customer questions and complaints. Also, today's Internet users are less patient about figuring out how to make a site do what it promises. They won't wait ten minutes for a video clip to download or click through five different pages to complete a purchase.

After making content decisions and designing the site, the next step is connecting to the Internet by placing the required computer files on a server. Companies can have their own dedicated Web servers or contract to place their Web sites on servers at ISPs or other host companies. Most small businesses lack the necessary expertise to set up and run their own servers; they are better off outsourcing to meet their hosting and maintenance needs. They also need to draw business to their site. This usually requires a listing with the major search engines, such as Google and Yahoo!.

## Costs and Maintenance

As with any technological investment, Web site costs are an important consideration. The highly variable cost of a Web site includes not only development expenses but also the cost of placing the site on a Web server, maintaining and updating it, and promoting it. A reasonably tech-savvy employee with off-the-shelf software can create a simple piece of brochureware for a few hundred dollars. A Web site that can handle e-business will cost at least $10,000. Creating it requires understanding of how to link the Web site to the company's other information systems.

Although developing a commercial Web site with interactive features can cost tens of thousands of dollars, putting it online can cost as little as $11.95 a month for a spot on the server of a **Web host** server such as Yahoo!

It's also important for a Web site to stay current. Visitors don't return to a site if they know the information never changes or that claims about inventory or product selection are

Figure

7.8

Measures of Web Site Effectiveness

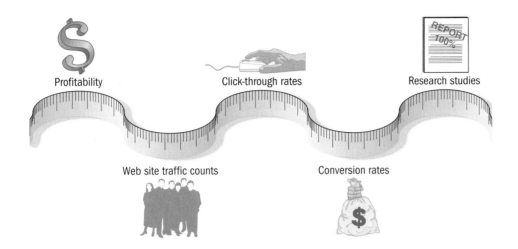

not current. Consequently, updating design and content is another major expense. In addition, site maintenance should include running occasional searches to test that links to the company's Web site are still active.

## Measuring Web Site Effectiveness

How does a company gauge the return from investing in a Web site? Measuring the effectiveness of a Web site is a tricky process, and the appropriate process often depends on the purpose of the Web site. Figure 7.8 lists some measures of effectiveness. Profitability is relatively easy to measure in companies that generate revenues directly from online product orders, advertising, or subscription sales. As noted earlier, Southwest Airlines generates more than $3 billion annually in revenue from Southwest.com. However, what's not clear is how many of those tickets Southwest would have sold through other channels if Southwest.com did not exist. Moreover, and as noted earlier, evidence shows that so-called **Web-to-store** shoppers— a group that favors the Internet primarily as a research tool and time-saving device for retail purchases made in stores—are a significant consumer niche.[43]

For many companies, revenue is not a major Web site objective. Most company Web sites are classified as corporate Web sites, not shopping sites. For such companies, online success is measured by increased brand awareness and brand loyalty, which presumably translates into greater profitability through offline transactions.

Some standards guide efforts to collect and analyze traditional consumer purchase data, such as how many Ohio residents bought new Honda Accords the previous year, watched ABC's series *Lost*, or tried McDonald's new chicken sandwiches. Still, the Internet presents several challenges for businesses. Although information sources are getting better, it is difficult to be sure how many people use the Internet, how often, and what they actually do online. Some Web pages display counters that measure the number of visits. However, the counters can't tell whether someone has spent time on the page or skipped over it on the way to another site, or whether that person is a first-time or repeat viewer.

Advertisers typically measure the success of their ads in terms of **click-through rates,** meaning the percentage of people presented with a banner ad who click on it, thereby linking to a Web site or a pop-up page of information related to the ad. Recently, the average click-through

**click-through rate** percentage of people presented with a Web banner ad who click on it.

rate has been declining to about 0.5 percent of those viewing an ad. This rate is much lower than the 1.0 to 1.5 percent response rate for direct-mail advertisements. Low click-through rates have made Web advertising less attractive than it was when it was novel and people were clicking on just about anything online. Selling advertising has therefore become a less reliable source of e-business revenues.

As e-business gains popularity, new models for measuring its effectiveness are being developed. A basic measurement is the **conversion rate,** the percentage of Web site visitors who make purchases. A conversion rate of 3 to 5 percent is average by today's standards. A company can use its advertising cost, site traffic, and conversion rate data to find out the cost to win each customer. E-business companies try to boost their conversion rates by ensuring that their sites download quickly, are easy to use, and deliver on their promises. Many are turning to one of several firms that help companies improve the performance of their Web sites. For instance, CompUSA—a computer and electronics retailer—turned to Web consultants Coremetrics to help it improve the overall performance of its Web site. Using Coremetrics Online Analytics, CompUSA identified the specific online shopping tools that helped create loyal, high-volume customers. By improving these tools and making them more accessible on its Web site, CompUSA increased revenues by more than $2 million.[44]

Besides measuring click-through and conversion rates, companies can study samples of consumers. Research firms such as Media Metrix and RelevantKnowledge recruit panels of computer users to track Internet site performance and evaluate Web activity; this service works in much the same way that television rating firm ACNielsen monitors television audiences. WebTrends provides information on Web site visitors, including where they come from; what they see; and the number of "hits," or visits to the site, during different times of the day. Other surveys of Web users investigate their brand awareness and their attitudes toward Web sites and brands.

**assessment check**

1. What are the first three questions a company should ask itself when planning a Web site?
2. How does the type of Web site affect measures of effectiveness?
3. Explain the difference between click-through and conversion rates.

## THE GLOBAL ENVIRONMENT OF E-BUSINESS

For many companies, future growth is directly linked to a global strategy that incorporates e-business. While the United States still leads the world in technology, communications infrastructure, and ownership of PCs and other consumer technology products, other countries are rapidly catching up. This is also the case when it comes to Internet use. Figure 7.9 shows the top ten nations in terms of number of Internet users and Internet penetration. As the figures show, while the United States leads the world in the number of Internet users—more than 200 million—it ranks only fifth in Internet penetration, at less than 68 percent. Sweden leads the world in Internet penetration, with an estimated 74 percent. Moreover, Internet usage in the United States is growing more slowly than it is in other countries. For instance, in a recent year the average amount of time spent online by U.S. Internet users barely changed. By contrast, average time spent online was up 25 percent in Hong Kong, 19 percent in France, and 12 percent in Japan.[45]

When it comes to e-business, the United States still leads, but the rest of the world is making major strides forward. Forrester Research, an e-business research firm, estimates that online shopping currently accounts for around 5 percent of total retail sales in the United Kingdom, increasing to over 11 percent by 2008. While broadband penetration in Europe and Asia is lower than it is in the United States, the rate of growth in broadband in other countries and regions appears to be accelerating. As we've discussed earlier, people with broadband connections typically spend more online than those with narrowband connections. Moreover, U.S. firms cannot expect that their earlier experience with the Internet and e-business gives

Figure

7.9

## World Internet Statistics

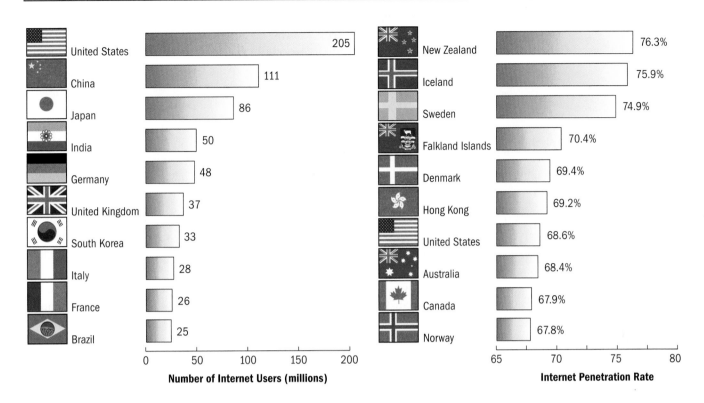

**Source:** Internet World Stats, accessed July 20, 2006, http://www.internetworldstats.com.

them a natural and permanent edge in foreign markets. According to recent statistics, Web sites run by U.S. firms still make up eight of the ten most popular e-business Web sites in Europe, with eBay and Amazon leading the way. However, Fnac.com—the online subsidiary of giant French retailing group PPR—is now more popular than Amazon in both France and Spain, and it is growing rapidly in other European countries. [46]

With so many users and so much buying power, the Internet creates an enormous pool of potential customers. Companies can market their goods and services internationally and locate distribution sources and trading partners abroad. Customers can search for products at their convenience, browsing through online catalogs that always show current information. Many companies divide their Web sites internationally. For instance, when you visit software company Symantec's Web site, you are first asked your country of origin; after entering the information, you are automatically taken to that country-specific portion of the Web site. A list of the products available for your country are listed, along with local distributors and service centers. And the information on the site is presented in the local language.

One practical implication of this global marketplace is the different languages that buyers and sellers speak. Reflecting the Internet's origins, more than half of users now communicate in English. However, the remainder use other languages, led by Japanese, German, Chinese, Spanish, and French. So far, roughly three of every four Web pages are still in English, slowing the adoption of the Internet in non-English-speaking countries. Other international differences are important, too. Auction site eBay initially goofed in the United Kingdom by launching an auction site with prices stated in U.S. dollars. After realizing that its British audience was offended and confused, the company quickly switched to British pounds.

**assessment check**

1. How do language differences affect global e-business?
2. How does e-business heighten global competition?

E-business can heighten competition. In the virtual global marketplace, many manufacturers use the Internet to search online catalogs for the lowest-priced parts. No longer can local suppliers assume that they have locked up the business of neighboring firms. Furthermore, the Internet is a valuable way to expand a company's reach, especially for small businesses that would otherwise have difficulty finding customers overseas.

# WHAT'S AHEAD

The Internet is revolutionizing the way we communicate, obtain information, seek entertainment, and conduct business. It has created tremendous opportunities for B2B and B2C e-business. So far, B2B transactions are leading the way online. B2C e-business is growing and attracting new buyers every year. Companies are just beginning to harness the communication power of the Web to help achieve higher levels of customer satisfaction and loyalty. In spite of the challenges and roadblocks, the future of e-business looks bright.

In upcoming chapters, we look at other trends that are reshaping the business world of the 21st century. For example, in the next part we explore the critical issues of how companies organize, lead, and manage their work processes; manage and motivate their employees; empower their employees through teamwork and enhanced communication; handle labor and workplace disputes; and create and produce world-class goods and services.

## Summary of Learning Goals

**1 Define e-business and discuss how it can help achieve business success.**

E-business involves targeting customers by collecting and analyzing business information, conducting customer transactions, and maintaining online relationships with customers, suppliers, and other interested parties by means of the Internet. It consists of e-tailing, business-to-business transactions, electronic data interchanges, business-to-business exchange of data, and the use of Web-enabled communication tools such as e-mail. E-business increases a company's global reach, increases personalization, is interactive, offers right-time and integrated marketing, and can reduce costs.

Assessment Check Answers

**1.1 Define e-business.**
E-business refers to conducting business via the Internet.

**1.2 List some benefits of e-business.**
Benefits of e-business include global reach, personalization, interactivity, right-time and integrated marketing, and cost savings for both buyers and sellers.

**2 Distinguish between a corporate Web site and a marketing Web site.**

Virtually all businesses have Web sites. Generally, these sites can be classified as either corporate Web sites or marketing Web sites. Corporate Web sites are designed to increase the firm's visibility, promote their offerings, and provide information to interested parties. Marketing Web sites are also designed to communicate information and build customer relationships, but the main purpose of marketing Web sites is to increase purchases by site visitors.

## Assessment Check Answers

**2.1 Briefly identify the differences between a corporate Web site and a marketing Web site.**
A corporate Web site is designed to increase a firm's visibility, promote its offerings, and provide information for interested parties. A marketing Web site generally includes the same information found on a corporate Web site but is also designed to increase sales to site visitors.

**2.2 Visit the Specialized Web site** (http://www .specialized.com). **Is this site a corporate Web site or a marketing Web site?**
Specialized.com is a marketing Web site. It includes an online store where visitors can purchase Specialized products.

**3** **List the major forms of business-to-business (B2B) e-business.**
Electronic data interchange was an early use of technology to conduct business transactions. E-business is the process of selling goods and services through Internet-based exchanges of data. It includes product information; ordering, invoicing, and payment processes; and customer service. In a B2B context, e-business uses Internet technology to conduct transactions between two organizations via extranets, private exchanges, electronic exchanges, and e-procurement.

## Assessment Check Answers

**3.1 What is B2B e-business? How large is it relative to B2C e-business?**
B2B e-business is the use of the Internet for business transactions between organizations. By some estimates, around 80 percent of all e-business activity consists of B2B e-business.

**3.2 What is an EDI? An extranet? A private exchange?**
An EDI is a computer-to-computer exchange of invoices, purchase orders, price quotations, and other sales information between buyers and sellers. An extra-

net is a secure network accessible through a firm's Web site by authorized users. A private network is a secure Web site at which a company and its suppliers share all types of data from product design to the delivery of orders.

**3.3 Briefly explain how e-procurement works.**
E-procurement consists of Web-based systems that enable all types of organizations to improve the efficiency of their procurement processes.

**4** **Explain business-to-consumer (B2C) e-business and identify the products most often sold online.**
After a rocky start, business-to-consumer (B2C) e-business is maturing. B2C uses the Internet to connect companies directly with consumers. E-tailing and electronic storefronts are the major forms of online sales to consumers. Online shoppers are young, highly educated, affluent, and urban. However, in the coming years, online consumers will begin to look more like offline shoppers, and the kinds of products sold online will change as well. Benefits of B2C e-business include lower prices, increased convenience, and personalization. Payment methods include electronic cash, electronic wallets, and online transfers of cash.

## Assessment Check Answers

**4.1 Outline the differences between shopping Web sites and informational sites. Visit the Web site of Cross pens** (http://www.cross.com). **Is this site a shopping or informational B2C Web site?**
An informational site provides product information, technical support, and links to local retailers. A shopping Web site allows visitors to buy a firm's products. The Cross Web site is a shopping site.

**4.2 Discuss the characteristics of the typical online buyer, how those characteristics are changing, and the potential impact on the types of products sold online.**
While the typical online buyer is still relatively urban, young, and affluent, growing evidence shows that online shoppers are beginning to look more like offline shoppers. As these trends continue, the types of products sold online will likely change. For instance, as online shoppers get older, online sales of pharmaceuticals will likely increase. As the number of

female online shoppers has increased, so too have online sales of shoes, clothing, and kitchen products.

### 4.3 List some ways online merchants try to ensure secure payment systems.

Online shopping sites use encryption—the process of encoding data for security purposes. Major firms involved in all aspects of e-business use Secure Sockets Layer (SSL) technology, an industry-wide standard for secure Internet payment transactions. Electronic wallets are secure data files at Web sites that contain customer information so customers don't have to retype personal information each time they make a purchase.

**5** **Describe some of the challenges associated with e-business.**

The growth of e-business has been hampered by consumer security and privacy concerns, fraud, and system overload. In addition, poor Web design and service, unreliability of delivery and returns, and lack of retail expertise has limited e-business success. The Internet can also generate conflict among buyers and sellers.

## Assessment Check Answers

### 5.1 List the major challenges to e-business.

Challenges to e-business include protecting consumer privacy, fraud, unreliable and hard-to-use Web sites, problems with deliveries and returns, and potential channel conflicts.

### 5.2 Most cases of Internet-related fraud come from what category of online activity?

The largest number of cases of Internet-related fraud come from online auctions.

### 5.3 What is a channel conflict?

A channel conflict is a dispute between a producer, wholesaler, and/or retailer.

**6** **Discuss how organizations use the communication functions of the Internet to advance their objectives.**

Communication remains the most popular function of the Internet. Companies have long used e-mail to communicate with customers, suppliers, and other partners. Online communities are groups of people who share common interests. Companies use online communities such as forums and electronic bulletin boards to communicate with and obtain feedback from customers and other partners. Blogs are online journals that have gained popularity in recent years. Companies have just begun to explore the potential of blogs. Web-based promotions include advertising on other Web sites, search marketing, and online coupons.

## Assessment Check Answers

### 6.1 What are online communities? Explain how online communities can help companies market their products and improve customer service.

Online communities can take several forms and include Internet discussion groups and electronic bulletin boards. Users log in and participate by sending comments and questions, or receiving information from other forum members. Companies use online communities to ask questions and exchange information with customers.

### 6.2 What is a blog? A wiki? A podcast?

A blog, short for a *Web log,* and is Web page that serves as a publicly accessible journal for an individual or organization. A wiki is a Web page that anyone can edit, and a podcast is a video blog.

### 6.3 Explain the difference between a banner ad, a pop-up ad, and search marketing.

Banner ads are small messages placed in high-visibility areas of frequently visited Web sites. A pop-up ad is a separate window that pops up containing an advertising message. Search marketing is an arrangement by which a firm pays a search engine—such as Google—a fee to make sure that the firm's listing appears toward the top of the search results.

**7** **List the steps involved in developing successful Web sites and identify methods for measuring Web site effectiveness.**

Businesses establish Web sites to expand their customer bases, increase buyer awareness of their products, improve consumer communications, and provide better service. Before designing a Web site, a company's decision makers must first determine what they want to achieve with the site. Other important decisions include who should create, host, and manage the site; how to promote it; and how much funding to allocate. Successful Web sites contain informative, up-to-date, and visually appealing content. Sites should also download quickly and be easy to use. Finally, management must develop ways to measure how well a site accomplishes its objectives.

## Assessment Check Answers

**7.1 What are the first three questions a company should ask itself when planning a Web site?**
The first question deals with the purpose of the Web site. The second deals with whether the firm should develop the site itself or outsource it to a specialized firm. The third question is determining the name of the site.

**7.2 How does the type of Web site affect measures of effectiveness?**
For a shopping site, profitability is an important measure of effectiveness, though profitability can be difficult to measure given the presence of so-called Web-to-store shoppers. For company Web sites, online success is measured by increased brand awareness and loyalty, which presumably translates into greater profitability through offline transactions.

**7.3 Explain the difference between click-through and conversion rates.**
The click-through rate is the percentage of viewers who, when presented with a banner ad, click on it. The conversion rate is the percentage of Web site visitors who actually make purchases.

**8 Explain the global scope of e-business.**
Technology allows companies to compete in the global market and workplace. Even the smallest firms can sell products and find new vendors in international markets. Through its own Web site, a company can immediately reach customers all over the world. Improved communications among employees in different locations create new ways to collaborate on projects.

## Assessment Check Answers

**8.1 How do language differences affect global e-business?**
Most Web pages, including e-business sites, are still in English, which inhibits the growth of e-business in other countries. Also, online retailers need to be sensitive to cultural differences.

**8.2 How does e-business heighten global competition?**
In the virtual global marketplace, companies can search online catalogs to find the lowest-priced goods and services. The Internet is also a valuable tool for expanding a company's reach, especially for smaller businesses that would otherwise have difficulty finding overseas customers.

## Business Terms You Need to Know

electronic business (e-business) 215
corporate Web site 217
marketing Web site 218
business-to-business (B2B)
   e-business 219

business-to-consumer (B2C)
   e-business 221
electronic storefront 222
phishing 228
spam 231

blog 231
search marketing 234
click-through rate 237
conversion rate 238

## Other Important Business Terms

electronic data interchange
   (EDI) 219
quick response 219
extranet 220
private exchange 220
electronic exchange 220
e-procurement 221
electronic shopping cart 222

bot 224
encryption 225
Secure Sockets Layer (SSL) 225
electronic wallet 225
electronic signatures 226
firewall 228
channel conflict 230
electronic bulletin board 231

wiki 232
podcast 232
banner ad 233
pop-up ad 233
Web host 236
Web-to-store 237

1. List the five e-business categories.
2. Explain how a Web presence can improve the performance of traditional brick-and-mortar operations.
3. Describe the type and purpose of information found on a corporate Web site.
4. Which is larger, B2B or B2C e-business?
5. Explain how an electronic data interchange operates. What is rapid response?
6. What is an electronic exchange? Why have they proven to be less successful than many originally projected?
7. What is a bot and how do consumers use it to find the lowest price for a product online?

8. Define encryption and Secure Sockets Layer technology.
9. Describe some of the privacy concerns of online shoppers.
10. What is phishing?
11. Discuss how companies can use blogs.
12. Assume a company spends $100,000 to attract 25,000 visitors to its Web site. If the conversion rate is 5 percent, how much did the company spend to acquire each customer?
13. What are the challenges and benefits of e-commerce in the global business environment?

1. Discuss how the profile of online buyers and sellers is changing. What are some of the implications of these trends for B2C e-business?
2. Communication is still the most popular Web function; team up with a partner and describe how a travel company could take advantage of online communication to market its travel services.
3. Compared with brick-and-mortar retailers, what are the advantages and disadvantages of so-called pure-play e-business companies? Why have so many pure-play e-business companies failed?
4. Assume the role of an online shopper who wishes to purchase a pair of jeans over the Internet. Two leading online clothing retailers are Old Navy (http://www.oldnavy.com) and Eddie Bauer (http://www.eddiebauer.com). Visit both sites and learn enough so that you can describe each to your class, including which of the two you'd be most likely to purchase from and why.
5. Identify a local company that has a significant online presence. Arrange to interview the person in charge of the company's Web site. Ask the following questions:
   a. How was the Web site developed?
   b. Did the company develop the site in-house or did it outsource the task?
   c. How often does the company make changes to the site?
   d. In the opinion of your respondent, what are the advantages and disadvantages of going online?
6. Many consumers are reluctant to purchase online products that are perishable or that consumers typically like to touch, feel, or smell before buying. Working in a small group, suggest ways an e-business company might be able to reduce this reluctance.
7. Identify a local company that operates with little or no online presence. Outline a proposal that explains the benefits to the firm of either going online or significantly expanding its online presence. Sketch out what the firm's Web site should look like and the functions it should perform.
8. Choose one of the following types of companies and describe how it could take advantage of the communication power of the Internet to market its products:
   a. a travel agency that specializes in adventure travel.

b. a real estate firm.

c. a firm that ships gourmet foods—such as lobster, cheeses, or exotic coffees—nationwide.

d. a minor-league hockey team.

9. IBM offers extensive consulting services, software, and hardware (such as servers) for organizations engaged in e-business. Working with a partner, assume you're entrepreneurs and you'd like to expand your presence in the B2B market. Visit the IBM e-business Web site (http://www.ibm .com). Read about the services offered and review some of the case studies in which IBM has assisted firms in their B2B activities. Prepare a report on what you have learned.

10. Using a search engine such as Google (http://www.google.com), identify two or three company-sponsored blogs. Read some of the recent entries and prepare a report summarizing the goals of each blog and your assessment of its effectiveness.

## Case 7.1

### eBay Backs Off a Price Hike

One of the most popular sites on the Internet, giant auctioneer eBay earns most of its profits by charging sellers modest fees for membership and collecting a small percentage of the final selling price of certain items. The formulas for these fees were usually seen as fair, and sellers prospered. Buyers paid only for their purchases. Then in early 2005 the company announced a new fee structure affecting sellers in the United States, Canada, Australia, and the United Kingdom. The basic monthly subscription fee that sellers would pay to list items on eBay Stores rose from $9.95 to $15.95; the fee for ten-day listings would double to 40 cents; and "Buy It Now" sellers would pay 8 to 16 percent of an item's selling price, instead of a flat fee as before.

"We carefully evaluate the pricing structure and, from time to time, we'll change prices when it's the right thing to do to ensure the vibrancy of the marketplace," an eBay spokesperson told a reporter. "We implement these changes to spur the market in certain categories." Auction industry experts agree that eBay routinely uses its pricing power to draw profit from the features of the site that are most popular every year.

Sellers weren't pleased. To some, the fee hikes—in particular the increase in "Buy It Now" charges—were an attempt to cash in on heavily used site features just to add to the company's coffers at their expense. Loyal sellers bombarded eBay with e-mail protests, threatening to raise their own prices, which would drive buyers away; close their e-stores; or switch to other auction sites such as Overstock.com, which trails eBay in transaction volume by a wide margin. But in a well-timed move, Overstock.com slashed its own fees following eBay's announcement and saw a sharp spike in sales on its site.

One letter-writing campaign was led by a seller of historical costumes and bridal wear, who had never participated in eBay's seller communities before. Others wondered whether it was time for the government to regulate what eBay could charge, especially to protect small sellers who stood to lose the most revenue from the new fees.

EBay responded quickly to its members' unhappiness. "We're listening to everything you have to say," wrote eBay president Bill Cobb in a weekend e-mail sent to all the firm's sellers less than a month later. "I've been taking it all in and thinking hard about how we can make sure eBay remains a fun, safe place to trade, and a prosperous home for our many dedicated sellers."

Putting sentiments into action, the company announced it would issue a credit of $15.95—the price of a one-month subscription—to all its eBay Stores small-business owners of record as of the preceding month. It also reduced the minimum fee for inexpensive auction items and replaced its automated customer service response system with live customer service agents, who would answer questions in real time and for a broader population of sellers than had ever qualified for customer service support before. Some observers called the expanded support an important gesture that would go a long way toward offsetting the effect of price increases for small-business owners. But eBay held firm on the biggest increases.

Many still thought lessons could be learned from the firm's experience. "A price increase is always going to be painful," said one retail analyst. "Companies need to think strategically and communicate to their consumers the value and benefit of what they are getting in exchange for the price increases."

## Questions for Critical Thinking

1. Do you think eBay handled its price increase in the best possible way? Why or why not? What, if any-

thing, do you think eBay should do differently next time it needs to communicate price changes to its customers? Why?
2. Can improvements in customer service really offset price increases? Would you answer differently for a brick-and-mortar retailer than for an online retailer like eBay? Why or why not?

---

**Sources:** "eBay Eats Humble Pie on Fee Hikes," CBS News, accessed July 20, 2006, http://www.cbsnews.com; Jennifer LeClaire, "eBay Responds to Price Hike Outcry," *MacNewsWorld*, accessed July 20, 2006, http://www.macnewsworld.com; Tim Richardson, "eBay Backtracks as It Cuts Some Fees," *The Register*, accessed July 20, 2006, http://www.theregister.co.uk; Rick Aristotle Munarriz, "eBay, Hike, and Other 4-Letter Words," Motley Fool, accessed July 20, 2006, http://www.fool.com; Ryan Naraine, "eBay Flexes Pricing Muscle," eWeek.com, accessed July 20, 2006, http://www.eweek.com.

---

## VIDEO | Case 7.2

### Manifest Digital: Putting the User First

This video case appears on page 615. A recently filmed video, designed to expand and highlight the written case, is available for class use by instructors.

# Second City: An Entrepreneurial Experience from Stage to Strategic Planning

Over the last 50 years, the entrepreneurial spirit of The Second City (SC) has been found in its stock-in-trade: its style of comedy. Its comedic and business philosophy is to *listen and react*. Much like true entrepreneurship, improvisational comedy requires vision, energy, self-confidence, creativity, accountability, a tolerance for ambiguity, and the boldness to plunge ahead in the face of failure.

When a hip group of University of Chicago students began performing comedy shows in 1959, they offered a satirical, uniquely subversive take on society. It was a society beginning to wake from a decade of political docility. Improvisation, an art form based on risk and off-the-cuff reaction, excited audiences of the day. Like the momentum of a good scene, Second City used its innovations in comedy to spawn an amazing variety of related business ventures. Student training centers, corporate training, TV shows, national touring companies, and theaters in Chicago, Toronto, Las Vegas, Detroit, and Denver are all successful extensions of Second City's entrepreneurial character.

The founding of Second City was a collaborative artistic effort. Using improvisation as an entrepreneurial technique, Second City continued to form partnerships on the-

atrical and corporate stages. Notably, SC's first producer, Bernard Sahlins, saw the groundbreaking nature of the SC style and offered the group a needed skill: the ability to balance a checkbook. SC's comedy spoke to a changing cultural climate. Sahlins claimed they "[violated] taboos up to the point of bad taste, without crossing it." Within eight months of opening, Second City grabbed national attention. Second City continued to refine its message and mission. By listening and reacting to public themes and material, their product, Second City comedy, began to take shape as a creative innovation worthy of more expansive entrepreneurial ventures.

Bernie Sahlins took the show to Toronto, where one of Second City's most significant partnerships was formed. After only a short, unsuccessful run in 1973, the Toronto cast arrived at their theater to see the doors padlocked shut. Without the legal ability to sell liquor in the theater, the show had gone bankrupt. The spirit of Second City comedy had, however, unknowingly met the heart of yet another entrepreneur, who faced this supposed "failure" with both confidence and business savvy. Andrew Alexander, a Canadian promoter, bought the Canadian rights to SC from Bernie

Sahlins—a monthly royalty deal was struck between the two men and was signed on a cocktail napkin. This turnaround strategy was risky but in step with the SC personality, and Alexander had prepared practical solutions for improvement. He borrowed money and beckoned a hesitant cast back to Toronto with one such solution—an acquired liquor license. The Toronto branch cultivated and exposed a new generation of talent that continues to be a commodity for SC today. Looking to cast a new sketch TV show, *Saturday Night Live,* Lorne Michaels picked talent right off the Toronto stage—thereby offering SC a new level of fame. In fact, when *Saturday Night Live (SNL)* started, Second City attendance boomed. Alumni such as John Candy, Dan Aykroyd, and Gilda Radner further cemented the Second City legacy.

Second City encountered a series of changes in the entertainment industry that tested its ability to listen and react, just like the comedic timing of its performers. As talent moved into the TV medium, co-owners Sahlins and Alexander felt a need to respond. Concerned that they would continue to lose talent to *SNL,* they decided to give television a try themselves. Andrew Alexander's business partner, Len

Stuart, provided the capital needed to launch SC from the stage to the screen. With only $35,000 for seven episodes, the cast and producers used their underfinanced reality as a backdrop for the program. Self-referenced as a low-budget show, the inexperienced crews and performers became the theme. After an eight-year run, *SCTV* had earned two Emmys for writing, thirteen Emmy nominations, and a place in comedy history. *SCTV* spotlighted more future stars, including Harold Ramis, Rick Moranis, and Martin Short.

The art of improvisation now dominates the comedic world and integrates the artistic and entrepreneurial work of Second City. Its theaters promote innovation within the structure of the business. Second City now boasts training centers in Chicago, Los Angeles, New York, Toronto, and Detroit, offering students of all ages a curriculum based on listening and reacting, team building, communication, and the most subversive of Second City's techniques, humor.

The Second City is a corporation, owned by Andrew Alexander and Len Stuart, who bought SC from Bernie Sahlins in 1984. Today, Second City's senior management team continues to base the company's business ventures on the seemingly undisciplined attitude of improvisational comedy. Vice president Kelly Leonard says that The Second City remains "true to the core" of its lineage. According to

Leonard, "Second City is all about making the new—so entrepreneurship is at the core—both on a creative and business level. You can see that by the expansion of the business into new and lucrative areas of training, touring, education, television, radio, etc." With an abundance of creative proposed ventures to consider, Second City takes professional risks and picks interesting advancements over merely lucrative endeavors. SC's latest undertaking is a deal Leonard brokered with Norwegian Cruise Lines. Second City Theatricals has a select partnership with Norwegian, placing Second City's adventurous style of comedy on the bow of a new performance venue, accessing a new demographic of audience members.

Second City Communications is another branch of the company that other businesses seek out for help in fostering a creative corporate atmosphere. Using improvisational techniques such as confidence, teamwork, and relationship building, Second City Communications trains business professionals and contemporary entrepreneurs in a variety of business practices. SC listens to the needs of its clients and responds accordingly. Mock business encounters are set up in which professionals can learn and experience firsthand how to handle business situations. Corporate events feature customized comedic material. The tried-and-true methods of improvisational comedy

are taught, along with a few other secrets to Second City's charm.

Each of Second City's business and nonprofit ventures appears on its Web site. SC finds the greatest profit return in selling tickets to its theatrical revues. Other creative elements, including blogs and podcasts, are compelling features that routinely increase site traffic. According to Leonard, the trickiest aspect of managing http://www.secondcity.com seems to be making the electronic medium as funny as SC's live comedy.

While the lights come up on future ventures for The Second City, its visionaries will continue to look back on the principals of improv for guidance: *to listen and react.* They teach this method to an impressive variety of interested students from all backgrounds. Anyone can be inspired by the innovative approach of The Second City, but especially talented young actors destined for the footlights and courageous entrepreneurs entering the market.

## QUESTIONS

1. What challenges might Second City's entrepreneurial managers face as they continue to field proposals and generate business endeavors?
2. How are a comedic improviser and an entrepreneur similar?
3. How does collaboration and the forming of partnerships benefit the growth of Second City or any business?

# Part 2: Launching Your Entrepreneurial Career

In Part 2, "Starting and Growing Your Business," you learned about the many ways that business owners have achieved their dreams of owning their own company and being their own boss. The part's three chapters introduced you to the wide variety of entrepreneurial or small businesses; the forms they can take—sole proprietorship, partnership, corporation, or franchise and the reasons that some new ventures succeed and others fail. You learned that entrepreneurs are visionaries who build firms that create wealth and that they share traits such as vision and creativity, high energy, optimism, a strong need to achieve, and a tolerance for failure. Finally, you learned about the impact of computer technology in making e-business possible and about the importance of the Internet for business operations. By now you might be wondering how you can make all this information work for you. Here are some career ideas and opportunities in the small-business and e-business areas.

First, whatever field attracts you as a future business owner, try to acquire experience by working for someone else in the industry initially. The information and skills you pick up will be invaluable when you start out on your own. Lack of experience is often cited as a leading reason for small-business failure.[1]

Next, look for a good fit between your own skills, abilities, and characteristics and a market need or niche. For instance, the U.S. Department of Labor reports that opportunities in many healthcare fields are rising with the nation's increased demand for health services.[2] As the population of older people rises, and as young families find themselves increasingly pressed for time, the need for child care and elder services will also increase—and so will the opportunities for new businesses in those areas. So keep your eyes on trends to find ideas that you can use or adapt.

Another way to look for market needs is to talk to current customers. Patrick Martucci, founder of United Asset Coverage (UAC), discovered that sometimes the best opportunities for

entrepreneurs are customers whose needs aren't being met. As a sales representative for a firm that maintained only Rolm telephone equipment, Martucci realized that what his client, JCPenney, really needed was a firm to service its entire phone system. The $1.5 million JCPenney contract would have been worth $10 million if Martucci's employer had offered the right service. Shortly after that, Martucci launched UAC, a network of technicians to offer maintenance and repair of any brand of office equipment, at any location. From its first contract covering a single copy machine at a TGI Friday's in St. Louis, UAC has become the largest telecom-maintenance company in the world, with annual earnings of about $40 million.[3]

Are you intrigued by the idea of being your own boss but worried about risking your savings to get a completely new and untried business off the ground? Then owning a franchise, such as Quiznos or Dunkin' Donuts, might be for you. The Small Business Administration advises aspiring entrepreneurs that while franchising can be less risky than starting a new business from scratch, it still requires work and sacrifice. In addition, you need to completely understand both the resources to which you'll be entitled and the responsibilities you'll assume under the franchise agreement. Again, filling a market need is important for success. To find more information about franchising, access the Federal Trade Commission's consumer guide to buying a franchise at http://www.ftc.gov/bcp/conline/pubs/invest/buyfran.htm.

Are you skilled in a particular area of business, technology, or science? The consulting industry will be a rapidly growing area for several years, according to the Bureau of Labor Statistics.[4] Consulting firms offer their expertise to clients in private, government, not-for-profit, and even foreign business operations. Business consultants influence clients' decisions in marketing, finance, manufacturing, information systems, e-commerce, human resources, and many other areas including corporate strategy and organization. Technology consultants support businesses in all fields, with services ranging from setting up a secure Web site or training employees in the use of new software to managing an off-site help desk or planning for disaster recovery. Science consulting firms find plenty of work in the field of environmental consulting, helping businesses deal with pollution cleanup and control, habitat protection, and compliance with government's environmental regulations and standards.

But perhaps none of these areas appeal to you quite so much as tinkering with gears and machinery or with computer graphics and code. If you think you have the insight and creativity to invent something completely new, you need to make sure you're informed about patents, trademarks, and copyright laws to protect your ideas.[5] Each area offers different protections for your work, and none will guarantee success. Here again, hard work, persistence, and a little bit of luck will help you succeed.

## Career Assessment Exercises in Entrepreneurship and Business Ownership

1. Find out whether you have what it takes to be an entrepreneur. Review the material on the SBA's Web site http://www.sba.gov/starting_business/startup/basics.html or take the Brigham Young University's Entrepreneurial Test at http://marriottschool.byu.edu/cfe/startingout/test.cfm. Answer the questions there. After you've finished, use the scoring guides to determine how ready you are to strike out on your own. What weak areas did your results disclose? What can you do to strengthen them?

2. Find an independent business or franchise in your area, and make an appointment to talk to the owner about his or her start-up experience. Prepare a list of questions for a ten- to fifteen-minute interview, and remember to ask about details such as the number of hours worked per week, approximate start-up costs, goals of the business, available resources, lessons learned since opening, and rewards of owning the business. How different are the owner's answers from what you expected?

3. Search online for information about how to file for a patent, trademark, or copyright. (A good starting point is http://www.firstgov.gov.) Assume you have an invention you wish to protect. Find out what forms are required; what fees are necessary, if any; how much time is typically needed to complete the legal steps; and what rights and protections you will gain.

# Management: Empowering People to Achieve Business Objectives

# Part 3

DIGITAL VISION

# Chapter 8

## Management, Leadership, and the Internal Organization

### Learning Goals

1. Define *management* and the three types of skills necessary for managerial success.

2. Explain the role of vision and ethical standards in business success.

3. Summarize the major benefits of planning and distinguish among strategic planning, tactical planning, and operational planning.

4. Describe the strategic planning process.

5. Contrast the two major types of business decisions and list the steps in the decision-making process.

6. Define *leadership* and compare different leadership styles.

7. Discuss the meaning and importance of corporate culture.

8. Identify the five major forms of departmentalization and the four main types of organization structures.

Microsoft is the world's most profitable technology company, with revenues of nearly $40 billion a year. Its reach is global, employing 60,000 people around the world, and the company receives almost that many job applications every month. Microsoft loses only about 9 percent of its employees a year, lower than the industry average, and of those lucky enough to be offered a job at the software giant, about 90 percent accept.

Yet the company has had its troubles, aside from the long-running legal battles stemming from antitrust charges in the United States and Europe. Its stock price has recently stagnated. And as it has grown, so has its internal bureaucracy, bringing new procedures and more meetings that some workers feel are stifling the creativity

© LOU DEMATTEIS/CORBIS

## How Does Bill Gates Plan Microsoft's Future?

that made the company an unbeatable innovator in the past.

A couple of Microsoft researchers recently jotted down "Ten Crazy Ideas to Shake Up Microsoft," a twelve-page memo packed with suggestions to change the company. Some CEOs might not like receiving such advice, but at Microsoft, the memo made its way directly to the desk of founder and chairman Bill Gates.

Twice a year Gates leaves his headquarters office and heads for an undisclosed location in the Pacific Northwest, where he spends one week completely alone to read, think, and plan. His "Think Weeks" are legendary within the firm, and the general manager of the company's MapPoint group says Gates's open call for employee input at those times is "the world's coolest suggestion box." A few weeks before each Think Week, Gates's assistant sorts through papers submitted from every corner of the company and collects those that are priorities for his boss to consider. This year, "Ten Crazy Ideas" was one of them, even though breaking up the company was one of the ideas.

Gates pores over employees' submissions for new products and other input including books, articles, research papers, and industry reports. What began as a

stack of paper when he first started his Think Weeks—at his grandmother's in the 1980s—has now been transformed into a computerized interactive library in which he can enter comments and link entries. Paper versions serve as backup. By the end of the week, Gates has begun firing off e-mails to employees around the world, green-lighting new Microsoft projects, rejecting others, reordering priorities, changing direction, or asking for follow-up or a meeting. The general manager of Microsoft's education group posted Gates's comments on the group's internal Web site to spark further discussion of the team's initiatives. The general manager of MapPoint called a brainstorming meeting to fine-tune plans in response to the chairman's reactions to his group's proposal. The Virtual Earth team was asked to meet with Gates and discuss security issues as a follow-up to its 62-page paper on mapping services.

Planning is, of course, an ongoing activity at Microsoft, as it is in all organizations. But Gates is a firm believer in the value of his Think Weeks for Microsoft. They consist of long days interrupted only by 5-minute breaks to play online bridge or 30-minute walks on the beach. Two meals a day are brought in, and by installing a bathroom and refrigerator in the upstairs office of his hideaway,

Gates can save the time it would have taken him to go up and down the stairs and devote it to thinking and planning.

His technique does seem to produce results. A 1995 Think Week inspired Microsoft's famous decision to overtake Netscape and dominate the Internet with its Web browser, and later sessions led to the creation of the Tablet PC and to strategies designed to improve the secu-

rity of Microsoft's software, better integrate the company's offerings, and enter the online video game market. Perhaps that's why another of the "Ten Crazy Ideas" submitted by the two researchers was that, like Gates, *every* employee should be given a slice of unscheduled time to think creatively about new ideas and innovations. After all, Google does it.[1]

A management career brings challenges that appeal to many students in introductory business courses. When asked about their professional objectives, many students say, "I want to be a manager." You may think that the role of a manager is basically being the boss. But in today's business world, companies are looking for much more than bosses. They want managers who understand technology, can adapt quickly to change, skillfully motivate subordinates, and realize the importance of satisfying customers. Managers who can master those skills will continue to be in great demand because their performance strongly affects their firms' performance.

This chapter begins by examining how successful organizations use management to turn visions into reality. It describes the levels of management, the skills that managers need, and the functions that managers perform. The chapter explains how the first of these functions, planning, helps managers such as Microsoft's Bill Gates meet the challenges of a rapidly changing business environment and develop strategies that guide a company's future. Other sections of the chapter explore the types of decisions that managers make, the role of managers as leaders, and the importance of corporate culture. The chapter concludes by examining the second function of management—organizing.

# WHAT IS MANAGEMENT?

**management** process of achieving organizational objectives through people and other resources.

**Management** is the process of achieving organizational objectives through people and other resources. The manager's job is to combine human and technical resources in the best way possible to achieve the company's goals.

Management principles and concepts apply to not-for-profit organizations as well as profit-seeking firms. A city administrator, a Salvation Army major, and the CEO of your local United Way organization all perform the managerial functions described later in this chapter. Managers preside over organizations as diverse as Miami-Dade Community College, the New York Stock Exchange, and the Starbucks coffee shop down the street.

## The Management Hierarchy

A local fast-food restaurant such as McDonald's typically works through a very simple organization that consists of an owner-manager and a few assistant managers. By contrast, large organizations develop more complex management structures. Southwest Airlines manages its activities through a chairperson of the board, a vice chairperson and chief executive officer, a president and chief operating officer, three executive vice presidents, a senior vice president, and 23 vice presidents, plus an array of managers and supervisors. All of these people are managers because they combine human and other resources to achieve company objectives. Their jobs differ, however, because they work at different levels of the organization.

A firm's management usually has three levels: top, middle, and supervisory. These levels of management form a management hierarchy, as shown in Figure 8.1. The hierarchy is the traditional structure found in most organizations. Managers at each level perform different activities.

The highest level of management is **top management.** Top managers include such positions as chief executive officer (CEO), chief financial officer (CFO), and executive vice president. Top managers devote most of their time to developing long-range plans for their organizations. They make decisions such as whether to introduce new products, purchase other companies, or enter new geographical markets. Top managers set a direction for their organization and inspire the company's executives and employees to achieve their vision for the company's future.

Michael Bloomberg once headed a media conglomerate—Bloomberg LP—that primarily sells financial data via leased computer terminals. This business made Bloomberg a billionaire. Then he decided to move on to a new CEO position. Today, Michael Bloomberg has what is often called the second toughest job in the United States—mayor of New York City. Instead of building wealth, as mayor he works at building the city's infrastructure, resolving budget problems, and keeping firms from fleeing to the suburbs or elsewhere. Bloomberg still follows the leadership style he used in the corporate world. At Bloomberg LP, he sat in the corner of his TV studio. Now in his second term as mayor, Bloomberg operates out of an open cubicle in a big hall resembling the brokerage trading room where he got his start. The official mayor's office is used only for interviews and similar events. Mayor Bloomberg is providing hands-on direction to his staff—situated in nearby cubicles. The leadership pattern that proved successful at Bloomberg LP is now at work in New York's City Hall.[2]

**Middle management,** the second tier in the management hierarchy, includes positions such as general managers, plant managers, division managers, and branch managers. Middle managers' attention focuses on specific operations, products, or customer groups within an organization. They are responsible for developing detailed plans and procedures to implement the firm's strategic plans. If top management decided to broaden the distribution of a product, a sales manager would be responsible for determining the number of salespeople required. Middle managers are responsible for targeting the products and customers who are the source of the sales and profit growth expected by their CEOs. To achieve these goals, middle managers might budget money for product development, identify new uses for existing products, and improve the ways they train and motivate salespeople. Middle managers are also responsible for solving unique company problems. After a hurricane destroyed five miles of railroad tracks outside New Orleans, Jeff McCracken of Norfolk Southern managed a team of 100 employees and dozens of engineers who rebuilt the tracks in less than a week. McCracken said, "It was a colossal job that took more than 400 moves with heavy equipment." But McCracken was happiest about "working with people from all parts of the company—and getting the job done without anyone getting hurt."[3]

Figure

8.1

The Management Hierarchy

| Top Management | → | Chief Executive Officer, Chief Financial Officer, Governor, Mayor |
| Middle Management | → | Regional Manager, Division Head, Director, Dean |
| Supervisory (First-Line) Management | → | Supervisor, Group Leader, Section Chief |

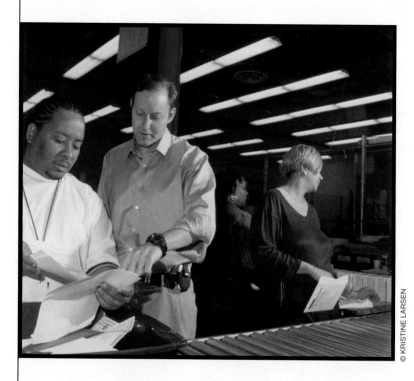

Supervisory management, or first-line management, includes positions such as supervisor, section chief, and team leader. These managers are directly responsible for assigning nonmanagerial employees to specific jobs and evaluating their performance. Managers at this first level of the hierarchy work directly with the employees who produce and sell the firm's goods and services. They are responsible for implementing middle managers' plans by motivating workers to accomplish daily, weekly, and monthly goals. For instance, Charles Lee, who is a production supervisor at an American Airlines' maintenance center in Fort Worth, is responsible for motivating employees such as Fred Amato to reduce the cost of replacement parts for planes. Amato did just that when he replaced a $146 part about the size of a quarter with a $5.24 part made in American's machine shop.[4]

## Skills Needed for Managerial Success

Managers at every level in the management hierarchy must exercise three basic types of skills: technical, human, and conceptual. All managers must acquire these skills in varying proportions, although the importance of each skill changes at different management levels.

**Technical skills** are the manager's ability to understand and use the techniques, knowledge, and tools and equipment of a specific discipline or department. Technical skills become less important at higher levels of the management hierarchy, but most top executives started out as technical experts. The résumé of a vice president for information systems probably lists experience as a computer analyst, and that of a vice president for marketing usually shows a background in sales. And, as you read at the beginning of the chapter, Microsoft's founder, Bill Gates, is the company's chairman *and* chief software architect. During his weeklong "Think Weeks," Gates typically reads 100 papers and proposals, nearly all of which deal with technological products or strategies for Microsoft. Not surprisingly, 31 of the 100 papers at his last "Think Week" addressed technological issues related to Internet and computer security.[5]

Supervisory managers, such as Ozzie Guillen of the Chicago White Sox, are responsible for carrying out the day-to-day activities that help their organizations reach their goals. Guillen needs to assess each player's ability, determine who is available to play, and juggle lineups to compete against each day's opponents.

David Steinberg, CEO of InPhonic, a company that sells cell phone handsets over the Internet, succeeds in this business by using his human skills. Steinberg began his career as an insurance salesperson, where he mastered the art of give-and-take with clients. Then he moved into the new cell phone industry during its early growth stages, working with company managers to create 350 jobs.

**Human skills** are interpersonal skills that enable managers to work effectively with and through people. Human skills include the ability to communicate with, motivate, and lead employees to complete assigned activities. Managers need human skills to interact with people both inside and outside the organization. It would be tough for a manager to succeed without such skills, even though they must be adapted to different forms today—for instance, mastering and communicating effectively with staff through e-mail, cell phones, pagers, faxes, and even instant messaging, all of which are widely used in today's offices. And, as you'd expect, all that communication means many interruptions. See the "Business Etiquette" feature for steps managers can take to handle the constant interruptions that are a part of their jobs.

**Conceptual skills** determine a manager's ability to see the organization as a unified whole and to understand how each part of the overall organization interacts with other parts. These skills involve an ability to see the big picture by acquiring, analyzing, and interpreting information. Conceptual skills are especially important for top-level managers, who must develop long-range plans for the future direction of their organization. For three decades, Microsoft has made its money by building software that was purchased and then installed on people's personal computers. However, facing challenges from Internet companies such as Google and eBay, Microsoft will begin developing a "next-generation Internet services platform" to deliver products, such as Microsoft Office, via the Internet and, perhaps, Internet-based advertising. In terms of Microsoft's need to change its business model, chief technical officer Ray Ozzie said, "It's clear that if we fail to do so, our business as we know it is at risk. We must respond quickly and decisively."[6]

## Managerial Functions

In the course of a typical day, managers spend time meeting and talking with people,

---

## (b)usiness (e)tiquette

### Handling Interruptions

Managers at all levels of an organization are interrupted every few minutes every day to deal with important—and sometimes not-so-important—issues. Interruptions are part of a manager's day, and they simply can't be avoided. So here are some suggestions for dealing with them tactfully.

1. If someone stops by just to chat, say something friendly but unmistakable such as, "I don't have time to talk right now. Can we catch up later?"
2. Discourage persistent visitors by getting up and moving away from your desk, by picking up some work or positioning yourself in front of your computer, or even by excusing yourself to go to the restroom.
3. Remove extra chairs from your office or cubicle to make it a less inviting place for others to kill time.
4. If you really need a block of time without interruptions, ask your staff and co-workers to respect that time, forward your phone calls, turn off your cell phone and pager, and, if you have a door, close it.
5. When unintentional interruptions such as the noise of others in the hallway interfere with a meeting or phone call, consider requesting the use of a conference room for a set period of time. Once there, turn off your cell phone and close the door.
6. When an interruption to a meeting or interview is expected and can't be avoided, explain in advance to those attending and arrange to make the break as short as possible.
7. If you can handle phone interruptions to a meeting only by answering the phone, answer promptly, thank the person for calling, get a call-back number, and say, "I'm meeting with someone now, but I'll get back to you right after the meeting," and be sure to do so.
8. Avoid letting interruptions make the person standing or sitting in front of you feel less important.
9. Keep your pager in "vibrate" mode and wear it. Noisy vibrations against a table or desktop defeat the purpose of silencing the device.
10. Avoid creating interruptions for others by asking yourself before phoning them whether they really need to hear from you right now. If not, call later.

**Sources:** Rebecca L. Morgan, "Handling Interruptions in a High-Tech Environment," iVillage, accessed June 27, 2006, http://www.ivillage.co.uk; "Business Etiquette," Newspaper Association of America, accessed June 27, 2006, http://www.naa.org; Bob Lang, "Proper Business Etiquette for Using Electronic Communicating Devices," accessed June 27, 2006, http://www.baltimoremd.com; "Peter Post," *Boston Globe,* accessed July 31, 2005, http://www.boston.com.

reading, thinking, and sending e-mail messages. As they perform these activities, managers are carrying out four basic functions: planning, organizing, directing, and controlling. Planning activities lay the groundwork, and the other functions are aimed at carrying out the plans.

**planning** process of anticipating future events and conditions and determining courses of action for achieving organizational objectives.

*Planning*   **Planning** is the process of anticipating future events and conditions and determining courses of action for achieving organizational objectives. Effective planning helps businesses crystallize their visions, which are described in the next section, avoid costly mistakes, and seize opportunities. Effective planning requires an evaluation of the business environment and a well-designed road map of the actions needed to lead a firm forward. For example, Alcoa, the world's largest aluminum company, has been hard hit by skyrocketing energy prices, which increased its costs by almost half a billion dollars in less than a year. Consequently, Alcoa is closing aluminum smelting plants in the United States, where energy costs are high. But, it is building plants in Iceland, Trinidad, and Brunei and buying plants in Russia, where energy costs are much cheaper.[7] In a later section of this chapter, we elaborate on the planning process.

*Organizing*   Once plans have been developed, the next step in the management process typically is **organizing**—the means by which managers blend human and material resources through a formal structure of tasks and authority. This activity involves classifying and dividing work into manageable units by determining specific tasks necessary to accomplish organizational objectives, grouping tasks into a logical pattern or structure, and assigning them to specific personnel. Managers also must staff the organization with competent employees capable of performing the necessary tasks and assigning authority and responsibility to these individuals. Often organizing involves studying a company's existing structure and determining whether to reorganize it so that the company can better meet its objectives. The organizing process is discussed in detail later in this chapter.

*Directing*   Once plans have been formulated and an organization has been created and staffed, the management task focuses on **directing,** or guiding and motivating employees to accomplish organizational objectives. Directing includes explaining procedures, issuing orders, and seeing that mistakes are corrected. Managers may also direct in other ways, such as getting employees to agree on how they will meet objectives and inspiring them to care about customer satisfaction or their contribution to the company.

The directing function is a vital responsibility of supervisory managers. To fulfill their responsibilities to get things done through people, supervisors must be effective leaders. In addition, middle and top managers must be good leaders and motivators, and they must create an environment that fosters such leadership. A later section of this chapter discusses leadership, and Chapter 9 discusses motivating employees and improving performance.

**assessment check**

1. What is management?
2. How do the jobs of top managers, middle managers, and supervisory managers differ?
3. What is the relationship between the manager's planning and controlling functions?

*Controlling*   **Controlling** is the function of evaluating an organization's performance to determine whether it is accomplishing its objectives. The basic purpose of controlling is to assess the success of the planning function. Controlling also provides feedback for future rounds of planning.

The four basic steps in controlling are to establish performance standards, monitor actual performance, compare actual performance with established standards, and take corrective action if required. Under the provisions of the Sarbanes-Oxley Act, for example, CEOs and CFOs must monitor the performance of the firm's accounting staff more closely. They must personally attest to the truth of financial reports filed with the Securities and Exchange Commission.

# SETTING A VISION AND ETHICAL STANDARDS FOR THE FIRM

As Chapter 1 discusses, business success usually begins with a **vision,** a perception of market-place needs and the methods an organization can use to satisfy them. Vision serves as the target for a firm's actions, helping direct the company toward opportunities and differentiating it from its competitors. Michael Dell's vision of selling custom-built computers directly to consumers helped distinguish Dell from many other computer industry start-ups. John Schnatter, founder of Papa John's Pizza, keeps his vision—and his menu—focused to satisfy his pizza-loving customers.

A company's vision must be focused and yet flexible enough to adapt to changes in the business environment. The vision for Merck, which develops and manufactures pharmaceuticals, is "to provide society with superior products and services by developing innovations and solutions that improve the quality of life and satisfy customer needs." In the long run, Merck's vision is the same, to develop drugs ("innovations and solutions") that improve people's health. However, it is adaptable to changes as Merck's managers and researchers can accomplish that vision using natural or synthetic chemical compounds or high-tech gene-splicing equipment or low-tech Petri dishes.

Also critical to a firm's long-term success are the ethical standards that top executives set. As we saw in Chapter 2, a company's top managers can take an organization down a slippery slope to bankruptcy—and even criminal—court if they operate unethically. Avoiding that path requires executives to focus on the organization's success, not merely personal gain, like Tyco's former CEO Dennis Kozlowski and Tyco's former chief financial officer, Mark Swartz, who were found guilty of taking at least $150 million for themselves from the company to finance their extravagant lifestyles. Kozlowski and Swartz were sentenced to between $8^1/_3$ and 25 years in prison and must pay $240 million in fines and restitution. Both men are awaiting their appeals in jail.[8] Holding the welfare of the company's constituencies—customers, employees, investors, and society in general—as the top priority can build lasting success for a firm. For more on a related issue, see the "Solving an Ethical Controversy" feature, which discusses whether CEOs should get "golden handshakes," that is, lucrative severance packages when they are fired by the company.

The ethical tone that a top management team establishes can also reap nonmonetary rewards. Setting a high ethical standard does not merely restrain employees from doing wrong, but it encourages, motivates, and inspires them to achieve goals they never thought possible. Such satisfaction creates a more productive, stable workforce—one that can create a long-term competitive advantage for the organization.

Still, a leader's vision and ethical conduct are only the first steps along an organization's path to success. Turning a business idea into reality takes careful planning and actions. The next sections take a closer look at the planning and implementation process.

**assessment check**

1. What is meant by a vision for the firm?
2. Why is it important for a top executive to set high ethical standards?

# IMPORTANCE OF PLANNING

When you think of Wal-Mart, you think of low prices. But in a nod to Target, which is growing twice as fast by selling higher-quality products, Wal-Mart has created a new store prototype with a more attractive layout, with fake wood floors, wider aisles, lower shelves, more

# SHOULD CEOS GET GOLDEN HANDSHAKES?

*Executive compensation continues to raise eyebrows as departing CEOs walk away with massive financial rewards from companies that may be struggling.*

Gary Rodkin, PepsiCo's former North American CEO, received $4.56 million for "consultancy services" on his resignation. Carly Fiorina, deposed CEO of Hewlett-Packard, took home a $21.2 million severance package. Eugene S. Kahn, former CEO of May Department Stores, which is now part of the Federated Department Stores chain, resigned with a payout worth almost $11 million. The average severance package for ex-CEOs is $4.5 million, and surprisingly, those who are dismissed are more likely to receive generous payouts than those who resign.

Should top executives receive multimillion-dollar severance packages when they leave or are fired from their jobs?

## PRO

1. Such "golden handshakes" compensate executives for taking risks and encourage visionary leaders to accept these jobs—and the additional risk of losing them.
2. The scarcity of jobs at the top level means it is more difficult for an ex-CEO to find another job, and firings are more likely today than ever before.

## CON

1. The size of these payouts is seldom linked to the CEO's actual performance, which means they can be generously rewarded for doing a poor job.
2. Large severance packages cost shareholders money and set unwelcome precedents throughout the corporate world.

## Summary

Financial scandals and the passage of the Sarbanes-Oxley Act have focused more attention on internal corporate policies and forced some companies to reexamine their executive compensation practices. More corporate boards have stepped up to fire their CEOs for poor performance, wrongdoing, and even poor ethical decisions. On the other hand, because CEOs often sit on the compensation boards of other corporations, overall executive compensation is still on the rise.

**Sources:** Marcy Gordon, "SEC Moves for More Exec Pay Disclosure," Associated Press, accessed June 27, 2006, http://news.yahoo.com; Tim McLaughlin, "Golden Parachutes Are Soaring to Platinum Levels," *St. Louis Post-Dispatch*, accessed June 27, 2006, http://www.stltoday.com; Joanne S. Lublin, "CEO Compensation Survey," *Wall Street Journal*, accessed June 27, 2006, http://online.wsj.com; Gary Strauss and Barbara Hansen, "CEO Pay Packages 'Business as Usual'," *USA Today*, accessed June 27, 2006, http://www.usatoday.com.

solving an **ETHICAL** controversy

attractive product displays, and higher-quality goods that appeal to slightly more upscale shoppers. With that in mind, Wal-Mart is now focusing on fashion by spending $12 million to advertise in *Vogue* and opening a strategic planning office for apparel and home furnishings in New York City, not at Wal-Mart's Bentonville, Arkansas, headquarters.[10] Will Wal-Mart's plans work? Shopper Caroline Geppert's comments suggest it will be a challenge: "I've been surprised going to Target and seeing some things that I would buy and wear, whereas in Wal-Mart I usually wouldn't buy anything other than socks or underwear or a basic T-shirt." Let's take a closer look at the various types of planning that businesses do to achieve their goals.

## Types of Planning

Planning can be categorized by scope and breadth. Some plans are very broad and long range, while others are short range and very narrow, affecting selected parts of the organization rather than all. Planning can be divided into the following categories: strategic, tactical, operational, and contingency, with each step including more specific information than the last. From the mission statement (described in the next section) to objectives to specific plans, each phase must fit into a comprehensive planning framework. The framework also must include narrow, functional plans aimed at individual employees and work areas relevant to individual

# HIT & MISS

## When Wal-Mart Was the Only Lifeline

Months and years will pass before the full story of Hurricane Katrina's devastation is told. But in the days immediately following the disaster, one thing was clear: Wal-Mart's emergency plans worked where others failed.

In the wake of the chaos of Hurricane Charlie, which had hit Florida the year before, Wal-Mart decided to prepare for emergencies and specifically for hurricanes in vulnerable states. With its disaster plans in place, the firm was able to act even before the pattern of Katrina's movements became clear. The chain's one-room Emergency Operations Center began moving trucks and supplies into position six days before the storm hit. That action enabled it to respond quickly with basic items that often reached victims before government agencies could and that sometimes made the difference between survival and disaster. Once managers were warned by the company's own meteorologists that the storm had unexpectedly shifted toward New Orleans, the giant retailer started shipping huge quantities of bottled water, packaged food, and other supplies to Louisiana. Fuel, generators, and dry ice were shipped to the stores in the path of the storm. Based on its research into buying patterns in hurricane-vulnerable areas, Wal-Mart's information systems division even knew that in addition to water, food, batteries, flashlights, tarps, chain saws, and mops, customers in stricken areas also bought Pop-Tarts. So employees loaded them up and shipped them with everything else. The company's headquarters also acts as an information clearinghouse in the early stages of emergencies, coordinating store evacuations and passing data among store managers.

When the magnitude of the emergency became clear, many employees made on-the-spot decisions that their communities will long remember. Jessica Lewis, co-manager of a Wal-Mart store in Georgia that was severely damaged by hurricane floodwaters, salvaged shoes, clothing, diapers, food, water, and even medicines from her store and handed them out free to her barefoot and homeless neighbors in the store's parking lot. "This is the right thing to do," she remembers thinking.

### Questions for Critical Thinking

1. How effective do you think set plans can be when it comes to natural disasters?
2. What elements of Wal-Mart's plans could not be set ahead of time? How do you think an organization can ensure that on-the-spot decisions are appropriate in emergencies?

**Sources:** "Wal-Mart Support of the Hurricane Relief Efforts," accessed June 27, 2006, http://www.walmartfacts.com; Thomas Sowell, "Observe Private Businesses' Quick Response to Katrina," *Deseret Morning News*, accessed June 27, 2006, http://deseretnews.com; Devin Leonard, "After Katrina: Crisis Management," *Fortune*, accessed June 27, 2006, http://www.fortune.com; Christopher Leonard, "Katrina Puts Wal-Mart on Alert," *Arkansas Democrat Gazette*, acessed August 30, 2005, http://www.ardemgaz.com.

---

tasks. These plans must fit within the firm's overall planning framework, and help it reach objectives and achieve its mission.

*Strategic Planning* The most far-reaching level of planning is **strategic planning**—the process of determining the primary objectives of an organization and then acting and allocating resources to achieve those objectives. At Dell, managers maintain this long-range view. "You may have a great day today and the stock goes down, and you may have a horrible day tomorrow and the stock goes up," says CEO Michael Dell. "But over a long period of time you build a great company."[11]

*Tactical Planning* **Tactical planning** involves implementing the activities specified by strategic plans. Tactical plans guide the current and near-term activities required to implement overall strategies. Craig Knouf, CEO of Associated Business Systems, which sells office equipment in Portland, Oregon, examines his company's 30-page business plan every month, with additional semiannual and annual reviews, making tactical changes when needed. After one of

> ## "They Said It"
>
> "If you chase two rabbits, both will escape."
> —*Anonymous*

those reviews, he noticed an unexpected increase in sales of high-volume document scanners. So he changed his business plan to put a greater emphasis on scanners and scanning software. As a result, sales of scanning products have doubled and now account for one-third of all sales. Working without his business plan, says Knouf, "would be like driving a car with no steering wheel."[12]

*Operational Planning* **Operational planning** creates the detailed standards that guide implementation of tactical plans. This activity involves choosing specific work targets and assigning employees and teams to carry out plans. Unlike strategic planning, which focuses on the organization as a whole, operational planning deals with developing and implementing tactics in specific functional areas. For example, as part of its larger strategy to sell more expensive, higher-quality goods, the electronics departments in Wal-Mart's new prototype stores are stocking 27-inch to 42-inch plasma HD TVs costing between $1,700 and $2,000. Brent Allen, who manages a new Wal-Mart in McKinney, Texas, is seeing "high-double-digit percentage" sales increases in flat-screen TVs, compared with sales in the old Wal-Mart store he operated across the street.[13]

*Contingency Planning* Planning cannot foresee every possibility. Major accidents, natural disasters, and rapid economic downturns can throw even the best-laid plans into chaos. To handle the possibility of business disruption from events of this nature, many firms use **contingency planning,** which allows them to resume operations as quickly and as smoothly as possible after a crisis while openly communicating with the public about what happened. This planning activity involves two components: business continuation and public communication. Many firms have developed management strategies to speed recovery from accidents such as airline crashes, fires and explosions, chemical leaks, package tampering, and product failures.

A contingency plan usually designates a chain of command for crisis management, assigning specific functions to particular managers and employees in an emergency. Contingency planning also involves training workers to respond to emergencies, improving communications systems, and using advanced technology. As discussed in the "Hit & Miss" feature, companies with well-defined disaster recovery plans generally fared better in the aftermath of Hurricane Katrina than those that didn't develop and implement plans.

## Planning at Different Organizational Levels

Although managers spend some time on planning virtually every day, the total time spent and the type of planning done differ according to the level of management. As Table 8.1 points

Table 8.1 | Planning at Different Management Levels

| Primary Type of Planning | Managerial Level | Examples |
| --- | --- | --- |
| Strategic | Top management | Organizational objectives, fundamental strategies, long-term plans |
| Tactical | Middle management | Quarterly and semiannual plans, departmental policies and procedures |
| Operational | Supervisory management | Daily and weekly plans, rules, and procedures for each department |
| Contingency | Primarily top management, but all levels contribute | Ongoing plans for actions and communications in an emergency |

out, top managers, including a firm's board of directors and CEO, spend a great deal of time on long-range planning, while middle-level managers and supervisors focus on short-term, tactical planning. Employees at all levels can benefit themselves and their company by making plans to meet their own specific goals.

**assessment check**

1. Outline the planning process.
2. Describe the purpose of tactical planning.
3. Compare the kinds of plans made by top managers and middle managers. How does their focus differ?

# THE STRATEGIC PLANNING PROCESS

Strategic planning often makes the difference between an organization's success and failure. Strategic planning has formed the basis of many fundamental management decisions:

- Recognizing the devotion that TiVo-watching consumers had to their personal digital recorders, which record their favorite TV shows to be watched whenever they want at a cost of $10 to $15 a month, cable companies such as Comcast now provide similar on-demand services that let viewers watch TV shows whenever they want—all without purchasing a personal digital recorder.[14]
- With well-established women's beauty products, but a poor selection of men's grooming products, Procter & Gamble paid $54 million to buy Gillette and its market-leading razors and number-two-ranked men's deodorants.[15]

Successful strategic planners typically follow the six steps shown in Figure 8.2: defining a mission, assessing the organization's competitive position, setting organizational objectives, creating strategies for competitive differentiation, implementing the strategy, and evaluating the results and refining the plan.

## Defining the Organization's Mission

The first step in strategic planning is to translate the firm's vision into a **mission statement.** A mission statement is a written explanation of an organization's business intentions and aims. It is an enduring statement of a firm's purpose, possibly highlighting the scope of operations, the market it seeks to serve, and the ways it will attempt to set itself apart from competitors. A mission statement guides the actions of people inside the firm and informs customers and

**mission statement** written explanation of an organization's business intentions and aims.

**Figure 8.2**

Steps in the Strategic Planning Process

KEVIN P. CASEY/BLOOMBERG NEWS/LANDOV

Starbucks CEO Howard Schultz (above right) is involved in all details of his company's operations, including daily contact with employees and customers. Guiding his actions are his concerns for high ethical standards and for consistent quality in his products. Schultz says he refers to his heart and conscience to ensure that decisions are true to the company's mission and cause.

other stakeholders of the company's underlying reasons for existence. The mission statement should be widely publicized among employees, suppliers, partners, shareholders, customers, and the general public.

Merck's mission statement was outlined earlier in the section on establishing an organization's vision. Mission statements can vary in complexity and length.

- A Birmingham, Alabama, securities firm has a very straightforward mission statement: "The mission of Sterne, Agee, and Leach, Inc. is to build wealth for our clients."
- Google's mission is "to organize the world's information and make it universally accessible and useful."[16]
- German chemical company Bayer's mission statement is "Bayer: Science for a better life." According to Bayer's CEO, "We have set our course for the future. This new mission statement defines our future perspectives, our goals and our values, and guides our strategy at a time of sweeping change. It outlines to our stockholders, our customers, the public and especially our employees how we think and behave as a company."[17]

Developing a mission statement can be one of the most complex and difficult aspects of strategic planning. Completing these statements requires detailed considerations of a company's values and vision. Effective mission statements indicate specific, achievable, inspiring principles. They avoid unrealistic promises and statements.

## Assessing Your Competitive Position

Once a mission statement has been created, the next step in the planning process is to assess the firm's current position in the marketplace. This phase also involves examining the factors that may help or hinder the organization in the future. A frequently used tool in this phase of strategic planning is SWOT analysis.

A **SWOT analysis** is an organized approach to assessing a company's internal strengths and weaknesses and its external opportunities and threats. SWOT is an acronym for *strengths, weaknesses, opportunities,* and *threats.* The basic premise of SWOT is that a critical internal and external reality check should lead managers to select the appropriate strategy to accomplish their organization's objectives. SWOT analysis encourages a practical approach to planning based on a realistic view of a firm's situation and scenarios of likely future events and conditions. When gas prices rose to more than $3 a gallon in some areas, sales of large sport-utility vehicles dropped by nearly 10 percent, and automakers immediately began designing family vehicles, which make up more than one-fourth of all car sales, that held five or six people rather than seven or eight and were more fuel efficient.[18] The framework for a SWOT analysis appears in Figure 8.3.

To evaluate a firm's strengths and weaknesses, the planners may examine each functional area such as finance, marketing, information technology, and human resources. Entrepreneurs may focus on the individual skills and experience they bring to a new business. Large firms may also examine strengths and weaknesses of individual decisions and geographical opera-

Figure

8.3

Elements of SWOT Analysis

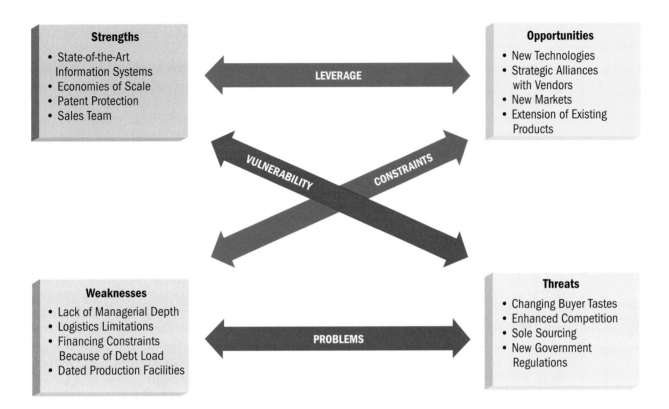

| Strengths | LEVERAGE | Opportunities |

**Strengths**
- State-of-the-Art Information Systems
- Economies of Scale
- Patent Protection
- Sales Team

**LEVERAGE**

**Opportunities**
- New Technologies
- Strategic Alliances with Vendors
- New Markets
- Extension of Existing Products

**VULNERABILITY**  **CONSTRAINTS**

**Weaknesses**
- Lack of Managerial Depth
- Logistics Limitations
- Financing Constraints Because of Debt Load
- Dated Production Facilities

**PROBLEMS**

**Threats**
- Changing Buyer Tastes
- Enhanced Competition
- Sole Sourcing
- New Government Regulations

tions. Usually, planners attempt to look at their strengths and weaknesses in relation to those of other firms in the industry.

For Starbucks, a key strength is consumers' positive image of the company's brand, which gets them to stand in line to pay premium prices for coffee. That positive image comes from Starbucks's being one of the best 100 companies to work for in the United States, according to *Fortune,* and from its socially responsible corporate policies. The company's strategic plans have included various ways to build on Starbucks' strong brand loyalty by attaching it to new products expanding into new markets. The expansion efforts have included creating a Web site, selling bottled Frappuccino iced coffee in supermarkets, and opening thousands of Starbucks outlets in Europe, Asia, and the Middle East.

SWOT analysis continues with an attempt to define the major opportunities and threats the firm is likely to face within the time frame of the plan. Possibilities include environmental factors such as market growth, regulatory changes, and increased competition. Starbucks saw an opportunity in the growth of the Internet and the interest in online shopping. Its Web site sells coffee and related accessories. In addition, Starbucks' experience in Japan, where its outlets' average sales top those in the United States, suggested that international expansion presented a solid opportunity. A threat is that consumers could tire of paying $3.50 or so for cappuccinos and lattés and switch to something else. The company has begun addressing that threat with the introduction of gourmet tea products.

Some aspects of Starbucks' strategy have succeeded better than others. Initially, Starbucks tried selling gourmet foods, music, and even furniture on its Web site. Sales were disappointing, and the firm quickly dropped the least successful offerings. Recently, Starbucks has shifted more of its attention to its retail units, where sales remain strong. Furthermore, Starbucks is now co-branding alcohol products with Jim Beam Brands to sell Starbucks Cream Liqueur and has moved aggressively into selling music, partnering with XM Satellite Radio, Sony BMG, and Virgin Records to sell music in its stores and online at http://www.starbucks.com/hearmusic.[19]

If a firm's strengths and opportunities mesh successfully, as at the Starbucks retail stores, it gains competitive leverage in the marketplace. On the other hand, if internal weaknesses prevent a firm from overcoming external threats, as in the case of the Starbucks Web site, it may face major difficulties. SWOT analysis is useful in the strategic planning process because it forces management to look at factors both inside and outside the organization and determine which steps it must take in the future to minimize external threats and take advantage of strategic opportunities.

## Setting Objectives for the Organization

After defining the company's mission and examining factors that may affect its ability to fulfill that mission, the next step in planning is to develop objectives for the organization. **Objectives** set guideposts by which managers define the organization's desired performance in such areas as profitability, customer service, growth, and employee satisfaction. While the mission statement delineates a company's goals in general terms, objectives are more concrete statements. For instance, Toyota wants to sell 600,000 hybrid gas/electric cars in the United States by 2010. Today, however, out of the 1.1 million cars per year that Toyota sells in the United States, only 80,000, or roughly 7 percent, are hybrids. Because Toyota plans to sell 2 million cars in the United States by 2010, one of every three cars that it sells will have to be a hybrid to reach that goal. Today, while Toyota only offers three hybrid models—the Toyota Prius and Highlander and the Lexus RX400h SUV—it plans to reach its sales goal of 600,000 hybrids a year by eventually offering 50 different hybrid models.[20]

Also, more and more businesses are setting explicit objectives for performance standards other than profitability. As public concern about environmental issues mounts, many firms find that operating in an environmentally responsible manner pays off in good relations with customers. Others channel some of their profits into socially responsible causes, such as funding educational programs and scholarships.

## Creating Strategies for Competitive Differentiation

Developing a mission statement and setting objectives point a business toward a specific destination. To get there, however, the firm needs to map the strategies it will follow to compete with other companies pursuing similar missions and objectives. The underlying goal of strategy development is **competitive differentiation,** the unique combination of a company's abilities and approaches that sets it apart from competitors. Common sources of competitive differentiation include product innovation, technology, and employee motivation.

Home Box Office (HBO), the subscription cable TV movie channel, uses a differentiation strategy to set itself apart from its competitors such as Starz and Showtime. Like its competitors, HBO spends half a billion dollars a year to acquire the rights to broadcast first-run movies. But it differentiates itself by spending an additional half billion dollars to develop its own programming, such as *Six Feet Under, Sex and the City,* and *The Sopranos,* among others. As a result, 90 percent of cable and satellite customers who pay for premium TV services subscribe to HBO. In turn, HBO is more profitable than the ABC, CBS, NBC, and Fox television networks put together. Chris Albrecht, HBO's chairman, said, "HBO is the most profitable network in the world and will continue to be as long as anybody can see."[21]

## Implementing the Strategy

Once the first four phases of the strategic planning process are complete, managers face even bigger challenges. They must put strategic plans into action by identifying specific action stops and deploying the resources needed to implement the intended plans.

Capital One Financial—headquartered in Falls Church, Virginia—is a major player in the credit card industry. Capital One's "information strategy" is based on the idea that it can make more money and serve customers better when it has detailed data about customers, their finances, and their spending habits. For example, thanks to its extensive database, when customers phone Capital One, the person they talk to knows exactly how profitable each customer is to the bank, whether they are likely to accept or reject a particular credit card or banking product, and what types of concessions, such as lower rates or forgiving fees, they've received in the past. Also, Capital One constantly adds to its customer database, which is between 180 and 200 terabytes of information (a terabyte is the same as 500 million pages of single-spaced text), by running 65,000 different market tests a year (a test is a unique combination of credit card features, terms, and market promotions), with each test being sent to between 5,000 and 10,000 customers. Why conduct so many tests and collect so much information? Because, says vice president Mike Rowen, "We are the ultimate pack rats. You never know what's valuable. We like to keep things, and we go look at them."[22]

## Monitoring and Adapting Strategic Plans

The final step in the strategic planning process, which naturally follows implementation, is to monitor and adapt plans when actual performance fails to match expectations. Monitoring involves establishing methods of securing feedback about actual performance. Common methods include comparing actual sales and market share data with forecasts, compiling information from supplier and customer surveys, monitoring complaints from the firm's customer hot line, and reviewing reports prepared by production, finance, marketing, and other company units.

Ongoing use of such tools as SWOT analysis and forecasting can help managers adapt objectives and functional plans as changes occur. An increase in the price of a key product component, for instance, could dramatically affect the firm's ability to maintain planned prices and still earn acceptable profits. An unexpected UPS strike may disrupt shipments of products to retail and business customers. In each instance, the original plan may require modification to continue to guide the firm toward achievement of its objectives.

**assessment check**

1. What is the purpose of a mission statement?
2. Which of the firm's characteristics does a SWOT analysis compare?
3. How do managers use objectives?

# MANAGERS AS DECISION MAKERS

In carrying out planning and the other management functions, executives must make decisions every day. **Decision making** is the process of recognizing a problem or opportunity and then dealing with it. Managers make two basic kinds of decisions, programmed decisions and nonprogrammed decisions.

## Programmed and Nonprogrammed Decisions

A **programmed decision** involves simple, common, and frequently occurring problems for which solutions have already been determined. Examples of programmed decisions include assigning a starting salary for the new marketing assistant, reordering raw materials needed in

**decision making** process of recognizing a problem or opportunity, evaluating alternative solutions, selecting and implementing an alternative, and assessing the results.

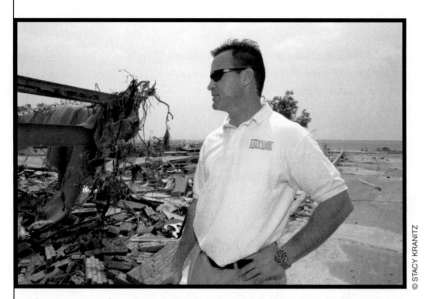

Ed Weingartner's firm, Dynamic Restoration, specializes in repairs and reconstruction after disasters, such as the hurricanes that devastated the Gulf Coast. Making quick decisions is crucial so that buildings can be saved, dried out, and restored instead of being demolished. Weingartner must determine whether to hire additional staff to meet expected demand before he has signed contracts, decide where to position teams before storms hit so that they are in place when needed, and estimate the amount of equipment to move or rent for the teams to do their work.

the manufacturing process, and setting a discount schedule for large-volume customers. For these types of decisions, organizations develop rules, policies, and detailed procedures that managers apply to achieve consistent, quick, and inexpensive solutions to common problems. Because such solutions eliminate the time-consuming process of identifying and evaluating alternatives and making new decisions each time a situation occurs, managers can devote their time to the more complex problems associated with nonprogrammed decisions. For example, routine review of the inventory of fresh produce might allow the buyer at Whole Foods Market more time to seek other merchandising opportunities.

A **nonprogrammed decision** involves a complex and unique problem or opportunity with important consequences for the organization. Examples of nonprogrammed decisions include entering a new geographical market, acquiring another company, or introducing a new product. For example, when Microsoft introduced its new Xbox 360 game console, it was the responsibility of Todd Holmdahl, Microsoft's vice president of Xbox manufacturing, to coordinate the flow and manufacture of the Xbox's 1,700 different parts. Approximately 25,000 employees working for 250 suppliers make the parts in China, Japan, Korea, Taiwan, Canada, and La Crosse, Wisconsin, which are assembled in two key plants in China. Says Holmdahl, "With 1,700 components all it takes is one not being there and it's an issue." And not only was the number of parts and the number of suppliers an issue, so was the scale of production, as Microsoft expected to sell 3 million consoles within 90 days and 5.5 million within 8 months. Over time as the bugs were worked out of the production process, Holmdahl switched from making the thousands of unique, nonprogrammed decisions related to the start-up to making the programmed decisions needed to tweak and improve the Xbox manufacturing process. And when those decisions had to be made, said Holmdahl, "Everybody has my phone number here."[23]

## How Managers Make Decisions

In a narrow sense, decision making involves choosing among two or more alternatives with the chosen alternative becoming the decision. In a broader sense, decision making involves a systematic, step-by-step process that helps managers make effective choices. This process begins when someone recognizes a problem or opportunity; it proceeds by developing potential courses of action, evaluating the alternatives, selecting and implementing one of them, and assessing the outcome of the decision. The steps in the decision-making process are illustrated in Figure 8.4. This systematic approach can be applied to all decisions, with either programmed or nonprogrammed features.

The decision-making process can be applied in both for-profit and not-for-profit organizations. Consider how Michael Miller built the Portland, Oregon, Goodwill Industries retail business of selling donated items. Miller knew that he had to locate stores where Goodwill's donors and customers meshed. Surveys uncovered that the typical donor was female, age 35 to

Figure

8.4

Steps in the Decision-Making Process

Recognize Problem or Opportunity → Develop Alternative Courses of Action → Evaluate Alternatives → Select and Implement Chosen Alternative → Follow Up to Determine Effectiveness of Decision

44, with an income of $50,000. In contrast, Miller's customers were women age 25 to 54 with two kids. Their average income was roughly $30,000. Miller then got some help from the locally based Fred Meyer supermarket chain (part of Kroger). Fred Meyer's database contained gender and income demographics by neighborhood. Miller's decision to open stores was then based on where his two target clients intersected. To make customers more comfortable, Miller's 28 stores even feature bookstores and coffee bars.[24]

Making good decisions is never easy, however, because it involves taking risks that can influence a firm's success or failure. Managers' decisions often have complex legal and ethical dimensions. An executive research firm recently tested 1,400 managers to assess their integrity and found that one in eight "believe the rules do not apply to them" and they "rarely possess feelings of guilt."[25]

**assessment check**

1. Compare and contrast programmed and nonprogrammed decisions.

2. What are the steps in the decision-making process?

# MANAGERS AS LEADERS

The most visible component of a manager's responsibilities is **leadership,** directing or inspiring people to attain organizational goals. Leadership is how former CEO Gordon Bethune turned around Continental Airlines and its previously poisonous labor-management relations. Bethune explained it this way: "When I was a mechanic, I knew how much faster I could fix an airplane when I wanted to fix it than when I didn't," he said. "I've tried to make it so our guys want to do it."[26] Because effective leadership is so important to organizational success, a large amount of research has focused on the characteristics of a good leader. Great leaders do not all share the same qualities, but three traits are often mentioned: empathy, which is the ability to imagine yourself in another's position; self-awareness; and objectivity in dealing with others. Many great leaders share other traits, including courage, ability to inspire others, passion, commitment, flexibility, innovation, and willingness to experiment.

Leadership involves the use of influence or power. This influence may come from one or more sources. One source of power is the leader's position in the organization. A national sales manager has the authority to direct the activities of the sales force. Another source of power is a leader's expertise and experience. A first-line supervisor with expert machinist skills will most likely be respected by employees in the machining department. Some leaders derive power from their personalities. Employees may admire a leader because they recognize an exceptionally kind and fair, humorous, energetic, or enthusiastic person.

A well-known example is Herb Kelleher, the retired CEO and now chairman of Southwest Airlines. Kelleher's legendary ability to motivate employees to outperform those at rival airlines came from his dynamic personality, boundless energy, love of fun, and sincere concern for his employees. Kelleher led by example, modeling the behavior he wanted to see in his

**leadership** ability to direct or inspire people to attain organizational goals.

**"They Said It"**

"A great leader is not one who does the greatest things. He's the one who gets the people to do the greatest things."
—Ronald Reagan
(1911–2004)
40th president
of the United States

employees. He pitched in to help serve snacks to passengers and load luggage. Employees, inspired by his example, now unload and reload a plane in 20 minutes—one-half of the average time for other airlines.

## Leadership Styles

The way a person uses power to lead others determines his or her leadership style. Researchers have identified a continuum of leadership styles based on the amount of employee participation allowed or invited. At one end of the continuum, **autocratic leadership** is centered on the boss. Autocratic leaders make decisions on their own without consulting employees. They reach decisions, communicate them to subordinates, and expect prompt implementation of instructions. An autocratic sales manager might assign quotas to individual salespeople without consulting them.

**Democratic leadership** involves subordinates in making decisions. Located in the middle of the continuum, this leadership style centers on employees' contributions. Democratic leaders delegate assignments, ask employees for suggestions, and encourage participation. An important trend that has developed in business during the past decade is the concept of **empowerment,** a practice in which managers lead employees by sharing power, responsibility, and decision making with them.

Sometimes the sharing of power is institutionalized, as in a company like Southwest Airlines. Southwest has the highest proportion of union members among all U.S. air carriers and is the only one of the country's top eight airlines to consistently post a profit. Rules governing contract negotiations in unionized firms require labor and management to sit down together and discuss wages, hours, and benefits each time the contract is up for renewal. Typically, such negotiations are contentious, stressful, and difficult. At Southwest Airlines, however, they are much less so because of the positive way in which management treats workers. Colleen Barrett, who started as a legal secretary and is now company president, comments: "Our industry is unionized, and we are too. [Eighty-one percent of Southwest's employees belong to a union.] If you don't have the basic altruistic and caring attitude toward your employees at all times, then, when you have heavy-duty contract negotiations, people won't believe anything that you do if it is out of the norm when there wasn't a contract negotiation. It is so simple to me. We approach labor relations in a totally different way. We approach them as a team. We acknowledge we are going to have strong disagreements. But it is like politicians: We all have our constituents, but there should be common goals and behaviors and expectations that must be met."[27]

At the other end of the continuum from autocratic leadership is **free-rein leadership.** Free-rein leaders believe in minimal supervision. They leave most decisions to their subordinates. Free-rein leaders communicate with employees frequently, as the situation warrants.

## Which Leadership Style Is Best?

The most appropriate leadership style depends on the function of the leader, the subordinates, and the situation. Some leaders cannot work comfortably with a high degree of subordinate participation in decision making. Some employees lack the ability or the desire to assume responsibility. In addition, the specific situation helps determine the most effective style of interactions. Sometimes managers must handle problems that require immediate solutions without consulting employees. When time pressure is less acute, participative decision making may work better for the same people.

Democratic leaders often ask for suggestions and advice from their employees but make the final decisions themselves. A manager who prefers the free-rein leadership style may be forced by circumstances to make a particular decision in an autocratic manner. A manager may involve employees in interviewing and hiring decisions but take complete responsibility for firing an employee.

After years of research intended to determine the best types of leaders, experts agree that they cannot identify any single best style of leadership. Instead, they contend that the most effective style depends on the leader's base of power, the difficulty of the tasks involved, and the characteristics of the employees. Both extremely easy and extremely difficult situations are best suited to leaders who emphasize the accomplishment of assigned tasks. Moderately difficult situations are best suited to leaders who emphasize participation and good working relationships with subordinates.

**assessment check**

1. How is leadership defined?
2. Identify the styles of leadership as they appear along a continuum of greater or lesser employee participation.

# CORPORATE CULTURE

The best leadership style to adopt often depends on the organization's **corporate culture**, its system of principles, beliefs, and values. Managerial philosophies, communications networks, and workplace environments and practices all influence corporate culture. At Home Depot, the corporate culture is based on the belief that employees should fully understand and be enthusiastic about the core business of serving do-it-yourselfers. All newly hired employees, including top managers, must spend their first two weeks working on the sales floor of a Home Depot store. Even CEO Robert Nardelli spends time at an Atlanta-area store helping customers. By working at stores, all employees are exposed to the company's customers and, the company hopes, will soak up some of their can-do spirit. The company also encourages employees to get involved in service projects, such as building homes for Habitat for Humanity, which brings them closer to their community while seeing the stores' products in use. In addition, Home Depot gets employees excited about the business by granting them stock options. This benefit has made millionaires of many Home Depot employees. Stories like that of Franc Gambatse, who started as a sales clerk and less than a decade later was managing a Home Depot store and enjoying prosperity he "never could have imagined," inspire other employees to give their all. The retailer even has a company cheer: "Gimme an H!" and on through the store's name, as the troops reply, ready to support the company's continued growth in stores, sales, and profits.[28]

A corporate culture is typically shaped by the leaders who founded and developed the company and by those who have succeeded them. One generation of employees passes on a corporate culture to newer employees. Sometimes this transfer is part of formal training. New managers who attend sessions at McDonald's Hamburger University may learn skills in management, but they also acquire the basic values of the organization's corporate culture established by McDonald's founder Ray Kroc: quality, service, cleanliness, and value.[29] Employees can absorb corporate culture through informal contacts, as well as by talking with other workers and through their experiences on the job.

Managers use symbols, rituals, ceremonies, and stories to reinforce corporate culture. San Antonio–based Valero Energy Corporation, an oil refining company, has a tough corporate culture—dress codes for managers and regular drug testing to ensure employee safety—but it also puts employees first with its no-layoff policy and by firing managers for cursing at subordinates. When Hurricane Katrina hit, the dedication of Valero's staff shone through—they repaired its severely damaged facilities weeks and months faster than its competitors did. The company had stationed a 50-person "ride-out" crew at its St. Charles refinery, which is near New Orleans. One maintenance supervisor used his personal credit card to stock food for the crew before the storm hit and then stayed up round the clock to cook gumbo for them afterward as

**corporate culture** organization's system of principles, beliefs, and values.

they completed their repairs. CEO Bill Greehey praised his employees' extra efforts, saying, "We got this refinery running, [and] it will be weeks before the refinery across the street is running. . . . How you jump-started and got this thing done—I guarantee it, no one else could do what you did. No one."[30]

Corporate cultures can be changed. When Paul Pressler became the CEO of Gap Inc. several years ago, one of his goals was to change what his managers thought and valued, in other words, the culture. In particular, Pressler wanted his managers and workers to stop thinking and caring just about their business units, such as Gap, Banana Republic, Old Navy, and Forth & Towne and to begin working together across units, functions, brands, and international borders. Pressler began this cultural change by introducing Gap's Purposes, Values, and Behaviors (PVBs), which described what was important in the new culture. The first step was to introduce the PVBs to Gap's 2,000 top managers at numerous full-day meetings called "Leadership Summits." Only then did Gap roll out the PVBs to its 150,000 employees, along with posters, coffee cups, an internal employee-only Gap Web site, and a newsletter, all of which were used to highlight stories and examples critical to Gap's new cooperative, company-wide culture.[31]

In an organization with strong culture, everyone knows and supports the same principles, beliefs, and values. A company with weak or constantly shifting culture lacks a clear sense of purpose. To achieve goals, a business must also provide a framework that defines how employees should accomplish their tasks. This framework is the organization structure, which results from the management function of organizing.

**assessment check**

1. What is the relationship between leadership style and corporate culture?
2. What is a strong corporate culture?

**organization** structured grouping of people working together to achieve common goals.

UPI PHOTO/D. VAN/LANDOV

# ORGANIZATIONAL STRUCTURES

The management function of organizing is the process of blending human and material resources through a formal structure of tasks and authority. It involves arranging work, dividing tasks among employees, and coordinating them to ensure implementation of plans and accomplishment of objectives. The result of this process is an **organization,** a structured grouping of people working together to achieve common goals. An organization features three key elements: human interaction, goal-directed activities, and structure. The organizing process should result in an overall structure that permits interactions among individuals and departments needed to achieve company goals.

The steps involved in the organizing process are shown in Figure 8.5. Managers first determine the specific activities needed to implement plans and achieve goals. Next, they group these work activities into a logical structure. Then they assign work to specific employees and give the people the resources they need to complete it. Managers coordinate the work of different groups and employees within the firm. Finally, they evaluate the results of the organizing process to ensure effective and efficient progress toward planned goals. Evaluation often results in changes to the way work is organized.

Many factors influence the results of organizing. The list includes a firm's goals and competitive strategy, the type of product it offers, the way it uses tech-

Oprah Winfrey's success is legendary. But she learned the hard way that she couldn't rely on an informal structure for her business—employees didn't have the same assumptions that she had about the company's direction. So she developed a formal communication system and structure to let all employees know her expectations for their performance.

Figure

8.5

Steps in the Organizing Process

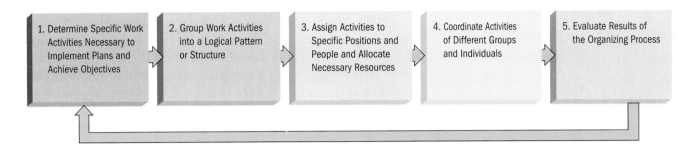

1. Determine Specific Work Activities Necessary to Implement Plans and Achieve Objectives → 2. Group Work Activities into a Logical Pattern or Structure → 3. Assign Activities to Specific Positions and People and Allocate Necessary Resources → 4. Coordinate Activities of Different Groups and Individuals → 5. Evaluate Results of the Organizing Process

nology to accomplish work, and its size. Small firms typically create very simple structures. The owner of a dry-cleaning business generally is the top manager, who hires several employees to process orders, clean the clothing, and make deliveries. The owner handles the functions of purchasing supplies such as detergents and hangers, hiring and training employees and coordinating their work, preparing advertisements for the local newspaper, and keeping accounting records.

As a company grows, its structure increases in complexity. With increased size comes specialization and growing numbers of employees. A larger firm may employ many salespeople, along with a sales manager to direct and coordinate their work, or organize an accounting department and hire employees to work as payroll clerks and cost accountants.

The organizing process should result in a well-defined structure so that employees know what expectations their jobs involve, to whom they report, and how their work contributes to the company's effort to meet its goals. To help employees understand how their work fits within the overall operation of the firm, managers prepare an **organization chart,** which is a visual representation of a firm's structure that illustrates job positions and functions. Figure 8.6 illustrates a sample organization chart. Each box in the chart would show a specific position. An organization chart depicts the division of a firm into departments that meet organizational needs.

Figure

8.6

Sample Organization Chart

Not-for-profit organizations also have specific structures. The Catholic Church, for example, is a hierarchy with clearly defined levels and a strict reporting structure. The head of the church is the pope, based at the Vatican in Rome. The pope is held to be preeminent in matters of church doctrine, but responsibility for administering the church's many other functions is dispersed downward in the hierarchy. Looking only at the U.S. church, we find 13 cardinals appointed by the pope. The cardinals advise the pope and are responsible for electing a new pope when the current one dies. Reporting to the U.S. cardinals are 45 archbishops, who preside over major dioceses or congregational areas. Next in rank are 290 bishops, about half of whom head the country's dioceses. Bishops are teachers of doctrine and ministers of the church's government. Priests are the final level of the church hierarchy.[32]

## Departmentalization

**departmentalization**
process of dividing work activities into units within the organization.

**Departmentalization** is the process of dividing work activities into units within the organization. This arrangement lets employees specialize in certain jobs to promote efficient performance. The marketing effort may be headed by a sales and marketing vice president, who directs the work of salespeople, marketing researchers, and advertising and promotion personnel. A human resources manager may head a department made up of people with special skills in such areas as recruiting and hiring, employee benefits, and labor relations. The five major forms of departmentalization subdivide work by product, geographical area, customer, function, and process:

- *Product departmentalization.* This approach organizes work units based on the goods and services a company offers. The "Hit & Miss" feature explains how IBM, which once struggled to turn its research and development ideas into competitive products, is now using independent divisions, called "emerging business opportunities" or EBOs, to take ideas from the research lab to the marketplace. EBOs are a special kind of product departmentalization.
- *Geographical departmentalization.* This form organizes units by geographical regions within a country or, for a multinational firm, by region throughout the world. Some retailers, such as Dillard's, are organized by divisions that serve different parts of the country. Railroads and gas and oil distributors also favor geographical departmentalization.
- *Customer departmentalization.* A firm that offers a variety of goods and services targeted at different types of customers might structure itself based on customer departmentalization. Management of 3M's 50,000 products is divided among seven business units: consumer and office; display and graphics; electro and communications; healthcare; industrial; safety, security, and protection services; and transportation.[33]
- *Functional departmentalization.* Some firms organize work units according to business functions such as finance, marketing, human resources, and production. An advertising agency may create departments for creatives (say, copywriters), media buyers, and account executives.
- *Process departmentalization.* Some goods and services require multiple work processes to complete their production. A manufacturer may set up separate departments for cutting material, heat-treating it, forming it into its final shape, and painting it.

As Figure 8.7 on page 276 illustrates, a single company may implement several different departmentalization schemes. The departments initially are organized by functions and then subdivided by geographical areas, which are further organized according to customer types. In deciding on a form of departmentalization, managers take into account the type of product they produce, the size of their company, their customer base, and the locations of their customers.

# HIT & MISS

## IBM Refocuses on Emerging Business Opportunities

Sometimes it's difficult for a large organization to move quickly. With 300,000 people creating $80 billion in annual revenue, IBM is among the world's largest and most successful companies. Yet a few years ago, it watched nimble start-up companies such as Cisco and Oracle turn its own innovations, such as the relationship database and the router, into profitable real-world applications.

Lou Gerstner Jr., then chairman and CEO, decided to change the pattern. IBM's researchers won record-breaking numbers of awards and patents every year, but the company's short-term focus on cutting department costs hampered them in developing their concepts. "Everything was based on the current period, not on the future," says one of the company's strategic planners. Another problem was that inexperienced employees were put in charge of developing risky new ideas. "We were not putting the best and brightest talent on this," says the company's senior vice president for strategy.

Now, however, star performers such as Ron Adkins, who once ran the $4 billion Unix computing division, are given the job of growing specific new ideas into businesses in what IBM calls "emerging business opportunities," or EBOs. Begun in 2000 with the goal of creating about $2 billion of new revenue a year, the EBO program has launched 22 successful projects out of 25 started, with combined annual revenues of $15 billion. Growing at about 40 percent a year, the program is not only attracting talented managers but also changing the company's culture. "Through EBOs, IBM has become more of a learning organization," says one EBO leader. "We've become more willing to experiment, more willing to accept failure, learn from it, and move on. It's more a part of our culture and our official processes. Now being an EBO leader is a really desirable job at IBM."

That's quite a change from Ron Adkins's reaction to being placed in charge of the pilot EBO in 2000. His operation now earns $2.4 billion a year in sales of wireless technology applications. But stripped of his 35,000 Unix employees and his operating budget, Adkins at first thought he'd been fired. "Geez," he recalls thinking. "What do I tell my mom?"

### Questions for Critical Thinking

1. Do you think the creation of the EBO program shifted IBM's corporate strategy? Why or why not?
2. How would you characterize the relationship between corporate strategy and corporate culture, using IBM as an example?

**Sources:** "Background," accessed June 27, 2006, IBM http://www.ibm.com/us; Alan Deutschman, "Building a Better Skunk Works," *Fast Company*, accessed June 27, 2006, http://www.fastcompany.com; Martin LaMonica, "Does IBM's Success Herald a Software Comeback?" CNet News.com, accessed June 27, 2006, http://news.com.com; Michael Kanellos, "Research: From Lab to Market," CNet News.com, accessed June 27, 2006, http://news.com.com.

## Delegating Work Assignments

After grouping activities into departments, managers assign this work to employees. The act of assigning activities to employees is called **delegation.** Managers delegate work to free their own time for planning and decision making. Subordinates to whom managers assign tasks thus receive responsibility, or obligations to perform those tasks. Along with responsibilities, employees also receive authority, or the power to make decisions and to act on them so they can carry out their responsibilities. Delegation of responsibility and authority makes employees accountable to their supervisor or manager. *Accountability* means that employees are responsible for the results of the ways they perform their assignments; they must accept the consequences of their actions.

Authority and responsibility tend to move downward in organizations, as managers and supervisors delegate work to subordinates. However, accountability moves upward, as managers assume final accountability for performance by the people they manage.

**delegation** act of assigning work activities to subordinates.

Figure

**Span of Management** The **span of management,** or *span of control,* is the number of subordinates a manager supervises. The subordinates are often referred to as *direct reports.* First-line managers have wider spans of management, monitoring the work of many employees. The span of management varies considerably depending on many factors, including the type of work performed and employees' training. In recent years, a growing trend has brought ever wider spans of control, as companies have reduced their layers of management to flatten their organizational structures, in the process increasing the decision-making responsibility they give employees.

**span of management** number of subordinates a manager can supervise effectively.

*Centralization and Decentralization* How widely should managers disperse decision-making authority throughout an organization? A company that emphasizes **centralization** retains decision making at the top of the management hierarchy. A company that emphasizes **decentralization** locates decision making at lower levels. A trend toward decentralization has pushed decision making down to operating employees in many cases. Firms that have decentralized believe that the change can enhance their flexibility and responsiveness in serving customers. Christine Poon is executive vice chairman at Johnson & Johnson in charge of pharmaceuticals and biotechnology. With more than 220 different business units worldwide, Johnson & Johnson has to rely on decentralization. Says Poon, "The most important thing a leader can do is find good people and match them with what they like to do and what they're good at." Why this employee focus? Because "you can't run a company of more than 100,000 people waiting for the [people at the] top to tell them what to do."[34]

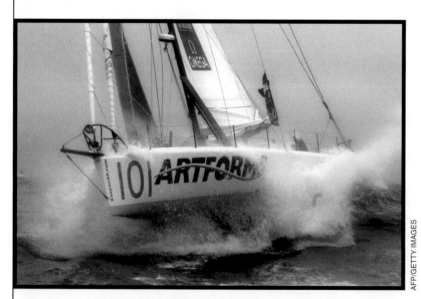

Kip Stone founded his T-shirt design and production business, Artforms, in West-brook, Maine, and worked for fifteen years to build it into a first-class company. Once Artforms was on stable footing, he decided to pursue his other passion—competitive ocean sailing. So instead of hiring hard workers that he would manage, he focused on hiring managers with expertise in accounting, production, inventory, and sales to whom he could delegate daily decision-making authority. Both Artforms and Stone have thrived as a result.

## Types of Organization Structures

The four primary types of organization structures are line, line-and-staff, committee, and matrix structures. These terms do not specify mutually exclusive categories, though. In fact, most modern organizations combine elements of one or more of these structures.

*Line Organizations* A **line organization,** the oldest and simplest organization structure, establishes a direct flow of authority from the chief executive to subordinates. The line organization defines a simple, clear **chain of command**—a set of relationships that indicates who gives direction to whom and who reports to whom. This arrangement helps prevent buck passing. Decisions can be made quickly because the manager has authority to control subordinates' actions.

A line organization has an obvious defect, though. Each manager must accept complete responsibility for a number of activities and cannot possibly be an expert in all of them. This defect is apparent in midsize and large firms, where the pure line structure fails to take advantage of the specialized skills that are so vital to business today. Managers become overburdened with details and paperwork, leaving them little time for planning.

As a result, the line organization is an ineffective model in any but the smallest organizations. Hair-styling salons, so-called mom-and-pop grocery stores, and small law firms can operate effectively with simple line structures. The Coca-Cola Company, General Electric, and ExxonMobil cannot.

*Line-and-Staff Organizations*  A **line-and-staff organization** combines the direct flow of authority of a line organization with staff departments that support the line departments. Line departments participate directly in decisions that affect the core operations of the organization. Staff departments lend specialized technical support. Examples of staff departments include labor relations, legal counsel, and information technology. Figure 8.8 illustrates a line-and-staff organization. Accounting, engineering, and human resources are staff departments that support the line authority extending from the plant manager to the production manager and supervisors.

A line manager and a staff manager differ significantly in their authority relationships. A **line manager** forms part of the primary line of authority that flows throughout the organization. Line managers interact directly with the functions of production, financing, or marketing—the functions needed to produce and sell goods and services. A **staff manager** provides information, advice, or technical assistance to aid line managers. Staff managers do not have authority to give orders outside their own departments or to compel line managers to take action.

The line-and-staff organization is common in midsize and large organizations. It is an effective structure because it combines the line organization's capabilities for rapid decision making and direct communication with the expert knowledge of staff specialists.

*Committee Organizations*  A **committee organization** is a structure that places authority and responsibility jointly in the hands of a group of individuals rather than a single manager. This model typically appears as part of a regular line-and-staff structure. Examples of the committee structure emerge throughout organizations at one point in time. Nordstrom, the department store chain, once had an "office of the co-presidency" in which six members of the Nordstrom family shared the top job.

Committees also work in areas such as new-product development. A new-product committee may include managers from such areas as accounting, engineering, finance, manufacturing, marketing, and technical research. By including representatives from all areas involved in creating and marketing products, such a committee generally improves planning and employee morale because decisions reflect diverse perspectives.

**chain of command** set of relationships that indicates who directs which activities and who reports to whom.

**"They Said It"**

"The university is incapable of ordering blackboard erasers in quantities of more than six without a committee."
—Lawrence H. Summers (b. 1954)
Former President, Harvard University

**Figure**

**8.8**

Line-and-Staff Organization

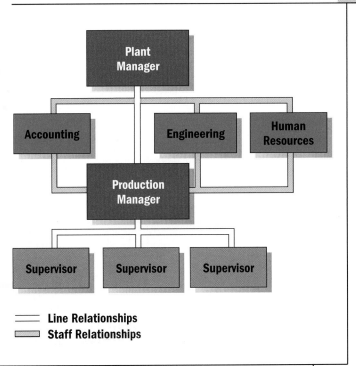

— Line Relationships
▭ Staff Relationships

Committees tend to act slowly and conservatively, however, and they often make decisions by compromising conflicting interests rather than by choosing the best alternative. The definition of a camel as "a racehorse designed by committee" provides an apt description of some limitations of committee decisions. At Nordstrom, the six-person office of the co-presidency was eventually abandoned for a more traditional structure.

*Matrix Organizations*   Some organizations use the **matrix,** or project management, **structure.** This structure links employees from different parts of the organization to work together on specific projects. Figure 8.9 diagrams a matrix structure. For a specific project, a project manager assembles a group of employees from different functional areas. The employees retain their ties to the line-and-staff structure, as shown in the vertical white lines. As the horizontal gold lines indicate, however, employees are also members of project teams. Upon completion of a project, employees return to their "regular" jobs.

In the matrix structure, each employee reports to two managers: one line manager and one project manager. Employees who are selected to work on a special project, such as development of a new product, receive instructions from the project manager (horizontal authority), but they continue as employees in their permanent functional departments (vertical authority). The term *matrix* comes from the intersecting grid of horizontal and vertical lines of authority.

**Figure**

8.9   Matrix Organization

The matrix structure has become popular at high-technology and multinational corporations, as well as hospitals, consulting firms, and aerospace firms. Dow Chemical and Procter & Gamble have both used matrix structures. The National Aeronautics and Space Administration used the matrix structure for its Mercury and Apollo space missions.

The major benefits of the matrix structure come from its flexibility in adapting quickly to rapid changes in the environment and its capability of focusing resources on major problems or products. It also provides an outlet for employees' creativity and initiative, giving them opportunities that their functional jobs may deny them. However, it challenges the project manager to integrate the skills of specialists from many departments into a coordinated team. Another disadvantage is that employees may be confused and frustrated in reporting to two bosses. Dick Nicholson, who worked for a packaging manufacturer that used a matrix design, found it frustrating. Nicholson said, "Everyone who could fog a mirror thought he was my boss." When asked whether that simplified who was in charge, he responded, "It didn't in my experience. Everyone just became a boss."[35]

# WHAT'S AHEAD

In the next chapter, we sharpen our focus on the importance of people—the human resource—in shaping the growth and profitability of the organization. We examine how firms recruit, select, train, evaluate, and compensate employees in their attempts to attract, retain, and motivate a high-quality workforce. The concept of motivation is examined, and we will discuss how managers apply theories of motivation in the modern workplace. The next chapter also looks at the important topic of labor–management relations.

## Summary of Learning Goals

**1 Define *management* and the three types of skills necessary for managerial success.**

Management is the process of achieving organizational objectives through people and other resources. The management hierarchy depicts the levels of management in organizations: Top managers provide overall direction for company activities, middle managers implement the strategies of top managers and direct the activities of supervisors, and supervisors interact directly with workers. The three basic managerial skills are technical skills, or the ability to apply the techniques, tools, and knowledge of a specific discipline or department; human skills, which involve working effectively with and through people; and conceptual skills, or the capability to see an overall view of the organization and how each part contributes to its functioning.

### Assessment Check Answers

**1.1 What is management?**

Management is the process of achieving organizational objectives through people and other resources. The manager's job is to combine human and technical resources in the best way possible to achieve the company's goals.

**1.2 How do the jobs of top managers, middle managers, and supervisory managers differ?**

Top managers develop long-range plans, set a direction for their organization, and inspire managers and employees to achieve the company's vision. Middle managers focus on specific operations, products, or customer groups and develop detailed plans and procedures to implement the firm's strategic plans. Supervisory managers are directly responsible for evaluating the performance of nonmanagerial employees who produce and sell the firm's goods and services. They are responsible for implementing the plans developed by middle managers and motivating workers to accomplish daily, weekly, and monthly goals.

### 1.3 What is the relationship between the manager's planning and controlling functions?

Controlling is evaluating an organization's performance to determine whether it is accomplishing its objectives. The basic purpose of controlling is to assess the success of the planning function. Controlling also provides feedback for future rounds of planning.

### 2 Explain the role of vision and ethical standards in business success.

Vision is the ability to perceive the needs of the marketplace and develop methods for satisfying those needs. Vision helps new businesses pinpoint the actions needed to take advantage of opportunities. In an existing firm, a clear vision of company purpose helps unify the actions of far-flung divisions, keep customers satisfied, and sustain growth. Setting high ethical standards helps a firm survive and be successful over the long term. Behaving ethically places an organization's constituents—those to whom it is responsible—at the top of its priorities. It also goes beyond avoiding wrongdoing to encouraging, motivating, and inspiring employees.

## Assessment Check Answers

### 2.1 What is meant by a vision for the firm?

A vision serves as the target for a firm's actions, helping direct the company toward opportunities and differentiating it from its competitors. Vision must be focused and yet flexible enough to adapt to changes in the business environment.

### 2.2 Why is it important for a top executive to set high ethical standards?

When top managers engage in unethical behavior, their actions encourage others to do the same. Legal charges, fines, prison time, financial losses, and bankruptcy can result. Because they set the standards for others, executives need to focus on achieving personal and organizational success in ethical ways.

### 3 Summarize the major benefits of planning and distinguish among strategic planning, tactical planning, and operational planning.

The planning process identifies organizational goals and develops the actions necessary to reach them. Planning helps a company turn vision into action, take advantage of opportunities, and avoid costly mistakes. Strategic planning is a far-reaching process. It views the world through a wide-angle lens to determine the long-range focus and activities of the organization. Tactical planning focuses on the current and short-range activities required to implement the organization's strategies. Operational planning sets standards and work targets for functional areas such as production, human resources, and marketing.

## Assessment Check Answers

### 3.1 Outline the planning process.

Some plans are very broad and long range, focusing on key organizational objectives; others are more detailed and specify how particular objectives will be achieved. From the mission statement to objectives to specific plans, each phase must fit into a comprehensive planning framework.

### 3.2 Describe the purpose of tactical planning.

The purpose of tactical planning is to determine which short-term activities should be implemented to accomplish the firm's overall strategy.

### 3.3 Compare the kinds of plans made by top managers and middle managers. How does their focus differ?

Top managers focus on long-range, strategic plans. In contrast, middle-level managers and supervisors focus on short-term, tactical planning.

### 4 Describe the strategic planning process.

The first step of strategic planning is to translate the firm's vision into a mission statement that explains its overall intentions and aims. Next, planners must assess the firm's current competitive position, using tools such as SWOT analysis—which weighs the firm's strengths, weaknesses, opportunities, and threats—and forecasting. Based on this information, managers set specific objectives that elaborate what the organization hopes to accomplish. The next step is to develop strategies for reaching objectives that will differentiate the firm from its competitors. Managers then develop an action plan that outlines the specific methods for implementing the strategy. Finally, the results achieved by the plan are evaluated, and the plan is adjusted as needed.

## Assessment Check Answers

### 4.1 What is the purpose of a mission statement?
A mission statement is a public declaration of a firm's purpose, the reason it exists, the customers it will serve, and the way it is different from competitors. A mission statement guides the actions of company managers and employees.

### 4.2 Which of the firm's characteristics does a SWOT analysis compare?
A SWOT analysis determines a firm's strengths, weaknesses, opportunities, and threats relative to its competitors. In other words, SWOT analysis helps determine a firm's competitive position in the marketplace.

### 4.3 How do managers use objectives?
Objectives, which are derived from the firm's mission statement, are used to define desired performance levels in areas such as profitability, customer service, and employee satisfaction.

**5** **Contrast the two major types of business decisions and list the steps in the decision-making process.**

A programmed decision applies a company rule or policy to solve a frequently occurring problem. A nonprogrammed decision forms a response to a complex and unique problem with important consequences for the organization. The five-step approach to decision making includes recognizing a problem or opportunity, developing alternative courses of action, evaluating the alternatives, selecting and implementing an alternative, and following up the decision to determine its effectiveness.

## Assessment Check Answers

### 5.1 Compare and contrast programmed and nonprogrammed decisions.
Because programmed decisions are simple and common and recur frequently, rules and policies can be established to eliminate the time-consuming process of identifying and evaluating alternatives and making new decisions each time a programmed situation occurs. By using rules and procedures to save time with programmed decisions, managers can devote more of their time to more complex nonprogrammed decisions.

### 5.2 What are the steps in the decision-making process?
The decision-making process begins when someone recognizes a problem or opportunity, develops potential courses of action to solve the problem, evaluates the alternatives, selects and implements one of them, and assesses the outcome of the decision.

**6** **Define *leadership* and compare different leadership styles.**

Leadership is the act of motivating others or causing them to perform activities designed to achieve specific objectives. The basic styles are autocratic, democratic, and free-rein leadership. The best leadership style depends on three elements: the leader, the followers, and the situation. Today's leaders tend increasingly to involve employees in making decisions about their work.

## Assessment Check Answers

### 6.1 How is leadership defined?
Leadership means directing or inspiring people to attain organizational goals. Effective leaders share several traits, such as empathy, self-awareness, and objectivity in dealing with others. Leaders also use the power of their jobs, expertise, and experience to influence others.

### 6.2 Identify the styles of leadership as they appear along a continuum of greater or lesser employee participation.
At one end of the continuum, autocratic leaders make decisions without consulting employees. In the middle of the continuum, democratic leaders ask employees for suggestions and encourage participation. At the other end of the continuum, free-rein leaders leave most decisions to their subordinates.

**7** **Discuss the meaning and importance of corporate culture.**

Corporate culture refers to an organization's principles, beliefs, and values. It is typically shaped by a firm's founder and perpetuated through formal programs such as training, rituals, and ceremonies, as well as through informal discussions among employees. Corporate culture can influence a firm's success by giving it a competitive advantage.

## Assessment Check Answers

### 7.1 What is the relationship between leadership style and corporate culture?

The best leadership style to adopt often depends on the organization's corporate culture and its system of principles, beliefs, and values. Managerial philosophies, communications networks, and workplace environments and practices all influence corporate culture.

### 7.2 What is a strong corporate culture?

A corporate culture is an organization's system of principles, beliefs, and values. In an organization with a strong culture, everyone knows and supports the same principles, beliefs, and values. A company with weak or constantly shifting culture lacks a clear sense of purpose.

### 8 Identify the five major forms of departmentalization and the four main types of organization structures.

The subdivision of work activities into units within the organization is called *departmentalization*. It may be based on products, geographical locations, customers, functions, or processes. Most firms implement one or more of four structures: line, line-and-staff, committee, and matrix structures. Each structure has advantages and disadvantages.

## Assessment Check Answers

### 8.1 What is the purpose of an organization chart?

An organization chart is a visual representation of a firm's structure that illustrates job positions and functions.

### 8.2 What are the five major forms of departmentalization?

Product departmentalization organizes units by the different goods and services a company offers. Geographical departmentalization organizes units by geographical regions within a country or, for a multinational firm, by regions throughout the world. Customer departmentalization organizes units by different types of customers. Functional departmentalization organizes units by business functions such as finance, marketing, human resources, and production. Process departmentalization organizes units by the steps or work processes it takes to complete production or provide a service.

### 8.3 What does *span of management* mean?

The span of management, or span of control, is the number of subordinates a manager supervises.

## Business Terms You Need to Know

| | | |
|---|---|---|
| management 254 | decision making 267 | delegation 275 |
| planning 258 | leadership 269 | span of management 276 |
| vision 259 | corporate culture 271 | chain of command 277 |
| mission statement 263 | organization 272 | |
| objectives 266 | departmentalization 274 | |

## Other Important Business Terms

top management 255
middle management 255
supervisory management 256
technical skills 256
human skills 257
conceptual skills 257
organizing 258
directing 258
controlling 258
strategic planning 261

tactical planning 261
operational planning 261
contingency planning 261
SWOT analysis 264
competitive differentiation 266
programmed decision 267
nonprogrammed decision 268
autocratic leadership 270
democratic leadership 270
empowerment 270

free-rein leadership 270
organization chart 273
centralization 276
decentralization 276
line organization 276
line-and-staff organization 277
line manager 277
staff manager 277
committee organization 277
matrix structure 278

## Review Questions

1. What is a management hierarchy? In what ways does it help organizations develop structure? In what ways could it be considered obsolete?

2. What are the three basic types of skills that managers must possess? Which type of skill is most important at each management level?

3. Identify and describe the four basic functions of managers.

4. Why is a clear vision particularly important for companies that have numerous operations around the country or around the world? Cite an example.

5. Which type of planning is most far-reaching? How does this type of planning affect other types of planning?

6. Suppose you planned a large cookout for your friends, but when you woke up on the morning of the party, it was pouring rain. What type of plan would allow you to cope with this situation? Specifically, what could you do?

7. As a student, you have a mission in school. Write your own mission statement for your education and program, including your goals and the ways you plan to accomplish them.

8. Identify each of the following as a programmed or nonprogrammed decision:
   a. reordering printer cartridges
   b. selecting a cell phone provider
   c. buying your favorite toothpaste and shampoo at the supermarket
   d. selecting a college to attend
   e. filling your car with gasoline

9. Identify the traits that are most often associated with great leaders. Which trait would be most important in the leader of a large corporation? A small company? Why?

10. Why is a strong corporate culture important to a company's success? Relate your answer to a specific firm.

1. Create a résumé for yourself, identifying your technical skills, human skills, and conceptual skills. Which set of skills do you think is your strongest? Why?

2. Think of a company with which you are familiar—either one you work for or one with whom you conduct business as a customer. Consider ways in which the organization can meet the needs of its marketplace. Then write a sentence or two describing what you think the organization's vision is—or should be.

3. Conduct your own SWOT analysis for a company with which you are familiar. Visit the organization's Web site to learn as much about the company as you can before stating your conclusions. Be as specific as possible in identifying your perceptions of the company's strengths, weaknesses, opportunities, and threats.

4. Identify a classmate or college friend who you think is a good leader. Describe the traits that you think are most important in making this person an effective leader.

5. Your school has its own organizational culture. Describe what you perceive to be its characteristics. Is the culture strong or weak? How does the culture affect you as a student?

## Case 8.1

### Kraft's Recipe for Success

Imitation is said to be the sincerest form of flattery, but when copycats undercut your prices and take business away, it's hard to feel complimented. Frustration over market losses to competitors who "borrow" ideas and create cheaper products is one reason Kraft Foods has doubled the number of patent lawyers on its staff. The company is fighting private-label food manufacturers that copy its popular products and sell them for less. Kraft figures that it takes competitors only six to twelve months to copy its new ideas, and part of its drive to nurture its development process and creative packaging ideas is to stem the flow of imitators.

New ideas are the lifeblood of any company, and for Northfield, Illinois–based Kraft, they are a key component of its strategy to be number one in every business it is in. The biggest food company in North America, second in the world only to Nestlé, Kraft has recently been reshaping itself to meet its ambitious goal, following a restructuring plan it calls the Sustainable Growth Plan. Although earnings increases have not been steady, so far the plan seems to be working. The company spent $19 billion to acquire ten competitors in the last few years. But it divested noncore businesses such as Life Savers candies and Altoid mints, selling them to Wrigley for a cool $12.5 billion.

In its new, streamlined form, the company plans to focus on powdered beverages, including those using proprietary technologies that are designed to address vitamin, mineral, and protein deficiencies; cracker chips, led by Ritz Chips in a single-serve package and a new BBQ flavor; a new microwave frozen pizza debuting in several flavors under the DiGiorno Thin Crust brand name; health and wellness products such as the new South Beach Diet line, which is introducing 27 items; and its proprietary Tassimo hot-beverage system, which makes coffeeshop-quality cappuccinos, lattes, and hot tea and hot chocolate at home. Says CEO Roger K. Deromedi, "We want the products that consumers and retailers are more excited about." In other words, Kraft wants to concentrate on the blockbuster brands that can rise to the top of their categories worldwide.

Because consolidation in the retail market has left manufacturers such as Kraft with fewer customers to sell to, Kraft also wants what giant retailers such as Wal-Mart want, which increasingly means fast-selling products that dominate their market. For instance, weight-conscious shoppers are expected to appreciate innovations such as the 100-calorie packages of favorite brands Chips Ahoy, Cheese Nips, Honey Maid Cinnamon Grahams, Ritz crackers, and Wheat Thins. Not merely repackaged snacks in single servings, these products feature reduced sugar and fat content that makes them more like crackers than cookies. Kraft also hopes the new DiGiorno pizza line will hit it big and bring in $75 million in sales, and its South Beach brand has a goal of reaping another $100 million. To reach those numbers, Kraft has increased its marketing budget by about $550 million and has committed to continue increasing its outlays for advertising and product development.

One potential stumbling block to Kraft's new strategy is that in the past it has risked saturating stores with too many variations of existing products, such as multiple varieties of Oreo cookies, instead of delivering truly new products as other consumer goods companies such as Procter & Gamble consistently manage to do. And, like all food producers, Kraft struggles with rising costs, driven by increased prices for raw materials such as coffee and nuts and for essentials such as energy and packaging materials. Hikes here could cost the company $600 million a year and force it to raise its own prices. Meanwhile, competitor Proc-

ter & Gamble is introducing reduced-fat Pringles chips in 100-calorie packs, and Kraft's drive to differentiate itself and reach number one in every category continues.

## Questions for Critical Thinking

1. What strategies can Kraft adopt that will allow it to succeed in the market for calorie-controlled foods such as its 100-calorie packs and South Beach Diet products? How can the company ensure that they do not undercut sales of its traditional snack products or lose out to competitors' efforts?

2. What are some of the possible downsides of the company's restructuring plan of selling off marginal or secondary businesses and acquiring competitors? What are some of the immediate and long-term advantages?

**Sources:** Melanie Warner, "Goodies in Small Packages Prove to Be a Big Hit," *New York Times*, accessed June 27, 2006, http://www.nytimes.com; "Brand Close-Ups," Kraft Foods, accessed January 17, 2006, http://www.kraft.com; Shirley A. Lazo, "The Big Cheese: Kraft Foods Slices Costs and Serves a Payout Hike," *Barron's*, August 29, 2005, http://online.barrons.com; "Kraft to Double Patent Lawyers," *Food & Drug Packaging*, accessed June 1, 2005, http://www.fdp.com; Michael Arndt, "Why Kraft Is on a Crash Diet," *BusinessWeek*, November 29, 2004, http://www.businessweek.com.

## VIDEO Case 8.2

### Made in the U.S.A.: American Apparel

This video case appears on page 616. A recently filmed video, designed to expand and highlight the written case, is available for class use by instructors.

# Chapter 9

Human Resource Management, Motivation, and Labor–Management Relations

Growing economies need raw materials. But there's a critical labor shortage in the world's mines just as demand is rapidly climbing in expanding markets such as China and India. Both of these countries—with populations of more than 1 billion each—are investing heavily in airports, roads, commercial buildings, and communication systems. As they build, their need for iron ore, coal, and other materials produced by mines is increasing at an unprecedented pace. Meanwhile, mining firms such as Virginia-based Massey Energy are scrambling to hire enough employees to fill their customers' needs, both in the United States and overseas.

Recruiting, hiring, training, and managing a world-class workforce is the goal of every company, and Massey Energy is no exception. To meet increased skilled workers. "It's a very high-tech business now with a lot of intellectual challenge and opportunities to do interesting things," says Mike Nelson, an associate professor

PHOTODISC/GETTY IMAGES

# Massey Energy: Mining for Employees

demand for its products, the company must attract qualified employees who possess specialized skills—or who can learn them—and who are willing to live in remote areas and face physical danger, such as the Sago Mine explosion in West Virginia that killed a dozen miners. In addition, a generation of well-trained engineers, electricians, and miners is beginning to retire. "In order to replace those who are retiring over the next 10 years, we'll have to triple our production of engineers," predicts Kim McCarter, chairman of the University of Utah's mining department. "That's not assuming any kind of growth. That's just replacing those who are retiring." Currently, only about 100 mining engineers graduate each year from U.S. colleges. Katharine Kenny, vice president at Massey, echoes this concern. "In this industry, it's tough enough just to maintain your [existing] workforce," she says. The shortage of labor is "the most difficult business issue we face."

To boost enrollment, institutions that offer mining programs are providing scholarships and job placement assistance for mining engineers with starting salaries ranging from $50,000 to $60,000. The industry wants students to understand that mining is not an "old" profession; instead, it uses the latest technologies and needs

of mining engineering at the University of Utah. Louis Cononelos of Kennecott Utah Copper emphasizes the career opportunities for recent graduates. "As the industry now has started to pick up, you have fewer candidates to choose from. It's really a great labor market for these recent graduates because now they have the pick of the jobs." In addition to existing college programs, several specialized training academies have opened near the sites of mining companies to help fill the urgent need for workers. Two such academies with programs designed to train coal miners recently opened in West Virginia. "There is an immediate need to train 1,800 to 2,500 miners in the next 18 months," explains Chris Hamilton of the West Virginia Coal Association.

At Massey Energy, recruitment and training efforts are progressing steadily. "We have a workforce in place which is up about 600 [or] 700 persons over where it was," reports chairman and CEO Don Blankenship. "And it's a matter of getting them trained and getting the equipment in place and beginning the mining. We're gaining ground on it in general, although we fell back a little in [one recent] quarter. But we still believe that the numbers we're projecting will be achieved."[1]

The importance of people to the success of any organization is the very definition of **management:** the use of people and other resources to accomplish organizational objectives. In this chapter, we address the critical issues of human resource management and motivation. We begin with a discussion of the ways organizations attract, develop, and retain employees. Then we describe the concepts behind motivation and the way human resource managers apply them to increase employee satisfaction and organizational effectiveness.

We also explore the reasons for labor unions and focus on legislation that affects labor–management relations. The process of collective bargaining is then discussed, along with tools used by unions and management in seeking their objectives.

# HUMAN RESOURCE MANAGEMENT IS VITAL TO ALL ORGANIZATIONS

**human resource management** function of attracting, developing, and retaining enough qualified employees to perform the activities necessary to accomplish organizational objectives.

As you saw with Massey Energy at the opening of the chapter, most organizations devote considerable attention to **human resource management,** the function of attracting, developing, and retaining enough qualified employees to perform the activities necessary to accomplish organizational objectives. Human resource managers are responsible for developing specific programs and activities as well as creating a work environment that generates employee satisfaction and efficiency.

The core responsibilities of human resource management include planning for staffing needs, recruitment and selection, training and evaluating performance, compensation and benefits, and employee separation. In accomplishing these five tasks, shown in Figure 9.1, human resource managers achieve their objectives of (1) providing qualified, well-trained employees for the organization, (2) maximizing employee effectiveness in the organization, and (3) satisfying individual employee needs through monetary compensation, benefits, opportunities to advance, and job satisfaction.

One of the key ways in which human resource managers accomplish those tasks is to develop *human resource plans* based on their organization's competitive strategies. They forecast the number of employees their firm will need and determine the types of skills necessary to implement its plans. Human resource managers are responsible for adjusting their company's workforce to meet the requirements of expanding in new markets; reducing costs, which may require laying off employees; or adapting to new technology. They formulate both long- and short-term plans to provide the right number of qualified employees.

Human resource managers also must plan how to attract and keep good employees with the right combination of pay, benefits, and working conditions. At Trilogy Software, this aspect of human resource planning is at the core of the company's strategy. Trilogy develops software that handles information processing related to sales and marketing, an industry in which only fast-moving, highly sophisticated companies can succeed. So the company has a strategy to expand its staff of software developers. Knowing that it is competing for talent with software giants such as Microsoft and Cisco Systems, Trilogy targets college campuses, recruiting the brightest, most energetic students it can find. As a substitute for work experi-

## "They Said It"

"This may sound soft and mushy, but happy people are better for business. They are more creative and productive, they build environments where success is more likely, and you have a much better chance of keeping your best players."
—*Shelly Lazarus (b. 1947) Chairwoman and CEO, Ogilvy & Mather Worldwide*[2]

Figure 9.1

Human Resource Management Responsibilities

ence, the company sends these young recruits to an intense three-month orientation program called Trilogy University, where they work on the firm's products as they learn about the software industry and the company culture. Trilogy appeals to recruits by emphasizing that their contribution to the company matters. "By hiring great people and giving them mission-critical responsibilities from the first day on the job, Trilogy ensures our ability to respond to competitive challenges and to achieve the goal of building a high-impact company," states the company Web site.[3]

# RECRUITMENT AND SELECTION

In recruiting and selecting employees, human resource managers strive to hire applicants who have skills the organization needs. To ensure that potential employees bring the necessary skills or have the capacity to learn them, most firms implement the recruitment and selection process shown in Figure 9.2.

Core Responsibilities of Human Resource Management

- Employee Recruitment and Selection
- Employee Training and Performance Evaluation
- Employee Compensation and Benefits
- Employee Separation
- Planning for Staffing Needs

## Finding Qualified Candidates

Finding the right candidate for a job isn't as simple as it sounds. For example, more than eight in ten manufacturers report facing moderate or severe shortages of the highly skilled workers they need to run today's computerized factories.[4] In addition, with 77 million baby boomers in their mid-40s to early 60s beginning to retire in the next five years and with only 46 million so-called Generation X workers, who are age 24 to 40, to take their places, finding talented workers is going to get even more difficult.[5] So human resource managers must be creative in their search for qualified employees. Businesses look to both internal and external sources to find the best candidates for specific jobs. Policies of hiring from within emphasize internal sources, so many employers consider their own employees first for job openings. Internal recruiting is less expensive than external methods, and it helps boost employee morale. But if recruiters cannot find qualified internal candidates, they must look for people outside the organization. Recruitment from external sources involves advertising on the Internet and in newspapers and trade magazines, placing radio and television ads, and working through state and private employment agencies, college recruiting and internship offices, retiree job banks, and job fairs. One of the most effective external sources is employee referrals, in which employers ask current employees to recommend applicants, rewarding them with bonuses or prizes for new hires.

To recruit new workers, firms' Web sites often contain career sections that provide general employment information and list open positions. Applicants may even be able to submit a résumé and apply for an open position online. As the "Launching Your Business Career" feature in the front matter pointed out, some firms also post job openings at employment Web sites, such as Monster.com. Internet recruiting is such a quick, efficient, and inexpensive way to reach a large pool of job seekers that between 82 and 92 percent of companies currently use the Internet to fill job openings. In fact, Internet recruiting is now second to newspaper advertising in terms of the number of applicants it generates. And, with the addition of a new ".jobs" Internet suffix (for example, http://cocacola.jobs/ for jobs at The Coca-Cola Company), more and more companies will now use their Web sites to attract, recruit, and screen job applicants.[6]

**assessment check**

1. Why do human resource managers need to develop staffing plans?
2. How do human resource managers attract and keep good employees?

## 9.2 Steps in the Recruitment and Selection Process

- **Identify Job Requirements**

⬇

- **Choose Sources of Candidates**
  - Internet
  - Schools
  - Employee Referrals
  - Promotion from Within
  - Colleges
  - Want Ads

⬇

- **Review Applications and Résumés**

⬇

- **Interview Candidates**

⬇

- **Conduct Employment Tests and Check References**

⬇

- **Conduct Follow-Up Interviews**

⬇

- **Select a Candidate and Negotiate an Offer**
  - Compensation and Benefits
  - Job Performance Expectations
  - Accommodations for Disabilities

# Selecting and Hiring Employees

In selecting and hiring employees, human resource managers must follow the requirements set out by federal and state laws. Title VII of the Civil Rights Act of 1964 prohibits employers from discriminating against applicants based on their race, religion, color, sex, or national origin. The Americans with Disabilities Act of 1990 prohibits employers from discriminating against disabled applicants. The Civil Rights Act created the Equal Employment Opportunity Commission (EEOC) to investigate discrimination complaints. The EEOC also helps employers set up affirmative action programs to increase job opportunities for women, minorities, disabled people, and other protected groups. The Civil Rights Act of 1991 expanded the alternatives available to victims of employment discrimination by including the right to a jury trial, punitive damages, and damages for emotional distress.

Failure to comply with equal employment opportunity legislation can expose an employer to fines and other penalties, negative publicity, and poor employee morale. The EEOC files hundreds of cases each year, with damages paid by businesses in the tens of millions annually. For example, Morgan Stanley, an investment bank, agreed to pay $54 million in damages after the EEOC filed a gender discrimination suit on behalf of 300 of Morgan Stanley's female employees. The women were paid less and promoted less often than comparable male employees with whom they worked.[7] At the same time, opponents to such laws have launched initiatives to restrict affirmative action standards and protect employers against unnecessary litigation. In one instance, California voters passed a proposition that prohibits the state from granting hiring preferences to minorities.

Increases in discrimination lawsuits have elevated the importance of human resource managers in the hiring process. To prevent violations, human resource personnel must train managers involved in interviewing to follow employment law. For example, the law prohibits an interviewer from asking an applicant any questions relating to marital status, number of children, race, nationality, religion, or age. Interviewers also may not ask questions about applicants' criminal records, mental illness histories, or alcohol-related problems. For more information about employment litigation issues, visit the Web sites of the Society for Human Resource Management (http://www.shrm.org) and the EEOC (http://www.eeoc.gov).

Employers must also observe various other legal restrictions governing hiring practices. Some firms try to screen out high-risk employees by requiring drug testing for job applicants, particularly in industries in which employees are responsible for public safety,

AP PHOTO/CHARLIE NEIBERGALL

Recognizing the technology and leadership skills of returned Iraq War veterans, many publicly traded businesses are partnering with veterans organizations to actively recruit vets. Private organizations such as the Coalition to Salute America's Heroes, whose spokesperson Robert Jackson is shown here, also provide disabled veterans with job counseling, support, and raise funds and awareness through golf outings and other events.

# HOW MUCH INFORMATION SHOULD JOB APPLICANTS REVEAL?

*The Americans with Disabilities Act makes it illegal for a company to ask about job applicants' health when they are applying for a job—unless the condition directly affects the person's ability to perform the job.*

But suppose a candidate has a chronic illness or condition that means the employer will be paying higher-than-average medical costs through insurance coverage, sick leave, and other related expenses. Even though it is legal to refrain from disclosing the condition, is it ethical?

Should job applicants reveal chronic illnesses or conditions to potential employers?

## PRO

1. To be fair, an applicant should tell a potential employer. The law prohibits discrimination, so nothing is lost—and the disclosure may go a long way toward building trust. "If employers feel like they've been duped, they have much less reason to be supportive about your missing work," warns one newspaper reporter who has a chronic condition.
2. It is better for the candidate and the employer to be prepared for any situations that might arise due to the employee's health. By bringing it up ahead of time, both can discuss the situation and make a plan to cope with it.

## CON

1. Despite the law, many firms favor candidates who appear to be 100 percent healthy. "It's a fact of life," says a graphic artist who has scleroderma, a chronic skin disorder.
2. If the condition will not hinder the applicant's job performance, it is his or her right to keep personal information private. Even if the employer does not discriminate, co-workers might do so.

## Summary

Every situation is different—for both medical conditions and job activities. A person who has arthritis may be able to design a direct marketing campaign but not lift 50-pound boxes. One type of cancer could be classified as a disability while another might not. "There's no right or wrong," says Rosalind Joffee, a chronic illness coach. Instead, most experts recommend the use of common sense alongside one's moral compass. It is fair to disclose what a potential employer needs to know—but perhaps foolish to disclose too much more.

**Sources:** "Avoid Disability Discrimination When Hiring New Employees," Nolo, accessed July 2, 2006, http://www.nolo.com; Joann S. Lublin, "Should Job Hunters Reveal Chronic Illness? The Pros and Cons," *Wall Street Journal*, accessed July 2, 2006, http://online.wsj.com. "Questions and Answers about Cancer in the Workplace and Americans with Disabilities Act," States News Service, July 26, 2005, http://www.states.com; Carole Kanchier, "Working," *Vancouver Sun*, July 23, 2005, http://www.canada.com.

## solving an ETHICAL controversy

such as airlines and other public transportation. But drug testing is controversial because of concerns about privacy. Also, positive test results may not accurately indicate drug use, and traces of legal drugs, such as prescribed medications, may chemically resemble traces of illegal substances. For more on the issue of employee privacy, see the "Solving an Ethical Controversy" feature, which examines the pros and cons behind job applicants' revealing chronic illnesses or other conditions.

Recruitment and selection are expensive processes because firms incur costs for advertising job openings, interviewing applicants, and conducting background checks, employment tests, and medical exams. A bad hiring decision is even more expensive, though. A hiring mistake causes a firm to spend money to train and motivate a less-than-optimal employee, as well as risk the potential costs of poor decisions by that employee. Other costs resulting from a bad hiring decision may include lawsuits, unemployment compensation claims, recruiting and training a replacement, and reductions in productivity and employee morale.

To avoid the costly results of a bad hiring decision, many employers require applicants to complete employment tests. These tests help verify the skills that candidates list on their application forms or résumés to ensure that they meet the performance expectations of the job.

A variety of tests is available to gauge applicants' knowledge of mechanical, technical, language, and computer skills. One example is the Wonderlic Basic Skills Test, which measures basic math and verbal skills. The Wonderlic, and others like it, are **cognitive ability tests,** which measure job candidates' abilities in perceptual speed, verbal comprehension, numerical aptitude, general reasoning, and spatial aptitude. In other words, these tests indicate how quickly and how well people understand words, numbers, and logic. Cognitive ability tests accurately predict job performance in almost all kinds of jobs. Why is this so? Because people with strong cognitive or mental abilities are usually good at learning new things, processing complex information, solving problems, and making decisions, and these abilities are important in almost all jobs. As a result, if you were allowed to use just one selection test, cognitive ability tests would be the one to use. The Wonderlic test is such an effective way to determine whom to hire that even the National Football League uses it when screening players for its annual draft. Floyd Reese, general manager of the Tennessee Titans, believes that players with higher Wonderlic scores are quicker and better able to understand the complex coverage and alignments typical of today's sophisticated defenses. The St. Louis Rams always rely on the Wonderlic. One NFL head coach said, "So long as he plays at a high level, we'll always choose a guy that is smarter."[8]

# ORIENTATION, TRAINING, AND EVALUATION

Once hired, employees need information about what is expected of them and how well they are performing. Companies provide this information through orientation, training, and evaluation. A newly hired employee often completes an orientation program administered jointly by the human resource department and the department in which the employee will work. During orientation, employer representatives inform employees about company policies regarding their rights and benefits. Many organizations give new hires copies of employee manuals that describe benefits programs and working conditions and expectations. They also provide different types of training to ensure that employees get a good start at the company.

## Training Programs

Employees are increasing their requests for training so that they can build skills and knowledge that will prepare them for new job opportunities. Training is also a good investment from the employer's perspective. A firm should view employee training as an ongoing process throughout each employee's tenure with the company. Companies such as Trilogy, which was mentioned earlier, make training a vital part of selecting and hiring employees, as well as developing their careers. Houston-based David Weekley Homes, which *Fortune* ranks as one of the best small companies to work for, spends a minimum of $4,500 a year training each of its employees.[9] At Rochester, New York–based Wegmans Food Markets, which *Fortune* consistently ranks near the top as among the best companies to work for, regardless of size, the company spends as much as $5 million training workers before opening a new store. Why? Because according to *Fortune,* "The company never opens a store until its employees are fully prepared."[10]

### On-the-Job Training
One popular instructional method is **on-the-job training,** which prepares employees for job duties by allowing them to perform tasks under the guidance of experienced employees. A variation of on-the-job training is apprenticeship training, in which an employee learns a job by serving for a time as an assistant to a trained worker. Patio Enclo-

sures, a construction firm based in Ohio, made its employees more productive and more committed to the company by setting up an apprenticeship program. Apprenticeship programs are much more common in Europe than in the United States. While American apprenticeships usually focus on blue-collar trades—such as plumbing and heating services and blacksmithing—in Europe, many new entrants to white-collar professions complete apprenticeships.

*Classroom and Computer-Based Training*   Off-the-job training involves some form of classroom instruction such as lectures, conferences, audiovisual aids, computer instruction, and special machines to teach employees everything from basic math and language skills to complex, highly skilled tasks. Cisco Systems, for instance, offers 4,500 e-learning courses to its managers and employees.[11]

Many firms are replacing classroom training with computer-based training programs. These programs can save employers money by reducing travel costs and employee time away from work. For example, British Telecom used a computer-generated instructor in an online program to train 4,500 salespeople in a little more than a month. Traditional classroom training would have cost twice as much and taken twice as long to deliver.[12] In addition, computer-based training offers consistent presentations, because the training content won't vary with the quality of the instructor. Audio and visual capabilities help these systems simulate the work environment better than some classroom training could, and employees benefit from greater control over the learning process. They can learn at their own pace and convenience, and they generally do not have to wait for the company to schedule a class. Despite these advantages, firms also offer traditional classroom training because it usually provides more opportunities for employees to interact with the instructor and with one another. Some people learn better through human interaction, and some have difficulty completing a computer-based learning program on their own.

Off-the-job training frequently involves use of the Internet. The Web provides a convenient means of delivering text, audio, and video training materials to employees wherever they are located. Online training programs also can offer interactive learning, such as simulations in which employees see the results of their decisions. When CDW account manager Danielle Paden took an online sales course, the computerized instructor would describe a situation, such as an unhappy customer whose computer won't make a high-speed Internet connection. Then a picture of the customer appeared on the screen, along with audio of the customer speaking. Finally, with the program's help, Paden decided what to do and then received feedback and another response from the hypothetical customer. Paden said that the training was "the closest thing you can get to [actual] client interactions."[13] The "Hit & Miss" feature provides more information on how companies are using computer games to improve training.

*Management Development*   A **management development program** provides training designed to improve the skills and broaden the knowledge of current and potential executives. The share of the workforce in their mid-20s to mid-30s, who traditionally have been developing their management skills, is shrinking, and many members of the workforce are approaching retirement age. It's estimated that the largest 500 companies in the United States will lose half of their senior managers in the next five years.[14] Without the luxury of developing executive talent slowly over the years, organizations instead must provide programs that help managers quickly learn how to lead a fast-moving company through turbulent times.

The content of management development programs may involve reviews of issues facing the company, as well as *benchmarking,* or learning the best practices of the best companies so they can serve as performance standards. The teachers may be the company's own executives. At other times, managers may be encouraged to receive counseling from an outside management coach, who helps them improve their skills. At GE, Robert Cancalosi is one of five executives in

## Cisco Systems Plays Games to Improve Training

Unfortunately, many traditional training programs are just too dull. Savvy human resource managers know this and have begun to encourage the use of electronic games in training programs to generate interest and excitement. The U.S. military is one organization that does so, using complex computer games to simulate field situations.

In the corporate sector, Cisco Systems has a Creative Learning Studio. This unit develops training programs using games and high-quality video to bolster the programs' interest level. Cisco now has a stock of about 4,500 e-learning training programs—incorporating games—in its files. One such game is SAN Rover (shorthand for Storage Area Network), which requires trainees to race against the clock to gather the "pieces" of the computer network—hard drives, switches, and the like—and correctly assemble them. Sound a little dull? It's not—learners have to complete the game while dodging crashing asteroids. SAN Rover reinforces skills and teaches trainees how the network actually works. "More and more people are learning that gaming can be useful in training in the corporate environment," says Marcia Sitscoske, head of Cisco's Creative Learning Studio.

Some firms encourage competition through gaming, even awarding prizes to winners. Borland Software uses games for training and continued learning of its sales staff. Winners are entered in a drawing for Apple iPods. The grand prize winner receives a cash award of $3,000. "The competition is a motivator," reports Wynn Johnson, director of field readiness. ERC Properties uses software called Game Show Pro to train its property managers in Internal Revenue Service regulations for affordable housing tax credits. The advantages of using the game are simple, according to corporate training director Candace Armstrong. "Most training is very boring, especially if it's government related. The difference was pretty obvious. People learn more when they laugh."

### Questions for Critical Thinking

1. Does the idea of using gaming in training programs appeal to you? Why or why not?
2. Would the use of gaming be successful with employees of all ages and backgrounds? Why or why not?

**Sources:** Holly Dolezalek, "Building Better Learners," Training Mag.com, accessed July 2, 2006, http://www.trainingsupersite .com; Rob Faulkner, "Playing Video Games at Work Could Make You Smarter," *Hamilton Spectator,* accessed July 2, 2006, http://www.hamiltonspectator.com; Michael Totty, "Better Training through Gaming," *Wall Street Journal,* accessed July 2, 2006, http://online.wsj.com.

---

charge of leadership development. Says Cancalosi, "We are known and benchmarked as the world's greatest leadership development company, and my job is to make us better at that." As part of his responsibilities in that position, Cancalosi personally coaches promising managers and has them sign contracts pledging to accept his feedback, which often pushes them out of their comfort zone. However, many of GE's managers, such as regional sales manager Cathy Neville, thrive on Cancalosi's developmental feedback. Says Neville, "He's a total motivator, and he's very engaging; he'll challenge you in front of people." In the end, says Cancalosi, "My deep-down passion is helping people get better."[15]

## *Performance Appraisals*

**performance appraisal**
evaluation of an employee's job performance that compares actual results with desired outcomes.

Organizations also help employees improve their performance by providing feedback about their past performance. A **performance appraisal** is an evaluation of an employee's job performance that compares actual results with desired outcomes. Based on this evaluation, managers make objective decisions about compensation, promotions, additional training needs, transfers, or terminations. Rating employees' performance and communicating perceptions of their strengths and weaknesses are important elements in improving a firm's effectiveness, productivity, or profits. Government agencies, not-for-profit organizations, and academic institutions also conduct performance appraisals.

Some firms conduct peer reviews, in which employees assess the performance of coworkers, while other firms allow employees to review their supervisors and managers. One type of performance appraisal is the **360-degree performance review,** a process that gathers feedback from a review panel of eight to twelve people, including co-workers, supervisors, team members, subordinates, and sometimes customers. The idea is to get as much frank feedback from as many perspectives as possible. However, this approach to performance appraisal tends to generate considerable work for both employees and managers—each of whom may have to review 20 or more people—and volumes of paperwork. Fortunately, though, companies such as Halogen Software offer computer programs that automate the procedures and "paperwork" associated with 360-degree feedback.[16] A potential weakness of 360-degree performance reviews is that because the evaluations are anonymous, staff members might try to use the system to their advantage in personal disputes.

Still, the 360-degree system appears to be gaining in popularity. A survey of large U.S. firms found that a majority are using the multirater system, compared with 40 percent a decade ago. It's not enough, however, to just gather 360-degree feedback. For real change to occur, managers who receive 360-degree feedback must acknowledge their weaknesses and then commit to improving. One of the best ways to do that is to have managers work through their 360-degree feedback with a coach. Manager Jim Moore has worked with Marshall Goldsmith, a leading executive coach, several times. When his 360-degree feedback indicated that Moore was too critical in his comments about others, Goldsmith got him to agree to put $5 in a jar every time he made overly critical comments. Moore, who successfully changed this behavior thanks to the feedback and coaching, said, "The money went into a beer fund for the people I worked with. In the first few weeks, we had a lot of beer sessions."[17]

**assessment check**

1. Describe some aids in off-the-job training.
2. What is a management development program?
3. What is the main way an organization provides employees with feedback about their performance?

# COMPENSATION

Human resource managers work to develop an equitable compensation system spanning wages and salaries plus benefits. Because human resource costs represent a sizable percentage of any firm's total product costs, excessive wage rates may make its goods and services too expensive to compete effectively in the marketplace. Inadequate wages, however, lead to difficulty in attracting qualified people, high turnover rates, poor morale, and inefficient production.

The terms *wages* and *salary* are often used interchangeably but are different. **Wages** represent compensation based on an hourly pay rate or the amount of output produced. Firms pay wages to production employees, maintenance workers, and sometimes retail salespeople. **Salaries** represent compensation calculated periodically, such as weekly or monthly. Office personnel, executives, and professional employees usually receive salaries.

An effective compensation system should attract well-qualified workers, keep them satisfied in their jobs, and inspire them to succeed. Most firms base their compensation policies on the following five factors:

1. Salaries and wages paid by other companies that compete for the same people
2. Government legislation, including the federal, state, or local minimum wage
3. The cost of living
4. The firm's ability to pay
5. Worker productivity

**wage** compensation based on an hourly pay rate or the amount of output produced.

**salary** compensation calculated on a periodic basis, such as weekly or monthly.

## How to Negotiate a Raise

When you are offered your first entry-level job, there isn't much room for negotiation in pay. Your employer is assuming that, although you will bring some natural ability and skills to the job, you will need to be trained. So you will start at the bottom of the salary ladder. Eventually, though, you'll have opportunities for an increase. Some raises occur automatically, according to a specific scale and after a designated period of time. But others don't. In these cases, you'll probably have to do some negotiating. Don't be intimidated; you can learn to negotiate smoothly and successfully. Here are a few tips:

- If salary discussion is not part of your performance review, make an appointment with your supervisor to discuss your salary.
- Before the meeting, review your own salary and benefits package so that you know exactly how much you are being compensated. If possible, ask the human resource department for the salary range for your position.
- List your major achievements on the job. Include ways in which your initiative has helped support your work unit beyond the basic job description. Also, include any training or education you have pursued on your own. These points will help support your negotiation. When you meet with your supervisor, be prepared to present your list of accomplishments. "Good companies pay for performance. The biggest single thing that gets you a raise is perfor-

mance," says one training consultant.
- Discuss any other reasons why you deserve a raise. Have you been covering for a colleague who has left or is on leave, doing the job of two people? Are you already handling the responsibilities of the next-level job? In this case, you might be a candidate for a promotion and the raise that comes with it.
- Be realistic in your expectations. Consider the general economic environment and your company's current performance in the marketplace. Keep in mind the salary range for your job. "If you are out of step with reality, at worst you might find yourself in a position where you have to leave and, at best, your boss might question your street smarts," warns one career counselor.
- Discuss your request calmly, intelligently, and politely. If you have done your homework, the meeting shouldn't take more than 20 minutes or so. If your request is denied, ask for specific reasons and listen carefully. Ask what you can do on the job to earn the raise—and do it.

Sources: "Negotiating for a Raise," LifeTips, accessed July 2, 2006, http://career.lifetips.com; Virginia Galt, "Deserve a Raise?" *Globe and Mail*, accessed July 2, 2006, http://www.theglobeandmail.com; Matt Villano, "The Smallest Raise in the Office Was Yours," *New York Times*, accessed July 2, 2006, http://www.nytimes.com; Perri Capell, "How Does Your Current Pay Stack Up against a New Offer?" *CareerJournal*, accessed July 2, 2006, http://www.careerjournal.com.

If you're wondering how to increase your salary, read the "Business Etiquette" feature on how to negotiate a raise.

Many employers balance rewarding workers with maintaining profits by linking more of their pay to superior performance. They try to motivate employees to excel by offering some type of incentive compensation in addition to salaries or wages. Today, almost one-tenth of the compensation of salaried workers is some form of variable pay. These programs include the following:

- Profit sharing, which awards bonuses based on company profits
- Gain sharing, when companies share the financial value of productivity gains, cost savings, or quality improvements with their workers
- Lump-sum bonuses and stock options, which reward one-time cash payments and the right to purchase stock in the company based on performance
- Pay for knowledge, which distributes wage or salary increases as employees learn new job tasks

Figure 9.3 summarizes the four types of incentive compensation programs.

## Employee Benefits

In addition to wages and salaries, firms provide benefits to employees and their families as part of their compensation. **Employee benefits,** such as retirement plans, health and disability insurance, sick leave, child-care and elder care, and tuition reimbursement, are paid entirely or in part at the company's expense. Benefits represent a large component of an employee's total compensation. Although wages and salaries account for around 70 percent of the typical employee's earnings, the other 30 percent takes the form of employee benefits.[18]

**employee benefits** rewards such as retirement plans, health insurance, vacation, and tuition reimbursement provided for employees either entirely or in part at the company's expense.

Historically, many companies have picked up most of the tab for health-care benefits, with employees paying little of the cost. However, with costs increasing nearly 15 percent per year, employers are requiring employees to pay a larger share of their healthcare benefits. For example, in terms of costs, General Motors recently spent $5.6 billion for healthcare, or about $1,525 for every car that it produces.[19] As a result, GM's unionized autoworkers are paying healthcare premiums for the first time. Other companies, such as GE, Halliburton, and IBM, have placed caps on what they will pay for employee and retiree health benefits. After the caps are reached, individuals are responsible for the remaining costs.

Other companies have begun charging unhealthy employees more for their healthcare coverage. For example, Gannett, the nationwide newspaper publisher, charges smokers an additional $50 per month if they don't attend smoking cessation programs.[20] One increasingly used, but highly controversial, technique involves not hiring unhealthy workers at all. A public-relations storm erupted when an internal Wal-Mart memo on this issue became public. The memo stated, "It will be far easier to attract and retain a healthier work force than it will be to change behavior in an existing one. [These policy changes] would also dissuade unhealthy people from coming to work at Wal-Mart."[21] While many believe that such strategies are illegal or unethical, particularly under the Americans with Disabilities Act, companies such as Union Pacific are already refusing to hire smokers in states where that is legal.

Some benefits are required by law. U.S. firms are required to make Social Security and Medicare contributions, as well as payments to state unemployment insurance and workers' compensation programs, which protect workers in case of job-related injuries or illnesses. The Family and Medical Leave Act of 1993 requires covered employers to offer up to twelve weeks of unpaid, job-protected leave to eligible employees. Firms voluntarily provide other employee benefits, such as child care and health insurance, to help them attract and retain employees. Recently, California became the first state to make paid family leave into law.[22]

Pensions and other retirement plans have been another area of concern for U.S. companies. Some companies have reduced the amount of matching contributions they will make to workers' **401(k) plans,** retirement savings plans to which employees can make pretax contributions to retirement accounts. Some companies have been cutting back on cash contributions to their employees' plans and are contributing company stock instead. Others, such as United Airlines, have gone bankrupt and defaulted on employees' pensions, which originally had guaranteed workers a set monthly payment in retirement. When this occurs, the U.S. government's Pension Benefit Guaranty Corporation pays employees' pensions, but retirement benefits are limited to $45,614 per year, which is sometimes well below the amount promised by their company pension plans.[23] Such defaults are rare so far.

Figure 9.3

Four Forms of Incentive Compensation

| Profit Sharing | Gain Sharing |
|---|---|
| Bonus based on company profits | Bonus based on productivity gains, cost savings, or quality improvements |
| **Lump-Sum Bonus** One-time cash payment or option to buy shares of company stock based on performance | **Pay for Knowledge** Salary increase based on learning new job tasks |

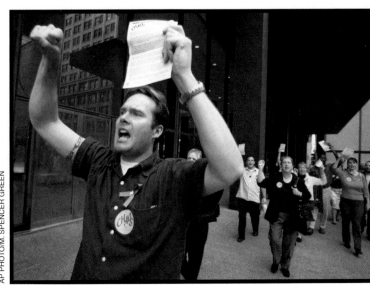

Facing severe competition from lower-cost air carriers, United Airlines defaulted on its pension obligations to 120,000 workers and retirees. The Pension Benefit Guarantee Corporation stepped in to provide some retirement assistance, but workers will not receive the benefits they thought they had earned.

AP PHOTO/M. SPENCER GREEN

## Flexible Benefits

In response to the increased diversity of the workplace, human resource managers are developing creative ways to tailor their benefit plans to the varying needs of employees. One approach sets up **flexible benefit plans,** also called *cafeteria plans.* Such a benefit system offers employees a range of options from which they can choose, including different types of medical insurance, dental and vision plans, and life and disability insurance. This flexibility allows one working spouse to choose his or her firm's generous medical coverage for the entire family, and the other spouse can allocate benefit dollars to purchasing other types of coverage. "Employees don't want all the same benefits," explains Jamie Berge, owner of a tax and financial services firm in Anchorage that administers cafeteria plans for small businesses. "With cafeteria plans, you pick and choose."[24] Typically, each employee receives a set allowance (called *flex dollars* or *credits*) to pay for purchases from the benefits menu. A healthy, single employee might choose to allocate fewer flex dollars to health insurance, say, by choosing a higher deductible, and put more flex dollars toward an optional dental or vision plan. By contrast, an older employee might earmark some flex dollars to pay for elder care for aging parents.

Contributions to cafeteria accounts are commonly made by both the employee and employer. Cafeteria plans also offer tax benefits to both employees and employers. Employee contributions are made using so-called *pretax dollars,* meaning that employees don't pay taxes on their contributions. Also, employers don't have to pay unemployment taxes or Social Security and Medicare taxes on the amount deducted from employee paychecks.

When it comes to offering employees benefit choices, many companies now recognize the importance of offering "family-friendly" benefits that help employees care for children, aging parents, or other dependents. Such benefits—ranging from child-care facilities to paid time off and flexible work hours—help employees juggle responsibilities. Almost nine out of ten large U.S. companies offer dependent-care spending accounts to help pay for child care, and almost half offer some form of elder-care program. SAS Institute offers employees an excellent on-site child-care facility for a monthly fee of only $300, a cafeteria with pianists, an on-site health clinic, and a huge fitness center. Men's Wearhouse, which sells men's suits and jackets, offers workers three-week paid sabbaticals every five years, while Starbucks provides domestic partner benefits.[25] For more on how companies are using employee sabbaticals, see the "Hit & Miss" feature on whether corporate sabbaticals pay off.

Another way of increasing the flexibility of employee benefits involves time off from work. Instead of establishing set numbers of holidays, vacation days, and sick days, some employers give each employee a bank of **paid time off (PTO)**. Employees use days from their PTO accounts without having to explain why they need the time. At Republic Bancorp, employees get 35 days of paid time off, or seven weeks per year, to use however they like.[26] CUNA Mutual Group takes a partial approach to paid time off by letting employees use unused sick, vacation, and personal leave days to care for sick children, parents, or

COURTESY OF THE TIMBERLAND COMPANY

Timberland is widely known for its community service efforts. Employees can take service sabbaticals to work in communities both in the United States and throughout the world. In its most recent "Serv-a-palooza" program, Timberland employees completed projects at 100 U.S. sites from coast to coast and in 27 countries ranging across the globe—from China to Turkey to the Dominican Republic.

## HIT & MISS

### Corporate Sabbaticals: Do They Pay Off?

Imagine having several months or even a year off from your job—paid. This type of time off with pay is known as a *sabbatical,* which stems from a Hebrew word meaning "to rest." Sabbaticals have been around in academic circles for a long time. But increasingly, U.S. companies are recognizing the value of sabbaticals in reducing employee turnover and increasing productivity and loyalty. Firms such as Procter & Gamble, Nike, Intel, *Newsweek,* and Timberland offer sabbaticals to employees. So does publisher Bertelsmann AG's Random House division.

Eligibility requirements for and benefits of the programs vary widely from firm to firm. At Procter & Gamble, employees are eligible for up to 12 weeks of unpaid sabbatical after only 1 year and every 7 years after that. At *Newsweek,* reporters and editors can take 6 months of sabbatical at half their salaries after 15 years. At Random House, full-time employees may take 4 paid weeks off at the end of 10 years; after 20 years, they may take 5 weeks of sabbatical.

Peter Olson, CEO of Random House, admits that the sabbatical plan was "initially met with skepticism by several senior executives." Legitimate concerns included calculating the cost of sabbaticals and figuring out how the work would be accomplished while employees were gone. But Olson believed that sabbaticals would be a simple, low-cost way to motivate and retain his best employees—to encourage them to explore avenues that could result in innovation for the company—so he went ahead with the program. To date, more than 800 Ran-

dom House employees have participated in the sabbatical program. One editor returned to work with an idea for a new list of books, which is now being launched. An unexpected benefit to the program has been the opportunity for lower-level employees to fill in for their supervisors, giving them a chance to broaden their knowledge and skills on the job. "It's become a developmental opportunity," reports Olson.

Human resource experts agree that sabbaticals can motivate employees to return better than ever. Sabbaticals combat a culture "where being overworked is seen as a red badge of courage," reports the Families and Work Institute.

#### Questions for Critical Thinking

1. Do you think the benefits of a sabbatical outweigh the costs to a firm? Explain.
2. What challenges might a firm face in establishing and maintaining a sabbatical program?

**Sources:** "Are Employee Sabbaticals Worth the Hassle?" Vault, accessed July 2, 2006, http://www.vault.com; Erin White and Jeffrey A. Trachtenberg, "Sabbaticals Can Be The Pause That Refreshes," *Wall Street Journal,* accessed July 2, 2006, http://online.wsj.com; Kelley M. Butler, "Faced with Worker Burnout, Employers Pay Employees to Get Away," *Employee Benefit News,* accessed July 2, 2006, http://www.benefitnews.com; Alan R. Earls, "Sabbaticals Aren't Just for Academia Anymore," *Boston Globe,* accessed July 2, 2006, http://www.boston.com.

spouses.[27] And 58 percent of companies reward employees who don't use all of their paid time off by "buying back" that time in cash.[28] One recent trend involves giving employees paid time off for volunteer service. Timberland is well known for doing this. The boot and apparel maker gives every employee 40 hours of paid time a year for volunteer work, and its New Hampshire headquarters actually closes one day a year so that Timberland employees can build playgrounds, work at the local SPCA, and assist the elderly. Employees are also eligible for six months of "social service leave" at full pay.[29]

## Flexible Work

Another part of the trend toward responsiveness to employee needs is the option of **flexible work plans.** Flexible work plans are benefits that allow employees to adjust their working hours and places of work to accommodate their personal needs. Flexible work plan options include flextime, compressed workweeks, job sharing, and home-based work. By implementing these benefit programs, employers have reduced employee turnover and absenteeism and boosted productivity and job satisfaction.

**Flextime** is a scheduling system that allows employees to set their own work hours within constraints specified by the firm. Rather than requiring everyone to work the regular work hours of 8 a.m. to 5 p.m., an employer may require employees to be at work between the core hours of 10 a.m. and 3 p.m. but vary their start times. Outside the core hours, employees can choose when to start and end their workdays, opting either to arrive at work early, say at 6 a.m., and leave early, or to arrive later and work later. Flextime works well in jobs in which employees can work relatively independently, but not so well when they must work together in teams, such as in manufacturing, or must provide direct customer service. The practice is common in European countries; an estimated 40 percent of the Swiss workforce and 25 percent of German workers have flextime schedules. Growing numbers of U.S. firms—particularly those that are not involved in manufacturing—are offering flextime, and increasing numbers of employees are taking advantage of this benefit.

The **compressed workweek** is a scheduling option that allows employees to work the regular number of weekly hours in fewer than the typical five days. Employees might work four ten-hour days and then have three days off each week. Such arrangements not only reduce the number of hours employees spend commuting each week but can stretch out the company's overall workday, providing more availability to customers in other time zones. Hospitals, police and fire departments, and airlines often offer work schedules that allow several long days matched by several days off. Six years ago, PNC Financial Services in Philadelphia switched to a compressed workweek of four ten-hour days after an initial seven-month study found strong increases in productivity, an 85 percent drop in absenteeism, and a reduction in turnover costs (costs associated with employees leaving the company) of nearly $6,000 per worker. Kathleen D'Appolonia, PNC's senior vice president for corporate recruiting, said, "If you engage employees and provide them with flexibility, they will be more committed to [the] business and serve customers better."[30]

A **job sharing program** allows two or more employees to divide the tasks of one job. This plan appeals to a growing number of people who prefer to work part time rather than full time—such as older workers, students, working parents, and people of all ages who want to devote time to personal interests or leisure—so companies are offering this option and even suggest these arrangements to help attract and retain valuable employees. Job sharing requires a high degree of cooperation and communication between the partners, but it can let a company benefit from the talents of people who do not want to work full time. At AT&T, Mary Kay Ross and Sharon Snyder share one phone number, one e-mail address, one cubicle, and one résumé, with each working 25 hours a week, or three days a week (they both work on Wednesdays). Said Ross, "We're able to hold challenging jobs together that as individual part-timers we might not be able to secure."[31] A successful job sharing arrangement requires partners who work well together, ongoing communication, and dedication to making the partnership work. That's been the case for Ross and Snyder, who have shared four jobs, including a promotion, for more than a decade. Said Ross, "I just feel very, very fortunate that we've had this opportunity for so long."[32]

A *home-based work program* allows employees to perform their jobs from home instead of at the workplace. Home-based workers are sometimes called *teleworkers* or **telecommuters** because many "commute" to work via telephones, e-mail, computers, and fax machines. Working from home has great appeal to employees with disabilities, older workers, and parents with small children. Forty-five million Americans have telecommuted from home at some point. However, with the advent of high-speed Internet connections in home offices, more than

26 million telecommute from home one day per month, and more than 22 million telecommute from home at least once a week.[33]

Because telecommuters work with minimal supervision, they need to be self-disciplined and reliable employees. They also need managers who are comfortable with setting goals and managing from afar.

**assessment check**

1. Explain the difference between wage and salary.
2. What is another name for a cafeteria plan?
3. What types of organizations typically use a compressed workweek?

# EMPLOYEE SEPARATION

Employee separation is a broad term covering the loss of an employee for any reason, voluntary or involuntary. It also includes businesses' efforts to control the cost of their workforces, such as downsizing or outsourcing.

## Voluntary and Involuntary Turnover

Either employer or employee can decide to terminate employment. *Voluntary turnover* occurs when employees leave firms to start their own businesses, take jobs with other firms, move to another city, or retire. Some firms ask employees who leave voluntarily to participate in *exit interviews* to find out why they decided to leave. These interviews give employers a chance to learn about problems in the workplace, such as unreasonable supervisors or unfair work practices. Because of recruitment and replacement costs, as well as lost productivity, the best companies actively work to minimize turnover by creating a positive work environment, training bosses to be good managers, and offering competitive compensation and benefits. In addition, successful companies are clearly focused on retaining their best workers. At Schlumberger, a multinational oil-field services company based in Houston, crew manager Eric Bartz, who manages an office in Victoria, Texas, said that because employees "are a big investment . . . , we essentially treat attrition, especially if someone has a high potential, as a catastrophic incident."[34] Consequently, each time an employee leaves Schlumberger, an exit interview is conducted to find out why they are leaving and what they were dissatisfied with, and the results are then posted online so that any manager in the company can view them.

*Involuntary turnover* occurs when employers terminate employees because of poor job performance, negative attitudes toward work and co-workers, or misconduct such as dishonesty or sexual harassment. Terminating poor performers is necessary because they lower productivity and employee morale. Co-workers resent employees who receive the same pay and benefits as they do without contributing fairly to the company's work. But employers need to carefully document reasons when terminating employees. Protests against wrongful dismissal are often involved in complaints filed by the EEOC or by lawsuits brought by fired employees.

## Downsizing

During the early years of the 21st century, employers terminated thousands of employees, including many middle managers, through downsizing. **Downsizing** is the process of reducing the number of employees within a firm by eliminating jobs. Many downsizing firms have reduced their workforces by offering early retirement plans, voluntary severance programs, and opportunities for internal reassignment to different jobs. Employers who value their employees have helped them find jobs with other companies and set up job counseling centers.

Companies downsize for many reasons. The two most common objectives of downsizing are to cut overhead costs and streamline the organizational structure. In a move to reduce costs

**downsizing** process of reducing the number of employees within a firm by eliminating jobs.

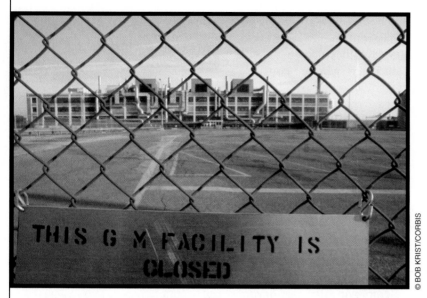

Once the largest corporation in the world, General Motors has fallen on hard times recently. To survive, the company had to lay off 25,000 employees and close plants amongst other actions.

by 70 billion yen, Sanyo Electric of Japan announced that it would cut 14,000 jobs, 8,000 of those within Japan, and close or sell 20 percent of its factories. The reason, said Sanyo's president, Toshimasa Iue, is that "We will no longer conduct operations that don't produce profits."[35]

While some firms report improvements in profits, market share, employee productivity, quality, and customer service after downsizing, studies show that downsizing doesn't guarantee those improvements. Why? A big reason is that eliminating jobs through downsizing can have devastating effects on employee morale. Workers who remain after a downsizing worry about job security and become angry when they have to work harder for the same pay. As commitment to their jobs and their firms weakens, many employees will leave to seek employment offering greater job security. In general, corporate downsizing has encouraged employees to put individual career success before employer loyalty, which has declined in the last two decades.

Employee surveys reveal that many workers are more interested in career security than job security. Specifically, the typical employee may seek training to improve the skills needed for the next job. People are willing to work hard at their current jobs, but they also want to share in the success of their companies in the form of pay-for-performance and stock options. For human resource managers, the new employee-employer relationship requires developing continuous training and learning programs for employees.

## Outsourcing

**outsourcing** contracting with another business to perform tasks or functions previously handled by internal staff members.

In their continuing efforts to remain competitive against domestic and international rivals, a growing number of firms hold down costs by evolving into leaner organizations. Functions that were performed previously by company employees may be contracted to other firms whose employees will perform them in a practice called **outsourcing.** Outsourcing began on a small scale, with firms contracting out services such as maintenance, cleaning, and delivery. Services commonly outsourced today include housekeeping; architectural design; grounds, building, utility, and furniture maintenance; food service; security; and relocation services. Today, outsourcing has expanded to include outside contracting of many tasks once considered fundamental internal functions.

Outsourcing complements today's focus on business competitiveness and flexibility. It allows a firm to continue performing the functions it does best, while hiring other companies to do tasks that they can handle more competently and cost-effectively. Another benefit of outsourcing is the firm's ability to negotiate the best price among competing bidders and the chance to avoid the long-term resource costs associated with in-house operations. Firms that outsource also gain flexibility to change vendors at the end of contract periods if they desire. The key to successful outsourcing is a strong commitment by both parties to form a partnership from which each derives benefits. Having had previous success with outsourcing, Dallas-based Electronic Data Systems (EDS), which provides computer and data services to major companies and has 117,000 employees worldwide, is planning to double the number of jobs that it outsources overseas to lower-wage workers in companies in India and Asia.[36]

**assessment check**

1. What is the difference between voluntary and involuntary turnover?
2. What is downsizing? How is it different from outsourcing?

# MOTIVATING EMPLOYEES

Employee motivation is the key to effective management. And motivation starts with good employee morale. **Morale** is the mental attitude of employees toward their employer and jobs. It involves a sense of common purpose among the members of work groups and throughout the organization as a whole. High morale is a sign of a well-managed organization because workers' attitudes toward their jobs affect the quality of their work. One of the most obvious signs of poor manager-worker relations is poor morale. It lurks behind absenteeism, employee turnover, and strikes. It shows up in falling productivity and rising employee grievances.

In contrast, high employee morale occurs in organizations in which employees feel valued and heard and can contribute what they do best. This climate reinforces a human tendency—that people perform best when they believe they are capable of succeeding. High morale also results from an organization's understanding of human needs and its success at satisfying those needs in ways that reinforce organizational goals.

Each person is motivated to take action designed to satisfy needs. A need is simply a lack of some useful benefit. It reflects a gap between an individual's actual state and his or her desired state. A motive is an inner state that directs a person toward the goal of satisfying a felt need. Once the need—the gap between where a person is now and where he or she wants to be—becomes important enough, it produces tension. The individual is then moved—the root word for *motive*—to reduce the tension and return to a condition of equilibrium. Figure 9.4 depicts the principle behind this process. A need produces a motivation, which leads to goal-directed behavior, resulting in need satisfaction.

## Maslow's Hierarchy-of-Needs Theory

The studies of psychologist Abraham H. Maslow suggest how employers can motivate employees. **Maslow's hierarchy of needs** has become a widely accepted list of human needs based on these important assumptions:

- People's needs depend on what they already possess.
- A satisfied need is not a motivator; only needs that remain unsatisfied can influence behavior.
- People's needs are arranged in a hierarchy of importance; once they satisfy one need, at least partially, another emerges and demands satisfaction.

**Maslow's hierarchy of needs** theory of motivation proposed by Abraham Maslow. According to the theory, people have five levels of needs that they seek to satisfy: physiological, safety, social, esteem, and self-actualization.

**Figure 9.4**

The Process of Motivation

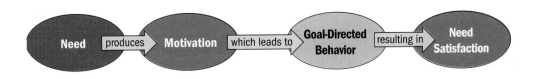

Need → produces → Motivation → which leads to → Goal-Directed Behavior → resulting in → Need Satisfaction

In his theory, Maslow proposed that all people have basic needs such as hunger and protection that they must satisfy before they can consider higher-order needs such as social relationships or self-worth. He identified five types of needs:

1. *Physiological needs.* These basic human needs include food, shelter, and clothing. In the workplace, employers satisfy these needs by paying salaries and wages and establishing comfortable working environments.
2. *Safety needs.* These needs refer to desires for physical and economic protection. Employers satisfy these needs by providing benefits such as retirement plans, job security, and safe workplaces.
3. *Social (belongingness) needs.* People want to be accepted by family and other individuals and groups. At work, employees want to maintain good relationships with their coworkers and managers and to participate in group activities.
4. *Esteem needs.* People like to receive attention, recognition, and appreciation from others. Employees feel good when they are recognized for good job performance and respected for their contributions.
5. *Self-actualization needs.* These needs drive people to seek fulfillment, realizing their own potential and fully using their talents and capabilities. Employers can satisfy these needs by offering challenging and creative work assignments and opportunities for advancement based on individual merit.

According to Maslow, people must satisfy the lower-order needs in the hierarchy (physiological and safety needs) before they are motivated to satisfy higher-order needs (social, esteem, and self-actualization needs). Table 9.1 elaborates on employers' efforts to motivate employees by satisfying each level of needs.

## Goal-Setting Theory

As shown in Figure 9.4, a need produces motivation, which leads to goal-directed behavior, which results in need satisfaction. In other words, needs motivate people to direct their behavior toward something that will satisfy their needs. That something is a goal. A **goal** is a target, objective, or result that someone tries to accomplish. **Goal-setting theory** says that people will be motivated to the extent to which they accept specific, challenging goals and receive feedback that indicates their progress toward goal achievement. As shown in Figure 9.5 on page 306, the basic components of goal-setting theory are goal specificity, goal difficulty, goal acceptance, and performance feedback.

*Goal specificity* is the extent to which goals are detailed, exact, and unambiguous. Goals such as "we want to lower our costs" are not as motivating as goals that are more specific, such as "we want to lower our costs by 2 percent." *Goal difficulty* is the extent to which a goal is hard or challenging to accomplish. More difficult goals, such as "we want to lower costs by 5 percent," are more motivating than less difficult goals, such as "we want to lower costs by 2 percent." *Goal acceptance* is the extent to which people consciously understand and agree to goals. If the stated goal was to "lower costs by 20 percent," people might not accept or be committed to that goal because they view it as unreasonable and unattainable. Finally, *performance feedback* is information about the quality or quantity of past performance and indicates whether progress is being made toward accomplishing a goal. When people know how near they are to their goals, they adjust their strategies to reach them. Goal setting typically won't work unless performance feedback is provided.

How does goal setting work? To start, challenging goals focus employees' attention—their direct effort—on the critical aspects of their jobs and away from unimportant areas. Goals also energize behavior, motivating employees to develop plans and strategies to reach them. Goals

**"They Said It"**

"I wanted and was excited by the challenge [of a new type of job]. If you don't know how to do something or if something scares you or looks impossible, you're going to work a lot harder, and in the end you're going to be gratified."
—Anne Sweeney (b. 1957) TV executive[37]

**goal** target, objective, or result that someone tries to accomplish.

**goal-setting theory** theory that people will be motivated to the extent to which they accept specific, challenging goals and receive feedback that indicates their progress toward goal achievement.

Table

9.1

Maslow's Hierarchy of Human Needs

| Human Needs | Key Ingredients | Example |
|---|---|---|
| 1. Physiological needs | Wages and working environment | Dallas-based Container Store has one of the highest pay scales in the retail industry. Entry-level sales professionals' salaries top $37,000, and entry-level hourly distribution center workers earn more than $20,000. Not surprisingly, the company enjoys low turnover. |
| 2. Safety needs | Protection from harm, employee benefits | After a study revealed that Transportation Security Administration baggage screeners suffered an unusually high number of back strains, cuts, bruises, and even broken bones, the TSA spent hundreds of millions of dollars to improve the mechanical baggage-handling systems and to provide employees with training in proper lifting techniques. |
| 3. Social (belongingness) needs | Acceptance by other employees | Valassis Communications, which prints coupon inserts for newspapers, sends employees memos introducing new hires. The employees, including the president of the company, then write "welcoming" notes to the new employee. "On your first day on the job, you're so nervous and you feel uncomfortable, and it just really makes a difference and makes you feel comfortable," says one new employee. |
| 4. Esteem needs | Recognition and appreciation from others | Entrepreneur Candace Bryan, chief executive of Kendle, a firm that designs clinical tests for drugs, keeps a photo gallery of her employees engaged in their favorite outside activities from scuba diving to grandparenting. The recognition boosts employee morale and helps make Bryan an inviting supervisor for prospective employees. |
| 5. Self-actualization needs | Accomplishment, opportunities for advancement, growth, and creativity | Ohio-based J. M. Smucker allows its employees to take unlimited paid time off to volunteer and better their communities. Some of the programs with which employees are involved are the Orrville, Ohio, Heartland Education community, which focuses on improving high school education; Adopt-a-School programs; Junior Achievement classroom volunteers; and Secondary Education Partnerships with local colleges. |

also create tension between the goal, which is the desired future state of affairs, and the employee's or company's current state. This tension can be satisfied in only two ways: by achieving or abandoning the goal. Finally, goals influence the persistence of employee efforts. Because goals "go away" only when they are accomplished, employees are more likely to persist in their attempts when they have goals.

Although goal setting is one of the most effective ways to motivate people, managers often make the mistake of setting unreachable goals or of setting short-term goals that hurt a company's long-term performance. Commenting on the effect of unreachable goals, a Texas manager wrote, "I'm watching this happen in my wife's company. She made President's Club last year for being 220% above quota, and her whole team did well and was recognized as tops in the company. Their reward: The VP raised their overall quota by 65% this year, an impossible target. Teams in adjacent areas that did not do nearly as well had their quotas raised 15%. Her whole team is out looking for new jobs and is very discouraged. For my wife,

**Figure**

**9.5**   Components of Goal-Setting Theory

| Goal Specificity | Goal Difficulty |
| Performance Feedback | Goal Acceptance |

**job enlargement** job design that expands an employee's responsibilities by increasing the number and variety of tasks assigned to the worker.

**job enrichment** change in job duties to increase employees' authority in planning their work, deciding how it should be done, and learning new skills.

it means she will not make as much this year, and in fact will have a hard time even making quota."[38]

## Job Design and Motivation

In their search for ways to improve employee productivity and morale, a growing number of firms are focusing on the motivation inherent in the job itself. Rather than simplifying the tasks involved in a job, employers are broadening tasks to add meaning and satisfaction to employees' work. Two ways employers are applying motivational theories to restructure jobs are job enlargement and job enrichment.

**Job enlargement** is a job design that expands an employee's responsibilities by increasing the number and variety of tasks they entail. Some firms have successfully applied job enlargement by redesigning the production process. A typical approach is to replace assembly lines on which each worker repeats the same step on each product with modular work areas in which employees perform several tasks on a single item. Similarly, many companies have enlarged administrative assistants' jobs in areas such as communications.

**Job enrichment** is a change in job duties to increase employees' authority in planning their work, deciding how it should be done, and learning new skills that help them grow. Many companies have developed job enrichment programs that empower employees to take responsibility for their work. The Pampered Chef, a direct seller of kitchen products that is owned by Berkshire Hathaway, gives its managers and consultants the power to make decisions about many aspects of their work. Kitchen consultants, who organize selling and demonstration parties at customers' homes, can choose how much or how little they want to work and receive various incentive rewards for performance. "Over the years, thousands of people from all walks of life have joined our Pampered Chef family. They've found a truly unlimited opportunity and life-changing possibilities," notes founder and chairman Doris Christopher.[39]

## Managers' Attitudes and Motivation

The attitudes that managers display toward employees also influence worker motivation. Managers' traditional view of workers as cogs in the production process—much like lathes, drill presses, and other equipment—led them to believe that money was the best way to motivate employees. Maslow's theory has helped managers understand that employees feel needs beyond those satisfied by monetary rewards.

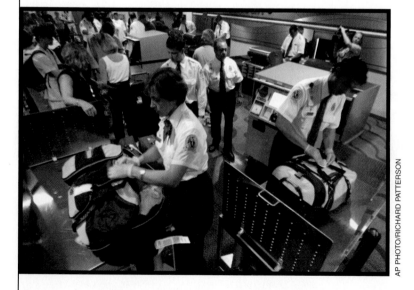

To provide more variety and prevent boredom in their jobs, security screeners working for the Transportation Security Administration are rotated to other tasks. These workers are checking bags from a Miami cruise ship for passengers headed to flights home.

*AP PHOTO/RICHARD PATTERSON*

Psychologist Douglas McGregor, a student of Maslow, studied motivation from the perspective of how managers view employees. After observing managers' interactions with employees, McGregor coined the terms *Theory X* and *Theory Y* as labels for the assumptions that different managers make about worker behavior and how these assumptions affect management styles.

**Theory X** assumes that employees dislike work and try to avoid it whenever possible. So managers must coerce or control them or threaten punishment to achieve the organization's goals. Managers who accept this view feel that the average person prefers to receive direction, wishes to avoid responsibility, has relatively little ambition, and can be motivated only by money and job security. Managers who hold these assumptions are likely to keep their subordinates under close and constant observation, hold out the threat of disciplinary action, and demand that they adhere closely to company policies and procedures.

**Theory Y** assumes that the typical person likes work and learns, under proper conditions, to accept and seek responsibilities to fulfill social, esteem, and self-actualization needs. Theory Y managers consider the expenditure of physical and mental effort in work as an ordinary activity, as natural as play or rest. They assume that most people can think of creative ways to solve work-related problems but that most organizations do not fully utilize the intelligence that most employees bring to their jobs. Unlike the traditional management philosophy that relies on external control and constant supervision, Theory Y emphasizes self-control and self-direction.

Theory Y requires a different management approach that includes worker participation in decisions that Theory X would reserve for management. If people actually behave in the manner described by Theory X, they may do so because the organization satisfies only their lower-order needs. If the organization instead designs ways to satisfy their social, esteem, and self-actualization needs as well, employees may be motivated to behave in different ways.

Another perspective on management proposed by management professor William Ouchi has been labeled **Theory Z**. Organizations structured on Theory Z concepts attempt to blend the best of American and Japanese management practices. This approach views worker involvement as the key to increased productivity for the company and improved quality of work life for employees. Many U.S. firms have adopted the participative management style used in Japanese firms by asking workers for suggestions to improve their jobs and then giving them the authority to implement proposed changes.

**assessment check**

1. In an organization, what conditions are likely to produce high morale?
2. Explain how goal setting works.
3. Identify two ways that employers structure jobs for motivation.
4. Compare and contrast Theory X, Theory Y, and Theory Z.

# LABOR-MANAGEMENT RELATIONS

In nations throughout the world, employees have joined together to increase their power to achieve the goals of improved wages and benefits, fewer working hours, and better working conditions. These efforts have succeeded, especially in the United States; today's workplace is far different from that of a century ago, when child labor, unsafe working conditions, and a 72-hour workweek (six 12-hour days a week) were common. In this section, we review the development of labor unions, labor legislation, the collective bargaining process, settling labor-management disputes, and competitive tactics of unions and management.

## Development of Labor Unions

A **labor union** is a group of workers who have banded together to achieve common goals in the areas of wages, hours, and working conditions. Workers gradually learned that bargaining

**labor union** group of workers who have banded together to achieve common goals in the areas of wages, hours, and working conditions.

as a unified group could bring them improvements in job security, wages, working conditions, and other areas. The organized efforts of Philadelphia printers in 1786 resulted in the first U.S. minimum wage—$1 a day. After 100 more years, New York City streetcar conductors were able to negotiate a reduction in their workday from seventeen to twelve hours.

Labor unions can be found at the local, national, and international levels. A *local union* represents union members in a specific area, such as a single community, while a *national union* is a labor organization consisting of numerous local chapters. An *international union* is a national union with membership outside the United States, usually in Canada. Large national and international unions in the United States include the United Auto Workers, the National Education Association, the Teamsters, the International Brotherhood of Electrical Workers, the International Association of Machinists and Aerospace Workers, the United Steelworkers of America, and the American Federation of Teachers. Over half of U.S. union members belong to one of these giant organizations.

Almost 16 million U.S. workers—close to 13 percent of the nation's full-time workforce—belong to labor unions.[40] Although only about 8 percent of workers in the private sector are unionized, more than one in three government workers belong to unions. The 1.8-million-member Service Employees International Union (SEIU) is the largest union in the United States. In addition to a wide range of service workers—clerical staff, nurses' aides, and janitors—SEIU has also organized such professionals as nurses, doctors, engineers, and librarians. Other large unions include the 1.4 million members of the United Food and Commercial Workers, the 1.4 million members of the International Brotherhood of Teamsters, and the 710,000 members of the United Auto Workers.

## Labor Legislation

Government attitudes toward unions have varied considerably over the past century. These shifting attitudes influenced major pieces of legislation enacted during this period. Let's look at the major pieces of labor legislation:

- *National Labor Relations Act of 1935 (Wagner Act):* Legalized collective bargaining and required employers to negotiate with elected representatives of their employees. Established the National Labor Relations Board (NLRB) to supervise union elections and prohibit unfair labor practices such as firing workers for joining unions, refusing to hire union sympathizers, threatening to close if workers unionize, interfering with or dominating the administration of a union, and refusing to bargain with a union.
- *Fair Labor Standards Act of 1938:* Set the initial federal minimum wage (25 cents an hour, with exceptions for farm workers and retail employees) and maximum basic workweek for workers employed in industries engaged in interstate commerce. Outlawed child labor.
- *Taft-Hartley Act of 1947 (Labor-Management Relations Act):* Limited unions' power by prohibiting such practices as coercing employees to join unions; coercing employers to discriminate against employees who are not union members, except for failure to pay union dues under union shop agreements; discrimination against nonunion employees; picketing or conducting secondary boycotts or strikes for illegal purposes; featherbedding; and excessive initiation fees under union shop agreements.
- *Landrum-Griffin Act of 1959 (Labor-Management Reporting and Disclosure Act):* Amended the Taft-Hartley Act to promote honesty and democracy in running unions' internal affairs. Required unions to set up a constitution and bylaws and to hold regularly scheduled elections of union officers by secret ballot. Set forth a bill of rights for members. Required unions to submit certain financial reports to the U.S. secretary of labor.

# The Collective Bargaining Process

Labor unions work to increase job security for their members and improvement of wages, hours, and working conditions. These goals are achieved primarily through **collective bargaining,** the process of negotiation between management and union representatives for the purpose of arriving at mutually acceptable wages and working conditions for employees.

Issues covered in collective bargaining include wages, work hours, benefits, union activities and responsibilities, grievance handling and arbitration, layoffs, and employee rights and seniority. As in all types of negotiations, the collective bargaining process involves demands, proposals, and counterproposals that ultimately result in compromise and agreement. The initial demands represent a starting point in negotiations. They are rarely, if ever, accepted by the other party without some compromise. The final agreement depends on the negotiating skills and relative power of management and union representatives.

Union contracts, which typically cover a two- or three-year period, are often the result of weeks or more of discussion, disagreement, compromise, and eventual agreement. Once agreement is reached, union members must vote to accept or reject the contract. If the contract is rejected, union representatives may resume the bargaining process with management representatives, or union members may strike to obtain their demands.

## Settling Labor-Management Disputes

Although strikes make newspaper and television headlines, most labor-management negotiations result in a signed agreement without a work stoppage. Approximately 140,000 union contracts are currently in force in the United States. Of these, on average no more than 20 labor-management contract negotiations involve a work stoppage of some kind.[41] The courts are the most visible and familiar vehicle for dispute settlement, but most disputes are settled by negotiations. Dispute resolution mechanisms, such as grievance procedures, mediation, and arbitration, are quicker, cheaper, and less complicated procedurally and receive less publicity.

The union contract serves as a guide to relations between the firm's management and its employees. The rights of each party are stated in the agreement. But no contract, regardless of how detailed, will eliminate the possibility of disagreement. Such differences can be the beginning of a **grievance,** a complaint—by a single employee or by the entire union—that management is violating some provision of the union contract. Almost all union contracts require these complaints to be submitted to a formal grievance procedure similar to the one shown in Figure 9.6.

The procedure typically begins with the employee's supervisor and then moves up the company's chain of command. If the highest company officer cannot settle the grievance, it is submitted to an outside party for mediation or arbitration.

**Mediation** is the process of settling labor-management disputes through recommendations of an impartial third party. Although the mediator does not serve as a decision maker, union and management representatives can be assisted by the mediator's suggestions, advice, and compromise solutions.

> **collective bargaining** process of negotiation between management and union representatives for the purpose of arriving at mutually acceptable wages and working conditions for employees.

**Figure**

**9.6**

Steps in the Grievance Procedure

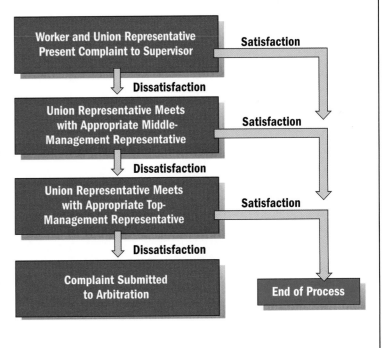

Worker and Union Representative Present Complaint to Supervisor → **Satisfaction**

↓ **Dissatisfaction**

Union Representative Meets with Appropriate Middle-Management Representative → **Satisfaction**

↓ **Dissatisfaction**

Union Representative Meets with Appropriate Top-Management Representative → **Satisfaction**

↓ **Dissatisfaction**

Complaint Submitted to Arbitration

**End of Process**

When disputes cannot be solved voluntarily through mediation, the parties can turn to **arbitration**—bringing in an impartial third party, called an *arbitrator,* who renders a legally binding decision. The arbitrator must be acceptable both to the union and to management, and his or her decision is legally enforceable. In essence, the arbitrator acts as a judge, making a decision after listening to both sides of the argument. Most union contracts call for the use of arbitration if union and management representatives fail to reach an agreement.

## Competitive Tactics of Unions and Management

Although most differences between labor and management are settled through the collective bargaining process or through a formal grievance procedure, both unions and management occasionally resort to various tactics to make their demands known.

*Union Tactics*   The chief tactics of unions are strikes, picketing, and boycotts. The **strike,** or *walkout,* is one of the most effective tools of the labor union. It involves a temporary work stoppage by employees until a dispute has been settled or a contract signed. Although strikes are relatively rare, they do make headlines. In recent years, strikes have involved workers at Supervalu, Ralphs (a supermarket chain owned by Kroger's), home health care agencies in New York City, and hotel and casino employers in Atlantic City.[42]

Although the power to strike represents unions' ultimate tactic, they do not wield it lightly because strikes can do damage in a number of ways, affecting not only one company but an

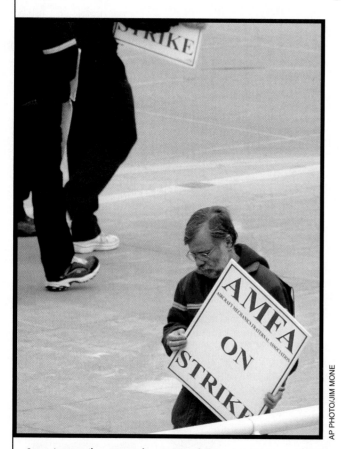

AP PHOTO/JIM MONE

Sometimes strikes cannot be prevented. But when they occur, they are costly to both employees and companies. Shown here are members of the Aircraft Mechanics Fraternal Association picketing against Northwest Airlines.

entire industry, as well as related businesses. When 60,000 southern California grocery store workers went on a four-month strike, Safeway, Kroger, and Supervalu lost tens of millions of dollars. However, because profits were weak and the companies were losing business to Wal-Mart, the unions still had to make cost concessions, dropping the pay of new workers from $17.90 to $15.10. Plus, new workers no longer receive free healthcare.[43]

**Picketing**—workers marching at the entrances of the employer's business as a public protest against some management practice—is another effective form of union pressure. As long as picketing does not involve violence or intimidation, it is protected under the U.S. Constitution as freedom of speech. Picketing may accompany a strike, or it may be a protest against alleged unfair labor practices. When union workers for Boeing, the airplane manufacturer, went on strike and began picketing, it cost the company $70 million a day in lost production. The union and Boeing management eventually agreed on a new contract after a monthlong strike.[44] Because members of other unions often refuse to cross picket lines, the picketed firm may be unable to obtain deliveries and other services. Unions occasionally stage "informational" picketing during contract negotiations to pressure management while still working.

A **boycott** is an organized attempt to keep the public from purchasing the products of a firm. Some unions have been quite successful in organizing boycotts, and some unions even fine members who defy a primary boycott. The United Food and Commercial Workers International Union, which would like to unionize Wal-Mart's workers, created a "Wake Up Wal-Mart" campaign in which it encouraged schoolteachers, many of whom are members of teachers' unions, to boycott Wal-Mart for back-to-school purchases.[45]

*Management Tactics*   Management also has tactics for dealing with organized labor. In the past, it has used the **lockout**—in effect, a management strike to put pressure on union members by closing the firm. However, other than a few high-profile cases, the lockout is not commonly used unless a union strike has partially shut down a plant or engaged in a work slowdown. Firms can easily recruit strikebreakers in high-status fields such as professional sports and in high-paying industries located in areas of high unemployment. Yet even in favorable conditions, management frequently has difficulties securing enough replacement workers with required skills. Some employers get around these difficulties by using supervisors and nonunion replacement employees to continue operations during strikes. When Northwest Airline's 4,400 mechanics went on strike after company management demanded a 25 percent wage cut, Northwest temporarily hired 1,200 replacement workers, employed 300 managers who had been formally trained as mechanics, and relied on 400 mechanics from outside vendors. Northwest's replacement mechanics were so effective that it was able to fly 98 percent of its normal flights during the strike.[46]

# The Future of Labor Unions

Union membership and influence grew through most of the 20th century by giving industrial workers a voice in decisions about their wages, benefits, and working conditions. Today, however, union members and influence are declining. As the United States, western Europe, and Japan have shifted from manufacturing economies to information and service economies, the makeup of the workforce has become less favorable for unions. While almost 8 percent of private-sector workers are union members today, that's down from nearly 17 percent in 1983. Likewise, unions have won only 7,224 of the 13,144 union votes (in which employees decide whether they want to be represented by a union) over the last five years.[47] That is a historically low percentage. In fact, unions have been unable to organize any of the Japanese-owned automobile plants in the United States (Toyota, Honda, Nissan) or those of Mercedes Benz, BMW, and Hyundai. Their biggest lack of success has been their inability to organize Wal-Mart's 1.2 million U.S. workers.

Why are unions shrinking and why are they having difficulty attracting members? Debbie Moore, who was in a union fourteen years ago when she worked in a manufacturing plant, now works for Wal-Mart in an automotive repair department, where she and her co-workers voted 19–0 to reject union representation. Said Moore, "Right now, in this day and era, I don't think I need a union to pay for anybody to protect me. Years ago, I believe work conditions were bad, and unions had their place of bringing standards up and making jobs safe. Unions are headed downward now. And the government is there to help."[48] Mary Gilleece, director of an information technology school in Somerville, Massachusetts, summarizes the thoughts of many of today's workers when she says, "If it's a decent company, you don't need a union."[49]

At nonunion companies, management often offers a compensation and benefit structure comparable to those of unionized firms in the area. Willingness to offer comparable wages and working conditions, coupled with effective communications, emphasis on promotions from within, employee empowerment, and employee participation in goal setting and grievance handling clearly helps employers avert unionization. Satisfied workers such as Mary Gilleece conclude that they would receive few additional benefits for the union dues they would have to pay.

How will labor unions have to change to maintain their relevance? More than anything else, with manufacturing jobs shrinking from increasing productivity and overseas outsourcing,

**assessment check**

1. How many U.S. workers are represented by labor unions?
2. Identify the major issues covered in the collective bargaining process.
3. Explain picketing, boycotts, and lockouts.

labor unions are reaching out to nonmanufacturing workers, such as healthcare, high-tech, and service workers. Another possibility is offering affiliate or partial memberships, which offer the same benefits as full memberships except for collective bargaining or grievance issues.[50] Finally, labor unions will have to overcome the widespread belief that they can't succeed unless company management loses. Today, most workers realize that they prosper when their companies prosper, and that it's better for management and workers to work together and to have positive rather than adversarial relationships.

# WHAT'S AHEAD

Treating employees well by enriching the work environment will continue to gain importance as a way to recruit and retain a highly motivated workforce. In addition, managers can tap the full potential of their employees by empowering them to make decisions, leading them to work effectively as teams, and fostering clear, positive communication. The next chapter covers these three means of improving performance. By involving employees more fully through empowerment, teamwork, and communication, companies can benefit from their knowledge while employees enjoy a more meaningful role in the company.

## Summary of Learning Goals

**1 Explain the importance of human resource management, the responsibilities of human resource managers, and the role of human resource planning in an organization's competitive strategy.**
Organizations devote considerable attention to attracting, training, and retaining employees to help maintain their competitiveness. Human resource managers are responsible for recruiting, selecting, training, compensating, terminating, and motivating employees. They accomplish these tasks by developing specific programs and creating a work environment that generates employee satisfaction and efficiency. A human resource plan is designed to implement a firm's competitive strategies by providing the right number of employees, training them to meet job requirements, and motivating them to be productive and satisfied workers.

### Assessment Check Answers

**1.1 Why do human resource managers need to develop staffing plans?**
Staffing plans help managers determine how many employees their firms will need and the kinds of skills those employees will need.

**1.2 How do human resource managers attract and keep good employees?**
Using the right combination of pay, benefits, and working conditions helps managers attract and keep good employees.

**2 Describe how recruitment and selection contribute to placing the right person in a job.**
Firms use internal and external methods to recruit qualified employees. For needs that the company cannot meet with existing employees, it may find candidates by encouraging employee referrals, advertising, accepting résumés at its Web site, and using job search Web sites. In selecting qualified candidates, human resource managers must follow legal requirements designed to promote equal employment opportunity. Employment tests, such as cognitive ability tests, are often used to assess job candidates' capabilities and help companies hire more qualified workers.

### Assessment Check Answers

**2.1 What are some of the costs associated with recruitment and selection?**
Firms incur costs for advertising job openings, interviewing applicants, and conducting background checks,

employment tests, and medical exams. Hiring mistakes increase training costs, can result in lawsuits and unemployment compensation claims, and reduce productivity and employee morale.

## 2.2 What key federal and state laws apply to recruitment and selection?

Recruitment and selection practices must adhere to Title VII of the Civil Rights Act of 1964, the Americans with Disabilities Act of 1990, the Civil Rights Act of 1991, and other regulations of the Equal Employment Opportunity Commission.

**3** **Explain how training programs and performance appraisal help companies grow and develop their employees.**

Human resource managers use a variety of training techniques, including on-the-job training, computerized training programs, and classroom methods. In addition, management development programs help managers make decisions and improve interpersonal skills. Companies conduct performance appraisals to assess employees' work, as well as their strengths and weaknesses.

## Assessment Check Answers

### 3.1 Describe some aids in on-the-job training.

In on-the-job training, you learn how to perform tasks under the guidance of experienced employees. A variation of on-the-job training is apprenticeship training, in which an employee learns a job by serving for a longer time as an assistant to a trained worker.

### 3.2 What is a management development program?

A management development program provides training designed to improve the skills and broaden the knowledge of current and potential executives.

### 3.3 What is the main way an organization provides employees with feedback about their performance?

The main method is a performance appraisal, in which an employee's job performance is compared with desired outcomes. Peer reviews and 360-degree performance reviews are also used to provide feedback.

**4** **Outline the methods employers use to compensate employees through pay systems and benefit programs.**

Firms compensate employees with wages, salaries, and incentive pay systems, such as profit sharing, gain sharing, lump-sum bonuses, stock options, and pay-for-knowledge programs. Benefit programs vary among firms, but most companies offer healthcare programs, insurance, retirement plans, paid time off, and sick leave. A growing number of companies are offering flexible benefit plans and flexible work plans, such as flextime, compressed workweeks, job sharing, and home-based work.

## Assessment Check Answers

### 4.1 Explain the difference between wage and salary.

Wages represent compensation based on an hourly pay rate or the amount of output produced. Salaries represent compensation calculated periodically, such as weekly or monthly.

### 4.2 What is another name for a *cafeteria plan?*

Cafeteria plans are also called *flexible benefit plans.*

### 4.3 What types of organizations typically use a compressed workweek?

Hospitals, police and fire departments, airlines, and manufacturing organizations often use compressed workweeks. However, many other kinds of companies are now finding success with compressed workweeks.

**5** **Discuss employee separation and the impact of downsizing and outsourcing.**

Either employers or employees can decide to terminate employment (called *involuntary turnover* and *voluntary turnover,* respectively). Downsizing reduces a company's workforce to reduce labor costs in an effort to improve the firm's competitive position. The company may transfer some responsibilities to contractors, a practice called *outsourcing.* The goals of outsourcing are to reduce costs by giving work to more efficient specialists and to allow the company to focus on the activities it does best.

## Assessment Check Answers

### 5.1 What is the difference between voluntary and involuntary turnover?

Voluntary turnover occurs when employees leave firms to start their own businesses, take jobs with other firms, move to another city, or retire. Involuntary turnover occurs when employers terminate employees because of poor job performance, negative attitudes toward work and co-workers, or misconduct.

### 5.2 What is downsizing? How is it different from outsourcing?

Downsizing is the process of reducing the number of employees within a firm by eliminating jobs.

Downsizing is done to cut overhead costs and streamline the organizational structure. With outsourcing, companies contract with other firms to perform non-core jobs or business functions, such as housekeeping, maintenance, or relocation services. This allows companies to focus on what they do best, and can result in a downsized workforce.

**6** **Explain how Maslow's hierarchy-of-needs theory, goal setting, job design, and managers' attitudes relate to employee motivation.**

Employee motivation starts with good employee morale. Maslow's hierarchy-of-needs theory states that all people have basic needs (physiological and safety) that they must satisfy before they can consider higher-order needs (social, esteem, and self-actualization). Goal-setting theory, job enlargement, and job enrichment are three ways in which managers can motivate employees and satisfy various levels of needs. Managers' attitudes can also affect employee motivation. Theory X managers keep their subordinates under close and constant observation. Theory Y managers emphasize workers' self-control and self-direction. Theory Z managers believe that worker involvement is the key to increased productivity for the company and improved quality of work life for employees.

## Assessment Check Answers

**6.1 In an organization, what conditions are likely to produce high morale?**

High employee morale occurs when employees feel valued and heard and can contribute what they do best. High morale also results from an organization's understanding of human needs and its success at satisfying those needs in ways that reinforce organizational goals.

**6.2 Explain how goal setting works.**

People will be motivated to the extent to which they accept specific, challenging goals and receive feedback that indicates their progress toward goal achievement.

**6.3 Identify two ways that employers structure jobs for motivation.**

Two ways that employers apply motivational theories to restructure jobs are job enlargement and job enrichment. Job enlargement is a job design that expands an employee's responsibilities by increasing the number and variety of tasks they entail. Job enrichment is a change in job duties to increase employees' authority in planning their work, deciding how it should be done, and learning new skills that help them grow.

**6.4 Compare and contrast Theory X, Theory Y, and Theory Z.**

Theory X assumes that employees dislike work and try to avoid it whenever possible. Theory Y assumes that the typical person likes work and learns, under proper conditions, to accept and seek responsibilities to fulfill social, esteem, and self-actualization needs. Theory Z views worker involvement as the key to increased productivity for the company and improved quality of work life for employees.

**7** **Summarize the role of labor unions and the tactics of labor-management conflicts.**

A labor union is a group of workers who have banded together to achieve common goals in the key areas of wages, working hours, and working conditions. Labor unions exist at local, national, and international levels. Government attitudes toward unions have varied considerably during the past century and are reflected in the major pieces of labor legislation enacted during this period. Labor unions work to achieve their goals of increased job security and improvements in wages, hours, and working conditions through a process known as *collective bargaining*. Most labor-management negotiations result in a signed agreement without a work stoppage. Even after an agreement is signed, disputes can arise. A grievance is a complaint that management is violating some provision of the union contract. Mediation is the process of settling labor-management disputes through recommendations of an impartial third party. Arbitration is a process in which an impartial third party renders a legally binding decision. Some tactics available to labor unions during disputes include strikes (walkouts), picketing, and boycotts. Tactics available to management include lockouts and hiring replacement workers.

## Assessment Check Answers

**7.1 How many U.S. workers are represented by labor unions?**

Almost 16 million U.S. workers—close to 13 percent of the nation's full-time workforce—belong to labor unions. Although only about 8 percent of workers in the private sector are unionized, more than one in three government workers belong to unions.

**7.2 Identify the major issues covered in the collective bargaining process.**

The major issues covered in collective bargaining include wages, work hours, benefits, union activities and responsibilities, grievance handling and arbitration, layoffs, and employee rights and seniority.

## 7.3 Explain picketing, boycotts, and lockouts.

Picketing is when workers march at the entrances of the employer's business to protest against some management practice. A boycott is an organized attempt to keep the public from purchasing the products of a firm. A lockout is a management strike, in which company management pressures labor union members by locking them out of the company and closing the firm.

## Business Terms You Need to Know

human resource management 288
performance appraisal 294
wage 295
salary 295
employee benefits 296

downsizing 301
outsourcing 302
Maslow's hierarchy of needs 303
goal 304
goal-setting theory 304

job enlargement 306
job enrichment 306
labor union 307
collective bargaining 309

## Other Important Business Terms

management 288
cognitive ability tests 292
on-the-job training 292
management development
    program 293
360-degree performance
    review 295
401(k) plan 297
flexible benefit plan 298

paid time off (PTO) 298
flexible work plan 299
flextime 300
compressed workweek 300
job sharing program 300
telecommuter 300
morale 303
Theory X 307
Theory Y 307

Theory Z 307
grievance 309
mediation 309
arbitration 310
strike 310
picketing 310
boycott 310
lockout 311

## Review Questions

1. What are the core responsibilities of human resource management? What are the three main objectives of human resource managers?
2. What methods do companies use to recruit and select employees?
3. What types of training programs are popular today? How does 360-degree feedback work?
4. On what five factors are compensation policies usually based? Name at least three employee benefits that are required by law and three more that are provided voluntarily by many firms.
5. Describe four types of flexible work plans. Identify an industry that would be well suited to each type of plan and explain why.
6. Outline the major reasons for terminating employees. Why do companies downsize? What are some of the difficulties they may encounter in doing so?

7. Explain Maslow's hierarchy-of-needs theory. How do companies attempt to satisfy employee needs at each level in the hierarchy?

8. How is goal setting related to need satisfaction? What mistakes need to be avoided when setting goals?

9. How do companies use job design to motivate employees?

10. What are the chief tactics of unions and management in their contract negotiations? Are they usually effective? Why or why not?

## Projects and Teamwork Applications

1. Choose one of the following organizations (or select one of your own) and write a memo outlining a plan for outsourcing some of the tasks currently performed by employees. Cite reasons for your choices.
   a. summer resort in Wisconsin
   b. regional high school in Arizona
   c. software development firm in California
   d. major hospital in Massachusetts
   e. manufacturing plant in Kentucky

2. Would you accept a job you didn't particularly like because the firm offered an attractive benefits package? Why or why not? Do you think your answer would change as you get older? Why or why not?

3. Not every unionized worker has the right to strike. All federal employees and many state and municipal employees—such as police officers and firefighters—cannot strike. Suppose you were a teacher or an airline pilot. Do you think members of your union should be allowed to strike? Why or why not?

4. Do you think the downward trend in union membership will continue? In what ways might this trend change the relationship between companies and employees over the next decade?

5. Suppose you are a human resource manager and you have determined that your company would benefit from hiring some older workers. Write a memo explaining your reasons for this conclusion.

## Case 9.1

### Best Buy's Workers Thrive with Flexible Scheduling

Best Buy wasn't always the best place to work. Despite the firm's mission to "make life fun and easy for millions of people across North America," its employees were pressured to work long hours and sacrifice themselves for the company. One store manager used to award a plaque to the employee who "turns on the lights in the morning and turns them off at night." But things have changed at the company with the big yellow price tag.

More than 90,000 people work at Best Buy in distribution centers and stores. Employees perform a variety of tasks: designing advertisements, selling products, installing computer software, and ensuring efficient shipping. To provide superior service to customers, the firm must find ways to motivate its workforce to do their best, without burning them out. Recently, Best Buy launched a new program that centers on flexible scheduling for employees. Called a Results Oriented Work Environment (ROWE), the program allows employees to work when and where they prefer—as long as they get their jobs done. The new focus is a breakthrough for many employees—working parents, students, and those who live a long commuting distance away.

Carrying out a program like ROWE takes planning and flexibility on the part of managers. They had to learn to relax their control over employees, trusting that they would get the job done. "Trust doesn't cost me anything," said one manager, who discovered that the morale of his workers increased dramatically.

Each department found its own way to make the transition and obtained input from all employees. The public-relations group decided to get pagers so everyone could be reached when necessary. The finance department purchased software that transcribes voice mail into e-mails that can be accessed from anywhere. Many teams decided immediately that they needed far fewer meetings than they'd been required to hold before the ROWE program. By using more phone calls and e-mails, they discovered that much less time was wasted.

Not surprisingly, some blips have occurred at Best Buy. Some managers are more resistant to the change than others. And some jobs simply don't lend themselves to as much flexibility as others. For instance, administrative assistants need to be at their workstations when their supervisors are in the office; security guards need to be on-site; and salespeople need to be on hand during store hours. And some workers struggle to determine how to make their performance stand out under the new system. "I had all this panic," says one employee who had grown accustomed to arriving first at work and leaving last. "Everything we knew about success was suddenly changing." Employees who thrive on set routines have felt somewhat lost without the time clock. The new system is "harder for people who want order in their lives," explains sociologist Phyllis Moen. And some employees just still can't let go—they check their e-mail and voice mail messages on their days off.

Despite these challenges, Best Buy managers are reporting higher productivity among their employees, along with rising morale. Employees like the idea of being evaluated on their job performances, not how long they toil. Hourly employees still track their hours, but they enjoy more freedom in scheduling their work time. Turnover and absenteeism have begun to drop as well. Employees who previously considered leaving the firm to achieve a better balance between family and career have decided to stay. Best Buy now expects more training and increased initiative from its employees—and the company is getting it. All of this bodes well for the firm, which needs its employees in order to remain competitive in the marketplace. "We can embrace that reality and ride it," says executive vice president Shari Ballard, "or we can fight it." Best Buy has chosen the reality.

## Questions for Critical Thinking

1. How might Best Buy's recruitment, selection, training, and evaluation processes be different under the new ROWE program?
2. In what ways would you expect employee–management relations at Best Buy to change under the ROWE program?

**Sources:** Best Buy Web site, accessed July 2, 2006, http://www.bestbuy.com; Leah Carlson, "Flexibility Proves Profitable for Large Firms," *Employee Benefit News,* accessed July 2, 2006, http://www.benefitnews.com; Jyoti Thottam, "Reworking Work," *Time,* accessed July 2, 2006, http://www.time.com; Charlotte Huff, "With Flex-time, Less Can Be More," *Workforce Management,* accessed July 2, 2006, http://www.workforce.com; Leah Carlson, "Flex Benefits: Swinging away from 9 to 5," *Employee Benefit News,* accessed July 2, 2006, http://www.benefitnews.com.

 **Case 9.2**

### Allstate Employees Are in Good Hands

This video case appears on page 617. A recently filmed video, designed to expand and highlight the written case, is available for class use by instructors.

# Chapter 10

## Improving Performance through Empowerment, Teamwork, and Communication

1. Describe why and how organizations empower employees.

2. Distinguish among the five types of teams in the workplace.

3. Identify the characteristics of an effective team.

4. Summarize the stages of team development.

5. Relate team cohesiveness and norms to effective team performance.

6. Describe the factors that can cause conflict in teams and how to manage conflict.

7. Explain the importance and process of effective communication.

8. Compare the different types of communication.

9. Explain external communication and how to manage a public crisis.

PHOTODISC/GETTY IMAGES

When Diane Davidson accepted a job at W. L. Gore & Associates, she found a corporate structure and culture very different from what she'd experienced in her fifteen years in the apparel industry. Gore makes the famous Gore-Tex fabric and other leading products, which generate about $1.3 billion in sales. Innovation is key to the company's continuing success, and that focus is reflected in its teamwork.

"When I arrived at Gore, I didn't know who did what," Davidson remembers. "I wondered how anything got done here. It was driving me crazy." Struggling with the concept of having a mentor called a "starting sponsor" instead of a manager to report to, Davidson kept asking, "Who's my boss?"

To which her sponsor replied, "Stop using the B-word."

AP PHOTO/ROBERTO BOREA

Associates are free to pursue ideas on their own, to communicate about them with anyone in the firm, to figure out what to do to make the ideas work, and then to attract other associates to

## W. L. Gore Frees Its Workers to Perform

Gore's unique combination of self-managed teams, employee empowerment, and employee ownership has kept it on *Fortune*'s list of "100 Best Companies to Work For" every year since the list' debut in 1984, a distinction only seven other companies have ever achieved. Gore is also one of the country's 100 largest companies that are 50 percent or more employee owned. All 7,000 Gore employees own shares in the firm. But the company has no hierarchy, no bosses, and no job titles. As Davidson eventually found out, "Your team is your boss, because you don't want to let them down. Everyone's your boss, and no one's your boss."

Instead of job descriptions, Gore employees—who are called "associates"—have individual sets of "commitments" they make to their teams. Those commitments often allow the person to create a nontraditional work role that bridges several different functions such as sales, marketing, product design, and product sponsorship. It usually takes new team members as much as a year or more to get used to the process, create their roles, and build credibility. During that period, they are also encouraged to spend about 10 percent of their time on developing new ideas.

develop the ideas with them in small teams. Gore believes this practice fosters "natural leadership" and credits it with forming a remarkable environment in which employees work together because of internal motivation, rather than from a sense of duty imposed from the outside. About half the company's employees consider themselves leaders.

Despite the focus on teamwork and independent thinking, not all new initiatives at the company succeed, of course. But those that are axed get a celebratory send-off, the same as is given to ideas that succeed. That endorsement encourages risk taking, as does the pay structure at the firm. Each year, a committee of team members decides the value of an individual's contribution, counting past and present performance as well as future potential.

The company resembles a set of small task forces, with few corporate ranks or titles. In fact, job titles are optional at Gore. Responsibility is "pushed out" to the individual team member, not consolidated in a leader who is defined by a predetermined corporate structure. Some organization, however, is reflected in the company's division into four product areas: (1) fabrics, including the famous breathable waterproof textile;

(2) medical; (3) industrial; and (4) electronic. The firm also has several support functions such as human resources and information technology. Each of these areas has a leader, and CEO Terri Kelly oversees the entire operations as president.

But as Kelly says, "Leaders need to be approachable and real. They can't only fly at 50,000 feet." As for her own job, Kelly says that at Gore, "It's never about the CEO. You're an associate, and you just happen to be the CEO."[1]

**Chapter Overview**

Top managers at most firms recognize that teamwork and communication are essential for encouraging employees and helping them improve organizational performance. This chapter focuses on how organizations involve employees by sharing information and empowering them to make critical decisions, allowing them to work in teams, and fostering communication. We begin by discussing the ways managers are expanding their employees' decision-making authority and responsibility. Then we explain why and how a growing number of firms rely on teams of workers rather than individuals to make decisions and carry out assignments. Finally, we discuss how effective communication allows workers to share information that improves decision making.

# EMPOWERING EMPLOYEES

**empowerment** giving employees authority and responsibility to make decisions about their work without traditional managerial approval and control.

An important component of effective management is **empowerment** of employees. Managers promote this goal by giving employees authority and responsibility to make decisions about their work without traditional managerial approval and control. Empowerment seeks to tap the brainpower of all workers to find improved ways of doing their jobs and executing their ideas. Empowerment frees managers from hands-on control of subordinates. It also motivates workers by adding challenges to their jobs and giving them a feeling of ownership. Managers empower employees by sharing company information and decision-making authority and by rewarding them based on company performance.

## Sharing Information and Decision-Making Authority

One of the most effective methods of empowering employees is to keep them informed about the company's financial performance. Companies such as Virginia-based Anderson & Associates provide regular reports to their employees on key financial information, such as profit-and-loss statements. Anderson, an engineering firm that designs roads, water and sewer lines, and water treatment facilities, posts financial statements, training schedules, policy documents, and other information on the company's internal Web site.[2] Any employee can visit the site and look up the company's cash flow, design standards, and photos of co-workers in other cities, as well as basic measures of financial performance. Senior vice president Brad Stipes says, "I can open up [CEO] Ken Anderson's time sheet. I'm not just accountable to Ken Anderson. I'm accountable to everybody. We're judged on the numbers, and everyone [in the company] can see those numbers."[3]

# HIT & MISS

## Hampton Inn Empowers Front-Line Employees

Would you spend a dollar to get $7 back? Hampton Inn, a division of the Hilton hotel group, does it regularly. Each year, the chain of 1,300 hotels refunds about 0.5 percent of its total room revenues to guests who aren't satisfied with their rooms or service. For every dollar refunded, the company estimates it gets back about $7 in new business, either from a new customer or from an unhappy one who was won over when the chain stood by its commitment to service. Hampton Inn guarantees total guest satisfaction in all its hotels throughout the United States, Canada, and Latin America with this statement: "If you're not 100% satisfied, we don't expect you to pay. That's our promise and your guarantee."

What makes the policy so effective is that every employee in the hotel—whether a front desk clerk, a housekeeper, a maintenance worker, or a restaurant hostess—is empowered to offer guests a free stay on the spot if they are unhappy for any reason. Guests don't have to send their complaints to the manager, call an 800 number, answer a lot of questions, or fill out a response card and then wait for a refund. All they need to do is tell someone why they're unhappy, and not only is the problem corrected immediately, but their room is also free.

Recent Hampton Inn guests included Tom Taylor, a Michigan auditor who told the front desk clerk about the incorrect directions on the hotel's Web site, room lights that were left unplugged, and air conditioning that was too cold. Taylor was immediately offered both nights of his stay free, but he was so impressed by the response that one free night was enough to keep him a happy guest; he insisted on paying for the second one himself. Chris Byrd, a pharmaceutical industry consultant from Arizona, found crumbs in a chair and hair in the bathroom of his Hampton Inn room. Even though he left without complaining, the hotel found out about the problems through Byrd's response to the customer satisfaction e-mail it sent him. Offered a free room to apply to his next stay, Byrd, who hadn't planned to use Hampton Inn again, instead became a fan of the chain. "I wouldn't have come back if they didn't come up with an offer," he said.

### Questions for Critical Thinking

1. Could Hampton Inn's guarantee work for other service firms? Why or why not?
2. If you managed employees who were empowered as Hampton Inn's are, how would you ensure that they make appropriate decisions on their own about when and how to satisfy customers?

**Sources:** Hampton Inn Web site, accessed July 2, 2006, http://hamptoninn.hilton.com; Gerri Willis, "Trip from Hell? It's Payback Time," CNN/Money, accessed July 2, 2006, http://money.cnn.com; Gary Stoller, "Companies Give Front-Line Employees More Power," USA Today, accessed July 2, 2006, http://www.usatoday.com.

Like other companies that practice this strategy of open-book management, Anderson also trains its employees to interpret financial statements so they can understand how their work contributes to company profits. Using information technology to empower employees does carry some risks. One is that information may reach competitors. Although Anderson & Associates considered this problem, management decided that sharing information was essential to the company's strategy.

The second way in which companies empower employees is to give them broad authority to make workplace decisions that implement a firm's vision and its competitive strategy. Even among nonmanagement staff, empowerment extends to decisions and activities traditionally handled by managers. Employees might be responsible for such tasks as purchasing supplies, making hiring decisions, scheduling production or work hours, overseeing the safety program, and granting pay increases. At Mission Controls Automation, a manufacturing company in Costa Mesa, California, employees not only receive the same financial information as company management but also are responsible for hiring. Every job applicant is reviewed by a team called SNAGs, which stands for Screening New Applicant Groups. No one is hired unless every SNAG member gives his or her approval.[4] For more on employee empowerment, see the "Hit & Miss" feature, which explains how Hampton Inn empowers its employees.

## Linking Rewards to Company Performance

Perhaps the ultimate step in convincing employees of their stake in the continuing prosperity of their firm is worker ownership, which makes employees financial participants in company performance. Two widely used ways that companies provide worker ownership are employee stock ownership plans and stock options. Table 10.1 compares these two methods of employee ownership.

*Employee Stock Ownership Plans*   Around 10 million workers at 11,500 different companies participate in **employee stock ownership plans (ESOPs)** worth half a trillion dollars.[5] These plans benefit employees by giving them ownership stakes in their companies, leading to potential profits as the value of their firm increases. Under ESOPs, the employer buys shares of the company stock on behalf of the employee as a retirement benefit. The accounts continue to grow in value tax-free, and when employees leave the company, they can cash in their stock shares. Employees are motivated to work harder and smarter than they would without ESOPs because, as part owners, they share in their firm's financial success. Ryan Till is a salesperson for Chicago-based Anson Industries, a construction firm completely owned by its managers and employees. Till says that without the ESOP plan, "I definitely wouldn't work Saturdays and Sundays and holidays like I do now. It helps to motivate you that last little bit, just when you're starting to think, 'Why am I here?'"[6]

As retirement plans, ESOPs must comply with government regulations designed to protect pension benefits. Because ESOPs can be expensive to set up, they are more common in larger firms than in smaller ones. Public companies with ESOPs average around 14,000 employees.[7] ESOPs work incredibly well. Productivity jumps by 4 percent in the first year alone when ESOPs are introduced. Moreover, a review of 70 studies from the past 25 years shows that profits rise an average of 14 percent with ESOPs, compared with traditional companies.[8]

*Stock Options*   Another popular way for companies to share ownership with their employees is through the use of **stock options**, or rights to buy a specified amount of company stock at a given price within a given time period. In contrast to an ESOP, in which the company holds stock for the benefit of employees, stock options give employees a chance to own the stock themselves if they exercise their options by completing the stock purchase. According to the National Center for Employee Ownership, stock options work like this: "A stock option

**Table 10.1**   Employee Stock Ownership Plans and Stock Options

| ESOP | Stock Options |
|---|---|
| Company-sponsored trust fund holds shares of stock for employees | Company gives employees the option to buy shares of its stock |
| Usually covers all full-time employees | Can be granted to one, a few, or all employees |
| Employer pays for the shares of stock | Employees pay a set price to exercise the option |
| Employees receive stock shares (or value of stock) upon retiring or leaving the company | Employees receive shares of stock when (and if) they exercise the option, usually during a set period. |

**Source:** Based on "Employee Stock Options Fact Sheet," "How an Employee Stock Ownership Plan (ESOP) Works," and "A Comprehensive Overview of Employee Ownership," National Center for Employee Ownership, accessed July 2, 2006, http://www.nceo.org/library.

plan grants employees the right to buy company stock at a specified price during a specified period once the option has vested. So if an employee gets an option on 100 shares at $10 and the stock price goes up to $20, the employee can 'exercise' the option and buy those 100 shares at $10 each, sell them on the market for $20 each, and pocket the difference. But if the stock price never rises above the option price, the employee will simply not exercise the option."[9]

Though options were once limited to senior executives and members of the board of directors, some companies now grant stock options to employees at all levels. Moreover, federal labor laws allow stock options to be granted to hourly and salaried employees. Stock options have turned hundreds of employees at firms such as Home Depot, Microsoft, and Google into millionaires.

Some argue, however, that to be most effective as motivators, stock options need to be granted to a much broader base of employees. About one-third of all stock options issued by U.S. corporations go to the top five executives at each firm. Much of the remainder goes to other executives and managers, who make up only about 2 percent of the U.S. workforce. Yet there is solid evidence that stock options motivate regular employees to perform better.

## TEAMS

A **team** is a group of people with complementary skills who are committed to a common purpose, approach, and set of performance goals. All team members hold themselves mutually responsible and accountable for accomplishing their objectives. Teams are widely used in business and in many not-for-profit organizations such as hospitals and government agencies. Teams are one of the most frequently discussed topics in employee training programs, in which individuals often learn team-building skills. Many firms emphasize the importance of teams during their hiring processes, asking job applicants about their previous experiences as team members. Why? Because companies want to hire people who can work well with other people and pool their talents and ideas to achieve more together than they could achieve working alone. Today, as shown in Figure 10.1, there are five basic types of teams: work teams, problem-solving teams, self-managed teams, cross-functional teams, and virtual teams.

About two-thirds of U.S. firms currently use **work teams,** which are relatively permanent groups of employees. In this approach, people with complementary skills perform the day-to-day work of the organization. Most of Wal-Mart's major vendors maintain offices near its headquarters in Bentonville, Arkansas. Typically, the vendor offices

**team** group of employees who are committed to a common purpose, approach, and set of performance goals.

**work team** relatively permanent group of employees with complementary skills who perform the day-to-day work of organizations.

**Figure 10.1**

Five Species of Teams

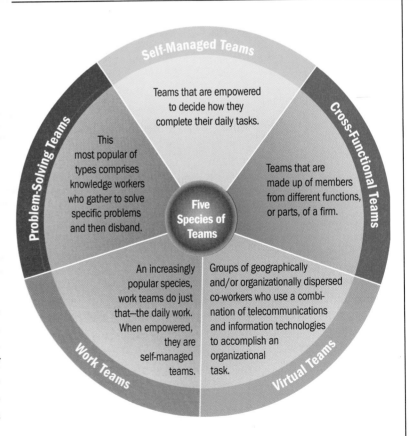

- **Self-Managed Teams** — Teams that are empowered to decide how they complete their daily tasks.
- **Problem-Solving Teams** — This most popular of types comprises knowledge workers who gather to solve specific problems and then disband.
- **Cross-Functional Teams** — Teams that are made up of members from different functions, or parts, of a firm.
- **Work Teams** — An increasingly popular species, work teams do just that—the daily work. When empowered, they are self-managed teams.
- **Virtual Teams** — Groups of geographically and/or organizationally dispersed co-workers who use a combination of telecommunications and information technologies to accomplish an organizational task.

Five Species of Teams

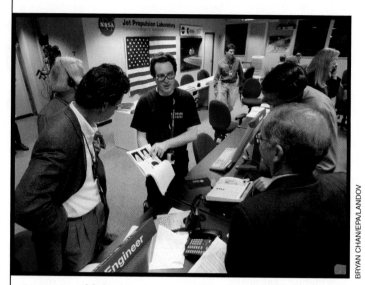

In a survey of federal government employees conducted by Partnership for Public Service, the National Aeronautics and Space Administration (NASA) ranked high on its support for and use of teams.

BRYAN CHAN/EPA/LANDOV

**problem-solving team** temporary combination of workers who gather to solve a specific problem and then disband.

**self-managed team** work team that has the authority decide how its members complete their daily tasks.

**cross-functional team** team made up of members from different functions, such as production, marketing, and finance.

operate as work teams, and the head of these vendor offices often has the title of "team leader."

In contrast to work teams, a **problem-solving team** is a temporary combination of workers who gather to solve a specific problem and then disband. They differ from work teams in important ways, though. Work teams are permanent units designed to handle any business problem that arises, but problem-solving teams pursue specific missions. These missions can be broadly stated, such as finding out why customers are satisfied or how to transition from one major computer system to another, or narrowly defined, such as solving the overheating problem in Generator 4 or determining the best way and time to move from an old office location to a new one. Once the team completes its task by solving the assigned problem, it usually disbands.

A work team empowered with the authority to decide how its members complete their daily tasks is called a **self-managed team.** A self-managed team works most effectively when it combines employees with a range of skills and functions. Members are cross-trained to perform each other's jobs as needed. Distributing decision-making authority in this way can free members to concentrate on satisfying customers. Whole Foods Market, a national chain of upscale food stores, has a structure based on self-managed work teams. Company managers decided that Whole Foods could be most innovative if employees made decisions themselves. Every employee is part of a team, and each store has about ten teams handling separate functions, such as groceries, bakery, and customer service. Each team handles responsibilities related to setting goals, hiring and training employees, scheduling team members, and purchasing goods to stock. Teams meet at least monthly to review goals and performance, solve problems, and explore new ideas. Whole Foods awards bonuses based on the teams' performance relative to their goals.[10]

A team made up of members from different functions, such as production, marketing, and finance, is called a **cross-functional team.** Most often, cross-functional teams work on specific problems or projects, but they can also serve as permanent work team arrangements. The value of cross-functional teams comes from their ability to bring many different perspectives to a work effort. When Hypertherm, a Hanover, New Hampshire–based maker of metal cutting machines, experienced conflict between its engineering and marketing departments, CEO Richard Couch reorganized the company into five cross-functional teams, one for each line of products. To strengthen the teams, he rearranged offices so that the salespeople, engineers, marketers, and researchers for each product sat next to each other in nearby cubicles. An engineer griped about "sitting next to this marketing guy. I don't have anything to say to him." Couch remembered, "I thought precisely my point. Maybe you will actually say something to him," now that you sit together.[11] For more on cross-functional teams, see the "Hit & Miss" feature describing GE's action learning teams.

**Virtual teams** are groups of geographically or organizationally dispersed co-workers who use a combination of telecommunications and information technologies to accomplish an organizational task. Because of the availability of e-mail, videoconferencing, and group communication software, members of virtual teams rarely meet face-to-face. For example, consulting firm PricewaterhouseCoopers (PWC) has 190 employees in its training department in the United States located in 70 different offices. One-fourth of those staff members work at home, never setting foot in the office. Yet these employees regularly work together in virtual teams as they write proposals, put together training programs, or offer advice to PWC consultants.

## GE's Action Learning Teams

General Electric combines cross-functional and problem-solving teams by having managers and employees from different parts of the company work together to apply their specialized knowledge to a challenge posed by upper-level executives. Top management often acts on these teams' suggestions to solve puzzling questions and problems within the firm.

GE makes wide use of such teams, gathering people from manufacturing, sales, marketing, legal, and finance, for example, to tackle specific problems. Because GE also fast-tracks its most promising young employees, the younger members of its action learning teams have a unique opportunity to work with and learn from more experienced personnel. As GE's chief learning officer says, team members "get exposed to very big projects and issues, but with a safety net. You learn by doing, and you get continuous feedback on your performance." And the teams "encourage people to learn a lot about a lot of things, not just their own jobs. It reduces the likelihood that when boomers do retire, you'll be left saying, 'Gee, old Alex was the only person here who knew how to do this.'"

Another characteristic of action learning teams is that time to reflect and discuss the assigned task is built into their structure. While "learning by doing" is one of the major benefits employees get from participation in the team, learning from reflection, from ambiguity, and even from coping with small failures along the way are also hallmarks of action learning.

At GE, action learning teams seem certain to remain a popular magnet for up-and-coming managers. Todd Wyman, 37, has risen through nine different positions since joining the company right after college. At 33, he was managing the supply chain for GE's Mexican manufacturing operations, worth $1 billion a year. Action learning teams gave him the chance to work in Romania, Belgium, Qatar, and Latin America. Now manager of GE's rail transportation global supply chain, Wyman highlights a very personal benefit of action learning: "Giving people really challenging jobs early in their careers is important for companies that want to retain them."

### Questions for Critical Thinking

1. How would you select members of a successful action learning team? What criteria would you use?
2. Explain why most recommendations of action learning teams are accepted by top management. What do you think accounts for their successful track record?

**Sources:** Damon Darlin, "Growing Tomorrow," *Business 2.0,* accessed July 2, 2006, http://www.business2.com; Anne Fisher, "How to Battle the Coming Brain Drain," *Fortune,* accessed July 2, 2006, http://www.fortune.com; Udo Dierk and Scott Saslow, "Action Learning in Management Development Programs," *Chief Learning Officer,* May 2005, pp. 20–25.

---

Manager Peter Nicolas says, "Virtual teaming is the norm for us." But when Nicolas leads a new virtual team that has never worked together before, he says, "I always try to do the kick-off meeting face-to-face. If we can put people in the same room, we do," because it is the best way to build "enthusiasm and to get clear about everyone's roles and responsibilities." Then, over time, "We also try to bring the group back together for major milestones in a project."[12] The principal advantage of virtual teams is that they are very flexible. Employees can work with each other regardless of physical location, time zone, or organizational affiliation. But as PWC's experience shows, the give-and-take that naturally occurs in face-to-face meetings is much more difficult to achieve in virtual teams. Thus, bringing virtual team members together on a regular basis is one of the best ways to overcome this difficulty.

**virtual team** group of geographically and/or organizationally dispersed co-workers who use a combination of telecommunications and information technologies to accomplish an organizational task.

## TEAM CHARACTERISTICS

Effective teams share a number of characteristics. They must be an appropriate size to accomplish their work. In addition to size, teams also can be categorized

**assessment check**

1. What is a team?
2. What are the five types of teams and how are they different?

according to the similarities and differences among team members, called *level* and *diversity*. We discuss these three characteristics next.

## Team Size

Teams can range in size from as small as two people to as large as 150 people. In practice, however, most teams have fewer than twelve members. Although no ideal size limit applies to every team, research on team effectiveness indicates that they achieve maximum results with about six or seven members.[13] A group of this size is big enough to benefit from a variety of diverse skills, yet small enough to allow members to communicate easily and feel part of a close-knit group.

Certainly, groups smaller or larger than this ideal size can do effective work, but they can create added challenges for a team leader. Participants in small teams of two to four members often show a desire to get along with each other. They tend to favor informal interactions marked by discussions of personal topics, and they make only limited demands on team leaders. A large team with more than twelve members poses a different challenge for team leaders because decision making may work slowly and participants may feel less committed to team goals. Larger teams also tend to foster disagreements, absenteeism, and membership turnover. Subgroups may form, leading to possible conflicts among various functions. As a general rule, a team of more than 20 people should be divided into subteams, each with its own members and goals.

## Team Level and Team Diversity

**team level** average level of ability, experience, personality, or any other factor on a team.

**Team level** is the average level of ability, experience, personality, or any other factor on a team. For example, a high level of team experience means that a team has members who, on average, are very experienced. This does not mean that *every* member of the team has considerable experience but that enough team members do to significantly raise the average level of experience on the team. Businesses consider team level when they need teams with a particular set of skills or capabilities to do their jobs well.

**team diversity** variances or differences in ability, experience, personality, or any other factor on a team

While team level represents the average level or capability on a team, **team diversity** represents the variances or differences in ability, experience, personality, or any other factor on a team. In other words, strong teams not only have talented members (as demonstrated by their team level) but also members who are different in terms of ability, experience, or personality. Team diversity is an important consideration for teams that must complete a wide range of different tasks or particularly complex tasks. A cross-functional team establishes one type of diversity by bringing together the expertise of members from different functions in the organization. For instance, many financial companies are moving away from using individual financial advisors to using diverse teams of financial advisors. At Wachovia Services, Don DeWees Jr. is part of a ten-member team that advises 800 wealthy clients. The members of this team are specialists in investments, retirement planning, strategies to reduce taxes, and trust and estate planning. Said DeWees, "We look at ourselves as the families' CFO [chief financial officer], the go-to guys to help answer all the questions."[14] Wachovia's use of diverse teams is part of a growing trend; half of Merrill Lynch's financial advisors now work on diverse teams, as do 40 percent of those at Smith Barney and 38 percent of those at UBS.

## Stages of Team Development

Teams typically progress through five stages of development: forming, storming, norming, performing, and adjourning. Although not every team passes through each of these stages, teams that do tend to be better performers. These stages are summarized in Figure 10.2.

**Stage 1: Forming** The first stage, forming, is an orientation period during which team members get to know each other and find out what behaviors are acceptable to the group. Team members begin with curiosity about expectations of them and whether they will fit in with the group. An effective team leader provides time for members to become acquainted.

**Stage 2: Storming** The personalities of team members begin to emerge at the storming stage as members clarify their roles and expectations. Conflicts may arise, as people disagree over the team's mission and jockey for position and control of the group. Subgroups may form based on common interests or concerns. At this stage, the team leader must encourage everyone to participate, allowing members to work through their uncertainties and conflicts Teams must move beyond this stage to achieve real productivity.

**Stage 3: Norming** During the norming stage, members resolve differences among them, accept each other, and reach broad agreement about the roles of the team leader and other participants. This stage is usually brief, and the team leader should use it to emphasize the team's unity and the importance of its objectives.

Stages of Team Development

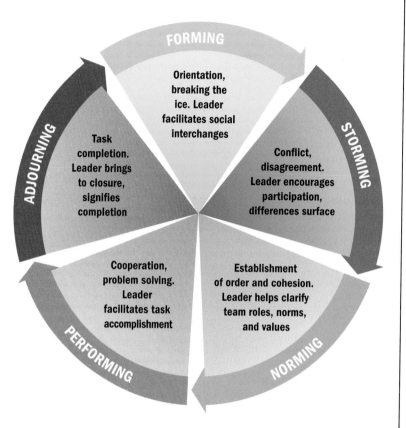

**Stage 4: Performing** Team members focus on solving problems and accomplishing tasks at the performing stage. They interact frequently and handle conflicts in constructive ways. The team leader encourages contributions from all members. He or she should attempt to get any nonparticipating team members involved.

**Stage 5: Adjourning** The team disbands at the adjourning stage after members have completed their assigned task or solved the problem. During this phase, the focus is on wrapping up and summarizing the team's experiences and accomplishments. The team leader may recognize the team's accomplishments with a celebration, perhaps handing out plaques or awards.

**assessment check**

1. Explain how teams progress through the stages of team development.
2. Explain the difference between the storming and performing stages.

## Team Cohesiveness and Norms

Teams tend to maximize productivity when they form into highly cohesive units. **Team cohesiveness** is the extent to which team members feel attracted to the team and motivated to remain part of it. This cohesiveness typically increases when members interact frequently, share common attitudes and goals, and enjoy being together. When cohesiveness is low, morale suffers. By contrast, cohesive groups have a better chance of retaining their members. As a result, cohesive groups typically experience lower turnover. In addition, team cohesiveness promotes cooperative behavior, generosity, and a willingness on the part of team members to help each other. When team cohesiveness is high, team members are more motivated to contribute to

**team cohesiveness** extent to which team members feel attracted to the team and motivated to remain part of it.

New Age Transportation's employees spend most of their days staring at computer screens to track customer orders, their shipments, and their invoices. To break the sometimes stressful work environment at the Lake Zurich, Illinois firm, top managers suggested twice-a-day dance breaks. The ten-minute breaks were a hit—they fostered team cohesiveness by getting employees from different departments, who normally wouldn't interact, to talk with one another.

**team norm** informal standard of conduct shared by team members that guides their behavior.

**assessment check**

1. How does cohesiveness affect teams?
2. Explain how team norms positively and negatively affect teams.

the team, because they want the approval of other team members. Not surprisingly, studies have clearly established that cohesive teams quickly achieve high levels of performance and consistently perform better.

A **team norm** is a standard of conduct shared by team members that guides their behavior. Norms are not formal written guidelines; they are informal standards that identify key values and clarify team members' expectations. Not all norms, though, are positive. For example, the norm in most operating rooms is that the surgeon is clearly in charge. At first look, there doesn't seem to be anything wrong with that. After all, if the surgeon weren't in charge, who would be? However, at 20 hospitals, 60 percent of the operating room staffers—nurses, technicians, and other doctors—agreed with this statement: "In the ORs here, it is difficult to speak up if I perceive a problem with patient care."[15] And when nurses and other operating room staffers don't speak up, serious mistakes can occur.

In highly productive teams, however, norms contribute to constructive work and the accomplishment of team goals. In fact, many hospitals are trying to change the norms in their operating rooms so that surgeons will be more team-oriented and other operating room personnel will speak up when there are problems. VHA, which helps 2,400 hospitals coordinate best practices, has a new program called "Transformation of the Operating Room," in which operating teams use "safety pauses" and "time-outs." The surgical team pauses for a moment, is asked if anyone has concerns or comments, and then addresses them if need be. Studies show that programs such as this are not only changing the norms in operating rooms but also reducing mistakes, such as operating on the wrong leg or noticing that key surgical instruments are missing prior to beginning surgery.[16]

## Team Conflict

**Conflict** is an antagonistic interaction in which one party attempts to thwart the intentions or goals of another. Conflict and disagreement are inevitable in most teams. But this shouldn't surprise anyone. People who work together are naturally going to disagree about what and how things are done. What causes conflict in teams? Although almost anything can lead to conflict—casual remarks that unintentionally offend a team member or fighting over scarce resources—the primary cause of team conflict is disagreement over team goals and priorities. Other common causes of team conflict include disagreements over task-related issues, interpersonal incompatibilities, and simple fatigue.

Though most people view conflict negatively, the key to dealing with it is not avoiding it, but making sure that the team experiences the right kind of conflict. **Cognitive conflict** focuses on problem-related differences of opinion, and reconciling these differences strongly improve team performance. With cognitive conflict, team members disagree because their different experiences and expertise lead them to different views of the problem and its solutions. Cognitive conflict is also characterized by a willingness to examine, compare, and reconcile differences to produce the best possible solution. By contrast, **affective conflict** refers to the emotional reactions that can occur when disagreements become personal rather than professional, and these differences strongly decrease team performance. Because affective conflict

**"They Said It"**

"The team that trusts—their leader and each other—is more likely to be successful."
—Mike Krzyzewski (b. 1947)
Head basketball coach, Duke University

**conflict** antagonistic interaction in which one party attempts to thwart the intentions or goals of another.

often results in hostility, anger, resentment, distrust, cynicism, and apathy, it can make people uncomfortable, cause them to withdraw, decrease their commitment to a team, lower the satisfaction of team members, and decrease team cohesiveness. So unlike cognitive conflict, affective conflict undermines team performance by preventing teams from engaging in activities that are critical to team effectiveness.

What can managers do to manage team conflict? Emphasizing cognitive conflict alone isn't enough, because cognitive and affective conflict can occur together in the same teams. Attempts to agree on a difficult issue can quickly deteriorate from cognitive to affective conflict if the discussion turns personal and tempers and emotions flare. So while cognitive conflict is clearly the better approach to take, encouraging conflict of any type should be approached with caution. Perhaps the team leader's most important contribution to conflict resolution can be facilitating good communication so that teammates respect each other and are free to disagree with each other. Ongoing, effective communication ensures that team members perceive each other accurately, understand what is expected of them, and obtain the information they need. Improved communication increases the chances of working cooperatively as a team. The remainder of this chapter discusses the importance of effective communication and the development of good communication skills.

**assessment check**

1. What is cognitive conflict and how does it affect teams?
2. Explain affective conflict and its impact on teams.

# THE IMPORTANCE OF EFFECTIVE COMMUNICATION

Andrea Tam is the production manager of a small clothing design company in Vancouver, British Columbia. When she asked her boss what to do with 1,100 yards of unused fabric, she hoped for a quick answer. She waited, and waited, and waited for her boss to communicate his wishes. He never told her, so she eventually decided to let the fabric sit in a warehouse in China, costing the company storage fees and lost revenue.[17]

**Communication** can be defined as a meaningful exchange of information through messages. Few businesses, including the clothing design company that Andrea Tam works for, can succeed without effective communication. Managers spend about 80 percent of their time—six hours and 24 minutes of every eight-hour day—in direct communication with others, whether on the telephone, in meetings, via e-mail, or in individual conversations. Company recruiters consistently rate effective communication, such as listening, conversing, and giving feedback, as the most important skill they're looking for when hiring college graduates. In this last half of the chapter, you'll learn about the communication process, the basic forms of communication, and ways to improve communication within organizations.

**communication** meaningful exchange of information through messages.

The importance of communication was in a glaring spotlight after Hurricane Katrina devastated New Orleans and the Mississippi Gulf Coast. Because cell phone towers were damaged during the storm, emergency responders did not know who was in trouble or where they were. The teams also could not communicate with headquarters staff.

© JASON REED/REUTERS/CORBIS

# The Process of Communication

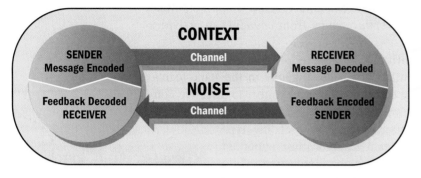

Every communication follows a step-by-step process that involves interactions among six elements: sender, message, channel, audience, feedback, and context. This process is illustrated in Figure 10.3.

In the first step, the *sender* composes the message and sends it through a communication carrier, or channel. Encoding a message means that the sender translates its meaning into understandable terms and a form that allows transmission through a chosen channel. The sender can communicate a particular message through many different channels, including written messages, face-to-face conversations, and electronic mail. A promotional message to the firm's customers may be communicated through such forms as radio and television ads, billboards, magazines, and sales messages. The *audience* consists of the people who receive the message. In decoding, the receiver of the message interprets its meaning. *Feedback* from the audience—in response to the sender's communication—helps the sender determine whether the audience has correctly interpreted the intended meaning of the message.

Every communication takes place in some sort of situational or cultural context. The *context* can exert a powerful influence on how well the process works. A conversation between two people in a quiet office, for example, may be a very different experience from the same conversation held in a crowded and noisy restaurant. A request by an American to borrow a flashlight from an Australian friend might produce only confusion; what Americans call *flashlights,* Australians call *torches.* Anthropologists classify cultures as low context and high context. Communication in **low-context cultures** tends to rely on explicit written and verbal messages. Examples include Switzerland, Austria, Germany, and the United States. In contrast, communication in **high-context cultures**—such as those of Japan, Latin America, and India—depends not only on the message itself but also on the conditions that surround it, including nonverbal cues, past and present experiences, and personal relationships between the parties. Westerners must carefully temper their low-context style to the expectations of colleagues and clients from high-context countries. Although Americans tend to favor direct interactions and want to "get down to business" soon after shaking hands or sitting down to a business dinner, businesspeople in Mexico and Asian countries prefer to become acquainted before discussing details. When conducting business in these cultures, wise visitors allow time for relaxed meals during which business-related topics are avoided.

Senders must pay attention to audience feedback, even requesting it if none is forthcoming, because this response clarifies whether the communication has conveyed the intended message. Feedback can indicate whether the receiver paid attention to a message and was able to decode it accurately. Even when the receiver tries to understand, the communication may fail if the message was poorly encoded with difficult or ambiguous words. Managers sometimes become fond of using fuzzy language such as *transparency, forward leading,* and *paradigm shift.* Feedback can indicate whether the sender's audience succeeded in decoding this jargon—or even bothered to try.

Even with the best of intentions, sender and audience can misunderstand each other. The Episcopal Church Medical Trust, which provides insurance coverage for 17,000 people, wanted to lower its costs by discouraging unnecessary visits to emergency rooms. Being the sender, it communicated the simple message that its health plan members would now have to pay an extra $50 co-pay when visiting the emergency room for nonemergency treatment. That simple communication was easily understood by its health plan members, who made fewer trips to emergency rooms. However, the Medical Trust's computer programmers misunderstood this simple communication and wrote computer code that charged the health plan members $50 for each emergency room doctor who treated them, resulting in inaccurate co-pays as high as $200 per visit. Vice president for plan administration Tim Hanover said, "Sometimes what your intent was isn't what comes across when the claims actually come in. Now whenever we want to make changes, we discuss [with our claims administrator] first how it's really going to work out."[18]

*Noise* during the communication process is some type of interference that influences the transmission of messages and feedback. Noise can result from simple physical factors such as poor reception of a cell phone message or static that drowns out a radio commercial. It can also be caused by more complex differences in people's attitudes and perceptions. Consequently, even when people are exposed to the same communications, they can end up with very different perceptions and understandings because of communication noise. This is why communication can be so difficult and frustrating for managers. It's also why executives have to purposefully stick to and repeat their messages to cut through the noise. Bill Zollars, CEO of Yellow Roadway, a trucking firm based in Overland Park, Kansas, says, "When I first got to Yellow, we were in a bad state. So I spent 85% of my time on the road talking to people one-on-one or in small groups. I would start off in the morning with the sales force, then talk to drivers, and then the people on the docks. At the end of the day, I would have a customer dinner. I would say the same thing to every group and repeat it ad nauseam. The people traveling with me were ready to shoot me. But you have to be relentless in terms of your message."[19]

## Basic Forms of Communication

People communicate in many different ways. Some obvious methods include calling a meeting of team members or writing a formal mission statement. Other much less obvious methods include gestures and facial expressions during a conversation or leaning forward when speaking to someone. These subtle variations can significantly influence the reception of the message. As Table 10.2 points out, different communications can assume various forms: oral and written, formal and informal, and verbal and nonverbal.

**assessment check**

1. What is the difference between communication in low-context and high-context cultures?
2. In the context of the communication process, what is noise?

**Table 10.2**

Forms of Communication

| Form | Description | Examples |
|------|-------------|----------|
| Oral communication | Communication transmitted through speech | Personal conversations, speeches, meetings, voice mail, telephone conversations, videoconferences |
| Written communication | Communication transmitted through writing | Letters, memos, formal reports, news releases, e-mail, faxes, online discussion groups, Internet messaging |
| Formal communication | Communication transmitted through the chain of command within an organization to other members or to people outside the organization | Internal—memos, reports, meetings, written proposals, oral presentations, meeting minutes; External—letters, written proposals, oral presentations, speeches, news releases, press conferences |
| Informal communication | Communication transmitted outside formal channels without regard for the organization's hierarchy of authority | Rumors spread informally among employees via the grapevine |
| Verbal communication | Transmission of messages in the form of words | Meetings, telephone calls, voice mail, videoconferences |
| Nonverbal communication | Communication transmitted through actions and behaviors rather than through words | Gestures, facial expressions, posture, body language, dress, makeup |

## Minding Your Telephone Manners

It's all too easy to forget the importance of the impression we make over the telephone. But that link is as critical for businesses as communicating face-to-face. To ensure that your telephone conversations at work send the right message about you and your firm, check out the following guidelines.

1. Answer your own phone whenever possible, and answer promptly—by the third ring.
2. Say, "Hello, this is [your name] speaking," or a variation that is preferred in your workplace or department.
3. If the caller has the wrong number, be gracious when acknowledging the error and hanging up. If you think you can redirect the call for the person, offer to do so first. Likewise, if you dial a wrong number, apologize briefly and hang up.
4. Reduce background noise when using the phone to avoid distractions and to convey the message that the caller is your first priority.
5. Return all calls within 24 hours. The only exception is urgent calls, which you should return immediately.
6. Speak slowly, clearly, and in a pleasant tone. Smile when

you speak—it conveys a positive attitude even if the other person can't see you.

7. If you are taking a call for someone else who is out, give as little detail as possible about where the person is and offer to either take a message or transfer the caller to a voice-mail system. If you take a message, get complete information, including the time of the call; write clearly; and make sure the message is delivered promptly.
8. When you make a call, dial carefully, identify yourself, and ask for the party to whom you wish to speak.
9. Prepare what you need to say ahead of time and get to the point. Be considerate of others' time.
10. Remember that you may be working with people who live in different time zones from yours. Make sure you call during their regular working hours, not yours.

**Sources:** "Telephone Etiquette," Essortment, accessed July 2, 2006, http://mt.essortment.com; "Telephone Etiquette Guide," California State University, Fullerton: Information Technology, accessed July 2, 2006, http://www.fullerton.edu; Lewena Bayer and Karen Mallett, "Telephone Etiquette," accessed August 15, 2005, Lifewise, http://www.canoe.ca.

### Oral Communication

**Oral Communication** Managers spend a great deal of their time engaged in oral communication, both in person and on the phone. Some people prefer to communicate this way, believing that oral channels more accurately convey messages. Face-to-face oral communication allows people to combine words with such cues as facial expressions and tone of voice. Oral communication over the telephone lacks visual cues, but it offers some of the advantages of face-to-face communication, such as opportunities to hear the tone of voice and provide immediate feedback by asking questions about anything the receiver doesn't understand or raising new issues related to the message. For more on oral communication, see the "Business Etiquette" feature on minding your telephone matters.

Procter & Gamble's CEO, A. G. Lafley, believes strongly in the benefits of oral communication. Lafley says, "I'm not a big e-mailer. I prefer face-to-face whenever possible. And usually we're in a cafeteria or an auditorium somewhere, and I talk briefly, and then I spend half to two-thirds of the time on comments and questions and answers, which is when you really get at what's on people's minds."[20]

In any medium, a vital component of oral communication is **listening**—receiving a message and interpreting its genuine meaning by accurately grasping the facts and feeling conveyed. Although listening is the first communication skill that people learn and the one they use most often, it is also the one in which they receive the least formal training.

Listening may seem easy, because the listener makes no obvious effort. This apparent passivity creates a deceptive picture, however. The average person talks at a rate of roughly 150 words per minute, but the

**listening** receiving a message and interpreting its intended meaning by grasping the facts and feelings it conveys.

brain can handle up to 400 words per minute. This discrepancy can lead to boredom, inattention, and misinterpretation. In fact, immediately after listening to a message, the average person can recall only half of it. After several days, the proportion of a message that a listener can recall falls to 25 percent or less.

Certain types of listening behaviors are common in both business and personal interactions:

- *Cynical listening.* This defensive type of listening occurs when the receiver of a message feels that the sender is trying to gain some advantage from the communication.

- *Offensive listening.* In this type of listening, the receiver tries to catch the speaker in a mistake or contradiction.
- *Polite listening.* In this mechanical type of listening, the receiver listens to be polite rather than to communicate. Polite listeners are usually inattentive and spend their time rehearsing what they want to say when the speaker finishes.
- *Active listening.* This form of listening requires involvement with the information and empathy with the speaker's situation. In both business and personal life, active listening is the basis for effective communication.

Learning how to be an active listener is an especially important goal for business leaders, because effective communication is essential to their role.

*Written Communication*  Channels for written communication include reports, letters, memos, online discussion boards, and e-mail messages. Most of these channels permit only delayed feedback and create a record of the message. So it is important for the sender of a written communication to prepare the message carefully and review it to avoid misunderstandings.

Effective written communication reflects its audience, the channel carrying the message, and the appropriate degree of formality. When writing a formal business document, such as a complex report, a manager must plan in advance and carefully construct the document. The process of writing a formal document involves planning, research, organization, composition and design, and revision. Written communication via e-mail may call for a less-formal writing style, including short sentences, phrases, and lists.

E-mail can be a very effective communication channel, especially for delivering straightforward messages and information. But e-mail's effectiveness also leads to its biggest problem: too much e-mail! Scott McNealy, former CEO of Sun Microsystems, averaged 150 e-mails a day—and that was just from his own employees. Henry McKinnell, Jr., CEO of New York–based Pfizer, the largest pharmaceuticals company in the world, says, "I don't look out the window [when being driven to meetings]. I use my BlackBerry and answer my e-mail." Finally, James Rogers, CEO of Cinergy, a Cincinnati-based provider of gas and electricity, keeps his BlackBerry next to his bed. Before you go to bed, says Rogers, "you don't say your prayers. You check your e-mail."[21]

Another problem with e-mail is security. Because e-mail messages are often informal, senders occasionally forget that they are creating a written record. Also, even if the recipient deletes an e-mail message, other copies exist on company e-mail servers. And if e-mails are available on company servers, they can be used against you and your firm in a lawsuit. Nancy Flynn, executive director of the ePolicy Institute of Columbus, Ohio, says, "You can take it to the bank that your employee e-mail is going to be subpoenaed. If you can't produce the e-mail that the court wants you to produce, then you're going to face court sanctions. And you may even get into a situation where the court gives instructions to the jury to go ahead and draw negative inferences because your organization wasn't able to produce e-mail."[22] So be careful about what you say in your e-mails—someone is probably watching.

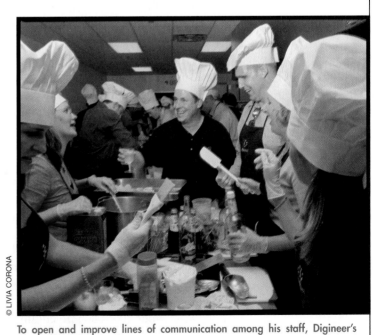

© LIVIA CORONA

To open and improve lines of communication among his staff, Digineer's CEO Michael Lacey held an Iron Chef cook-off. Lacey, who previously had prepared elaborate meals for his staff, had his employees split themselves into teams to create a three-course meal. Lacey judged the results as both fun and delicious.

### Formal Communication

A **formal communication channel** carries messages that flow within the chain of command structure defined by an organization. The most familiar channel, downward communication, carries messages from someone who holds a senior position in the organization to subordinates. Managers may communicate downward by sending employees e-mail messages, presiding at department meetings, giving employees policy manuals, posting notices on bulletin boards, and reporting news in company newsletters. The most important factor in formal communication is to be open and honest. "Spinning" bad news to make it look better almost always backfires. Yvonne Hunt, vice president for worldwide internal communications at Hewlett-Packard, said, "When companies spin internally, it is very difficult to build credibility since most news delivered to an internal audience (especially difficult news) is often communicated externally. When there is a disparity between what employees hear from their manager and what they see in the media, it leads to distracted, de-motivated employees who feel a lack of trust caused by a lack of transparency—whether that is real or perceived."[23]

Many firms also define formal channels for upward communications. These channels encourage communication from employees to supervisors and upward to top management levels. Some examples of upward communication channels are employee surveys, suggestion boxes, and systems that allow employees to propose new projects or voice complaints.

### Informal Communication

**Informal communication channels** carry messages outside formally authorized channels within an organization's hierarchy. A familiar example of an informal channel is the **grapevine,** an internal channel that passes information from unofficial sources. Research shows that many employees cite the grapevine as their most frequent source of information. Grapevines rapidly disseminate information. A message sent through formal channels may take days to reach its audience, but messages that travel via grapevines can arrive within hours. Grapevines also are surprisingly reliable links. They pass on accurate information 70 to 90 percent of the time.[24] Workplace psychologist Nicholas DiFonzo, who spent months in *Fortune* 500 companies tracking rumors, says, "The main focus of rumor [and the grapevine] is to figure out the truth." When rumors began about downsizing at one of the companies he was studying, "The rumor mill produced a list of people that would be laid off that was 100% accurate."[25] For more on a unique case of information communication, holiday office parties, see the "Solving an Ethical Controversy" feature.

The spontaneity of informal communication may diminish when a company's employees are spread among many locations. Employees who telecommute or travel frequently may miss opportunities to build smooth working relationships or exchange ideas. In those situations, communication technology can help firms promote informal communication. Some companies establish online chat areas for employees, so they can visit each other during breaks. Some also encourage their workers to create home pages that describe their interests and hobbies. In fact, surveys reveal that even among people in the same office, workplace instant messaging is used for personal discussions and work-related gossip. A survey of U.S. and British workers found that 80 percent of workplace instant messages were for gossiping and that nearly two-thirds contained complaints to managers about co-workers.[26]

### Verbal and Nonverbal Communication

So far, this section has considered different forms of verbal communication, or communication that conveys meaning through words. Equally important is **nonverbal communication,** which transmits messages through actions and behaviors. Gestures, posture, eye contact, tone of voice, and even clothing choices are all nonverbal actions that become communication cues. Nonverbal cues can strongly influence oral communication by altering or distorting intended meanings.

Nonverbal cues can have a far greater impact on communications than many people realize. One study divided face-to-face conversations into three sources of communication cues: verbal cues (the actual words spoken), vocal cues (pitch or tone of a person's voice), and

**grapevine** internal information channel that transmits information from unofficial sources.

# SHOULD COMPANIES HOLD HOLIDAY OFFICE PARTIES?

*Holidays are times for getting together, renewing relationships, and celebrating with colleagues. Office parties, whether lavish or small, serve all these functions and are a staple of organizational life.*

But if inappropriate actions such as excessive drinking or unprofessional behavior occur at office holiday parties, or if nonparticipants feel slighted or left out because they don't observe certain holidays, can such parties really foster better work relationships and improve teamwork? Or will they have the opposite effect?

Should companies hold holiday office parties?

## PRO

1. Many people view office parties as a reward for their hard work during the year, and they deserve the chance to gather for social reasons, let down some organizational barriers, and have fun with their co-workers. Parties are also great morale builders.
2. With well-publicized guidelines and safeguards, inappropriate or unsafe behavior can be reduced to a minimum or even eliminated. Holding luncheons is another option to help ensure a safer environment to celebrate. Most people know how to behave and just want to enjoy themselves; most employees are not a problem.

## CON

1. It's too difficult to agree on what holidays should be acknowledged and celebrated in the office. It's fairer and less divisive to allow everyone to celebrate their own particular holidays at home with their families and not to single any out at work.
2. Employers may be held legally liable for the actions of drunk drivers or other alcohol-related accidents following an office party where drinks were served. But employees tend to expect alcohol at parties. So it's better to avoid both accidents and liability by not having office parties.

## Summary

Some possible solutions for avoiding the drawbacks of holiday parties are to restrict or even ban the flow of liquor. Stopping alcohol service an hour or so before the end of a party and offering coffee, tea, and other nonalcoholic beverages is another option. Companies can also provide transportation home for employees who attend. As for cultural differences, with a little creative effort, businesses can make their parties unique by looking for new themes and traditions that give everyone a reason to celebrate.

**Sources:** Jessica M. Walker, "Should Auld Acquaintance Forget Themselves at the Office Holiday Party," *New Jersey Law Journal,* accessed July 3, 2006, http://www.law.com/nj; Diane E. Lewis, "Party Like It's Not Quite 9 to 5," *Boston Globe,* accessed July 3, 2006, http://www.boston.com; Mitch Moxley, "Parties No Excuse for Bad Behaviour," *Financial Post,* accessed January 3, 2005, http://www.canada.com/national/nationalpost.

solving an **ETHICAL** controversy

facial expressions. The researchers found some surprising relative weights of these factors in message interpretation: verbal cues (7 percent), vocal cues (38 percent), and facial expressions (55 percent).[27]

Even personal space—the physical distance between people who are engaging in communication—can convey powerful messages. Figure 10.4 shows a continuum of personal space and social interaction with four zones: intimate, personal, social, and public. In the United States, most business conversations occur within the social zone, roughly between four and twelve feet apart. If one person tries to approach closer than that, the other will likely feel uncomfortable or even threatened.

Interpreting nonverbal cues can be especially challenging for people with different cultural backgrounds. Concepts of appropriate personal space differ dramatically throughout most of the world. Latin Americans conduct business discussions in positions that most Americans and Northern Europeans would find uncomfortably close. Americans often back away to preserve their personal space, a gesture that Latin Americans perceive as a sign of cold and unfriendly relations. To protect their personal space, some Americans separate themselves across desks or tables from their Latin American counterparts—at the risk of challenging their colleagues to maneuver around those obstacles to reduce the uncomfortable distance.

## 10.4  Influence of Personal Space in Nonverbal Communication

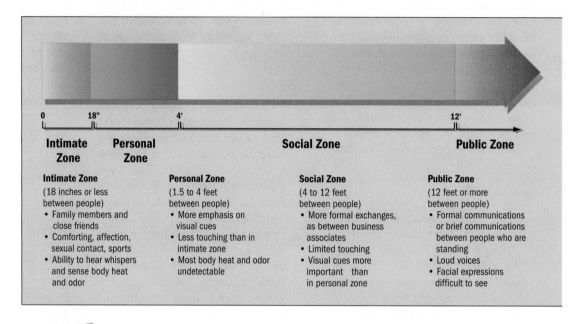

| 0 | 18" | 4' | | 12' |
|---|---|---|---|---|
| **Intimate Zone** | **Personal Zone** | **Social Zone** | | **Public Zone** |

| **Intimate Zone** | **Personal Zone** | **Social Zone** | **Public Zone** |
|---|---|---|---|
| (18 inches or less between people) | (1.5 to 4 feet between people) | (4 to 12 feet between people) | (12 feet or more between people) |
| • Family members and close friends | • More emphasis on visual cues | • More formal exchanges, as between business associates | • Formal communications or brief communications between people who are standing |
| • Comforting, affection, sexual contact, sports | • Less touching than in intimate zone | • Limited touching | • Loud voices |
| • Ability to hear whispers and sense body heat and odor | • Most body heat and odor undetectable | • Visual cues more important  than in personal zone | • Facial expressions difficult to see |

People send nonverbal messages even when they consciously try to avoid doing so. Sometimes nonverbal cues convey a person's true attitudes and thoughts, which may differ from spoken meanings. Generally, when verbal and nonverbal cues conflict, receivers of the communication tend to believe the nonverbal content. This is why Southwest Airlines, which seeks to hire people with good attitudes and a team orientation, closely watches nonverbal behavior during job interviews in which job applicants participate in group sessions with other job candidates applying for the same job. If in those group interviews an applicant frowns or looks discouraged when a competing candidate gives a good answer, Southwest concludes from that nonverbal behavior that this person may not be strongly team oriented.[28]

# EXTERNAL COMMUNICATION: CRISIS MANAGEMENT

**external communication**
meaningful exchange of information through messages transmitted between an organization and its major audiences.

**External communication** is a meaningful exchange of information through messages transmitted between an organization and its major audiences, such as customers, suppliers, other firms, the general public, and government officials. Businesses use external communication to keep their operations functioning, to maintain their positions in the marketplace, and to build customer relationships by supplying information about topics such as product modifications and price changes. Every communication with customers—including sales presentations, customer orders, and advertisements—should create goodwill and contribute to customer satisfaction. However, all of this is threatened when companies experience a public crisis that threatens their reputation or goodwill. For example, Wendy's restaurants saw an immediate decline in sales after reports that a severed finger was found served in a bowl of chili at a Wendy's in San Jose, California. In northern California alone, sales declined by $2.5 million, which resulted in layoffs and reduced working hours. However, one month later, police arrested the woman who "found" the finger, charging her with perpetrating a hoax to win a lawsuit or financial settlement from the company. Joseph Desmond, owner of the Wendy's restaurant in which this all took place, said, "It's been 31 days, and believe me it's been really tough. My thanks also go out to all the little people who were hurt in our stores. They lost a lot of wages because we had to cut back because our business has been down so badly."[29]

So what steps can companies and their managers or spokespersons take when dealing with a public crisis? First, companies must respond quickly when a crisis occurs and with a prepared statement. During the initial news contact, which might be a press conference or simply an interview with a print or TV reporter, prepare by writing a statement—no matter how short—and stick to it. The statement should mention the time, place, initial description of what occurred (not the cause), and the number and status of the people involved.

Second, as soon as possible, put top company management in front of the press. Because the public will hold top management accountable, it's best to have top managers responding to reporters' questions. For instance, after a Southwest Airlines flight ran off the runway in a snowstorm at Chicago's Midway airport, hitting a car and killing a 6-year-old boy, Southwest had CEO Gary Kelly in Chicago the next morning to represent and speak for the company.[30]

Third, when answering reporters' questions, stick to the facts. Don't wing it. If you don't know the details about what happened, then don't speculate. If you speculate and are proven wrong, it will look like you were lying. So tell people only what you know.

Fourth, if you don't know, offer to find out. You don't have to know the answer to each question off the top of your head. When you don't know, say so: "I don't know the answer to that question." When you can find out an answer, say that, too. But then be sure to deliver the answer in a timely manner.

Fifth, never say "no comment." "No comment" is perceived as a statement of guilt. It's better to say, "I don't know."

Sixth, identify and speak to your audience. In the Wendy's case, there were several audiences, among them people who watch TV news and people who like to eat at fast-food restaurants. When speaking to an audience, it's important to recognize that what you say is likely to be only a small part of a TV, print, or radio story. Accordingly, you can speak more effectively to your audience by using visual or word images instead of facts. Most people don't have the time or are reluctant to immerse themselves in the details of a story. Facts are easily forgotten. Images are easily remembered. For instance, when a hypodermic needle was "found" in a can of Pepsi, the company quickly took reporters to their bottling plants where they showed (1) that Pepsi bottles and cans were washed and then dried *upside down* on a high-speed assembly line a split second before being turned right side up and filled with Pepsi, and (2) that the cans were then weighed and any can that didn't correspond to the standard weight was automatically kicked out of the production process.[31]

Finally, acknowledge problems and explain solutions. If a question or factual statement puts your organization in a negative light, acknowledge the problem, and then explain how you're correcting it.

**assessment check**

1. What is external communication?
2. During a company crisis, why is it dangerous for a spokesperson to say "no comment" when answering reporters' questions?

# WHAT'S AHEAD

Today's consumers expect the products they buy to be of the highest value for the price. Firms ensure this value by developing efficient systems for producing goods and services, as well as maintaining high quality. The next chapter examines the ways in which businesses produce world-class goods and services, efficiently organize their production facilities, purchase what they need to produce their goods and services, and manage large inventories to maximize efficiency and reduce costs.

### 1 Describe why and how organizations empower employees.

By empowering employees, a firm finds better ways to perform jobs, motivates people by enhancing the challenges and satisfaction in their work, and frees managers from hands-on control so that they can focus on other tasks. Employers empower workers by sharing information, distributing decision-making authority and responsibility, and linking rewards to company performance through employee stock ownership plans and stock options.

### Assessment Check Answers

**1.1 What is empowerment?**
Empowerment is giving employees authority and responsibility to make decisions about their work without traditional managerial approval and control.

**1.2 What kinds of information can companies provide employees to help them share decision-making responsibility?**
Sharing information about company performance, particularly financial performance, is one of the best ways to share decision-making responsibility.

**1.3 What are some of the risks of sharing this information?**
One risk is that proprietary competitive or financial information may reach competitors.

**1.4 How do employee stock ownership plans and stock options reward employees and encourage empowerment?**
Employee stock ownership plans (ESOPs) benefit employees by giving them ownership stakes in their companies. Employees are motivated to work harder and smarter than they would without ESOPs because they share in their firm's financial success. In contrast to an ESOP, in which the company holds stock for the benefit of employees (when employees leave the company, they cash in their stock), stock options give employees a chance to own the stock themselves if they exercise their options by completing the stock purchase.

### 2 Distinguish among the five types of teams in the workplace.

The five basic types of teams are work teams, problem-solving teams, self-managed teams, cross-functional teams, and virtual teams. Work teams are permanent groups of co-workers who perform the day-to-day tasks necessary to operate the organization. Problem-solving teams are temporary groups of employees who gather to solve specific problems and then disband. Self-managed teams have the authority to make decisions about how their members complete their daily tasks. Cross-functional teams are made up of members from different functions, such as production, marketing, and finance. Virtual teams are groups of geographically or organizationally dispersed co-workers who use a combination of telecommunications and information technologies to accomplish an organizational task.

### Assessment Check Answers

**2.1 What is a team?**
A team is a group of employees who are committed to a common purpose, approach, and set of performance goals.

**2.2 What are the five types of teams and how are they different?**
Work teams are permanent, while problem-solving teams are temporary. Unlike work teams, self-managed teams have the authority to change how they get their work done. Cross-functional teams are composed of people from different backgrounds, while virtual teams are composed of people from different locations.

### 3 Identify the characteristics of an effective team.

Three important characteristics of a team are its size, team level, and team diversity. Effective teams typically contain between five and twelve members, with about six or seven members being the ideal size. Team level is the average level of ability, experience, personality, or any other factor on a team. For example, a high level of team experience means that members have, on average, particular expertise in some area. Instead of considering similarities, team diversity represents the variances or differences in ability, experience, personality, or any other factor on a team. In other words, strong teams not only have talented members (i.e., team level) but also benefit from the differences in terms of ability, experience, or personality of individual members. Diverse teams tend to display broader ranges of viewpoints and produce more innovative solutions to problems than do homogeneous teams.

## Assessment Check Answers

**3.1 Teams reach maximum effectiveness, diversity, and communication flow with how many members?**
Six or seven members is typically the best size for a team.

**3.2 Explain team level and team diversity.**
While team level represents the average level or capability on a team, team diversity represents the variances or differences in ability, experience, personality, or any other factor on a team.

**4 Summarize the stages of team development.**
Teams pass through five stages of development: (1) Forming is an orientation period during which members get to know each other and find out what behaviors are acceptable to the group. (2) Storming is the stage during which individual personalities emerge as members clarify their roles and expectations. (3) Norming is the stage at which differences are resolved, members accept each other, and consensus emerges about the roles of the team leader and other participants. (4) Performing is characterized by problem solving and a focus on task accomplishment. (5) Adjourning is the final stage, with a focus on wrapping up and summarizing the team's experiences and accomplishments.

## Assessment Check Answers

**4.1 Explain how teams progress through the stages of team development.**
Teams pass through five stages of development: forming, storming, norming, performing, and adjourning.

**4.2 Explain the difference between the storming and performing stages.**
The primary difference is how teams handle conflict in these stages. In the storming stage, people disagree over the team's mission and jockey for position and control of the group. But in the performing stage, those issues have been settled, so team members handle conflicts in constructive ways; in other words, they encourage cognitive conflict to solve problems.

**5 Relate team cohesiveness and norms to effective team performance.**
Team cohesiveness is the extent to which team members feel attracted to the team and motivated to remain on it. Team norms are standards of conduct shared by team members that guide their behavior.

Highly cohesive teams whose members share certain standards of conduct tend to be more productive and effective.

## Assessment Check Answers

**5.1 How does cohesiveness affect teams?**
Members of cohesive teams interact more often, share common attitudes and goals, have higher morale, and are more likely to help each other. Cohesive teams also perform better.

**5.2 Explain how team norms positively and negatively affect teams.**
Norms are informal standards that identify key values and clarify team members' expectations. But those norms can be positive or negative. Positive norms contribute to constructive work and the accomplishment of team goals. Negative norms can, for example, contribute to reduced work effort, reduced quality, and poor job attendance.

**6 Describe the factors that can cause conflict in teams and how to manage conflict.**
Conflict and disagreement are inevitable in most teams. Conflict can stem from many sources: disagreements about goals and priorities, task-related issues, interpersonal incompatibilities, scarce resources, and simple fatigue. Though most people view conflict negatively, the key to dealing with team conflict is not avoiding it, but making sure that the team experiences the right kind of conflict. Cognitive conflict focuses on problem-related differences of opinion and, when reconciled, strongly improves team performance. By contrast, affective conflict refers to the emotional reactions that can occur when disagreements become personal rather than professional, and these differences strongly decrease team performance. A team leader can limit conflict by focusing team members on broad goals, clarifying participants' respective tasks and areas of authority, acting as mediator, and facilitating effective communication.

## Assessment Check Answers

**6.1 What is cognitive conflict and how does it affect teams?**
With cognitive conflict, team members disagree because their different experiences and expertise lead them to different views of the problem and its solutions. Cognitive conflict is characterized by a willingness to

examine, compare, and reconcile differences to produce the best possible solution.

### 6.2 Explain affective conflict and its impact on teams.

Because affective conflict often results in hostility, anger, resentment, distrust, cynicism, and apathy, it can make people uncomfortable, cause them to withdraw, decrease their commitment to a team, lower the satisfaction of team members, and decrease team cohesiveness.

### 7 Explain the importance and process of effective communication.

Managers and employees spend much of their time exchanging information through messages. Communication helps all employees understand the company's goals and values and the parts they play in achieving those goals. Every communication follows a step-by-step process that involves interactions among six elements: sender, message, channel, audience, feedback, and context.

## Assessment Check Answers

### 7.1 What is the difference between communication in low-context and high-context cultures?

Communication in low-context cultures tends to rely on explicit written and verbal messages. By contrast, communication in high-context cultures depends not only on the message itself but also on the conditions that surround it, including nonverbal cues, past and present experiences, and personal relationships between the parties.

### 7.2 In the context of the communication process, what is noise?

Noise interferes with the transmission of messages and feedback. Noise can result from physical factors such as poor reception of a cell phone message or differences in people's attitudes and perceptions.

### 8 Compare the different types of communication.

People exchange messages in many ways: oral and written, formal and informal, verbal and nonverbal communication. Effective written communication reflects its audience, its channel, and the appropriate degree of formality. Formal communication channels carry messages within the chain of command. Informal communication channels, such as the grapevine, carry messages outside the formal chain of command.

Nonverbal communication plays a larger role than most people realize. Generally, when verbal and nonverbal cues conflict, the receiver of a message tends to believe the meaning conveyed by nonverbal elements.

## Assessment Check Answers

### 8.1 What are four common listening behaviors? Characterize each.

Cynical listening occurs when the receiver of a message feels that the sender is trying to gain some advantage from the communication. Offensive listening occurs when the receiver tries to catch the speaker in a mistake or contradiction. Polite listening occurs when the receiver acts politely but, rather than listening, is rehearsing what he or she wants to say when the speaker finishes. Active listening requires involvement with the information and empathy with the speaker's situation.

### 8.2 What are some advantages of e-mail as a communication medium? What are some disadvantages?

E-mail can be a very effective communication channel, especially for delivering straightforward messages and information. But too much e-mail and poor security, meaning that it's easy for people who weren't intended to read a particular e-mail to do so, are some of its disadvantages.

### 8.3 What are the differences between formal and informal communication?

Formal communication occurs within the formal chain of command defined by an organization, whereas informal communication occurs outside the organization's hierarchy.

### 8.4 Why do we pay more attention to nonverbal communication cues than to verbal communication cues?

Nonverbal cues can reveal what senders are really thinking or feeling, particularly when nonverbal cues don't match verbal communication.

### 9 Explain external communication and how to manage a public crisis.

External communication is a meaningful exchange of information through messages transmitted between an organization and its major audiences, such as customers, suppliers, other firms, the general public, and government officials. Every communication with customers should create goodwill and contribute to customer satisfaction. However, all of this is threatened when companies experience a public crisis that threatens their reputations or goodwill. To manage a public crisis, businesses should respond quickly when a crisis occurs with a prepared statement; quickly put top company management in front of the press; answer reporters' questions with facts; offer to find out answers; never say, "No comment"; identify and speak to their audience by using visual or word images instead of facts; and acknowledge problems and explain solutions.

## Assessment Check Answers

**9.1 What is external communication?**
External communication occurs when organizations communicate with and receive messages from key external groups, such as customers, suppliers, other firms, the general public, and government officials.

**9.2 During a company crisis, why is it dangerous for a spokesperson to say "no comment" when answering reporters' questions?**
"No comment" is perceived as a statement of guilt. It's better to say, "I don't know."

## Business Terms You Need to Know

empowerment 320
team 323
work team 323
problem-solving team 324
self-managed team 324
cross-functional team 324

virtual team 324
team level 326
team diversity 326
team cohesiveness 327
team norm 328
conflict 328

communication 329
listening 332
grapevine 334
external communication 336

## Other Important Business Terms

employee stock ownership plan
   (ESOP) 322
stock options 322
cognitive conflict 328
affective conflict 328

low-context culture 330
high-context culture 330
formal communication
   channel 334

informal communication
   channel 334
nonverbal communication 334

## Review Questions

1. Describe the ways employers can empower their employees. Give a specific example of each.
2. Identify and briefly explain the approaches companies use to provide for worker ownership. What are the main differences between them?
3. How does each of the five team types function? In what instances might a company use each type?
4. How do team level and team diversity affect team performance?
5. What are the characteristics of an effective team? Why are these features so significant?
6. Identify and briefly describe the five stages of team development. At what stages might a team get "stuck" and not be able to move forward?
7. How does affective conflict hinder group effectiveness?
8. What are the major elements in the communication process? Briefly define each element.
9. Outline the two channels for formal communication. Give an example of each.
10. What is the central focus of a company's external communication?

1. Consider your current job or one you have held in the past. Did your employer practice any kind of employee empowerment? If so, what? If not, why not? Or think of your family as a company. Did your parents empower their children? If so, in what ways? In either scenario, what do you think were the consequences of empowerment or nonempowerment?

2. Identify a firm that makes extensive use of teams. Then interview someone from the firm to assess how their teams operate.

3. Do you consider yourself a good listener? First, identify which listening style you think you practice. Then describe the listening styles outlined in this chapter to a friend, family member, or classmate and ask that person what type of listening style he or she thinks you practice. Finally, compare the two responses. Do they agree or dis-

agree? *Note:* You can take this exercise a step further by asking more than one person what type of listening style you practice and then comparing all of the responses.

4. The grapevine is one of the strongest communication links in any organization, from large corporation to college classroom to family. Do you rely on information that travels along the grapevine? Why or why not?

5. Take a seat in the library or dorm lounge, in a mall, in a restaurant, or wherever there is a flow of people whom you can watch unobtrusively. For at least fifteen minutes, observe and jot down the nonverbal cues that you see pass between people. Then try to interpret these cues. How would your interpretation affect any actual communication you might have with one of these people?

## Case 10.1

### Communicating and Listening at Cabela's

Cabela's, a premier outdoors and sporting-goods supplier founded in 1961, has transformed itself over the last few years from a catalog retailer to a string of a dozen gigantic "destination" stores. And more are on the way. It's not unusual for shoppers to spend two to three hours browsing, testing products, asking questions, and shopping. The stores each hold tens of thousands of products for enthusiasts of fishing, hunting, hiking, and camping. And they feature attractions like gun libraries, shooting galleries, indoor archery ranges, three-dimensional scenes of the African plains, ice-fishing seminars, and exotic sandwiches filled with wild boar, ostrich, bison, and elk meat. Cabela's newest outlet, in Austin, Texas, spans 185,000 square feet on 126 acres and has more stuffed and mounted animals on display than it has employees—571 versus 517.

"People will drive 200 to 300 miles to visit a Cabela's store," says a commercial real estate broker. "It's crazy. But they will."

Unique product offerings, unbeatable entertainment value, and competitive prices have helped the chain grow rapidly in the tough brick-and-mortar world of retail. In a recent year, Cabela's shipped more than 8 million orders through its catalog operation, for sales of more than $970 million, and logged nearly $500 million in revenues from its stores. But with that growth have come new needs: an urgent need for temporary workers to handle the phones at Cabela's five call centers and for salespeople to work in the stores. In one recent busy period, from the fall hunting season through the winter holidays, the number of phone agents doubled to 4,000, and the opening of each new store—six more are in the works—requires the addition of about 500 employees.

"Taking all those people onto staff has become more of a challenge as we've continued to grow," says the company's CFO. "It is hard to manage the people, and it is expensive to continue to retrain them."

How does Cabela's solve the problem of communicating information about its thousands of products to its new recruits? How does it do that successfully enough not only to satisfy its demanding customers but also to avoid costly rehiring and retraining efforts?

One major strategy is Cabela's reliance on a huge and innovative knowledge-sharing system it calls "Item Notes," which puts at their fingertips the product information in-store and call-center employees need to quickly and efficiently answer customers' questions. Do you need to know what to bring on your first hunting trip? Are you worried about whether a camouflage seat cover will fit on your golf cart? Any employee at Cabela's can tell you.

The database of Item Notes has been built up from the experiences of the store's dedicated employees, most of whom are outdoor enthusiasts themselves and who borrow, take home and test, and then report on many of its products. The loans are free, of course, but there is a catch—after returning the item, employees are required to report on its features and benefits, both pros and cons, and explain what they've learned about it to other employees or to customers. The information base grows as other employees learn about the products, even including notes about possible typos in the product's instructions, tips on its use, or unexpected quirks or bugs in its operation. Because there is no rigid format for the information, anything and everything of importance can be included in the database, such as customer feedback.

Select, trusted customers who are outdoor guides or fish and wildlife biologists are also tapped for their contributions to the Item Notes database. They borrow products just as the salespeople do and return them with similar feedback and reports. Customer comments are fed in, whether they come by phone or e-mail, and these reports are also sent to the responsible departments for resolution, if any is needed. Jim Cabela, founder and vice chairman of the firm, reads every e-mail message.

## Questions for Critical Thinking

1. Why is it important for Cabela's to collect the kind of information stored in its Item Notes? If the store didn't have this database, what other sources of product information could it tap? Would they be inferior to Item Notes, and if so, why?
2. What are some possible sources of "noise" in a communication system like the Item Notes database? How can they be overcome?

**Sources:** Michael A. Prospero, "Leading Listener: Cabela's," *Fast Company,* Anthony Lonetree, "Cabela's Makes Rogers a Destination," *Minneapolis–St. Paul Star-Tribune,* accessed July 3, 2006, http://www.startribune .com; Chris Serres, "Big Store for the Big Outdoors," *Minneapolis–St. Paul Star-Tribune,* accessed July 3, 2006, http://www.startribune.com; J. Bonasia, "Managing for Success," *Investor's Business Daily,* accessed July 3, 2006, http://www.investors.com; Patrick Beach, "Cabela's Fans Finally Get to See the Great Indoors," *Austin American-Statesman,* accessed July 3, 2006, http://www.statesman.com.

# VIDEO Case 10.2
## Meet the People of BP

This video case appears on page 618. A recently filmed video, designed to expand and highlight the written case, is available for class use by instructors.

# Chapter 11

## Production and Operations Management

egardless of where you live, you'll remember the names—Katrina and Rita. They were two of the largest and most devastating hurricanes to ever hit U.S. shores. Lives, homes, and businesses were lost in their floods and high winds.

Offshore in the Gulf of Mexico, the storms pounded oil and natural-gas drilling rigs and platforms, destroying or severely damaging more than 100 of them. Chevron's giant Typhoon platform actually capsized and drifted 70 miles. Two of Global Santa Fe's drilling rigs were found lying in shallow coastal waters, about 80 miles from their original location. About 99 percent of the gulf's daily oil production and 80 percent of its natural-gas production were knocked out during a time when demand was already extremely high. "The impact on the rigs is something that's never been seen by this country before," said

CHRIS ZUPPA/EPA/LANDOV

Will it be more expensive? Yes. Will the end product cost more? You bet," warned Al Reese Jr., CFO of ATP Oil &

# Hurricanes and the U.S. Fuel Industry

Daniel Naatz, director of federal resources for the Independent Petroleum Association of America. On land, damaged refineries lost production of about 1.7 million barrels a day of refined products.

Within days, it became apparent that a lack of workers, helicopters, and equipment would deter efforts to evaluate the damage to oil and natural-gas facilities offshore in the gulf, and a timeline for restarting production was nonexistent. "A lot of dock facilities that boats would leave from are gone. [Air transportation] hangars are messed up. Helicopter availability is tight," said Tony Lentini, a spokesperson for oil exploration company Apache. The longer it took to assess the situation, make repairs, and begin producing again, the higher the prices would rise. "Will it be more difficult to drill? Yes.

Gas. In addition to lack of workers and equipment, widespread power outages made start-up of the refineries along the coast impossible.

The federal government predicted that average heating-oil and natural-gas bills could climb 50 percent higher than they had the year before. "We think consumers need to know this now so they can take steps to do something about it," noted David Garman, undersecretary of energy. Meanwhile, some experts observed that worldwide demand for oil has grown faster than supply in recent years, thanks in part to developing economies such as China's and consumers' devotion to large cars and trucks. With one-third of the nation's refining capacity located in the Gulf Coast region, all sights are set on finding every drop of liquid gold in the gulf.[1]

By producing and marketing desired goods and services, businesses satisfy their commitment to society as a whole. They create what economists call *utility*—the want-satisfying power of a good or service. Businesses can create or enhance four basic kinds of utility: time, place, ownership, and form. A firm's marketing operation generates time, place, and ownership utility by offering goods and services to customers when they want to buy at convenient locations where ownership of the products can be transferred.

Production, by contrast, creates form utility by converting raw materials and other inputs into finished products, as the oil companies described in the opening vignette do. **Production** applies resources such as people and machinery to convert materials into finished goods and services. The task of **production and operations management** is to oversee the application of people and machinery in converting materials into finished goods and services. Figure 11.1 illustrates the production process.

People sometimes use the terms *production* and *manufacturing* interchangeably, but doing so ignores an important difference. Production is a broader term that spans both manufacturing and nonmanufacturing industries. For instance, companies in extractive industries

such as fishing, lumber, and mining engage in production, and so do service providers. Services are intangible outputs of production systems. They include outputs as diverse as trash hauling, education, haircuts, tax accounting, dental care, mail delivery, transportation, and lodging. Figure 11.2 lists five examples of production systems for a variety of goods and services.

But whether the production process results in a tangible good or an intangible service, it always converts inputs into outputs. This conversion process may make major changes in raw materials or simply combine already finished parts into new products. A cabinetmaker combines wood, tools, and skill to create finished kitchen cabinets for a new home. A transit system combines buses, trains, and employees to create its output: passenger transportation. Both of these production processes create utility.

This chapter describes the process of producing goods and services. It looks at the importance of production and operations management and discusses the new technologies that are transforming the production function. It then discusses the tasks of the production and operations manager, the importance of quality, and the methods businesses use to ensure high quality.

**production** application of resources such as people and machinery to convert materials into finished goods and services.

**production and operations management** managing people and machinery in converting materials and resources into finished goods and services.

**11.1**  The Production Process: Converting Inputs to Outputs

Figure

11.2

| Example | Primary Inputs | Transformation | Outputs |
|---|---|---|---|
| **Computer Factory** | Hard drives, computer memory, computer chips, keyboards, cases, power supply, DVD drives, central circuit board, boards for network and Internet access and graphics, monitors, and sofware | Assembles components to meet customer orders, including specialized orders for hardware and software | Desktop or laptop computers |
| **Trucking Firm** | Trucks, personnel, buildings, fuel, goods to be shipped, packaging supplies, truck parts, utilities | Packages and transports goods from sources to destinations | Delivered goods |
| **Department Store** | Buildings, displays, scanners, merchandise, personnel, supplies, utilities | Attracts customers, stores goods, sells products | Merchandise sold |
| **Automobile Body Shop** | Damaged autos, paints, supplies, machines, tools, buildings, personnel, utilities | Transforms damaged auto bodies into facsimiles of the originals | Repaired automobile bodies |
| **County Sheriff's Department** | Personnel, police equipment, automobiles, office furniture, buildings, utilities | Detects crimes and brings criminals to justice | Lower crime rates and peaceful communities |

# STRATEGIC IMPORTANCE OF THE PRODUCTION FUNCTION

Along with marketing and finance, production is a vital business activity. Without a good or service to sell, companies cannot generate money to pay their employees, lenders, and stockholders. And without the profits from products, firms quickly fail. The production process is just as crucial in nonprofit organizations, such as the Mayo Clinic and Goodwill Industries, because the goods or services they offer justify their existence. Effective production and operations management can lower a firm's costs of production, boost the quality of its goods and services, allow it to respond dependably to customer demands, and enable it to renew itself by providing new products. Let's look at the differences between mass, flexible, and customer-driven production.

## Mass Production

Workers on an automobile assembly line use specialization of labor tasks for maximum efficiency.

From its beginnings as a colonial supplier of raw materials to Europe, the United States evolved into an industrial giant. Much of this remarkable change resulted from **mass production,** a system for manufacturing products in large amounts through effective combinations of employees with specialized skills, mechanization, and standardization. Mass production makes outputs available in large quantities at lower prices than individually crafted items would cost.

Mass production begins with specialization of labor, dividing work into its simplest components so that each worker can concentrate on performing one task. Secondly, by separating jobs into small tasks, managers create conditions for high productivity through mechanization, in which machines perform much of the work previously done by people. Standardization, the third element of mass production, involves producing uniform, interchangeable goods and parts. Standardized parts simplify the replacement of defective or worn-out components. For instance, if your car's windshield wiper blades wear out, you can easily buy replacements at a local auto parts store such as AutoZone.

**assembly line** manufacturing technique that carries the product on a conveyor system past several workstations where workers perform specialized tasks.

A logical extension of these principles of specialization, mechanization, and standardization led to development of the **assembly line.** This manufacturing technique moves the product along a conveyor belt past a number of workstations, where workers perform specialized tasks such as welding, painting, installing individual parts, and tightening bolts. Henry Ford's application of this concept revolutionized auto assembly. Before the assembly line, it took Ford's workers 12 hours to assemble a Model T car. But with an assembly line, it took just 1.5 hours to make the same car. Not surprisingly, dozens of other industries soon adopted the assembly line technique.

Although mass production has important advantages, it has limitations, too. While mass production is highly efficient for producing large numbers of similar products, it is highly inefficient when producing small batches of different items. This trade-off tempts some companies to focus on efficient production methods rather than on making what customers really want. In addition, the labor specialization associated with mass production can lead to boring jobs, because workers keep repeating the same task. To improve their competitive capabilities, many firms adopt flexible production and customer-driven production systems. These techniques may not replace mass production altogether but may simply improve a company's use of mass production.

## Flexible Production

While mass production efficiently creates large batches of similar items, flexible production can cost-effectively produce smaller batches. Flexible production can take many forms, but it generally involves using information technology to share the details of customer orders, programmable equipment to fulfill the orders, and skilled people to carry out whatever tasks are needed to fill a particular order. This arrangement is useful when combined with lean production methods that use automation and information technology to reduce requirements for workers and inventory. Flexible production also requires a high degree of communication and cooperation among customers and employees throughout the organization.

DaimlerChrysler is switching its U.S. auto plants from mass to flexible production. This change will allow it to move from producing one type of car at each automobile plant to being able to produce three kinds of cars at each plant. Because a typical auto plant can make 200,000 to 240,000 cars a year, auto plants lose money if the sales of the one car they make fall below those levels. For instance, in its first year, the new Dodge Charger sold an average of 7,000 cars a month, or just 84,000 for the year, almost two-thirds fewer cars than the capability of a typical DaimlerChrysler auto plant. However, by using flexible production to make the Dodge Charger, the Chrysler 300, and the Dodge Magnum at the same auto plant, Daimler-Chrysler can continue to sell these small-market cars and make money at that production facility, which is now used to its full capacity.[2]

NikeID shoes are manufactured to customer specifications. Customers can either visit the NikeID Web site to order their shoes electronically or go to a nearby Nike ID lab store. Approximately three weeks later, a unique pair of shoes arrives.

## Customer-Driven Production

A customer-driven production system evaluates customer demands to link what a manufacturer makes with what customers want to buy. Many firms have implemented this approach with great success. One method is to establish computer links between factories and retailers' scanners, using data about sales as the basis for creating short-term forecasts and designing production schedules to meet those forecasts.

Another approach to customer-driven production systems is simply not to make the product until a customer orders it. For example, a new computer is produced every five seconds at Dell's new Winston-Salem, North Carolina, manufacturing plant, which uses one of the most advanced customer-driven production operations in the computer business. But every one of those different computers—Dell makes each one to customer orders—has already been purchased. Ray Archer, Dell's vice president of Americas manufacturing, said, "If we don't have an order, we don't have a customer."[3] Because Dell doesn't order parts from suppliers until machines are purchased, its computers always have the latest, most advanced components. And because the prices of computer components tend to fall, Dell can immediately pass those lower prices on to its customers, too.

**assessment check**

1. What are the advantages and disadvantages of mass production?
2. What are the characteristics of flexible production?
3. Describe a customer-driven production system.

# PRODUCTION PROCESSES

Not surprisingly, the production processes and time required to make an Apple iPod and a gallon of gasoline are different. Production processes use either an analytic or synthetic system, and time requirements call for either a continuous or an intermittent process.

An *analytic production system* reduces a raw material to its component parts in order to extract one or more marketable products. For example, petroleum refining breaks down crude oil into several marketable products, including gasoline, heating oil, and aviation fuel. When corn is processed further, the resulting marketable products include animal feed and corn sweetener.

By contrast, a *synthetic production system* is the reverse of an analytic system. It combines a number of raw materials or parts or transforms raw materials to produce finished products. Dell's assembly line produces personal computers by assembling the various components ordered by each customer. Ford's assembly line uses a variety of metal, plastic, and rubber

Synthetic production systems assemble raw materials and other components into finished products, such as these Ford Mustangs being welded in Flat Rock, Michigan.

components to produce cars and trucks. Other synthetic production systems make drugs, chemicals, computer chips, and canned soup.

A *continuous production process* generates finished products over a lengthy period of time. The steel industry provides a classic example. Its blast furnaces never completely shut down except for malfunctions. Petroleum refineries, chemical plants, and nuclear power facilities also practice continuous production. A shutdown can damage sensitive equipment, with extremely costly results.

An *intermittent production process* generates products in short production runs, shutting down machines frequently or changing their configurations to produce different products. Most services result from intermittent production systems. For instance, accountants, plumbers, and dentists traditionally have not attempted to standardize their services because each service provider confronts different problems that require individual approaches. However, some companies, including Jiffy Lube (auto service) and Terminix (pest control services), offer standardized services as part of a strategy to operate more efficiently and compete with lower prices. In contrast, McDonald's has moved toward a more intermittent production model. The fast-food chain invested millions in new cooking equipment to set up kitchens for preparing sandwiches quickly to order, rather than producing large batches ahead of time and then keeping them warm under heat lamps.

# TECHNOLOGY AND THE PRODUCTION PROCESS

Like other business functions, production has changed dramatically as computers and related technologies have developed. For example, in manufacturing, a "lights out" factory is completely automated. In other words, because of computers, software, robots, and other kinds of integrated technology systems, no workers are needed to make what a "lights out" factory produces. You could literally turn all the lights off, and the factory would keep producing finished products. IBM has a "lights out" factory in East Fishkill, New York, at its most advanced computer chip fabrication (fab) plant. Perry Hartswick, IBM's manager of semiconductor automation and integration, said, "We consider our fab's automation system architecture an example of a true business transformation. We had to take hundreds of very complex inputs, consider them in conjunction with hundreds of operational scenarios, and come up with an architecture that could run our fab in a fully automated mode."[4] Compared with IBM's other fab plants, IBM's fab plant in East Fishkill has 59 percent higher productivity.

In addition to boosting efficiency in the production process, automation and information technology allow firms to redesign their current methods to enhance flexibility. These changes allow a company to design and create new products faster, modify them more rapidly, and meet customers' changing needs more effectively than it could achieve with traditional methods. Important production technologies today include robots, computer-aided design and manufacturing, flexible manufacturing systems, and computer-integrated manufacturing.

## Robots

**robot** reprogrammable machine capable of performing numerous tasks that require manipulation of materials and tools.

A growing number of manufacturers have freed people from boring, sometimes dangerous assignments by replacing them with robots. A **robot** is a reprogrammable machine capable of performing a variety of jobs that require manipulation of materials and tools. Robots can repeat the same tasks many times without varying their movements. Many factories use robots today to "palletize" their products for shipping. This means stacking finished products on a wood, plastic, or steel pallet and then shrink-wrapping the items onto the pallet with plastic. Not only do robots lift pallets into place, they also use their gripping "hands" and lifting "arms" to put products into neat rows and layers for shipping. At Ohio-based JTM, a maker of industrial lubricants, a robot places 3,300 twenty-five-pound containers of finished product onto 70 pallets a day. Larry Wilson, JTM's director of operations, said, "In the old facility without the robot, I would have had to add two people to get up to this volume." In the past, said Wilson, "We had people picking up 1,800 or 1,900 pails a day. That's a long day."[5]

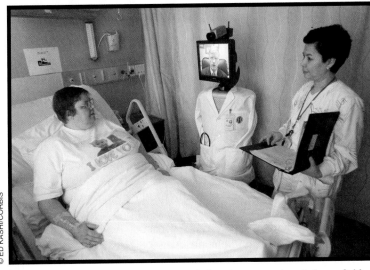

To help reduce the effects of a shortage of physicians, some hospitals use field robots to perform patient rounds. The doctor's face is visible on the robot's monitor, and patients can discuss their conditions directly with him or her in real time.

Initially, robots were most common in automotive and electronics manufacturing, but growing numbers of industries, such as JTM's, are adding robots to production lines as improvements in technology make them less expensive and more useful. Firms operate many different types of robots. The simplest kind, a *pick-and-place robot,* moves in only two or three directions as it picks up something from one spot and places it in another. The robot, which "palletizes" Murphy's Oil Soap at JTM, is a pick-and-place robot. So-called *field robots* assist people in nonmanufacturing, often hazardous, environments such as nuclear power plants, the space station, and even battlefields. For instance, police use robots to remotely dispose of suspected bombs. However, the same technology can be used in factories. Using vision systems, infrared sensors, and bumpers on mobile platforms, robots can automatically move parts or finished goods from one place to another, while either following or avoiding people, whichever is necessary to do the job.

## Computer-Aided Design and Manufacturing

A process called **computer-aided design (CAD)** enables engineers to design parts and buildings on computer screens faster and with fewer mistakes than they could achieve working with traditional drafting systems. Using an electronic pen, an engineer can sketch 3-D designs on an electronic drafting board or directly on the screen. The computer then provides tools to make major and minor design changes and to analyze the results for particular characteristics or problems. Engineers can put a new car design through a simulated road test to project its real-world performance. If they find a problem with weight distribution, for example, they can make the necessary changes virtually—without actually test-driving the car. In other words, with advanced CAD software, prototyping is as much "virtual" as it is "hands-on." Actual prototypes or parts aren't built until the engineers are satisfied that the required structural characteristics in their virtual designs have been met.

The process of **computer-aided manufacturing (CAM)** picks up where the CAD system leaves off. Computer tools enable a manufacturer to analyze the steps that a machine must take to produce a needed product or part. Electronic signals transmitted to processing equipment provide instructions for performing the appropriate production steps in the correct order. Both CAD and CAM technologies are now used together at most modern production facilities.

**computer-aided design (CAD)** system for interactions between a designer and a computer to create a product, facility, or part that meets predetermined specifications.

**computer-aided manufacturing (CAM)** electronic tools to analyze CAD output and determine necessary steps to implement the design, followed by electronic transmission of instructions to guide the activities of production equipment.

## HIT & MISS

### Toyota and the Product Life Cycle

Every product goes through stages in its life cycle. A firm will probably make different choices about production in the beginning stages of a product's life than it would later on. Product life-cycle management (PLM) is an approach that companies use to make these decisions. Not surprisingly, enterprise software is available to help managers create, develop, produce, promote, and sell their products. PLM software provides a framework that companies can use to construct new ideas and convert them to tangible products quickly. "PLM is becoming the enabling tool for innovation," predicts Navi Radjou, a consultant with Forrester Research.

Toyota has embraced the concept of PLM, as well as the supporting software. Using PLM software, Toyota can ensure right from the beginning that the design of a new or updated vehicle is directly linked to manufacturing, supply chain, and beyond. Using software called Pro/ENGINEER, Toyota achieved improvements in the design cycle of its powertrains with PLM software that aided in 3-D engineering, analysis, manufacturing planning, and the creation of drawings. Toyota—which is already known for its innovative engineering and manufacturing—has become a true believer in PLM. Toyota president Fujio Cho predicts that PLM will be the mechanism by which the firm's production system is transformed into a digital manufacturing system.

With PLM, Toyota can design quality into a vehicle, build it well, and roll it off the line in record time. Because of its reputation for quality and engineering, Toyota can also command a higher price than some of its competitors can. By using product development software called Value Opportunity Six, Toyoya built and marketed such successes as the Lexus, the Sienna minivan, and the Highlander. The popularity of these models translates to actual dollars; the Lexus RX300 SUV commands a price that is $17,000 above the average price of an SUV, while the Toyota 4-Runner pulls in $9,000 above the average.

#### Questions for Critical Thinking

1. How might a firm such as Heinz or Nikon use PLM software to gain a competitive edge?
2. How would PLM software help ensure quality?

**Sources:** Gene Bylinsky, "Not Your Grandfather's Assembly Line," *Fortune*, accessed July 5, 2006, http://www.fortune.com; Kevin P. Hopkins, "Value Opportunity Six," *Business-Week*, accessed July 5, 2006, http://www.businessweek.com; "Better by Design," *The Economist*, accessed July 5, 2006, http://www.economist.com.

---

For more on CAD and CAM technologies, see the "Hit & Miss" feature, which explains how Toyota is using product life-cycle management software to develop, produce, promote, and sell its products.

## Flexible Manufacturing Systems

A **flexible manufacturing system (FMS)** is a production facility that workers can quickly modify to manufacture different products. The typical system consists of computer-controlled machining centers to produce metal parts, robots to handle the parts, and remote-controlled carts to deliver materials. All components are linked by electronic controls that dictate activities at each stage of the manufacturing sequence, even automatically replacing broken or worn-out drill bits and other implements.

Flexible manufacturing systems have been enhanced by powerful new software that allows machine tools to be reprogrammed while they are running. This allows the same machine to make hundreds of different parts without the operator having to shut the machine down each time to load new programs for making different parts. The software also connects to the Internet to receive updates or to control machine tools at other sites. And because the software resides on a company's computer network, engineers can use it to diagnose production problems anytime, from anywhere they can access the network.

## Computer-Integrated Manufacturing

Companies integrate robots, CAD/CAM, FMS, computers, and other technologies to implement **computer-integrated manufacturing (CIM),** a production system in which computers help workers design products, control machines, handle materials, and control the production function in an integrated fashion. This type of manufacturing does not necessarily imply more automation and fewer people than other alternatives. It does, however, involve a new type of automation organized around the computer. The key to CIM is a centralized computer system running software that integrates and controls separate processes and functions. For example, VistaPrint, an international printing company with state-of-the-art printing factories in the Netherlands and Windsor, Ontario, uses proprietary CIM software to coordinate 300,000 separate printing jobs each month. Each day, VistaPrint gets 10,000 small printing orders from 20 different companies. VistaPrint's software automates the entire printing process from ordering to delivery. With so many small orders, it saves money as the software automatically combines similar small print jobs into one larger job. CIM software automates the product design used by customers, as well as all parts of the printing process; from prepress to plate changing to delivery, it controls the machines that assemble, package, sort, and ship printing orders.[6]

**assessment check**

1. List some of the reasons businesses invest in robots.
2. Distinguish among computer-aided design, computer-aided manufacturing, flexible manufacturing, and computer-integrated manufacturing.

# THE LOCATION DECISION

The decision of where to locate a production facility hinges on transportation, human, and physical factors, as shown in Table 11.1. Transportation factors include proximity to markets and raw materials, along with availability of alternative modes for transporting both inputs and outputs. For instance, automobile assembly plants are located near major rail lines. Inputs—

Factors in the Location Decision

**Table 11.1**

| Location Factor | Examples of Affected Businesses |
| --- | --- |
| **Transportation** | |
| Proximity to markets | Baking companies and manufacturers of other perishable products, dry cleaners, hotels, other services |
| Proximity to raw materials | Paper mills |
| Availability of transportation alternatives | Brick manufacturers, retail stores |
| **Physical Factors** | |
| Water supply | Computer chip fabrication plants |
| Energy | Aluminum, chemical, and fertilizer manufacturers |
| Hazardous wastes | All businesses |
| **Human Factors** | |
| Labor supply | Auto manufacturers, software developers |
| Local zoning regulations | Manufacturing and distribution companies |
| Community living conditions | All businesses |

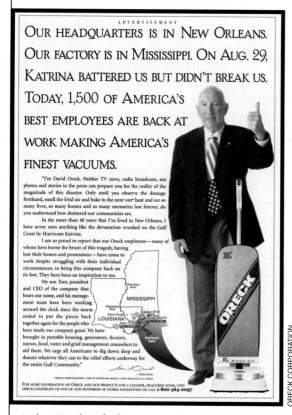

In locating their facilities, companies often take advantage of convenient transportation, such as a seaport or rail lines in New Orleans, to obtain raw materials or parts and ship finished products. But Oreck found that its employees were a distinct advantage after Hurricane Katrina hit. Despite their personal tragedies or difficulties, Oreck employees returned to their jobs to help the company get back on its feet within weeks.

such as engines, plastics, and metal parts—arrive by rail, and the finished vehicles are shipped out by rail. Shopping malls are often located adjacent to major streets and freeways in urban and suburban areas, because most customers arrive by car.

Physical variables involve such issues as weather, water supplies, available energy, and options for disposing of hazardous waste. Theme parks, such as Walt Disney World, are often located in warm climates so they can be open, and attract visitors, year-round. A firm that wants to locate near a community often must prepare an **environmental impact study** that analyzes how a proposed plant would affect the quality of life in the surrounding area. Regulatory agencies typically require these studies to cover topics such as the impact on transportation facilities; energy requirements; water and sewage treatment needs; natural plant life and wildlife; and water, air, and noise pollution.

Human factors include an area's labor supply, local regulations, and living conditions. Management considers local labor costs, as well as the availability of workers with needed qualifications. For instance, software makers and other computer-related firms concentrate in areas with the technical talent they need, including Silicon Valley in and around San Jose, California; Boston; and Austin, Texas. Likewise, Toyota built a new automobile assembly plant in Ontario, Canada, instead of Georgia because Ontario had more highly skilled workers.[7] By contrast, some labor-intensive industries have located plants in rural areas with readily available labor pools and limited high-wage alternatives. And some firms with headquarters in the United States and other industrialized countries have moved production offshore in search of low wages. Apparel is a classic example. But no matter what business you're in, studies show that labor productivity, the availability of skilled labor, and labor costs are the three most important factors in deciding where to locate a new office or facility.[8]

In the United States, this trend, coupled with automation, has shrunk manufacturing's share of the nation's gross domestic product. However, manufacturing continues to be an important segment of the U.S. economy, with total output greater than it ever has been. During the past ten years, U.S. manufacturing output grew much faster than the number of people employed by manufacturing companies, largely because of increases in productivity that allow fewer workers to produce more. However, many foreign companies locate facilities in the United States precisely because U.S. workers are extremely productive. Output per hour has risen steadily and is higher than most other industrialized nations.

# THE JOB OF PRODUCTION MANAGERS

Production and operations managers oversee the work of people and machinery to convert inputs (materials and resources) into finished goods and services. As Figure 11.3 shows, these managers perform four major tasks. First, they plan the overall production process. Next, they determine the best layout for the firm's facilities. Then they implement the production plan. Finally, they control the manufacturing process to maintain the highest possible quality. Part

**PRODUCTION MANAGEMENT TASKS**

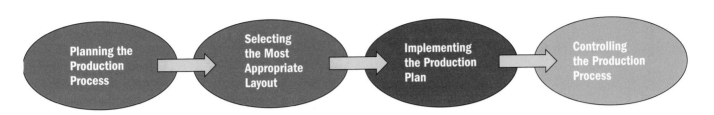

of the control process involves continuous evaluation of results. If problems occur, managers return to the first step and make adjustments.

## Planning the Production Process

Production planning begins by choosing what goods or services to offer to customers. This decision is the essence of every company's reason for operating. Other decisions such as machinery purchases, pricing decisions, and selection of retail outlets all grow out of product planning. But with product planning, it's not enough to plan products that satisfy customers. Products must satisfy customers *and* be produced as efficiently and inexpensively as possible. So while marketing research studies determine consumer reactions to proposed products and estimate potential sales and profitability levels, production departments focus on planning the production process when they (1) convert original product ideas into final specifications and (2) design the most efficient facilities to produce those products.

Earlier in the chapter, you learned that DaimlerChrysler is switching from mass production, in which it makes one kind of car in each production facility, to flexible production, in which it makes three different cars in the same production facility. Toyota has been using flexible production in its North American auto plants for some time but still finds the complexity of making multiple cars in the same factory "daunting." At Toyota's Georgetown, Kentucky, plant, where it builds the Toyota Camry and Toyota Avalon, workers had just a few seconds to choose from 24 kinds of visors or 9 kinds of seat belts, depending on which version of the Camry or Avalon was coming down the assembly line. But after redesigning its production processes to reduce workers' choices, increase quality, and lower costs, Toyota has simplified its process by placing the right "parts kits" in each vehicle so that workers don't have to waste time deciding which parts to use.[9]

## Determining the Facility Layout

Once managers have established the activities needed in their firm's production process, they can determine the best layout for the facility. This decision requires them to consider all phases of production and the necessary inputs at each step. Figure 11.4 shows three common layout designs: process, product, and fixed-position layouts. It also shows a customer-oriented layout typical of service providers' production systems.

A process layout groups machinery and equipment according to their functions. The work in process moves around the plant to reach different workstations. A process layout often facilitates production of a variety of nonstandard items in relatively small batches. Honda also uses a version of a process layout to build its Civic. The company organizes into several workstations, or

**a**ssessment **c**heck

1. What is the key responsibility of production managers?
2. List the four major tasks of production and operations managers.

Figure

11.4 | Basic Facility Layouts

### (A) Process Layout

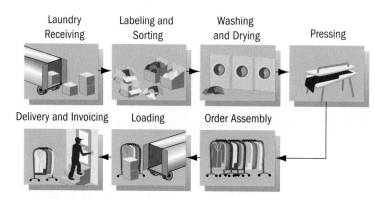

Laundry Receiving → Labeling and Sorting → Washing and Drying → Pressing

Delivery and Invoicing ← Loading ← Order Assembly ←

### (B) Product Layout

### (C) Fixed-Position Layout

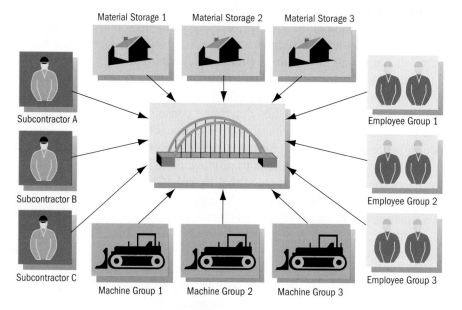

Material Storage 1    Material Storage 2    Material Storage 3

Subcontractor A

Subcontractor B

Subcontractor C

Machine Group 1    Machine Group 2    Machine Group 3

Employee Group 1

Employee Group 2

Employee Group 3

### (D) Customer-Oriented Layout

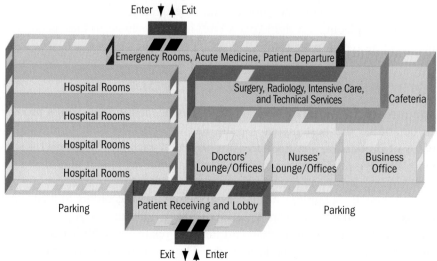

Enter ▼ ▲ Exit

Emergency Rooms, Acute Medicine, Patient Departure

Hospital Rooms

Surgery, Radiology, Intensive Care, and Technical Services

Cafeteria

Hospital Rooms

Hospital Rooms

Hospital Rooms

Doctors' Lounge/Offices

Nurses' Lounge/Offices

Business Office

Parking

Patient Receiving and Lobby

Parking

Exit ▼ ▲ Enter

"zones," grouping activities related to the interior, chassis, and wiring and tubing. At the end of each zone, workers perform an inspection before sending the car to the next zone. Nonstandard activities, such as preparing tanks for natural gas–powered vehicles, take place in a subassembly area.[10]

A product layout sets up production equipment along a product-flow line, and the work in process moves along this line past workstations. This type of layout efficiently produces large numbers of similar items, but it may prove inflexible and able to accommodate only a few product variations. Although product layouts date back at least to the Model T assembly line, companies are refining this approach with modern touches. In Saarlouis, Germany, the Ford Focus assembly plant uses a conveyor belt to move workers along the assembly line, rather than having them trudge from car to car. The resulting productivity increase allowed the company to transfer workers from the assembly line to other jobs. Based on the success of this idea, Ford has since installed similar conveyor belts in other factories.[11]

Boeing's Everett, Washington, assembly line now tows huge planes along a track during assembly to make production more efficient.

A fixed-position layout places the product in one spot, and workers, materials, and equipment come to it. This approach suits production of very large, bulky, heavy, or fragile products. An example is building a bridge. Airplanes were also traditionally assembled using the fixed-position layout approach. Alan Mulally, head of Boeing's commercial aircraft division, said, "We always thought airplanes were different because they had four million parts. Well, airplanes aren't different. This is manufacturing."[12] So Boeing modified its Everett, Washington, production facility to be more like an automobile factory. Now giant jetliners move, although at the rate of one foot an hour, from workstation to workstation, as the aircraft is assembled. This approach saves both time and money. For instance, workers used to spend up to two hours per shift walking around the huge plant gathering tools, parts, and other materials.[13]

Service organizations also must decide on appropriate layouts for their production processes. A service firm should arrange its facilities to enhance the interactions between customers and its services—also called *customer-oriented layout*. If you think of patients as inputs, a hospital implements a form of the process layout. In other service organizations, direct contact with the recipient of services is a less significant part of production. For example, much of a law or accounting firm's work takes place away from clients. Access to colleagues and the Internet, as well as a quiet environment, is often vital for such processes.

**assessment check**

1. Differentiate between the three most common layout designs: process, product, and fixed-position.
2. Describe a customer-oriented layout that is typically used by service providers.

## Implementing the Production Plan

After planning the manufacturing process and determining the best layout, a firm's production managers begin to implement the production plan. This activity involves (1) deciding whether to make, buy, or lease components; (2) selecting the best suppliers for materials; and (3) controlling inventory to keep enough, but not too much, on hand.

### Make, Buy, or Lease Decision
One of the fundamental issues facing every producer is the **make, buy, or lease decision**—choosing whether to manufacture a needed product or component

in house, purchase it from an outside supplier, or lease it. This decision is critical in many contemporary business situations.

Several factors affect the make, buy, or lease decision, including the costs of leasing or purchasing parts from vendors compared with the costs of producing them in house. The decision sometimes hinges on the availability of outside suppliers that can dependably meet a firm's standards for quality and quantity. The need for confidentiality sometimes affects the decision, as does the short- or long-term duration of the firm's need for supplies.

Even when the firm decides to purchase from outside vendors, production managers should maintain access to multiple supply sources. An alternative supplier ensures that the firm can obtain needed materials despite strikes, quality-assurance problems, or other situations that may affect inputs. Of course, not everything can be outsourced. In particular, companies are advised not to outsource the core or central parts of their businesses. For example, Toyota, which produces the most reliable cars in the world, designs all of its autos and runs all of its manufacturing facilities. Following this general rule, it would be a mistake for Toyota to outsource the design and assembly of its cars. Using this same reasoning, would it be advisable for airlines to outsource their maintenance? See the "Solving an Ethical Controversy" feature for more on this issue.

*Selection of Suppliers*   Once a company decides what inputs to purchase, it must choose the best vendors for its needs. To make this choice, production managers compare the quality, prices, dependability of delivery, and services offered by competing companies. Different suppliers may offer virtually identical quality levels and prices, so the final decision often rests on factors such as the firm's experience with each supplier, speed of delivery, warranties on purchases, and other services.

For a major purchase, negotiations between the purchaser and potential vendors may stretch over several weeks or even months, and the buying decision may rest with a number of colleagues who must say yes before the final decision is made. The choice of a supplier for an industrial drill press, for example, may require a joint decision by the production, engineering, purchasing, and quality-control departments. These departments often must reconcile their different views to settle on a purchasing decision.

The Internet has given buyers powerful tools for finding and comparing suppliers. Buyers can log on to business exchanges to compare specifications, prices, and availability. Ariba Spend Management, at http://freemarkets.com, offers organizations software and other tools that allow them to source $35 billion worth of goods and services from suppliers around the world. Ariba Spend Management claims that it saves customers more than $12 billion per year.[14]

### assessment check

1. What factors affect the make, buy, or lease decision?
2. What factors should firms consider when selecting vendors?

Firms often purchase raw materials and component parts on long-term contracts. If a manufacturer requires a continuous supply of materials, a one-year or two-year contract with a vendor helps ensure availability. Today, many firms are building long-term relationships with suppliers and slashing the number of companies with which they do business. At the same time, they are asking their vendors to expand their roles in the production process.

*Inventory Control*   Production and operations managers' responsibility for **inventory control** requires them to balance the need to keep stocks on hand to meet demand against the costs of carrying inventory. Among the expenses involved in storing inventory are warehousing costs, taxes, insurance, and maintenance. Firms waste money if they hold more inventory than they need. On the other hand, having too little inventory on hand means a shortage of raw materials, parts, or goods for sale that often leads to delays and unhappy customers. Firms lose business when they consistently miss promised delivery dates or turn away orders. There-

# SHOULD AIRLINES OUTSOURCE THEIR MAINTENANCE?

*Every firm makes certain decisions about which tasks it must fulfill itself and which can—or should—be purchased from an outside supplier.*

This is true in the airline industry, in which airlines must decide whether they can best serve customers and monitor quality by performing their own maintenance on passenger jets or outsource the job to other companies that are maintenance specialists. But the ultimate question is which method benefits passengers and their safety the most.

Should airlines outsource their maintenance?

## PRO

1. It is much more cost-effective for airlines to hire outside specialists. In an industry that is suffering tremendous economic losses, the savings may be passed along to customers and could mean the difference between staying in business and going under.

2. Outside maintenance experts can perform the job more efficiently and objectively, increasing the safety of passengers.

## CON

1. Airlines can control safety and maintenance standards much more closely if they have their own workers perform such work.
2. The Federal Aviation Administration (FAA) is unable to monitor safety as closely when maintenance is outsourced.

## Summary

Airlines have contracted out maintenance tasks for many years, yet the debate continues. Some reports note potential problems with air carriers that try to adhere to short gate turn-around times, maintenance work that is done overnight, and the growth of discount airlines and the shortage of FAA inspectors. Currently, US Airways outsources 60 percent of its maintenance; United Airlines, 54 percent; American, 42 percent; and Delta, 35 percent.

**Sources:** Laura Meckler, "Airline Turmoil Poses Safety Issues," *Wall Street Journal,* accessed July 5, 2006, http://online.wsj.com; Russell Grantham, "Delta CEO Looks to Rebuild Ties with Workers," *Atlanta Journal-Constitution,* accessed July 5, 2006, http://www.ajc.com; Susan Carey and Alex Frangos, "New Destination: Airlines, Facing Cost Pressure, Outsource Crucial Safety Tasks," *Wall Street Journal,* accessed July 5, 2006, http://online.wsj.com.

solving an **ETHICAL** controversy

fore, managers must balance this threat against the cost of holding inventory to set acceptable stocking levels.

Efficient inventory control can save a great deal of money. In one common technique, many firms maintain **perpetual inventory** systems to continuously monitor the amounts and locations of their stocks. Such inventory control systems typically rely on computers, and many automatically generate orders at the appropriate times. Many supermarkets link their scanning devices to perpetual inventory systems that reorder needed merchandise without human interaction. As the system records a shopper's purchase, it reduces the inventory count stored in the computer. Once inventory on hand drops to a predetermined level, the system automatically reorders the merchandise.

Some companies go further and hand over their inventory control functions to suppliers. This concept is known as *vendor-managed inventory.* Best Buy, the consumer electronics retailer, is switching its vendors to a vendor-managed inventory system. For instance, instead of shipping DVDs and CDs to Best Buy's Franklin, Indiana, music and video distribution center, music and video vendors are now expected to ship their product directly to Best Buy stores. Two things must happen for that to occur. First, vendors must directly link their electronic ordering systems to Best Buy's store-level data so that only stores that need more inventory get it. Second, the vendors must make their products shelf-ready by affixing Best Buy stickers, codes, and pricing to their DVDs and CDs.[15]

**just-in-time (JIT) system** management philosophy aimed at improving profits and return on investment by minimizing costs and eliminating waste through cutting inventory on hand.

**materials requirement planning (MRP)** computer-based production planning system by which a firm can ensure that it has needed parts and materials available at the right time and place in the correct amounts.

*Just-in-Time Systems*  A just-in-time (JIT) system implements a broad management philosophy that reaches beyond the narrow activity of inventory control to influence the entire system of production and operations management. A JIT system seeks to eliminate all sources of waste—anything that does not add value—in operations activities by providing the right part at the right place at just the right time—right before it is needed in production.

Production using JIT shifts much of the responsibility for carrying inventory to vendors, which operate on forecasts and keep stocks on hand to respond to manufacturers' needs. Suppliers that cannot keep enough high-quality parts on hand are often assessed steep penalties by purchasers. Navistar International, which makes trucks, assesses fines that can run tens of thousands of dollars per minute. Why? Because running out of parts effectively shuts down the entire product line. Consequently, in an emergency, some firms even bring in parts by helicopter, because it's still cheaper than paying the fine.[16]

Another risk of using JIT systems is what happens if manufacturers underestimate demand for a product. Strong demand will begin to overtax JIT systems, as suppliers and their customers struggle to keep up with orders with no inventory cushion to tide them over.

*Materials Requirement Planning*  Besides efficiency, effective inventory control requires careful planning to ensure the firm has all the inputs it needs to make its products. How do production and operations managers coordinate all of this information? They rely on **materials requirement planning (MRP)**, a computer-based production planning system that lets a firm ensure that it has all the parts and materials it needs to produce its output at the right time and place and in the right amounts.

Production managers use MRP programs to create schedules that identify the specific parts and materials required to produce an item. These schedules specify the exact quantities needed and the dates on which to order those quantities from suppliers so that they are delivered at the correct time in the production cycle. A small company might get by without an MRP system. If a firm makes a simple product with few components, a telephone call may ensure overnight delivery of crucial parts. For a complex product, however, such as a car or a Joint Strike Fighter aircraft, MRP becomes an invaluable tool.

**assessment check**

1. What balance must managers seek when controlling inventory?
2. Explain perpetual inventory and vendor-managed inventory.
3. What is a just-in-time inventory system, and what are some of its advantages?
4. What is MRP used for?

## Controlling the Production Process

The final task of production and operations managers is controlling the production process to maintain the highest possible quality. **Production control** creates a well-defined set of procedures for coordinating people, materials, and machinery to provide maximum production efficiency. Suppose that a watch factory must produce 80,000 watches during October. Production control managers break down this total into a daily production assignment of 4,000 watches for each of the month's 20 working days. Next, they determine the number of workers, raw materials, parts, and machines the plant needs to meet the production schedule. Similarly, a manager in a service business such as a restaurant must estimate how many dinners the outlet will serve each day and then determine how many people are needed to prepare and serve the food, as well as what food to purchase.

Figure 11.5 illustrates production control as a five-step process composed of planning, routing, scheduling, dispatching, and follow-up. These steps are part of the firm's overall emphasis on total quality management.

*Production Planning*  The phase of production control called **production planning** determines the amount of resources (including raw materials and other components) an organization needs to produce a certain output. The production planning process develops a bill of

Figure

11.5

materials that lists all needed parts and materials. By comparing information about needed parts and materials with the firm's perpetual inventory data, purchasing personnel can identify necessary purchases. Employees or automated systems establish delivery schedules to provide needed parts and materials when required during the production process. Production planning also ensures the availability of needed machines and personnel. Although material inputs contribute to service-production systems, production planning for services tends to emphasize human resources more than materials.

*Routing*   Another phase of production control, called **routing,** determines the sequence of work throughout the facility and specifies who will perform each aspect of the work at what location. Routing choices depend on two factors: the nature of the good or service and the facility layouts discussed earlier in the chapter—product, process, fixed-position, or customer-oriented.

Observing production activities can improve routing decisions. At the Fenton, Michigan, factory of TRW Chassis Systems, a team of employees charged with improving work processes on an assembly line discovered that one worker's job consisted of simply moving parts from the end of a conveyor line to a test stand. The team moved the test stand, placing it next to the end of the assembly line so that the tester could unload the items. The unnecessary worker moved to another—probably more gratifying—job in a different part of the plant.[17]

*Scheduling*   In the **scheduling** phase of production control, managers develop timetables that specify how long each operation in the production process takes and when workers should perform it. Efficient scheduling ensures that production will meet delivery schedules and make efficient use of resources.

Scheduling is an extremely important activity for a manufacturer of a complex product with many parts or production stages. Think of all the component parts needed to make a computerized tomography (CT) or magnetic resonance imaging (MRI) scanner or other complex hospital equipment. Scheduling must make each one available in the right place at the right time and in the right amounts to ensure a smooth production process.

Scheduling practices vary considerably in service-related organizations. Printing shops or hair stylists may use relatively unsophisticated scheduling systems, resorting to such devices as "first come, first served" rules, appointment schedules, or take-a-number systems. They may call in part-time workers and use standby equipment to handle demand fluctuations. On the other hand, hospitals typically implement sophisticated scheduling systems similar to those of manufacturers.

Production managers use a number of analytical methods for scheduling. One of the oldest methods, the *Gantt chart,* tracks projected and actual work progress over time. Gantt charts like the one in Figure 11.6 remain popular because they show at a glance the status of a particular project. However, they are most effective for scheduling relatively simple projects. In a technical field such as production management, people often use specialized terms such as *Gantt charts* and *just-in-time inventory.* Use of technical jargon may improve communication, but

**scheduling** development of timetables that specify how long each operation in the production process takes and when workers should perform it.

Figure

11.6 Sample Gantt Chart

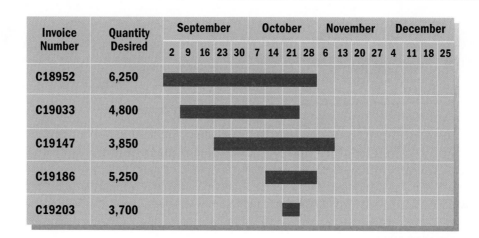

| Invoice Number | Quantity Desired | September | | | | | October | | | | November | | | | December | | | |
|---|---|---|---|---|---|---|---|---|---|---|---|---|---|---|---|---|---|---|
| | | 2 | 9 | 16 | 23 | 30 | 7 | 14 | 21 | 28 | 6 | 13 | 20 | 27 | 4 | 11 | 18 | 25 |
| C18952 | 6,250 | | | | | | | | | | | | | | | | | |
| C19033 | 4,800 | | | | | | | | | | | | | | | | | |
| C19147 | 3,850 | | | | | | | | | | | | | | | | | |
| C19186 | 5,250 | | | | | | | | | | | | | | | | | |
| C19203 | 3,700 | | | | | | | | | | | | | | | | | |

sometimes it doesn't. The "Business Etiquette" feature discusses when and when not to use technical jargon in business situations.

A complex project might require a **PERT (Program Evaluation and Review Technique)** chart, which seeks to minimize delays by coordinating all aspects of the production process. First developed for the military, PERT has been modified for industry. The simplified PERT diagram in Figure 11.7 summarizes the schedule for obtaining a new computer system for a business. The red line indicates the **critical path**—the sequence of operations that requires the longest time for completion. The dotted line shows work that can be done simultaneously.

In practice, a PERT network may consist of thousands of events and cover months of time. Complex computer programs help production managers develop such a network and find the critical path among the maze of events and activities. The construction of a huge sky-

Figure

11.7 PERT Diagram for Obtaining a New Computer System

scraper requires complex production planning of this nature.

*Dispatching*  The phase of production control in which the manager instructs each department on what work to do and the time allowed for its completion is called **dispatching.** The dispatcher authorizes performance, provides instructions, and lists job priorities. Dispatching may be the responsibility of a manager or a self-managed work team.

*Follow-Up*  Because even the best plans sometimes go awry, production managers need to be aware of problems that arise. **Follow-up** is the phase of production control in which employees and their supervisors spot problems in the production process and determine needed changes. Problems take many forms: machinery malfunctions, delayed shipments, and employee absenteeism can all affect production. The production control system must detect and report these delays to managers or work teams so they can adjust schedules and correct the underlying problems.

## assessment check

1. What five steps are involved in controlling the production process?
2. What is the difference between a PERT chart and a Gantt chart?
3. What is the critical path?

# IMPORTANCE OF QUALITY

Although "quality" can be defined several ways, perhaps the most common definition of quality is a good or service free of deficiencies. Quality matters because fixing deficient products is costly. If Seagate makes a defective computer hard drive, it has to either fix the drive or replace it to keep a customer happy. If an airline books

## When—and When Not— to Use Technical Jargon

The business world is filled with technical jargon. Just flip through this chapter. What's CAD? What is a PERT diagram used for? What is a critical path? If you are like most people, you recoil from technical jargon when you aren't sure what it means. Worse yet, it may have negative effects on a business conversation because it can cloud the meaning of a message. You can quickly lose a listener who is trying to decipher what you mean. On the other hand, jargon can serve as a kind of shorthand in a conversation between two people who understand clearly what is being said. In general, it's best to use common sense—and err on the side of clarity. Here are a few tips on when—and when *not*—to use technical jargon.

*When to use technical jargon:*

- Use an abbreviation without explanation if you are certain everyone with whom you are communicating knows it. Only use a term such as *CAD*, which stands for *computer-aided design*, if you are communicating with people who work in the special field and already know what computer-aided design is.
- Use a technical term such as *perpetual inventory* if necessary, but surround it with conventional phrases and concrete words to help listeners. Keep technical terms to a minimum so that the necessary ones have impact.

*When not to use technical jargon:*

- Avoid technical jargon when communicating with an audience outside your industry. This includes consumers who are customers. Instead of referring to an "output device" on a computer, simply say "printer."
- Avoid jargon when you are speaking or writing to someone from another country or who speaks a different language.
- Don't use acronyms that are specific to your own organization when you are communicating externally. Everyone who works for Midwest Engineering might refer to the firm as ME, but it's best to use the full name elsewhere. However, exceptions can be made for firms like IBM and GE because they are so well known.
- Don't use an abbreviation if its common interpretation is something other than what you intend. Most businesspeople understand *PC* to be a personal computer, so it's best not to use it to refer to Private Council or Principal Control.

**Sources:** Michael Bernhardt, "Seven Sins to Avoid with Your Next Public Speaking Engagement," accessed July 5, 2006, http://www.refresher.com/!sevensins.html; Nancy Halligan, Technical Writing, accessed July 5, 2006, http://www.technical-writing-course.com/avoid-jargon.html; Joe Fleischer, "You Don't Need a Hero," *Call Center Magazine*, accessed July 5, 2006, http://www.callcentermagazine.com.

**benchmarking** process of determining other companies' standards and best practices.

**quality control** measuring goods and services against established quality standards.

too many passengers for a flight, thus overselling its service, it has to offer vouchers worth several hundred dollars to encourage passengers to give up their seats and take a later flight.

For most companies, the costs of poor quality can amount to 20 percent of sales revenue, if not more. Some typical costs of poor quality include downtime, repair costs, rework, and employee turnover. Production and operations managers must set up systems to track and reduce such costs.

One process that companies use to ensure that they produce high-quality products from the start is **benchmarking**—determining how well other companies (and not just competitors) perform business functions or tasks. In other words, benchmarking is the process of determining other companies' standards and best practices. Automobile companies routinely purchase each other's cars and then take them completely apart to examine and compare the design, components, and materials used to make even the smallest part. They then make improvements to match or exceed the quality found in their competitors' cars. But benchmarking is helpful for service organizations, too. David Clayden, director of information technology for the Salvation Army in the United Kingdom, sums up why his organization and others should use benchmarking: "We use benchmarking to demarcate where we are underperforming, where we are effective, and where we have deficiencies."[18]

## Quality Control

**Quality control** involves measuring output against established quality standards. Firms need such checks to spot defective products and to avoid delivering inferior shipments to customers. Standards should be set high enough to meet customer expectations. A 90 or 95 percent success rate might seem to be a good number, but consider what your phone service or ATM network would be like if it operated for that share of time. Every year, it would be out of service for 438 hours (5 percent of the year) to 875 hours (10 percent).

Manufacturing firms can monitor quality levels through visual inspections, electronic sensors, robots, and X-rays. For service businesses surveys can provide quality-control information. Negative feedback from customers or a high rejection rate on a product or component sends a danger signal that production is not achieving quality standards.

Because the typical factory can spend up to half its operating budget identifying and fixing mistakes, companies cannot rely solely on inspections to achieve its quality goals. Instead, quality-driven production managers identify all processes involved in producing goods and services and work to maximize their efficiency. The causes of problems in the processes must be found and eliminated. If a company concentrates its efforts on improving processes, it can minimize production mistakes and make defect-free products.

General Electric, Ford, DuPont, Nokia, and Sony are just five of the growing number of major manufacturers using the Six Sigma concept to achieve quality goals. *Six Sigma* means a company tries to make error-free products 99.9997 percent of the time—a tiny 3.4 errors per million opportunities. The goal of Six Sigma programs is for companies to eliminate virtually all defects in output, processes, and transactions. While Six Sigma has obvious benefits and applications in manufacturing settings, it can be equally helpful in service organizations. Acosta is a Jacksonville, Florida–based sales and marketing agency that helps consumer goods companies such as Nestlé, Clorox, and Heinz get their products into supermarkets and convenience stores. Basically, Acosta's company representatives act as sales representatives and travel to stores to persuade managers to carry their clients' products. With 5,500 cars for its representatives, the company was spending $15,500 per vehicle each year, or more than $85 million a year. But by using Six Sigma techniques and charting the number of stores visited by each representative, the distances between those stores, and the sales made from each trip, Acosta was able to reduce its fleet to just 2,500 cars, saving millions in the process.[19] The

# HIT & MISS

## It's No Mystery: Quality at Bank of America

At Bank of America, achieving quality goals may boil down to one word: *listen*. It's a simple concept that has been around in business for a long time. But companies often do more talking than listening to their customers. Bank of America, in contrast, is all ears.

Several years ago, Bank of America adopted the Six Sigma approach to quality, meaning that it will attempt to provide top-quality, error-free service 99.9997 percent of the time. Manufacturers such as Ford and GE have adopted the approach, but Bank of America was the first major financial institution to do so. "It's often harder to measure some of the attributes of financial services," comments senior vice president James Buchanan. "It's not as tangible a product." But the firm has found some ways that do work.

Bank of America sends "mystery shoppers" to its banking centers to make sure employees greet customers warmly, connect with them, and process their requests efficiently. In addition, the firm surveys 10,000 existing customers quarterly by phone, and it calls about 90,000 customers who have recently visited a branch to find out about their experience with the bank. Both methods of collecting information require listening. "It's a great learning tool and a building block for us to deliver better processes," says senior vice president Randall King.

These and other initiatives require training. So far, about 10,000 Bank of America employees have been trained in different aspects of the Six Sigma quality initiative. In just a few years, different programs have resulted in a $6.6 million reduction in losses from identity theft and a $10 million increase in revenue from tellers referring customers to additional bank products. In addition, one survey revealed that the number of customers who considered themselves "highly satisfied" with Bank of America's services rose from 43 percent to slightly more than 53 percent since the quality initiative. At Bank of America, someone is always listening.

### Questions for Critical Thinking

1. How might Bank of America use benchmarking as part of its quality initiative?
2. Do you think it is possible to achieve virtually error-free service, or is the attempt doomed to fail? Explain your view.

**Sources:** Liam McGee, "Sweating the Small Stuff: How Six Sigma Enables the Future," Bank of America, accessed July 5, 2006, http://www.bankofamerica.com/newsroom/speeches; Chris Costanzo, "Business Management: BofA Tackles Six Sigma," American Banker-Bond Buyer, accessed July 5, 2006, http://www.us-banker.com; "Bank of America—Hoshin Kanri & Six Sigma," Six Sigma Companies, accessed July 5, 2006, http://www.sixsigmacompanies.com.

---

"Hit & Miss" feature explains how Bank of America is using Six Sigma to minimize mistakes and provide better service to its customers.

## ISO Standards

For many goods, an important measure of quality is to meet the standards of the **International Organization for Standardization**, known as **ISO** for short—not an acronym but a shorter name derived from the Greek word *isos*, meaning "equal." Established in Europe in 1947, ISO includes representatives from more than 146 nations. Its mission is to promote the development of standardized products to facilitate trade and cooperation across national borders. ISO standards govern everything from the format of banking and telephone cards to freight containers to paper sizes to metric screw threads. The U.S. member body of ISO is the American National Standards Institute.

The ISO 9000 family series of standards sets requirements for quality processes; these standards define how a company should ensure that its products meet customers' requirements. The ISO 14000 series sets standards for operations that minimize harm to the environment.

> **International Organization for Standardization (ISO)** organization whose mission is to promote the development of standardized products to facilitate trade and cooperation across national borders.

**assessment check**

1. What are some ways in which a company can monitor the quality level of its output?
2. What does Six Sigma mean?
3. List some of the benefits of acquiring ISO 9000 certification.

ISO accredits organizations in member countries to evaluate performance against these standards. To receive an ISO 9000 family certification, a company must undergo an on-site audit. The audit ensures that documented quality procedures are in place and that all employees understand and follow the procedures. Production managers meet these requirements through an ongoing process involving periodic recertification.

Nearly half a million ISO 9000 family certificates have been awarded to companies around the world. Their numbers are growing rapidly, with the fastest growth occurring in China, Italy, and Japan. Over half the certificates have been awarded in Europe. Why should companies achieve ISO 9000 certification? Because studies clearly show that customers prefer to buy from companies that are ISO 9000 certified. Companies, in turn, believe that being ISO 9000 certified helps them keep customers who might otherwise leave to work with an ISO 9000–certified corporation.[20]

# WHAT'S AHEAD

Maintaining high quality is an important element of satisfying customers. Product quality and customer satisfaction are also objectives of the business function of marketing. The next part consists of three chapters that explore the many activities involved in customer-driven marketing. These activities include product development, distribution, promotion, and pricing.

## Summary of Learning Goals

### 1 Outline the importance of production and operations management.

Production and operations management is a vital business function. Without a quality good or service, a company cannot create profits, and it soon fails. The production process is also crucial in a not-for-profit organization, because the good or service it produces justifies the organization's existence. Production and operations management plays an important strategic role by lowering the costs of production, boosting output quality, and allowing the firm to respond flexibly and dependably to customers' demands.

### Assessment Check Answers

**1.1 What are the advantages and disadvantages of mass production?**
Mass production leads to high productivity, mechanization, and standardization, all of which make outputs available in large quantities at lower prices than individually crafted items would cost. The disadvantages are inefficiency when making small batches of items and specialized tasks leading to boring, repetitive jobs.

**1.2 What are the characteristics of flexible production?**
Flexible production is characterized by cost-effective production of small batches, use of information technology to share the details of customer orders, programmable equipment to fulfill the orders, and skilled people to carry out whatever tasks are needed to fill a particular order.

**1.3 Describe a customer-driven production system.**
Customer-driven production systems directly link what manufacturers make with what customers want to buy. One way to do this is to establish computer links between factories and retailers' scanners. Another is to not make a product until a customer orders it.

### 2 Explain the roles of computers and related technologies in production.

Computer-driven automation allows companies to design, create, and modify products rapidly and produce them in ways that effectively meet customers' changing needs. Important design and production technologies include robots, computer-aided design (CAD), computer-aided manufacturing (CAM), and computer-integrated manufacturing (CIM).

## Assessment Check Answers

**2.1 List some of the reasons businesses invest in robots.**

Businesses use robots to free people from boring, sometimes dangerous assignments and to move heavy items from one place to another in a factory.

**2.2 Distinguish among computer-aided design, computer-aided manufacturing, flexible manufacturing, and computer-integrated manufacturing.**

Computer-aided design (CAD) enables engineers to design parts and buildings on computer screens faster and with fewer mistakes than they could achieve working with traditional drafting systems. Computer-aided manufacturing (CAM) uses the CAD specifications to determine the steps that machines must take to produce products or parts. CAD and CAM are typically used together. Computer-integrated manufacturing (CIM) is a system in which companies integrate robots, CAD/CAM, FMS, computers, and other technologies to design products, control machines, handle materials, and control the production function in an integrated fashion.

**3 Identify the factors involved in a plant location decision.**

Criteria for choosing the best site for a production facility fall into three categories: transportation, human, and physical factors. Transportation factors include proximity to markets and raw materials, along with availability of transportation alternatives. Physical variables involve such issues as water supply, available energy, and options for disposing of hazardous wastes. Human factors include the area's labor supply, local regulations, and living conditions.

## Assessment Check Answers

**3.1 What is the purpose of an environmental impact study, and how does it influence the location decision?**

The purpose is to analyze how a proposed plant would affect the quality of life in the surrounding area. The effects on transportation facilities, energy requirements, water and sewage treatment needs, natural plant life and wildlife, and water, air, and noise pollution are studied.

**3.2 What human factors are relevant to the location decision?**

Human factors include an area's labor supply, labor costs, local regulations, and living conditions.

**4 Explain the major tasks of production and operations managers.**

Production and operations managers use people and machinery to convert inputs (materials and resources) into finished goods and services. Four major tasks are involved. First, the managers must plan the overall production process. Next, they must pick the best layout for their facilities. Then they implement their production plans. Finally, they control the production process and evaluate results to maintain the highest possible quality.

## Assessment Check Answers

**4.1 What is the key responsibility of production managers?**

Production managers must oversee the work of people and machinery to convert inputs (materials and resources) into finished goods and services.

**4.2 List the four major tasks of production and operations managers.**

The four tasks are planning overall production, laying out the firm's facilities, implementing the production plan, and controlling manufacturing to achieve high quality.

**5 Compare alternative layouts for production facilities.**

Process layouts effectively produce nonstandard products in relatively small batches. Product layouts are appropriate for the production of a large quantity of relatively similar products. Fixed-position layouts are common when production involves very large, heavy, or fragile products. Customer-oriented layouts are typical for service facilities where success depends on interaction between customers and service providers.

## Assessment Check Answers

**5.1 Differentiate between the three most common layout designs: process, product, and fixed-position.**

A process layout groups machinery and equipment according to their functions. The work in process moves around the plant to reach different workstations. A product layout sets up production equipment along a product-flow line, and the work in process moves along this line past workstations. A fixed-position layout places the product in one spot, and workers, materials, and equipment come to it.

**5.2 Describe a customer-oriented layout that is typically used by service providers.**

A customer-oriented layout enhances the interactions between a company and its customers. For example, a hospital can make sure that the nurses' station is close to all of the patients' beds in a hospital wing.

**6** **List the steps in the purchasing process.**

In the make, buy, or lease decision, production and operations managers determine whether to manufacture needed inputs in house, purchase them, or lease them from an outside supplier. Managers determine the correct materials to purchase, select appropriate suppliers, and develop an efficient ordering system. The objective is to buy the right materials in the right amounts at the right time and in the right place.

## Assessment Check Answers

**6.1 What factors affect the make, buy, or lease decision?**

The costs of leasing or purchasing parts from vendors, versus producing them in house, the availability of dependable, outside suppliers, and the need for confidentiality affect this decision.

**6.2 What factors should firms consider when selecting vendors?**

Firms should compare quality, prices, speed, warranties, and the dependability of delivery and services offered by vendors.

**7** **Outline the advantages and disadvantages of maintaining large inventories.**

The task of inventory control is to balance the need to maintain adequate supplies against the need to minimize funds invested in inventory. Excessive inventory results in unnecessary expenditures for warehousing, taxes, insurance, and maintenance. Inadequate inventory may mean production delays, lost sales, and inefficient operations.

## Assessment Check Answers

**7.1 What balance must managers seek when controlling inventory?**

Managers must balance the need to keep stocks on hand to meet demand against the costs of carrying inventory.

**7.2 Explain perpetual inventory and vendor-managed inventory.**

Perpetual inventory systems continuously monitor the amount and location of inventory and automatically generate orders at the appropriate times. Vendor-managed inventory is a system in which companies have their suppliers control and manage their inventory.

**7.3 What is a just-in-time inventory system, and what are some of its advantages?**

With a just-in-time inventory system, component parts arrive from suppliers just as they are needed at each stage of production. By having parts arrive "just in time," the manufacturer keeps little inventory on hand and thus avoids the costs associated with holding inventory.

**7.4 What is MRP used for?**

Production managers use MRP programs to create schedules that identify the specific parts and materials required to produce an item. These schedules specify the exact quantities required and when to order those quantities from suppliers so that needed inventory is delivered at the best time within the production cycle.

**8** **Identify the steps in the production control process.**

The production control process consists of five steps: planning, routing, scheduling, dispatching, and follow-up. Quality control is an important consideration throughout this process. Coordination of each of these phases should result in high production efficiency and low production costs.

## Assessment Check Answers

**8.1 What five steps are involved in controlling the production process?**

The five steps are planning, routing, scheduling, dispatching, and follow-up.

**8.2 What is the difference between a PERT chart and a Gantt chart?**

PERT charts, which seek to minimize delays by coordinating all aspects of the production process, are used for more complex projects; Gantt charts, which track projected and actual work progress over time, are used for scheduling relatively simple projects.

**8.3 What is the critical path?**

In a PERT chart, a red line indicates the critical path, which is the sequence of steps or operations that will take the longest time to complete.

**9** **Explain the benefits of quality control.**

Quality control involves evaluating goods and services against established quality standards. Such checks are necessary to spot defective products and to see that they are not shipped to customers. Devices for monitoring quality levels of the firm's output include visual inspection, electronic sensors, robots, and X-rays. Companies are increasing the quality of their goods and services by using Six Sigma techniques and by becoming ISO 9000 and 14000 certified.

## Assessment Check Answers

**9.1 What are some ways in which a company can monitor the quality level of its output?**

Benchmarking, quality control, Six Sigma, and ISO standards are ways of monitoring quality.

**9.2 What does Six Sigma mean?**
Six Sigma means a company tries to make error-free products 99.9997 percent of time—just 3.4 errors per million opportunities.

**9.3 List some of the benefits of acquiring ISO 9000 certification.**
These standards define how a company should ensure that its products meet customers' requirements. Studies show that customers prefer to buy from companies that are ISO 9000 certified.

## Business Terms You Need to Know

production 346
production and operations
    management 346
assembly line 348
robot 350
computer-aided design (CAD) 351

computer-aided manufacturing
    (CAM) 351
just-in-time (JIT) system 360
materials requirement planning
    (MRP) 360
scheduling 361

benchmarking 364
quality control 364
International Organization for
    Standardization (ISO) 365

## Other Important Business Terms

mass production 348
flexible manufacturing system
    (FMS) 352
computer-integrated manufactur-
    ing (CIM) 353
environmental impact study 354

make, buy, or lease decision 357
inventory control 358
perpetual inventory 359
production control 360
production planning 360
routing 361

PERT (Program Evaluation and
    Review Technique) 362
critical path 362
dispatching 363
follow-up 363

## Review Questions

1. What is utility? Define and briefly describe the four different types of utility.
2. Distinguish between production and manufacturing. In what ways does each of the following perform a production function?
   a. delicatessen
   b. dentist
   c. local transit system
   d. Tower Records music store

3. Why is production such an important business activity? In what ways does it create value for the company and its customers?
4. How does mass production work? Describe a good or service that would lend itself well to mass production and one that would not lend itself well to mass production.
5. How does flexible production compare with mass production?

6. Briefly describe the four different production systems. Give an example of a good or service that is produced by each.
7. Describe the four major tasks of production and operations managers: planning the production process, selecting the most appropriate layout, implementing the production plan, and controlling the production process.
8. What would be the best facility layout for each of the following?
   a. card shop
   b. chain of economy motels
   c. car wash
   d. accountant's office
   e. large auto dealer's service facility
9. Describe a flexible manufacturing system.
10. What are the benefits of producing a quality product? Briefly describe the International Organization for Standardization (ISO).

## Projects and Teamwork Applications

1. Imagine that you have been hired as a management consultant for one of the following types of service organizations to decide on an appropriate layout for its facility. Select one and sketch or describe the layout that you think would be best.
   a. chain of dry-cleaning outlets
   b. doctor's office
   c. small, elegant lakeside restaurant
   d. coffee house
2. Imagine that you have been hired as production manager for a snowboard manufacturer (or choose another type of manufacturer that interests you). What type of inventory control would you recommend for your company? Write a brief memo explaining why.
3. Nissan and Hyundai have built auto assembly plants in Mississippi and Alabama, respectively. What factors do you think Nissan and Hyundai considered when choosing their plant location?
4. Suggest two or three ways in which each of the following firms could practice effective quality control:
   a. pharmaceutical firm
   b. miniature golf course
   c. Internet florist
   d. agricultural packing house

## Case 11.1

### Apple Faces Shortages of iPods, iPod Shuffles, and Nanos

When consumers are clamoring for a popular product, what happens when the manufacturer can't deliver it? That's the situation recently faced by Apple, and it's not just a case of one product. Consumers who wanted the firm's iPods, iPod Shuffles, and Nanos were left empty handed. Just as one holiday season reached its peak—along with the demand for the players—supply dwindled to almost nothing. Target, Best Buy, and other retailers reported complete sell-outs. Even Amazon's supply was gone. Nearly a year later, more shortages occurred. What went wrong?

No one predicted how popular the iPod line would be. Within a year, the iPod represented nearly 25 percent of Apple's total sales. "It's right up there with the most highly demanded products I've seen, and I've been in this business since '87," observed David Weisman, senior director of home merchandising at electronics retailer Crutchfield. Apple executives say that many of the shortages were due to a scarcity of component parts. Some experts criticized Apple's lack of preparedness for demand. "Apple has this history of introducing a new product and then immediately failing to meet demand for it," said one retailer. Others pointed to the reality of the situation. "Given how strong demand has been . . . , you would have thought [Apple] would have gotten every last [player] they could into the stores," said Stephen Baker of marketing research firm NPD Group. "I suspect they have. It may just be they can't build them fast enough." Some of the shortages could be traced to the outsourcing of manufacturing to factories in China that, while offering lower costs, also had longer production times, longer supply chains, and more downtime due to energy shortages.

Nearly the same shortages have occurred with each new version of the iPod, including the Nano, which eventually replaced the Mini. Within days of its initial release, Microwarehouse—one of Apple's distributors located in the Philippines—began receiving thousands of orders for the new iPod. The orders far exceeded the distributor's original targets. "These are the less than 1,000-song market," said sales manager Cecilio Tuanquin Jr. "These kinds of buyers usually just want a limited number of songs in their devices especially when they couldn't listen to all the other songs in an iPod with bigger capacity." Tuanquin also said that Microwarehouse had a backlog of at least a month's worth of orders.

Apple did its best to appease customers, but in the end most just had to wait. "To try to meet the high demand, we're making and shipping iPods as fast as we can," the firm said in a written statement. "So, if one store has run out, you may find iPods in another authorized iPod reseller." Meanwhile, the firm continued to roll out new products, including its video iPod. The screen remained tiny—only $2\frac{1}{2}$ inches wide—indicating that music is still the priority of that device. But consumers who wanted to catch a quick clip of music video or a friend's podcast while sitting in traffic, waiting for a flight, or walking to class could do so.

## Questions for Critical Thinking

1. What are some of the pitfalls of Apple's decision to outsource production of its iPods to factories in other countries?
2. Describe two or three steps that Apple might take to avoid shortages of popular products in the future.

**Sources:** Rob Pegoraro, "With Video iPod, the Music Still Comes First," *Washington Post,* accessed July 5, 2006, http://www.washingtonpost.com; "Apple Expected to Unveil Video iPod," Associated Press, accessed July 5, 2006, http://news.yahoo.com; Peter Burrows, "What's the Next Verse in Apple's Song?" *BusinessWeek,* accessed July 5, 2006, http://www.businessweek.com; Yossi Sheffi, "Business Life Summer School: Day Sixteen," *Financial Times,* accessed July 5, 2006, http://www.ft.com; Nick Wingfield, "Out of Tune: iPod Shortage Rocks Apple," *Wall Street Journal,* accessed July 5, 2006, http://online.wsj.com; Alexander Villafania, "iPod Nano Waiting List: Two Months," INQ7, accessed September 22, 2005, http://www.inq7.net.

## ᴠɪᴅᴇᴏ Case 11.2
### Washburn Guitars: Sound Since 1883

This video case appears on page 620. A recently filmed video, designed to expand and highlight the written case, is available for class use by instructors.

**The Second City**

# The Second City Theater Continuing Case
# Management: Empowering People to Achieve Business Objectives

The most important asset of The Second City is its talent. Well known as the creative launch pad for comedy greats such as John Belushi, Bill Murray, and Mike Myers, the success of The Second City continues to depend on the quality of its performers. Second City managers are adept at finding and cultivating comedians, then producing and presenting that special brand of comedy, which continues to attract and please the paying audience.

In front of the Chicago Second City entrance is a chronological list of names, those of every performer who has opened a new revue on one of Second City's stages. This nondescript list is the first step in Second City's customer-oriented layout. Inside the Second City building, a visitor can see how these names came to life on stage and screen. Large black-and-white pictures capture famous Second City comedians in the costumes and characters that made them famous and the Second City tradition uniquely identifiable. The spirit of creation and off-the-cuff humor are part of the atmosphere in this building. Ascending the spiral staircase, patrons are met with pictures of today's Second City Main Stage cast, the newest generation of comedy mavericks. Once inside the theater, audience members witness a newly created Second City revue

that speeds through both engaging sketch comedy and biting cultural and political satire. The experience is full of energy and based on an intimate relationship between ensemble and audience. Finally, a night at the Second City ends where its tradition began—with a thirty-minute set of completely improvised comedy based on audience suggestions and the momentum of their laughter. The experience has a similar impact at the four other Second City theaters.

The Second City became famous in 1959 with its first cast of characters, called The Compass Players, and has since been able to garner impressive reviews and profitable returns on a regular basis. The Second City comprises a growing comedy dynasty that includes three stages in Chicago, along with stages in Toronto, Las Vegas, Denver, and Detroit. It also has numerous touring companies performing around the world and multiple shows being produced on cruise lines or specifically created for various businesses. In total they have nearly one hundred performers representing the best in comedy. So how does The Second City control the quality of all of its productions? CEO Andrew Alexander, who has produced more than 200 Second City revues since joining the company in 1974, says that SC "looks for individuals that are

intelligent, have a point of a view, and the potential to become a good actor. And a comedic sensibility doesn't hurt." This general welcoming of talent has brought hundreds of performers of all ages to Second City's door. Creating a diverse cast of eight people who can function as a creative team six nights a week, however, calls for a certain kind of vision. This vision and this approach originated with the Compass Players themselves. "SC was founded . . . with the goal to use improvisational techniques developed in the late 1930's by Viola Spolin to create satirical revues for commercial audiences," says Alexander. The Second City ensemble uses improvisational techniques such as risk taking, acceptance, and communication to create comedic material and form a cohesive foundation for the team. Similarly, Second City fosters a relationship with its audience such that new material can be tried out on a nightly basis. Hot topics and sensitive issues are broached by the fearless Second City cast, a collection of scenes, songs, characters, and improvisations that unite the ensemble's creative endeavors under the heading of a new revue. The most successful works are archived for further study and entertainment.

According to Kelly Leonard, vice president of Second City, the corporation's top management continues to advance with the culture of improvisational comedy in mind. "Second City's culture is built upon improvisation. We 'Yes, and . . .' to ideas, we are always creating. We trade ideas, build upon what makes us laugh or think." The concept of affirming an idea ("Yes"), and building on it ("and") has developed a strong cultural infrastructure for the organization. "In the Second City," says Leonard, "authority and the norm are to be disturbed—creativity and originality are to be celebrated."

The Second City actively devotes itself to a variety of endeavors and functions as a markedly departmentalized corporation. The company's initiatives are separated geographically, functionally, and in relation to its customers. It has stages in two countries and touring companies around the world. They function with The Second City Business Company, operating specifically for the corporate community; in regard to its customers, The Second City gains a significant revenue from its box office and its Training Center. External communication, which is usually related to the specific department undertaking, is overseen by management staff working with performers/ teachers to build an appropriate business relationship with the client.

The Second City communicates internally through a large e-mail list created for anyone who chooses to be a "Second Citizen" while on the SC website. This list informs patrons and students about news, show openings, reviews, special events, and other interesting happenings in the Second City community. This is the most formal way that management disseminates information to others involved with the theater. With a high number of aspiring actors filling in the Second City environment, an active grapevine enriches the culture with news of upcoming shows and staff openings for performers . . . or cocktail waitresses.

The Second City functions primarily as a comedy club, and most of the employees who staff its bar, box office, and theater house are current or former students of the Training Center. While resident performers are granted Equity Actor Benefits, these lower-level employees are granted flexible, part-time schedules to accommodate their thespian lifestyles and the motivating knowledge that alumni such as Tina Fey, Chris Farley, and Stephen Colbert have all trained at the same institution. A variety of class levels all focus on team-building skills, active listening, and the quick, confident reactions necessary for the Second City brand

of comedy. Exposing its students to the true method of the Second City, the Training Center offers plenty of performance opportunities. Graduates of the Second City Training Program are produced in their own SC style revue, complete with a seasoned Second City director empowering them to use every skill at their disposal.

As new generations of Second City fans come up to the second floor of the concrete building on North Avenue and Wells Street in Chicago, Second City visionaries will cling to its black-and-white photos as the core symbols of success. Meanwhile, the next wave of Second City talent and the newest faces in comedy could be the employees tearing your ticket and serving your beverage.

## QUESTIONS

1. How does Second City's management differ from that of a traditional company?
2. How would you summarize the culture of Second City?
3. Why is it important for Second City to maintain its caliber of comedy? How does it do so?
4. How does ensemble play a role in the managerial techniques of Second City?

# Part 3: Launching Your Management Career

Part 3, "Management: Empowering People to Achieve Business Objectives," covers Chapters 8 through 11, which discuss management, leadership, and the internal organization; human resource management, motivation, and labor-management relations; improving performance through empowerment, teamwork, and communication; and production and operations management. In those chapters, you read about top managers and company founders such as Michael Bloomberg of Bloomberg LP, who is also mayor of New York City; middle manager Jeff McCracken, a chief engineer at Norfolk Southern who managed a team of 100 employees and dozens of engineers who rebuilt miles of railroad tracks destroyed by a hurricane; and supervisory manager Charles Lee, a production supervisor at an American Airlines maintenance center responsible for motivating airplane mechanics to repair and maintain passenger jets, all while finding ways to cut company costs. As these managers show, an incredible variety of jobs is available to those choosing management careers. And the demand for managers will continue to grow. The U.S. Department of Labor estimates that managerial jobs will grow by 11 percent over the next decade.[1]

So what kinds of jobs might you be able to choose from if you launch a management career? As you learned in Chapter 8, three types of management jobs exist: supervisory managers, middle managers, and top managers. Supervisory management, or first-line management, includes positions such as supervisor, office manager, department manager, section chief, and team leader. Managers at this level work directly with the employees who produce and sell a firm's goods and services.

Middle management includes positions such as general managers, plant managers, division managers, and regional or branch managers. They are responsible for setting objectives consistent with top management's goals and planning and implementing strategies for achieving those objectives.

Top managers include such positions as chief executive officer (CEO), chief operating officer (COO), chief financial officer (CFO), chief information officer (CIO), and executive vice president. Top managers devote most of their time to developing long-range plans, setting a direction for their organization, and inspiring a company's executives and employees to achieve their vision for the company's future. Top managers travel frequently between local, national, and global offices as they meet and work with customers, suppliers, and company managers and employees.

Most managers start their careers in areas such as sales, production, or finance, so you likely will start in a similar entry-level job. If you do that job and other jobs well, you may be considered for a supervisory position. Then, if you are interested and have the technical, human, and conceptual skills to succeed, you'll begin your management career at the supervisory level. But what kinds of supervisory management jobs are typically available? Let's review the exciting possibilities.

*Administrative service managers* manage basic services—such as clerical work, payroll, travel, printing and copying, data records, telecommunications, security, parking, and supplies—without which no organization could operate. On average, administrative service managers earn $60,000 a year.[2]

*Construction managers* plan, schedule, and coordinate the building of homes, commercial buildings such as offices and stores, and industrial facilities such as manufacturing plants and distribution centers. Unlike administrative service managers, who work in offices, construction managers typically work on building sites with architects, engineers, construction workers, and suppliers. On average, construction managers earn $70,000 a year.[3]

*Food service managers* run restaurants and services that prepare and offer meals to customers. They coordinate workers and suppliers in kitchens, dining areas, and banquet operations; are responsible for those who order and purchase food inventories; maintain kitchen equipment; and recruit, hire, and train new workers. Food service managers can work for chains such as Ruby Tuesday or Olive Garden, for local restaurants, and for corporate food service departments in organizations. On average, food service managers earn $40,000 a year.[4]

*Human resource managers* help organizations follow federal and local labor laws; effectively recruit, hire, train, and retain talented workers; administer corporate pay and benefits plans; develop and administer organizational human resource policies; and, when necessary, participate in contract negotiations or handle disputes. Human resource management jobs vary widely, depending on how specialized the requirements are. On average, human resource managers earn from $66,000 to $93,000 a year, depending on the area in which they specialize.[5]

*Lodging managers* work in hotels and motels but also help run camps, ranches, and recreational resorts. They may oversee guest service, front desk, kitchen, restaurant, banquet, house cleaning, and maintenance workers. Because they are expected to help satisfy customers 24/7, they often work long hours and may be on call when not at work. On average, lodging managers earn $38,000 a year.[6]

*Medical and health service managers* work in hospitals, nursing homes, doctors' offices, and corporate and university settings. They run departments that offer clinical services; ensure that state and federal laws are followed; and handle decisions related to the management of patient care, nursing, surgery, therapy, medical records, and financial payments. On average, medical and health service managers earn $67,000 a year.[7]

*Purchasing managers* lead and control organizational supply chains that ensure that companies have needed materials to produce the goods and services they sell, purchase materials at reasonable prices, and oversee deliveries when and where they are needed. Purchasing managers work with wholesale and retail buyers, buying goods that are then resold to others; purchasing agents, who buy supplies and raw materials for their organizations; and contract specialists, who negotiate and supervise purchasing contracts with key suppliers and vendors. On average, purchasing managers earn $72,000 a year.[8]

*Production managers* direct and coordinate operations that manufacture goods. They work with employees who produce parts and assemble products, help determine which new machines should be purchased and when existing machines need maintenance, and are responsible for achieving production goals that specify the quality, cost, schedule, and quantity of units to be produced. On average, production managers earn $73,000 a year.[9]

## Career Assessment Exercises in Management

1. The American Management Association is a global, not-for-profit professional organization that provides a range of management development and educational services to individuals, companies, and government agencies. Access the AMA's Web site at http://www.amanet.org. Explore the "Free Resources" link there (you will have to register). Pick an article or research area that interests you. Provide a one-page summary of the management issues discussed in the feature.

2. Go online to a business news service, such as Yahoo! News or Google News, or look at the business section of your local newspaper. Find a story relating to a first-line supervisor, middle manager, or top executive. Summarize that person's duties. What decisions does that

person make and how do those decisions affect his or her organization?

3. Pick a supervisory management position from the descriptions provided here that interests you. Research the career field. What skills do you possess that would make you a good candidate for a management position in that field? What work and other experience do you need to help you get started? Create a list of both your strengths and weaknesses and formulate a plan to add to your strengths.

# Marketing Management

# Part
## 4

# Chapter 12

## Customer-Driven Marketing

DIGITAL VISION/GETTY IMAGES

The words *natural food* used to conjure up images of bins filled with sprouts, tofu, and cardboard-dry wheat bread. People who actually knew what to do with dried beans purchased in bulk shopped at these markets. Not anymore. Whole Foods Market, which was founded in Austin, Texas, in 1978 by John Mackey and his girlfriend, admittedly had its share of sandal-clad customers driving VW buses. Today, Whole Foods's 168 stores welcome well-heeled customers, along with their Lexuses and Range Rovers, to its parking lots. Whole Foods has figured out what consumers want and how to offer it. "Americans love to eat. And Americans love to shop," says CEO John Mackey. "But we don't like to shop for food. . . . Whole Foods thinks shopping should be fun.

# Whole Foods Market: A Whole New Kind of Grocery Store

With this store, we're pioneering a new lifestyle that synthesizes health and pleasure. We don't see a contradiction."

The Whole Foods experience is better than any spa or theme park. Consumers can stroll along aisles of heirloom tomatoes, wander past the lobster and crab tanks, dip a fresh strawberry into a flowing chocolate fountain, sample any of 350 varieties of cheese, or order a salad while they sip a glass of Chardonnay. They can pick up dinner to go—sushi, goat cheese lasagna, or Indian *aloo mattar.* They can rest assured that it's all offered to promote their good health; Whole Foods specializes in organic foods, those produced without unwanted extras such as pesticides and hormones. Chickens raised for Whole Foods, the firm promises, have never ingested antibiotics or growth hormones. The pasta comes from an Italian farmer who grows acres of organic durum wheat to produce his Montebello brand. Fish is caught fresh every day.

Whole Foods also caters to local and ethnic taste preferences. When the manager of the Whole Foods store in Santa Monica, California, learned that some of his Buddhist customers were unable to eat foods containing onion or garlic, he began posting "No Onion, No Garlic" signs above prepared dishes that did not contain these ingredients. In Glendale, California, customers of

Iranian descent can purchase their pilaf staple by the pound, while Asian customers can pick up gai choy and chicken feet. Hispanic customers have a wide choice of tamale fixings at the same store. Manager Dave Aebersold appreciates the freedom he has to offer selections specific to his customer base. "I'm empowered to run this like it's my own store," he says.

Not surprisingly, all of these delicacies come at a price. A pound of brie that sells for $3.99 at a regular supermarket will cost you $6.23 at Whole Foods, and a half gallon of orange juice that goes for $1.99 elsewhere will set you back $2.69. If you really want to splurge, you can pick up a pound of French aged goat cheese for $25 or a bottle of Villa Manodori balsamic vinegar for $27. That strawberry you dip in the chocolate fountain will cost you $1.59—as much as a pint of strawberries at another store. While some might argue that high prices could drive consumers away, Mackey claims that the quality of his goods attracts shoppers. "If Americans want to eat higher quality, they can pay for it," he remarks. Whole Foods customers are loyal, even if it costs them a little more. "Business is simple," Mackey explains. "Management's job is to take care of employees. The employees' job is to take care of the customers. Happy customers take care of the shareholders. It's a virtuous circle."[1]

Business success in the 21st century is directly tied to a company's ability to identify and serve its target markets. In fact, all organizations—profit-oriented and not-for-profit, manufacturing and retailing—*must* serve customer needs to succeed, just as Whole Foods Market does by providing a wide array of healthful foods tailored to its customers. Marketing is the link between the organization and the people who buy and use its goods and services. It is the way organizations determine buyer needs and inform potential customers that their firms can meet those needs by supplying a quality product at a reasonable price. And it is the path to developing loyal, long-term customers.

Although consumers who purchase goods for their own use and enjoyment or business purchasers seeking products to use in their firm's operation may seem to be huge, undifferentiated masses, marketers see distinct wants and needs for each group. To understand buyers, from huge manufacturers to Web surfers to shoppers in the grocery aisles, companies gather mountains of data on every aspect of consumer lifestyles and buying behaviors. Marketers use the data to understand the needs and wants of both final customers and business buyers so that they can

better satisfy them. Satisfying customers goes a long way toward building relationships with them. It's not always easy. To establish links with the buying public, Whole Foods CEO John Mackey invites e-mails from consumers who may—or may not—be customers. After several weeks of electronic debate with an animal welfare activist over Whole Foods's practice of selling duck meat from a particular source, Mackey asked the activist to help rewrite his firm's policies on farm animal treatment. "It made me fall out of my chair," recalls activist Lauren Ornelas. "Now we're working together."[2] This relationship, which developed through direct communication between the CEO and a consumer, has helped Whole Foods cement its relationship with customers who are vegetarian or have other food-source concerns.

This chapter begins with an examination of the marketing concept and the way businesspeople develop a marketing strategy. We then turn to marketing research techniques, leading to an explanation of how businesses apply data to market segmentation and understanding customer behavior. The chapter closes with a detailed look at the important role played by customer relationships in today's highly competitive business world.

# *WHAT IS MARKETING?*

Every organization—from profit-seeking firms such as Costco and Johnson & Johnson to such not-for-profits as the United Way and the M. D. Anderson Cancer Center—must serve customer needs to succeed. Perhaps retail pioneer J. C. Penney best expressed this priority when he told his store managers, "Either you or your replacement will greet the customer within the first 60 seconds."

According to the American Marketing Association, **marketing** is "an organizational function and a set of processes for creating, communicating, and delivering value to customers and for managing customer relationships in ways that benefit the organization and its stakeholders."[3] In addition to selling goods and services, marketing techniques help people advocate ideas or viewpoints and educate others. The American Diabetes Association mails out questionnaires that ask, "Are you at risk for diabetes?" The documents help educate the general public about this widespread disease by listing its risk factors and common symptoms and describing the work of the association.

Department store founder Marshall Field explained marketing quite clearly when he advised one employee to "give the lady what she wants." The phrase became the company motto, and it remains a business truism today. The best marketers not only give consumers what they want but even anticipate consumers' needs before those needs surface. Ideally, they can get a jump

**marketing** organizational function and set of processes for creating, communicating, and delivering value to customers and for managing customer relationships in ways that benefit the organization and its stakeholders.

on the competition by creating a link in consumers' minds between the new need and the fulfillment of that need by the marketers' products. Principal Financial Group markets employee retirement plans to other firms as a strategy for retaining the best employees. NetJets offers fractional jet ownership to executives who want the luxury and flexibility of private ownership at a reduced cost. Samsung offers its next generation of high-definition TV with its trademarked Cinema Smooth Light Engine. "Stop watching TV," says its latest promotion. "Start living it."

As these examples illustrate, marketing is more than just selling. It is a process that begins with discovering unmet customer needs and continues with researching the potential market; producing a good or service capable of satisfying the targeted customers; and promoting, pricing, and distributing that good or service. Throughout the entire marketing process, a successful organization focuses on building customer relationships.

When two or more parties benefit from trading things of value, they have entered into an **exchange process.** When you purchase a cup of coffee, the other party may be a convenience store clerk, a vending machine, or a Starbucks barista. The exchange seems simple—some money changes hands, and you receive your cup of coffee. But the exchange process is more complex than that. It could not occur if you didn't feel the need for a cup of coffee or if the convenience store or vending machine were not available. You wouldn't choose Starbucks unless you were aware of the brand. Because of marketing, your desire for a latte, cappuccino, or plain black coffee is identified, and the coffee manufacturer's business is successful.

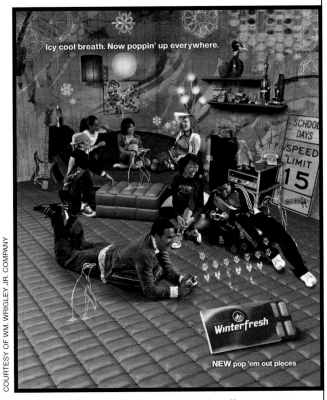

Icy cool breath. Now poppin' up everywhere.

Winterfresh
NEW pop 'em out pieces

COURTESY OF WM. WRIGLEY JR. COMPANY

Wrigley's facilitates the exchange process by offering its Winterfresh gum at many outlets, including convenience stores and grocery stores. The bubble packaging keeps each piece fresh until you're ready to share with your friends.

**exchange process** activity in which two or more parties give something of value to each other to satisfy perceived needs.

## How Marketing Creates Utility

Marketing affects many aspects of an organization and its dealings with customers. The ability of a good or service to satisfy the wants and needs of customers is called **utility.** A company's production function creates *form utility* by converting raw materials, component parts, and other inputs into finished goods and services. But the marketing function creates time, place, and ownership utility. **Time utility** is created by making a good or service available when customers want to purchase it. **Place utility** is created by making a product available in a location convenient for customers. **Ownership utility** refers to an orderly transfer of goods and services from the seller to the buyer. Firms may be able to create all three forms of utility. Putting a new spin on the traditional drive-through restaurant, firms such as Applebee's, Outback Steakhouse, and Ruby Tuesday have begun offering curbside service. Customers phone in their orders and then drive to designated spots in the restaurants' parking lots, where employees deliver the food. The service creates time utility by making the food available when customers want to purchase it, place utility by offering a convenient location, and ownership utility by providing the food that customers desire. Industry experts report that this is the fastest-growing trend in casual dining. "It may have started out as a convenience, but it's becoming a complete necessity," says a president of a restaurant consulting firm.[4]

**utility** want-satisfying power of a good or service.

**assessment check**

1. What is utility?
2. Identify ways in which marketing creates utility.

# EVOLUTION OF THE MARKETING CONCEPT

Marketing has always been a part of business, from the earliest village traders to large 21st-century organizations producing and selling complex goods and services. Over time, however, marketing activities evolved through the four eras shown in Figure 12.1: the production, sales, and marketing eras, and now the relationship era. Note that these eras parallel some of the business eras discussed in Chapter 1.

For centuries, organizations of the *production era* stressed efficiency in producing quality products. Their philosophy could be summed up by the remark, "A good product will sell itself." Although this production orientation continued into the 20th century, it gradually gave way to the *sales era,* in which businesses assumed that consumers would buy as a result of energetic sales efforts. Organizations didn't fully recognize the importance of their customers until the *marketing era* of the 1950s, when they began to adopt a consumer orientation. This focus has intensified in recent years, leading to the emergence of the *relationship era* in the 1990s, which continues to this day. In the relationship era, companies emphasize customer satisfaction and building long-term relationships with customers.

## Emergence of the Marketing Concept

**marketing concept**
company-wide consumer orientation to promote long-run uccess.

The term **marketing concept** refers to a company-wide customer orientation with the objective of achieving long-run success. The basic idea of the marketing concept is that marketplace success begins with the customer. A firm should analyze each customer's needs and then work backward to offer products that fulfill them. The emergence of the marketing concept can be explained best by the shift from a *seller's market,* one with a shortage of goods and services, to a *buyer's market,* one with an abundance of goods and services. During the 1950s, the United States became a strong buyer's market, forcing companies to satisfy customers rather than just producing and selling goods and services. Today, much competition among firms centers on the effort to satisfy customers. Recently, Apple Computer opened an iTunes store in Japan, which has long been considered Sony's domain. But the iPod has already been a hit in

**12.1** Four Eras in the History of Marketing

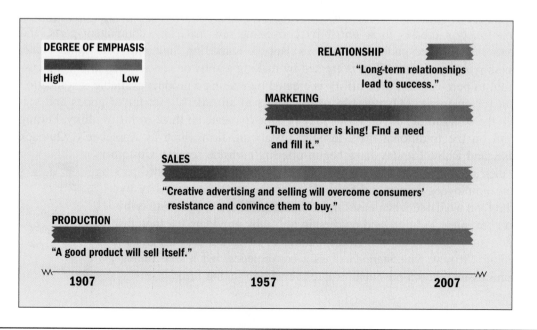

Japan, despite Sony's alternative MP3 offerings. Apple marketers see the move as a way to reach and satisfy the Japanese market. "We think this is going to change the experience of discovering and buying and enjoying music in Japan," predicts CEO Steve Jobs. "Together with the iPod, we think we are ushering in a new age of digital music."[5]

## Delivering Added Value through Customer Satisfaction and Quality

What is the most important sale for a company? Some assume that it's the first, but many marketers argue that the second sale is the most important, because repeat purchases are concrete evidence of **customer satisfaction.** The concept of a good or service pleasing buyers because it has met or exceeded their expectations is crucial to an organization's continued operation. A company that fails to match the customer satisfaction that its competitors provide will not stay in business very long. In contrast, increasing customer loyalty by just 5 percent translates into significant increases in lifetime profits per customer.[6]

The best way to keep a customer is to offer more than just products. Customers today want value, their perception that the quality of goods or services is in balance with the prices charged. When a company exceeds value expectations by adding features, lowering its price, enhancing customer service, or making other improvements that increase customer satisfaction, it provides a **value-added** good or service. As long as customers believe they have received value—good quality for a fair price—they are likely to remain satisfied with the company and continue their relationships. Cereality, the firm described in the "Hit & Miss" feature, offers value to its customers. Providing superior customer service can generate long-term success. FedEx, United Parcel Service, Hewlett-Packard, Nordstrom, and Target are all firms noted for superior customer service. Singapore Airlines is another such firm. Despite service cutbacks in other airlines, Singapore Airlines continues to provide top-notch service to its travelers, winning frequent international awards for doing so. The firm achieves this level of service by sticking to a clear mission and values; requiring continuous training of its employees; and maintaining constant communication with customers.[7]

*Quality*—the degree of excellence or superiority of an organization's goods and services—is another way firms enhance customer satisfaction. In an intensely competitive industry, Singapore Airlines constantly seeks methods to serve customers better and "get ahead of the pack." The company not only observes its direct competitors but also watches for ways in which hotels, banks, and restaurants improve service and adapts them to its own business.[8]

While a reputation for high quality enhances a firm's competitiveness, a slip in quality can damage a firm's image. Firms such as Ford, Firestone, and even McDonald's have suffered from quality slips and have worked hard to rebuild their reputations. Hyundai used to be viewed by the auto industry—and consumers—as producing a lower-quality vehicle than its competitors did. Now the firm advertises its high quality as well as "America's Best Warranty."

Although quality relates to physical product traits, such as durability and reliability, it also includes customer service. For a firm to be truly successful at providing customer service, the focus must come from the top.

## Customer Satisfaction and Feedback

One of the best ways to find out whether customers are satisfied with the goods and services provided by a company is to obtain *customer feedback* through toll-free telephone hotlines, customer satisfaction surveys, Web site message boards, or written correspondence. Some firms find out how well they have satisfied their customers by calling them or making personal visits to their businesses or residences.

**customer satisfaction** ability of a good or service to meet or exceed a buyer's needs and expectations.

# HIT & MISS

## One Company Makes a Cereal Killing

David Roth noticed something about U.S. consumers—they eat a lot of cereal. But they don't just eat it for breakfast; they seem to like it for lunch and dinner, and even snacks in between. "They were eating it everywhere, at different times of day," he recalls of his initial observation. Roth and his friend, designer Rick Bacher, knew they were on to something. Backed by marketing research that told them 95 percent of U.S. consumers like cereal, they decided to figure out a way to make this favorite food available in unusual places.

Roth and Bacher first targeted college students because "they basically live on cereal," says Roth. The two entrepreneurs set up a kiosk at Arizona State University's food court, where students could dish up their favorites—in any combination they wanted. The kiosk was a hit, and Cereality quickly expanded to Philadelphia, Chicago, and other locations near universities.

Here's how a Cereality bar and café works. Customers select from among 30 different types of brand-name cereal and 30 toppings—yes, toppings, including bananas and marshmallows. They can mix and match their Corn Pops and Captain Crunch, then choose what kind of milk they want, such as skim or soy. They can even have Quaker hot cereals made to order. All the cereals are served in individual fold-over boxes by servers wearing pajamas. The boxes even come with long straws to reach milk at the bottom. "You never

have a bad bowl of cereal, because you create it," explains Nelson Diaz, a Cereality café manager. In some of the larger cafés, customers can even lounge on couches and use free Internet connections. The experience also fits a college budget—for about $3, a cereal-hungry student can get a meal.

Cereality customers are loyal. The only downside, they say, is that some of the cafés aren't open late enough—when students are pulling all-nighters. "This would be a great study break," says one senior. "It would be smart for them to be open later."

Roth and Bacher are listening. They are also thinking big. Their next targets will be airports, hospitals, and train stations. Roth looks at cereal this way: "[It is] the great equalizer. It crosses all demographics, all races, all ages. People see it as a happy thing."

### Questions for Critical Thinking

1. In what ways does Cereality deliver customer satisfaction? How might it improve?
2. Describe two ways in which Cereality could obtain customer feedback.

**Sources:** April Y. Pennington, "Breakfast of Champions," *Entrepreneur,* accessed July 12, 2006, http://www.entrepreneur.com; "The Loop Gets Ready for Froot Loops Plus 29 Other Cereals," PR Newswire, February 22, 2005, http://biz.yahoo.com; Craig Wilson, "A Whole New Bowl Game," *USA Today,* December 8, 2004, http://www.usatoday.com.

## assessment check

1. What is the marketing concept?
2. How does customer satisfaction result in a value-added good or service?

Customer complaints are excellent sources of customer feedback, because they present companies with an opportunity to overcome problems and improve their services. Customers often feel greater loyalty after a conflict has been resolved than if they had never complained at all. Complaints can also allow firms to gather innovative ideas for improvement.

## EXPANDING MARKETING'S TRADITIONAL BOUNDARIES

The marketing concept has traditionally been associated with products of profit-seeking organizations. Today, however, it is also being applied to not-for-profit sectors and other nontraditional areas ranging from religious organizations to political campaigns.

# Not-for-Profit Marketing

Residents of every continent benefit in various ways from the approximately 20 million not-for-profit organizations currently operating around the globe. Some 1.5 million of them are located in the United States, where they employ about 8.6 million workers and benefit from another 7.2 million volunteers. Worldwide, the not-for-profit sector accounts for nearly 5 percent of the gross domestic product.[9] The largest not-for-profit organization in the world is the Red Cross/Red Crescent. Others range from Habitat for Humanity and Save the Children to the National Science Foundation and the World Food Program. These organizations all benefit by applying many of the strategies and business concepts used by profit-seeking firms. They apply marketing tools to reach audiences, secure funding, improve their images, and accomplish their overall missions. Marketing strategies are important for not-for-profit organizations because they are all competing for dollars—from individuals, foundations, and corporations—just as commercial businesses are.

Not-for-profit organizations operate in both public and private sectors. Public groups include federal, state, and local government units as well as agencies that receive tax funding. A state's department of natural resources, for instance, regulates land conservation and environmental programs; the local animal control officer enforces ordinances protecting people and animals; a city's public health board

STAMP OUT BREAST CANCER
WITH YOUR FEET.

Up to 75% of the net proceeds from our Race are spent locally, supporting the fight against breast cancer in your community. For more information, visit komen.org or call 1.888.603.RACE.

The Susan G. Komen Breast Cancer Foundation

RACE FOR THE CURE

Presented by

©2006, The Susan G. Komen Breast Cancer Foundation

THE SUSAN G. KOMEN BREAST CANCER FOUNDATION

Not-for-profit organizations conduct major marketing campaigns. The Susan G. Komen Breast Cancer Foundation holds races and walks around the country to raise funds for research for a cure.

ensures safe drinking water for its citizens. The private not-for-profit sector comprises many different types of organizations, including California State University–Fullerton's baseball team, the Adirondack Mountain Club, and Portsmouth, New Hampshire–based Cross Roads House for homeless families. Although some private not-for-profits generate surplus revenue, their primary goals are not earning profits. If they earn funds beyond their expenses, they invest the excess in their organizational missions.

In some cases, not-for-profit organizations form a partnership with a profit-seeking company to promote the firm's message or distribute its goods and services. This partnership usually benefits both organizations. Large corporations may form their own not-for-profit charitable organizations. McDonald's is well known for its Ronald McDonald Charities. Designer Ralph Lauren has partnered with the U.S. Tennis Association to market an exclusive line of tennis gear, including tennis balls imprinted with pink polo players on ponies. Sales from the tennis balls help benefit breast cancer research.[10]

In addition, wealthy athletes and other celebrities sometimes form their own not-for-profit organizations to support causes that are personally meaningful to them. Hockey player Mario Lemieux established a foundation that assists hospitals in Pittsburgh and funds neonatal and anticancer research. Tennis star Andre Agassi established an organization to fund an academy for underprivileged children in Las Vegas.[11]

## Nontraditional Marketing

Not-for-profit organizations often engage in one or more of five major categories of nontraditional marketing: person marketing, place marketing, event marketing, cause marketing, and organization marketing. Figure 12.2 provides examples of these types of marketing. Through each of these types of marketing, an organization seeks to connect with the audience that is most likely to offer time, money, or other resources. In some cases, the effort may reach the market the organization intends to serve.

## 12.2 Categories of Nontraditional Marketing

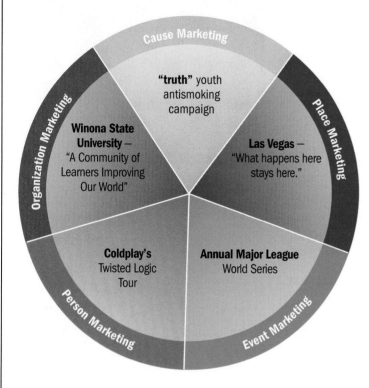

*Cause Marketing*

"**truth**" youth antismoking campaign

*Organization Marketing*

**Winona State University** — "A Community of Learners Improving Our World"

*Place Marketing*

**Las Vegas** — "What happens here stays here."

**Coldplay's** Twisted Logic Tour

**Annual Major League** World Series

*Person Marketing*

*Event Marketing*

**Person Marketing** Efforts designed to attract the attention, interest, and preference of a target market toward a person are called **person marketing.** Campaign managers for a political candidate conduct marketing research, identify groups of voters and financial supporters, and then design advertising campaigns, fund-raising events, and political rallies to reach them. Celebrities such as cyclist Lance Armstrong, who won the *Tour de France* a record seven times, engage in person marketing to expand their audience, attract viewers to events, and enhance their images with the public.

Many successful job seekers apply the tools of person marketing. They research the wants and needs of prospective employers, and they identify ways they can meet them. They seek employers through a variety of channels, sending messages that emphasize how they can benefit the employer.

**Place Marketing** As the term suggests, **place marketing** attempts to attract people to a particular area, such as a city, state, or nation. It may involve appealing to consumers as a tourist destination or to businesses as a desirable business location. A strategy for place marketing often includes advertising.

Place marketing may be combined with event marketing, such as the Olympics. Beijing, host of the 2008 Summer Olympics, has combined its marketing efforts to attract visitors and businesses to China for more than the athletic events. "For many of China's new brands and leading companies, the Games . . . provide a unique international platform to showcase themselves to the world. For leading global companies, the Games . . . open the gates to the most important market in the world," noted Jacques Rogge, president of the International Olympic Committee.[12]

**Event Marketing** Marketing or sponsoring short-term events such as athletic competitions and cultural and charitable performances is known as **event marketing.** The No Limits Tour of BMX bike and skateboarding stunts involved event marketing by Skippy peanut butter, *Sports Illustrated Kids,* and Six Flags. Target recently sponsored the first women's junior professional surfing competition.

Event marketing often forges partnerships between not-for-profit and profit-seeking organizations. Many businesses sponsor events such as 10K runs to raise funds for health-related charities. These occasions require a marketing effort to plan the event and attract participants and sponsors. Events may be intended to raise money or awareness, or both.

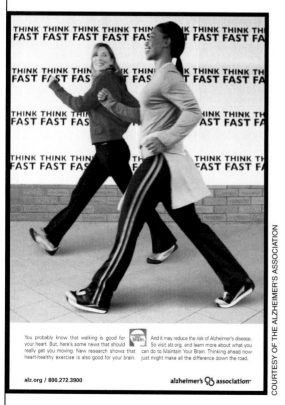

THINK THINK THINK THINK THINK THINK THINK
FAST FAST FAST FAST FAST FAST FAST

You probably know that walking is good for your heart. But, here's some news that should really get you moving. New research shows that heart-healthy exercise is also good for your brain. And it may reduce the risk of Alzheimer's disease. So visit alz.org, and learn more about what you can do to Maintain Your Brain. Thinking ahead now just might make all the difference down the road.

alz.org / 800.272.3900          alzheimer's association

The Alzheimer's Association encourages people to learn more about this crippling and progressive brain disorder. Recent studies show that exercise is good for your brain and may help reduce the risk of Alzheimer's disease, so the association is spreading the word with this promotion.

The United Nations' Food and Agriculture Organization sponsors World Food Day on October 16 each year to raise awareness of worldwide poverty and hunger and to promote sustainable agriculture. More than 150 countries hold national events to observe the day.[13]

*Cause Marketing*   Marketing that promotes a cause or social issue, such as preventing child abuse, antilittering efforts, and antismoking campaigns, is **cause marketing.** Cause marketing seeks to educate the public and may or may not attempt to directly raise funds. An advertisement often contains a phone number or Web site address through which people can obtain more information.

Profit-seeking companies look for ways to give back to their communities by joining forces with charities and causes, providing financial, marketing, and human resources. Timberland is well known for its City Year and Bikes for Tikes programs. NBC has underwritten its "The More You Know" public-service announcements for nearly two decades. Celebrities who have participated in the announcements include business mogul Donald Trump and actors Mariska Hargitay and James Caan.

*Organization Marketing*   The final category of nontraditional marketing, **organization marketing,** influences consumers to accept the goals of, receive the services of, or contribute in some way to an organization. The U.S. Postal Service, the U.S. military, the American Red Cross, and the Tiger Woods Foundation are all examples of organizations that engage in marketing. Organizations such as the American Heart Association and the Disabled American Veterans send out printed return-address labels with donation requests enclosed. These groups hope that consumers will be willing to pay for the customized labels with donations.

**assessment check**

1. Why do not-for-profit organizations engage in marketing?
2. What are the five types of nontraditional marketing used by not-for-profit organizations?

# DEVELOPING A MARKETING STRATEGY

Decision makers in any successful organization, for-profit or not-for-profit, follow a two-step process to develop a *marketing strategy*: First, they study and analyze potential target markets and choose among them. Second, they create a marketing mix to satisfy the chosen market. Figure 12.3 shows the relationship among the target market, the marketing mix variables, and the marketing environment. Later discussions refer back to this figure as they cover each topic. This section describes the development of a marketing strategy.

**Figure 12.3**

Target Market and Marketing Mix within the Marketing Environment

MARKETING ENVIRONMENT

Political/Legal · Competitive · MARKETING MIX · Product · Distribution · TARGET MARKET · Promotion · Price · Social/Cultural · Technological · Economic

Earlier chapters of this book introduced many of the environmental factors that affect the success or failure of a firm's business strategy, including today's rapidly changing and highly competitive world of business, a vast array of social-cultural factors, economic challenges, political and legal factors, and technological innovations. Although these external forces frequently operate outside managers' control, marketers must still consider the impact of environmental factors on their decisions.

A marketing plan is a key component of a firm's overall business plan. The marketing plan outlines its marketing strategy and includes information about the target market, sales and revenue goals, the marketing budget, and the timing for implementing the elements of the marketing mix.

## Selecting a Target Market

The expression "find a need and fill it" is perhaps the simplest explanation of the two elements of a marketing strategy. A firm's marketers find a need through careful and continuing study of the individuals and business decision makers in its potential market. A market consists of people with purchasing power, willingness to buy, and authority to make purchase decisions.

Markets can be classified by type of product. **Consumer products**—often known as business-to-consumer (B2C) products—are goods and services, such as DVDs, shampoo, and dental care, that are purchased by end users. **Business products**—or business-to-business (B2B) products—are goods and services purchased to be used, either directly or indirectly, in the production of other goods for resale. Some products can fit either classification depending on who buys them and why. A computer or checking account, for example, can be either a consumer or business product.

**target market** group of people toward whom an organization markets its goods, services, or ideas with a strategy designed to satisfy their specific needs and preferences.

An organization's **target market** is the group of potential customers toward whom it directs its marketing efforts. Customer needs and wants vary considerably, and no single organization has the resources to satisfy everyone. *Forbes* is geared toward businesspeople and consumers who are interested in business, while *Teen Vogue* is aimed at teenagers who are interested in fashion.

Decisions about marketing involve strategies for four areas of marketing activity: product, distribution, promotion, and pricing. A firm's **marketing mix** blends the four strategies to fit the needs and preferences of a specific target market. Marketing success depends not on the four individual strategies but on their unique combination.

**marketing mix** blending the four elements of marketing strategy—product, distribution, promotion, and pricing—to satisfy chosen customer segments.

*Product strategy* involves more than just designing a good or service with needed attributes. It also includes decisions about package design, brand names, trademarks, warranties, product image, new-product development, and customer service. Think, for instance, about your favorite soft drink. Do you like it for its taste alone, or do other attributes, such as clever ads, attractive packaging, and overall image, also contribute to your brand preference? *Distribution strategy,* the second marketing mix variable, ensures that customers receive their purchases in the proper quantities at the right times and locations. *Promotional strategy,* another marketing mix element, effectively blends advertising, personal selling, sales promotion, and public relations to achieve its goals of informing, persuading, and influencing purchase decisions.

*Pricing strategy,* the final mix element, is also one of the most difficult areas of marketing decision making in setting profitable and justifiable prices for the firm's product offerings. Such actions are sometimes subject to government regulation and considerable public scrutiny. They also represent a powerful competitive weapon and frequently produce responses by the other firms in the industry, who match price changes to avoid losing customers.

Barbara Kavovit used a variety of marketing mix elements to launch her company, called Barbara K!, to success. Already the owner of a construction firm, Kavovit targeted a specific market—women—and developed a product line of household tools and kits that were easy for women to use. Barbara K! tools are distributed online and through stores where women are likely to shop, including Bed Bath & Beyond, Target.com, and TheKnot.com. They are priced affordably—customers can pick up a 30-piece tool kit for $49.99, the roadside safety kit for $29.99, and the jewelry repair kit for $9.99. They can also purchase single tools, such as the Power-Lite cordless drill for $49.99. Kavovit's promotional strategy includes appearances on ABC's *Good Morning America;* advertisements in magazines and on cable television; and online instruction in home décor, home repair, and automotive care. Kavovit has also published her first book, *Room for Improvement.* Kavovit's marketing efforts are filled with messages of empowerment. "If I can do it, so can you," is the Barbara K! slogan.[14]

## Developing a Marketing Mix for International Markets

Marketing a good or service in foreign markets means deciding whether to offer the same marketing mix in every market (*standardization*) or to develop a unique mix to fit each market (*adaptation*). The advantages of standardizing the marketing mix include reliable marketing performance and low costs. This approach works best with B2B goods, such as steel, chemicals, and aircraft, that require little sensitivity to a nation's culture.

Adaptation, on the other hand, lets marketers vary their marketing mix to suit local competitive conditions, consumer preferences, and government regulations. Consumer tastes are often shaped by local cultures. Because consumer products generally tend to be more culture dependent than business products, they more often require adaptation. This has been the case with Kentucky Fried Chicken in China. Chinese consumers love chicken—more than burgers and fries—which is one reason KFC has been so successful in the world's most populous country. KFC serves up buckets of its Original Recipe chicken, but it has also adapted some of its choices to satisfy Chinese taste buds. For instance, one sandwich is styled along the lines of Peking duck but with fried chicken instead. And while coleslaw hasn't become popular in China, customers can choose side dishes such as seasonal vegetables including bamboo shoots, lotus roots, and rice porridge. "We are really positioned as a part of the fabric of life in China," says David Novak, chairman and CEO of Yum brands, the parent company of KFC.[15]

Marketers also try to build adaptability into the designs of standardized goods and services for international and domestic markets. *Mass customization* allows a firm to mass-produce goods and services while adding unique features to individual or small groups of orders. The Smart Car is a tiny two-person vehicle that has been cruising along the roads of Europe and Asia for several years. Taking a marketing risk, the California firm Zap began importing the cars to the United States in the hope that they would compete with the popular Mini Cooper. Marketed to urban dwellers who need a car that can squeeze into tight spaces, the Smart Car can be customized to suit personal color preferences. Instead of painting each car a different hue, the basic car is sold with different-colored door panels that can be snapped on and off. Zap is aiming big with its Smart Car. "If we can create a California car company, it would be great for consumers and the world," says Zap spokesman Alex Campbell.[16]

Audi promotes its A3 Sportback to the Spanish-language market. The ad mentions the company's forward—thinking technology but appeals to a universal human characteristic—the need for a fun and exciting driving experience.

**assessment check**

1. Distinguish between consumer products and business products.
2. What are the steps in developing a marketing strategy?

# MARKETING RESEARCH

Marketing research involves more than just collecting data. Researchers must decide how to collect data, interpret the results, convert the data into decision-oriented information, and communicate those results to managers for use in decision making. **Marketing research** is the process of collecting and evaluating information to help marketers make effective decisions. It links business decision makers to the marketplace by providing data about potential target markets that help them design effective marketing mixes.

## Obtaining Marketing Research Data

Marketing researchers need both internal and external data. Firms generate *internal data* within their organizations. Financial records provide a tremendous amount of useful information, such as changes in unpaid bills, inventory levels, sales generated by different categories of customers or product lines, profitability of particular divisions, or comparisons of sales by territories, salespeople, customers, or product lines.

Researchers gather *external data* from outside sources, including previously published data. Trade associations publish reports on activities in particular industries. Advertising agencies collect information on the audiences reached by various media. National marketing research firms offer information through subscription services. Some of these professional research firms specialize in specific markets, such as Teenage Research Unlimited, which recently reported that American teenagers spend $155 billion on goods and services each year—valuable information for firms interested in reaching these consumers.[17]

For years, retail giant Wal-Mart relied on its suppliers to determine what was fashionable in clothing, but it had no way to determine whether they were correct. As a result, clothing sales languished—although 100 million customers shop at Wal-Mart every week, only about one in three buys apparel there. In an effort to revamp its clothing image and increase sales, Wal-Mart created a marketing research arm called Trend Office and placed it in New York's fashion center, Fifth Avenue. The ten staff members research the latest trends and colors and suggest new product lines for Wal-Mart stores to carry. If the research effort succeeds, the company will be able to add more lucrative, style-conscious customers to its traditional base of shoppers looking for rock-bottom prices.[18]

*Secondary data,* or previously published data, are low cost and easy to obtain. Federal, state, and local government publications are excellent data sources, and most are available online. The most frequently used government statistics include census data, which contain the population's age, gender, education level, household size and composition, occupation, employment status, and income. Even private research firms such as Teenage Research Unlimited provide some free information on their Web sites. This information helps firms evaluate consumers' buying behavior, anticipate possible changes in the marketplace, and identify new markets.

Even though secondary data represent a quick and inexpensive resource, marketing researchers sometimes discover that this information isn't specific or current enough for their needs. If so, researchers may conclude that they must collect *primary data*—data collected firsthand through such methods as observation and surveys.

Marketing researchers sometimes collect primary data through observational studies, in which they view the actions of consumers either directly or through mechanical devices. Once Famous, a retail laboratory, observes the actions of shoppers in a "real" store setting. Online sites also measure traffic, typically by counting the number of new visitors to a Web site during a given time period. Web-based data collection can also track which links each visitor clicks while at a Web site, as well as what a visitor orders and how much money the visitor spends.

Simply observing customers cannot provide some types of information. A researcher might observe a customer buying a red sweater, but have no idea why the purchase was made—or for whom. When researchers need information about consumers' attitudes, opinions, and motives, they need to ask the consumers themselves. They may conduct surveys by telephone, in person, online, or in focus groups.

A focus group gathers eight to twelve people in a room or over the Internet to discuss a particular topic. A focus group can generate new ideas, address consumers' needs, and even point out flaws in existing products. Teenage Research Unlimited frequently uses focus groups, called Trendwatch Panels, to learn what teens are thinking. Recently, by combining a panel discussion with a broader survey, the firm learned that the current generation of teens is practical and willing to work toward attainable goals. They are well grounded and family oriented, although they want to find their own "voice" in the world. How might marketers use this information? When asked which factors would be most important to them in the purchase of a car, the teens answered: price and style.[19]

## Applying Marketing Research Data

As the accuracy of information collected by researchers increases, so does the effectiveness of resulting marketing strategies. General Motors gathered five groups of Jeep Cherokee and Chevy Blazer owners to critique early sketches of the new Hummer. The groups came one at a time, and researchers revised the drawings for the next group based on the comments of the previous one. GM was looking for the perfect design for the third-generation Hummer. When the H3 hit the market, design changes in the grille, headlights, and doors, all made on the basis of the groups' responses, were evident.[20]

## Data Mining

Computer searches through customer data to detect patterns and relationships is referred to as **data mining.** These patterns may suggest predictive models of real-world business activities. Accurate data mining can help researchers forecast recessions, weed out credit card fraud, and pinpoint sales prospects.

**data mining** computer searches of customer data to detect patterns and relationships.

Data mining uses **data warehouses,** which are sophisticated customer databases that allow managers to combine data from several different organizational functions. Wal-Mart's data warehouse, considered the largest in the private sector, contains more than 500 terabytes (trillions of characters) of data. The retail giant uses data mining to assess local preferences for merchandise so that it can tailor the inventory of each store to the tastes of its neighborhood. By identifying patterns and connections, marketers can increase the accuracy of their predictions about the effectiveness of their strategy options. Harrah's casino in Las Vegas tracks customers' purchases and activities to tailor pricing for its hotel rooms. Harrah's also uses the data to predict what its repeat customers want and then customize its offerings—such as free steak dinners, spa treatments, and show tickets.[21]

**assessment check**

1. What is the difference between primary data and secondary data?
2. Why is marketing research important to business?

# MARKET SEGMENTATION

**Market segmentation** is the process of dividing a market into several relatively homogeneous groups. Both profit-seeking and not-for-profit organizations use segmentation to help them reach desirable target markets. Market segmentation is often based on the results of marketing research.

**market segmentation** process of dividing a total market into several relatively homogeneous groups.

Market segmentation attempts to isolate the traits that distinguish a certain group of customers from the overall market. However, segmentation doesn't automatically produce marketing success. Table 12.1 lists several criteria that marketers should consider. The effectiveness of a segmentation strategy depends on how well the market meets these criteria. Once marketers identify a market segment to target, they can create an appropriate marketing strategy.

For years, bread manufacturers have known that kids like white bread, despite the fact that bread made from whole grains is more nutritious. As a result, firms have spent millions of dollars trying to develop a more nutritious bread that would satisfy two targeted markets at once—children and their parents, who buy the bread. Sara Lee Corporation recently launched its new Soft & Smooth bread—made with Ultragrain, a product manufactured by ConAgra, which looks white but contains 30 percent whole grain. As a result, Wonder Bread has announced a new loaf that is made with 100 percent whole grain—but is still white.[22]

## How Market Segmentation Works

An immediate segmentation distinction involves whether the firm is offering goods and services to customers for their own use or to purchasers who will use them directly or indirectly in providing other products for resale (the so-called B2B market). Depending on whether their firms offer consumer or business products, marketers segment their target markets differently. Four common bases for segmenting consumer markets are geographical segmentation, demographic segmentation, psychographic segmentation, and product-related segmentation. Business markets can segment on only three criteria: customer-based segmentation, end-use segmentation, and geographical segmentation. Figure 12.4 illustrates the segmentation methods for these two types of markets.

## Segmenting Consumer Markets

Market segmentation has been practiced since people first began selling products. Tailors made some clothing items for men and others for women. Tea was imported from India for tea drinkers in Europe and England. In addition to demographic and geographical segmentation, today's marketers also define customer groups based on psychographic criteria as well as product-related distinctions.

*Geographical Segmentation*   The oldest segmentation method is **geographical segmentation**—dividing a market into homogeneous groups on the basis of their locations. Geographical location does not guarantee that consumers in a certain region will all buy the same kinds of products, but it does provide some indication of needs. For instance, suburbanites usually

**Table**

**12.1**   Criteria for Market Segmentation

| Criterion | Example |
|---|---|
| A segment must be a measurable group. | Data can be collected on the dollar amount and number of purchases by college students. |
| A segment must be accessible for communication. | A growing number of seniors are going online, so they can be reached through Internet channels. |
| A segment must be large enough to offer profit potential. | In a small community, a store carrying only large-size shoes might not be profitable. Similarly, a specialty retail chain may not locate in a small market. |

**Figure**

**12.4**

Methods of Segmenting Consumer and Business Markets

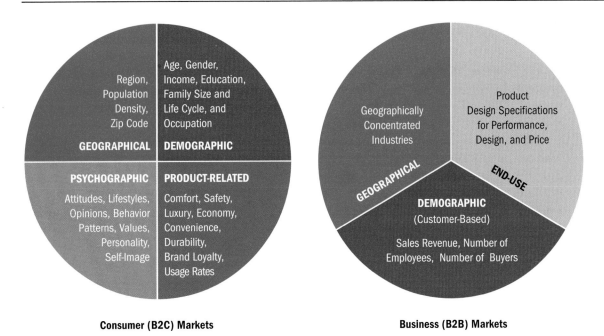

**Consumer (B2C) Markets**                     **Business (B2B) Markets**

buy more lawn care products than central-city dwellers. However, many suburbanites choose instead to purchase the services of a lawn maintenance firm. Consumers who live in northern states, where winter is more severe, are more likely to buy ice scrapers, snow shovels, and snowblowers than those who live in warmer climates. They are also more likely to contract with firms who plow driveways. Marketers also look at the size of the population of an area, as well as who lives there—are residents old or young? Do they reflect an ethnic background? What is the level of their income?

General Motors's sales have lagged on both the East and West Coasts. It has captured less than 15 percent of auto sales there, compared with its nearly 26 percent share elsewhere. In investigating the problem, the company found out that its product lines, featuring pickup trucks and sport-utility vehicles, were not as popular on the coasts. So GM marketers are revising the company's leasing deals, which Easterners favor, and promoting its sportier Saturn Sky roadster and Pontiac Solstice in California.[23]

Job growth and migration patterns are important considerations as well. Some businesses combine areas or even entire countries that share similar population and product-use patterns instead of treating each as an independent segment.

*Demographic Segmentation*  By far the most common method of market segmentation, **demographic segmentation** distinguishes markets on the basis of various demographic or socioeconomic characteristics. Common demographic measures include gender, income, age, occupation, household size, stage in the family life cycle, education, and ethnic group. The U.S. Census Bureau is one of the best sources of demographic information for the domestic market.

Gender used to be a simple way to define markets for certain products—cosmetics and kitchen appliances for women, hammers and drills for men. Much of that has changed—dramatically. Men buy skin care products, and women buy tools. Bath and Body Works, a popular retailer of skin care products and fragrances for women, also has a men's line of products—soothing face conditioner, shower gel, and cologne sprays in scents named Woodland

and Glacier Bay.[24] In a recent marketing research survey, the Lowe's home-improvement chain learned that 67 percent of women are ready to be entirely responsible for the care and maintenance of their own homes. This percentage rose even higher among Hispanic women— 79 percent. Also, 78 percent of all female homeowners own a combination of hand tools and power tools.[25] In addition to a shift in the types of products that men and women buy, there has been a tremendous shift in purchasing power. Women now control an estimated 85 percent of the $7 trillion spent each year on personal consumption items, and one expert predicts that women will control 60 percent of all wealth in the United States by 2010, in part because of their tendency to live longer than men.[26]

Age is perhaps the most volatile factor in demographic segmentation in the United States, with our rapidly aging population. By 2020, one of every three Americans will be over age 50, and smart companies will focus their attention on reaching this growing part of the market. Marketers who conducted research on baby boomers—Americans born between 1946 and 1964—discovered that 42 percent of these consumers want to combine work and leisure; 17 percent want to leave work completely behind; and 13 percent want to start their own businesses.[27] Based on these statistics, marketers for travel and leisure products, as well as retirement and business investments, are working hard to attract the attention of this age group. However, some businesses haven't yet recognized the opportunity, as described in the "Hit & Miss" feature.

As mentioned earlier, teens are another rapidly growing market. The purchases that the average teen makes—or influences—add up to about $116 a week. Marketers always want to know what teens like to do and buy. According to a recent survey by *Time,* 13-year-olds would rather use an Xbox or PS2 than watch TV; iPod Minis and flip cell phones are in; and Snickers, Doritos, Snapple drinks, and Ben & Jerry's ice cream rank high with teen taste buds.[28]

Minority groups hold a combined purchasing power of more than $1 trillion a year in the United States alone, an amount that marketers must not overlook. The three largest minority groups—Hispanic Americans, African Americans, and Asian Americans—number almost one out of every three U.S. residents. By 2050, the nation's population will be more than 50 percent minorities. Already, four states in the United States—California, New Mexico, Hawaii, and Texas—have nonwhite majority populations. Maryland, Mississippi, Georgia, New York, and Arizona each have about 40 percent minority populations.[29] Hispanic buying power is expected to hit nearly $1 billion in the next few years, about equal to that of African Americans. The buying power of Asian Americans hovers around $500 million.[30] Another important group of consumers is Native Americans, who currently number about 2.5 million across the United States. Clearly, these unique markets represent significant business opportunities.

To avoid stereotyping, marketers try to break large groups of minorities into smaller segments. For instance, the Hispanic market is made up of many smaller segments, based not only on country of origin but also on lifestyle. Best Buy recently ran Spanish-language commercials and print ads targeting Hispanic adults age 40 and older because marketing research revealed that while household heads had the most buying power, they also had the least information. So the ads were designed to provide more information about Best Buy products.[31]

Entrepreneurs who are members of minority groups may start their own businesses out of frustration at not being able to find food, clothing, entertainment, or other goods and services that fit their tastes and needs. Parry Singh did exactly that. He established a series of Web sites to cater to the demand for ethnic foods. The first site, Namaste.com, came about because of his sister's inability to find Indian groceries. Later he founded EthnicGrocer.com, an online global grocery market. Visitors may browse among the culinary treats of fifteen countries including China, Italy, Greece, Mexico, India, Vietnam, and others. Or they can select what they need by category, such as spices, oils, pasta, or baking needs. They can purchase exotic seasonings such as seaweed and spice paste, download international recipes, and get tips on

# HIT & MISS

how to use various products. EthnicGrocer is not just for expert ethnic cooks; the site seeks to educate anyone who is interested in and willing to try different styles of cooking.[32]

*Psychographic Segmentation* Lifestyle is the sum of a person's needs, preferences, motives, attitudes, social habits, and cultural background. In recent years, marketing researchers have tried to formulate lifestyle portraits of consumers. This effort has led to another strategy for segmenting target markets, **psychographic segmentation,** which divides consumer markets into groups with similar psychological characteristics, values, and lifestyles.

Psychographic studies have evaluated motivations for purchases of hundreds of goods and services, ranging from soft drinks to healthcare services. Using the resulting data, firms tailor their marketing strategies to carefully chosen market segments. A frequently used method of developing psychographic profiles involves the use of *AIO statements*—verbal descriptions of various activities, interests, and opinions. Researchers survey a sample of consumers, asking them whether they agree or disagree with each statement. The answers are then tabulated and analyzed for use in identifying various lifestyle categories.

Another way to get current information from consumers about their lifestyles is to create *blogs,* as described in Chapter 7, to which consumers respond. Companies ranging from Stonyfield Farm to Microsoft have hired full-time corporate bloggers to run online Web journals as a way to connect with and receive information from consumers. Other firms encourage employees at all levels to use blogs to communicate with consumers. General Motors vice chairman Bob Lutz even has his own blog, through which he shares ideas and viewpoints with the car-buying public.[33]

Although demographic classifications such as age, gender, and income are relatively easy to identify and measure, researchers also need to define psychographic categories. Often marketing research firms conduct extensive studies of consumers and then share their psychographic data with clients. In addition, businesses look to studies done by sociologists and psychologists to help them understand their customers. A group of scientists at UCLA spent the last several years following the lives of several U.S. families and identified some important lifestyle trends. Families tend to engage in many organized activities, including sports and music lessons, limiting the time for spontaneous outings, games, or meals. They also spend more time in their cars, where kids may actually do homework and eat meals. Children and parents stay in constant contact via cell phones and pagers.[34] These are just a few trends identified by the researchers, but they provide valuable information to firms that may be considering developing convenience foods, designing the interiors of family vehicles, or implementing new wireless plans.

### Product-Related Segmentation

Using **product-related segmentation,** sellers can divide a consumer market into groups based on buyers' relationships to the good or service. The three most popular approaches to product-related segmentation are based on benefits sought, usage rates, and brand loyalty levels.

Segmenting by *benefits sought* focuses on the attributes that people seek in a good or service and the benefits they expect to receive from it. In Johnson & Johnson's ad for BAND-AID® Brand TOUGH-STRIPS® adhesive bandages, consumers learn that they can soak an adhesive bandage with a garden hose, and it still won't peel off the skin.

Consumer markets can also be segmented according to the amounts of a product that people buy and use. Segmentation by *product usage rate* usually defines such categories as heavy users, medium users, and light users. The 80/20 principle states that roughly 80 percent of a product's revenues come from only 20 percent of its buyers. Companies can now pinpoint which of their customers are the heaviest users—and even the most profitable customers—and direct their heaviest marketing efforts to those customers.

The third technique for product-related segmentation divides customers by *brand loyalty*—the degree to which consumers recognize, prefer, and insist on a particular brand. Marketers define groups of consumers with similar degrees of brand loyalty. They then attempt to tie loyal customers to a good or service by giving away premiums, which can be anything from a logo-emblazoned T-shirt to a pair of free tickets to a concert or sports event.

Take me fishing.
Because you're the
coolest grandpa ever.

Take me fishing.
So you can tell me
stories about my dad.

Take me fishing.
And show me how
to drive the boat.

Take me fishing.
So I'll always remember you.

"takemefishing"
GET INFORMATION AND GET GOING AT
TAKEMEFISHING.ORG

COURTESY OF THE RECREATIONAL BOATING AND FISHING FOUNDATION

Capitalizing on the psychographic value of family time together and the interest in fishing and boating, the Recreational Boating and Fishing Foundation developed its "takemefishing" promotion and Web site. The not-for-profit organization hopes to involve families in recreational boating and fishing while increasing the public's awareness of the need to protect and restore the U.S.'s natural water resources.

## Segmenting Business Markets

In many ways, the segmentation process for business markets resembles that for consumer markets. However, some specific methods differ. Business markets can be divided through geographical segmentation; demographic, or customer-based, segmentation; and end-use segmentation.

*Geographical segmentation* methods for business markets resemble those for consumer markets. Many B2B marketers target geographically concentrated industries, such as aircraft manufacturing, automobiles, and oil field equipment. Especially on an international scale, customer needs, languages, and other variables may require differences in the marketing mix from one location to another.

*Demographic,* or *customer-based, segmentation* begins with a good or service design intended to suit a specific organizational market. Ciao Bella Gelato, a gourmet ice cream maker, sells its Italian ice cream and sorbet to high-end grocery stores and restaurants. The firm, which creates such exotic flavors as strawberry chardonnay and white chocolate lavender, has a loyal following among its business customers, including Whole Foods Market.[35]

To simplify the process of focusing on a particular type of business customer, the federal government has developed a system for subdividing the business marketplace into detailed segments. The six-digit *North American Industry Classification System (NAICS)* provides a common classification system used by the member nations of NAFTA: the United States, Canada, and Mexico. It divides industries into broad categories such as agriculture, forestry, and fishing; manufacturing; transportation; and retail and wholesale trade. Each major category is further subdivided into smaller segments—such as gas stations with convenience food and warehouse clubs—for more detailed information and to facilitate comparison among the member nations.

Another way to group firms by their demographics is to segment them by size based on their sales revenues or numbers of employees. Consolidated Freightways collects data from visitors to its Web site and uses the data to segment customers by size. Modern information processing also enables companies to segment business markets based on how much they buy, not just how big they are.

**End-use segmentation** focuses on the precise way a B2B purchaser will use a product. Resembling benefits-sought segmentation for consumer markets, this method helps small and midsize companies target specific end-user markets rather than competing directly with large firms for wider customer groups. A company might also design a marketing mix based on certain criteria for making a purchase.

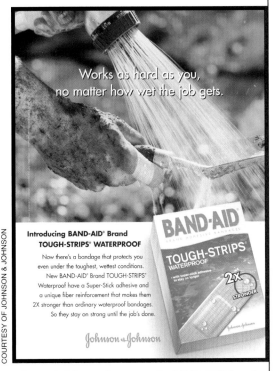

COURTESY OF JOHNSON & JOHNSON

Works as hard as you, no matter how wet the job gets.

Introducing BAND-AID® Brand TOUGH-STRIPS® WATERPROOF

Now there's a bandage that protects you even under the toughest, wettest conditions. New BAND-AID® Brand TOUGH-STRIPS® Waterproof have a Super-Stick adhesive and a unique fiber reinforcement that makes them 2X stronger than ordinary waterproof bandages. So they stay on strong until the job's done.

*Johnson & Johnson*

Johnson & Johnson focuses on its BAND-AID® Brand TOUGH-STRIPS® product features and benefits: its fiber-reinforced strength and waterproof Super-Stick adhesive. The company says this makes its bandages twice as strong as the run-of-the-mill bandage.

**assessment check**

1. What is the most common form of segmentation for consumer markets?

2. What are the three approaches to product-use segmentation?

3. What is end-use segmentation in the B2B market?

# CONSUMER BEHAVIOR: DETERMINING WHAT CUSTOMERS WANT

A fundamental marketing task is to find out why people buy one product and not another. The answer requires an understanding of consumer behavior, the actions of ultimate consumers directly involved in obtaining, consuming, and disposing of products and the decision processes that precede and follow these actions.

## Determinants of Consumer Behavior

**consumer behavior** actions of ultimate consumers directly involved in obtaining, consuming, and disposing of products and the decision processes that precede and follow these actions.

By studying people's purchasing behavior, businesses can identify consumers' attitudes toward and uses of their products. This information also helps marketers reach their targeted customers. Both personal and interpersonal factors influence the way buyers behave. Personal influences on **consumer behavior** include individual needs and motives, perceptions, attitudes, learned experiences, and self-concept. For instance, today people are constantly looking for ways to save time, so firms do everything they can to provide goods and services designed for convenience. Betty Crocker offers Slow Cooker Helper—all the ingredients for beef stroganoff or beef stew, except for the meat—that can be mixed together in a slow cooker for a complete meal. The brand also has a line of individual, microwaveable cake desserts called Warm Delights. Insurance firm Liberty Mutual provides "hassle-free guaranteed auto repairs" to customers whose cars have been damaged in accidents. And Cingular launched the Black-Berry 7100g, which provides capabilities ranging from international voice roaming to Bluetooth wireless connections for instant access to e-mail, calendar entries, and other data—all designed for the busy businessperson.[36]

The interpersonal determinants of consumer behavior include cultural, social, and family influences. In the area of convenience foods, cultural, social, and family influences come into play as much as an individual's need to save time. Understanding that many consumers value the time they spend with their families and want to care for them by providing good nutrition, marketers often emphasize these values in advertisements for convenience food products.

Sometimes external events influence consumer behavior. When crude oil prices spiked to $71 a barrel, forcing hikes at the gas pump, consumers responded by cutting back on clothing purchases, eating out in restaurants, vacations and trips, and the number of channels they receive on their cable service. Especially hard hit were low-income consumers, who used more and more of their budgets for gasoline. "You can't go out and have a good time. Gas is too expensive to go out and do things," said one hard-hit San Jose resident.[37]

**Figure**

| 12.5 | Steps in the Consumer Behavior Process |

FEEDBACK

## Determinants of Business Buying Behavior

Because a number of people can influence purchases of B2B products, business buyers face a variety of organizational influences in addition to their own preferences. A design engineer may help set the specifications that potential vendors must satisfy. A procurement manager may invite selected companies to bid on a purchase. A production supervisor may evaluate the operational aspects of the proposals that the firm receives, and the vice president of manufacturing may head a committee making the final decision.

## Steps in the Consumer Behavior Process

Consumer decision making follows the sequential process outlined in Figure 12.5, with interpersonal and personal influences affecting every step. The process begins when the consumer recognizes a problem or opportunity. If someone needs a new pair of shoes, that need becomes a problem to solve. If you receive a promotion at work and a 20 percent salary increase, that change may also become a purchase opportunity.

To solve the problem or take advantage of the opportunity, the consumer seeks information about his or her intended purchase and evaluates alternatives, such as available brands. The goal is to find the best response to the problem or opportunity.

Eventually, the consumer reaches a decision and completes the transaction. Later, he or she evaluates the experience by making a postpurchase evaluation. Feelings about the experience serve as feedback that will influence future purchase decisions. The various steps in the sequence are affected by both interpersonal and personal factors.

**assessment check**

1. Define consumer behavior.
2. What are some determinants of consumer behavior?

# CREATING, MAINTAINING, AND STRENGTHENING MARKETING RELATIONSHIPS

The past decade has brought rapid change to most industries, as customers have become better informed and more-demanding purchasers through closely comparing competing goods and services. They expect, even demand, new benefits from the companies that supply them, making it harder for firms to gain a competitive advantage based on product features alone.

In today's hypercompetitive era, businesses need to find new ways of relating to customers if they hope to maintain long-term success. Businesses are developing strategies and tactics that draw them into tighter connections with their customers, suppliers, and even employees. As a result, many firms are turning their attention to the issues of relationship marketing. **Relationship marketing** goes beyond an effort toward making the sale. Instead, it develops and maintains long-term, cost-effective exchange relationships with partners. These partners include individual customers, suppliers, and employees. As its ultimate goal, relationship marketing seeks to achieve customer satisfaction. Sometimes businesses fall short in their attempts to create relationships with consumers, as discussed in the "Solving an Ethical Controversy" feature.

Managing relationships instead of simply completing transactions often leads to creative partnerships. However, customers enter into relationships with firms only if they are assured that the relationship will somehow benefit them. As the intensity of commitment increases, so does the likelihood of a business continuing a long-term relationship with its customers. Businesses are building relationships by partnering with customers, suppliers, and other businesses. Timberland, maker of footwear and clothing, creates many partnerships that foster long-term relationships. The firm partners with not-for-profit organizations such as CARE, City Year, and Clean Air–Cool Planet to complete service projects for communities and the environment. Through its Serve-a-Palooza, hundreds of Timberland employees engage in volunteer tasks in their communities. Those opportunities even extend to customers who have expressed interest in participating in programs in their own regions. If you want to be volunteer for a food drive or to help restore a marsh, just log on to the Timberland Web site to see what's available. All of these activities help build relationships with customers, communities, and other organizations.[38]

**relationship marketing** developing and maintaining long-term, cost-effective exchange relationships with partners.

## Benefits of Relationship Marketing

Relationship marketing helps all parties involved. In addition to providing mutual protection against competitors, businesses that forge solid links with suppliers and customers are often

# ARE GIFT CARDS REALLY A GIFT?

*Gift cards seem like the perfect present—to give or receive. Recipients have no worries about returning wrong size pajamas, odd-colored bath towels, or the book they've already read.*

But some gift cards come with strings attached—purchase or inactivity fees, expiration dates, limited locations for use, or no way to replace them if they are lost or stolen. Consumer advocates, including attorneys general in several states, are beginning to look into the drawbacks of gift cards.

Are gift cards truly beneficial to consumers?

## PRO

1. Gift cards are convenient and portable, and they guarantee the right choice of gift.
2. Companies use the gift card to add value to consumers' experiences. McDonald's and Starbucks, along with other retailers, issue "stored value" cards that consumers can reload when the balance gets too low.

## CON

1. Most people are not aware of hidden fees such as activation charges, monthly service fees, and expiration dates when they purchase a gift card. When the recipient tries to redeem the card and learns that the amount has been reduced, it creates frustration and embarrassment.
2. There is no standardization among businesses when it comes to their gift card practices and policies, which adds to consumers' confusion about whether they are protected.

## Summary

Gift cards are big business. The National Retail Federation estimates that by 2007, gift card sales will top $85 billion. Lawsuits have been filed in California, Massachusetts, New Hampshire, and Connecticut over the sale of gift cards by Simon Property Group, which owns, operates, and manages regional malls. Simon levied such charges as a $2.50 monthly service fee, a $.50 fee each time a balance was checked, and $5 for replacing a lost card. In addition, the gift card expired after one year. Despite such cases, the National Retail Federation reports that 50 percent of consumers "would like to receive a gift card."

**Sources:** "Gift Cards: OCC Provides Holiday Tips for Consumers," accessed July 12, 2006, http://www.occ.treas.gov/ftp/release/2004-108a.pdf; Krysten Crawford, "Got a Gift Card? Know the Risks," CNN Money, accessed May 8, 2005, http://money.cnn.com; Rhonda Abrams, "Gift Cards for Small Business?" *Rhonda Report,* accessed May 8, 2005, http://www.rhonda online.com.

 solving an ETHICAL controversy

rewarded with lower costs and higher profits than they would generate on their own. Long-term agreements with a few high-quality suppliers frequently reduce a firm's production costs. Unlike onetime sales, these ongoing relationships encourage suppliers to offer customers preferential treatment, quickly adjusting shipments to accommodate changes in orders and correcting any quality problems that might arise. In your own business career, you can develop good relationships with customers, co-workers, and others by thanking them when they have done something special for you, as described in the "Business Etiquette" feature.

Good relationships with customers can be vital strategic weapons for a firm. By identifying current purchasers and maintaining positive relationships with them, organizations can efficiently target their best customers. Studying current customers' buying habits and preferences can help marketers identify potential new customers and establish ongoing contact with them. Attracting a new customer can cost five times as much as keeping an existing one. Not only do marketing costs go down, but long-term customers usually buy more, require less service, refer other customers, and provide valuable feedback. Together, these elements contribute to a higher **lifetime value of a customer**—the revenues and intangible benefits (referrals and customer feedback) from the customer over the life of the relationship, minus the amount the company must spend to acquire and serve that customer.

Businesses also benefit from strong relationships with other companies. Purchasers who repeatedly buy from one business may find that they save time and gain service quality as the business learns their specific needs. Some relationship-oriented companies also customize items based on customer preferences. Because many businesses reward loyal customers with discounts or bonuses, some buyers may even find that they save money by developing long-term relationships. Alliances with other firms to serve the same customers also can be rewarding. The partners combine their capabilities and resources to accomplish goals that they could not reach on their own. In addition, alliances with other firms may help businesses develop the skills and experience they need to successfully enter new markets or improve service to current customers.

## Tools for Nurturing Customer Relationships

Although relationship marketing has important benefits for both customers and businesses, most relationship-oriented businesses quickly discover that some customers generate more profitable business than others. If 20 percent of a firm's customers account for 80 percent of its sales and profits—the 80/20 principle mentioned earlier in the chapter—a customer in that category undoubtedly has a higher lifetime value than a customer who buys only once or twice or who makes small purchases.

While businesses shouldn't ignore any customer, they need to allocate their marketing resources wisely. A firm may choose to customize goods or services for high-value customers while working to increase repeat sales of stock products to less-valuable customers. Differentiating between these two groups also helps marketers focus on each in an effort to increase their commitment.

*Frequency Marketing and Affinity Marketing Programs* Popular techniques through which firms try to build and protect customer relationships include frequent buyer or user programs. These so-called **frequency marketing** programs reward purchasers with cash, rebates, merchandise, or other premiums. Frequency programs have grown more sophisticated over the years. They offer more personalization and customization than in the past. Airlines, hotel groups, restaurants, and many retailers including supermarkets offer frequency programs. Customers who join the Marriott Rewards

### Thank-You Notes Do Count

When someone gives you a gift—whether it is an item wrapped and tied with a bow, a home-cooked meal, or even some career advice on the phone—it is appropriate to acknowledge the person's time and effort with a thank-you note. After a job interview, it is customary to write a thank-you as well. A well-written thank-you may not land you the job, but it is certain to set you apart from other candidates in the mind of an employer.

If you're like many people, you're hit with a huge case of writer's block the minute you sit down with a blank thank-you note. Maybe you're tempted to delay your note writing until you've forgotten what you were thanking the person for, or until so much time has passed that you are embarrassed to write at all. But "thank you" may be the two most important words you'll ever say to someone, and you can write a brief note in just a few minutes. You'll be glad you did, and so will the recipient. Here are a few tips to help:

1. Handwrite your note, even if it is career related. A handwritten note takes a bit more time and effort, so it conveys both warmth and sincerity. Use simple notepaper and blue or black ink.
2. Don't know what to say? Get straight to the point, and specifically name the gift or favor. "Thank you so much for the green coffee mug" or "Thank you very much for the time you took to interview me yesterday" are good starters. Then say how you plan to use the gift, how much you learned during the interview, or something similar. If appropriate, relate a personal anecdote such as, "I just broke my favorite coffee mug" or "I have always wanted to work for a company like this." End with a final thank-you and suitable closing, such as "Best wishes" or "Yours truly."
3. If you didn't like the gift or the meal, or you don't think you'd like to work for this particular company, write a thank-you note anyway. Remember, the person spent time and effort on you.
4. Write a note immediately, or at least within two weeks. Otherwise, the person may wonder whether you received or liked the gift; an interviewer may forget you altogether.

**Sources:** Leslie Harpold, "How to Write a Thank-You Note," *The Morning News*, accessed July 12, 2006, http://www.themorningnews.org; Linda Kulman, "Thank-You-Note Writing 101," *U.S. News & World Report*, May 9, 2005, p. D12; Nisha Ramachandran, "Office Manners," *U.S. News & World Report*, April 25, 2005, p. EE8.

program have the option to spend their earned points at any of 2,400 hotels, resorts, spas, and golf locations.

**Affinity programs** are another tool for building emotional links with customers. An affinity program is a marketing effort sponsored by an organization that solicits involvement by individuals who share common interests and activities. Affinity programs are common in the credit card industry. For instance, a person can sign up for a credit card emblazoned with the logo of a favorite charity, a sports or entertainment celebrity, or a photograph of his or her college. MBNA offers credit cards featuring the logos of all the Major League Baseball teams.

Many businesses also use comarketing and cobranding. In a **comarketing** deal, two businesses jointly market each other's products. When two or more businesses link their names to a single product, **cobranding** occurs. When two seemingly unlikely businesses team up, the marketing sparks fly—and two very different groups of consumers may come together to buy the same product. Cobranding agreements include Adidas and Goodyear, Nickelodeon and Holiday Inn, and Apple and Swarovski. The new Adidas Tuscany shoes sport soles made from Goodyear Eagle F1 tire treads. Families can opt to stay at Holiday Inn's Nickelodeon Family Suites—which offer water parks, arcades, and other attractions. Music buffs who really want to sparkle can pick up an Apple iPod mini studded with 1,000 Swarovski crystals—exactly the same as the number of songs the iPod can store.[39]

*One-on-One Marketing* The ability to customize products and rapidly deliver goods and services has become increasingly dependent on technology such as computer-aided design and manufacturing (CAD/CAM). The Internet offers a way for businesses to connect with customers in a direct and intimate manner. Companies can take orders for customized products, gather data about buyers, and predict what goods or services a customer might want in the future. Computer databases provide strong support for effective relationship marketing. Marketers can maintain databases on customer tastes, price-range preferences, and lifestyles, and they can quickly obtain names and other information about promising prospects. Amazon.com greets each online customer with a list of suggested books he or she might like to purchase. Many online retailers send their customers e-mails about upcoming sales, new products, and special events.

Small and large companies often rely on *customer relationship management (CRM)* software technology that helps them gather, sort, and interpret data about customers. John Deere, a manufacturer of heavy equipment ranging from lawn mowers to farm tractors, uses such software to keep track of its sales force, dealerships, suppliers, and customers. "The farms are getting bigger and bigger, and accounts are getting fewer and fewer, so salespeople need to know what's going on with an account and get out into the field and sell," says a John Deere spokesman.[40]

**assessment check**

1. What is the lifetime value of a customer?
2. Discuss the increasing importance of one-on-one marketing efforts.

# WHAT'S AHEAD

The next two chapters examine each of the four elements of the marketing mix that marketers use to satisfy their selected target markets. Chapter 13 focuses on products and their distribution through various channels to different outlets. Chapter 14 covers promotion and the various methods marketers use to communicate with their target customers, along with strategies for setting prices for different products.

## Summary of Learning Goals

**1** **Summarize the ways in which marketing creates utility.**

Utility is the ability of a good or service to satisfy the wants and needs of customers. The production function creates form utility by converting inputs to finished goods and services. Marketing creates time, place, and ownership utility by making the product available when and where consumers want to buy and by arranging for orderly transfers of ownership.

### Assessment Check Answers

**1.1 What is utility?**
Utility is the ability of a good or service to satisfy the wants and needs of customers.

**1.2 Identify ways in which marketing creates utility.**
Marketing creates time utility by making a good or service available when customers want to purchase it; place utility by making the product available in a convenient location; and ownership utility by transferring the product from the buyer to the seller.

**2** **Explain the marketing concept and relate how customer satisfaction contributes to added value.**

The marketing concept refers to a company-wide customer orientation with the objective of achieving long-run success. This concept is essential in today's marketplace, which is primarily a buyer's market, meaning buyers can choose from an abundance of goods and services. Customer satisfaction contributes to added value of a good or service by delivering more than buyers expect in the form of added features, reduced prices, enhanced customer service, a strengthened warranty, or other marketing mix improvements.

### Assessment Check Answers

**2.1 What is the marketing concept?**
The marketing concept is a company-wide customer orientation with the objective of achieving long-run success. According to the marketing concept, success begins with the customer.

**2.2 How does customer satisfaction result in a value-added good or service?**
When a firm makes improvements that increase customer satisfaction, it may result in a value-added good

or service. If customers believe they have received value, they are likely to remain satisfied with the firm's goods or services.

**3** **Describe not-for-profit marketing, and identify the five major categories of nontraditional marketing.**

Not-for-profit organizations must engage in marketing just as for-profit firms do. Not-for-profit organizations operate in both the public and private sectors, and use marketing to obtain volunteers and donations, make people aware of their existence, achieve certain goals for society, and so on. Not-for-profit organizations may engage in several types of nontraditional marketing—person, place, event, cause, or organization marketing. They may rely on one type or a combination.

### Assessment Check Answers

**3.1 Why do not-for-profit organizations engage in marketing?**
Not-for-profit organizations use marketing to attract volunteers and donors, communicate their message, and achieve their societal goals.

**3.2 What are the five types of nontraditional marketing used by not-for-profit organizations?**
The five types of nontraditional marketing are person, place, event, cause, and organization marketing.

**4** **Outline the basic steps in developing a marketing strategy.**

All organizations develop marketing strategies to reach customers. This process involves analyzing the overall market, selecting a target market, and developing a marketing mix that blends elements related to product, distribution, promotion, and pricing decisions. Often company marketers develop a marketing plan that expresses their marketing strategy.

### Assessment Check Answers

**4.1 Distinguish between business and consumer products and business products.**
Business products are goods and services purchased to be used, either directly or indirectly, in the production of other goods for resale. Consumer products are purchased by end users.

## 4.2 What are the steps in developing a marketing strategy?

The steps in developing a marketing strategy are to analyze the overall market, select a target market, and develop a marketing mix.

**5** **Describe the marketing research function.**

Marketing research is the information-gathering function that links marketers to the marketplace. It provides valuable information about potential target markets. Firms may generate internal data or gather external data. They may use secondary data or conduct research to obtain primary data. Data mining, which involves computer searches through customer data to detect patterns and relationships, is one helpful tool in forecasting various trends such as sales revenues and consumer behavior.

### Assessment Check Answers

**5.1 What is the difference between primary data and secondary data?**

Secondary data are previously published facts that are low cost to retrieve and easy to obtain. Primary data are collected firsthand through observation or surveys.

**5.2 Why is marketing research important to business?**

Marketing research is important because it provides vital information about existing or potential target markets.

**6** **Identify and explain each of the methods available for segmenting consumer and business markets.**

Consumer markets can be divided according to four criteria: demographic characteristics, such as age and family size; geographical factors; psychographic variables, which involve behavioral and lifestyle profiles; and product-related variables, such as the benefits consumers seek when buying a product or the degree of brand loyalty they feel toward it. Business markets are segmented according to three criteria: geographical characteristics, customer-based specifications for products, and end-user applications.

### Assessment Check Answers

**6.1 What is the most common form of segmentation for consumer markets?**

Demographics is the most commonly used consumer market segmentation method.

## 6.2 What are the three approaches to product-use segmentation?

The three approaches to product-use segmentation are by benefits sought, product usage rate, and brand loyalty.

## 6.3 What is end-use segmentation in the B2B market?

End-use segmentation focuses on the precise way a B2B purchaser will use a product.

**7** **Outline the determinants of consumer behavior.**

Consumer behavior refers to the actions of ultimate consumers with direct effects on obtaining, consuming, and disposing of products, as well as the decision processes that precede and follow these actions. Personal influences on consumer behavior include an individual's needs and motives, perceptions, attitudes, learned experiences, and self-concept. The interpersonal determinants include cultural influences, social influences, and family influences. A number of people within a firm may participate in business purchase decisions, so business buyers must consider a variety of organizational influences in addition to their own preferences.

### Assessment Check Answers

**7.1 Define** *consumer behavior.*

Consumer behavior refers to the actions of ultimate consumers directly involved in obtaining, consuming, and disposing of products, along with the decision processes surrounding these actions.

**7.2 What are some determinants of consumer behavior?**

Determinants of consumer behavior include both personal influences and interpersonal influences. Personal influences include an individual's needs and motives; perceptions, attitudes, experiences; and self-concept. Interpersonal influences include cultural, social and family influences.

**8** **Discuss the benefits of and tools for relationship marketing.**

Relationship marketing is an organization's attempt to develop long-term, cost-effective links with individual customers for mutual benefit. Good relationships with customers can be a vital strategic weapon for a firm. By identifying current purchasers and maintaining a positive relationship with them, an organization can efficiently target its best customers, fulfill their needs, and create loyalty. Information technologies, frequency and affinity programs, and one-on-one efforts all help build relationships with customers.

## Assessment Check Answers

**8.1 What is the lifetime value of a customer?**
The lifetime value of a customer incorporates the revenues and intangible benefits from the customer over the life of the relationship with a firm, minus the amount the company must spend to acquire and serve the customer.

**8.2 Discuss the increasing importance of one-on-one marketing efforts.**
One-on-one marketing is increasing in importance as consumers demand more customization in goods and services. It is also increasingly dependent on technology such as computer-aided design and manufacturing (CAD/CAM). The Internet also offers a way for businesses to connect with customers in a direct and personal manner.

## Business Terms You Need to Know

| | | |
|---|---|---|
| marketing 380 | customer satisfaction 383 | data mining 391 |
| exchange process 381 | target market 388 | market segmentation 391 |
| utility 381 | marketing mix 388 | consumer behavior 397 |
| marketing concept 382 | marketing research 390 | relationship marketing 399 |

## Other Important Business Terms

| | | |
|---|---|---|
| time utility 381 | organization marketing 387 | end-use segmentation 397 |
| place utility 381 | consumer (B2C) product 388 | lifetime value of a customer 400 |
| ownership utility 381 | business (B2B) product 388 | frequency marketing 401 |
| value-added 383 | data warehouse 391 | affinity program 402 |
| person marketing 386 | geographical segmentation 392 | comarketing 402 |
| place marketing 386 | demographic segmentation 393 | cobranding 402 |
| event marketing 386 | psychographic segmentation 395 | |
| cause marketing 387 | product-related segmentation 396 | |

## Review Questions

1. Define the four different types of utility and explain how marketing contributes to the creation of utility. Then choose one of the following companies and describe how it creates each type of utility with its goods or services:
   a. Cold Stone Creamery
   b. Sea World
   c. Borders Books
   d. Flynn's Car Wash

2. Why was the shift from a seller's market to a buyer's market important to marketers?

3. Suppose you walk into a pizza restaurant to order a mushroom and pepperoni pizza. Describe three ways in which the restaurant could create a value-added service for you.

4. Identify at least three ways a firm can obtain customer feedback. How might a complaint actually strengthen customer loyalty?

5. Identify the five types of nontraditional marketing and give an example of each.

6. Identify each of the following as a consumer product or a business product, or classify it as both:
   a. loaf of bread
   b. laptop computer
   c. electricity
   d. cell phone
   e. concert tickets
   f. lawn-mowing service

7. What four strategies blend to create a marketing mix?
8. What is a target market? Why is target market selection the first step performed in marketing strategy development?
9. Describe the types of data that someone who is thinking of starting a restaurant might choose to gather. How might this businessperson apply the data to create the business?
10. Explain each of the methods used to segment consumer and business markets. Which methods do you think would be most effective for each of the following and why? (Note that a combination of methods might be applicable.)
   a. supermarket featuring Mexican foods
   b. air conditioning units
   c. motorcycles
   d. line of pet food
   e. dental insurance
   f. spa treatments
11. What are the three major determinants of consumer behavior? Give an example of how each one might influence a person's purchasing decision.
12. Explain two ways that firms rely on relationships to increase or benefit business. What are the benefits, both to businesses and their customers, of relationship marketing?

## Projects and Teamwork Applications

1. On your own or with a classmate, choose one of the following businesses and come up with a plan for the owner to add value to the goods or services offered. Present your plan to the class and ask for a response—would your classmates conduct business with your firm with its value-added goods or services?
   a. hair salon
   b. for-profit career placement service
   c. online apparel retailer
   d. coffee shop
2. Choose one of the following nonprofit organizations or find one of your own. Research the organization online to learn more about it. Outline your proposed contents for a fund-raising event based on the chapter discussion of nontraditional marketing, such as cause marketing or organization marketing.
   a. World Wildlife Fund
   b. American Cancer Society
   c. Toys for Tots
   d. Habitat for Humanity
3. Marketers are always looking for ways to reach new customers. On your own or with a classmate, choose a product that has been targeted for one market—say, teens or women—and develop a plan for marketing it to a new group of consumers. For example, Home Depot and Lowe's have been marketing home improvement tools and other products to women, although men are the traditional market for these items.
4. Think of two situations in which you have been a customer: one in which you have been satisfied with the merchandise you received and one in which you have not. Make a list of the reasons you were satisfied in the first case and another list of the reasons you were not satisfied in the second case. Would you say that the failure was the result of the seller not understanding your needs?
5. Two techniques for building long-term relationships with customers are frequency marketing programs and affinity programs. On your own or with a classmate, visit a so-called big-box retailer such as Wal-Mart, Target, or Menards. If you can't make the trip, access one of these firms online. Make yourself familiar with the range of products your retailer offers, including any special services such as free delivery or gift wrapping. Then design a frequency marketing program or affinity program for the retailer to build relationships with the consumers who shop at the store. Finally, present your program to the class and ask your classmates whether it would encourage them to shop at the store—and why or why not.

## Native Americans: A New American Market

Despite being acknowledged as the first civilization to populate the United States, Native Americans have emerged only recently as a target market for businesses. They have also emerged as new business owners, offering goods and services to their own segment of the population and broader segments. While the success of the major casinos run by Native American tribes is well known—Foxwoods Resort Casino in Connecticut rakes in $1.5 billion in revenues each year—Native American firms, and the consumers they serve, reach much farther afield than gambling and entertainment.

Native Americans are making an impact both as businesspeople and as valued customers. Banker John Chapman, based in Oklahoma and a member of the Chickasaw Nation, helps other tribal nations establish banks—which, in turn, provide loans to small businesses, provide mortgages to individuals and families, and help tribes diversify their investments. In the past decade, the newspaper industry has begun targeting Native American readership in certain geographic areas. The *Great Falls Tribune* of Montana and the *Bellingham Herald* of Washington have greatly expanded their coverage of issues and events concerning local tribes. Recently, Cavco Industries, a producer of manufactured housing, donated a building for the new Piestewa Native American Veterans' Center on the Navajo Reservation in Tuba City, Arizona. The building was featured on ABC Television's *Extreme Makeover: Home Edition*. "We consider this as a great opportunity to assist the Native American community and to recognize their importance to our culture and their service to our country. This facility will be a place for their veterans to call their own," declared Joe Stegmayer, CEO of Cavco Industries.

Congress is considering a bill to amend the Small Business Act to provide more help to groups of native peoples, including those in the continental United States, Alaska Natives, and Native Hawaiians. States would be able to apply for grants each year to pass on to Native Americans as recommended by local tribal councils. Because about 60 percent of tribal members live near regions with high unemployment, efforts to develop business in these areas are especially important. However, small businesses owned by Native Americans already generate about $34 billion in revenues each year.

As consumers and businesspeople, Native Americans look for ways to blend traditional with modern cultural values and lifestyles. "For a huge long time, it was not a good thing to be an Indian in this country," explains Tex Hall, president of the National Congress of American Indians. "But it's starting to be a good thing again."

### Questions for Critical Thinking

1. Suppose you have been hired as the manager of a department store in an area with a growing population of Native American consumers. What steps might you take to research the market?
2. Describe how marketers might approach developing relationships with Native American consumers.

**Sources:** "Udall Sponsors Bill to Foster More Native American Businesses," *New Mexico Business Weekly*, accessed July 12, 2006, http://albuquerque.bizjournals .com; Dennis Coyle, "Native American Readership Has Potential," *Inland Press*, accessed July 12, 2006, http://www.inlandpress.org; "Cavco Homes Builds New Veterans' Center for Native Americans," Builder Online, April 18, 2005, http://www.builderonline.com; Thomas Hayden, "A Modern Life," *U.S. News & World Report*, October 4, 2004, pp. 46–50.

VIDEO Case 12.2

## Harley-Davidson: An American Icon Cruises into Its Second Century

This video case appears on page 621. A recently filmed video, designed to expand and highlight the written case, is available for class use by instructors.

# Chapter 13

## Product and Distribution Strategies

### Learning Goals

1. Explain marketing's definition of a product and list the components of a product strategy.

2. Describe the classification system for consumer and business goods and services.

3. Distinguish between a product mix and a product line.

4. Briefly describe each of the four stages of the product life cycle.

5. List the stages of the new-product development process.

6. Explain how firms identify their products.

7. Outline and briefly describe each of the major components of an effective distribution strategy.

8. Identify the various categories of distribution channels and discuss the factors that influence channel selection.

PHOTODISC/GETTY IMAGES

Customers can easily determine what makes one toothpaste or detergent better for them. Most of us don't have much trouble choosing a DVD or a new outfit, and we can quickly come up with criteria for choosing a new car. But how does the airline industry decide which jets to buy? Two competitors—Airbus and Boeing—have distinctly different views of what airlines need now and in the future.

Airbus, which is owned by a partnership of French, German, and British companies, and U.S.-based Boeing have been intense rivals for years. While both companies supply planes of all sizes to airlines and freight carriers around the world, their projections for the future of air travel have led them each to create new jets that fill very different needs.

## Boeing vs. Airbus: Battle for the Skies

Airbus has invested $13 billion in developing its giant A380, a double-decker superjumbo jet weighing more than 300 tons, with a 262-foot wingspan. The plane is as tall as a seven-story building and carries 555 passengers in three separate cabin classes, about a third more people than one of Boeing's largest planes—the 747—in twice as much space. In fact, the interior of the A380 is roomy enough to include shops, bars, casinos, and nurseries for passengers' use and entertainment.

Airbus thinks that the next 20 years will see air travel become concentrated between big hubs in Asia and other stopover cities, called spokes. The international flights will foster use of jumbo jets for more passenger comfort, and flights will be concentrated among the busiest airports, those that can handle the large number of passengers on each jumbo flight. Some airports, such as Dallas–Fort Worth, are already constructing special hangars and cargo facilities to accommodate the giant craft. The A380 is so large that it can't dock at a regular gate.

The Airbus jet can travel about 5 percent farther than Boeing's longest-range jumbo, a factor projected to reduce operating costs below what buyers of Boeing planes will pay. All these features don't come cheap—the A380 costs $280 million. But before the plane had flown a mile, Airbus already had orders for 149 units from more than a dozen airline and freight transport customers, most of whom attended the plane's recent grand unveiling in France. That's considered an extraordinary advance sale, and Airbus hopes to move about 600 more planes. Many observers believe the jet heralds a new era in flying, a milestone not surpassed since the dawn of the supersonic Concorde.

Boeing, on the other hand, sees a very different trend in global air travel. Boeing anticipates that airline deregulation will increase competition among airlines, which will opt to entice passengers with more direct flights and invest in smaller, long-range planes to bypass the congested hub-and-spoke cities Airbus hopes to capitalize on. Boeing thinks worldwide demand for planes larger than the 747, like the A380, won't exceed 400 units over the next 20 years. Smaller planes can also be built more quickly than the A380 and will be more fuel-efficient and cheaper for airlines to buy.

As a result, Boeing is producing a new midsize passenger jet it calls the 787 Dreamliner. Boeing already has about 250 advance orders for the 787 and tentative commitments for more than 400 more planes. The new plane is designed to be extremely efficient, using 20 percent less fuel than a traditional airplane of comparable size. With skyrocketing fuel costs, that efficiency could ease airlines' tight budgets. The 787 is also constructed of high-tech composite materials that are lighter than aluminum and stronger than steel. The plane is constructed in large sections through a revolutionary manufacturing process using carbon-fiber reinforced plastics, which are commonly used in military aircraft. These composites can be shaped into huge barrel pieces, avoiding the labor of bolting the typical aluminum plates together. Like the A380, the 787 is expected to be an aviation milestone—if Boeing can succeed in leveraging its revolutionary manufac-

turing process to save the thousands of hours it used to spend stocking and assembling small parts. If it can, then the company will reap billions of dollars in manufacturing savings. That should help Boeing price the 787, which carries 230-some passengers, competitively enough to allow airlines to make money flying it. Boeing is also cutting manufacturing costs by distributing manufacturing operations around the world, making plane parts in Europe and Asia and assembling them in Seattle.

With these two different visions of the aviation future, one question remains: Who will win the battle for the world's airlines?[1]

In this chapter we examine ways in which organizations design and implement marketing strategies that address customers' needs and wants. As the story of Airbus and Boeing illustrates, companies in the same industry can draw very different conclusions about the needs and wants of the same set of customers. Airbus believes commercial airlines will be looking to concentrate passengers in huge planes that fly from hub to hub around the world, and it expects the airlines that buy its A380 to use major airports in Europe and Asia as well as North America. As one industry consultant said, "The economics of the A380 are going to be great as long as you can put a lot of bodies on them. This is not a plane that's going to fly to [smaller airports]."

Boeing, however, with access to the same information about its customers, has drawn very different conclusions about what kind of product they will buy, and it is designing, manufacturing, and pricing its new jet accordingly. Boeing is betting that to serve the needs of their own customers, airlines will want to fly to smaller airports directly, and that requires smaller planes.

The creation of new products, from shampoo to furniture to jumbo jets, is the lifeblood of an organization. Because products do not remain economically viable forever, new ones must be developed to ensure the survival of an organization. If either the 787 Dreamliner or the A380 fails, for instance, airline industry observers predict that their companies will be in serious financial trouble.

This chapter focuses on the first two elements of the marketing mix: product and distribution. Our discussion of product strategy begins by describing the classifications of goods and services, customer service, product lines and the product mix, and the product life cycle. Companies often shape their marketing strategies differently when they are introducing a new product, when the product has established itself in the marketplace, and when it is declining in popularity. We also discuss product identification through brand name and distinctive packaging, and the ways in which companies foster loyalty to their brands to keep customers coming back for more.

Distribution, the second mix variable discussed, focuses on moving goods and services from producer to wholesaler to retailer to buyers. Managing the distribution process includes making decisions such as what kind of wholesaler to use and where to offer products for sale. Retailers can range from specialty stores to factory outlets and everything in between, and they must choose appropriate customer service, pricing, and location strategies in order to succeed. The chapter concludes with a look at logistics, the process of coordinating the flow of information, goods, and services among suppliers and on to final consumers.

# *PRODUCT STRATEGY*

**product** bundle of physical, service, and symbolic attributes designed to satisfy buyers' wants.

Most people respond to the question "What is a product?" by listing its physical features. By contrast, marketers take a broader view. To them, a **product** is a bundle of physical, service, and symbolic attributes designed to satisfy consumer wants. The chief executive officer of a major tool manufacturer once startled his stockholders with this statement: "Last year our customers bought over 1 million quarter-inch drill bits, and none of them wanted to buy the product. They all wanted quarter-inch holes." Product strategy involves considerably more than just producing a good or service; instead, it focuses on benefits. The marketing conception of a product includes decisions about package design, brand name, trademarks, warranties, product image, new-product development, and customer service. Think, for instance, about your favorite soft drink. Do you like it for its taste alone, or do other attributes, such as clever ads, attractive packaging, ease of purchase from vending machines and other convenient locations, and overall image, also attract you? These other attributes may influence your choice more than you realize.

**assessment check**

1. What is a product?
2. What is the marketing view of a product?

## Classifying Goods and Services

Marketers have found it useful to classify goods and services as either B2C or B2B depending on whether the purchasers of the particular item are consumers or businesses. These classifications can be subdivided further, and each type requires a different competitive strategy.

**Classifying Consumer Goods and Services** The classification typically used for ultimate consumers who purchase products for their own use and enjoyment and not for resale is based on consumer buying habits. **Convenience products** are items the consumer seeks to purchase frequently, immediately, and with little effort. Items stocked in 7-Eleven stores, vending machines, and local newsstands are usually convenience products—for example, newspapers, milk, disposable diapers, and bread.

**Shopping products** are those typically purchased only after the buyer has compared competing products in competing stores. A person intent on buying a new sofa or dining room table may visit many stores, examine perhaps dozens of pieces of furniture, and spend days making the final decision. **Specialty products,** the third category of consumer products, are those that a purchaser is willing to make a special effort to obtain. The purchaser is already familiar with the item and considers it to have no reasonable substitute. The nearest Jaguar dealer may be 75 miles away, but if you have decided you want one—and can afford it—you will make the trip. See the "Solving an Ethical Controversy" feature for a discussion of foie gras, a specialty food product made from goose liver.

Note that a shopping product for one person may be a convenience item for someone else. Each item's product classification is based on buying patterns of the majority of people who purchase it.

The interrelationship of the marketing mix factors is shown in Figure 13.1. By knowing the appropriate classification for a specific product, the marketing decision maker knows much about how the other mix variables will adapt to create a profitable, customer-driven marketing strategy.

**Classifying Business Goods** *Business products* are goods and services such as paycheck services and huge multifunction copying machines used in operating an organization; they

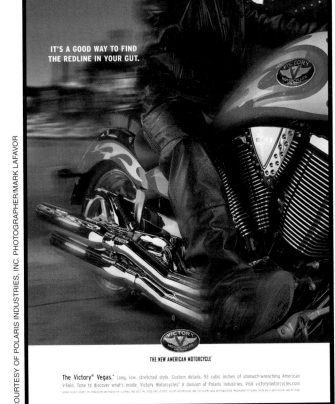

COURTESY OF POLARIS INDUSTRIES, INC. PHOTOGRAPHER/MARK LAFAVOR

IT'S A GOOD WAY TO FIND THE REDLINE IN YOUR GUT.

THE NEW AMERICAN MOTORCYCLE

The Victory® Vegas." Long, low, stretched style. Custom details. 92 cubic inches of stomach-wrenching American V-Twin. Time to discover what's inside. Victory Motorcycles. A division of Polaris Industries. Visit victorymotorcycles.com

Consumers spend quite a bit of time selecting the perfect motorcycle, so it is a specialty product. But if you've set your mind on a low-slung custom-detailed Victory Vegas cycle, then you'll find the dealer to get one.

# SHOULD SOME PRODUCTS BE BANNED?

*Foie gras is a delicacy usually spread on toast or crackers as a paste, or pâté. In fact, foie gras means "fat liver." It is produced by force-feeding animals, usually geese, in order to artificially fatten their livers to several times their normal size.*

Several European countries, including Germany, Luxembourg, and Italy, as well as Israel have outlawed force-feeding on the grounds that it is cruel to the animals. The city of Chicago has also created an ordinance banning restaurants and retailers from serving and selling *foie gras*. The ordinance, which took effect in July 2006, is the first of its kind taking effect in the United States. California has also instituted a ban on force-feeding, which effectively bans *foie gras*. The California ban takes effect in 2012, and Oregon may soon follow suit, along with several other states, among them New York and Massachusetts.

Should some animal products like *foie gras* that pose no danger to humans be banned?

## PRO

1. Any product produced by cruel means such as force-feeding should be banned.

2. The feeders at farms that produce *foie gras*, geese, and ducks (the majority of whom are Mexican immigrants), are required to work 30 days in a row for the last four and a half weeks of the animals' lives. If they took a day off, the feeding process would be disrupted and the ducks would become stressed. So, this is an issue of not only animal cruelty but also of human rights violations.

## CON

1. Farmers in France, where the dish originated, claim that only industrial force-feeding is cruel and that its traditional feeding practices neither distress nor frighten the animals.
2. State legislators should be paying more attention to health, human services, and education than to bans on specialty food items enjoyed by only a few.

## Summary

Strong arguments will continue to be made over *foie gras* by animal rights activists as well as by farmers, chefs, and restaurateurs. The debates need to address not only the question of the feeding practices some find cruel but also the question of whether legislating against food products best serves the needs of the residents.

**Sources:** Nicole Niebisch with Amy Tarr, "Ducking It Out: The Debate on Foie Gras," StarChefs.com, accessed August 8, 2006, http://www.starchefs.com; Tamiko Thomas, "California Decides to Permanently Pull Foie Gras off the Menu," Humane Society of the United States, accessed July 14, 2006, http://www.hsus.org; Matthew Hemming, "Charlie Trotter Abandons Foie Gras," Decanter.com, accessed July 14, 2006, http://www.decanter.com; Nick Vagnoni, "Chicago Bans Foie Gras," accessed June 29, 2006, http://www.slashfood.com; Fran Spielman, "City Council Approves Foie Gras Ban," *Chicago Sun-Times,* accessed June 29, 2006, http://www.suntimes.com; Julie Boorstin, "A Wild Goose Chase," *Fortune,* May 2, 2005, p. 26.

solving an **ETHICAL** controversy

also include machinery, tools, raw materials, components, and buildings used to produce other items for resale. While consumer products are classified by buying habits, business products are classified based on how they are used and by their basic characteristics. Products that are long-lived and relatively expensive are called *capital items*. Less costly products that are consumed within a year are referred to as *expense items*.

Five basic categories of B2B products exist: installations, accessory equipment, component parts and materials, raw materials, and supplies. *Installations* are major capital items, such as new factories, heavy equipment and machinery, and custom-made equipment. Installations are expensive and often involve buyer and seller negotiations that may last for more than a year before a purchase actually is made. Purchase approval frequently involves a number of different people—production specialists, representatives from the purchasing department, and members of top management—who must agree on the final choice.

Although *accessory equipment* also includes capital items, they are usually less expensive and shorter lived than installations and involve fewer decision makers. Examples include hand tools and fax machines. *Component parts and materials* are finished business goods that

Figure

13.1

Marketing Impacts of Consumer Product Classifications

| Marketing Strategy Factor | Convenience Product | Shopping Product | Specialty Product |
|---|---|---|---|
| • Purchase Frequency | • Frequent | • Relatively infrequent | • Infrequent |
| • Store Image | • Unimportant | • Very important | • Important |
| • Price | • Low | • Relatively high | • High |
| • Promotion | • By manufacturer | • By manufacturer and retailers | • By manufacturer and retailers |
| • Distribution Channel | • Many wholesalers and retailers | • Relatively few wholesalers and retailers | • Very few wholesalers and retailers |
| • Number of Retail Outlets | • Many | • Few | • Very small number; often one per market area |

become part of a final product, such as disk drives that are sold to computer manufacturers or batteries purchased by automakers. *Raw materials* are farm and natural products used in producing other final products. Examples include milk, iron ore, leather, and soybeans. *Supplies* are expense items used in a firm's daily operation that do not become part of the final product. Often referred to as MRO (maintenance, repair, and operating supplies), they include paper clips, lightbulbs, and copy paper.

*Classifying Services*   Services can be classified as either B2C or B2B. Child- and eldercare centers and auto detail shops provide services for consumers, while the Pinkerton security patrol at a local factory and Kelly Services' temporary office workers are examples of business services. In some cases, a service can accommodate both consumer and business markets. For example, when ServiceMaster cleans the upholstery in a home, it is a B2C service, but when it spruces up the painting system and robots in a manufacturing plant, it is a B2B service.

Like tangible goods, services can also be convenience, shopping, or specialty products depending on the buying patterns of customers. However, they are distinguished from goods in several ways. First of all, services, unlike goods, are intangible. In addition, they are perishable because firms cannot stockpile them in inventory. They are also difficult to standardize, because they must meet individual customers' needs. Finally, from a buyer's perspective, the service provider is the service; the two are inseparable in the buyer's mind.

## Marketing Strategy Implications

The consumer product classification system is a useful tool in marketing strategy. As described in Figure 13.1, once a new appliance has been classified as a shopping good, marketers have a better idea of its promotion, pricing, and distribution needs.

Each group of business products, however, requires a different marketing strategy. Because most installations and many component parts frequently are marketed directly from manufacturer to business buyer, the promotional emphasis is on personal selling rather than on advertising. By contrast, marketers of supplies and accessory equipment rely more on advertising, because their products often are sold through an intermediary, such as a wholesaler. Producers of installations and component parts may involve their customers in new-product development, especially when the business product is custom made. Finally, firms selling supplies and accessory equipment place greater emphasis on competitive pricing strategies than do other B2B marketers, who tend to concentrate more on product quality and customer service.

## Product Lines and Product Mix

Few firms operate with a single product. If their initial entry is successful, they tend to increase their profit and growth chances by adding new items to offer their customers. Some goods producers are even able to branch out into services. Dell, for instance, recently emerged from the slowdown in PC sales not only by adding printers, personal digital assistants, and a new featherweight laptop to its product line but also by marketing technical services to its business customers.[2]

A company's **product line** is a group of related products marked by physical similarities or intended for a similar market. A **product mix** is the assortment of product lines and individual goods and services that a firm offers to consumers and business users. Although the Kellogg Company first appeared in 1906 with a single product—Kellogg's Corn Flakes—today its product mix has several product lines, including milk bars mixed with different cereals, Real Fruit Winders, Rice Krispies Squares, and Eggo Toaster Swirlz. Eddie Bauer extended its casual-clothing product line by moving into home furnishings and furniture.[3]

Marketers must assess their product mix continually to ensure company growth, to satisfy changing consumer needs and wants, and to adjust to competitors' offerings. To remain competitive, marketers look for gaps in their product lines and fill them with new products or modified versions of existing ones. A helpful tool that is frequently used in making product decisions is the product life cycle.

**assessment check**

1. Differentiate among convenience, shopping, and specialty products.
2. How do business products differ from consumer items?

**product line** group of related products that are physically similar or are intended for the same market.

**product mix** company's assortment of product lines and individual offerings.

**assessment check**

1. What is a product line?
2. What is a product mix?

**product life cycle** four basic stages—introduction, growth, maturity, and decline—through which a successful product progresses.

# PRODUCT LIFE CYCLE

Once a product is on the market, it usually goes through a series of four stages known as the **product life cycle:** introduction, growth, maturity, and decline. As Figure 13.2 shows, industry sales and profits vary depending on the life-cycle stage of an item.

Product life cycles are not set in stone; not all products follow this pattern precisely, and different products may spend different periods of time in each

Baby Gap is just one of the product lines offered by the Gap clothing chain. The retail group also offers traditional Gap casual clothing, Old Navy's stylish but low-priced line, and Banana Republic's upscale clothing.

Stages in the Product Life Cycle

stage. The concept, however, helps the marketing planner anticipate developments throughout the various stages of a product's life. Profits assume a predictable pattern through the stages, and promotional emphasis must shift from dispensing product information in the early stages to heavy brand promotion in the later ones.

## Stages of the Product Life Cycle

In the *introduction stage,* the firm tries to promote demand for its new offering, inform the market about it, give free samples to entice consumers to make a trial purchase, and explain its features, uses, and benefits. Dreyer's, the largest ice cream maker in the United States, promoted an essay contest as a first step to giving away 1,500 free ice cream parties to get people to try its lower-fat ice cream called Slow Churned.[4] New-product development costs and extensive introductory promotional campaigns to acquaint prospective buyers with the merits of the innovation, though essential to later success, are expensive and commonly lead to losses in the introductory stage. Losses also occur due to the relatively low sales and high costs of promotions, establishing distribution channels, and training the sales force about the new product's advantages. It is not uncommon for firms to spend $30 million to introduce new packaged-goods products such as detergents, bottled waters, and candies. But such expenditures are necessary if the firm is to profit later.

During the *growth stage,* sales climb quickly as new customers join early users who now are repurchasing the item. Word-of-mouth referrals and continued advertising and other special promotions by the firm induce others to make trial purchases. At this point, the company begins to earn profits on the new product. This success encourages competitors to enter the field with similar offerings, and price competition appears. Digital cameras are in the growth stage, and film suppliers such as Eastman Kodak are struggling to continue their century-long record of sales and revenue growth in the wake of the greatest challenge ever to their market. Another technology in the growth stage is radio-frequency identification devices, discussed later in this chapter.

In the *maturity stage,* industry sales at first increase, but eventually reach a saturation level at which further expansion is difficult. Competition also intensifies, increasing the availability of the product. Firms concentrate on capturing competitors' customers, often dropping prices to further the appeal. Cell phones are in the maturity stage: Competitors compete not only on price but also on features such as calendars, e-mail and attachments, messaging capability, full-color screens, keyboards, and fax and word processing functions. New capabilities may still be in the works. C-Sam, a small tech firm headquartered in Chicago, is about to introduce a test of its technology to transmit shoppers' credit card information from their cell phones to the cash register.[5] A mature business environment also faces the world's largest personal computer marketers, who compete in an increasingly saturated U.S. market. More than half of all homes already have a PC, and virtually all businesses are computerized.

Sales volume fades late in the maturity stage, and some of the weaker competitors leave the market. During this stage, firms promote mature products aggressively to protect their market share and to distinguish their products from those of competitors.

Sales continue to fall in the *decline stage,* the fourth phase of the product life cycle. Profits decline and may become losses as further price-cutting occurs in the reduced overall market for the item. Competitors gradually exit, making some profits possible for the remaining firms in the shrinking market. The decline stage usually is caused by a product innovation or a shift in consumer preferences. Sometimes technology change can hasten the decline stage for a product. One of every three U.S. residences contains at least one DVD player, and DVDs have surpassed videocassettes in both sales and rental revenue. Releases of both new and older films on DVD have long since overtaken the VHS format, which some film studios—and a growing number of rental outlets—have abandoned.

## Marketing Strategy Implications of the Product Life Cycle

Like the product classification system, the product life cycle is a useful concept for designing a marketing strategy that will be flexible enough to accommodate changing marketplace characteristics. These competitive moves may involve developing new products, lowering prices, increasing distribution coverage, creating new promotional campaigns, or any combination of these approaches. In general, the marketer's objective is to extend the product life cycle as long as the item is profitable. Some products can be highly profitable during the later stages of their life cycle, because all the initial development costs already have been recovered.

A commonly used strategy for extending the life cycle is to increase customers' frequency of use. Wal-Mart and Target have added grocery sections to their stores in order to increase the frequency of shopper visits. Another strategy is to add new users. With cigarette sales in decline, Zippo Manufacturing marketed a new Zippo Multi-Purpose Lighter for igniting candles, fireplaces, and grills. It boasts an advanced ignition system, a patented childproof safety lock, and a sturdy metal case. Sales have stabilized despite a continuing drop in the number of U.S. smokers.[6] Arm & Hammer used a third approach: finding new uses for its products. The original use of the firm's baking soda in baking has been augmented by its newer uses as a toothpaste, refrigerator freshener, and flame extinguisher. A fourth product life cycle extension strategy—changing package sizes, labels, and product designs—inspired Sony to develop PlayStation Portable, with a display screen just over $3 \times 2$ inches that boasts resolution high enough to do justice not only to video games but also to blockbuster movies.[7]

**assessment check**

1. What are the stages of the product life cycle?
2. What are the marketing implications of each stage?

## Stages in New-Product Development

New-product development is expensive, time-consuming, and risky, because only about one-third of new products become success stories. Products can fail for many reasons. Some are not properly developed and tested, some are poorly packaged, and others lack adequate promotional support or distribution or do not satisfy a consumer need or want. Even successful products eventually reach the end of the decline stage and must be replaced with new-product offerings.

Most of today's newly developed items are aimed at satisfying specific consumer demands. New-product development is becoming increasingly efficient and cost-effective because marketers use a systematic approach in developing new products. As Figure 13.3 shows, the new-product development process has six stages. Each stage requires a "go/no-go" decision by management before moving on to subsequent stages. Because items that go through each development stage only to be rejected at one of the final stages involve significant investments in both money and time, the sooner decision makers can identify a marginal product and drop it from further consideration, the less time and money will be wasted.

The starting point in the new-product development process is generating ideas for new offerings. Ideas come from many sources, including customer suggestions, suppliers, employees, research scientists, marketing research, inventors outside the firm, and competitive products. The most successful ideas are directly related to satisfying customer needs. Chicago chef Homaro Cantu experiments with all sorts of food ideas. One that he hopes to market to the U.S. armed forces is a spoon with a detachable cartridge, whose chemicals when mixed can heat the preserved food. Cantu hopes the invention will make meals in the battlefield more palatable for troops.[8]

In the second stage, screening eliminates ideas that do not mesh with overall company objectives or cannot be developed given the company's resources. Some firms hold open discussions of new-product ideas with specialists who work in different functional areas in the organization.

During the concept development and business analysis phase, further screening occurs. The analysis involves assessing the new product's potential sales, profits, growth rate, and competitive strengths and whether it fits with the company's product, distribution, and promotional resources. *Concept testing*—marketing research designed to solicit initial consumer reaction to new-product ideas—may be used at this stage. For example, potential consumers might be asked about proposed brand names and other methods of product identification. *Focus groups* are formal sessions in which consumers meet with marketers to discuss what they like or dislike about current products and perhaps test or sample a new offering to provide some immediate feedback.

Next, an actual product is developed, subjected to a series of tests, and revised. Functioning prototypes or detailed descriptions of the product may be created. These designs are the joint responsibility of the firm's development staff and its marketers, who provide feedback on consumer reactions to the proposed product design, color, and other physical features.

**Test marketing** introduces a new product supported by a complete marketing campaign to a selected city or TV coverage area. Marketers look for a location or television coverage area with a manageable size, where residents match their target market's demographic profile, to test their product. During the test marketing stage, the item is sold in a limited area while the company examines both consumer responses to the new offering and the marketing effort used to support it. Test market results can help managers

**test marketing** introduction of a new product supported by a complete marketing campaign to a selected city or TV coverage area to examine both consumer responses to the new offering and the marketing effort used to support it.

**Figure**

Process for Developing New Goods and Services

**13.3**

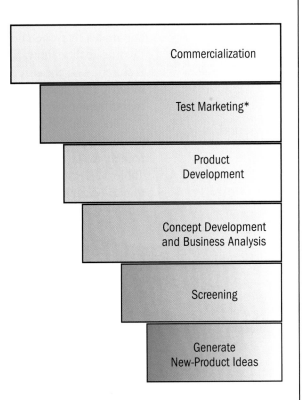

Commercialization

Test Marketing*

Product Development

Concept Development and Business Analysis

Screening

Generate New-Product Ideas

*Some firms skip this step and move directly from product development to commercialization.

Table

13.1   The Five Worst Cars in the Last 100 Years

| Rank | Auto | Typical Owner Comment |
|------|------|------------------------|
| 1 | Yugo | "At least it had heated rear windows—so your hands would stay warm while you pushed." |
| 2 | Chevy Vega | "Burned so much oil, it was singlehandedly responsible for the formation of OPEC." |
| 3 | Ford Pinto | "The car would do 75 mph in 2nd gear, shaking apart and sounding like a bat out of hell. In 4th gear, the top speed was 70 mph. What's wrong with this picture? You do the math." |
| 4 | AMC Gremlin | "Calling it a pregnant roller skate would be kind." |
| 5 | Chevy Chevette | "If I got on the Interstate without being run over, the car would creep towards 55. About an hour later, I'd reach it. Then the shaking would begin." |

**Source:** Reported in "Car Talk," accessed August 7, 2006, http://www.cartalk.com.

determine the product's likely performance in a full-scale introduction. Some firms skip test marketing, however, because of concerns that the test could reveal their product strategies to the competition. Also, the expense of doing limited production runs of complex products such as a new auto or refrigerator is so high that the test marketing stage is skipped and the development process moves directly to the next stage.

In the final stage, commercialization, the product is made generally available in the marketplace. Sometimes this stage is referred to as a product launch. Considerable planning goes into this stage, because the firm's distribution, promotion, and pricing strategies must all be geared to support the new product offerings. Osaka, Japan–based Sharp Corporation has developed a new liquid crystal display (LCD) television screen that lets two viewers see completely different images on the same screen. The viewers must look at the screen from different angles, but one could watch a soccer match while another surfs the Internet or watches a favorite reality show. Sharp is launching the product worldwide and is supplying other manufacturers with the displays. The company says the screens could be used in cars for maps and movies, on billboards for two promotions, and in stores to show sales personnel and customers two different images.[9]

The need for a steady stream of new products to offer the firm's customers, the chances of product failure, and the tens of millions of dollars needed to complete a successful new-product launch make new-product development a vital process for 21st-century firms. However, as Table 13.1 illustrates, success is not guaranteed until the new-product offering achieves customer acceptance. General Motors witnessed this principle in action when the company launched its much-ridiculed Aztek sport-utility vehicle. The design had started out as a smaller vehicle, like a tall station wagon meant to appeal to younger drivers. But for cost considerations, the design was adapted to fit GM's minivan platform and then further modified to fit Pontiac's aggressive image. In testing, markets were divided in their opinion, but GM delivered a crushing blow to the Aztek by pricing it at the high end of what its younger target market could afford. Following the product launch, instead of taking to the back roads, Azteks sat quietly on dealers' lots.

**assessment check**

1. What are the stages of the new product development process?
2. Where do ideas for new products come from?

## PRODUCT IDENTIFICATION

A major aspect of developing a successful new product involves methods used for identifying a product and distinguishing it from competing offerings. Both tangible goods and intangible services are identified by brands, brand names, and trademarks. A **brand** is a name, term, sign, symbol, design, or some combination thereof used to identify the products of one firm and to differentiate them from competitive offerings. Tropicana, Pepsi, and Gatorade are all made by PepsiCo, but a unique combination of name, symbol, and package design distinguishes each brand from the others.

A **brand name** is that part of the brand consisting of words or letters included in a name used to identify and distinguish the firm's offerings from those of competitors. The brand name is the part of the brand that can be vocalized. Many brand names, such as Coca-Cola, McDonald's, American Express, Google, and Nike, are famous around the world. Likewise, the "golden arches" brand mark of McDonald's also is widely recognized.

A **trademark** is a brand that has been given legal protection. The protection is granted solely to the brand's owner. Trademark protection includes not only the brand name but also design logos, slogans, packaging elements, and product features such as color and shape. A well-designed trademark, such as the Nike "swoosh," can make a definite difference in how positively consumers perceive a brand.

**brand** name, term, sign, symbol, design, or some combination that identifies the products of one firm and differentiates them from competitors' offerings.

## Selecting an Effective Brand Name

Good brands are easy to pronounce, recognize, and remember: Crest, Visa, and Avis are examples. Global firms face a real problem in selecting brand names, because an excellent brand name in one country may prove disastrous in another. Most languages have a short *a*, so Coca-Cola is pronounceable almost anywhere. But an advertising campaign for E-Z washing machines failed in the United Kingdom because the British pronounce *z* as "zed."

Brand names should also convey the right image to the buyer. One effective technique is to create a name that links the product with its positioning strategy. The name Dial reinforces the concept of 24-hour protection; Dove soap and beauty products give an impression of mildness, and Taster's Choice instant coffee supports the promotional claim "Tastes and smells like ground roast coffee."

Brand names also must be legally protectable. Trademark law specifies that brand names cannot contain words in general use, such as *television* or *automobile*. Generic words—words that describe a type of product—cannot be used exclusively by any organization. On the other hand, if a brand name becomes so popular that it passes into common language and turns into a generic word, the company can no longer use it as a brand name. Once upon a time, aspirin, linoleum, and zipper were exclusive brand names, but today they have become generic terms and are no longer legally protectable.

## Brand Categories

A brand offered and promoted by a manufacturer is known as a **manufacturer's** (or **national**) **brand.** Examples are Tide, Jockey, Gatorade, Swatch, and Reebok. But not all brand names belong to manufacturers; some are the property of retailers or distributors. A **private** (or **store**) **brand** identifies a product that is not linked to the manufacturer but instead carries a wholesaler's or retailer's label. Sears's DieHard batteries and Wal-Mart's Ol' Roy dog food are examples.

Another branding decision marketers must make is whether to use a family branding strategy or an individual branding strategy. A **family brand** is a single brand name used for several related products. KitchenAid, Johnson & Johnson, Hewlett-Packard, and Dole use a family name for their entire line of products. When a firm using family branding introduces a new product, both customers and retailers recognize the familiar brand name. The promotion of individual products within a line benefits all the products because the family brand is well known.

KitchenAid uses a family branding strategy for its products. Along with its traditional standing mixers, the company now uses the brand for its food processors, coffee makers, and kitchen utensils.

CURTIS COMPTON/BLOOMBERG NEWS /LANDOV

Other firms use an **individual branding** strategy by giving each product within a line a different name. For example, Procter & Gamble has individual brand names for its different laundry detergents, including Tide, Cheer, and Dash. Each brand targets a unique market segment. Consumers who want a cold-water detergent can choose Cheer over Tide or Dash, instead of purchasing a competitor's brand. Individual branding also builds competition within a firm and enables the company to increase overall sales.

## Brand Loyalty and Brand Equity

Brands achieve varying consumer familiarity and acceptance. While a homeowner may insist on Anderson windows when renovating, the consumer buying a loaf of bread may not prefer any brand. Consumer loyalty increases a brand's value, so marketers try to strengthen brand loyalty. When a brand image suffers, marketers try to re-create a positive image.

**Brand Loyalty** Marketers measure brand loyalty in three stages: brand recognition, brand preference, and brand insistence. *Brand recognition* is brand acceptance strong enough that the consumer is aware of the brand, but not strong enough to cause a preference over other brands. A consumer might have heard of L'Oréal hair care products, for instance, without necessarily preferring them to Redken. Advertising, free samples, and discount coupons are among the most common ways to increase brand recognition.

*Brand preference* occurs when a consumer chooses one firm's brand over a competitor's. At this stage, the consumer usually relies on previous experience in selecting the product. Automobiles and apparel fall into this category. A shopper who knows that Dockers slacks fit him well is likely to choose the brand again. *Brand insistence* is the ultimate degree of brand loyalty, in which the consumer will accept no substitute for a preferred brand. If the desired product is not available, the consumer will look for it at another outlet, special-order it from a dealer, order by mail, or search the Internet. Few sellers achieve brand insistence for their products, though cosmetics are one product that sometimes inspires this degree of loyalty.

A recent study found that retail Web sites are another means of building brand loyalty. About 4,000 consumers who had made recent purchases of gifts, apparel, electronics, and toys were asked about their experiences. The consumers bought merchandise from retailers that had several different outlet options, such as department stores, smaller boutiques, and e-business sites. Those who used the Web as a research tool not only were more satisfied with their purchases but were also more likely to repeat them.[10]

Brand-building strategies were once limited to the consumer realm, but now they are becoming more important for B2B brands as well. Intel, Xerox, IBM, and service providers such as Manpower and ServiceMaster are among the suppliers who have built brand names among business customers.

**Brand Equity** Brand loyalty is at the heart of **brand equity**, the added value that a respected and successful name gives to a product. This value results from a combination of factors, including awareness, loyalty, and perceived quality, as well as any feelings or images the customer asso-

**brand equity** added value that a respected and successful name gives to a product.

ciates with the brand. High brand equity offers financial advantages to a firm, because the product commands a relatively large market share and sometimes reduces price sensitivity, generating higher profits. Figure 13.4 shows the world's ten most valuable brands and their estimated worth.

*Brand awareness* means the product is the first one that comes to mind when a product category is mentioned. For instance, if someone says "diapers," you may instantly think of Pampers. Brand association is a link between a brand and other favorable images. When you think of getting together with friends over coffee, for example, you may associate that image with Starbucks.

Large companies have typically assigned the task of managing a brand's marketing strategies to a *brand manager,* who may also be called a *product manager* at some firms. This marketing professional plans and implements the balance of promotional, pricing, distribution, and product arrangements that leads to strong brand equity. A **category manager,** a newer concept, oversees an entire group of products. Unlike traditional brand or product managers, category managers have profit responsibility for their product group. These managers are assisted by associates, usually called *analysts.* Part of the shift to category management was initiated by large retailers, which realized they could benefit from the marketing muscle of large grocery and household goods producers such as Kraft and Procter & Gamble. As a result, producers began to focus their attention on in-store merchandising instead of mass-market advertising. A few years ago, Kraft reorganized its sales force so that each representative was responsible for a retailer's needs instead of pushing a single brand.

A **category advisor** functions in the B2B context. This vendor is the major supplier designated by a business customer to assume responsibility for dealing with all the other suppliers for a project and presenting the entire package to the business buyer.

Figure

13.4

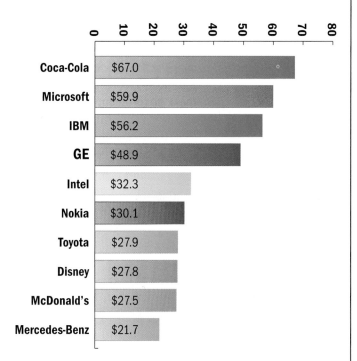

The World's Ten Most Valuable Brands (millions)

| | |
|---|---|
| Coca-Cola | $67.0 |
| Microsoft | $59.9 |
| IBM | $56.2 |
| GE | $48.9 |
| Intel | $32.3 |
| Nokia | $30.1 |
| Toyota | $27.9 |
| Disney | $27.8 |
| McDonald's | $27.5 |
| Mercedes-Benz | $21.7 |

**Source:** "The Top 100 Brands 2006," *BusinessWeek,* accessed August 7, 2006, http://www.businessweek.com/brand/2006/.

**category advisor** vendor that is designated by the business customer as the major supplier to deal with all other suppliers for a special purchase and to present the entire package to the business buyer.

## Packages and Labels

Packaging and labels are important in product identification. They also play an important role in a firm's overall product strategy. Packaging affects the durability, image, and convenience of an item and is responsible for one of the biggest costs in many consumer products. Customers have often been annoyed by the small paper stickers pasted to each piece of fruit, which also takes the peel or skin with it. So the produce industry developed a new technology to laser-tattoo fruits and vegetables instead, making labeling and packaging more efficient and cost-effective.[11]

Choosing the right package is especially crucial in international marketing, because marketers must be aware of such factors as language variations and cultural preferences. Consumers in African nations often prefer bold colors, but use of the country's flag colors may be problematic. Some countries frown on other uses of their flag. Also, in Africa red is often associated with death or witchcraft. Package size can vary according to the purchasing patterns and market conditions of a country. In countries with small refrigerators, people may want to buy their beverages one at a time rather than in six-packs. Package weight is another important issue, because shipping costs are often based on weight.

Labeling is an integral part of the packaging process as well. In the United States, labeling must meet federal laws requiring companies to provide enough information to allow consumers to make value comparisons among competitive products and, in the case of food packaging, provide nutrition information on the label. Marketers who ship products to other countries have to comply with labeling requirements in those nations. This means knowing the answers to such questions as the following: Should the labels be in more than one language? Should ingredients be specified? Do the labels give enough information about the product to meet government standards? A recent lawsuit against McDonald's hinged on the amount of nutritional information the company provides about its products.

Another important aspect of packaging and labeling is the *Universal Product Code (UPC)*, the bar code read by optical scanners that print the name of the item and the price on a receipt. For many stores, these identifiers are useful not just for packaging and labeling but also for simplifying and speeding retail transactions and for evaluating customer purchases and controlling inventory. Radio-frequency identification (RFID) technology—embedded chips that can broadcast their product information to receivers—may soon replace UPC bar codes, however, as we'll discuss later in this chapter.

# DISTRIBUTION STRATEGY

The next element of the marketing mix, **distribution strategy,** deals with the marketing activities and institutions involved in getting the right good or service to the firm's customers. Distribution decisions involve modes of transportation, warehousing, inventory control, order processing, and selection of marketing channels. Marketing channels typically are made up of intermediaries such as retailers and wholesalers that move a product from producer to final purchaser.

The two major components of an organization's distribution strategy are distribution channels and physical distribution. **Distribution channels** are the paths that products—and title to them—follow from producer to consumer or business user. They are the means by which all organizations distribute their goods and services. **Physical distribution** is the actual movement of these products from the producer to the user. Physical distribution covers a broad range of activities, including customer service, transportation, inventory control, materials handling, order processing, and warehousing.

## Distribution Channels

In their first decision for distribution channel selection, marketers choose which type of channel will best meet both their firm's marketing objectives and the needs of their customers. As shown in Figure 13.5, marketers can choose either a **direct distribution channel,** which carries goods directly from producer to consumer or business user, or distribution channels that involve several different marketing intermediaries. A *marketing intermediary* (also called a *middleman*) is a business firm that moves goods between producers and consumers or business users. Marketing intermediaries perform various functions that help the distribution channel operate smoothly, such as buying, selling, storing, and transporting products; sorting and grading bulky items; and providing information to other channel members. The two main categories of marketing intermediaries are wholesalers and retailers.

The large number of goods and services distributed through so many different channels is enough to convince most observers that no one channel suits every product. The best choice

**distribution channel**
path through which products—and legal ownership of them—flow from producer to consumers or business users.

**physical distribution**
actual movement of products from producer to consumers or business users.

Figure 13.5

Alternative Distribution Channels

depends on the circumstances of the market and on customer needs. The most appropriate channel choice may also change over time as new opportunities arise and marketers strive to maintain their competitiveness. The Kodak Picture Maker, for instance, is a freestanding kiosk that consumers can use to make their own reprints and enlargement, to print pictures from digital cameras, and to create photo IDs. With 35,000 units installed worldwide, the Picture Maker remains one of the top applications of a uniquely flexible distribution method.[12]

*Direct Distribution* The shortest and simplest means of connecting producers and customers is direct contact between the two parties. This approach is most common in the B2B market. It also serves consumers who buy fresh fruits and vegetables at rural roadside stands. Services ranging from banking and ten-minute oil changes to ear piercing employ direct distribution, as does Mary Kay Cosmetics.

Direct distribution is commonly found in the marketing of relatively expensive, complex products that may require demonstrations. Most major B2B products such as installations, accessory equipment, component parts, business services, and even raw materials are typically marketed through direct contacts between producers and business buyers. The Internet has also made direct distribution an attractive option for many retail companies and service providers. Netflix allows movie enthusiasts to rent DVDs through its Web site; each disc arrives in the mail a few days later in an envelope that converts to a return mailer. Tom Online, an Internet and wireless service provider in China, has become the sole distributor for Warner Brothers games and animation that Tom Online's more than 60 million wireless customers can download to their cell phones.[13]

**Figure**

**13.6** Reducing Transactions through Marketing Intermediaries

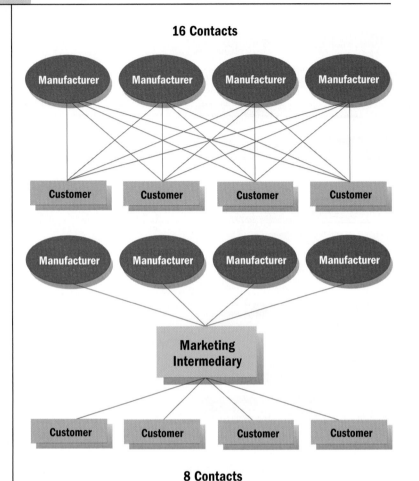

**16 Contacts**

**8 Contacts**

***Distribution Channels Using Marketing Intermediaries*** Although direct channels allow simple and straightforward connections between producers and their customers, the list of channel alternatives in Figure 13.5 suggests that direct distribution is not the best choice in every instance. Some products sell in small quantities for relatively low prices to thousands of widely scattered consumers. Makers of such products cannot cost-effectively contact each of their customers, so they distribute products through specialized intermediaries called *wholesalers* and *retailers*.

Although you might think that adding intermediaries to the distribution process would increase the final cost of products, more often than not this choice actually lowers consumer prices. Intermediaries such as wholesalers and retailers often add significant value to a product as it moves through the distribution channel. They do so by creating utility, providing additional services, and reducing costs.

Marketing utility is created when intermediaries help ensure that products are available for sale when and where customers want to purchase them. If you want something warm to eat on a cold winter night, you don't call up Campbell Soup and ask them to ship a can of chicken noodle soup. Instead, you go to the nearest grocery store, where you find utility in the form of product availability. In addition, intermediaries perform such important services as transporting merchandise to convenient locations. Finally, by representing numerous producers, a marketing intermediary can cut the costs of buying and selling. As Figure 13.6 shows, if four manufacturers each sold directly to four consumers, this would require sixteen separate transactions. Adding a marketing intermediary, such as a retailer, to the exchange cuts the number of necessary transactions to eight.

# WHOLESALING

**wholesaler** distribution channel member that sells primarily to retailers, other wholesalers, or business users.

A **wholesaler** is a distribution channel member that sells primarily to retailers, other wholesalers, or business users. For instance, Sysco is a wholesaler that buys food products from producers and then resells them to restaurants, hotels, and other institutions in the United States and Canada.

Wholesaling is a crucial part of the distribution channel for many products, particularly consumer goods and business supplies. Wholesaling intermediaries can be classified on the basis of ownership; some are owned by manufacturers, some are owned by retailers, and others are independently owned. The United States has more than 450,000 wholesalers, most of which are independent businesses.[14]

## Manufacturer-Owned Wholesaling Intermediaries

A manufacturer's marketing manager may decide to distribute goods directly through company-owned facilities to control distribution or customer service. Firms operate two main types of manufacturer-owned wholesaling intermediaries: sales branches and sales offices.

*Sales branches* stock the products they distribute and fill orders from their inventories. They also provide offices for sales representatives. Sales branches are common in the chemical, petroleum products, motor vehicle, and machine and equipment industries.

A *sales office* is exactly what its name implies: an office for a producer's salespeople. Manufacturers set up sales offices in various regions to support local selling efforts and improve customer service. Some kitchen and bath fixture manufacturers maintain showrooms to display their products. Builders and decorators can visit these showrooms to see how the items would look in place. Unlike sales branches, however, sales offices do not store any inventory. When a customer orders from a showroom or other sales office, the merchandise is delivered from a separate warehouse.

## Independent Wholesaling Intermediaries

An independent wholesaling intermediary is a business that represents a number of different manufacturers and makes sales calls on retailers, manufacturers, and other business accounts. Independent wholesalers are classified as either merchant wholesalers or agents and brokers, depending on whether they take title to the products they handle.

*Merchant wholesalers,* like apparel wholesaler WholesaleSarong.com, are independently owned wholesaling intermediaries that take title to the goods they handle. Within this category, a *full-function merchant wholesaler* provides a complete assortment of services for retailers or industrial buyers, such as warehousing, shipping, and even financing. A subtype of full-function merchant is a *rack jobber,* such as Ohio-based Arrow Distributing, which handles distribution of CDs and DVDs to retail stores. This type of firm stocks, displays, and services particular retail products, such as paperback books or greeting cards in a drugstore or supermarket. Usually, the retailer receives a commission based on actual sales as payment for providing merchandise space to a rack jobber.

A *limited-function merchant wholesaler* also takes legal title to the products it handles, but it provides fewer services to the retailers to which it sells. Some limited-function merchant wholesalers only warehouse products but do not offer delivery service. Others warehouse and deliver products but provide no financing. One type of limited-function merchant wholesaler is a *drop shipper* such as Kate Aspen, an Atlanta-based wholesaler of wedding favors. Drop shippers also operate in such industries as coal and lumber, characterized by bulky products for which no single producer can provide a complete assortment. They give access to many related goods by contacting numerous producers and negotiating the best possible prices. Cost considerations call for producers to ship such products directly to the drop shipper's customers.

Another category of independent wholesaling intermediaries consists of *agents* and *brokers*. They may or may not take possession of the goods they handle, but they never take title, working mainly to bring buyers and sellers together. Stockbrokers such as Piper Jaffray and real estate agents such as RE/MAX perform functions similar to those of agents and brokers, but at the retail level. They do not take possession of or title to the sellers' property; instead, they create time and ownership utility for both buyer and seller by helping carry out transactions.

*Manufacturers' reps* act as independent sales forces by representing the manufacturers of related but noncompeting products. These agent intermediaries, sometimes referred to as *manufacturers' agents,* receive commissions based on a percentage of the sales they make.

## Retailer-Owned Cooperatives and Buying Offices

Retailers sometimes band together to form their own wholesaling organizations. Such organizations can take the form of either a buying group or a cooperative. The participating retailers set up the new operation to reduce costs or to provide some special service that is not readily available in the marketplace. To achieve cost savings through quantity purchases, independent retailers may form a buying group that negotiates bulk sales with manufacturers. One such buying group is Florida-based Retail Advantage Group, which buys products for its member hospital gift shops and gift shop chains. Members join for a year at a time and can receive up to 10 percent discounts on orders they place, while remaining free to buy from any other vendors.[15] In a cooperative, an independent group of retailers may decide to band together to share functions such as shipping or warehousing.

# RETAILING

**retailer** channel member that sells goods and services to individuals for their own use rather than for resale.

**Retailers,** in contrast to wholesalers, are distribution channel members that sell goods and services to individuals for their own use rather than for resale. Consumers usually buy their food, clothing, shampoo, furniture, and appliances from some type of retailer. The supermarket where you buy your groceries may have bought some of its items from a wholesaler such as Unified Western Grocers and then resold them to you.

Retailers are the final link—the so-called last three feet—of the distribution channel. Because they are often the only channel members that deal directly with consumers, it is essential that retailers remain alert to changing shopper needs. For instance, the soaring price of gas affects consumers' budgets, so they may make fewer trips to the mall or cut back on nonessential purchases. As a result, retailers may need to offer special sales or events to lure customers to their shops. It is also important for retailers to keep pace with developments in the fast-changing business environment, such as the disruption in delivery of supplies from Hurricane Katrina.

## Nonstore Retailers

Two categories of retailers exist: store and nonstore. As Figure 13.7 shows, nonstore retailing includes four forms: direct-response retailing, Internet retailing, automatic merchandising, and direct selling. *Direct-response retailing* reaches prospective customers through catalogs, telemarketing, and even magazine, newspaper, and television ads. Shoppers order merchandise by mail, telephone, computer, and fax machine and then receive home delivery or pick the merchandise up at a local store. Lands' End has long stood out as a highly successful direct-response retailer; its famous clothing catalog and stellar customer service have set the standard for this type of distribution channel. With the retailer's purchase by Sears, however, customers can now see, feel, and try on Lands' End's classic clothing at selected stores around the country.

**Figure**

**13.7** Types of Nonstore Retailing

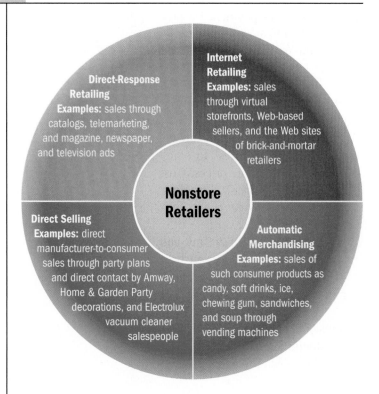

**Direct-Response Retailing**
**Examples:** sales through catalogs, telemarketing, and magazine, newspaper, and television ads

**Internet Retailing**
**Examples:** sales through virtual storefronts, Web-based sellers, and the Web sites of brick-and-mortar retailers

**Nonstore Retailers**

**Direct Selling**
**Examples:** direct manufacturer-to-consumer sales through party plans and direct contact by Amway, Home & Garden Party decorations, and Electrolux vacuum cleaner salespeople

**Automatic Merchandising**
**Examples:** sales of such consumer products as candy, soft drinks, ice, chewing gum, sandwiches, and soup through vending machines

NORDSTROM, INC.

USED WITH PERMISSION. NORDSTROM, INC.

Nordstrom offers customers shopping convenience at both its traditional brick-and-mortar stores (left) and its Web site. The retailer's Web site offers more than 400 brands to choose from.

*Internet retailing,* the second form of nonstore retailing, has grown rapidly. Tens of thousands of retailers have set up shop online, with total sales increasing 15 to 25 percent annually.[16] A severe shakeout saw hundreds of Internet enterprises shut down during the first few years of the 21st century, but firms that survived have stronger business models than those that failed. Two examples of success by pure dot-coms are Amazon and eBay. A major shift in retailing has seen traditional brick-and-mortar retailers competing with pure dot-com start-ups by setting up their own Web sites as an option for shoppers. Nordstrom, JCPenney, and Wal-Mart report strong online sales. Shopping sites are among the most popular Internet destinations, and sales of clothing and DVDs in particular have risen.

The last two forms of nonstore retailing are automatic merchandising and direct selling. *Automatic merchandising* provides convenience through the use of vending machines. ATMs may soon join the ranks of vending machines as banks find new ways to compete for customers. Some ATMs offer extra services such as check cashing and stamps, as well as concert tickets and road maps. Future ATMs will be able to connect wirelessly to Palm Pilots and cell phones to allow customers to download and pay for games and music. *Direct selling* includes direct-to-consumer sales by Pampered Chef kitchen representatives and salespeople for Longaberger (baskets and gifts) and Luxe Jewels (jewelry) through party-plan selling methods. Both are forms of direct selling.

Companies that previously relied heavily on telemarketing in generating new customers have encountered consumer resistance to intrusive phone calls. Among the growing barriers are caller ID, call-blocking devices such as the TeleZapper, and the National Do Not Call list, which made it illegal for most companies to call people who registered. As a result, dozens of companies, including telecommunications and regional utilities, have sent direct-mail pieces to promote such services as phones, cable television, and natural gas distributors.

## Store Retailers

In-store sales still outpace nonstore retailing methods like direct-response retailing and Internet selling. Store retailers range in size from tiny newsstands to multistory department stores and multiacre warehouselike retailers such as Sam's Club. Table 13.2 lists the different types

Table

13.2 | Types of Retail Stores

| Store Type | Description | Example |
|---|---|---|
| Specialty store | Offers complete selection in a narrow line of merchandise | Cabela's sports store, Coconuts music store, Calyx & Corolla flower store |
| Convenience store | Offers staple convenience goods, easily accessible locations, long store hours, and rapid checkouts | 7-Eleven, QuikTrip, Kum & Go |
| Discount store | Offers wide selection of merchandise at low prices; off-price discounters offer designer or brand-name merchandise | Target, Wal-Mart, Nordstrom Rack, Marshall's |
| Warehouse club | Large, warehouse-style store selling food and general merchandise at discount prices to membership cardholders | Costco, Sam's Club, BJ's |
| Factory outlet | Manufacturer-owned store selling seconds, production overruns, or discontinued lines | Adidas, Reebok, Coach, Pottery Barn, Gap |
| Supermarket | Large, self-service retailer offering a wide selection of food and nonfood merchandise | Safeway, Whole Foods Market, Kroger |
| Supercenter | Giant store offering food and general merchandise at discount prices | Wal-Mart Supercenter, Super Target |
| Department store | Offers a wide variety of merchandise selections (furniture, cosmetics, housewares, clothing) and many customer services | Kohl's, Dillard's, Nordstrom, Belk, Neiman Marcus |

of store retailers, with examples of each type. Clearly, there are many approaches to retailing and a variety of services, prices, and product lines offered by each retail outlet. For a look at one unique retailer, see the "Hit & Miss" feature on page 430.

Figure

13.8 | The Wheel of Retailing

**Mid-1900s**
Supermarkets;
Discount
Stores

**Early 1900s**
Self-Service
Grocers;
Sears
Catalog

**Early 2000s**
Internet Retailers;
Big-Box Stores;
Lifestyle Shopping
Centers

**Late 1800s**
Department
Stores;
Five & Dime
Variety Stores

*The Wheel of Retailing* Retailers are subject to constant change as new stores replace older establishments. In a process called the **wheel of retailing,** new retailers enter the market by offering lower prices made possible through reductions in service. Supermarkets and discount houses, for example, gained their initial market footholds through low-price, limited-service appeals. These new entries gradually add services as they grow and ultimately become targets for new retailers.

As Figure 13.8 shows, most major developments over time in retailing appear to fit the wheel pattern. The low-price, limited-service strategy characterized supermarkets, catalog retailers, discount stores, and most recently, Internet retailers and giant "big-box" stores, such as PetsMart, Borders, and Office Depot. Most of these retailers have raised price levels gradually as they added new services. Corner grocery stores gave way to supermarkets and then to warehouse clubs such as Costco or discount supermarkets such as Kansas City–based Hy-Vee. Department stores lost market share to discount clothing retailers such as Target and T. J. Maxx. Independent bookstores have lost business to giant chains like Barnes & Noble, Books-A-Million, Borders, and, more recently, such online sellers as Amazon.com and Buy.com.

Even though the wheel of retailing does not fit every pattern of retail evolution—for example, automatic merchandising has always been a relatively high-priced method of retailing—it does give retail managers a general idea of what is likely to occur during the evolution of retailing. It also shows that business success involves the "survival of the fittest." Retailers that fail to change fail to survive.

## How Retailers Compete

Retailers compete with each other in many ways. Nonstore retailers focus on making the shopping experience as convenient as possible. Shoppers at stores such as the Nature Company, on the other hand, enjoy maximum atmosphere in the form of soothing background music and ready access to environmentally oriented products like telescopes, globes, and books.

Like manufacturers, retailers must develop marketing strategies based on goals and strategic plans. Successful retailers convey images that alert consumers to the stores' identities and the shopping experiences they provide. To create that image, all components of a retailer's strategy must complement each other. After identifying their target markets, retailers must choose merchandising, customer service, pricing, and location strategies that will attract customers in those market segments.

*Identifying a Target Market*  The first step in developing a competitive retailing strategy is to select a target market. This choice requires careful evaluation of the size and profit potential of the chosen market segment and the current level of competition for the segment's business. Bargain stores such as Family Dollar target consumers who are extremely price conscious, for example, while convenience stores like 7-Eleven target consumers who want an easy way to purchase items they buy frequently. Hoping to revive sluggish sales, Gap opened a new flagship chain called Forth & Towne, which targets women age 35 and older and is aimed at competitors like rapidly growing Chico's.[17]

*Selecting a Product Strategy*  Next, the retailer must develop a product strategy to determine the best mix of merchandise to carry to satisfy that market. Retail strategists must decide on the general product categories, product lines, and variety to offer. Seven of ten products carried in Home Depot stores were suggested by customers, for example.

*Shaping a Customer Service Strategy*  A retailer's customer service strategy focuses on attracting and retaining target customers to maximize sales and profits. Some stores offer a wide variety of services, such as gift wrapping, alterations, returns, interior design services, and delivery. Other stores offer bare-bones customer service, stressing low price instead. Some grocery shoppers, for instance, can find convenience online through a service like Peapod, which handles product selection, packing, and delivery. They can visit a supermarket and make their own selections. Or they can go to a discount supermarket like Minnesota-based Cub Foods, where they not only assemble their orders but also bag their purchases.

*Selecting a Pricing Strategy*  Retailers base their pricing decisions on the costs of purchasing products from other channel members and offering services to customers. Pricing can play a major role in consumers' perceptions of a retailer, and not just because they appreciate low prices. For instance, Costco limits markups on branded items to no more than 14 percent and on private-label items to no more than 15 percent. For comparison, supermarkets use markups of 25 percent, and in department stores 50 percent or more is the rule. Yet according to Jim Sinegal, Costco's CEO, what keeps his generally well-off customers coming back to the store is their perception that its employees aren't paying for those low prices with poor compensation. Costco workers in fact are paid well compared with rival discounters and have

# HIT & MISS

## The Wizard of Odd

Not many retailers would buy up old amusement park trains on a whim, but James "Jungle Jim" Bonaminio did. He followed up his initial investment of $1 for the eight trains with $1 million worth of renovations and track, and soon the sprawling Jungle Jim's International Market, an offbeat supermarket and specialty foods store north of Cincinnati, will connect to the parking lot with its own two-mile monorail.

Despite a less-than-ideal location, Jungle Jim's, which occupies about 280,000 square feet in Fairfield, Ohio, has become highly profitable, drawing 50,000 shoppers a week from miles around. In his efforts to make shopping fun—and stave off competition—Bonaminio is just as likely to roller-skate through the aisles in a wizard suit as to splurge on 40,000 scrapped highway guardrails to be incorporated into the multibuilding structure. Since entering the food business with a roadside stand in the 1970s, Bonaminio, who never finished college, has grown a very successful business.

The store offers novelty, entertainment, and variety, with an enormous selection of foods from 75 countries. High-margin specialty foods provide most of the profits, but a full stock of necessities such as milk and bread, which recently moved to a prominent place at the front of the store, supports another of the store's strategies—to attract local customers doing their routine shopping.

But fun is still key to the retailer's success. Bonaminio is adding a shopping center he hopes will house a dozen restaurants, alongside a two-story "events center" where cooking demonstrations and food and wine tastings and festivals will be held. He already has a cooking school and garden center, but he's hoping to attract a hotel to the site.

"Jungle seems wacky on the outside," says one Ohio developer, "but he has a consumer brilliance about him. He really understands his market."

### Questions for Critical Thinking

1. Jungle Jim's is a specialty retailer located several traffic-filled miles from the nearest major highway. How successful do you think its strategy of attracting shoppers in search of convenience goods such as bread will be? Why?
2. Which type of products is Jungle Jim's providing its customers by leasing retail space to a U.S. post office, a bank, a pharmacy, Starbucks, an ice cream parlor, and Buck$ Dollar Stores?

**Sources:** Jungle Jim's International Market Web site, accessed July 15, 2006, http://www.junglejims.com; "Jungle Jim's Expansion Project," City of Fairfield (Ohio) Web site, accessed July 15, 2006, http://www.fairfield-city.org; Anthony Biano, "The Wizard of Odd," *BusinessWeek*, accessed July 15, 2006, http://www.businessweekasia.com.

a generous health plan, resulting in very low theft and turnover. "This is not altruistic," says Sinegal. "This is good business."[18] As at Costco, pricing strategy must support the retailer's overall marketing objectives and policies. Pricing strategy is covered in more detail in Chapter 14.

*Choosing a Location*   A good location often makes the difference between success and failure in retailing. The location decision depends on the retailer's size, financial resources, product offerings, competition, and, of course, its target market. Traffic patterns, the visibility of the store's signage, parking, and the location of complementary stores also influence the choice of a retail location. One reason Target's in-store grocery departments have proved less successful than Wal-Mart's is that many of them are located in urban areas where heavy traffic tends to limit shopping trips and where rival grocery chains already dominate the market.

A *planned shopping center* is a group of retail stores planned, coordinated, and marketed as a unit to shoppers in a geographical trade area. By providing single convenient locations with free parking, shopping centers have largely replaced downtown shopping in many urban areas. But time-pressed consumers are increasingly looking for more efficient ways to shop, including catalogs, Internet retailers, and one-stop shopping at large free-standing stores such as Wal-Mart Supercenters. To lure more customers, shopping centers are recasting themselves as entertainment destinations, with art displays, carousel rides, and musical entertainment. The giant Mall of America in Bloomington, Minnesota, features a seven-acre amusement park and an aquarium.

In recent years, large regional malls have also witnessed a growing shift in shopping center traffic to smaller strip centers, name-brand outlet centers, and *lifestyle centers,* open-air complexes containing retailers that often focus on specific shopper segments and product interests. Lifestyle centers such as Kierland Commons in Scottsdale, Arizona, have a distinctly urban, but residential feel, with open-air plazas, bandshells, flowered walkways, and special restaurants and cafés.[19] They also cater to those who prefer to browse online before shopping; they are usually designed for quick access to and exit from each individual store, with next-door parking and landscaped walkways. Instead of being anchored by a giant department store, lifestyle centers generally have a small-town feel and feature movie theaters or nice restaurants to encourage shoppers to stay.[20]

*Building a Promotional Strategy*   A retailer designs advertisements and develops other promotions to stimulate demand and to provide information such as the store's location, merchandise offerings, prices, and hours. In a publicity coup to promote a renovation, Marshall Field's flagship store staged the first "Vertical Fashion Show," complete with models rappelling down the store's façade in the latest fashions. Nonstore retailers provide their phone numbers and Web site addresses. More recently, online retailers have scaled back their big advertising campaigns and worked to build traffic through word of mouth and clever promotions. Promotional strategy is also discussed in depth in Chapter 14.

*Creating a Store Atmosphere*   A successful retailer closely aligns its merchandising, pricing, and promotion strategies with *store atmospherics,* the physical characteristics of a store and its amenities, to influence consumers' perceptions of the shopping experience. Atmospherics begin with the store's exterior, which may use eye-catching architectural elements and signage to attract customer attention and interest. Interior atmospheric elements include store layout, merchandise presentation, lighting, color, sound, and cleanliness. A high-end store such as Nordstrom's, for instance, features high-ceilinged selling areas that spotlight tasteful and meticulously cared-for displays of a few carefully chosen items of obvious quality. Old Navy, on the other hand, crams an ever-changing array of inexpensive items into its warehouselike settings furnished with industrial-style display hardware.

**assessment check**

1. Define distribution channels.
2. What is a marketing intermediary?
3. Differentiate between a merchant wholesaler and an agent or broker in terms of title to the goods.
4. What are the elements of a retailer's marketing strategy?

# DISTRIBUTION CHANNEL DECISIONS AND LOGISTICS

Every firm faces two major decisions when choosing how to distribute its goods or services: selecting a specific distribution channel and deciding on the level of distribution intensity. In deciding which distribution channel is most efficient, business managers need to consider four factors: the market, the product, the producer, and the competition. These factors are often interrelated and may change over time. Because so many companies are now doing business on a global basis, they are finding it important to meet and greet customers, suppliers, and distribution partners in other countries. See the "Business Etiquette" feature for some tips about introducing yourself abroad.

# (b)usiness (e)tiquette

## How Do You Do?

Retailers and wholesalers work with large numbers of people, not just their customers but also suppliers and other partners in the supply chain. Every industry and country has its own conventions to help people meet others and establish good working relationships. Here are some tips for introducing and addressing people when you meet them for the first time.

1. In the United States, once you have been introduced to a person, you can use first names for almost everyone in your own company no matter how many layers of management are between you.
2. First names are considered too familiar even between colleagues in Europe, unless you are invited to use them. Instead, use the person's courtesy title (such as *Herr* or *Madame*) and last name.
3. Be aware that introductions are more formal and more important in Europe and Asia than in the United States.
4. Always introduce the less senior person to the more senior first. If Ms. Ricci is the CEO, for example, you would introduce the new receptionist by saying, "Ms. Ricci, I'd like you to meet Mr. Hanover. Mr. Hanover, this is Ms. Ricci."
5. In the United States or abroad, always stand to introduce or be introduced to anyone, and smile. It shows you are interested in and respect them.
6. If it is appropriate to shake hands, do so firmly. Find out what gestures are considered appropriate overseas. In Japan a bow often accompanies a handshake, and in France a handshake may conclude with an embrace.
7. Begin meetings by making sure everyone present is known to all the others, and perform the appropriate introductions if not.
8. Find out the correct business titles of those you will be meeting or introducing, and if necessary, practice the proper pronunciation of their names. Mistakes in such matters are not well tolerated, especially abroad.
9. Be informed and understanding about the acceptable physical distances between people in other cultures. Some stand closer together when conversing than is common in the United States, and others a little farther apart.
10. Business cards are more important abroad than in the United States. Accept them graciously and treat them with care. Print your own cards in English on one side and on the other side in the language of the country you are visiting; present the foreign-language side up.

**Sources:** Paula Gamonal, "Doing Business in Europe," *Ravenwerks*, accessed July 15, 2006, http://www.ravenwerks.com; "Social/Conversational Etiquette," San Jose State University Career Center, accessed July 15, 2006 http://www.sjsu.edu; Susan Witt, "International Business: Learn Your Client's Cultural Sensitivities Before You Travel," WomensMedia.com, http://www.womensmedia.com, accessed July 15, 2006.

## Selecting Distribution Channels

Market factors may be the most important consideration in choosing a distribution channel. To reach a target market with a small number of buyers or buyers concentrated in a geographical area, the most feasible alternative may be a direct channel. In contrast, if the firm must reach customers who are dispersed or who make frequent small purchases, then the channel may need to incorporate marketing intermediaries to make goods available when and where customers want them.

In general, products that are complex, expensive, custom made, or perishable move through shorter distribution channels involving few—or no—intermediaries. On the other hand, standardized products or items with low unit values usually pass through relatively long distribution channels. Levi's tried selling its basic jeans products through its Web site but quickly realized it was impractical to fill orders for a single order of pants available at local stores. Greek entrepreneur Stelios Haji-Ioannou, however, finds the Internet the perfect channel for each of his multimillion-dollar firms, including easyJet, a European airline; easyCar rental; and the easyInternetcafe chain. Each firm offers a no-frills service that consumers can order online with few choices. EasyCar, for instance, rents only one kind of car, and drivers must return it, clean, to the original rental location. EasyJet is one of Europe's biggest Internet retailers, selling 95 percent of its seats online. Phil Jones, chief technology officer of parent company easyGroup, says, "We don't aspire to be all things to all people. We do one thing very well at low cost."[21]

Producers that offer a broad product line, with the financial and marketing resources to distribute and promote it, are more likely to choose a shorter channel. Instead of depending on marketing intermediaries, financially strong manufacturers with broad product lines typically use their own sales representatives, warehouses, and credit departments to serve both retailers and consumers.

In many cases, start-up manufacturers turn to direct channels because they can't persuade intermediaries to carry their products. Direct Focus launched production of an exercise bench called Bowflex, designed to be easier to store and use than competing products. But fitness and sporting goods stores, wary of the "fad of the month" mentality of their industry, passed on the product, forcing the company to offer it directly to consumers. Bowflex was promoted through thousands of television ads featuring product benefits and the company's toll-free telephone number. With this direct distribution combined with an effective promotion, Bowflex sales skyrocketed.[22]

Competitive performance is the fourth key consideration when choosing a distribution channel. A producer loses customers when an intermediary fails to achieve promotion or product delivery. Channels used by established competitors as well as new market entries also can influence decisions.

Sirius and XM are two pioneering satellite radio networks. Although neither has turned a profit yet, satellite radio is expected to change the way Americans receive radio broadcasts over the next decade. Each network broadcasts more than 100 specialized channels for a small monthly subscription fee, offering all kinds of music as well as sports and talk-show programming. Sirius boasts controversial talk host Howard Stern, a hip-hop channel programmed by Eminem, and an all-Elvis channel. XM, the larger firm, also markets a handheld receiver for capturing its broadcasts anywhere and even for storing up to five hours of programming. Most satellite receivers are being installed in cars for now, but handheld receivers are rented out at some sporting events, such as golf tournaments, to keep fans posted on the latest news. Both networks already have millions of subscribers, and traditional radio broadcasters are taking note.[23]

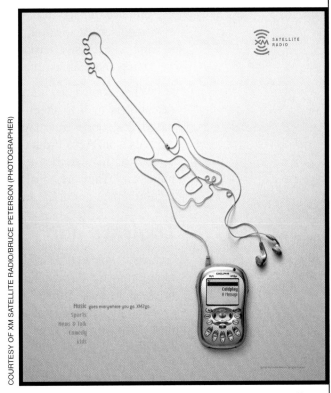

COURTESY OF XM SATELLITE RADIO/BRUCE PETERSON (PHOTOGRAPHER)

Using satellites as a new distribution channel, XM Radio offers hand-held receivers for its on-the-go customers. For a subscription fee, customers get music, sports, news, talk, comedy, and kids programming.

## Selecting Distribution Intensity

A second key distribution decision involves *distribution intensity*—the number of intermediaries or outlets through which a manufacturer distributes its goods. Only one BMW dealership may be operating in your immediate area, but you can find Coca-Cola everywhere—in supermarkets, convenience stores, gas stations, vending machines, and restaurants. BMW has chosen a different level of distribution intensity than Coca-Cola. In general, market coverage varies along a continuum with three different intensity levels:

1. **Intensive distribution** involves placing a firm's products in nearly every available outlet. Generally, intensive distribution suits low-priced convenience goods such as milk, newspapers, and soft drinks. This kind of market saturation requires cooperation by many intermediaries, including wholesalers and retailers, to achieve maximum coverage.
2. **Selective distribution** is a market-coverage strategy in which a manufacturer selects only a limited number of retailers to distribute its product lines. Selective distribution can reduce total marketing costs and establish strong working relationships within the channel.
3. **Exclusive distribution,** at the other end of the continuum from intensive distribution, limits market coverage in a specific geographical region. The approach suits relatively expensive specialty products such as Rolex watches. Retailers are carefully selected to enhance the

product's image to the market and to ensure that well-trained personnel will contribute to customer satisfaction. Although producers may sacrifice some market coverage by granting an exclusive territory to a single intermediary, the decision usually pays off in developing and maintaining an image of quality and prestige.

When companies are offloading excess inventory, even high-priced retailers may look to discounters to help them clear the merchandise from their warehouses. One reason Dallas-based discounter Tuesday Morning was able to land a shipment of discontinued Deluxe Airbeds from Aero Products International, which was launching a new version of the product, is that the retailer tries to specialize in hip or trendy items that customers like to "treasure hunt" for. "They are considered a closeout retailer," said an Aero spokesperson, "but they have a good reputation in the market. So they don't hurt the brand."[24]

## Logistics and Physical Distribution

A firm's choice of distribution channels creates the final link in the **supply chain**, the complete sequence of suppliers that contribute to creating a good or service and delivering it to business users and final consumers. The supply chain begins when the raw materials used in production are delivered to the producer and continues with the actual production activities that create finished goods. Finally, the finished goods move through the producer's distribution channels to end customers.

The process of coordinating the flow of goods, services, and information among members of the supply chain is called **logistics.** The term originally referred to strategic movements of military troops and supplies. Today, however, it describes all of the business activities involved in the supply chain with the ultimate goal of getting finished goods to customers. For a look at how UPS is planning to provide logistics to global customers, see the "Hit & Miss" feature.

*Physical Distribution* A major focus of logistics management—identified earlier in the chapter as one of the two basic dimensions of distribution strategy—is *physical distribution,* the activities aimed at efficiently moving finished goods from the production line to the consumer or business buyer. As Figure 13.9 shows, physical distribution is a broad concept that includes transportation and numerous other elements that help link buyers and sellers. An effectively managed physical distribution system can increase customer satisfaction by ensuring reliable movements of products through the supply chain. For instance, Wal-Mart studies the speed with which goods can be shelved once they arrive at the store because strategies that look efficient at the warehouse, such as completely filling pallets with goods, can actually be time-consuming or costly in the aisles.

A new technology called *radio-frequency identification (RFID)* relies on a computer chip implanted somewhere on a product or its packaging that emits a low-frequency radio signal identifying the item. The radio signal doesn't require a line of sight to register on the store's computers the way a bar code does, so a handheld RFID reader can scan crates and cartons without unloading them. Because the chip can store information about the product's progress through the distribution channel, retailers can efficiently manage inventories, maintain stocking levels, reduce loss, track stolen goods, and cut costs. The technology is similar to that already used to identify lost pets and speed vehicles through toll booths. Wal-Mart, Target, the U.S. Department of Defense, and the German retailer Metro Group already require their suppliers to use RFID technology, and there's little doubt that its use will spread.[25]

*Warehousing* is the physical distribution activity that involves the storage of products. *Materials handling* is moving items within factories, warehouses, transportation terminals, and stores. Inventory control involves managing inventory costs, such as storage facilities, insurance, taxes, and handling. The physical distribution activity of *order processing* includes preparing orders for shipment and receiving orders when shipments arrive.

## HIT & MISS

### UPS Delivers More

Already the world's largest package distribution company, Atlanta-based UPS hopes to quickly grow into a global provider of a wide range of transportation and related services, particularly in Asia's rapidly expanding business markets. As its chief information officer says, "We build a global network so our customers don't have to."

A big part of UPS's push to become a major logistics provider to other firms is information technology, a billion-dollar annual budget item for the company, which it uses both to cut costs and to better serve its business customers around the world. The UPS Web site, for instance, supports 22 languages. Its strategy for expanding into large and growing new markets such as China and India includes the same handheld devices its drivers in Europe and the United States use. To support the handhelds, UPS has already invested in new telecommunications infrastructures in cities such as Shanghai and Beijing. It also opened three new warehouse and distribution centers in China and plans to expand to at least 20 other major cities in the near future.

More new technologies are undoubtedly on the way. Already successful in the United States is a new label-printing system that UPS expects will save $600 million a year and reduce both loading time at U.S. distribution centers and delivery times for the company's well-known brown trucks. Saving even a few minutes can make a difference when multiplied by 3 billion items a day. Given the infrastructures it's building in Asia, UPS will be well positioned to transfer successful new technologies abroad as its business grows.

In addition to technology hurdles, working with China's highly centralized government is just one of the challenges UPS faces in the Chinese market. To overcome cultural and other barriers, the firm is recruiting Chinese students at U.S. universities to learn its U.S. operations and then return home to China and help run operations there. With a new slogan, "Deliver More," designed to emphasize its intention to expand its services beyond package delivery, UPS is set to enter more than 100 business markets around the world.

#### Questions for Critical Thinking

1. What advantages do you think UPS can offer overseas businesses looking for logistics providers?
2. What are some of the distribution problems customers in Asia might want UPS to help them solve?

**Sources:** "UPS Has Big Plans for China and the World," *InformationWeek*, accessed July 15, 2006, http://www .informationweek.com; "UPS Launches 'Deliver More' Tagline," *Atlanta Business Chronicle*, accessed July 15, 2006, http:// atlanta.bizjournals.com; Anna Maria Virzi, "United Parcel Service: Sticky Fix," *Baseline*, accessed July 15, 2006, http:// www.baselinemag.com; "HP: Packaging a Dual Data Warehouse Solution for UPS," Hewlett Packard, accessed July 25, 2005, http://www.hp.com.

---

The wide use of electronic data interchange (EDI) and the constant pressure on suppliers to improve their response time have led to **vendor-managed inventory,** in which the producer and the retailer agree that the producer (or the wholesaler) will determine how much of a product a buyer needs and automatically ship new supplies when needed.

The form of transportation used to ship products depends primarily on the kind of product, the distance involved, and the cost. The logistics manager can choose from a number of companies and modes of transportation. As Table 13.3 shows, the five major transport modes are—in order of total expenditures—trucks (with about 75 percent of total expenditures), railroads (approximately 12 percent), water carriers (6 percent), air freight (4 percent), and pipelines (3 percent). The faster methods typically cost more than the slower ones.

**Figure**

**13.9**

Elements of a Physical Distribution System

**Physical Distribution**

Marketer → Customer Service • Transportation • Warehousing • Materials Handling • Inventory Control • Order Processing → Customers

Table

13.3 | Comparison of Transportation Modes

| Mode | Speed | Dependability in Meeting Schedules | Frequency of Shipments | Availability in Different Locations | Flexibility in Handling | Cost |
|------|-------|-----------------------------------|------------------------|------------------------------------|-------------------------|------|
| Rail | Average | Average | Low | Low | High | Average |
| Water | Very slow | Average | Very low | Limited | Very high | Very low |
| Truck | Fast | High | High | Very extensive | Average | High |
| Pipeline | Slow | High | High | Very limited | Very low | Low |
| Air | Very fast | High | Average | Average | Low | Very high |

Speed, reliable delivery, shipment frequency, location availability, handling flexibility, and cost are all important considerations when choosing the most appropriate mode of transportation.

About 15.5 million trucks operate in the United States, carrying most finished goods all or part of the way to the consumer.[26] But railroads, which compete with many truck routes despite their recent loss of market share, are trying to improve both their efficiency and their service by cutting costs, using tighter controls, and adding consulting services to help clients achieve efficient distribution and lower costs in their own businesses.[27]

*Customer Service*   Customer service is a vital component of both product and distribution strategies. *Customer service standards* measure the quality of service a firm provides for its customers. Managers frequently set quantitative guidelines—for example, that all orders be processed within 24 hours after they are received or that salespeople approach shoppers within two minutes after they enter the store. Sometimes customers set their own service standards and choose suppliers that meet or exceed them.

The customer service components of product strategy include warranty and repair service programs. *Warranties* are firms' promises to repair a defective product, refund money paid, or replace a product if it proves unsatisfactory. Repair services are also important. Consumers want to know that help is available if something goes wrong. Those who shop for home computers, for example, often choose retailers that not only feature low prices but also offer repair services and tech support centers. Products with inadequate service backing quickly disappear from the market as a result of word-of-mouth criticism.

Consumers' complaints of the impersonal service they received at Web sites led dot-coms to take a number of steps to "humanize" their customer interactions and deal with complaints. Many Web sites contain button help icons that link the visitor to a representative. Lands' End offers immediate customer feedback through chat rooms.

**assessment check**

1. What is distribution intensity?
2. Define supply chain.
3. What do customer service standards measure?

# WHAT'S AHEAD

This chapter covered two of the elements of the marketing mix: product and distribution. It introduced the key marketing tasks of developing, marketing, and packaging want-satisfying goods and services. It also focused on the three major components of an organization's distribution strategy: the design of efficient distribution channels; wholesalers and retailers who make up many distribution channels; and logistics and physical distribution. We turn to the remaining two—promotion and pricing—in Chapter 14.

**1** **Explain marketing's definition of a product and list the components of a product strategy.**

A product is a bundle of physical, service, and symbolic attributes designed to satisfy consumer wants. The marketing conception of a product includes the brand, product image, warranty, service attributes, packaging, and labeling, in addition to the physical or functional characteristics of the good or service.

### Assessment Check Answers

**1.1 What is a product?**

A product is a bundle of physical, service, and symbolic attributes designed to satisfy consumer wants.

**1.2 What is the marketing view of a product?**

The marketing view of a product includes the brand, product image, warranty, service attributes, packaging, and labeling, in addition to the physical or functional characteristics of the good or service.

**2** **Describe the classification system for consumer and business goods and services.**

Goods and services can be classified as consumer (B2C) or business (B2B) products. Consumer products are those purchased by ultimate consumers for their own use. They can be convenience products, shopping products, or specialty products depending on consumer habits in buying them. Business products are those purchased for use either directly or indirectly in the production of other goods and services for resale. They can be classified as installations, accessory equipment, component parts and materials, raw materials, and supplies. This classification is based on how the items are used and product characteristics. Services can be classified as either consumer or business services.

### Assessment Check Answers

**2.1 Differentiate among convenience, shopping, and specialty products.**

Convenience products are items the consumer seeks to purchase frequently, immediately, and with little effort. Shopping products are typically purchased after the buyer has compared competing products in competing stores. Specialty products are those a purchaser is willing to make a special effort to obtain.

**2.2 How do business products differ from consumer items?**

Business products, such as drill presses, are sold to firms or organizations. Consumer products, such as personal care items, are sold to final users.

**3** **Distinguish between a product mix and a product line.**

A product mix is the assortment of goods and services a firm offers to individual consumers and B2B users. A product line is a series of related products.

### Assessment Check Answers

**3.1 What is a product line?**

A product line is a series of related products.

**3.2 What is a product mix?**

A product mix is the assortment of goods and services a firm offers to individual consumers and B2B users.

**4** **Briefly describe each of the four stages of the product life cycle.**

Every successful new product passes through four stages in its product life cycle: introduction, growth, maturity, and decline. In the introduction stage, the firm attempts to elicit demand for the new product. In the product's growth stage, sales climb, and the company earns its initial profits. In the maturity stage, sales reach a saturation level. In the decline stage, both sales and profits decline. Marketers sometimes employ strategies to extend the product life cycle, including increasing frequency of use, adding new users, finding new uses for the product, and changing package size, labeling, or product quality.

### Assessment Check Answers

**4.1 What are the stages of the product life cycle?**

In the introduction stage, the firm attempts to elicit demand for the new product. In the product's growth stage, sales climb, and the company earns its initial profits. In the maturity stage, sales reach a saturation level. In the decline stage, both sales and profits decline.

**4.2 What are the marketing implications of each stage?**

Marketers sometimes employ strategies to extend the product life cycle, including increasing frequency of use, adding new users, finding new uses for the product, and changing package size, labeling, or product quality.

**5  List the stages of the new-product development process.**

Six stages exist in the new-product development process for most products: idea generation, screening, business analysis, product development, test marketing, and commercialization. At each stage, marketers must decide whether to continue to the next stage, modify the new product, or discontinue the development process. Some new products skip the test marketing stage due to the desire to quickly introduce a new product with excellent potential, a desire not to reveal new-product strategies to competitors, and the high costs involved in limited production runs characteristic of expensive items.

## Assessment Check Answers

**5.1 What are the stages of the new-product development process?**

Six stages exist in the new-product development process for most products: idea generation, screening, business analysis, product development, test marketing, and commercialization.

**5.2 Where do ideas for new products come from?**

New product ideas come from many sources including customer suggestions, suppliers, employees, research scientists, marketing research, investors outside the firm, and competitive products.

**6  Explain how firms identify their products.**

Products are identified by brands, brand names, and trademarks, which are important elements of product images. Effective brand names are easy to pronounce, recognize, and remember, and they project the right images to buyers. Brand names cannot contain generic words. Under certain circumstances, companies lose exclusive rights to their brand names if common use makes them generic terms for product categories. Some brand names belong to retailers or distributors rather than to manufacturers. Brand loyalty is measured in three degrees: brand recognition, brand prefer-

ence, and brand insistence. Some marketers use family brands to identify several related items in a product line. Others employ individual branding strategies by giving each product within a line a different brand name.

## Assessment Check Answers

**6.1 Differentiate between a brand, a brand name, and a trademark.**

A brand is a name, term, sign, symbol, design, or some combination thereof used to identify the products of one firm and differentiate them from competitive offerings. A brand name is that part of the brand consisting of words or letters included in a name used to identify and distinguish the firm's offerings from those of competitors. A trademark is a brand that has been given legal protection.

**6.2 Define *brand equity*.**

Brand equity is the added value that a respected and successful brand name gives to a product.

**7  Outline and briefly describe each of the major components of an effective distribution strategy.**

A firm must consider whether to move products through direct or indirect distribution. Once the decision is made, the company needs to identify the types of marketing intermediaries, if any, through which it will distribute its goods and services. The Internet has made direct distribution an attractive option for many retail companies. Another component is distribution intensity. The business must decide on the amount of market coverage—intensive, selective, or exclusive—needed to achieve its marketing strategies. Finally, attention must be paid to managing the distribution channel. It is vital to minimize conflict between channel members.

## Assessment Check Answers

**7.1 Define *distribution channels*.**

Distribution channels are the paths that products, and title to them, follow from producer to consumer or business user.

**7.2 What is a marketing intermediary?**

A marketing intermediary (also called a middleman) is a business firm that moves goods between producers and consumers or business users.

**7.3 Differentiate between a merchant wholesaler and an agent or broker in terms of title to the goods.**
Merchant wholesalers are independently owned wholesaling intermediaries that take title to the goods they handle. Agents and brokers may or may not take possession of the goods they handle, but they never take title, working mainly to bring buyers and sellers together.

**7.4 What are the elements of a retailer's marketing strategy?**
After identifying their target markets, retailers must choose merchandising, customer service, pricing, and location strategies that will attract customers in those market segments.

**8** Identify the various categories of distribution channels and discuss the factors that influence channel selection.
Marketers can choose either a direct distribution channel, which moves goods directly from the producer to the consumer, or indirect distribution channels, which involve marketing intermediaries in the paths through which products—and legal ownership of them—flow from producer to the final customer. Ideally, the choice of a distribution channel should support a firm's overall marketing strategy. Before selecting distribution channels, firms must consider their target markets, the types of goods being distributed, their own internal systems and concerns, and competitive factors.

## Assessment Check Answers

**8.1 What is distribution intensity?**
Distribution intensity is the number of intermediaries or outlets through which a manufacturer distributes its goods.

**8.2 Define *supply chain*.**
A supply chain is the complete sequence of suppliers that contribute to creating a good or service and delivering it to business users and final consumers.

**8.3 What do customer service standards measure?**
Customer service standards measure the quality of service a firm provides for its customers.

## Business Terms You Need to Know

product 410
product line 414
product mix 414
product life cycle 414
test marketing 417

brand 419
brand equity 420
category advisor 421
distribution channel 422
physical distribution 422

wholesaler 424
retailer 426
supply chain 434
logistics 434

## Other Important Business Terms

convenience product 411
shopping product 411
specialty product 411
brand name 419
trademark 419
manufacturer's (national)
   brand 419

private (store) brand 419
family brand 419
individual branding 420
category manager 421
distribution strategy 422
direct distribution channel 422
wheel of retailing 428

intensive distribution 433
selective distribution 433
exclusive distribution 433
vendor-managed inventory 435

1. Classify each of the following business-to-consumer (B2C) and business-to-business (B2B) products:
   a. *Time* or *Newsweek* magazine
   b. six-pack of bottled water
   c. Case forklift truck
   d. Mississippi river barge
   e. lumber
2. What is the relationship between a product line and a product mix?
3. Identify and briefly describe the six stages of new-product development.
4. What are some strategies for extending the product life cycle?
5. What are the three stages of brand loyalty?

6. What are the advantages of direct distribution? When is a producer most likely to use direct distribution?
7. What is the wheel of retailing? How has the Internet affected the wheel of retailing?
8. Identify and briefly describe the four different types of nonstore retailers. Give an example of at least one type of good or service that would be suited to each type of nonstore retailer.
9. What are the three intensity levels of distribution? Give an example of two products for each level.
10. Describe the strengths and weaknesses of each transport mode and explain how companies can improve their competitiveness through effective distribution.

1. Suggest an appropriate brand name for each of the following goods. Defend your choices.
   a. laundry detergent
   b. sport-utility vehicle
   c. backpack
   d. outdoor boots
   e. fresh-fruit drink
2. As a marketer, review your five-brand list in question 1. What steps you would take to build brand loyalty for three of those products?
3. Which type of distribution intensity would best suit the following products?
   a. Ferrari sports cars
   b. retail shelving units
   c. facial tissue
   d. earth-moving equipment
   e. Altoid flavored mints
4. Think of your favorite store. If it is near where you live or go to school, stop by for a visit. If not, rely on your memory. Describe the store in terms of its atmospherics. What features contribute to your positive experiences and feelings about the store?

5. Suggest the best method for transporting each of the following goods. Explain your choices.
   a. natural gas
   b. oranges and grapefruit
   c. teak furniture from Thailand
   d. redwood lumber from California
   e. industrial machine parts
6. Many products must adhere to a prescribed set of standards. One example is ice hockey equipment. Visit the two Web sites listed and review the basic requirements ice hockey equipment must meet. How do these standards affect manufacturers of ice hockey equipment?
   http://www.usahockey.com
   http://www.iihf.com
7. The International Trademark Association is a worldwide not-for-profit organization of trademark owners and advisors. Visit the association's Web site (http://www.inta.org) and select "Information Center" and then "Learn the Basics." Prepare a brief oral report on the process of selecting and registering a domain name.

## Case 13.1

### American Eagle Hopes to Soar

American Eagle Outfitters is currently riding a wave of popularity among its teen and young-adult market. With trendy but high-quality clothing in affordable price ranges, the chain of almost 850 stores is a top destination for 15- to 25-year-olds.

American Eagle appeals to teens looking for a casual but preppy look. In price range and style choices, it fills a middle ground in the teen and young adult market.

American Eagle's long-standing partnership with MTV began with the hit show *Road Rules,* for which it provided cast wardrobes. The relationship was recently expanded to include American Eagle's sponsorship of MTV's wildly popular Spring Break promotion, recently held in Cancun. "Spring Break is more than just a vacation for our customers—it is a lifestyle. Memories are made on spring break, and our goal with MTV is to make sure this Spring Break is the best ever and the most memorable," said American Eagle's chief marketing officer of the Cancun bash.

The company is far from taking a vacation, however. After a couple of difficult years when its fickle market shopped elsewhere and sales plunged, American Eagle Outfitters has been beating sales projections in a comeback that brought an increase in sales of nearly 32 percent.

But despite the good news at the mall, with 850 locations management knows the chain is about to run out of room to spread its wings. It is considering expanding the American Eagle brand into Asian markets and is also expected to soon start testing a new store concept at home for a slightly older market that will provide fresh avenues for continued growth.

### Questions for Critical Thinking

1. American Eagle Outfitters has not yet released the name of the new retail clothing chain it plans to test, or any details about the store concept it's considering. What product mix strategies do you think would help ensure the new chain's success? Do you think American Eagle would be wise to try to leverage any brand loyalty among its current customers to win them over to the new stores? Why or why not?

2. Why do retailers in the faddish teen market make their brand names and logos so prominent on many of their T-shirts, polos, jeans, and sweats? Why are customers willing to wear these items? Do you think brand names are the only feature that distinguishes one teen retailer's product line from another's? Why or why not?

**Sources:** American Eagle Outfitters Web site, accessed July 15, 2006, http://www.ae.com; Teresa F. Lindeman, "'Hot' American Eagle Heats Up Profits, Stock," *Pittsburgh Post-Gazette,* accessed July 15, 2006, http://www.post-gazette.com; Teresa F. Lindeman, "Soaring Eagle Hopes to Avoid Plunging Back to Earth," *Pittsburgh Post-Gazette,* accessed July 15, 2006, http://www.post-gazette.com; "American Eagle Outfitters Makes a Splash at MTV Spring Break," press release, March 3, 2005.

## Video Case 13.2

### High Sierra Climbs to New Heights

This video case appears on page 622. A recently filmed video, designed to expand and highlight the written case, is available for class use by instructors.

# Chapter 14

## Promotion and Pricing Strategies

There's nothing cuter than a puppy. But as cuddly and adorable as puppies are, the business of promoting products such as pet food, heartworm medicine, and flea and tick repellent is serious—and highly competitive.

One of the best places to advertise is in veterinary clinics. Pet owners are already a captive audience, and they want to feed and treat their animal companions with the best products. So sales reps for various manufacturers often call on veterinary hospitals to promote their goods. Sometimes they leave free samples; other times they offer discount coupons. Bayer Healthcare, which manufactures K9 Advantix (for dogs) and Advantix (for cats), recently launched a new promotional campaign for its popular flea and tick repellent. The firm introduced three-dimensional promotional cards that sit on counters or tables in 14,000 vets' offices nationwide.

# Companies Promoting Pet Products: It's Not Puppy Love

The cards display key images that also appear in Advantix commercials on television. For instance, the card for K9 Advantix shows a puppy asleep in a tent. The tagline reads, "Get rid of fleas, ticks, and mosquitoes and you're left with one happy camper." The cards are easy to ship and simple for veterinary staff to set up. They arrive flat in a box and pop up to create a shadow-box display on the counter. Why put such effort into designing this type of display? "Our number-one goal with this year's program was to have our P-O-P [point-of-purchase] match identically with our visuals," explains marketing manager Drew Mantek. "We wanted to enhance our brand recognition in the clinics, which can be difficult. Even if they don't remember the name of the product, consumers can connect the images from the TV ads to the pieces they see in the clinic."

Pet owners may also watch a K9 Advantix advertising DVD on PetCARE television while they are waiting in the reception area of a vet clinic. PetCARE TV focuses on veterinary healthcare issues and is obtained through a yearly subscription. DVDs like the K9 commercial are shipped to veterinarians monthly.

Sometimes the pet care industry bares its teeth. Recently Meriel, maker of Frontline Plus, which competes directly with Bayer's Advantix, filed a lawsuit against Bayer, alleging unfair competition. The manufacture of flea and tick medicines is part of a multibillion-dollar market—more than $8.5 billion of nonfood pet supplies are sold in one year in the United States. With more than 146 million pets living with U.S. families, the market keeps growing—and every company wants its share. Because pet owners rely heavily on the opinions of their veterinarians, these companies want to create every advantage they can with vets and other animal health professionals. "If a vet tells [an owner] one thing over another, it's the gospel," notes an appointment supervisor for an office of nine vets. The Meriel lawsuit centered on Bayer's use of comparison advertising. As a result, Bayer agreed to withdraw its comparison of Advantix and Frontline in its advertising campaign. But the sleeping puppy remains, and consumers can pick up coupons for free products with another purchase when they read the counter cards at the vet's office. Marketer Drew Mantek says the campaign has been an early success. "The [displays] are appreciated for being appropriately sized for the clinic," he remarks. "And everyone gets a chuckle out of the images."[1]

This chapter focuses on the different types of promotional activities and the way prices are established for goods and services. **Promotion** is the function of informing, persuading, and influencing a purchase decision. This activity is as important to not-for-profit organizations such as the Boys and Girls Clubs and the Huntington's Disease Society of America as it is to profit-seeking companies such as Nationwide Insurance and the Boston Red Sox.

Some promotional strategies try to develop *primary demand,* or consumer desire for a general product category. The objective of such a campaign is to stimulate sales for an entire industry so that individual firms benefit from this market growth. A popular example is the dairy industry's "Got Milk?" campaign. Print and television messages about the nutritional benefits of milk show various celebrities, including Green Bay Packers quarterback Brett Favre and TV host Meredith Vieira. The American Heart Association has also become a part of these ads. Other promotional campaigns aimed at hiking per-capita consumption have been commissioned by the California Strawberry Commission and the National Cattlemen's Beef Association.

Most promotional strategies, in contrast, seek to stimulate *selective demand*—desire for a specific brand. Every driver needs some type of car insurance, and the Geico gecko wants consumers to pick its firm for the best rates.

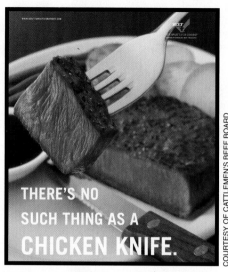

THERE'S NO SUCH THING AS A CHICKEN KNIFE.

America's Beef Producers hope to stimulate the overall demand for beef with this advertisement. So it helps increase primary demand.

COURTESY OF CATTLEMEN'S BEEF BOARD

Sean "P. Diddy" Combs appears in Diet Pepsi commercials, which encourages his fans to choose that brand over competitors. Sales promotions that offer teens a free iTunes song download for trying on a pair of Gap jeans also encourage shoppers to purchase a specific brand.

Marketers choose among many promotional options to communicate with potential customers. Each marketing message a buyer receives—through a television or radio commercial, newspaper or magazine ad, Web site, direct-mail flyer, or sales call—reflects on the product, place, person, cause, or organization promoted in the content. In a process of **integrated marketing communications (IMC),** marketers coordinate all promotional activities—advertising, sales promotion, personal sales presentations, and public relations—to execute a unified, customer-focused promotional strategy. This coordination is designed to avoid confusing the consumer and to focus positive attention on the promotional message.

This chapter begins by explaining the role of IMC and then discusses the objectives of promotion and the importance of promotional planning. Next, it examines the components of the promotional mix: advertising, sales promotion, personal selling, and public relations. Finally, the chapter addresses pricing strategies for goods and services.

**promotion** the function of informing, persuading, and influencing a purchase decision.

**integrated marketing communications (IMC)** coordination of all promotional activities—media advertising, direct mail, personal selling, sales promotion, and public relations—to produce a unified customer-focused message.

**"They Said It"**

"Doing business without advertising is like winking at a girl in the dark. You know what you are doing, but nobody else does."
—Steuart Henderson Britt (1907–1979)
American educator

# *INTEGRATED MARKETING COMMUNICATIONS*

An integrated marketing communications strategy focuses on customer needs to create a unified promotional message in the firm's ads, in-store displays, product samples, and presentations by company sales representatives. To gain a competitive advantage, marketers that implement IMC need a broad view of promotion. Media options continue to multiply, and marketers cannot simply rely on traditional broadcast and print media and direct mail. Plans must include all forms of customer contact. Packaging, store displays, sales promotions, sales presentations, and online and interactive media also communicate information about a brand or organization. With IMC, marketers create a unified personality and message for the good, brand, or service they promote. Coordinated activities also enhance the effectiveness of reaching and serving target markets.

Marketing managers set the goals and objectives for the firm's promotional strategy with overall organizational objectives and marketing goals in mind. Based on these objectives, marketers weave the various elements of the strategy—personal selling, advertising, sales promotion, publicity, and public relations—into an integrated communications plan. This document becomes a central part of the firm's total marketing strategy to reach its selected target market. Feedback, including marketing research and sales reports, completes the system by identifying any deviations from the plan and suggesting improvements.

With hundreds of different soft drink brands and flavors lining store shelves around the world, how does Coca-Cola manage to stay on top? When the firm rolled out its new flavored soft drink—Coca-Cola with Lime—it relied on IMC to get the word out to consumers. The company used TV advertising, billboards, and tie-ins to the popular *American Idol* TV show, which has had a long-running partnership with Coke. One of the ads featured an adaptation of the 1971 hit song *Coconut* by Harry Nilsson. The words for the Coke ad sang, "You put the lime in the Coke, you nut." Bottlers also used promotional strategies at the local level—offering free samples at fairs and festivals, sponsoring music or sporting events, and the like.[2]

# THE PROMOTIONAL MIX

Just as every organization creates a marketing mix combining product, distribution, promotion, and pricing strategies, each also requires a similar mix to blend the many facets of promotion into a cohesive plan. The **promotional mix** consists of two components—personal and nonpersonal selling—that marketers combine to meet the needs of their firm's target customers and effectively and efficiently communicate its message to them. **Personal selling** is the most basic form of promotion: a direct person-to-person promotional presentation to a potential buyer. The buyer-seller communication can occur during a face-to-face meeting or via telephone, videoconference, or interactive computer link.

**Nonpersonal selling** consists of advertising, sales promotion, direct marketing, and public relations. Advertising is the best-known form of nonpersonal selling, but sales promotion accounts for about half of these marketing expenditures. Spending for sponsorships, which involves marketing messages delivered in association with another activity such as a golf tournament or a benefit concert, is on the rise as well. Marketers need to be careful about the types of promotion they choose or risk alienating the very people they are trying to reach.

Each component in the promotional mix offers its own advantages and disadvantages, as Table 14.1 demonstrates. By selecting the most effective combination of promotional mix elements, a firm may reach its promotional objectives. Spending within the promotional mix varies by industry. Manufacturers of many business-to-business (B2B) products typically spend more on personal selling than on advertising because those products—such as a new telecommunications system—may require a significant investment. Consumer-goods marketers may focus more on advertising and sponsorships. Later sections of this chapter discuss how the parts of the mix contribute to effective promotion.

**promotional mix** combination of personal and nonpersonal selling techniques designed to achieve promotional objectives.

**personal selling** interpersonal promotional process involving a seller's face-to-face presentation to a prospective buyer.

Table

14.1

Comparing the Components of the Promotional Mix

| Component | Advantages | Disadvantages |
|---|---|---|
| Advertising | Reaches large consumer audience at low cost per contact<br>Allows strong control of the message<br>Message can be modified to match different audiences | Difficult to measure effectiveness<br>Limited value for closing sales |
| Personal selling | Message can be tailored for each customer<br>Produces immediate buyer response<br>Effectiveness is easily measured | High cost per contact<br>High expense and difficulty of attracting and retaining effective salespeople |
| Sales promotion | Attracts attention and creates awareness<br>Effectiveness is easily measured<br>Produces short-term sales increases | Difficult to differentiate from similar programs of competitors<br>Nonpersonal appeal |
| Public relations | Enhances product or company credibility<br>Creates a positive attitude about the product or company | Difficult to measure effectiveness<br>Often devoted to nonmarketing activities |
| Sponsorships | Viewed positively by consumers<br>Enhances brand awareness | Difficult to control message |

Figure

14.1

Five Major Promotional Objectives

DIFFERENTIATE PRODUCT
Example: Television ad comparing performance of two leading laundry detergents

PROVIDE INFORMATION
Example: Print ad describing features and availability of a new breakfast cereal

STABILIZE SALES — Example: Even out sales patterns by promoting low weekend rates for hotels, holding contests during slow sales periods, or advertising cold fruit soups during summer months

INCREASE SALES
Example: End-of-aisle grocery displays, or "end caps," to encourage impulse purchases

ACCENTUATE PRODUCT VALUE
Example: Warranty programs and guarantees that make a product more attractive than its major competitors

## Objectives of Promotional Strategy

Promotional strategy objectives vary among organizations. Some use promotion to expand their markets, and others use it to defend their current positions. As Figure 14.1 illustrates, common objectives include providing information, differentiating a product, increasing sales, stabilizing sales, and accentuating a product's value.

Marketers often pursue multiple promotional objectives at the same time. To promote its Microsoft Office software, Microsoft has to convince business owners, who buy the software, and their employees, who use the software, that the product is a worthwhile investment.

Marketers need to keep their firm's promotional objectives in mind at all times. Sometimes the objectives are obscured by a fast-paced, creative ad campaign. In this case, the message—or worse, the brand name or image—is lost. One example is a series of ads run by Vonage for its voice-over Internet protocol telephone services. The ads contain segments of home videos showing silly capers that are so distracting it's hard to remember the message—that the service allows consumers to make unlimited phone calls in the United States and Canada for $24.99 a month.[3]

**Providing Information** A major portion of U.S. advertising is information oriented. Credit card ads provide information about benefits and rates. Ads for hair-care products include information about benefits such as shine and volume. Ads for breakfast cereals often contain nutritional information. Based on new informational guidelines developed by the pharmaceutical industry, drug manufacturer Pfizer has pledged to submit all new TV ads to the U.S. Food and Drug Administration for review and will refrain from advertising new drugs directly to consumers for the first six months. The firm also plans to create more disease-awareness ads that do not mention branded products, along with ads that increase awareness of its discount programs for people without insurance coverage.[4]

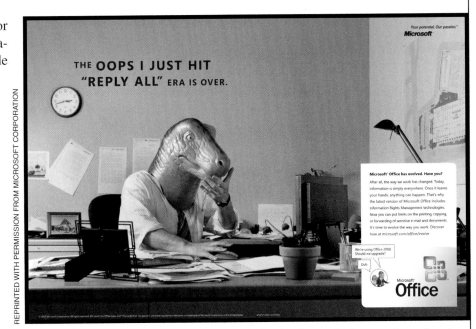

REPRINTED WITH PERMISSION FROM MICROSOFT CORPORATION

Microsoft promotes its latest upgrade to Microsoft Office by showing both companies and workers the benefits of its new features. Mistakes such as sending e-mails to everyone is a practice it considers prehistoric.

**Differentiating a Product** Promotion can also be used to differentiate a firm's offerings from the competition. Applying a concept called **positioning,** marketers attempt to establish their products in the minds of customers. The idea is to communicate to buyers meaningful distinctions about the attributes, price, quality, or use of a good or service.

When you set out to purchase a car, you have hundreds from which to choose. How do you decide which one to buy? Carmakers do their best to differentiate their vehicles by style, performance, safety features, and price. They must make their vehicles stand out to individual consumers. "Just going out there . . . with a big broad market message can mean a company runs the risk of speaking to everyone and speaking to no one at the same time," warns Rick Wainschel, vice president of marketing research at Kelley Blue Book, the organization that provides pricing information for new and used cars. Recent studies show that fuel efficiency, price, durability, and style are important distinguishing factors for U.S. consumers.[5]

**Increasing Sales** Increasing sales volume is the most common objective of a promotional strategy. Naturalizer became the third-largest seller of women's dress shoes by appealing to baby boomers. But as these women have grown older, they have bought fewer pairs of shoes each year. Naturalizer wants to keep these customers but also attract the younger generation. So the firm developed a new line of trendy shoes. The promotional strategy included ads in magazines read by younger women—such as *Elle* and *Marie Claire*—featuring young women in beach attire and Naturalizer shoes. The response to this strategy was a substantial increase in Naturalizer's sales through department stores.

**Stabilizing Sales** Sales stabilization is another goal of promotional strategy. Firms often use sales contests during slack periods, motivating salespeople by offering prizes such as vacations, TVs, camera phones, and cash to those who meet certain goals. Companies distribute sales promotion materials—such as calendars, pens, and notepads—to customers to stimulate sales during the off-season. Jiffy Lube puts that little sticker on your windshield to remind you when to have your car's next oil change—the regular visits help stabilize sales. A stable sales pattern brings several advantages. It evens out the production cycle, reduces some management and production costs, and simplifies financial, purchasing, and marketing planning. An effective promotional strategy can contribute to these goals.

7-Eleven has been advertising its Slurpee to a whole new generation hooked on smoothies and Frappuccinos. The Slurpee is 40 years old but is just as fun as it always was—producing colored tongues and brain freezes. "We've kept it fun with the interesting flavors we've had over the years," says CEO Jim Keyes. "At the heart of it, it's just a fun product that people enjoy." Since 1965, more than 6 billion Slurpees have been sold in seventeen countries. Sales in the United States alone top $170 million each year.[6]

*Accentuating the Product's Value*  Some promotional strategies enhance product values by explaining hidden benefits of ownership. Carmakers offer long-term warranty programs; life insurance companies promote certain policies as investments. The creation of brand awareness and brand loyalty also enhances a product's image and increases its desirability. Advertising with luxurious images supports the reputation of premium brands like Jaguar, Tiffany, and Rolex.

## Promotional Planning

Today's marketers can promote their products in many ways, and the lines between the different elements of the promotional mix are blurring. Consider the practice of **product placement.** A growing number of marketers pay placement fees to have their products showcased in various media, ranging from newspapers and magazines to television and movies. Martha Stewart's new syndicated show features General Electric kitchen appliances and food products from Procter & Gamble.[7] The "Hit & Miss" feature describes the leap of product placement from movies into video games. However, television shows and movies account for 90 percent of all product placements.[8]

Another type of promotional planning must be considered by firms with small budgets. **Guerrilla marketing** is innovative, low-cost marketing efforts designed to get consumers' attention in unusual ways. Guerrilla marketing is an increasingly popular tactic for marketers, especially those with limited promotional budgets. Attleboro, Massachusetts–based Willow Tree Poultry Farm hired a well-known chef to develop new recipes and menus featuring its chicken salad and pot pies. Entrepreneur Mark Vinci used guerrilla marketing to launch his own marketing business, K9 Billboards. Vinci lives in New York, and everywhere he takes his Akita puppy, Ling Ling, passersby seem to want to stop to pet her or talk with him. So many people were drawn to his dog it occurred to him that if he could put a brand banner on her, maybe people would be drawn to the brand. He started with a banner for a local ski resort, which was a huge hit with skiers.

Marketers for larger companies have caught on and are using guerrilla approaches as well. Nissan turned six locations in New York and Los Angeles into movie sets with melted props—parking meters, trash cans, and bicycles—near a "hot" Maxima. Called its "Touch" campaign, Nissan wanted passersby to walk past the display and touch the car. "The street scene ties it all together," explained Fred Suckow, director of Nissan marketing.[9]

From this overview of the promotional mix, we now turn to discussions of each of its elements. The following sections detail the major components of advertising, sales promotion, personal selling, and public relations.

**assessment check**

1. Which component of the promotional mix reaches the largest audience?
2. Why do firms pursue multiple promotional objectives at the same time?
3. What are product placement and guerrilla marketing?

## HIT & MISS

### Product Placement—A Virtual Success

Product placement has been around for decades. E.T. ate Reese's Pieces simply because Mars turned down the opportunity to have him eat M&M's. Hungry *Survivor* contestants descend on a variety of branded snacks and soft drinks after winning a challenge. Pepsi has been placed in more top films than any other soft drink brand. Product placement has become its own business, so it stands to reason that the practice has taken the next big leap—a virtual one.

Products are now appearing in video games. Electronic Arts, the world's largest video game publisher, made product placements for its Need for Speed Underground 2 game for companies such as Best Buy, Cingular Wireless, Burger King, and even Old Spice. The company reports that its ad revenues have increased 60 percent since it began placing products in its games. In EA's Sims Online, game players use computers that emit familiar Intel tones, and they can buy McDonald's burgers for their hungry Sims characters.

Product placement in video games has become so popular that firms such as Massive are developing software that allows advertisers to update their ads even after a game has been released. If the product comes in a new version or updated package, the advertiser can make the change. In addition, the software allows for customized ads aimed at each player who is using the computer. You might encounter a product placement ad for a CD or a snowboard; your dad might come across one for retirement investments.

Some firms have actually encountered too much of a good thing, though. Vivendi Universal Games found itself turning companies away from product placement opportunities. When alcohol advertisers tried to place their products in Vivendi's Leisure Suit Larry game, the firm said no. Vivendi also denied requests for footwear companies to have the characters wear branded shoes.

Naturally, product placement comes at a price. When determining the fee for product placement, marketers consider such factors as how prominent the product will be, how often a character uses the product, and why the product is being placed in the game or show.

### Questions for Critical Thinking

1. Do you think product placement is more effective than traditional advertising? Why or why not?
2. Describe two or three factors—in addition to those already mentioned—that might determine the price of a virtual product placement ad.

**Sources:** Apryl Duncan, "Product Placement Makes a Virtual Leap," About.com, accessed July 18, 2006, http://advertising.about.com; Abram Sauer, "Brand Channel's 2004 Product Placement Awards," Brandchannel.com, accessed July 18, 2006, http://www.brandchannel.com; Ellen Neuborne, "Ready for Your Product's Close-Up?" *Inc.*, October 2004, pp. 48–50.

## ADVERTISING

Consumers receive somewhere between 3,500 and 5,000 marketing messages each day, many of them in the form of advertising.[10] Advertising is the most visible form of nonpersonal promotion—and the most effective for many firms. **Advertising** refers to paid nonpersonal communication usually targeted at large numbers of potential buyers. Although U.S. citizens often think of advertising as a typically American function, it is a global activity. Seven of the top 20 advertisers in the United States are headquartered in other countries: DaimlerChrysler, GlaxoSmithKline, Toyota, Sony, Nissan, L'Oréal, and Unilever. The top five advertisers in the United States are, in order, General Motors, Procter & Gamble, Time Warner, Pfizer, and AT&T.[11]

**advertising** paid nonpersonal communication delivered through various media and designed to inform, persuade, or remind members of a particular audience.

Advertising expenditures vary among industries, companies, and media. Automotive, retail, and telecommunications take top honors for spending in the United States—carmakers spend a whopping $20 billion per year. Top advertiser General Motors—an auto manufacturer—spends nearly $4 billion a year. Network TV still ranks highest in advertising media

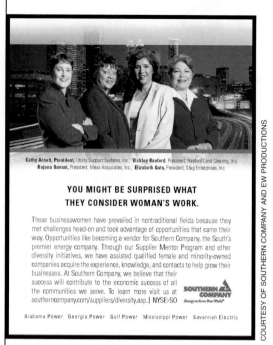

**Cathy Arnett, President,** Utility Support Systems, Inc.; **Vickley Raeford,** President, Raeford Land Clearing, Inc. **Rajana Savant,** President, Mesa Associates, Inc.; **Elizabeth Gats,** President, Stag Enterprises, Inc.

**YOU MIGHT BE SURPRISED WHAT
THEY CONSIDER WOMAN'S WORK.**

These businesswomen have prevailed in nontraditional fields because they met challenges head-on and took advantage of opportunities that came their way. Opportunities like becoming a vendor for Southern Company, the South's premier energy company. Through our Supplier Mentor Program and other diversity initiatives, we have assisted qualified female and minority-owned companies acquire the experience, knowledge, and contacts to help grow their businesses. At Southern Company, we believe that their success will contribute to the economic success of all the communities we serve. To learn more visit us at southerncompany.com/suppliers/diversity.asp. | NYSE>SO

**SOUTHERN COMPANY**
*Energy to Serve Your World®*

Alabama Power   Georgia Power   Gulf Power   Mississippi Power   Savannah Electric

Energy firm Southern Company promotes its commitment to cultivating women's careers through its Supplier Mentor Program, as well as other diversity initiatives. Such a promotion is an example of institutional advertising.

revenues, at $22 billion.[12] Because advertising expenditures are so great, and because consumers are bombarded with so many messages, firms need to be more and more creative and efficient at getting consumers' attention.

## Types of Advertising

The two basic types of ads are product and institutional advertisements. **Product advertising** consists of messages designed to sell a particular good or service. Advertisements for Nantucket Nectars, iPods, and Capital One credit cards are examples of product advertising. **Institutional advertising** involves messages that promote concepts, ideas, philosophies, or goodwill for industries, companies, organizations, or government entities. Each year, the Juvenile Diabetes Research Foundation promotes its "Walk for the Cure" fund-raising event, and your college may place advertisements in local papers or news shows to promote its activities.

A form of institutional advertising that is growing in importance, **cause advertising,** promotes a specific viewpoint on a public issue as a way to influence public opinion and the legislative process about issues such as literacy, hunger and poverty, and alternative energy sources. Both not-for-profit organizations and businesses use cause advertising, sometimes called *advocacy advertising.* The massive destruction to Louisiana, Mississippi, and Alabama caused by Hurricane Katrina spawned a slew of cause advertisements to raise funds for aid to victims of the storm. Within days, telethons were announced by major networks and their local affiliates. A special program, "A Concert for Hurricane Relief," was aired on NBC, MSNBC, and CNBC, featuring musicians such as Tim McGraw, Harry Connick Jr., Wynton Marsalis, and Green Day. The concert raised funds for the American Red Cross and other relief organizations.[13]

## Advertising and the Product Life Cycle

Both product and institutional advertising fall into one of three categories based on whether the ads are intended to inform, persuade, or remind. A firm uses *informative advertising* to build initial demand for a product in the introductory phase of the product life cycle. Highly publicized new-product entries attract the interest of potential buyers who seek information about the advantages of the new products over existing ones, warranties provided, prices, and places that offer the new products. When Motorola and Apple introduced their Rokr iTunes cell phone, the companies immediately provided the public with the product's details—that it could store up to 100 songs and had a color screen, stereo speakers, stereo headphones, and a camera.[14]

*Persuasive advertising* attempts to improve the competitive status of a product, institution, or concept, usually in the growth and maturity stages of the product life cycle. One of the most popular types of persuasive product advertising, *comparative advertising,* compares products directly with their competitors—either by name or by inference. Tylenol advertisements mention the possible stomach problems that aspirin could cause, stating that its pain reliever does not irritate the stomach. But advertisers need to be careful when they name competing brands in comparison ads because they might leave themselves open to controversy or even legal action by competitors. Possibly for that reason, Tylenol does not mention a specific aspirin brand in its promotions.

*Reminder-oriented advertising* often appears in the late maturity or decline stages of the product life cycle to maintain awareness of the importance and usefulness of a product, concept, or institution. Triscuits have been around for a long time, but Nabisco is attempting to mobilize sales with up-to-date advertising that appeals to health and fitness–conscious consumers.

## Advertising Media

Marketers must choose how to allocate their advertising budgets among various media. All media offer advantages and disadvantages. Cost is an important consideration in media selection, but marketers must also choose the media best suited for communicating their message. As Figure 14.2 indicates, advertising on television, through direct mail, in newspapers, and in magazines represent the four leading media outlets. However, online interactive advertising is growing fast. Consumers now receive ads when they download news and other information to their handheld wireless devices.

Advertising executives agree that firms need to rethink traditional ad campaigns to incorporate new media as well as updated uses of traditional media. "Today you need a great idea, and you can work out which media types will reflect it," says John Hunt, chief creative officer of international advertising firm TBWA/Chiat/Day. Some ad agencies have developed ways to incorporate adaptive technology with which advertisers can digitally alter television commercials for different markets. Other advertisers are placing more emphasis on the Internet. "The consumer that comes to your Web site is actively looking for you, and that's the best media deal you can make," says Bob Lachky, head of marketing for Anheuser-Busch.[15]

*Television* Television is still one of America's leading national advertising media. Television advertising can be classified as network, national, local, and cable ads. The four major national networks—ABC, CBS, NBC, and Fox—along with CW, broadcast almost one-fifth of all television ads. Despite a decline in audience share and growing competition from cable, network television remains the easiest way for advertisers to reach large numbers of viewers—10 million to 20 million with a single commercial. Automakers, fast-food restaurants, and food manufacturers are heavy users of network TV advertising.

Nearly two-thirds of U.S. households with TVs now subscribe to cable, drawn to the dozens or even hundreds of channels available through cable or satellite services.[16] As these services broaden their offerings to Internet and interactive programming, their audience is expected to continue growing. The variety of channels on cable and satellite networks lets advertisers target specialized markets and reach selected demographic groups, such as consumers who watch the Outdoor Life Network. BMW, maker of the Mini Cooper, has combined interactive Internet advertising with traditional TV ads that appear on the cable channels E!, History Channel, ESPN, and MTV.[17] Cable companies such as Comcast, Time Warner, Cox, and Charter are launching technologies that send different advertising messages to different neighborhoods.[18] Even TiVo, once famous for making it possible to help consumers skip commercials, is now promoting them. The firm plans to insert symbols that identify advertisers during commercial breaks so that viewers can watch commercials if they choose. "TiVo's proprietary advertising technology presents a real opportunity for advertisers to enhance the effectiveness of traditional television advertising," claims its CFO, David Courtney.[19]

Although television reaches the greatest number of consumers at once, it is the most expensive advertising medium. The price to air a 30-second ad during weeknight prime time

**14.2**

Carving up the Advertising Media Pie

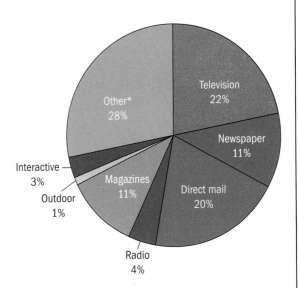

*An additional 28 percent is spent on such miscellaneous media as Yellow Pages listings, Spanish-language media, business papers, transit displays, point-of-purchase displays, cinema advertising, and regional farm papers.

**Source:** Advertising Age, "Domestic Advertising Spending Totals," *Special Report: Profiles Supplement, 100 Leading National Advertisers,* June 27, 2005, p. 4.

on network television generally ranges from $100,000 to more than $500,000 for the most popular shows. Super Bowl ads have been known to command prices of more than $2 million. So marketers want to be certain that their commercials reach the greatest number of viewers. Because of the high cost, advertisers may demand guarantees of audience size and receive compensation if a show fails to deliver the promised number of viewers.

*Newspapers* Daily and weekly newspapers continue to dominate local advertising. Marketers can easily tailor newspaper advertising for local tastes and preferences. Advertisers can also coordinate advertisements with other promotional efforts such as discount coupons from supermarkets and one-day sales at department stores. A disadvantage comes from the relatively short life span; people usually discard their newspapers soon after reading. Retailers and automobile dealers rank first among newspaper advertisers. Most newspapers now maintain Web sites, some of which offer separate material and features, to complement their print editions.

*Radio* Despite the proliferation of other media, the average U.S. household owns five radios—including those in cars—a market penetration that makes radio an important advertising medium. Advertisers like the captive audience of listeners as they commute to and from work. As a result, morning and evening drive-time shows command top ad rates. In major markets, many stations serve different demographic groups with targeted programming. The potential of the Internet to deliver radio programming also offers opportunities for yet more focused targeting. "Many companies have built their businesses on radio advertising," says Hugh Dow, president of media company M2 Universal. "It's a very important medium for many advertisers, particularly many retail advertisers."[20]

Satellite stations have great potential for advertisers. Although Sirius satellite radio—which offers 120 stations to consumers' cars, home, and boats—promises 100 percent commercial-free programming, the station's Web page contains promotions such as sweepstakes and rebates for subscribers. [21]

*Magazines* Magazines include consumer publications and business trade journals. *Time, Reader's Digest,* and *Sports Illustrated* are consumer magazines, whereas *Advertising Age* and *Oil & Gas Journal* fall into the trade category.

Magazines may customize their publications and target advertising messages to different regions of the country. One method places local advertising in regional editions of the magazine. Other magazines attach wraparounds—half-size covers on top of full-size covers—to highlight articles inside that relate to particular areas; different wraparounds appear in different parts of the country.

Magazines are a natural choice for targeted advertising. Media buyers study demographics of subscribers and select magazines that attract the desired readers. American Express advertises in *Fortune* and *Forbes* to reach businesspeople, while PacSun clothes and Clearasil skin medications are advertised in *teenVogue*.

*Direct Mail* The average American household receives about 550 pieces of direct mail each year, including 100 catalogs. The huge growth in the variety of direct-mail offerings combined with the convenience they offer to today's busy, time-pressed shoppers has made direct-mail advertising a multibillion-dollar

Etnies Girl Skate Shoes targets fashion-conscious teens with ads in magazines like *teenVogue* and *Seventeen*.

business. Even consumers who like to shop online often page through a catalog before placing an online order. Although direct mail is expensive per person, a small business may be able to spend less on a limited direct-mail campaign than on a television or radio ad. For businesses with a small advertising budget, a carefully targeted direct-mail effort can be highly effective. E-mail is a low-cost form of direct marketing. Marketers can target the most interested Internet users by offering Web site visitors an option to register to receive e-mail. Companies like Amazon.com, Spring Hill Nurseries, and Abercrombie & Fitch routinely send e-mail to regular customers.

Address lists are at the heart of direct-mail advertising. Using data-mining techniques to segment markets, direct-mail marketers create profiles that show the traits of consumers who are likely to buy their products or donate to their organizations. Catalog retailers sometimes experiment by sending direct-mail pieces randomly to people who subscribe to particular magazines. Next, they analyze the orders received from the mailings and develop profiles of purchasers. Finally, they rent lists of additional subscriber names that match the profiles they have developed.

Studies have shown that most U.S. consumers are annoyed by the amount of "junk mail" they receive every day, including catalogs, advertising postcards, and flyers. Among Internet users, a major pet peeve is *spam,* or junk e-mail. Many states have outlawed such practices as sending e-mail promotions without legitimate return addresses, although it is difficult to track down and catch offenders.

The Direct Marketing Association (DMA; http://www.the-dma.org) helps marketers combat negative attitudes by offering its members guidelines on ethical business practices. The DMA also provides consumer information at its Web site, as well as services that enable consumers to opt out of receiving unsolicited offers. In addition, new Federal Trade Commission regulations have taken effect for direct mail in certain industries. Now when you receive that unsolicited, preapproved credit card application in the mail, it must be accompanied by a prominent notice telling you how to get off the bank's mailing list. This law will affect millions of consumers, because 5.8 applications are received by each household every month—or 1.4 billion applications per quarter.[22]

***Outdoor Advertising*** Outdoor advertising accounts for about $3.2 billion in advertising expenditures. The majority of spending on outdoor advertising is for billboards, but spending for other types of outdoor advertising, such as signs in transit stations, stores, airports, and sports stadiums, is growing fast. Advertisers are exploring new forms of outdoor media, many of which involve technology: computerized paintings, video billboards, "trivision" that displays three revolving images on a single billboard, and moving billboards mounted on trucks. Other innovations include displaying ads on the Goodyear blimp, using an electronic system that offers animation and video. And there's the traditional banner flying behind a plane, or skywriting.[23] There's also K9 Billboards, described earlier in the chapter. Outdoor advertising suffers from several disadvantages, however. The medium requires brief messages, and billboards are subject to opposition by preservation and conservation groups.

***Online and Interactive Advertising*** Marketing experts predict that sales from online advertising will double by 2010. Search engine marketing, display ads, and even classified ads are expected to surge.[24]

Online and interactive media have already changed the nature of advertising. Starting with simple banner ads, Internet advertising has become much more complex and sophisticated. Burger King created a media buzz when its Web site featured a Subservient Chicken—a man in a silly chicken suit—who responded to commands typed in by consumers. The ad campaign was such an Internet hit that the company followed it will a boxing match on DirecTV between boxers dressed as chickens—representing different BK chicken sandwiches. Russ

Klein, Burger King's chief marketing officer, is realistic about the future of the nontraditional ad. "In another 10 to 15 years all this stuff will be as normal as talking 30-second ads," he predicts.[25] Before that happens, marketers will be well on their way to coming up with something new.

Subservient Chicken is an example of *viral advertising,* which creates a message that is novel or entertaining enough for consumers to forward it to others, spreading it like a virus. The great advantage is that spreading the word costs the advertiser nothing. Another fast-food restaurant chain, Long John Silver's, recently launched a Web site called ShrimpBuddy.com to promote its Popcorn Shrimp. The site features a two-minute film about a road trip by a guy and his best buddy—who happens to be a shrimp. The ad appealed to young, hip consumers who are Web savvy and have a sense of humor—just the target market that the company hoped to reach.[26]

However, not all online advertising is well received. Like spam, many consumers resent the intrusion of *pop-up ads* that suddenly appear on their computer screen. These ads can be difficult to ignore, remove, or pass by. Some Internet service providers, such as Earthlink, have turned this problem into a marketing advantage by offering service that comes without pop-ups. "You'll never log-on and be greeted by an Earthlink pop-up ad. Your address comes with spam-reducing tools and eight mailboxes," its ads promise.

*Sponsorship*    One of the hottest trends in promotion offers marketers the ability to integrate several elements of the promotional mix. **Sponsorship** involves providing funds for a sporting or cultural event in exchange for a direct association with the event. Sports sponsorships attract two-thirds of total sponsorship dollars in the U.S. alone. Entertainment, festivals, causes, and the arts divide up the remaining third of sponsorship dollars.

NASCAR, the biggest spectator sport in the United States, thrives on sponsorships. Because it can cost as much as $20 million a year to run a top NASCAR team, drivers depend on sponsorships from companies to keep the wheels turning. Firms may also sponsor charitable or other not-for-profit awards or events. In conjunction with sports network ESPN, Gatorade sponsors its High School Athlete of the Year award, presented to the top male and female high school athletes who "strive for their best on and off the field."

Sponsors benefit in two major ways: exposure to the event's audience and association with the image of the activity. If a celebrity is involved, sponsors usually earn the right to use his or her name along with the name of the event in advertisements. They can set up signs at the event, offer sales promotions, and the like. Sponsorships play an important role in relationship marketing, bringing together the event, its participants, and the sponsoring firms.

AP PHOTO/DAMIAN DOVARGANES

For two decades, Gatorade has sponsored the High School Athlete of the Year awards. The awards are given to the top male and female who strive to be the best both on and off the field.

*Other Media Options*    As consumers filter out familiar advertising messages, marketers look for novel ways to catch their attention. In addition to the major media, firms promote through many other vehicles such as infomercials and specialized media. **Infomercials** are a form of broadcast direct marketing, also called *direct response television (DRTV).* These 30-minute programs resemble regular television programs, but are devoted to selling goods or services such as exercise equipment, skin-care products, or kitchenware. The long format allows an advertiser to thoroughly present product benefits, increase awareness, and make an impact on consumers. Advertisers also receive immediate responses in the form of sales or inquiries because most infomercials feature toll-free phone numbers. Infomercial stars may become celebrities in their own right, attracting more customers wherever they go. That's what happened to John Carleo, featured in infomercials for the Total Gym. Carleo can be seen demonstrating the exercise machine alongside supermodel Christie Brinkley and actor Chuck Norris. "It got me national recognition," says Carleo. "No matter where I go, someone will come up and say, 'Hey I know you, you're the Total Gym Guy.'" The recognition keeps the Total Gym in the minds of consumers, long after the infomercial is over.[27]

Advertisers use just about any medium they can find. They place messages on subway tickets in New York City and toll receipts on the Massachusetts Turnpike. A more recent development is the use of ATMs for advertising. Some ATMs can play 15-second commercials on their screens, and many can print advertising messages on receipts. An ATM screen has a captive audience because the user must watch the screen to complete a transaction. Directory advertising includes the familiar Yellow Pages listings in telephone books and thousands of other types of directories, most presenting business-related promotions. About 6 percent of total advertising revenue goes to Yellow Pages ads. Besides local and regional directories, publishers also have produced special versions of the Yellow Pages that target ethnic groups.

**assessment check**

1. What are the two basic types of advertising? Into what three categories do they fall?
2. What is the leading advertising medium in the United States?
3. In what two major ways do firms benefit from sponsorship?

# SALES PROMOTION

Traditionally viewed as a supplement to a firm's sales or advertising efforts, sales promotion has emerged as an integral part of the promotional mix. Promotion now accounts for close to half as many marketing dollars as are spent on advertising, and promotion spending is rising faster than ad spending. **Sales promotion** consists of forms of promotion such as coupons, product samples, and rebates that support advertising and personal selling.

Both retailers and manufacturers use sales promotions to offer consumers extra incentives to buy. Beyond the short-term advantage of increased sales, sales promotions can also help marketers build brand equity and enhance customer relationships. Examples include samples, coupons, contests, displays, trade shows, and dealer incentives.

## Consumer-Oriented Promotions

The goal of a consumer-oriented sales promotion is to get new and existing customers to try or buy products. In addition, marketers want to encourage repeat purchases by rewarding current users, increase sales of complementary products, and boost impulse purchases. Figure 14.3 shows how marketers allocate their consumer-oriented spending among the categories of promotions.

**Premiums, Coupons, Rebates, and Samples** Two of every five sales promotion dollars are spent on *premiums*—items given free or at a reduced price with the purchase of another product. Cosmetics companies such as Clinique offer sample kits with purchases of their products. Fast-food restaurants are also big users of premiums. McDonald's and Burger King include a toy with every children's meal—the toys often tie in with new movies or popular

**sales promotion** nonpersonal marketing activities other than advertising, personal selling, and public relations that stimulate consumer purchasing and dealer effectiveness.

**Figure**

**14.3**

Spending on Consumer-Oriented Promotions

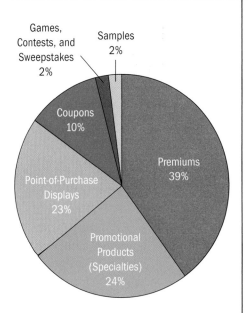

- Games, Contests, and Sweepstakes 2%
- Samples 2%
- Coupons 10%
- Point-of-Purchase Displays 23%
- Premiums 39%
- Promotional Products (Specialties) 24%

cartoon shows. In general, marketers choose premiums that are likely to get consumers thinking about and caring about the brand and the product. People who purchase health foods at a grocery store may find an offer for a free personal training session at a local health club printed on the back of their sales receipt.

Customers redeem *coupons* for small price discounts when they purchase the promoted products. Such offers may persuade a customer to try a new or different product. Some large supermarket chains double the face value of manufacturers' coupons. Coupons have the disadvantage of focusing customers on price rather than brand loyalty. Other discounters such as Wal-Mart prefer to lure customers with their own low-priced brands. While some consumers complain that clipping coupons is too time-consuming, others relish the savings, particularly when prices seem to be high. "Coupons are an age-old solid tactic to engage consumers to purchase products," says Claire Rosenzweig, president of the Promotion Marketing Association."[28]

*Rebates* offer cash back to consumers who mail in required proofs of purchase. Rebates help packaged-goods manufacturers increase purchase rates, promote multiple purchases, and reward product users. Other types of companies also offer rebates, especially for electronics, computers and their accessories, and automobiles. Processing rebates gives marketers a way to collect data about their customers. Recently, Aetna Insurance and drugstore chain Walgreens announced a plan to pass along rebates to companies that have employee prescription programs through the two firms.[29]

A *sample* is a gift of a product distributed by mail, door to door, in a demonstration, or inside packages of another product. On any given day you might receive a sample CD for Internet service, a bar of soap, or a packet of laundry detergent. Three of every four consumers who receive samples will try them.

### Games, Contests, and Sweepstakes

Contests, sweepstakes, and games offer cash, merchandise, or travel as prizes to participating winners. Firms often sponsor these activities to introduce new goods and services and to attract additional customers. Games and contests require entrants to solve problems or write essays and sometimes provide proof of purchase. Sweepstakes choose winners by chance and require no product purchase. Consumers typically prefer them because games and contests require more effort. Companies like sweepstakes, too, because they are inexpensive to run and determine the number of winners from the beginning. With games and contests, the company cannot predict the number of people who will correctly complete a puzzle or gather the right number of symbols from scratch-off cards. Sweepstakes, games, and contests can reinforce a company's image and advertising message, but consumer attention may focus on the promotion rather than the product.

In recent years, court rulings and legal restrictions have limited the use of games and contests. Companies must proceed carefully in advertising their contests and games and the prizes they award. Marketers must indicate the chances of winning and avoid false promises such as implying that a person has already won.

### Specialty Advertising

Do you have any pens, T-shirts, or refrigerator magnets imprinted with a business name that you received for free? These offers are examples of **specialty advertising** or *advertising specialties*. This type of sales promotion involves the gift of useful merchandise carrying the name, logo, or slogan of a profit-seeking business or a not-for-profit organization. Because those products are useful and sometimes personalized with recipients' names, people tend to keep and use them, giving advertisers repeated exposure. Originally designed to identify and create goodwill for advertisers, advertising specialties now generate sales leads and develop traffic for stores and trade show exhibitors. Like premiums, these promotions should reinforce the brand's image and its relationship with the recipient.

## Trade-Oriented Promotions

Sales promotion techniques can also contribute to campaigns directed to retailers and wholesalers. **Trade promotion** is sales promotion geared to marketing intermediaries rather than to consumers. Marketers use trade promotion to encourage retailers to stock new products, continue carrying existing ones, and promote both new and existing products effectively to consumers. Successful trade promotions offer financial incentives. They require careful timing, attention to costs, and easy implementation for intermediaries. These promotions should bring quick results and improve retail sales. Major trade promotions include point-of-purchase advertising and trade shows.

**Point-of-purchase (POP) advertising** consists of displays or demonstrations that promote products when and where consumers buy them, such as in retail stores. When the Swiffer floor cleaner was being introduced, Procter & Gamble used in-store demonstrations to show consumers how it worked. Marketing research has shown that consumers are more apt to purchase certain products when such displays are present. Sunscreen, painting supplies, and snacks are typically displayed this way. A high-tech version of POP advertising is the use of kiosks that display product information and promotional offers. Whether cardboard or electronic, POP advertising takes advantage of many shoppers' tendencies to make purchase decisions in the store.

Manufacturers and other sellers often exhibit at *trade shows* to promote goods or services to members of their distribution channels. These shows are often organized by industry trade associations, typically during annual meetings or conventions. Each year, thousands of trade shows attract millions of exhibitors and hundreds of millions of attendees. Such shows are particularly important in fast-changing industries like those for computers, toys, furniture, and fashions. The annual electronics show, which is held in Las Vegas and attracts more than 100,000 visitors, is the nation's largest. But shows in the medical and healthcare, RV and camping, and even woodworking machinery fields remain strong.[30] These shows are especially effective for introducing new products and generating sales leads.

# PERSONAL SELLING

Many companies consider personal selling—a person-to-person promotional presentation to a potential buyer—the key to marketing effectiveness. Unless a seller matches a firm's goods or services to the needs of a particular client or customer, none of the firm's other activities produce any benefits. Today, sales and sales-related jobs employ about 13.5 million Americans.[31] Businesses often spend five to ten times as much on personal selling as on advertising. Given the significant cost of hiring, training, benefits, and salaries, businesses are very concerned with the effectiveness of their sales personnel. One of the key tasks for a salesperson is to remember the names of customers and other contacts. The "Business Etiquette" feature provides some tips on remembering names.

How do marketers decide whether to make personal selling the primary component of their firm's marketing mix? In general, firms are likely to emphasize personal selling rather than advertising or sales promotion under four conditions:

1. Customers are relatively few in number and geographically concentrated.
2. The product is technically complex, involves trade-ins, and requires special handling.
3. The product carries a relatively high price.
4. It moves through direct-distribution channels.

A perfect example of the right situation for personal selling is when selling to the federal government or to the military, both of which have large purchasing requirements and follow

## How to Remember Names

It happens to everyone. You bump into someone on the street, in the library, or in the dorm lounge—and you draw a complete blank. You *know* this person, and yet you can't remember his or her name! So you fumble around, look at the floor, and mumble "hi." In business, it is especially important to remember people's names—not just your boss and co-workers, but customers, suppliers, and colleagues in other divisions. Since most of us aren't magicians, here are a few tips for pulling that elusive name out of the hat:

1. When you first meet someone, repeat his or her name several times, which will help emblazon the name and face together in your memory. You don't have to be obvious about it. You can say, "It's a pleasure to meet you, Gabrielle," and "I hope to see you again, Luis."

2. If appropriate, ask the person one or two questions that will help secure details in your memory. Questions such as, "Do you live in town?" or even "Where did you go to college?" help establish a more complete image of the person.

3. Try associating the person with other people—for example, was he or she part of a group when you were introduced? Do you have mutual friends or colleagues? Also try to associate the location or circumstances of your introduction—at a restaurant, in a conference room, outside the office building.

4. Without staring, pick a feature about the person that stands out—jet-black hair, a prominent nose, a bright red tie, an unusual purse. Later you can mentally attach the feature to the name. This will help you create a mental picture of the person.

5. If you scroll through your mental picture, association with others, and individual details and you still can't come up with the person's name, simply reintroduce yourself. Say, "Hello, I'm Chris Montgomery," and chances are the person will respond with a similar reintroduction. If not, and you've only met the person briefly once before, go ahead and ask for his or her name again. Be sure to listen carefully and apply some of the memory cues listed, so next time that name won't be stuck on the tip of your tongue.

**Sources:** Kate Lorenz, "Tricks to Remembering Names," CNN.com, accessed July 18, 2006, http://www.cnn.com; "How Do I Remember People's Names?" LearnThat, accessed August 15, 2005, http://www.learnthat.com; Tom Weber, "How to Remember Names," The Sideroad, http://www.sideroad.com, accessed August 15, 2005; Valencia P. Higuera, "Techniques to Remember Names," FineTuning.com, accessed July 25, 2005, http://www.finetuning.com.

complex purchasing rules. Recently Sigarms was awarded a five-year, $23.7 million contract to supply Immigration and Customs Enforcement (ICE) with 65,000 handguns. "There were 74 pages of specifications with 50 characteristics," recalls Peter Kujawski, vice president of military and government sales. As part of the selection process, each bidder sent a shooting team to a federal facility to fire its pistols for performance. To ensure that its team members' performance was top-notch, Sigarms sent along a master sergeant from the U.S. Army Reserve as a coach. Taking this initiative, as well as meeting all the specifications, got Sigarms the contract. "It was a long, arduous process," says Kujawski.[32]

The sales functions of most companies are experiencing rapid change. Today's salespeople are more concerned with establishing long-term buyer-seller relationships and acting as consultants to their customers than in the past.

Personal selling can occur in several environments, each of which can involve business-to-business or business-to-consumer selling. Sales representatives who make sales calls on prospective customers at their homes or businesses are involved in *field selling*. Companies that sell major industrial equipment typically rely heavily on field selling. *Over-the-counter selling* describes sales activities in retailing and some wholesale locations, where customers visit the seller's facility to purchase items. *Telemarketing* sales representatives make their presentations over the phone. A later section reviews telemarketing in more detail.

## Sales Tasks

All sales activities involve assisting customers in some manner. Although a salesperson's work can vary significantly from one company or situation to another, it usually includes a mix of three basic tasks: order processing, creative selling, and missionary selling.

***Order Processing*** Although both field selling and telemarketing involve this activity, **order processing** is most often related to retail and wholesale firms. The salesperson identifies customer needs, points out merchandise to meet them, and processes the order. Route sales personnel process orders for such consumer goods as bread, milk, soft drinks, and snack foods. They check each store's stock, report inventory needs to the store manager, and complete the sale. Most of these jobs include at least minor order-processing functions.

*Creative Selling*   Sales representatives for most business products and some consumer items perform **creative selling,** a persuasive type of promotional presentation. Creative selling promotes a good or service whose benefits are not readily apparent or whose purchase decision requires a close analysis of alternatives. Sales of intangible products such as insurance rely heavily on creative selling, but sales of tangible goods benefit as well.

Many retail salespeople just process orders, but many consumers are looking for more in the form of customer service, which is where creative selling comes in. Trained sales staff at Talbots women's clothing stores hold seasonal wardrobe-building workshops at the stores, helping customers select and purchase coordinating clothing, accessories, and shoes from the Talbots line—which they might not have purchased without such advice.

*Missionary Selling*   Sales work also includes an indirect form of selling in which the representative promotes goodwill for a company or provides technical or operational assistance to the customer; this practice is called **missionary selling.** Many businesses that sell technical equipment, such as Oracle and Fujitsu, provide systems specialists who act as consultants to customers. These salespeople work to solve problems and sometimes help their clients with questions not directly related to their employers' products. Other industries also use missionary selling techniques. Pharmaceutical company representatives—called *detailers*—visit physicians to describe the firm's latest products. The actual sales, however, are handled through pharmacies, which fill the prescriptions. Such sales calls have created a public debate, as the "Solving an Ethical Controversy" feature describes.

*Telemarketing*   **Telemarketing,** personal selling conducted by telephone, provides a firm's marketers with a high return on their expenditures, an immediate response, and an opportunity for personalized two-way conversation. Many firms use telemarketing because expense or other obstacles prevent salespeople from meeting many potential customers in person. Telemarketers can use databases to target prospects based on demographic data. Telemarketing takes two forms. A sales representative who calls you is practicing *outbound telemarketing*. On the other hand, *inbound telemarketing* occurs when you call a toll-free phone number to get product information or place an order.

Outbound telemarketers must abide by the Federal Trade Commission's 1996 Telemarketing Sales Rule. Telemarketers must disclose that they are selling something and on whose behalf they are calling before they make their presentations. The rule also limits calls to between 8 a.m. and 9 p.m., requires sellers to disclose details on exchange policies, and requires them to keep lists of people who do not want to receive calls. In some states, it is also against the law for telemarketers to leave messages on consumers' answering machines. Despite opposition from the Direct Marketing Association, Congress enacted another law in 2003 creating a national "do not call" registry intended to help consumers block unwanted telemarketing calls. Consumers who want to be on the list must call a special number or visit a Web site to register. Telemarketers must check the list every three months and update their own lists or face stiff fines of up to $11,000 for each violation. Charities, surveys, and political campaign calls are exempt from these restrictions. Businesses with which consumers already have a relationship, such as the bank where they have accounts or the dealership where they buy their cars, may conduct telemarketing calls under the guidelines of the Telemarketing Sales Rule.

# DRUG SALES CALLS TO PHYSICIANS: PROVIDING INFORMATION OR SIMPLY SELLING?

*Pharmaceutical companies have traditionally employed large numbers of sales representatives—typically called detailers. Their job is to visit physicians' offices to make them aware of new products that could help their patients and to provide special dosage information.*

But as the number of drug salespeople tripled to more than 100,000 in a decade and the frequency of visits increased, doctors became increasingly skeptical—and annoyed—with the continual toll on their time schedules. Physicians and the public also wondered whether the purpose of the visits was geared simply toward increasing sales, instead of benefiting patients.

Should the number of direct sales calls to physicians' offices be limited or stopped altogether?

## PRO

1. Some drug reps offer free lunches, small tokens such as candies, and free drug samples to physicians who agree to see them. They often befriend office staff to gain entry. Such freebies and behavior can bias a doctor in favor of a product, regardless of its true merits.
2. With the number of drug sales calls expanding, doctors spend more time on calls and less on face time with patients. Such intrusions are burdens to an already stressed healthcare system.

## CON

1. Drug company reps can provide doctors with quick, detailed knowledge about a new drug and its uses. Cutting back on this information source limits doctors' awareness of new developments.
2. Pharmaceutical companies deny that their motives are simply to sell more drugs. One company explained that its "longstanding policy is to communicate the benefits and limitations of its products in a fair and balanced manner."

## Summary

The American Medical Association offers its member doctors guidelines about limiting the value of the gifts they receive, but it leaves the decision of whether to admit reps to the doctors themselves. Some physicians have become so fed up with the number of calls, they have closed their doors to drug reps or severely limited their access. As part of its ongoing investigation into the pharmaceutical industry, the U.S. Congress is taking a closer look at companies' sales practices to see whether legislation should be passed. Meanwhile, several big pharmaceutical firms, such as Pfizer, Merck, and Wyeth, are already voluntarily limiting their sales calls to physicians. Time will tell whether these efforts will change a well-established sales practice.

**Sources:** Scott Hensley and Barbara Martinez, "To Sell Their Drugs, Companies Increasingly Rely on Doctors," accessed August 7, 2006, http://www.josmc.org; University of Washington "Drug Sales Pitches Have Little Effect on Physicians, Study Shows," *University Week*, accessed August 7, 2006, http://www.admin.urel.washington.edu; Bruce Japsen, "Drug Sales Calls Wear on Doctors," *Chicago Tribune*, May 8, 2005, section 1, pp. 1, 12; Book review of *Hard Sell: The Evolution of a Viagra Salesman*, *Fortune*, May 2, 2005, p. 26.

 solving an **ETHICAL** controversy

## The Sales Process

The sales process typically follows the seven-step sequence shown in Figure 14.4: prospecting and qualifying, the approach, the presentation, the demonstration, handling objections, the closing, and the follow-up. Remember the importance of flexibility, though; a good salesperson is not afraid to vary the sales process based on a customer's responses and needs. The process of selling to a potential customer who is unfamiliar with a company's products differs from the process of serving a longtime customer.

### Prospecting, Qualifying, and Approaching
At the prospecting stage, salespeople identify potential customers. They may seek leads for prospective sales from such sources as existing customers, friends and family, and business associates. The qualifying process identifies potential customers who have the financial ability and authority to buy.

Companies use different tactics to identify and qualify prospects. Some companies rely on business development teams to do this legwork. They use the responses from direct mail to provide leads to sales reps. Other companies believe in personal visits from sales representatives.

Successful salespeople make careful preparations, analyzing available data about a prospective customer's product lines and other pertinent information before making the initial contact. They realize the importance of a first impression in influencing a customer's future attitudes toward the selling company and its products.

**Presentation and Demonstration**  At the presentation stage, salespeople communicate promotional messages. They may describe the major features of their products, highlight the advantages, and cite examples of satisfied consumers. A demonstration helps reinforce the message that the salesperson has been communicating—a critical step in the sales process. Department-store shoppers can get a free makeover at the cosmetics counter. Anyone looking to buy a car will take it for a test drive before deciding whether to purchase it.

Some products are too large to transport to prospective buyers or require special installation to demonstrate. Using laptop computers and multimedia presentations, sales representatives can demonstrate these products for customers. Others, such as services, are intangible. So a presentation including testimonials from satisfied customers or graphs illustrating results may be helpful.

**Figure**

**14.4**

Seven Steps in the Sales Process

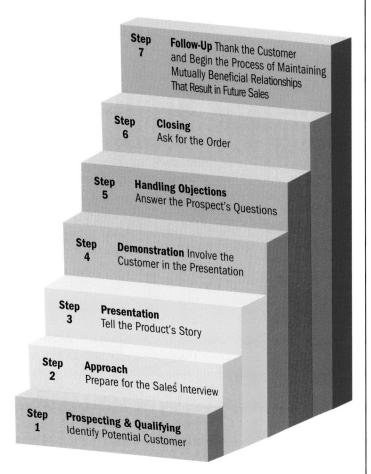

Step 7  **Follow-Up** Thank the Customer and Begin the Process of Maintaining Mutually Beneficial Relationships That Result in Future Sales

Step 6  **Closing** Ask for the Order

Step 5  **Handling Objections** Answer the Prospect's Questions

Step 4  **Demonstration** Involve the Customer in the Presentation

Step 3  **Presentation** Tell the Product's Story

Step 2  **Approach** Prepare for the Sales Interview

Step 1  **Prospecting & Qualifying** Identify Potential Customer

**Handling Objections**  Some salespeople fear potential customers' objections because they view the questions as criticism. But a good salesperson can use objections as an opportunity to answer questions and explain how the product will benefit the customer. As a general rule, the key is to sell benefits, not features: How will this product help the customer?

**Closing**  The critical point in the sales process—the time at which the salesperson actually asks the prospect to buy—is the closing. If the presentation effectively matches product benefits to customer needs, the closing should be a natural conclusion. If there are more bumps in the process, the salesperson can try some different techniques, such as offering an alternative product, offering a special incentive for purchase, or restating the product benefits. Closing the sale—and beginning a relationship in which the customer builds loyalty to the brand or product—is the ideal outcome of this interaction. But even if the sale is not made at this time, the salesperson should regard the interaction as the beginning of a potential relationship anyway. The prospect might very well become a customer in the future.

**Follow-Up**  A salesperson's actions after the sale may determine whether the customer will make another purchase. Follow-up is an important part of building a long-lasting relationship. After closing, the salesperson should process the order efficiently. By calling soon after a purchase, the salesperson provides reassurance about the customer's decision to buy and creates an opportunity to correct any problems.

## Public Relations

A final element of the promotional mix, public relations (PR)—including publicity—supports advertising, personal selling, and sales promotion, usually by pursuing broader objectives. Through PR, companies attempt to improve their prestige and image with the public by distributing specific messages or ideas to target audiences. Cause-related promotional activities are often supported by PR and publicity campaigns. In addition, PR helps a firm establish awareness of goods and services, then builds a positive image of them.[33]

**public relations** organization's communications and relationships with its various audiences.

**Public relations** refers to an organization's communications with its various public audiences, such as customers, vendors, news media, employees, stockholders, the government, and the general public. Many of these communication efforts serve marketing purposes. Public relations is an efficient, indirect communications channel for promoting products. It can publicize products and help create and maintain a positive image of the company.

The PR department links a firm with the media. It provides the media with news releases and video and audio clips, as well as holding news conferences to announce new products, the formation of strategic alliances, management changes, financial results, and similar developments. Publications issued by the PR department include newsletters, brochures, and reports.

## Publicity

**publicity** stimulation of demand for a good, service, place, idea, person, or organization by disseminating news or obtaining favorable unpaid media presentations.

The type of public relations that is tied most closely to promoting a company's products is **publicity**—nonpersonal stimulation of demand for a good, service, place, idea, event, person, or organization by unpaid placement of information in print or broadcast media. Press releases generate publicity, as does news coverage. Entrepreneur Eric Anderson, CEO of Space Adventures, held a press conference to announce that his firm, along with its Russian partners, would be offering "around the moon" space travel to anyone willing to pay $100 million for the trip. That's $80 million more than the $20 million the group is charging for trips to the International Space Station. Naturally, the announcement generated plenty of buzz in the news media.[34] Not-for-profit organizations benefit from publicity when they receive coverage of events such as the Boston Marathon, in which thousands of runners participate to raise money for sixteen charities, such as the Doug Flutie Foundation for Autism. When a for-profit firm teams up with a not-for-profit firm in a fund-raising effort, the move usually generates good publicity for both organizations.

While good publicity can promote a firm's positive image, negative publicity can cause problems. When home decorating and entertaining expert Martha Stewart was convicted in a stock-trading case, her image as well as that of her company, Martha Stewart Living, suffered. But Stewart took steps to improve her image, even while serving a prison sentence. When she returned to public life, she already had contracts for two television shows.

**assessment check**

1. Why do retailers and manufacturers use sales promotions?
2. When does a firm use personal selling instead of nonpersonal selling?
3. How does public relations serve a marketing purpose?

# PROMOTIONAL STRATEGIES

Many of this chapter's examples demonstrate the considerable overlap among the elements of the promotional mix. Clear boundaries no longer distinguish advertising from sales promotion. By blending advertising, sales promotion, personal selling, and public relations, marketers create an integrated promotional mix that reflects the market, product type, stage in the product life cycle, price, and promotional budget. Then they implement one of two promotional alternatives: pulling or pushing strategies.

## Pushing and Pulling Strategies

Marketers can choose between two general promotional strategies: a pushing strategy or a pulling strategy. A **pushing strategy** relies on personal selling to market an item to wholesalers and retailers in a company's distribution channels. So companies promote the product to members of the marketing channel, not to end users. Sales personnel explain to marketing intermediaries why they should carry particular merchandise, usually supported by offers of special discounts and promotional materials. Marketers also provide **cooperative advertising** allowances, in which they share the cost of local advertising of their firm's product or line with channel partners. All of these strategies are designed to motivate wholesalers and retailers to push the good or service to their own customers.

A **pulling strategy** attempts to promote a product by generating consumer demand for it, primarily through advertising and sales promotion appeals. Potential buyers will then request that their suppliers—retailers or local distributors—carry the product, thereby pulling it through the distribution channel. Dove used this strategy when it launched a highly popular advertising campaign—called "Campaign for Real Beauty"—for its products featuring real women instead of professional models. The ads for soap, shampoo, and lotions were placed in magazines, on billboards and buildings, and even along the sides of buses. The strategy was so successful that it also generated good publicity—including a segment on NBC's *Today Show.*[35]

Most marketing situations require combinations of pushing and pulling strategies, although the primary emphasis can vary. Consumer products usually depend more heavily on pulling strategies than do B2B products, which favor pushing strategies.

COURTESY OF UNILEVER USA, INC

☐ grey?
☐ gorgeous?

Why can't more women feel glad to be grey? Join the beauty debate.

campaignforrealbeauty.com ➥ | *Dove*

Dove's popular ad campaign used a pulling strategy—featuring women with whom consumers could identify—to promote its new line of beauty products.

**assessment check**

1. Give an example of a pushing strategy.
2. Give an example of a pulling strategy.

# ETHICS IN PROMOTION

Of all the elements in a 21st-century business organization, promotion probably raises the most ethical questions. Many people view advertising with a cynical eye, criticizing its influence on consumers, its potential for creating unnecessary needs and wants, its overemphasis on sex and beauty, and its delivery of inappropriate messages to children.

This section examines three controversial issues related to the promotion element of the firm's marketing mix: puffery and deception, promotion to children and teens, and promotion in public schools and on college campuses.

## Puffery and Deception

Claims such as "bigger," "best," "most advanced," and "number one" are examples of **puffery.** Puffery is exaggeration about the benefits or superiority of a product. It literally means "puffed up." Puffery is legal because it doesn't guarantee anything, but it certainly raises ethical questions.

Can an advertiser be absolutely certain that every consumer knows the difference between exaggeration and reality? Some advertisers argue that consumers don't take the claims literally, but others disagree. Engaging in puffery may ultimately undermine the credibility of a firm's marketing messages.[36] Manufacturers of cosmetics and personal care products seem to be particularly prone to criticism for puffery in their ads. Procter & Gamble faced the problem when the Advertising Standards Authority challenged certain claims about its Pantene Pro-V shampoo.[37]

The Uniform Commercial Code, which standardizes laws for business practices throughout the United States, distinguishes puffery from specific or quantifiable statements about product quality or performance. Those statements amount to an "express warranty," for which the company must stand behind its claim. General boasts of product superiority and vague claims are considered puffery, not warranties. A marketer's quantifiable statement, on the other hand, implies a certain level of performance. Tests can establish the validity of a claim that one brand of batteries outlasts a rival brand.

Deception involves deliberately making promises that are untrue, such as guaranteed weight loss in five days, get-rich-quick schemes for would-be entrepreneurs, or promised return on investments. Today's climate of skepticism among consumers may actually present an opportunity for ethical companies to shine.

## Promotion to Children and Teens

Children and teens possess huge purchasing power, whether they are doing their own shopping or influencing the buying decisions of their families. It is tempting for some marketers to try anything to influence these young consumers. Although young children are certainly accustomed to promotional messages, they are not sophisticated at analyzing them. "Because younger children do not understand persuasive intent in advertising, they are easy targets for commercial persuasion," warns psychologist Brian Wilcox.[38] In addition, to woo young consumers, advertisers often make ads as unadlike as possible—designing messages that resemble entertainment. With modern media companies owning a variety of broadcast, print, Internet, and other outlets, U.S. children watching cartoons and other shows are exposed to an integrated marketing effort that combines advertising for related videos, books, and video games, as well as licensed merchandise from toys to backpacks to T-shirts.

However, sometimes marketing to children can be socially responsible. With children's health—in particular, obesity—at stake, firms are beginning to use their influence toward a more positive outcome. Nickelodeon, which sponsors *SpongeBob SquarePants* and *Dora the Explorer,* has begun licensing its characters to the distributors of fruits and vegetables, in an effort to get kids to eat more healthful foods. Kids whose parents buy spinach from Boskovich Farms will find peel-off SpongeBob tattoos in the bags.[39]

As children grow older and become more sophisticated, so does the marketing effort. The U.S. teen population is large, and marketers are working harder than ever to learn about them. In their search for insights into their market's special needs and wants, MTV marketers even borrowed the techniques of anthropology to visit teens and observe their lives firsthand.

## Promotion in Public Schools and on College Campuses

A related ethical issue is the placement of promotional messages in schools, from kindergartens through university campuses. The idea of school as a place where students are free from marketing messages is long gone. Some schools have brought in millions in income by signing contracts that give certain brands exclusive access to their students.

In-school promotions have begun to generate a backlash, however. Several states have considered laws that would limit or ban such promotions, particularly those that feature snack foods and soft drinks.[40] On its own, Coca-Cola decided to include healthier products—bottled water, juice, and other beverages—in school vending machines. In addition, Coke began to replace corporate logos on the machines with images of students exercising and playing.

College students are older and generally considered more educated consumers than younger children. With a total of $122 billion in on-campus spending power in the United States, they remain an attractive market for marketers. Figure 14.5 reveals some facts about these consumers.

# PRICING OBJECTIVES IN THE MARKETING MIX

When Hurricanes Katrina and Rita slammed into the U.S. Gulf Coast, pouring destruction across the shores of Louisiana, Mississippi, Alabama, and Texas, within days the already high price of gas spiked to record levels. Economists predicted a 30 percent hike in gasoline prices, a 52 percent increase in the price of natural gas, and a 21 percent rise in the cost of jet fuel. A week later, they warned of "hidden" increases in the price of coffee and bananas, detergent and paint, tires and roofing shingles, and even paper goods because of increased delivery costs.[41]

These and other products offer utility, or want-satisfying power. However, we as consumers determine how much value we associate with each one. In the aftermath of a storm, we may value electricity and food and water above everything else. If we commute a long distance or are planning a vacation, fuel may be of greater concern. But all consumers have limited amounts of money and a variety of possible uses for it. So the **price**—the exchange value of a good or service—becomes a major factor in consumer buying decisions.

Businesspeople attempt to accomplish certain objectives through their pricing decisions. Pricing objectives vary from firm to firm, and many companies pursue multiple pricing objectives. Some try to improve profits by setting high prices; others set low prices to attract new business. As Figure 14.6 shows, the four basic categories of pricing objectives are (1) profitability, (2) volume, (3) meeting competition, and (4) prestige.

## Profitability Objectives

**Profitability objectives** are perhaps the most common objectives included in the strategic plans of most firms.

**Figure**

**14.5**

College-Age Consumers: An Attractive Market

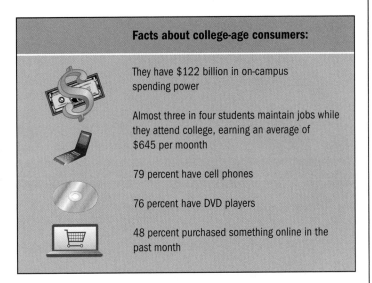

**Facts about college-age consumers:**

They have $122 billion in on-campus spending power

Almost three in four students maintain jobs while they attend college, earning an average of $645 per moonth

79 percent have cell phones

76 percent have DVD players

48 percent purchased something online in the past month

**Source:** Data from 360 Youth/Harris Interactive College Explorer Study, cited in Paul Soltoff, "E-Mail Marketing to College Students 101," ClickZ Network, accessed July 18, 2006, http://www.click.com.

**assessment check**

1. Define puffery.
2. Why is promoting to young children potentially unethical?

**price** exchange value of a good or service.

Gas prices, already high due to hurricane damage, soared after the Middle East conflict.

Figure

14.6 | Pricing Objectives

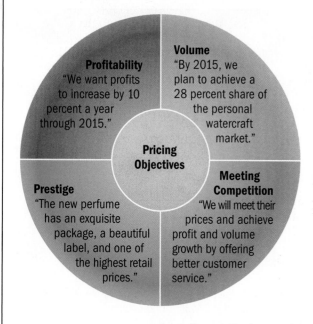

**Profitability**
"We want profits to increase by 10 percent a year through 2015."

**Volume**
"By 2015, we plan to achieve a 28 percent share of the personal watercraft market."

**Pricing Objectives**

**Prestige**
"The new perfume has an exquisite package, a beautiful label, and one of the highest retail prices."

**Meeting Competition**
"We will meet their prices and achieve profit and volume growth by offering better customer service."

## "They Said It"

"Free is good—but read the fine print."
—*Anonymous*

Marketers know that profits are the revenue the company brings in, minus its expenses. Usually a big difference exists between revenue and profit. Large automakers try to produce at least one luxury vehicle for which they can charge $50,000 or more instead of relying entirely on the sale of $15,000 to $25,000 models, thus making a greater profit typical of luxury models.

Some firms maximize profits by reducing costs rather than through price changes. Companies can maintain prices and increase profitability by operating more efficiently or by modifying the product to make it less costly to produce. One strategy is to maintain a steady price while reducing the size or amount of the product in the package—something that manufacturers of candy, coffee, and cereal have done over the years.

## Volume Objectives

A second approach to pricing strategy—**volume objectives**—bases pricing decisions on market share, the percentage of a market controlled by a certain company or product. One firm may seek to achieve a 25 percent market share in a certain industry, and another may want to maintain or expand its market share for particular products. As a market becomes saturated—like the PC market—firms need to find ways to get consumers to upgrade or try new products. Setting a lower price can accomplish that objective, as long as the firm still makes a profit. Many PC makers—and retailers—have begun to offer their products at lower prices, particularly at the start of the school year.

## Pricing to Meet Competition

A third set of pricing objectives seeks simply to meet competitors' prices so that price essentially becomes a nonissue. In many lines of business, firms set their own prices to match those of established industry leaders. However, companies may not legally work together to agree on prices or force retailers to sell at a set price. As more and more manufacturers of flat-panel televisions began to enter the market, prices tumbled as much as 35 percent in one year. Lesser-known brands such as Westinghouse Electric and Norcent Micro cut their prices in order to compete against better-known brands like Sharp and Sony. In turn, the big-name firms dropped their prices as well. Not everyone followed suit, though. Some major retailers held out for higher prices on plasma and liquid crystal display (LCD) televisions, pocketing 25 percent profits from customers willing to pay for the luxury.[42]

Because price is such a highly visible component of a firm's marketing mix, businesses may be tempted to use it to obtain an advantage over competitors. But sometimes the race to match competitors' prices results in a *price war*, which has happened periodically in the airline and fast-food industries. The ability of competitors to match a price cut leads many marketers to try to avoid price wars by favoring other strategies, such as adding value, improving quality, educating consumers, and establishing relationships.

## Prestige Objectives

The final category of objectives encompasses the effect of prices on prestige. **Prestige pricing** establishes a relatively high price to develop and maintain an image of quality and exclusiveness. Marketers set such objectives because they recognize the role of price in communicating an overall image for the firm and its products. People expect to pay more for a Hummer vehicle, a Louis Vuitton purse, or a vacation on St. Kitts or Nevis in the Caribbean.

Scarcity can create prestige. Products that are limited in distribution or so popular that they become scarce generate their own prestige—allowing businesses to charge more for them. Banana Republic and J. Crew have been cashing in on the lure of scarcity. Although Banana Republic has more than 450 stores, its Café Society Collection of women's clothing and accessories is being carried by only 30 of them. Men can hunt for the Heritage Collection, from which they may purchase a leather blazer for $450 and a pair of "antiqued" jeans for $128. J. Crew is taking the scarcity trend a step further—at certain stores, privileged shoppers may pick up a hand-beaded skirt for $800 and a pair of crocodile pumps for $600.[43]

EXPERIENCE THE *exceptional nature* OF BALD HEAD ISLAND

*North Carolina's premier second home community.*
Homes from $500,000 to over $4,000,000.
Homesites from $200,000 to over $2,500,000.
For real estate information, please call Bald Head Island Limited Real Estate Sales at 1-800-411-6130 or visit us online at www.discoverbhi.com.

This promotion attracts customers with appeals to prestige. Consumers who want to purchase a home in the North Carolina community of Bald Head Island can expect to pay between $500,000 and $4,000,000—and that's for a vacation home.

# PRICING STRATEGIES

People from different areas of a company contribute their expertise to set the most strategic price for a product. Accountants, financial managers, and marketers provide relevant sales and cost data, along with customer feedback. Designers, engineers, and systems analysts all contribute important data as well.

Prices are determined in two basic ways: by applying the concepts of supply and demand discussed in Chapter 3, and by completing cost-oriented analyses. Economic theory assumes that a market price will be set at the point at which the amount of a product desired at a given price equals the amount that suppliers will offer for sale at that price. In other words, this price occurs at the point at which the amount demanded and the amount supplied are equal. Online auctions, such as those conducted on eBay, are a popular application of the demand-and-supply approach.

**a**ssessment **c**heck

1. Define price.
2. Which pricing objective actually results in diverting consumer attention from price?

## Price Determination in Practice

Economic theory might lead to the best pricing decisions, but most businesses do not have all the information they need to make those decisions, so they adopt **cost-based pricing** formulas. These formulas calculate total costs per unit and then add markups to cover overhead costs and generate profits.

Cost-based pricing totals all costs associated with offering a product in the market, including research and development, production, transportation, and marketing expenses. An added amount, the markup, then covers any unexpected or overlooked expenses and provides a profit. The total becomes the price. Manufacturers, wholesalers, and retailers usually practice markup pricing. Although the actual markup used varies by such factors as brand image and type of store, the typical markup for clothing is determined by doubling the wholesale price (the cost to the merchant) to arrive at the retail price for the item. The "Hit & Miss" feature describes one way businesses have attempted to lower their costs and improve their bottom line.

**cost-based pricing** adding a percentage (markup) to the base cost of a product to cover overhead costs and generate profits.

# HIT&MISS

## Offering Lower Prices: The Temptation to Outsource to China

Outsourcing—particularly to China—is tempting for many businesses that are looking for better prices. Manufacturing overseas often allows firms to reduce their costs and be more competitive in the eyes of their own customers. So as consumers continue to demand lower prices for goods, businesses are looking for ways to cut costs. With lower labor costs, a large labor pool, and an ability to mass produce goods, China has become an attractive supplier site for U.S. businesses.

But some firms are finding drawbacks—much higher costs than they had anticipated. One reason is that it costs a lot more to set up and manage trade with China than it does to actually manufacture the goods. So the price quoted by a supplier does not reflect all the costs associated with obtaining raw materials, delivery of finished goods, customs inspection, and other activities. "If you just [outsource] based on pricing negotiations and have not thought through the logistics of delivery, assurance of supply, flexibility of supply and quality, your total cost very quickly outweighs the price savings you made in the negotiations up front," warns Richard McCluney, vice president of account operations for E2open, a global supply-chain management firm. Customs regulations alone can eat up a big chunk of savings—in time and dollars. Traffic-choked or impassable roads in China are another cost-increasing headache. "Because of the huge increase in traffic, you now have to rethink where you have your suppliers based," explains McCluney.

Another challenge is the design of products themselves. One study also warns companies, "When they look only to outsourcing for cost reduction, [businesses] run the risk of becoming myopic in the design process." Instead, an effective redesign might save more than cheaper prices overseas. "I think a lack of real involvement of the purchasing or supply chain group in that early design process has some impact on getting a full understanding of what the costs are," says Nicholas Dewhurst, a coauthor of the study.

As a result, many experts advise firms to consider all of the implications of outsourcing to China—product design, manufacturing, inventory management, and final shipping. If outsourcing still makes sense, then it is the best alternative in the long run. But basing a decision solely on low manufacturing costs may come back to haunt a business: After all, costs in China are bound to increase in the long run also.

### Questions for Critical Thinking

1. How does the breakeven point figure into a firm's decision to outsource some of its processes?
2. Describe two or three steps that a firm might take to avoid the pitfalls of outsourcing to China.

**Sources:** Lisa Harrington, "Small Companies Take on the World," *Inbound Logistics*, accessed August 7, 2006, http://www.inboundlogistics.com; Ed Frauenheim, "Outsourcing Moving to China?" ZDNet News, accessed July 18, 2006, http://news.zdnet.com; Wayne Forrest, "Analyzing the Pros and Cons of Outsourcing to China," Purchasing.com, accessed July 18, 2006, http://www.purchasing.com.

## Breakeven Analysis

**breakeven analysis** pricing technique used to determine the minimum sales volume a product must generate at a certain price level to cover all costs.

Businesses often conduct a **breakeven analysis** to determine the minimum sales volume a product must generate at a certain price level to cover all costs. This method involves a consideration of various costs and total revenues. *Total cost* is the sum of total variable costs and total fixed costs. *Variable costs* change with the level of production, as labor and raw materials do, while *fixed costs* such as insurance premiums and utility rates charged by water, natural gas, and electric power suppliers remain stable regardless of the production level. *Total revenue* is determined by multiplying price by the number of units sold.

**Finding the Breakeven Point** The level of sales that will generate enough revenue to cover all of the company's fixed and variable costs is called the breakeven point. It is the point at which total revenue just equals total costs. Sales beyond the breakeven point will generate profits; sales volume below the breakeven point will result in losses. The following formulas give the breakeven point in units and dollars:

$$\text{Breakeven point (in units)} = \frac{\text{Total Fixed}}{\text{Contribution to Fixed Costs per Unit}}$$

$$\text{Breakeven point (in dollars)} = \frac{\text{Total Fixed Costs}}{1 - \text{Variable Cost per Unit/Price}}$$

A product selling for $20 with a variable cost of $14 per unit produces a $6 per-unit contribution to fixed costs. If the firm has total fixed costs of $42,000, then it must sell 7,000 units to break even on the product. The calculation of the breakeven point in units and dollars is as follows:

$$\text{Breakeven point (in units)} = \frac{\$42,000}{\$20 - \$14} = \frac{\$42,000}{\$6} = 7,000 \text{ units}$$

$$\text{Breakeven point (in dollars)} = \frac{\$42,000}{1 - \$14/\$20} = \frac{\$42,000}{1 - 0.7} = \frac{\$42,000}{0.3} = \$140,000$$

Figure 14.7 illustrates this breakeven point in a graph.

Marketers use breakeven analysis to determine the profits or losses that would result from several different proposed prices. Because different prices produce different breakeven points, marketers could compare their calculations of required sales to break even with sales estimates from marketing research studies. This comparison can identify the best price—one that would attract enough customers to exceed the breakeven point and earn profits for the firm.

Most firms add consumer demand—determining whether enough customers will buy the number of units the firm must sell at a particular price to break even—by developing estimates through surveys of likely customers, interviews with retailers that would be handling the product, and assessments of prices charged by competitors. Then the breakeven points for several possible prices are calculated and compared with sales estimates for each price. This practice is referred to as *modified breakeven analysis.*

## Alternative Pricing Strategies

The strategy a company uses to set its prices should grow out of the firm's overall marketing strategy. In general, firms can choose from four alternative pricing strategies: skimming, penetration, discount or everyday low pricing, and competitive pricing.

**Skimming Pricing** A **skimming pricing** strategy sets an intentionally high price relative to the prices of competing products. The term comes from the expression "skimming the cream." This pricing strategy often works for the

**Figure**

14.7

Breakeven Analysis

Wal-Mart has long relied on everyday low pricing, a strategy that has consistently won it a place as the world's #1 retailer.

introduction of a distinctive good or service with little or no competition, although it can be used at other stages of the product life cycle as well. A skimming strategy can help marketers set a price that distinguishes a firm's high-end product from those of competitors. It can also help a firm recover its product development costs before competitors enter the field. This is often the case with prescription drugs.

*Penetration Pricing* By contrast, a **penetration pricing** strategy sets a low price as a major marketing weapon. Businesses may price new products noticeably lower than competing offerings when they enter new industries characterized by dozens of competing brands. Once the new product achieves some market recognition through consumer trial purchases stimulated by its low price, marketers may increase the price to the level of competing products. However, stiff competition might prevent the price increase.

*Everyday Low Pricing and Discount Pricing* **Everyday low pricing (EDLP)** is a strategy devoted to maintaining continuous low prices rather than relying on short-term price-cutting tactics such as cents-off coupons, rebates, and special sales. This strategy has been used successfully by retailers such as Wal-Mart to consistently offer low prices to consumers; manufacturers also use EDLP to set stable prices for retailers.

With *discount pricing,* businesses hope to attract customers by dropping prices for a set period of time. Recently the three major U.S. automakers offered consumers the "employee discount" on most or all of their vehicles. But experts warn that discounting must be done carefully, or profits can disappear. Businesses should offer discounts only for a specified period of time and with a clear understanding of what they are trying to accomplish with the strategy. They should advertise the discount, so customers know it is a special deal. When the time period has elapsed, so should the discount.[44]

**assessment check**

1. What is a cost-based pricing formula?
2. What might be considered the most stable of the alternative pricing strategies?

*Competitive Pricing* Although many organizations rely heavily on price as a competitive weapon, even more implement **competitive pricing** strategies. They try to reduce the emphasis on price competition by matching other firms' prices and concentrating their own marketing efforts on the product, distribution, and promotional elements of the marketing mix. In fact, in industries with relatively homogeneous products, competitors must match one another's price reductions to maintain market share and remain competitive. By pricing their products at the levels of competing offerings, marketers largely negate the price variable in their marketing strategies.

## CONSUMER PERCEPTIONS OF PRICES

How do you perceive prices for certain products? Marketers must consider this. If large numbers of potential buyers consider a price too high or too low, businesses must correct the situation. Price-quality relationships and the use of odd pricing are important considerations in setting prices.

## Price-Quality Relationships

Research shows that a consumer's perception of product quality is closely related to an item's price. Most marketers believe that this perceived price-quality relationship remains steady over a relatively wide range of prices, although extremely high or low prices have less credibility. The price-quality relationship can critically affect a firm's pricing strategy.

Many consumers associate prestige, quality, and high price together—believing that paying a high price for an item such as an Infiniti car or a Kate Spade bag not only conveys prestige but also ensures quality. Others believe that eating at an expensive restaurant automatically means the food will be better than food served at a fast-food chain. Conversely, consumers may view an extremely low price as an indication that corners have been cut and quality will suffer.

### "They Said It"

"Price is what you pay. Value is what you get."
—Warren Buffett (b. 1930)
American investor

## Odd Pricing

Have you ever wondered why retailers set prices like $1.99 instead of $2 or $9.99 instead of $10? Before the age of cash registers and sales taxes, retailers reportedly followed this practice of odd pricing to force clerks to make correct change as part of cash control efforts. But now **odd pricing** is commonly used because many retailers believe that consumers favor uneven amounts or amounts that sound less than they really are: It's easier to justify a purchase of $299 than one of $300. However, some retailers also use this method to identify items that have been marked down. The odd price lets sales personnel—and customers—know the item is on sale.

### assessment check

1. How does the price-quality relationship affect a firm's pricing strategy?
2. Why is odd pricing used?

# WHAT'S AHEAD

The chapters in Part 4 have explained the main principles underlying marketing management and described how each fits a firm's overall business strategy. The next few chapters will help you understand how companies manage the technology and information that are available to businesses to create value for their customers and enhance their competitiveness in the marketplace. You'll also learn how firms manage their financial resources.

## Summary of Learning Goals

**1** Discuss how integrated marketing communications relates to a firm's overall promotional strategy.

In practicing integrated marketing communications, a firm coordinates all promotional activities to produce a unified, customer-focused message. IMC identifies consumer needs and then shows how a company's products meet those needs. Marketers select the promotional media that best target and reach customers. Teamwork and careful promotional planning to coordinate IMC strategy components are important elements of these programs.

### Assessment Check Answers

**1.1 What is the objective of an integrated marketing communications program?**

An integrated marketing communications strategy focuses on customer needs to create a unified promotional message about a firm's goods or services.

**1.2 What types of media are used in integrated marketing communications?**

Media used in integrated marketing communications include broadcast, print, direct mail, packaging and store displays, sales promotions, presentations, and online and interactive media.

## 2 Explain the concept of a promotional mix and outline the objectives of promotion.

A company's promotional mix integrates two components: personal selling and nonpersonal selling, which includes advertising, sales promotion, and public relations. By selecting the appropriate combination of promotional mix elements, marketers attempt to achieve the firm's five major promotional objectives: provide information, differentiate a product, increase demand, stabilize sales, and accentuate the product's value.

### Assessment Check Answers

**2.1 Which component of the promotional mix reaches the largest audience?**
Nonpersonal selling reaches the largest audience.

**2.2 Why do firms pursue multiple promotional objectives at the same time?**
Firms pursue multiple promotional objectives because they may need to convey different messages to different audiences.

**2.3 What are product placement and guerrilla marketing?**
Product placement involves paying a fee to have a product showcased in certain media, such as movies and television. Guerrilla marketing is innovative, low-cost marketing efforts designed to get consumers' attention in unusual ways.

## 3 Summarize the different types of advertising and advertising media.

Advertising, the most visible form of nonpersonal promotion, is designed to inform, persuade, or remind. Product advertising promotes a good or service, while institutional advertising promotes a concept, idea, organization, or philosophy. Television, newspapers, and direct mail represent the largest advertising media categories. Others include magazines, radio, and outdoor advertising. Interactive media such as the Internet represent the fastest-growing type of advertising. Interactive advertising directly involves the consumer, who controls the flow of information.

### Assessment Check Answers

**3.1 What are the two basic types of advertising? Into what three categories do they fall?**
The two basic types of advertising are product and institutional. They fall into the categories of informative, persuasive, and reminder-oriented advertising.

**3.2 What is the leading advertising medium in the United States?**
According to the most recent numbers listed in Figure 14.2, television is the leading advertising medium in the United States, slightly edging out direct mail.

**3.3 In what two major ways do firms benefit from sponsorship?**
Firms benefit from sponsorship in two ways: they gain exposure to the event's audience and are associated with the image of the activity.

## 4 Outline the roles of sales promotion, personal selling, and public relations in promotional strategy.

Sales promotion accounts for greater expenditures than does advertising. Consumer-oriented sales promotions such as coupons, games, rebates, samples, premiums, contests, sweepstakes, and promotional products offer an extra incentive to buy a product. Point-of-purchase advertising displays and trade shows are sales promotions directed to the trade markets. Personal selling involves face-to-face interactions between seller and buyer. The primary sales tasks are order processing, creative selling, and missionary selling. The seven-step sales process entails prospecting and qualifying, approach, presentation, demonstration, handling objections, closing, and follow-up. Public relations is nonpaid promotion that seeks to enhance a company's public image through press releases, news conferences, articles, and news broadcasts.

### Assessment Check Answers

**4.1 Why do retailers and manufacturers use sales promotions?**
Retailers and manufacturers use sales promotions to offer consumers extra incentives to buy their products.

**4.2 When does a firm use personal selling instead of nonpersonal selling?**
Personal selling is generally used when customers are few and geographically concentrated, the product is technically complex or requires special handling, the price is high, or the product moves through direct-distribution channels.

**4.3 How does public relations serve a marketing purpose?**
Public relations can be an efficient, indirect communications channel for promoting products. It can pub-

licize products and help create and maintain a positive image of the company.

## 5 Describe pushing and pulling promotional strategies.

A pushing strategy relies on personal selling to market a product to wholesalers and retailers in a company's distribution channels. Marketers promote the product to members of the marketing channel, not to end users. A pulling strategy promotes the product by generating consumer demand for it, through advertising and sales promotion.

### Assessment Check Answers

**5.1 Give an example of a pushing strategy.**
A classic example of a pushing strategy is drug manufacturers, who used to market solely to physicians and hospitals. (Today, they also use a pulling strategy by marketing directly to patients through advertising, which encourages patients to ask their doctors about medications.)

**5.2 Give an example of a pulling strategy.**
Pulling strategies are used by retailers and by manufacturers of consumer goods like cosmetics, automobiles, and clothing.

## 6 Discuss the major ethical issues involved in promotion.

Many consumers believe that advertising exerts too much influence on buyers and that it deceives customers by exaggerating product claims through puffery and consciously blurring the line between promotion and entertainment through deception. Many consumers also question the appropriateness of marketing to children and through schools.

### Assessment Check Answers

**6.1 Define *puffery*.**
Puffery is the exaggeration of product claims.

**6.2 Why is promoting to young children potentially unethical?**
Young children do not understand persuasive intent and are not sophisticated at analyzing advertising messages, so they are often not capable of determining the truth of promotional claims.

## 7 Outline the different types of pricing objectives.

Pricing objectives can be classified as profitability, volume, meeting competition, and prestige. Prof-

itability objectives are probably the most common. Volume objectives base pricing decisions on market share. Meeting competitors' prices makes price a nonissue in competition. Prestige pricing establishes a high price to develop and maintain an image of quality or exclusiveness.

### Assessment Check Answers

**7.1 Define *price*.**
Price is the exchange value of a good or service.

**7.2 Which pricing objective actually results in diverting consumer attention from price?**
Pricing to meet the competition diverts consumer attention from price.

## 8 Discuss how firms set prices in the marketplace, and describe the four alternative pricing strategies.

Although economic theory determines prices by the law of demand and supply, most firms use cost-based pricing, which adds a markup after costs. They usually conduct a breakeven analysis to determine the minimum sales volume a product must generate at a certain price in order to cover costs. The four alternative pricing strategies are skimming, penetration, everyday low pricing and discounting, and competitive pricing. A skimming strategy sets a high price initially to recover costs and then lowers it; a penetration strategy sets a lower price to attract customers and then raises it later. Discounting offers a lower price for a certain period of time. Competitive pricing matches other firms' prices and emphasizes nonprice benefits of a product.

### Assessment Check Answers

**8.1 What is a cost-based pricing formula?**
A cost-based pricing formula calculates the total costs per unit and then adds markups to cover overhead costs and generate profits.

**8.2 What might be considered the most stable of the alternative pricing strategies?**
Everyday low pricing or discount pricing would be the most stable pricing strategy by offering consistently low prices.

## 9 Discuss consumer perceptions of price.

Marketers must consider how consumers perceive the price-quality relationship of their products. Consumers may be willing to pay a higher price if they perceive a product to be of superior quality. However, extreme prices—either high or low—may turn consumers away. Marketers often use odd pricing to convey a message to consumers.

## Assessment Check Answers

**9.1 How does the price-quality relationship affect a firm's pricing strategy?**
Consumers must believe that the price of an item reflects its quality, except in extreme cases. So a firm must try to set its prices accordingly.

**9.2 Why is odd pricing used?**
Odd pricing is commonly used because retailers believe that consumers favor uneven amounts or amounts that sound less than they really are. Odd pricing may also be used to indicate a sale item.

## Business Terms You Need to Know

promotion 444

integrated marketing
    communications (IMC) 444

promotional mix 445

personal selling 445

advertising 449

sales promotion 455

public relations 462

publicity 462

price 465

cost-based pricing 467

breakeven analysis 468

## Other Important Business Terms

nonpersonal selling 445
positioning 447
product placement 448
guerrilla marketing 448
product advertising 450
institutional advertising 450
cause advertising 450
sponsorship 454
infomercial 454
specialty advertising 456

trade promotion 457
point-of-purchase (POP) advertising 457
order processing 458
creative selling 459
missionary selling 459
telemarketing 459
pushing strategy 463
cooperative advertising 463
pulling strategy 463

puffery 463
profitability objectives 465
volume objectives 466
prestige pricing 466
skimming pricing 469
penetration pricing 470
everyday low pricing (EDLP) 470
competitive pricing 470
odd pricing 471

## Review Questions

1. What is the purpose of integrated marketing communications?
2. What are the five major objectives of a promotional strategy?
3. Identify and define each of the three categories of advertising based on their purpose. Which type of advertising might marketers use for the following products?
   a. aspirin
   b. camera phone
   c. six-pack of yogurt for kids
   d. healthcare insurance
4. What are the benefits of online and interactive advertising? What might be some drawbacks?
5. For each of the following, describe potential benefits and drawbacks of a sponsorship relationship:
   a. Extreme Pizza and extreme sports
   b. World Cup Soccer and Corona
   c. Wrangler and the Wrangler Football Golf Classic (a golf tournament that raises money for high school football programs)
6. If you were a marketer for General Mills, what kind of sales promotion might you use for your line of prepackaged chicken and pasta dinners?
7. Under what circumstances are firms likely to emphasize personal selling?
8. Describe the seven-step sales process.
9. Identify and define the four basic categories of pricing objectives.
10. What are the four alternative pricing strategies used by marketers? Give an example of the circumstances under which each might be selected.

## Projects and Teamwork Applications

1. On your own or with a classmate, choose a product that one or both of you purchased recently. Identify the various media that were used to promote the product and analyze the promotional mix. Do you agree with the company's marketing strategy, or would you recommend changes to the mix? Why? Create your own print ad for the product you chose, using any business strategies or knowledge you have learned in this course so far.
2. Evaluate the price of the product you selected in the preceding exercise. What appears to be the pricing strategy used by its manufacturer? Do you think the price is fair? Why or why not? Choose a different strategy and develop a new price for the product based on the strategy. Poll your classmates to learn whether they would purchase the product at the new price—and why.
3. Some schools have received financial benefits by allowing companies to promote their goods and services to students within the school. Others have decided against the practice, and some states are even considering laws banning this type of promotion. With your class, discuss the pros and cons of promotion in public schools and on college campuses. In your view, is there a distinction between a public school and a college campus? Why or why not?
4. On your own or with a classmate, research a recent situation that has caused a business, a not-for-profit organization, or a government agency to suffer from bad publicity. Evaluate the situation and create a program outlining steps the firm or organization might take to obtain better publicity and build good public relations.
5. Imagine that the town where your college or university is located has decided to build and develop a new baseball stadium for a minor-league team. The park will be small—about 7,500 seats. As a marketer, what kind of approach would you take for establishing ticket prices?

## Lunesta: The Price of Sleep

Consumers are accustomed to seeing advertisements and other promotions for prescription medications. Television commercials, Internet ads, and magazine promotions with toll-free numbers offering coupons are commonplace. As consumers become increasingly educated about purchasing medications, how do marketers create competitive messages and pricing structures for their products?

Insomnia has been called an epidemic in the United States. Every night, millions of people toss and turn without getting the sleep they need. The market for sleep aids has existed for a long time and has been filled with all kinds of remedies sold by prescription and over the counter. They have a wide range of effectiveness and side effects. Recently, the Food and Drug Administration approved a prescription sleep aid manufactured by Sepracor, called Lunesta. The drug is considered a breakthrough because studies have shown that most patients who take it do not experience drowsiness the next day and its effectiveness does not decrease over time. Because Lunesta is the first such medication to be approved for long-term use, the choices that Sepracor makes for promotion and pricing are critical.

The Lunesta launch was accompanied by a series of ads explaining the benefits of the medication, as well as cautions regarding its correct use. For instance, one ad says, "Lunesta works quickly, so you should only take it right before bed." The ads contain a toll-free number and Web site address so that consumers can learn more about the drug. In the ads, a luminescent butterfly accompanies the image of a sleeping person; that way, consumers will begin to associate the butterfly with the Lunesta brand.

Lunesta comes in different strengths, at different prices. The average price for 30 tablets—a one-month supply of the lowest dose—is $99. The average price for the same number of tablets in the highest dose is $332. The top three nonprescription, natural sleep aids sell for around $30—a large difference in price. Lunesta must compete not only with other prescription medications but also with those that are sold over the counter, so its marketing messages must be strong.

So far, the Lunesta launch has been successful from a business standpoint. "The . . . data suggest that the launch is meeting the already high expectations for the drug," reported investment firm Morgan Stanley just a few months after the drug reached the market. If the drug's track record continues to be positive and doctors continue to provide prescriptions for their patients, then there may be a lot fewer sleepless nights—both for patients and for Sepracor.

### Questions for Critical Thinking

1. Identify two or three ethical issues that marketers of prescription drugs such as Lunesta must consider when developing their promotional efforts.
2. How would you describe the pricing objectives of the makers of Lunesta? What do you think would be the best pricing strategy? Why?

Sources: Lunesta Web site, accessed July 18, 2006, http://www.lunesta.ws; "Sepracor Announces Launch Timing for Lunesta Brand Eszopiclone for Treatment of Insomnia," ImmuneSupport.com, accessed July 18, 2006, http://www.immunesupport.com; "Sepracor's Seamless Lunesta Launch," Forbes, accessed July 18, 2006, http://www.forbes.com; Cassandra Walters, "Is Lunesta (Eszolpiclone) Right for You?" Consumer Health Digest.com, accessed May 10, 2005, http://consumerhealthdigest.com.

## VIDEO Case 14.2

### Wild Oats Promotes Local Foods

This video case appears on page 623. A recently filmed video, designed to expand and highlight the written case, is available for class use by instructors.

# The Second City Theater Continuing Case
# Marketing: This Company Is More Than Just Funny Business

Consider for a moment the various options you might have while visiting Chicago. You may want to go to a Cubs or White Sox game. You could visit Sue, the world's most complete T-Rex at the Field Museum, or perhaps go to the top of Sears Tower and gaze upon one of the largest cities in America. Or . . . you could see why Chicago has been dubbed the comedy capital of the world. The Second City is vastly celebrated in the entertainment industry and continues to attract audiences from around the globe. In fact, since its founding in 1959, SC Chicago has consistently played to sold-out crowds. It first got the term *Second City* from a series of *New Yorker* articles disparaging Chicago. It was a brilliant marketing move, inspired by news and propelled by bold jest.

Tourists coming to the Windy City provide the most significant customer base for Second City. The innovative, fast-paced comedy is a unique experience for travelers who then return home and promote the company by word of mouth. This is Second City's primary form of advertising. With an impressive list of famous performers and the ability to produce quality local shows, Second City has gained extensive brand equity. Because Second City is unparalleled in the comedic theater industry, cable television and cinema are the competition. Second City has evolved into a family brand, distributing the company through a variety of channels and thereby capitalizing on its position in the market. Its numerous performance venues, touring companies, training centers, productions on cruise lines, and business communications branch are all marketed as Second City brand endeavors.

Whether you visit Chicago, Detroit, Toronto, Denver, or Las Vegas, the Second City Theater will be decorated with its now famous logo and photos of its famous graduates filling the walls. The cast and everything created before your eyes will be an authentically new experience. Second City's marketing strategies are customized to the character of the locale. In Toronto, the theater deals with a struggling economy by creating a more localized show; in Las Vegas, Second City stands out as a comparatively understated venue in an otherwise overstated city; in Detroit and Denver, the two newer establishments, shows and promotion, are building a core audience in the community; and in Chicago, the theater supplements its flagship Main Stage with additional eclectic shows designed to reattract the local audience. Each theater uses personalized comedy and marketing to build a relationship with the community.

Kelly Leonard, Second City's vice president, attributes Second City's success in forming long-term relationships with consumers through "our expanded services. We offer kids' classes now, so we have 5-year-olds getting in touch with Second City. We offer workshops and shows in the high schools; we play the colleges; we provide corporate entertainment—basically, we're creating a series of 'ins' that cross over a variety of ages and experiences. The more stuff we can create that is pure to what we do, the better we are positioning ourselves for the future." Across its marketing landscape, The Second City handles their principal product of comedy. For the SC Communications Company, this can foster a limiting perception for a corporate client that may benefit from more than just laughs. Collaborating with clients in the creation process has enriched the relationship. The ability to understand its consumers has provided Second City with various lucrative connections to the business world.

Second City's partnership with Norwegian Cruise Lines illustrates an understanding of its target market. Building on its appeal to tourists, Second City has seized an opportunity to reach a group with similar lifestyles and cultural backgrounds. Naming the group as its exclusive provider of sketch comedy, the exotic cruise line has brought Second City an exciting new platform for product distribution.

Back on land, Second City attracts two primary constituents to its sizable Training Center. The high visibility of the Second City brand throughout the entertainment industry has led aspiring performers from all over the country to learn the art of improvisation. There are also classes intended for the casual humor hobbyist or anyone who would like to relieve stress with what is commonly known as "the best medicine." These students continue to market the institution to their friends and family. The more serious participants find a certain "specialty product" within the unique training. By training with Second City, performers might find themselves graduating from the program and getting hired for one of the touring companies, a cruise ship, or even SC's coveted Main Stage. With the reputation of Second City as the liftoff stage for talent, training at the famous theater can be a key accomplishment. Even

multigenre actors such as Halle Berry and Alan Arkin have benefited from the cherished comedic education.

The Second City touring companies showcase emerging talent in two markets: performing arts centers and colleges. The company performs the signature combination of SC sketch comedy and live improvisation inspired by audience suggestions. A booking agent manages the financial agreements through various conferences and networking. For Kelly Leonard, the touring companies represent the organization's true appeal. "For the performing arts centers we position ourselves as a trusted and respected theatrical brand. For the colleges, we're the cutting-edge comedians," says Leonard. Second City offers a convenient product with the help of these ensembles.

No matter how you might have heard of Second City, its Web site is the most inclusive marketing tool. SecondCity.com includes a full list of alumni, posters, reviews of shows up and running on all its stages, training center information and virtual shorts that market the theatre's services to the corporate industry. The Internet is one place where the family of Second City brands unites.

Now if you wander up to Second City's management offices, you won't find an extensive collection of marketing research studies. They've only recently begun using market research. Second City has distributed its brand by reacting quickly to the ideas fostered in the creative atmosphere that has been with it since the beginning. Its inventive approach to marketing has widely extended its product while preserving its recognizable brand. So if visiting Chicago might not be on your schedule this year, a visit from a Second City touring company might be just around the corner.

## QUESTIONS

1. How has Second City been able to maintain its strong brand identity?
2. How does Second City vary its marketing strategies across the company?
3. What is Second City's target market and how is it related to the location of the theater? What are some marketing challenges that Second City faces with its family branding?

# Part 4: Launching Your Marketing Career

In Part 4, "Marketing Management," you learned about the goals and functions of marketing. The three chapters in this part emphasized the central role of customer satisfaction in defining value and developing a marketing strategy in traditional and nontraditional marketing settings. You learned about the part played by marketing research and the need for relationship marketing in today's competitive environment. You discovered how new products are developed and how they evolve through the four stages of the product life cycle, from introduction through growth and maturity to decline. You also learned about the role of different channels in creating effective distribution strategies. Finally, you saw the impact of integrated marketing communications on the firm's promotional strategy, the role of advertising, ethical issues in promotion, and the way pricing influences consumer behavior. Perhaps you came across some marketing tasks and functions that sounded especially appealing to you. Here are a few ideas about careers in marketing that you may want to pursue.

The first thing to remember is that, as the chapters in this part made clear, marketing is about a great deal more than personal selling and advertising. For instance, are you curious about why people behave the way they do? Are you good at spotting trends? *Marketing research analysts* seek answers to a wide range of questions about business competition, customer preferences, market trends, and past and future sales. They often design and conduct their own consumer surveys, using the telephone, mail, the Internet, or personal interviews and focus groups. After they analyze the data they've collected, their recommendations form input for managerial decisions about whether to introduce new products, revamp current ones, enter new markets, or abandon products or markets where profitability is low. As members of a new-product development team, marketing researchers often work directly with members of other business departments such as scientists, production and manufacturing personnel, and

finance employees. Also, marketing researchers are increasingly asked to help clients implement their recommendations. With today's highly competitive economy, jobs in this area are expected to grow. Annual earnings for marketing research analysts average $56,000.[1]

Another career path in marketing is sales. Do you work well with others and read their feelings accurately? Are you a self-starter? Being a *sales representative* might be for you. Selling jobs exist in every industry, and because many use a combination of salary and performance-based commissions, they can pay handsomely. Sales jobs are often a first step on the ladder to upper-management positions as well. Sales representatives work for wholesalers and manufacturing companies (and even for publishers such as the one that produces this book). They sell automobiles, computer systems and technology, pharmaceuticals, advertising, insurance, real estate, commodities and financial services, and all kinds of consumer goods and services.

If you're interested in mass communications, note that magazines, newspapers, and broadcast companies such as ESPN and MTV generate most of their revenue from advertising, so sales representatives who sell space and time slots in the media contribute a great deal to the success of these firms.[2] And if you like to travel, consider that travel agents are salespeople, too.

*Advertising, marketing management, and public relations* are other categories of marketing. In large companies, marketing managers, product managers, promotion managers, and public-relations managers often work long hours under pressure; they may travel frequently or transfer between jobs at headquarters and positions in regional offices. Their responsibilities include directing promotional programs, overseeing advertising campaigns and budgets, and conducting communications such as press releases with the firm's publics. Thousands of new positions are expected to open up in the next several years; the field is expected to grow 22 percent over the next decade.

Growth of the Internet and new media has especially increased demand for advertising and public-relations specialists. [3]

Advertising and public-relations firms employed about 425,000 people in a recent year.[4] About one in five U.S. advertising firms are located in New York or California, and more than a quarter of advertising industry workers live in those two states. Most advertising firms develop specialties; many of the largest are international in scope and earn a major proportion of their revenue abroad. Online advertising is just one area in which new jobs will be opening in the future, as more and more client firms expand their online sales operations.

## Career Assessment Exercises in Marketing

1. Select a field that interests you. Use the Internet to research types of sales positions available in that field. Locate a few entry-level job openings and see what career steps that position can lead to. (You might wish to start with a popular job-posting site such as Monster.com.) Note the job requirements, the starting salary, and the form of compensation—straight salary? salary plus commission?—and write a one-page summary of your findings.

2. Use the Internet to identify and investigate two or three of the leading advertising agencies in the United States, such as Young & Rubicam or J. Walter Thompson. What are some of their recent ad campaigns, or who are their best-known clients? Where do the agencies have offices? What job openings do they currently list, and what qualifications should applicants for these positions have? Write a brief report comparing the agencies you selected, decide which one you would prefer to work for, and give your reasons.

3. Test your research skills. Choose an ordinary product, such as toothpaste or soft drinks, and conduct a survey to find out why people chose the brand they most recently purchased. For instance, suppose you wanted to find out how people choose their shampoo. List as many decision criteria as you can think of, such as availability, scent, price, packaging, benefits from use (conditioning, dandruff-reducing, and so on), brand name, and ad campaign. Ask eight to ten friends to rank these decision factors, and note some simple demographics about your research subjects such as their age, gender, and occupation. Tabulate your results. What did you find out about how your subjects made their purchase decision? Did any of your findings surprise you? Can you think of any ways in which you might have improved your survey?

# Part 5

# Chapter 15

## Using Technology to Manage Information

Less than a decade ago, Larry Page and Sergey Brin came up with a brilliant—and ambitious—idea. What if they could organize all the information in the world *and* make it accessible to anyone with a computer? And what if they could somehow turn this idea into a business? With these lofty goals, Google was born.

"Googol" is the mathematical term for a 1 followed by 100 zeros. The term was created by Milton Sirotta, nephew of American mathematician Edward Kasner. Google's use of the term reflects the company's mission to organize the vast amount of information available on the Internet. Founders Page and Brin have been true to their company's name: Google's Internet search engine is so powerful that it has "essentially tamed the Web," writes one industry watcher. And the name is already so pervasive in everyday life and lan-

Google pulls in revenues from the text ads that appear next to search results. When a user clicks the ad, the advertiser is charged a fee. These revenues allow the firm to hire engineers and designers to develop new search products. "The number of new [Google] products is related

# Google: How to Succeed without Really Selling

guage that it has become a verb. People routinely say, "I'll Google that." Why has Google become this successful this quickly?

First, Google's search products are easy to access and use. Second, they are free. Both consumers and businesses like Google's convenience. Its index now consists of more than 8 billion Web pages. Whether you are looking for information on an obscure artist or a list of Web sites that sell gourmet coffee, you'll find what you need through Google. Specialized Google search products include inboxes (Gmail) and photos (Picasa). If you've forgotten what you searched for in the past, you can click My Search History. Google will hold the data for you until you decide to delete it—an important feature in many people's security-conscious minds. With Google Earth, you can pinpoint just about any location on the planet, including your own home. In fact, the launch of this most recent product has some government officials worried that it could actually provide satellite photos of potential terrorist targets. The governments of India, South Korea, Thailand, and the Netherlands have already expressed concern about Google Earth's capabilities. But Google insists that its software uses only information that is already available to the public.

to the number of engineers—it's a linear function," explains Marissa Mayer, director of the firm's consumer Web products. With more than 4,000 employees, Google is poised to grow much larger. In fact, some industry watchers warn that it is already nipping at the heels of Microsoft, which employs 61,000 workers and holds $38 billion in cash. "When we see a remarkable new company that redefines the technology industry, we either fear it because of all the things it might do or we expect more from it than it can possibly deliver," notes business author John Battelle.

What's next for Google? Engineers are currently working on ways to remove language barriers from the Internet. Currently, Google can automatically translate Web pages from English into German, Spanish, French, Italian, Japanese, Chinese, and several other languages. But Google engineers are developing the technology for all search results to return automatically in a user's native language, regardless of what it is. "The goal is to make the Internet language-independent," explains Alan Eustace, head of Google's research. "In the long term, if you can create technology that can unify information around the world and remove the language barrier, that would be very special."

**ChapterOverview**

This chapter explores how businesses manage information as a resource, particularly how they use technology to do so. The chapter begins by differentiating information and data, and describing management information systems. It then looks at ways companies use information systems to organize and use information, including databases and information system programs. Because computers drive information systems, the chapter also discusses computer types and their applications in business settings. Today, specialized networks make information access and transmission function smoothly, so the chapter examines new types of networks to see how businesses are applying them for competitive advantage. Finally, the chapter explores the importance of protecting valuable information and recovering from information system disasters.

**data** raw facts and figures that may or may not be relevant to a business decision.

**information** knowledge gained from processing data.

**management information system (MIS)** organized method for providing past, present, and projected information on internal operations as well as external intelligence to support decision making.

## "They Said It"

"You can give people responsibility and authority, but without information they are helpless."
—Bill Gates (b. 1955)
Co-founder, Microsoft Corporation

# MANAGEMENT INFORMATION SYSTEMS

Every day, businesspeople ask themselves questions such as the following:

- How well is our brand selling in Seattle compared with Charlotte? How has the bird flu epidemic affected sales of poultry products in Asia? In Europe?
- If we raise the price of our products by 2 percent, how will the change affect sales in each city? In each country?
- What impact have higher energy prices had on the cost of raw materials?
- If employees can access the benefits system through our network, will it increase or decrease benefits costs?

An effective information system can help answer these and many other questions. **Data** consist of raw facts and figures that may or may not be relevant to a business decision. **Information** is knowledge gained from processing those facts and figures. So although businesspeople need to gather data about the demographics of a target market or the specifications of a certain product, the data are useless unless they are transformed into relevant information that can be used to make a competitive decision. Technology has advanced so quickly that all businesses, regardless of size or location, now have access to data and information that can make them competitive in a global arena.

A **management information system (MIS)** is an organized method for providing past, present, and projected information on internal operations as well as external intelligence to support decision making. A large organization typically assigns responsibility for directing its MIS and related computer operations to an executive called the **chief information officer (CIO)**. Often the CIO reports directly to the firm's chief executive officer (CEO). But small companies rely just as much on an MIS as do large ones, even if they do not employ a manager assigned to this area on a full-time basis. An effective CIO can understand and harness technology so that the company can communicate internally and externally in one seamless operation.

The role of the CIO is both expanding and changing as the technology to manage information continues to develop. According to one recent survey, around half of all CIOs stated that their job responsibilities have broadened significantly in recent years.[2] CIOs are also well compensated. The Gartner Group, an information technology consulting company, found that annual compensation for CIOs today exceeds $300,000 on average, with many CIOs at larger firms earning more than $1 million per year.[3]

The importance of managing information can also be seen in the growth in demand for college graduates with degrees in information systems. According to the Bureau of Labor Statistics, the number of people employed in information systems and related fields will grow by around 55 percent between now and 2012.[4] Starting salaries for those with undergraduate degrees in information systems average more than $43,000 per year.[5]

Information systems can be tailored to assist many business functions and departments—providing reports for everything from marketing and manufacturing, to finance and accounting. They can manage the overwhelming flood of information by organizing data in a logical and accessible manner. Through the system, a company can monitor all components of its business strategy, identifying problems and opportunities. Information systems gather data from inside and outside the organization; they then process the data to produce information that is relevant to all aspects of the organization. Processing steps could involve storing data for later use, classifying and analyzing it, and retrieving it easily when needed. Computerized location systems are a booming technology that has many applications.

Many companies—and nations—combine high-tech and low-tech solutions to manage the flow of information. E-mail, wireless communications, and videoconferencing haven't totally replaced paper memos, phone conversations, and face-to-face meetings, but they are increasingly common. Information can make the difference between staying in business and going bankrupt. Keeping on top of changing consumer demands, competitors' actions, and the latest government regulations will help a firm fine-tune existing products, develop new winners, and maintain effective marketing.

## Databases

The heart of a management information system is its **database,** a centralized integrated collection of data resources. A company designs its databases to meet particular information processing and retrieval requirements that its decision makers encounter. Businesses create databases in many ways. They can hire a staff person to build them on site, hire an outside source to do so, or buy readily available database programs. A database serves as an electronic filing cabinet, capable of storing massive amounts of data and retrieving it within seconds. A database should be continually updated; otherwise, a firm may find itself with data that are outdated and possibly useless. One problem with databases is that they can contribute to information overload—too much data for people to absorb or data that are not relevant to decision making. Because computer processing speed and storage capacity are both increasing rapidly, and as data have become more abundant, businesspeople need to be careful that their databases contain only the facts they need, so they do not waste time wading through unnecessary data.

Decision makers can also look up online data. Online systems give access to enormous amounts of government data, such as economic data from the Bureau of Labor Statistics and the Department of Commerce. One of the largest online databases is that of the U.S. Census Bureau. The census of population, conducted every ten years, attempts to collect data on more than 120 million households across the United States. Selected participants fill out forms containing questions about marital status, place of birth, ethnic background, citizenship, workplaces, commuting time, income, occupation, type of housing, number of telephones and vehicles, even grandparents as caregivers. Households receiving the most recent questionnaire could

**database** centralized integrated collection of data resources.

The U.S. Census Bureau's Web site is a large, searchable online database with all sorts of information. The "Reference Maps" link in the American Factfinder topic area contains information on states, such as major roads, bodies of water, and other details. Visitors can zoom in and out for different sets of data.

respond in English as well as a variety of other languages including Spanish, Chinese, Vietnamese, and Korean. Not surprisingly, sifting through all the collected data takes time. Although certain restrictions limit how businesspeople can access and use specific census data, the general public may access the data via the American FactFinder on the Census Bureau's Web site (http://www.census.gov), as well as at state data centers and public libraries.

Another source of free information is company Web sites. Interested parties can visit firms' home pages to look for information about customers, suppliers, and competitors. Trade associations and academic institutions also maintain Web sites with information on topics of interest.

Companies also subscribe to commercial online services that provide fee-for-service databases on particular topics. In addition to broad-based online databases available through such services as LexisNexis and Infotrac, firms can also access specialized databases geared to particular industries and functions. Many professional groups and trade associations have set up electronic bulletin board systems on the Internet where data and information are available. For instance, *Bicycle Retailer* maintains an bulletin board on its Web site where bike shop owners and employees can exchange ideas and information. It also provides data to members on bike sales and other industry trends. Businesspeople who gather data online should always try to verify the reliability of their sources, however.

## Business Intelligence

Once a company has built a database, its managers need to be able to analyze the data in it. As discussed in Chapter 12, *data mining,* or *business intelligence,* is the task of using computer-based technology to retrieve and evaluate data in a database to identify useful trends. It focuses on identifying relationships that are not obvious to businesspeople—in a sense, answering questions that they may not even have thought to ask. Data mining is an efficient way to sort through huge databases and to make sense of that data. Among other things, data mining can help create customer profiles, pinpoint reasons for customer loyalty, analyze the impact of pricing changes, and forecast sales.

Specialized data mining and business intelligence software is available from a variety of companies such as Oracle and SAP. IBM offers a software product called DB2 Intelligent Miner for Data. Customers use the program to gain new business insights and to harvest valuable business intelligence from all of a company's data, such as high-volume transaction data generated by point-of-sale, ATM, and credit card transactions or call center and e-commerce activities. With Intelligent Miner for Data, executives are better equipped to make insightful decisions, whether the problem is how to develop more precisely targeted marketing campaigns, reduce customer attrition, or increase revenue generated by online shopping.[6]

Some consulting firms, such as Boston-based Data Miners, specialize in data mining for their clients. Recently, Data Miners was asked to

SAS Institute offers business intelligence software to companies to help them analyze their data.

investigate transaction-level data from loyalty cardholders of a New England health food supermarket. Data Miners found that 50 percent of the supermarket's customers were meat eaters, and this group was among the store's most valuable customers. Had the supermarket eliminated meat, assuming that its customers were vegetarians, it would have lost a very profitable business segment. The data clearly showed that meat-eating customers were interested in, and willing to pay for, health food.[7] As this example illustrates, successful data mining can help a business discover patterns in the sale of certain goods and services, find new customers, track customer complaints and requests, and evaluate the cost of materials.

**assessment check**

1. What is the difference between data and information?
2. Define management information system.
3. What is the purpose of business intelligence?

# INFORMATION SYSTEMS FOR DECISION MAKING

So much data clogs the Internet, databases, and other data sources that the challenge for businesses has shifted from acquiring data to sorting through it to find the most useful elements, which can then be turned into valuable information. New types of information system software are being developed all the time. These range from tools that help users look up data on various topics to specialized systems that track costs, sales, inventory levels, and other data. Businesses can develop and implement their own systems or hire someone else to do so. Many also hire an outside service to manage data for them.

## Decision Support System

A **decision support system (DSS)** is an information system that quickly provides relevant data to help businesspeople make decisions and choose courses of action. It includes software tools that help decision makers generate the type of information they need. These DSS tools may vary from company to company, but they typically include retrieval features that help users obtain needed information from a database, simulation elements that let decision makers create computer models to evaluate future company performance under different conditions, and presentation tools that create graphs and charts.

**decision support system (DSS)** information system that quickly provides relevant data to help businesspeople make decisions and choose courses of action.

An information interface is a software program between the user and the underlying information system. Advances in information interfaces have simplified and synthesized data into useful information for a variety of users. For instance, visitors to the *Cooking Light* Web site (http://www.cookinglight.com) can access recipes through an easy-to-use interface. Visitors can search the magazine's vast database by main ingredient, cooking technique, ethnicity, and even special dietary requirements. Comments from users are also available. With a few mouse clicks visitors can create an entire menu, accompanied by a shopping list. Such sophisticated interfaces make information retrieval more efficient.

**Executive Support Systems** Although the trend is increasingly toward employee empowerment and decision making at all levels of an organization, sometimes companies need to create specialized information systems to address the needs of executives. An **executive support system (ESS)** lets top managers access the firm's primary databases, often by touching the computer screen, pointing with a mouse, or even speaking via voice recognition. The typical ESS allows users to choose from many kinds of data, such as the firm's financial statements and sales figures as well as stock market trends for the company and for the industry as a whole. If they wish, managers can start by looking at summaries and then proceed toward more detailed information.

**executive support system (ESS)** system that allows top managers to access a firm's primary databases.

*Expert Systems* An **expert system** is a computer program that imitates human thinking through complicated sets of "if-then" rules. The system applies human knowledge in a specific subject area to solve the problem. Expert systems are used for a variety of business purposes: determining credit limits for credit card applicants, monitoring machinery in a plant to predict potential problems or breakdowns, making mortgage loans, and determining optimal plant layouts. They are typically developed by capturing the knowledge of recognized experts in a field whether within a business itself or outside it.

## Trends in Information Systems

New information systems are being developed all the time. Today's computer systems help businesspeople obtain and share information in real time, across departments, across the country, and around the world through networks.

*Local Area Networks and Wide Area Networks* Most organizations connect their offices and buildings by creating **local area networks (LANs),** computer networks that connect machines within limited areas, such as a building or several buildings near one another. LANs are useful because they link personal computers and allow them to share printers, documents, and information, as well as provide access to the Internet. Figure 15.1 shows what a small business computer network might look like.

Wide area networks (WANS) tie larger geographical regions together by using telephone lines and microwave and satellite transmission. One familiar WAN is long-distance telephone service. Companies such as AT&T and Verizon provide WAN services to businesses and con-

**Figure**

**15.1** A Local Area Network

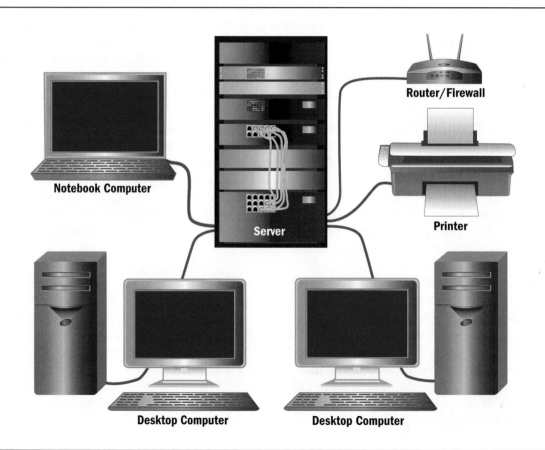

Notebook Computer

Router/Firewall

Server

Printer

Desktop Computer      Desktop Computer

sumers. Firms also use WANs to conduct their own operations. Typically, companies link their own network systems to outside communications equipment and services for transmission across long distances. Later in the chapter, we discuss other specialized networking systems.

*Wireless Local Networks*    A wireless network allows computers, printers, and other devices to be connected without the hassle of stringing cables in traditional office settings. The current standard for wireless networks is called **Wi-Fi.** Wi-Fi—short for *wireless fidelity*—is a wireless network that connects various devices and allows them to communicate with one another through radio waves. Any PC with a Wi-Fi receptor can connect with the Internet at so-called *hot spots*—locations with a wireless router and a high-speed Internet modem. By one estimate, the number of registered hot spots worldwide now exceeds 70,000.[8] They are found in a variety of places including airports, libraries, and coffee shops. For instance, virtually all Starbucks locations throughout the United States, and in many other countries, are Wi-Fi hot spots. Some hot spots provide free Internet access; others charge fees. AT&T, for example, offers the Freedom Network, a collection of hot spots throughout the nation. Access requires either an annual subscription or the payment of a onetime access fee.

> **Wi-Fi** wireless network that connects various devices and allows them to communicate with one another through radio waves; short for *wireless fidelity.*

Many believe that the successor to Wi-Fi will be **Wi-Max**, a new wireless standard. Wi-Max recently got a huge boost when Intel announced that it would begin producing computer chips incorporating this new wireless standard.[9] Unlike Wi-Fi's relatively limited geographic coverage area—generally around 300 feet—a single Wi-Max access point can provide coverage over many miles. Hundreds of cities, including San Francisco and Philadelphia, have announced plans to build Wi-Max networks that will, in essence, turn these cities into giant hot spots. Wi-Max also has the potential to bring high-speed Internet access to rural areas where traditional forms of broadband access are too expensive or impractical. For instance, Morrow County, Oregon, has only 11,000 people but covers more than 2,000 square miles. Wi-Max is the only practical and cost-effective way to provide broadband access to this sparsely populated region. So Morrow County became one of the first rural areas in the country to be blanketed by a Wi-Max network. Now onion farmer Bob Hale can open his laptop to check his e-mail, find out the current price of onions, send digital photographs of his crop to restaurant buyers throughout the country, or adjust his irrigation sprinklers. And Hale can accomplish these tasks sitting in the cab of his truck in the middle of his vast onion fields.[10]

## Application Service Providers and On-Demand Computing

Because of the increasing cost and complexity of obtaining and maintaining information systems, many firms hire an **application service provider (ASP)**, an outside supplier that provides both the computers and the application support for managing an information system. An ASP can simplify complex software for its customers so that it is easier for them to manage and use. When an ASP relationship is successful, the buyer can then devote more time and resources to its core businesses instead of struggling to manage its information systems. Other benefits include stretching the firm's technology dollar farther and giving smaller companies the kind of information power that in the past has been available only to much larger organizations. Even large companies turn to ASPs to manage some or all of their information systems. Recently, the Walt Disney Company decided to outsource much of its IT functions to IBM and Affiliated Computer Services to save money. Around 1,000 Disney employees moved into new jobs with the two vendors.[11]

> **application service provider (ASP)** specialist in providing both the computers and the application support for managing information systems for clients.

Another recent trend is **on-demand computing,** also called **utility computing.** Instead of purchasing and maintaining expensive software, firms essentially rent the software time from application providers and pay only for their usage of the software, similar to purchasing

# HIT&MISS

## How Does Dell Do It?

When is a computer company not a computer company? When it changes its name—as Dell did several years ago, shifting from Dell Computer Corp. to Dell Inc.—and when it creates a new name for an existing category of products. Dell is still the largest PC vendor in the United States, and its total PC sales make up the majority of its revenues. But in a business environment in which PC sales are generally flat or declining, Dell has fashioned a new term for the category of products it sells the most: *mobility*.

Dell's mobility products include laptops, wireless devices, handheld computers, and digital music players. These items account for about 20 percent of Dell's sales, mostly from laptops. While some skeptics wonder about the firm's distinction between desktop computers and laptops as two different types of products, Michael Dell believes the distinction is important to his company's new direction. Dell believes that wireless technology has created a new type of demand for laptops, making them completely different from the way desktops are used. Then there's the obvious distinction: laptops are portable, while desktops are not.

Dell is still very much in the PC business. The packages it sells, which include software, printers, monitors, storage devices, and services, all surround the PC itself. But these additional products truly help bolster the firm during a time when the industry itself is sluggish. For instance, Dell entered the services marketplace focusing on what it does best—offering flexibility and a low price. "Dell has been flexible in defining the level of service. There are different levels of service even in one data center," says one business customer. In addition, Dell offers a nearly unbeatable financing service, following its original direct-sales business model. Loans or leases made by Dell Financial Services to Dell customers have increased more than 35 percent annually in recent years.

Meanwhile, Dell has also made inroads overseas, particularly in Asia—Japan, South Korea, India, China, and Vietnam—where it is focusing on its business customers. Dell faces two formidable competitors in Asia: Hewlett-Packard and Lenovo Group. But it's not backing down. "Everyone wants to be number one," says one analyst who follows the companies.

### Questions for Critical Thinking

1. Do you agree with Dell's distinction between laptops and desktops? Why or why not?
2. Describe ways in which Dell might market its "mobility" category of products.

**Sources:** Stan Gibson, "Dell Makes Services Inroads," *eWeek,* accessed July 21, 2006, http://www.eweek.com; "Sales Hiccup as Dell Gobbles Market Share," Datamonitor, accessed July 21, 2006, http://www.datamonitor.com; Satish Shankar and Ravi Vijayaraghavan, "It Can Pay to Be a Copycat," *Financial Times,* accessed July 21, 2006, http://www.financialtimes.com; Gretchen Morgenson, "Dude, You're Getting a Loan," *New York Times,* accessed July 21, 2006, http://www.nytimes.com; Sumner Lemon, "Dell Wants More Satisfaction in Asia," IT World.com, accessed September 23, 2005, http://www.itworld.com; Crayton Harrison, "Dell Sees Much of its Future Grow in Mobility Products," *Dallas Morning News,* accessed April 8, 2005, http://www.dallasnews.com.

---

electricity from a utility. On-demand computing is particularly useful for firms that experience annual peaks in demand or seasonal spikes in customer usage of their applications. By renting the service they need only when they need it, they can avoid buying equipment and software that is not routinely required. On-demand computing can also help companies remain current with the most efficient software on the market without purchasing huge upgrades.

Companies that decide to use ASPs should check the backgrounds and references of these firms before hiring them to manage critical systems. In addition, customers should try to ensure that the service provider has taken appropriate measures to block computer hackers or other unauthorized access to the data, that its data centers are up and running consistently, and that adequate backups are maintained.

Although information systems can help a company run smoothly and efficiently, the firm must carefully plan and organize them. Otherwise, it can lose control of a critical function—and tremendous amounts of time and money. Issues of privacy and security also arise. Should everyone in the company be able to access all of the company's data? What about confidential human resources files or the corporation's payroll system? These issues are explored later in the chapter.

# COMPUTER HARDWARE AND SOFTWARE

Just a few decades ago, computers were considered exotic curiosities, used only for very specialized applications and understood by only a few people. Up until the 1980s, the idea of a computer on every desk, or in every home, seemed far-fetched. Today they have become indispensable not only to businesses but also to households. Who can imagine daily life without sending e-mails to friends and co-workers, booking airline tickets over the Internet, preparing reports with a word-processing program, or balancing a checkbook using a personal money management program? Computers have become not only much more powerful and faster over the past 25 years but less expensive as well. IBM's first personal computer, introduced in the early 1980s, cost close to $5,000 (fully configured) and yet its computing power was only a small fraction of that of today's PCs. Today's PCs also cost thousands less than IBM's original PC. According to one recent survey, the average desktop sells for less than $800 today.[12]

As the price of computers continues to drop, so have profit margins for computer manufacturers. IBM, which along with Apple pretty much invented the personal computer, recently sold its PC business to concentrate on servers, larger computers, software, and technology services. Many of the remaining manufacturers such as Gateway and HP struggle to make money. The one exception is Dell, the world's largest PC maker. Its success is profiled in the "Hit & Miss" feature.

## Types of Computer Hardware

**Hardware** consists of all tangible elements of a computer system—the input devices, the components that store and process data and perform required calculations, and the output devices that present the results to information users. Input devices allow users to enter data and commands for processing, storage, and output. Common input devices include the keyboard, mouse, scanner, modem, microphone, and touch screen. Storage and processing components consist of the hard drive as well as various other storage components, including CD and DVD drives and flash memory devices. Most computers today have CD and DVD drives that allow users to create (or burn) CDs and DVDs as well as read them. Flash memory devices are becoming increasingly popular because they are small, hold large amounts of data—as much as two gigabytes or more—and fit in a pocket. They can be plugged into an unused USB (universal serial bus) port found on virtually all of today's computers.

Output devices are the hardware elements that transmit or display documents and other results of a computer system's work. Examples include the monitor, printer, fax machine, modem, and audio system. Notice that some devices, such as the monitor and modem, can perform both input and output functions. While CRT monitors are still in use, most new desktop computers today come with so-called *flat-panel LCD monitors*. (Notebook computers use LCD displays.) LCD monitors take up much less desk space, and use less electricity, than CRT monitors.

USED WITH PERMISSION. SAMSUNG ELECTRONICS AMERICA, INC.

Samsung displays. Turn business on.

The Samsung 242MP display. Explore more of what's out there.

SAMSUNG

**LCD monitors are now standard with many of today's PCs.**

Different types of computers incorporate widely varying memory capacities and processing speeds. As shown in Figure 15.2, these differences define three broad classifications: mainframes, minicomputers, and personal computers. A **mainframe** computer is the largest type of computer system with the most extensive storage capacity and the fastest processing speeds. Especially powerful mainframes called *supercomputers* can handle extremely rapid, complex calculations involving thousands of variables. A **minicomputer** is an intermediate-size computer—more compact and less expensive than a mainframe but also somewhat slower and with less memory. These intermediate computers often toil in universities, factories, and research labs. Minicomputers also appeal to many small businesses that need more power than personal computers can offer to handle specialized tasks. IBM, Sun Microsystems, and Silicon Graphics are major manufacturers of minicomputers.

Personal computers (PCs) are everywhere today—in homes, schools, businesses, nonprofit organizations, and government agencies. For example, an estimated two-thirds of American households have at least one personal computer. They have earned increasing popularity because their ever-expanding capability to handle many of the functions that cumbersome mainframes performed only a few decades ago. These advances were made possible by the development of powerful chips—thin silicon wafers that carry integrated circuits (networks of transistors and electronic circuits). A microprocessor is a fingernail-size chip that contains the PC's entire central processing unit. Intelligent functions of today's new cars, toys, watches, and other household items also rely on microprocessors. Additional chips provide instruction and memory to convert a microprocessor into a PC.

As technology continues to advance, computers have diminished in size. Desktop computers are still the standard PC seen in offices and homes. However, notebook computers are

**Figure**

**15.2** Types of Computers

COMPUTERS

Mainframes

Supercomputers

Minicomputers

Personal Computers

Desktop Computers

Notebook Computers

Tablet Computers

Handheld Devices

gaining an increasing share of the PC market each year. While sales of desktop computers have remained relatively flat in recent years, sales of notebook computers are growing at double-digit rates. Recently, for instance, sales of notebook computers exceeded sales of desktop computers for the first time.[13] The increasing popularity of notebook computers is due to many factors, including the increased computing power of notebooks, better displays, expansion in wireless access, and, perhaps most important, a shrinking of the price gap between notebooks and desktops, although notebooks still cost more on average.

A more recent innovation in personal computers is the tablet PC, which looks like a notebook computer but with a difference. The screen is detachable. Users can write on the screen using a special-purpose pen. The handwriting is then digitized and can be converted into a format that can be read by word-processing programs. The pen can also be used to edit existing documents. When tablet PCs were first introduced in 2002, some thought that they would quickly be embraced by a wide variety of users. So far, however, that hasn't happened. Tablet PCs make up less than 5 percent of the notebook computers sold worldwide, although they have taken hold in some markets such as education and healthcare. Experts cite higher prices and the mediocre performance of many handwriting recognition software applications as reasons for slow start to tablet PC sales. However, tablet PC prices are falling, along with notebook prices, and handwriting recognition is improving. So many of these same experts are more optimistic about the future of tablet PCs.[14]

**Handheld devices**—made by companies such as BlackBerry, Nokia, Palm, HP, Toshiba, and Dell—are even smaller. They fit in a shirt pocket and run on rechargeable batteries. Two kinds of handheld devices are available to most business and consumer users. The original type is the personal digital assistant (PDA). PDAs keep schedules and contact information and have limited software applications such as word processing and spreadsheets. Most PDAs today allow users to access the Internet through wireless networks. The other type of handheld device is the so-called *smart phone*. A smart phone is essentially a device that combines a cell phone with a PDA. Many users like the added features offered by smart phones; consequently, sales of smart phones are growing rapidly. Gartner Research estimates that annual sales of smart phones exceed 20 million units, while the number of PDAs sold per year has declined to less than 13 million units.[15]

Notebook computers are gaining a larger share of the PC market.

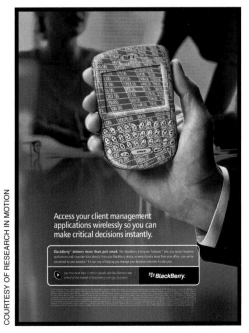

Access your client management applications wirelessly so you can make critical decisions instantly.

The BlackBerry, made by Research In Motion, is one of the most popular handheld devices.

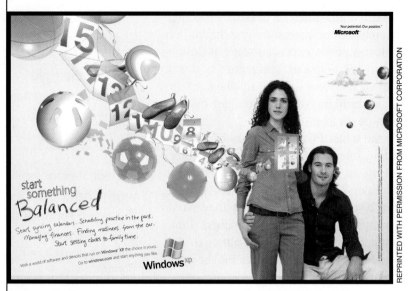

REPRINTED WITH PERMISSION FROM MICROSOFT CORPORATION

**Microsoft Windows runs the majority of PCs.**

**software** set of instructions that tell the computer hardware what to do.

In addition to PDAs and smart phones, specialized handheld devices are used in a variety of businesses for a variety of applications. For instance, DHL, UPS, and FedEx drivers use special handheld devices to track package deliveries. The driver scans each package as it is delivered, and the information is transmitted to the delivery firm's network. Within a few minutes, the sender, using an Internet connection, can obtain the delivery information.

## Types of Computer Software

**Software** includes all of the programs, routines, and computer languages that control a computer and tell it how to operate. The software that controls the basic workings of a computer system is its **operating system.** Moe than 80 percent of personal computers use a version of Microsoft's popular Windows operating system. Personal computers made by Apple use the Mac operating system. Most handheld devices use either the Palm operating system or a special version of Windows called Windows Mobile. Other operating systems include Unix, which runs many minicomputers, and Linux.

A program that performs the specific tasks that the user wants to carry out—such as writing a letter or looking up data—is called **application software.** Examples of application software include Oracle Supply Chain Management Suite, Microsoft Excel, Adobe Acrobat, and QuickBooks. Realtor Trevor Thirsk uses Microsoft Outlook to control his e-mail and organize client paperwork and Microsoft Publisher to create marketing materials. Using these and other software programs helps Thirsk save time—he estimates up to an hour a day—and become one of the top producers at John L. Scott Real Estate, a large residential real estate company in the Pacific Northwest. Even more impressive, Thirsk is one of the youngest, least experienced real estate agents at the firm.[16] The next section discusses the major categories of application software used by business.

**assessment check**

1. How are computers classified?
2. What are the two major categories of computer software?

# HOW COMPUTERS HELP BUSINESSPEOPLE

Computers and their related technologies continue to revolutionize the methods by which businesses manage information. These technologies affect contemporary business in three important ways. First, the enhanced speed and quantity of information available improves the speed and effectiveness of decision making. Second, computers make accurate, unbiased data available to everyone. Third, their information-sharing capabilities support team decision making at low levels of an organization's hierarchy. Every industry has felt at least some impact as computers and information systems have spread.

Consider the Great Harvest Bread Company, headquartered in Dillon, Montana, which operates more than 200 franchised bakeries. Unlike other franchise operations, Great Harvest believes that its franchise operators should be free—after a one-year apprenticeship—to run their stores as they see fit. They aren't required to use the same bread recipe or paint their storefronts the same color. But they are required to share information with each other, which they do via computers. The Great Harvest internal Web site, called the Breadboard, contains announcements of equipment for sale, ongoing electronic charts among franchisees, new recipes, tips for maintaining certain ovens, and archives of other information. Computers help people manage information in an industry that has historically been considered low tech.[17]

Some of the most widely used business applications of computers include enterprise resource planning, word processing, spreadsheets, electronic mail, presentation graphics, and multimedia and interactive media, which are discussed shortly. Users once acquired applications such as these as individual software packages. Today, however, they normally buy integrated software, or *software suites,* which combine several applications into a single package that can share modules for data handling and processing. For personal computer users, the most popular software suite is Microsoft Office, a package that includes word-processing, database management, spreadsheet, presentation, electronic mail, and personal information management software. Businesspeople, for instance, can import data from Access, the database program, into Excel, the spreadsheet program, to create reports and graphs. As another example, you're likely to use PowerPoint—the presentation program—to create dynamic classroom presentations containing text, figures, and even multimedia elements, in many of the classes you take in the coming years.

Some integrated software packages help businesses handle more specific tasks. For example, Palo Alto Software has several software packages that help businesspeople create customized advertising campaigns, marketing plans, and even overall business plans. These programs contain such features as spreadsheet templates designed to evaluate a company's competitiveness in the marketplace.[18]

Today's network technology and software allows multiple users to collaborate on reports and other projects even if they're separated by thousands of miles. Say Ashley and Juan are working on a project. Ashley—who works in the Denver office—writes a preliminary draft using Microsoft Word. She then sends the electronic document to Juan in the Chicago office by e-mail. Juan reviews the document, inserts several figures he created using Microsoft Excel, electronically marks some changes in the Word document, and returns the entire document, including the figures, to Ashley. The process is repeated until they agree on the finished product.

Despite all the advantages of computers, they do have their limitations and should be used to serve the mission of the organization, not just for their own sake. Many businesses have found that their use of computers is actually enhanced by maintaining a human touch—or adding it—to the process. Computers will never replace such face-to-face interactions as phone conversations and meetings.

## Enterprise Resource Planning System

As information systems developed in organizations, they were at first contained within functional departments. Soon managers noticed that the data collected about customers during order processing were reentered by inventory control and shipping. The same duplication was found in human resources management systems and finance and accounting. To avoid such rework, eliminate mistakes or inconsistencies in data, and streamline processes, businesses began to demand a system to unify these separate systems. An **enterprise resource planning (ERP) system** is a set of integrated programs designed to collect, process, and provide information about all business operations. Firms such as Microsoft, Oracle, and SAP offer enterprise software programs and suites to help companies run factories, keep track of accounting, manage the human resources function, and assist in marketing efforts.

Oracle, for instance, offers a variety of ERP software suites and programs, each tailored to specific business applications. One is called Oracle Internet Expenses, part of the company's

enterprise resource planning (ERP) system information system that collects, processes, and provides information about an organization's various functions.

# HIT & MISS

## Nobody Does It Better: Oracle

Oracle founder Larry Ellison has been described as "a slightly grizzled survivor," having weathered all kinds of storms in the software industry. His reputation for being brash and aggressive hasn't changed, but it has mellowed somewhat as the 60-something entrepreneur continues to run the database company he started in 1977.

In an era when the software industry has become increasingly fragmented, Ellison remains focused—providing his customers with the best business application software in the world and on acquiring the companies he believes he needs in order to do so. Consolidation could be termed Ellison's mantra. "The industry is maturing. It is going to consolidate," maintains Ellison. In fact, Oracle had begun to snap up other companies long before Ellison made the prediction. In a highly publicized takeover, Oracle acquired PeopleSoft, a large human resources ERP software company. Recently, Oracle also acquired Siebel Systems, producer of customer relationship management (CRM) applications. CRM applications collect and navigate through all customer interactions so that businesses can better understand and fulfill their customers' needs. The move was huge for Oracle. "In a single step, Oracle becomes the number one CRM applications company in the world," boasted Ellison.

Even with its acquisitions, Oracle still lags behind Cisco, Google, IBM, Intel, and Microsoft in size. And its largest direct ERP competitor is SAP, a German firm. But some industry experts note that hundreds of small software companies are still out there in the market for Oracle—which has plenty of cash—to purchase. And the point of all this acquisition isn't size alone; its ultimate goal is to allow Oracle to surge ahead as the best in the business of providing software applications to companies. The CRM market alone accounts for nearly $10 billion.

Some analysts give Ellison credit for anticipating the next trend in corporate software as well as the move toward consolidation in the industry. "Larry Ellison is a technology visionary and someone who has taken a long-term perspective," notes one industry analyst. Others warn that it will be years before Ellison's strategy proves itself. Bill McDermott, CEO of SAP America, notes that Oracle is only poising itself for larger battles. "The games begin when Microsoft and Oracle lock horns," he predicts. "That's the big looming battle: Oracle versus Microsoft. You've got IBM in there, too."

### Questions for Critical Thinking

1. Oracle seeks to dominate the business software industry. What challenges do you think the firm will face in the next five years?
2. How can a firm like Oracle help its customers improve their own businesses?

**Sources:** Glen Fest, "Battle of Tech Titans: Oracle vs. SAP: Smoke, but No Fire," *Bank Technology News,* accessed July 21, 2006, http://www.banktechnews.com; Daniel Gross, "The J. P. Morgan of Silicon Valley," *Slate,* accessed July 21, 2006, http://slate.msn.com; Benjamin Pimentel, "Top CEO: Larry Ellison Convinced That the Future in High Tech Depends on Consolidation," *San Francisco Chronicle,* accessed July 21, 2006, http://www.sfgate.com.

---

E-Business Suite. It is designed to improve the efficiency of travel and entertainment expense reporting and approval. MasterCard International uses Internet Expenses to process the company's own travel and entertainment transactions. The online application quickly validates and approves expense reports while flagging unusual transactions for further investigation. According to MasterCard, since it started using Internet Expenses, productivity increased by 118 percent and reporting costs dropped by more than 50 percent.[19] Through a series of recent acquisitions, Oracle has become one of the world leaders in ERP software. The firm is profiled in the "Hit & Miss" feature.

**word processing** software that uses a computer to input, store, retrieve, edit, and print various types of documents.

## Word Processing

One of the original business applications—and currently one of the most popular—**word processing** uses computers to input, store, retrieve, edit, and print various types of documents.

With word processing, users can revise sentences, check spelling, correct mistakes, and move copy around quickly and cleanly.

Word processing helps a company handle huge volumes of correspondence, process numerous documents, and personalize form letters. Today virtually all companies use general-purpose computers running word-processing software. By far the most popular word-processing software is Microsoft Word, part of the firm's Office suite. Other word-processing programs include Corel's WordPerfect. These programs enable users to include graphics and spreadsheets from other programs in their documents and to create Web sites by translating documents into hypertext markup language (HTML), the language of the World Wide Web.

Many businesses extend word-processing capabilities to create sophisticated documents. **Desktop publishing** employs computer technology to allow users to design and produce attractively formatted printed material themselves rather than hiring professionals. Desktop publishing software combines high-quality type, graphics, and layout tools to create output that can look as attractive as documents produced by professional publishers and printers. Advanced equipment can scan photos and drawings and duplicate them on printed pages. Documents created through desktop publishing can not only be printed on paper but also published on the Web. Two popular desktop publishing programs are Microsoft Publisher and Adobe InDesign.

Many firms use desktop publishing systems to print newsletters, reports, form letters, and Web pages. Advertising and graphic arts departments often use desktop publishing systems to create brochures and marketing materials. A good desktop publishing system can save a company money by allowing staff members to produce such documents, whether they are for internal or external use.

Word processing and desktop publishing can also be used to reduce the amount of paper generated by the typical office. While a true "paperless" office may never become a reality, many businesses realize that cutting down on paper can improve efficiency and save money. For instance, Minnesota-based Farmers Home Mutual Insurance uses the Intelligent Document Platform from Adobe as part of a Web-based system to improve client service and reduce administrative costs. Instead of using a paper application, agents enter client information electronically. Farmers estimates that it saves more than $500,000 per year by eliminating paper application forms. Moreover, the electronic application shortens the time needed to process applications by 70 percent and virtually eliminates errors.[20]

## Spreadsheets

An electronic **spreadsheet** is the computerized equivalent of an accountant's worksheet. This software permits businesspeople to manipulate decision variables and determine their impact on such outcomes as profits and sales. With a spreadsheet, a manager can have an accurate answer to a question in seconds and can often glance at the whole financial picture of a company on a single page. Not surprisingly, Microsoft Excel, part of the Office suite, is by far the most popular spreadsheet program. Another popular spreadsheet program is Corel Quattro Pro. Spreadsheet programs can also be used to create graphs and charts, and they have statistical analysis capabilities. Spreadsheets aren't just for accountants or finance professionals; people in other business areas such as marketing, human resources, and production rely on spreadsheet programs as well.

Figure 15.3 demonstrates how a manager uses a spreadsheet to set a price for a proposed product. Note that the manager can analyze alternative decisions using a spreadsheet. For instance, he or she can estimate the impact on sales given a change in the product's price. A more complex spreadsheet may stretch across many more columns and rows and even contain multiple worksheets, but the software still makes new calculations as fast as the manager can change the variables.

**spreadsheet** software package that creates the computerized equivalent of an accountant's worksheet, allowing the user to manipulate variables and see the impact of alternative decisions on operating results.

Figure

15.3 | How a Spreadsheet Works

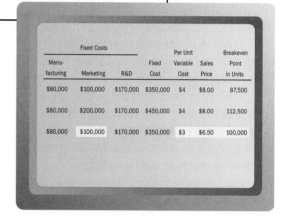

## Electronic Mail

Businesspeople need to communicate directly with associates as well as customers, suppliers, and others outside their organization. Increasingly, they turn to their computers for this function, replacing much of their regular mailings (jokingly called *snail mail*) by sending messages via e-mail. Popular e-mail programs include Microsoft Outlook, Outlook Express, and Eudora. While e-mail may be a regular part of your business day, it is important to understand clearly when and how to use it—and the Internet in general—as described in the "Business Etiquette" feature.

As discussed in Chapter 7, a popular adaptation of e-mail is instant messaging. Instant messaging allows users to create private chat rooms with other individuals on their personal lists. The instant messaging system alerts a user whenever somebody on his or her list is online. The user can then initiate a chat session with that individual. There are several different instant messaging systems, including AOL Instant Messenger, Yahoo! Messenger, and Windows Messenger. To communicate, however, all users must use the same instant messaging system.

E-mail and instant messaging are rapid ways to communicate both inside and outside the organization. As a means of internal communication, e-mail is especially useful in organizations with employees located in different parts of the country or in different countries altogether. Employees can typically access their organization's e-mail anytime, anywhere. All it takes is a Web connection.

Certainly e-mail can help companies reduce paperwork, time wasted in playing telephone tag, and similar inefficiencies. But e-mail does have its limitations. It works best for short unemotional messages. Longer documents are best sent as attachments to e-mail or via fax. And e-mail users should be aware that messages are not private; employers may be monitoring messages, so employees should refrain from sending personal messages or jokes to each other. Some messages, such as those containing potentially emotional news or those that may need an explanation, are best transmitted by telephone or in person. Also, as we noted in Chapter 7, some of the benefits of e-mail have been undermined by the proliferation of spam, or junk e-mail.

## Presentation Graphics

Analyzing columns of numbers can be a tedious task. But when people see data displayed as charts or graphs, they can often identify patterns and relationships that raw data do not reveal. Businesspeople once had to labor to create charts and graphs or send the data or rough sketches to professional artists and then wait for the finished products. Computer software has greatly simplified the process of creating graphics. As noted earlier, spreadsheet programs can create dozens of types of high-quality graphs. **Presentation software,** the most popular of which is Microsoft PowerPoint, goes one step further. These programs create entire presentations. Users can create bulleted lists, charts, graphs, pictures, audio, and even short video clips. Examples are shown in Figure 15.4. By combining these elements in ways that are easy to read, a user can prepare presentations and handouts for a business meeting. To persuade management to fund a new project, an employee might create a series of graphs and charts to illustrate how the project will benefit the organization over time.

## Multimedia and Interactive Media

Today's computers have leaped beyond numbers, text, and graphs to encompass multimedia and interactive media capabilities.

**presentation software** computer program that includes graphics and tools to produce a variety of charts, graphs, and pictures.

### When—and How—to Use Your Computer at Work

Just about anywhere you work, you are bound to have access to a computer. Whether you're in sales, marketing, finance, or human resources, a computer will be nearby—if not actually on your desk. You already know what your computer is for: work. Despite this fact, one recent survey revealed that 93 percent of workers who had a computer at work also used it for personal purposes—e-mailing or accessing the Web. The most popular sites accessed were news, personal e-mail, online banks, travel companies, and shopping. Gaming has also soared in popularity. Microsoft's game site, Zone.com, reports that its busiest time of day is midafternoon Eastern time—when most people are at work.

While this practice may seem harmless, businesses that allow employees to surf the Internet freely may face serious consequences. An employer may be held legally responsible for employees' misuse of e-mail—bullying, threatening, or making sexually explicit comments. A firm is also vulnerable to disclosure of its private information, as well as viruses spread via e-mail. Then there's the lost productivity of employees who are gaming and shopping during work time. So before you log on at work, consider the following:

- Make sure you know your company's policy about computer and Internet use. One firm might allow casual e-mailing or shopping during lunch hours; another might not. If you violate the policy, you could find yourself un-

employed. If your firm doesn't have a formal policy, ask your supervisor for guidelines before you log on. Then use common sense.

- If you may use your computer for some personal messages, be aware that most firms can monitor employee e-mail. "[Employees] should avoid pretty much anything they wouldn't want to print out and hang up on their cubicle walls," warns one technology consultant.

- Be honest about whether you really need to use the Internet during the workday. If you need to make a quick bank deposit online or check the time of your next flight, fine. But if you're surfing the Web for a great pair of shoes to wear next weekend, save it for after work.

Every firm is different, but "the solution lies in balancing employees' needs for personal use of the Web at work without draining overall productivity," advises Geoff Haggart of Internet firm Websense.

**Sources:** "Monitoring Employees' Use of Company Computers and the Internet," *Texas Workforce,* accessed July 21, 2006, http://www.twc.state.tx.us; Mimi Ho, "Internet Surfing at the Workplace," *CIO,* accessed July 21, 2006, http://www2.cio.com; Michele Marrinan, "Beware the Wandering Mouse," Monster.com, accessed July 21, 2006, http://wlb.monster.com; Bureau of Labor Statistics, "Most Common Uses for Computers at Work," U.S. Department of Labor, accessed July 21, 2006, http://www.bls.gov; "Web Surfing as Addictive as Coffee," CNN.com, accessed July 21, 2006, http://edition.cnn.com.

Figure

15.4 Examples of Presentation Graphics Software

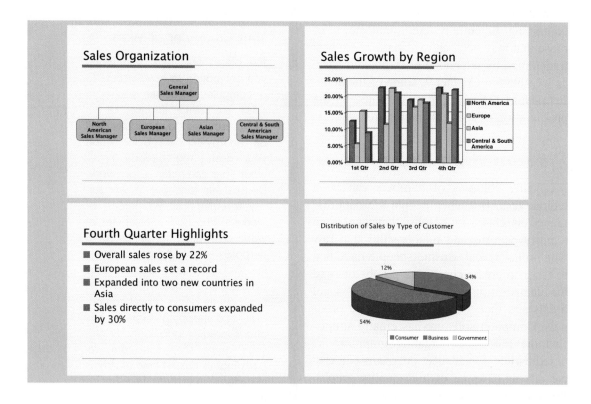

Multimedia computing refers to technologies that integrate two or more types of media, such as text, voice, sound, full-motion video, still video, graphics, and animation into computer-based applications. Many popular business applications have multimedia computing capabilities. For example, as we just noted, Microsoft PowerPoint users can add audio and video clips to their presentations.

One of the growing business applications for multimedia computing is employee business presentations and conferences. The Internet has made transmission of these meetings widely available. Many companies routinely provide multimedia Webcasts of their annual meetings for viewing on their Web sites. Salespeople use their notebook computers to make presentations to customers in the field.

Many applications of multimedia computing use interactive media—programs that allow users to interact with computer displays. Home Depot's Expo Design Centers interactive software allows customers to plan and design home remodeling and building projects either online or at Home Depot stores. Customers can view a variety of 3D products, enter their room dimensions, create orders, and track the installation of their projects on a computer screen.

**assessment check**

1. What is enterprise resource planning software?

2. Explain the difference between word-processing and desktop publishing software.

3. Briefly discuss how a spreadsheet program might be used to help solve a common business problem.

# INTRANETS, VIRTUAL PRIVATE NETWORKS, AND VoIP

A previous section discussed the use of LANs and WANs to allow businesses to communicate, transmit and print documents, and share data. These networks require businesses to install special equipment and connections between office sites. But Internet technology has also been applied to internal company communications and business tasks, tapping a ready-made network. Among these new Internet-based applications are intranets, virtual private networks (VPNs), and voice over Internet protocol (VoIP). Each has contributed to the effectiveness and speed of business processes.

## Intranets

A broad approach to sharing information in an organization is to establish a company network patterned after the Internet. Such a network, called an **intranet,** links employees through Internet tools such as e-mail and searches using Web browsers. Intranets are similar to the Internet, but they limit access to employees or other authorized users. An intranet blocks outsiders without valid passwords from entering its network by incorporating software or hardware known as a **firewall.** Firewalls limit data transfers to certain locations and log system use so that managers can identify attempts to log on with invalid passwords and other threats to a system's security. Highly sophisticated packages immediately alert system administrators about suspicious activities and permit authorized personnel to use smart cards to log on from remote terminals.

> **intranet** a computer network that links employees and other authorized users.

Intranets solve the problem of linking different types of computers. Like the Internet, intranets can integrate computers running all kinds of operating systems. In addition, intranets are relatively easy and inexpensive to set up because most businesses already have some of the required hardware and software. For instance, a small business can simply purchase a DSL router and a few cables and create an intranet using phone jacks and internal phone lines. All the business's computers will be linked with each other as well as with the Internet.

Intranets also support teamwork among employees who travel or work from home. Any intranet member with the right identification, a PC, and some sort of Internet access—either dial-up or broadband—can access the intranet and gain access to group calendars, e-mail, documents, and other files. Intranets can also be used for videoconferencing and other forms of virtual meetings.

Global financial services firm Rothschild uses intranet services provided by Interwoven. Interwoven replaced the firm's ad hoc shared network drives and various filing systems with a uniform document management system. The intranet allows access and sharing of financial dealings and client data. Documents, financial models, agreements, reports, and market data can be accessed securely by Rothschild bankers anywhere in the world. This speeds research, facilitates knowledge sharing, and, in the end, provides more consistent client relationships.[21]

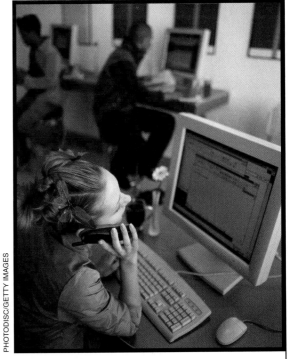

Network management and security are increasing concerns of businesses.

## Virtual Private Networks

To gain increased security for Internet communications, companies often turn to **virtual private networks (VPNs),** secure connections between two points on the Internet. These VPNs use firewalls and programs that encapsulate data to make them more secure during transit. Loosely defined, a VPN can include a range of networking technologies, from secure Internet connections to private networks from service providers like IBM and AT&T. A VPN is cheaper for a company to use than leasing several of its own lines. It can also take months to install a leased line in some parts of the world, but a new user can be added to a VPN in a day. Because a VPN uses the Internet, it can be wired, wireless, or a combination of the two.

Singapore's Nanyang Technological University (NTU) uses a VPN provided by Juniper Networks. The VPN enables the university's IT staff to remotely manage 85 e-learning servers, which make up the university's e-learning operations center. This eliminates the need for the company's information technology (IT) staff to be physically near the servers, greatly reducing the amount of time and expense needed for server maintenance. Chye Seng of NTU says, "instead of working on the server console in the data center, staff members now have the option to work remotely, saving us time and money, and improving the quality of our e-learning service."[22]

## VoIP

**VoIP**—which stands for *voice over Internet protocol*—is an alternative to traditional telecommunication services provided by companies such as Verizon and Qwest. The VoIP telephone is not connected to a traditional phone jack but rather is connected to a personal computer with any type of broadband connection. Special software transmits phone conversations over the Internet, rather than through telephone lines. A VoIP user dials the phone as usual. Recipients can receive calls made using VoIP through regular telephone connections (land or wireless). Moreover, you can call another person who has VoIP using a regular landline or cell phone.

A growing number of consumers and businesses have embraced VoIP, mainly due to the cost savings and extra features offered by VoIP. For instance, Skype—owned by eBay—has around 6 million users.[23] Home Care Delivered, a Virginia-based healthcare supply firm, decided to go with VoIP when it opened a new facility recently. For CEO Gordy Fox, it made perfect sense because a corporate data network was already in place. Fox believes that the company will save thousands of dollars by bypassing the public phone network. VoIP allows the company to set up an office anywhere there's a fast Internet connection.[24]

In spite of VoIP's apparent advantages, there are several potential drawbacks to replacing traditional telephony with Internet telephony. For one thing, your Internet phone service will be only as reliable as your broadband connection. If your broadband connection goes out, so will your phone service. For another, without extensive safeguards, VoIP can expose a phone system to the havoc affecting the rest of the Internet, such as worms and viruses. Gary Heller, deputy CIO for the Arizona Healthcare Cost Containment System, recently helped install VoIP in system offices throughout the state. Before installing VoIP, Heller focused hard on security and didn't go ahead with VoIP until he thought that all the potential security issues had been resolved. "You'll be sorry if security is an afterthought with VoIP," he says.[25]

### assessment check

1. Explain the differences between an intranet and a virtual private network.
2. What are some of the major advantages and disadvantages of VoIP?

# PROTECTING INFORMATION SYSTEMS

As information systems become increasingly important business assets, they also become progressively harder to replace. When computers are connected to a network, a problem at any individual computer can affect the entire network. Although many computer security issues go beyond the scope of this book, the following sections discuss three important security threats: computer crime, or e-crime; viruses; and disasters that may damage information systems.

# E-Crime

Computers provide efficient ways for employees to share information. But they may also allow people with more malicious intentions to access information. Or they may allow pranksters—who have no motive other than to see whether they can hack into a system—to gain access to classified information. Common e-crimes involve stealing or altering data in several ways:

- Employees or outsiders may change or invent data to produce inaccurate or misleading information.
- Employees or outsiders may modify computer programs to create false information or illegal transactions or to insert viruses.
- Unauthorized people can access computer systems for their own illicit benefit or knowledge or just to see if they can get in.

E-crime is on the rise. According to a recent survey of IT professionals and managers conducted by *CSO* magazine in cooperation with the U.S. Secret Service and Carnegie Mellon University's CERT Coordination Center, 70 percent of respondents reported at least one e-crime and almost half reported an increase in e-crimes compared with the prior year. The typical respondent reported more than 130 e-crimes during the year. The total cost of these crimes was estimated at around $700 million. Of course, the statistics don't include the number of incidents that were not reported, so the total number and cost are probably higher.

Individuals, businesses, and government agencies are all vulnerable to computer crime. Computer hackers—unauthorized users—sometimes work alone and sometimes in groups. Sometimes hackers break into computer systems just to show that they can do it; other times they have more sinister motives. Along a stretch of highway in a shopping area near downtown Miami, hackers obtained credit card information for thousands of customers at four major stores. The thieves identified stores with strong wireless signals and weakly protected data networks. For more than a month, hackers gained access to the stores' computer systems and obtained sensitive financial information from their databases. Security experts and law enforcement officials estimated that more than 1.4 million customer accounts were exposed. The exact dollar amount of losses is not known.[26] In another recent incident, hackers gained access to a LexisNexis database. The security of thousands of Social Security numbers, driver's license data, and other personal information may have been compromised.[27]

Information system administrators implement two basic protections against computer crime: they try to prevent access to their systems by unauthorized users and the viewing of data by unauthorized system users. To prevent access, the simplest method requires authorized users to enter passwords. The company may also install firewalls, described earlier. To prevent system users from reading sensitive information, the company may use encryption software, which encodes, or scrambles, messages. To read encrypted messages, users must use an electronic key to convert them to regular text. But as fast as software developers invent new and more elaborate protective measures, hackers seem to break through their defenses. So security is an ongoing battle. Debate continues over whether stronger laws are needed to protect the sensitive personal information contained in many computer databases. This debate is summarized in the "Solving an Ethical Controversy" feature.

Another form of computer theft is as old as crime itself: theft of equipment. As the size of computer hardware diminishes, it becomes increasingly vulnerable to theft. Handheld devices, for instance, can vanish with a pickpocket or purse snatcher. And because these machines may contain all kinds of important information for a business, employees need to be especially careful not to leave them unattended or out of reach. The recent theft, and subsequent recovery, of a

# DOES DATABASE SECURITY EXIST?

*Everywhere you go, companies obtain information about you—enough for just about anyone to steal your identity. Firms vow to keep your information secure, but increasingly, those promises are broken by technologically savvy thieves, who in one fell swoop may gain access to a single database containing information about millions of individuals.*

Businesses, consumer groups, and the U.S. Congress continue to debate who is ultimately responsible for database security. New legislation and regulations have been proposed.

Are companies doing enough to protect their customer database information?

## PRO

1. Companies that engage in financial transactions are already required to establish and enforce information security programs to prevent identify theft. In addition, new legislation strengthens customer notification requirements when security is breached.
2. Companies that make security a top priority have professional support staff who constantly review any possible compromises in the system. This type of vigilance is the best way to maintain security.

## CON

1. Experts warn that identity theft is often committed by a company's own workers, vendors, and sup-

pliers, who have access to passcodes, passwords, or key codes. "We're creating this façade that we can protect this information, and in reality we can't," warns Pete Lindstrom of Spire Security LLC. "There are too many people who have legitimate access to this stuff."
2. Although well intentioned, many companies focus too much on outdated methods of security such as encryption. While encryption was once enough protection, experts now advise that it is merely one layer of defense.

## Summary

Database security has become increasingly critical as large companies have admitted to massive losses of personal data. ChoicePoint, which collects and sells personal information to government agencies and private firms, announced the potential exposure of information on 35,000 consumers in California. Data provider LexisNexis discovered a security breach of data on more than

310,000 consumers. Organizations as diverse as Bank of America, San Jose Medical Group, and Boston College have also reported security breaches. As a result, financial institutions have agreed to work more closely with the Federal Trade Commission to solve—and ultimately thwart—identity theft crimes.

**Sources:** Jon Oitsik, "The Truth about Database Security," CNet News.com, accessed July 21, 2006, http://news .com.com; Charles Garry, "Taking a Trip Down Denial," *eWeek*, accessed July 21, 2006, http://www.eweek .com; Lisa Vaas, "Congress Nears Final Identity Theft Legislation," *eWeek*, accessed July 21, 2006, http://www .eweek.com; Karen D. Schwartz, "Financial Institutions to Share Identity-Theft Data," *eWeek*, accessed July 21, 2006, http://www.eweek.com; Judith M. Collins, "Identity Theft: An Inside Job," *eWeek*, accessed July 21, 2006, http:// www.eweek.com; Jon Swartz, "Personal Info about 310,000 at Risk," *USA Today*, accessed July 21, 2006, http://www.usatoday.com; Bob Sullivan, "Database Giant Gives Access to Fake Firms," MSNBC, accessed July 21, 2006, http://www.msnbc.com.

## solving an ETHICAL controversy

notebook computer belonging to an official of the Department of Veterans Affairs, containing sensitive information on millions of veterans and active duty military personnel, illustrates the vulnerability of these devices. Many notebook computers and handheld devices contain special security software that makes it difficult for a thief or any unauthorized person to access the data stored in the computer's memory.

## Computer Viruses, Worms, Trojan Horses, and Spyware

Rather than directly tampering with a company's data or computers, computer hackers may create viruses, worms, or Trojan horses to infect computers at random. Attacks by these and other forms of malicious software cost consumers and businesses billions of dollars annually.

Computer *viruses* are programs that secretly attach themselves to other programs (called *hosts*) and change them or destroy data. Viruses can be programmed to become active immediately or to remain dormant for a period of time, after which the infections suddenly activate themselves and cause problems. A virus can reproduce by copying itself onto other programs stored in the same drive. It spreads as users install infected software on their systems or exchange files with others, usually by exchanging e-mail, accessing electronic bulletin boards, trading disks, or downloading programs or data from unknown sources on the Internet.

A *worm* is a small piece of software that exploits a security hole in a network to replicate itself. A copy of the worm scans the network for another machine that has a specific security hole. It copies itself to the new machine using the security hole and then starts replicating from there as well. Unlike viruses, worms don't need host programs to damage computer systems.

A *Trojan horse* is a program that claims to do one thing, but in reality does something else, usually something malicious. For example, a Trojan horse might claim, and even appear, to be a game. When an unsuspecting user clicks the Trojan horse, the program might erase the hard drive or steal any personal data stored on the computer.

*Spyware* is software that covertly gathers user information through the user's Internet connection without his or her knowledge, usually for advertising purposes. Spyware applications are typically bundled with other programs downloaded from the Internet. Once installed, the spyware monitors user activity on the Internet and transmits that information in the background to someone else.

Attacks by viruses, worms, Trojan horses, and spyware are not limited to computers and computer networks; handheld devices, including cell phones, have been affected as well. Recently, for example, a Trojan horse was discovered that turned Sony's popular PSP (PlayStation Portable) into what one expert referred to as a "brick." The program—which posed as a patch allowing a user to run games not approved by Sony—actually deleted four critical system files, rendering the PSP inoperable. The owner had little choice but to send the infected PSP into Sony for expensive repairs.[28]

As viruses, worms, and Trojan horses become more complex, the technology to fight them must increase in sophistication as well. The simplest way to protect against computer viruses is to install one of the many available antivirus software programs, such as Norton AntiVirus and McAfee VirusScan. These programs, which also protect against worms and some Trojan horses, continuously monitor systems for viruses and automatically eliminate any they spot. Users should regularly update them by downloading the latest virus definitions. In addition, computer users should also install and regularly update antispyware programs because many Trojan horses are forms of spyware.

But management must begin to emphasize security at a deeper level: software design, corporate servers, Web gateways, and Internet service providers. Because more than 80 percent of the world's PCs run on Microsoft operating systems, a single virus, worm, or Trojan horse can spread quickly among them. Individual computer users should carefully choose the files they load onto their systems, scan their systems regularly, make sure their antivirus software is up-to-date, and install software only from known sources. They should also be very careful when opening attachments to e-mails, because many viruses, worms, and Trojan horses are spread that way.

**assessment check**

1. List some examples of e-crime.
2. Explain the differences between a virus, a worm, and a Trojan horse.

# DISASTER RECOVERY AND BACKUP

Natural disasters, power failures, equipment malfunctions, software glitches, human error, and terrorist attacks can disrupt even the most sophisticated computer systems. These disruptions can cost businesses and other organizations billions of dollars.

Recently flooding from the Delaware River damaged a bakery and café owned by Jane and Joel Vitart in New Hope, Pennsylvania. The flood caused about $120,000 in damage and cleanup costs, but the biggest blow was the loss of the business's computer system. As Jane Vitart noted, "I ran my whole business on that computer—all my financial data, inventory, vendor bills, my marketing materials, customer lists, menus." She had backed up some of her financial data, but the backup disk turned out to be defective. The business was closed for six weeks and then reopened only after the couple stretched their credit to the limit and used all their personal savings. Jane Vitart said "I feel like I'm starting from scratch." Now, at the first hint of flooding, she makes sure the computer system is among the first items evacuated.[29]

Software glitches are no less serious. Recently, a software glitch shut down the systems running the New York Stock Exchange. The shutdown halted all trading for about twelve minutes right before the market closed, creating havoc in the financial markets throughout the country. Another recent software glitch at Bank of America resulted in teachers in several California districts not getting paid on time. And a software glitch at a Baltimore Gas and Electric computer caused about 7,000 customers to be overcharged for electricity, some for many years.[30]

Disaster recovery planning—deciding how to prevent system failures and continue operations if computer systems fail—is a critical function of all organizations. Disaster prevention programs can avoid some of these costly problems. The most basic precaution is routinely backing up software and data—at the organizational and individual levels.

Disaster planning helped the Veterans Health Information System get back to normal quickly following Hurricane Katrina. The hurricane affected Veterans Affairs (VA) facilities in New Orleans and in Jackson and Biloxi, Mississippi. However, within a couple of days, the patient database was operating as it did the day before the hurricane. Any patient who was being treated by VA facilities in the affected areas could walk into any VA provider, anywhere in the country, and his or her records could be pulled up on the screen.[31]

Companies can now back up data at such online storage services as Iron Mountain or Network Associates. Technology planners may decide to respond to the possibility of a natural disaster such as an earthquake or flood by paying for extra hardware installation in a secure location that can be accessed during an emergency. PSS/World, a medical equipment distributor based in Jacksonville, uses disaster recovery services from SunGard Availability Services, which cost the company around $500,000 per year. Among other items, PSS/World stores its data in the vendor's Philadelphia facility. As Katrina neared the Gulf Coast, PSS/World decided that its Jackson, Mississippi, call center might be affected. Losing the call center would cost the firm an estimated $3 million a day. The firm alerted SunGard that it was putting its emergency plan into effect. The storm did knock out the Jackson call center for several days, but thanks to its disaster plan and the services provided by SunGard, PSS/World's business wasn't hurt.[32]

**assessment check**

1. What is a software glitch?
2. Explain disaster recovery planning as it relates to information systems.

# WHAT'S AHEAD

This is the first of two chapters devoted to managing technology and information. Chapter 16, "Understanding Accounting and Financial Statements," focuses on the functions of accounting, steps in the accounting process, functions and components of financial statements, and the role of budgets in an organization.

## Summary of Learning Goals

**1 Distinguish between data and information and explain the role of management information systems in business.**

It is important for businesspeople to know the difference between data and information. Data are raw facts and figures that may or may not be relevant to a business decision. Information is knowledge gained from processing those facts and figures. An effective information system can help answer many management questions. A management information system (MIS) is an organized method for providing past, present, and projected information on internal operations as well as external intelligence to support decision making. The heart of an MIS is its database, which serves as an electronic filing cabinet for facts and figures.

### Assessment Check Answers

**1.1 What is the difference between data and information?**
Data consist of raw facts and figures that may or may not be relevant to a business decision. Information is the knowledge gained from processing data.

**1.2 Define *management information system.***
A management information system is an organized method for providing past, present, and projected information on internal operations as well as external intelligence to support decision making.

**1.3 What is the purpose of business intelligence?**
Business intelligence is the task of using computer-based technology to retrieve and evaluate data in a database to identify useful trends.

**2 Identify and briefly describe the different types of information system programs.**

The key to a useful information system is the program that links users to data. Different types of information system programs include decision support systems (DSSs), which provide relevant data to help businesspeople make decisions and choose courses of action; executive support systems, which allow top managers to access the firm's primary databases; and expert systems, which imitate human thinking. Trends in information systems include local area and wide area networks (LANs and WANs); wireless local networks (Wi-Fi and Wi-Max); and application service

providers (ASPs), outside firms that provide both computers and application support for managing an information system.

### Assessment Check Answers

**2.1 What is a decision support system?**
A decision support system is an information system that quickly provides relevant data to help businesspeople make decisions and choose courses of action.

**2.2 Why do some organizations use application service providers?**
The major advantages of using application service providers are cost and added expertise. Many organizations find it much more cost-effective to outsource information technology than to try to handle it in house.

**3 Describe the hardware and software used in managing information.**

Hardware consists of all tangible elements of a computer system, including input and output devices. Major categories of computers include mainframes, supercomputers, minicomputers, and personal computers (PCs). Newer developments in PCs include notebooks, tablet PCs, and handheld devices. Computer software provides the instructions that tell the hardware what to do. The software that controls the basic workings of the computer is its operating system. Other programs, called *application software,* perform specific tasks that users want to complete.

### Assessment Check Answers

**3.1 How are computers classified?**
Computers are classified as being either mainframes, minicomputers, or personal computers. Personal computers are divided into desktop computers, notebook computers, tablet computers, and handheld devices (PDAs and smart phones).

**3.2 What are the two major categories of computer software?**
Operating systems control the basic workings of a computer. A program that performs a specific task is called *application software.*

**4** **Identify how different types of software can help businesspeople.**

Individual types of software can help businesses in a variety of ways. Word processing helps a company handle massive volumes of correspondence, reports, and other documents. Desktop publishing allows users to design and produce attractively formatted printed material. Spreadsheets calculate and present information clearly. Electronic mail allows businesspeople to communicate rapidly anywhere in the world. Presentation graphics provide graphs and charts that help businesspeople see patterns in data. Multimedia integrates two or more types of media. Interactive media are programs that allow users to interact with computer displays. Integrated software combines several applications into a single package that can share modules for data handling and processing.

## Assessment Check Answers

**4.1 What is enterprise resource planning software?**
Enterprise resource planning software is a set of integrated programs designed to collect, process, and provide information about all business operations.

**4.2 Explain the difference between word-processing and desktop publishing software.**
Word-processing software uses computers to input, store, retrieve, edit, and print various types of documents. Desktop publishing takes word processing one step further by combining high-quality type and graphics. Documents can be printed or published on the Web.

**4.3 Briefly discuss how a spreadsheet program might be used to help solve a common business problem.**
A spreadsheet is a computerized equivalent of an accountant's worksheet. The software helps businesspeople manipulate decision variables and determine their impact on such outcomes as profits and sales. For example, a marketing manager might use a spreadsheet to evaluate the impact of increased promotional expenditures on sales and profits.

**5** **Explain the importance of special network technologies.**

Intranets allow employees to share information on a ready-made company network. Access to an intranet is restricted to authorized users and is protected by a firewall. Virtual private networks (VPNs) help save companies money by providing a secure Internet con-

nection between two or more points. VoIP—voice over Internet protocol—uses a personal computer running special software and a broadband Internet connection to make and receive telephone calls over the Internet rather than over traditional telephone networks. VoIP is usually cheaper than traditional telephony and offers users added flexibility.

## Assessment Check Answers

**5.1 Explain the differences between an intranet and a virtual private network.**
An intranet is a physical network that links an organization's computers, allowing them to share documents, printers, and other devices. A virtual private network links two or more computers over a secure Internet connection.

**5.2 What are some of the major advantages and disadvantages of VoIP?**
The major advantages of VoIP are lower cost, increased communications flexibility, and additional features. Security and reliability are two drawbacks of VoIP.

**6** **List the ways that companies can protect themselves from computer crimes.**

Companies can protect themselves from computer crime by requiring users to enter passwords, installing firewalls or encryption software, and keeping up to date on new security methods. In addition, managers should install antivirus security programs on all computers and networks.

## Assessment Check Answers

**6.1 List some examples of e-crime.**
Examples of e-crime include the stealing or altering of data and the theft of computer hardware.

**6.2 Explain the differences between a virus, a worm, and a Trojan horse.**
A virus is a program that secretly attaches itself to other programs and changes the host program or destroys data. A worm is a small piece of software that exploits a security hole in a network and duplicates itself. Worms don't require host programs. A Trojan horse is a program that claims to do one thing but in reality does something else, usually something malicious.

**7** **Explain the steps that companies go through in anticipating, planning for, and recovering from information system disasters.**

Businesses can avoid the results of disaster by routinely backing up software and data, both at an organizational level and at an individual level. They can back up data at online storage services or pay for extra hardware installation in a secure location. They may also want to invest in extra hardware and software sites, which can be accessed during emergencies.

## Assessment Check Answers

**7.1 What is a software glitch?**
A software glitch is an error in a computer program that has an unintended consequence, such as shutting down a system at the wrong time.

**7.2 Explain disaster recovery planning as it relates to information systems.**
Disaster recovery planning involves deciding how to prevent system failures and to continue operations if computer systems fail because of natural disasters or human error. A basic precaution is routinely backing up data and software and storing the backups in a secure location.

## Business Terms You Need to Know

data 484
information 484
management information
    system (MIS) 484
database 485
decision support system (DSS) 487
executive support system (ESS) 487

Wi-Fi 489
application service provider
    (ASP) 489
software 494
enterprise resource planning
    (ERP) system 495
word processing 496

spreadsheet 497
presentation software 499
intranet 501

## Other Important Business Terms

chief information officer
    (CIO) 484
expert system 488
local area network (LAN) 488
wide area network (WAN) 488
Wi-Max 489

on-demand (utility)
    computing 489
hardware 491
mainframe 492
minicomputer 492
handheld devices 493

operating system 494
application software 494
desktop publishing 497
firewall 501
virtual private network (VPN) 501
VoIP 502

## Review Questions

1. Distinguish between data and information. Why is the distinction important to businesspeople in their management of information?
2. What is business intelligence?
3. Describe three different types of information system programs and give an example of how each might help a particular business.
4. Explain decision support systems, executive support systems, and expert systems.

5. What are the major categories of computers? What is a smart phone?
6. How might a hotel chain use desktop publishing to manage its marketing program?
7. What is enterprise resource planning? How has it streamlined business processes?
8. What is an intranet? Give specific examples of benefits for firms that set up their own intranets.

9. Briefly explain how VoIP works. Why might a business switch from regular telephony to Internet telephony?
10. What steps can organizations and individuals take to prevent computer crime?
11. How does a computer virus work? What can individuals and organizational computer users do to reduce the likelihood of acquiring a computer virus?
12. Why is disaster recovery important for businesses? Relate your answer to a natural disaster such as a hurricane.

## Projects and Teamwork Applications

1. Do you believe that information overload is a serious problem in your life? What steps do you (or can you) take to reduce this overload so that you can function more effectively in all areas of your life?

2. Suppose you were chief information officer for Great Harvest Bread Company. Describe the different parts of an integrated software package (in addition to the intranet described in the chapter) that would help your company manage its flow of information. Give an example of how each application you choose would help the company.

3. Working with a partner, research the current status of Wi-Max. Prepare a short report on its growth, its current uses, and its future for business computing.

4. Do you think computer hacking is a serious crime? Defend your answer.

5. What information-related technology lessons do you think businesses learned from Hurricanes Katrina, Rita, and Wilma? How will these lessons help firms respond to other disasters—natural as well as those caused by humans?

6. Assume you're in the market for a new personal computer. First, make a list of your needs. Needs represent the basic configuration that will meet your individual computing requirements. Next, make a list of your wants. Wants represent features you'd like to have in your new PC but don't necessarily need. Finally, decide between a notebook computer and a desktop computer. List the reasons why you chose a desktop or a notebook.
   a. Visit the CNet (http://www.cnet.com) or ZDNet (http://www.zdnet.com) Web site. Research different computer makes and models that meet your specifications. Make a list of the five top-rated systems. What criteria did CNet or ZDNet consider when developing the rankings?
   b. Decide where you will buy your new computer. Will you order it from a direct seller, such as Dell, or will you buy it at a retail store, such as Best Buy? What are the advantages and disadvantages of each option?
   c. Finally, working in a small group, repeat the exercise, assuming you're buying a computer for your job. Explain any differences between a computer purchased for personal and school use and one purchased for business use.

7. Computer viruses and worms pose a major problem for computer users and systems. Software publishers constantly scramble to update their antivirus software programs in response to newly discovered viruses and worms. Searching online, research the current status of worms and viruses and then answer the following questions:
   a. Approximately how many different computer viruses have been discovered?
   b. How many new viruses are discovered each month?
   c. What are the names of the most recently discovered viruses?
   d. What is the best way to protect a computer from viruses?

8. After the terrorist attacks of September 11, 2001, and the more recent string of major hurricanes, interest in data backup and recovery software for critical computer data increased dramatically. Visit the following Web sites and, working with a partner, prepare a report outlining some of the key features of these programs with the goal of convincing the owner of a small business that he or she should invest in critical data backup and recovery software.

   http://www.baymountain.com
   http://www.unitrends.com

### Compaq and Hewlett-Packard: Can They Live Happily Ever After?

Business mergers between companies sometimes seem nearly as common as marriages between people. And like marriages, they may or may not result in happy relationships. The merger between Hewlett-Packard and Compaq—the largest so far in the computer industry—has proved to be rocky. HP's acquisition of Compaq was orchestrated by HP's former CEO, Carly Fiorina. The move met its greatest resistance from HP director Walter Hewlett, son of HP's co-founder William Hewlett. Hewlett argued that the match would dilute HP's profits, trigger layoffs, and not benefit either firm in the long run.

After the first year, HP reported that it had obtained some valuable service contracts, including a $243 million deal to provide help desk and other services to Telecom Italia. Later it announced a contract with Procter & Gamble worth $3 billion over the next decade. But in technological innovation, HP continued to move too slowly, and the acquisition of Compaq failed to satisfy investors. HP's once-healthy market share in printers began to falter because it was devoting resources to its PC business. So far the HP merger with Compaq has yet to produce effective integration between the two organizations and their products—and Fiorina has left the company.

HP is trying to recover its image as a force for innovation and engineering, blend with Compaq, and offer products such as desktop computers at lower prices to consumers and business customers through its HP Compaq division. Industry experts warn that the firm will also have to jump ahead of its competitors—such as Dell—in developing whole new categories of goods and services. It's a task nearly as large as reinventing the wheel.

### Questions for Critical Thinking

1. Visit the HP Web site to learn more about HP products and services. Select a new offering that you think will be successful, and explain why.
2. Do you think that eventually the relationship between HP and Compaq will be successful? Why or why not?

**Sources:** John Gallant, "The Firing of Fiorina: Overdue or Premature?" *Network World*, accessed August 16, 2006, http://www.networkworld.com; John Spooner, "HP Does Desktop PC Price Limbo," *PC Magazine*, accessed July 21, 2006, http://www.PCMagazine.com; "Fallen Star," Online NewsHour, accessed July 21, 2006, http://www.pbs.org/newshour; Robert X. Cringely, "What Carly Will Be Missing," Public Broadcasting Service, accessed July 21, 2006, http://www.pbs.org/cringely; "Hewlett-Packard Top Executive Ousted," MSNBC, accessed July 21, 2006, http://www.msnbc.msn.com.

## VIDEO Case 15.2

### Peet's Coffee & Tea: Just What the Customer Ordered

This video case appears on page 624. A recently filmed video, designed to expand and highlight the written case, is available for class use by instructors.

# Chapter 16

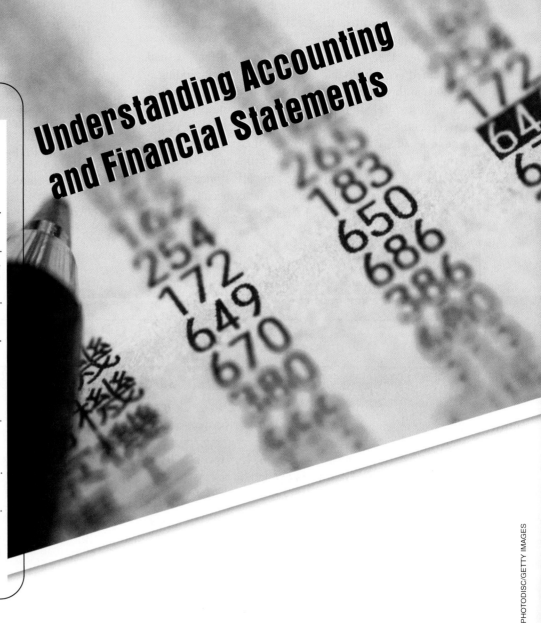

## Understanding Accounting and Financial Statements

PHOTODISC/GETTY IMAGES

**K**eeping the books of large corporations is a complicated task. So most big companies, such as General Motors and Sun Microsystems, have traditionally relied on the giants of the auditing industry, known as the Big Four. These huge accounting firms—Pricewaterhouse Coopers, Ernst & Young, Deloitte & Touche, and KPMG—all have long histories and multinational operations. They are considered the top tier of their industry. But recently, smaller accounting companies have begun to take some of their prestigious, and lucrative, business away. The change came about partly because of a long list of accounting scandals that involved leading audit and consulting firms such as Arthur Andersen, which was virtually destroyed by its association with some law-breaking clients, such as Enron. Other reasons why organizations are giving a second look to relatively small accounting

## Who Is Grant Thornton?

practices include their nimbleness in responding to legal and technological changes, their ability to deliver personalized service, their specialization in particular industries, and their stain-free records. The lower fees charged by these "second-tier" firms, such as Grant Thornton, BDO Seidman, McGladrey & Pullen, and Crowe Group, are another big factor.

For instance, Hercules, a Delaware chemicals producer with $2 billion in sales, considered PricewaterhouseCoopers for its audit needs but settled instead on the far smaller firm BDO Seidman. In addition to BDO's speedy decision making and reasonable fees, the firm impressed Hercules with its experience in the chemical industry. And finally, "There was a sense that we would be important to BDO, that there will be top management attention if we have problems," says Hercules's chairman.

Hercules's perception of receiving more personal attention is very real. The Big Four accounting firms are actually giving up some of their clients, sometimes unwillingly, because they often lack the resources to maintain their current client list under the demanding new requirements of the Sarbanes-Oxley Act. These stringent audit reforms lengthen the time required for the typical audit process at a publicly traded company by as much as a

third. That means the bigger firms must work with fewer clients or risk doing an inadequate job for some. A shortage of seasoned auditing professionals has also limited their ability to add staff in the last few years, so all of the Big Four have reduced their number of clients.

As a result of this pressure on the Big Four to reduce their client load, in addition to clients' desire to combine good accounting services with lower professional fees, almost 250 firms earning $100 million a year or more switched auditors in one recent year—away from the top tier. That's about double the number from the year before. BDO was a big winner, netting 71 new clients, while Grant Thornton, McGladrey & Pullen, and Crowe Group added a total of 46.

Some businesses that are required to follow Sarbanes-Oxley guidelines also hire separate accounting services to help them comply. They are performing the act's mandated audits of their own internal controls to prevent financial wrongdoing. Because federal law prohibits a firm from using its own financial auditing staff to assess its accounting controls, the act has created a flood of new work for outside accounting companies at firms of all sizes. Smaller accounting companies are benefiting from the new business, from the new contacts and leads they are getting from their new clients, from the opportunity to specialize in Sarbanes-Oxley compliance or in a particular industry, and even from the new employees they have hired—often from the Big Four and from Arthur Andersen.

Meanwhile, as the accounting industry continues to struggle back from the scandal-ridden years to meet growing new demands for its expertise, starting salaries for managers and large accounting firms are expected to jump to a high of $92,000. More people are taking the CPA exam than ever before, and it's no wonder.[1]

**chapteroverview**

Accounting professionals prepare the financial information that organizations present in their annual reports. Whether you begin your career by working for a company or by starting your own firm, you need to understand what accountants do and why their work is so important in contemporary business.

**Accounting** is the process of measuring, interpreting, and communicating financial information to enable people inside and outside the firm to make informed decisions. Accounting is the language of business. Accountants gather, record, report, and interpret financial information in a way that describes the status and operation of an organization and aids in decision making.

Millions of men and women throughout the world describe their occupation as accountant. In the United States alone, more than 1.1 million people, more than half of whom are women, work as accountants. According to the Bureau of Labor Statistics, the number of accounting-related jobs is expected to increase by at least 20 percent between now and 2012.[2] The availability of jobs and relatively high starting salaries for talented graduates—starting salaries for accounting graduates average around $45,000 per year—have made accounting one of the most in-demand majors on college campuses.[3]

This chapter begins by describing who uses accounting information. It discusses business activities involving accounting statements: financing, investing, and operations. It explains the accounting process and then discusses the development of accounting statements from information about financial transactions. It presents the methods of interpreting these statements and examines the roles of budgeting in planning and controlling a business.

---

**accounting** process of measuring, interpreting, and communicating financial information to support internal and external business decision making.

## USERS OF ACCOUNTING INFORMATION

People both inside and outside an organization rely on accounting information to help them make business decisions. Figure 16.1 lists the users of accounting information and the applications they find for that information.

Managers with a business, government agency, or not-for-profit organization are the major users of accounting information, because it helps them plan and control daily and long-range operations. Business owners and boards of directors of not-for-profit groups also rely on accounting data to determine how well managers are operating the organizations. Union officials use accounting data in contract negotiations, and employees refer to it as they monitor their firms' productivity and profitability performance.

To help employees understand how their work affects the bottom line, many companies share sensitive financial information with their employees and teach them how to understand and use financial statements. Proponents of what is often referred to as **open book management** believe that allowing employees to view financial information helps them better understand how their work contributes to the company's success which, in turn, benefits them. The "Hit & Miss" feature discusses how one small Missouri manufacturer has profited by using open-book management.

Outside a firm, potential investors evaluate accounting information to help them decide whether to buy a firm's securities. As we'll discuss in more detail later in the chapter, any

**"They Said It"**

"There's no business like show business, but there are several businesses like accounting."
—David Letterman
(b. 1947)
Comedian

## Opening the Books Opens the Door to Success at Trinity Products

Robert Griggs, president of Trinity Products, has been running his company on an open-book basis since its founding in 1979, but for most of that time, he didn't realize what it was called. Now, thanks in part to a grant from Missouri's state government, Griggs's construction industry supply company can run a formal employee training program to support and continue the open-book management policy he began.

Griggs describes his practice this way: "Open-book management means you open your entire books to everybody in the company, and you require them to learn how to read a financial statement, how to do budgeting, and this is from the guy who sweeps the floor to the gal that answers the phone." Trinity's 50 employees attend financial meetings twice a month and take a financial literacy course that teaches them about balance sheets, sales forecasting, and income statements. Everyone contributes to the forecasting of sales and expenses. Through this form of ownership, as Griggs calls it, "they have a stake in how much money they make by how much money we make."

Setting goals together allows employees to feel invested in the business and in the need to meet goals, monitor costs, and satisfy customers. Even the bonus plan is put together by mutual agreement. Says Griggs, "We agreed that we would share 20 percent of the profit if we hit 5 percent net return on sales. [The industry average is 3.5 percent.] This year we'll split up $200,000 among 50 employees."

The company has enjoyed an astonishing growth rate of about 80 percent a year since 1993, with sales rocketing from $2.2 million that year to an estimated $25 million. Griggs and his crew's new target is $39 million. "The biggest contribution to that success is the open-book managing policy," says Trinity's CFO, Brian Davis. "We teach people how to read the books."

### Questions for Critical Thinking

1. In what specific way does Trinity's open-book policy contribute to its financial success? What other factors might account for its rapid growth?
2. Can you think of any situations in which open-book management might not improve a firm's financial performance? Why?

**Sources:** Trinity Products Web site, accessed July 21, 2006, http://www.trinityinc.com; Ellyn Spragins, "The Open-Book CEO," *Fortune Small Business*, accessed July 21, 2006, http://www.fortune.com; Robin Seaton Jefferson, "Trinity Products Hangs Success on Open-Book Management," *St. Charles County Business Record*, July 21, 2005, p. 1.

company whose stock is traded publicly is required to report its financial results on a regular basis. So anyone, for example, can find out what PepsiCo's sales were last year or how much money Starbucks made during the past three months. Bankers and other lenders use accounting information to evaluate a potential borrower's financial soundness. The Internal Revenue Service (IRS) and state tax officials use it to determine a company's tax liability. Citizens' groups and government agencies use such information in assessing the efficiency of operations such as the Cleveland Clinic; the Boulder, Colorado, school system; and the American Museum of Natural History.

Accountants play fundamental roles not only in business but also in other aspects of society. Their work influences each of the business environments discussed earlier in this book. They clearly contribute important information to help managers deal with the competitive and economic environments. Less obvious contributions

**Figure**

**16.1**

Users of Accounting Information

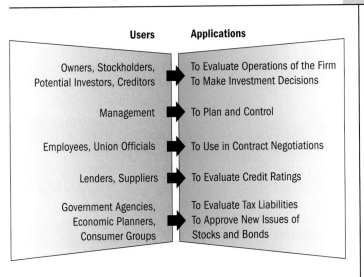

**a**ssessment **c**heck

1. Define accounting.
2. Who uses accounting information?

help others understand, predict, and react to the technological, regulatory, and social and cultural environments.

For instance, thousands of people volunteer each year to help people with their taxes. One of the largest organized programs is Tax-Aide, sponsored by AARP (formally known as American Association of Retired Persons), which is the leading nonprofit, nonpartisan membership organization for people age 50 and over in the United States. Its program has in excess of 30,000 volunteers helping more than 1.5 million low- and middle-income senior citizens file their state and federal tax returns.[4]

# BUSINESS ACTIVITIES INVOLVING ACCOUNTING

The natural progression of a business begins with financing. Subsequent steps, including investing, lead to operating the business. All organizations, profit oriented and not-for-profit, perform these three basic activities, and accounting plays a key role in each one:

- *Financing activities* provide necessary funds to start a business and expand it after it begins operating.
- *Investing activities* provide valuable assets required to run a business.
- *Operating activities* focus on selling goods and services, but they also consider expenses as important elements of sound financial management.

**a**ssessment **c**heck

1. List the three business activities that involve accounting.
2. Give an example of one of the business activities that involves accounting.

Bob Parsons performed these three activities during the start-up and growth of Go Daddy Group, a provider of Web domain registration services. He financed his new company with the proceeds from the sale of another firm he founded, Parsons Technology. Parsons invested these funds in computer systems and other office equipment. His operating activities involved hiring professional and clerical staff and promoting the company's services to a variety of clients. Parsons is also keenly aware of the importance of cost control, because lower costs mean he can charge lower prices for his products and still turn a profit. The role of accounting has increased considerably since GoDaddy was founded in 1997, driven by the firm's rapid growth. The company ranks in the top ten of *Inc.* magazine's 500 fastest-growing companies. The firm's revenues have increased by more than 7,500 percent since its first year in operation. GoDaddy now has around 350 employees and annual revenues of more than $40 million.[5]

# ACCOUNTING PROFESSIONALS

Accounting professionals work in a variety of areas in and for business firms, government agencies, and not-for-profit organizations. They can be classified as public, management, government, and not-for-profit accountants.

## Public Accountants

**public accountant**
accountant who works for an independent accounting firm.

A **public accountant** provides accounting services to individuals or business firms for a fee. Most public accounting firms provide three basic services to clients: (1) auditing, or examining, financial records; (2) tax preparation, planning, and related services; and (3) management consulting. Because public accountants are not employees of a client firm, they can provide unbiased advice about the firm's financial condition.

While there are hundreds of public accounting firms in the United States, the industry is heavily concentrated at the top. The four largest public accounting firms noted earlier—Deloitte & Touche, Ernst & Young, KPMG, and PricewaterhouseCoopers (PWC)—collect close to $20 billion annually from U.S. clients. By contrast, the nation's fifth-largest accounting firm, Chicago-based Grant Thornton, has annual revenues of less than $500 million.[6]

Several years ago, public accounting firms came under sharp criticism for providing management consulting services to many of the same firms they audited. Critics contended that when a public accounting firm does both—auditing and management consulting— an inherent conflict of interest is created. In addition, this conflict of interest may undermine confidence in the quality of the financial statements accounting firms audit. The bankruptcies of such high-profile firms as Enron and WorldCom increased pressure on public accounting firms to end the practice. Legislation also established strict limits on the types of consulting services auditors can provide. For example, an accounting firm that audits a company's books cannot provide *any* other services to that company, including tax services. As a result, three of the four largest public accounting firms either sold large portions of their consulting practices or spun them off into separate companies, and they now concentrate on providing auditing and tax services. PWC, for instance, sold much of its consulting business to IBM.

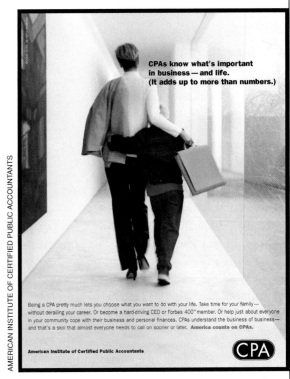

The certified public accountant (CPA) is the highest professional designation for a public accountant.

**Certified public accountants (CPAs)** demonstrate their accounting knowledge by meeting state requirements for education and experience and successfully completing a number of rigorous tests in accounting theory and practice, auditing, law, and taxes. Other accountants who meet specified educational and experience requirements and pass certification exams carry the title *certified management accountant* or *certified internal auditor.*

**certified public accountant (CPA)** accountant who meets specified educational and experiential requirements and has passed a comprehensive examination on accounting theory and practice.

## Management Accountants

An accountant employed by a business other than a public accounting firm is called a **management accountant.** Such a person collects and records financial transactions and prepares financial statements used by the firm's managers in decision making. Management accountants provide timely, relevant, accurate, and concise information that executives can use to operate their firms more effectively and more profitably than they could without this input. In addition to preparing financial statements, a management accountant plays a major role in interpreting them. A management accountant should provide answers to many important questions:

- Where is the company going?
- What opportunities await it?
- Do certain situations expose the company to excessive risk?
- Does the firm's information system provide detailed and timely information to all levels of management?

Management accountants frequently specialize in different aspects of accounting. A cost accountant, for example, determines the cost of goods and services and helps set their prices. An internal auditor examines the firm's financial practices to ensure that its records include accurate data and that its operations comply with federal, state, and local laws and regulations. A tax accountant works to minimize a firm's tax bill and assumes responsibility for its federal, state, county, and city tax returns.

**"They Said It"**

"I don't know technology and engineering. I don't know accounting."
—Bernie Ebbers (b. 1941) Former CEO, WorldCom MCI

## Tips for Gift Giving

Gifts to clients and prospective clients are a well-established business tradition that can yield long-lasting positive results. But because the practice of giving can be tricky, many industries and individual firms have established rules and guidelines to prevent missteps and backfires. Here are a few general suggestions.

1. Before you give a gift, find out what the gift policy and limit on gift value are at the company where the recipient works. If individual gifts are frowned on or even prohibited because management fears undue influence, you might still make a group gift, make a charitable contribution in the company's name, or contribute to a gift-matching program.

2. Avoid giving gifts when negotiating or bidding for new business.

3. Give only to those you know well; otherwise, the gesture may backfire.

4. Present the gift with taste and care. Wrap it or have it wrapped and include a handwritten note.

5. If possible, deliver the gift yourself—in person.

6. Be creative about when you give. In addition to traditional gift-giving holidays, consider the date of contract renewal or the anniversary of a business relationship. Or give to commemorate a joint achievement or to celebrate a client's promotion.

7. Be thoughtful and choose a practical gift that you're sure will be appreciated. Know your recipient's taste and interests (sports, hobbies, food, or music preferences) and choose accordingly.

8. Avoid giving a gift that makes the recipient uncomfortable for any reason—steer clear of a gift that is too large, too small, inappropriate, poorly timed, humorous, or too personal.

9. Use restraint. Giving too many gifts reduces their effect and can embarrass the recipient.

10. Recognize that gifts with your company's logo on them may be seen as tacky or impersonal. If you must include it, use the logo in the wrapping and not the gift.

---

**Sources:** "Gift Giving Etiquette," American Express, accessed August 16, 2006, http://www.133.americanexpress.com; Mike Hetherington, "Client Gifts That Keep on Giving," *Bozeman (MT) Daily Chronicle*, accessed July 21, 2006, http://www.bozemandailychronicle.com; "Holiday Etiquette," Eticon, accessed July 21, 2006, http://www.eticon.com.

One small way in which taxes affect a firm is under the IRS ruling that a business can deduct the value of business gifts to individuals, but only up to $25 during a given tax year. The "Business Etiquette" feature provides some further tips on business gift giving.

## Government and Not-for-Profit Accountants

Federal, state, and local governments also require accounting services. **Government accountants** and those who work for not-for-profit organizations perform professional services similar to those of management accountants. Accountants in these sectors concern themselves primarily with determining how efficiently the organizations accomplish their objectives. Among the many government agencies that employ accountants are NASA, the Federal Bureau of Investigation, the IRS, the Commonwealth of Pennsylvania, and the City of Fresno, California. Not-for-profit organizations, such as churches, labor unions, political parties, charities, schools, hospitals, and universities, also hire accountants. In fact, the not-for-profit sector is one of the fastest-growing segments of accounting practice. An increasing number of not-for-profits publish financial information because contributors want to know how the groups spend the money that they donate.

### assessment check

1. What is the difference between a public accountant and a management accountant?

2. What services does the typical public accounting firm provide to clients? How has the mix of services changed in recent years?

# THE ACCOUNTING PROCESS

Accounting deals with financial transactions between a firm and its employees, customers, suppliers, and owners; bankers; and various government agencies. For example, payroll checks result in a cash outflow to compensate employees. A payment to a vendor results in receipt of

Figure

16.2

needed materials for the production process. Cash, check, and credit purchases by customers generate funds to cover the costs of operations and to earn a profit. Prompt payment of bills preserves the firm's credit rating and its future ability to earn a profit. The procedure by which accountants convert data about individual transactions to financial statements is called the **accounting process.** Figure 16.2 illustrates the activities involved in the accounting process: recording, classifying, and summarizing transactions in order to produce financial statements for the firm's management and other interested parties.

The Accounting Process

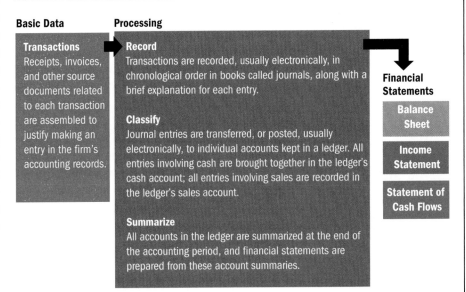

**Basic Data**

**Transactions**
Receipts, invoices, and other source documents related to each transaction are assembled to justify making an entry in the firm's accounting records.

**Processing**

**Record**
Transactions are recorded, usually electronically, in chronological order in books called journals, along with a brief explanation for each entry.

**Classify**
Journal entries are transferred, or posted, usually electronically, to individual accounts kept in a ledger. All entries involving cash are brought together in the ledger's cash account; all entries involving sales are recorded in the ledger's sales account.

**Summarize**
All accounts in the ledger are summarized at the end of the accounting period, and financial statements are prepared from these account summaries.

**Financial Statements**

Balance Sheet

Income Statement

Statement of Cash Flows

## The Impact of Computers and the Internet on the Accounting Process

For hundreds of years, bookkeepers recorded, or posted, accounting transactions through manual entries in journals. They then transferred the information, or posted it, to individual accounts listed in ledgers. Computers have simplified the process, making it faster and easier than the manual method. For instance, point-of-sale terminals perform a number of functions each time they record sales. These terminals not only recall prices from computer system memory and maintain constant inventory counts of individual items in stock but also automatically perform accounting data entry functions.

Accounting software programs are used widely in both large and small businesses today. They allow a do-it-once approach, in which a single input leads to automatic conversion of a sale into a journal entry, which then is stored until needed. Decision makers can then request up-to-date financial statements and financial ratios when needed. Improvements in accounting software continue to make the process even faster and easier.

Because the accounting needs of entrepreneurs and small businesses differ from those of larger firms, accounting software makers have designed programs that meet specific user needs. Some examples of accounting software programs designed for entrepreneurs and small businesses, and designed to run on personal computers, include QuickBooks, Peachtree, and BusinessWorks. Software programs designed for larger firms, often requiring more sophisticated computer systems, include products from Computer Associates, Oracle, and SAP.

For firms that conduct business worldwide, software producers have introduced new accounting programs that handle all of a company's accounting information for every country in which it operates. The software handles different languages and currencies, as well as the financial, legal, and tax requirements of each nation in which the firm conducts business.

The Internet also influences the accounting process. Several software producers offer Web-based accounting products designed for small and medium-sized businesses. One example is the series of products from Sage Software. Among other benefits, these products allow users to access their complete accounting systems from anywhere using a standard Web browser. Witt Industries—a Cincinnati-based manufacturer of a proprietary line of metal waste receptacle products—uses one Sage product, Insight, for fast and accurate managerial

**accounting process** set of activities involved in converting information about individual transactions into financial statements.

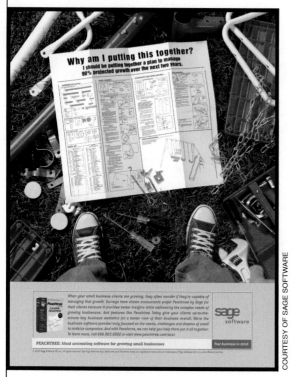

Accounting software is available to help small businesses.

reporting and analyses of accounting data. Gregg Battaglia, the firm's vice president and CFO, comments, "It used to take us a long time to create spreadsheets, print reports, and send them out. Now we generate information in a fraction of the time and distribute it company-wide electronically."[7]

## The Foundation of the Accounting System

To provide reliable, consistent, and unbiased information to decision makers, accountants follow guidelines, or standards, known as **generally accepted accounting principles (GAAP).** These principles encompass the conventions, rules, and procedures for determining acceptable accounting practices at a particular time. In the United States, the **Financial Accounting Standards Board (FASB)** is primarily responsible for evaluating, setting, or modifying GAAP. Accountants adhere to GAAP to create uniform financial statements for comparison between firms. Using GAAP ensures a solid basis for sound business decision making. FASB carefully monitors changing business conditions, enacting new rules and modifying existing rules when necessary. One major change in accounting rules recently dealt with the expensing of executive and employee stock options. Stock options give the holder the right to buy stock at a fixed price. FASB now requires that firms who give employees stock options calculate the cost of the options and treat the cost as an expense, similar to salaries.

FASB is also proposing new rules in the area of pension accounting—how firms with pensions account for pension obligations. These rules are quite controversial and are strongly opposed by many corporate executives. The pros and cons of the new rules for pension accounting are debated in the "Solving an Ethical Controversy" feature.

In response to cases of accounting fraud, and questions about the independence of auditors, the Sarbanes-Oxley Act—commonly known as SOX—created the Public Accounting Oversight Board. The five-member board has the power to set audit standards and to investigate and sanction accounting firms that certify the books of publicly traded firms. Members of the Public Accounting Oversight Board are appointed by the Securities and Exchange Commission (SEC)—the chief federal regulator of the securities markets and the accounting industry—to serve staggered five-year terms. No more than two of the five members of the board can be certified public accountants.

In addition to creating the Public Accounting Oversight Board, SOX also added to the reporting requirements for publicly traded companies. Senior executives including the CEO and chief financial officer (CFO), for example, have to personally certify that the financial information reported by the company is correct. These requirements have increased the demand for accounting professionals, especially managerial accountants. One result of this increased demand has been higher salaries. The "Hit & Miss" feature describes the growing need for managerial accountants.

Two financial statements form the foundation of the accounting system: the balance sheet and the income statement. The information found in these statements is calculated using the accounting equation and the double-entry bookkeeping system. A third statement, the statement of cash flows, is also prepared to focus specifically on the sources and uses of cash for a firm from its operating, investing, and financing activities.

# DOES ACCOUNTING FOR PENSION OBLIGATIONS TELL THE REAL STORY?

*A new report by the publisher of* The Analyst's Accounting Observer *reveals that General Motors, with the country's largest corporate pension fund, would have negative shareholder equity if it fully accounted for its pension obligations. GM's net worth would fall by about $38 billion, reducing shareholder equity to −$10 billion, if its balance sheet were adjusted to show pension-related items realistically. The study "shows the General without its clothes, and it's not pretty," says the study's author.*

GM defends its financial reporting by claiming, correctly, that it has not violated any rules nor done anything unusual or improper by representing its obligations with balance sheet "placeholders." It says its pension fund is in no danger of running dry, and the company is a very long way from having negative value. As one accounting consultant says, "It's the rules that are wrong."

Should companies be required to show the true market value of their pension fund obligations on their balance sheets?

## PRO

1. Investors and employees have a right to full disclosure and deserve to see the real numbers.
2. Accurate accounting will force managers to ensure the safety of the company's pension funds and prevent failures such as United Airlines' recent historic default on its employee pension plan.

## CON

1. Accurate numbers are kept elsewhere in companies' financial reports; the balance sheet numbers are used for convenience.
2. A pension fund is a long-term entity whose ups and downs net out over time and therefore have little meaning for investors on a year-to-year basis.

## Summary

According to the study, other companies that fared poorly with adjusted pension numbers inserted into their balance sheets included Boeing, Goodyear, Lucent Technologies, Delta Air Lines, Maytag, Qwest, and to a lesser degree General Electric. GM has been scrupulous about complying with the rules for *funding* its pension system, which are unconnected with the rules for accounting for it. But—inspired partly by the pension default of United Airlines—separate inquiries are under way in Congress and at the Securities and Exchange Commission, and a pension reporting rule change could result. In fact, the FASB began a review of the rules for how a company must show the true economic value of its retirement plans on its balance sheet. But at the moment, it has decided to defer a more comprehensive examination of the effects on a firm's earnings.

**Sources:** Mary Williams Walsh, "Thorny Issue for Board: How to Value Pension Plans," *New York Times,* accessed July 21, 2006, http://www.nytimes.com; Mary Williams Walsh, "GM Tops List as Study Questions Pension Accounting," *New York Times,* accessed July 21, 2006, http://www.nytimes.com; Jane Tisdale, "PBGC Woes Galvanize U.S. Pension Reform," State Street Global Advisors, accessed July 21, 2006, http://www.ssga.com; Douglas Fore, "Changes in Accounting Practices Will Drive Pension Paradigm Shift," Position Research Council, *working paper,* Wharton School, 2004, accessed July 21, 2006, http://prc.wharton.upenn.edu/prc/prc.html.

solving an **ETHICAL** controversy

# The Accounting Equation

Three fundamental terms appear in the accounting equation: assets, liabilities, and owners' equity. An **asset** is anything of value owned or leased by a business. Assets include land, buildings, supplies, cash, accounts receivable (amounts owed to the business as payment for credit sales), and marketable securities.

**asset** anything of value owned or leased by a business.

Although most assets are tangible assets, such as equipment, buildings, and inventories, intangible possessions such as patents and trademarks are often some of a firm's most important assets. This kind of asset is especially essential for many companies, including computer software firms, biotechnology companies, and pharmaceutical companies. For instance, Johnson & Johnson—which has both biotechnology and pharmaceutical operations—reported close to $12 billion in intangible assets in one recent year, compared with around $43 billion in tangible assets.[8]

# HIT & MISS

## Accounting Jobs on the Rise in the Wake of SOX

Tired of hearing how tight the job market is? Joe McCann, dean of Sykes College of Business at the University of Tampa, says this about jobs in the accounting profession: "There's no question that demand is up for accounting graduates—and in particular those interested in, or having a background in, anything related to forensic accounting and auditing. From a student's standpoint, accounting is back, and it's back in a big way."

The Bureau of Labor Statistics reports that the number of accountants and accounting jobs is increasing. In some areas, the number of accountants has grown while the size of the overall workforce has remained the same. Demand for accounting expertise is expanding rapidly in the wake of the Sarbanes-Oxley Act (SOX), which was passed to regulate publicly owned firms after financial scandals at fraud-riddled companies such as Enron and WorldCom. With numerous new requirements, such as annual audits of internal financial controls that must be performed by a third-party accounting firm, the act has fueled not just better management practices but also a big jump in employment and growth opportunities for managerial accountants. There's more work to be done, and more people are needed to do it.

Accountants will find themselves well compensated for expertise in the newest areas of accounting regulation and technology. A recent survey by the Institute of Management Accountants (available at http://www.imanet.org)

found salaries and other compensation rising, especially for certified management accountants (CMAs) but also for certified public accountants (CPAs). Each can earn at least $90,000 a year, and those with both a CMA and CPA can make $105,000 or more. Salary gains occurred at all levels in the profession. "These changes in salary and overall compensation are a direct result of Sarbanes-Oxley," says IMA's president and chief executive officer, "and we expect this trend to continue."

### Questions for Critical Thinking

1. What unanticipated effects has the Sarbanes-Oxley Act had on the accounting profession and on accounting education and certification?
2. Do you think that the application of Sarbanes-Oxley (or similar legislation) will eventually widen to include not-for-profit and private organizations or that legal demands on smaller companies will be reduced? What impact would each possibility have on the accounting profession and why?

**Sources:** Bruce Pounder, "The Overworked Accountant, Part 1," CareerBank.com, accessed July 21, 2006, http://www.careerbank.com; "Sarbanes-Oxley Requirements Boost Value of CMA Certification; New Survey Reveals Salaries for Management Accountants Rising," PR Newswire, accessed July 16, 2006, http://www.prnewswire.com; Dave Simanoff, "Accountants Can Count On More Job Offers," *Tampa Tribune*, June 30, 2006, http://www.tampatrib.com.

---

**liability** claim against a firm's assets by a creditor.

**owners' equity** all claims of the proprietor, partners, or stockholders against the assets of a firm, equal to the excess of assets over liabilities.

**basic accounting equation** relationship that states that assets equal liabilities plus owners' equity.

There are two claimants to the assets of a firm: creditors and owners. A **liability** of a business is anything owed to creditors—that is, the claims of a firm's creditors. When a firm borrows money to purchase inventory, land, or machinery, the claims of creditors are shown as accounts payable, notes payable, or long-term debt. Wages and salaries owed to employees also represent liabilities (known as wages payable or accrued wages).

**Owners' equity** represents the owners' initial investment in the business plus profits that were not paid out to owners over time in the form of cash dividends. A strong owners' equity position often is used as evidence of a firm's financial strength and stability.

The **basic accounting equation** states that assets equal liabilities plus owners' equity. This equation reflects the financial position of a firm at any point in time:

$$\text{Assets} = \text{Liabilities} + \text{Owners' Equity}$$

Because financing comes from either creditors or owners, the right side of the accounting equation also represents the business's financial structure.

The basic accounting equation also illustrates **double-entry bookkeeping**—the process by which accounting transactions are recorded. Because assets must always equal liabilities plus equity, each individual transaction must have an offsetting transaction. For example, if a company increases an asset, either another asset must decrease, a liability must increase, or owners' equity must increase. So if a company uses cash to purchase inventory, one asset (inventory) is increased while another (cash) is decreased by the same amount. Similarly, a decrease in an asset must be offset by either an increase in another asset, a decrease in a liability, or a decrease in owners' equity. If a company uses cash to repay a bank loan, both an asset (cash) and a liability (bank loans) decrease, and by the same amount.

The relationship expressed by the accounting equation underlies development of the balance sheet and income statement. These two statements reflect the firm's current financial position and the most recent report of its incomes, expenses, and profits for interested parties inside and outside the firm. They provide a fundamental basis for planning activities and help companies attract new investments, secure borrowed funds, and complete tax returns.

**double-entry bookkeeping** process by which accounting transactions are entered; each individual transaction always has an offsetting transaction.

**assessment check**

1. Briefly describe the accounting process.
2. Define GAAP. What is the role of the Financial Accounting Standards Board?
3. Describe the basic accounting equation.

# FINANCIAL STATEMENTS

Financial statements provide managers with essential information they need to evaluate the liquidity position of an organization—its ability to meet current obligations and needs by converting assets into cash; the firm's profitability; and its overall financial health. The balance sheet, income statement, and statement of cash flows provide a foundation on which managers can base their decisions. By interpreting the data provided in these statements, the appropriate information can be communicated to internal decision makers and to interested parties outside the organization.

## The Balance Sheet

A firm's **balance sheet** shows its financial position on a particular date. It is similar to a photograph of the firm's assets together with its liabilities and owners' equity at a specific moment in time. Balance sheets must be prepared at regular intervals, because a firm's managers and other internal parties often request this information every day, every week, or at least every month. On the other hand, external users, such as stockholders or industry analysts, may use this information less frequently, perhaps every quarter or once a year.

The balance sheet follows the accounting equation. On the left side of the balance sheet are the firm's assets—what it owns. These assets, shown in descending order of liquidity (in other words, convertibility to cash), represent the uses that management has made of available funds. On the right side of the equation are the claims against the firm's assets. Liabilities and owners' equity indicate the sources of the firm's assets and are listed in the order in which they are due. Liabilities reflect the claims of creditors—financial institutions or bondholders that have loaned the firm money, suppliers that have provided goods and services on credit, and others to be paid, such as federal, state, and local tax authorities. Owners' equity represents the owners' claims (those of stockholders, in the case of a corporation) against the firm's assets. It also amounts to the excess of all assets over liabilities.

Figure 16.3 shows the balance sheet for Shasta Outfitters, a California-based chain of retail stores selling fitness gear and clothing. The basic accounting equation is illustrated by the three classifications of assets, liabilities, and owners' equity on the company's balance sheet. Remember, total assets must always equal the sum of liabilities and owners' equity.

**"They Said It"**

"I never get the accountants in before I start up a business."
—*Richard Branson*
*(b. 1950)*
*Businessman and entrepreneur*

**balance sheet** statement of a firm's financial position—what it owns and the claims against its assets—at a particular point in time.

Figure

16.3  Balance Sheet for Shasta Outfitters

**① Current Assets:**
Cash and other liquid assets that can or will be converted to cash or used within one year.

**② Fixed Assets:**
Plant, property, equipment, and other assets expected to last for more than one year. Accumulated depreciation represents the cumulative value of fixed assets that have been expensed, or depreciated.

**③ Current Liabilities:**
Claims of creditors that are to be repaid within one year.

**④ Long-Term Debt:**
Debts that come due one year or longer after the date on the balance sheet.

**⑤ Owners'(Shareholders') Equity:** Claims of the proprietor, partners, or stockholders against the assets of the firm; the difference between total assets and total liabilities.

### Shasta Outfitters

**Balance Sheet**
Year Ending January 31

| ($ millions) | 2007 | 2006 |
|---|---|---|
| Current Assets | | |
| Cash and equivalents | 23.50 | 20.40 |
| Short-term investments | 65.50 | 52.30 |
| ① Accounts receivable | 13.90 | 12.30 |
| Inventory | 100.50 | 90.00 |
| Total current assets | 203.40 | 175.00 |
| | | |
| ② Fixed assets | 382.00 | 285.00 |
| (Accumulated depreciation) | (142.30) | (104.00) |
| Net fixed assets | 239.70 | 181.00 |
| | | |
| Total Assets | 443.10 | 356.00 |
| | | |
| ③ Current Liabilities | | |
| Accounts payable | 32.50 | 18.50 |
| Accruals | 22.56 | 19.40 |
| Short-term debt | 45.23 | 38.00 |
| Total current liabilities | 100.29 | 75.90 |
| | | |
| ④ Long-term debt | 20.31 | 10.80 |
| Total Liabilities | 120.60 | 86.70 |
| | | |
| ⑤ Owner's Equity | 322.50 | 269.30 |
| Total Assets and Equity | 443.10 | 356.00 |

## The Income Statement

**income statement** financial record of a company's revenues, expenses, and profits over a period of time.

Whereas the balance sheet reflects a firm's financial situation at a specific point in time, the income statement represents the flow of resources that reveals the performance of the organization over a specific time period. Resembling a video rather than a photograph, the **income statement** is a financial record summarizing a firm's financial performance in terms of revenues, expenses, and profits over a given time period, say a quarter or a year.

**① Sales:**
Funds received from the sale of goods and services over a specified period of time.

**② Cost of Goods Sold:**
Cost of merchandise or services that generate the firm's sales.

**③ Operating Expenses:**
Salaries, advertising, and other operational expenses not directly related to the acquisition, production, or sale of the firm's output.

### Shasta Outfitters

**Income Statement**
Year Ending January 31, 2007

| ($ millions) | 2007 | 2006 |
|---|---|---|
| ① Net sales | 713.00 | 615.00 |
| ② Cost of sales | 410.00 | 375.30 |
| Gross profit | 303.00 | 239.70 |
| ③ Operating expenses | 175.60 | 152.30 |
| ④ Operating income | 127.40 | 87.40 |
| ⑤ Depreciation | 38.30 | 32.00 |
| Net interest | 3.70 | 2.70 |
| Taxable income | 85.40 | 52.70 |
| Taxes | 25.62 | 15.81 |
| ⑥ Net income | 59.78 | 36.89 |
| Dividends | 6.58 | 5.30 |

**④ Operating Income (EBIDTA):**
Gross income minus operating expenses; also called EBIDTA (earnings before interest, depreciation, taxes, and amortization).

**⑤ Depreciation:**
Noncash expense that reflects the systematic reduction in the value of the firm's fixed assets.

**⑥ Net Income:**
Sales minus total expenses; profit after taxes.

In addition to reporting the firm's profit or loss results, the income statement helps decision makers focus on overall revenues and the costs involved in generating these revenues. Managers of a not-for-profit organization use this statement to determine whether its revenues from contributions and other sources will cover its operating costs. Finally, the income statement provides much of the basic data needed to calculate the financial ratios managers use in planning and controlling activities. Figure 16.4 shows the income statement for Shasta Outfitters.

An income statement (sometimes called a profit-and-loss, or P&L, statement) begins with total sales or revenues generated during a year, quarter, or month. Subsequent lines then deduct all of the costs related to producing the revenues. Typical categories of costs include costs involved in producing the firm's goods or services, operating expenses, interest, and taxes.

After all of them have been subtracted, the remaining net income may be distributed to the firm's owners (stockholders, proprietors, or partners) or reinvested in the company as retained earnings. The final figure on the income statement—net income after taxes—is the so-called **bottom line.**

Keeping costs under control is an important part of running a business. Too often, however, companies concentrate more on increasing revenue than controlling costs. Regardless of how much money a company collects in revenues, it wouldn't stay in business for long unless it eventually earns a profit.

## The Statement of Cash Flows

In addition to the income statement and the balance sheet, most firms prepare a third accounting statement—the statement of cash flows. Public companies are required to prepare and publish a statement of cash flows. In addition, commercial lenders often require a borrower to submit a statement of cash flows. The **statement of cash flows** provides investors and creditors with relevant information about a firm's cash receipts and cash payments for its operations, investments, and financing during an accounting period. Figure 16.5 shows the statement of cash flows for Shasta Outfitters.

Companies often prepare a statement of cash flows due to the widespread use of **accrual accounting.** Accrual accounting recognizes revenues and costs when they occur, not when actual cash changes hands. As a result, there can be differences between what is reported as sales, expenses, and profits, and the amount of cash that actually flows into and out of the business during a period of time. An example is depreciation. Companies depreciate fixed assets—such as machinery and buildings—over a specified period of time, meaning that they systematically reduce the value of the asset. Depreciation is reported as an expense on the firm's income statement—see Figure 16.4—but does not involve any actual cash. The fact that depreciation is a noncash expense means that what a firm reports as net income (profits after tax) for a particular period actually understates the amount of cash the firm took in, less expenses, during that period of time. Consequently, depreciation is added back to net income to obtain **cash flow.**

The fact that cash flow is the lifeblood of every organization is evidenced by the business failure rate. Many owners of firms that fail blame inadequate cash flow. Proponents of the statement of cash flows hope that its preparation and scrutiny by affected parties will prevent financial distress for otherwise profitable firms, too many of which are forced into bankruptcy due to a lack of cash needed to continue day-to-day operations.

Even for firms for which bankruptcy is not an issue, the statement of cash flows can provide investors and other interested parties with vital information. For instance, assume that a firm's income statement reports rising earnings. At the same time, however, the statement of cash flows shows that the firm's inventory is rising faster than sales—often a signal that demand for the firm's products is softening, which may in turn be a sign of impending financial trouble.

## FINANCIAL RATIO ANALYSIS

Accounting professionals fulfill important responsibilities beyond preparing financial statements. In a more critical role, they help managers interpret the statements by comparing data about the firm's current activities to that for previous periods and to results posted by other companies in the industry. **Ratio analysis** is one of the most commonly used tools for measur-

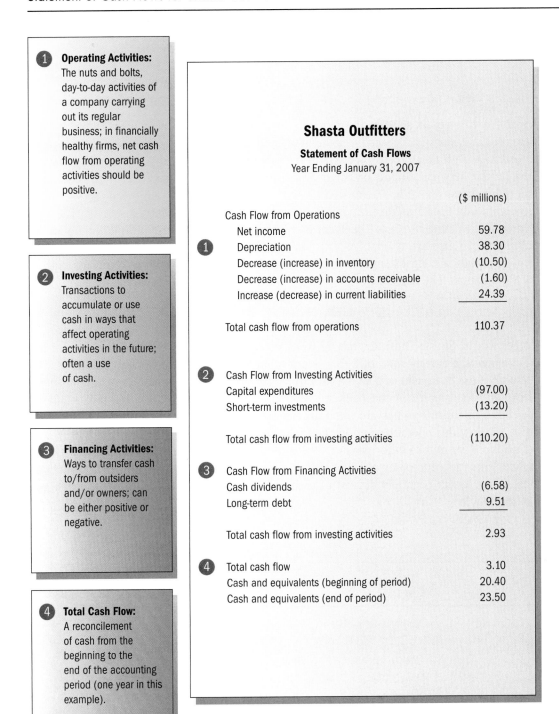

**Operating Activities:**
The nuts and bolts, day-to-day activities of a company carrying out its regular business; in financially healthy firms, net cash flow from operating activities should be positive.

**Investing Activities:**
Transactions to accumulate or use cash in ways that affect operating activities in the future; often a use of cash.

**Financing Activities:**
Ways to transfer cash to/from outsiders and/or owners; can be either positive or negative.

**Total Cash Flow:**
A reconcilement of cash from the beginning to the end of the accounting period (one year in this example).

### Shasta Outfitters
#### Statement of Cash Flows
Year Ending January 31, 2007

($ millions)

| | |
|---|---|
| Cash Flow from Operations | |
| Net income | 59.78 |
| Depreciation | 38.30 |
| Decrease (increase) in inventory | (10.50) |
| Decrease (increase) in accounts receivable | (1.60) |
| Increase (decrease) in current liabilities | 24.39 |
| | |
| Total cash flow from operations | 110.37 |
| | |
| Cash Flow from Investing Activities | |
| Capital expenditures | (97.00) |
| Short-term investments | (13.20) |
| | |
| Total cash flow from investing activities | (110.20) |
| | |
| Cash Flow from Financing Activities | |
| Cash dividends | (6.58) |
| Long-term debt | 9.51 |
| | |
| Total cash flow from investing activities | 2.93 |
| | |
| Total cash flow | 3.10 |
| Cash and equivalents (beginning of period) | 20.40 |
| Cash and equivalents (end of period) | 23.50 |

ing the firm's liquidity, profitability, and reliance on debt financing, as well as the effectiveness of management's resource utilization. This analysis also allows comparisons with other firms and with the firm's own past performance.

Ratios assist managers by interpreting actual performance and making comparisons to what should have happened. Comparisons with ratios of similar companies help managers understand their firm's performance relative to competitors' results. These industry standards serve as important yardsticks and help pinpoint problem areas as well as areas of excellence. Ratios for the current accounting period also may be compared with similar calculations for previous periods to spot developing trends. Ratios can be classified according to their specific purposes. The four major categories of financial ratios are summarized in Table 16.1.

## Liquidity Ratios

A firm's ability to meet its short-term obligations when they must be paid is measured by **liquidity ratios.** Increasing liquidity reduces the likelihood that a firm will face emergencies caused by the need to raise funds to repay loans. On the other hand, firms with low liquidity may be forced to choose between default or borrowing from high-cost lending sources to meet their maturing obligations.

Two commonly used liquidity ratios are the current ratio and the acid-test ratio. The current ratio compares current assets to current liabilities, giving managers information about the firm's ability to pay its current debts as they mature. The current ratio compares current assets to current liabilities, giving executives information about the firm's ability to pay its current debts as they mature. The current ratio of Shasta Outfitters can be computed as follows:

$$\text{Current ratio} = \frac{\$203.40}{\$100.29} = 2.03$$

In other words, Shasta Outfitters has $2.03 of current assets for every $1.00 of current liabilities. In general, a current ratio of 2 to 1 is considered to indicate satisfactory liquidity. This rule of thumb must be considered along with other factors, such as the nature of the business, the season, and the quality of the company's management team. Shasta Outfitters' management and other interested parties are likely to evaluate this ratio of 2.03 to 1 by comparing it with ratios for previous operating periods and with industry averages.

The acid-test (or quick) ratio measures the ability of a firm to meet its debt payments on short notice. This ratio compares quick assets—the most liquid current assets—against current liabilities. Quick assets generally consist of cash and equivalents, short-term investments, and accounts receivable.

**Table 16.1** Major Financial Ratios

| Ratio Category | Ratio | How Defined | Shasta Outfitters Ratio |
|---|---|---|---|
| **Liquidity** | Current ratio | Current assets divided by current liabilities | 2.03 |
| | Acid-test ratio | Current assets (less inventory) divided by current liabilities | 1.03 |
| **Activity** | Inventory turnover | Sales divided by average inventory | 7.49 |
| | Asset turnover | Sales divided by average assets | 1.78 |
| **Profitability** | Gross profit margin | Gross profit divided by sales | 42.5% |
| | Net profit margin | Net income divided by sales | 8.4% |
| | Return on assets | Net income divided by average assets | 15.0% |
| | Return on equity | Net income divided by average equity | 44.4% |
| **Leverage** | Debt ratio | Total liabilities divided by total assets | 27.2% |
| | Long-term debt to equity | Long-term debt divided by equity | 6.3% |

Shasta Outfitters' current balance sheet lists the following quick assets: cash and equivalents ($23.50 million), short-term investments ($65.50 million), and accounts receivable ($13.90 million). The firm's acid-test ratio is computed as follows:

$$\text{Acid-test ratio} = \frac{\$102.90}{\$100.29} = 1.03$$

Because the traditional rule of thumb for an adequate acid-test ratio is around 1 to 1, Shasta Outfitters appears to have a reasonable level of liquidity. However, the same cautions apply here as for the current ratio. The ratio should be compared with industry averages and data from previous operating periods in determining whether it is adequate for the firm.

## Activity Ratios

**Activity ratios** measure the effectiveness of management's use of the firm's resources. One of the most frequently used activity ratios, the inventory turnover ratio, indicates the number of times merchandise moves through a business:

$$\text{Inventory turnover} = \frac{\$713.00}{\$95.25} = 7.49$$

Average inventory for Shasta Outfitters is determined by adding the inventory as of January 31, 2007 ($100.50 million) with the inventory as of January 31, 2006 ($90.00 million) and dividing it by 2. Comparing the 7.49 inventory turnover ratio with industry standards gives a measure of efficiency. It's important to note, however, that inventory turnover can vary substantially depending on the products a company sells and the industry in which in operates. For instance, grocery retailer Supervalu has an inventory turnover of almost 13. By contrast, clothing retailer the Gap has an inventory turnover of around 9.

Another measure of efficiency is total asset turnover. It measures how much in sales each dollar invested in assets generates:

$$\text{Total asset turnover} = \frac{\$713.00}{\$399.55} = 1.78$$

Average total assets for Shasta Outfitters equals total assets as of January 31, 2007 ($443.10 million) plus total assets as of January 31, 2006 ($356.00 million) divided by 2.

Shasta Outfitters generates about $1.78 in sales for each dollar invested in assets. Although a higher ratio generally indicates that a firm is operating more efficiently, care must be taken when comparing firms that operate in different industries.

Some industries simply require higher investment in assets than do other industries. For example, American Electric Power has an asset turnover ratio of around 0.45, meaning that every dollar AEP invests in assets generates only 45 cents in revenue. While this figure seems low, it is actually relatively high compared with other electric utilities.

## Profitability Ratios

Some ratios measure the organization's overall financial performance by evaluating its ability to generate revenues in excess of operating costs and other expenses. These measures are called **profitability ratios.** To compute these ratios, accountants compare the firm's earnings with total sales or investments. Over a period of time, profitability ratios may reveal the effectiveness of management in operating the business. Four important profitability ratios are gross profit margin, net profit margin, return on assets, and return on equity:

$$\text{Gross profit margin} = \frac{\$303.00 \text{ million}}{\$713.00 \text{ million}} = 42.5\%$$

$$\text{Net profit margin} = \frac{\$59.78 \text{ million}}{\$713.00 \text{ million}} = 8.4\%$$

$$\text{Return on assets} = \frac{\$59.78 \text{ million}}{\$399.55 \text{ million}} = 15.0\%$$

$$\text{Return on equity} = \frac{\$59.78 \text{ million}}{\$295.90 \text{ million}} = 20.2\%$$

All of these ratios support positive evaluations of the current operations of Shasta Outfitters. For example, the net profit margin indicates that the firm realizes a profit of about 8.4 cents on each dollar of merchandise it sells. Although this ratio varies widely among business firms, Shasta Outfitters compares favorably with retailers in general, which have an average net profit margin of around 5 percent. However, this ratio, like the other profitability ratios, should be evaluated in relation to profit forecasts, past performance, or more specific industry averages to enhance the interpretation of results. Similarly, while the firm's return on equity of more than 20 percent appears outstanding, the degree of risk in the industry also must be considered.

## Leverage Ratios

**Leverage ratios** measure the extent to which a firm relies on debt financing. They provide particularly interesting information to potential investors and lenders. If management has assumed too much debt in financing the firm's operations, problems may arise in meeting future interest payments and repaying outstanding loans. Relying too heavily on debt financing can lead to bankruptcy. More generally, both investors and lenders may prefer to deal with firms whose owners have invested enough of their own money to avoid overreliance on borrowing. The total liabilities to total assets ratio and long-term debt to equity ratio help analysts evaluate these concerns:

$$\text{Total liabilities to total assets} = \frac{\$120.60 \text{ million}}{\$443.10 \text{ million}} = 27.2\%$$

$$\text{Long-term debt to equity} = \frac{\$20.31 \text{ million}}{\$322.50 \text{ million}} = 6.3\%$$

A total liabilities to total assets ratio greater than 50 percent indicates that a firm is relying more on borrowed money than owners' equity. Because Shasta Outfitters' total liabilities to total assets ratio is 27.2 percent, the firm's owners have invested considerably more than the total amount of liabilities shown on the firm's balance sheet. Moreover, the firm's long-term debt to equity ratio is only 6.3%, indicating that Shasta Outfitters has only about 6.3 cents in long-term debt to every dollar in equity. The long-term debt to equity ratio also indicates that Shasta Outfitters hasn't relied very heavily on borrowed money.

The four categories of financial ratios relate balance sheet and income statement data to one another, help management pinpoint a firm's strengths and weaknesses, and indicate areas in need of further investigation. Large, multiproduct firms that operate in diverse markets use their information systems to update their financial ratios every day or even every hour. Each company's management must decide on an appropriate review schedule to avoid the costly and time-consuming mistake of overmonitoring.

In addition to calculating financial ratios, managers, investors, and lenders should pay close attention to how accountants applied a number of accounting rules when preparing financial statements. GAAP gives accountants leeway in reporting certain revenues and expenses. Public companies are required to disclose, in footnotes to the financial statements, how the various accounting rules were applied.

**budget** planning and control tool that reflects a firm's expected sales revenues, operating expenses, and cash receipts and outlays.

# BUDGETING

Although the financial statements discussed in this chapter focus on past business activities, they also provide the basis for planning in the future. A **budget** is a planning and controlling tool that reflects the firm's expected sales revenues, operating expenses, and cash receipts and outlays. It quantifies the firm's plans for a specified future period. Because it reflects management estimates of expected sales, cash inflows and outflows, and costs, the budget serves as a financial blueprint and can be thought of as a short-term financial plan. It becomes the standard for comparison against actual performance.

Budget preparation is frequently a time-consuming task that involves many people from various departments within the firm. The complexity of the budgeting process varies with the size and complexity of the organization. Large corporations such as United Technologies, Clorox, and Motorola maintain complex and sophisticated budgeting systems. Their budgets help managers integrate their numerous divisions in addition to serving as planning and controlling tools. But budgeting in both large and small firms is similar to household budgeting in its purpose: to match income and expenses in a way that accomplishes objectives and correctly times cash inflows and outflows.

Because the accounting department is an organization's financial nerve center, it provides much of the data for budget development. The overall master, or operating, budget is actually a composite of many individual budgets for separate units of the firm. These individual budgets typically include the production budget, cash budget, capital expenditures budget, advertising budget, and sales budget.

Technology has improved the efficiency of the budgeting process. The accounting software products discussed earlier—such as Quick-Books—all include budgeting features. Moreover, modules designed for specific businesses are often available from third parties. The University of Missouri, for example, has developed a series of QuickBooks modules designed to meet the budgeting needs of dairy farmers.[9]

One of the most important budgets prepared by firms is the **cash budget.** The cash budget, usually prepared monthly, tracks the firm's cash inflows and outflows. Figure 16.6 illustrates a sample cash budget for Velo Mart—a Texas-based chain of bicycle shops. The company has set a $350,000 target cash balance. The cash budget indicates months in which the firm will need temporary loans—May, June, and July in the

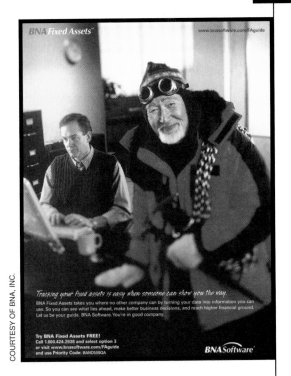

COURTESY OF BNA, INC.

Specialized accounting software can serve individual business needs.

**Velo Mart**
Four-Month Cash Budget

| | May | June | July | August |
|---|---|---|---|---|
| **Sales** | 800.0 | 1,500.0 | 1,800.0 | 1,500.0 |
| Cash sales | 560.0 | 1,050.0 | 1,260.0 | 1,050.0 |
| Collection of credit sales | | | | |
| One month prior | 140.0 | 160.0 | 300.0 | 360.0 |
| Two months prior | 60.0 | 70.0 | 80.0 | 150.0 |
| Other cash inflows | | | | |
| Total cash inflows | 760.0 | 1,280.0 | 1,640.0 | 1,560.0 |
| | | | | |
| **Purchases** | 1,050.0 | 1,260.0 | 1,050.0 | 840.0 |
| Cash purchases | 525.0 | 630.0 | 525.0 | 420.0 |
| Payment of credit purchases | | | | |
| One month prior | 140.0 | 262.5 | 315.0 | 262.5 |
| Two months prior | 122.5 | 140.0 | 262.5 | 315.0 |
| Rent and utilities | 100.0 | 100.0 | 100.0 | 100.0 |
| Salaries | 175.0 | 175.0 | 175.0 | 175.0 |
| Other cash outflows | | 50.0 | | 25.0 |
| Total cash outflows | 1,062.5 | 1,357.5 | 1,377.5 | 1,297.5 |
| | | | | |
| **Net cash flow** | (302.5) | (77.5) | 262.5 | 262.5 |
| Beginning cash balance | 350.0 | 47.5 | (30.0) | 232.5 |
| Ending cash balance | 47.5 | (30.0) | 232.5 | 495.0 |
| Surplus (deficit) | (302.5) | (380.0) | (117.5) | 145.0 |
| Cumulative surplus (deficit) | (302.5) | (682.5) | (497.5) | 27.2 |

case of Velo Mart. The document also indicates months in which the firm can invest excess funds in securities to earn interest rather than leaving them idle in a bank account—August in the case of Velo Mart. Finally, the cash budget produces a tangible standard against which to compare actual cash inflows and outflows.

**assessment check**

1. What is a budget?
2. Describe how a cash budget is organized.

# INTERNATIONAL ACCOUNTING

Today, accounting procedures and practices must be adapted to accommodate an international business environment. The Coca-Cola Company and McDonald's both generate more than half their annual revenues from sales outside the United States. Nestlé, the giant chocolate and food products multinational, operates throughout the world. It derives 98 percent of its revenues from outside Switzerland, its home country. International accounting practices for global firms must reliably translate the financial statements of the firm's international affiliates, branches, and subsidiaries and convert data about foreign currency transactions to dollars. Also, foreign currencies and exchange rates influence the accounting and financial reporting processes of firms operating internationally.

## Exchange Rates

As defined in Chapter 4, an exchange rate is the ratio at which a country's currency can be exchanged for other currencies. Currencies can be treated as goods to be bought and sold. Like the price of any product, currency prices change daily according to supply and demand. So exchange rate fluctuations complicate accounting entries and accounting practices.

Accountants who deal with international transactions must appropriately record their firms' foreign sales and purchases. Today's sophisticated accounting software helps firms handle all of their international transactions within a single program. An international firm's consolidated financial statements must reflect any gains or losses due to changes in exchange rates during specific periods of time. Financial statements that cover operations in two or more countries also need to treat fluctuations consistently to allow for comparison.

In the United States, GAAP requires that firms make adjustments to their earnings reflecting changes in exchange rates. In general, a weakening dollar increases the earnings of a U.S.

firm that has international operations because the same units of a foreign currency will translate into more U.S. dollars. By the same token, a strengthening dollar will have the opposite effect on earnings—the same number of units of a foreign currency will translate into fewer dollars. Over a recent three-year period, foreign currency adjustments effectively added more than $1.5 billion to Procter & Gamble's earnings.[10]

## International Accounting Standards

The International Accounting Standards Committee (IASC) was established in 1973 to promote worldwide consistency in financial reporting practices. The IASC is recognized worldwide as the body with the sole responsibility and authority to issue pronouncements on international accounting standards. The International Federation of Accountants supports the work of the IASC and develops international guidelines for auditing, ethics, education, and management accounting. Every five years, an international congress is held to judge progress in achieving consistency in standards and works toward increasing comparability among nations' financial data and currencies.

The European Union and NAFTA have led to widespread recognition of the necessity for comparability and uniformity of international accounting standards. An increasing number of investors are buying shares in foreign multinational corporations. In response to global investors' needs, more and more firms are beginning to report their financial information according to international accounting standards. This practice helps investors compare the financial results of firms in different countries. Moreover, the SEC and FASB are working with the IASC with the goal of eventually creating one worldwide set of accounting rules.

**assessment check**

1. Assume the U.S. dollar gets stronger relative to the euro. What impact would that have on a U.S. firm with extensive operations in Europe?
2. What is the IASC?

# WHAT'S AHEAD

This chapter describes the role of accounting in an organization. Accounting is the process of measuring, interpreting, and communicating financial information to interested parties both inside and outside the firm. The next chapter discusses the finance function of an organization. Finance deals with planning, obtaining, and managing the organization's funds to accomplish its objectives in the most efficient and effective manner possible.

## Summary of Learning Goals

**1** **Explain the functions of accounting and its importance to the firm's management, investors, creditors, and government agencies.**

Accountants measure, interpret, and communicate financial information to parties inside and outside the firm to support improved decision making. Accountants gather, record, and interpret financial information to management. They also provide financial information on the status and operations of the firm for evaluation by such outside parties as government agencies, stockholders, potential investors, and lenders.

### Assessment Check Answers

**1.1 Define accounting.**
Accounting is the process of measuring, interpreting, and communicating financial information in a way that describes the status and operation of an organization and aids in decision making.

**1.2 Who uses accounting information?**
Managers of all types of organizations use accounting information to help them plan, assess performance, and control daily and long-term operations. Outside

users of accounting information include government officials, investors, creditors, and donors.

### 2 Identify the three basic business activities involving accounting.

Accounting plays key roles in financing activities, which help start and expand an organization; investing activities, which provide the assets it needs to continue operating; and operating activities, which focus on selling goods and services and paying expenses incurred in regular operations.

## Assessment Check Answers

**2.1 List the three business activities that involve accounting.**

The three activities involving accounting are financing, investing, and operations.

**2.2 Give an example of one of the business activities that involves accounting.**

Financing activities provide the necessary funds to start a business and expand it after it begins operating. Investing activities determine what type of assets the business needs in order to operate. Operating activities focus on selling products as well as other activities such as cost control.

### 3 Describe the roles played by public, management, government, and not-for-profit accountants.

Public accountants provide accounting services to other firms or individuals for a fee. They are involved in such activities as tax statement preparation, management consulting, and accounting system design. Management accountants collect and record financial transactions, prepare financial statements, and interpret them for managers in their own firms. Government and not-for-profit accountants perform many of the same functions as management accountants, but they analyze how effectively the organization or agency is operating rather than its profits and losses.

## Assessment Check Answers

**3.1 What is the difference between a public accountant and a management accountant?**

A public accountant provides accounting services to individuals and organizations for a fee. A manage-

ment accountant is employed by an organization other than a public accounting firm.

**3.2 What services does the typical public accounting firm provide to clients? How has the mix of services changed in recent years?**

Public accounting firms provide audit, tax, and consulting services to clients. In recent years, some of the largest public accounting firms, such as PWC, sold their consulting businesses in order to focus mainly on tax and auditing services.

### 4 Outline the steps in the accounting process.

The accounting process involves recording, classifying, and summarizing data about transactions and then using this information to produce financial statements for the firm's managers and other interested parties. Transactions are recorded chronologically in journals, posted in ledgers, and then summarized in accounting statements. Today much of this takes place electronically. The foundation of the accounting system is GAAP (generally accepted accounting principles), a set of guidelines or standards that accountants follow. In the United States, the Financial Accounting Standards Board (FASB) is primarily responsible for evaluating, setting, and modifying GAAP. The basic accounting equation states that assets (what a firm owns) must always equal liabilities (what a firm owes creditors) plus owners' equity. This equation also illustrates double-entry bookkeeping—the process by which accounting transactions are recorded. Under double-entry bookkeeping, each individual transaction must have an offsetting transaction.

## Assessment Check Answers

**4.1 Briefly describe the accounting process.**

The accounting process involves recording, classifying, and summarizing transactions in order to produce financial statements.

**4.2 Define GAAP. What is the role of the Financial Accounting Standards Board?**

GAAP stands for generally accepted accounting principles and consists of guidelines or standards that accountants follow when recording, classifying, and summarizing transactions. In the United States the Financial Accounting Standards Board (FASB) is primarily responsible for evaluating, setting, and modifying GAAP.

### 4.3 Describe the basic accounting equation.

The basic equation states that assets (what a firm owns) always equals liabilities (what a firm owes creditors) plus owners' equity.

### 5 Explain the functions and major components of the three principal financial statements: the balance sheet, the income statement, and the statement of cash flows.

The balance sheet shows the financial position of a company on a particular date. The three major classifications of balance sheet data represent the components of the accounting equation: assets, liabilities, and owners' equity. The income statement shows the results of a firm's operations over a specific period. It focuses on the firm's activities—its revenues and expenditures—and the resulting profit or loss during the period. The major components of the income statement are revenues, cost of goods sold, expenses, and profit or loss. The statement of cash flows indicates a firm's cash receipts and cash payments during an accounting period. It shows the sources and uses of cash in the basic business activities of financing, investing, and operating.

## Assessment Check Answers

### 5.1 Explain how a company's balance sheet is organized and its overall purpose.

The purpose of a balance sheet is to show a company's financial position at a point in time—say the end of the fiscal year. Assets are listed on one side in order of liquidity (how easily and quickly the asset could be converted into cash). Liabilities are listed on the other side in the order in which they are due. Owners' equity is listed after liabilities.

### 5.2 What is an income statement?

The income statement lists all sales (or revenues) and expenses that occurred during a period of time (such as a quarter or year). The bottom line of the income statement is net income.

### 5.3 Why do firms prepare a statement of cash flows? Explain accrual accounting.

The statement of cash flows lists the sources and uses of cash during a period of time. Public companies are required to prepare and report a statement of cash flows. Cash flow can differ from income because of the widespread use of accrual accounting. Accrual accounting records transactions when they occur, not necessarily when cash changes hands.

### 6 Discuss how financial ratios are used to analyze a firm's financial strengths and weaknesses.

Liquidity ratios measure a firm's ability to meet short-term obligations. Examples are the current ratio and the acid-test ratio. Activity ratios, such as the inventory turnover ratio and the total asset turnover ratio, measure how effectively a firm uses its resources. Profitability ratios assess the overall financial performance of the business. The gross profit margin, net profit margin, return on assets, and return on owners' equity are examples. Leverage ratios, such as the total liabilities to total assets ratio and the long-term debt to equity ratio, measure the extent to which the firm relies on debt to finance its operations. Financial ratios help managers and outside evaluators compare a firm's current financial information with that of previous years and with results for other firms in the same industry.

## Assessment Check Answers

### 6.1 What is the purpose of financial ratio analysis?

Financial ratios provide managers and outside investors and creditors with information concerning the financial health of a company. They allow comparisons of a company's financial information with that of previous years and with results for similar firms.

### 6.2 List the categories of financial ratios. Give an example of each.

The major categories of financial ratios are liquidity, activity, profitability, and leverage. Examples include current ratio (liquidity), inventory turnover (activity), net profit margin (profitability), and debt ratio (leverage).

### 7 Describe the role of budgets in a business.

Budgets are financial guidelines for future periods reflecting expected sales revenues, operating expenses, and/or cash receipts and outlays. They represent management expectations for future occurrences based on plans that have been made. Budgets serve as important planning and controlling tools by providing standards against which actual performance can be measured.

## Assessment Check Answers

### 7.1 What is a budget?

A budget is a planning and control tool that reflects the firm's expected sales revenues, operating expenses, cash receipts, and cash outlays.

### 7.2 Describe how a cash budget is organized.

Cash budgets are generally prepared monthly. Cash receipts are listed first. They include cash sales as well as the collection of past credit sales. Cash outlays are listed next. These include cash purchases, payment of past credit purchases, and operating expenses. The difference between cash receipts and cash outlays is net cash flow.

**8** **Explain how exchange rates influence international accounting practices and the importance of uniform financial statements for global business.**
An exchange rate is the ratio at which a country's currency can be exchanged for other currencies. Daily changes in exchange rates affect the accounting entries for sales and purchases of firms involved in international markets. These fluctuations create either losses or gains for particular companies. Data about international financial transactions must be translated into the currency of the country in which the parent company resides. The International Accounting Standards Committee was established to provide worldwide consistency in financial reporting practices and comparability and uniformity of international accounting standards.

## Assessment Check Answers

### 8.1 Assume the U.S. dollar gets stronger relative to the euro. What impact would that have on a U.S. firm with extensive operations in Europe?

European profits have to be converted from euros to dollars. If the value of the dollar rises relative to the euro, the dollar value of European profits declines. This decline will hurt the firm's earnings.

### 8.2 What is the IASC?

The IASC (International Accounting Standards Committee) provides worldwide consistency in financial reporting practices and comparability and uniformity of accounting standards worldwide.

## Business Terms You Need to Know

| | | |
|---|---|---|
| accounting 514 | liability 522 | income statement 524 |
| public accountant 516 | owners' equity 522 | statement of cash flows 526 |
| certified public accountant (CPA) 517 | basic accounting equation 522 | accrual accounting 526 |
| accounting process 519 | double-entry bookkeeping 523 | budget 531 |
| asset 521 | balance sheet 523 | |

## Other Important Business Terms

| | | |
|---|---|---|
| open-book management 514 | Financial Accounting Standards | liquidity ratios 528 |
| management accountant 517 | Board (FASB) 520 | activity ratios 529 |
| government accountant 518 | bottom line 526 | profitability ratios 529 |
| generally accepted accounting | cash flow 526 | leverage ratios 530 |
| principles (GAAP) 520 | ratio analysis 526 | cash budget 531 |

## Review Questions

1. Define *accounting*. Who are the major users of accounting information?
2. What are the three major business activities in which accountants play a major role? Give an example of each.
3. Explain the differences between a public accountant, a management accountant, and a government accountant. What services do public accounting firms provide for clients?
4. What does the term *GAAP* mean? Briefly explain the role of the Financial Accounting Standards Board.
5. List the three major financial statements.
6. Explain the basic accounting equation.
7. What is double-entry bookkeeping? Give an example.

8. What is the difference between a current asset and a long-term asset? Why is cash typically listed first on a balance sheet?
9. What is accrual accounting? Give an example of how accrual accounting affects a firm's financial statements.
10. List the four categories of financial ratios and give an example of each. What is the purpose of ratio analysis?
11. What is a cash budget? Briefly outline what a simple cash budget might look like.
12. What financial statements are affected by exchange rates for firms with global operations? What are the benefits of uniform international accounting standards?

## Projects and Teamwork Applications

1. Your grandmother sends you a large check for your birthday, asking that you use the money to buy shares of stock in a company. She recommends that you review the company's financial statements before investing. What can a company's financial statements tell you about the investment potential of its stock?
2. Contact a local public accounting firm and set up an interview with one of the firm's partners. Ask the individual what his or her educational background is, what attracted the individual to the accounting profession, and what he or she does during a typical day. Prepare a brief report on your interview. Do you now want to learn more about the accounting profession? Are you more interested in possibly pursuing a career in accounting?
3. Suppose you work for a U.S. firm that has extensive European operations. You need to restate data from the various European currencies in U.S. dollars in order to prepare your firm's financial statements. Which financial statements and which components of these statements will be affected? Has the adoption of the euro made your job easier or more difficult?

4. The collapse of Enron, WorldCom, and other firms raised a number of questions concerning the ethical standards of outside auditors. As a result, a number of new rules and laws were adopted. Some complain that these rules have increased audit fees and even make it more difficult for firms to find auditors. Working with a small group, research these new rules and laws, and write a two-page report summarizing them.
5. Working with a partner, identify a public company you've heard of. Collect at least three years' worth of financial statements for the company. Calculate the financial ratios listed in Table 16.1. Prepare an oral report summarizing your findings.
6. Suppose you are offered a job with a small, private company. Because the company isn't required to publish its financial information—as public companies are—you ask the owner if you could review the financial statements prior to accepting the job. The owner refuses and says that only the firm's accountant and banker are allowed to see the statements. What could you say that might persuade the company's owner to share financial information with employees?

7. You've been appointed treasurer of a local not-for-profit organization. You would like to improve the quality of the organization's financial reporting to existing and potential donors. Describe the kinds of financial statements you would like to see the organization's accountant prepare. Why do you think better-quality financial statements might help reassure donors?

8. Adapting the format of Figure 16.6, prepare on a separate sheet of paper your personal cash budget for next month. Keep in mind the following suggestions as you prepare your budget:

   a. *Cash Inflows.* Your sources of cash would include your salary/wages, gifts, scholarship monies, tax refunds, dividends and interest, and income from self-employment.

   b. *Cash Outflows.* When estimating next month's cash outflows, include any of the following that may apply to your situation:
      i. Household expenses (mortgage/rent, utilities, maintenance, home furnishings, telephone/cell phone, cable TV, household supplies, groceries)
      ii. Education (tuition, fees, textbooks, supplies)
      iii. Work (transportation, meals)
      iv. Clothing (purchases, cleaning, laundry)
      v. Automobile (auto payments, fuel, repairs)
      vi. Insurance (life, auto, homeowner's, renter's, health, and dental)
      vii. Taxes (income, property, Social Security, Medicare)
      viii. Savings and investments
      ix. Entertainment/recreation (health club, vacation/travel, dining, movies)
      x. Debt (credit cards, installment loans)
      xi. Miscellaneous (charitable contributions, child care, gifts, medical expenses)

   c. *Beginning Cash Balance.* This amount could be based on a minimum cash balance you keep in your checking account and should include only the cash available for your use; therefore, money such as that invested in a 401(k) retirement plan should not be included.

More than half of all accountants and auditing professionals today are women, according to the American Institute of Certified Public Accountants (AICPA). A generation ago, women represented less than half of the profession, but with more than half of all new accountants coming from the ranks of working females, including many with young children, the work-life balance at many accounting firms has been getting a big overhaul. The results are positive enough to land the profession's Big Four on *Working Mother* magazine's list of 100 best companies for working mothers for several years in a row.

To earn a place on the prestigious roster, Deloitte & Touche USA, PricewaterhouseCoopers, KPMG, and Ernst & Young had to stand out by offering family-friendly benefits such as flextime, compressed workweeks, job sharing, telecommuting, extended parental leave, backup child care, and adoption benefits. But they also provided other innovations such as women's networks and mentoring programs. Finally, they had to demonstrate that taking advantage of such benefits would not harm the career paths of their female accountants.

At Ernst & Young, for instance, more than 2,300 employees rely on flexible work schedules; more than 100 of them are partners, principals, and directors. "This demonstrates to all our people that it is possible to succeed personally and reach the highest levels of our organization," says the firm's director of gender equity and flexibility, "even for those trying to balance work and family." *Working Mother* saluted Deloitte for being "one of the organizations working to eliminate . . . bias against flextime workers by offering its working mother employees, not just flexibility, but advancement opportunities as well."

PricewaterhouseCoopers says fully half its new hires in the last twelve to fifteen years have been women. The firm believes that "work and life shouldn't be mutually exclusive" and that employees should not be judged for the choices they make about their personal priorities. About 6 percent of its accountants work part time, and their salaries and benefits are adjusted accordingly. Says the company's director of diversity and work/life, "It's a retention tool for high performers."

The push to make the demanding environment of public accounting, with its 70- and 80-hour workweeks, more adaptable to family needs isn't limited to the top-tier firms, however, and many benefits, such as free or subsidized breakfast and lunch, are intended for all employees, not just women and parents. At Plante & Moran, which has been a leader in instituting family-friendly benefits such as mentors for all employees, a dedicated runner was allowed a flexible schedule during tax season in order to train for a marathon, for instance.

But there's no question that women are big beneficiaries of many innovative work/life perks, such as on-site day care, lactation rooms, free breast pumps for nursing moms, and reserved parking for pregnant employees. "We know it's critical that we have to do some of these things and do them right," says Pricewaterhouse. At KPMG, nearly half of front-line managers are female. Dara Bazanno, senior audit manager, juggles four children and a two-hour commute. "I live 140 miles from the office," she says, "and I would have had to quit five years ago, because I just can't afford 15 or 20 hours a week on the road given the number of hours we work." The home office KPMG set up for her makes it all possible.

At the same time, however, women's salaries for accounting and auditing jobs still lag behind those of men, running at only about 75 percent of men's pay nationwide, according to the U.S. Department of Labor. Women also enjoy a smaller share of nonfinancial benefits such as automobile allowances, stock options, bonuses, profit sharing, and overtime.

Some industry observers point out that even though fewer than one in five public accounting firm partners is a woman, women have entered accounting in larger numbers only within the last fifteen years or so, which means there are still fewer women than men with the experience to reach partner. One encouraging trend reported by the *Journal of Accountancy,* however, is that nearly a third of the partnership promotions made within the last three years went to women.

## Questions for Critical Thinking

1. Some critics of work-life programs say they disproportionately benefit women and parents. Do you

think policies designed to retain valued employees can have a downside? Why or why not? If yes, what can companies do to minimize problems that can arise for other employees who aren't eligible for such benefits because they are male and/or single?

2. Long hours and crushing work flows created by the annual tax season are common fare for accountants. In what ways can accounting firms ease the burden on all employees at such times? How would such actions help improve the firms' performance?

**Sources:** Michelle Cater Rash, "Women Outpacing Men in Accounting," *Birmingham Business Journal,* accessed August 16, 2006, http://www.bizjournals.com; Joyce Gannon, "Balancing a Lifestyle," Pittsburgh Post-Gazette, accessed August 16, 2006, http://www.post-gazette.com; "Ernst & Young LLP Marks Its Eighth Consecutive Year as One of the '100 Best Companies for Working Mothers,'" PR Newswire, accessed July 21, 2006, http://www.prnewswire.com; "Sarbanes-Oxley Requirements Boost Value of CMA Certification," PR Newswire, accessed July 21, 2006, http://www.prnewswire.com; "*Working Mother* 2005 100 Best Companies," accessed July 21, 2006, http://www.workingmother.com; Jena McGregor, "Balance and Balance Sheets," *Fast Company,* accessed July 21, 2006, http://www.fastcompany.com; Dona DeZube, "Perks Keep Public Accountants at Work," Monster.com, accessed September 23, 2005, http://monster.com.

## VIDEO  Case 16.2

### Taking Account: The Little Guys

This video case appears on page 625. A recently filmed video, designed to expand and highlight the written case, is available for class use by instructors.

# The Second City Theater Continuing Case
# Comedy, Theater, Technology: Where These Three Shall Meet

A comedy show requires only two things: performers and an audience. When you see the lights come up on the cast and hear the rock music played between scenes, it's clear that The Second City hasn't let technology get in the way of an authentically theatrical experience. In a recent interview, Bernie Sahlins, co-founder of Second City, attributed the company's success to its dedication as a live theater venue. Television, cinema, radio, and the Internet have inundated the American public. Part of Second City's charm is that the core of the theater will always remain on the stage. Monitoring its success in the modern world has, however, required technical strength. Its use of technology to manage information has built a digital evolution for Second City, and has also given its fast-paced comedy the power to move at lightning speed.

Information management at Second City is both systematic and improvised. The company monitors everything from the high volume of students coming through the Training Center to the profit margins of its productions. Handling this information in a way that can benefit decisions calls for some impromptu organization. The company responds to the particular needs of each branch, or division, when designing appropriate technologies. Primarily, Second City has developed a series of databases that track figures and trends.

As the audience shuffles into Chicago's Mainstage theater on a Friday night, or fills up the e.t.c. stage for an edgier night of satire, the company keeps track of its market. Audience View is a brand new database system that monitors ticketing for the company. This helps the company see trends in seasonal and weekly purchase ratios. This type of database can calculate the success of certain revues over time and give the company a perspective on its earnings. The theater occasionally decides to react to sold-out nights by producing additional shows to meet demand.

Rob Chambers, director of the Training Center, uses software that organizes hundreds of students throughout dozens of classes. Keeping an eye on the popularity of certain classes helps Second City decide how to expand its curriculum. It has developed its own databases for the Training Center to keep the software accessible to the staff and suitable for its program. Because the Training Center has attracted a body of contributors who train, work, teach, and perform for the company, Second City created an informal intranet.

A large e-mail list updates the e-community on shows, tuition updates, new class offerings, and links to new material on the Second City Web site.

Second City's Web site has become one of its most innovative tools for external marketing and gathering information. Using a variety of broadband technologies, http://www.secondcity.com is the modern media center for the company. To compete in the digital age, Second City has partnered with media distribution agencies that help it maximize its impact in the market. The theater has always created an impressive amount of comedy entertainment material. Up-to-date information systems release this creative content to a younger, electronic audience. Among other features, the Web site showcases interviews with alumni, clips from shows, Training Center information, theater history, hiring information, and a new series of podcasts that the company hopes will bring some direct revenue for the site. Second City monitors how many hits the site gets and for which pages. This helps it make decisions about what creative material to put on the Web, how and when to update the site, and which offerings seem to get the most attention. Working with leading Internet media agencies, Second City uses its Web site as a forerunner for creative advances in the company.

Excited by the new frontier, Second City's Kelly Leonard reports that "technology becomes an increasingly prominent part of The Second City business every year." Second City is currently looking for an IT director who can integrate recent tech advances in the company throughout the organization. The company benefits from technical savvy even in its communications branch. Electronic prowess is an important tool for the branch, which provides *Fortune* 500 companies with modern, interactive consultation services. When working with a technically adept client, Second City must be able to communicate effectively. If asked to do a piece on a recent computer-virus-related disaster, the ensemble must even know now to use the correct technical jargon to make light of whatever has been "bugging" the client.

Second City has its own accounting department and also uses an outside firm. It strives to keep ticket prices under the traditional price of Equity (the theater actors' union) costs. However, Second City has realized, after analyzing its accounting data, that in order to thrive when demand is high, it can easily sell tickets at a higher price for weekend shows without any frustration from its customers. Classes at the Training Center are around the cost of similar services in the entertainment or arts industry.

Managing all the information that travels through Second City's doors is a big job. Though it is growing and already uses information technology in many ways throughout the company, Second City has seen the rising importance of having one person in charge of all electronic business systems. Until they find an information director, SC has the advantage of being a small organization in which information systems have been designed with its specific needs in mind. Second City will continue to explore the benefits of information management as its Web site and theaters attract the increasingly computer-proficient consumer. As long as improvisation is the heart of the matter, no Second City techie will ever feel too far from home.

## QUESTIONS

1. What makes Second City stand out as a technically integrated organization?
2. What is Second City's primary management information system? Do you think this is the most effective system for this company?
3. What challenges face Second City in the modern computerized age?
4. In what ways is Second City on the cutting edge of technology? In what ways does it still have to grow?

# Part 5: Launching Your Information Technology and Accounting Career

Part 5, "Managing Technology and Information," includes Chapters 15 and 16, which discuss using computers and related technology to manage information and accounting and financial statements. In Chapter 15, we profiled well-known technology companies such as Google and Oracle, as well as a host of smaller organizations, such as Great Harvest Bread Company and Singapore's Nanyang Technological University, that use computer technology to manage information. In Chapter 16, you read about giant accounting firms such as Ernst & Young and a variety of public and private organizations, large and small, that generate and use accounting data. These examples illustrate that all organizations need to manage technology and information. And with the complexity and scope of technology and information likely to increase in the years ahead, the demand for accounting and information systems professionals is expected to grow. According to the U.S. Department of Labor, employment in occupations such as accounting, computer support specialists, and systems administrators is expected to grow faster than the average for all occupations in the next decade.[1] In addition, recent graduates with bachelor's degrees in accounting and information systems have among the highest average starting salaries of all business graduates. The most recent survey from the National Association of Colleges and Employers listed the average starting salary for graduates with bachelor's degrees in accounting at more than $43,000 per year; starting salaries for those with undergraduate degrees in information systems averaged around $45,000.[2]

What types of jobs are available in information systems and accounting? What are the working conditions like? What are the career paths? Information systems and accounting are both fairly broad occupations and encompass a wide variety of jobs. In some cases you'll work in the accounting or information systems department of a business such as Procter & Gamble or Shell. In other cases, you'll work for a specialized accounting or information systems firm, such as PricewaterhouseCoopers or IBM, that provides these services to governments, not-for-profit organizations, and businesses.

Accounting and information systems are popular business majors, and many entry-level positions are available each year. For instance, many accounting graduates start their careers working for a public accounting firm. Initially, their job duties involve auditing or tax services, usually working with more senior accountants. As their careers progress, accounting graduates take on more and more supervisory responsibilities. Some may move from public accounting firms to take accounting positions at other organizations. Many accounting and information systems graduates spend their entire careers in these fields, while others move into other areas. People who began their careers in accounting or information systems are well represented in the ranks of senior management today. Let's look briefly at some of the specific jobs you might find after earning a degree in accounting or information systems.

*Public accountants* perform a broad range of accounting, auditing, tax, and consulting services for their clients, which include businesses, governments, not-for-profit organizations, and individuals. Auditing is one of the most important services offered by public accountants, and many accounting graduates begin their careers in auditing. Auditors examine a client's financial statements and accounting procedures to make sure they conform with all applicable laws and regulations. Public accountants either own their own businesses or work for public accounting firms. Many public accountants are certified public accountants (CPAs). To become a CPA, you have to meet educational and experience requirements and pass a comprehensive examination.

*Management accountants* work for an organization other than a public accounting firm. They record and analyze financial information and financial statements for their organizations. Management accountants are also involved in budgeting, tax preparation, cost management, and asset management. Internal auditors verify the accuracy of their organization's internal controls and check for irregularities, waste, and fraud.

*Technical support specialists* are troubleshooters who monitor the performance of computer systems; provide technical support and solve problems for computer users; install, modify, clean, and repair computer hardware and software; and write training manuals and train computer users.

*Network administrators* design, install, and support an organization's computer networks, including its local area network, wide area network, Internet, and intranet systems. They provide administrative support for software and hardware users and ensure that the design of an organization's computer networks and all of the components fit together efficiently and effectively.

*Computer security specialists* plan, coordinate, and implement an organization's information security. They educate users about how to protect computer systems, install antivirus and similar software, and monitor the networks for security breaches. In recent years, the role and importance of computer security specialists have increased in response to the growing number of attacks on networks and data.

## Career Assessment Exercises in Information Systems and Accounting

1. The American Institute of Certified Public Accountants is a professional organization dedicated to the enhancement of the public accounting profession. Visit the organization's Web site (http://www.aicpa.org). Review the information on CPA standards and examinations. Write a brief summary on what you learned about how to become a CPA.

2. Assume you're interested in a career as a systems administrator. Go to the following Web site: http://www.sage.org. Prepare a brief report outlining the responsibilities of a systems administrator, who hires for these positions, and what kind of educational background you need to become one.

3. Identify a person working in your local area in the accounting field and arrange an interview with that person (your college career center may be able to help you). Ask that person about his or her job responsibilities, educational background, and the best and worst aspects of his or her job as an accountant.

# Managing Financial Resources

# Part 6

# chapter 17

## Financial Management and Institutions

Fannie Mae and Freddie Mac are two of the largest financial institutions in the United States. Their odd names are shortened forms of their official titles, the Federal National Mortgage Association and the Federal Home Loan Mortgage Corporation. Both were created by the federal government and have special charters, even though they are stockholder owned. Their purpose is to increase the supply of mortgage credit available to the public, especially to low- and moderate-income families in all areas of the country and under all economic conditions. Fannie and Freddie, as they are known, buy mortgage loans from banks, mortgage bankers, and other private sources. They finance these purchases by selling bonds and a variety of other types of securities.

Over the years Fannie and Freddie have helped millions of new homeowners and worked to ensure fair

the results were that the validity of its past financial reports was called into question. A report by the Office of Federal Housing Enterprise Oversight found what it called "pervasive misapplication of accounting rules" in the

## Reining in Fannie and Freddie

lending practices. They help finance half the home mortgage loans granted in the United States each year and make money from the difference in value between the mortgages they buy and their cost of financing. Thanks to them, says one congressional representative, "we have the strongest, most dynamic housing market in the world."

But recently members of Congress, the Federal Reserve chairman, and some prominent economists have expressed concern that Fannie and Freddie are too loosely regulated. First, Freddie Mac was found to be improperly accounting for its use of certain exotic financial instruments called *derivatives,* and the company was slapped with a $125 million fine. A management shake-up followed.

A few months later, government investigators turned their attention to Fannie Mae. Soon Fannie was criticized too for also using improper accounting methods; among

company's records, some of which allowed Fannie Mae's managers to receive bonuses in a recent year that would not otherwise have been paid. The company was accused of maintaining a corporate culture that encouraged such problems to continue unchecked. Fannie Mae was fined $400 million, one of the largest penalties in an accounting fraud case.

The Senate Banking Committee passed a bill to rein in the two companies with tighter controls as well as by shrinking their investment portfolios, which add up to about $1.5 trillion, by forcing the companies to sell assets that are not related to their mortgage businesses. Passage of the bill in the House remains in doubt, however, and both Fannie Mae and Freddie Mac have criticized its provisions.[1]

Previous chapters discuss two essential functions that a business must perform. First, the company must produce a good or service or contract with suppliers to produce it. Second, the firm must market its good or service to prospective customers. This chapter introduces a third, equally important function: a company's managers must ensure that it has enough money to perform its other tasks successfully, in both the present and the future. Adequate funds must be available to buy materials and equipment, pay bills, purchase additional facilities, and compensate employees. This third business function is **finance**—planning, obtaining, and managing the company's funds in order to accomplish its objectives effectively and efficiently.

An organization's financial objectives include not only meeting expenses but also maximizing its overall worth, often determined by the value of the firm's common stock. Financial managers are responsible for meeting expenses and increasing profits to shareholders.

This chapter focuses on the role of financial managers, the reasons businesses need funds, and the various types and sources of funds. It discusses the role of money and measures of the money supply. The chapter explains the purpose and structure of the financial system, the operations of financial institutions, and the way the Federal Reserve System functions. A discussion of the role of the financial system in the global business environment concludes the chapter.

**finance** business function of planning, obtaining, and managing a company's funds in order to accomplish its objectives effectively and efficiently.

**financial manager** executive who develops and implements the firm's financial plan and determines the most appropriate sources and uses of funds.

# THE ROLE OF THE FINANCIAL MANAGER

Organizations are placing greater emphasis on measuring and reducing the costs of conducting business as well as increasing revenues and profits. As a result, **financial managers**—executives who develop and implement their firm's financial plan and determine the most appropriate sources and uses of funds—are among the most vital people on the corporate payroll.

The finance organization of a typical company might look like this: at the top is the chief financial officer (CFO). The CFO usually reports directly to the company's chief executive officer (CEO) or chief operating officer (COO), if the firm has one. In some companies, the CFO is also a member of the board of directors. Robert Wayman, for instance, is CFO of Hewlett-Packard and is also a member of the HP board of directors. Reporting directly to the CFO are often three senior managers. While titles can vary, these three executives are commonly called the **vice president for financial management** (or **planning**), the **treasurer,** and the **controller.** The vice president for financial management or planning is responsible for preparing financial forecasts and analyzing major investment decisions. Major investment decisions include new products, new production facilities, and acquisitions. The treasurer is responsible for all of the company's financing activities, including cash management, tax planning and preparation, and shareholder relations. The treasurer also works on the sale of new security issues to investors. The controller is the chief accounting manager. The controller's functions include keeping the company's books, preparing financial statements, and conducting internal audits.

The growing importance of financial professionals is reflected in an expanding number of CEOs promoted from financial positions. By one estimate, around 20 percent of all newly appointed CEOs during a recent year spent time in the finance ranks. A recent example is Louis Raspino. Prior to becoming CEO of oil services firm Pride International, Raspino served as the firm's CFO.[2] The importance of finance professionals is also reflected in how much CFOs earn today. According to a recent survey, annual compensation for CFOs averages around $2.4 million.[3]

In performing their jobs, financial professionals continually seek to balance risks with expected financial returns. Risk is the uncertainty of gain or loss; return is the gain or loss that results from an investment over a specified period of time. Financial managers strive to maximize the wealth of their firm's shareholders by striking the optimal balance between risk and return. This balance is called the **risk-return trade-off.** For example, heavy reliance on borrowed funds may increase the return to shareholders, but the more money a firm borrows, the greater the risks to shareholders. An increase in a firm's cash on hand reduces the risk of meeting unexpected cash needs. However, because cash does not earn any return, failure to invest surplus funds in an income-earning asset—such as in marketable securities—reduces a firm's potential return or profitability.

**risk-return trade-off** optimal balance between the expected payoff from an investment and the investment's risk.

Every financial manager must perform this risk-return balancing act. For example, in the late 1990s, Airbus wrestled with a major decision: whether to begin development and production of the giant A380 jetliner. The development costs for the aircraft—to be the world's largest jetliner—were initially estimated at more than $10 billion. Before committing to such a huge investment, financial managers had to weigh the potential profits of the A380 with the risk that the profits would not materialize. With its future on the line, Airbus decided to go ahead with the development of the A380. After spending more than $14 billion, Airbus rolled out the first A380 in 2005. Airbus has orders for approximately 150 jetliners at a list price of around $285 million each. It's unclear, however, whether the A380 investment turns out to be a smart, and profitable, decision.[4]

## The Financial Plan

Financial managers develop their organization's **financial plan,** a document that specifies the funds needed by a firm for a period of time, the timing of inflows and outflows, and the most appropriate sources and uses of funds. The financial plan is based on forecasts of production costs, purchasing needs, and expected sales activities for the period covered. Financial managers use forecasts to determine the specific amounts and timing of expenditures and receipts. They build a financial plan based on the answers to three questions:

1. What funds will the firm require during the appropriate period of operations?
2. How will it obtain the necessary funds?
3. When will it need more funds?

**financial plan** document that specifies the funds a firm will need for a period of time, the timing of inflows and outflows, and the most appropriate sources and uses of funds.

Some funds flow into the firm when it sells its goods or services, but funding needs vary. The financial plan must reflect both the amounts and timing of inflows and outflows of funds. Even a profitable firm may well face a financial squeeze as a result of its need for funds when sales lag, when the volume of its credit sales increases, or when customers are slow in making payments.

The cash inflows and outflows of a business are similar to those of a household. The members of a household may depend on weekly or monthly paychecks for funds, but their expenditures vary greatly from one pay period to the next. The financial plan should indicate when the flows of funds entering and leaving the organization will occur and in what amounts.

A good financial plan also involves financial control, a process of checking actual revenues, costs, and expenses and comparing them against forecasts. If this process reveals significant differences between projected and actual figures, it is important to discover them early to take timely corrective action.

Paula Brock, CFO of the Zoological Society of San Diego (which operates the famous San Diego Zoo), credits the zoo's financial plan and planning process with helping it weather a recent outbreak of an exotic bird disease in Southern California. When the disease first appeared, the zoo took immediate action to protect its valuable bird collection. Thanks to these actions, no birds got sick, and the damage to the zoo's finances were minimal, even though the zoo spent more than half a million dollars. The financial plan raised the alarm as resources were redirected to fight the disease, allowing managers to make the necessary adjustments.[5]

**"They Said It"**

"When I was young, I used to think that money was the most important thing in life; now that I am older, I know it is."
—Oscar Wilde (1854–1900)
Humorist and playwright

**assessment check**

1. Define finance and explain the role of the financial manager.
2. What are the three questions on which a financial plan is based?

# CHARACTERISTICS AND FUNCTIONS OF MONEY

Playwright George Bernard Shaw once said that the lack of money is the root of all evil. Added comedian Woody Allen, "Money is better than poverty, if only for financial reasons." Most businesspeople would agree, because money is the lubricant of contemporary business.

## Characteristics of Money

**Money** is anything generally accepted as payment for goods and services. Most early forms of money imposed a number of serious disadvantages on users. For example, a cow is a poor form of money for an owner who wants only a loaf of bread and some cheese. Exchanges based on money permit economic specialization and provide a general basis for purchasing power, provided that the form of money used has certain characteristics. Money must be divisible, portable, durable, difficult to counterfeit, and stable in value.

*Divisibility*   A U.S. dollar is divided into cents, nickels, dimes, and quarters. The Canadian dollar is divided similarly, except that Canada has a 20-cent coin and no quarter. Mexico's nuevo peso is broken down into centavos (100 centavos equals one nuevo peso). People can easily exchange these forms of money for products ranging from a cup of coffee to automobiles. Today, most economic activity involves making and spending money.

*Portability*   The light weight of modern paper currency facilitates the exchange process. Portability is an important characteristic, because a typical dollar bill changes hands around 400 times during its lifetime, staying in the average person's pocket or purse fewer than two days.

*Durability*   U.S. dollar bills survive an average of twelve to eighteen months, and they can survive folding some 4,000 times without tearing. Coins, on the other hand, can last 30 years or longer. Most countries have replaced small-denomination paper currency with coins. For instance, there are no one-euro or two-euro bills—only one- and two-euro coins. In the United States there have been several attempts to get Americans to switch to dollar coins, none of which have met with much success. Americans, it appears, are reluctant to give up the dollar bill—the greenback is one of the great icons of American culture. This hasn't stopped the government from trying again. The latest attempt to wean Americans from the paper dollar bill is described in the "Hit & Miss" feature.

*Difficulty in Counterfeiting*   Widespread distribution of counterfeit money undermines a nation's monetary system and economy by ruining the value of legitimate money. For this reason, governments consider counterfeiting a serious crime and take elaborate steps to prevent it. Among counterfeiters, U.S. currency is the most popular. To increase the difficulty of counterfeiting U.S. currency in this age of sophisticated computers and color printers, the U.S. Treasury has redesigned paper bills. The new design adds a letter to each bill's serial number along with the seal of the Federal Reserve, larger portraits that are off-center, and polymer threads that run vertically through the bills and glow under ultraviolet light.

*Stability*   Money should also maintain a relatively stable value. If the value of money fluctuates too much, people hesitate to use it. They begin to abandon it and look for safer means of storing their wealth. Businesses start to demand that bills be paid in other, more stable currencies.

As part of a broad economic reform program, Argentina pegged the value of its currency, the peso, to the U.S. dollar in the early 1990s; one peso equaled one dollar. This policy

## Getting Americans to Break the Dollar Habit

Unless you're a coin collector, the first thing that comes to mind about the U.S. dollar coin is probably how you lost 75 cents when you spent it by mistaking it for a quarter. Despite failing twice to get U.S. consumers to adopt the dollar coin as money and not a collectible, starting in 2007 Congress is trying again with a plan to introduce four dollar coins a year, bearing likenesses of the presidents. Like the series of quarters commemorating the states, the new dollars are likely to be hoarded instead of spent. The U.S. Mint isn't worried about that, however; it costs just pennies to mint dollar coins, which last 30 years compared with twelve to eighteen months for a dollar bill. So even if the bid to get them into circulation fails, the new dollars will save money for the government.

Silver dollars were minted from 1794 to the 1930s, and a copper-and-nickel dollar was made in the 1970s. In 1978 the mint unveiled the Susan B. Anthony dollar to great fanfare, but the public rejected it, partly owing to its resemblance to a quarter. A similar fate befell the golden or Sacagawea dollar (named for Lewis and Clark's Shoshone guide) in 2000, despite its more distinctive look.

Critics of the dollar coin say the government has not done a good enough job promoting the new currency—particularly the Sacagawea dollar—and suggest taking paper dollars out of circulation to force consumers to stop hoarding the coins. Canada, for example, stopped printing one- and two-dollar bills after coins were introduced. Mint officials say it takes a year to build awareness of the dollar, and the next step is to get people to use it. The question remaining is, will the third time do the trick?

### Questions for Critical Thinking

1. Do consumers really need a dollar coin? Does the government? Why or why not?
2. How do you think the government could do a better job of changing consumers' perception of the dollar coin from curiosity to currency? Would taking the paper dollar out of circulation be a wise move? Why or why not?

**Sources:** "United States Dollar," Answers.com, accessed July 27, 2006, http://www.answers.com; "The Golden Dollar, One Year Later," About.com, accessed July 27, 2006, http://collectibles.about.com; Gordon T. Anderson, "Congress Tries Again for a Dollar Coin," CNN Money, accessed July 27, 2006; http://money.cnn.com.

worked well for a while as inflation fell sharply and economic growth accelerated. However, a strong U.S. dollar meant a strong peso. This made Argentinean products more expensive and hurt exports. The country's economy started to unravel. The government was forced to close banks and limit cash withdrawals. Finally, it allowed its currency to float independently of the dollar. The peso promptly lost 70 percent of its value relative to the dollar as Argentineans scrambled to convert their pesos into dollars.

## Functions of Money

Money performs three basic functions, shown in Figure 17.1. First, it serves primarily as a medium of exchange—a means of facilitating economic transactions and eliminating the need for a barter system. For example, assume you work part time and are paid $10 per hour—money is being used as the medium of exchange: payment for your labor. Second, money functions as a unit of account—a common standard for measuring the value of goods and services. For example, assume the cost of renting an apartment off campus is $500 per month. This standardized unit of account allows you to compare the cost of renting an off-campus apartment to the cost of on-campus housing. Third, money acts as a temporary store of value—a way of keeping accumulated wealth until the owner needs it to make new purchases. Money offers one big advantage as a store of value: its high liquidity allows people to obtain it and dispose of it in quick and easy transactions. Money is immediately available for purchasing products or paying debts. You purchase $200 worth of goods from the bookstore. You can pay for your purchases using cash, a credit or debit card, or a check. In each case you're using money as a temporary store of value.

### assessment check

1. What characteristics should money have?
2. List the three basic functions of money.

## THE MONEY SUPPLY

Ask someone on the street to define the money supply, and he or she might answer that the money supply is the total value of all currency and coins in circulation. That answer, however, is only half right. One measure of the U.S. money supply consists of coins and currency as well as financial assets that also serve as a medium of exchange: traveler's checks, bank checking accounts, and other so-called **demand deposit** accounts (such as NOW accounts and credit union share draft accounts). Government reports and business publications use the term **M1** to refer to the total value of coins, currency, traveler's checks, bank checking account balances, and the balances in other demand deposit accounts. The current breakdown of M1 is shown on the right in Figure 17.2.

Another, broader definition of the money supply is also widely used. Called **M2,** this measure of the money supply includes M1 plus a number of other financial assets that are

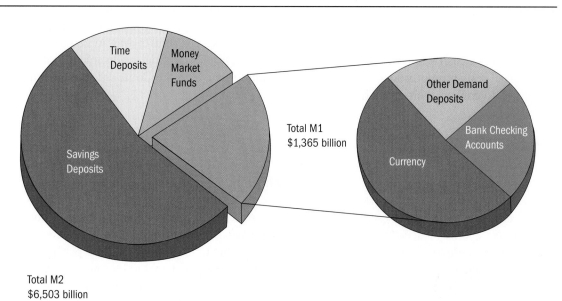

**Sources:** Federal Reserve, accessed August 3, 2006, http://www.federalreserve.gov.

# CREDIT CARDS HIT CAMPUS AND DEBTS FOLLOW

*Today's college students often graduate with a heavy load of debt, whether they borrowed for tuition expenses or not. More than half have at least one consumer credit card and many are already in debt in their freshman year, carrying an average balance of more than $2,000, often at interest rates up to 15 percent.*

This amount may not seem too large, but it can take several years to pay off after graduation. Some students are further burdened by annual fees, by penalties and higher interest rates on delinquent or late monthly payments, or by the even higher fees and rates attached to cash advances.

New college students are bombarded with credit card offers, promoted by "free gifts" such as T-shirts and sunglasses, and many are woefully unprepared for the financial consequences of charging pizza and beer for several years. Parents are not required to cosign the credit applications, and some can't afford to pick up the resulting debt. Debtors age 18 to 24 are among the fastest-growing group of bankruptcy filers. "Abuse of credit cards is a serious problem for young people," said a federal bankruptcy judge in San Diego.

Should the government restrict the marketing of credit cards to college students?

## PRO

1. Students can ruin their credit rating in college, making it hard to rent an apartment or even get a job.
2. Credit card companies are taking unfair advantage of students' inexperience with budgeting and managing their money.

## CON

1. Most students eventually pay their bills, learning an important lesson from their credit card experience.
2. Many students are responsible about spending, and credit cards offer them a way to pay for necessities without carrying cash.

## Summary

Following in the footsteps of hundreds of colleges and universities, Washington State's house of representatives is reviewing a bill to regulate credit companies operating on state campuses. The bill has few teeth—it only requires campuses to set policies, such as limiting the times and places cards can be marketed or forbidding free gift offers. But given the snowballing debt that student cards can create, the bill might be a step in the right direction.

**Sources:** Amy L. Cooper, "Credit Card Debt: A Survival Guide for College Students," *Young Money*, accessed July 27, 2006, http://www.youngmoney.com; "Senate Approves Bill Restricting Credit Card Marketing to College Students," *News Target*, accessed July 27, 2006, http://www.newstarget.com; Michael Kinsman, "Debt-Loaded Message," *San Diego Union-Tribune*, May 19, 2005, p. C-1.

**solving an ETHICAL controversy**

almost as liquid as cash but do not serve directly as a medium of exchange. These assets include various savings accounts, certificates of deposit, and money market mutual funds. Users must complete some sort of transaction before these assets can fulfill all the functions of money. The current breakdown of M2 is shown on the left in Figure 17.2.

The use of credit cards—often referred to as plastic money—has increased significantly. Over the past 20 years, for instance, the amount of outstanding credit card debt has risen by more than 400 percent.[6] Credit card companies spend billions of dollars each year trying to attract new customers. Recently, many credit card companies have targeted college students in their marketing efforts. Consequently, the percentage of college students with at least one credit card now exceeds 50 percent. Concerns over rising credit card balances among college students have led some states to restrict the marketing of credit cards to college students. The issue of marketing credit cards to college students is debated in the "Solving an Ethical Controversy" feature.

MasterCard and Visa, issued by banks, dominate the credit card market, though the Discover Card has made some inroads. In addition, American Express offers several credit cards. However, its flagship American Express card is not really a credit card but rather a charge

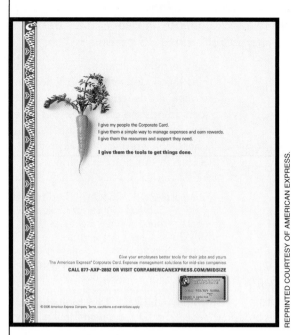

Corporate credit cards are issued to companies. Employees use the cards to pay for business-related expenses.

REPRINTED COURTESY OF AMERICAN EXPRESS.

card; that is, balances must be paid in full each month. Customers do not have the option of carrying a balance from month to month. American Express, MasterCard, Visa, and Discover card issue credit cards to both individuals as well as businesses. Authorized employees use business, or corporate credit cards to pay for business-related expenses such as travel.

Even though all MasterCard and Visa credit cards are issued by banks, so-called *branded credit cards* have become popular in recent years. Corporations, not-for-profit organizations, and college alumni associations have partnered with banks to issue branded credit cards. The partner receives a payment from the bank based on how much the card is used. Branded cards often provide perks to the cardholder. For instance, holders of an American Express Delta Sky Miles credit card receive Delta Sky Miles for each purchase made with the card.

Another recent trend has been the emergence of prepaid shopping cards. Consumers buy the cards in varying denominations—such as $25, $50, or $100—from retailers such as Barnes & Noble, Best Buy, and Target and then use them to make purchases up to that amount. The cards are reusable, meaning that the consumer can put more money on them anytime. Many cards can also be used to make online purchases. Some cards offer users perks such as special discounts. If you use a Wal-Mart shopping card to buy gas as a station located at a Wal-Mart store, you receive a 3 cent per gallon discount.

Many entrepreneurs rely on credit cards, as mentioned in Chapter 6, to provide seed capital in financing their new ventures. Movie director Spike Lee, for example, reportedly used his American Express card to finance his first film.

Although credit cards are convenient and easy to use, they are a very expensive source of business or consumer credit, with annual interest rates averaging around 15 percent. Another problem with credit cards is fraud. As discussed in Chapter 7, online purchases are especially vulnerable to fraud and cost credit card issuers, merchants, and consumers billions of dollars each year. The credit card industry is experimenting with a variety of ways to improve security and reduce fraud.

**assessment check**

1. Explain the differences between M1 and M2.
2. Who issues Visa and MasterCard credit cards? Explain the difference between a credit card and a charge card.

USED WITH PERMISSION. VISA USA

Visa's approach to credit card security to reduce fraud.

## WHY ORGANIZATIONS NEED FUNDS

Organizations require funds for many reasons. They need money to run day-to-day operations, compensate employees and hire new ones, pay for inventory, make interest payments on loans, pay dividends to shareholders, and purchase property, facilities, and equipment. A firm's financial plan identifies the amount and time of its specific cash needs.

By comparing these needs with expenditures and expected cash receipts (from sales, payments made by credit purchasers, and other sources), financial managers determine precisely what additional funds they must obtain at any given time. If inflows exceed cash needs, financial managers invest the surplus to earn interest. On the other hand, if inflows do not meet cash needs, they seek additional sources of funds. Figure 17.3 illustrates this process.

## Generating Funds from Excess Cash

Many financial managers invest most of their firms' excess cash balances in marketable securities. These financial instruments are very close to cash because they are, by definition, marketable and easy to convert into cash. Four of the most popular marketable securities are U.S. Treasury bills, commercial paper, repurchase agreements, and certificates of deposit.

Treasury bills are short-term securities issued by the U.S. Treasury and backed by the full faith and credit of the U.S. government. Treasury bills are sold with a maturity of either 30, 90, 180, or 360 days and have a minimum denomination of $10,000. They are considered virtually risk-free and easy to resell. Commercial paper is securities sold by corporations, such as General Electric, maturing anywhere from 1 to 270 days from the date of issue. Although slightly riskier than Treasury bills, commercial paper is generally still considered a very low-risk security. Repurchase agreements, or *repos,* are an arrangement in which one party sells a package of U.S. government securities to another party, agreeing to buy back, or repurchase, the securities at a higher price on a later date. Repos are also considered low-risk securities.

A certificate of deposit (CD) is a time deposit at a financial institution, such as a commercial bank, savings bank, or credit union. The sizes and maturity dates of CDs vary considerably and can often be tailored to meet the needs of purchasers. CDs with denominations of $100,000 or less per depositor are federally insured. CDs with larger denominations are not federally insured but can be sold more easily prior to maturity.

**EXPENDITURES**
- Day-to-Day Activities
- Inventory
- Dividends to Stockholders
- Purchases of Land, Facilities, and Equipment

If the firm has insufficient funds:
- Evaluate alternative sources for additional funds

**CASH RECEIPTS**
- Product Sales
- Payments from Credit Purchasers
- Sales of Stock
- Additional Funds from Venture Capitalists
- Private Placement Financing

If the firm has excess funds:
- Seek interest-producing investments

**assessment check**

1. Why do organizations need funds?
2. List several alternatives to holding large cash balances.

# SOURCES OF FUNDS

To this point, the discussion has focused on half of the definition of finance—the reasons why organizations need funds and how they use them. A firm's financial plan must give equal importance, however, to the choice of the best sources of needed funds. Sources of funds fall into two categories: debt capital and equity capital.

**Debt capital** represents funds obtained through borrowing (referred to as *debt financing* in Chapter 6). **Equity capital** consists of funds provided by the firm's owners when they reinvest earnings, make additional contributions, liquidate assets, issue stock to the general public, or raise capital from venture capitalists and other investors (an approach referred to as *equity financing* in Chapter 6). A firm also obtains equity capital whenever it makes a profit.

A company's cash needs vary from one time period to the next, and even an established firm may not generate sufficient funds from operations to cover all costs of a major expansion

**debt capital** funds obtained through borrowing.

**equity capital** funds provided by the firm's owners when they reinvest earnings, make additional contributions, or issue stock to investors.

Table

17.1    Characteristics of Debt and Equity Capital

| Characteristics | Debt Capital | Equity Capital |
|---|---|---|
| 1. Payments to security holders | Contractual payment of interest and repayment of principal. | No contractual payments. |
| 2. Maturity | Pays a fixed amount of principal at a set future date. | No maturity. |
| 3. Claim on assets | Lenders have a prior claim on assets in the event of bankruptcy. | In the event of bankruptcy, equity holders receive nothing unless all creditors are repaid. |
| 4. Control | As long as payments are made when due and other terms of the lending contract are followed, debt holders have no control over the company. | Equity holders are owners of the company and usually have the right to vote on major company issues and elect the board of directors. |

**assessment  check**

1. What are the two major sources of funds?
2. Do different companies take different approaches to the mix between debt and equity capital?

**"They Said It"**

"A bank is a place that will lend you money if you can prove that you don't need it."
—Bob Hope (1903–2003)
Actor and comedian

or a significant upgrade of equipment. In these instances, financial managers must evaluate the potential benefits and drawbacks of seeking funds by borrowing. As an alternative to borrowing, the firm may raise new equity capital. A financial manager's job includes determining the most cost-effective balance between equity and borrowed funds and the proper blend of short-term and long-term funds. Table 17.1 compares debt capital and equity capital on the basis of four important criteria.

Different companies can take very different approaches to the mix between debt and equity capital. For instance, Home Depot and Lowe's are both large, profitable, and fast-growing home improvement retailers. Home Depot, however, relies less on debt capital than does Lowe's. For each dollar in debt capital, Home Depot has about $1.64 in equity capital. By contrast, Lowe's has less than $1.19 in equity capital for each dollar in debt capital.[7]

## Short-Term Sources of Funds

Many times throughout a year, an organization may discover that its cash needs exceed its available funds. For example, retailers generate surplus cash for most of the year, but they need to build up inventory during the late summer and fall to get ready for the holiday shopping season. Consequently, they often need funds to pay for merchandise until holiday sales generate revenue. Then retailers use the incoming funds to repay the borrowed funds. In these instances, financial managers evaluate short-term sources of funds. By definition, short-term sources of funds are repaid within one year.

Three major sources of short-term funds exist: trade credit, short-term loans, and commercial paper. Trade credit is extended by suppliers when a firm receives goods or services, agreeing to pay for them at a later date. Short-term loans can be either unsecured, meaning the firm does not pledge any assets as collateral, or secured, meaning that specific assets such as inventory are pledged as collateral. A major source of short-term loans is commercial banks such as PNC Bank and Sun Trust. Commercial paper was briefly described earlier in the chapter. The interest cost on commercial paper is typically 1 or 2 percent lower than the interest rate on short-term bank loans, and firms can raise large amounts of money in the commercial paper market. However, only large firms with considerable financial strength and stability can sell commercial paper.

# Long-Term Sources of Funds

Funds from short-term sources can help a firm meet current needs for cash or inventory. A larger need, however, such as acquiring another company or making a major investment in real estate or equipment, often requires funds for a much longer period of time. Unlike short-term sources, long-term sources are repaid over many years.

Organizations acquire long-term funds from three sources. One is long-term loans obtained from financial institutions such as commercial banks, life insurance companies, and pension funds. A second source is **bonds**—certificates of indebtedness sold to raise long-term funds for firms and governments. A third source is equity financing acquired by selling stock in the firm or reinvesting company profits (known as *retained earnings*).

**bond** certificate of indebtedness sold to raise long-term funds for a corporation or government agency.

## Public Sale of Stocks and Bonds

Sales of stocks and bonds represent a major source of funds for corporations. Such sales provide cash inflows for the issuing firm and either a share in its ownership (for a stock purchaser) or a specified rate of interest and repayment at a stated time (for a bond purchaser). Because stock and bond issues of many corporations are traded in the securities markets, stockholders and bondholders can easily sell these securities. The decision of whether to issue stock or bonds to finance a firm's plans is an important decision discussed in more detail in Chapter 18.

## Private Placements

Some new stock or bond issues may not be sold publicly but rather only to a small group of large investors such as pension funds and insurance companies. These sales are referred to as **private placements.** Most private placements involve corporate debt issues. In a typical year, about one-third of all new corporate debt issues are privately placed. Recent private placements include a $200 million debt issue by SC Johnson and a $300 million debt issue by media company Hearst.[8]

It is often cheaper for a company to sell a security privately than publicly, and there is less government regulation with which to contend. Institutions buy private placements because they typically carry slightly higher interest rates than publicly issued bonds. In addition, the terms of the issue can be tailored to meet the specific needs of both the issuer and the institutional investors. Of course, the institutional investor gives up liquidity. Privately placed securities do not trade in securities markets.

## Venture Capitalists

Venture capitalists are an important source of long-term financing, especially to new companies. **Venture capitalists** raise money from wealthy individuals and institutional investors and invest these funds in promising firms. Venture capitalists also provide management consulting advice as well as funds. In exchange for their investment, venture capitalists become part owners of the business. If the business succeeds, venture capitalists can earn substantial profits. US Venture Partners is one of many venture capital firms operating today. Over the past fifteen years, California-based US Venture Partners has invested close to $2 billion in 370 companies, including Sun Microsystems and Check Point Software.[9]

## Leverage

Raising needed cash by borrowing allows a firm to benefit from the principle of **leverage,** a technique of increasing the rate of return on funds invested through the use of borrowed funds. The key to managing leverage is ensuring that a company's earnings remain larger than its interest payments, which increases the leverage on the rate of return on shareholders' investment. Of course, if the company earns less than its interest payments, shareholders lose money on their original investments.

**leverage** technique of increasing the rate of return on an investment by financing it with borrowed funds.

Figure 17.4 shows the relationship between earnings and shareholder returns for two identical hypothetical firms that choose to raise funds in different ways. Leverage Company obtains 50 percent of its funds from lenders who purchase company bonds (Leverage Company pays

## 17.4 The Impact of Leverage on Risk and Return

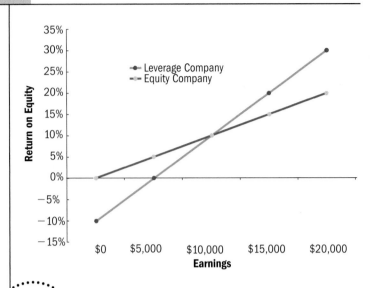

10 percent interest on its bonds). Equity Company raises all of its funds through sales of company stock.

Notice that if earnings double, from say $10,000 to $20,000, returns to shareholders of Equity Company also double (from 10 percent to 20 percent). On the other hand, returns to shareholders of Leverage Company more than double (from 10 percent to 30 percent). However, leverage works in the opposite direction as well. If earnings fall from $10,000 to $5,000, a decline of 50 percent, returns to shareholders of Equity Company also fall by 50 percent (from 10 percent to 5 percent). By contrast, returns to shareholders of Leverage Company fall from 10 percent to zero. Thus, leverage increases potential returns to shareholders but also increases risk. Another problem with borrowing money is that an overreliance on borrowed funds reduces management's flexibility in future financing decisions.

### assessment check

1. List the three sources of short-term funds.
2. Define leverage and explain how leverage increases both potential returns and potential risks to owners.

**financial system** system by which funds are transferred from savers to users.

### "They Said It"

"It is well that the people of the nation do not understand our banking and monetary system, for if they did, I believe there would be a revolution before tomorrow morning."

—Henry Ford (1863–1947)
American industrialist

# THE FINANCIAL SYSTEM AND FINANCIAL INSTITUTIONS

Households, businesses, government, financial institutions, and financial markets together form what is known as the financial system. The **financial system** is the process by which money flows from savers to users. A simple diagram of the financial system is shown in Figure 17.5.

On the left are savers—those with excess funds. For a variety of reasons, savers choose not to spend all of their current income, so they have a surplus of funds. Users are the opposite of savers; their spending needs exceed their current income so they have a deficit. They need to obtain additional funds to make up the difference. Savings are provided by households, businesses, and government. At the same time, borrowers also consist of households, businesses, and government. Households need money to buy automobiles or homes. Businesses need money to purchase inventory or build new production facilities. Governments need money to build highways and new schools or to fund budget deficits.

Generally, in the United States, households are net savers—meaning that in the aggregate they save more funds than they use—while businesses and governments are net users—meaning that they use more funds than they save. The fact that most of the net savings in the U.S. financial system are provided by households may be a bit of a surprise initially, because Americans do not have the reputation of being thrifty. Yet even though the savings rate of American households is low compared with those of other countries, American households still save hundreds of billions of dollars each year.

Funds can be transferred between savers and users in two ways. One is through the financial markets. For example, whenever a company sells stocks or bonds publicly or privately, funds are transferred between savers and users. Savers expect to receive some sort of return from the firm for the use of their money. The role and functioning of the financial markets will be described in more depth in the next chapter.

The other way in which funds can be transferred is through financial institutions—for example, a commercial bank such as Cincinnati-based Fifth Third or Cleveland-based Key Corporation. For instance, whenever a consumer or business deposits money into a bank account,

Figure

17.5

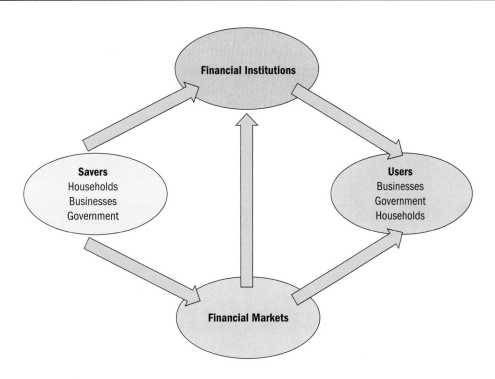

Financial Institutions

Savers
Households
Businesses
Government

Users
Businesses
Government
Households

Financial Markets

**depository institutions**
financial institutions that
accept deposits that can
be converted into cash
on demand.

money is transferred indirectly to users. The bank pools customer deposits and uses the funds to make loans to businesses and consumers. These borrowers pay the bank interest, and it, in turn, pays depositors interest for the use of their money.

Financial institutions greatly increase the efficiency and effectiveness of the transfer of funds between savers and users. Because of financial institutions, savers earn more, and users pay less, than they would without financial institutions. Indeed, it is difficult to imagine how any modern economy could function without well-developed financial institutions. Think about how difficult it would be for a businessperson to obtain inventory financing or a consumer to purchase a new home without financial institutions. Prospective borrowers would have to identify and negotiate terms with each saver individually.

Traditionally, financial institutions have been classified into **depository institutions**—institutions that accept deposits that customers can withdraw on demand—and nondepository institutions. Examples of depository institutions include commercial banks (such as Regions and Wells Fargo), savings banks (such as Golden West and Ohio Savings), and credit unions (such as the State Employees Credit Union of North Carolina). Nondepository institutions include life insurance companies (such as Northwestern Mutual), pension funds (such as the Florida state employee pension fund), and the various government-sponsored financial institutions such as Fannie Mae and Freddie Mac (profiled in the chapter's opening vignette). In total, financial institutions have trillions of dollars in assets. Figure 17.6 shows the relative sizes of the major types of financial institutions in the United States.

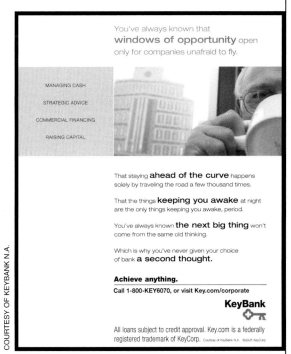

Commercial banks such as KeyBank offer many services to businesses, such as managing cash, strategic advice, commercial financing, and raising capital.

## 17.6 Total Assets of Major Types of Financial Institutions

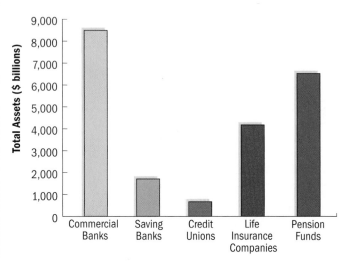

**Source:** Insurance Information Institute, *Financial Services Facts*, accessed August 2, 2006, http://www.financialservicesfacts.org.

## 17.7 Distribution of Outstanding Commercial Bank Loans

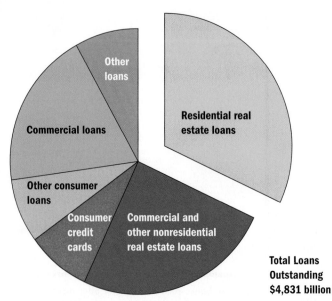

Total Loans Outstanding $4,831 billion

**Source:** FDIC, *Statistics on Banking*, accessed August 3, 2006, http://www.fdic.gov.

# Commercial Banks

Commercial banks are the largest and probably most important financial institution in the United States, and in most other countries as well. In the United States today, the approximately 7,600 commercial banks have total assets of almost $8.5 trillion.[10] Commercial banks offer the most services of any financial institution. These services include a wide range of checking and savings deposit accounts, consumer loans, credit cards, home mortgage loans, business loans, and trust services. Commercial banks also sell other financial products, including securities and insurance.

Although 7,600 may sound like a lot of banks, the number of banks has actually declined dramatically in recent years; 25 years ago there were 14,000 commercial banks. At the same time, banks have gotten larger: today, the typical commercial bank is about five times as large as it was ten years ago. Both changes can be explained by the fact that larger banks are buying smaller banks. In one recent year, almost 300 banks were acquired by other banks.[11]

While the overall trend in the banking industry has been toward fewer, larger banks, a countertrend has also emerged: the growth of small *community banks.* More than 100 such banks began operation during a recent year.[12] Community banks typically serve a single city or county and have millions, rather than billions, of dollars in assets and deposits. Many consumers and small-business owners prefer smaller banks because they feel they're offered a higher level of personal service and often pay lower fees. As the "Hit & Miss" feature illustrates, this segment of the banking industry is thriving.

*How Banks Operate* Banks raise funds by offering a variety of checking and savings deposits to customers. The banks then pool these deposits and lend most of them out in the form of a variety of consumer and business loans. At the end of a recent year, banks held than $5.5 trillion in deposits and had almost $5 trillion in outstanding loans.[13] The distribution of outstanding loans is shown in Figure 17.7. As the figure shows, banks lend a great deal of money to both households and businesses, for a variety of purposes. Commercial banks are an especially important source of funds for small businesses.

Banks make money primarily because the interest rate they charge borrowers is higher than the rate of interest they pay depositors. Banks also make money from other sources, such as fees charged customers for checking accounts and using automated teller machines. Fees and other so-called *noninterest income* now makes up around one-third of total bank revenue.[14]

*Electronic Banking* More and more funds each year move through **electronic funds transfer systems** (EFTSs), computerized systems for conducting financial transactions over electronic links. Millions of businesses and con-

# HIT & MISS

## Small Banks Thriving in the Land of the Giants

Have you received a free bottle of water lately at your bank? If you're like most customers of the country's increasingly large banks, you bank online, by phone, or by machine, and you haven't seen a human bank teller in months. But tiny Western National Bank in Phoenix is bucking the trend toward bank consolidation and automation. At its single ground-floor location in the city's business district, a curbside teller greets you by name and hands you a free bottle of spring water.

"Our customers absolutely love it," says Bill Hinz II, the bank's owner. That's just one of the personal touches the bank offers to customers tired of faceless giants with billions in assets. Western National, with about 400 accounts and $32 million in assets, understands that customers with a few thousand in savings or a small-business loan want to be treated as if they were important, by a bank that's part of their community. Big banking networks aren't set up to do that, says Hinz.

The Federal Deposit Insurance Corporation (FDIC) says community banks are on the rise, with 112 charters for such institutions issued in a recent year. "We're seeing more small community banks popping up," reports a banking consultant in Houston. "People want

to bank with people, not machines." Thanks in part to recent low interest rates that increased the demand for loans, the uptick in community banking also reflects small banks' ability to cater to market niches such as ethnic or religious minorities and small-business owners. "The stock-in-trade of small banks is customization," says the FDIC's chief economist.

### Questions for Critical Thinking

1. Why do small banks do a better job of personalizing the banking experience for their customers?
2. With higher interest on savings, lower fees, extended hours, online banking, and a wider variety of banking services, large banks offer depositors many advantages. What are some of their disadvantages? How important are they to you as a banking customer?

Sources: Eve Tahmincioglu, "Small Business: Small Banking in a Big Bank World," *New York Times*, accessed August 9, 2006, http://www.nytimes.com; Chris Taylor, "Restoring Success," *Sales and Marketing Management*, accessed July 27, 2006, http://www.salesandmarketing.com; Péralte C. Paul, "Banking on Small Success," *Atlanta Journal-Constitution*, accessed July 27, 2006, http://www.ajc.com.

---

sumers now pay bills and receive payments electronically. Most employers, for example, directly deposit employee paychecks in their bank accounts, rather than issuing employees paper checks. Today nearly all Social Security checks and other federal payments made each year arrive as electronic data rather than paper documents.

One of the original forms of electronic banking, the automated teller machine (ATM), continues to grow in popularity. ATMs allow customers to make banking transactions 24 hours a day, 7 days a week by inserting an electronic card into the machine and entering a personal identification number. Networked systems enable ATM users to access their bank accounts in distant states and even throughout the world. In the United States alone, there are around 400,000 ATMs, which process almost 11 billion transactions annually.[15] Bank of America alone has almost 17,000 ATMs located in around 30 states.[16]

Most banks now offer customers debit cards—also called *check cards*—which allow customers to make purchases directly from their checking or savings account. A debit card looks like a credit card but acts like a check and replaces the customer's ATM card. A growing number of retailers—including Supervalu, Target, and Walgreen's—have installed special terminals that allow customers to use their ATM or debit cards to make purchases. Customers are required to enter their personal identification numbers and can often get cash back. Consumers enjoy the convenience of this feature; at the same time, it eliminates the problem of bad checks for retailers.

*Online Banking* Today, many consumers do some or all of their banking on the Internet. According to one survey, more than one-third of American households use some online banking

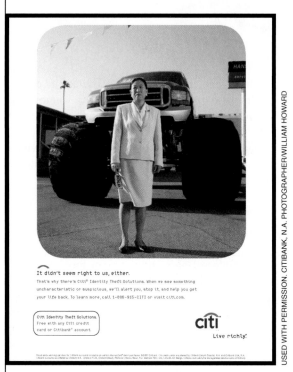

USED WITH PERMISSION. CITIBANK, N.A. PHOTOGRAPHER/WILLIAM HOWARD

Online banking offers safety features, such as checking purchases that don't seem quite right.

services on a regular basis.[17] Almost 5 million Bank of America customers annually pay more than $80 billion worth of bills online.[18] Two types of online banks exist: Internet-only banks (such as ING Direct) and traditional brick-and-mortar banks with Web sites (such as Wachovia and Citibank). A major reason people are attracted to online banking is convenience. Customers can transfer money, check account balances, and pay bills 24 hours a day, 7 days a week on their PCs. Making customers comfortable is one of the intangible personal services banks can still offer at local branches. See the "Business Etiquette" feature for tips on using small talk to make customers feel at home.

## Bank Regulation

Banks are among the nation's most heavily regulated businesses. The main purpose of bank regulation is to ensure public confidence in the safety and security of the banking system. Banks are critical to the overall functioning of the economy, and a collapse of the banking system can have disastrous results. Many believe that one of the major causes of the Great Depression was the collapse of the banking system starting in the late 1920s.

### Who Regulates Banks?
All banks are either state or federally chartered. Most banks are state chartered; however, federally chartered banks control more than half of all banking assets. State-chartered banks are regulated by the appropriate state banking authorities; federally chartered banks are regulated by the Federal Reserve, the Federal Deposit Insurance Corporation (FDIC), and the Comptroller of the Currency. Furthermore, state banks that are federally insured—and virtually all are—are also subject to FDIC regulation.

Banks are subject to periodic examination by state and/or federal regulators. Examinations ensure that the bank is following safe and sound banking practices and is complying with all applicable regulations. Bank examinations include the review of detailed reports on the bank's operating and financial condition, as well as on-site inspections.

### Federal Deposit Insurance
A cornerstone of bank regulation is deposit insurance. Deposits up to a set amount—currently $100,000 per depositor—are insured by the FDIC. Deposit insurance means that, in the event the bank fails, depositors are paid in full by the FDIC, up to $100,000. Federal deposit insurance was enacted by the Banking Act of 1933 as one of the measures designed to restore public confidence in the banking system. Before deposit insurance, so-called runs were common as people rushed to withdraw their money from a bank, often just on a rumor that the bank was in precarious financial condition. At some point, the bank was unable to meet withdrawal demands and closed its doors. Remaining depositors often lost most of the money they had in the bank. Deposit insurance shifts the risk of bank failures from individual depositors to the FDIC. While banks still fail today, no insured depositor has ever lost any money.

### Recent Changes in Banking Laws
In addition to establishing the FDIC, depression-era banking legislation also restricted the kinds of activities in which banks could engage, including restricting their role in the securities markets. Believing that some of these restrictions were outdated, Congress passed a law that allows banks to enter the securities and insurance businesses. In return, other financial services firms may now offer banking services.

## Savings Banks and Credit Unions

While commercial banks are by far the largest depository financial institution in the United States, savings banks and credit unions are also important financial institutions. Today savings banks and credit unions offer many of the same services as commercial banks.

Savings banks used to be called savings and loan associations or thrift institutions. They were originally established in the early 1800s to make home mortgage loans. Savings and loans originally raised funds by accepting only savings deposits and then lent these funds to consumers to buy homes. Today, there are around 1,300 savings banks with total assets of about $1.7 trillion.[19] Although the typical savings bank offers many of the same services as a commercial bank, including checking accounts, savings banks are not major lenders to businesses. More than 70 percent of their outstanding loans are still home mortgage loans. Washington Mutual, the nation's largest savings bank, is also the nation's largest mortgage lender. Deposits in savings banks are now FDIC insured, and savings banks are regulated in much the same way as commercial banks.

Credit unions are unique financial institutions. They are cooperative financial institutions that are owned by their depositors, all of whom are members. Around 85 million Americans belong to one of the nation's approximately 9,200 credit unions. Combined, credit unions have more than $650 billion in assets.[20] By law, credit union members must share similar occupations, employers, or membership in certain organizations. This law effectively caps the size of credit unions. In fact, the nation's largest bank—Bank of America—holds more deposits than all the country's credit unions combined. The Navy Federal Credit Union is the largest credit union in the country, with around 2.5 million members and $25 billion in deposits.[21] Membership is open to active-duty personnel in the Navy and Marine Corps, retired personnel, civilian employees of the Navy Department, and members of their immediate families.

## (b)usiness (e)tiquette

### Mastering the Art of Small Talk

When people sit down with a bank employee to discuss the very personal topic of their money, they want to feel comfortable. It is up to the banker to offer the personal warmth that creates trust, and that begins with the art of small talk.

Here are a few tips for establishing common ground with a few minutes of polite conversation before getting to the business reason for a meeting.

1. Always greet clients by looking them in the eye, smiling, saying their name, and offering a firm handshake and a chair.
2. Eliminate any possible distractions such as phone calls or music playing in the office.
3. Offer tea, coffee, or other refreshments, if available.
4. You can never go wrong by asking, "How are you today?"
5. If asked how you are, always respond briefly and turn the conversation back to your customer. Avoid saying anything about being ill or having any personal problems.
6. If you are already acquainted with the customer and his or her family, inquire about other family members. You might want to keep a brief file of personal information about your regular customers for this purpose. If not, ask whether they have any family, how many, where they live, and so on.
7. Remember that people are nearly always eager to talk about their children and grandchildren.
8. Even more, people like to talk about themselves. Sometimes all they need is an opening such as a question about their work, their interests and hobbies, recent travels, and so on.
9. Borrow a trick from Eleanor Roosevelt, who would mentally run through the alphabet thinking of topics to introduce in conversation. For instance, A might remind you of animals, and you can ask whether the person has any pets; B might suggest books, and you can inquire whether the person has read a popular best-seller; C could suggest cuisine, as in, "Have you tried the new restaurant around the corner?"
10. Know when to stop. Use observation and empathy to help you determine when the person has started to relax and feel comfortable. Then it's time to ask, "How may I help you today?"

**Sources:** "Learning Small Talk," Mannersmith, accessed August 16, 2006, http://www.mannersmith .com; Melissa Leonard, "Avoid the 'Fatal' Faux Pas," ABA Banking Online, accessed July 27, 2006, http://www.ababj.com; "How to Master Small Talk," Canadian Business Online, accessed July 3, 2006, http://www.canadianbusiness.com.

Credit unions, such as Navy Federal, provide a variety of services to members.

Credit unions are designed to serve consumers, not businesses. Credit unions raise funds by offering members a number of demand and saving deposits—checking accounts at credit unions are referred to as *share draft accounts*—and then, in turn, lend these funds to members. Because credit unions are not-for-profit institutions, they often pay savers higher rates of interest, charge lower rates of interest on loans, and have fewer fees than other financial institutions. Credit unions can have either state or federal charters, and deposits are insured by a federal agency, the National Credit Union Administration (NUCU), which functions essentially the same as the FDIC.

## Nondepository Financial Institutions

Nondepository financial institutions accept funds from businesses and households, much of which they then invest. Generally, these institutions do not offer checking accounts or other types of demand deposits. Three examples of nondepository financial institutions are insurance companies, pension funds, and finance companies.

*Insurance Companies* Households and businesses buy insurance to transfer risk from themselves to the insurance company. The insurance company accepts the risk in return for a series of payments, called *premiums*. **Underwriting** is the process insurance companies use to determine whom to insure and what to charge. During a typical year, insurance companies collect more in premiums than they pay in claims. After they pay operating expenses, they invest this difference. Insurance companies are a major source of short- and long-term financing for businesses. Life insurance companies alone have total assets of more than $4 trillion invested in everything from bonds and stocks to real estate.[22] Examples of life insurers include Prudential and New York Life.

*Pension Funds* Pension funds provide retirement benefits to workers and their families. They are set up by employers and are funded by regular contributions made by employers and employees. Because pension funds have predictable long-term cash inflows and very predictable cash outflows, they invest heavily in long-term assets, such as common stocks and real estate. By some estimates, more than 25 percent of all common stocks are owned by pension funds. In total, pension funds have more than $6.5 trillion in assets.[23] General Motors, General Electric, and IBM have the largest private-employer pension funds. The largest public-employer pension funds are the California and New York state employee pension funds and the federal employee pension fund.[24]

Most private-employer pension funds are insured by the Pension Benefit Guaranty Corporation (PBGC), a federal agency. Employers pay premiums to the PBGC in return for pension insurance. Should an employer default on its pension obligations or go bankrupt, PBGC will continue to provide limited pension benefits to affected employees. PBGC currently insures the pensions of around 44 million Americans.[25] Recently, some have raised concerns about the financial health of the PBGC, noting that the agency's assets are only a fraction of insured pension obligations. When United Airlines recently terminated its employee pension plans, the PBGC was forced to pick up around $6.8 billion in pension obligations for over 100,000 current and retired United employees.[26]

*Finance Companies* Consumer and commercial finance companies, such as Ford Credit, John Deere Capital Corporation, and Pennsylvania-based Dollar Financial, offer short-term loans to borrowers. A commercial finance company supplies short-term funds to businesses that pledge tangible assets such as inventory, accounts receivable, machinery, or property as collateral for the loan. A consumer finance company plays a similar role for consumers. Finance companies raise funds by selling securities or borrowing funds from commercial banks. Many finance companies, such as GMAC, are actually subsidiaries of a manufacturer, such as General Motors. GMAC finances dealer inventories of new cars and trucks, as well as providing loans to consumers and other buyers of GM products.

# THE FEDERAL RESERVE SYSTEM

Created in 1913, the **Federal Reserve System,** or Fed, is the central bank of the United States and is an important part of the nation's financial system. The Fed has four basic responsibilities: regulating commercial banks, performing banking-related activities for the U.S. Treasury, providing services for banks, and monetary policy. Not all banks belong to the Fed. Banks with federal charters are required to belong to the Fed, but membership is optional for state-chartered banks. Because the largest banks in the country are all federally chartered, the bulk of banking assets are controlled by Fed members. The Fed acts as the banker's bank for members. It provides wire transfer facilities, clears checks, replaces worn-out currency, and even lends banks money.

**Federal Reserve System**
U.S. central bank.

## Organization of the Federal Reserve System

The nation is divided into twelve federal reserve districts, each with its own federal reserve bank. Each district bank supplies banks within its district with currency and facilitates the clearing of checks. District banks are run by a nine-member board of directors, headed by a president.

The governing body of the Fed is the board of governors. The board consists of seven members, including a chair and vice chair, appointed by the president and confirmed by the Senate. A full term for a Fed governor is fourteen years. If a governor serves a full term, he or she cannot be reappointed. A governor can be reappointed if he or she was initially appointed to an unexpired term. The chair and vice chair serve in that capacity for four years and can be reappointed. The chair of the board of governors is a very important position. Some have commented, only half jokingly, that the Fed chair is the second most powerful person in the nation.

The Fed is designed to be politically independent. Terms for Fed governors are staggered in such a way that a president could not appoint a majority of members, assuming that all members serve their entire terms. The Fed also has its own sources of revenue and does not depend on congressional appropriations.

An important part of the Fed is the Federal Open Markets Committee (FOMC). The FOMC sets most policies concerning monetary policy and interest rates. It consists of twelve members—the seven Fed board governors plus five representatives of the district banks who serve on a rotating basis. The Fed chair is also chair of the FOMC.

**"They Said It"**

"Most Americans have no real understanding of the operation of the international money lenders. The accounts of the Federal Reserve System have never been audited. It operates outside the control of Congress and manipulates the credit of the United States."
—Barry Goldwater
(1909–1998)
U.S. senator

## Check Clearing and the Fed

As mentioned earlier, one of the Fed's responsibilities is to help facilitate the clearing of checks. Even in this age of electronic and online banking, Americans still write billions of paper checks each year. The clearing of a check is the process by which funds are transferred from the check writer to the recipient.

Assume the owner of Gulf View Townhouses of Tampa buys a $600 carpet cleaner from the local Home Depot and writes a check. If Home Depot has an account at the same bank as Gulf View, the bank will clear the check in house. It will decrease the balance in the owner's account by $600 and increase the balance in Home Depot's account by $600. If Home Depot has an account at another bank in Tampa, the two banks may still clear the check directly with one another. This process is cumbersome, however, so it is more likely that the banks will use the services of a local check clearinghouse.

On the other hand, if Home Depot has its account with a bank in another state—perhaps in Atlanta, where Home Depot is based—the check will likely be cleared through the Federal Reserve System. Home Depot will deposit the check in its Atlanta bank account. Its bank, in turn, will deposit the check in the Federal Reserve Bank of Atlanta. The Atlanta Federal Reserve bank will present the check to Gulf View's bank for payment, which pays the check by deducting $600 from Gulf View's account. Regardless of the method used, the *Check Clearing for the 21st Century Act* allows banks and the Fed to use electronic images of checks—rather than the paper documents themselves—during the clearing process. Because these images are transferred electronically, the time it takes to clear a check has been reduced substantially.

## Monetary Policy

monetary policy using interest rates and other tools to control the supply of money and credit in the economy.

The Fed's most important function is controlling the supply of money and credit, or **monetary policy.** The Fed's job is to make sure that the money supply grows at an appropriate rate, allowing the economy to expand and inflation to remain in check. If the money supply grows too slowly, economic growth will slow, unemployment will increase, and the risk of a recession will increase. If the money supply grows too rapidly, inflationary pressures will build. The Fed uses its policy tools to push interest rates up or down. If the Fed pushes interest rates up, the growth rate in the money supply will slow, economic growth will slow, and inflationary pressures will ease. If the Fed pushes interest rates down, the growth rate in the money supply will increase, economic growth will pick up, and unemployment will fall. The Fed has three major policy tools: reserve requirements, the discount rate, and open market operations.

The Fed requires that banks maintain reserves—defined as cash in their vaults plus deposits at district Federal Reserve banks—equal to some percentage of what the banks hold in deposits. For example, if the Fed sets the reserve requirement at 5 percent, a bank that receives a $500 deposit must reserve $25, so it has only $475 to invest or lend out. By changing the reserve requirement, the Fed can affect the amount of money available for making loans. The higher the reserve requirement, the less banks can lend out to consumers and businesses. The lower the reserve requirement, the more banks can lend out. Because any change in the reserve requirement can have a sudden and dramatic impact on the money supply, the Fed rarely uses this tool. In fact, the Fed has not changed reserve requirements in more than ten years. Reserve requirements range from 0 to 10 percent, depending on the type of account.

Another policy tool is the so-called **discount rate,** the interest rate at which Federal Reserve banks make short-term loans to member banks. A bank might need a short-term loan if transactions leave it short of reserves. If the Fed wants to slow the growth rate in the money supply, it increases the discount rate. This increase makes it more expensive for banks to borrow funds. Banks, in turn, raise the interest rates they charge on loans to consumers and businesses. The end result is a slowdown in economic activity. Lowering the discount rate has the opposite effect.

The third policy tool, and the one used most often, is **open market operations,** the technique of controlling the money supply growth rate by buying or selling U.S. Treasury securities. If the Fed buys Treasury securities, the money it pays enters circulation, increasing the

Table 17.2

**Tools Used by the Federal Reserve to Regulate the Growth in the Money Supply**

| Tool | Brief Description | Impact on the Growth Rate of the Money Supply | Impact on Interest Rates and the Economy | Frequency of Use |
|---|---|---|---|---|
| 1. Reserve requirements | Change in the percentage of deposits held as reserves. | Increases in reserve requirements slow the growth rate in the money supply. | Increases in reserve requirements push interest rates up and slow economic growth. | Rarely used. |
| 2. Discount rate | Change in the rate the Fed charges banks for loans. | An increase in the discount rate slows the growth rate in the money supply. | An increase in the discount rate pushes interest rates up and slows economic growth. | Used only in conjunction with open market operations. |
| 3. Open market operations | Buying and selling government securities to increase or decrease bank reserves. | Selling government securities reduces bank reserves and slows the growth rate in the money supply. | Selling government securities pushes interest rates up and slows economic growth. | Used frequently. |

money supply and lowering interest rates. When the Fed sells Treasury securities, money is taken out of circulation and interest rates rise. When the Fed uses open market operations it employs the so-called *federal funds rate*—the rate at which banks lend money to one another overnight—as its benchmark. Table 17.2 illustrates how the tools used by the Federal Reserve can stimulate or slow the economy.

The Federal Reserve also has the authority to exercise selective credit controls when it feels the economy is growing too rapidly or too slowly. These credit controls include the power to set margin requirements—the percentage of the purchase price of a security that an investor must pay in cash on credit purchases of stocks or bonds.

Transactions in the foreign exchange markets also affect the U.S. money supply and interest rates. The Fed can lower the exchange value of the dollar by selling dollars and buying foreign currencies, and it can raise the dollar's exchange value by doing the opposite—buying dollars and selling foreign currencies. When the Fed buys foreign currencies, the effect is the same as buying securities because it increases the U.S. banking system's reserves. Selling foreign currencies, on the other hand, is like selling securities, in that it reduces bank reserves.

**assessment check**

1. How is the Federal Reserve organized?
2. List and briefly explain the various methods by which the fed can control the supply of money and credit. Which method is used most frequently?

# U.S. FINANCIAL INSTITUTIONS: A GLOBAL PERSPECTIVE

Financial institutions have become a global industry, and any review should consider U.S. financial institutions in their international context. Major U.S. banks—such as Citibank, J. P. Morgan Chase, and Bank of America—have extensive international operations. They have offices, lend money, and accept deposits from customers throughout the world. According to recent statistics, U.S. banks have more than $200 billion in outstanding loans to international customers.[27]

While most Americans recognize large U.S. banks such as Citibank among the global financial giants, only 3 of the 20 largest banks in the world (measured by total assets) are U.S.

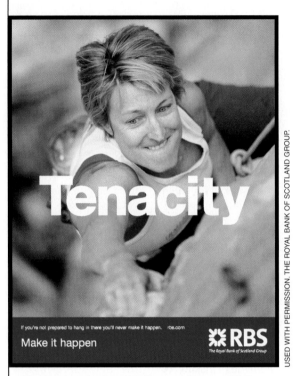

Tenacity

If you're not prepared to hang in there you'll never make it happen.   rbs.com

Make it happen

**RBS**
The Royal Bank of Scotland Group

The Royal Bank of Scotland is one of the world's largest banks.

institutions—Bank of America, Citibank, and J. P. Morgan Chase. The other 17 are based in France, Germany, Holland, Japan, Switzerland, and the United Kingdom. The world's largest bank is Japan's Mitsubishi UFJ Holdings, with more than $1.7 trillion in assets.[28] These international banks also operate worldwide, including in the United States.

Virtually all nations have some sort of a central bank, similar to the U.S. Federal Reserve. Examples include the Banks of Canada, England, and Japan, and the European Central Bank. These central banks play roles much like the Fed, such as controlling the money supply and regulating banks. Policy makers at other nations' central banks often respond to changes in the U.S. financial system by making similar changes in their own systems. For example, if the Fed pushes U.S. interest rates lower, central banks in Japan and Europe may also push their interest rates lower. These changes can influence events in countries around the world. Lower U.S. and European interest rates not only decrease the cost of borrowing for U.S. and European firms but also increase the amount of money available for loans to borrowers in other countries such as Chile and India.

International banks and other providers of financial services play important roles in global business. They help transfer purchasing power from buyers to sellers and from lenders to borrowers. They also provide credit to importers and reduce the risk associated with changes in exchange rates.

## assessment check

1. How does the size of U.S. banks compare to the size of banks located in other countries?

2. Do other countries have organizations that play roles similar to those played by the Federal Reserve?

# WHAT'S AHEAD

This chapter introduced the finance function of contemporary business. Finance deals with planning, obtaining, and managing the company's funds to accomplish its objectives effectively and efficiently. The chapter also described the role of money, where and how firms obtain funds, and what the financial system does. The next chapter explores how securities—stocks and bonds—are bought and sold. It also describes the investment characteristics of stocks and bonds and the ways investors choose specific securities. Chapter 18 also outlines how securities' market regulations protect investors.

## Summary of Learning Goals

### 1  Identify the functions performed by a firm's financial managers.

The major responsibility of financial managers is to develop and implement a financial plan for their organization. The firm's financial plan is based on forecasts of expenditures and receipts for a specified period and reflects the timing of cash inflows and outflows. The financial managers systematically determine their company's need for funds during the period

and the most appropriate sources from which it can obtain them. In short, the financial manager is responsible for both raising and spending money.

### Assessment Check Answers

**1.1 Define *finance* and explain the role of the financial manager.**
Finance deals with planning, obtaining, and managing a company's funds to accomplish objectives efficiently

and effectively. The financial manager is the executive who develops and implements the firm's financial plan and determines the most appropriate sources and uses of funds.

### 1.2 What are the three questions on which a financial plan is based?

A financial plan revolves around the answers to three questions: How much money will the firm require for a specific period of time? Where will the necessary funds come from? When will the company need additional funds?

### 2 Describe the characteristics a form of money should have, and list the functions of money.

Money should be divisible, portable, durable, difficult to counterfeit, and stable in value. Money in countries with modern economies have all of these characteristics. The functions of money are as a medium of exchange, a store of value, and a unit of account.

## Assessment Check Answers

### 2.1 What characteristics should money have?

Money should be divisible, portable, durable, difficult to counterfeit, and stable in value.

### 2.2 List the three basic functions of money.

The functions of money are as a medium of exchange, a store of value, and a unit of account.

### 3 Identify the various measures of the money supply.

The two most commonly used measures of the money supply are M1 and M2. M1 is defined as anything generally accepted as payment for goods and services, such as coins, paper money, and checks. M2 consists of M1 plus other assets that are almost as liquid as money but do not function directly as a medium of exchange, such as savings deposits and money market mutual funds. The use of credit cards—also known as plastic money—has increased sharply in recent years. While credit cards are convenient and easy to use, they are a very expensive source of consumer and business credit.

## Assessment Check Answers

### 3.1 Explain the differences between M1 and M2.

M1 consists of anything that is generally accepted as payment for goods and services. M2 consists of M1 plus other assets that are almost as liquid as currency and demand deposits but do not function directly as a medium of exchange.

### 3.2 Who issues Visa and MasterCard credit cards? Explain the difference between a credit card and a charge card.

All Visa and MasterCard credit cards are issued by banks. A credit card gives the holder the option of paying part or all of the balance due each month. Finance charges are levied on the portion of the balance not paid each month. A charge card requires that the balance be paid in full each month.

### 4 Explain how a firm uses funds.

Organizations use funds to run their day-to-day operations, pay for inventories, make interest payments on loans, pay dividends to shareholders, and purchase land, facilities, and equipment. If a firm finds itself with a surplus of cash, most financial managers invest that excess cash in marketable securities.

## Assessment Check Answers

### 4.1 Why do organizations need funds?

Companies need funds for a variety of purposes, including paying for daily operations, compensating employees, paying suppliers, making interest payments on loans, paying dividends to shareholders, and purchasing new assets.

### 4.2 List several alternatives to holding large cash balances.

Many financial managers hold excess cash balances in marketable securities, because these securities pay interest but are easy to convert into cash. Examples of marketable securities include Treasury bills, commercial paper, repurchase agreements, and large certificates of deposit.

### 5 Compare the two major sources of funds for a business.

Debt capital and equity capital are the two major sources from which businesses acquire funds. Debt capital represents funds obtained through borrowing. Equity capital comes from several sources, including the sale of stock, additional investments by the firm's owners, and reinvested earnings.

## Assessment Check Answers

### 5.1 What are the two major sources of funds?

Debt capital and equity capital are the major sources from which businesses acquire funds. Debt capital consists of borrowed funds, while equity capital represent funds provided by owners and reinvested earnings.

**5.2 Do different companies take different approaches to the mix between debt and equity capital?**
Yes, some companies rely more on debt financing than other companies.

### 6 Identify the likely sources of short- and long-term funds for business operations.

Sources of short-term funds include trade credit (accounts payable), unsecured loans, secured loans (for which the firm must pledge collateral), and sales of commercial paper by large, financially sound firms. Sources of long-term funds include long-term loans repaid over one year or longer, bonds, equity funds (ownership obtained from selling stock, accumulating additional contributions from owners, or reinvesting earnings in the firm). Leverage—the use of borrowed funds—increases the potential returns to shareholders (owners) but also increases risk.

### Assessment Check Answers

**6.1 List three sources of short-term funds.**
The three sources of short-term funds are trade credit; loans from financial institutions, such as banks; and commercial paper.

**6.2 Define leverage and explain how leverage increases both potential returns and potential risks to owners.**
Leverage is the technique of increasing the rate of return on owners' funds through the use of borrowed funds. As long as the company's earnings are higher than its interest payments, leverage increases the return to owners. However, if earnings are less than interest payments, the owners lose some of their original investment.

### 7 Describe the financial system and the major financial institutions.

The financial system is the process by which funds are transferred between savers and users of funds. Funds can be transferred either through the financial markets or through financial institutions. Depository institutions—commercial banks, savings banks, and credit unions—accept deposits from customers that can be redeemed on demand. Depository institutions are closely regulated by state and federal authorities. Nondepository institutions include pension funds and insurance companies. Nondepository institutions invest a large portion of their funds in stocks, bonds, and real estate.

### Assessment Check Answers

**7.1 Describe the financial system. How are funds transferred between savers and borrowers?**

The financial system is the process by which funds are transferred between savers (households, businesses, and governments) and users (also households, businesses, and governments). While funds can move directly between savers and users, most funds are transferred indirectly through the financial markets or through financial institutions.

**7.2 What is the difference between a depository financial institution and a nondepository institution? Give an example of each.**
A depository institution accepts deposits that are payable on demand—such as checking accounts. Nondepository institutions do not accept these types of deposits. A commercial bank is an example of a depository institution; a life insurance company is an example of a nondepository institution.

**7.3 Who regulates commercial banks?**
Banks with federal charters are regulated by the Federal Reserve; banks with state charters are regulated by state banking authorities. Any bank—regardless of charter—that is a member of the FDIC is subject to FDIC regulation as well. Virtually all banks are members of the FDIC.

### 8 Explain the functions of the Federal Reserve System and the tools it uses to control the supply of money and credit.

The Federal Reserve System is the central bank of the United States. The Federal Reserve regulates banks, performs banking functions for the U.S. Treasury, and acts as the banker's bank (clearing checks, lending money to banks, and replacing worn-out currency). It controls the supply of credit and money in the economy to promote growth and control inflation. The Federal Reserve's tools include reserve requirements, the discount rate, and open market operations. Selective credit controls and purchases and sales of foreign currencies also help the Federal Reserve manage the economy.

### Assessment Check Answers

**8.1 How is the Federal Reserve organized?**
The Federal Reserve System divides the nation into twelve districts, each with a district bank. The governing body is the board of governors, consisting of seven members appointed by the president and confirmed by the Senate. The governors serve for staggered terms and are headed by the Fed chair. Another important part of the Fed is the Federal Open Markets Committee, consisting of the seven Fed governors plus

five district bank presidents (who serve on a rotating basis). The Fed has its own sources of revenue and doesn't depend on congressional appropriations.

**8.2 List and briefly explain the various methods by which the Fed can control the supply of money and credit. Which method is used most frequently?**
The Fed has three policy tools to control the supply of money and credit: reserve requirements (the percentage of deposits banks must maintain as reserves), the discount rate (the rate the Fed charges member banks for loans), and open market operations (adding or subtracting bank reserves through the sale of U.S. government securities). The Fed relies most frequently on open market operations to control the supply of money and credit.

**9** **Describe the global financial system.**
Large U.S. banks and other financial institutions have a global presence. They accept deposits, make loans, and have branches throughout the world. Foreign banks also operate worldwide. The average Euro-pean or Japanese bank is much larger than the average American bank. Virtually all nations have central banks that perform the same roles as the U.S. Federal Reserve System. Central bankers often act together, raising and lowering interest rates as economic conditions warrant.

## Assessment Check Answers

**9.1 How does the size of U.S. banks compare to the size of banks located in other countries?**
Only 3 of the world's 20 largest banks are located in the United States. The others are located in Japan and Europe.

**9.2 Do other countries have organizations that play roles similar to those played by the Federal Reserve?**
Virtually all countries have central banks that function essentially like the U.S. Federal Reserve and perform the same functions.

## Business Terms You Need to Know

finance 548
financial manager 548
risk-return tradeoff 549
financial plan 549
money 550

debt capital 555
equity capital 555
bond 557
leverage 557
financial system 558

depository institutions 559
Federal Reserve System 565
monetary policy 566

## Other Important Business Terms

**vice-president for financial management 548**
**treasurer 548**
**controller 548**
**demand deposits 552**
**M1 552**

**M2 552**
**private placements 557**
**venture capitalist 557**
**electronic funds transfer systems 560**
**underwriting 564**

**discount rate 566**
**open market operations 566**

## Review Questions

1. Define *finance*. Briefly explain the risk-return trade-off in finance.
2. What is a financial plan? In building a financial plan, what three questions must be answered?
3. What characteristics should money have? List the three functions of money.
4. Explain the difference between M1 and M2. What is a demand deposit?
5. What are some of the reasons organizations need funds? What do many companies do if they find themselves with excess cash?

6. What is the difference between debt capital and equity capital? List several examples of each.
7. Define *leverage*. Construct a simple numerical example to illustrate the effect of leverage.
8. What is the financial system? Why is the direct transfer of funds between savers and users rare?
9. Explain the difference between a depository and a nondepository financial institution. Give several examples of each type of financial institution.
10. Briefly outline how a commercial bank operates. Why is deposit insurance so important?
11. Compare and contrast a commercial bank, a savings bank, and a credit union. Give an example of each.
12. Explain the role of life insurance companies and pension funds in the financial system.
13. How is the Federal Reserve System organized? Discuss the process by which a check clears.
14. Explain how open market operations work.
15. Briefly discuss the global perspective of U.S. financial institutions.

## Projects and Teamwork Applications

1. Assume you would like to start a business. Put together a rough financial plan that addresses the three financial planning questions listed in the text.
2. Your business has really grown, but now it needs a substantial infusion of capital. A venture capital firm has agreed to invest the money you need. In return, the venture capital firm will own 75 percent of the business. You will be replaced as board chairman and CEO, but retain the title of company founder and president, and the venture capital firm will provide a new CEO. Would you be willing to take the money but lose control of your business?
3. The owner of your company is trying to decide how to raise an additional $1.5 million, and she has asked for your advice about whether the firm should use debt capital or equity capital. Working in a small group, prepare a brief memo to the owner outlining the advantages and disadvantages of both debt capital and equity capital. Be sure to explain the concept of leverage. Assume your company can borrow $1.5 million at an annual interest rate of 8 percent. It currently has $1.5 million in equity and no debt.
4. As noted in the prior chapter, a company whose stock is publicly traded is required to report financial results on a regular basis. Working with a partner, choose three public companies. Collect recent balance sheets, determine how levered each company is, and decide whether each company has become more or less levered in recent years. Why do some companies appear to rely more heavily on debt financing than other companies? (Note: A good source of financial statements is MSN Money Central, http://moneycentral.msn.com.)
5. Compared with most businesses, is a bank more vulnerable to failure? Why or why not? Why does federal deposit insurance help protect the soundness of the banking system?
6. Working in a small team, identify a large bank. Visit that bank's Web site and obtain its most recent financial statements. Compare the bank's financial statements to those of a nonfinancial company, such as a manufacturer or retailer. Report on your findings.
7. An exchange rate is the rate at which one currency can be exchanged for another. Working with a partner, use the Internet to find the current exchange rate between the U.S. dollar and the following currencies: Australian dollar, euro, British pound, Japanese yen, and Brazilian real. Has the dollar been rising or falling in value relative to these currencies? Assume that there was general agreement that the dollar was "undervalued." Why would an increase in U.S. interest rates help increase the value of the dollar relative to other currencies? Explain how the Federal Reserve could push U.S. interest rates higher.
8. Choose one of the following countries: Canada, the United Kingdom, or Japan. Research that country's central bank. How is the bank organized? Who appoints the members of the central bank? What functions does the central bank perform? How is the central bank similar to the U.S. Federal Reserve? How does it differ from the Fed?

## At Giant Bank of America, Small Businesses Rule

Bank of America is the nation's largest bank in terms of deposits. But small-business lending is still its primary mission, and it maintains a commitment to building local communities with investment and loans.

The Bank of America was recently named Lender of the Year for Oregon and Southwest Washington by the government's Small Business Administration (SBA), for approving 183 loans worth more than $5.5 million. It was also named co-winner of the Minority Lender of the Year award for making loans worth more than $1.2 million to minority-owned small businesses in the area. Such awards are not unusual for the bank, which has also been ranked the number one SBA lender in California, where its average small-business loan is worth $35,000. "The strength of our SBA lending, combined with our conventional lending, is a clear indicator that we intend to be known as 'the' small business bank," says the bank's small-business banking president.

Bank of America is the lender for about 20 percent of the small businesses in the 29 states and the District of Columbia in which it does business. With nearly 3.3 million clients, it is the largest small-business bank in the country.

The bank provides more services than just loans, of course, and among its clients it also counts individual consumers and large corporations, including nearly all the *Fortune* 500 companies. It offers banking, investing, asset management, and risk management services through its roughly 5,800 retail banking offices.

The bank is also broadening its commitment to community development, with an ambitious plan covering the next decade. Working primarily in low- and moderate-income communities, Bank of America plans to focus on lending and investment to support affordable housing, small-business/small-farm loans, consumer loans, and economic development. It will lend and invest about $750 billion as its Community Goal, one of the largest in U.S. commercial banking history, unfolds across the country.

Conventional loans and lines of credit will be available for small businesses and small farms, which the bank calls "the economic engines of local communities." Personal, car, and student loans will be available (excluding credit card borrowing), and in fulfillment of its economic development goal, Bank of America will work with government agencies, nonprofit developers, and financial intermediaries to promote neighborhood redevelopment, job creation, and core neighborhoods in rural and urban areas.

To maintain its good record of accountability, Bank of America will report regularly on the results of its plan, both through its Web site (http://www.bankofamerica.com) and directly to shareholders.

### Questions for Critical Thinking

1. What kind of image do you think Bank of America conveys to its small-business customers? What is the source of their loyalty to the bank?

2. What are some of the benefits to local areas of the bank's Community Goal? What are the benefits to the bank?

---

**Sources:** Kennedy Smith, "SBA Recognizes Lenders of the Year for Oregon and Southwest Washington," *All-Business,* accessed August 16, 2006, http://www.allbusiness.com; "Bank of America Retains Top SBA Lender Status in California," PR Newswire, accessed July 27, 2006, http://www.prnewswire.com; "Bank of America Releases Targets for $750 Billion Community Development Goal," PR Newswire, accessed July 27, 2006, http://www.prnewswire.com.

---

## JPMorganChase Lends a Hand to Small Business

This video case appears on page 627. A recently filmed video, designed to expand and highlight the written case, is available for class use by instructors.

# chapter 18

## Financing and Investing through Securities Markets

### Learning Goals

**1** Distinguish between the primary market for securities and the secondary market.

**2** Compare money market instruments, bonds, and common stock, and explain why particular investors might prefer each type of security.

**3** Identify the five basic objectives of investors and the types of securities most likely to help them reach each objective.

**4** Describe the characteristics of the major stock exchanges.

**5** Explain the process of buying or selling a security listed on an organized securities exchange and the information included in stock and bond quotations and stock indexes.

**6** Discuss the role of mutual funds and exchange-traded funds in the securities markets.

**7** Evaluate the major features of regulations and laws designed to protect investors.

Every day, companies do exactly what you do as an individual: figure out how much money is needed to cover expenses and still have some left over to invest for the future. Like you, they must determine where and how to obtain any financing to survive and thrive. While you are looking for a job, companies are searching for ways to keep their enterprises operating. One way of finding funds is to take a firm public by selling shares of stock to investors. But recently a number of public corporations have been reversing this trend: they have reverted to private status. Going private has several advantages: the firm no longer has to worry about dips in its stock prices, it no longer has to answer to shareholders or pay out dividends, and it is not required to report financial results.

# Cable Companies Leave Public Life

Two cable television companies—Cablevision and Cox Communications—have decided to privatize. By doing so, they can avoid the intense scrutiny of investors and the public eye and exert more internal control. With money borrowed from such sources as Merrill Lynch and Bank of America, Cablevision plans to buy back its stock from shareholders and then spin off two divisions into one smaller public company—Rainbow Media cable and Madison Square Garden. Cox Communications accomplished its move to private status when its controlling shareholder, Cox Enterprises, paid $8.5 billion for the 38 percent of Cox Communications that it didn't already own—effectively taking it off the stock market. Cox Communications is the third-largest cable television provider in the United States, with 6.3 million basic cable subscribers. The firm also offers digital cable, digital telephone, and high-speed Internet services and is now focused on encouraging subscribers to purchase bundled services. Going private cuts the cost of public financial reporting requirements and takes the firm out of the Wall Street spotlight, where investors often focus on short-term performance.

Rumors continue to circulate that cable companies—and Cablevision in particular—are ripe for acquisition. Some industry experts believe that Cablevision, run by the Dolan family, is open to offers. Cablevision, a smaller company than its larger rivals Comcast and Time Warner, is located in the suburbs of New York. But despite its size, the firm has shown an uncanny ability to dominate its market. It also maintains a steady and substantial flow of cash. With its high profile and solid financial standing, Cablevision could be attractive to buyers. But others believe that taking the firm private makes a potential sale more complicated. "Once private, the lack of a public market trading value for [Cablevision] would appear to make an acquisition more complicated," explains one industry analyst, "with the buyer having far less information." It would probably be more expensive, as well. Either way, cable companies are rewriting the script for their industry, and viewers will need to tune in to see what ultimately happens.[1]

The previous chapter discussed two sources of funds for long-term financial needs: debt capital and equity capital. Long-term debt capital takes the form of U.S. government bonds, municipal bonds, and corporate bonds. Equity capital takes the form of common and preferred stock—ownership shares in corporations. Stocks and bonds are commonly called **securities,** because both represent obligations on the part of issuers to provide purchasers with expected or stated returns on the funds invested or loaned.

This chapter examines how securities are bought and sold in two financial markets—the primary market and the secondary market. The primary market involves the initial sale of new securities to investors, and the secondary market consists of the sale of existing securities between investors. As we discussed in Chapter 17, financial markets are an important part of the overall financial system, the system by which funds are transferred from savers to users. Next, we explore the characteristics of stocks, bonds, and money market instruments (short-term debt securities) and the way investors choose specific securities. We then examine the role of organized securities exchanges, such as the New York Stock Exchange, in the financial sector and outline the information included in reports of securities transactions. This section is followed by a discussion of mutual funds—an especially popular option for individual investors. Finally, we review the laws that regulate the securities markets and protect investors.

---

## *PRIMARY VERSUS SECONDARY MARKETS*

**securities** financial instruments such as stocks and bonds.

**primary market** market in which new security issues are first sold to investors; issuers receive the proceeds from the sale.

In the **primary market**, firms and governments issue securities and sell them initially to the public. When a company needs capital to purchase inventory, expand a plant, make major investments, acquire another firm, or pursue other business goals, it may sell a bond or stock issue to the investing public. For example, Wal-Mart Stores recently sold about $800 million in bonds. It used the proceeds to build new stores.[2] Similarly, when Washington State needs capital to build a new highway, to buy a new ferry, or to fulfill other public needs, its leaders may also decide to sell bonds.

A stock offering gives investors the opportunity to purchase ownership shares in a firm such as well-known drug maker Amgen and to participate in its future growth, in exchange for providing current capital. When a company offers stock for sale to the general public for the first time, it is called an **initial public offering (IPO)**. During a recent twelve-month period, around 180 initial public offerings raised a total of more than $30 billion. These companies, on average, had been in existence for seven years prior to going public.[3]

Both profit-seeking corporations and government agencies also rely on primary markets to raise funds by issuing bonds. For example, the federal government sells Treasury bonds to finance part of federal outlays such as interest on outstanding federal debt. State and local governments sell bonds to finance capital projects such as the construction of sewer systems, streets, and fire stations.

Announcements of new stock and bond offerings appear daily in business publications such as the *Wall Street Journal*. These announcements are often in the form of a simple black-and-white ad called a *tombstone.*

Securities are sold to the investment public in two ways: in open auctions and through investment bankers. Virtually all securities sold through open auctions consist of U.S. Treasury securities. A week before an upcoming auction, the Treasury announces the type and number of securities it will be auctioning. Treasury bills are auctioned weekly, whereas longer-term Treasury securities are auctioned once a month or once a quarter. Prospective buyers submit bids to the Treasury. Two types of bids are allowed: competitive and noncompetitive. A competitive bid specifies how much the investor wishes to purchase and the price. The higher the price specified, the lower the return to the investor, and the lower the cost to the

Treasury. In a typical auction the Treasury accepts about half of the competitive bids submitted. An investor submitting a noncompetitive bid only specifies the amount he or she wishes to purchase (up to a limit of $5 million) and agrees to pay a price equal to the average price on accepted competitive bids. Investors may submit bids directly to the Treasury or through banks and investment firms.

Sales of most corporate and municipal securities are made via financial specialists called **investment bankers.** Merrill Lynch, Goldman Sachs, Lehman Brothers, and Crédit Suisse First Boston (CSFB) are examples of well-known investment banking firms. An investment banker is a financial intermediary that purchases the issue from the firm or government and then resells the issue to investors. This process is known as **underwriting.**

Investment bankers underwrite stock and bond issues at a discount, meaning that they pay the issuing firm or government less than the price the investment banker charges investors. This discount is compensation for services rendered, including the risk investment bankers incur whenever they underwrite a new security issue. Although the size of the discount is often negotiable, they usually average around 5 percent for all types of securities. The size of the underwriting discount, however, is generally higher for stock issues than it is for bond issues. For instance, the average underwriting discount for IPOs is close to 7 percent.[4]

Corporations and governments are willing to pay for the services provided by investment bankers because they are financial market experts. In addition to locating buyers for the issue, the underwriter typically advises the issuer on such details as the general characteristics of the issue, its pricing, and the timing of the offering. Several investment bankers commonly participate in the underwriting process. The issuer selects a lead, or primary, investment banker, which in turn forms a syndicate consisting of other investment banking firms. Each member of the syndicate purchases a portion of the security issue, which it resells to investors.

Media reports of stock and bond trading are most likely to refer to trading in the **secondary market,** a collection of financial markets in which previously issued securities are traded among investors. The corporations or governments that originally issued the securities being traded are not directly involved in the secondary market. They neither make any payments when securities are sold nor receive any of the proceeds when securities are purchased. The New York Stock Exchange (NYSE) and the Nasdaq stock market are both secondary markets. In terms of the dollar value of securities bought and sold, the secondary market is four to five times as large as the primary market. During a typical trading day, more than $50 billion worth of stock changes hands on the NYSE alone.[5] We describe secondary markets in more depth later in the chapter.

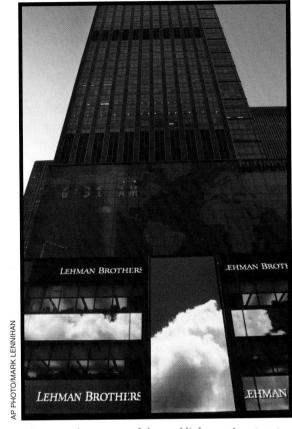

Lehman Brothers is one of the world's largest investment banking firms.

**secondary market** market in which existing security issues are bought and sold by investors.

**assessment check**

1. Distinguish between the primary and secondary markets for securities. Is the primary market or secondary market larger?

2. Explain the two ways in which securities are sold in the primary market.

# TYPES OF SECURITIES

Securities can be classified into three categories: money market instruments, bonds, and stock. Money market instruments and bonds are both debt securities, and stocks are units of ownership in corporations like General Electric, Best Buy, 3M, and PepsiCo.

## Money Market Instruments

**money market instruments** short-term debt securities issued by corporations, financial institutions, and governments.

**Money market instruments** are short-term debt securities issued by governments, financial institutions, and corporations. By definition, all money market instruments mature within one year from the date of issue. Investors are paid interest by the issuer for the use of their funds. Money market instruments are generally low-risk securities and are purchased by investors when they have surplus cash. As noted in the prior chapter, financial managers often invest surplus cash in money market instruments because they are low risk and are easily convertible into cash. For example, Microsoft has more than $15 billion currently invested in money market instruments.[6] Examples of money market instruments include U.S. Treasury bills, commercial paper, and bank certificates of deposit. These securities were described in the prior chapter.

## Bonds

Bondholders are creditors of a corporation. By selling bonds, a firm obtains long-term debt capital. Federal, state, and local governments also acquire funds in this way. Bonds are issued in various denominations (face values), usually between $1,000 and $25,000. Each issue indicates a rate of interest to be paid to the bondholder—stated as a percentage of the bond's face value—as well as a maturity date on which the bondholder is paid the bond's face value. Because bondholders are creditors, they have a claim on the firm's assets that must be satisfied before any claims of stockholders in the event of the firm's bankruptcy, reorganization, or liquidation. For example, when California and Bermuda–based Global Crossing emerged from bankruptcy, existing creditors received about 35 percent of the shares of the newly reorganized company to satisfy their claims. Those who owned shares of Global Crossing at the time of its bankruptcy filing, by contrast, received nothing, losing about $50 billion.[7]

**Types of Bonds**   A prospective bond investor can choose among a variety of bonds. Major types of bonds are summarized in Table 18.1.

**Government bonds** are bonds sold by the U.S. Treasury. Because government bonds are backed by the full faith and credit of the U.S. government, they are considered the least risky of all bonds. The Treasury sells bonds that mature in 2, 3, 5, 7, 10, and 30 years from the date of issue. The Treasury stopped selling new 30-year bonds in 2001 but recently reintroduced sales of the so-called *long bond.* The "Hit & Miss" feature on page 580 discusses some of the reasons why the sale of 30-year bonds was resumed.

**Municipal bonds** are bonds issued by state or local governments. There are two types of municipal bonds. A revenue bond is a bond issue whose proceeds are to be used to pay for a project that will produce revenue—such as a toll road or bridge. The Oklahoma Turnpike Authority has issued such bonds. A general obligation bond is a bond whose proceeds are to be used to pay for a project that will not produce any revenue—such as a new Indiana state police post. General obligation bonds can be sold only by states such as Oregon or local governmental units such as Toledo, Ohio, or Bergen County, New Jersey, that have the power to levy taxes. An important feature of municipal bonds is the exemption of interest payments from federal income tax. Because of this attractive feature, municipal bonds generally carry lower interest rates than either corporate or government bonds.

Corporate bonds are a diverse group and often vary based on the collateral backing the bond. A **secured bond** is backed by a specific pledge of company assets. For example, mortgage bonds are backed by real and personal property owned by the firm, such as machinery or furniture, and collateral trust bonds are backed by stocks and bonds of other companies owned by the firm. In the event of default, bondholders may receive the proceeds from selling these

Table 18.1

Types of Bonds

| Issuer | Types of Securities | Risk | Special Features |
|---|---|---|---|
| U.S. Treasury (government bonds) | Notes: Mature in 10 years or fewer from date of issue.<br><br>Bonds: Mature in 30 years from date of issue | Treasury bonds and notes have virtually no risk. | Interest is exempt from state income taxes. |
| State and local governments (municipal bonds) | General obligation: Issued by state or local governmental units with taxing authority; backed by the full faith and credit of the state where issued.<br><br>Revenue: Issued to pay for projects that generate revenue—such as water systems or toll roads; revenue from project used to pay principal and interest. | Risk varies depending on the financial health of the issuer.<br><br>Most large municipal bond issues are rated in terms of credit risk (AAA or Aaa is the highest rating). | Interest is exempt from federal income taxes and may be exempt from state income taxes. |
| Corporations | Secured bonds: Bonds are backed by specific assets.<br><br>Unsecured bonds (debentures): Backed by the financial health and reputation of the issuer. | Risk varies depending on the financial health of the issuer.<br><br>Most corporate bond issues are rated in terms of credit risk (AAA or Aaa is the highest rating). | A few corporate bonds are convertible into shares of common stock of the issuing company. |
| Financial institutions (such as Fannie Mae and Freddie Mac) | Mortgage pass-through securities | Generally very low risk. | They pay monthly income consisting of both interest and principal. |

assets. Because bond purchasers want to balance their financial returns with their risks, bonds backed by pledges of specific assets are less risky than those without such collateral. Consequently, a firm can issue secured bonds at lower interest rates than it would have to pay for comparable unsecured bonds. However, many firms do issue unsecured bonds, called **debentures.** These bonds are backed only by the financial reputation of the issuing corporation.

Another popular type of bond is the **mortgage pass-through security.** Mortgage pass-through securities are sold by Fannie Mae, Freddie Mac, and other financial institutions. The securities are backed by a self-liquidating pool of mortgage loans purchased from lenders such as savings banks. As borrowers make their monthly mortgage payments, these payments are "passed through" to the holders of the pass-through securities. Mortgage pass-through securities are popular because they are relatively safe (mortgages have to be insured) and provide monthly income.

*Quality Ratings for Bonds* Two factors determine the price of a bond: its risk and its interest rate. Bonds vary considerably in terms of risk. One tool used by bond investors to assess the risk of a bond is its so-called **bond rating.** Two investment firms—Standard & Poor's (S&P) and Moody's—rate most corporate and municipal bonds. The bonds with the least risk are assigned a rating of either AAA (S&P) or Aaa (Moody's). The ratings descend as

# HIT & MISS

## An Old Investment Makes a Comeback

Treasury bonds aren't glamorous, especially ones with long-range maturity dates. In fact, the U.S. Treasury put a hold on the sale of 30-year bonds for several years because the federal government had a budget surplus and didn't need to borrow the money. But the Treasury recently announced their return to the marketplace. Who's not yawning about the announcement? In the investment industry, it's the fixed-income specialists who are cheering the comeback. "It's like having an old friend back," explains Clifford A. Gladson, a senior vice president for fixed-income investments at USAA Investment Management.

Thirty-year bonds carry with them a reputation for long-term security in the form of guaranteed rates for mutual funds and pension funds, which tend to make long-range investments. But most individuals don't hang onto the same investments for three decades—they can usually do better with shorter-term, slightly riskier investments. And as interest rates in general climb, the value of a long-term bond may diminish even though it pays a higher fixed interest rate than short-term bonds. Still, the 30-year bond has been a benchmark for many investment professionals. "There's a love affair out there for some people," quips one manager of fixed-income portfolios for Vanguard. The 30-year bond provides a guaranteed rate of return and is free of state income taxes, two features that attract investors. It also gives them one more option they did not have for several years.

Anyone interested in making an investment should do the homework before purchasing. Individuals must consider their own needs and goals. An 80-year-old retiree is unlikely to buy a 30-year bond, but a 45-year-old might want this type of investment as part of his or her retirement portfolio. "I think it's good for [investment] portfolios," notes a financial economist at Wachovia Securities. "It adds to the diversification component." So you make the purchase and then hit the snooze button—several times.

### Questions for Critical Thinking

1. Would you purchase a 30-year Treasury bond during your career? If so, when and why? If not, why not?

2. If you plan to participate in a firm's pension plan or other investments made on your behalf by your employer, what steps might you take to learn about the types of investments being made?

**Sources:** Avrum D. Lank, "30-Year Treasury Bonds May Come Up Short for Individual Investors," *Milwaukee Journal Sentinel,* accessed August 16, 2006, http://www.jsonline.com; Elizabeth Harris, "The 30-Year Bond Is Back, and So Is Romance," *New York Times,* accessed July 28, 2006, http://www.nytimes.com; Kathleen Lynn, "Investors, Take Note: The 30-Year Treasury Bond Is Back," *The Record,* accessed August 4, 2005, http://www.recordnet.com; Mike Meyers, "30-Year's Revival May Help Taxpayer," *(Minneapolis) Star Tribune,* accessed August 4, 2005, http://startribune.com.

---

risk increases. Table 18.2 lists the S&P and Moody's bond ratings. Bonds with ratings of BBB (or Baa) and above are classified as **investment-grade bonds.** Examples of investment-grade bonds include Royal Dutch Shell (rated AA by Standard and Poor's) and the Illinois State Building Authority (rated AAA by Standard & Poor's). By contrast, bonds with ratings of BB (or Ba) and below are classified as speculative, or so-called **junk bonds.** Junk bonds attract investors by offering high interest rates in exchange for greater risk. Today, junk bonds pay about 50 percent more in interest than do investment-grade corporate bonds. An example of speculative-grade bonds is those issued by Ford Motor Company (rated BB by Standard and Poor's).

The second factor affecting the price of a bond is its interest rate. Other things being equal, the higher the interest rate, the higher the price of a bond. However, everything else usually is not equal; the bonds may not be equally risky, or one may have a longer maturity. Investors must evaluate the trade-offs involved.

Another important influence on bond prices is the market interest rate. Because bonds pay fixed rates of interest, as market interest rates rise, bond prices fall, and vice versa. For instance, the price of a ten-year bond, paying 5 percent per year, would fall by about 8 percent if market interest rates rose from 5 percent to 6 percent.

Table

18.2

Bond Ratings

| Standard & Poor's Rating | Moody's Rating | |
|---|---|---|
| AAA | Aaa | |
| AA | Aa | Investment-grade bonds |
| A | A | |
| BBB | Baa | |
| BB | Ba | |
| B | B | Speculative-grade bonds (junk bonds) |
| CCC | Caa | |
| CC | Ca | |
| C | C | |

Note: Any bond with a rating below is C is currently in default, meaning it is not paying interest or repaying principal.

*Retiring Bonds* Because bonds in an issue mature on a specific date, borrowers such as Bed Bath & Beyond or Harris County, Texas, must have the necessary funds available to repay the principal at that time. In some instances, this can create a cash flow problem. To ease the repayment problem, some borrowers issue serial bonds. A serial bond issue consists of bonds that mature on different dates. For example, assume a corporation issues $20 million in serial bonds for a 30-year period. None of the bonds mature during the first 20 years. However, beginning in the 21st year, $2 million in bonds mature each year until all the bonds are repaid at the end of the 30 years.

A variation of the concept of serial bonds is the sinking fund bond, or prerefunded bond. Under this arrangement, the issuer, such as the city of Oakland, California, makes annual deposits to accumulate funds for use in redeeming the bonds when they mature. These deposits are made to the bond's trustee—usually a large bank—who represents bondholders. The deposits must be large enough that their total, plus accrued interest, will be sufficient to redeem the bonds at maturity.

Most corporate and municipal bonds, and some government bonds, are callable. A **call provision** allows the issuer to redeem the bond before its maturity at a prespecified price. Not surprisingly, issuers tend to call bonds when market interest rates are declining. For example, if York County, Pennsylvania, had $50 million in bonds outstanding with a 6 percent annual interest rate, it would pay $3 million annually in interest. If interest rates decline to 4 percent, the county may decide to call the 6 percent bonds, repaying the principal from the proceeds of newly issued 4 percent bonds. Calling the 6 percent bonds, and issuing 4 percent bonds, will save the county $1 million a year in interest payments. The savings in annual interest expense should more than offset the cost of retiring the old bonds and issuing new ones.

## Stock

The basic form of corporate ownership is embodied in **common stock.** Purchasers of common stock are the true owners of a corporation. Holders of common stock vote on major company decisions, such as purchasing another company or electing a board of directors. In return for

**common stock** shares of ownership in a corporation.

the money they invest, they expect to receive some sort of return. This return can come in the form of cash dividend payments and/or expected price appreciation. Dividends vary widely from stock to stock. DuPont, for instance, pays an annual dividend of almost $1.50 per share. By contrast, Starbucks pays no annual dividend to its shareholders. As a general rule, faster-growing companies pay less in dividends because they need more funds to finance their growth. Consequently, investors expect stocks paying little or no cash dividends to show greater price appreciation compared with stocks paying more generous cash dividends.

Common stockholders benefit from company success, and they risk the loss of their investments if the company fails. If a firm dissolves, claims of creditors must be satisfied before stockholders receive anything. Because creditors have a senior claim to assets, holders of common stock are said to have a residual claim on company assets.

Sometimes confusion arises over the difference between the book value and a stock's market value. *Book value* is determined by subtracting the company's liabilities from its assets. When this net figure is divided by the number of shares of common stock outstanding, the book value of each share is known. Recently, Johnson & Johnson had a book value of around $12 per share.

The *market value* of a stock is the price at which the stock is currently selling. Johnson & Johnson had a recent market price of $68 per share. It is easily found by referring to the financial section of daily newspapers or on the Internet and may be more or less than the book value. What determines market value, however, is more complicated. However, while many variables cause stock prices to fluctuate up and down in the short term, in the long run stock prices tend to follow a company's profits. For instance, over the last ten years, both Johnson & Johnson's earnings and stock price have risen by more than 300 percent.

**Preferred Stock**   In addition to common stock, a few companies also issue **preferred stock**—stock whose holders receive preference in the payment of dividends. General Motors and Bank of America are examples of firms with preferred stock outstanding. Also, if a company is dissolved, holders of preferred stock have claims on the firm's assets that are ahead of the claims of common stockholders. On the other hand, preferred stockholders rarely have any voting rights, and the dividend they are paid is fixed, regardless of how profitable the firm becomes. Therefore, although preferred stock is legally equity, many investors consider it to be more like a bond than common stock.

**Convertible Securities**   Companies may issue bonds or preferred stock that contains a conversion feature. This feature gives the bondholder or preferred stockholder the right to exchange the bond or preferred stock for a fixed number of shares of common stock. For example, credit card issuer Providian Financial has a convertible bond outstanding that allows its holder to exchange the bond (which has a face value of $1,000) for around 77 shares of Providian common stock. So if Providian's stock was selling for $20 per share, the convertible bond would be worth at least $1,540 (77 × $20). Convertible bonds pay lower interest rates than those lacking conversion features, helping reduce the interest expense of the issuing firms. Investors are willing to accept these lower interest rates because they value the potential for additional gains if the price of the firm's stock increases.

# SECURITIES PURCHASERS

Two general types of investors buy securities: institutions and individuals. An **institutional investor** is an organization that invests its own funds or those it holds in trust for others. Insti-

**preferred stock** stock whose holders have priority over common stockholders in the payment of dividends but usually have no voting rights.

**assessment check**

1. Explain the difference between a money market instrument and a bond.
2. What are the two types of bonds issued by state and local governments? Describe the difference between a secured and unsecured bond.
3. Discuss the major investment characteristics of common stock.

tutional investors include insurance companies such as New York Life, pension funds such as Alabama's state employee pension fund, T. Rowe Price mutual funds, and not-for-profit organizations such as the American Cancer Society. Many institutional investors are huge. As noted in Chapter 17, pension funds have more than $6.5 trillion in assets, and the total assets of life insurance companies exceed $4.2 trillion.[8] Institutional investors buy and sell large quantities of securities, often in blocks of 10,000 or more shares per transaction. Such block trading represents about half of the total daily volume on the major securities exchanges.[9]

The number of individual investors who own shares through mutual funds or their employer's retirement plans is steadily rising, and the firms that manage their funds control more than half of all U.S. equities.[10] More than half of all Americans now own stocks, either directly or by investing in stock mutual funds. By contrast, 30 years ago, less than one-third of American households owned any stocks at all.[11]

## Investment Motivations

Why do individuals and institutions invest? In general, individuals and institutions have five primary motivations for investing: growth in capital, stability of principal, liquidity, current income, and income growth. All investors must rank each motivation in terms of importance, and all investments involve trade-offs. For example, an investment that has the potential for substantial growth in capital may provide no current income. By contrast, an investment that has very stable principal may have little potential for capital growth. The bottom line is this: Some investments are more appropriate for certain investors than for others. Table 18.3 provides a useful guide for evaluating money market instruments, bonds, and stocks.

**Growth in Capital**   When it comes to potential growth in capital over time, especially over long periods of time, common stocks are the clear winner. For example, over a recent 20-year period, $10,000 invested in common stocks would have grown to more than $64,000. A similar investment in bonds made during the same period would have grown to less than $35,000. This example does not imply, however, that the prices of all common stocks go up all the time, nor do they go up by the same amount. Not surprisingly, stock performance varies considerably. For instance, over the past decade $10,000 invested in Procter & Gamble's common stock would have grown to more than $37,000. By contrast, over the same period, a $10,000 investment in Ford's common stock would have grown to less than $13,500.

**Stability of Principal**   Treasury bills and other money market instruments are the clear winner when it comes to stability of principal. The odds that the price of a money market

**"They Said It"**

"Successful investing is anticipating the anticipations of others."
—John Maynard Keynes (1883–1946)
Economist

Table 18.3

Comparing Investment Alternatives

| Investment Motivation | Money Market Instruments | Bonds | Common Stocks |
|---|---|---|---|
| Growth in capital | * | ** | *** |
| Stability of principal | *** | ** | * |
| Liquidity | *** | ** | * |
| Current income | * | *** | ** |
| Growth in income | ** | * | *** |

Note: *** = best or highest.

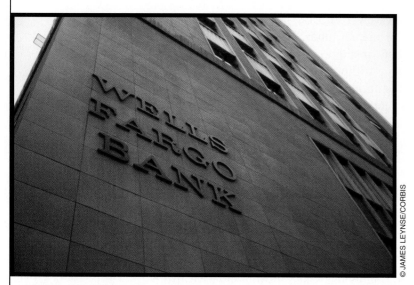

A key to successful investing is finding a strategy that has an appropriate level of risk. Banks and investment firms such as Wells Fargo often provide investment advice.

investment will fall below the price the investor originally paid are virtually zero. Furthermore, when an investor buys a Treasury bill or other money market instrument, the investor can be pretty sure the original investment will be returned. For example, a 90-day Treasury bill has a face value of $10,000. If you buy the T-bill today, you're virtually ensured that you'll receive $10,000 in three months. With stocks, there is no such guarantee.

**Liquidity**   Because the prices of stocks, and to a lesser extent bonds, can vary widely, investors cannot count on making profits whenever they decide or need to sell. Liquidity is a measure of the speed at which assets can be converted into cash. Because money market instruments such as a CD issued by Wells Fargo have short maturities and stable prices, they offer investors the highest amount of liquidity.

**Current Income**   Historically, bonds have provided the highest current income of any security. Interest rates on bonds are usually higher than money market interest rates or the dividends paid on common stocks. For instance, Lowe's has an outstanding bond that pays about 5 percent interest per year. By contrast, the company's common stock has a current dividend yield (annual dividend divided by the stock price) of less than 1 percent. Also, money market interest rates vary, but the interest rate on a bond remains constant. Investors looking for high current income should invest a large portion of their funds in bonds.

**Income Growth**   When you buy a bond, the interest you receive is fixed for the life of the bond. Interest rates on money market instruments can increase over time, but they can decrease as well. On the other hand, common stock dividends have historically risen at a rate that exceeds the rate of inflation. Over the past 20 years, for instance, Johnson & Johnson's common stock dividend has risen at an average annual rate exceeding 10 percent. There is, however, no guarantee that a company's common stock dividend will *always* increase and can, in fact, decrease. For instance, over the past four years Kodak has cut its common stock dividend by more than 75 percent.[12]

## Taxes and Investing

**assessment check**

1. Who purchases securities?
2. What are the five motivations for investing? On which of the five motivations for investment do common stocks rank highest?
3. Discuss the tax implications of investing. Are all sources of investment returns taxed equally?

Interest received from government and corporate bonds is considered ordinary income and is taxed at the investor's marginal tax rate. (Interest received from municipal bonds is usually exempt from federal income taxes, although not always from state income taxes.) Dividends received from common and most preferred stocks is taxed at a lower rate than ordinary income. Furthermore, investors who sell securities at a profit owe so-called capital gains taxes on the difference between the selling price and the purchase price.

Taxes can influence investment decisions in a number of ways. Investors in high marginal tax brackets, for instance, are more likely to hold municipal bonds than investors in lower tax brackets. Because capital losses (selling a security for less than the purchase price) offset capital gains, an investor might decide to take a capital loss at the end of the year rather than waiting until the following year.

# SECURITIES EXCHANGES

Securities exchanges are centralized marketplaces where stocks and bonds are traded. Most of the largest and best-known securities exchanges are commonly called **stock exchanges,** or *stock markets,* because most securities traded are common-stock issues. Stock exchanges are secondary markets. The securities have already been issued by firms, which received proceeds from the issue when it was sold in the primary market. Sales in a securities exchange occur between individual and institutional investors.

Stock exchanges exist throughout the world and most countries today have at least one stock market. The five largest stock exchanges, based on the market value of the stocks traded, are shown in Figure 18.1. As the figure shows, the two largest stock exchanges are located in the United States.

## The New York Stock Exchange

The New York Stock Exchange—sometimes referred to as the Big Board—is arguably the most famous and one of the oldest stock markets in the world, having been founded in 1792. Today, more than 3,000 common- and preferred-stock issues are listed on the NYSE. These stocks represent most of the largest, best-known companies in the United States and have a total market value exceeding $13 trillion.[13] In terms of the total value of stock traded, the NYSE is the world's largest stock market.

For a company's stock to be traded on the NYSE, the firm must apply to the exchange for listing and meet certain listing requirements. In addition, the firm must continue to meet requirements each year to remain listed on the NYSE. Corporate bonds are also traded on the NYSE, but bond trading makes up less than 1 percent of the total value of securities traded there during a typical year.

Trading on the NYSE takes place face-to-face on a trading floor. Buy and sell orders are transmitted to a specific post on the floor of the exchange. Buyers and sellers then bid against one another in an open auction. Only investment firms that are members of the NYSE are allowed to trade, meaning that the firm owns at least one of 1,366 "seats." Seats are occasionally bought and sold. Recently a seat on the NYSE sold for $2.8 million.[14]

Each NYSE stock is assigned to a specialist firm. Specialists are unique investment firms that maintain an orderly and liquid market in the stocks assigned to them. Specialists must be willing to buy when there are no other buyers and sell when there are no other sellers. Specialists also act as auctioneers and catalysts, bringing buyers and sellers together.

Some observers portray the NYSE and its trading practices as somewhat old-fashioned, especially in this technological age. Most

The New York Stock Exchange is one of the oldest stock exchanges in the world.

**Figure**

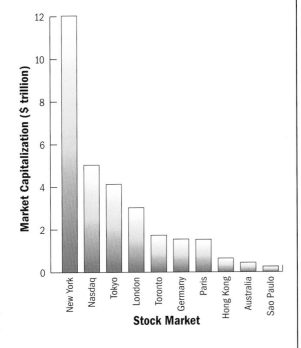

**Source:** *NYSE Fact Book* (interactive edition), New York Stock Exchange, accessed August 22, 2005, http://www.nyse.com.

**stock exchange** financial market where stocks are traded.

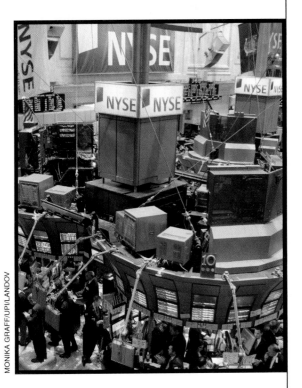

MONIKA GRAFF/UPI/LANDOV

markets, they note, have abandoned their trading floors in favor of electronic trading. However, even though the NYSE still retains a trading floor, the exchange has become highly automated in recent years. Its computer systems automatically match and route most orders, which are typically filled within a few seconds.

## The Nasdaq Stock Market

The world's second-largest stock market is the Nasdaq Stock Market. It is very different from the NYSE. Nasdaq—which stands for National Association of Securities Dealers Automated Quotations—is actually a computerized communications network that links member investment firms. It is the world's largest intranet.[15] All trading on Nasdaq takes place through its intranet, rather than on a trading floor. Buy and sell orders are entered into the network and executed electronically. All Nasdaq-listed stocks have two or more market makers—investment firms that perform essentially the same functions as NYSE specialists.

Around 5,000 companies have their stocks listed on Nasdaq. Compared with firms listed on the NYSE, Nasdaq-listed corporations tend to be smaller, less well-known firms. Some are relatively new businesses and cannot meet NYSE listing requirements. It is not uncommon for firms eventually to transfer the trading of their stocks from Nasdaq to the NYSE—sixteen did so in a recent year.[16] However, dozens of major companies currently trade on Nasdaq—such as Amgen, Cisco Systems, Dell, Intel, and Microsoft—that would easily meet NYSE listing requirements. For a variety of reasons, these firms have decided to remain listed on Nasdaq.

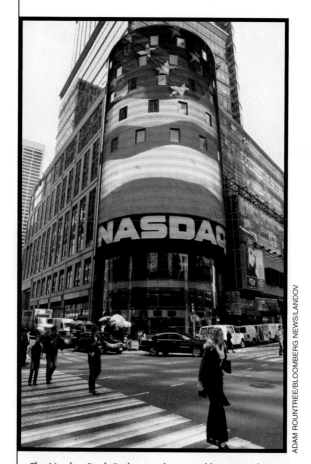

The Nasdaq Stock Exchange, the second-largest exchange in the world, conducts trading through a computerized network.

ADAM ROUNTREE/BLOOMBERG NEWS/LANDOV

## Other U.S. Stock Markets

In addition to the NYSE and Nasdaq Stock Market, several other stock markets operate in the United States. The American Stock Exchange, or AMEX, is also located in New York. It focuses on the stocks of smaller firms, as well as other financial instruments such as options. In comparison with the NYSE and Nasdaq, the AMEX is tiny. Daily trading volume is only around 60 million shares compared with the one-billion-plus shares on each of the larger two exchanges.[17]

Several regional stock exchanges also operate throughout the United States. They include the Chicago, Pacific (San Francisco), Boston, Cincinnati, and Philadelphia Stock Exchanges. Originally established to trade the shares of small, regional companies, the regional exchanges now list securities of many large corporations as well. In fact, more than half of the companies listed on the NYSE are also listed on one or more regional exchanges.

## Foreign Stock Markets

As noted earlier, stock markets exist throughout the world. Virtually all developed countries and many developing countries have stock exchanges. Examples include Bombay, Helsinki, Hong Kong, Mexico City, Paris, and Toronto. One of the largest stock exchanges outside the United States is the London Stock Exchange. Founded in the early 17th century, the London Stock Exchange lists approximately 2,900 stock and bond issues, more than 500 of which are shares of companies located outside the U.K. and Ireland. Trading on the London Stock Exchange takes place using a Nasdaq-type computerized communications network.

The London Stock Exchange is very much an international market. Around two-thirds of all cross-border trading in the world—for example, the trading of stocks of American companies outside the United States—takes place in London. It is not uncommon for institutional investors in the United States to trade NYSE- or Nasdaq-listed stocks in London. These investors claim they often get better prices and faster order execution in London than they do in the United States.

## ECNs and the Future of Stock Markets

For years a so-called *fourth market* has existed. The fourth market is the direct trading of exchange-listed stocks off the floor of the exchange, in the case of NYSE-listed stocks, or outside the network, in the case of Nasdaq-listed stocks. For the most part, trading in the fourth market was limited to institutional investors buying or selling large blocks of stock.

Now the fourth market has begun to open up to smaller, individual investors through markets called **electronic communications networks (ECNs).** Buyers and sellers meet in a virtual stock market in which they trade directly with one another. No specialist or market maker is involved. ECNs have become a significant force in the stock market in recent years. Around half of all trades involving Nasdaq-listed stocks take place on INET or Archipelago—the two largest ECNs—rather than directly through the Nasdaq system.[18] Some have suggested that ECNs represent the future for stock markets. In fact, INET and Archipelago were recently acquired by Nasdaq and the NYSE, respectively. Industry watchers now speculate that NYSE's acquisition of Archipelago could eventually lead to the exchange's abandoning its centuries-old trading floor and becoming an electronic market.

**assessment check**

1. Compare and contrast the NYSE and Nasdaq stock markets.
2. Explain the role of specialists and market makers.
3. What is an ECN?

# BUYING AND SELLING SECURITIES

Unless an investor is a member of one of the stock exchanges, the investor must use the services of a brokerage firm that is a member of one or more stock exchanges. A **brokerage firm** is a financial intermediary that buys and sells securities for individual and institutional investors. Examples include A. G. Edwards, Raymond James, Morgan Stanley, and Wachovia Securities. Brokerage firms are usually members of most major stock markets. Choosing a brokerage firm, and a specific stockbroker in some cases, is one of the most important decisions investors make. The "Business Etiquette" feature discusses one aspect of developing good business relations—networking.

**brokerage firm** financial intermediary that buys and sells securities for individual and institutional investors.

## Placing an Order

An investor who wants to purchase shares of a stock typically initiates the transaction by contacting his or her brokerage firm. The firm transmits the order to the appropriate market, completes the transaction, and confirms the transaction with the investor, all within a few minutes.

An investor's request to buy or sell stock at the current market price is called a market order. A **market order** instructs the brokerage firm, such as Edward Jones, to obtain the highest price possible, if the investor is selling, or the lowest price possible, if the investor is buying. By contrast, a **limit order** instructs the brokerage firm not to pay more than a specified price for a stock, if the investor is buying, or not to accept less than a specified price, if the investor is selling. If Edward Jones is unable to fill a limit order immediately, it is left with either an NYSE specialist or Nasdaq market maker. If the price reaches the specified price, the order is carried out. Limit orders are often recommended during periods of extreme price volatility.

**"They Said It"**

"There's always a bull market somewhere."
—Jim Cramer (b. 1955)
Host of Mad Money on CNBC

# (b)usiness (e)tiquette

## Networking for Successful Business Contacts

Networking is a fact of business life. But there is no need to feel intimidated by it—networking is really a matter of connecting with people and communicating effectively, which is something you do in your life as a student, friend, and family member. Networking helps you reach the right people at the right time to obtain a job, learn more about customers, or close a deal. It involves moving beyond your immediate circle of colleagues and friends. Here are a few suggestions for how to network smoothly and successfully.

1. Be clear about the purpose of your networking. Are you looking for a job in the financial industry? Do you want to develop customers in a certain region? Understanding your purpose will direct your search for the right person or people.
2. When you contact someone, introduce yourself and state your reasons for the contact. Ask for a few minutes of the person's time—a brief phone conversation or e-mail. If you set up a meeting or phone conference, be prompt and respect the person's time.
3. Ask clear questions, and listen carefully to the answers. Give the person an opportunity to give advice or voice an opinion.
4. Build on common ground— you might have attended the same college, grown up in the same region, or cheered for the same sports teams. However, don't stray far off the path of the visit.
5. Thank the person for his or her time and effort, even if the contact was not as helpful as you hoped. The contact may still be helpful at a later date. Offer to reciprocate, if appropriate.
6. When the meeting is over, be sure to respect any confidentiality implied or agreed on. Networking relationships are built on trust.

**Sources:** Lawrence K. Jones, "Practice Networking Etiquette," Career Key, accessed July 28, 2006, http://www.careerkey.org; Randall S. Hansen, "Online Discussion Group Networking Etiquette Do's and Don'ts," Quintessential Careers, accessed July 28, 2006, http://www.quintcareers.com; "Networking Etiquette," Massachusetts Institute of Technology, accessed July 28, 2006, http://web.mit.edu.

## Costs of Trading

When investors buy or sell securities through a brokerage firm, they pay a fee for the related services. Today, these costs vary widely among brokerage firms. A trade that costs less than $20 using E*Trade might cost more than $50 using Smith Barney. Often, the cost depends on what type of brokerage firm the investor uses. A full-service firm—such as NatCity—provides extensive client services and offers considerable investment advice, but charges higher fees. Brokers at full-service firms make recommendations and provide general advice to investors.

By contrast, a discount firm—such as Charles Schwab and Fidelity—charges lower fees but offers less advice and fewer services. However, most discount firms provide a variety of research tools to customers to help them make better decisions, and some offer investment-planning advice for an additional fee. All investors need to weigh the appropriate trade-off between cost, advice, and services when choosing a brokerage firm.

Online brokerage firms—such as Ameritrade—charge among the lowest fees of all brokerage firms. Investors enter buy and sell orders on their PCs or wireless devices. Most online firms also give customers access to a wide range of investment information, although they do not directly provide advice to investors. As online trading increased in popularity, most discount and full-service brokerage firms started offering online trading services. Merrill Lynch, for instance, now offers a wide range of online trading services. In addition, the company's 15,000 brokers—called financial advisors—now offer clients more comprehensive personal financial planning advice.[19]

## Reading the Financial News

At least four or five pages of most daily newspapers are devoted to reporting current financial news. This information is also available on countless Web sites. Much of the financial news coverage focuses on the day's securities transactions. Stocks and bonds traded on the various securities markets are listed alphabetically in the newspaper, with separate sections for each of the major markets. Information is provided on the volume of sales and the price of each security.

Today all major stock markets throughout the world quote prices in decimals. In the United States, stock prices are quoted in U.S. dollars and cents per share. In London, stock prices are quoted in pence, and in Japan they are quoted in yen.

*Stock Quotations*  To understand how to read the stock tables found in newspapers, you need to understand how to interpret the symbols in the various columns. As Figure 18.2 explains, the symbol in column 1 is the 52-week indicator. An arrow pointing up means that a stock hit its 52-week high during the day, and an arrow pointing down means that a stock hit its 52-week low. Column 2 gives the stock's highest and lowest trading prices during the past 52 weeks. Column 3 contains the abbreviation for the company's name, footnotes that provide information about the stock (*pf,* for instance, refers to preferred stock), and the stock's ticker symbol. Column 4 lists the dividend, usually an annual payment based on the last quarterly declaration. Column 5 presents the yield, the annual dividend divided by the stock's closing price.

Column 6 lists the stock's **price-earnings (P/E) ratio,** the current market price divided by the annual earnings per share. The stock's trading volume in 100-share lots is in column 7, and its highest and lowest prices for the day appear in column 8. Column 9 gives the closing price for the day, and column 10 summarizes the stock's net change in price from the close of the previous trading day.

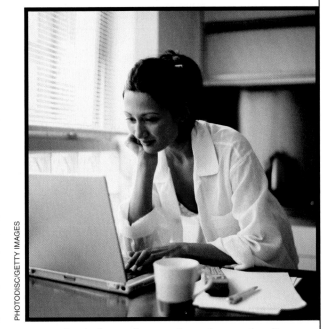

Using online brokerage firms can lower the cost of trading.

PHOTODISC/GETTY IMAGES

## How to Read Stock Quote Tables

**Figure 18.2**

| 52-Weeks | | Stock | Sym | Div | Yld % | PE | Vol (100s) | High | Low | Close | Net Chg |
|---|---|---|---|---|---|---|---|---|---|---|---|
| High | Low | | | | | | | | | | |
| $50^{70}$ | $29^{45}$ | AAAComp | AAC | 1.00 | 2.00 | 20 | 15800 | $50^{70}$ | $49^{50}$ | $50^{00}$ | + 50 |
| $30^{00}$ | $14^{00}$ | AAElec | AAE | | ... | 26 | 510 | $22^{00}$ | $19^{45}$ | $21^{06}$ | $-1^{34}$ |
| $78^{23}$ | $65^{00}$ | AaronInc. | AAI | .25 | .38 | 17 | 890 | $66^{56}$ | $65^{00}$ | $65^{00}$ | $-1^{78}$ |
| $51^{55}$ | $48^{00}$ | AaronInc. pf. | | 3.50 | 7.00 | ... | 54 | $50^{10}$ | $49^{75}$ | $50^{00}$ | + 05 |

① **52-Week Indicators:** ↑ = Hit 52-week high during the day. ↓ = Hit 52-week low.

② **52-Week High/Low:** Highest and lowest per-share trading prices in the past 52 weeks, adjusted for splits (dollars and cents—78.$^{23}$ means $78.23 per share).

③ **Stock, Sym, and Footnotes:** The company's name abbreviated. A capital letter usually means a new word. AAA-Comp, for example, is AAA Computer. The stock ticker symbol is expressed in capital letters. For AAA Computer, it is AAC. Stock footnotes include the following: **n**—new issue, **pf**—preferred stock, **rt**—rights, **s**—stock split within the past 52 weeks, **wi**—when issued, **wt**—warrant, **x**—ex-dividend.

④ **Div:** Dividends are usually annual payments based on the most recent quarterly declaration.

AAA Computer, for instance, declared a dividend of $0.25 per share in the most recent quarter.

⑤ **Yld %:** Percentage return from a dividend based on the stock's closing price.

⑥ **PE:** Price/earnings ratio, calculated by taking the last closing price of the stock and dividing it by the earnings per share for the past fiscal year.

⑦ **Vol:** Trading volume in 100-share lots. A listing of 510 means that 51,000 traded during the day. A number preceded by **z** is the actual number of shares traded.

⑧ **High/Low:** The high and low for the day (dollars and cents).

⑨ **Close:** Closing price (dollars and cents).

⑩ **Net Chg:** Change in price from the close of the previous trading day.

**Figure**

18.3 How to Read Bond Quote Tables

① **Bond:** Abbreviation of company name.

② **Annual Interest Rate:** Annual percentage rate of interest specified on the bond certificate.

③ **Maturity Date:** Year in which the bond matures and the issuer repays the face value of each bond.

④ **Cur Yld:** Annual interest payment divided by current price; **cv** means a convertible bond.

⑤ **Vol:** Number of bonds traded during the day.

| ① ② ③ Bond | ④ Cur Yld | ⑤ Vol | ⑥ Close | ⑦ Net Chg |
|---|---|---|---|---|
| AAA 9s20 | 7.8 | 15 | 104 3/4 | − 1 1/8 |
| ABGasElec 6.5s10 | 6.6 | 10 | 98 1/2 | + 3/4 |
| AlbertoPharm 5s15 | cv | 20 | 109 1/2 | + 1/2 |

⑥ **Close:** Closing price.

⑦ **Net Chg:** Change in the price from the close of the previous trading day.

**Bond Quotations** To learn how to read corporate bond quotations, pick a bond listed in Figure 18.3 and examine the adjacent columns of information. Most corporate bonds are issued in denominations of $1,000, so bond prices must be read a little differently from stock prices. The closing price of the first AAA bond reads 104 3/4, but this does not mean $104.75. Because bond prices are quoted as a percentage of the $1,000 price stated on the face of the bond, the 104 3/4 means $1,047.50.

The notation following the bond name—such as 6.5s10 in the case of AB Gas and Electric—indicates the annual interest rate stated on the bond certificate, 6.5 percent, and the maturity date of 2010. The *s* means that the bonds pays half of its annual interest every six months, so the investor would receive $32.50 every six months. The current yield for the AB Gas and Electric bond is 6.6 percent, slightly more than the 6.5 percent interest rate because the bond is selling for slightly less than $1,000. The price of a bond rises and falls to keep the current yield in line with market interest rates. The *cv* notation means that the bond is convertible.

The next column indicates the total trading volume for the day. The volume of 15 listed for the AAA bond means that $15,000 worth of bonds were traded. The closing bond price is listed next, followed by the change in price since the previous day's closing price.

## Stock Indexes

A feature of most financial news reports is the report of current stock indexes or averages. The most familiar is the *Dow Jones Average* (or *Dow*). Two other widely reported indexes on U.S. stocks are the Standard & Poor's 500 and Nasdaq Composite indexes. In addition, there are numerous indexes on foreign stocks, including the DAX (Germany); the FT-100, or "Footsie" (London); and the Nikkei (Tokyo). All of these indexes have been developed to reflect the general activity of specific stock markets.

While several Dow Jones indexes exist, the most widely followed is the so-called *Dow Jones Industrial Average,* consisting of 30 stocks of large, well-known companies. The S&P 500 is made up of 500 stocks, including industrial, financial, utility, and transportation stocks, and is considered a broader measure of overall stock market activity than the Dow. The Nasdaq Composite index consists of all the approximately 5,000 stocks that trade on the Nasdaq Stock Market. Because technology companies—such as Oracle and Intel—make up a substantial portion of the Nasdaq Stock Market, the Nasdaq Composite is considered a bellwether of the "tech" sector of the economy.

The Dow Jones Industrial Average has served as a general measure of changes in overall stock prices and a reflection of the U.S. economy since it was developed by Charles Dow, the original editor of the *Wall Street Journal,* in 1884. The term *industrial* is somewhat of a misnomer today, because the index now combines industrial corporations such as Alcoa, Boeing, General Motors, and United Technologies with such nonindustrial firms as American Express, Citigroup, Home Depot, and Walt Disney.

Periodic changes in the Dow reflect changes in the U.S. economy and composition of the stock market. In fact, General Electric is the only original member of the Dow industrials that remains in the index today. In the most recent changes, American International Group, Pfizer, and Verizon Communications were added and AT&T, Eastman Kodak, and International Paper were dropped from the Dow.

# MUTUAL FUNDS AND EXCHANGE-TRADED FUNDS

Many investors choose to invest through mutual funds or exchange-traded funds (ETFs). **Mutual funds** are financial institutions that pool money from purchasers of their shares and use it to acquire diversified portfolios of securities consistent with their stated investment objectives. While mutual funds and exchange-traded funds have similarities, important differences distinguish the two. Let's examine each.

## Mutual Funds

Investors who buy shares of a mutual fund become part owners of a large number of securities, thereby lessening their individual risk. Mutual funds also allow investors to purchase part of a diversified portfolio of securities for a relatively small investment, $250 to $3,000 in most cases. Mutual funds are managed by experienced investment professionals whose careers are based on success in analyzing the securities markets and choosing the right mix of securities for their funds. Mutual fund ads often stress performance or highlight the fund's investment philosophy. Most mutual funds are part of mutual families, a number of different funds sponsored by the same organization. The largest mutual fund families in the United States include Dreyfus, Fidelity, Janus, T. Rowe Price, and Vanguard.

Mutual funds have become extremely popular in recent years. Today mutual fund assets exceed $8 trillion. The number of American households owning mutual fund shares has increased from less than 5 million in 1980 to close to 55 million. Mutual funds are not limited to the United States either. Mutual funds in Europe have more than $5 trillion in assets.[20]

Today's mutual fund investors choose among around 8,000 funds in the United States. Some mutual funds invest only in stocks, some invest only in bonds, and others invest in money market instruments. The approximate breakdown of mutual fund assets by stock, bond, and money market funds is shown in Figure 18.4. Most funds pursue more specific goals within these broad categories. Some stock funds concentrate on small companies; others concentrate more on the shares of larger firms. Some bond funds limit their investments to municipal bonds; other bond funds invest in only investment-grade corporate bonds.

Unlike stocks, mutual funds don't trade on stock exchanges. Investors purchase shares directly from the fund. Moreover, an investor who wishes to sell shares of a mutual fund simply sells the shares back to the fund (the technical

**mutual fund** financial institution that pools money from purchases of its shares and uses the money to acquire diversified portfolios of securities consistent with the fund's investment objectives.

**Figure**

Distribution of U.S. Mutual Fund Assets by Type of Fund  **18.4**

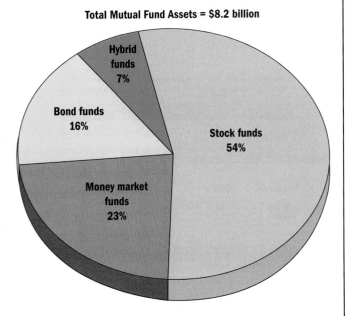

**Total Mutual Fund Assets = $8.2 billion**

Hybrid funds 7%
Bond funds 16%
Money market funds 23%
Stock funds 54%

Note: Hybrid funds invest in both stocks and bonds.

**Source:** "Trends in Mutual Fund Investing," Investment Company Institute, accessed July 3, 2006, http://www.ici.org.

## Figure
### 18.5 How to Read Mutual Fund Tables

| Issuer | NAV | Net Chg | YTD % ret |
|---|---|---|---|
| Zardoz Funds: | | | |
| AggreGro | 34.45 | −0.37 | +3.5 |
| Gro | 55.09 | −0.45 | +1.8 |
| GroInc | 20.17 | +0.05 | +6.9 |

(1) **Issuer:** Financial organization issuing and managing the mutual fund. Under the Zardoz family of funds are the different funds developed for investors with different objectives.

(2) **NAV:** Net asset value. Market value of fund's assets divided by the number of outstanding shares. Also the purchase price for no-load funds. (Load funds assess a sales charge on top of the NAV.)

(3) **Net Chg:** The change in NAV from the previous day's close.

(4) **YTD % ret:** The fund's total return for the year to date, from December 31 of the previous year. The percentage return assumes that all cash distributions were reinvested.

term is *redemption of shares*). Consequently, the size of a mutual fund, and the number of shares outstanding, can change daily. Another important feature of mutual funds is how investment returns are taxed. Mutual funds themselves don't pay taxes on investment profits (dividends, interest payments, or realized capital gains). Instead, the fund passes the profits to shareholders in the form of cash distributions. Shareholders then pay any taxes due.

A number of mutual funds have been developed for investors who want their religious or personal philosophies reflected in the management of the fund. For instance, there are funds designed for Catholics, conservative Christians, Lutherans, Mennonites, and Muslims. All attempt to follow investment philosophies that don't conflict with their religious teachings. Certain Muslim funds, for instance, don't invest in bank stocks because banks charge interest, which some believe is contrary to Islamic teachings. So-called *socially responsible mutual funds* limit their investments to companies meeting certain standards in areas such as environmental protection, ethical behavior, and labor relations. The Calvert Fund and the Domini Fund are both examples of socially responsible mutual funds.

Reading mutual fund tables is a relatively simple task. The first two columns in Figure 18.5 list the organization issuing and managing the fund, the different types of funds offered for investors, and footnotes. The NAV column lists the fund's net asset value (the market value of fund assets divided by the number of outstanding shares), the price at which investors can buy shares if the fund is a no-load fund. Purchasers of shares of load funds pay a fee called a *load charge* on top of the NAV. The net change column shows gains or losses in the NAV from the previous day's close. The figures in the last column, the year-to-date percentage return, indicate each funds' total return from the beginning of the year.

Spiders are examples of exchange-traded funds that track the S&P 500 index.

USED WITH PERMISSION. INVESTOPEDIA, INC.

## Exchange-Traded Funds

A relatively new investment option is the **exchange-traded fund** (or **ETF**). As described in the "Hit and Miss" feature, an ETF is similar to a mutual fund in that it raises funds by selling shares to investors and then uses those funds to purchase a portfolio of securities. Unlike mutual funds, however, an ETF sells a fixed number of shares to investors in what is effectively an initial public offering. Then ETF shares trade on stock exchanges much like shares of individual companies. Most ETFs are sponsored by investment companies and other financial institutions. ETFs have grown rapidly since the first one was introduced in 1993, and today there are close to 200 ETFs with total assets of around $250 billion.[21]

# HIT & MISS

## Investors Get Their Hands on Spiders and Diamonds

If "spiders and diamonds" sounds to you like the title of a new CD, check the financial pages of your newspaper. There's a new type of investment on the market called *exchange-traded funds (ETF)*, and investors have been scooping them up at a rapid pace. ETFs are funds that are listed and traded like equity investments. Like index mutual funds, they track the indexes of stocks, bonds, or other assets, but they are priced several times a day rather than just once, at the close of the market. In addition, their annual operating fees are usually lower than those of traditional mutual funds, and their tax liability is less. Where do the spiders and diamonds come in? Spiders are ETFs that track the Standard & Poor's 500 index, while diamonds are those that track the Dow 30.

ETFs have become so popular in the United States that they now account for about 25 percent of U.S. trading volume in stocks. In Europe, they represent just 1 percent. Still, U.S. investors are using ETFs to get into a global market because they work as a kind of shortcut. "Investors are increasingly using ETFs to gain exposure to international benchmarks," explains a global ETF strategist for Morgan Stanley. As the jobs of portfolio managers increase in complexity, they may not have the time or resources to enter each market in each country, so they turn to ETFs.

As with any investment, ETFs have both benefits and drawbacks. Because they are a newer type of investment, long-term results won't be known for a while. Because of their complexity, ETFs may be more difficult for the average individual investor to understand. And firms that are interested in getting into the market may have trouble because the number of indexes is limited—they must be linked to Dow Jones, S&P, Morgan Stanley Composite, or the like. With each purchase or sale, the investor must pay a broker's commission, which is why ETFs work best for investors who want to buy and hold them for a period of time. Finally, investors must remember that ETFs aren't fail-safe; they are vulnerable to the ups and downs of the stock market. They may sparkle like a diamond or bite like a spider.

### Questions for Critical Thinking

1. For what type of investor would an ETF work best? Why?
2. What might be the benefits and drawbacks of using an ETF to enter an international market?

**Sources:** Matt Ackermann, "ETF Sales Grow Rapidly as Sellers Dwindle," *Financial-Planning.com*, accessed August 16, 2006, http://www.financial-planning.com; Carla Fried, "Exchange-Traded Funds, in a Rainbow of Choices," *New York Times*, accessed July 28, 2006, http://www.nytimes.com; Susan Morris, "Exchange-Traded Funds Still Going Strong," *Pittsburgh Tribune-Review*, accessed July 28, 2006, http://www.pittsburghlive.com; M. Stanely, "Global ETF Trading Volume Surges in H1" Yahoo! News, accessed July 18, 2005, http://news.yahoo.com.

---

Another characteristic of ETFs is the fact that most are not actively managed, unlike the typical mutual fund. Rather, the ETF is designed to track a well-known stock or bond index, such as the Dow or the S&P 500. As the index rises or falls, so does the price of the ETF's shares. Dividends or interest payments are passed through to ETF shareholders on a prorated basis.

Exchange-traded funds appeal to many investors for two reasons. First, shareholders of ETFs are charged little, if anything, for annual operating expenses. By contrast, the typical stock mutual fund charges shareholders around 1.5 percent of the net asset value each year to pay for annual operating expenses. Operating expenses are paid before investment income is distributed to shareholders. Second, for some investors ETFs are more tax efficient. Because the typical ETF doesn't trade (buy or sell securities) very often, they don't generate a lot of taxable capital gains. Mutual funds, by contrast, usually trade frequently and generate more capital gains that are passed on to shareholders in the form of taxable distributions.

## assessment check

1. What is a mutual fund? Why are mutual funds popular investments?
2. Explain how an exchange-traded fund differs from a mutual fund.

# LEGAL AND ETHICAL ISSUES IN SECURITIES TRADING

As the number of Americans owning securities has increased, so have concerns about illegal and unethical trading practices. Practices such as churning (excessive trading), giving misleading investment advice to clients, conflicts of interest, insider trading, disclosing false information, and outright fraud are just some of the practices that concern investors, the securities industry, and government regulators. Government laws and regulations, as well as industry self-regulation, are designed to protect investors.

## Government Regulation of the Securities Markets

Regulation of U.S. securities markets is primarily a function of the federal government, although states also regulate the securities markets. Federal regulation grew out of various trading abuses during the 1920s. During the Great Depression, in an attempt to restore confidence and stability in the financial markets after the 1929 stock market crash, Congress passed a series of landmark legislative acts that have formed the basis of federal securities regulation ever since.

As noted in Chapter 16, the U.S. Securities and Exchange Commission (SEC), created in 1934, is the principal federal regulatory overseer of the securities markets. The SEC's mission is to administer securities laws and protect investors in public securities transactions. The SEC has broad enforcement power. It can pursue civil action against individuals and corporations, but actions requiring criminal proceedings are referred to the U.S. Justice Department. For instance, the SEC recently settled civil fraud charges against a former columnist for the popular investment Web site CBS MarketWatch.com. According to the SEC, the columnist made more than $400,000 by buying shares of companies and then writing highly favorable stories about the companies. After the prices of the shares rose—in part based on his recommendations—the individual quickly sold his shares.[22] The SEC argued that by not disclosing that he held a position in the stocks he was recommending, the columnist was committing securities fraud.

The SEC requires that virtually all new public issues of corporate securities be registered. Before offering securities for sale, an issuer must file a registration statement with the SEC. As part of the registration process for a new security issue, the issuer must prepare a *prospectus*. The typical prospectus gives a fairly detailed description of the company issuing the securities, including financial data, products, research and development projects, and pending litigation. It also describes the stock or bond issue and underwriting agreement in detail. The registration process seeks to guarantee **full and fair disclosure.** The SEC does not rule on the investment merits of a registered security. It is concerned only that an issuer gives investors enough information to make their own informed decisions.

**full and fair disclosure** requirement that investors should be told all relevant information by stock or bond issuers so they can make informed decisions.

Besides primary market registration requirements, SEC regulation extends to the secondary markets as well, keeping tabs on trading activity to make sure it is fair to all participants. Every securities exchange, including Nasdaq, must by law follow a set of trading rules that have been approved by the SEC. In addition, the *Market Reform Act* of 1990 gave the SEC emergency authority to halt trading and restrict practices such as program trading (when computer systems are programmed to buy or sell securities if certain conditions arise) during periods of extreme volatility.

**insider trading** use of material, nonpublic information to make investor profits.

One area to which the SEC pays particular attention is so-called insider trading. **Insider trading** is defined as the use of material nonpublic information about a company to make investment profits. Examples of material nonpublic information include a pending merger or a major oil discovery. The SEC's definition of insider trading goes beyond corporate insiders—people such as the company's officers and directors. It includes lawyers, accountants, investment bankers, and even reporters—anyone who uses nonpublic information to profit in the stock market at the expense of ordinary investors. In a recent case, the SEC filed complaints against several individuals who, it claims, had advance knowledge of the acquisition of Reebok by German footwear company Adidas. The SEC alleges that these individuals purchased Reebok stock before the acquisition announcement was made public.[23] While some actions or communications are clearly insider trading, others are more ambiguous. Consequently, all employees of public companies have to be mindful of what is and isn't permitted.

**Regulation FD** requires firms to share information with all investors at the same time. It prohibits selective disclosure of information by companies to favored investment firms. Clients of these firms often received the information sooner than other investors. The SEC recently settled charges against Flowserve Corporation—an oil services firm—and two of its executives. The complaint alleged that a private meeting Flowserve held with security analysts in which future company earnings were discussed violated Regulation FD.[24]

Securities laws also require every public corporation to file several reports each year with the SEC; the contents of these reports become public information. The best known, of course, is the annual report. Public corporations prepare annual reports for their shareholders, and they file another report containing essentially the same information, Form 10-K, with the SEC. The SEC requires additional reports each time certain company officers and directors buy or sell a company's stock for their own accounts (Form 4) or anytime an investor accumulates more than 5 percent of a company's outstanding stock (Form 13-d). All of these reports are available for viewing and download at the Free Edgar Web site (http://www.freeedgar.com). As we discussed in Chapter 16, the Sarbanes-Oxley Act increased the reporting requirements of public companies. Not surprisingly, complaints over the escalating cost of SEC-required reports has increased in recent years. The "Solving an Ethical Controversy" feature debates whether it is time to rethink the reporting requirements of public companies.

## Industry Self-Regulation

The securities markets are also heavily self-regulated by professional associations and the major financial markets. The securities industry recognizes that rules and regulations designed to ensure fair and orderly markets promote investor confidence to the benefit of all participants. Two examples of self-regulation are the rules of conduct established by the various professional organizations and the market surveillance techniques used by the major securities markets.

**Professional Rules of Conduct**   Prodded initially by federal legislation, the National Association of Securities Dealers (NASD) established and periodically updates rules of conduct for members (both individuals and firms). These rules try to ensure that brokers perform their basic functions honestly and fairly, under constant supervision. Failure to adhere to rules of conduct can result in disciplinary actions. The NASD also established a formal arbitration procedure through which investors can attempt to resolve disputes with brokers without litigation.

**Market Surveillance**   All securities markets use a variety of techniques to spot possible violations of trading rules or securities laws. For example, the NYSE continuously monitors trading activity throughout the trading day. A key technical tool used by the NYSE is called Stock Watch, an electronic monitoring system that flags unusual price and volume activity. The NYSE then seeks explanations for unusual activity from the member firms and companies involved. In addition, all market participants must keep detailed records of every aspect of every trade (called an *audit trail*). The NYSE's enforcement division may impose a variety of penalties on members for rule violations. In addition, the exchange turns over evidence to the

# SARBANES-OXLEY: TOO FAR OR JUST ABOUT RIGHT?

*Many consider the Sarbanes-Oxley Act the largest change in corporate regulations since the 1930s. Passed in response to accounting scandals of the early 21st century, the law known in the business world as SOX was designed to protect the stakeholders in a corporation from inadequate and unethical documentation of finances by management.*

No one would argue with the good intentions of SOX, but it seems that the hardest hit are the smallest companies, who may spend more than $1 million to implement the new accounting law.

Do the benefits of implementing changes mandated by the Sarbanes-Oxley Act outweigh the hardships for some companies?

## PRO

1. "Sarbanes-Oxley has recognized fairness toward shareholders—that a company is not run just for the benefit of management," says Ron Weinberg, chairman and CEO of a medium-sized firm.
2. Sarbanes-Oxley has raised the standards for all company directors. "Finding qualified directors has become a new growth indus-

try in the recruiting world," remarks one legal expert.

## CON

1. "Criminals find ways to take advantage of whatever system exists," argues Ted Frank, president of Axentis LLC, which makes software that helps companies comply with the new law.
2. The initial costs of compliance with SOX can be hard to bear. It "took us from making money to losing money," says Richard Leone of RTI International Metals Inc.

## Summary

Sarbanes-Oxley has forced public companies to examine their boards of directors for any conflicts of interest and to rethink many of their financial practices. In doing so, many

believe that the law has helped rebuild investor confidence in the stock market. But others say it is too early to claim results. "The jury is still out as to whether the internal control review processes are a cost-effective way to improve investor confidence," notes one CFO.

**Sources:** Barbara Hagenbaugh and Matt Krantz, "New Accounting Rules Raise Price of Audits," *USA Today,* accessed July 28, 2006, http://www.usatoday.com; Steven Martin, "Gaining Strength from Sarbox," *Information Week,* accessed July 28, 2006, http://www.informationweek.com; Alison Grant and Mary Vanac, "The Hefty Costs of Compliance," *Cleveland Plain Dealer,* accessed July 28, 2006, http://www.cleveland.com/plaindealer.

solving an **ETHICAL** controversy

**assessment check**

1. Is securities regulation primarily a state or federal responsibility? When was the SEC created?
2. Define insider trading.

SEC for further action if it believes that violations of federal securities laws may have occurred. In one recent case, the NYSE fined Merrill Lynch $10 million for various violations of exchange rules regarding the timely delivery of documents to clients, improper record keeping, and other actions inconsistent with proper business practices.[25]

# WHAT'S AHEAD

*Contemporary Business* concludes with three appendixes. Appendix A examines risk management and insurance. It discusses the concept of risk, alternative ways of dealing with risk, and various kinds of insurance available for businesses and individuals. Appendix B discusses some of the important components of personal financial planning such as budgeting, credit, and retirement planning. Finally, Appendix C describes how to write a business plan.

### 1 Distinguish between the primary market for securities and the secondary market.

The primary market for securities serves businesses and governments that want to sell new security issues to raise funds. Securities are sold in the primary market either through an open auction or via a process called underwriting. The secondary market handles transactions of previously issued securities between investors. The business or government that issued the security is not directly involved in secondary market transactions. In terms of the dollar value of trading volume, the secondary market is about four times as large as the primary market.

### Assessment Check Answers

**1.1 Distinguish between the primary and secondary markets for securities. Is the primary market or secondary market larger?**

In the primary market, securities are sold to investors for the first time, and the issuing corporation or government receives the proceeds from the sale. The secondary market involves trades between investors of previously issued securities. The secondary market is far larger than the primary market.

**1.2 Explain the two ways in which securities are sold in the primary market.**

The two ways in which securities are sold in the primary market are in open auctions and through a process called underwriting. The U.S. Treasury sells securities through open auctions. It announces before the auction what types of securities it wants to sell and solicits bids from investors. The higher the bid, the lower the interest rate. Corporate and municipal securities are sold via underwriting. The securities are sold to a specialized investment firm called an investment banker, which then sells the securities to investors. Investment bankers charge for their services by paying the issuer less than they charge investors. Investment bankers are specialists in the securities markets, and issuers find it more efficient and easier to use the services of investment bankers.

### 2 Compare money market instruments, bonds, and common stock, and explain why particular investors might prefer each type of security.

Money market instruments and bonds are debt instruments. Money market instruments are short-term debt securities and tend to be low-risk securities. Bonds are longer-term debt securities and pay a fixed amount of interest each year. Bonds are sold by the U.S. Treasury (government bonds), state and local governments (municipal bonds), and corporations. Financial institutions such as Fannie Mae and Freddie Mac sell mortgage pass-through securities—bonds backed by a self-liquidating pool of mortgage loans. Most municipal and corporate bonds have risk-based ratings. Common stock represents ownership in corporations. Common stockholders have voting rights and a residual claim on the firm's assets.

### Assessment Check Answers

**2.1 Explain the difference between a money market instrument and a bond.**

All money market instruments mature within one year from the date of issue. Bonds mature anywhere from 2 to 30 years from the day of issue.

**2.2 What are the two types of bonds issued by state and local governments? Describe the difference between a secured and unsecured bond.**

The two types of bonds issued by state and local governments are general obligation bonds and revenue bonds. General obligation bonds can be issued only by governmental units that have taxing authority (such as cities or states) and are backed by the full faith and credit of the state in which they are issued. Revenue bonds are issued to pay for public projects that generate revenue, such as toll roads. Only revenue from the project is used to pay interest and to repay principal. A secured bond is backed by specific collateral. An unsecured bond is backed only by the financial reputation of the issuer.

**2.3 Discuss the major investment characteristics of common stock.**

Common stock represents ownership claims in firms. Common stockholders are often paid cash dividends, but the amount of dividends varies widely from stock to stock. However, the major motivation for buying common stock is expected price appreciation. As a firm's profits grow, so too should the value of its stock.

### 3 Identify the five basic objectives of investors and the types of securities most likely to help them reach each objective.

The five basic objectives are growth in capital, stability of principal, liquidity, current income, and growth in income. Common stocks are the most likely to meet the objectives of growth in capital and growth in income. Historically, common-stock investments have had far higher returns on average than either bonds or money market instruments. Common-stock dividends have also generally risen over time. Money market instruments are the most stable in price and rarely lose value. Money market instruments are also the most liquid security. Bonds tend to provide the highest current income of any security. Investment income from government bonds, corporate bonds, common stocks, and realized capital gains are usually taxed at the federal level but often at different rates. Interest income from municipal bonds is exempt from federal income taxes but may be subject to state income taxes.

## Assessment Check Answers

### 3.1 Who purchases securities?
Securities are purchased by institutions—such as pension funds and life insurance companies—and individuals. Many individuals purchase securities indirectly through institutions.

### 3.2 What are the five motivations for investing? On which of the five motivations for investment do common stocks rank highest?
The five motivations are growth in capital, stability of principal, liquidity, current income, and growth in income. Common stocks have historically ranked highest in growth in capital and growth in income.

### 3.3 Discuss the tax implications of investing. Are all sources of investment returns taxed equally?
Income received from government and corporate bonds is taxed as ordinary income. Common-stock dividends, for most individuals, are taxed at a lower rate, as are realized capital gains, which result when a security is sold for more than its purchase price.

### 4 Describe the characteristics of the major stock exchanges.
Exchanges exist throughout the world. The two largest—the New York Stock Exchange and Nasdaq—are located in the United States. The NYSE is larger, measured in terms of the total value of stock traded. Larger and better-known companies dominate the NYSE. Buy and sell orders are transmitted to the trading floor for execution. The Nasdaq Stock Market is an electronic market in which buy and sell orders are entered into a computerized communication system for execution. Most of the world's major stock markets today use similar electronic trading systems. Electronic communication networks are electronic markets in which buyers and sellers trade directly without the use of a specialist or market maker.

## Assessment Check Answers

### 4.1 Compare and contrast the NYSE and Nasdaq stock markets.
The NYSE still maintains a trading floor, and all trading takes place on the floor, even though the trading process has become much more automated in recent years. Larger, better-known companies tend to be listed on the NYSE. The Nasdaq Stock Market is an electronic market—it is considered the world's largest intranet—and all trading takes place electronically. Nasdaq-listed stocks tend to be smaller, newer companies. Technology companies especially tend to be listed on Nasdaq. Each NYSE-listed stock has one specialist assigned to it. By contrast, each Nasdaq listed stock has at least two market makers.

### 4.2 Explain the role of specialists and market makers.
Specialists and market makers maintain an inventory of their stocks and act as buyers when no other buyers are present and sellers when no other sellers are present. This function adds liquidity to stock markets. Specialists and market makers also track unfilled limit orders.

### 4.3 What is an ECN?
*ECN* stands for *electronic communications network*. An ECN is a virtual stock market in which buyers and sellers trade with each other without the presence of a market maker or specialist.

### 5 Explain the process of buying or selling a security listed on an organized securities exchange and the information included in stock and bond quotations and stock indexes.
Investors use the services of a brokerage firm that is a member of one of the stock exchanges. After a broker receives a customer's order, it is sent electronically to the appropriate stock exchange for execution. A market order instructs the broker to obtain the best possible price, but a limit order limits the transaction price. Full-service brokers provide the most advice but charge the highest fees. Customers at discount firms and online trading firms have to make their own deci-

sions but are charged lower fees. Information in a stock quote includes the highest and lowest trading prices during the previous 52 weeks, the dividend, the dividend yield, the price/earnings ratio, the trading volume, the stock's highest and lowest prices for the day, and the closing price for that day. A bond quotation includes the maturity date and interest rate, the current yield, the trading volume, and a comparison of the day's closing price with that of the previous day. Stock indexes measure the overall direction of a particular market or particular types of stocks.

## Assessment Check Answers

**5.1 Explain the difference between a market order and a limit order.**
A market order instructs the broker to get the "best" price (lowest if buying or highest if selling). By contrast, a limit order specifies the highest price the investor will pay (if buying) or the lowest price he or she will accept (if selling).

**5.2 Distinguish between full-service and discount brokerage firms.**
Full-service firms provide order execution, record keeping, and extensive investment advice. By comparison, discount firms provide order execution and record keeping but don't necessarily provide investment advice. Most, however, give their clients access to a wide range of independent investment research so that clients can make their own investment decisions. Discount brokerage firms charge lower commissions than full-service firms.

**5.3 List some of the information contained in stock price quotations.**
Information contained in stock price quotations includes the 52-week high and low prices, the dividend, the price-to-earnings ratio, and the closing price.

**5.4 What are the two most closely followed stock market indexes?**
The two most closely followed stock market indexes are the Dow Jones Industrial Average (known as the Dow 30) and the Standard & Poor's 500 (S&P 500).

**6** **Discuss the role of mutual funds and exchange-traded funds in the securities markets.**
Mutual funds are professionally managed investment companies that own securities consistent with their overall investment objectives. Investors purchase shares of a mutual fund, which make them part owners of a diversified investment portfolio. Investors can purchase shares of mutual funds for relatively small amounts. Mutual funds have become extremely popular in recent years. More than half of all American households own mutual fund shares. Exchange-traded funds (ETFs) are sponsored by investment companies that sell a fixed number of shares and use the proceeds to buy a portfolio of securities. Shares of ETFs trade on the major stock markets and are generally unmanaged.

## Assessment Check Answers

**6.1 What is a mutual fund? Why are mutual funds popular investments?**
A mutual fund is an investment company that sells shares to investors and uses these funds to purchase securities consistent with the fund's investment objectives. Mutual funds are popular because they allow small investors to purchase a piece of a diversified portfolio of securities, thereby reducing the risk associated with holding an individual security. Most mutual funds are professionally managed.

**6.2 Explain how an exchange-traded fund differs from a mutual fund.**
An exchange-traded fund is similar to a mutual fund in that an ETF sells shares to investors and uses these funds to purchase securities. However, most ETFs sell only a fixed number of shares in an initial public offering. Afterward, shares of ETFs trade on the major stock markets like individual common stocks. In addition, most ETFs are unmanaged, and many are designed to track one of the major indexes such as the S&P 500 or Dow.

**7** **Evaluate the major features of regulations and laws designed to protect investors.**
In the United States, financial markets are regulated at both the federal and state levels. Markets are also heavily self-regulated by the financial markets and professional organizations. The chief regulatory body is the Securities and Exchange Commission. It sets forth a number of requirements for both primary and secondary market activity, prohibiting a number of practices, including insider trading. The SEC also requires public companies to disclose financial information regularly. Professional organizations and the securities markets also have rules and procedures that all members must follow.

## Assessment Check Answers

**7.1 Is securities regulation primarily a state or federal responsibility? When was the SEC created?**
In the U.S., securities regulation is primarily a federal responsibility, although the states do have some regulatory authority. The SEC (Securities & Exchange Commission) was created in the 1930s.

**7.2 Define *insider trading*.**
Insider trading is the use of material, nonpublic information to make investment profits.

## Business Terms You Need to Know

securities 576
primary market 576
secondary market 577
money market instruments 578

common stock 581
preferred stock 582
stock exchange 585
brokerage firm 587

mutual fund 591
full and fair disclosure 594
insider trading 594

## Other Important Business Terms

initial public offering (IPO) 576
investment banker 577
underwriting 577
government bond 578
municipal bond 578
secured bond 578
debenture 579

mortgage pass-through
  security 579
bond rating 579
investment-grade bond 580
junk bond 580
call provision 581
institutional investors 582

electronic communications
  network (ECN) 587
market order 587
limit order 587
price-earnings (P/E) ratio 589
exchange-traded fund (ETF) 592
Regulation FD 595

## Review Questions

1. Explain the differences between a primary market and a secondary market. In what two ways are securities sold in the primary market?
2. Outline the underwriting process. Why do corporations and state and local governments use the services of investment bankers?
3. What are the major characteristics of money market instruments? How do money market instruments differ from bonds?
4. What is the difference between a government bond and a municipal bond? What is the difference between a secured bond and an unsecured bond?
5. Explain the purpose of bond ratings. What is a junk bond?
6. What is common stock, and how does it differ from preferred stock? Over the long run, what does a company's stock price tend to follow?
7. What are the primary investment motivations or objectives? Which security best meets each objective?
8. Explain the difference between a market order and a limit order. What are the differences between full-service, discount, and online brokerage firms?

9. How does the New York Stock Exchange operate? Compare the operations of the NYSE with those of the Nasdaq stock market.
10. What is an ECN? Why did the NYSE and Nasdaq purchase the two largest ECNs?
11. Explain how a mutual fund operates. What are the benefits of investing in mutual funds?

12. What is an exchange-traded fund? How does an ETF differ from a mutual fund?
13. Define *insider trading* and cite an example. List some ways in which the securities industry is self-regulated.

## Projects and Teamwork Applications

1. Assume you just inherited $50,000 from your uncle and his will stipulates that you must invest all the money until you complete your education. Prepare an investment plan. What are your primary investment objectives? How much would you invest in money market instruments, bonds, and common stocks? Compare your results with those of a classmate.
2. Would you feel comfortable investing the $50,000 you inherited in Question 1 using a discount (or online) broker, or would you use a full-service firm? Discuss the reasons behind your choice.
3. Working with a partner, review the trading activity on the NYSE and the Nasdaq Stock Market for the past five trading days. Which market was more active? By how much did major indexes rise or fall? Which stocks were the most active? Prepare a brief report discussing your findings.
4. Assume you are considering buying shares of Lowe's or Home Depot. Describe how you would go about analyzing the stocks and deciding which, if either, you would buy.
5. Visit the Standard & Poor's Web site (http://www.standardandpoors.com) and click "Indexes" and then "S&P 500." Answer the following questions:
   a. What stocks have recently been added to the S&P 500? Which stocks did they replace?
   b. Which five stocks have the highest market values?
   c. Identify and briefly describe three other S&P indexes.

6. You've probably heard of U.S. savings bonds—you may even have received some bonds as a gift. What you may not know is that there are two different types of savings bonds. Do some research and compare and contrast the two types of savings bonds. What are their features? Their pros and cons? Assuming you were interested in buying savings bonds, which of the two do you find more attractive?
7. Go to the MSN Money Web Site (http://money central.msn.com). Click "fund screener." Assume you're investing money for retirement. Specify several investment criteria you believe are most important. Identify at least three mutual funds that best meet your criteria. Choose one of the funds and research it. Answer the following questions:
   a. What was the fund's average annual return for the past five years?
   b. How well did the fund perform relative to its peer group and relative to an index such as the S&P 500?
   c. What are the fund's ten largest holdings?
   d. Did your research change your opinion of the fund as an appropriate investment for your retirement savings? Why or why not?
8. Visit the SEC's Web site (http://www.sec.gov) and review five recent enforcement actions. How many dealt with cases of suspected insider trading? What actions did the SEC propose taking?

# Case 18.1

## The Future of the New York Stock Exchange

An investment community has existed in New York even before it was New York. When Dutch settlers arrived on the island of Manhattan in the mid-1600s, their purpose was commerce. They named their settlement New Amsterdam and set about building an economic empire. Four hundred years later, New York is a commercial powerhouse of global proportions, and many would claim that the center of this powerhouse is the New York Stock Exchange. With company listings worth $20 trillion, the NYSE has historically banked on its name and the ability of its trading floor specialists to guarantee their investors liquidity. But in the wake of tighter regulations from the Securities and Exchange Commission (SEC) and rapidly evolving technology that threatens to leave the NYSE in the dust, the exchange is poised for change.

When the SEC decided to tighten up the "trade-through" rule that links America's markets, it meant that all investors must have equal access to the best prices available on a given day. The only way to achieve this parity is electronically—something that other stock exchanges had already begun to implement. This put the NYSE—and its customers—at a disadvantage. Nasdaq and the Chicago Mercantile Exchange were already using some form of electronic trading, as were large institutional investors, who often rely on electronic communication networks (ECNs) for rapid trading. NYSE's customers began to complain.

In a radical move, the NYSE acquired Archipelago Holdings, owner of ArcaEx, a large ECN that already handled 25 percent of the trading in Nasdaq-listed shares and had recently acquired the Pacific Stock Exchange, which specializes in high-risk investments called *derivatives*. The merger means some big changes at the NYSE. First, it became a public company—it can raise a huge amount of capital, but it must also answer to shareholders. Second, it now has a way to compete for Nasdaq shares and accept listings from smaller companies that previously did not qualify for listing on the NYSE. Third, the NYSE can now participate more fully in the growing derivatives and ETF markets.

The merger seems to plant the NYSE squarely in the 21st century. But it does have its detractors. Some experts warn that the NYSE and Archipelago are like two different species and that their organizational cultures will not integrate very well. Others worry that the NYSE does not yet know how to use the trading technology used by ArcaEx. Still others point out that Nasdaq has actually acquired a better-fitting company—the electronic trading division of Instinet, which is owned by Reuters. But NYSE's entrance into the electronic trading market should step up competition, which in the long term should decrease costs for investors, speed up transactions, and even encourage more innovation—which is what commerce is all about.

### Questions for Critical Thinking

1. Describe at least two regulations that apply to NYSE's acquisition of Archipelago and its future methods of trading.
2. Do you think that the NYSE and Nasdaq will become more similar in the next few years? How might they differentiate themselves?

**Sources:** "The Cyberbuttonwood Arrives," Economist.com, accessed April 16, 2003, http://www .economist.com; Donna Block, "What NASDAQ Sees in Instinet," *Daily Deal,* accessed August, 2006, http://www .thedeal.com; Jenny Anderson, "Big Changes at the Exchanges Bring Their Self-Regulation into Question," *New York Times,* accessed July 28, 2006, http://www .nytimes.com.

# Case 18.2

## A.G. Edwards: Helping Businesses Grow

This video case appears on page 628. A recently filmed video, designed to expand and highlight the written case, is available for class use by instructors.

# The Second City Theater Continuing Case
## Managing Financial Resources: Keeping Creativity in the Money

When Second City Communications negotiates a deal with Motorola, or the Chicago Cubs, or Chicago's Steppenwolf Theatre, keeping an eye on the finances is chief financial officer Lou Carbone. Joining the company at its Toronto location in 1998, Carbone became CFO for the entire organization in 2005. He currently operates out of Second City's Chicago office as a strategist, a liaison, a treasurer, and, in his own words, "the father figure who may have to say 'no, you can't play with that toy.'" Behind a desk stacked full of project proposals, Lou Carbone manages Second City's unyielding creation of business ventures. He watches the risk-return trade-offs and designs accurate financial plans to turn concepts into reality. The reality for Lou Carbone is that a company as creative and well recognized as Second City needs a CFO with a practical disposition and an appreciation for the art of acting and the entrepreneurial spirit.

Second City has excelled as a company based on creative mission. As CFO, Lou Carbone approaches the company's lofty ambitions from a pragmatic angle. "My primary function" says Carbone, "is to ensure that there is accurate and timely financial reporting." He does this by developing financial statements with his team and distributing them regu-

larly to top management. Carbone's staff consists of four professionals: a senior accountant, a payroll administrator, a junior accountant, and the building manager. Though a small financial team, they operate as a close-knit crew, well suited for a for-profit business, functioning with a not-for-profit attitude. They have a variety of challenges. For instance, the company is stretched across North America with disparately functioning theaters. Revenue also fluctuates unpredictably throughout the year, and new projects encounter unforeseen costs. Meeting one-on-one with department heads, Lou Carbone has streamlined financial reporting within the organization to improve on past practices in which each department did its own budget. This is just one way in which Lou Carbone has helped Second City evolve financially.

Lou Carbone keeps the Second City stages lit, its actors paid, and its new ideas funded through his relationships with outside agencies. As a liaison for the comedy theater, Carbone meets with Second City's bank, lawyers, and insurance firms to ensure compliance and confirm that there are adequate reserves. Keeping a strong relationship with Second City's bank has been vital for the organization. Amid changes in revenue and struggling project starts

over the last 28 years, Second City has come across times in which bank loans have allowed it to develop as planned. Impressively, Lou Carbone and SC's financial team have maintained a strong alliance with the same bank that it has used since its start.

For all its growth and corresponding challenges, Second City remains a small business choosing to stay private for the foreseeable future. It is owned by three shareholders, two of whom are still closely involved with business operations and maintain a recognizable character throughout the organization.

Second City is clearly an unconventional business. In fact, its five theaters are structured with financial and organizational differences. Second City's Detroit stage is a franchise; Denver has been designed as a limited run to test the market; Las Vegas is a partnership. Chicago and Toronto are the only stages fully owned by the three sole investors, though Toronto operates as a separate legal entity.

Second City's financial management team must oversee all operations while paying close attention to these organizational differences. Overall, Second City's different U.S. bank accounts fuse into a whole that can be used flexibly throughout the organization. This enables Second City to fund start-up operations such as new Theatricals produced in performing arts centers with revenue garnered from mainstage ticket sales. This effort keeps the Second City mission intact across the board.

As the numbers fly around Second City and fall on the desk of Lou Carbone, putting them together to forecast and develop strategic plans is what he finds most interesting. Carbone balances available funds, needed funds, the costs of expansion, and pricing specifics to help inform the top management team about which ventures seem most reasonable. Through this analysis Second City has, for example, determined that new theater expansion should be put on hold. There won't be new Second City Theaters opening any time soon, but finding Second City's style of comedy in the business world is increasingly likely. It has seen its most significant growth in the corporate division over the past five years. Tom Yorton, president of Second City Inc., and Lou Carbone collaborate regularly in negotiations with corporate clients for SC Communications, the division of Second City that provides entertainment, training, and creative and multimedia services to businesses. Companies are looking to foster a more creative atmosphere within the workplace, and SC Communications finds itself increasingly relevant to contemporary business.

Carbone brings financial savvy to a company that is otherwise focused on creating an ideal environment for excellent acting. Yorton says, "Thank God for Lou. The fact is that none of us really have a finance background. He can help educate us to make the place run better. We're an improv theater, so we make it up as we go along. Finance is one area where you really can't make it up as you go along."

The hardest part of Lou Carbone's job isn't finding ways for Second City to increase revenue but to watch where all of it is going. With Detroit operating as a franchise, its status as a locally owned business means less exposure for Second City, and separate accounting practices present less concern for the company's home base. Second City's center, in Chicago, is busy monitoring the other operations around the country. Both Las Vegas and Denver are far enough away that accurate monitoring is a consistent dilemma. Toronto has its own two accountants, and they've been challenged by a struggling economy in their region throughout the last decade. Second City Chicago pulled from reserves and credit lines to back the operation. With so many divisions, Carbone must pay strict attention to monthly reports and annual audits.

At Second City, 40 to 50 percent of all revenue goes toward covering labor costs. Second City's profit fluctuates throughout the fiscal year as demands change, so funds must be carefully managed to meet payroll and cover fixed expenses. For example, the touring companies experience a decrease in sales over the summer, when most schools and colleges are not in full operation. Economic climate and real estate costs present consistent challenges. The company aptly chooses to rent its property, which makes a change of locations easier should its real estate needs change.

Through a small door adjacent to Second City's box office, up a staircase adorned with caricatures of SC alumni and tucked into an office overlooking the famous corner of North and Wells, Lou Carbone can be seen smiling as he wrestles with new project proposals. "I have to be the one to pull in the reins," he says. Carbone sifts through an assortment of inspired business ventures and evaluates the financial and social needs of the project. Inspired and innovative ideas are met with practical evaluation, considering all the costs involved. Perhaps the most innovative use of SC's widely used improv technique "Yes, and," comes from Lou Carbone. In a top management meeting a new idea may come up, to which Carbone must find a way to say "Yes, and . . . then we'd be out of business." Luckily, Second City has listened to its CFO, and the organization can continue to be as creative as possible.

## QUESTIONS

1. What are some of the challenges faced by Second City's CFO?
2. If Second City were to create more theaters, would you suggest franchising, partnerships, or another organizational format?
3. Would it be a sound financial decision for Second City to become a public company?
4. What is Lou Carbone's most important function at Second City? Why?

# Part 6: Launching Your Finance Career

Part 6, "Managing Financial Resources," describes the finance function in organizations. Finance deals with planning, obtaining, and managing an organization's funds to accomplish its objectives in the most effective way possible. In Chapter 17, we discussed financial plans, sources of funds, and financial institutions, such as commercial banks. In Chapter 18, we examined the structure of the financial, or securities, markets. Throughout both chapters we described the finance functions of a variety of businesses, governments, and not-for-profit organizations. As Part 6 illustrates, finance is a very diverse profession and encompasses many different occupations. According to the U.S. Department of Labor, over the next decade most finance-related occupations are expected to experience employment growth that is at least as fast as the average for all occupations. However, employment in several finance occupations is expected to grow faster than average.[1] Computers and related technology have affected the finance function significantly in recent years.

In most business schools, finance is either the most popular or second most popular major among undergraduates. Combining finance with accounting is a common double major. Those with degrees in finance also enjoy relatively high starting salaries. A recent survey found that the average starting salary for a person with an undergraduate degree in finance was more than $42,000 per year.[2]

All organizations need to obtain and manage funds, so they employ finance professionals. Financial institutions and other financial services firms employ a large percentage of finance graduates. These businesses provide important finance-related services to businesses, governments, and not-for-profit organizations. Some graduates with finance degrees take jobs with financial services firms such as Bank of America and Merrill Lynch, while others begin their careers working in the finance departments of businesses in other indus-tries such as 3M and Boeing, governments, or not-for-profit organizations. You may begin your career evaluating commercial loan applications for a bank, analyzing capital investments for a business, or helping a not-for-profit organization decide how to invest its endowment. Often finance professionals work as members of a team, advising top management. Some individuals spend their entire careers working in finance-related occupations; others use their finance experience to move into other areas of the firm. Today, the chief financial officer—the senior finance executive—holds one of the most critical jobs in any organization. In addition, the number of CEOs who began their careers in finance is growing.

Finance is a diverse, exciting profession. Here are a few of the specific occupations you might find after earning a degree in finance.

*Financial managers* prepare financial reports, direct investment activities, raise funds, and implement cash management strategies. Computer technology has significantly reduced the time needed to produce financial reports. Many financial managers spend less time preparing reports and more time analyzing financial data. All organizations employ financial managers, although roughly 30 percent of all financial managers work for financial services firms such as commercial banks and insurance companies.[3] Specific responsibilities vary with titles. For instance, credit managers oversee the firm's issuance of credit, establish standards, and monitor the collection of accounts. Cash managers control the flow of cash receipts and disbursements to meet the needs of the organization.

Most *loan officers* work for commercial banks and other financial institutions. They find potential clients and help them apply for loans. Loan officers typically specialize in commercial, consumer, or mortgage loans. In many cases, loan officers act in a sales capacity, contacting individuals and organizations about their need for funds and trying to persuade them to borrow the funds from the loan officer's institution. So loan officers often need marketing as well as finance skills.

*Security analysts* generally work for financial services firms such as Fidelity or Wachovia. Security analysts review economic data, financial statements, and other information to determine the outlook for securities such as common stocks and bonds. They make investment recommendations to individual and institutional investors. Many senior security analysts hold a CFA (Chartered Financial Analyst) designation. Obtaining a CFA requires a specific educational background, several years of related experience, and a passing grade on a comprehensive, three-stage examination.

*Portfolio managers* manage money for an individual or institutional client. Many portfolio managers work for pension funds or mutual funds for which they make investment decisions to benefit the funds' beneficiaries. Portfolio managers generally have extensive experience as financial managers or security analysts, and many are CFAs.

*Personal financial planners* help individuals make decisions in areas such as insurance, investments, and retirement planning. Personal financial planners meet with their clients, assess their needs and goals, and make recommendations. Approximately 40 percent of personal financial planners are self-employed, and many hold CFP (Certified Financial Planner) designations. Like the CFA, obtaining a CFP requires a specific educational background, related experience, and passing a comprehensive examination.

## Career Assessment Exercises in Finance

1. Assume you're interested in pursuing a career as a security analyst. You've heard that the CFA is an important designation and can help enhance your career. Visit the CFA's Web site (http://www.cfainstitute.org) to learn more about the CFA. Specifically, what are the requirements to obtain a CFA and what are the professional benefits of having a CFA?

2. Arrange for an interview with a commercial loan officer at a local bank. Ask the loan officer about his or her educational background, what a typical day is like, and what the loan officer likes and doesn't like about his or her job.

3. Ameriprise Financial offers financial planning services to individuals and organizations. Visit the firm's Web site (http://www.ameriprise.com) and click the "Careers" link. Review the material and write a brief summary of what you learned about being a personal financial planner. Does such a career interest you? Why or why not?

# Video Case Contents

## Peet's Coffee & Tea Brews Good Business

More than 40 years ago, Alfred Peet opened the door to his new shop in Berkeley, California, letting the rich scent of roasting coffee beans waft out to the sidewalk. Passersby were curious. Some couldn't resist. They came in to taste a cup of whatever was being offered. Peet had grown up in his family's coffee business in Holland. Later, he learned the tea trade in Indonesia. By the time he landed in California, he knew the best way to roast and brew both beverages. An entrepreneur at heart, he decided he could offer the very best cup of coffee or tea to customers, so he founded his own business. He chose Berkeley, where a collection of European-style shops and bistros serving fresh cheeses and breads, along with other gourmet delicacies, was beginning to gain popularity with consumers. The original Peet's location—at the corner of Vine and Walnut—is still there, serving up a variety of fresh, deep-roasted coffees, hand-selected teas, and bags of coffee beans ready to be ground and brewed at home.

Today, Peet's operates 111 retail stores in California, Illinois, Massachusetts, Oregon, and Washington. In addition, consumers can find Peet's products at Safeway, Supervalu, Ralphs, and Whole Foods Markets. Loyal fans who don't want to leave their homes in search of Peet's products can visit the firm's Web site. There they can order their favorites through the Home Delivery program, learn how to brew the perfect cup, find out where their coffee beans were grown, and discover how their tea leaves were selected. Customer service representatives are always available to answer questions or help with ordering. Finally, Peet's provides service to offices, restaurants, and food service distributors. "No matter where you buy Peet's, we make sure that all of our coffee [and tea] meets our exceptional standards for quality and freshness," promises the company's Web site.

To control its steady growth, Peet's executives must manage a variety of relationships—with growers who supply coffee beans and tea leaves, with the firm's own employees, with retailers and restaurant owners, with distributors, and with consumers. Peet's works closely with small and cooperative growers in Mexico, Central America, and Africa, where it believes it can obtain the highest-quality beans and leaves. As part of its mission, Peet's also develops programs to improve the lives of people who live in these communities, through education and economic growth. Peet's relationship with its customers is legendary—many have been enjoying Peet's coffees and teas for decades, passing the tradition along to children and grandchildren. The original Peet's fans, who visited the Berkeley shop every morning for their cup of coffee and conversation, were dubbed "Peetniks" (a takeoff on the word *beatnik*) by a Berkeley policeman—and the nickname stuck. Eventually, the nickname evolved to refer to Peet's employees, who are as passionate about their products as the original Peetniks themselves.

Peet's views its workforce as one of its most valuable resources—it is this group of people who roasts the coffee beans, tastes the tea, and packs and ships it to customers across the country. Roasters know exactly what Peet's proprietary blends should taste like—a knowledge base that Peet's believes cannot be duplicated by any other method. "Many coffee companies use computers to roast their coffees," explains the Web site. "But we believe no computer can roast beans like a skilled roaster can." Because it takes skill and experience to achieve this level of expertise, Peet's asks for a ten-year employment commitment from its roasters—an unusual request in an economy in which employers and employees typically part ways after much shorter periods of time. But Peet's believes it takes at least three or four years to learn the craft, and senior master roaster John Weaver points out that "a roaster's education is a continuous, ceaselessly fascinating process."

While nothing replaces the knowledge and experience of a worker, Peet's does rely on technology for some of its operations. Recently, the firm installed a high-speed Flo-Shipper system, which allows Peet's to ship coffee the same day it is roasted. The system sorts and routes verified parcels to the appropriate shipping lane, confirms data on bar code labels, and visually identifies any problems. This system has cut the time to fulfill orders in half—from two work shifts to one. What this means is simple: if you order a pound of Peet's coffee beans, they'll be roasted and shipped to you the same day. You may not hear the delivery truck driving up your street, but you might smell the fresh scent of coffee on its way to your door.

### Questions for Critical Thinking

1. In what ways was Alfred Peet an entrepreneur?
2. Peet's was founded during the marketing era. Today it operates in the relationship era. Describe its focus during each era.
3. Describe the employer-employee partnership at Peet's.
4. Would you characterize Peet's as an admired company? Why or why not?

**Sources:** Peet's Web site, accessed August 8, 2006, http://www.peets.com; "Peet's Coffee & Tea, Inc.," Google Finance Profile, accessed August 8, 2006, http://finance .google.com; Lori Corbin, "Peet's Coffee & Tea Tutorials," KABC-TV Los Angeles, accessed August 8, 2006, http://
abclocal.go.com; "National Coffee Roaster Streamlines B2C Fulfillment System," *FloStor Engineering*, accessed August 8, 2006, http://www.floStor.com; "Peet's Coffee & Tea Celebrates 40 Years of Craftsmanship," *Badgett's Coffee eJournal*, accesssed August 8, 2006, http://www.aboutcoffee.net.

# Video Case 2.2

## Ford Turns Green with Clean Energy

When the first Ford vehicles rolled off Henry Ford's pioneering assembly line, they were all black. Consumers didn't care—they wouldn't have thought of a car in another color. They also didn't worry about details such as gasoline emissions, as those Model T's and Model A's bounced along dirt roads spewing exhaust. They were more concerned about breakdowns, flat tires, and collisions with horse-drawn wagons.

Today, however, consumers are educated about fuels, pollution, and a responsibility to the environment. And Ford Motor Company is concerned about them, too. Consumers can now buy Ford trucks and cars in all kinds of colors. But perhaps the most innovative—and most important—color isn't the paint chip chosen for the exterior of a vehicle. Instead, it's the "green" that refers to Ford's new clean engines, including the gas-electric hybrid Escape, an SUV designed for consumers who want fuel efficiency without giving up safety, convenience, and style.

The Escape is a full hybrid, meaning that it can run on either its gasoline engine or its electric motor, with a fuel economy of 33 mpg or above in the city and 29 mpg on the highway (depending on the model). In addition, the Escape produces 97 percent less hydrocarbon and nitrogen oxide emissions than other vehicles that meet the current national emissions standards. So far, the new Escape has been a huge success—consumers have been willing to wait months to receive one after placing an order. "When we began work on an Escape Hybrid, we made a commitment to delivering a no-compromise, authentic Ford SUV that's fun to drive, spacious, comfortable and capable, with substantially lower fuel use and emissions," reports Mary Ann Wright, director of Sustainable Mobility Technologies and Hybrid Programs for Ford. "Mission accomplished! It's wonderful to see the vehicle we originally envisioned resonating so strongly with customers."

Ford Motor Company takes its role in protecting the environment and other aspects of social responsibility seriously. While the Escape receives accolades from the public and the industry—it was named "Truck of the Year" at a recent international auto show—Ford continues to design other types of clean engines, including the Ford Focus PZEV (Partial Zero Emissions Vehicle). A PZEV contains a gasoline-powered engine that is "so clean that the exhaust coming [directly] out of the tailpipe is often cleaner than freeway air," says the company. Still, the Focus delivers 130 horsepower—so consumers lose nothing in terms of power and gain by eliminating pollution. Ford doesn't manufacture only clean engines; it also produces a Continuously Variable Transmission (CVT), which allows the engine to operate at its most efficient speed, resulting in greater fuel economy. The CVT also provides a smoother ride than a traditional transmission, because it offers more gear ratios. The Freestyle, Mercury, Five Hundred, and Montego models contain CVTs.

Not much would be accomplished if the manufacturing processes for these new, cleaner engines continued to dump pollutants into the environment. Ford recently redesigned its Dearborn truck plant near Detroit to implement a range of innovations in "green" manufacturing. The plant has a "living" roof that is home to ten acres of plants called sedum, which help prevent stormwater runoff, improve the air quality around the plant by trapping dust and dirt, absorb carbon dioxide and release oxygen, and insulate the building. Sedum also provides a rich habitat for birds, insects, and butterflies; because it insulates the building, Ford uses less energy to heat and cool the manufacturing plant. Inside, Ford scientists have developed a Fumes-to-Fuel technology, which uses fumes from truck paint to power fuel cells, producing electricity. "It's a living laboratory," says Andy Acho, worldwide director of Environmental Outreach

& Strategy for Ford. "As we learn more, we'll find places to apply these technical and environmental initiatives." Consumers are encouraged to visit the plant to view for themselves Ford's environmental innovations.

Ford's environmental initiatives aren't limited to the United States. In Sweden, a Ford dealership is experimenting with the GreenZone project, an alliance with McDonald's and Statoil that encompasses three buildings—a car dealership, a restaurant, and a fuel station. The idea of GreenZone is to reduce energy requirements among the three businesses by installing lantern skylights, redirecting excess heat (say, from the restaurant kitchen to the car showroom), and applying the sedum technology for climate control and water circulation.

Ford continues to establish and take part in a wide range of sustainable energy projects around the world. Once a leader in producing black cars, Ford is now a leader in producing just about anything green.

**Questions for Critical Thinking**

1. How might Ford's commitment to the environment affect its business ethics?
2. How would you measure Ford's social responsibility?
3. Identify ways in which you think Ford is responsible to its customers, employees, investors, and society.
4. Create an advertisement for a Ford Escape Hybrid, a Ford Focus PZEV, or one of the CVT models that uses green marketing to promote its message.

**Sources:** Ford Web site, accessed September 8, 2006, http://www.ford.com; "Ford Motor Company Hybrid Sales up 115 Percent," Auto Channel, accessed August 8, 2006, http://www.theautochannel.com; "Ford Escape Hybrid," *Business-Week,* accessed September 8, 2006, http://www.businessweek.com; "Line Up for a Hybrid," *Kiplinger Magazine,* accessed May 19, 2006, http://biz.yahoo.com/Kiplinger; Mark K. Solheim, "Too Many Greenbacks," *Kiplinger Magazine,* accessed May 19, 2006, http://biz.yahoo.com/Kiplinger.

 **Case 3.2**

## BP Meets Global Energy Challenges Head-On

One industry is headlined in the world news almost every day: oil. Whether in a story on rising or falling prices, a prediction about rates of production, worries about U.S. dependency on foreign oil, or a discussion of alternative energy sources, oil is a daily topic of reporters and broadcasters. London-based BP (British Petroleum) is one of those companies featured in the news. Founded a century ago as the Anglo Persian Oil Company, BP is one of the world's largest energy companies, employing more than 100,000 workers in 100 countries. The firm sells 6.4 million barrels of refined petroleum products every day, serving millions of customers through its retail outlets. Those numbers are astounding, but they also mean that BP faces enormous challenges to serve its global customers, among them a continued search for oil, aggressive development for alternative energies, and the many environmental, political, and economic issues that affect the industry.

Fluctuations in the availability and production of oil have a ripple effect throughout nearly every economy in the world. Changes in political situations in places such as Iraq and Nigeria also affect the flow of oil—and the world economy. Even the free flow of news stories, commentary, and predictions about oil can affect the entire business environment. "Expectations, perceptions often affect the price more than physical changes," notes Manouchehr Takin of the Centre for Global Energy Studies. In an important sign of stability, BP has managed to replace its oil reserves for more than thirteen years in a row. In addition, the company adds as much as 2 billion new barrels each year, anticipating increased use. Despite the closure of refineries because of natural disasters such as Hurricane Katrina, BP manages to survive from a business standpoint because it engages in a number of cost-efficiency programs and continues to invest profits in the business.

BP executives know that fossil fuels such as oil are not renewable—eventually, they will run out. In addition, more and more evidence points to damage to the environment, including climate change, from overuse of these fuels. BP is at the center of a global challenge of the greatest magnitude: how to provide the world's businesses and consumers with the fuel they need, at a profit, without causing further changes to the natural environment. So through its various divisions devoted to exploration, research, and development, BP is pursuing alternative forms of energy. In India, BP has funded a $9.4 million project led by The Energy and Resources Institute (TERI) to research and demonstrate the feasibility of producing a biodiesel fuel from a nonedible oil-bearing crop called *Jatropha curcas* The plant can be easily grown in India, which has spare land to devote to such projects. "In some parts of the world there is only limited availability of land to produce food crops and therefore no surplus which can be used for energy crops," explains Phil New, senior vice president of BP's fuel management group. Both organizations will be keeping a sharp eye on the bottom line of this project.

"Recent developments have made green fuels economically attractive," says TERI director general R. K. Pachauri.

Closer to home, BP is developing the world's first industrial-scale capacity to generate electricity using hydrogen power. By creating this decarbonized fuel, BP could reduce carbon dioxide emissions by as much as 90 percent. The technologies involved already exist, but BP is the first to combine them to create decarbonized fuel. The process converts natural gas from wells beneath the North Sea into hydrogen and carbon dioxide, then "captures" the carbon dioxide separately and uses the hydrogen as a power source. Hydrogen is a clean fuel that produces only water—not pollutants—as a byproduct when burned.

The success of these and other energy projects depends on the health of economies—globally and locally. It also depends to some degree on the support of governments. While many agree that worldwide consumption of oil must be reduced, few agree on how to achieve this objective. The Rocky Mountain Institute in the United States recommends encouraging consumers to buy hybrid cars and trucks such as those made by Toyota, Honda, and Ford. The institute also suggests levying special fees on consumers who continue driving gasoline-only vehicles, with tax breaks for those who buy hybrids. While no single answer exists, BP continues to pursue many possibilities.

Meanwhile, the firm is tapping new markets. Already a huge investor in China, BP has entered into a joint venture with Sinopec, an arm of China Petroleum Chemical Corporation. Conducting business in China can be a complicated but ultimately profitable process. China represents an enormous market. Currently, there is now one car per 1,000 Chinese. Experts predict that number will grow to one car per 25 people within 25 years. With China's huge population, that represents a massive market opportunity. And BP isn't waiting around for others to grab it.

## Questions for Critical Thinking

1. Describe several supply and demand factors that could affect BP specifically and the oil industry as a whole.
2. What macroeconomic factors might affect a firm such as BP?
3. What challenges and opportunities does BP face as it enters a market such as China with a planned economy?
4. Why is it economically important for BP to research alternative energies?

**Sources:** British Petroleum Web site, accessed September 8, 2006, http://www.bp.com; Kevin G. Hall, "The Struggle to Quit Oil," *Philadelphia Inquirer,* accessed September 8, 2006, http://www.philly.com; Nick Mathiason, "China Paves Way for £14bn BP Oil Stake," *The Observer,* accessed September 8, 2006, http://observer.guardian.co.uk; Ben Richardson, "Oil Looms Large over a World Stage," BBC News, accessed September 8, 2006, http://news.bbc.co.uk; Timothy Gardner, "US Hopes to Reverse Oil Decline by Burying $CO_2$," Reuters, accessed March 13, 2006, http://news.yahoo.com.

---

## VIDEO · Case 4.2

## Cold Stone Creamery Cools Off Consumers around the World

On a steamy summer day, there's nothing like a cold, creamy dish of ice cream. Perhaps you are one of those ice cream connoisseurs who has favorite mix-ins or toppings—candy, nuts, fresh fruit, or good old-fashioned sprinkles. Maybe you prefer the clean taste of frozen yogurt or sorbet to help you chill. Cold Stone Creamery has it all, plus the most important ingredient: top-quality ice cream. Cold Stone uses fresh ingredients and churns its ice cream with very low air content, which makes it dense and creamy. Kids and adults love it, flocking to the nearly 1,000 stores (company-owned and franchises) across the country to order their favorites—whether it's Birthday Cake Remix, a blend of cake batter ice cream, rainbow sprinkles, brownies, and fudge, or Paradise Found, white chocolate ice cream with coconut, pineapples, and bananas mixed in.

Cold Stone Creamery was founded in 1988 in Tempe, Arizona, by Don and Susan Sutherland. It's *hot* in Arizona, especially in the summer, and people there like ice cream to cool off, too. Cold Stone serves 12 flavors of its own super-premium ice cream, waffle cones, and brownies—all made fresh daily at its stores. Its employees—called crew members—learn exactly how to scoop the ice cream onto a stone-cold slab and add any of the 38 mix-ins to create a custom confection for each customer. Some stores even feature singing crew members who entertain customers while they wait. A Cold Stone cone doesn't come cheap—it can cost $5 or more. And lines may snake around the block. But consumers don't seem to mind. "Consumers are willing to pay more and wait a little longer perceiving they're getting more of an upscale experience along with more 'made for me,'" explains industry analyst Ron Paul.

Cold Stone is not content to stop at U.S. shores. Instead, the firm's leaders have taken their passion for ice cream overseas, starting with the Caribbean and Guam, then on to Japan. Japanese consumers were ready and waiting for Cold Stone's arrival—Japan actually celebrates a national Ice Cream Day. Cold Stone started with five stores in the first seven months, and the lines quickly formed out the door and down the street, attracting more than 1,000 customers each day. The firm expects to have 150 stores open in Japan by the year 2010, helped along by an agreement with a local Japanese company that will help develop Cold Stone's presence in that country.

Cold Stone tweaks some of the favorite flavors for Japanese customers, whose tastebuds prefer flavors such as green tea and adzuki bean. Crew members often serve up creations such as Blushing Mango Cloud, mango ice cream with mango-strawberry whipped cream, and Joy Nut Club, coconut ice cream with almonds, coconut, and Oreo cookies, to Japanese ice-cream lovers. "Japanese people really appreciate quality and freshness," notes Lee Knowlton, vice president of international development for Cold Stone. "And that's Cold Stone's wheelhouse." The formula works.

Cold Stone wasn't the first to arrive in Japan. Rival Baskin-Robbins has been in Japan for 30 years, currently operates 750 stores there, and expects to grow to more than 1,000 shops there by 2010—compared with Cold Stone's projected 150 shops. But the ice cream market is changing. Consumers want innovation. They want more than new flavors; they are insisting on the best and freshest ingredients, the newest ideas in blending flavors, textures, and mix-ins. And they want their ice cream prepared in a fun, different way. So far, Cold Stone has created the buzz it needs to enter the marketplace in Japan, despite Baskin-Robbins's dominance. Häagen-Dazs, owned by General Mills, is also a presence in Japan—the firm has had stores there since 1984. Häagen-Dazs CFO Jim Lawrence remarks that entering the Japanese market is very expensive. "The advertising is more like what you would expect from a cosmetics company or a jewelry company," he says. A Baskin-Robbins executive echoes the difficulty of entering this expensive market that demands the best from businesses. "Starting and staying are two different things," he admits.

But Cold Stone isn't melting. The Japanese economy, where consumer goods are expensive, can support a premium ice-cream industry. And Cold Stone CEO Doug Ducey believes his firm can revolutionize its industry just as another famous food company revolutionized the coffee industry. "One of my favorite companies that expanded its . . . strategy into a revolutionary new industry approach is Starbucks," he says. By giving Japanese—and, in fact, all—consumers something new and different they can sink their teeth into, Ducey and the rest of Cold Stone's executives feel confident about winning them over. "I hope that people here will think of ice cream when they want to have a dessert," says Cold Stone Japan's president, Kazuhiro Ishihara. That would be sweet news for Cold Stone.

## Questions for Critical Thinking

1. Japan's economy—including the exchange rate—is such that doing business in that country is often expensive for U.S. companies such as Cold Stone Creamery. If the value of the U.S. dollar declines, how might that affect Cold Stone's business in Japan? If the value of the Japanese yen declines, how might that affect the firm's business?

2. Describe some of the barriers facing Cold Stone as it enters the Japanese market.

3. Describe the level of involvement Cold Stone has used for entering the Japanese market.

4. Does Cold Stone practice a global business strategy or a multidomestic business strategy? Explain your answer.

**Sources:** Cold Stone Creamery Web site, accessed September 8, 2006, http://www.coldstonecreamery.com; "Cold Stone Creamery," *Entrepreneur,* accessed September 8, 2006, http://www.entrepreneur.com; "Cold Stone Creamery," *Hoover's,* accessed September 8, 2006, http://www.hoovers .com; Corey Hajim and Cindy Kano, "Japan's Ice Cream Wars," *Fortune,* accessed September 8, 2006, http://money .cnn.com; "From Mom & Pop to Professional Op," Inc.com, accessed September 8, 2006, http://www.inc.com; Bob Hirschfield, "What's Hot in Ice Cream?" *Retail Traffic,* accessed September 8, 2006, http://retailtrafficmag.com.

## VIDEO Case 5.2

### The UL Mark of Approval

You've seen the little UL mark of approval on countless products. Maybe you've never paid attention to it, or maybe you've wondered briefly what the "UL" stood for. In fact, "UL" represents Underwriters Laboratories, a not-for-profit organization that has existed for more than a century. Founded by Chicago electrical inspector William Merrill in 1894—in response to the constant fires in the Palace of Electricity at the Chicago World's Fair—Underwriters

Laboratories has been devoted to inspecting and testing billions of products for safety and quality assurance ever since. UL conducts more than 100,000 product evaluations each year, and only those that pass the organization's rigorous examination get the coveted UL mark. UL tests everything, including computers, electric blankets, and commercial ice cream makers. Currently, 20 billion products from more than 71,000 manufacturers bear the UL mark.

UL started out small. In the first few years, two experts joined Merrill in his enterprise, and they performed 75 tests on a $3,000 budget. By the tenth year, UL's budget had increased to $300,000, with 7,500 test reports issued. UL inspectors had spread out over 67 cities, conducting evaluations and helping set safety standards. In 1916, a team was dispatched to London to monitor England's exports to the United States. By 1958, UL testing centers had spread across Europe. Three decades years later, UL opened facilities in Asia.

Underwriters Laboratories has grown like many other small businesses into a huge international organization. With 5,000 scientists, engineers, and safety specialists, the firm faces daily challenges. Yet UL has not lost sight of William Merrill's original mission—to provide product safety assurance to consumers. And UL continues to develop new standards for the products it tests. So the coffeepot you click on in the morning, the air conditioner that cools your bedroom, and the hair dryer that blows just the right amount of heated air were most likely tested by UL specialists before they ever reached the store shelves—or your home.

Here is how the process works. A firm submits a product to be tested, ideally sometime during its development. UL assigns the product to the correct testing division, where engineers and other specialists will see it through the evaluation. As part of the submission, the firm answers all kinds of questions about the product—what it is, how and when it will be used and by whom, what materials will be used in manufacturing it, and how the product is wired (with diagrams, if applicable). Then UL plans a testing program, tests the product for safety and reliability, and returns a formal report to the manufacturer. The standards for testing are developed by experts from UL, as well as by people from the industry and the public. For instance, standards for testing a fire extinguisher might be developed by UL specialists, members of the manufacturing industry, and firefighting personnel. If a product passes the tests, it gets the UL mark. If it doesn't, a manufacturer can modify the design and resubmit it or appeal the decision.

UL is not the only product-testing organization in existence; it has international competitors such as SGS, Intertek, and Bureau Veritas. Because of this rivalry, UL must remain innovative and current, constantly finding new ways to serve its clients and the general public. The UL program helps retailers by giving them a standard by which to evaluate the products they want to sell to consumers. And, although not *every* manufactured product must be tested, many states and towns do have ordinances or codes requiring a UL listing for certain items such as smoke alarms and electrical wiring. The certification program helps consumers identify the safest products on the market. The organization's Web site, which is easy for manufacturers, retailers, and consumers to use, also helps UL remain competitive by adding instant and easy access to information. In addition to providing safety standards on products, the UL Web site offers safety tips for a whole range of everyday situations at home, in the office, and elsewhere. Consumers can visit the site to learn more about child safety, college dorm safety, smoke alarms, ladders, lawn mowers, and Christmas lights. The next time you plug in the toaster oven or heat up your dinner in the microwave, check for the UL mark on your appliance—chances are, it's there.

## Questions for Critical Thinking

1. How might the Underwriters Laboratories team up with a business incubator? What might be the benefits to both?
2. UL is a not-for-profit organization. Describe its objectives, as well as the business concepts it shares with for-profit companies.
3. Look around your dorm room or apartment, and make a list of all the products with the UL mark on them. Also list those that don't have it, if any. How do you think the UL testing process affects the way manufacturing businesses operate?
4. Think of yourself as an entrepreneur starting a business. Imagine a product that you would like to make or sell. Then visit the UL Web site to learn the procedure for testing your product. Create a plan for your business that includes the way you would organize your business—such as sole proprietorship or partnership—and include a strategy to develop your product and have it tested.

**Sources:** UL Web site, accessed September 8, 2006, http://www.ul.com; "Underwriters Laboratories Inc.," *Hoovers,* accessed September 8, 2006, http://www.hoovers.com; "Underwriters Laboratories," eNotes.com, accessed September 8, 2006, http://business.enotes.com; Mark Thornton, "The Market for Safety," accessed September 8, 2006, http://www.westga.edu.

## Culver's: Great Food from a Good Business

Culver's isn't a typical fast-food burger joint. Yes, the smiling staff cooks up burgers, and the food is served fast. But the minute you walk in the door, you know something's different. Maybe it's the retro décor, which looks like a family diner from the 1950s or 1960s. Maybe it's the entire mouthwatering menu, which includes such specialties as the Wisconsin Swiss Melt sandwich and creamy frozen custard. Perhaps what makes Culver's unique is its signature ButterBurger—seared on a hot grill as soon as an order is placed, smothered with fresh toppings, and finished with Wisconsin cheese. Maybe it's the staff, which is genuinely swift—and friendly. Then there's the price—you can eat at Culver's for around $10 or even less. Or maybe all of these qualities rolled into one dining experience make you want to return. Culver's mission is simple: "Every guest who chooses Culver's leaves happy."

Despite the old-fashioned charm that makes you feel as though Culver's has been around for half a century or more, the business was founded just two decades ago in Sauk City, Wisconsin, by the Culver family. Currently, George and Ruth Culver, along with their son Craig and his wife, Lea, own five Culver's restaurants and oversee 315 franchise restaurants in fifteen states, cutting a swath right through the Midwest. Over the next few years, the family plans to focus its expansion on states such as Arizona, Texas, and Wyoming.

Culver's began as a family firm and remains true to that model today. The Culvers are dedicated to their business and to providing their customers with the best service. CEO Craig Culver has been working in restaurants since childhood. "I started in this business when I was 10 or 11," he recalls. "When other people were on vacation or on holidays, we were putting smiles on their faces. It was normal, and we loved doing it." When he was growing up, Culver's parents operated an A&W drive-in. "It was a fun environment, yet [my parents] had high expectations for everybody," he says. "It was a great learning ground." Culver notes that he still goes to his father—George Culver, now in his mid-80s—for business advice. For his part, George continues to monitor quality at his own Culver's stores, and approves every new frozen custard flavor.

Both Culvers enjoy experimenting in order to find new menu offerings that will appeal to their customers. "I believe it gives you a competitive edge to come out with new products that are exciting and different from our competitors," notes Craig. "I like to be the first on the block with new things." But the restaurant's signature frozen custard and trademarked ButterBurger are what keep the customers coming through the doors. "The ButterBurger is a brand in itself," says Craig, observing that although food trends have changed, the ButterBurger remains a staple. "If I started this business over again, I'm not certain I would call it a Butter-Burger, but 20 years ago I thought it was the neatest name. And it's been pretty good to us over the years."

The Culvers have chosen to expand their business through franchise opportunities. Culver's franchises are tightly controlled and awarded carefully. Potential franchisees must have at least $300,000 in liquid assets, complete a rigorous application and interview, and undergo the training process. "Our owner/operator philosophy is one of the core elements to our success," explains the company Web site. "We require each franchisee to personally manage and operate their restaurant in a full-time capacity. He or she cannot delegate management or operation responsibilities without written consent." Craig Culver personally approves all franchise applications. "We look at them to see if they fit our culture and our value system," he explains. As part of the selection process, each applicant is required to put in a 60-hour workweek at Culver's. "They decide at the end of the week if they want to stay or not," says Craig.

Despite close monitoring—and the fact that Culver's allows each franchisee to own and operate only one restaurant—Culver's promotes intrapreneurship among its franchisees, whom Craig Culver calls "franchise partners." In fact, Culver credits the firm's franchisees with much of Culver's current success. He believes that the contribution that franchisees make to the overall culture of the organization is vital to Culver's future. "Continuing to build on that culture is a great opportunity. The businesses with the best people are the businesses that are going to win. We get that through great leadership from my franchise partners. They have a passion for what they do."

Culver's continues to serve good food consistently—something its customers appreciate. "Taste How Much We Care," the firm's slogan invites. One bite of a hot Butter-Burger—or a lick of an ice-cold frozen custard in a cone—is likely to convince you.

## Questions for Critical Thinking

1. How has the environment for entrepreneurship over the past 20 years shaped the Culvers' business?
2. How would you classify the Culver family as entrepreneurs? What personality traits do the Culvers have that you believe have contributed to their success?

3. What are the risks and benefits to owning a Culver's franchise?
4. Do you predict that intrapreneurship will play an important role in Culver's future growth and development? Why or why not?

**Sources:** Culver's Web site, accessed September 8, 2006, http://www.culvers.com; Nathan Leaf, "Culver's," *Wisconsin State Journal*, June 4, 2006, pp. B1, B2; Carolyn Walkup, "Craig Culver," *Nation's Restaurant News*, September 19, 2005, pp. 78–80; Kathleen Gallagher, "All in the Family," *Milwaukee Journal Sentinel*, July 4, 2004.

## VIDEO Case 7.2

### Manifest Digital: Putting the User First

What would you be willing to do to win a 61" plasma display projector? Would you be willing to test your ability to hurl office equipment farther than your opponents can? Would you make a mad dash through a busy office, leaping over co-workers, filing cabinets, and copy machines? Would you roll down a hallway in a runaway office chair, dodging stacks of boxes, office furniture, and pesky janitors? This is what scores of information technology professionals did during the IT Guy Games, an online game developed to promote technology company NEC Visual Systems.

The IT Guy Web site was created by Manifest Digital, Inc., a user-centered marketing and design firm located in Chicago. The firm was founded by Jim Jacoby and Mike Davidson in 2001. According to Jacoby, Manifest Digital was "born of the dotcom fallout." After the dot-com bubble burst in 2000, the two joined forces to launch a company that would design and build Web sites based on "usability"—the ease with which a user can access, understand, and use a Web site. Although there are many Internet design firms, and a growing number of usability companies, Manifest Digital puts the target audience at the center of every decision they make. Clients such as Sony, Texas Instruments, and Wynn Las Vegas have taken advantage of Manifest Digital's capabilities.

In order to serve the audience, Manifest Digital must learn about them. The company does this through research and testing. Research may start with purchasing data and sales analysis. Who is buying the product now? Who is the company trying to reach? This was the starting point when the company redesigned the Baseball section of the Wilson Sporting Goods Web site. Wilson knew that its audience was primarily teen and preteen boys. But the existing Web site was similar to a catalog. There was little on the site to involve the user. Manifest Digital redesigned the site around players at five different positions: pitcher, catcher, first base, infield, and outfield. Each position featured several Major League Baseball players. This gave users a chance to learn about Wilson's products through their favorite players. In addition, Manifest Digital made the site more active and interactive. They added animation, downloads, and video to engage the audience. Sales grew, and Wilson asked Manifest Digital to redesign other elements of their Web site.

Unlike many Internet design firms, which don't test their Web sites until late in the design process, Manifest Digital tests during every stage. Testing involves bringing in users and gives them tasks to accomplish, such as finding, comparing, and purchasing products online. Designers observe the users in action to see where they succeed and where they have trouble. This helps Manifest Digital make the structure of the site clearer. "You have to be careful not to ask them what they need or what they want," warns Carolyn Chandler, a User Experience professional at Manifest Digital. "You end up with many different solutions to the same problem, but none of them address what the real need is."

To discover the real need, Manifest Digital uses "contextual inquiry." This involves observing users in their "real world" environment. While developing an Intranet for YMCA, Jacoby noticed that the employees were "scrapbooking"—collecting information from a variety of sources and putting it into binders. Although no one had asked for this capability, once Manifest Digital built it into the Web site, the client realized it was exactly what they needed.

Creating a relationship with users helps attract and retain an audience. Manifest Digital experienced the growth of a vibrant community when they built the NEC IT Guy site. The site was publicized by banner ads featuring the IT Guy. The character was so popular, the games were so much fun, and the prize was so good that IT managers—the target audience—flocked to the site. Manifest Digital built a message board into the site, and users posted voraciously, offering tips to their fellow competitors about how to win the games. The campaign was so effective that NEC, which expected to spend $67 per click in advertising, ended up spending less than $3 per click. Even after the competition ended, the site remained online, because the community surrounding the game was so strong.

Web design has gone through several stages as the Internet has grown. During the past ten years, standards of design and functionality have developed. Now designers are innovating around those standards. Jim Jacoby sees usability as the latest way for companies to differentiate themselves. "Technology is a commodity," he says, "but usability is an art."

## Questions for Critical Thinking

1. Describe ways in which Manifest Digital helps its business customers achieve success.
2. Manifest Digital must understand the consumers who will buy its clients' goods and services. Describe ways in which you think Manifest Digital demonstrates this understanding.
3. Why is usability an important component of Web design? What sites have you encountered that are not "user friendly?"
4. Why do you think the NEC IT Guy site and the Wilson Baseball site are successful?

**Sources:** Jim Jacoby and Carolyn Chandler, personal interview, July 20, 2006; Manifest Digital Web site, accessed September 8, 2006, http://www.manifestdigital.com; NEC IT Guy Games Web site, accessed September 8, 2006, http://www.necitguy.com/home.html; Wilson Baseball Web site, accessed September 8, 2006, http://www.wilson.com/wilson/baseball/index.jsp; "NEC's AdverGame Campaign Delivers Big Rewards" Eyeblaster Newsletter, accessed September 8, 2006, http://www.eyeblaster.com.

## Case 8.2

## Made in the USA: American Apparel

American Apparel is on the cutting edge of fashion. Its hip T-shirts are designed specifically for a young, urban crowd. All are made in the United States by workers who earn far better wages than most others in the garment industry. A sign at the doorway to one of the firm's stores promises to "pioneer an industry standard in social responsibility." Founder Dov Charney likes to project an image of free expression. Yet all of these qualities have a familiar ring—they sound very much like concerns of the late 1960s and early 1970s. Dov Charney even sports the look—a mustache and muttonchop sideburns.

Charney has a vision—to provide young, urban consumers with logo-free cotton clothing made in the United States and *not* sold in shopping malls. He wants to accomplish this objective by running a factory with a safe and innovative working environment. He prices his clothing between $15 and $45, so his core customers can afford it. And he locates his stores in areas where young consumers are likely to shop, such as New York City's Lower East Side. Charney knows who his customers are, and he is interested in serving only his target group. "We don't design clothes for a 50-year-old," he says without apology. "We don't even care about them."

To achieve his goals, several years ago Charney tapped Marty Bailey, who had already worked in the T-shirt industry for 20 years, including a stint at Fruit of the Loom. Bailey knew how to make the vision become a reality. Having watched most of the country's T-shirt production move offshore, he agreed with Charney that American Apparel should stay on American soil. But the manufacturing process itself needed to be streamlined and improved. "There were a lot of operators on the floor," recalls Bailey. "There was a lot of work in process. Material was sitting around for months. That means a lot of cash was tied up on the sewing floor. At Fruit of the Loom, I had instituted work teams. I did the same thing here." Over a period of about nine months, Bailey converted the entire operation to teams of four to twelve workers. Each worker would have responsibility for one portion of a garment—say, a sleeve or a neck—but the team would produce the final product. Each team would have access to a supervisor and a mechanic to help minimize delays. "We went from producing 30,000 pieces a day to 90,000, with no unfinished work in process," Bailey says of the conversion.

A successful company needs a leader and effective management. Dov Charney is clearly the leader of American Apparel. Sometimes he is called charismatic, sometimes controversial. But American Apparel is very much his company—he developed the style and continues to oversee all aspects of design, development, and marketing. Charney likes to visit American Apparel's 131 retail stores as often as he can; another 60 stores are planned for next year. "Dov is a huge part of the company," says Marty Bailey. "He is the face of the company, the passion, the drive. He's also the best marketer I've ever been associated with."

Bailey is also a top-notch manager. "I spend time in the stores, too. But I manage operations, which includes running the plant and handling distribution." Bailey acknowledges the difference in their two styles of leadership and management. "Dov is very animated, which is a huge part of our company. I'm pretty low key. But when I change pace, people know it's time to get serious." Yet Bailey points out that his goals and philosophies of leadership are really similar to Charney's. "I believe in managing people, not personnel," he says. "You ask people, you don't tell them."

Both men emphasize the importance of treating workers with respect. "My job is to support people, to train people, to listen to people, and to give them every opportunity to be successful," says Charney. Workers at American Apparel not only are paid better than the industry average but also have unique opportunities. Because the factory is located in Los Angeles, it attracts a substantial number of Hispanic employees. So the firm offers free English and citizenship classes, low-cost lunches, and free use of bicycles for commuting to and from work. A new health clinic has opened right at the factory to encourage employees to use their healthcare benefits.

Communication is also an important part of the American Apparel culture. "One of the main reasons people get upset is lack of information," Bailey observes. "You need to inform [employees], you let them know what's going on, and you let them know that they're needed. As a manager,

the three most important things I can ever do is say please, thank you, and ask, 'What do you think?'"

## Questions for Critical Thinking

1. Describe the skills that you think Marty Bailey has that enable him to manage American Apparel's operations.
2. Based on what you have learned about the company, its leader, and its top manager, write your own mission statement for American Apparel.
3. Using the five-step approach to decision making, describe how American Apparel might make the non-programmed decision to add a new product to its line.
4. How would you describe Dov Charney's leadership style? How does it help shape the corporate culture?

**Sources:** Jennifer Ordonez, "California Hustlin'," *Newsweek,* accessed September 8, 2006, http://www.msnbc.msn.com; American Apparel Web site, accessed September 8, 2006, http://www.americanapparel.net; "Living on the Edge at American Apparel," *BusinessWeek,* accessed September 8, 2006, http://www.businessweek.com; Stephen Franklin, "More Pay Americans' Way," *Chicago Tribune,* May 30, 2006, sec. 3, pp. 1, 3.

---

## ⅤⅠⅮⅇⅯ   *Case 9.2*

### Allstate Employees Are in Good Hands

At some point in your TV viewing life, you have probably seen an ad for Allstate Insurance that ends with the tagline, "You're in good hands with Allstate." An Allstate commercial may follow the case of a driver who's had a fender bender or a homeowner whose house has been hit by a tree. Allstate projects the image of the good caretaker, the quiet hero who makes things right when everything seems to go wrong. But what you don't see in the ad is the people who work behind the scenes to serve Allstate's customers. Allstate can do its job because it recruits and selects top-notch employees, trains them well, and provides important benefits for their well-being.

Founded in 1931 as a subsidiary of Sears, Roebuck (the name Allstate came from a brand of tire that was in the Sears catalog), Allstate has since become an independent firm and is now the largest publicly held personal insurer in the nation—providing auto, life, and homeowners' insurance as well as investment products. The firm has received many top awards for its working environment, including making *Working Mother* magazine's list of top "100 Best Companies for Working Mothers" for more than fourteen years in a row. These two factors go hand-in-hand at All-

state—financial success and success as an employer. The company's human resources (HR) managers, such as divisional senior vice president Joan M. Crockett—who has won several individual HR awards—understand that the firm's approach to attracting and retaining employees is vital to its competitive strategy. "It's simply a good business strategy," says Crockett about Allstate's development of an effective work environment. "I believe Allstate's work environment has a direct relationship with the company's success."

As the workforce changes, and as expectations between companies and their employees change, HR managers must think and work creatively to keep morale high and motivate employees to perform their best. Allstate does this in a variety of ways. First is a compensation package that includes base pay, incentive pay, a wide range of benefits, and learning opportunities. But the firm is perhaps best known for its commitment to helping employees balance work and family needs. Anise Wiley-Little, director of Diversity and Work/Life, explains that young people who are entering the workforce already accept that the "current business environment is a 24-7 business culture. But they also pay attention to work-life balance. That is a priority to them, and we have to accommodate that type of flexibility within our workforce." So Allstate offers on-site child care, employee discounts for other national day-care providers, monetary adoption assistance, flexible work hours, and support for the care of aging parents—all in an effort to create a family-friendly work environment. "We need to fit different lifestyles and different needs," says Wiley-Little. "Families are constantly changing, so you can adjust your benefits to reflect that. Domestic partners are covered, and our time-away policies cover family leave for adoptions."

But Allstate doesn't stop there. Because training and education are critical to the development of employees' careers, as well as their contributions to the firm, other benefits include on-site education and mentoring, tuition reimbursement, and comprehensive job training programs that include classroom and online teaching as well as coaching assistance. These education and training programs are designed to create opportunities for advancement within the company so that employees feel motivated and committed to a long-term work relationship with Allstate.

Diversity has long been a focus at Allstate. The firm began hiring women as claims adjusters in 1942, and it established an affirmative action policy in the 1960s. According to its HR managers, this practice simply makes good business sense. Not only does it provide a wider pool of qualified job candidates, but it also helps Allstate understand and serve a diverse customer base. "Diverse means more than just hiring women and people of color," says Wiley-Little. "True diversity includes a variety of values,

beliefs, and education." Wiley-Little and others in her department believe that hiring, training, and retaining a diverse workforce gives their company a competitive advantage.

Catherine Brune is a senior vice president and chief technology officer at Allstate. She supports Allstate's commitment to diversity and work-life balance, noting that as a working mother, she understands the pressures that all working parents feel. "At the same time we need to deliver a high-quality product to our customers in a timely fashion," she says. "At Allstate, we have the perfect equation." At Allstate, customers—and employees—are in good hands.

## Questions for Critical Thinking

1. In what ways do Allstate's HR managers contribute to the firm's overall competitive strategy?
2. Why is a focus on work-family life so important for today's companies?
3. How would you characterize the morale at Allstate? What factors might contribute to it?
4. Describe how Allstate succeeds or fails in satisfying each of the five needs outlined in Maslow's hierarchy.

**Sources:** Allstate Web site, accessed September 8, 2006, http://www.allstate.com; "100 Best Companies Hall of Fame," *Working Mother,* accessed September 8, 2006, http://www .workingmother.com; "*Working Mother* Magazine Recognizes Allstate," *NetAssets,* accessed September 8, 2006, http://www .hrms-netassets.net; Maria Schafer, "Why Workforce Management Is Back in Style," *Optimize,* accessed September 8, 2006, http://www.optimizemag.com.

 **Case 10.2**

### Meet the People of BP

London-based BP (British Petroleum) is a major player in the oil and energy industry, with more than 100,000 workers in 100 countries. Imagine what 100,000 workers can accomplish if they all perform at the highest level. From human resources managers, to sales and marketing managers, to finance executives, to retail store managers, to geologists, BP employees are part of an organizational culture that fosters empowerment, communication, and effective teamwork. "Experience isn't essential to join us . . . it's your attitude that's important to us," says one part of the careers section of the BP Web site. This outlook prevails throughout the many BP divisions.

BP recently instituted a training program designed to build better communication and teamwork among its top-

level managers. Called the Projects Academy, the program—based at the Massachusetts Institute of Technology (MIT)—provided top managers with new ways to examine complex problems, work with colleagues and staff, and find solutions for developing new products. Program director Jim Breson observed that getting these individuals to work together as a group was initially a challenge—they simply weren't accustomed to it. "When we were creating the program, we noted the high-level managers were rather like the Tom Cruise character in the movie *Top Gun.*" These managers, he says, were already highly competent, but they needed to find ways to perform even better, through teamwork and communication. The managers who emerged from the course say they are better for having taken it. "I think what Projects Academy provides is a framework that gives us the best of what we can learn from others while preserving the best of BP's unique approach," remarks David Dalton, a geologist who recently became BP's general manager in Abu Dhabi. "What's happening here is a real effort to keep people engaged and linked together on an ongoing basis. My classmates and I are focused . . . on how we, as a broad community of project people, can learn from each other and create new insights into how we perform our jobs." Dalton and his colleagues now communicate regularly from anywhere around the world. He likes the fact that he can call on the expertise of others who have similar concerns and responsibilities to his own. "It's positively wonderful to be part of a growing connectivity that allows us to share and communicate these responsibilities," he says.

Far from the oil fields of the Middle East—and from MIT—management trainees for BP's retail stores, which include convenience stores and cafes adjacent to BP stations, are learning the same concepts. During their training, they become familiar with the BP culture of empowerment. As part of the Customer Assistant team, they develop skills in working with others. They learn the norms of the team, including how to communicate with each other and with customers.

As a large firm, BP operates teams that serve different purposes; however, they all share the goal of communicating effectively and taking personal responsibility to improve performance, provide customer service, and gain a competitive advantage. Teams are so important to the firm that it gives awards to those that perform especially well. One award-winning problem-solving team found a better way to predict pressure in deep-water drilling operations, thus avoiding dangerous accidents and oil spills. A cross-functional team with members from refining and marketing worked together to launch Masana Petroleum Solutions in South Africa, a firm owned and run by local residents. Still another team found a new way to reduce $CO_2$ emissions at the Salah Gas Project in Algeria.

One of the more unusual BP teams is known as Operation People. During a time when the firm was cutting costs and morale was beginning to sag, BP convened an Operation People group to turn things around. They developed some corporate initiatives—and they also started a band, which took popular songs and rewrote the lyrics to apply to BP. The band played at one meeting and were a hit. So they began to perform at other venues, including the Rock and Roll Hall of Fame. With this creative form of communication, they spread the word about their company.

Not long ago, BP introduced a new global management framework that gives the financial controllers more independence to run their units. This change meant the firm needed to retrain the controllers in their new roles. So BP

created a training course that put participants in teams in which they had to solve real-work problems together, even if it meant resolving personal conflicts. BP spokesperson Sarah Harvey explains, "The program is designed to help our people develop a deeper knowledge of their role and accountabilities and also the interpersonal awareness to build the right relationships with their business partners so that they can remain connected yet independent." One team leader in the program notes the importance of understanding his teammates' behavior so that he could manage their relationships. But all of the relationship building took place within the context of real situations that BP financial controllers would face.

BP uses nearly every available medium of communication, including publishing its own very substantial magazine, called *The BP Magazine*. The publication is filled with all types of articles that focus on economics, culture, the environment, and even the foods of the nations in which BP does business. Not only does the magazine help BP employees around the world stay connected, but it also provides a forum for good publicity, such as announcements of awards the firm has won or achievements particular divisions or employees have accomplished. New events are happening somewhere every day at BP—and the company wants all 100,000 employees, and its many customers, to know.

## Questions for Critical Thinking

1. Describe ways that BP empowers its employees. Do you think this approach is effective in such a large company? Why or why not?
2. BP uses a variety of teams to accomplish many of its goals. What makes them effective? What are the benefits of this approach?
3. A company as large as BP must rely on many forms of communication. How might managers use teams as a basis for managing informal communication?
4. External communication is vital to a firm such as BP. Suppose an environmental accident such as an oil spill occurred involving BP. What steps would you recommend the firm take to communicate the circumstances of the incident and maintain goodwill with its customers and the general public?

**Sources:** British Petroleum Web site, accessed September 8, 2006, http://www.bp.com; Stephanie Johnson, "Meet the Elite," *Massachusetts Institute of Technology*, accessed September 8, 2006, http://web.mit.edu/bp-mit; "Helping BP's Controllers Stay Connected—Yet Independent," Pricewaterhouse-Coopers, accessed September 8, 2006, http://www.pwcglobal.com; *The BP Magazine*, Issue 1, 2005.

## Washburn Guitars: Sound Since 1883

Well-run businesses tend to stay sound for a long time. They grow, they change, they add and delete products, they open and close manufacturing plants, they streamline and expand their operations. But their basic business foundation remains strong, no matter what happens.

Washburn Guitars has been making beautiful sounds since it was founded in Chicago in 1883. Location has always been a key component of the company's overall strategy; when the firm became Washburn International nearly 100 years later, it wasn't long before its manufacturing, office headquarters, and warehouse divisions were consolidated into a single 130,000-square-foot facility outside Mundelein, Illinois. This allowed the firm to incorporate its SoundTech speaker division, which had been operating elsewhere, into the same facility. Perhaps the most important reason for the move, however, was the availability of a skilled workforce nearby. Company president Rudy Schlacher explained that moving to the new location allowed the firm to "tap into an exceptional local workforce." About three years after the move, Washburn International morphed again—into U.S. Music Corporation—which now includes even more divisions, such as Randall Amplifiers, Vinci Strings and Accessories, SoundTech Professional Audio, and Oscar Schmidt folk instruments. The organizational change "gives us the opportunity to clearly separate the parent corporation [U.S. Music] from the name of its producing division, Washburn Guitars," explained Schlacher.

Building fine musical instruments is an art in itself, and the production crew at Washburn takes its job seriously. "Every guitar that is shipped from the Chicago area factory is constructed with passion only a musician can feel," says the Washburn Web site. Each acoustic guitar is built by one craftsperson—called a luthier—from start to finish. "These guitars are crafted with the hard-working spirit and quality standards of the luthiers that have crafted Washburn guitars since the late 1800s for musicians and songwriters around the world."

"I like working with wood, taking it from raw lumber to an actual musical instrument with its own voice," says luthier John Stover. Stover has built acoustic guitars for such musical stars as Dolly Parton and Dan Donegan of Chicago-based metal band Disturbed.

Even though the guitars are built by hand, Washburn uses computer-aided design and manufacturing (CAD/CAM) technologies in its manufacturing process. A CAD/CAM engineer helps design and draw new guitar models. The electric models that are built on an assembly line are still guided by expert craftspeople whose jobs may be assembly lead or neck lead (the worker in charge of building and assembling guitar necks).

Building only 2,500 guitars a year for the general public while maintaining Washburn's high quality standards is expensive. But Washburn finds ways to save in production costs so that it can charge customers reasonable prices for its products; many of its models retail for between $500 and $1,000. Some models are manufactured in Indonesia, where labor is less expensive. Also, although Washburn accepts customized requests through dealers on its current line of guitars and basses made in the United States, the firm does not offer individual custom designs. So a customer could ask for a different paint finish or a left-handed conversion—but not an entirely different design. This system means that customers generally get what they want—without paying exorbitant prices. And it allows Washburn to carefully control its inventory of raw materials and components.

Occasionally Washburn creates an alliance with a musician such as Dan Donegan for a particular series of instruments. Together with Washburn's luthiers and production team, Donegan designed a new series of guitars called Maya (after Donegan's daughter). "Washburn really went above and beyond to make sure my guitars are to my exact specification. I really wanted to create a guitar that is somewhat unique but appeals to artists of all musical genres," said Donegan of his experience with Washburn. The Maya standard and Maya Pro guitars are both built in the United States and come with a range of components. The Maya standard is made of poplar and retails at about $1,500, while the Pro is made of mahogany and retails for just under $2,700. Washburn is also producing a limited customized edition of the Maya line that will be available through select dealers.

Building a guitar is clearly a labor of love for those who work at Washburn. These craftspeople understand the needs of their customers because most of them are musicians themselves. So working with someone like Dan Donegan is as smooth a process as strumming an old tune. Production manager Gil Vasquez explains his job at Washburn this way: "My knowledge of guitars is vast, and I am constantly searching for the ultimate tone, whether it is in the way the guitar is constructed or in the electronics that are being used." Vasquez knows what he is talking about; his customers include Lenny Kravitz, Eric Clapton, Jimmy Page—and Dan Donegan.

1. How do production and operations management contribute to the long-term success of Washburn Guitars?
2. Describe the manufacturing technique(s) you think are applicable to Washburn. Also, explain how CAD and CAM contribute to the design and production processes at Washburn.
3. Describe the physical variables and human factors involved in Washburn's choice of location for its headquarters and production facility in Mundelein, Illinois.

4. What are the benefits of quality control at Washburn? What methods might the firm use for controlling quality?

**Sources:** Washburn Web site, accessed September 8, 2006, http://www.washburn.com; Dan Moran, "U.S. Music Corp.'s Washburn Guitars No Strangers to Fame," *Suburban Chicago News,* accessed September 8, 2006, http://www.suburban chicagonews.com; "Washburn Guitars," Answers.com, accessed September 8, 2006, http://www.answers.com; "Disturbed's Dan Donegan Signature Series Washburn Guitar at Winter NAMM," All About Jazz, September 8, 2006, http://www.allaboutjazz.com; Washburn's 2006 Winter Catalog.

## VIDEO Case 12.2

## Harley-Davidson: An American Icon Cruises into Its Second Century

Freedom. Adventure. Fun. These three words best describe the experience of riding a Harley-Davidson motorcycle, and the Milwaukee-based company wants to keep it that way. Harley-Davidson has been manufacturing its heavyweight motorcycles for more than a century—so long, in fact, that they are woven into America's automotive heritage. From the telltale pop and roar of their engines to their signature teardrop-shaped gas tanks, Harley "hogs" have been a key part of America's motorcycle racing and touring culture. Elvis Presley even appeared on the cover of the company's *Enthusiast* magazine. So how did Harley-Davidson become so popular with its riders? By treating them as part of a family—one they can choose to join.

Through market segmentation, Harley-Davidson researched who its customers are. The company knows that the largest customer segment of Harley owners—its target market—is a 40-something male with a median income of a little more than $80,000 who probably owned a Harley-Davidson motorcycle previously. The company's Web site lists the statistical breakdown of its purchasers as 89 percent male and 11 percent female. Approximately 43 percent have already owned a Harley, 29 percent have owned a competitor's motorcycle, and 28 percent have not owned a motorcycle before. Marketers at the company use this information to help them design their products and programs.

To make sure that customers can find exactly the type of bike they want, the company manufactures 36 Harley-Davidson models and 8 Buell sport motorcycle models. And it makes sure that the bikes are ready where and when customers are ready to purchase them, committing its manufacturing plants to producing a record of roughly 350,000 motorcycles in a recent year. With such production rates, company finances have been roaring ahead. In fact, over

the past decade Harley-Davidson's annual growth rates for revenues and earnings have been climbing steadily. To make purchasing its motorcycles even more convenient, the company offers its Harley-Davidson Financial Services program, which provides financing and insurance programs for both its dealers and customers.

A key part of developing long-term relationships with customers is the Harley Owners Group (HOGs), with more than 1 million members worldwide. A one-year full membership is automatically given to anyone who purchases a new, unregistered Harley-Davidson motorcycle. Full HOG memberships cost $45 a year, with discounts for two- or three-year memberships. The company also offers associate memberships for HOG family members and passengers and life memberships for those die-hard Harley owners. What do members get for enrolling? Entry into the members-only portion of the HOG Web site, three to four issues of *Enthusiast* magazine a year, a subscription to the company's *Hogtales* member publication, a membership manual, access to a toll-free number with customer-service representatives available during daytime hours, and a touring handbook for trip planning. In addition, Harley-Davidson sponsors local chapters in the United States, Canada, Europe, Australia, New Zealand, and Japan. The company also sponsors events such as touring rallies, Pin Stops at which members can receive commemorative pins, Pit Stops where members can relax and socialize with other Harley owners at motorcycle races, open houses, parades and charity functions, and a HOG Hospitality area at Daytona Bike Week and the Sturgis Rally and Races.

For those wanting to take extended bike trips to faraway places, the company provides a travel service through its Web site, where members can schedule a Fly & Ride vacation. With a three-week advance reservation and payment of a deposit, full HOG members can fly to 41 locations throughout the United States, Canada, Europe, and Australia and pick up a Harley-Davidson motorcycle from a local dealership to tour in style. Or members can simply rent cycles through selected dealerships. And because the company wants riders for life, it also sponsors a safe rider skills program, through which it reimburses HOG members with a $50 coupon for successfully completing an accredited Motorcycle Safety Foundation training program.

Once customers have purchased a Harley-Davidson motorcycle, they may need some gear to go with it—a black leather jacket, T-shirt, or other equipment emblazoned with the familiar orange-and-black bar-and-shield logo. In addition to the more than 1,300 dealerships in 60 countries worldwide, satellite stores in shopping malls and other retail areas can outfit customers from head to toe. The company also offers collectible patches and pins for special events throughout the calendar year.

Harley-Davidson says its mission is to fulfill dreams through motorcycling experiences. Many HOGs across the globe would agree that it is succeeding.

## Questions for Critical Thinking

1. How does Harley-Davidson provide customers with form, time, place, and ownership utility for its motorcycles?
2. Would you say that Harley-Davidson creates customer satisfaction with its products? Support your answer.
3. What are the characteristics of Harley-Davidson's target market? Should the company's marketers focus solely on that market segment?
4. In what ways does Harley-Davidson practice relationship marketing?

**Sources:** Harley-Davidson Web site, accessed September 8, 2006, http://www.harley-davidson.com; Harley Owners Group Web site, accessed September 8, 2006, http://www.hog.com; Harley-Davidson Motor Company brochure, downloaded from the company Web site; Library of Congress "Hog Heaven: Celebrating 100 Years of the Harley-Davidson," accessed September 8, 2006, http://www.loc.gov.

# VIDEO Case 13.2

## High Sierra Climbs to New Heights

Long gone are the days when only hikers carried backpacks into the mountains or stuffed duffels with climbing gear and lashed them to the back of a mule or llama. Today, these bags are the gear of choice for students and savvy travelers of all types. They are lightweight and durable and can be stowed easily under an airplane seat, on a bus, or in the back of an SUV. High Sierra Sport Company is one of the premier manufacturers of adventure bags—regardless of how you define *adventure*—and in less than 30 years has become the tenth largest outdoor company in the United States.

High Sierra manufactures an impressive array of day packs, backpacks, and duffels. But the firm also makes book bags specifically for students, business and computer cases, bike messenger bags, yoga bags, hydration packs (packs with water reservoirs), lumbar packs, and ski and snowboard packs. Many of these items also come in wheeled models for easy transport. In short, whatever activity you do, High Sierra probably has a pack or bag made specifically for it. The firm even has a "Build-a-Bag" service for customers who can't find exactly what they want.

High Sierra distributes its goods through more than 1,500 retailers—both online and in brick-and-mortar stores—including such outlets as MC Sports, Modell's, Bag'n Baggage, eBags, TravelGizmos.com, Kittery Trading Post, and Fogdog Sports. You can't buy your bag directly from the company, but you can visit the site to view every single bag they make, read about the features, and even get some tips on how to get the perfect fit. In addition to retailers, High Sierra also has corporate accounts, providing bags and packs to companies. And the firm has a strong presence at the Travel Goods Association (TGA) convention, where travel industry experts eagerly examine more than 2,000 new product lines every year.

High Sierra is always innovating with its designs and construction techniques. Its executives—including top officer Hank Bernbaum—and employees are travelers who use the products they make, and they constantly look for ideas to create new products and improve existing ones. New colors, lighter and more durable fabrics, additional security features, multiuse bags, and trendy accessories are often on the list of improvements. "Consumers are driving this continuing surge of innovation," explains TGA president

Michele Marini Pittenger. "They want to travel more safely and securely, with greater comfort. And manufacturers and retailers have learned just how fast they can adapt to those changing needs. Rather than a year to get a new product to market, they're realizing they can do it in months."

High Sierra added to its reputation for quality and cutting-edge design a few years ago, when it became the official supplier of bags to the U.S. Olympic Ski Team and U.S. Olympic Snowboarding Team. The firm manufactures customized backpacks, boot bags, ski and board bags, and duffels for these teams. In addition, High Sierra makes a limited number of these models available for sale to consumers—with the official team logos—including the Loop Pack, the Jackknife Pack, the Mia Messenger Bag, and the Kahuna 70 Hydration Pack. So a few lucky skiers and snowboarders can own the same bags the U.S. Olympians carry. All of these models and more are available through the U.S. Ski Team and Snowboarding Team Web sites. High Sierra has also won various awards for design and for customer service.

High Sierra continues to reach new heights in supplying goods to travelers, students, skiers and boarders, hikers, and everyone else who wants durable, fashionable packs and bags. "You provide the adventure, we provide the gear," says the company slogan. Whether you're standing on a mountain summit or a street corner, High Sierra's got a bag for you.

## Questions for Critical Thinking

1. How would you classify High Sierra's products? Explain your choice.
2. Visit High Sierra's Web site at http//www.highsierrasport.com to view the firm's products. Briefly describe High Sierra's overall product mix. Then choose a product line and outline the features that make it unique as well as those that make it fit the mix.
3. Describe the factors that contribute to High Sierra's brand equity.
4. High Sierra sells its products through retailers and through the U.S. Ski and Snowboarding Teams. Do you view this as an effective distribution strategy? Why or why not?

**Sources:** U.S. Ski Team Web site, accessed September 8, 2006, http://www.ussa.org; High Sierra Web site, accessed September 8, 2006, http://www.highsierrasport.com; "Great Gifts for Grads," *USA Shopping News,* accessed September 8, 2006, http://www.usa101.com; "High Sierra Sport Company," Google Finance, accessed September 8, 2006, http://www.google.com/finance; Gear Trends, accessed September 8, 2006, http://www.geartrends.com; "Cyber Sidebar/Leader of the Pack," *Hemispheres,* accessed September 8, 2006, http://www.zipitgear.com; "About High Sierra," Luggage.com, accessed September 8, 2006, http://www.luggage.com; "High Sierra Sport Company Wins Microsoft Pinnacle Award," Sikich Worldwide, September 8, 2006, http://www.icsadvantage.com.

## VIDEO Case 14.2

## Wild Oats Promotes Local Foods

Whether or not you shop at organic food stores, by now you have seen entire sections of organic foods in even the biggest supermarket chains. Organic foods range from the more typical fresh produce to packaged goods such as corn chips and macaroni and cheese. Although organic and natural foods still make up only 8 percent of the grocery market, they are the fastest-growing food segment in the United States. According to the U.S. Department of Agriculture, the number of farmers' markets has increased 79 percent in just over a decade, and 75 percent of consumers surveyed want to know more about what is in—and on—the food they buy.

Wild Oats Markets is part of this trend. Founded in 1987 with a single store, the Boulder, Colorado–based firm now operates more than 110 stores in 25 states and Canada. Wild Oats sells only natural, organic, premium, and gourmet foods. Its fruit and vegetables are grown without syn-

thetic pesticides, herbicides, or fertilizers. Its seafood is chemical free, not soaked or dipped to increase its weight or alter its appearance. Its candy is naturally sweetened without refined sugar. Its meat and poultry are raised without antibiotics, artificial hormones, or other growth-promoting drugs. Its breads are baked fresh daily with all-natural ingredients. All of this means healthful foods for consumers—and a brand identity for Wild Oats. "Because we are a specialty retailer, we think of ourselves as a brand, not as a grocery store," says company spokesperson Laura Copeland. "The sort of items we offer are not available in many stores." Copeland observes that Wild Oats promotes to a specific market. "Our customers tend to be more educated, with a higher income," she observes. "Education is the biggest driver for the consumption of natural and organic foods."

Knowing who its customers are is the basis for Wild Oats's promotional strategy. Instead of spending a lot of time and money on television advertising, Wild Oats focuses much of its mass media promotion on print advertising—because its customers tend to be readers. "Our print ads have vibrant food images, but they tend to be text heavy," says Copeland. "We provide a lot of information about the products and services we offer. Generally we'll run a recipe, and we might feature one of our employees." In addition, Wild Oats publishes a monthly magazine insert distributed in newspapers. The magazine has full-color photographs, recipes, information about products, and a calendar of store events. It also lists sale items.

Wild Oats reaches out to the communities in which it operates—or where its products are grown—building good public relations. One of its community programs is called "Choose Local," which features fresh, organic produce from local growers, farmers, and artisans in each of its stores during the month of July. "We believe strongly in supporting the local communities where we do business, and we're dedicated to providing high-quality, local products whenever possible," says Perry Odak, president and CEO. "This local focus boosts area economies, reduces negative environmental impacts, and supports sustainable agriculture. Our commitment to these efforts is long term; it's part of our mission."

Each Wild Oats store has its own marketing person and budget, so many of the promotional efforts are local and rely on grassroots marketing. The local marketer attends community events, helping build awareness of Wild Oats and its products. Wild Oats also takes a visible stance on food issues, which generates publicity. "We have a high profile, so we get a lot of exposure in that area," notes Laura Copeland. "Public relations is very important. The power of the written word is most effective when it is not purchased." Wild Oats was recently praised for donating $55,000 to the Sierra Club in recognition of Earth Day and for announcing that it would begin sales of eggs from hens that are certified as humanely raised.

Having an in-store marketer means that store promotions can be tailored to meet the needs of each location and its customers. Education is the main focus of many of the promotional materials—the company reasons that customers who know and understand the products will buy them. "We have a lot of in-store signage," says Copeland, "but it's more about information than price. There are a lot of informational and educational posters and signs and shelf takers—giant signs that attach to the front of the shelf. Instead of featuring coupons, they feature information." Savvy customers find store coupons at the Wild Oats Web site. The staff is trained to provide more information and suggestions to customers, who often act on those suggestions by making purchases. Wild Oats also does a lot of in-store sampling—if customers try a specialty cheese or take a bite of grilled, marinated chicken, they are more likely to buy it.

All of this effort comes at a price—Wild Oats products may cost a bit more, but loyal customers are evidence that the expense is worthwhile. A bowl of fresh blueberries, a warm loaf of crusty bread, and a decadent chocolate cake all speak for themselves. They're all good food.

## Questions for Critical Thinking

1. How does Wild Oats use integrated marketing communications to create a unified promotional strategy?
2. Describe the components of the Wild Oats promotional mix and the way they contribute to the firm's objectives of promotion.
3. Why are personal selling and public relations such an important part of Wild Oats's promotional strategy?
4. What ethical issues might arise for Wild Oats in its promotional activities?

**Sources:** Wild Oats Web site, accessed September 8, 2006, http://www.wildoats.com; "Wild Oats Markets Redefines Green Grocer," The marketing info, accessed September 8, 2006, http://the-marketing.info; "Wild Oats Urges Customers to Choose Local," IDFA Smart Brief, accessed September 8, 2006, http://smartbrief.com/news; "Food Fest at Wild Oats," *Saugus Advertiser,* accessed September 8, 2006, http://www.townonline.com; "Wild Oats to Sell Eggs Certified as Humanely Raised," *New Mexico Business Weekly,* accessed September 8, 2006, http://www.bizjournals.com; "Wild Oats Donates $55K-Plus to Sierra Club for Earth Day," *Progressive Grocer,* accessed September 8, 2006, http://www.progressivegrocer.com.

 **Case 15.2**

### Peet's Coffee & Tea: Just What the Customer Ordered

A freshly brewed cup of coffee is one of life's simple pleasures; there's nothing high-tech about it. Or is there? California-based Peet's Coffee & Tea has specialized in offering consumers the richest, freshest coffee beans and select teas for more than 40 years. Although Peet's roasts its coffee beans in small batches by hand—every day—technology is still involved in the way the firm handles customer orders, processes information, and sends out shipments.

Peet's sells 32 different kinds of coffee—single bean, blends, and decaffeinated. It also sells a variety of teas. The coffee beans are roasted daily, and some are then ground to order in a variety of styles. Each order, large or small, is packaged and shipped the same day for freshness. Managing information in order to accomplish these tasks quickly and sell through five different channels—the company's 100-plus retail stores, mail order, the Internet, grocery stores, and corporate food services—requires the right technology. An individual customer may place an order through Peets.com, while grocery stores use an extranet at Peets.net. Or a customer may phone the call center, which transfers the order to the company's intranet. The firm also offers the Peetniks program, which automatically generates reorders for customers. Online customers have until midnight Pacific Standard Time to place an order for the next day.

Peet's relies on an order-fulfillment system designed by software producer Great Plains and modified over the years to meet the changing needs of the firm as it has grown. The system creates a roasting spreadsheet, which shows the roasters how many pounds of each kind of coffee to roast on a given day. The system also generates reports that show how big the order size of each type of coffee is and where it is going, which determines which roasting machine will be used. Once the coffee has finished the roasting process, the system indicates how much of each type of coffee will go to each channel. Because each channel uses different packaging, the system diverts the right amount of each coffee to the correct order-fulfillment department for packaging. A spreadsheet tells workers how much coffee goes into grocery packaging, how much goes into 5-pound "pillow packs" for Peet's retail stores, and how much goes into 1-pound bags for mail-order and Internet customers.

Finally, the system produces labels for the packages and shipping labels. The labels designate the type of coffee and the roasting date, so groceries and Peet's stores can monitor their inventory for freshness. This ordering process takes place continually throughout the day, with the system sorting information and directing the right coffee to the right place. "Before we had this system, the roasting staff just estimated what they needed to roast each day," recalls Mike Cloutier of Peet's. "This system is far more efficient."

Computer software can't physically transport a package of coffee from one location to another. So Peet's uses the FloShipper system, an automated conveyor system that boxes and tapes each packaged order of coffee, weighs it, and slots it into the appropriate shipping lane. The system is designed specially to handle individual orders from consumers. The hand-roasted coffee then gets to customers more quickly. Before Peet's adopted this system, Peet's workers took two shifts to complete an order manually; now the time is down to one shift. "We could not meet our same day roast-and-ship standards without the FloShipper system," says Peet's director of plant operations.

Throughout the Peet's organization, technology meets craftsmanship every day. Without the order-fulfillment software and automated shipping systems, customers would not receive the freshest coffee—which is still roasted by hand every day, the way it was 40 years ago.

## Questions for Critical Thinking

1. What are some of the data that Peet's order-fulfillment system gathers? What kind of information does it provide to workers?
2. How does technology help Peet's devote more time and resources to its core business?
3. How might Peet's use an enterprise resource planning (ERP) system?
4. How might Peet's use desktop publishing systems to communicate with consumers and business customers?

**Sources:** Peet's Web site, accessed September 8, 2006, http://www.peets.com; "National Coffee Roaster Streamlines B2C Fulfillment System," FloStor, accessed September 8, 2006, http://www.flostor.com; "Peet's Coffee & Tea, Inc.," Google Finance, accessed September 8, 2006, http://finance.google.com; "Peet's Coffee & Tea Celebrates 40 Years of Craftsmanship," *Badgett's Coffee Journal,* accessed September 8, 2006, http://www.aboutcoffee.net.

## VIDEO Case 16.2

### Taking Account: The Little Guys

Accounting is a vital part of every business, large and small. The Little Guys—an independent retailer based in the Chicago suburbs that specializes in selling and installing home theater equipment—is no exception. How does The Little Guys stay ahead of big guys such as Best Buy and Circuit City? By focusing carefully on what its customers want and purchasing and stocking merchandise wisely. The firm has made a name for itself through customer service, including hiring a friendly, knowledgeable staff that is eager to educate customers on the latest high-tech equipment. And it has adapted to changes in the market. "The biggest change in the industry is that five years ago brands drove people to our store," observes co-founder David Wexler. "Today, the manufacturers' brands are everywhere, so the brand is now us. It's 'The Little Guys' name that's most important." In fact, industry surveys confirm that consumers now care more about customer service and financial incentives than they do about big brand names in consumer electronics.

Making decisions about such issues as merchandise and staff payroll is all part of accounting—both short term and long term. Co-founder Evie Wexler handles most of the day-to-day accounting for The Little Guys with the help of the software program QuickBooks. Many small-business owners use such commercially available programs to help run their firms. Wexler reports that QuickBooks simplifies many accounting tasks, automatically placing data in the correct category. "[QuickBooks] writes all the checks, so that when you balance the checkbook, it's all there," she says. "When we started, we were small enough that someone could have kept the books by hand. What we've grown into—the amount of things we receive each day, the amount that goes out, the number of employees we have—it's too complex. The program gives us a better picture of what goes on in the business every day."

For more complex accounting issues, the Wexlers turn to an outside accountant, whom they view as a business consultant—not just someone who fills out forms and reports. They have relied on their accountant's expertise from the beginning. "When we first opened the store, we worked with the accountant as a consultant," recalls David. "He helped us understand some of the technicalities of opening a business. We wrote out a business plan." The business plan specified how much they would spend on advertising, rent, utilities, payroll, and other expenses.

Operating expenses such as payroll and overhead must be tracked carefully. Payroll in particular is a complicated accounting task for The Little Guys. The sales staff is paid based on a percentage of sales, providing an incentive for each salesperson to perform. "Because we pay on a percentage, payroll is difficult," explains Evie Wexler. "There are percentages and base pay. There are lots of idiosyncracies—401k, federal tax, [state] tax, Social Security, and Medicare. You have to track all of this." Overhead expenses such as warehousing and truck maintenance are another part of the accounting puzzle. And the retail store also needs to be insured. "When you look at your profit/loss statement, you can see how much it costs you to do business every day," says Evie.

The Wexlers and their business partner meet to review financial statements for each quarter. They evaluate each expense category to determine whether they are spending too much or not enough to get the results they want. David focuses on the sales figures for each month and compares them with the same month of the previous year. He notes that when they started their business, he tried to look at the sales figures for every day. But he learned that "you can't

do that—you'll drive yourself crazy. Now I'll look every week or ten days. You need a bigger slice of time." He points out that variables such as snowstorms, five Saturdays in a month, or a major sale can all skew the numbers. But he explains that they examine overall trends to make decisions. Perhaps surprisingly, Evie says, "We don't set financial goals. We look at how we did for the year. Then we'll decide how much better we're doing this year."

The Little Guys prides itself on offering customers the latest, highest-quality home theater products. With those high-end products come high prices. But the firm's customers don't pay the ticket price. Instead, they negotiate a deal for a full home theater system, including installation. This customization affects the firm's cash flow. "Sometimes we find ourselves in hot water, and then we react," says Evie. During one season, customers were placing special orders for items that The Little Guys had to pay the manufacturers for up front. Meanwhile, in-stock items were sitting on the shelves. So the Wexlers instructed the sales staff to concentrate on selling those in-stock items in order to improve the store's cash flow.

Because The Little Guys is—yes—little, it can be more flexible in the way it handles buying decisions than larger firms can. "Most businesses are more structured," says Evie. "Because we own the business, we don't buy new things without talking to each other. We have to be a little bit risky in order to be flexible and offer our customers the best products." As a result, the business doesn't have a rigid budget for the products it purchases. But the Wexlers wouldn't operate any other way. Evie admits that worrying about bills sometimes keeps her up at night. But years of experience have taught these business owners that they can compete successfully against the big guys.

## Questions for Critical Thinking

1. What role does an outside accountant play for a small firm like The Little Guys?
2. How might accounting help The Little Guys grow as a business?
3. For The Little Guys, create a table with three columns and list the major classifications of data in the accounting equation—assets, liabilities, and owners' equity—that could be used later in the firm's balance sheet.
4. Evie Wexler says that her firm does not have a rigid budget for purchasing items to sell in the store. But what role does a budget play in planning and providing standards by which The Little Guys can measure its performance?

**Sources:** The Little Guys Web site, accessed September 8, 2006, http://www.thelittleguys.com; Alan Wolf, "Consumers Cutting Back on CE Purchases This Summer," *This Week in Consumer Electronics,* accessed September 8, 2006, http://www.twice.com; Lisa Johnston, "Study: Brand-Name Importance Drops for CE Shoppers," *This Week in Consumer Electronics,* accessed September 8, 2006, http://www.twice.com; Alan Wolf, "Glikes to HTSA: Stay Ahead of the Curve," *This Week in Consumer Electronics,* accessed September 8, 2006, http://www.twice.com.

## JPMorganChase Lends a Hand to Small Business

If you own a small business or are thinking of starting one, you can get help from a big name in banking: JPMorgan-Chase. Ranked seventeenth on a recent *Fortune* 500 list, the bank is the third-largest in the United States in terms of revenues. JPMorganChase has assets of $1.3 trillion and operates in more than 50 countries worldwide. In short, the bank has considerable clout in the financial world. So you might think that it would concentrate only on serving huge corporations and the very wealthy. Not true: through its U.S. consumer and commercial banking subsidiary, Chicago-based Chase, the company reaches out to small businesses—those with revenues up to $10 million—with a variety of financial services and the latest technology.

Noting the importance of service to individual customers, CEO James Dimon says, "Huge companies operating in . . . fiercely competitive industries like ours can only achieve and sustain their success by competing where 'the rubber hits the road'—at the level of the store, the product, and the banker—not at corporate headquarters." So Chase works hard to offer small businesses both service and convenience. The firm's Chase Online for Small Business site allows companies to manage their checking and savings accounts, review their account history, make payments such as employee payroll via direct deposit, pay certain federal taxes, download account transactions into their business accounting software, reorder checks, stop payments, and even change their address—all with security protection. Chase also offers ATM/ debit cards, which companies can use to access ATM terminals or to make payments without writing checks. Customers who have personal as well as business accounts can manage them online through their personal account linkage. For those doing business globally, Chase also offers a foreign exchange transfer service. All of these services are available to clients using personal computers or Macs and standard browsers with security features called 128-bit encryption. You can even check your browser's encryption capability at the Chase Web site.

To fund daily expenses or major expansions, a small-business owner can obtain credit and loans from Chase. Through its Business Line of Credit, Business Overdraft Line of Credit, and Business Credit Card services, Chase allows firms to meet short-term cash needs. The line of credit service allows firms to borrow $10,000 or more through a revolving account, by which borrowers repay principal and interest on the funds used. Credit lines can be accessed by writing checks, using a company card, or telephoning a personal banker, and customers repay the borrowed funds via monthly installments. The overdraft line of credit covers a firm's checking account, protecting it if the account is overdrawn. But if a business owner never overdraws the account, he or she pays nothing, and there is no annual fee. The Chase Business Credit Card services offer a variety of products; some have low introductory rates and no annual fees, while others give cash back for purchases or travel rewards.

Long-term loans can be obtained to purchase major equipment or expand the business in other ways. Loans range upward from $5,000 and carry either fixed or variable rates. Payments can be deducted automatically from the company's business checking account. Chase also provides real estate loans starting at $50,000 and, if firms qualify, Small Business Administration Loans, which have longer repayment terms and higher borrowing limits. If the company wants to lease capital equipment, it can set up a True Lease or Motor Vehicle Lease for large transportation, manufacturing, and construction equipment or furniture, fixtures, and computers. At the end of the lease term, the firm has the option to purchase the equipment or return it to the owner.

When a business earns profits, it can turn to Chase to invest those funds to generate additional revenue or even to set up a retirement plan. Chase also provides Merchant Services that allow retail companies to accept payments 24/7 in many forms.

If you're just starting out and need assistance in writing a business plan or completing financial statements, Chase can help through its Business Resource Center. That link on the Web site explains financial terms used in the industry, details what a business plan should contain, and provides sample calculations for key financial statements.

Of course, offering all of these technical services to small businesses does not mean that Chase isn't interested in the owners themselves. The bank has spent hundreds of millions of dollars to open 150 new branches in a recent year, added more retail loan officers, and hired additional personal bankers. So if you feel like strolling into a Chase bank and getting to know your banker face to face, someone will be close by, ready to give you a handshake and discuss your financial needs.

### Questions for Critical Thinking

1. If you were a small-business owner, how might Chase help you organize and track day-to-day income and expenses? Why is it important to track these items?

2. What types of short-term funds does Chase offer to small businesses? What types of long-term funds?

3. As a financial institution, how would you classify JPMorganChase? Explain your reasoning.

4. What types of electronic banking services does Chase offer? How could they help a small-business owner?

**Sources:** JPMorganChase Web site, accessed September 8, 2006, http://www.jpmorganchase.com; Chase Web site, accessed September 8, 2006, http://www.chase.com; "J.P. Morgan Chase & Co.," *Fortune* 500 2006, http://money.cnn.com, accessed September 8, 2006; JPMorganChase, Annual Report 2005, accessed September 8, 2006, http://www.jpmorganchase.com.

## VIDEO Case 18.2

## A.G. Edwards: Helping Businesses Grow

Your first experience with money undoubtedly was a piggy bank. By now, you may have tried your hand at investing in a few securities. Businesses also save and invest their funds. To grow, they invest some of their profits in a variety of financial instruments. A.G. Edwards is a full-service brokerage firm that helps businesses—and individuals— select and manage their investments. A member of the New York Stock Exchange (NYSE), A.G. Edwards employs nearly 7,000 consultants in more than 700 offices in the U.S. and abroad. As the firm reaches its 120th year in business, it continues to focus on its mission to "furnish financial services of value to our clients."

A.G. Edwards was founded by General Albert Gallatin Edwards upon his retirement from the post of assistant secretary of the treasury in St. Louis, to which he was appointed by President Abraham Lincoln. His founding partner was his son, Benjamin Franklin Edwards. Later, the small firm helped middle-class investors purchase Liberty Bonds, and unlike other firms, it suffered only minor losses in the stock crash of 1929. In the 1970s, A.G. Edwards became one of the first publicly held brokerage firms. By the 21st century, Edwards had been on *Fortune*'s list of "100 Best Companies to Work For" many times.

Edwards conducts business in a couple of ways. Although the firm usually acts as a broker-dealer in the purchasing and selling of securities, it also takes the role of investment advisor for certain designated accounts. Edwards's financial consultants do not have instructions to sell their company's products and do not fulfill sales quotas for those products. Investors—large or small—are not required to maintain a minimum balance in their accounts.

Technology has transformed the financial industry— instead of emptying your piggy bank to make an investment, you can make your purchase online. Clients can buy and sell securities at any time of the day, seven days a week. To accomplish these transactions and all of its other services—reporting and tracking tasks, and manipulation of

data required to run an investment business—A.G. Edwards must have state-of-the-art information technology (IT) systems. In the last few years, Chief Technology Officer John Parker has revamped the firm's entire IT department, including the software and methodologies it uses to complete new projects. Parker credits the success of this technology update to top management's commitment to innovation. "If you try to fix [IT] project management without fixing the top first, you're not going to have much success," he explains. But upper management gave him the go-ahead to make the necessary changes. The IT department now boasts an 88 percent success rate in completing systems projects on time and on budget—a remarkable track record.

These new information systems translate to greater efficiency—and personalization—for clients. Clients who are new to A.G. Edwards receive their own home page at the firm's Web site. Brokers can post customized information on their clients' home pages, while the clients can access detailed spreadsheets showing activity on all their accounts. The A.G. Edwards site provides research information and analysis such as its Market Monitor column and real-time market quotes, with online stock and option trading on the near horizon. Tech support is always available. Business clients may use customized financial systems to implement employee benefit plans, invest cash for the short term, provide insurance for the business and employees, and research financing.

Do you think you want to be a financial consultant? A.G. Edwards emphasizes the importance of discipline, perseverance, accountability, and a positive attitude. The firm recognizes that it is handling people's life savings and businesses' opportunities to soar or crash. So Edwards searches carefully for people who are organized and focused, who don't mind working long hours for clients, who take responsibility for their own decisions, and whose positive outlook attracts clients.

Edwards has survived economic upswings and downturns for more than a century. Visitors to the Web site learn quickly that the firm expects to be in the business for the long term, helping individual and institutional investors achieve the most they can with their money. Says the firm, "We've been making sure we put our clients' needs first for more than 118 years, and we plan to continue this mission for another 118."

## Questions for Critical Thinking

1. Describe the goals of an individual investor that A.G. Edwards might serve. Describe the goals of an institutional investor that A.G. Edwards might serve.
2. A.G. Edwards is a full-service brokerage firm. How would its services differ from those of a discount firm?
3. Why is it important for potential employees of A.G. Edwards to possess the qualities of discipline, perseverance, accountability, and a positive attitude described in the case?
4. Suppose you had started your own business in the last year. How might A.G. Edwards help your firm grow?

**Sources:** A.G. Edwards Web site, accessed September 8, 2006, http://www.agedwards.com; "A.G. Edwards, *Fortune* 100 Best Companies to Work For 2006," CNN Money.com, accessed September 8, 2006, http://money.cnn.com; Jocelyn Drake, "Financials Find Their Footing," *Forbes*, accessed September 8, 2006, http://www.forbes.com; Meredith Levinson, "When Failure Is Not an Option," *CIO Magazine*, accessed September 8, 2006, http://www.cio.com.

# Risk Management and Insurance

## NEED INSURANCE? AISLE 4, ON THE RIGHT

Consumers have long been accustomed to buying everything from disposable razors to caviar and kayaks at "big box" stores such as Sam's Club and Costco. So these retailers have decided that insurance is another good product to offer for one-stop shoppers.

Costco, which has more than 400 warehouse-style stores in 36 states, has been offering its small-business customers PacifiCare Health System's health insurance coverage for a few years now. The company's assistant vice president of insurance services says that the discount retailer's recent decision to sell individual policies as well grew naturally out of the success of the small-business offering. "A lot of our business members have very small businesses, including sole proprietorships and husband-and-wife teams," she explains. "It's a logical extension of that program."

The individual coverage is being offered on a trial basis in the greater Los Angeles area. Costco hasn't set a date for a national rollout, which would require new partnerships with all the other insurers it works with outside California. Further complicating the possibility of expansion beyond California is the fact that health insurance regulations vary from state to state. But Costco hopes that the response in California will be big. To enroll in the individual plan, a shopper must have an executive membership card at Costco, which costs $100 a year and already includes such extras as long-distance phone service and auto financing. Almost half the company's 3.4 million executive members live in California.

Individual health insurance customers will be able to choose one of two plans: One has a deductible—the amount you must pay out of pocket for medical fees before your benefits kick in—of $1,500 a year, and the other has a deductible of $3,000. Each allows patients to see their doctors of choice for $35 per office visit.

The cost of the premiums—what people pay to sign up for the insurance—are in the neighborhood of 5 to 20 percent cheaper than comparable plans, depending on the buyer's age, location, number of dependents, and health history. The discount reflects lower commissions for sales agents and lower administrative costs because there are only two plans from which to choose. Costco and PacifiCare are hoping the plan's low cost may attract not only people interested in a cheaper plan than what they already have but also some of the country's 43 million people who have no insurance at all to cover their risk of high medical bills. With healthcare costs rising faster than most families' incomes, Costco just might be on to something.[1]

## APPENDIX OVERVIEW

Risk is a daily fact of life for both individuals and businesses. Sometimes it appears in the form of a serious illness or premature death. In other instances, it takes the form of property loss, such as the extensive damage to homes and businesses due to forest fires in Idaho or hurricanes in Louisiana. Risk can also occur as the result of the actions of others—such as a pizza delivery driver running a red light and striking another vehicle. In still other cases, risk may occur as a result of our own actions—we may not eat as many healthful foods as we should or decline an extended service warranty on a new computer.

Businesspeople must understand the types of risk they face and develop methods for dealing with them. One approach to risk is to shift it to specialized firms called *insurance companies.* This appendix discusses the concept of insurance in a business setting. It begins with a definition of risk. We then describe the various ways in which risk can be managed. Next, we list some of the major insurance concepts, such as what constitutes an insurable risk. The appendix concludes with an overview of the major types of insurance.

## THE CONCEPT OF RISK

**risk** uncertainty about loss or injury

**Risk** is uncertainty about loss or injury. Consider the risks faced by a typical business. A factory or warehouse faces the risk of fire, burglary, water damage, and physical deterioration. Accidents, judgments due to lawsuits, and natural disasters are just some of the risks faced by businesses. Risks can be divided into two major categories: speculative risk and pure risk.

**Speculative risk** gives the firm or individual the chance of either a profit or a loss. Purchasing shares of stock on the basis of the latest hot tip from an acquaintance at the local health club can result in profits or losses. Expanding operations into a new market may result in higher profits or the loss of invested funds.

**Pure risk,** on the other hand, involves only the chance of loss. Motorists, for example, always face the risk of accidents. If they occur, both financial and physical losses may result. If they do not occur, however, drivers do not profit. Insurance often helps individuals and businesses protect against financial loss resulting from pure risk.

## RISK MANAGEMENT

Because risk is an unavoidable part of business, managers must find ways to deal with it. The first step in any risk management plan is to recognize what's at risk and why it's at risk. After that, the manager must decide how to handle the risk. In general, businesses have four alternatives in handling risk: avoid it, minimize it, assume it, or transfer it.

Executives must consider many factors when evaluating the risks, both at home and abroad. These factors include a nation's economic stability; social and cultural factors, such as language; available technologies; distribution systems; and government regulations. International businesses are typically exposed to less risk in countries with stable economic, social and cultural, and political and legal environments.

### Avoiding Risk

Some of the pure risks facing individuals can be avoided by taking a healthy approach to life. Abstaining from smoking, getting regular exercise and staying physically fit, and not driving during blizzards and other hazardous conditions are three ways of avoiding personal risk. By the same token, businesses can also avoid some of the pure risks they face. For example, a manufacturer can locate a new production facility away from a flood-prone area.

## Reducing Risk

Managers can reduce or even eliminate many types of risk by removing hazards or taking preventive measures. Many companies develop safety programs to educate employees about potential hazards and the proper methods of performing certain dangerous tasks. For instance, any employee who works at a hazardous waste site is required to have training and medical monitoring that meet the federal Occupational Safety and Health Administration (OSHA) standards. The training and monitoring not only reduce risk but pay off on the bottom line. Aside from the human tragedy, accidents cost companies time and money.

Employees working at a hazardous waste site are required to have proper training and medical monitoring. This helps companies reduce risk.

Although many actions can reduce the risk involved in business operations, they cannot eliminate risk entirely. Most major business insurers help their clients avoid or minimize risk by offering the services of loss-prevention experts to conduct thorough reviews of their operations. These health and safety professionals evaluate customers' work environments and recommend procedures and equipment to help firms minimize worker injuries and property losses.

## Self-Insuring against Risk

Instead of purchasing insurance against certain types of pure risk, some companies accumulate funds to cover potential losses. So-called *self-insurance funds* are special funds created by periodically setting aside cash reserves that the firm can draw on in the event of a financial loss resulting from a pure risk. A firm makes regular payments to the fund, and it charges losses to the fund. Such a fund typically accompanies a risk-reduction program aimed at minimizing losses.

One of the most common forms of self-insurance is employee health insurance. Most companies provide health insurance coverage to employees as a component of their fringe benefit programs. Some firms, especially large ones, find it more economical to create a self-insurance fund covering employee healthcare expenses, as opposed to purchasing a health insurance policy from an insurance provider.

## Shifting Risk to an Insurance Company

Although a business or not-for-profit organization can take steps to avoid or reduce risk, the most common method of dealing with it is to shift it to others in the form of **insurance**—a contract by which an insurer, for a fee, agrees to reimburse another firm or individual a sum of money if a loss occurs. The insured party's fee to the insurance company for coverage against losses is called a **premium.** Insurance substitutes a small, known loss—the insurance premium—for a larger, unknown loss that may or may not occur. In the case of life insurance, the loss—death—is a certainty; the main uncertainty is the date when it will occur.

It is important for the insurer to understand the customer's business, risk exposure, and insurance needs. Firms that operate in several countries usually do business with insurance companies that maintain global networks of offices.

**insurance** contract by which the insurer, for a fee (the premium), agrees to reimburse another firm or individual a sum of money if a loss occurs

**premium** amount paid by the insured to the insurance company in exchange for insurance coverage

# BASIC INSURANCE CONCEPTS

Figure A.1 illustrates how an insurance company operates. The insurer collects premiums from policyholders in exchange for insurance coverage. The insurance company uses some of these funds to pay current claims and operating expenses. What's left over is held in the form of reserves, which are in turn invested. Reserves can be used to pay for unexpected losses. The returns from insurance company reserves may allow the insurer to reduce premiums, generate profits, or both. By investing reserves, the insurance industry represents a major source of long-term financing for other businesses.

An insurance company is a professional risk taker. For a fee, it accepts risks of loss or damage to businesses and individuals. Three basic principles underlie insurance: the concept of insurable interest, the concept of insurable risk, and the law of large numbers.

## Insurable Interest

**insurable interest** demonstration that a direct financial loss will result if some event occurs

**insurable risk** requirement that a pure risk must meet for the insurer to agree to provide protection

**underwriting** process used by an insurance company to determine who, or what, to insure and how much to charge for an insurance policy

To purchase insurance, an applicant must demonstrate an **insurable interest** in the property or life of the insured. In other words, the policyholder must stand to suffer a loss, financial or otherwise, due to fire, storm damage, accident, theft, illness, death, or lawsuit. A homeowner, for example, has an insurable interest in his or her home and its contents. In the case of life insurance coverage purchased for someone providing the bulk of a household's income, the policyholder's spouse and minor children have a clear insurable interest.

A firm can purchase property and liability insurance on physical assets—such as offices and factories—to cover losses due to such hazards as fire and theft because the company can demonstrate an obvious insurable interest. Similarly, because top managers are important assets to a company, a business often purchases key person life insurance, which compensates the business should an important manager die. By contrast, a businessperson cannot collect on insurance to cover damage to property of competitors because that person cannot demonstrate an insurable interest.

## Insurable Risk

**Insurable risk** refers to the requirements that a risk must meet in order for the insurer to provide protection. Only some pure risks, and no speculative ones, are insurable. Insurance companies impose five basic requirements for a pure risk to be considered an insurable risk:

1. The likelihood of loss should be reasonably predictable. If an insurance company cannot reasonably predict losses, it has no way of setting affordable premiums.
2. The loss should be financially measurable.
3. The loss should be accidental, or fortuitous.
4. The risk should be spread over a wide geographic area.
5. The insurance company has the right to set standards for accepting risk. This process of setting these standards is known as **underwriting.**

**Figure A.1** How an Insurance Company Operates

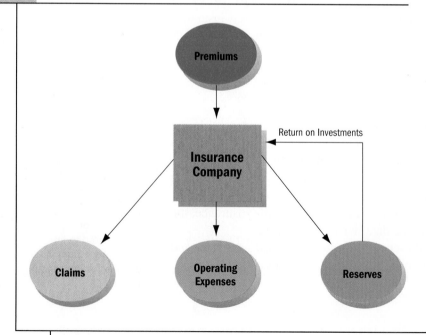

# The Law of Large Numbers

Insurance is based on the law of averages, or statistical probability. Insurance companies simply cannot afford to sell insurance policies unless they can reasonably predict losses. As a result, insurance companies have studied the chances of occurrences of deaths, injuries, property damage, lawsuits, and other types of hazards. Table A.1 is an example of the kind of data insurance companies examine. It shows the number of automobile accidents, by the age of the driver, for a recent year. From their investigations, insurance companies have developed **actuarial tables,** which predict the number of fires, automobile accidents, or deaths that will occur in a given year. Premiums charged for insurance coverage are based on these tables. Actuarial tables are based on the **law of large numbers.** In essence, the law of large numbers states that seemingly random events will follow a predictable pattern if enough events are observed.

An example can demonstrate how insurers use the law of large numbers to calculate premiums. Previously collected statistical data on a city with 50,000 homes indicates that the city will experience an average of 500 fires a year, with damages averaging $30,000 per occurrence. What is the minimum annual premium an insurance company would charge to insure a house against fire?

To simplify the calculations, assume that the premiums would not produce profits or cover any of the insurance company's operating expenses—they would just produce enough income to pay policyholders for their losses. In total, fires in the city would generate claims of $15 million (500 homes damaged × $30,000). If these losses were spread over all 50,000 homes, each homeowner would be charged an annual premium of $300 ($15 million divided by 50,000 homes). In reality, though, the insurance company would set the premium at a higher figure to cover operating expenses, build reserves, and earn a reasonable profit.

Some losses are easier for insurance companies to predict than others. Life insurance companies, for example, can pretty accurately predict the number of policyholders who will die within a specified period of time. Losses from such hazards as automobile accidents and weather events are much more difficult to predict. Insured losses resulting from a major hurricane—such as Katrina—can easily exceed $15 to $20 billion, but hurricanes are notoriously unpredictable.

**actuarial table** probability calculation of the number of specific events—such as deaths, injuries, fire, or windstorm losses—expected to occur within a given year

**law of large numbers** concept that seemingly random events will follow a predictable pattern if enough events are observed

**Table A.1**

Relationship between the Age of Driver and the Number of Motor Vehicle Accidents

| Age of Driver | Accidents per 100 Drivers |
| --- | --- |
| Under 19 | 46 |
| Between 20 and 24 | 22 |
| Between 25 and 34 | 11 |
| Between 35 and 44 | 8 |
| Between 45 and 54 | 6 |
| Between 55 and 64 | 5 |
| Between 65 and 74 | 5 |
| 75 and older | 5 |

**Source:** *Statistical Abstract of the United States (2006 edition),* accessed July 19, 2006, http://www.census.gov.

# SOURCES OF INSURANCE COVERAGE

The insurance industry includes both for-profit companies, such as Prudential, State Farm, and GEICO (part of famed investor Warren Buffett's Berkshire Hathaway), and a number of public agencies that provide insurance coverage for business firms, not-for-profit organizations, and individuals. Let's look at the primary features of this array of insurers.

## Public Insurance Agencies

A **public insurance agency** is a state or federal government unit established to provide specialized insurance protection for individuals and organizations. It provides protection in such areas as job loss (unemployment insurance) and work-related injuries (workers' compensation). Public insurance agencies also sponsor specialized programs, such as deposit, flood, and crop insurance.

*Unemployment Insurance* Every state has an unemployment insurance program that assists unemployed workers by providing financial benefits, job counseling, and placement services. Compensation amounts vary depending on workers' previous incomes and the states in which they file claims. These insurance programs are funded by payroll taxes paid by employers.

*Workers' Compensation* Under state laws, employers must provide workers' compensation insurance to guarantee payment of wages and salaries, medical care costs, and such rehabilitation services as retraining, job placement, and vocational rehabilitation to employees who are injured on the job. In addition, workers' compensation provides benefits in the form of weekly payments or single, lump-sum payments to survivors of workers who die as a result of work-related injuries. Premiums are based on the company's payroll, the on-the-job hazards to which it exposes workers, and its safety record.

*Social Security* The federal government is the nation's largest insurer. The Social Security program, established in 1935, provides retirement, survivor, and disability benefits to millions of Americans. **Medicare** was added to the Social Security program in 1965 to provide health insurance for people age 65 and older and certain other Social Security recipients. More than nine out of ten workers in the United States and their dependents are eligible for Social Security program benefits. The program is funded through a payroll tax, half of which is paid by employers and half by workers. Self-employed people pay the full tax.

## Private Insurance Companies

Much of the insurance in force is provided by private firms. These companies provide protection in exchange for the payment of premiums. Some private insurance companies are stockholder owned, and therefore are run like any other business, and others are so-called *mutual associations.* Most, though not all, mutual insurance companies specialize in life insurance. Technically, mutual insurance companies are owned by their policyholders, who may receive premium rebates in the form of dividends. In spite of this, however, there is no evidence that an insurance policy from a mutual company costs any less than a comparable policy from a stockholder-owned insurer. In recent years some mutual insurance companies have reorganized as stockholder-owned companies, including Prudential, one of the nation's largest insurers.

# TYPES OF INSURANCE

property and liability insurance general category of insurance that protects against financial losses due to a number of perils

Individuals and businesses spend hundreds of billions of dollars each year on insurance coverage. All too often, however, both business firms and individual households make poor decisions when buying insurance. Several commonsense tips for buying insurance are offered in Table A.2. Although insurers offer hundreds of different policies, they all fall into three broad categories: property and liability insurance, health and disability insurance, and life insurance.

## Property and Liability Insurance

Insurance that protects against fire, accident, theft, or other destructive events is called **property and liability insurance.** Examples of this insurance category include homeowners' insurance, auto insurance, business or commercial insurance, and liability insurance.

***Homeowners' Insurance***  Homeowners' insurance protects homeowners from damage to their homes due to various perils. If a home is destroyed by fire, for example, the homeowners' policy will pay to replace the home and its contents. Although standard policies cover a wide range of perils, most do not cover damage from widespread catastrophes such as floods and earthquakes. The federal government, through the National Flood Insurance Program, offers flood insurance as a supplement to a standard homeowners' policy. At an average cost of around $350 a year, flood insurance is often a wise purchase. Many of the homes in Florida, Louisiana, and Mississippi were damaged or destroyed by floods—not wind—as a result of Hurricane Katrina.

Homeowners in earthquake-prone areas can purchase earthquake insurance from a private insurer as an add-on to their homeowners' policy. However, earthquake coverage is expensive—the annual

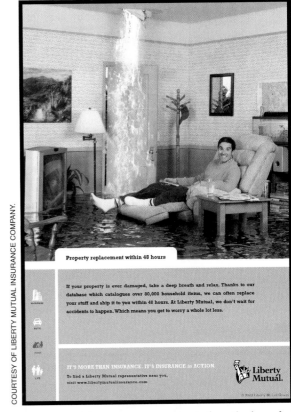

Property replacement within 48 hours

If your property is ever damaged, take a deep breath and relax. Thanks to our database which catalogues over 80,000 household items, we can often replace your stuff and ship it to you within 48 hours. At Liberty Mutual, we don't wait for accidents to happen. Which means you get to worry a whole lot less.

IT'S MORE THAN INSURANCE. IT'S INSURANCE *in* ACTION.
To find a Liberty Mutual representative near you, visit www.libertymutualinsurance.com

**Liberty Mutual.**

Homeowners' insurance protects people from the loss of what is usually their largest asset.

**Table**

**A.2**

## Some Commonsense Tips When Buying Insurance

- *Insure against big losses, not small ones.* Buy insurance to protect against big potential losses, but don't buy insurance to protect against small losses. A good example of this tip in action is to select the highest deductible you can afford on your property and liability insurance policies.

- *Buy insurance with broad coverage, not narrow coverage.* For example, it is much more cost-effective to buy a comprehensive health insurance policy, one that covers a wide range of illnesses and accidents, rather than several policies that cover only specific illnesses and accidents. It is extremely expensive to buy insurance coverage one disease at a time.

- *Shop around.* Insurance premiums for the same coverage can vary substantially. Insurance premiums also change frequently, so make sure to compare rates before renewing a policy.

- *Buy insurance only from financially strong companies.* Insurance companies occasionally go bankrupt. If this happens, you'll be left with no coverage and little chance of getting your premiums back. Several organizations—such as A.M. Best and Standard & Poor's—rate the financial strength of insurance companies.

**Source:** Louis E. Boone, David L. Kurtz, and Douglas Hearth, *Planning Your Financial Future,* 4th ed. (Mason, OH: Thomson South-Western, 2006), pp. 256–259.

premium often exceeds $1,000 with a $5,000 deductible—and not always available. States in earthquake-prone areas, such as California, are working with the insurance industry to make earthquake coverage more widely available and more affordable.

### Auto Insurance

With more than $130 billion in annual premiums, automobile insurance is the country's largest single type of property and liability insurance. Automobile insurance policies cover losses due to automobile accidents, including personal and property claims that result from accidents, fire, or theft. Virtually all states require drivers to have a minimum amount of auto insurance.

### Commercial and Business Insurance

Commercial and business insurance protects firms from financial losses resulting from the interruption of business operations (**business interruption insurance**) or physical damage to property as a result of fires, accidents, thefts, or other destructive events. Commercial and business insurance policies may also protect employers from employee dishonesty or losses resulting from nonperformance of contracts.

### Liability Insurance

**Liability insurance** protects an individual or business against financial losses to others for which the individual or business was responsible. If a driver runs a red light and hits another car, his or her liability insurance would pay to repair the damage to the other car. If a business sells a defective product, the firm's liability insurance would pay for financial losses sustained by customers. A standard amount of liability coverage is usually attached to auto, homeowners', and commercial insurance policies. Additional amounts of liability insurance can be purchased if needed. Adequate liability insurance is critically important today for both businesses and individuals. Wal-Mart, for example, requires all of its suppliers to have at least $2 million in liability coverage for their products.

## Health and Disability Insurance

Each of us faces the risk of getting sick or being injured in some way. Even a relatively minor illness can result in substantial health-care bills. To guard against this risk, most Americans have some form of **health insurance**—insurance that provides coverage for losses due to sickness or accidents. With soaring costs in healthcare, this type of insurance has become an important consideration for both businesses and individuals.

Sources of health insurance include private individual policies, private group policies, and the federal government, through Medicare and Medicaid (health insurance for lower-income people). More than 60 percent of Americans are covered by private group health insurance provided by their employer as an employee benefit. Four of every five U.S. employees work for businesses and not-for-profits that offer some form of group health insurance. Group policies resemble individual health insurance policies but are offered at lower premiums. Individual health insurance policies are simply too expensive for most people. Of every ten dollars spent by employers on employee compensation (wages, salaries, and employee benefits), more than one dollar goes to cover the cost of health insurance. As noted in the opening vignette, health insurance costs have soared in recent years and employers have responded by cutting back on benefits, requiring employees to pay more of the premium, or even dropping coverage altogether.

---

**business interruption insurance** insurance that protects firms from financial losses resulting from the interruption of business operations

**health insurance** insurance that covers losses due to illness or accidents

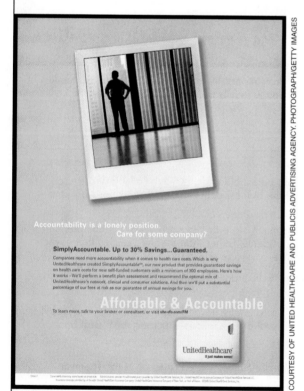

COURTESY OF UNITED HEALTHCARE AND PUBLICIS ADVERTISING AGENCY. PHOTOGRAPH/GETTY IMAGES

Providing health insurance is a major decision for employers.

Private health insurance plans fall into one of two general categories: fee-for-service plans and managed care plans. In a **fee-for-service plan,** the insured picks his or her doctor and has almost unlimited access to specialists. Fee-for-service plans charge an annual deductible and copayments. By contrast, a **managed care plan** pays most of the insured's healthcare bills. In return, the program has a great deal of say over the conditions of healthcare provided for the insured. Most managed care plans, for example, restrict the use of specialists and may specify which hospitals and pharmacies can be used. Some employers offer employees a choice between a fee-for-service and a managed care plan. (Some even offer multiple managed care plans.) Table A.3 compares the pros and cons of both types of healthcare plans.

Managed care plans have become extremely popular in recent years. More than 150 million Americans are enrolled in some form of managed care plan, and many fee-for-service plans have adopted some elements of managed care. A primary reason for the popularity of managed care is simply cost: managed care plans generally cost employers and employees less than fee-for-service plans. Managed care, however, is not without its critics. The effort to control costs has caused a backlash because of restrictions placed on doctors and patients. Legislation at both the federal and state level has forced managed care plans to give patients and physicians more control over medical decisions.

*Types of Managed Care Plans*   Two types of managed care plans can be found in the United States: health maintenance organizations and preferred provider organizations. Although both manage healthcare, important differences exist between the two.

**Health maintenance organizations (HMOs)** do not provide health insurance, they provide healthcare. An HMO supplies all of the individual's healthcare needs, including prescription drugs and hospitalization. The individual must use the HMO's own doctors and approved treatment facilities in order to receive benefits. Doctors and other healthcare professionals are actually employees of the HMO. Individuals pick a primary care physician and cannot see a specialist without a referral. An HMO charges no deductibles and only a low, fixed-dollar copayment.

**Table A.3**

Comparing Fee-for-Service Plans and Managed Care Health Plans

|  | Fee-for-Service Plan | Managed-Care Plan |
|---|---|---|
| Pros | • Almost unlimited choice of healthcare providers | • Little or no paperwork |
|  | • Easy access to medical specialists | • Lower out-of-pocket expenses |
|  | • Fewer limits on tests and diagnostic procedures | • No wait in getting reimbursed |
|  |  | • Pays for routine physicals and immunizations |
| Cons | • Higher out-of-pocket expenses (deductible and copayment) | • Choice of healthcare providers limited |
|  | • Some plans involve more paperwork and delays in getting reimbursed | • More difficult to change doctors |
|  | • Potentially more disputes with insurance company over charges | • Access to specialists restricted |
|  | • Some plans do not pay for routine physicals and immunizations | • Limits on tests and diagnostic procedures |

**Source:** Louis E. Boone, David L. Kurtz, and Douglas Hearth, *Planning Your Financial Future*, 4th ed. (Mason, OH: Thomson South-Western, 2006), p. 289.

The second type of managed care plan is the **preferred provider organization (PPO).** Although PPOs may get less publicity than HMOs, they actually cover more people. A PPO is an arrangement in which an employer negotiates a contract between local healthcare providers (physicians, hospitals, and pharmacies) to provide medical care to its employees at a discount. These plans have low fixed-dollar copayments. They are generally much more flexible than HMOs. Members can choose their primary care physician from a list of doctors. If a referral is given or hospitalization is required, the member again chooses from a list of approved healthcare providers. A member who obtains treatment from a healthcare provider outside the PPO network will likely be reimbursed for part of the cost.

*Disability Income Insurance*  Not only is disability income insurance one of the most overlooked forms of insurance, but many workers don't have enough coverage. The odds of a person developing a disability are considerably higher than most people realize. Take a group of five randomly selected 45-year-olds. There is approximately a 95 percent chance that one of the five will develop some form of a disability during the next 20 years. **Disability income insurance** is designed to replace lost income when a wage earner cannot work due to an accident or illness.

**life insurance** insurance that protects people against the financial losses that occur with premature death

Two sources of disability income insurance exist: Social Security and private disability insurance policies. Social Security disability benefits are available to virtually all workers, but they have very strict requirements. Private disability insurance is available on either an individual or group basis. As with health insurance, a group policy is much cheaper than an individual policy. Many employers provide at least some disability coverage as an employee benefit. Employees often have the option of obtaining additional coverage by paying more.

*Imagine a World Without Her...*

Prudential Financial
Growing and Protecting Your Wealth®

COURTESY OF PRUDENTIAL FINANCIAL INC.

Life insurance helps protect families against the loss of premature death. With the advent of two-income families and the soaring cost of child care, more and more women are obtaining life insurance policies.

## Life Insurance

**Life insurance** protects people against the financial losses that occur with premature death. Three of every four Americans have some form of life insurance. The main reason people buy life insurance is to provide financial security for their families in the event of their death. With assets totaling more than $4 trillion, the life insurance industry is one of the nation's largest businesses.

*Types of Life Insurance*  As with health and disability insurance, both individual and group life insurance policies are available. Many employers offer life insurance to employees as a component of the firm's benefit program. However, unlike health and disability insurance, an individual life insurance policy is usually cheaper than a group policy for younger people.

The different types of life insurance fall neatly into two categories: **term policies** and so-called **cash value policies.** Term policies provide a death benefit if the policyholder dies within a specified period of time. It has no value at the end of that period. Cash value policies—such as whole and universal life—combine life insurance protection with a savings or investment feature. The cash value represents the savings or investment portion of the life insurance policy. Although there are arguments in favor of cash value policies, many experts believe that term life insurance is a better choice for most consumers. For one thing, a term policy is much cheaper than a cash value policy, especially for younger people.

*How Much Life Insurance Should You Have?* People can purchase life insurance policies for almost any amount. Life insurance purchases are limited only by the amount of premiums people can afford and their ability to meet medical qualifications. The amount of life insurance a person needs, however, is a very personal decision. The general rule of thumb is that a person needs life insurance if he or she has family members who financially depend on that individual. A young parent with three small children could easily need $500,000 or more of life insurance. A single person with no dependents would reasonably see little or no need for a life insurance policy.

Businesses, as well as individuals, buy life insurance. The death of a partner or a key executive is likely to result in a financial loss to an organization. Key person insurance reimburses the organization for the loss of the services of an essential senior manager and to cover the executive search expenses needed to find a replacement. In addition, life insurance policies may be purchased for each member of a partnership to be able to repay the deceased partner's survivors for his or her share of the firm and permit the business to continue.

## Business Terms You Need to Know

risk A-2
insurance A-3
premium A-3
insurable interest A-4

insurable risk A-4
underwriting A-4
actuarial table A-5
law of large numbers A-5

property and liability insurance A-7
business interruption insurance A-8
health insurance A-8
life insurance A-10

## Other Important Business Terms

**speculative risk A-2**
**pure risk A-2**
**public insurance agency A-6**
**Medicare A-6**
**liability insurance A-8**
**fee-for-service plan A-9**

**managed care plan A-9**
**health maintenance organization (HMO) A-9**
**preferred provider organization (PPO) A-10**

**disability income insurance A-10**
**term policy A-10**
**cash value policy A-10**

## Projects and Teamwork Applications

1. Assume you're the owner of a small manufacturing facility. Working with a partner, list some of some of the major risks your business faces. How should each risk be handled (avoided, reduced, assumed, or transferred)? What types of insurance will your business likely have to have, including those types of insurance required by law?

2. For many people one frustrating aspect of insurance is deciphering insurance terminology. The following Web site provides a lexicon of insurance terms: http://www.insweb.com/learningcenter/glossary/general-a.htm. Visit the Web site and look up the following terms:

   accommodation line
   fortuitous
   housekeeping
   earned premium
   tickler

3. Many companies currently sell insurance online. Two prominent companies that sell auto insurance policies online are GEICO (http://www.geico.com) and Progressive (http://www.progressive.com). Visit both Web sites and write a brief report on your experience. Would you consider buying insurance online? What are the advantages and disadvantages?

4. Several insurance-oriented Web sites have interactive worksheets to help you determine whether you need life insurance and, if so, how much you need. Visit the MSN Money Web site (http://moneycentral.msn.com/investor/calcs/n_life/main.asp). Complete the interactive worksheet. If you need life insurance, what kind of policy should you buy? How much will it cost?

5. If you own a car, you know how expensive auto insurance is. There are several commonsense ways to reduce your auto insurance bill. Visit http://www.pueblo.gsa.gov/cic_text/cars/autoinsu/autoinsu.htm and prepare a brief report on reducing the cost of auto insurance.

# Appendix B

# Personal Financial Planning

## PILOTING YOUR OWN FINANCIAL SHIP

Gone are the days when employees started work after receiving their education, stayed with a firm for 30 years, and then retired with a gold watch and a company-funded pension plan. From businesses' current perspective, large pension set-asides are a drag on their profitability, especially when they are competing against newer start-ups that do not carry such obligations. For instance, United Airlines recently defaulted on $6.6 billion in pension payments it was to make to retired employees, which the court allowed because its pension debt would hinder United's recovery from bankruptcy. Meanwhile, the government's backup fund—the Pension Benefit Guaranty Corporation, which assumes the pensions of private companies that default—is stretched to its limits. So, lacking the means to pay their future obligations, other firms are freezing or terminating traditional defined-benefit pension plans more frequently. Defined-benefit plans promise a specific monthly payment to retirees.

From employees' perspective, few workers want to remain with an employer for their entire lifetime. They change jobs and even career paths more frequently to gain skills, seek fulfillment, and accept new challenges. And with the current frantic pace of mergers and acquisitions, they may not want to link their future success too closely with one firm's fortunes. So they want their pension plans to be portable and flexible, not tied to a specific employer. Increasingly, workers are planning ahead, taking control, and saving money to ensure a comfortable retirement.

As a result of this fundamental shift in the workplace, businesses now typically offer defined-contribution plans, such as 401k savings programs. Under these plans, employees set aside certain percentages of their annual wages, and employers often match funds up to a set level. Those funds are then invested and accumulate during a worker's lifetime. Getting an early start in these programs is key so that the investment can be compounded and grow over many years.

Still, nine out of ten Americans worry about saving enough for retirement, according to a recent study by banking and securities giant Wachovia. So what can today's workers do to ensure a secure retirement? In short, save—and start now. The saving habit can be acquired, and the sooner it is started, the easier and the more profitable it will be. Some financial planners suggest that young workers start saving at least 10 percent of their income. Others recommend as much as 20 to 25 percent. Although those numbers may seem high, they advise that workers will never look back and wish they had saved less. And the savings vehicles people use in this new do-it-yourself retirement environment range from the 401k plans mentioned earlier to individual retirement accounts (IRAs), which employees set up on their own and contribute to yearly. But those plans may soon be just the tip of the iceberg as flexible new retirement savings plans are developed to encourage employees to take their financial future into their own hands. With a little advance planning and periodic reassessment and fine-tuning, creating and managing your own retirement fund need not become a burden. You just need to plan and start early.[1]

# APPENDIX OVERVIEW

You are studying business, but much of what you learn in this course will also apply to your personal life. For instance, you learn about each of the important functions of a business—from accounting to marketing, from finance to management. Learning about each business function will help you choose a career, and a career choice is one of the most important personal financial decisions you will make. You will learn why firms prepare budgets and financial statements. But budgets and financial statements are also important tools for individuals.

Everyone, regardless of age or income, can probably do a better job of managing his or her finances. As a group, Americans are much better at making money than they are at managing money. This appendix introduces you to personal financial management. **Personal financial management** deals with a variety of issues and decisions that affect a person's financial well-being. It includes basic money management, credit, tax planning, major consumer purchases, insurance, investing, and retirement planning.

The appendix will draw from many of the topics you will learn while studying business, but it introduces you to some new concepts as well. It is hoped that after completing the appendix, you will be a better-informed financial consumer and personal money manager and that you will be motivated to learn more about personal finance. The rewards, in both monetary and nonmonetary terms, can be tremendous.

**personal financial management** study of the economic factors and personal decisions that affect a person's financial well-being

# THE MEANING AND IMPORTANCE OF PERSONAL FINANCE

Personal finance is the study of the economic factors and personal decisions that affect a person's financial well-being. Personal finance affects, and is affected by, many things we do and many decisions we make throughout our lives.

On one level, personal finance involves money know-how. It is essential to know how to earn money, as well as how to save, spend, invest, and control it in order to achieve goals. The reward of sound money management is an improvement in one's **standard of living.** Standard of living consists of the necessities, comforts, or luxuries an individual seeks to attain or maintain.

On another level, personal finance is intertwined with each person's **lifestyle**—the way we live our daily lives. Our choice of careers, friends, hobbies, communities, and possessions is determined by personal finances, and yet our personal finances can also be determined by our lifestyles. If, for example, you're a college student living independently on a shoestring budget, you will probably have to make many financial sacrifices to achieve your educational goals. Where you live is determined by what school you attend and how much you can afford to pay for rent; your vacation is set by your academic schedule and your checkbook balance; your clothing depends on the climate and your budget. All these lifestyle decisions are partially determined by your personal finances.

**standard of living** necessities, comforts, and luxuries one seeks to obtain or to maintain

## The Importance of Personal Finance Today

Good money management has always been important, but major changes in the external environment over the past couple of decades have made personal finance even more important today. And this is true whether you're a 20-year-old college student, a 40-year-old parent with a mortgage, or a 60-year-old thinking about retirement. Let's look at three reasons why personal financial planning is so important in today's environment.

*Sluggish Growth in Personal Income* Personal income in the United States has grown very slowly in recent years. For instance, over the last ten years, wages and salaries, by far the largest component of personal income, have increased at an average annual rate that has barely exceeded the annual rate of inflation. In other words, when measured in so-called *real terms,* the wages and salaries of the average American worker have remained virtually unchanged. Will this trend continue? Perhaps. Many economists forecast that annual increases in wages and salaries will barely keep pace with the rate of inflation in the coming years.

The sluggish growth in personal income makes sound money management very important. You cannot count on rising personal income to improve your standard of living. Rather, you need to save and invest more money, stick to a budget, and make major purchases wisely.

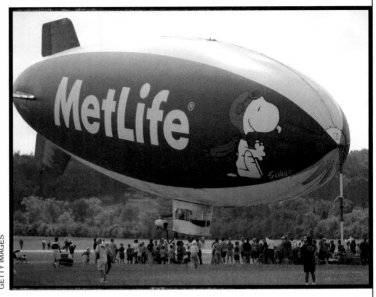

Financial planning advice is available from life insurance companies and other financial service firms.

*Changes in the Labor Market* Job security and the notion of work have changed in recent years. The traditional model of working for the same company for one's entire career is very rare today. Many people entering the workforce today will change jobs and employers several times during their working lives. Some will end up working part time or on a contract basis, with little job security and fewer benefits. Others will take time off to care for small children or elderly parents. And a goal many people have today is to start their own business and work for themselves.

Furthermore, it is estimated that one in four workers today will be unemployed at some point during their working lives. Frankly, you never know when your employer will "downsize," taking your job with it, or "outsource" your job to someone else. Just review today's headlines, and you will see that announcements of prominent companies downsizing and outsourcing are common.

These changes make sound personal financial management even more important. You have to keep your career skills up-to-date and accumulate sufficient financial resources to weather an unexpected crisis.

*More Options* The number of choices today in such areas as banking, credit, investments, and retirement planning can be bewildering. Today you can do most of your banking with a brokerage firm and then buy mutual fund shares at a bank. Even the simple checking account has become more complicated. The typical bank offers several different types of checking accounts, each with its own features and fees. Choosing the wrong account could easily cost you a hundred dollars or more in unnecessary fees each year.

Fifteen years ago, few college students carried credit cards, and those who did typically carried cards tied to their parents' accounts. The situation is much different today. Most college students have their own credit card accounts; many have multiple accounts. Approximately half of all college students carry a balance from month to month, and credit problems are a major reason why some students drop out of college. Today, you can choose whether to use credit properly.

One of the first things you'll do when you start a new job is make decisions concerning employee benefits. The typical employer may offer lots of choices in such areas as health

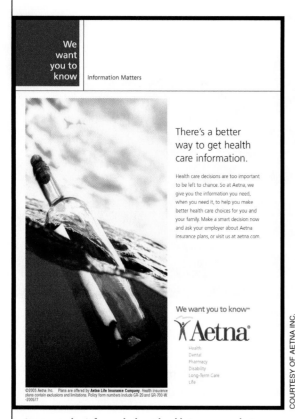

It pays to be informed about health insurance choices.

insurance, disability insurance, group life insurance, and retirement plans. Select the wrong health insurance plan, for example, and you could end up paying thousands of dollars more in out-of-pocket costs. Making the wrong decisions concerning retirement, even if you're still in your 20s, could make it difficult to achieve a financially secure retirement.

Most people believe that choice is a good thing, and having more choices in the personal finance arena means the consumer is likely to find what he or she seeks. At the same time, however, a longer menu of choices means it's easier to make mistakes. The more informed you are, the better choices and fewer costly mistakes you are likely to make.

## Personal Financial Planning— A Lifelong Activity

Personal financial planning is as important an activity whether you're 20, 40, or 60; whether you're single or married with children; and whether your annual income is $20,000 or $200,000. Many experts say that if you can't stick to a budget and control your spending when you're making $25,000 a year, you'll find it difficult to live within your means even if your income doubles or triples.

The fact that sound planning is a lifelong activity, of course, doesn't mean your financial goals and plans remain constant throughout your life—they won't. The major goal when you're young may be to buy your first home or pay off your college loans. For older people, the major goal is probably making their retirement funds last for the rest of their lives.

Also, the importance of personal finance goals will change as you go through life. Although we should all begin planning for retirement as soon as we begin our careers, the relative importance of retirement and estate planning increases as retirement nears. Choosing the right life insurance policy is a major decision for a 30-year-old father of two, but not for a 65-year-old grandfather. On the other hand, estate planning may be far more important for the 65-year-old than it is for the 30-year-old.

For many people, getting started toward a better financial future is one of the hardest tasks of all. Table B.1 lists, in rough order, what the experts believe your financial priorities should be. As always, the first step is to figure out exactly where you currently stand financially.

## Getting Professional Help

Many people believe they need professional help when it comes to managing their finances. The world is full of people and organizations who are willing to give you advice on everything from preparing a budget to estate planning. More than a few colleges and universities, for instance, offer credit counseling and other basic financial services to students who find themselves in financial trouble. When you are older, you may find it prudent to use the services of a certified public accountant (CPA) when preparing your tax returns or a professional investment advisor when choosing the right investments to fund your retirement. Dozens of financial self-help books are published annually. A great deal of financial information and advice is also available online. Two of the better personal finance Web sites are Quicken.com (http://www.quicken.com) and MSN Money (http://moneycentral.msn.com).

Getting Started: Your Financial Priorities

Okay, let's assume you're in your early 20s, recently graduated from college, and just got your first "real" job. Congratulations; you're probably making more money than you ever have before. However, you're also likely spending more money than ever, and probably came out of college with some debts—student loans, credit cards, an auto loan, and so forth. You know you need to start managing your money, but where do you start? You start by establishing some financial priorities. According to the experts, those in their 20s should do the following (in rough order):

- Figure out where you currently stand financially.
- Put yourself on a budget.
- Insure yourself against financial ruin.
- Get your debts under control.
- Start saving for retirement.
- Set up a regular savings program.

You may not be able to do everything immediately, but you do need to get started. Take it one step at a time. The worst mistake you can make is to procrastinate.

**Source:** Adapted from Louis Boone, David Kurtz, and Douglas Hearth, *Planning Your Financial Future,* 4th ed. (Mason, OH: Thomson South-Western, 2006), p. 6.

One thing you must recognize is that almost anyone can call himself or herself a financial planner, regardless of background or training. While financial planners must have certain federal and state licenses to sell many financial products, there are almost no standards governing financial planners. However, a professional organization—called the Certified Financial Planner Board—certifies financial planners. Anyone who obtains the Certified Financial Planner (CFP) designation has met a set of educational and professional requirements and passed a comprehensive examination.

# A PERSONAL FINANCIAL MANAGEMENT MODEL

A **financial plan** is a guide to help you reach targeted goals in the future. These goals could include buying a home, starting your own business, sending children to college, or retiring early. Developing a personal financial plan consists of several steps, as illustrated in Figure B.1.

The first step in the financial planning process is to develop a series of short- and long-term goals. These goals should be influenced by your values, as well as an assessment of your current financial situation. The next step is to establish a set of financial strategies—in each of the personal planning areas—designed to help close the gap between where you are now and where you want to be in the future. Next, put your plan into action and closely monitor its performance. Periodically evaluate the effectiveness of your financial plan and make adjustments when necessary.

Financial plans cannot be developed in a vacuum. They should reflect your available resources—especially salary and fringe benefits, such as health insurance and retirement

Banks offer a wide range of financial products and advice today.

**financial plan** guide to help a person reach desired goals

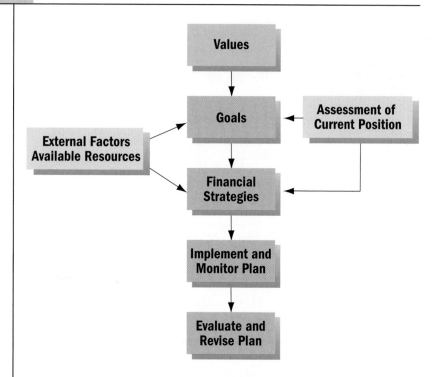

**Source:** Adapted from Louis Boone, David Kurtz, and Douglas Hearth, *Planning Your Financial Future,* 4th ed. (Mason, OH: Thomson South-Western, 2006), p. 7.

plans. For example, your goals and financial strategies must be based on a realistic estimate of your future income. If you cannot reach your financial goals through your present career path, you will have to scale back your goals or consider switching careers.

In addition, external factors—such as economic conditions and government policy—will influence your financial plan and decisions. For instance, assume you're in the market for a new car, much of which you will have to finance. Obviously, interest rates affect the size of your monthly payment and how much car you can afford. So you will need to keep track of interest rates. If interest rates appear to be falling, a smart financial decision may be to postpone the purchase in order to get a better rate on a new-car loan.

## General Themes Common to All Financial Plans

Regardless of the specifics, all financial plans revolve around three general themes: (1) maximizing income and wealth, (2) using money more effectively, and (3) monitoring expenditures.

**Maximizing Income and Wealth**  Maximizing your income and wealth means getting more money. Work smarter; seek retraining for a better, higher-paying job; take career risks that may pay off in the long run; make sound investment decisions—all these are examples of the implementation of the first step. The amount of money you earn is a vital part of any financial plan, and it is up to you to make the most of your opportunities.

**Using Money More Effectively**  Money has two basic uses: consumption and savings. Even if you are a regular saver, you'll still spend most of your income, probably more than 90 percent. You must try to spend every dollar wisely and make every major buying decision part of your overall financial plan. Avoid impulsive spending or giving in to the hard sell.

And it's not just big expenditures you need to watch. Cutting back your spending on small items can make a difference. Little purchases do add up. For example, taking your lunch a couple of times a week rather than eating out could save about $15 a week. Invest that savings at 6 percent interest (per year) and you'll have more than $65,000 in 30 years.

**Monitoring Expenditures**  Budgeting is the key to controlling expenditures. A budget focuses on where the money is going and whether a person's goals are being met. It also suggests appropriate times for reevaluating priorities. If your budget doesn't reflect what you want from life both now and in the future, change it.

Information also helps you keep your expenditures under control. The more you know about real estate, consumer loans, insurance, taxes, and major purchases, the more likely you are to spend the least money to purchase the greatest value.

## The Pitfalls of Poor Financial Planning

Unfortunately, too many people fail to effectively plan their financial future. Not only do many of these people find it difficult to improve their standard of living, but quite a few also find themselves with mounting debts and a general inability to make ends meet. In a recent year, more than 1.5 million Americans filed for bankruptcy. What happens to people when they cannot meet their debt obligations?

Creditors will not ignore missed or consistently late payments. First, they will send written inquiries concerning your failure to make required payments on time. Unless you make the payment or contact them about making other arrangements, your creditors are likely to take further actions. Examples of actions creditors can take include repossessing your property, garnishing your wages, or even sending you into personal bankruptcy. At the very least, your ability to obtain credit will be seriously damaged.

# SETTING PERSONAL GOALS

Whatever your personal financial goals, they should reflect your values. Values are a set of fundamental beliefs of what is important, desirable, and worthwhile in your life. Your values will influence how you spend your money and, therefore, should be the foundation of your financial plan. Each person's financial goals will be determined by the individual's values because every individual considers some things more desirable or important than others. Start by asking yourself some questions about your values, the things that are most important to you, and what you would like to accomplish in your life.

Your goals are also influenced by your current financial situation. Prepare a set of current financial statements for yourself. An income statement is a statement of income and expenditures. A balance sheet is a statement of what you own (assets) and what you owe (liabilities). For an individual or household, the difference between assets and liabilities is called **net worth.**

Figure B.2 shows a set of financial statements for a hypothetical couple, Brian and Michelle. Notice that on their income statement, which reflected income and expenditures for an entire year, Brian and Michelle divided their expenses into several major categories (such as housing, transportation, and child care). Because they spent less than they made, Brian and Michelle added money to their savings during the year.

Their balance sheet was prepared at the end of the year. Note that Brian and Michelle divided their assets into current financial assets, long-term financial assets, and nonfinancial or real assets. Likewise, they divided their liabilities into those that are due within a short amount of time and those that are not.

After reviewing your current financial statements, you should prepare a budget. Most households prepare budgets on a monthly basis. A budget is an excellent tool for monitoring your expenditures and cash flow and permits you to track past and current expenditures and plan future ones.

A sample budget is shown in Figure B.3. Expenses are divided into fixed expenses (those that vary little from month to month) and variable expenses (those that vary from month to month).

Next, establish a series of financial goals based on your values and current financial situation. Separate your goals into short-term goals (those you would like to accomplish within the next year or so) and long-term goals (those you would like to accomplish within the next several years). An example of a short-term goal is "pay off the outstanding balance on my Visa

# Balance Sheet

| Assets | | | Liabilities & Net Worth | | |
|---|---|---|---|---|---|
| **Current financial assets** | | | **Current liabilities** | | |
| Checking account | $2,500 | | Utilities | $200 | |
| Savings account | 5,000 | | Insurance | 250 | |
| Money market funds | 4,500 | | Credit card | 500 | |
| Total | $12,000 | | Other | 0 | |
| **Long-term financial assets** | | | Total | $950 | |
| Mutual funds | $12,000 | | **Long-term liabilities** | | |
| Stocks and bonds | $0 | | Auto loan | $8,000 | |
| Pension | $0 | | Student loans | 3,500 | |
| 401k | 30,000 | | Mortgage | 130,000 | |
| IRAs | 2,500 | | Other | 0 | |
| Other | 1,500 | | Total | $141,500 | |
| Total | $46,000 | | | | |
| **Fixed assets** | | | **Total Liabilities** | 142,450 | |
| Home | $165,000 | | | | |
| Auto 1: | 13,000 | | **Net Worth** | **$127,050** | |
| Auto 2: | 8,500 | | | | |
| Furniture | 15,000 | | | | |
| Personal property | 5,000 | | | | |
| Other | 5,000 | | | | |
| Total fixed | $211,500 | | | | |
| **Total Assets** | **$269,500** | | | | |

# Income Statement

| | |
|---|---|
| **Wages earned** | |
| Brian | 38,500 |
| Michelle | 43,000 |
| Other income | |
| Bonuses | 2,500 |
| Interest & dividends | 1,000 |
| Tax refunds | 500 |
| Other | 0 |
| Total income | $85,500 |
| Income and FICA taxes | $16,000 |
| **Net income** | **$69,500** |
| **Expenditures** | |
| Housing | |
| House payment | 12,000 |
| Utilities | 3,500 |
| Property taxes | 1,800 |
| Maintenance | 2,500 |
| Insurance | 500 |
| Other housing | 3,500 |
| Total housing | $23,800 |
| Transportation | |
| Car payments | 3,600 |
| Gas & repairs | 1,500 |
| Insurance | 1,000 |
| Registration | 200 |
| Other transportation | 300 |
| Total transportation | $6,600 |
| Food & clothing | 8,000 |
| Medical & dental expenses | 1,500 |
| Child care | 5,000 |
| Vacation & entertainment | 3,500 |
| Student loan payments | 2,000 |
| Credit card interest | 0 |
| Life insurance premiums | 1,500 |
| Cash allowances | 5,000 |
| Other expenses | 2,500 |
| **Total expenditures** | **$59,400** |
| **Amount available for savings** | **$10,100** |

Josh and Ellie's Monthly Budget

| | **July** | | | | **August** | | |
| | Budget | Actual | Difference | | Budget | Actual | Difference |
|---|---|---|---|---|---|---|---|
| **Cash Inflows** | | | | | | | |
| Net salary (Josh) | 2,800 | 2,800 | — | | 2,800 | 2,800 | — |
| Net salary (Ellie) | 2,300 | 2,300 | — | | 2,300 | 2,300 | — |
| Dividends and interest | 100 | 125 | 25 | | 100 | 100 | — |
| Bonus | — | — | — | | 1,500 | 2,000 | 500 |
| Other | — | — | — | | — | — | — |
| **Total inflows** | **5,200** | **5,225** | **25** | | **6,700** | **7,200** | **500** |
| **Cash Outflows** | | | | | | | |
| **Fixed expenses** | | | | | | | |
| Mortgage/rent | 1,100 | 1,100 | — | | 1,100 | 1,100 | — |
| Auto loan | 350 | 350 | — | | 350 | 350 | — |
| Student loan | 300 | 300 | — | | 300 | 300 | — |
| Credit card payments | — | — | — | | — | — | — |
| Automatic savings transfer | 500 | 500 | — | | 500 | 500 | — |
| **Variable expenses** | | | | | | | |
| Utilities | 325 | 375 | 50 | | 300 | 250 | (50) |
| Food | 500 | 550 | 50 | | 400 | 400 | — |
| Medical and dental | 100 | 200 | 100 | | 100 | — | (100) |
| Clothing and personal care | 250 | 325 | 75 | | 150 | 100 | (50) |
| Entertainment and recreation | 200 | 125 | (75) | | 1,200 | 1,500 | 300 |
| Transportation expenses | 200 | 200 | — | | 150 | 100 | (50) |
| Gifts and contributions | 100 | 175 | 75 | | 100 | 150 | 50 |
| Personal spending money | 400 | 475 | 75 | | 400 | 350 | (50) |
| Life insurance | 50 | 50 | — | | — | — | — |
| Auto insurance | 350 | 325 | (25) | | — | — | — |
| Homeowners' insurance | — | — | — | | 450 | 475 | 25 |
| Other expenses | — | — | — | | 800 | 600 | (200) |
| **Total cash outflows** | **4,725** | **5,050** | **325** | | **6,300** | **6,175** | **(125)** |
| **Net cash flow** | **475** | **175** | **(300)** | | **400** | **1,025** | **625** |

card by this time next year." A long-term goal might be to buy a house by age 30. It is important, of course, that your short-term goals support your long-term goals. For instance, if your long-term goal is to buy a house, short-term goals should include starting a regular savings program and paying off credit card debt.

In addition, some of your goals will be monetary in nature—meaning you can put a price tag on them—while other goals will be nonmonetary. If you want to pay off the outstanding balance on your Visa card by this time next year, and the current balance is $1,000, that is an example of a monetary goal. A goal of constructing and following a monthly budget is an example of a nonmonetary goal.

Whether short-term or long-term, monetary or nonmonetary, your financial goals should be defined as specifically as possible and focus on results. Goals should also be realistic and attainable. Paying off the $1,000 balance on your Visa card within the next twelve months may be realistic; paying it off in the next two months may not be. If your monthly take-home pay is $3,000, and your fixed monthly expenses—such as rent, utilities, transportation, and loan payments—amount to $2,000, setting a goal of saving $750 per month is probably not very realistic. On the other hand, setting a monthly savings goal of $250 may be reasonable.

Financial goals change throughout a person's lifetime, and for this reason they should be written down and reviewed periodically. To be effective, goals should reflect changes in

### Short-Term Financial Goals

| Description | Actions | Target Date | Estimated Cost | Priority |
|---|---|---|---|---|
| Example: Establish regular savings program. | Set up automatic monthly transfer between checking and savings accounts. | Immediate | $250 per month | High |

### Long-Term Financial Goals

| Description | Actions | Target Date | Estimated Cost | Priority |
|---|---|---|---|---|
| Example: Pay off credit card balance. | 1. Pay $250 more than minimum payment each month.<br>2. Use card only in emergencies. | 2008 or 2009 | $250 per month | High |

### Nonfinancial Goals

| Description | Actions | Target Date |
|---|---|---|
| Example: Create a monthly budget. | Categorize expenses; estimate income and expenses; compare estimate to current income and spending levels. | One month |

circumstances, such as education, family, career, the economic environment, and even your emotional and physical well-being. The worksheet shown in Figure B.4 is one way of formulating and tracking your personal financial goals. Notice that it separates short-term from long-term goals and monetary from nonmonetary goals. It also divides goals into major categories—such as saving, spending, and credit. The worksheet also asks you to estimate the cost of each goal, if monetary, and establish each goal's priority. Your worksheet should be updated regularly as you achieve short-term goals or your life situation changes.

# YOUR PERSONAL FINANCIAL DECISIONS

An individual's economic future is charted via financial strategies in such personal planning areas as career choice, credit management, and tax planning. These strategies should reflect your goals and be designed to close the gap between where you are and where you want to be.

## Career Choice

No factor exerts as strong an influence on an individual's personal finances as does a career choice. Virtually all of your income, especially when you're just starting out, will come from wages and salaries. It is through work that all of us acquire the income needed to build a lifestyle; to buy goods and services, including insurance protection; to save and invest; and to plan for retirement. Your job is also the source of many important fringe benefits, such as health insurance and retirement savings plans, that are important components of your financial future. Throughout *Contemporary Business,* we've discussed ways to select a career that fits your skills and interests, find a job, and perform in that job.

## Basic Money Management

Basic money management involves managing checking and savings accounts. Properly managing these relatively simple financial assets is an important first step toward proper management of more complicated financial assets such as investment and retirement accounts. You must choose a bank or other financial institution and then select the right checking account. Banks today offer several different types of checking accounts, each with its own set of features and fees. Table B.2 lists several tips for selecting and managing a checking account. Managing a savings account involves understanding the importance of savings, setting savings goals, and picking the best savings option.

## Credit Management

Not surprisingly, credit is the area of personal finance that gets more people into financial difficulties than any other area. Credit allows a person to purchase goods and services by borrowing the necessary funds from a lender, such as a bank. The borrower agrees to repay the loan over a specified period of time, paying a specified rate of interest. Credit is available from many sources today, but rates vary, so it pays to shop around.

**credit** receiving money, goods, or services on the basis of an agreement between the lender and the borrower that the loan is for a specified period of time with a specified rate of interest

There are two broad types of consumer credit: revolving (or open-end) credit and installment credit. Revolving credit is a type of credit arrangement that enables consumers to make a number of different purchases up to a credit limit, specified by the lender. The consumer has the option of repaying some or all of the outstanding balance each month. If the consumer carries a balance from month to month, finance charges (interest) are levied. An example of revolving credit is a credit card, such as Visa or MasterCard. An installment loan is a credit arrangement in which the borrower takes out a loan for a specified amount, agreeing to repay the loan in regular installments over a specified period of time. The installments include the finance charge. Student loans, auto loans, and home mortgage loans are examples of installment loans.

Keeping a Lid on Bank Fees

Banks today charge customers fees for a variety of services, but the amount can vary substantially. If you are not careful, you can end up paying a couple of hundred dollars a year, or more, in unnecessary fees. Here are some tips for keeping bank fees under control.

- Choose the right checking account.
- Shop around.
- Regularly balance your checkbook.
- Watch how you use your ATM card.
- Sign up for overdraft protection.
- Understand how your bank computes the minimum balance.
- Consider using your personal computer to pay bills electronically.
- Read the fine print in your monthly statement.

Source: Adapted from Louis Boone, David Kurtz, and Douglas Hearth, *Planning Your Financial Future,* 4th ed. (Mason, OH: Thomson South-Western, 2006), p. 96.

**Table B.2**

People have good reasons for borrowing money. They include purchasing large, important goods and services (cars, homes, or a college education), dealing with financial emergencies, taking advantage of opportunities or of convenience, and establishing or improving your credit rating. All of these reasons are appropriate uses of credit *if* you can repay the loans in a timely manner.

However, a wrong reason for borrowing money is using credit to live beyond your means. For instance, you may want to go to Cancun for vacation but really cannot afford to, so you charge the trip. Using credit to live beyond your means often leads to credit problems. Watch for these warning signs:

- You use credit to meet basic living expenses.
- You use credit to make impulse purchases.
- You take a cash advance on one credit card to repay another, and the unpaid balance increases month after month.

Consumers who think of credit purchases as a series of small monthly payments are fooling themselves. Today most college students have credit cards, and most carry balances from month to month averaging more than $2,000.[2] How long would it take someone with the average balance to become debt free, assuming he or she made only the minimum payment each month (the minimum payment is typically $25 or 2.5 percent of the outstanding balance, whichever is greater) and is charged the average rate of interest (around 16 percent)? The answer is almost *11 years* (129 months to be exact), during which time the borrower would pay almost $2,000 in interest. What's more, the preceding example assumes that the person does not charge anything else while paying off the balance.

If you feel as though you have a problem with credit, or may be developing one, you should seek help as soon as possible. Your college or university may offer credit counseling services. If not, contact a local not-for-profit credit counseling service or the National Federation for Credit Counseling (800-388-2227 or http://www.nfcc.org). According to the experts, one of the keys to the wise use of credit is education. Learning about the pros and cons of borrowing money, as well as learning about responsible spending, can help people avoid future problems with credit.

## Tax Planning

Everyone pays a variety of taxes to federal, state, and local governments. The major taxes paid by individuals include federal and state income taxes, FICA (Social Security and Medicare) taxes, property taxes, and sales taxes. The median-income family paid almost 38 percent of its income in taxes during a recent year. Think about your own situation and the taxes you pay. If you work, you have federal income taxes withheld from each paycheck. In addition, if you live in one of the 41 states with a state income tax, you have state income tax withheld also. Social Security and Medicare taxes amount to 15.3 percent of your wages split between you and your employer (you pay the entire amount if you're self-employed). If you rent an apartment, part of your monthly rent goes to pay the landlord's property tax bill. Every time you buy something, you likely pay sales tax to your state and local governments.

Unfortunately, there is very little you can do to reduce some of the taxes you pay. The only tax over which you have some control is the federal income tax. But even with the federal income tax, people have only a handful of ways to legally reduce their tax bill. Still, you need to understand the federal income tax system and know what kinds of tax records to keep. Even though millions of Americans pay someone else to do their taxes, many people have relatively simple returns. Preparing a tax return is one of the best ways of learning more about your personal finances. The Internal Revenue Service (IRS) has several excellent publications to help you prepare a federal income tax return. One of the best is IRS Publication #17 (*You and Your Federal Income Tax*). This and all other IRS publications are available free of charge from local IRS offices or the IRS Web site (http://www.irs.gov). We also strongly suggest that you use one of the tax preparation software programs (TurboTax or TaxCut) and your personal computer to prepare your federal and state income tax returns.

## Major Purchases

Even if you are a great budgeter and saver, you will still spend most of your income each year. Effective buying is an important part of your financial plan. Within personal budget limits, an individual exercises his or her rights as a consumer to select or reject the wide range of goods and services that are available. As you purchase an automobile, a home, or any other major item, you need to carefully evaluate alternatives, separate needs from wants, and determine how you are going to finance the purchase. Your goal is to make every dollar you spend count.

Americans spend more than $500 billion annually on transportation, most of which goes to purchasing and maintaining automobiles. Given that new vehicles average more than $20,000 today, and even good used cars can cost in excess of $12,000, buying an automobile is a substantial purchase. On top of that, most car purchases are financed. Buying a car involves weighing many factors, including whether you want a new or used car, what makes and models appeal to you, and how much you can afford to pay.

For most people, housing consumes the largest share of their monthly budgets. Most Americans—more than 70 percent—own their own homes, and home ownership is a goal of most people. Owning a home has a number of advantages, both financial and nonfinancial. Some of the financial benefits include tax savings (home mortgage interest and property taxes are both tax deductible) and the potential increase in the home's value. Nonfinancial benefits include pride of ownership. For those who don't own homes, the major barrier to home ownership is the down payment required to get a mortgage loan, along with other so-called *closing costs.* Even a modestly priced home will require that the buyer have around $20,000 in cash.

The other major housing option is renting. Renting also offers a number of advantages, including cost savings (the landlord takes care of maintenance and repairs) and mobility. It is much easier to move if you rent than if you own a home. People who plan on staying in a area for a short period of time are usually better off renting. The choice between buying and renting is obviously a major financial decision that needs to be approached rationally, not emotionally—especially true for first-time home buyers.

## Insurance

Another important personal planning area is insurance. Insurance is an admittedly expensive—Americans spend more than $125 billion each year on auto insurance alone—but necessary purchase. Some of the basic principles and the various types of insurance are described in Appendix A of *Contemporary Business.* Although the focus of that appendix is business insurance, much of what is discussed applies to your personal insurance needs as well.

Your goal is to have adequate and appropriate coverage in each of the major insurance types—life, health, disability, and property and liability. Insurance needs can vary substantially from individual to individual. For instance, what are the insurance needs of Karen (a single 25-year-old who rents an apartment) and Bill (a divorced 40-year-old with custody of young children who owns a home)? Their individual insurance needs are listed in Figure B.5. Notice that they both need health, disability, and auto coverage, but only Bill needs life insurance. Bill's children are financially dependent on him, but Karen has no financial dependents. Karen should have renters' insurance, while Bill needs homeowners' insurance.

| Personal Characteristics | Bill | Karen |
|---|---|---|
| Age | 43 | 26 |
| Annual income | $75,000 | $40,000 |
| Marital status | Divorced | Single |
| Number of dependent children | 2 (has custody) | 0 |
| Own automobile (yes/no) | Yes | Yes |
| Homeowner (yes/no) | Yes | No |

| Type of Insurance | Bill's Needs | Karen's Needs |
|---|---|---|
| Life | Needs life insurance amounting to several times his annual salary; perhaps $500,000 or more. | Needs no life insurance. |
| Health | Major medical plan that covers Bill and his children is required. Obtain from employer. | Karen should be covered by a major medical plan. Obtain from employer. |
| Disability | Should have a policy that pays an annual benefit of between $45,000 and $50,000. Obtain from employer. | Should have a policy that provides an annual benefit of between $30,000 and $33,000 per year. Obtain from employer. |
| Auto | Should have substantial liability coverage and, depending on the age and value of his car, collision and comprehensive as well. Uninsured driver coverage is strongly recommended. | Should have as much liability coverage as she can afford. Collision and comprehensive are recommended, depending on the age and value of her car. Uninsured driver coverage is strongly recommended. |
| Homeowners' | Should have comprehensive, full replacement coverage on both the structure and contents of his home. | Should have a renters' policy covering her personal property. |
| Personal liability | Liability portions of auto and homeowner's policies probably sufficient. | Liability portions of auto and renters' policies probably sufficient. |

As noted earlier in *Contemporary Business,* some types of insurance are provided to employees as fringe benefits. They typically include health insurance, disability insurance, and life insurance. In the standard arrangement, the premium is split between the employee and employer. A few employers contract with insurance companies to offer employees auto and homeowners' insurance at discounts.

## *Investment Planning*

Investing is a process by which money acquired through work, inheritance, or other sources is preserved and increased. Sound investment management is an important component of the financial plan and can make it easier to attain other personal goals, such as buying a home, sending children to college, starting a business, or retiring comfortably. Furthermore, it is very difficult today to substantially increase wealth without investing. And, given the changes to the external environment—such as employer-sponsored retirement plans—it is likely that everyone will have to make investment decisions at some point during his or her life.

The investment process consists of four steps. The first step is to complete some preliminary tasks, including setting overall personal goals, having a regular savings program, and managing credit properly. The second step is to establish a set of investment goals—why you want to invest, what you want to accomplish, and what kind of time frame you have. Obviously, your investment goals should be closely related to your overall personal goals. Next, you need to assess risk and return. You invest because you expect to earn some future rate of return. At the same time, however, all investing exposes you to a variety of risks. You need to find the proper balance between risk and return because investments offering the highest potential returns also expose you to more risk. Your age, income, and short- or long-term investment time frames all have an impact on the risk/return trade-off.

The final step is to select the appropriate investments. As discussed in Chapter 18 of *Contemporary Business,* there are three general types of investments: money market instruments, bonds, and common stock. The proper mix of these three investments depends on such factors as your investment goals and investment time horizon. For instance, a 25-year-old investing for retirement should have close to 100 percent of his or her funds invested in common stocks because growth in capital is the overriding investment objective. Over longer periods of time, stocks tend to outperform money market instruments and bonds. On the other hand, if the 25-year-old is investing to have sufficient funds for a down payment on a house within the next couple of years, the investor should have most of his or her funds invested in money market instruments and bonds. Liquidity, current income, and stability of principal are the most important investment objectives. Even after selecting the appropriate investments, the investor must monitor their performance and be prepared to make changes when necessary.

## *Financial Planning for Tomorrow*

The last major personal planning area deals with future financial issues, such as sending children to college and retirement and estate planning. As you know, college is expensive and is likely to become even more expensive in the coming years. By beginning a college savings program early, parents can ensure that they will have sufficient financial resources to send their children to college when the time comes. Today a variety of college savings programs exist, some of which provide parents with tax benefits.

Most people want to eventually retire with sufficient funds to ensure a degree of financial security. Social Security will provide only a fraction of what you will need; you will be responsible for the rest. According to the experts, you will need to have a savings nest egg of at least $1.5 million by the time you retire. Four important principles apply when it comes to saving for retirement: start early, save as much as you can each month, take advantage of all tax-deferred retirement savings plans to which you are entitled, and invest your retirement savings appropriately.

Aside from Social Security, two other major sources of retirement income exist: employer-sponsored retirement plans and individual retirement plans. Most employers offer their workers a retirement plan; many offer more than one plan. For most people, employer-sponsored retirement plans will likely provide the bulk of their retirement income. Essentially, two types of employer-sponsored retirement plans exist. A

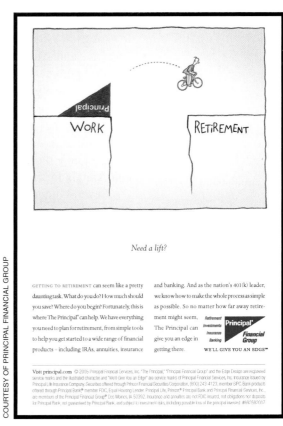

*Need a lift?*

GETTING TO RETIREMENT can seem like a pretty daunting task. What do you do? How much should you save? Where do you begin? Fortunately, this is where The Principal® can help. We have everything you need to plan for retirement, from simple tools to help you get started to a wide range of financial products – including IRAs, annuities, insurance and banking. And as the nation's 401(k) leader, we know how to make the whole process as simple as possible. So no matter how far away retirement might seem, The Principal can give you an edge in getting there.

**WE'LL GIVE YOU AN EDGE™**

Visit principal.com © 2005 Principal Financial Services, Inc. "The Principal," "Principal Financial Group" and the Edge Design are registered service marks and the illustrated character and "We'll Give You an Edge" are service marks of Principal Financial Services, Inc. Insurance issued by Principal Life Insurance Company. Securities offered through Princor Financial Services Corporation, (800) 243-4123, member SIPC. Bank products offered through Principal Bank® member FDIC, Equal Housing Lender. Principal Life, Princor® Principal Bank and Principal Financial Services, Inc., are members of the Principal Financial Group® Des Moines, IA 50392. Insurance and annuities are not FDIC insured, not obligations nor deposits for Principal Bank, nor guaranteed by Principal Bank, and subject to investment risks, including possible loss of the principal invested. #8975920517

**Retirement is a major personal goal.**

*defined benefit plan* guarantees a worker a certain retirement benefit each year. The size depends on a number of factors, including the worker's income and the length of time he or she worked for the employer. Pension plans are classified as defined benefit plans.

The other type of employer-sponsored retirement plan is the *defined contribution plan.* In this type of retirement plan, you contribute to your retirement account and so does your employer. You are given some choice of where your retirement funds can be invested. Often you are given a list of mutual funds in which to invest your money. A 401k is an example of a defined contribution plan. Defined contribution plans are becoming more common and, as the opening vignette notes, are in many cases replacing defined benefit plans.

Millions of Americans have some sort of individual retirement plan, which they often set up and administer and are not tied to any employer. These workers may be self-employed or may merely want to supplement their retirement savings. Examples of individual retirement plans include regular IRAs (individual retirement accounts), Roth IRAs, Keogh plans, and SEP plans. To set up one of these retirement plans, you must meet certain eligibility requirements.

Another element of financial planning for tomorrow is estate planning. Of all the personal planning areas, estate planning is probably the least relevant for you, although your parents and grandparents probably face some estate-planning issues. However, *all* adults, regardless of age, need to have two documents: a valid will (naming a guardian if you have any minor children) and a durable power of attorney (the name varies from state to state, but it is a document that gives someone else the power to make financial and medical decisions if you are incapacitated).

# AN EXAMPLE OF A FINANCIAL PLAN

Alberto and Anita Mendoza are a married couple in their late 20s. They have one child and live outside Cincinnati, Ohio. Alberto works as an assistant brand manager at Procter & Gamble, and Anita works for Fifth Third Bank. Their combined annual income is around $95,000 per year, and they own their own home. Sam and Anita put together their first financial plan shortly before they were married. They review it at least once a year, or after a major change in their lives. For example, Alberto and Anita substantially revised their financial plan shortly after their daughter was born. Parts of their current financial plan are shown in Figure B.6. Notice that all three general themes of a financial plan—increasing wealth, using money more effectively, and monitoring expenditures—are present throughout Alberto and Anita's financial plan.

Several other noteworthy items appear in Alberto and Anita's financial plan. First, they've divided it into several categories—spending, credit, investments, insurance, and other personal goals. This makes the plan easier to follow and generally more organized. Second, notice how they have established a time frame for each of their goals and how short-term goals support long-term goals. Third, Alberto and Anita have put a dollar value on each goal, if possible. Reducing nonmortgage debt to zero, for instance, will cost around $20,000. Finally, a strategy (or strategies) is attached to each goal. For example, paying off their nonmortgage debt by 2008 will require that they double up on their car and student-loan payments. Doing so requires that the couple cut back on nonessential spending.

Alberto and Anita's financial plans also reflects the couple's dreams. They want to have another child within the next couple of years. Anita would like to be able to cut back on her work schedule and begin working from home. They'd also like to remodel their kitchen, and Alberto would like to start working on his MBA. Without sound planning today, these and other dreams will be more difficult to achieve.

Financial Plan for Alberto and Anita Mendoza

| Goal | Time Frame | Estimated Cost or Dollar Goal | Strategy |
|------|-----------|------------------------------|----------|
| **A. Spending** | | | |
| 1. Cut nonessential spending by 5% | Ongoing | $2,000 to $3,000 annually | Review budget quarterly; keep better track of cash. |
| 2. Buy new bedroom set | 2009 | $3,000 | Wait for sale; use money from savings. |
| 3. Buy a new car | 2009 or 2010 | $25,000 | Save $200 a month toward down payment; save bonuses. |
| **B. Debt** | | | |
| 1. Reduce nonmortgage debt to zero | 2009 | $20,000 | Double up on loan payments. |
| 2. Refinance mortgage | Ongoing | $1,500 (estimated closing costs) | Refinance once fixed-rate loans decrease to 6%; use savings to pay refinancing costs. |
| **C. Investments and Savings** | | | |
| 1. Build emergency fund | Ongoing | $15,000 by 2008 | Cut spending by 5%. |
| 2. Build nonretirement savings | Ongoing | $65,000 by 2009 | Cut spending by 5%; try to save/invest all pay increases. |
| 3. Build retirement savings | Ongoing | $150,000 by 2010 | Maximum contribution to retirement accounts; invest appropriately. |
| 4. Build college fund | Ongoing | $75,000 by 2025 | Cut spending by 5%; try to save/invest all pay increases. |
| **D. Insurance** | | | |
| 1. Life | Ongoing | Depends | Regularly review coverage; increase if necessary. |
| 2. Health and disability | Ongoing | Depends | Regularly review coverage. |
| 3. Property and liability | Ongoing | Depends | Regularly review coverage; drop unnecessary coverage; raise deductibles. |
| **E. Other goals** | | | |
| 1. Have second child | 2009 or 2011 | $20,000 in lost income; $5,000 in additional expenses per year. | Build financial cushion; budget for additional expenses. |
| 2. Pursue MBA | 2011 or 2012 | $5,000 per year | Keep spending under control; invest regularly and wisely. |

# WHAT'S AHEAD

This appendix has just scratched the surface of personal financial planning. We hope it has encouraged you to learn more. Dozens of helpful books, Web sites, and other resources are available. If you can fit it into your class schedule, consider taking a class in personal financial planning. Your college or university probably offers one. Taking such a class may be one of the smartest decisions you make while you're in college.

personal financial management B-2     financial plan B-5
standard of living B-2                credit B-11

**lifestyle B-2**
**net worth B-7**

1. Prepare a current set of financial statements for yourself using a format similar to the one shown in Figure 2. What do you think your financial statements will look like a year from now? Five years from now?

2. One of the most important tools for managing your personal finances is a budget. The earlier you learn to prepare and follow a budget, the better off you will be. If Figure 3 looks a bit intimidating, there are a variety of interactive budget forms available on the Internet. Go to http://www.nelliemae.com/calc/calc10.asp and fill out the budget worksheet. Compare your entries with the guidelines listed. Remember, a budget has to be realistic and support your overall goals. How difficult will it be for you to follow the budget you prepared?

3. You have probably heard of credit files (or reports). In fact, if you have a credit card, a student loan, or some other form of credit, you already have a credit file. Working with a partner, visit the Federal Trade Commission's website (http://ftc.gov/), searching under the "consumer" category, and the TransUnion Bank website (http://truecredit.com/), searching under the "Credit Learning Center." Review the materials that these websites provide on credit files and credit reporting.
   a. What is a credit file?
   b. What information is contained in a credit file?
   c. Who compiles the information contained in a credit file?
   d. Who has access to a credit file?
   e. Regarding your credit file, what rights do you have?

4. Even though you are still in college, you face a number of important financial issues, everything from paying college expenses to dealing with credit cards. Visit http://www.nhheaf.org/pdfs/10steps.pdf listed here and click "10 Steps to Financial Fitness." What are the ten steps? Which of these will be easiest for you to complete? Which will be the most difficult?

5. Analyze your current credit situation. What are your existing debts? How much are you paying each month? Did you borrow for the right reasons? List some steps you think you should start taking to improve your management of credit. Compare your findings with those of a classmate.

# Developing a Business Plan

## *DRAPER FISHER JURVETSON SEARCHES FOR BILLION-DOLLAR IDEAS—MAYBE YOURS?*

Every would-be entrepreneur dreams of hatching the next hot business idea, one that changes the world as we know it forever. And every venture capitalist's wish is to find that upcoming entrepreneur first, before competitors. That's what venture capitalists do—take risks, invest in new firms, and help get them off the ground and soaring to new heights for a hoped-for big payoff. Tim Draper of Silicon Valley–based Draper Fisher Jurvetson (DFJ) has had uncanny success in backing high-tech start-ups that go on to revolutionize business. Heard of Hotmail? That was one of Draper's early investments. The company was eventually purchased for $400 million by none other than Microsoft.

More recent successes have included Internet telephony company Skype, which eBay purchased for $2.6 billion, and Chinese search engine Baidu, whose shares skyrocketed more than 350 percent in its first day of trading. DFJ had a 10 percent share in Skype and a 28 percent share in Baidu, which together are worth nearly $1.5 billion for the VC firm. Of course, not all investments pay off, and that's where the risk part of the equation comes into play. But Draper prefers not to dwell on the failures.

So how does DFJ learn about new companies and decide whether they are worth their investment? By talking with entrepreneurs and studying their business plans. Draper says he does a lot of reading—including technical journals, philosophy, science fiction, and history—to help him understand the world and the way it works. But, he adds, "The overwhelming amount of reading I do is business plans and e-mails." He also searches the world through affiliate companies in developing markets such as Ukraine, China, and India for the best new ideas. To cast its net even wider, DFJ put a blog on the Internet encouraging businesspeople to "pitch Tim Draper on your billion-dollar idea." The company narrowed the responses it received to eleven ideas, and those entrepreneurs discussed their plans with Draper via a video conference. One was eventually funded. DFJ has held several of these conferences.

Other areas of interest for the company are memory devices, nanotechnology and life sciences, and alternative, clean energies. The firm aims to be on the cutting edge of the high-tech world because Draper believes that business fuels many more of the solutions to society's problems than government does. He maintains, "The next big energy breakthrough will happen through a business. . . . Medicine has been advanced through business. It turns out that it's the businesspeople that tend to be the ones who solve all this stuff."

Such enthusiasm got Draper's own business off the ground. He got his start with a $6 million loan from the U.S. Small Business Administration. The first three years were rocky, and Draper thought his company might fail. But in 1990, "We had a series of about five IPOs [initial public offerings]. It went from near disaster to the best-performing fund of its ilk. Now there's a picture of me in the lobby of the SBA."

Do you have a great idea for a high-tech start-up—one that can dominate its market? Draper would love to hear about it. The company's Web site features a "Submit Business Plan" link to make it simple. So do your research, go to your computer, and get busy. This appendix can help you plan for your new business adventure, whatever it may be.[1]

# APPENDIX OVERVIEW

Many entrepreneurs and small-business owners have written business plans to help them organize their businesses, get them up and running, and raise money for expansion. In this appendix, we cover the basics of business planning: what business plans are, why they're important, and who needs them. We also explain the steps involved in writing a good plan and the major elements it should contain. Finally, we cover additional resources to get you started with your own business plan—to help you bring your unique ideas to reality with a business of your own.

# WHAT IS A BUSINESS PLAN?

You may wonder how the millions of different businesses operating in the United States and throughout the world today got their start. Often it is with a formal business plan. A business plan is a written document that articulates what a company's objectives are, how these objectives will be achieved, how the business will be financed, and how much money the company expects to bring in. In short, it describes where a company is, where it wants to go, and how it intends to get there. Elizabeth Wasserman, writing in the magazine MBA Jungle, states that a business plan has to be "a compelling story with drama (a demonstrated need), hope (how your product can fill that need), heroes (the management team), and a happy ending (return on investment)."[2]

## Why a Business Plan Is So Important

A well-written business plan can be used for many purposes, but it serves two key functions:

1. It organizes the business and validates its central idea.
2. It summarizes the business and its strategy to obtain funding from lenders and investors.

First, a business plan gives a business formal direction, whether it is just starting, going through a phase of growth, or struggling. The business plan forces the principals—the owners—through rigorous planning, to think through the realities of running and financing a business. In their planning, they consider many details. How will inventory be stored, shipped, and stocked? Where should the business be located? How will the business use the Internet? And most important, how will the business make enough money to make it all worthwhile?

A business plan also gives the owners a well-reasoned blueprint to refer to when daily challenges arise, and it acts as a benchmark by which successes and disappointments can be measured. Additionally, a solid business plan will sell the potential owner on the validity of the idea. In some cases, the by-product of developing the plan is demonstrating to a starry-eyed person that he or she is trying to start a bad business. In other words, the process of writing a plan benefits a would-be businessperson as much as the final plan benefits potential investors.

Finally, a business plan articulates the business's strategy to financiers who can fund the business, and it is usually required to obtain a bank loan. Lenders and venture capitalists need to see that the business owner has thought through the critical issues and presented a promising idea before they will consider investing in it. They are, after all, interested in whether it will bring them significant returns.

## Who Needs a Business Plan?

Some people mistakenly believe that they need a business plan only if it will land on the desk of a venture capitalist or the loan committee of the company's bank. Others think that writing a plan is unnecessary if their bank or lending institution doesn't require it. Such assumptions miss the point of planning, because a business plan acts as a map to guide the way through the often tangled roads of running a business. The answer to the question of who needs a plan is anyone who is serious abut being successful. Every small-business owner should develop a business plan because it empowers that person to take control.

# HOW DO I WRITE A BUSINESS PLAN?

Developing a business plan should mean something different to everyone. Think of a business plan as a clear statement of a business's identity. A travel agency has a different identity from a newly launched magazine, which has yet a different identity from a restaurant hoping to expand its share of the market. Each business has unique objectives and processes, and each faces different obstacles.

At the same time, good business plans contain some similar elements no matter who the business owner is, what he or she sells, or how far the owner is into the venture. A savvy business owner molds the elements of a business plan into a professional and personal representation of the firm's needs and goals. The plan should also realistically assess the risks and obstacles specific to the business and present solutions for overcoming them.

Because the document is important, it takes time to collect needed information and organize it. Don't be misled into believing that you will simply sit down and begin writing. Before any writing begins, the business owner must become an expert in his or her field. Readying important information about the company and the market will make the writing easier and faster. Some critical pieces of information to have on hand are the following items:

- The company's name, legal form of organization, location, financial highlights, and owners or shareholders (if any).
- Organization charts, list of top managers, consultants or directors, and employee agreements.
- Marketing research, customer surveys, and information about the company's major competitors.
- Product information, including goods and services offered; brochures; patents, licenses, and trademarks; and research and development plans.
- Marketing plans and materials.
- Financial statements (both current and forecasted).

The business owner also must do a lot of soul searching and brainstorming to answer important questions necessary to build the backbone of a healthy business. Figure C.1 lists some critical questions to ask yourself.

Once equipped with these answers, you can begin writing the document, which can be anywhere between 10 and 50 pages long. The length of the plan depends on the complexity of the company, whether the company is a start-up (established companies have longer histories to detail), and what the plan will be used for. Regardless of size, the document should be well organized and easy to use, especially if the business plan is intended for external uses, such as

> ## "They Said It"
>
> "Good plans shape good decisions. That's why good planning helps to make elusive dreams come true."
> —Lester R. Bittel (b. 1918)
> In The Nine Master Keys of Management

**Figure**

C.1 | Self-Evaluation Questions

**Take a few minutes to read and answer these questions.
Don't worry about answering in too much detail at this point.
The questions are preliminary and
intended to help you think through your venture.**

1. In general terms, how would you explain your idea to a friend?

2. What is the purpose or objective of your venture?

3. What service are you going to provide, or what goods are you going to manufacture?

4. Is there any significant difference between what you are planning and what already exists?

5. How will the quality of your product compare with competitive offerings?

6. What is the overview of the industry or service sector you are going to enter? Write it out.

7. What is the history, current status, and future of the industry?

8. Who is your customer or client base?

9. Where and by whom will your good or service be marketed?

10. How much will you charge for the product you are planning?

11. Where is the financing going to come from to initiate your venture?

12. What training and experience do you have that qualifies you for this venture?

13. Does such training or experience give you a significant edge?

14. If you lack specific experience, how do you plan to gain it?

to secure financing. Number all pages, include a table of contents, and make sure the format is attractive and professional. Include two or three illustrative charts or graphs and highlight the sections and important points with headings and bulleted lists. Figure C.2 outlines the major sections of a business plan.

The following paragraphs discuss the most common elements of an effective business plan. When you need additional instruction or information as you write, refer to the "Resources" section at the end of the appendix.

## Executive Summary

The primary purpose of an executive summary is to entice readers sufficiently to read more about the business. An **executive summary** is a one- to two-page snapshot of what the overall business plan explains in detail. Consider it a business plan within a business plan. Through its enthusiasm and quick momentum, the summary should capture the reader's imagination.

Describe your strategy for succeeding in a positive, intriguing, and realistic way and briefly yet thoroughly answer the first questions anyone would have about your business: who, what, why, when, where, and how. Financiers always turn to the executive summary first. If it isn't well presented or lacks the proper information, they will quickly move on to the next business plan in the stack. The executive summary is just as important to people funding the business with personal resources, however, because it channels their motivations into an articulate mission statement. It is a good idea to write the summary last, because it will inevitably be revised once the business plan takes final shape.

To write an effective executive summary, focus on the issues that are most important to your business's success and save the supporting matters for the body. The executive summary should describe the business's strategy and goals, the good or service it is selling, and the advantages it has over the competition. It should also give a snapshot of how much money will be required to launch the business, how it will be used, and how the lenders or investors will recoup their funds.

## Introduction

The **introduction** follows the executive summary. After the executive summary has offered an attractive synopsis, the introduction should begin to discuss the fine details of the business. It should be crafted to include any material the upcoming marketing and financing sections do not cover. The introduction should describe the company, the management team, and the product in detail. If one of these topics is particularly noteworthy for your business, you may want to present that topic as its own section. Listen to what you write and respond as the plan takes shape.

Include basic information about the company—its past, present, and future. What are the company's roots, what is its current status, and what actions need to be taken to achieve its goals? If you are starting a company, include a description of the evolution of the concept. Be sure to tie all of the business's goals and plans to the industry in which it will operate, and describe the industry itself.

A business doesn't run itself, of course. People are the heart of a business, so write an appealing picture of the business's management team. Who are the key players and how does their experience resonate with the company's goals? Describe their—or your, if you are a sole proprietor—education, training, and experience, and highlight and refer to their résumés included later in the plan. Be honest, however—not all businesses are started by experts. If you lack demonstrated experience in a certain area, explain how you plan to get it.

Also describe the product, the driving force behind the venture. What are you offering, and why is it special? What are the costs of the service or price tag on the good? Analyze the features of the offering and the effect these features have on the overall cost.

Figure

C.2

# The Business Plan

**I. Executive Summary**
  - Who, what, when, where, why, and how?

**II. Table of Contents**

**III. Introduction**
  - The concept and the company
  - The management team
  - The product

**IV. Marketing Strategy**
  - Demographics
  - Trends
  - Market penetration
  - Potential sales revenue

**V. Financing the Business**
  - Cash flow analysis
  - Pro forma balance sheet
  - Income statement

**VI. Résumés of Principals**

## Marketing Strategy

Next comes the marketing strategy section. The **marketing strategy** describes the market's need for the item and how the business will fulfill it. Marketing strategies are not based on informal projections or observations. They are the result of a careful market analysis. So formulating a marketing strategy allows the business owner to become familiar with every aspect of the particular market. If done properly, it will allow you to define your target market and position your business within that sector to get its share of sales.

The marketing strategy includes a discussion of the size of the customer base that will want to purchase your good or service and the projected rate of growth for the product or category. Highlight information on the demographics of your customers. **Demographics** are statistical characteristics of the segment of the market, such as income, gender, and age. What types of people will purchase your product? How old are they, and where do they live? What is their lifestyle like? For example, someone starting an interior design business will want to report how many homeowners live within a certain radius of the business, as well as their median income. Of course, this section of the marketing analysis will be quite different for a company that conducts all of its business online. You will want to know the types of people who will shop at your Web site, but your discussion won't be limited to one geographic area. It is also a good idea to describe the trends in your product category. **Trends** are consumer and business tendencies or patterns that business owners can exploit to gain market share in an industry.

The marketing strategy should also detail your distribution, pricing, and promotional goals. Discuss the average price of your offering and the reasons behind the price you have chosen. How do you intend to let your potential customers know that you have a product to sell? How will you sell it—through a catalog, in a retail location, online, or perhaps a combination of all three? The effectiveness of your distribution, pricing, and promotional goals determines the extent to which you will be able to garner market share.

Competitors are another important part of your marketing strategy. What companies are already selling products similar to yours? Include a list of your competitors to show that you know exactly who they are and what you are up against. Describe what you think are their major strengths and weaknesses and how successful they have been within your market.

Also include the **market penetration,** which is the percentage of total customers who have purchased a company's product. If there are 10,000 people in your market, and 5,000 have purchased your product, your market penetration is 50 percent. The **potential sales revenue,** also an important figure to include, is the total revenue of a company if it captured 100 percent market penetration. In other words, this figure represents the total dollar value of sales you would bring in if everyone who is a potential customer purchased your product.

## Financing the Business

The goal of a business is to make money. Everything in the business plan lays the foundation for the **financing section.** Business owners should not skip this section even if they are not seeking outside money. While it is crucial to have an accurate financial analysis to get financing, it also is a necessary exercise for business owners funding the venture themselves. The financing section demonstrates the cost of the product, operating expenses, expected sales revenue and profit, and the amount of the business owner's own funds that will be invested to get the business up and running. The financial projections should be compelling but accurate and based on realistic assumptions. The owner should be able to defend them.

Any assumptions made in the body of the business plan should be tied into the financial section. For instance, if you think you will need a staff of five, your cash flow analysis should explain how you are going to pay them. A cash flow analysis, a mandatory component of a financial analysis, shows how much money will flow through your business throughout the year. It helps you plan for staggered purchasing, high-volume months, and slow periods. Your business may be cyclical or seasonal, so the cash flow projection lets you know if you need to arrange a line of credit to cover periodic shortfalls. In addition, an income statement is a critical component. The income statement is a statement of income and expenses your company has accrued over a period of time.

Remember that leaving out important details can undercut your credibility, so be thorough. The plan must include your assumptions about the conditions under which your business will operate. It should cover details such as market strength; date of start-up; sales buildup; gross profit margin; equipment, furniture, and fixtures required; and payroll and other key expenses that will affect the financial plan. In addition, a banker will want a pro forma balance sheet, which provides an estimate of what the business owns (assets), what it owes (liabilities), and what it is worth (owner's equity). Refer to Chapters 16, 17, and 18 of *Contemporary Business* for additional details on accounting, financial statements, and financial management.

## Résumés of Principals

The final element of the business plan is the inclusion of the résumés of the principals behind the business: the management team. Each résumé should include detailed employment information and accomplishments. If applicable to your business, consider expanding on the traditional résumé by including business affiliations, professional memberships, hobbies, and leisure activities.

However you choose to develop a business plan, make sure that *you* develop the plan. It should sound as though it was written by the entrepreneur, not by some outside "expert."

# RESOURCES

A tremendous amount of material is available to help business owners (whether existing or prospective) write effective business plans. The biggest task is narrowing it down to which resources are right for you. The Internet delivers an abundance of sound business-planning tools and advice, much of which are free. It allows you to seek diverse examples and opinions, which is important because no one source will match your situation exactly. Your school library and career center also have a wealth of resources. Following are some helpful resources for business planning.

## Books

Dozens of books exist on how to write a business plan. Examples include the following:

- Joseph Covello and Brian Hazelgren, *The Complete Book of Business Plans,* 2nd ed. (Sourcebooks, Inc., 2006).
- Mike McKeever, *How to Write a Business Plan,* 7th ed. (Nolo Press, 2005)
- *Building a Successful Business Plan: Advice from the Experts* (Socrates Media, 2005)
- David Bangs and Mark Hendricks, *Business Plans Made Easy* (Entrepreneur Press, 2005)

## Web Sites

- *Entrepreneur* and *Inc.* magazines offer knowledgeable guides to writing a business plan. *Entrepreneur*'s Web site also contains sample business plans.

  http://www.entrepreneur.com
  http://www.inc.com

- Deloitte & Touche offers a useful document called "Writing an Effective Business Plan." It can be found on the firm's Web site.

  http://www.deloitte.com

- American Express offers several business planning tools on its Web site.

  http://www.americanexpress.com/open

- If you are hoping to obtain funding with your business plan, you should familiarize yourself with what venture capitalists are looking for in a business plan. An example can be found at the following site:

  http://cpvp.com/submit/businessplan.html

- New Enterprise Associates has a useful Web site.

  http://www.nea.com

## Software

Business-planning software can give an initial shape to your business plan. However, a word of caution is in order if you write a business plan using the software's template. Bankers and potential investors, such as venture capitalists, read so many business plans that those based on templates may sink to the bottom of the pile. Also, if you aren't looking for funding, using software can undercut a chief purpose of writing a plan—learning about your unique idea. So think twice before you deprive yourself of that experience. Remember, software is a tool. It can help you get started, stay organized, and build a professional-looking business plan, but it can't actually write the plan for you.

## Associations and Organizations

Many government and professional organizations provide assistance to would-be business owners. Here is a partial list:

- The U.S. Small Business Administration offers planning materials, along with other resources.

  http://www.sba.gov/starting_business

The SBA also has a center specifically designed for female entrepreneurs.

  http://www.onlinewbc.gov

- One of the missions of the Ewing Marion Kauffman Foundation is to encourage entrepreneurship across the U.S. The foundation's Web site offers an online resource center for new and growing businesses.

  http://entreworld.com

# Glossary

**360-degree performance review** employee performance review that gathers feedback from co-workers, supervisors, managers, and sometimes customers.

**401(k) plan** retirement savings plan to which employees can make pretax contributions; sometimes employers make additional contributions to the plan.

**accounting** process of measuring, interpreting, and communicating financial information to support internal and external business decision making.

**accounting process** set of activities involved in converting information about individual transactions into financial statements.

**accrual accounting** accounting method that records revenue and expenses when they occur, not necessarily when cash actually changes hands.

**acquisition** procedure in which one firm purchases the property and assumes the obligations of another.

**activity ratios** measures of how efficiently a firm utilizes its assets.

**actuarial table** probability calculation of the number of specific events—such as deaths, injuries, fire, or windstorm losses—expected to occur within a given year.

**advertising** paid nonpersonal communication delivered through various media and designed to inform, persuade, or remind members of a particular audience.

**affective conflict** disagreement that focuses on individuals or personal issues.

**affinity program** marketing effort sponsored by an organization that solicits involvement by individuals who share common interests and activities.

**agency** legal relationship whereby one party, called a principal, appoints another party, called an agent, to enter into contracts with third parties on the principal's behalf.

**alien corporation** firm incorporated in one nation and operating in another nation.

**angel investors** wealthy individuals who invest directly in a new venture in exchange for an equity stake.

**appellate courts** courts that hear appeals of decisions made at the general trial court level; both the federal and state systems have appellate courts.

**application service provider (ASP)** specialist in providing both the computers and the application support for managing information systems for clients.

**application software** programs that carry out a specific task such as word processing.

**arbitration** bringing in an impartial third party called an arbitrator to render a binding decision in a dispute.

**assembly line** manufacturing technique that carries the product on a conveyor system past several workstations where workers perform specialized tasks.

**asset** anything of value owned or leased by a business.

**autocratic leadership** management approach whereby leaders make decisions on their own without consulting employees.

**balance of payments** overall money flows into and out of a country.

**balance of trade** difference between a nation's exports and imports.

**balance sheet** statement of a firm's financial position—what it owns and the claims against its assets—at a particular point in time.

**balanced budget** situation in which total revenues raised by taxes and fees equal total proposed government spending for the year.

**bankruptcy** legal nonpayment of financial obligations.

**banner ad** ad placed by an organization on another organization's Web site; interested parties click the ad for more information.

**basic accounting equation** relationship that states that assets equal liabilities plus owners' equity.

**benchmarking** process of determining other companies' standards and best practices.

**blog** online journal written by a blogger.

**board of directors** elected governing body of a corporation.

**bond rating** tool used by investors to assess the credit risk of municipal and corporate bonds.

**bond** certificate of indebtedness sold to raise long-term funds for a corporation or government agency.

**bot** software program that allows online shoppers to compare the price of a particular product offered by several online retailers.

**bottom line** another term for net income or profits after taxes.

**boycott** effort to prevent people from purchasing a firm's goods or services.

**brand equity** added value that a respected and successful name gives to a product.

**brand name** part of a brand consisting of words or letters that form a name that identifies and distinguishes an offering from those of competitors.

**brand** name, term, sign, symbol, design, or some combination that identifies the products of one firm and differentiates them from competitors' offerings.

**branding** process of creating an identity in consumers' minds for a good, service, or company; a major marketing tool in contemporary business.

**breach of contract** violation of a valid contract.

**breakeven analysis** pricing technique used to determine the minimum sales volume a product must generate at a certain price level to cover all costs.

**brokerage firm** financial intermediary that buys and sells securities for individual and institutional investors.

**budget** organization's plan for how it will raise and spend money during a given period of time.

**budget deficit** funding shortfall in which government spends more than the amount of funds raised through taxes and fees.

**budget surplus** excess funding that occurs when government spends less than the amount of funds raised through taxes and fees.

**business** all profit-seeking activities and enterprises that provide goods and services necessary to an economic system.

**business (B2B) product** good or service purchased to be used, either directly or indirectly, in the production of other goods for resale.

**business ethics** standards of conduct and moral values involving right and wrong actions arising in the work environment.

**business incubator** organization that provides temporary low-cost, shared facilities to small start-up ventures.

**business interruption insurance** insurance that protects firms from financial losses resulting from the interruption of business operations.

**business law** aspects of law that most directly influence and regulate the management of business activity.

**business plan** written document that provides an orderly statement of a company's goals, the methods by which it intends to achieve those goals, and the standards by which it will measure achievements.

**business-to-business (B2B) e-business** electronic business transactions between organizations using the Internet.

**business-to-consumer (B2C) e-business** selling directly to consumers over the Internet.

**call provision** provision that allows a bond issuer to buy the bond back from investors before maturity.

**capital** production inputs consisting of technology, tools, information, and physical facilities.

**capitalism** economic system that rewards firms for their ability to perceive and serve the needs and demands of consumers; also called the private enterprise system.

**cash budget** accounting report that tracks the firm's cash inflows and outflows; usually prepared monthly.

**cash flow** sources of cash minus uses of cash during a specified period of time.

**cash value policy** type of life insurance that combines a death benefit with some sort of savings feature.

**category advisor** vendor that is designated by the business customer as the major supplier to deal with all other suppliers for a special purchase and to present the entire package to the business buyer.

**category manager** person who oversees an entire group of products and assumes profit responsibility for the product group.

**cause advertising** form of institutional advertising that promotes a specific viewpoint on a public issue as a way to influence public opinion and the legislative process.

**cause marketing** marketing that promotes a cause or social issue, such as preventing child abuse, antilittering efforts, and antismoking campaigns.

**Central American Free Trade Agreement (CAFTA)** agreement among the United States, Costa Rica, the Dominican Republic, El Salvador, Guatemala, Honduras, and Nicaragua to reduce tariffs and trade restrictions.

**centralization** decision making based at the top of the management hierarchy.

**certified public accountant (CPA)** accountant who meets specified educational and experiential requirements and has passed a comprehensive examination on accounting theory and practice.

**chain of command** set of relationships that indicates who directs which activities and who reports to whom.

**change agent** manager who revitalizes an established firm to keep it competitive.

**channel conflict** conflict between two or more members of a supply chain, such as manufacturers, wholesalers, and retailers.

**chief information officer (CIO)** executive responsible for managing a firm's information technology.

**Class-Action Fairness Act of 2005** law that moves most large, multistate class-action lawsuits to federal courts, ensures judicial oversight of plaintiffs' compensation, bases lawyers' compensation on awards actually distributed or actual time spent, and ensures that plaintiffs' interests are protected equally with their lawyers'.

**classic entrepreneur** person who identifies a business opportunity and allocates available resources to tap that market.

**click-through rate** percentage of people presented with a Web banner ad who click on it.

**cobranding** cooperative arrangement in which two or more businesses team up to closely link their names on a single product.

**code of conduct** formal statement that defines how the organization expects employees to resolve ethical issues.

**cognitive ability tests** tests that measure job candidates' abilities in perceptual speed, verbal comprehension, numerical aptitude, general reasoning, and spatial aptitude.

**cognitive conflict** disagreement that focuses on problem- and issue-related differences of opinion.

**collective bargaining** process of negotiation between management and union representatives for the purpose of arriving at mutually acceptable wages and working conditions for employees.

**comarketing** cooperative arrangement in which two businesses jointly market each other's products.

**committee organization** organizational structure that places authority and responsibility jointly in the hands of a group of individuals rather than a single manager.

**common law** body of law arising out of judicial decisions, some of which can be traced back to early England.

**common stock** shares of ownership in a corporation.

**communication** meaningful exchange of information through messages.

**communism** planned economic system in which private property is eliminated, goods are owned in common, and factors of production and production decisions are controlled by the state.

**competition** battle among businesses for consumer acceptance.

**competitive differentiation** unique combination of organizational abilities, products, and approaches that sets a company apart from competitors in the minds of customers.

**competitive pricing** pricing strategy that tries to reduce the emphasis on price competition by matching other firms' prices and concentrating marketing efforts on the product, distribution, and promotional elements of the marketing mix.

**compressed workweek** scheduling option that allows employees to work the regular number of hours per week in fewer than the typical five days.

**computer-aided design (CAD)** system for interactions between a designer and a computer to create a product, facility, or part that meets predetermined specifications.

**computer-aided manufacturing (CAM)** electronic tools to analyze CAD output and determine necessary steps to implement the design, followed by electronic transmission of instructions to guide the activities of production equipment.

**computer-integrated manufacturing (CIM)** production system that integrates computer tools and human workers to design products, control machines, handle materials, and control production.

**conceptual skills** ability to see the organization as a unified whole and to understand how each part interacts with others.

**conflict of interest** situation in which an employee must make a decision about a business's welfare versus personal gain.

**conflict** antagonistic interaction in which one party attempts to thwart the intentions or goals of another.

**conglomerate merger** combination of two or more unrelated firms, usually with the goal of diversification, spurring sales growth, or spending a cash surplus that might otherwise make the firm a tempting target for a takeover attempt.

**consumer (B2C) product** good or service that is purchased by end users.

**consumer behavior** actions of ultimate consumers directly involved in obtaining, consuming, and disposing of products and the decision processes that precede and follow these actions.

**consumer orientation** business philosophy that focuses first on determining unmet consumer needs and then designing products to satisfy those needs.

**Consumer Price Index (CPI)** monthly measure of changes in retail price levels by comparisons of changes in the prices of a "market basket" of goods and services most commonly purchased by urban consumers.

**consumerism** public demand that a business consider the wants and needs of its customers in making decisions.

**contingency planning** plans that allow a firm to resume operations as quickly and as smoothly as possible after a crisis while openly communicating with the public about what happened.

**contract** legally enforceable agreement between two or more parties regarding a specified act or thing.

**controller** chief accounting manager; the person who keeps the company's books, prepares financial statements, and conducts internal audits.

**controlling** function of evaluating an organization's performance to determine whether it is accomplishing its objectives.

**convenience product** item the consumer seeks to purchase frequently, immediately, and with little effort.

**conversion rate** percentage of visitors to a Web site who make a purchase.

**cooperative advertising** allowances provided by marketers in which they share the cost of local advertising of their firm's product or product line with channel partners.

**cooperative** organization whose owners join forces to collectively operate all or part of the functions in their business.

**copyright** protection of written material such as books, designs, cartoon illustrations, photos, and computer software.

**core inflation rate** the underlying inflation rate of the economy after energy and food prices are removed.

**corporate charter** legal document that formally establishes a corporation.

**corporate culture** organization's system of principles, beliefs, and values.

**corporate philanthropy** act of an organization giving something back to the communities in which it earns profits.

**corporate Web site** Web site designed to increase a firm's visibility, promote its offerings, and provide information to interested parties.

**corporation** business that stands as a legal entity with assets and liabilities separate from those of its owner(s).

**cost-based pricing** adding a percentage (markup) to the base cost of a product to cover overhead costs and generate profits.

**countertrade** barter agreement whereby trade between two or more nations involves payment made in the form of local products instead of currency.

**creative selling** personal selling that involves skillful proposals of solutions for the customer's needs.

**creativity** capacity to develop novel solutions to perceived organizational problems.

**credit** receiving money, goods, or services on the basis of an agreement between the lender and the borrower that the loan is for a specified period of time with a specified rate of interest.

**critical path** sequence of operations that requires the longest time for completion.

**critical thinking** ability to analyze and assess information to pinpoint problems or opportunities.

**cross-functional team** team made up of members from different functions, such as production, marketing, and finance.

**customer satisfaction** ability of a good or service to meet or exceed a buyer's needs and expectations.

**damages** financial payments to compensate for a loss and related suffering.

**data** raw facts and figures that may or may not be relevant to a business decision.

**data mining** computer searches of customer data to detect patterns and relationships.

**data warehouse** customer database that allows managers to combine data from several different organizational functions.

**database** centralized integrated collection of data resources.

**debenture** bond backed by the reputation of the issuer rather than by a specific pledge of a company's assets.

**debt capital** funds obtained through borrowing.

**debt financing** borrowed funds that entrepreneurs must repay.

**decentralization** decision making based at lower levels of the organization.

**decision making** process of recognizing a problem or opportunity, evaluating alternative solutions, selecting and implementing an alternative, and assessing the results.

**decision support system (DSS)** information system that quickly provides relevant data to help businesspeople make decisions and choose courses of action.

**deflation** falling prices caused by a combination of reduced consumer demand and decreases in the costs of raw materials, component parts, human resources, and other factors of production.

**delegation** act of assigning work activities to subordinates.

**demand** willingness and ability of buyers to purchase goods and services.

**demand curve** graph of the amount of a product that buyers will purchase at different prices; generally slopes downward to reflect larger quantities likely to be purchased as prices decline.

**demand deposits** deposits held in banks and other financial institutions that are payable on demand, such as checking accounts.

**democratic leadership** management approach whereby leaders delegate assignments, ask employees for suggestions, and encourage their participation.

**demographic segmentation** dividing markets on the basis of various demographic or socioeconomic characteristics such as gender, age, income, occupation, household size, stage in family life cycle, education, or ethnic group.

**demographics** statistical characteristics of the segment of the market that might purchase a product.

**departmentalization** process of dividing work activities into units within the organization.

**depository institutions** financial institutions that accept deposits that can be converted into cash on demand.

**deregulation** regulatory trend toward elimination of legal restraints on competition in industries previously served by a single firm in an attempt to improve customer service and lower prices through increased competition.

**desktop publishing** computer technology that allows users to design and produce attractively formatted documents.

**devaluation** reduction in a currency's value relative to other currencies or to a fixed standard.

**direct distribution channel** marketing channel that moves goods directly from producer to ultimate user.

**directing** guiding and motivating employees to accomplish organizational objectives.

**disability income insurance** insurance that pays benefits to those who cannot work due to some sort of a disability.

**discount rate** rate the Federal Reserve charges member banks for loans.

**dispatching** phase of production control in which the manager instructs each department on what work to do and the time allowed for its completion.

**distribution channel** path through which products—and legal ownership of them—flow from producer to consumers or business users.

**distribution strategy** planning that ensures that customers find their products in the proper quantities at the right times and places.

**diversity** blending individuals of different genders, ethnic backgrounds, cultures, religions, ages, and physical and mental abilities to enhance a firm's chances of success.

**domestic corporation** firm that operates in the state where it is incorporated.

**double-entry bookkeeping** process by which accounting transactions are entered; each individual transaction always has an offsetting transaction.

**downsizing** process of reducing the number of employees within a firm by eliminating jobs.

**dumping** selling products abroad at prices below production costs or below typical prices in the home market to capture market share from domestic competitors.

**economics** social science that analyzes the choices people and governments make in allocating scarce resources.

**electronic bulletin board** Internet chat room that allows users to post and read messages on a specific topic.

**electronic business (e-business)** conducting business via the Internet.

**electronic communications network (ECN)** computerized market that directly matches buyers and sellers.

**electronic data interchange (EDI)** computer-to-computer exchanges of invoices, purchase orders, price quotations, and other information between buyers and sellers.

**electronic exchange** online marketplace that caters to a specific industry's needs.

**electronic funds transfer systems** computerized systems for conducting financial transactions over electronic links.

**electronic shopping cart** file that holds items that the online shopper has chosen to buy.

**electronic signatures** form of electronic identification.

**electronic storefront** company Web site that sells products to customers.

**electronic wallet** computer data file set up by an online shopper at an e-business site's checkout counter that contains not only electronic cash but credit card information and owner identification.

**embargo** total ban on importing specific products or a total halt to trading with a particular country.

**employee benefits** rewards such as retirement plans, health insurance, vacation, and tuition reimbursement provided for employees either entirely or in part at the company's expense.

**employee ownership** business in which workers purchase shares of stock in the firm that employs them.

**employee stock ownership plan (ESOP)** plan that benefits employees by giving them ownership stakes in the companies for which they work.

**empowerment** giving employees authority and responsibility to make decisions about their work without traditional managerial approval and control.

**encryption** process of encoding data for security purposes, using software that encodes or scrambles messages.

**end-use segmentation** marketing strategy that focuses on the precise way a B2B purchaser will use a product.

**enterprise resource planning (ERP) system** information system that collects, processes, and provides information about an organization's various functions.

**entrepreneur** person who seeks a profitable opportunity and takes the necessary risks to set up and operate a business.

**entrepreneurship** willingness to take risks to create and operate a business.

**environmental impact study** study that analyzes how a proposed plant would affect the quality of life in the surrounding area.

**e-procurement** use of the Internet by businesses and government agencies to solicit bids and purchase goods and services from suppliers.

**Equal Employment Opportunity Commission (EEOC)** government agency created to increase job opportunities for women and minorities and to help end discrimination based on race, color, religion, disability, gender, or national origin in any personnel action.

**equilibrium price** prevailing market price; the point at which the quantity demanded of a product equals the quantity supplied.

**equity capital** funds provided by the firm's owners when they reinvest earnings, make additional contributions, or issue stock to investors.

**equity financing** funds invested in new ventures in exchange for part ownership.

**European Union (EU)** 25-nation European economic alliance.

**event marketing** marketing or sponsoring short-term events such as athletic competitions and cultural and charitable performances.

**everyday low pricing (EDLP)** pricing strategy devoted to maintaining continuous low prices rather than relying on short-term price cuts such as cents-off coupons, rebates, and special sales.

**exchange control** restriction on importation of certain products or against certain companies to reduce trade and expenditures of foreign currency.

**exchange process** activity in which two or more parties give something of value to each other to satisfy perceived needs.

**exchange rate** value of one nation's currency relative to the currencies of other countries.

**exchange-traded fund (ETF)** fund with a fixed number of shares outstanding that trades on a stock market; generally invests in the securities that make up a well-known index.

**exclusive distribution** distribution strategy involving limited market coverage by a single retailer or wholesaler in a specific geographical territory.

**executive summary** one- to two-page snapshot of what the overall business plan explains in detail.

**executive support system (ESS)** system that allows top managers to access a firm's primary databases.

**expert system** computer program that imitates human thinking through complicated sets of "if-then" rules.

**exports** domestically produced goods and services sold in other countries.

**external communication** meaningful exchange of information through messages transmitted between an organization and its major audiences.

**extranet** secure networks accessible from outside a firm, but only by authorized third parties.

**factors of production** four basic inputs for effective operation: natural resources, capital, human resources, and entrepreneurship.

**family brand** brand name used to identify several different, but related, products.

**family leave** granting up to 12 weeks of unpaid leave annually for employees who have or adopt a child, are becoming foster parents, are caring for a seriously ill relative or spouse, or are themselves seriously ill.

**Federal Reserve System** U.S. central bank.

**fee-for-service plan** traditional form of health insurance in which the insured chooses his or her healthcare provider, pays for treatment, and is reimbursed by the insurance company; also called an indemnity plan.

**finance** business function of planning, obtaining, and managing a company's funds in order to accomplish its objectives effectively and efficiently.

**Financial Accounting Standards Board (FASB)** organization that interprets and modifies GAAP in the United States.

**financial manager** executive who develops and implements the firm's financial plan and determines the most appropriate sources and uses of funds.

**financial plan** document that specifies the funds a firm will need for a period of time, the timing of inflows and outflows, and the most appropriate sources and uses of funds.

**financial system** system by which funds are transferred from savers to users.

**financing section** section of a business plan that demonstrates the cost of the product, operating expenses, expected sales revenue and profit, and the amount of the business owner's own funds that will be invested to get the business up and running.

**firewall** electronic barrier between a company's internal network and the Internet that limits access into and out of the network.

**fiscal policy** government spending and taxation decisions designed to control inflation, reduce unemployment, improve the general welfare of citizens, and encourage economic growth.

**flexible benefit plan** benefit system that offers employees a range of options from which they may choose the types of benefits they receive.

**flexible manufacturing system (FMS)** facility that workers can quickly modify to manufacture different products.

**flexible work plan** employment that allows personnel to adjust their working hours and places of work to accommodate their personal needs.

**flextime** scheduling system that allows employees to set their own work hours within constraints specified by the firm.

**follow-up** phase of production control in which employees and their supervisors spot problems in the production process and determine needed adjustments.

**foreign corporation** firm that operates in states where it is not incorporated.

**foreign licensing agreement** international agreement in which one firm allows another to produce or sell its product, or use its trade-mark, patent, or manufacturing processes, in a specific geographical area in return for royalties or other compensation.

**formal communication channel** messages that flow within the chain of command defined by an organization.

**franchise** contractual agreement in which a franchisee gains the right to produce and/or sell the franchisor's products under that company's brand name if they agree to certain operating requirements.

**franchisee** small-business owner who contracts to sell the good or service of a supplier (the franchisor) in exchange for a payment (usually a flat fee plus a percentage of sales).

**franchising** contractual agreement that specifies the methods by which a dealer can produce and market a supplier's good or service.

**franchisor** business owner who permits the franchisee to sell its products and use its name, as well as providing a variety of marketing, management, and other services in return for the payment of various fees and a percentage of sales.

**free-rein leadership** management style of leaders who believe in minimal supervision and leave most decisions to their subordinates.

**frequency marketing** marketing initiative that rewards frequent purchases with cash, rebates, merchandise, or other premiums.

**full and fair disclosure** requirement that investors should be told all relevant information by stock or bond issuers so they can make informed decisions.

**General Agreement on Tariffs and Trade (GATT)** international trade accord that substantially reduced worldwide tariffs and other trade barriers.

**generally accepted accounting principles (GAAP)** principles that encompass the conventions, rules, and procedures for determining acceptable accounting practices at a particular time.

**geographical segmentation** dividing an overall market into homogeneous groups on the basis of their locations.

**global business strategy** offering a standardized, worldwide product and selling it in essentially the same manner throughout a firm's domestic and foreign markets.

**goal** target, objective, or result that someone tries to accomplish.

**goal-setting theory** theory that people will be motivated to the extent to which they accept specific, challenging goals and receive feedback that indicates their progress toward goal achievement.

**government accountant** accountant who performs professional services similar to those of management accountants and determines how efficiently government agencies accomplish their objectives.

**government bond** bond issued by the U.S. Treasury.

**grapevine** internal information channel that transmits information from unofficial sources.

**green marketing** marketing strategy that promotes environmentally safe products and production methods.

**grievance** formal complaint filed by an employee or a union that management is violating some provision of a union contract.

**gross domestic product (GDP)** sum of all goods and services produced within a country's boundaries during a specific time period, such as a year.

**guerrilla marketing** innovative, low-cost marketing schemes designed to get consumers' attention in unusual ways.

**handheld devices** small computerized devices that operate on rechargeable batteries; includes personal digital assistants and smart phones.

**hardware** all tangible elements of a computer system.

**health insurance** insurance that covers losses due to illness or accidents.

**health maintenance organization (HMO)** organization that, in return for a monthly fee, provides all of the insured's healthcare.

**high-context culture** a society in which communication depends not only on the message itself but also on nonverbal cues, past and present experiences, and personal relationships between the parties.

**home-based business** company operated from the residence of the business owner.

**horizontal merger** combination of two or more firms in the same industry that wish to diversify, increase their customer bases, cut costs, or offer expanded product lines.

**human resource management** function of attracting, developing, and retaining enough qualified employees to perform the activities necessary to accomplish organizational objectives.

**human resources** production inputs consisting of anyone who works, including both the physical labor and the intellectual inputs contributed by workers.

**human skills** interpersonal skills that enable a manager to work effectively with and through people; the ability to communicate with, motivate, and lead employees to accomplish assigned activities.

**imports** foreign goods and services purchased by domestic customers.

**income statement** financial record of a company's revenues, expenses, and profits over a period of time.

**individual brand** different brand names given to each product within a line.

**inflation** rising prices caused by a combination of excess consumer demand and increases in the costs of raw materials, component parts, human resources, and other factors of production.

**infomercial** form of broadcast direct marketing; 30-minute programs that resemble regular TV programs, but are devoted to selling goods or services.

**informal communication channel** messages outside formally authorized channels within an organization's hierarchy.

**information** knowledge gained from processing data.

**infrastructure** basic systems of communication, transportation, and energy facilities in a country.

**initial public offering (IPO)** first sale of a firm's stock to the investing public.

**insider trading** use of material, nonpublic information to make investor profits.

**institutional advertising** promotion of concepts, ideas, philosophies, or goodwill for industries, companies, organizations, or government entities.

**institutional investors** large investors such as pension funds and life insurance companies that invest for the benefit of others.

**insurable interest** demonstration that a direct financial loss will result if some event occurs.

**insurable risk** requirement that a pure risk must meet for the insurer to agree to provide protection.

**insurance** contract by which the insurer, for a fee (the premium), agrees to reimburse another firm or individual a sum of money if a loss occurs.

**integrated marketing communications (IMC)** coordination of all promotional activities—media advertising, direct mail, personal selling, sales promotion, and public relations—to produce a unified customer-focused message.

**integrity** adhering to deeply felt ethical principles in business situations.

**intensive distribution** distribution strategy that involves placing a firm's products in nearly every available outlet.

**international law** regulations that govern international commerce.

**International Monetary Fund (IMF)** organization created to promote trade, eliminate barriers, and make short-term loans to member nations that are unable to meet their budgets.

**International Organization for Standardization (ISO)** organization whose mission is to promote the development of standardized products to facilitate trade and cooperation across national borders.

**intranet** a computer network that links employees and other authorized users.

**intrapreneur** entrepreneurially oriented person who develops innovations within a large organization.

**intrapreneurship** process of promoting innovation within the structure of an existing organization.

**introduction** section of a business plan that describes the company, the management team, and the product in detail.

**inventory control** management effort to balance the priority of limiting inventory costs with that of meeting customer demand.

**investment banker** financial intermediary that purchases an issue or securities from the firm or government and then resells the issue to investors.

**investment-grade bond** corporate or municipal bond with a rating of BBB or above.

**job enlargement** job design that expands an employee's responsibilities by increasing the number and variety of tasks assigned to the worker.

**job enrichment** change in job duties to increase employees' authority in planning their work, deciding how it should be done, and learning new skills.

**job sharing program** management decision that allows two or more employees to divide the tasks of one job.

**joint venture** partnership between companies formed for a specific undertaking.

**judiciary** branch of the government charged with deciding disputes among parties through the application of laws.

**junk bond** corporate or municipal bond with a rating of BB or below.

**just-in-time (JIT) system** management philosophy aimed at improving profits and return on investment by minimizing costs and eliminating waste through cutting inventory on hand.

**labor union** group of workers who have banded together to achieve common goals in the areas of wages, hours, and working conditions.

**law of large numbers** concept that seemingly random events will follow a predictable pattern if enough events are observed.

**law** standards set by government and society in the form of either legislation or custom.

**leadership** ability to direct or inspire people to attain organizational goals.

**leverage** technique of increasing the rate of return on an investment by financing it with borrowed funds.

**leverage ratios** measures of the extent to which a company relies on borrowed funds.

**liability** claim against a firm's assets by a creditor.

**liability insurance** insurance that protects against financial losses to others for acts for which the insured was responsible.

**life insurance** insurance that protects people against the financial losses that occur with premature death.

**lifestyle** expression of how one lives one's daily life.

**lifestyle entrepreneur** person who starts a business to reduce work hours and create a more relaxed lifestyle.

**lifetime value of a customer** revenues and intangible benefits (referrals and customer feedback) from a customer over the life of the relationship, minus the amount the company must spend to acquire and serve that customer.

**limit order** investor's request to buy or sell a security but specifying a maximum price (if buying) or a minimum price (if selling).

**limited liability company (LLC)** legal form of organization allowing business owners to secure the corporate advantage of limited liability while avoiding the double taxation characteristic of corporations.

**line manager** executive involved with the functions of production, financing, or marketing.

**line organization** organizational structure that establishes a direct flow of authority from the chief executive to subordinates.

**line-and-staff organization** structure that combines the direct flow of authority of a line organization with staff departments that support the line departments.

**liquidity ratios** measures of a firm's ability to meet its short-term obligations.

**listening** receiving a message and interpreting its intended meaning by grasping the facts and feelings it conveys.

**local area network (LAN)** computer network that connects machines within limited areas, such as one building or several buildings near each other; allows personal computers to share printers, documents, and information.

**lockout** management decision to put pressure on union members by closing the firm.

**logistics** activities involved in controlling the flow of goods, services, and information among members of the supply chain.

**low-context culture** a society in which communication tends to rely on explicit written and verbal messages.

**M1** measure of the money supply that equals the total of coins and currency in circulation plus checking and other demand deposit account balances.

**M2** a measure of the money supply that equals M1 plus savings account and money market mutual fund balances.

**macroeconomics** study of a nation's overall economic issues, such as how an economy maintains and allocates resources and how a government's policies affect the standards of living of its citizens.

**mainframe** computer system containing the most extensive storage capacity and the fastest processing speeds.

**make, buy, or lease decision** choosing whether to manufacture a needed product or component in house, purchase it from an outside supplier, or lease it.

**managed care plan** healthcare plan in which most, if not all, of the insured's healthcare bills are paid by the insurance company; in exchange, the insured has much less say over his or her treatment.

**management** process of achieving organizational objectives through people and other resources.

**management accountant** accountant who works for a company other than a public accounting firm.

**management development program** training designed to improve the skills and broaden the knowledge of current and potential executives.

**management information system (MIS)** organized method for providing past, present, and projected information on internal operations as well as external intelligence to support decision making.

**manufacturer's (national) brand** brand offered and promoted by a manufacturer or producer.

**market order** investor's request to buy or sell a security at the current market price.

**market penetration** percentage of the market that has purchased your product.

**market segmentation** process of dividing a total market into several relatively homogeneous groups.

**marketing** organizational function and set of processes for creating, communicating, and delivering value to customers and for managing customer relationships in ways that benefit the organization and its stakeholders.

**marketing concept** company-wide consumer orientation to promote long-run success.

**marketing mix** blending the four elements of marketing strategy—product, distribution, promotion, and pricing—to satisfy chosen customer segments.

**marketing research** collecting and evaluating information to support marketing decision making.

**marketing strategy** section of a business plan that presents information describing the market's need for a product and how the business will satisfy it.

**marketing Web site** Web site whose main purpose is to increase purchases by visitors.

**Maslow's hierarchy of needs** theory of motivation proposed by Abraham Maslow. According to the theory, people have five levels of needs that they seek to satisfy: physiological, safety, social, esteem, and self-actualization.

**mass production** system for manufacturing products in large amounts through effective combinations of specialized labor, mechanization, and standardization.

**materials requirement planning (MRP)** computer-based production planning system by which a firm can ensure that it has needed parts and materials available at the right time and place in the correct amounts.

**matrix structure** project management structure that links employees from different parts of the organization to work together on specific projects.

**mediation** dispute resolution process that uses a third party, called a mediator, to make recommendations for settling labor-management differences.

**Medicare** health insurance program for those age 65 and older.

**merger** combination of two or more firms to form one company.

**microeconomics** study of small economic units, such as individual consumers, families, and businesses.

**microloans** Small Business Administration–guaranteed loans of up to $35,000 made to start-ups and other very small firms.

**middle management** second tier in the management pyramid that focuses on specific operations within the organizations.

**minicomputer** intermediate-size computer—more compact and less expensive than a mainframe but more powerful and expensive than a personal computer.

**mission statement** written explanation of an organization's business intentions and aims.

**missionary selling** indirect selling in which specialized salespeople promote the firm's goodwill among customers, often by assisting them in product use.

**mixed market economy** economic system that combines characteristics of both planned and market economies in varying degrees, including the presence of both government ownership and private enterprise.

**monetary policy** using interest rates and other tools to control the supply of money and credit in the economy.

**money** anything generally accepted as payment for goods and services.

**money market instruments** short-term debt securities issued by corporations, financial institutions, and governments.

**monopolistic competition** market structure, like that for retailing, in which large numbers of buyers and sellers exchange relatively well-differentiated (heterogeneous) products, so each participant has some control over price.

**monopoly** market structure in which a single seller dominates trade in a good or service for which buyers can find no close substitutes.

**morale** mental attitude of employees toward their employer and jobs.

**mortgage pass-through security** security backed by a self-liquidating pool of mortgage loans.

**multidomestic business strategy** developing and marketing products to serve different needs and tastes of separate national markets.

**multinational corporation (MNC)** firm with significant operations and marketing activities outside its home country.

**municipal bond** bond issued by a state or local government.

**mutual fund** financial institution that pools money from purchases of its shares and uses the money to acquire diversified portfolios of securities consistent with the fund's investment objectives.

**national debt** money owed by government to individuals, businesses, and government agencies who purchase Treasury bills, Treasury notes, and Treasury bonds sold as a result of trade deficits and other expenditures.

**natural resources** all production inputs that are useful in their natural states, including agricultural land, building sites, forests, and mineral deposits.

**nearshoring** outsourcing production or services to locations near a firm's home base.

**negotiable instrument** commercial paper that is transferable among individuals and businesses.

**net worth** difference between what a person owns (assets) and what the person owes (liabilities).

**nonpersonal selling** promotion that includes advertising, sales promotion, direct marketing, public relations, and sponsorships—all conducted without face-to-face contact with the buyer.

**nonprogrammed decision** complex and unique problem or opportunity with important consequences for the organization.

**nonverbal communication** transmission of messages through actions and behaviors.

**North American Free Trade Agreement (NAFTA)** agreement among the United States, Canada, and Mexico to break down tariffs and trade restrictions.

**not-for-profit corporation** businesslike organization such as a charitable group, social welfare group, or religious congregation that pursues objectives other than returning profit to its owners.

**not-for-profit organization** organization that has primary objectives such as public service rather than returning a profit to its owners.

**objectives** guideposts by which managers define the organization's desired performance in such areas as profitability, customer service, growth, and employee satisfaction.

**odd pricing** pricing method using uneven amounts, which appear less than they really are to consumers.

**offshoring** the relocation of business processes to lower-cost locations overseas.

**oligopoly** market structure, like those in the airline and steel industries, in which relatively few sellers compete and high start-up costs form barriers that keep out most new competitors.

**on-demand (utility) computing** renting software time from an application provider rather than purchasing and maintaining the software.

**on-the-job training** training method that teaches an employee to complete new tasks by performing them under the guidance of an experienced employee.

**open market operations** buying and selling of government securities by the Federal Reserve to affect the money supply.

**open-book management** policy of giving all employees access to important financial information.

**operating system** software that controls a computer's basic functions.

**operational planning** detailed standards that guide implementation of tactical plans.

**order processing** form of selling, mostly at the wholesale and retail levels, that involves identifying customer needs, pointing them out to customers, and completing orders.

**organization** structured grouping of people working together to achieve common goals.

**organization chart** visual representation of a firm's structure that illustrates job positions and functions.

**organization marketing** marketing strategy that influences consumers to accept the goals of, receive the services of, or contribute in some way to an organization.

**organizing** process of blending human and material resources through a formal structure of tasks and authority; arranging work, dividing tasks among employees, and coordinating them to ensure implementation of plans and accomplishment of objectives.

**outsourcing** using outside vendors to produce goods or fulfill services and functions that were previously handled in-country or in-house.

**owners' equity** all claims of the proprietor, partners, or stockholders against the assets of a firm, equal to the excess of assets over liabilities.

**ownership utility** orderly transfer of goods and services from the seller to the buyer; also called possession utility.

**pacing program** company-initiated and -financed program to develop new products.

**paid time off (PTO)** bank of time that employees can use for holidays, vacation, and sick days.

**partnership** form of business ownership in which the company is operated by two or more people who are co-owners by voluntary legal agreement.

**patent** guarantee to an inventor exclusive rights to an invention for seventeen years.

**penetration pricing** pricing strategy that sets a low price as a major marketing tactic.

**performance appraisal** evaluation of an employee's job performance that compares actual results with desired outcomes.

**perpetual inventory** system that continuously monitors the amounts and locations of a company's stocks.

**person marketing** use of efforts designed to attract the attention, interest, and preference of a target market toward a person.

**personal financial management** study of the economic factors and personal decisions that affect a person's financial well-being.

**personal selling** interpersonal promotional process involving a seller's face-to-face presentation to a prospective buyer.

**PERT (Program Evaluation and Review Technique)** chart that seeks to minimize delays by coordinating all aspects of the production process.

**phishing** high-tech scam that uses authentic looking e-mail or pop-up ads to get unsuspecting victims to reveal personal information.

**physical distribution** actual movement of products from producer to consumers or business users.

**picketing** workers marching at a plant entrance to protest some management practice.

**place marketing** attempt to attract people to a particular area, such as a city, state, or nation.

**place utility** availability of a product in a location convenient for customers.

**planned economy** economic system in which strict government controls determine business ownership, profits, and resource allocation to accomplish government goals rather than those set by individual businesses.

**planning** process of anticipating future events and conditions and determining courses of action for achieving organizational objectives.

**podcast** online video blog.

**point-of-purchase (POP) advertising** displays or demonstrations that promote products when and where consumers buy them, such as in retail stores.

**pollution** environmental damage caused by a company's products or operating processes.

**pop-up ad** online ad that "pops up" as a separate window; interested parties click the ad for more information.

**positioning** concept in which marketers attempt to establish their own places in the minds of customers by communicating to prospective purchasers meaningful distinctions about the attributes, price, quality, or use of a good or service.

**potential sales revenue** amount of revenue the business would collect if its market penetration were 100 percent.

**preferred provider organization (PPO)** contract between local healthcare providers and employers to provide employee medical care at a discount.

**preferred stock** stock whose holders have priority over common stockholders in the payment of dividends but usually have no voting rights.

**premium** amount paid by the insured to the insurance company in exchange for insurance coverage.

**presentation software** computer program that includes graphics and tools to produce a variety of charts, graphs, and pictures.

**prestige pricing** establishing a relatively high price to develop and maintain an image of quality and exclusiveness.

**price** exchange value of a good or service.

**price-earnings (P/E) ratio** a stock's current price divided by its current earnings.

**primary market** market in which new security issues are first sold to investors; issuers receive the proceeds from the sale.

**private (store) brand** product that is not linked to the manufacturer, but instead carries the label of a retailer or wholesaler.

**private enterprise system** economic system that rewards firms for their ability to identify and serve the needs and demands of customers.

**private exchange** secure Web site at which a company and its suppliers share all types of data related to e-business, from product design through order delivery.

**private placements** private sale of securities to large institutional investors.

**private property** most basic freedom under the private enterprise system; the right to own, use, buy, sell, and bequeath land, buildings, machinery, equipment, patents, and various intangible kinds of property.

**privatization** recent international trend to convert government-owned and -operated companies into privately held businesses.

**problem-solving team** temporary combination of workers who gather to solve a specific problem and then disband.

**product** bundle of physical, service, and symbolic attributes designed to satisfy buyers' wants.

**product advertising** nonpersonal selling of a particular good or service.

**product liability** responsibility of manufacturers for injuries and damages caused by their products.

**product life cycle** four basic stages—introduction, growth, maturity, and decline—through which a successful product progresses.

**product line** group of related products that are physically similar or are intended for the same market.

**product mix** company's assortment of product lines and individual offerings.

**product placement** form of promotion in which marketers pay fees to have their products showcased in movies and television shows.

**production** application of resources such as people and machinery to convert materials into finished goods and services.

**production and operations management** managing people and machinery in converting materials and resources into finished goods and services.

**production control** process that creates a well-defined set of procedures for coordinating people, materials, and machinery to provide maximum production efficiency.

**production planning** phase of production control that determines the amount of resources (including raw materials and other components) a firm needs in order to produce a certain output.

**productivity** relationship between the number of units produced and the number of human and other production inputs necessary to produce them.

**product-related segmentation** dividing consumer markets into groups based on benefits sought by buyers and usage rates.

**profitability objectives** firm's goal to generate enough money (its revenues) through its pricing policies to cover its expenses.

**profitability ratios** measures of a company's overall financial performance by evaluating its ability to generate revenues in excess of expenses.

**profits** rewards for business-people who take the risks involved to offer goods and services to customers.

**programmed decision** simple, common, and frequently occurring problem for which a solution has already been determined.

**promotion** the function of informing, persuading, and influencing a purchase decision.

**promotional mix** combination of personal and nonpersonal selling techniques designed to achieve promotional objectives.

**property and liability insurance** general category of insurance that protects against financial losses due to a number of perils.

**psychographic segmentation** dividing consumer markets into groups with similar attitudes, values, and lifestyles.

**public accountant** accountant who works for an independent accounting firm.

**public insurance agency** government agency that provides certain types of insurance protection.

**public ownership** organization owned and operated by a unit or agency of government.

**public relations** organization's communications and relationships with its various audiences.

**publicity** stimulation of demand for a good, service, place, idea, person, or organization by disseminating news or obtaining favorable unpaid media presentations.

**puffery** exaggerated claims of a product's superiority or the use of subjective or vague statements that may not be literally true.

**pulling strategy** promotional effort by a seller to stimulate demand among final users, who will then exert pressure on the distribution channel to carry the good or service, pulling it through the distribution channel.

**pure competition** market structure, like that of small-scale agriculture, in which large numbers of buyers and sellers exchange homogeneous products and no single participant has a significant influence on price.

**pure risk** risk where there is no chance of gain, only a chance of loss.

**pushing strategy** promotional effort by a seller to members of the distribution channel intended to stimulate personal selling of the good or service, thereby pushing it through the channel.

**quality control** measuring goods and services against established quality standards.

**quick response** system that allows a retailer to buy just the merchandise from suppliers that its customers want and just when it needs to restock its shelves; the retailing equivalent of just-in-time inventory systems.

**quota** limit set on the amounts of particular products that can be imported.

**ratio analysis** commonly used tool for measuring the financial strength of a firm.

**recession** cyclical economic contraction that lasts for six months or longer.

**recycling** reprocessing used materials for reuse.

**Regulation FD** provision requiring that firms disclose information to all investors at the same time.

**relationship era** the business era in which firms seek ways to build long-term relationships with customers by managing every interaction.

**relationship management** collection of activities that build and maintain ongoing, mutually beneficial ties between a business and its customers and other parties.

**relationship marketing** developing and maintaining long-term, cost-effective exchange relationships with partners.

**retailer** channel member that sells goods and services to individuals for their own use rather than for resale.

**risk** uncertainty about loss or injury.

**risk-return trade-off** optimal balance between the expected payoff from an investment and the investment's risk.

**robot** reprogrammable machine capable of performing numerous tasks that require manipulation of materials and tools.

**routing** phase of production control that determines the sequence of work throughout the facility and specifies who will perform each aspect of production at what location.

**S corporation** modified form of the traditional corporate structure often used by firms with fewer than 75 shareholders; such businesses can elect to pay federal income taxes as partnerships while retaining the liability limitations typical of corporations.

**salary** compensation calculated on a periodic basis, such as weekly or monthly.

**sales law** law governing the sale of goods or services for money or on credit.

**sales promotion** nonpersonal marketing activities other than advertising, personal selling, and public relations that stimulate consumer purchasing and dealer effectiveness.

**Sarbanes-Oxley Act of 2002** federal legislation designed to deter and punish corporate and accounting fraud and corruption and to protect the interests of workers and shareholders through enhanced financial disclosures, criminal penalties on CEOs and CFOs who defraud investors, safeguards for whistle-blowers, and establishment of a new regulatory body for public accounting firms.

**scheduling** development of timetables that specify how long each operation in the production process takes and when workers should perform it.

**search marketing** paying search engines, such as Google, a fee to make sure that the company's listing appears toward the top of the search results.

**secondary market** market in which existing security issues are bought and sold by investors.

**Secure Sockets Layer (SSL)** technology that secures a Web site by encrypting information and providing authentication.

**secured bond** bond that is backed by specific assets as collateral.

**securities** financial instruments such as stocks and bonds.

**seed capital** initial funding needed to launch a new venture.

**selective distribution** distribution strategy in which a manufacturer selects only a limited number of retailers to distribute its product lines.

**self-managed team** work team that has the authority to decide how its members complete their daily tasks.

**serial entrepreneur** person who starts one business, runs it, and then starts and runs additional businesses in succession.

**set-aside program** component of a government contract specifying that certain government contracts (or portions of those contracts) are restricted to small businesses and/or to women- or minority-owned companies.

**sexism** discrimination against members of either sex, but primarily affecting women.

**sexual harassment** inappropriate actions of a sexual nature in the workplace.

**shopping product** item typically purchased only after the buyer has compared competing products in competing stores.

**skimming pricing** pricing strategy that sets an intentionally high price relative to the prices of competing products.

**skunkworks** project initiated by a company employee who conceives the idea, convinces top management of its potential, and then recruits human and other resources from within the firm to turn it into a commercial project.

**small business** firm that is independently owned and operated, is not dominant in its field, and meets industry-specific size standards for income or number of employees.

**Small Business Administration (SBA)** federal agency that aids small businesses by providing management training and consulting, financial assitance, and support in securing government contracts.

**Small Business Investment Company (SBIC)** business licensed by the Small Business Administration to provide loans to small businesses.

**social audit** formal procedure that identifies and evaluates all company activities that relate to social issues such as conservation, employment practices, environmental protection, and philanthropy.

**social responsibility** business's consideration of society's well-being and consumer satisfaction in addition to profits.

**socialism** planned economic system characterized by government ownership and operation of major industries.

**software** set of instructions that tell the computer hardware what to do.

**sole proprietorship** form of business ownership in which the company is owned and operated by one person.

**spam** popular name for junk e-mail.

**span of management** number of subordinates a manager can supervise effectively.

**specialty advertising** promotional items that prominently display a firm's name, logo, or business slogan.

**specialty product** item that a purchaser is willing to make a special effort to obtain.

**speculative risk** risk where there is a chance of gain as well as a chance of loss.

**sponsorship** funding a sporting or cultural event in exchange for a direct association with the event.

**spreadsheet** software package that creates the computerized equivalent of an accountant's worksheet, allowing the user to manipulate variables and see the impact of alternative decisions on operating results.

**staff manager** executive who provides information, advice, or technical assistance to aid line managers; does not have the authority to give orders outside his or her own department or to compel line managers to take action.

**standard of living** necessities, comforts, and luxuries one seeks to obtain or to maintain.

**statement of cash flows** statement of a firm's cash receipts and cash payments that presents information on its sources and uses of cash.

**statutory law** written law, including state and federal constitutions, legislative enactments, treaties of the federal government, and ordinances of local governments.

**stock exchange** financial market where stocks are traded.

**stock options** rights to buy a specified amount of company stock at a given price within a given time period.

**stockholder** person or organization who owns shares of stock in a corporation.

**strategic alliance** partnership formed to create a competitive advantage for the businesses involved; in international business, a business strategy in which a company finds a partner in the country where it wants to do business.

**strategic planning** process of determining the primary objectives of an organization and then acting and allocating resources to achieve those objectives.

**strike** temporary work stoppage by employees until a dispute is settled or a contract signed.

**subcontracting** international agreement that involves hiring local companies to produce, distribute, or sell goods or services in a specific country or geographical region.

**supervisory management** first-line management; includes positions such as supervisor, line manager, and group leader; responsible for assigning nonmanagerial employees to specific jobs and evaluating their performance every day.

**supply** willingness and ability of sellers to provide goods and services.

**supply chain** complete sequence of suppliers that contribute to creating a good or service and delivering it to business users and final consumers.

**supply curve** graph of the amount of a product that suppliers will offer for sale at different prices; generally slopes upward to reflect larger quantities likely to be offered for sale as prices increase.

**SWOT analysis** method of assessing a company's internal strengths and weaknesses and its external opportunities and threats.

**tactical planning** implementing the activities specified by strategic plans.

**target market** group of people toward whom an organization markets its goods, services, or ideas with a strategy designed to satisfy their specific needs and preferences.

**tariff** tax imposed on imported goods.

**tax** assessment by a governmental unit.

**team** group of employees who are committed to a common purpose, approach, and set of performance goals.

**team cohesiveness** extent to which team members feel attracted to the team and motivated to remain part of it.

**team diversity** variances or differences in ability, experience, personality, or any other factor on a team.

**team level** average level of ability, experience, personality, or any other factor on a team.

**team norm** informal standard of conduct shared by team members that guides their behavior.

**technical skills** manager's ability to understand and use techniques, knowledge, and tools and equipment of a specific discipline or department.

**technology** business application of knowledge based on scientific discoveries, inventions, and innovations.

**telecommuter** home-based employee.

**telemarketing** personal selling conducted entirely by telephone, which provides a firm's marketers with a high return on their expenditures, an immediate response, and an opportunity for personalized two-way conversation.

**term policy** pure type of life insurance providing only a death benefit.

**test marketing** introduction of a new product supported by a complete marketing campaign to a selected city or TV coverage area to examine both consumer responses to the new offering and the marketing effort used to support it.

**Theory X** assumption that employees dislike work and will try to avoid it.

**Theory Y** assumption that employees enjoy work and seek social, esteem, and self-actualization fulfillment.

**Theory Z** assumption that employee involvement is key to productivity and quality of work life.

**time utility** availability of a good or service when customers want to purchase it.

**top management** managers at the highest level of the management pyramid who devote most of their time to developing long-range plans for their organizations.

**tort** civil wrong inflicted on another person or the person's property.

**trade promotion** sales promotion geared to marketing intermediaries rather than to final consumers.

**trademark** brand with legal protection against another company's use, not only of the brand name but also of pictorial designs, slogans, packaging elements, and product features such as color and shape.

**transaction management** building and promoting products in the hope that enough customers will buy them to cover costs and earn profits.

**treasurer** executive responsible for all of the company's financing activities, including cash management, tax planning and preparation, and shareholder relations.

**trends** consumer and business tendencies or patterns that firms can exploit to gain market share in an industry.

**trial courts** federal and state courts of general jurisdiction.

**underwriting** the process insurance companies use to determine whom to insure and what to charge.

**unemployment insurance** benefits paid to workers who are currently unemployed.

**unemployment rate** indicator of a nation's economic health, typically expressed as a percentage of the total workforce who are actively seeking work but are currently unemployed.

**Uniform Commercial Code** the basis of U.S. business law; referred to as the UCC.

**utility** want-satisfying power of a good or service.

**value-added** describes a good or service that exceeds value expectation because the company has added features, lowered its price, enhanced customer service, or made other improvements that increase customer satisfaction.

**vendor-managed inventory** company's decision to hand over its inventory control functions to suppliers.

**venture capitalist** firm or group of individuals that invests in new and growing firms in exchange for an ownership share.

**vertical merger** combination of two or more firms operating at different levels in the production and marketing process.

**vice president for financial management** executive who prepares financial forecasts and analyzes major investment decisions.

**virtual private network (VPN)** linking of two or more computers over secure Internet connections.

**virtual team** group of geographically and/or organizationally dispersed co-workers who use a combination of telecommunications and information technologies to accomplish an organizational task.

**vision** perception of marketplace needs and the methods an organization can use to satisfy them.

**VoIP** technology that uses a personal computer, special software, and a broadband network connection to make and receive telephone calls over the Internet.

**volume objectives** pricing decisions based on market share—the percentage of a market controlled by a certain company or product.

**wage** compensation based on an hourly pay rate or the amount of output produced.

**Web host** company that provides server space to other commercial Web sites for a fee.

**Web-to-store** use of the Internet to aid shoppers at brick-and-mortar retailers.

**wheel of retailing** theory of retailing in which new retailers gain a competitive foothold by offering low prices and limited services and then add services and raise prices, creating opportunities for new low-price competitors.

**whistle-blowing** employee's disclosure to company officials, government authorities, or the media of illegal, immoral, or unethical practices committed by an organization.

**wholesaler** distribution channel member that sells primarily to retailers, other wholesalers, or business users.

**wide area network (WAN)** computer network that ties larger geographical regions together by using telephone lines and microwave and satellite transmission.

**Wi-Fi** wireless network that connects various devices and allows them to communicate with one another through radio waves; short for *wireless fidelity*.

**wiki** Web page that anyone can edit.

**Wi-Max** a new wireless standard that provides coverage over much larger geographic areas.

**word processing** software that uses a computer to input, store, retrieve, edit, and print various types of documents.

**work team** relatively permanent group of employees with complementary skills who perform the day-to-day work of organizations.

**worker's compensation insurance** benefits paid to workers who are injured on the job.

**World Bank** organization established by industrialized nations to lend money to less developed countries.

**World Trade Organization (WTO)** 149-member international institution that monitors GATT agreements and mediates international trade disputes.

# Notes

## Prologue

1. Penelope Wang, "Four Myths about College Costs," *Money,* February 2005, p. 49.

2. Virginia Gewin, "Making It in the Biotech Business," *Nature,* accessed August 2006, http://www.nature.com.

3. Elizabeth Levin, "Getting Hired Full Time after an Internship," *College Journal,* accessed August 2006, http://www.collegejournal.com.

4. Silpada Web site, accessed August 2006, http://www.silpada.com.

5. "Prepare Your Resume for E-Mailing or Posting on the Internet," *Riley Guide,* accessed August 2006, http://www.rileyguide.com.

6. Liz Ryan, "The Elephant in Your Résumé," *BusinessWeek,* accessed August 2006, http://www.businessweek.com.

7. Marshall Loeb, "Six Tips for Writing a Winning Cover Letter," *College Journal,* accessed August 2006, http://www.collegejournal.com.

8." Prepare Your Résumé for E-Mailing or Posting on the Internet."

9. Olivia Barker and Sarah Bailey, "Going Toe-to-Toe on Office Etiquette," *USA Today,* August 15, 2005, p. D1.

10. "Fifty Standard Interview Questions," CollegeGrad.com, accessed August 2006, http://www.collegegrad.com.

11. "Tomorrow's Jobs," *Occupational Outlook Handbook,* Bureau of Labor Statistics, accessed August 2006, http://www.bls.gov.

12. "Tomorrow's Jobs."

13. Anne Fisher, "Hot Careers for the Next 10 Years," *Fortune,* March 21, 2005, p. 131.

14. "Tomorrow's Jobs."

## Chapter 1

1. Procter & Gamble Web site, accessed August 2006, http://www.pg.com; Jerry Useem, "America's Most Admired Companies," *Fortune,* March 7, 2005, pp. 67–68; "It Was a No-Brainer," *Fortune,* February 21, 2005, pp. 97–102; Nanette Byrnes et al., "Branding: Five New Lessons," *BusinessWeek,* February 14, 2005, pp. 26–28; Robert Berner, Nanette Byrnes, and Wendy Zellner, "P&G Has Rivals in a Wringer," *BusinessWeek,* October 4, 2004, p. 74.

2. "U.S. Hospitality Industry Sees Boom through 2007," *Hotel Marketing,* accessed August 2006, http://www.hotelmarketing.com; "Fitch: Travel Rebound Fuels U.S. Lodging Sector 2005 Outlook," *Hospitality Net,* accessed August 2006, http://www.hospitality.org.

3. "Corp. Travel Rebound Contributes to Record Amex Quarter," *Business Travel News,* accessed August 2006, http://www.btnmag.com.

4. Ross Kerber, "Industry Invests in Students—Its Future Workers," *Boston Globe,* accessed August 2006, http://www.boston.com.

5. "Homeland Security and Traveler Safety Information," American Hotel & Lodging Association, accessed August 2006, http://www.ahla.com.

6. "Number of Nonprofit Organizations in the United States 1996–2004," National Center for Charitable Statistics at the Urban Institute, accessed August 2006, http://nccsdataweb.urban.org.

7. Stephen Kaufman, "Former Presidents' Visit to Tsunami-Affected Countries a Success," International Information Programs, August 2006, http://usinfo.state.gov.

8. Lance Armstrong Foundation, accessed August 2006, http://www.livestrong.org.

9. Peter Lewis, "The Keys to Happiness," *Fortune,* September 20, 2004, pp. 74–75.

10. "Get Ready for WiMax," *eWeek,* accessed August 2006, http://www.eweek.com.

11. David Neeleman, "Turn Managers into Leaders," *Business 2.0,* September 2004, p. 70.

12. Kathy Ireland Worldwide Web site, accessed August 2006, http://www.kathyireland.com; Elyssa Lee and Rob Turner, "Celebrity Entrepreneurs," *Inc.,* December 2004, p. 74.

13. "Carlos Gutierrez Biography," U.S. Department of Commerce Web site, accessed August 2006, http://www.commerce.gov; Matthew Boyle, "The Man Who Fixed Kellogg," *Fortune,* September 6, 2004, pp. 218–226.

14. Carrie Johnson, "Fifteen NYSE Traders Indicted," *Washington Post,* April 13, 2005, p. A1; Julie Creswell, "The Exchange Faces Change," *Fortune,* August 9, 2004, pp. 108–114.

15. U.S. Census Bureau, accessed August 2006, http://www.census.gov.

16. Blitz Web site, accessed August 2006, http://www.timetoblitz.com; Jeffrey Ressner, "Fighting for Fitness," *Time,* November 8, 2004, p.113.

17. Thorlo Web site, accessed August 2006, http://www.thorlo.com.

18. Granite Rock Web site, accessed August 2006, http://www.graniterock.com.

19. Lauren Gard, "Online Extra: Stonyfield Farm's Blog Culture," *BusinessWeek Online,* accessed August 2006, http://www.businessweek.com.

20. eBay Web site, accessed August 2006, http://www.ebay.com.

21. "Apple Eyes Fizz in Pepsi iTunes Giveaway," C/Net, accessed August 2006, http://www.news.com.com.

22. Barbara Rose, "Retirees Preparing to Step Back, Not Away," *Chicago Tribune,* January 16, 2005, section 1, pp. 1, 19.

23. Haya el Nasser, "Youthquakes Shake Up Gray-Haired States," *USA Today,* March 10, 2005, p. 3A.

24. Rose, "Retirees Preparing to Step Back, Not Away."

25. "The Immigrant Policy Project," National Conference of State Legislatures, accessed August 2006, http://www.ncsl.org.

26. "The Immigrant Policy Project."

27. "Diversity at UPS," UPS Web site, accessed August 2006, http://www.ups.com.

28. Jim Hopkins, "To Start Up Here, Companies Hire Over There," *USA Today,* accessed August 2006, http://www.usatoday.com.

29. John W. Miller, "Eastern Europe Becomes Hub for 'Nearshoring' Call-Center Jobs," *The Wall Street Journal*'s Career Journal Europe,

accessed August 2006, http://www.careerjournaleurope.com; Andy Reinhardt, "Forget India, Let's Go to Bulgaria," *Business-Week*, March 1, 2004, p. 93.

30. "How to Exploit Innovation," *Business 2.0*, December 2004, p. 104.

31. "Bose's Sound Strategy," *Chief Executive*, accessed August 2006, http://www.chiefexecutive.net; Brian Dumaine, "I'd Rather Be Inventing," in "14 Innovators," *Fortune*, November 15, 2004, p. 194.

32. "The Story," Kate Spade Web site, accessed August 2006, http://www.katespade.com; Julie Creswell, "You Can't Say, 'The Customer Doesn't Get It,'" in "14 Innovators," p. 196.

33. Abraham Lustgarten, "A Hot, Steaming Cup of Customer Awareness," in "14 Innovators," p. 192.

34. Andrew Martin, "What's Next for Fast Food? McTofu?" *Chicago Tribune*, accessed August 2006, http://www.chicagotribune.com; Matthew Boyle, "Can You Really Make Fast Food Healthy?" *Fortune*, August 9, 2004, pp. 134–140.

35. Jerry Useem, "America's Most Admired Companies," *Fortune*, March 7, 2005, pp. 67–70.

36. Useem, "America's Most Admired Companies."

## Chapter 2

1. Green Mountain Coffee Roasters Web site, accessed August 2006, http://www.greenmountaincoffee.com; "Green Mountain Coffee Roasters Brews an Optimized Workforce with Human Resources, Payroll and Time and Labor Solutions from Kronos," press release, May 2, 2005; Mark Pendergrast, "Green Mountain Coffee Roasters: Doing Well by Doing Good," *Tea & Coffee Trade Journal*, April 20, 2004, pp. 100ff.

2. "National Business Ethics Survey," Ethics Research Center, accessed August 2006, http://www.ethics.org.

3. Johnson & Johnson Web site, accessed August 2006, http://www.jnj.com.

4. David Teather, "GE Doubles Research on Clean Technology," *The Guardian*, accessed August 2006, http://www.guardian.co.uk; Marc Gunther, "Money and Morals at GE," *Fortune*, November 15, 2004, pp. 176–182.

5. "Where Americans and Business Leaders Agree/Disagree on Business Ethics," Public Agenda, accessed August 2006, http://www.publicagenda.org.

6. "Coors Ethics Program among Best in Nation," accessed August 2006, http://accounting.smartpros.com.

7. "Deskside Skiving Adds Up to Seven Days Holiday a Year," *Personnel Today*, accessed August 2006, http://www.personneltoday.com.

8. Scott Kirsner, "Reebok Offers Help Fighting Overseas Abuse," *Boston Globe*, accessed August 2006, http://www.boston.com; "Fair Factories Clearinghouse Created to Support Compliance with Workplace Conditions in Factories," FFC press release, January 13, 2005.

9. Paul Fireman, "What We Can Do about Burma," *Wall Street Journal Online*, accessed August 2006, http://online.wsj.com.

10. George Cahlink, "Ex-Pentagon Procurement Executive Gets Jail Time," *Government Executive*, accessed August 2006, http://www.govexec.com.

11. Peter Saalfield, "Internet Misuse Costs Businesses $178 Billion Annually," *Info World*, accessed August 2006, http://www.infoworld.com; Tim Higgins, "Workplaces Frown If Sex Pops up on a Computer," *Des Moines Register*, accessed August 2006, http://desmoinesregister.com.

12. Robin L. Wakefield, "Employee Monitoring and Surveillance: The Growing Trend," Information Systems Audit and Control Association, accessed August 2006, http://www.isaca.org.

13. Neil Weinberg, "The Dark Side of Whistleblowing," *Forbes*, accessed August 2006, http://www.forbes.com.

14. Nortel Networks Web site, accessed August 2006, http://www.nortel.com

15. Ronald J. Alsop, "B-Schools Still Seeking Ways to Stress Ethics," *CollegeJournal*, accessed August 2006, http://www.collegejournal.com.

16. Kavaljit Singh, "Citi Never Sleeps," Asia-Europe Dialogue, accessed February 6, 2005, http://www.ased.org; Mark Train, "Citigroup Embroiled in Bond Selling Scandal," *The Guardian*, accessed August 2006, http://www.guardian.co.uk.

17. Nortel Networks Web site, accessed August 2006, http://www.nortel.com

18. "100 Best Corporate Citizens: 2004," *Business Ethics*, accessed August 2006, http://www.business-ethics.com.

19. Council on Economic Priorities Web site, accessed August 2006, http://www.web.ca/~robrien/papers/sri/players/cep.html and http://www.geocites.com/CapitolHill/Senate/1777/cep.htm.

20. Center for Science in the Public Interest Web site, accessed August 2006, http://www.cspinet.org.

21. Judy Silber, "Chiron to Produce Less Vaccine," *(San Jose, CA) Mercury News*, accessed June 15, 2005, http://www.mercurynews.com; "U.S. Government Outlines Flu Vaccine Guidelines," MSNBC, accessed August 2006, http://www.msnbc.msn.com.

22. Michael E. Hochman, "New Drug Tests Try to Keep Up with Athletes," *Boston Globe*, accessed August 2006, http://www.boston.com; Mark Sappenfield, "States Taking on Teen Steroid Use," *Christian Science Monitor*, accessed August 2006, http://www.csmonitor.com; Nicholas Thompson, "Bud Selig," Slate, accessed August 2006, http://slate.com; Mark Madden, "Baseball's War on Steroids Probably Can't Be Won," *(Pittsburgh, PA) Post-Gazette*, accessed August 2006, http://www.post-gazette.com.

23. Lara Jill Rosenblith, "The Hidden Harm of the Technological Revolution," *Fact Sheet—Electronics Waste (E-Waste)*, http://environment.about.com; Ellen Simon, "'E-Junk' Recycling Still in Its Infancy," Yahoo! News, accessed December 6, 2004, http://www.yahoo.com.

24. Juliet Eilperin, "Dead Electronics Going to Waste," *Washington Post*, accessed August 2006, http://www.washingtonpost.com.

25. Dee-Ann Durbin, "Hybrid Car Sales Soar in U.S. in 2004," Yahoo! News, accessed April 25, 2005, http://www.yahoo.com.

26. "Scientists Make Phone that Turns into a Sunflower," Yahoo! News, accessed December 6, 2004, http://www.yahoo.com.

27. Ellen Simon, "'E-Junk' Recycling Still in Its Infancy."

28. Juliet Elperin, "Dead Electronics Going to Waste."

29. Leonard Anderson and Timothy Gardner, "U.S. Cities Eye Ocean Waves for Power Supplies," Yahoo! News, accessed February 14, 2005, http://www.yahoo.com.

30. "The Gift of a College Degree Lasts a Lifetime," *Princeton Review*, accessed August 2006, http://www.princetonreview.com; U.S. Department of Labor Web site, accessed August 2006, http://www.dol.gov.

31. Target Web site, accessed August 2006, http://www.target.com.

32. "Community Action," General Mills Web site, accessed August 2006, http://www.generalmills.com; Ellen P. Gabler, "Strategic Giving Provides Win-Win for Corporations," *Business Journal*, accessed August 2006, http://www.bizjournals.com/twincities.

33. David Henderson, "The Role of Business in the World of Today," *Journal of Corporate Citizenship*, accessed August 2006, http://www.greenleaf-publishing.com; Jessi Hempel and Lauren Gard, "The Corporate Givers," *BusinessWeek*, accessed August 2006, http://www.businessweek.com.

34. "GM Recalls 300,000 Vehicles to Repair Turn-Signal Problems," *The Wall Street Journal*, May 11, 2005, p. D5.

35. "Security and Resolution Center," eBay Web site, accessed August 2006, http://pages.ebay.com/securitycenter/buying_tips.html.

36. Jewel-Osco Web site, accessed August 2006, http://www.jewelosco.com.

37. Tatsha Robertson, "Between Work and Life There's Balance," *Boston Globe*, accessed August 2006, http://www.boston.com; Diane Brady, "Hopping aboard the Daddy Track," *BusinessWeek*, November 8, 2004, pp. 100–101.

38. Christine Larson, "Family Balance," *U.S. News & World Report*, March 21, 2005, pp. 44–46.

39. Hope Yen, "Court Issues Age Discrimination Ruling," Yahoo! News, accessed March 30, 2005, http://www.yahoo.com.

40. "Hands off the employees," *St. Louis Post-Dispatch*, accessed August 2006, http://www.stltoday.com.

41. Bureau of Labor Statistics, "Women in the Labor Force: A Databook," accessed August 2006, http://www.bls.gov.cps/wlf-databook2005.htm; Jenny Strasburg, "Equity: Losing Ground," *San Francisco Chronicle*, accessed August 2006, http://www.sfgate.com.

42. Jenny Strasburg, "Equity: Losing Ground."

### Chapter 3

1. "Chrysler Rolls Out New Dodge Charger Police Car," ConsumerAffairs.com, accessed August 2006, http://www.consumeraffairs.com; Sharon Silke Carty, "Crown Vic Challenged in Police Vehicle Arena," *USA Today*, March 28, 2005, p. 4B; "Arkansas Presses Ford Police Car Suit," ConsumerAffairs.com, accessed August 2006, http://www.consumeraffairs.com.

2. Shannon Dininny, "Apple Growers Happy about McDonald's Shift," Yahoo! News, accessed May 1, 2005, http://www.yahoo.com.

3. Steven Levy and Brad Stone, "Grand Theft Identity," *Newsweek*, July 4, 2005, pp. 38–47.

4. "Oil Prices Rise, with Focus on Hurricane Emily, Chinese Demand Concerns," Yahoo! News, accessed July 15, 2005, http://www.yahoo.com.

5. Christopher Calnan, "Summer Travel Not Expected to Cool," *(Jacksonville) Florida Times-Union*, accessed May 28, 2005, http://www.jacksonville.com.

6. Alexandra Marks and Robert Tuttle, "Oil Prices Spread to Grapes, TVs, Pizza," *Christian Science Monitor*, accessed August 2006, http://www.csmonitor.com.

7. "Oil Prices Rise, with Focus on Hurricane Emily, Chinese Demand Concerns."

8. Shannon Dininny, "Apple Growers Happy about McDonald's Shift."

9. "GM Announces Employee Pricing for Everyone," advertising section, *Sports Illustrated*, June 20, 2005.

10. Cemex Web site, accessed August 2006, http://www.cemex.com.

11. Anick Jesdanun, "Microsoft's Share of Browser Market Slips," Yahoo! News, accessed May 12, 2005, http://www.yahoo.com.

12. Air Canada Web site, accessed August 2006, http://www.aircanada.com.

13. David Wyss, "Productivity Won't Always Save the Day," *BusinessWeek*, accessed August 2006, http://www.businessweek.com.

14. Michael Mandel, "The Case of the Missing Trillion," *BusinessWeek*, accessed August 2006, http://www.businessweek.com.

15. Ron Scherer, "Inflation Flickers Again on Horizon," *Christian Science Monitor*, accessed August 2006, http://www.csmonitor.com.

16. Martin Crutsinger, "Greenspan Signals Further Rate Increases," Yahoo! News, accessed July 20, 2005, http://www.yahoo.com.

17. Steve Forbes, "Why Forgive Kleptocracy and Economic Incompetence?" *Forbes*, April 11, 2005, pp. 31–32.

18. Mortimer B. Zuckerman, "The Case of the 12 Zeros," *U.S. News & World Report*, March 21, 2005, p. 68.

19. Rama Lakshmi, "Indian Call Centers Cursed," *Morning News*, March 4, 2005, p. 3B.

### Chapter 4

1. Red Wing Web site, accessed August 2006, http://www.redwingshoe.com; Scott A. Briggs, "Change Is Afoot," *Twin Cities Business Monthly*, accessed May 2005, http://www.redwingshoe.com; Timothy Aeppel, "Red Wing Digs In Its Heels," *Wall Street Journal*, September 28, 2004, pp. B1, B6.

2. U.S. Census Bureau, "Foreign Trade Statistics: Annual Trade Highlights," accessed February 10, 2005, http://www.census.gov/foreign-trade; U.S. Census Bureau, "Foreign Trade Statistics: U.S. International Trade in Goods and Services Highlights," accessed May 11, 2005, http://www.census.gov/indicator/www/ustrade.html.

3. Anthony Faiola, "A Baby Bust Empties Out Japan's Schools," *Washington Post*, accessed August 2006, http://www.washingtonpost.com; Phillip Longman, "The Global Baby Bust," *Foreign Affairs*, accessed August 2006, http://www.foreignaffairs.org; "Lower Birth Rate, AIDS Deaths Help Slow World Population Growth," *San Francisco Chronicle*, accessed March 23, 2004, http://www.sfgate.com.

4. Data from Central Intelligence Agency, *World Factbook*, accessed August 9, 2005, http://www.cia.gov.

5. Associated Press, "Wal-Mart to Nearly Double Stores in China," accessed July 25, 2005, Yahoo! News, http://www.yahoo.com.

6. U.S. Census Bureau, "Top Ten Countries with Which the U.S. Trades," accessed April 2005, http://www.census.gov/foreign-trade/top/dst/current/balance.html.

7. TradeStats Express, "State Export Data," accessed August 2006, http://tse.export.gov.

8. "Saffron," Spice Advice Encyclopedia, accessed August 2006, http://www.spiceadvice.com.

9. Ron Scherer, "Imports Increasingly Burden U.S. Economy," *Christian Science Monitor*, accessed August 2006, http://www.csmonitor.com.

10. Chester Dawson, "Why the Dollar Is Blooming Again," *BusinessWeek*, accessed August 2006, http://www.businessweek.com.

11. Patrick O'Gilfoil Healy, "For Muslims, Loans for the Conscience," *New York Times*, accessed August 2006, http://www.nytimes.com;

Feisal Abdul Rauf, "Bringing Muslim Nations into the Global Century," *Fortune*, October 18, 2004, pp. 80–81.

12. George Obulutsa, "Kenyans Text Messaging Their Way to Jobs," Reuters Limited, accessed April 13, 2005, http://www.yahoo.com.

13. "News Analysis: Kids' TV Confronts Junk-food Fear," *PRWeek*, accessed May 5, 2005, http://www.prweek.com.

14. Organization for Economic Cooperation and Development, "The OECD Anti-Bribery Convention: How it Works," accessed August 2006, http://www.oecd.org.

15. En-Lai Yeoh, "Report: Software Piracy Cost $8B in Asia," Yahoo! News, accessed May 18, 2005, http://www.yahoo.com; Roy Mark, "U.S. Ups Pressure on China over IP Rights," Internet News.com, accessed August 2006, http://www.internetnews.com.

16. "How to Hurt American Business," *New York Times*, editorial, accessed August 2006, http://www.nytimes.com.

17. Martin Crutsinger, "White House Re-Imposes Quotas on China," Yahoo! News, accessed May 13, 2005, http://www.yahoo.com.

18. Elizabeth Wasserman, "Happy Birthday, WTO?" *Inc.*, January 2005, pp. 21–23

19. United States Mission to the European Union, "G8 Summit Ends with Commitment to Finalize World Trade Talks," accessed August 2006, http://www.useu.be.

20. Dana Bash and Robin Oakley, "Bush, Blair Push African Debt Relief," CNN.com, accessed August 2006, http://www.cnn.com.

21. Central Intelligence Agency, "Canadian, Mexican, and U.S. populations" and GDP data, *World Factbook*, http://www.cia.gov/cia/publications/factbook.

22. Central Intelligence Agency, "Canada," *World Factbook*, http://www.cia.gov/cia/publications/factbook.

23. Central Intelligence Agency, "Mexico," *World Factbook*, http://www.cia.gov/cia/publications/factbook.

24. Geri Smith, "A Border Transformed," *BusinessWeek*, accessed August 2006, http://www.businessweek.com.

25. Robert Manor, "CAFTA Called an Export Builder," *Chicago Tribune*, accessed August 2006, http://www.chicagotribune.com; "CAFTA Could Help Agri Companies," *Northwest Arkansas Business Journal*, July 18, 2005, p. 4.

26. Economic Research Service, "Briefing Room: European Union," U.S. Dept. of Agriculture, accessed August 2006, http://www.ers.usda.gov/Briefing/EuropeanUnion/basicinfo.htm.

27. John Chalmers, "Wounded EU Limps On after Double 'No' to Treaty," Yahoo! News, accessed June 2, 2005, http://www.yahoo.com.

28. Roots Canada Web site, accessed August 2006, http://www.roots.com; "Roots Canada Ltd.," accessed August 2006, www.hoovers.com; "Roots Canada Ltd.," Yahoo! Finance, accessed August 2006, http://finance.yahoo.com.

29. "Delivering at Domino's Pizza," *Fortune*, February 7, 2005, p. 28.

30. Michael Kanellos, "Hello Kitty's Guide to Business Success," CNet News.com, accessed August 2006, http://news.com.com.

31. Pacific Bridge Medical Web site, accessed August 2006, http://www.pacificbridgemedical.com.

32. Whirlpool Corporation Web site, accessed August 2006, http://www.whirlpoolcorp.com; Keith Bradsher, "Made in India vs. Made in China," *New York Times*, accessed August 2006, http://www.nytimes.com.

33. "Outsourcing: 100 U.S. Bills Target India," *Economic Times*, accessed August 2006, http://economictimes.indiatimes.com; Ed Frauenheim and Mike Yamamoto, "Reforms, Not Rhetoric, Needed to Keep Jobs on U.S. Soil," CNet News.com, accessed August 2006, http://news.com.com.

34. Rachel Konrad, "U.S. Interminable Workday," *Arizona Republic*, accessed May 15, 2005, http://www.azcentral.com.

35. "Lenovo's Long March," *BusinessWeek*, accessed August 2006, http://www.businessweek.com; Richard J. Newman, "Big Blue Goes Red," *U.S. News & World Report*, December 20, 2004, pp. 38–40.

36. "Heinz Acquires Majority Stake in Leading Russian Maker of Ketchup, Condiments, and Sauces," press release, accessed May 3, 2005, http://biz.yahoo.com.

37. Panasonic Web site, accessed August 2006, http://www.panasonic.com.

38. General Electric Web site, accessed August 2006, http://www.ge.com.

39. Toyota Web site, accessed August 2006, http://www.toyota.com.

40. Randall Frost, "Local Success on a Global Scale," *Brandchannel.com*, accessed August 2006, http://www.brandchannel.com; Geoffrey A. Fowler and Ramin Setoodeh, "Outsiders Get Smarter about China's Tastes," *Wall Street Journal*, August 5, 2004, p. B1.

## Part 1 Appendix

1. Mike France, "How to Fix the Tort System," *BusinessWeek*, March 14, 2005, pp. 70–78; Dan Zegart, "Tort Reform Triumphs," *The Nation*, accessed August 2006, http://www.thenation.com; "Bush Signs So-Called Class-Action Fairness Act of 2005," Legal News Watch, accessed August 2006, http://www.legalnewswatch.com; "President Signs Class-Action Fairness Act of 2005," The White House, accessed August 2006, http://www.whitehouse.gov.

2. Dan Ackman, "Bernie Ebbers Guilty," *Forbes*, accessed August 2006, http://www.forbes.com.

3. Tom Cole, "Frivolous Litigation, a Tax on Americans," press release, accessed August 2006, http://www.house.gov.

4. Howard Witt, "Much a Doodle-Doo about Nothing," *Chicago Tribune*, May 22, 2005, pp. 1, 10.

5. "U.S. Federal Laws," FindLaw, accessed August 2006, http://findlaw.com/casecode.

6. "Supreme Court of the United States," Encarta, accessed August 2006, http://www.encarta.msn.com.

7. Cain Burdeau, "Canada to Slap Surtax on American Oysters," *Seafood News*, accessed August 2006, http://www.seafood-norway.com.

8. Jeannine Aversa, "Pension Bailout Posed to Fed Boss," *The Cincinnati Enquirer*, accessed July 22, 2005, http://news.enquirer.com.

9. Glen Johnson, "House Votes to Extend Patriot Act," Yahoo! News, accessed July 22, 2005, http://www.yahoo.com.

10. Katie Merx and Kortney Stringer, "Drug Ad Changes Looming," *Detroit Free Press*, accessed June 20, 2005, http://www.freep.com; "Prescription Drug Advertising Will Get More Scrutiny, FDA Promises," News Target, accessed August 2006, http://www.newstarget.com.

11. Albert B. Crenshaw, "Retiree Benefits Can't Be Cut at 65, Judge Says," *Washington Post*, accessed August 2006, http://www.washingtonpost.com.

12. Hope Yen, "Court: File-Sharing Services May Be Sued," Yahoo! News, accessed June 27, 2005, http://www.yahoo.com.

13. "Uniform Commercial Code (UCC)," accessed August 2006, http://www.smartagreements.com.

14. "Uniform Commercial Code (UCC)."

15. *Kelo v. New London*, U.S Supreme Court Database, accessed August 2006, http://www.usscplus.com; Adam Karlin, "Property Seizure Backlash," *Christian Science Monitor*, accessed August 2006, http://www.csmonitor.com.

16. R. Subramanyam, "Wipro Accused of Infringement by German Company," *Economic Times*, accessed August 2006, http://economictimes.indiatimes.com.

17. Ben Mutzabaugh, "Today in the Sky," *USA Today*, accessed June 8, 2005, http://www.usatoday.com.

18. Michelle Kessler, "Pressure Mounts for Reform of Patent System," *USA Today*, accessed August 2006, http://www.usatoday.com.

19. Steven Musil, "This Week in Copyright Infringement," CNet News.com, accessed August 2006, http://news.com.com.

20. Hope Yen, "Court: File-Sharing Services May Be Sued."

21. Steven Musil, "This Week in Copyright Infringement."

22. Steven Musil, "This Week in Copyright Infringement."

23. Laura Parker, "When Pets Die at the Vet, Grieving Owners Call Lawyers," *USA Today*, March 15, 2005, pp. 1A, 2A.

24. Sandra Block, "Filing Chapter 7 Bankruptcy Will Get Tougher Soon," *USA Today*, April 21, 2005, p. 4B.

25. James Vicini, "Court Overturns Andersen Enron Conviction," Yahoo! News, accessed May 31, 2005, http://www.yahoo.com.

26. Gregory M. Lamb, "Creative Work Makes for Slippery Private Property Online," *Christian Science Monitor*, accessed August 2006, http://www.csmonitor.com; Emily Bazelon, "Grok around the Clock," *Slate*, accessed August 2006, http://slate.com.

## Part 1: Launching Your Global Business and Economics Career

1. U.S. Department of Labor, "Tomorrow's Jobs," *Occupational Outlook Handbook*, 2006–2007 edition, U.S. Bureau of Labor Statistics, accessed August 2006, http://www.bls.gov.

2. U.S. Department of Labor, "Economists," *Occupational Outlook Handbook*, 2006–2007 edition, U.S. Bureau of Labor Statistics, accessed August 2006, http://www.bls.gov.

3. Adapted from Michael R. Czinkota, Ilkka A. Ronkainen, and Michael H. Moffett, "Criteria for Selecting Managers for Overseas Assignments," in *International Business*, 7th ed. (Mason, OH: South-Western, 2005), Table 19.2, p. 634.

4. Del Jones, "New MBAs Finding Education Pays Off Big Time," *USA Today*, accessed August 2006, http://www.usatoday.com.

5. Erin White, "For M.B.A. Students, a Good Career Move Means a Job in Asia," *Wall Street Journal*, accessed August 2006, http://online.wsj.com.

6. Carol Hymowitz, "Diversity in a Global Economy—Ways Some Firms Get It Right," Career Journal, accessed August 2006, http://www.careerjournal.com.

## Chapter 5

1. Sherri Daye Scott, "The Phenomenon," *QSR Magazine*, accessed August 2006, http://www.qsrmagazine.com; Oscar Avila, "Nostalgia Served Piping Hot," *Chicago Tribune*, accessed August 2006, http://www.chicagotribune.com; Rebecca Flass, "Guatemalan Restaurant Chain Plays Chicken with Big Brands," *Los Angeles Business Journal*, accessed August 2006, http://www.findarticles.com; "Mayor Michael R. Bloomberg Cuts Ribbon for the First Pollo Campero Restaurant in New York City," New York City press release, accessed August 2006, http://www.nyc.gov; "Pollo Campero," Ahorre.com, accessed August 2006, http://www.hispanicmarket.net.

2. U.S. Census Bureau, "Statistics about Business Size," accessed August 2006, http://www.census.gov.

3. Ibid.

4. Office of Advocacy, U.S. Small Business Administration, "Frequently Asked Questions: Advocacy Small Business Statistics and Research," accessed August 2006, http://app1.sba.gov/faqs.

5. Office of Advocacy, U.S. Small Business Administration, "Women-owned Business Economic Research," accessed August 2006, http://www.sba.gov/advo.

6. Office of Advocacy, U.S. Small Business Administration, "Frequently Asked Questions."

7. Small Business Administration, "Frequently Asked Questions (FAQs) about Small Business Size Standards," accessed August 2006, http://www.sba.gov/size.

8. Allen Roberts, Jr., "How I Did It: Barbara K," *Inc.*, May 2005, p. 112.

9. Dee Gill, ". . . Or Your Money Back," *Inc.*, September 2005, p. 46.

10. Powell's Web site, accessed August 2006, http://www.powells.com; "They Said It" quotation from "Michael Powell," *Inc.*, accessed September 1, 2005, http://www.inc.com.

11. U.S. Department of Agriculture, Agriculture Fact Book, pp. 20, 23, accessed August 2006, http://www.usda.gov/factbook.

12. Office of Advocacy, U.S. Small Business Administration, "The Small Business Economy: A Report to the President," accessed August 2006, http://www.sba.gov/advo.

13. Gerald Oettinger, "The Growth in Home-Based Wage and Salary Employment in the United States, 1980-2000: How Much and Why?" University of Chicago Graduate School of Business, accessed September 3, 2005, http://gsb.uchicago.edu.

14. Allison Bruce, "Bead Business Booming for eBay-Using Camarillo Couple," *Ventura County (CA) Star*, June 5, 2005.

15. Salem Five Web site, accessed August 2006, http://www.salemfive.com.

16. Office of Advocacy, U.S. Small Business Administration, "Frequently Asked Questions."

17. Small Business Administration, "Small Business Statistics," accessed August 2006, http://www.sba.gov/advo.

18. Office of Advocacy, U.S. Small Business Administration, "U.S. Receipt Size of Firm by Major Industry Group," accessed August 2006, http://www.sba.gov/advo.

19. Small Business Administration, "Welfare to Work Program," accessed September 3, 2005, http://www.sba.gov.

20. Christopher Caggiano, "Insider Training," *Inc.*, accessed August 2006, http://www.inc.com; Tucker Technology Web site, accessed August 2006, http://www.tuckertech.com.

21. InterDigital Communications, "Profile," accessed August 2006, http://www.interdigital.com.

22. Netflix, "Fact Sheet," accessed August 2006, http://www.ir.netflix.com.

23. Daniel McGinn & Ramin Setoodeh, "Rewinding a Video Giant," *Newsweek*, June 27, 2005, p. 38; Wal-Mart, "What to Know about Wal-Mart DVD Rentals," accessed September 3, 2005, http://www.walmart.com.

24. "Interview with Thomas D'Ambra," accessed August 2006, https://secure.twst.com.

25. Chi Research, "Small Serial Innovators: The Small Firm Contribution to Technical Change," Small Business Administration, accessed August 2006, http://www.sba.gov/advo; "They Said It" quotation from "Zach Nelson," *Inc.*, February 2005, p. 71.

26. Small Business Administration, Office of Advocacy, "Financing Patterns of Small Firms," accessed August 2006, http://www.sba.gov/advo.

27. C. J. Prince, "Plastic Rap," *Entrepreneur*, accessed August 2006, http://www.entrepreneur.com.

28. "Precision Plastics: An Employee-Owned Company," accessed August 2006, http://www.pplastic.com.

29. U.S. Department of Labor, "As an Employer, Are You Engaged in Commerce or in an Industry or Activity Affecting Commerce?" elaws—Family and Medical Leave Act Advisor, accessed August 2006, http://www.dol.gov.

30. Small Business Administration, Office of Disaster Assistance, "Fact Sheet about U.S. Small Business Administration Disaster Loans," accessed August 2006, http://www.sba.gov.

31. Small Business Administration, "The Microloan Program for Entrepreneurs," accessed August 2006, http://www.sba.gov.

32. Active Capital, "Frequently Asked Questions," accessed August 2006, http://activecapital.org.

33. Small Business Administration, "Government Contracting: What We Do," accessed August 2006, http://www.sba.gov.

34. Small Business Administration, "SBA, OMB, GSA and DOD Work Together to Integrate PRO-Net and CCR Database and Simplify Contracting Process for Small Businesses," accessed August 2006, http://www.pro-net.sba.gov.

35. National Business Incubator Association, accessed August 2006, http://www.nbia.org.

36. National Foundation for Women Business Owners, "Top Facts about Women-Owned Businesses," accessed September 4, 2005, http://www.nfwbo.org; National Foundation for Women Business Owners, "Businesses Owned by Women of Color in the United States: A Fact Sheet," accessed September 4, 2005, http://www.nfwbo.org.

37. kemse & company, "About Us," accessed August 2006, http://www.kemseandcompany.com.

38. National Foundation for Women Business Owners, "Privately-Held, 50% or More Women-Owned Businesses in the United States: A Fact Sheet," accessed September 4, 2005, http://www.nfwbo.org.

39. Bridget McCrea, "Doing Her Part to Ensure the Safety of Children," AdvancingChildren Network, accessed August 2006, http://www.advancingwomen.com/_business/entpr_8.html.

40. Aliza Sherman, "The Opposite Sex: Women in Search of Money Still Face a Man's World," *Entrepreneur*, accessed August 2006, http://www.entrepreneur.com.

41. Forum for Women Entrepreneurs and Executives, accessed August 2006, http://www.fwe.org; Women Entrepreneurs, "Information . . . Action . . . Results," accessed August 2006, http://www.we-inc.org.

42. Robert Fairlie, "Self-Employed Business Ownership Rates in the United States: 1979–2003," Small Business Administration, accessed August 2006, http://www.sba.gov/advo.

43. Hispanic Trends, "Economic Clout," accessed August 2006, http://www.hispaniconline.com.

44. Robert Fairlie, "Self-Employed Business Ownership Rates in the United States."

45. Stephanie Clifford, "Business Ownership among Immigrant Women on the Rise," *Inc.*, accessed August 2006, http://www.inc.com.

46. Associated Press, "Arkansas Hispanics See Success in Business," July 30, 2005.

47. Cora Daniels, "Minority Entrepreneurs: Minority Rule," *Fortune*, accessed August 2006, http://www.money.cnn.com; Robert Lussier, Gregory Greenberg, and Joel Corman, "Bank Financing Discrimination against African-American Owned Small Business," Small Business Advancement National Center, University of Central Arkansas, accessed August 2006, http://www.sbaer.uca.edu; Karlyn Mitchell and Douglas K. Pearce, "Availability of Financing to Small Firms Using the Survey of Small Business Finances," Small Business Administration, accessed August 2006, http://www.sba.gov/advo.

48. "Testimony of Matthew R. Shay, President, International Franchise Association" Subcommittee on Economic Opportunity of the Committee on Veterans Affairs, U.S. House of Representatives, accessed September 5, 2005, http://www.franchise.org.

49. "Entrepreneur's 26th Annual Franchise 500," *Entrepreneur*, accessed August 2006, http://www.entrepreneur.com.

50. "Top Homebased Franchises 2005 Rankings," *Entrepreneur*, accessed August 2006, http://www.entrepreneur.com.

51. McDonald's, "New Restaurants," accessed August 2006, http://www.mcdonalds.com/corp; "McDonald's Franchise for Sale and McDonald's Franchise Information—Franchise Zone," *Entrepreneur*, accessed August 2006, http://www.entrepreneur.com; "Subway Franchise for Sale and Subway Franchise Information—Franchise Zone," *Entrepreneur*, accessed August 2006, http://www.entrepreneur.com.

52. "Welcome from Happy & Healthy Products Inc. and Our Fantastic Fruitfulls Franchisees!" Happy & Healthy Products Web site, accessed August 2006, http://www.fruitfull.com.

53. Gene Koprowski, "Successful Franchisees Embrace 'The System,'" *StartupJournal*, accessed August 2006, http://www.startupjournal.com.

54. David Welch, Dan Beucke, Kathleen Kerwin, Michael Arndt, Brian Hindo, Emily Thornton, and David Kiley, "Why GM's Plan Won't Work," *BusinessWeek Online*, accessed August 2006, http://www.businessweek.com.

55. Norihiko Shirouzu, "Dealers' Dilemma—Popular Asian Autos Seek More Space in Showrooms as U.S. Makers Try to Reduce," *Wall Street Journal*, 17 June 2005, p. B1.

56. Paulette Thomas, "Startup Q&A, Corporate Giants are Unlikely First Customers," *StartupJournal*, accessed August 2006, http://www.startupjournal.com.

57. Perri Capell, "Many Partnerships Form for the Wrong Reasons," *StartupJournal*, accessed August 2006, http://www.startupjournal.com.

58. "The 2005 *Fortune* 500: Full List," *Fortune*, accessed August 2006, http://www.money.cnn.com.

59. Internal Revenue Service, "IRS Launches Study of S Corporation Reporting Compliance," accessed August 2006, http://www.irs.gov.

60. Nolo Press, "Corporations FAQ: Who Should Form a Corporation?" accessed August 2006, http://www.nolo.com.

61. David Teather, "'Gimme a W, Gimme an A, Gimme an L . . . It's the Best Firm in the World': Retail Rocks at Annual Wal-Mart Rally," *The Guardian*, June 4, 2005, p. 27.

62. National Center for Employee Ownership, "Research and Statistics: A Statistical Profile of Employee Ownership," accessed August 2006, http://www.nceo.org.

63. National Center for Employee Ownership, "Largest Study Yet Shows ESOPs Improve Performance and Employee Benefits," accessed August 2006, http://www.nceo.org.

64. Information from San Francisco Ballet Web site, accessed August 2006, http://www.sfballet.org; Jesse Drucker and Almar Latour, "Verizon Wins Bidding for MCI; Qwest Drops Out," *Wall Street Journal*, May 3, 2005, p. A1.

65. Nikhil Deogun, Charles Forelle, Dennis K. Berman, and Emily Nelson, "Razor's Edge: P&G to Buy Gillette for $54 Billion," *Wall Street Journal*, January 28, 2005, p. A1.

66. Robert Weisman, "Merger Activity at Full Tilt, Even before Gillette: Number of Deals Up 8 Percent, in Part on Dollar's Weakness," *Boston Globe*, accessed August 2006, http://www.boston.com.

67. Christina Passariello, "Bacardi's Spirited Campaign—It Aims to Keep Grey Goose Vodka Flying above Rival Brands," *Wall Street Journal*, September 5, 2005, p. A4.

68. "Microsoft Acquires Teleo, Innovative VoIP Technology Company," Microsoft PressPass-Information for Journalists, accessed August 2006, http://www.microsoft.com.

69. Nikhil Deogun, Charles Forelle, Dennis K. Berman, and Emily Nelson, "Razor's Edge: P&G to Buy Gillette for $54 Billion."

70. "Transport4: What We Do," Transport 4 Web site, accessed August 2006, http://www.transport4.com.

71. David Fish, "Survey: Government-Owned Telecom Up 54 Percent," IT&T News, accessed August 2006, http://www.heartland.org.

## Chapter 6

1. Idealab Web site, accessed August 2006, http://www.idealab.com; Nadira A. Hira, "Idealab Reloaded: Surprise! Ex-Dot-Com-Wizard Bill Gross Is Back," *Fortune*, accessed August 2006, http://www.money.cnn.com; Michael Liedtke, "Search Engine Pioneer Raises $10 Million for Latest Quest," Associated Press, accessed July 19, 2005, http://www.ap.com; "Planned Online Ad System to Charge Only If Purchase Made," Dow Jones International News, accessed July 18, 2005, http://www.dowjones.com.

2. "Crunching the Numbers: Highlights From the *Inc.* 500 CEO Survey," *Inc. 500 Special Issue*, Fall 2005, p. 109.

3. Burt Helm, "How I Did It: Hall of Fame Profile, Jim Ansara—On the Importance of Growing with Your Company," *Inc. 500 Special Issue*, p. 10, accessed August 2006, http://www.inc.com.

4. Nadine Heintz, "Training Wheels," *Inc.*, October 2005, p. 51.

5. "The Portal Site for All easyGroup Companies," easyGroup, accessed August 2006, http://www.easy.com.

6. Dean Foust, "BofA's Happy Surprise," *BusinessWeek*, February 27, 2005, p. 68.

7. Zoltan Acs, Pia Arenius, Michael Hay, and Maria Minniti, "Global Entrepreneurship Monitor: Executive Report," Global Entrepreneurship Monitor Consortium, accessed August 2006, http://www.gemconsortium.org.

8. "America's Young Entrepreneurs: Trend Data at-a-Glance," National Association for the Self-Employed, accessed August 2006, http://www.nase.org.

9. Robert W. Fairlie, "Table 4, Kauffman Index of Entrepreneurial Activity by Age," Kauffman Index of Entrepreneurial Activity, Ewing Marion Kauffman Foundation, accessed August 2006, http://www.kauffman.org.

10. Nancy J. Lyons, "Moonlight over Indiana," Inc.com, accessed August 2006, http://www.inc.com/magazine.

11. Pallavi Gogoi, "Liz Lange's Labor of Love," *BusinessWeek Online*, accessed August 2006, http://www.businessweek.com.

12. Thomas Stanley and William Danko, "Chapter One: Meet the Millionaire Next Door," in *The Millionaire Next Door: The Surprising Secrets of America's Wealthy*, accessed August 2006, http://www.nytimes.com.

13. Luisa Kroll and Allison Fass, "Billionaires Rush to Riches," October 26, 2005, News.com.au via Forbes.com, accessed, http://www.finance.news.com.au.

14. Kerry Dolan, "From Buses to Planes; How to Build an Airline from Scratch: First, Steal Ideas from JetBlue and Southwest?" *Forbes*, October 21, 2005, p. 118.

15. Office of Advocacy, U.S. Small Business Administration, "Frequently Asked Questions: Advocacy Small Business Statistics and Research," accessed August 2006, http://app1.sba.gov/faqs; Amy Knaup, "Survival and Longevity in the Business Employment Dynamics Data," *Monthly Labor Review* (Bureau of Labor Statistics), May 2005, p. 50.

16. Alison Stein, "Are You Paying Yourself Enough?" *Inc.*, accessed August 2006, http://www.inc.com.

17. *Kiplinger's Personal Finance*, May, p. 21, accessed August 2006, http://www.kiplinger.com/magazine.

18. Office of Advocacy, U.S. Small Business Administration, "The Facts about Small Business," accessed November 2, 2005, http://www.sba.gov/advo.

19. Jim Hopkins, "The New Entrepreneurs: Americans over 50," *USA Today*, January 18, 2005, p. A1.

20. Martha Irvine, "Young and Self-Employed," *Associated Press Newswires*, November 10, 2004.

21. Joshua Kurlantzick, "About Face," *Entrepreneur*, accessed August 2006, http://www.entrepreneur.com.

22. Mark Henricks, "Some Entrepreneurs Can't Find the Slow Lane," *StartupJournal*, accessed August 2006, http://www.startupjournal.com.

23. Ibid.

24. Rainbow Play Systems Web site, accessed August 2006, http://www.rainbowplay.com; Joseph Conlin, "Natural Order," *Entrepreneur*, accessed August 2006, http://www.entrepreneur.com.

25. Paulette Thomas, "Now What . . . Make It: In a Global Economy, It Isn't Easy to Transform an Idea into a Product," *Wall Street Journal*, May 9, 2005, p. R6.

26. Zoltan Acs, Pia Arenius, Michael Hay, and Maria Minniti, "Global Entrepreneurship Monitor: Executive Report."

27. Michelle Henery, "Four out of Ten Business Owners Say 'Never Again in the UK,'" *The Times*, June 16, 2005, p. 61.

28. "Top 100 Entrepreneurial Colleges for 2005," *Entrepreneur,* accessed August 2006, http://www.entrepreneur.com.

29. "Hinman CEOs Overview," Hinman Campus Entrepreneurship Opportunities Program, accessed August 2006, http://www.hinmanceos.umd.edu.

30. "Students in Free Enterprise," SIFE, accessed August 2006, http://www.sife.org.

31. Mark Henricks, "Honor Roll," *Entrepreneur,* accessed August 2006, http://www.entrepreneur.com.

32. Mark Henricks, "Honor Roll"; "About Us," Float Tech, accessed August 2006, http://www.floattech.com.

33. Amy Chozick, "Managing Technology—Appearances Are Deceiving," *Wall Street Journal,* September 19, 2005, p. R7.

34. Gwendolyn Bounds, "You Have a Great Idea; Now What?" *Wall Street Journal,* May 9, 2005, p. R1.

35. David Kesmodel, "Beyond eBay: Small E-Tailers Discover Life Outside The Big Online Marketplaces," *Wall Street Journal,* July 18, 2005, p. R8.

36. "About Alere," Alere Medical, accessed August 2006, http://www.alere.com.

37. "Segway Tours by City Segway Tours," City Segway Tours, accessed August 2006, http://www.citysegwaytours.com.

38. Cynthia Yeldell, "Segway Finds Niche among People with Disabilities," *Pittsburgh Post-Gazette,* October 12, 2005, p. E-2.

39. George Gendron, "The Origin of the Entrepreneurial Species," *Inc.,* February 2000, p. 106.

40. Gilat Satellite Network Web site, accessed August 2006, http://www.gilat.com.

41. Rosie Del Campo, "It's Important to Strike Right Work-Life Mix," *Toronto Star,* 13 October 2005, p. J07; Eric Beauchesne, "Entrepreneurs Generally Enjoy Happier Work Life," Small Business Centre, accessed August 2006, http://www.canada.com.

42. Mark Henricks, "Parent Trap?" *Entrepreneur,* accessed August 2006, http://www.entrepreneur.com.

43. George Gendron, "The Origin of the Entrepreneurial Species," p. 110.

44. LuLu's Dessert Factory Web site, accessed August 2006, http://www.lulusdessert.com; Michele Prather, "Gettin' Jiggly with It," *Entrepreneur,* accessed August 2006, http://www.entrepreneur.com.

45. Sherri Cruz, "LuLu's Back in OC, Battling with Costs," *Orange County Business Journal,* March 7, 2005, p. 3.

46. Mike Hofman, "Inside Innovative Minds," *Inc.,* accessed August 2006, http://www.inc.com/magazine; Bill Atkinson, "CEO Finds Taking Risks Is Fast Track to Success," *Baltimore Sun,* accessed August 2006, http://www.baltimoresun.com.

47. John Anderson, "The Company That Grew Too Fast," *Inc.,* November 2005, p. 104.

48. Abrahm Lustgarten, Brian Dumaine, Julie Creswell, Christopher Tkaczyk, Matthew Boyle, Nadira A. Hira, Kate Bonamici, Fred Vogelstein, and Julia Boorstin, "14 Innovators," *Fortune,* accessed August 2006, http://www.money.cnn.com.

49. "A Scientist, as Humanitarian," FLAVORx, accessed November 6, 2005, http://www.flavorx.com.

50. Neil Adler, "A Conversation with Kenny Kramm," *Washington Business Journal,* accessed November 6, 2005, http://washington.bizjournals.com.

51. George Gendron, "The Origin of the Entrepreneurial Species," pp. 109–110.

52. Abrahm Lustgarten et al., "14 Innovators."

53. Brad Howarth, "Motivation Factor," *Business Review Weekly,* January 27, 2005, p. 64.

54. "Firefly Phone," Firefly Web site, accessed August 2006, http://www.fireflymobile.com.

55. Ann Zimmerman, "Do the Research: To Understand the Market—and the Competition—for Your Idea, You'll Have to Delve beyond the Obvious," *Wall Street Journal,* May 9, 2005, p. R3.

56. Ibid.

57. Richard Craver, "Made in the USA; Furniture-Maker Bucks Trend toward Imports by Retooling and Hiring Back Former Workers," *Winston-Salem (NC) Journal,* September 11, 2005, p. 1.

58. "In Good Company: CEO Survey, Part II," *Inc.,* November 2005, p. 140.

59. Sarah Bartlett, "Seat of the Pants," *Inc.,* accessed August 2006, http://www.inc.com/magazine.

60. Darren Dahl, "Start-up Capital: CEO Survey, Part II," *Inc.,* November 2005, p. 140.

61. Neil Young, "Commentary: Eye on the Entrepreneur: Baltimore Entrepreneur Delivers Nurses Now," *(Baltimore, MD) Daily Record,* October 14, 2005.

62. Ibid.

63. Diya Gullapalli, "What You Need to Know Before Selling Off Equity," *StartupJournal,* accessed August 2006, http://www.startupjournal.com.

64. Darren Dahl, "Start-Up Capital."

65. Larry Olmsted, "Nonstop Innovation," *Inc.,* July 2005, p. 34.

66. "About Us" and "Management Team," eCompanies and Business.com Web sites, accessed August 2006, http://www.ecompanies.com and http://www.business.com.

## Chapter 7

1. Lauri Giesen, "What Teens Want," *Internet Retailer,* accessed August 2006, http://internetretailer.com; Bob Tedeschi, "E-Commerce Report: Teenagers Are among Online Retailers' Most Sought-After Customers," *New York Times,* February 28, 2005, p. C3; Mark Albright, "Macy's Targets Young Women with Hip Web Site, Hot Fashions," *St. Petersburg (FL) Times,* accessed August 2006, www.sptimes.com; "Macy's to Launch New Website for Juniors," *Apparel Search,* accessed August 2006, http://www.apparelsearch.com.

2. "VeriSign Announces Valentine's Day-Related Online Shopping Activity," PR Newswire, LexisNexis Web site, accessed May 29, 2006, http://www.lexis-nexis.com.

3. "Web Integration: Then and Now," *Network World,* InfoTrac Web site, accessed March 16, 2005, http://www.infotrac.com.

4. Internet World Statistics, accessed August 2006, http://www.internetworldstats.com; Rob McGann, "Web Usage Growth Flatlines in U.S., Other Mature Markets," ClickZ Network, accessed August 2006, http://www.clickz.com.

5. Rob McGann, "Internet Edges Out Family Time More Than TV Time," ClickZ Network, accessed August 2006, http://www.clickz.com.

6. Rob McGann, "Broadband: High Speed, High Spend," ClickZ Network, accessed August 2006, http://www.clickz.com.

7. 2004 IBM Annual Report, accessed August 2006, http://www.ibm.com.

8. "Giving E-Procurement a Civic Twist," FCW.com, accessed March 23, 2005, http://www.fcw.com.

9. Laura Rush, "E-Commerce Growth Spurred by Maturation," ClickZ Network, accessed August 2006, http://www.clickz.com.

10. Betsey Streisand, "Make New Sales, But Keep the Old," *U.S. News & World Report*, accessed August 2006, http://www.usnews.com.

11. Amy Tsao, "Where Retailers Shop for Savings," BusinessWeek, accessed August 2006, http://www.businessweek.com.

12. Rob McGann, "Web-to-Store Consumers Spend, Shop More at Local Stores," ClickZ Network, accessed August 2006, http://www.clickz.com.

13. Timothy Mullaney, "The E Biz Surprise." *Business Week*, accessed August 2006, http://www.bwonline.com.

14. "More Businesses are Buying over the Internet," M2 Presswire, accessed May 29, 2006, http://www.lexis-nexis.com.

15. "About Us," Intelsat Business Network, accessed May 29, 2006, http://www.intelsat.com/aboutus/.

16. David Hannon, "Exchanges are Dead, but Collaboration Is Not," *Purchasing*, accessed August 2006, http://www.purchasing.com; Cara Cannella, "Why Online Exchanges Died," *Inc.*, accessed August 2006, http://www.inc.com; Arundhati Parmar, "A Focus on Services Helped Revive B2B E-Exchanges," *Marketing News*, accessed May 1, 2006, http://www.marketingpower.com.

17. "The Role of E-Marketplaces in Relationship-Based Supply Chains: A Survey," *IBM Systems Journal*, accessed May 29, 2006, http://www.infotrac.com.

18. "Ariba at Work: Customer Spotlight," Ariba, accessed May 29, 2006, http://www.ariba.com.

19. "General Information" and "Benefits," State of North Carolina E-Procurement Program, accessed August 2006, http://www.ncgov.com.

20. Estimate by Dr. Gene Huang, *Business Forecast 2005*, Sam M. Walton College of Business, University of Arkansas, January 28, 2005.

21. David Kaplan, "Internet Retailers Score Big," *Houston Chronicle*, accessed May 29, 2006, http://www.lexis-nexis.com.

22. Laura Rush, "E-Commerce Growth Spurred by Maturation," ClickZ Network, accessed August 2006, http://www.clickz.com.

23. Dan Reed, "Southwest Counters Cost Pressures with Longer Routes, Revved Growth," *USA Today*, accessed August 2006, http://www.usatoday.com.

24. "Southwest Airlines Sends Hottest Fares Directly to Customers' Computer Desktops," Southwest Airlines press release, accessed May 29, 2006, http://www.southwest.com.

25. "About Lands' End," Lands' End, accessed August 2006, http://www.landsend.com.

26. Rob McGann, "Broadband: High Speed, High Spend."

27. "Trends," Pew Internet and American Life Project, August 2006, http://www.pewinternet.org.

28. Laura Rush, "Women, Comparison Shopping Help Boost E-Commerce Holiday Revenues," ClickZ Network, accessed August 2006, http://www.clickz.com.

29. "Irrelevance through Constant Consumer Analysis," Jupiter Media Metrix, accessed March 6, 2005, http://www.jmm.com.

30. Robyn Greenspan, "E-Tailers Will See Green." ClickZ Network, accessed August 2006, http://www.clickz.com.

31. "About VeriSign," accessed August 2006, http://www.verisign.com.

32. Rob McGann, "Concerns over Online Threats this Holiday Season," ClickZ Network, accessed August 2006, http://www.clickz.com.

33. "Personal Data of 59,000 People Stolen," Associated Press, accessed March 22, 2005, http://www.yahoo.com.

34. Internet Crime Complaint Center, *Internet Fraud Crime Report*, Federal Bureau of Investigation, accessed August 2006, http://www.ic3.gov.

35. "How Not to Get Hooked by a Phishing Scam," FTC Consumer Alert, accessed August 2006, http://www.ftc.gov.

36. Bob Tedeschi, "Holiday Slowdowns and Crashes at Kmart.com, Amazon.com and Others Highlight the Web's Persistent Growing Pains," *New York Times*, accessed August 2006, http://www.nytimes.com.

37. Rob McGann, "Concerns over Online Threats This Holiday Season."

38. Kate Zernike, "Tired of TiVo? Beyond Blogs? Podcasts Are Here," *New York Times*, accessed August 2006, http://www.nytimes.com.

39. Riva Richmond, "Blogs Keep Internet Customers Coming Back," *Wall Street Journal*, March 1, 2005, p. B8.

40. "News Analysis: How Blogs Help Brands Build Trust Online," *Revolution*, accessed May 29, 2006, http://www.infotrac.com.

41. Amy Joyce, "More PR Than No-Holds-Barred on Bosses' Corporate Blogs," *Washington Post*, accessed August 2006, http://www.washingtonpost.com.

42. "Employee Blogs Can Be Good for Business," *PRWeek*, accessed March 3, 2005, http://www.infotrac.com.

43. Rob McGann, "Web-to-Store Consumers Spend, Shop More at Local Stores."

44. "Success Stories," Coremetrics, accessed August 2006, http://www.coremetrics.com.

45. Rob McGann, "Web Usage Growth Flatlines in U.S., Other Mature Markets," ClickZ Network, accessed August 2006, http://www.clickz.com.

46. Lucy Aitken, "E-Commerce: Survey of Surveys," *Management Today*, accessed August 29, 2006, http://www.infotrac.com.

## Part 2 Launching Your Entrepreneurial Career

1. Michael Ames in *Small Business Management*, cited in "Are You Ready?" Small Business Administration, accessed August 2006, http://www.sba.gov.

2. U.S. Department of Labor, *Occupational Outlook Handbook*, 2006–2007 edition, Bureau of Labor Statistics, accessed August 2006, http://www.bls.gov.

3. Paulette Thomas, "How One Employee Became an Entrepreneur," *CollegeJournal*, accessed August 2006, http://www.collegejournal.com.

4. U.S. Department of Labor, "Career Guide to Industries," Bureau of Labor Statistics, accessed August 2006, http://www.bls.gov.

5. U.S. Small Business Administration, "Protecting Your Ideas," accessed August 2006, http://www.sba.gov.

## Chapter 8

1. Ina Fried and Michael Kanellos, "Microsoft: We're in Fighting Shape," CNet News.com, accessed August 2006, http://news.com.com; Jay Greene, Steve Hamm, Diane Brady, and Mara Der Hovanesian, "Troubling Exits at Microsoft," *BusinessWeek*, accessed August 2006, http://www.businessweek.com; Robert A. Guth, "Think Pad: In Secret Hideaway, Bill Gates Ponders

Microsoft's Future," *Wall Street Journal*, accessed August 2006, http://online.wsj.com; Ina Fried, "Microsoft Gets Outside the Box with Software," CNet News.com, accessed August 2006, http://news.com.com.

2. Jared Sandberg, "The CEO in the Next Cube—Bosses Who Abandon Offices Win Kudos for Collegiality, But Make Neighbors Nervous," *Wall Street Journal*, June 22, 2005, p. B1.

3. Carol Hymowitz, "Middle Managers Are Unsung Heroes on Corporate Stage," *Wall Street Journal*, September 19, 2005, p. B1.

4. Melanie Trottman, "Nuts-and-Bolts Savings—To Cut Costs, Airlines Make More of Their Own Parts; Jettisoning a $719 Toilet Seat," *Wall Street Journal*, May 3, 2005, p. B1.

5. Robert A. Guth, "Think Pad."

6. Robert Guth, "Microsoft Revamp for Online Push Gains Urgency," *Wall Street Journal*, November 9, 2005, p. A3.

7. P. Glader, "Aluminum Foil: As Alcoa Struggles, O'Neill's Successor Tries New Direction," *Wall Street Journal*, October 12, 2005, p. A1.

8. Mark Maremont, "Tyco Figures Will Be Jailed at Least 7 Years—Judge Orders Kozlowski, Swartz to Also Pay Back $240 Million; CEO's 'Kleptocratic Management,'" *Wall Street Journal*, September 20, 2005, p. C1.

9. *Quoted in "Conscience in a Cup of Coffee,"* U.S. News & World Report, October 31, 2005, p. 48.

10. Ann Zimmerman and Kris Hudson, "Target Practice: Looking Upscale, Wal-Mart Begins a Big Makeover," *Wall Street Journal*, September 17, 2005, p. A1.

11. Del Jones, "Dell: Take Time to Build," *USA Today*, August 2006, http://www.usatoday.com.

12. Nicole Gull, "Plan B (and C and D and . . . )," *Inc.*, accessed August 2006, http://www.inc.com.

13. Ann Zimmerman and Kris Hudson, "Target Practice."

14. Peter Grant and Dionne Searcey, "How to Watch TV," *Wall Street Journal*, November 9, 2005, p. D1.

15. Nikhil Deogun, Charles Forelle, Dennis Berman, and Emily Nelson, "Razor's Edge: P&G to Buy Gillette for $54 Billion," *Wall Street Journal*, January 28, 2005, p. A1.

16. "Corporate Information: Company Overview," Google, accessed August 2006, http://www.google.com.

17. "Bayer: Science for a Better Life," Bayer Annual Report 2004, accessed January 17, 2006.

18. Jennifer Saranow, "Smaller Models; 43 Crossovers to Choose From," *Wall Street Journal*, October 27, 2005, p. D1.

19. Starbucks Corporation Annual Report, accessed August 2006, http://www.starbucks.com; press releases, Starbucks Web site, accessed August 2006, http://www.starbucks.com.

20. Jack Speer, "Automakers Unveil New Hybrids at Detroit Show," National Public Radio, accessed August 2006, http://www.npr.org; Neal Boudette and Ann Keeton, "Toyota Expects Surge in Sales of Hybrid Vehicles," *Wall Street Journal*, August 4, 2005, p. D3.

21. David Bauder, "Profits Are Big, but Ratings Slip as Its Unique Niche among Networks Appears to Fade," *Houston Chronicle*, June 20, 2005, p. 3.

22. Business Writers, "Hibernia to Boost Credit Card Business; Capitol One's Muscle to Grow with Merger," *Times-Picayune*, May 22, 2005, p.1.

23. Robert Guth, "Getting Xbox 360 to Market—Microsoft Must Coordinate Game Player's 1,700 Parts to Ensure Big Enough Supply," *Wall Street Journal*, November 18, 2005, p. B1.

24. Thomas Kellner, "One Man's Trash . . . , " *Forbes*, accessed August 2006, http://www.forbes.com.

25. Louis Lavelle, "Another Crop of Sleazy CEOs?" *BusinessWeek*, accessed August 2006, http://www.businessweek.com.

26. J. Helyar, "Why Is This Man Smiling?" *Fortune*, accessed August 2006, http://www.money.cnn.com.

27. Kim Clark, "Flying High after Disaster," *U.S. News & World Report*, accessed August 2006, http://www.usnews.com.

28. "Living Our Values," Home Depot Web site, accessed January 17, 2006, http://careers.homedepot.com; Lorrie Grant, "Home Depot's Chief Builds on Big Dreams," *USA Today*, accessed August 2006, http://www.usatoday.com; Daintry Duffy, "Cultural Evolution," *CIO Enterprise*, CIO Web site, August 2006, http://www.cio.com.

29. "Hamburger University," McDonald's Web site, accessed August 2006, http://www.mcdonalds.com.

30. Janet Guyon, "The Soul of a Moneymaking Machine," *Fortune*, October 3, 2005, p. 113.

31. Jill Nash, "A Comprehensive Campaign Helps Gap Employees Embrace Cultural Change," *Communication World*, November 1, 2005, p. 42.

32. "The State of the Church," *Time*, accessed August 2006, http://www.time.com.

33. "Products & Services," 3M, accessed August 2006, http://www.3M.com.

34. Scott Hensley, "Christine Poon: Women to Watch (A Special Report)—In Line to Lead," *Wall Street Journal*, October 31, 2005, p. R6.

35. Jared Sandberg, "Office Democracies: How Many Bosses Can One Person Have?" *Wall Street Journal*, November 22, 2005, p. B1.

## Chapter 9

1. Breakdown at Sago Mine: Trouble and Tragedy Two Miles In," *Pittsburgh Post-Gazette*, accessed August 2006, http://www.post-gazette.com; Ted David, "Massey Energy—Chairman & CEO Interview," CNBC/Dow Jones Business Video, accessed September 9, 2005, http://www.cnbc.com; Dave Anderson, "Few Graduates Dig Mining," *Deseret Morning News*, accessed August 26, 2005, http://deseretnews.com; Patrick Barta, "Lack of Qualified Workers Strains Mining Companies," *Wall Street Journal*, accessed August 2006, http://online.wsj.com; "Mining Schools Set to Open, Legislators Told," Associated Press, accessed August 9, 2005, http://www.ap.org.

2. Quoted in "My Golden Rule," *Business 2.0*, December 2005, p. 110.

3. Trilogy Web site, accessed August 2006, http://www.trilogy.com.

4. Timothy Aeppel, "Firms' New Grail: Skilled Workers—U.S. Manufacturers Report Shortages Are Widespread; Critics Cite Training Cuts," *Wall Street Journal*, November 22, 2005, p. A2.

5. Nanette Byrnes and Amy Barrett, "Star Search: How to Recruit, Train, and Hold On to Great People. What Works, What Doesn't," *BusinessWeek*, October 10, 2005, p. 68.

6. "New .jobs Suffix Approved for Worldwide Recruiting/Hiring," *Human Resource Department Management Report*, May 2005, p. 9.

7. D. Lewis, "EEOC: Damage Awards; Reach $420m in 2004," *Boston Globe*, February 20, 2005, p. D2.

8.  Sam Walker, "The NFL's Smartest Team," *Wall Street Journal*, September 30, 2005, p. W1.

9.  Robert Levering, Milton Moskowitz, Ann Harrington, Nadira Hira, and Christopher Tkaczyk, "The 100 Best Companies to Work For," *Fortune*, January 24, 2005, p. 72.

10. Matthew Boyler and Ellen Kratz, "The Wegmans Way," *Fortune*, January 24, 2005, p. 62.

11. M. Totty, "Better Training through Gaming," *CareerJournal*, April 25, 2005, p. R6.

12. J. Borzo, "Almost Human: Using Avatars for Corporate Training, Advocates Say, Can Combine the Best Parts of Face-to-Face Interaction and Computer-based Learning," *Wall Street Journal*, May 24, 2004, p. R4.

13. J. Borzo, "Almost Human."

14. Nanette Byrnes and Amy Barrett, "Star Search."

15. Kathleen Gallagher, "GE Investing in Future Leaders; Executive's Program Challenges a Select Few," *Milwaukee Journal Sentinel*, October 24, 2005, p. D1.

16. "Halogen eAppraisal Case Studies," Halogen Software, accessed August 2006, http://www.halogensoftware.com.

17. Michael Kinsman, "Coach for Executives," *San Diego Union-Tribune*, October 11, 2005, p. C-1.

18. "Employer Costs for Employee Compensation Summary," Bureau of Labor Statistics, accessed August 2006, http://www.bls.gov.

19. Lee Hawkins Jr., "As GM Battles Surging Costs, Workers' Health Becomes Issue," *Wall Street Journal*, April 7, 2005, p. A1.

20. Ann Zimmerman, Robert Matthews, and Kris Hudson, "Can Employers Alter Hiring Policies to Cut Health Costs?" *Wall Street Journal*, October 27, 2005, p. B1.

21. Ibid.

22. "Paid Family Leave Insurance," Employee Development Department, accessed August 2006, http://www.edd.ca.gov.

23. Jeff Opdyke and Kelly Greene, "Is Your Retirement Money Safe? UAL's Move to Default Highlights Range of Risks and Protections for Different Types of Plans," *Wall Street Journal*, May 12, 2005, p. D1.

24. Deborah Myers, "Cafeteria Plans Offer Flexible Insurance Options," *Alaska Business Monthly*, accessed December 4, 2005, http://akbizmag.com.

25. Robert Levering and Milton Moskowitz, "The 100 Best Companies to Work For," *Fortune*, January 24, 2005, p. 72.

26. Ibid.

27. Jill Carlson, "Employers Can Help Employee Caregivers Win on Two Fronts," *Capital Region Business Journal*, December 1, 2005, p. 36.

28. Knight Ridder/Tribune Business News, "Staffing Survey Reveals Rise in Employees' Personal Days Off," *Daily Oklahoman*, November 20, 2005.

29. Shirley Won, "Doing Good Helps You Do Well at Work; Corporate Volunteerism Grows as Companies Realize Host of Benefits for Staff and Themselves," *Globe and Mail*, January 19, 2005, p. C1.

30. Joyce Gannon, "Study Says Flex Time Boosts Morale While Reducing Turnover," *Pittsburgh Post-Gazette*, November 8, 2005.

31. Katherine Lewis, "This Time-Share Involves Working," *Grand Rapids (MI) Press*, November 27, 2005, p, H1.

32. Ibid.

33. "Annual Survey Shows Americans Are Working from Many Different Locations Outside Their Employer's Office," International Telework Association and Council, accessed August 2006, http://www.workingfromanywhere.org.

34. Nanette Byrnes and Amy Barrett, "Star Search."

35. Kazuhiro Shimamura, Arran Scott, and Ginny Parker, "Sanyo to Cut Staff 15%, Shut Factories," *Wall Street Journal*, July 6, 2005, p. A3.

36. Frank Byrt, "EDS to Double Jobs Outsourced to Low-Wage Regions in 2 Years," *Wall Street Journal*, December 1, 2005, p. B2.

37. Quoted in "How I Got There," *Newsweek*, October 24, 2005, p. 59.

38. Carol Hymowitz, "Readers Share Tales of Jobs Where Strategy Became Meeting Target," *Wall Street Journal*, March 22, 2005, p. B1.

39. Pampered Chef Web site, accessed August 2006, http://www.pamperedchef.com.

40. "Union Members in 2004," Bureau of Labor Statistics, accessed December 5, 2005, http://www.bls.gov.

41. "Major Work Stoppages in 2004," Bureau of Labor Statistics, accessed August 2006, http://www.bls.gov.

42. Ibid.

43. Gary Fields, Timothy Aeppel, Kris Maher, and Janet Adam, "Can the New Economy Be Organized?" *Wall Street Journal*, July 27, 2005, p. B1.

44. J. Lynn Lunsford, "Boeing, Idled for a Month, Agrees to Meet Most of Union's Demands," *Wall Street Journal*, September 26, 2005, p. A3.

45. Kris Maher, "Labor Leaders Say Multination Effort Targets Wal-Mart," *Wall Street Journal*, August 23, 2005, p. B2.

46. Amy Merrick and Kris Maher, "Using Temps Proves Potent at Northwest," *Wall Street Journal*, August 29, 2005, p. B1.

47. Robert Matthews and Kris Maher, "Labor's PR Problem—As More Workers Find Unions Weak and Irrelevant, Leaders Seek to Restore Positive Image," *Wall Street Journal*, August 15, 2005, p. B1.

48. Ibid.

49. Ibid.

50. Gary Fields, et al., "Can the New Economy Be Organized?"

## Chapter 10

1.  Alan Deutschman, "The Un-CEO," *Fast Company*, accessed August 2006, http://www.fastcompany.com; Richard Donkin, "New Angle on the Search for Workplace Flexibility," *Financial Times*, accessed August 2006, http://www.ft.com; Sara J. Welch, "The Fabric of Success," *Successful Meetings*, August 2006, http://www.mimegasite.com; Chris Markham, "Full Bore at Gore," accessed August 2006, *Arizona Daily Sun*, http://www.azdaily-sun.com; Alan Deutschman, "The Fabric of Creativity," *Fast Company*, accessed August 2006, http://www.fastcompany.com.

2.  "About A&A," Anderson & Associates, accessed August 2006, http://www.andassoc.com.

3.  Paul Dellinger, "Workers Buy Anderson & Associates," *Roanoke Times & World News*, May 8, 2005, p. 16.

4. Jan Norman, "People Power: A Costa Mesa Engineering Firm Empowers Its Workers with Financial Information to Build Business and Avoid Layoffs," *Orange County Register,* March 23, 2005, p. 1.

5. "A Statistical Profile of Employee Ownership," National Center for Employee Ownership, accessed August 2006, http://www.nceo.org.

6. Andrew Blackman, "You're the Boss: New Accounting Rules May Reduce the Number of Employee-Owned Firms; But Anson Industries Sees the Benefits Far Outweighing the Costs," *Wall Street Journal,* April 11, 2005, p. R5.

7. "A Statistical Profile of Employee Ownership."

8. Andrew Blackman, "You're the Boss."

9. "How to Choose an Employee Stock Plan for Your Company," National Center for Employee Ownership, accessed August 2006, http://www.nceo.org.

10. "Our Core Values," Whole Foods Market, accessed August 2006, http://www.wholefoodsmarket.com.

11. S. Thurm, "Teamwork Raises Everyone's Game—Having Employees Bond Benefits Companies More than Promoting 'Stars,'" *Wall Street Journal,* November 7, 2005, p. B8.

12. Jack Gordon, "Do Your Virtual Teams Deliver Only Virtual Performance?" *Training,* June 1, 2005, p. 20.

13. Mallory Stark, "The Five Keys to Successful Teams," Working Knowledge from Harvard Business School, PricewaterhouseCoopers, accessed August 2006, http://hbswk.hbs.edu.

14. Lingling Wei, "Brokers Increasingly Use Teamwork," *Wall Street Journal,* February 23, 2005.

15. Laura Landro, "The Informed Patient: Bringing Surgeons Down to Earth—New Programs Aim to Curb Fear that Prevents Nurses from Flagging Problems," *Wall Street Journal,* November 16, 2005, p. D1.

16. Ibid.

17. Jessica Mintz, "Career Journal: The Jungle," *Wall Street Journal,* August 30, 2005, p. B6.

18. Vanessa Fuhrmans, "Oops! As Health Plans Become More Complicated, They're Also Subject to a Lot More Costly Mistakes," *Wall Street Journal,* January 24, 2005, p. R4.

19. Christopher Tkaczyk and Matthew Boyle, "Follow These Leaders," *Fortune,* December 12, 2005, p. 125.

20. Ibid.

21. Joann Lublin, "The 'Open Inbox'—Some CEOs Stay Up Late Reading Employee E-Mails; Replies Can Be Brief: 'Thanks,'" *Wall Street Journal,* October 10, 2005, p. B1.

22. Peter Loftus, "Send and Save: Regulations on Storing Old E-Mails Can Be a Huge Burden for Small Firms," *Wall Street Journal,* September 19, 2005, p. R7.

23. Gretchen Hoover, "Maintaining Employee Engagement when Communicating Difficult Issues: An IABC Survey Shows That Companies That Take a Strong Position and Answer Questions as Forthrightly as Possible Reap the Benefits," *Communication World,* November 1, 2005, p. 25.

24. Sheri Rosen, "Carry on the Conversation: Helping Employees Make Sense of What Happens at Work," *Communication World,* March 1, 2005, p. 24.

25. Kevin Voigt, "Making the Rumor Mill Work for You," *Asian Wall Street Journal,* January 21, 2005, p. P1.

26. Ibid.

27. Albert Mehrabian, *Silent Messages* (Belmont, CA: Wadsworth, 1971); Albert Mehrabian, "Communication without Words," *Psychology Today,* September 1968, pp. 53–55.

28. Marilyn Much, "Stopping Workplace Incivility; More Companies Realize that On-the-Job Rudeness Can Mean Lower Revenue," *Investor's Business Daily,* February 28, 2005, p. A7.

29. Associated Press, "Wendy's Hopes Arrest Will Bring Back Customers: Investigators Call Finger Incident a Hoax," MSNBC, accessed August 2006, http://www.msnbc.msn.com.

30. Trebor Banstetter, "Crash Tests Southwest's Disaster Response," *Fort Worth Star-Telegram,* December 10, 2005, p. 1A.

31. "A 1993 Instance of Product Tampering Resulted in Syringes Being Found in Cans of Pepsi," Urban Legends Reference Pages, accessed August 2006, http://www.snopes.com.

## Chapter 11

1. Russell Gold and Michael M. Phillips, "Gulf Energy Facilities Get Off to a Slow Restart after Storms," *Wall Street Journal,* accessed August 2006, http://online.wsj.com; Chip Cummins, Bhushan Bahree, and Jeffrey Ball, "Gulf Coast: Why the World Is One Storm Away from Energy Crisis," *Wall Street Journal,* accessed August 2006, http://online.wsj.com; Jessica Resnick-Ault, Beth Heinsohn and Bhushan Bahree, "Gulf Coast Refineries Hunker Down," *Wall Street Journal,* accessed August 2006, http://online.wsj.com.

2. Neal Boudette and Norihiko Shirouzu, "Amid Price War, Chrysler to Revamp Manufacturing—Move to 'Flexible' Plants Aims to Improve Efficiency in Fragmented Auto Market," *Wall Street Journal,* August 2, 2005, p. A1.

3. William Hoffman, "Dell Beats the Clock," *Traffic World,* October 24, 2005.

4. Jennifer Yario, "2005 Top Fab: IBM," *Semiconductor International,* December 1, 2005, p. 55.

5. "Robotic Palletizing Leads to 55 Percent Productivity Gain at JTM Products," *Robotics World,* September 1, 2005, p. 14.

6. Allan Madrid, "Gang Run; VistaPrint Produces Thousands of Short-Run Jobs Daily on 400 Presses by Automating Combo Runs," *Graphic Arts Monthly,* August 1, 2005, p. 52.

7. James Salzer, "'Growing Jobs' No Snap: Perdue Finds Task Easier Said Than Done," *Atlanta Journal-Constitution,* August 10, 2005, p. C1.

8. Ed Anderson, "Workers Key to Luring Businesses; Executives Rank Work Force Issues as Most Important," *(New Orleans, LA) Times-Picayune,* January 27, 2005, p. 1.

9. Neal Boudette and Norihiko Shirouzu, "Amid Price War, Chrysler to Revamp Manufacturing."

10. Gary S. Vasilash, "Honda's Hat Trick," Automotive Manufacturing and Production, accessed August 2006, http://www.autofieldguide.com.

11. Ford Motor Company press releases, accessed August 2006, http://media.ford.com.

12. Daniel Michaels and J. Lynn Lunsford, "Streamlined Plane Making: Boeing, Airbus Look to Car Companies' Methods to Speed Up Jetliner Production," *Wall Street Journal,* April 1, 2005, p. B1.

13. Stephanie Fitch, "The Progress of Change—Inch by Inch," *Forbes,* accessed August 2006, http://www.forbes.com; Allison Linn, "Boeing Moving Right Along," *The Morning News,* April 12, 2002, p. 7C.

14. "Spend Management Overview," Ariba, accessed August 2006, http://www.ariba.com.

15. Ed Christman, "Retail Track: Best Buy to Rely on Vendor-Managed Pipeline," *Billboard,* January 29, 2005.

16. J. Bonasia, "Just-in-Time Cuts Costs, But Has Risks, as Dock Lockout Shows System Increases Rate of Deliveries," *Investor's Business Daily,* accessed December 16, 2005, http://www.investors.com.

17. Jeff Sabatini, "Turning Japanese," Automotive Manufacturing and Production, accessed August 2006, http://www.autofieldguide.com.

18. Nicholas Enticknapp, "Getting the Best Measure of the Business," *Computer Weekly,* November 15, 2005, p. 44.

19. J. Bonasia, "GE Black Belts to the Rescue; Consultants from Firm's Financial Arm Help Borrowers Improve Processes," *Investor's Business Daily,* April 25, 2005, p. A10.

20. J. Briscoe, S. Fawcett, and R. Todd, "The Implementation and Impact of ISO 9000 among Small Manufacturing Enterprises," *Journal of Small Business Management,* July 2005, p. 309.

## Part 3 Launching Your Management Career

1. U.S. Department of Labor, "Tomorrow's Jobs," *Occupational Outlook Handbook,* 2006–2007 edition, Bureau of Labor Statistics, accessed August 2006, http://www.bls.gov.

2. U.S. Department of Labor, "Administrative Services Managers," *Occupational Outlook Handbook,* 2006–2007 edition, Bureau of Labor Statistics, accessed August 2006, http://www.bls.gov.

3. U.S. Department of Labor, "Construction Managers," *Occupational Outlook Handbook,* 2006–2007 edition, Bureau of Labor Statistics, accessed August 2006, http://www.bls.gov.

4. U.S. Department of Labor, "Food Service Managers," *Occupational Outlook Handbook,* 2006–2007 edition, Bureau of Labor Statistics, accessed August 2006, http://www.bls.gov.

5. U.S. Department of Labor, "Human Resources, Training, and Labor Relations Managers and Specialists," *Occupational Outlook Handbook,* 2006–2007 edition, Bureau of Labor Statistics, accessed August 2006, http://www.bls.gov.

6. U.S. Department of Labor, "Lodging Managers," *Occupational Outlook Handbook,* 2006–2007 edition, Bureau of Labor Statistics, accessed August 2006, http://www.bls.gov.

7. U.S. Department of Labor, "Purchasing Managers, Buyers, and Purchasing Agents," *Occupational Outlook Handbook,* 2006–2007 edition, Bureau of Labor Statistics, accessed August 2006, http://www.bls.gov.

8. U.S. Department of Labor, "Medical and Health Services Managers," *Occupational Outlook Handbook,* 2006–2007 edition, Bureau of Labor Statistics, accessed January 25, 2006, http://www.bls.gov.

9. U.S. Department of Labor, "Industrial Production Managers," *Occupational Outlook Handbook,* 2006–2007 edition, Bureau of Labor Statistics, accessed August 2006, http://www.bls.gov.

## Chapter 12

1. Whole Foods Web site, accessed August 2006, http://www.wholefoodsmarket.com; Daniel McGinn, "The Green Machine," *Newsweek,* March 21, 2005, pp. E8–E12; Bruce Horovitz, "A Whole New Ballgame in Grocery Shopping," *USA Today,* March 9, 2005, pp. B1–B2; Seth Lubove, "Food Porn," *Forbes,* February 14, 2005, pp. 102–12.

2. Daniel McGinn, "The Green Machine."

3. American Marketing Association, "AMA Adopts New Definition of Marketing," MarketingPower.com, accessed August 2006, http://www.marketingpower.com.

4. "Crazy about Curbside," About.com, accessed August 16, 2005, http://houston.about.com; Bruce Horovitz, "Casual Dining Puts Spin on Drive-Thru," *USA Today,* September 20, 2004, p. B1.

5. Yuri Kageyama, "Apple Opens iTunes Music Store in Japan," Yahoo! News, accessed August 4, 2005, http://www.yahoo.com.

6. Andrew Mennie, "The Value of Customer Satisfaction," CRM Today, accessed August 2006, http://www.crm2day.com.

7. Ron Kaufman, "How Does Singapore Airlines Fly So High?" CRM Today, accessed July 11, 2005, http://www.crm2day.com.

8. Ibid.

9. "Social Enterprise," Harvard Business School, accessed August 2006, http://www.hbs.edu.

10. Betsy Kroll, "Fashion Statements," *Time,* August 8, 2005, p. 75.

11. Jonah Freedman, "The Fortunate 50," *Sports Illustrated,* July 4, 2005, pp. 65–69.

12. "Beijing 2008 Marketing Plan Officially Launched," PR Newswire, accessed August 8, 2005, http://www.news.com.com.

13. United Nations Food and Agriculture Organization, "About World Food Day," accessed August 2006, http://www.fao.org.

14. Barbara K! Web site, accessed August 2006, http://www.barbarak.com; Allen P. Roberts, "How I Did It: Barbara K," *Inc.,* May 2005, pp. 112–14; Penelope Green, "Home Improvement, Self-Improvement," *New York Times,* May 8, 2005, pp. 11-1, 11-4.

15. "KFC Hits Home Run in China," Fox News, accessed August 2006, http://www.foxnews.com.

16. John Gartner, "Smart Car Seeks Small Niche," Wired News, accessed August 2006, http://www.wired.com.

17. Teenage Research Unlimited, accessed August 2006, http://www.teenresearch.com.

18. Michael Barbaro, "Wal-Mart Trend Office Seeks Out What's Hip," *The Morning News,* August 14, 2005, pp. 1D, 3D.

19. Teenage Research Unlimited.

20. Melanie Wells, "Have It Your Way," *Forbes,* February 14, 2005, pp. 78–86.

21. Daniel McGinn, "From Harvard to Las Vegas," *Newsweek,* April 18, 2005, pp. E8–E14.

22. Emily Fredrix, "What's Brown and White and Bread All Over?" Yahoo! News, accessed August 9, 2005, http://www.yahoo.com.

23. David Welch, "GM Goes Gunning for the Coasts," *BusinessWeek,* June 27, 2005, p. 14.

24. Bath and Body Works Web site, accessed August 2006, http://www.bathandbodyworks.com.

25. "Miss Independent Steps Up to the D-I-Y Plate," Lowe's, accessed August 2006, http://www.lowes.mediaroom.com.

26. Nicholas Varchaver, "Pitchman for the Gray Revolution," *Fortune,* July 11, 2005, pp. 63–72.

27. Ibid.; statistics based on a Merrill Lynch survey of 3,448 Americans born between 1946 and 1964.

28. Jeremy Caplan, "Gotta Have It," *Time,* August 8, 2005, pp. 46–47.

29. Alicia A. Caldwell, "Texas Becomes a Majority-Minority State," Yahoo! News, accessed August 11, 2005, http://www.yahoo.com.

30. Deborah L. Vence, "Pick Up the Pieces," *Marketing News,* March 15, 2005, pp. 14–15.

31. Ibid.

32. Ethnic Grocer Web site, accessed August 2006, http://www.ethnicgrocer.com.

33. Mary Jacobs, "Corporate Blogging's All the Buzz," *Herald Sunday,* August 7, 2005, p. D1.

34. Joseph B. Verengia, "American Family Life in Flux," CBS News.com, accessed August 2006, http://www.cbsnews.com.

35. Chris Taylor, "One Pint at a Time," *BusinessWeek Online,* accessed August 2006, http://www.businessweek.com.

36. Cingular advertisements from *Time,* August 8, 2005.

37. Chris O'Brien and Matthai Chakko Kuruvila, "Gas Costs Cramping Consumer Spending," RedOrbit News, accessed August 2006, http://www.redorbit.com; Tenisha Mercer, "Gasoline Prices Sock Retail Sales," *Detroit News,* accessed August 2006, http://www.detnews.com.

38. Timberland Web site, accessed August 2006, http://www.timberland.com.

39. Jeremy Caplan, "Strange Bedfellows," *Time,* March 7, 2005.

40. "Agricultural News," John Deere Web site, accessed August 2006, http://www.deere.com; Julia Chang, "CRM at Any Size," *Sales & Marketing Management,* August 2004, pp. 30–35.

## Chapter 13

1. Vijay Verghese, "Mirror Mirror on the Wall," accessed August 2006, http://www.smarttravelasia.com; Marc E. Babej and Tim Pollak, "Boeing Versus Airbus," *Forbes,* accessed August 2006, http://www.forbes.com; "DFW International Airport Ready for Airbus A380 as International Terminal Opens," PR Newswire, accessed July 24, 2005, http://biz.yahoo.com; Jim DuPlessis, "Dreaming about the Future," The State.com, accessed July 19, 2005, http://www.thestate.com; Jorn Madslien, "Airbus v. Boeing: The Next Battle," *BBC News,* accessed August 2006, http://www.bbc.co.uk; David Greising and Michael Oneal, "The Global Factory," *Chicago Tribune,* February 23, 2005, section 1, pp. 1, 20–21; Laurence Frost, "World's Largest Passenger Plane Unveiled," Associated Press, accessed January 18, 2005, http://www.yahoo.com; Michael Oneal and David Greising, "Boeing Bets Big on a Plastic Plane," *Chicago Tribune,* January 12, 2005, section 1, pp. 1, 20–21.

2. Dell Web site, accessed August 2006, http://www.dell.com; Matt Slagle, "Cost-Conscious Dell Branches Out on Style," Yahoo! News, accessed July 14, 2005, http://www.yahoo.com.

3. Kellogg Web site, accessed August 2006, http://www.kelloggs.com; Eddie Bauer Web site, accessed August 2006, http://www.eddiebauer.com.

4. Ramin Setoodeh, "Corporate Last Licks," *Newsweek,* May 9, 2005, pp. 24–25.

5. Bruce Myerson, "Cell Phones Now Playing Role of Wallet," Yahoo! News, accessed June 18, 2005, http://www.yahoo.com.

6. Cool Zippos Web site, accessed August 2006, http://www.coolzippos.com; Ellen Neuborne, "The Problem: Zippo Has a Strong Brand Name . . . " *Inc.,* September 2004, pp. 42-44.

7. Kenneth Terrell, "The Whole World in Your Hand," *U.S. News & World Report,* March 28, 2005, p. 71.

8. Geoff Dougherty, "Spinoffs from the Kitchen?" *Chicago Tribune,* May 2, 2005, section 4, pp. 1, 4.

9. Yuri Kageyama, "Sharp Develops 'Two-Way Viewing-Angle' LCD," Yahoo! News, accessed July 15, 2005, http://www.yahoo.com.

10. Tony Kontzer, "Survey: Web Sites Building Better Brand Loyalty than Physical Stores," *InformationWeek,* accessed August 2006, http://www.informationweek.com.

11. Julia Moskin, "Tired of Prying Off Stickers? Tattooed Fruit Is on the Way," *New York Times,* July 19, 2005, p. A1.

12. "The Top 20 Greatest Kiosk Projects," *Kiosk Magazine Online,* accessed March 23, 2005, http://www.kiomag.com.

13. "China's Tom Online Signs Distribution Deal," Yahoo! News, accessed June 20, 2005, http://www.yahoo.com.

14. "Industry Statistics Sampler, NAICS 42, Wholesale Trade," U.S. Census Bureau, accessed August 2006, http://www.census.gov.

15. Retail Advantage Group Web site, accessed August 2006, http://www.retailadvantagegroup.com.

16. "Retail Industry Trends/Retail Trade Analysis," *Plunkett's Retail Industry Almanac,* accessed July 27, 2005, http://retailindustry.about.com.

17. Matt Krantz, "Gap's Newest Store, Forth & Towne, Opens Today," *USA Today,* accessed August 2006, http://www.usatoday.com.

18. Steven Greenhouse, "How Costco Became the Anti-Wal-Mart," *New York Times,* accessed August 2006, http://www.nytimes.com.

19. Andrew Blum, "The Mall Goes Undercover," *Slate,* accessed August 2006, http://www.slate.com.

20. Joseph Weber with Ann Therese Palmer, "How the Net Is Remaking the Mall," *BusinessWeek,* May 9, 2005, pp. 60–61.

21. Easy.com Web sites, accessed August 2006, http://www.easy.com, http://www.easyjet.com, and http://www.easycar.com; David Kirkpatrick, "How to Erase the Middleman in One Easy Lesson," *Fortune,* March 17, 2003, p. 122.

22. Bowflex Web site, accessed August 2006, http://www.bowflex.com.

23. Gregory M. Lamb, "Not Your Father's Radio," *Christian Science Monitor,* accessed July 25, 2005, http://www.csmonitor.com.

24. Chana R. Schoenberger, "The Morning After," *Forbes,* May 23, 2005, pp. 210–14.

25. Peter Henry, "Coming to a Store Near You," *Software Development,* accessed August 2006, http://www.cognizant.com; Matt Hines, "Companies' RFID Plans Fuzzy So Far," ZDNet News, accessed August 2006, http://news.zdnet.com.

26. "U.S. Statistics," Truckinfo.net, accessed August 2006, http://www.truckinfo.net.

27. Marianne Lavelle, "Railroad Revival," *U.S. News & World Report,* Executive Edition, March 28, 2005, pp. EE4–EE8.

## Chapter 14

1. K9 Advantix Web site, accessed August 2006, http://www.K9Advantix.com; Erin Moriarty, "A Dogfight over Fleas, Ticks," *Atlanta Business Chronicle,* accessed August 2006, http://www.bizjournals.com/atlanta; "Humans, Animals Are Susceptible to West Nile Disease," KVBC TV, accessed August 4, 2005, http://www.kvbc.com; Craig A. Shutt, "Bayer Integrates P-O-P TV, Advertising," Structural Graphics, accessed August 2006, http://www.structuralgraphics.com; "PetCARE Television Network

Inc. Signs Bayer as New Advertiser," *Business Wire,* accessed August 2006, http://www.findarticles.com.

2. Theresa Howard, "Coca-Cola Uses Island Inspiration," *USA Today,* accessed August 2006, http://www.usatoday.com; "Results Marketing," *Motivation Strategies,* accessed August 2006, http://www.motivationstrategies.com.

3. Bob Lamons, "Sales Pitch Often Gets Lost in Ads' Creativity," *Marketing News,* February 15, 2005, p. 8.

4. Theresa Agovino, "Pfizer Sets Guidelines on its Advertising," *Yahoo! News,* accessed August 11, 2005, http://www.yahoo.com.

5. Roland Jones "Reading the Minds of Car Consumers," *MSNBC News,* accessed August 2006, http://www.msnbc.msn.com.

6. Theresa Howard, "Slurpee Celebrates 40 Years of 'Brain Freeze'," *USA Today,* accessed August 2006, http://www.usatoday.com.

7. Jeff Greenfield, "Product Placement Report," *1st Approach,* accessed August 2006, http://www.productplacement.biz.

8. Joe Mandese, "Paid Product Placement Surges in Magazines, Newspapers, and Other Media," *Media Daily News,* accessed August 2006, http://publications.mediapost.com.

9. Nissan Web site, accessed August 2006, http://www.nissanusa.com; Alice T. Cuneo, "Nissan Plays with Fire," *Advertising Age,* October 11, 2004, p. 6.

10. Theresa Howard, "Advertisers Forced to Think Way outside the Box," *USA Today,* accessed August 2006, http://www.usatoday.com.

11. "National Advertisers Ranked 1 to 50," *Advertising Age's Special Report: Profiles Supplement,* June 27, 2005.

12. "Domestic Advertising Spending Totals," "Domestic Advertising Spending by Category," and "National Advertisers Ranked 1 to 50," *Advertising Age's Special Report: Profiles Supplement,* June 27, 2005.

13. Lynn Elber, "TV Telethons Announced for Katrina Victims," *Associated Press,* accessed September 1, 2005, http://www.yahoo.com.

14. "iPod Nano, iPod Phone Unveiled," *CNN.com,* accessed September 8, 2005, http://www.cnn.com.

15. Theresa Howard, "Advertisers Forced to Think Way outside the Box."

16. Richard R. Green, "Cable Television Technology Deployment," *National Information Infrastructure,* National Academies Press, accessed August 2006, http://darwin.nap.edu.

17. Theresa Howard, "Advertisers Forced to Think Way outside the Box."

18. David Leiberman, "Cable Firms Make You Easy Target for TV Ads," *USA Today,* February 21, 2005, p. B1.

19. Greg Sandoval, "TiVo Wants You to Watch Commercials," *Associated Press,* accessed July 18, 2005, http://www.yahoo.com.

20. Tara Perkins, "Satellite Radio Could Be a Problem for Advertisers Who Rely on Conventional Ads," *Canadian Press,* accessed June 19, 2005, http://www.yahoo.com.

21. Sirius Web site, accessed August 2006, http://www.sirius.com.

22. Bob Sullivan, "Deluged with Credit Card Mail? Help Is Coming," *MSNBC,* accessed August 2006, http://www.msnbc.com.

23. Teri Cettina, "When You Care Enough . . . Say it with Billboards," *Bankrate.com,* accessed August 2006, http://www.bankrate.com.

24. "Online Advertising to Skyrocket, Study Says," *CNet News.com,* accessed August 2006, http://news.com.com.

25. Theresa Howard, "Advertisers Forced to Think Way outside the Box."

26. Theresa Howard, "'Viral' Advertising Spreads through Marketing Plans," *USA Today,* accessed August 2006, http://www.usatoday.com.

27. Gregory Krupey, "John Carleo's Fitness Quest," *Pittsburgh Tribune-Review,* accessed August 2006, http://pittsburghlive.com.

28. Dahleen Glanton, "Coupon Clippers Clean Up," *Chicago Tribune,* May 8, 2005, section 1, pp. 1, 14.

29. Kerry Dooley Young, "Aetna and Walgreen to Pass on Drug Rebates," *Sun-Sentinel.com,* accessed August 2006, http://www.sun-sentinel.com.

30. "Growth Spurt Continues into the First Quarter," *Tradeshow Week,* accessed August 2006, http://www.tradeshowweek.com.

31. "Occupational Employment and Wages," U.S. Department of Labor, Bureau of Labor Statistics, accessed August 2006, http://www.bls.gov.

32. Brian L. Clark, "Targeting the DHS," *Inc.,* May 2005, pp. 44, 46.

33. Paul Christ, "New Roles and New Tools for PR," *KnowThis.com,* accessed August 2006, http://www.knowthis.com.

34. Otis Port, "Billionaires Blasting Off," *BusinessWeek,* accessed August 2006, http://www.businessweek.com.

35. Theresa Howard, "Real Women Have Curves, and Ads," *USA Today,* accessed August 2006, http://www.usatoday.com; Seth Stevenson, "When Tush Comes to Shove," *Slate,* accessed August 2006, http://slate.com.

36. Lew McCreary, "Lies, Damn Lies and Puffery," *CMO Magazine,* accessed August 2006, http://www.cmomaga-zine.com.

37. Jennifer Whitehead, "P&G Advertising Beauty Claims Dismissed as Non-Existent," *Brand Republic,* accessed August 2006, http://www.brandrepublic.com.

38. "Television Advertising Leads to Unhealthy Habits in Children, Says APA Task Force," American Psychological Association, accessed August 2006, http://www.apa.org.

39. Pallavi Gogoi, "SpongeBob SquareMeal?" *BusinessWeek,* accessed August 2006, http://www.businessweek.com.

40. Alison Leigh Cowan, "Connecticut Lawmakers Debate Strict Bill on School Nutrition," *New York Times,* accessed August 2006, http://www.nytimes.com.

41. Ron Scherer, "Coming in the Mail: Big Energy Bills," *Christian Science Monitor,* accessed August 2006, http://www.csmonitor.com; "Hurricane Rita to Compound Katrina's Dampening Impact on Economy," *Business Wire,* accessed September 28, 2005, http://biz.yahoo.com; *MSNBC News,* September 1, 2005, and September 6, 2005.

42. Greg Sandoval, "Flat-Screen TV Prices Finally Come Down," *Yahoo! News,* accessed August 15, 2005, http://www.yahoo.com.

43. Julia Boorstin, "What's in Fashion This Fall? Scarcity," *Fortune,* August 22, 2005, p. 19.

44. Alison Stein Wellner, "Taking the Guesswork out of Pricing," *Inc.,* June 2005, pp. 72–82.

## End of Part 4: Launching Your Marketing Career

1. U.S. Department of Labor, "Market and Survey Researchers," *Occupational Outlook Handbook,* 2006–2007 edition, Bureau of Labor Statistics, accessed August 2006, http://www.bls.gov.

2. U.S. Department of Labor, "Advertising Sales Agents," *Occupational Outlook Handbook,* 2006–2007 edition, Bureau of Labor Statistics, accessed August 2006, http://www.bls.gov.

3. U.S. Department of Labor, "Advertising and Public Relations Services," *Occupational Outlook Handbook,* 2006–2007 edition, Bureau of Labor Statistics, accessed August 2006, http://www.bls.gov.

4. U.S. Department of Labor, "Advertising and Public Relations Services."

## Chapter 15

1. Omer Farooq, "Google Satellite Photos Worry India Leader," *BusinessWeek,* accessed October 15, 2005, http://www.businessweek.com; Michael Liedtke, "Google Morphs into Multifaceted Juggernaut," Associated Press, accessed October 3, 2005, http://www.yahoo.com; Dwight Silverman, "Is Google Getting Too Big for Its Original Good Ideas?" *Houston Chronicle,* accessed August 2006, http://www.chron.com; Alan Deutschman, "Can Google Stay Google?" *Fast Company,* accessed August 2006, http://www.fastcompany.com; Harry McCracken, "A Google, Google, Google, Google World," *PC World,* accessed August 2006, http://www.pcworld.com; Ian Burrell, "The Interview with Nikesh Arora: We're Living in a Google World," *The Independent,* accessed August 2006, http://www.news.independent.co.uk.

2. Jodi Mardesich, "Getting the Pay You Deserve," CIO Strategy Center, accessed August 2006, http://www.ciostrategycenter.com.

3. Jodi Mardesich, "Getting the Pay You Deserve."

4. "Tomorrow's Jobs," *Occupational Outlook Handbook,* 2006–07 Edition, Bureau of Labor Statistics, accessed August 2006, http://www.bls.gov.

5. *Occupational Outlook Handbook,* Bureau of Labor Statistics.

6. DB2 Intelligent Miner for Data, IBM, accessed October 19, 2005, http://www.ibm.com.

7. Retailing Case Study, Data Miners, accessed August 2006, http://www.data-miners.com.

8. "Wi-Fi on the Farm," CNN, accessed October 19, 2005, http://www.cnn.com.

9. Kristen Kenedy, "Intel Endorses Wi-Max with New Line of Chips for Standard," *Computer Reseller News,* accessed August 2006, http://www.crn.com.

10. "Wi-Fi on the Farm."

11. Richard Verrier, "Disney IT Jobs to Be Unloaded," *Los Angeles Times,* accessed August 2006, http://www.latimes.com.

12. Scott Campbell, "Survey: Notebooks Surpass Desktop Sales for First Time," CRN News, accessed August 2006, http://www.crn.com.

13. Scott Campbell, "Survey: Notebooks Surpass Desktop Sales for First Time."

14. Thomas Fitzgerald, "Tablet PC's Reach for the Masses," *New York Times,* accessed August 2006, http://www.nytimes.com.

15. Karen Brown, "The PDA's Future: Where Art Thou?," *Wireless Week,* accessed August 2006, http://www.wirelessweek.com.

16. "Success Stories," Microsoft Small Business Center, accessed August 2006, http://www.microsoft.com.

17. "About Great Harvest," Great Harvest, accessed October 26, 2005, http://www.greatharavest.com.

18. "Palo Alto Software Products," Palo Alto Software, accessed August 2006, http://www.paloalto.com.

19. "Business Benefits Series," Oracle, accessed August 2006, http://www.oracle.com.

20. "Success Story," Adobe, accessed August 2006, http://www.adobe.com.

21. "Case Study," Interwoven, accessed August 2006, http://www.interwoven.com.

22. "Singapore University Deploys Juniper Networks SSL VPN Solution to Improve Efficiency of E-Learning System," press release, Juniper Networks, accessed August 2006, http://www.juniper.net.

23. "VoIP Grabs the Phone," *Newsweek,* November 14, 2005, p. E16.

24. Jeffrey Kelley, "New Protocol; Business Embrace Internet Telephone, Should You?" *Richmond Times-Dispatch,* accessed August 2006, http://www.timesdispatch.com.

25. Susannah Patton, "Dial VoIP for Vulnerability," *CIO,* accessed August 2006, http://www.cio.com.

26. Eric Dash, "Main Street in the Cross Hairs; Nation's 5 Million Retail Stores Prove an Easy Target for Data Thieves," *New York Times,* accessed August 2006, http://www.nytimes.com.

27. Jill Curcum and Richard Meryhew, "Privacy of Thousands Breached," *(Minneapolis) Star Tribune,* accessed August 2006, http://www.startribune.com.

28. Will Knight, "Malicious Software Turns PSP into a 'Brick'," NewScientist.com, accessed August 2006, http://www.newscientist.com.

29. Eve Tahmincioglu, "Small Business; Trying to Stay a Step Ahead of Murphy's Law," *New York Times,* accessed August 2006, http://www.nytimes.com.

30. "Malfunction Briefly Halts Trading on Big Board," *New York Times,* accessed August 2006, http://www.nytimes.com; Bethany Clough, "Some Madera County Teachers Don't Get Paid on Time Friday," *Fresno Bee,* accessed October 31, 2005, http://www.fresnobee.com; Paul Adams, "Software Glitch Causes Some Baltimore Gas & Electric Customers to Pay Too Much," *Baltimore Sun,* accessed October 31, 2005, http://www.baltimoresun.com.

31. "Agency IT Provides Relief after Katrina," *Government Computer News,* accessed August 2006, http://www.gcn.com.

32. "Disaster Planning: A Perfect Storm," *Baseline,* accessed October 17, 2005, http://www.baselinemag.com.

## Chapter 16

1. Nanette Byrnes, "The Little Guys Doing Large Audits," *BusinessWeek,* accessed August 2006, http://www.businessweek.com; Jack Naudi, "Sarbanes-Oxley Is Big Business Here," *St. Louis Post-Dispatch,* accessed August 2006, http://www.stltoday.com; Diya Gullapalli, "After the Accounting Scandals: More Work and Opportunity," *Wall Street Journal Online,* accessed August 2006, http://www.careerjournal.com.

2. Bureau of Labor Statistics, accessed August 2006, http://www.bls.gov.

3. American Institute of Certified Public Accountants, accessed August 2006, http://www.aicpa.org.

4. Tax-Aide, AARP, accessed August 2006, http://www.aarp.org/money/taxaide/.

5. "About GoDaddy.com," GoDaddy, accessed August 2006, http://www.godaddy.com.

6. "Public Accounting Firms," Government Accountability Office, accessed August 2006, http://www.gao.gov.

7. "Success Stories," ACCPAC, accessed August 2006, http://www.sageaccpac.com.

8. Johnson & Johnson financial statements, accessed September 23, 2005, http://moneycentral.msn.com.

9. Dairy Finance Tools, University of Missouri, accessed August 2006, http://agebb.missouri.edu.

10. Annual report, Procter & Gamble, accessed August 2006, http://www.pg.com.

## End of Part 5: Launching Your Information Technology and Accounting Career

1. U.S. Department of Labor, *Occupational Outlook Handbook,* 2006–2007 Edition, Bureau of Labor Statistics, accessed August 2006, http://www.bls.gov.

2. National Association of Colleges and Employers, "Salary Survey," accessed August 2006, http://www.jobweb.com.

## Chapter 17

1. "Fannie Mae Oversight Bill Approved by Senate Panel," Bloomberg.com, accessed August 2006, http://www.bloomberg.com; Brian Collins, "GSE Reform Headway Slow," *American Banker-Bond Buyer,* July 11, 2005, p. 1; "Tighter Leash on Freddie, Fannie Urged," CNNMoney.com, accessed August 2006, http://money.cnn.com; David S. Hilzenrath, "Report Slams Fannie Mae," *Washington Post,* accessed August 2006, http://www.washingtonpost.com.

2. "After Turnaround, Pride Promotes Its CFO," Oilgram News, July 1, 2005.

3. CFO.com Web site, accessed August 2006, http://www.cfo.com.

4. Peggy Hollinger, "Airborne: After 10 Years and US$ 14.2 Billion in Development Costs, Largest Airliner Ever Successfully Debuts," *Financial Post,* accessed July 27, 2005, http://www.lexis-nexis.com.

5. Tim Reason, "Budgeting in the Real World," CFO.com, accessed August 2006, http://www.cfo.com.

6. U.S. Census Bureau, *Statistical Abstract of the United States,* accessed August 2006, http://www.census.gov.

7. Home Depot and Lowe's financial statements, accessed August 1, 2005, http://moneycentral.msn.com.

8. "Representative Private Placements," Credit Suisse First Boston, accessed August 4, 2005, http://www.csfb.com.

9. "About USVP," US Venture Partners, accessed August 2006, http://www.usvp.com.

10. Federal Deposit Insurance Corporation, *Statistics on Banking,* accessed August 2006, http://www.fdic.gov.

11. Ibid.

12. Ibid.

13. Ibid.

14. Ibid.

15. *Financial Services Fact Book,* accessed August 2006, http://www.financialservicesfacts.org.

16. "Corporation Facts," Bank of America, accessed August 4, 2005, http://www.bankofamerica.com.

17. Online Banking Report, accessed August 2006, http://www.onlinebankingreport.com.

18. "Fast Facts," Bank of America, accessed August 2, 2005, http://www.bankofamerica.com.

19. FDIC, *Statistics on Banking.*

20. "Credit Union Facts," National Credit Union Administration, accessed August 2, 2005, http://www.ncua.gov.

21. Navy Federal Credit Union Web site, accessed August 2006, http://www.navyfcu.org.

22. Insurance Information Institute, Financial Services Facts, accessed August 2006, http://www.financialservicesfacts.org.

23. Ibid.

24. "Global Investment Review," Watson Wyatt, accessed August 2006, http://www.watsonwyatt.com.

25. "About PBGC," PBGC Web site, accessed August 2006, http://www.pbgc.gov.

26. Mary Williams Walsh, "How Wall Street Wrecked United's Pension," *New York Times,* accessed August 2006, http://www.nytimes.com.

27. FDIC, *Statistics on Banking.*

28. "Japanese Banks to Merge, Becoming World's Largest," *San Diego Union-Tribune,* accessed August 2006, http://www.signonsandiego.com.

## Chapter 18

1. Cox Web site, accessed August 2006, http://www.cox.com; Jay Sherman, "Cabler's Motives Under Question," *Television Week,* accessed August 2006, http://www.televisionweek.com; David Lieberman, "Cablevision Plans to Go Private, Split Firm," *USA Today,* accessed August 2006, http://www.usatoday.com; Jay Sherman, "Signs of M&A Return May Be Misinterpreted," *Television Week,* accessed August 2006, http://www.televisionweek.com.

2. David Russell, "Minority Firms Tapped for Bond Sale," *The Morning News,* August 9, 2005, p. 2D.

3. Jay Ritter, "Some Factoids about the 2005 IPO Market," accessed August 2006, http://bear.cba.ufl.edu.

4. Ibid.

5. "NYSE Exchange Market Statistics," New York Stock Exchange, accessed August 9, 2005, http://www.nyse.com.

6. Microsoft financial statements, accessed August 23, 2005, http://www.moneycentral.msn.com.

7. "Global Crossing Emerges from Chapter 11," PR Newswire, accessed August 2006, http://www.prnewswire.com.

8. Insurance Information Institute, Financial Services Facts, accessed August 2006, http://www.financialservicesfacts.org.

9. New York Stock Exchange, accessed August 2006, http://www.nyse.com.

10. *Mutual Fund Fact Book,* Investment Company Institute, accessed August 2006, http://www.ici.org.

11. *Survey of Consumer Finances,* Federal Reserve, accessed August 2006, http://www.federalreserve.gov.

12. Eastman Kodak financial statements, accessed August 23, 2005, http://www.moneycentral.msn.com.

13. *NYSE Fact Book* (interactive version), New York Stock Exchange, accessed August 2006, http://www.nyse.com.

14. Press release, New York Stock Exchange, accessed August 2006, http://www.nyse.com.

15. Nasdaq Stock Market, accessed August 2006, http://www.nasdaq.com.

16. *NYSE Fact Book* (interactive version), New York Stock Exchange.

17. AMEX Statistics, American Stock Exchange, accessed August 2006, http://www.amex.com.

18. "Instinet Group Announces Transaction Information," accessed August 24, 2005, http://www.investor.instinetgroup.com; "Archipelago Holdings Releases Transaction Volume Data," PR Newswire, accessed August 24, 2005, http://investor.archipelago.com.

19. Merrill Lynch, accessed August 2006, http://askmerrill.ml.com.

20. *Mutual Fund Fact Book,* Investment Company Institute.

21. Ibid.; "ICI Reports Exchange-Traded Fund Assets," Investment Company Institute, accessed August 2006, http://www.ici.org.

22. "SEC Brings Fraud Charges Against Former CBS Marketwatch Columnist Thom Calandra for Illegal Trading Scheme," press release, Securities and Exchange Commission, accessed August 2006, http://www.sec.gov.

23. "SEC Charges Eight More in Reebok Insider Trading Case," press release, Securities and Exchange Commission, accessed August 2006, http://www.sec.gov.

24. "SEC Files Settled Regulation FD Charges against Flowserve Corporation," press release, Securities and Exchange Commission, accessed August 2006, http://www.sec.gov.

25. "Exchange Hearing Panel Decision 05-87," New York Stock Exchange, accessed August 2006, http://www.nyse.com.

### End of Part 6: Launching Your Finance Career

1. U.S. Department of Labor, *Occupational Outlook Handbook,* 2006-07 Edition, accessed August 2006, http://www.bls.gov.

2. National Association of Colleges and Employers, Salary Survey, accessed August 2006, http://www.jobweb.com.

3. U.S. Department of Labor, Occupational Outlook Handbook, 2006-07 Edition.

### Appendix A

1. Margot Roosevelt with Logan Orlando, "Health Insurance? Turn Left at Aisle 6," *Time,* accessed August 2006, http://www.time.com, p. 14; Amy Reeves, "Health Insurance: Now Available at Your Local Costco," *Insurance Newsnet,* accessed August 2006, http://www.insurancenewsnet.com; Robert Jablon, "Costco to Sell Health Insurance in Calif.," accessed August 2006, http://www.cicaworld.com

### Appendix B

1. Randy Dotinga, "Are You Saving Too Much for Retirement?" *Christian Science Monitor,* accessed August 2006, http://www.csmonitor.com; Justin Fox, "You're on Your Own (and That's OK)," *Fortune,* July 19, 2006, pp. 19–21; "More Companies Froze, Terminated Pension Plans in 2004, Watson Wyatt Analysis Finds," *PR Newswire,* accessed August 2006, http://www.prnewswire.com; Jonathan Stempel, "Study: Nine in 10 Americans Worry about Retirement," Reuters, accessed February 8, 2005, http://www.yahoo.com.

2. "College Students Get Wise about Credit Cards," PR Newswire, accessed July 19, 2006, http://www.prnewswire.com.

### Appendix C

1. Draper Fisher Jurvetson Web site, accessed August 2006, http://www.dfj.com; Adam Lashinsky, "Venture Capital Is Not for Girlie Men," *Fortune,* October 17, 2005, p. 38; Michael Kanellos, "The Big Winner behind Skype and Baidu," CNet News.com, accessed August 2006, http://news.com.com; "Draper Fisher Jurvetson on the Record: Tim Draper," San Francisco Chronicle, accessed August 2006, http://www.sfgate.com.

2. Elizabeth Wasserman, "A Simple Plan," *MBA Jungle,* accessed August 2006, http://www.mbajungle.com.

# Name Index

Geico, 444
Gendron, George, N–8
General Agreement on Tariffs and Trade (GATT), 106–107
General Electric, 4, 25, 33, 84, 116, 117, 141, 168–169, 220, 277, 293–294, 297, 324, 325, 363, 364, 365, 421, 448, 521, 555, 564, 577, 590–591, N–4
General Mills, 9, 28, 47, 53, N–3
General Motors (GM), 7, 45, 48, 50, 70, 89, 165–166, 168, 297, 302, 391, 393, 396, 418, 449, 513, 521, 564, 565, 582, 590
Genuine Scooter, 210–211
Genzyme, 4
George, Jason, 187
Georgia Tech, 70
Geppert, Caroline, 260
Gerstner, Lou, Jr., 275
Getty, J. Paul, 555
Gewin, Virginia, N–1
G.I. Joe's, 29
Giant Eagle, 183
Gibson, Stan, 490
Giesen, Lauri, N–8
Gilat Satellite Networks, 196, N–8
Gill, Dee, N–5
Gilleece, Mary, 311
Gillette, 173, 174, 263
Glace, GB, 101
Glader, P., N–10
Gladson, Clifford A., 580
Glanton, Dahleen, N–15
GlaxoSmithKline, 449
Global Crossing, 32, 578
Global Santa Fe, 345
GM. *See* General Motors (GM)
GNOME, 74
Go Daddy Group, 516
Go2.com, 183
Gogoi, Pallavi, N–7, N–15
Gol Linhas Aéreas Inteligentes, 189
Gold, Russell, N–12
Golden West, 559
Goldman Sachs, 577
Goldsmith, Marshall, 295
Goldwater, Barry, 565
Goldwyn, Samuel, 132
Gomez, 229
Goodwill Industries, 268–269, 347
Goodyear, 402, 453, 521
Google, 21, 152, 183, 189, 233, 234, 235, 236, 245, 254, 264, 323, 375, 419, 483–484, 496, 542
Gorbachev, Mikhail, 75
Gordon, Jack, N–12
Gordon, Kim T., 395
Gordon, Marcy, 260
Government Accountability Office (GAO), 83, N–16
Graham, Benjamin, 586
Graham, Nicholas, 420
Granite Rock, 13, N–1
Grant, Alison, 596
Grant, Peter, N–10
Grant Thornton, 513, 517
Grantham, Russell, 359
Great Harvest Bread Company, 494–495, 510, 542, N–16
Great Plains Software, 79
Greehey, Bill, 272
Green, Penelope, N–13
Green, Richard R., N–15
Green Bay Packers, 444

Green Day, 450
Green Mountain Coffee Roasters, 31–32, 45, N–2
Greenberg, Gregory, N–6
GreenCine, 232
Greene, Jay, N–9
Greene, Kelly, N–11
Greenfield, Jeff, N–15
Greenhouse, Steven, N–14
Greenspan, Alan, 82, 141
Greenspan, Robyn, N–19
Greising, David, N–14
Grey Goose, 173
Griggs, Robert, 515
Grimand, Joe, 165
Grokster, 131, 138
Gross, Bill, 183
Gross, Daniel, 496
Gross, Larry, 183
Guillen, Ozzie, 256
Gulf View Townhouses of Tampa, 566
Gull, Nicole, 150, N–10
Gullapalli, Diya, N–8, N–16
Gunther, Marc, N–2
Guth, Robert A., N–9, N–10
Gutierrez, Carlos, 9
Gutierrez, Don Dionisio, 145
Gutierrez, Don Juan Bautista, 145
Gutierrez, Juan Jose, 145
Guyon, Janet, N–10

**H**
H. J. Heinz, 116
Habitat for Humanity, 5, 48, 406
Hagenbaugh, Barbara, 596
Haggart, Geoff, 499
Haji-Ioannou, Stelios, 186, 432
Hale, Bob, 489
Hall, Tex, 407
Halliburton, 297
Halligan, Nancy, 363
Halogen Software, 295
Halvorson, Christine, 16
Hamadeh, Samer, xxxix
Hamburger University, 165, 271
Hamilton, Chris, 287
Hamm, Steve, N–9
Hampton Inn, 321
Hancock & Moore, 202
Hannon, David, N–9
Hanover, Tim, 331
Hansen, Barbara, 260
Hansen, Randall S., 588
Happy & Healthy Products, 164, N–6
Hargitay, Mariska, 387
Harley-Davidson, 41, 407
Harpo, 20, 210
Harpold, Leslie, 401
Harrah's, 391
Harrington, Ann, N–11
Harrington, Lisa, 468
Harris, Barbara, 139
Harris, Elizabeth, 580
Harrison, Crayton, 490
Hartswick, Perry, 350
Harvard, 188, 277, N–13
Hastings, Reed, 152
Hatch, Orrin, 135
Hawkins, Lee, Jr., N–11
Hay, Michael, 192, N–7
Hay Group, 24
Hayden, Thomas, 407

HBO. *See* Home Box Office (HBO)
Healy, Patrick O'Gilfoil, N–3
Hearst, 557
Heartland Education community, 305
Hebert, H. Josef, 69
Heinsohn, Beth, N–12
Heintz, Nadine, N–7
Heinz, 364
Heller, Gary, 502
Helm, Burt, N–7
Helyar, J., N–10
Hemming, Matthew, 412
Hempel, Jessi, N–3
Henderson, David, N–3
Henery, Michelle, N–7
Henricks, Mark, N–7
Henry, Peter, N–14
Hensley, Scott, N–10
Herbert, Frank, 488
Hercules, 513
Hetherington, Mike, 518
Hewlett, Walter, 511
Hewlett-Packard, 45, 46, 260, 334, 383, 419, 435, 490, 493, 511, 548
Heyer, Raymond, 186
Higuera, Valencia P., 458
Higgins, Tim, N–2
Hilton, 28, 321
Hilzenrath, David S., N–17
Hindo, Brian, N–6
Hines, Matt, N–14
Hinman Campus Entrepreneurship Opportunities Program, N–8
Hinz, Bill II, 561
Hira, Nadira A., N–7, N–8, N–11
Hirshberg, Gary, 16
Hispanic Scholarship Fund, 47
Hispanic Trends, N–6
History Channel, 451
Ho, Mimi, 499
Hochman, Michael E., N–2
Hoffman, William, N–12
Hofman, Mike, N–8
Holiday Inn, 402
Hollinger, Peggy, N–17
Holmdahl, Todd, 268
Home Box Office (HBO), 266
Home Care Delivered, 502
Home Depot, 18, 147, 180, 271, 323, 406, 500, 556, 566, 590, 601, N–10, N–17
Honda, 7, 45, 49, 64, 211, 237, 311, 355, 357
Hoover, Gretchen, N–12
Hoover, Herbert, 64
Hope, Bob, 556
Hopkins, Jim, N–1, N–7
Hopkins, Kevin P., 352
Horovitz, Bruce, N–13
HotJobs.com, xli
Howard, Theresa, N–15
Howarth, Brad, N–8
Hrcareerpage.com, xli
HSBC Group, 92, 117
Huang, Gene, N–9
Huawei Technologies, 102
Hubbard, Connie, 186
Hudson, Kris, N–10, N–11
Huff, Charlotte, 317
Hughes, Karen, 447
Hugo, Victor, 111
Humane Society, 412
Hunt, John, 451

# Subject Index

People's Republic of China *(continued)*
   GDP of, 78, 94
   Hong Kong and, 122
   Huawei Technologies in, 102
   international marketplace, 93
   international regulations in, 105
   Internet users in, 239
   KFC in, 389
   Lenovo Group in, 116
   offshoring in, 114–115
   oil demand in, 66–67
   Olympics in, 386
   outsourcing and, 21, 371
   Panasonic in, 116
   political climate in, 103
   population in, 94
   Red Wing Shoe Company and, 91
   Republic of Tea and, 49
   United States and, 97, 104, 468
   UPS in, 435
   U.S. trade with, 94, 95
   Wal-Mart in, 94
   Whirlpool in, 114
   workforce in, 21
Performance, 318–343
   communication and, 329–337
   empowerment and, 320–323
   linking rewards to company, 322–323
   social, 43
   teamwork and, 323–329
**Performance appraisal, 294**–295
Performing, as team development stage, 327
**Perpetual inventory, 359**
**Person marketing, 386**
Personal computers (PCs), 492–494
Personal data form, for preparing job credentials, xli
Personal financial planners, 606
**Personal selling, 445,** 457–462, 463
Personal space, 335
Personalization, of e-business, 216, 225
Persuasive advertising, 450
PERT. *See* **Program Evaluation and Review Technique (PERT)**
Peru, 31, 192
Petroleum companies, 174
P&G. *See* Procter & Gamble (P&G)
Philadelphia Stock Exchange, 586
Philippines, Microwarehouse in, 371
**Phishing, 228**–229
**Physical distribution, 422, 434**–436
Physical factors in location decision, 353–354
Physiological needs, in Maslow's hierarchy of needs, 304, 305
Pick-and-place robot, 351
**Picketing, 310**
**Place marketing, 386**
**Place utility, 381**
**Planned economy, 70, 74**–75
Planned shopping center, 430–431
**Planning, 258,** 259–267. *See also* Business plan
   contingency, 261
   at different organizational levels, 261–263
   operational, 261
   production, 360–361
   production process, 355
   strategic, 261, 262, 263–267
   tactical, 261
   types of, 260–261
Plant managers, 255
PLM. *See* **Product life-cycle management (PLM)**
**Podcasts, 232**
**Point-of-purchase (POP) advertising,** 457

Poland
   entrepreneur statistics in, 192
   EU and, 109, 110
   political climate in, 103
Polite listening, 333
Political climate, barriers to trade and, 103
**Pollution, 44–45,** 107, 129
POP advertising. *See* **Point-of-purchase (POP) advertising**
Population, 18–20
   aging, 52
   in United States, xlix–l, 94, 485–486
   world, 18, 93, 94
**Pop-up ads, 233,** 454
Pop-up messages, Internet fraud and, 228–229
Portfolio managers, 606
Portugal, 192
**Positioning, 447**
Postconventional stage of ethical development, 36, 37
PR. *See* Public relations (PR)
Preconventional stage of ethical development, 36, 37
**Preferred stock, 171, 582,** 584, 585
Pregnancy Discrimination Act (1978), 53, 54
Premiums, 455–456, 564
Prepaid shopping cards, 554
Prerefunded bond, 581
Presentation, in sales process, 461
**Presentation software, 499,** 500
**Prestige pricing, 466**–467
**Price, 465.** *See also* Pricing; Pricing strategy
   as benefit of B2C e-business, 224
   issues at eBay, 245–246
**Price-earnings (P/E) ratio, 589**
Price war, 466
Price-level changes, 78–80
Pricing. *See also* **Price**
   competitive, 466, 470
   consumer perceptions of, 470–471
   discount, 470
   everyday low, 470
   markup, 467
   objectives in marketing mix, 465–467
   odd, 471
   penetration, 470
   prestige, 466–467
   at Second City, 604
   skimming, 469–470
   strategies for (*See* Pricing strategy)
Pricing strategy, 467–470. *See also* **Price;** Pricing
   in marketing mix, 388, 445
   for retailers, 429
Primary data, 390
Primary demand, 444
**Primary market, 576**–577
Privacy
   as e-business challenge, 226
   employee, 291
Private employment agencies, xlii
**Private enterprise system, 8, 9**–12, 70, 71–74, 76
**Private exchanges, 220**
Private ownership, 167, 174, 175
**Private placements, 557**
**Private property, 9**–10
**Private/store brand, 419**
**Privatization, 76**
Probate courts, 126
**Problem-solving team, 323, 324**
Process departmentalization, 274
Process layout, 355–357, 361
Procter & Gamble (P&G), as international company, 3–4
Producers
   distribution channels and, 432
   dumping and, 106

**Product advertising, 450**
Product departmentalization, 274
Product identification, 418–422
Product launch, 418
Product layout, 356, 357, 361
**Product liability, 48,** 136
**Product life cycle, 414**–418, 450–451
Product life-cycle management (PLM), 352
**Product line, 414**
Product manager, 421
**Product mix, 414**
**Product placement, 448,** 449
**Product** strategy, **410**–421, 429
   classifying goods and services in, 411–413
   in marketing mix, 388
   marketing strategy implications in, 413–414
   product identification in, 418–422
   product life cycle in, 414–418
Product usage, segmentation by, 396
**Production, 344**–371. *See also* Factors of production; Manufacturing; **Production and operations management/managers**
   customer-driven, 349
   defined, **346**
   flexible, 348–349
   importance of, 347–349
   location for, 353–354
   managers and, 354–363
   marketing era and, 14
   mass, 348
   processes of, 346, 349–350
   technology and, 350–354
**Production and operations management/managers, 346**–349, 354–363, 375. *See also* Production
   controlling production process as, 360–363
   facility layout as, 355–357
   implementing production plan as, 357–360
   planning the production process as, 355
   quality and, 364, 366
**Production control, 360**
Production equipment, 46
Production era in business, 13, 14
Production era in marketing, 382
**Production planning, 360**–361
**Productivity, 46, 78**
**Product-related segmentation, 396**
**Product(s), 410.** *See also* Business-to-business (B2B) products; Business-to-consumer (B2C) products; Product strategy
   business ethics of certain, 412
   distribution channels for, 432
   identification of, 418–422
   life cycle of, 414–418
   marketing mix and, 445
   placement of (*See* Product placement)
   puffery of, 463–464
   specialty, 411, 413
Profit sharing, 296, 297
**Profitability objectives, 465**–466
**Profitability ratios, 528, 529**–530
Profits, 5
   breakeven point and, 469
   corporations and, 169
   income statement and, 524–526
   joint venture and, 174
   private enterprise system and, 9, 10
   product life cycle and, 415, 416
   revenue *vs.,* 466
   social responsibility and, 43
   sole proprietorships and, 166
**Program Evaluation and Review Technique (PERT), 362**–363, 363

Team diversity, 326
Team leader, 256
Team level, 326
Team norm, 328
Teamwork, at W. L. Gore, 319
Technical jargon, 361–362, 363
Technical skills, 256
Technical support specialists, 543
Technology, 16, 482–511
    broadband, 222
    budgeting and, 531
    business ethics and, 35
    business success and, 7
    career in, 542–543
    computer hardware and software as, 491–494
    to deal with Internet privacy issues, 226
    disabilities and, 53
    disaster recovery and backup, 505–506
    entrepreneurship and, 111
    at Google, 483–484
    home-based businesses and, 149
    how computers help businesspeople and, 494–500
    information, 193–194
    information systems for decision making
        as, 487–490
    infrastructure and, 102
    intranets as, 501
    lifestyle entrepreneur and, 190
    management information systems as, 484–487
    managing relationships through, 16–17
    production and, 350–354
    productivity and, 78
    protecting information systems, 502–505
    RFID, 422, 434
    Second City and, 541–542
    SSL, 225
    supply and, 68
    VoIP as, 502
    VPNs as, 501–502
    workforce quality with, 46
Telecommunications Act, 129
Telecommunications protection, 131
Telecommuters, 300–301
Telemarketing, 458, 459
Telemarketing Sales Rule, 459
Television, as advertising media, 451–452
Terrorism, global economy and, 84
Test marketing, 417–418
Text messaging, 213, 214
Thailand, Panasonic in, 116
Theory X, 307
Theory Y, 307
Theory Z, 307
30-year bonds. See Government bonds
360-degree performance review, 295
Time deposit, 552, 555
Time utility, 381
Tipping, 71
Tobacco industry, social responsibility and,
    44, 52
Top management, 172, 255, 258, 262, 263, 309,
    337, 374
    at Second City, 373, 604
Tort, 135–136
Total asset turnover, 529
Total cost, 468
Total liabilities to total assets, 530
Total revenue, 468
Toyota, 7, 25, 45, 46, 64
Trade, 84, 92, 93
    administrative barriers to, 105–106
    balance of, 96

barriers to (See Trade barriers)
international law and, 127
measuring, 95–98
reducing barriers to, 106–110
regulation of, 128
research resources on Internet, 111
why nations, 93–95
Trade barriers, 98–110
    economic differences as, 101–102
    political/legal differences as, 102–105
    reducing, 106–110
    social/cultural differences as, 99–101
    types of, 105–106
Trade credit, 156, 556
Trade deficit, 96
Trade promotion, 457
Trade shows, 456, 457
Trade surplus, 96
Trade unions, 107
Trademarks, 103, 104, 114, 134–135, 411,
    419, 521
Trade-oriented promotions, 457
Trading, securities and, 594–596
Training programs, 292–294
Transaction management, 15
Transcripts, for preparing job credentials, xli
Transparency, 330
Transportation
    distribution and, 435–436
    as factor in location decision, 353–354
    infrastructure and, 102
Travel, 4, 104, 196, 217
    global air, 409–410
    by Southwest Airlines, 223
Treasurer, 548
Treasury bills, 555
Treaties, 103–104
Trial courts, 126
Trojan horse, 505
Truth, vs. loyalty, 37, 39
Tuition reimbursement, 296
Turkey, political climate in, 103
Turnaround entrepreneurs, 186

U

UCC. See Uniform Commercial Code (UCC)
Uganda, 192
Ukraine, international regulations in, 105
Underwriting, 564, 577
Unemployment, 80–81
    cyclical, 81, 82
    frictional, 80, 82
    seasonal, 80, 82
    structural, 81, 82
    types of, 82
Unemployment compensation, xlii
Unemployment insurance, 297
Unemployment rate, 80, 81, 82
    fiscal policy and, 82
    in North Dakota, 79
Uniform Commercial Code (UCC), 132–133
Uniform Partnership Act, 168
Uniformed Services Employment and Reemployment
    Rights Act of 1994, 54, 130
Union. See Labor union
Unit of account, money as, 551, 552
United Arab Emirates
    OPEC and, 73
    Second City and, 140
United Kingdom
    advertising in, 102–103, 104
    African debt relief from, 108

B2B e-business in, 219
benchmarking in, 364
business ethics in, 42
business history and, 12, 13
corporations in, 169
entrepreneur statistics in, 192
environmental issues in, 45
EU and, 110
euro in, 98
Internet users in, 239
multinationals in, 116
online shopping in, 238
Second City and, 139
Tacit Networks and, 153
transactions in, 98
U.S. trade with, 94, 95
world's leading companies in, 117
Yahoo! in, 111
United States
    advertising in, 449–450
    Afghanistan and, 123
    African debt relief from, 108
    aging in, 54–55, 84, 194, 394, 395
    business dinners in, 330
    business history in, 12–18
    buyer's market in, 382
    CAFTA and, 109
    China and, 97, 104, 468
    comparative advantage in, 95
    countertrade and, 113
    CPI in, 80
    debt in, 83
    employment in, 80
    entrepreneur statistics in, 192
    entrepreneurial spirit in, 10
    environmental issues in, 44, 45, 46
    ETFs in, 593
    exchange rate in, 97, 98
    exports and, 95, 96–97
    financial systems in, 102
    flextime in, 300
    GDP of, 78, 94
    global expansion and, 84, 85
    global perspective on financial institutions in,
        567–568
    home-based work programs in, 300–301
    imports and, 95, 96–97
    international law and, 127
    Internet penetration rate in, 239
    Internet users in, 214–215, 217,
        222–223, 238
    introducing/addressing people in, 432
    keeping manufacturing jobs in, 115
    labor shortage in parts of, 79
    as low-context culture, 330
    Microsoft antitrust charges in, 253
    monopolies in, 74
    multinationals in, 116
    NAFTA agreement and, 108, 110
    Native Americans in, 407
    oil supply in, 68, 69
    online shopping in, 221
    personal space in, 335
    political climate in, 103
    Pollo Campero in, 145
    population in, xlix–l, 94, 485–486
    products made in, 92
    Red Bull in, 113
    Second City in, 139
    small business statistics in, 146, 160, 162–163
    social/cultural differences in, 100
    Soviet Union and, 75

# International Index

Russia
    African debt relief from, 108
    copyright issues and, 135
    corruption and, 103
    countertrade and, 113
    etiquette in, 100
    Internet users in, 239
    joint ventures in, 116
    political climate in, 103
    population in, 94
    ruble in, 98

**S**

Saeco, 97
Safe Kids Cards, 194
San Marino
    wealth in, 94
Sanrio, 114
Saudi Arabia
    OPEC and, 73
    Second City and, 140
    social/cultural differences in, 100–101
SC. *See* Second City (SC)
Scotland
    Second City and, 139
Second City (SC), 139–140, 247–248, 372–373,
    477–478, 541–542
ServiceMaster Clean, 164
7-Eleven, 164
Singapore, 192
Slovakia, 109
Slovenia, 109, 192
Small business
    on global scale, 153
Snap-On Tools, 164
**Socialism, 75,** 76
Softa Bottling Company, 102
Solution Centre, 153
Sony, 382–383
South Africa
    entrepreneur statistics in, 192
    etiquette in, 100
    rand in, 98
    Republic of Tea and, 49
South America
    hyperinflation in, 79
South Korea
    Internet penetration rate in, 239
    Internet users in, 239
    trade restrictions and, 105
    U.S. trade with, 94, 95
    Yahoo! in, 111
Soviet Union
    communism in, 75
    hyperinflation in, 79
    political climate in, 103
Spain
    absolute advantage in, 95
    entrepreneur statistics in, 192
    Internet users in, 239
    translation issue in, 101
Starbucks, 265–266
Stock markets
    foreign, 586–587
**Strategic alliance, 17**–18
Subway, 164
**Supply, 65,** 70
    capitalism and, 71, 72
    currency and, 532
    factors driving, 68–69
    oil, 73
    pricing strategies and, 467

Sweden
    entrepreneur statistics in, 192
    euro in, 110
    Internet penetration rate in, 239
    socialism and, 75
    translation issue in, 101
Switzerland
    banks in, 568
    flextime in, 300
    as low-context culture, 330
    wealth in, 94
    world's leading companies in, 117

**T**

Tacit Networks, 153
Taiwan
    Domino's Pizza in, 114
    Panasonic in, 116
    U.S. trade with, 94, 95
**Tariffs, 104, 105,** 108
Terrorism
    global economy and, 84
Thailand
    Panasonic in, 116
Timberland, 298
Tobacco industry, social responsibility
    and, 44, 52
Toyota, 7, 25, 45, 46, 64, 101, 116, 117
Trade, 84, 92, 93
    administrative barriers to, 105–106
    balance of, 96
    barriers to (*See* Trade barriers)
    international law and, 127
    measuring, 95–98
    reducing barriers to, 106–110
    regulation of, 128
    research resources on Internet, 111
    why nations, 93–95
Trade barriers, 98–110
    economic differences as, 101–102
    political/legal differences as, 102–105
    reducing, 106–110
    social/cultural differences as, 99–101
    types of, 105–106
Trade credit, 156, 556
Trade deficit, 96
Trade-oriented promotions, 457
**Trade promotion, 457**
**Trade surplus, 96**
Trade unions, 107
**Trademarks,** 103, 104, 114, **134**–135, 411,
    **419,** 521
Trading, securities and, 594–596
Transparency International, 103, 104
Travel
    global air, 409–410
Treaties, 103–104
Turkey
    political climate in, 103
Turner Broadcasting, 102–103

**U**

UBS, 117
Uganda, 192
Ukraine
    international regulations in, 105
United Arab Emirates
    OPEC and, 73
    Second City and, 140
United Kingdom
    advertising in, 102–103, 104
    African debt relief from, 108

banks in, 568
B2B e-business in, 219
benchmarking in, 364
business ethics in, 42
business history and, 12, 13
corporations in, 169
entrepreneur statistics in, 192
environmental issues in, 45
EU and, 110
euro in, 98
Internet users in, 239
multinationals in, 116
online shopping in, 238
Second City and, 139
Tacit Networks and, 153
transactions in, 98
U.S. trade with, 94, 95
world's leading companies in, 117
Yahoo! in, 111
United Parcel Service (UPS), 434, 435
United States
    Afghanistan and, 123
    African debt relief from, 108
    aging in, 54–55, 84, 194, 394, 395
    business dinners in, 330
    CAFTA and, 109
    China and, 97, 104, 468
    comparative advantage in, 95
    countertrade and, 113
    environmental issues in, 44, 45, 46
    exchange rate in, 97
    exports and, 95, 96–97
    financial systems in, 102
    GDP of, 78, 94
    global expansion and, 84
    global perspective on financial institutions in,
        567–568
    imports and, 95, 96–97
    international law and, 127
    Internet penetration rate in, 239
    Internet users in, 214–215, 217,
        222–223, 238
    introducing/addressing people in, 432
    as low-context culture, 330
    multinationals in, 116
    NAFTA agreement and, 108, 110
    oil supply in, 68, 69
    personal space in, 335
    Pollo Campero in, 145
    population in, 94
    Red Bull in, 113
    social/cultural differences in, 100
    Soviet Union and, 75
    tariffs in, 105
    telecommunications technology in, 102
    trade and, 94, 95, 96, 106
    trade embargo on Cuba, 106
    travel and, 67, 196, 217
    wealth in, 94
    workforce and, 18–21, 46
    world's leading companies in, 117
UPS. *See* United Parcel Service (UPS)
Uruguay, 108

**V**

Vacation
    social/cultural differences in, 100
Values
    as barrier to trade, 100
Venezuela
    oil exports in, 68
    OPEC and, 73

Vietnam
    international regulations in, 104–105

**W**

Wal-Mart, 93, 94, 116
Walt Disney Company, 97
Wealth, world's top ten nations based on, 94
Web sites
    international trade informational, 111
    International Trademark Association, 440
    Livewire International, 180
    OPEC, 73
    social/cultural differences and, 99
    Wal-Mart, 222

Whirlpool, 114
Wipro, 134
Wipro Werbeagentur, 134
Women
    in Afghanistan, 123
    in Chili, 100
    Iraqi, 100
Workforce
    aging in, 18–19, 54–55
    outsourcing in, 20–21
**World Bank, 107**
**World Trade Organization (WTO), 106**–107, 111, 127, 135
WTO. *See* World Trade Organization (WTO)

**Y**

Yahoo!, 111
Yugoslavia, former
    political climate in, 103

**Z**

Zimbabwe
    international regulations in, 105